COMPARATIVE CONSTITUTIONA

RESEARCH HANDBOOKS IN COMPARATIVE LAW

Series Editors: Francesco Parisi, *Oppenheimer Wolff and Donnelly Professor of Law, University of Minnesota, USA and Professor of Economics, University of Bologna, Italy* and Tom Ginsburg, *Professor of Law, University of Chicago, USA*

The volumes in this series offer high-level discussion and analysis on particular aspects of legal systems and the law. Well-known scholars edit each handbook and bring together accessible yet sophisticated contributions from an international cast of top researchers. The first series of its kind to cover a wide range of comparative issues so comprehensively, this is an indispensable resource for students and scholars alike.

Titles in this series include:

Comparative Administrative Law
Edited by Susan Rose-Ackerman and Peter L. Lindseth

Comparative Constitutional Law
Edited by Tom Ginsburg and Rosalind Dixon

Comparative Constitutional Law

Edited by

Tom Ginsburg
University of Chicago, USA

and

Rosalind Dixon
University of Chicago, USA

RESEARCH HANDBOOKS IN COMPARATIVE LAW

Edward Elgar
Cheltenham, UK • Northampton, MA, USA

Published by
Edward Elgar Publishing Limited
The Lypiatts
15 Lansdown Road
Cheltenham
Glos GL50 2JA
UK

Edward Elgar Publishing, Inc.
William Pratt House
9 Dewey Court
Northampton
Massachusetts 01060
USA

Paperback edition 2012
Paperback edition reprinted 2014

A catalogue record for this book is available from the British Library

Library of Congress Control Number: 2010939197

ISBN 978 1 84844 539 0 (cased)
     978 0 85793 078 1 (paperback)

Typeset by Cambrian Typesetters, Camberley, Surrey
Printed and bound in Great Britain by TJ International Ltd, Padstow, Cornwall

Contents

List of contributors   viii
Acknowledgements   xi

1   Introduction   1
     Rosalind Dixon and Tom Ginsburg

PART I   CONSTITUTIONAL DESIGN AND REDESIGN

2   Drafting, design and gender   19
     Helen Irving
3   Participation in constitutional design   38
     Justin Blount
4   Transitional justice and the transformation of constitutionalism   57
     Ruti Teitel
5   Constitutional drafting and external influence   77
     Zaid Al-Ali
6   Constitutional amendment rules: a comparative perspective   96
     Rosalind Dixon
7   Constitutional endurance   112
     Tom Ginsburg

PART II   CONSTITUTIONAL IDENTITY

8   The formation of constitutional identities   129
     Gary J. Jacobsohn
9   Citizenship and the boundaries of the constitution   143
     Kim Rubenstein and Niamh Lenagh-Maguire
10   Comparative constitutional law and Indigenous peoples: Canada,
     New Zealand and the USA   170
     Claire Charters
11   A new global constitutional order?   189
     David Schneiderman

PART III   CONSTITUTIONAL STRUCTURE

12   Legislative-executive relations   211
     José Antonio Cheibub and Fernando Limongi
13   The separation of legislative and executive powers   234
     Ronald J. Krotoszynski, Jr.

14   Political parties and constitutionalism   254
     Richard H. Pildes
15   The rise of specialized constitutional courts   265
     Víctor Ferreres Comella
16   The interplay of constitutional and ordinary jurisdiction   278
     Frank I. Michelman
17   Constitutional experimentation: rethinking how a bill of rights functions 298
     Janet L. Hiebert
18   The rise of weak-form judicial review   321
     Mark Tushnet
19   Constitutions and emergency regimes   334
     Oren Gross
20   Federalism, devolution and secession: from classical to post-conflict
     federalism   356
     Sujit Choudhry and Nathan Hume

PART IV   INDIVIDUAL RIGHTS AND STATE DUTIES

21   The structure and scope of constitutional rights   387
     Stephen Gardbaum
22   The comparative constitutional law of freedom of expression   406
     Adrienne Stone
23   Comparative constitutional law and religion   422
     Ran Hirschl
24   Autonomy, dignity and abortion   441
     Donald P. Kommers
25   Human dignity in constitutional adjudication   459
     Paolo G. Carozza
26   Equality   473
     Kate O'Regan and Nick Friedman
27   The right to property   504
     Tom Allen
28   Socio-economic rights: has the promise of eradicating the divide between
     first and second generation rights been fulfilled?   519
     Dennis M. Davis
29   Comparative constitutional law and the challenges of terrorism law   532
     Kent Roach
30   Legal protection of same-sex partnerships and comparative constitutional
     law   551
     Nicholas Bamforth

PART V   COURTS AND CONSTITUTIONAL INTERPRETATION

31   Judicial engagement with comparative law   571
     Cheryl Saunders

32   Constitutional interpretation in comparative perspective: comparing
       judges or courts?   599
       Vicki C. Jackson and Jamal Greene
33   Docket control and the success of constitutional courts   624
       David Fontana

Index   643

Contributors

Zaid Al-Ali is Visiting Lecturer at the Institut d'Etudes Politiques (Sciences-Po), Paris, France; Senior Analyst at the International Crisis Group; PhD Candidate at the University of Paris II (Pantheon-Assas); and Outside Counsel (international commercial arbitration).

Tom Allen is Professor, Durham Law School (UK).

Nicholas Bamforth is Fellow in Law, Queen's College, University of Oxford (UK).

Justin Blount is Ph.D. candidate in the Department of Political Science, University of Illinois.

Paolo G. Carozza is Professor, University of Notre Dame Law School.

Claire Charters is Research Fellow, New Zealand Centre for Public Law, Victoria University of Wellington (New Zealand), and Human Rights Officer, United Nations Office of the High Commissioner for Human Rights.

José Antonio Cheibub is Professor in the Department of Political Science, University of Illinois at Urbana-Champaign.

Sujit Choudhry is Scholl Chair, University of Toronto Faculty of Law (Canada).

Dennis M. Davis is Judge of the High Court, Cape Town, South Africa.

Rosalind Dixon is Assistant Professor, University of Chicago Law School.

Víctor Ferreres Comella is Professor of Constitutional Law, Pompeu Fabra University (Barcelona).

David Fontana is Associate Professor, George Washington University Law School.

Nick Friedman is M.Phil Candidate, Centre for Socio-Legal Studies, University of Oxford (UK).

Stephen Gardbaum is MacArthur Foundation Professor of International Justice and Human Rights, University of California Los Angeles School of Law.

Tom Ginsburg is Professor, University of Chicago Law School.

Jamal Greene is Associate Professor, Columbia Law School.

Oren Gross is Irving Younger Professor of Law and Director, Institute for International Legal & Security Studies, University of Minnesota Law School.

Janet L. Hiebert is Professor of Political Studies, Queen's University (Canada).

Ran Hirschl is Professor of Law and Political Science, and Canada Research Chair in Constitutionalism, Democracy, and Development, University of Toronto (Canada).

Nathan Hume is an S.J.D. candidate at the University of Toronto Faculty of Law (Canada).

Helen Irving is Professor, University of Sydney Law School (Australia).

Vicki C. Jackson is Carmack Waterhouse Professor of Constitutional Law, Georgetown University Law Center.

Gary J. Jacobsohn is H. Malcolm Macdonald Professor of Constitutional and Comparative Law, Department of Government, University of Texas at Austin.

Donald P. Kommers is Joseph and Elizabeth Robbie Professor of Political Science and Professor of Law Emeritus, University of Notre Dame.

Ronald J. Krotoszynski, Jr. is John S. Stone Chairholder of Law and Director of Faculty Research, University of Alabama Law School.

Niamh Lenagh-Maguire is a Lawyer at the Australian Goverment Solicitor, Canberra (Australia).

Fernando Limongi is Professor, Universidade de São Paulo (Brazil).

Frank I. Michelman is Robert Walmsley University Professor, Harvard University.

Kate O'Regan is former Judge, Constitutional Court of South Africa (1994–2009); Honorary Professor, University of Cape Town; Visiting Professor, University of Oxford (UK).

Richard H. Pildes is Sudler Family Professor of Constitutional Law, New York University School of Law.

Kent Roach is Prichard-Wilson Chair of Law and Public Policy, University of Toronto Faculty of Law (Canada).

Kim Rubenstein is Professor and Director of the Centre for International and Public Law, Australian National University College of Law (Australia).

Cheryl Saunders is Laureate Professor, University of Melbourne Law School (Australia).

David Schneiderman is Professor, University of Toronto (Canada).

Adrienne Stone is Professor, University of Melbourne Law School (Australia).

Ruti Teitel is Ernst C. Stiefel Professor of Comparative Law, New York Law School.

Mark Tushnet is William Nelson Cromwell Professor of Law, Harvard Law School.

Acknowledgements

Our thanks to Dean Michael Schill and the Russell Baker Scholars Fund at the University of Chicago Law School for support for this project. We are also grateful to Chantelle Hougland, Youssef Kalad, Claudia Lai and Emily Winston for research assistance.

Some of the material in Chapter 13 first appeared as Ronald J. Krotoszynski, Jr., 'The Shot (Not) Heard 'Round the World: Reconsidering the Perplexing U.S. Preoccupation with the Separation of Legislative and Executive Powers', 51 *Boston College Law Review* 1 (2010). We gratefully acknowledge the permission of the *Boston College Law Review*.

1. Introduction

Rosalind Dixon and Tom Ginsburg

Comparative constitutional law is a newly energized field in the early 21st century. Never before has the field had such a broad range of interdisciplinary interest, with lawyers, political scientists, sociologists and even economists making contributions to our collective understanding of how constitutions are formed and how they operate. Never before has there been such demand from courts, lawyers and constitution-makers in a wide range of countries for comparative legal analysis. And never before has the field been so institutionalized, with new regional and international associations providing fora for the exchange of ideas and the organization of collaborative projects.

This *Handbook* is one such collaborative project, a small effort to provide an overview of the field. It is inherent that any such effort will be incomplete, and we surely recognize the limitations of any effort to distill such a rich field into a single volume. But we also believe that the time has come for some organization of the various issues and controversies that structure academic and legal debate. As the field matures, such efforts will help to advance scholarship to the next level, by focusing attention on outstanding questions as well as raising awareness of issues worth pursuing in under-analyzed jurisdictions.

This Introduction provides a brief history of the field, and wrestles with the definitional issues of the boundaries of the constitution. It then draws out the common themes that emerge from a reading of the chapters, particularly as they relate to patterns of constitutional similarity versus difference, or convergence versus divergence. The conclusion briefly speculates on future directions for the field.

1 COMPARATIVE CONSTITUTIONAL LAW: A THUMBNAIL HISTORY

The field of comparative constitutional studies can be traced back at least to Aristotle's *Politics*, which systematically evaluated the constitutions of the Greek city states to inform normative theorizing on optimal design. Classical thinkers in Imperial China, India and elsewhere also spent some time thinking about the fundamental principles of statecraft, arguing about matters that we would call constitutional. In the Western intellectual tradition, such analysis continued through many of the great political thinkers, from Machiavelli to Montesquieu to John Stuart Mill. In the 17th century, state-builders in the Netherlands undertook extensive study of ancient and contemporary models to resolve constitutional problems of the nascent Dutch republic, finding particular inspiration in the proto-federalism of the biblical Israelites (Boralevi 2002). In the 18th century, besides Montesquieu's foundational exploration, lesser known figures such as Gottfried Achenwall and Johann Heinrich Gottlieb von Justi undertook surveys of political forms (Marcos 2003: 313). Comparative constitutional study thus has a long and distinguished lineage.

It is the rise of the written constitutional form, conventionally understood to have emerged in full flower in the late 18th century, that spurred the field to develop more systematically and to become distinct from political theory *per se*. The enlightenment thinkers of the French, Polish and American projects saw written constitutions as acts of purposive institutional design, for which wide study was a desirable, even necessary, feature. They thus engaged in extensive examination and debate about the appropriateness of particular models. In turn, the models they produced, as channeled through the liberal 1812 Spanish Constitution of Cadiz, influenced the early constitutions of Latin America: the 1821 Constitution of Gran Colombia, the 1830 and 1832 Constitutions of New Granada, the 1830 Constitution of Venezuela, the 1823 and 1828 Constitutions of Peru, the Argentine Constitution of 1826, the Uruguayan Constitution of 1830, and the Chilean Constitution of 1828.

Throughout the 19th century, new state-builders, initially in Latin America and Western Europe but also in Japan, sought to adopt the new technology of the written constitution, and in doing so needed to engage in practical comparisons about which institutions were optimal. As a result, constitutional compilations became more popular, focusing on both European and Latin American countries (Marcos 2003: 314–16). The method involved a mix of normative and positive analysis, and in turn informed drafting exercises in new states and old (Takii 2007).

The 19th century also saw the rise of the academic discipline of comparative law, culminating in the International Congress of Comparative Law in 1900 (Riles 2001; Clark 2001). The zeitgeist was captured by the notion of legal science, an internal and autonomous study of law, using distinctively legal forms of reasoning to determine the answers to normative questions. Scholars sought to examine the scientific principles of law that provided a universal underlying structure to inform the drafting of civil codes. The comparative method was also used by those who sought to link legal science to social science, exemplified by Henry Sumner Maine's (1861) monumental efforts to discover the origins and development of legal institutions. Comparison, then, was a natural part of the milieu of 19th century jurisprudence, but the relative dearth of constitutional adjudication meant that there was little attention to that topic.

Perhaps as a legacy of this era, comparative law was to focus heavily on the private law core of Western legal systems for much of the next century. By and large, the great figures of Western comparative law did not place public law in their sights, preferring to ascribe to the public law a particularity and responsiveness to *local* values. In contrast, private law was seen as embodying common and universal features, derived ultimately from the Roman tradition. There was, to quote one such effort, a common core of private law (Bussani and Mattei 2002). The only comparable 'core' in the public law sphere was embodied in international human rights law, which formed a template of minimum content that constitutions were encouraged to adopt into local law. In the early 1950s, there was a burst of interest in the field in the United States, with many law schools offering a course in comparative constitutions, and such figures as Erwin Griswold and William Douglas writing on the topic (Fontana 2011). But for the bulk of the 20th century, comparative constitutional law was not a vigorous or prominent field for writing by academic lawyers.

Other disciplines, however, did focus on constitutional comparison. With the formation of political science as a modern discipline in the United States in the early 20th century, constitutional studies formed an important part of the core curriculum, with comparison being at least a part of the approach. The sub-discipline of public law spent a good deal of energy examining constitutional texts and describing the various political institutions they created, both to inform potential borrowing and also to understand how systems operated (Shapiro 1993).

With the behavioral revolution in the 1940s and 1950s, however, social scientists turned away from formal texts as objects of study, and instead sought to examine the 'science' of government decision-making. Public law scholars turned to judicial behavior, examining the micro-foundations of legal decisions rather than the broader structures within which judges were embedded. This necessarily involved a turn away from formal institutions and toward individual agents. Formal institutions such as law were seen to some degree as façades masking interests and 'real' politics.

Two developments in the late 20th century – one academic and one in the world – coalesced to provide a fruitful environment for the growth of comparative constitutional studies. The academic development was the revival of various institutionalisms in the social sciences (March and Olsen 1989; Powell and DiMaggio 1991; Clayton and Gilman 1998). Sociologists and some political scientists began to emphasize that individual agents were embedded in broader institutional structures, and that these structures helped to determine outcomes. From another angle, economists moving away from neoclassical models began to understand that rules were important (Buchanan and Tullock 1961; North 1991). Institutions were defined as the rules of the game that structured behavior. Constitutions, as the social devices that structure the creation of rules, were the ultimate institutions worthy of analysis. Hence there was a turn in economics to understanding constitutional structures. With some exceptions (Brennan and Pardo 1991; Voigt 1999), the literature in constitutional political economy focused more on theory than empirics, but it did provide a set of working assumptions and hypotheses for analyzing constitutions.

The late 20th century also saw epochal changes in the real world that made it hard for academics to ignore constitutions. The third wave of democracy beginning in the mid-1970s brought new attention to constitutions as instruments of democratization, and the emergence of new states following the end of the Cold War prompted a new round of efforts to theorize and analyze institutional design (Elster et al. 1998; Sunstein 2001; Holmes 1995). In particular, constitutional design became a central focus for ethnically diverse states in the hope that proper institutions could ameliorate conflict (Choudhry 2008; Ghai 2001; Horowitz 1991). There was a revival of interest in federalism and other design techniques (Le Roy and Saunders 2006).

A related development was the secular increase in the role of courts in many societies, a phenomenon known as judicialization (Tate and Vallinder 1995). Designated constitutional courts were prime locations for judicialization in many countries, and the phenomenon was examined by lawyers and political scientists interested in particular countries (Kommers 2002; Stone 1992; Volcansek 1990). The spread of judicialization and constitutionalization meant that there were both many more contexts in which the operation of the constitutional system 'mattered' as well as much more demand for comparative analysis. Some of this work was implicitly comparative, but most of the work in the 1990s considered a single jurisdiction (but see Baun and Franklin 1995).

With the rising prominence of constitutional courts as loci of major social and political decision-making, it became apparent that some of the problems courts were confronting were recurring in different countries. Many new democracies, for example, had to deal with lustration and other issues of transition (Teitel 2002), economic transformation, and electoral issues. These courts quite naturally began to pay attention to how the issues were resolved in other countries, especially the established democracies with well-developed jurisprudence on similar questions. Courts were also in dialogue about the interpretation of international human rights instruments, and what limitations might be acceptable within a free and democratic society. This phenomenon of transnational judicial dialogue was in fact quite old, but received renewed attention and was heavily criticized by judicial conservatives in the United States. The critique prompted a spate of work on the appropriate role for judicial borrowing across jurisdictions (see Chapter 31 by Saunders in this volume). Indeed, in part for this reason, the early 21st century has seen a veritable explosion of interest in the field.

2   COMPARATIVE CONSTITUTIONAL LAW: BOUNDARIES OF THE FIELD

An important question raised by the growth of the field of comparative constitutional law is how to define the outer boundaries of the phenomenon to be studied. The study of comparative constitutional law, most scholars agree, is something distinct from the study of comparative private law or non-constitutional law, but scholars also differ significantly in how they draw this distinction. Furthermore, the increasingly global context of constitution-making, in which norms are developed across borders, requires some attention to the relationship between constitutions and international law.

Perhaps the most straightforward way in which to define the constitutional domain is by reference to the text of legal instruments that are expressly labeled by their drafters as 'constitutional'. This is the approach taken, almost by necessity, by those scholars in the field who do large-scale empirical work: a good example in the *Handbook* is Chapter 7 by Tom Ginsburg on constitutional endurance. It is also an approach frequently adopted by scholars engaged in more qualitative research: the clearest examples of this are found in Part I of the *Handbook*, in those chapters dealing with questions relating to constitutional design and redesign, but such an approach is also an important definitional starting point for several later chapters, such as those by Sujit Choudhry and Nathan Hume, Dennis Davis, Donald Kommers, Ron Krotozynski, Vicki C. Jackson and Jamal Greene, and Kim Rubenstein and Niamh Lenagh-Maguire.

A second approach focuses on the idea of entrenchment, or the degree to which certain legal rules are immune from change by ordinary as opposed to super-majority legislative processes, either as a matter of legal form or political convention. While formal entrenchment may often coincide with a text-based approach (i.e. whether a norm is included in a written document labeled constitutional), other norms can be informally entrenched as a practical matter, and hence might be considered constitutional in some sense. A focus on the entrenchment criterion may offer quite distinctive answers as to the scope of the comparative constitutional field. Few contributions to the *Handbook* in fact adopt this approach, however, likely because it is difficult in the space of a short chapter to give detailed consideration to the degree to which such informal conventions exist.

A third approach, which is more common among contributors to the *Handbook*, is more functional, and defines the constitutional domain by reference to the role of constitutions in both 'checking' and 'creating' government power. This understanding is most explicit in Rick Pildes' contribution to the *Handbook*, but also runs through a number of other chapters, including those by Tom Allen, Nicholas Bamforth, Claire Charters, Oren Gross, Janet Hiebert, Kate O'Regan and Nick Friedman, Kent Roach, and Mark Tushnet. Perhaps the strongest evidence of this approach by these authors is their attention to statutes such as the UK Human Rights Act 1998, New Zealand Bill of Rights 1990 and the 1992 Israeli *Basic Law* on Human Dignity and Liberty, without detailed inquiry as to the informal entrenchment of such instruments. Another indication is the treatment of constitutions, or constitutionalism, as having an inherently 'pro-rights' orientation: this is implicit, for example, in Kent Roach's suggestion (following Kim Lane Scheppele 2006) that international law may have an 'anti-constitutional' dimension in the anti-terrorism context (see Chapter 29), and Tom Allen's suggestion that constitutional instruments tend to exhibit an intrinsic – as opposed to purely instrumental – commitment to individual rights (see Chaper 27). David Schneiderman, for his part, criticizes this kind of teleological approach to the definition of the field – which he labels 'global constitutionalism "as project" ' – but in doing so ultimately goes on to propose a functional definition of the 'constitutional' domain, whereby constitutional norms are defined by reference to their role in allocating political power.

A fourth approach is more sociological and open-textured, and linked to the way in which national actors understand domestic legal norms as constitutional. This approach is implicit in Gary Jacobsohn's chapter on constitutional identity; Victor Ferreres Comella's chapter on constitutional courts; Frank Michelman's chapter on the interplay between constitutional and ordinary jurisdiction; Stephen Gardbaum's chapter on the structure and scope of constitutional rights; Adrienne Stone's chapter on freedom of expression; Cheryl Saunders' chapter on comparative engagement by courts; and David Fontana's chapter on the way in which courts do (and ought to) control their docket.

Each of these approaches involves a somewhat different trade-off between objectivity and clarity, on the one hand, and the potential for under- and over-inclusiveness, on the other (compare Dixon and Posner (forthcoming). The lack of agreement, even at this preliminary definitional level, illustrates both the methodological pluralism of the field, but also our contention that significant work still remains to be done by scholars in the field.

3 COMPARATIVE CONSTITUTIONAL LAW: A STUDY IN DIFFERENCE OR SIMILARITY?

A central question almost all of the contributors to the *Handbook* take up is the degree to which, in various constitutional sub-fields, one observes patterns of constitutional similarity or even convergence over time.

For some authors, this is largely a question of identifying patterns of constitutional similarity, or difference, within a particular sub-group of countries. These authors' very careful and detailed consideration of the constitutional position in a number of countries makes it challenging to address the issue of convergence on a truly global scale (see e.g. the chapters by Jackson and Greene, and Rubenstein and Lenagh-Maguire). However, even for these authors, the different constitutional models or archetypes they identify may suggest at least some tentative conclusions about global constitutional patterns. Other authors explicitly aim to consider the degree to which there is general constitutional similarity or convergence, in a particular area, across the globe.

The most common pattern that authors in the *Handbook* identify is one of broad similarity at an abstract constitutional level, together with significant heterogeneity or polarization (i.e. similarity only among countries in a particular constitutional sub-group, and not across different sub-groups of countries) at a more concrete or specific level of constitutional comparison. For example, in Part I, Dixon notes that while almost all countries worldwide now include formal provision for constitutional amendment (Chapter 6), the frequency and function of formal constitutional amendment varies significantly across countries, as does the way in which countries' constitutions make it more difficult for legislatures to pass constitutional amendments as opposed to ordinary legislation. Ginsburg notes both a pattern of broad similarity across countries when it comes to the life-span or endurance of constitutions – most constitutions for most countries die quite young, but there is significant regional and other variation in both the observed and predicted rate of endurance (Chapter 7).

In Part II, in exploring questions of constitutional identity and membership, Gary Jacobsohn suggests important commonalities across countries in how they have forged a 'constitutional identity' over time, by confronting various sources of disharmony within their own constitutional system or traditions, but also notes important differences among countries in the role played by constitutional text, history, and different institutions and understandings of constitutionalism. Claire Charters identifies a similar pattern in constitutional responses to indigenous peoples: she notes the way in which, in all three countries she studies, there has been a period of 'official respect for indigenous peoples' sovereignty and control over their land' followed by a period of retreat in the state's willingness to recognize enforceable obligations towards indigenous people; a later period of expanded rights-based recognition, followed by political backlash; and the persistence of major differences on more specific constitutional questions, such as the status of treaties with indigenous peoples, issues of sovereignty and jurisdictional control. And Kim Rubenstein and Niamh Lenagh-Maguire again identify a pattern of only very abstract similarity among countries in their definition of citizenship and the boundaries of the constitution: they show that Australia, Canada and Israel all share a quasi-constitutional approach to the regulation of citizenship, as compared to the explicitly constitutional approach taken in the United States, but they also show that the jurisdictions vary greatly in how they see the relationship between statutory definitions of citizenship and constitutional norms.

In Part III, a number of authors reach similar conclusions in the context of questions of constitutional structure. In the context of legislative-executive relations, Ronald Krotoszynski suggests that 'even though concerns over the constitutional separation of powers are widely shared in other democratic republics, the specific US concern with the conflation of legislative [and executive] power, and the concomitant commitment of enforcement of this separation of powers by the federal judiciary, has failed to gain much traction' (Chapter 13). In the context of constitutional emergency regimes, Oren Gross likewise suggests that the pattern in democratic societies 'has almost invariably been [one based on] "models of accommodation"' (Chapter 19), and that, in most democracies, there is 'explicit constitutional reference to emergencies', but that there are also both clear exceptions to this pattern of explicit constitutional regulation (such as in the US, Japan and Belgium) and also significant differences among countries in their approach to questions such as which institutions are authorized to declare an emergency, and by what means; whether to adopt a unitary or multi-level approach to the definition of emergencies; and the effects of declaring an emergency, particularly on the enjoyment of individual rights.

In Part IV, in exploring constitutional rights protections, many authors identify a similar pattern. Donald Kommers, for example, in writing about abortion rights suggests that there is a seeming 'transnational consensus that unborn life (at some stage) and personal self-determination are both worthy of constitutional protection', and also increasing convergence among countries such as the US and Germany in exactly how they balance these competing commitments. But he also finds significant differences between Germany, the US, and Ireland in how they treat the constitutional status of the fetus and the nature of the right at stake for women: in Ireland, both the fetus and women are understood to enjoy a 'subjective' right to life; in Germany, women are understood to have a right to dignity or development of the person, whereas the fetus is protected by the state's duty to affirm the value of fetal life, as an objective constitutional value; and in the US, women's rights are understood largely in terms of liberty, rather than dignity, and the protection of fetal life as a compelling state interest – rather than constitutional duty. In the context of constitutional protections of human dignity, Paolo Carozza, in turn, notes a high degree of global consensus on the importance of respect for such a right, but also enormous variation among countries in how they understand the concept and its relationship to different sides of various rights debates.

Similarly, in writing about constitutional equality rights, while (former Justice) Kate O'Regan and Nick Friedman note that 'the right to equality is found in nearly all modern democratic constitutions' (Chapter 26), they also suggest that there is significant heterogeneity among countries in the way in which this right is implemented. They identify four distinct approaches in four different countries (i.e. the US, Canada, the UK and South Africa): in the US, at least under the 14th Amendment as opposed to statutory anti-discrimination provisions such as Title VII of the Civil Rights Act 1964, they note 'an equal treatment approach'; in Canada, a 'disparate impact' approach; in the UK a disparate impact plus 'ambit' test; and in South Africa, what they label a 'substantive equality' approach. In writing about constitutional responses to terrorism, post 9/11, Kent Roach likewise argues that there has been quite significant constitutional similarity – though in a quite different form to what many commentators suggest: rather than being generally deferential, courts have in fact, he suggests, not been particularly deferential in this area (Chapter 29). However, the precise way in which this has played out has also varied significantly by country with the use by various courts of administrative law and statutory interpretation tools, as well as more conventional forms of constitutional review. And in the context of gay rights, while Nicholas Bamforth devotes much of his attention to identifying institutional and substantive parallels between countries, he also stresses that 'the levels of moral controversy and social disagreement surrounding the legal recognition of same-sex partnerships var[ies] between jurisdictions' (Chapter 30).

In Part V, in writing about the way in which constitutional courts control access to their docket, David Fontana suggests the existence of broad – albeit hitherto under-appreciated – similarities among courts in their ability to control access to their docket, while also noting a range of more concrete differences among courts in the mechanisms they have for exercising such control.

Some authors put more emphasis on constitutional similarity across countries, arguing that there is in fact far greater similarity, in their particular field, than is generally thought to be the case. Helen Irving, for example, argues in Part I that when it comes to women's participation in constitution-making, there is a much longer history, and thus broader pattern of similarity, concerning such participation than many constitutional commentators appreciate: while (unlike modern constitutions) many older constitutions were drafted without direct female involvement, the US and Australian experience, she argues, shows that this was not universally so.

Stephen Gardbaum, in analyzing the scope and structure of constitutional rights in Part IV, argues that the US Supreme Court, rather than being a clear outlier in this context, is similar to almost all courts in approaching the justifiability of limitations on rights via the lens of 'balancing' or proportionality, and the 'horizontal' application of rights as a question of degree only (Chapter 21). Similarly, Adrienne Stone, in the context of freedom of expression, argues that there are important similarities among countries not simply in their recognition of this right, but also at a more concrete constitutional level. She finds similarities in the way in which courts generally give broad coverage to the right (for example, by including expressive activity in its scope), uphold implied as well as express limitations on the enjoyment of such rights, and in the way in which such rights have more or less direct horizontal effect (Chapter 22). And Tom Allen, in analyzing constitutional protection of property, suggests important similarities among countries not only in the sense that 'most constitutions impose restrictions on eminent domain' and 'follow a common structure' whereby 'government may only acquire property by a process laid down by law, for a public purpose, and on terms that provide the owner with compensation' (Chapter 27), but also in that, at a more concrete level, most courts tend to interpret such provisions in a way that distinguishes between 'takings' and other forms of regulatory interference with property rights, and to defer to the executive in its definition of the public interest.

Even these authors, however, still stress a range of ongoing constitutional differences among countries. Gardbaum, for example, notes a range of differences among countries at the more specific level of, for example, whether the limitation of rights is express or implied, is highly formalized or not, or includes attention to true cost-benefit judgments (Chapter 21); or whether their approach to horizontal application is so-called 'direct' versus 'indirect', or imposes duties on private individuals, and courts, as well as other government actors. Stone suggests that there are important differences in the way in which courts approach the justifiability of limitations on this right (Chapter 22), both in particular cases, and in their use of a 'categorical' as opposed to more open-ended 'balancing'-style approach. While the US is currently an outlier in preferring the latter to the former, Stone also hesitates to label this as a stable form of qualified similarity – given the potential for other countries to move toward a more heavily doctrinalized approach over time. And Allen notes significant variation among countries in how they define the 'minimum core' of a right to property, and thus also the line between takings and regulation.

Other contributors to the *Handbook* identify an even lesser degree of constitutional similarity across constitutional systems worldwide, even at the most abstract level – and instead, broad similarity only among distinct groups of countries (i.e. polarization).

In some cases, this pattern is one whereby countries can be divided into two rough categories or groups. In Part I, Justin Blount, for example, suggests (contra Helen Irving) that when it comes to norms of popular participation in constitution drafting there is a fairly clear distinction between old and new constitutions: in the former, there was limited provision for popular involvement in the drafting process; whereas in the latter, there has tended to be both a clear norm of and set of formal procedures for popular participation (Chapter 3). Zaid Al-Ali notes a similar difference between old and new constitutions when it comes to external influences in the constitutional drafting process, as well as a bifurcated pattern in the degree to which such influence tends to enforce, or depart, from international best practices in different contexts. And Ruti Teitel urges us to see constitution-making processes in terms of a parallel distinction between traditional state-centered forms of constitutionalism and newer, more civil society-focused forms of 'transformative' constitutionalism in societies facing challenges of transitional justice.

In Part III, Victor Ferreres Comella describes the two different canonical models of constitutional court structure – one in which ordinary courts exercise constitutional jurisdiction and the other in which constitutional courts are separate from the rest of the judiciary – and suggests that the latter model is common in Europe (18 out of 27 states in the European Union have such a model) and also Latin America, Africa and Asia, but not elsewhere. Frank Michelman, of course, asks us to think more critically about whether this pattern of polarization is in fact meaningful, given the instability inherent in any attempt strictly to divide constitutional from ordinary jurisdiction, but certainly also acknowledges the basic existence of such a pattern.

Rick Pildes suggests a bifurcation between old and new constitutions when it comes to the constitutional regulation of political parties (recent constitutions tend to reference political parties, older ones do not), as well as significant variation among more recent constitutions, such as in the degree to which they restrict or prohibit certain kinds of party, and recognize a general constitutional right to party autonomy (Chapter 14). Janet Hiebert and Mark Tushnet also note the increasing competition between two distinct models of constitutional rights protection: one based on judicial supremacy and another based on shared judicial and legislative responsibility for rights protection, or the idea of 'weak-form' judicial review (which, as Mark Tushnet notes, itself has at least three varieties).

In Part IV, in discussing constitutional rights protections, Dennis Davis suggests in the context of second generation rights that, while there are broad similarities among South Africa, India and Brazil in their courts' approach to the implementation of second generation rights (including a general pattern of restraint and commitment to 'fusing' positive and negative rights enforcement), this sub-set of countries remains a distinct minority even among signatories to the International Covenant on Economic, Social and Cultural Rights (ICESCR). (Indeed, one of Davis' key aims is to show how such a model could be extended to other countries, consistent with commitments to democracy and limits on judicial capacity.) Stephen Gardbaum also makes a similar observation, noting that while 'some constitutions contain no or very few positive rights, others include both negative and positive rights and some constitutional courts give positive interpretations to certain seemingly negatively-phrased rights but not others' (Chapter 21). In a similar vein, in Part V, in considering how courts themselves engage comparatively, Cheryl Saunders suggests that courts in common law countries are in fact quite likely to cite foreign law in the course of their opinions, whereas courts in civil law countries are less likely to do so (Chapter 31).

Some authors identify an even more diverse range of constitutional types in the context of constitutions' approach to questions of fundamental structure or rights protection. In Part III, for example, José Cheibub and Fernando Limongi note not only the prevalence of both presidential and parliamentary systems (the category of semi-presidential he regards as less useful), but also argues that both systems can be further sub-divided into those presidential systems that give strong legislative power to the president, versus those that do not (Chapter 12); and parliamentary systems that require formal assembly confidence for the executive to continue in office, versus those that do not. Sujit Choudhry and Nathan Hume likewise suggest in the context of constitutional federalism that, even among federal systems (which are far from the only model in global terms), there is significant variation between 'classical' and 'post-conflict' varieties (Chaper 20); and also between systems designed to address different forms of political conflict, such as those based on race/ethnicity, language and religion.

Ran Hirschl, in discussing the constitutional protection of religion, suggests in Part IV the existence of eight archetypal models governing relations between religion and state – (i) the atheist state; (ii) 'assertive secularism'; (iii) separation as state neutrality toward religion; (iv) weak religious establishment; (v) formal separation with de facto pre-eminence of one denomination; (vi) separation alongside multicultural accommodation; (vii) religious jurisdictional enclaves; and (viii) strong establishment. While he identifies at least one country in which each model is more or less dominant, he also suggests that there is significant cross-country variation in the interpretation of each model, so that there is meaningful constitutional similarity or convergence in this domain among countries only in the 'increasing reliance on constitutional law and courts to contain, tame and limit the spread and impact of religion-induced politics' (Chapter 23).

Vicki C. Jackson and Jamal Greene, in considering comparative approaches to constitutional interpretation in Part V, note at least three distinct approaches to interpretation: a 'historically focused positivist' approach; a 'purposive' approach; and a 'multi-valenced' approach; and suggest that while in the five countries they study (i.e. the US, Canada, Australia, Germany and France) there is 'considerable interpretive overlap' in various courts' approaches; there are also significant differences both 'within courts and their scholarly communities …. [and] across courts' and countries (Chapter 32).

Various authors also provide a number of explanations for these patterns of constitutional similarity and difference. As to patterns of constitutional similarity or convergence, while constitutional scholars have advanced a number of explanations for this (see e.g. Law 2008, Tushnet 2009, Dixon and Posner 2010), the most consistent explanation provided by contributors to the *Handbook* is the increasing influence on domestic constitutional practices of constitutional comparison itself – and also international law. Donald Kommers, for example, suggests that 'comparative constitutional law has come to play a central role in domestic constitutional adjudication', and that this is linked to patterns of legal harmonization or constitutional convergence (Chapter 24). Cheryl Saunders likewise notes the influence of both informal networks for constitutional comparison, such as transnational judicial networks, and the internationalization of constitutional law as 'catalysts' for what is likely an increasing pattern of comparative citation by many constitutional courts (Chapter 31). Ruti Teitel suggests that constitutionalism in societies facing issues of transitional justice has been influenced by 'the growing area of overlap' between constitutional norms and international law, particularly areas in which 'international law has been informed by precepts of international humanitarian law' (Chapter 4). In a less optimistic mode, Kent Roach notes the role of international law in prompting states to converge in their treatment of the assets of suspected terrorists (Chapter 29).

For some authors, the increasing overlap – and also parallel – between transnational and constitutional norms is such that comparative constitutional scholars should increasingly turn their attention toward the transnational domain. Victor Ferreres Comella, for example, suggests that while there are clear differences between transnational tribunals and domestic constitutional courts, the parallels are also sufficiently strong that it would be fruitful to include them in the scope of future comparative constitutional scholarship on constitutional courts. Kent Roach argues that 'the increased impact of the UN on domestic constitutional norms invites constitutional analysis of the UN itself' (Chapter 29). And David Schneiderman argues, in a similar vein, that because international trade law now plays a sufficiently central role in defining the scope of national government power, it too should be included in the scope of an appropriately critically-oriented form of comparative constitutionalism.

Some contributors in fact seem already to have heard this call: in thinking about gender equality and agency, Helen Irving, for example, engages in a fascinating analysis of the potential differences and similarities between federal/state and international/national juris-dictional divisions (Chapter 2). Tom Allen and Nicholas Bamforth also provide a similarly illuminating analysis of the comparative significance of the European Court of Human Rights jurisprudence on the right to property, and right to family life and non-discrimination (Chapters 27 and 30).

At the same time, as various authors show, there are also important limits in many areas on the degree to which international legal norms ultimately exert concrete influence on domestic constitutional norms. In the context of second generation rights, for example, while the ICESCR has been ratified at nearly the same rate as the International Covenant on Civil and Political Rights (with 160 as compared to 166 countries ratifying each covenant), at a constitutional level Dennis Davis notes, 'only first generation rights ... enjoy universal appeal' (Chapter 28). When it comes to the practice of constitutional law by courts and other domestic decision-makers, various authors also provide clear evidence that such a practice need not be convergent (see particularly Stone, Chapter 22).

When it comes to sources of ongoing constitutional difference among countries, contribu-tors to the *Handbook* also provide a number of explanations for such patterns. One factor that several authors point to is the persistence of differences in the background legal system. Victor Ferreres Comella, for example, suggests that, when it comes to the difference between systems with specialized constitutional courts and ordinary courts exercising constitutional jurisdiction, at least one logical explanation is the difference in training of judges in ordinary courts in the common law and civil law world, which makes the former better situated to exer-cising constitutional jurisdiction (Chapter 15). Tom Allen also notes the common law/civil-ian distinction as a central factor relevant to explaining differences in countries' approach to regulatory takings (Chapter 27). Cheryl Saunders makes a similar argument in connection with courts' approach to comparative constitutional materials, suggesting that differences in the reasoning style of courts in the two systems may also help explain differences in their approach to foreign law (Chapter 31).

A related factor, which several authors highlight, is the way in which the system of consti-tutional review is structured. Differences in how courts are structured and appointed seem an obvious explanation for ongoing polarization at a substantive or interpretive level (see e.g. Stone, Chapter 22; Saunders, Chapter 31). And even differences in the way in which consti-tutional opinions are structured may help explain differences at the level of interpretation, given clear differences in different countries' traditions in this regard. Vicki C. Jackson and Jamal Greene, for example, note that in Australia the High Court's seriatim opinion practice seems to contribute to it adopting a multi-valenced approach to constitutional interpretation (Chapter 32); whereas in France, the Conseil Constitutionnel's tradition of writing short, unanimous opinions seems to contribute to its more formalist, positivistic approach.

Conversely, as Frank Michelman notes, choices regarding judicial institutional arrange-ments may themselves also be influenced by parallel or prior substantive constitutional choices. For example, the broader the application of constitutional norms, the less sense it makes for a constitutional system to adopt a system of 'strict concentration and specialization of constitutional review powers' (Michelman, Chapter 16); whereas the narrower their scope, the more feasible it is for a country to create a stable system of either concentrated or specialized judicial review.

A quite different set of factors are cultural and historical, rather than institutional in nature. As authors such as Adrienne Stone, Ran Hirschl and Vicki Jackson and Jamal Greene note, history and past experience cast a long shadow over a constitution's text, as well as its subsequent interpretation. Cultural factors also play a central role in a constitution's drafting and how it is thereafter interpreted (see e.g. Stone; O'Regan and Friedman; and Kommers). Cultural understandings about the nature of the state and indeed even the constitution itself may also be important in this context. For example, as Donald Kommers notes, how a culture understands the nature of its own democratic commitments (e.g. as communal, social or liberal) may be an important factor influencing how it approaches the constitutional regulation of abortion (Chapter 24). The more particularistic a nation's constitution is understood to be by its citizens, the less support there will also tend to be, as Cheryl Saunders notes, for the kind of comparative and international engagement that can often lead to constitutional similarity (Saunders, Chapter 31).

In some areas, as Adrienne Stone argues in her chapter on freedom of expression, the 'sheer complexity' of constitutional law – and the commitments of members of the constitutional culture (see Post 2003) – also help explain constitutional heterogeneity (Stone, Chapter 22). An allegiance to multiple different constitutional values creates scope for significant disagreement on how to resolve constitutional questions even within countries, and across countries, the scope for such disagreement will be even larger (see Stone, Chapter 22; Dixon 2008).

Time is also an important factor in explaining constitutional differences in many areas. As Tom Ginsburg notes in his chapter in the *Handbook*, as well as elsewhere (see Elkins et al. 2010), constitutions have tended to have very different rates of endurance, so that even in mature democracies, there is significant variation in the time at which national constitutions were adopted. The time at which a constitution is adopted is an important predictor of many key formal features of a constitution (see e.g. Elkins et al. 2010). As Rick Pildes notes in Chapter 14 in the *Handbook*, this may reflect learning or 'transformations over time in the understanding of what the practice of democracy means in large societies', but also potentially the force of peer pressure or mere imitation on the part of constitutional drafters.

4   CONCLUSION: A MATURING FIELD OF INQUIRY

As the variety of these contributions helps demonstrate, comparative constitutional law is a rapidly maturing field. Yet as Venter (2000: 19) and other thoughtful observers have noted, the field is hardly complete. There are still numerous areas of constitutional law in which there is little truly comparative scholarship; and many areas in which, while there is a growing comparative literature, there is relatively little critical engagement among comparative scholars of the kind we generally associate with domestic constitutional scholarship, particularly in the US.

To some degree, this has constrained us in compiling the *Handbook*, so that there are some areas – such as the relationship between constitutions and the environment – in which there are obvious gaps in the *Handbook*'s coverage, even beyond those dictated by the constraints of space. In other respects, it has motivated us to use the *Handbook* as a means of challenging the current boundaries of the field.

One way in which we have done this is to invite several contributors to address topics that, more than in many volumes of this kind, overlap to some real degree. This is evident in the chapters by Janet Hiebert and Mark Tushnet (on alternatives to court-centered forms of constitutionalism); Victor Comella and Frank Michelman (on the idea of a court with specialized constitutional jurisdiction); Stephen Gardbaum and Dennis Davis (on the notion of state action and positive rights); and Oren Gross and Kent Roach (on constitutional emergencies and responses to terrorism). By encouraging this form of overlap among these authors with their diverse perspectives, we have hoped to show the possibilities for the future deepening, as well as broadening, of the current scope of the field.

By reading the *Handbook*, however, we also hope that comparative constitutional scholars will be encouraged to address gaps at both these levels. With this in mind we conclude with some suggestions for where the field might go in the future.

We certainly need a broader empirical base. It is probably the case that 90% of comparative work in the English language covers the same ten countries, for which materials are easily accessible in English. Some 'globalized' constitutional courts have made a special effort to have their decisions translated – South Korea is a good example here. But the field needs many more studies of the operation of constitutions and constitutional law in less well-studied contexts, including non-democracies (Barros 2002). A good example, as Kent Roach notes in his chapter, is the current gap in comparative constitutional scholarship on anti-terrorism law in the Arab world (Chapter 29). Indeed, work of this kind might help to inform broader theorizing on the nature of constitutions in general.

It is also the case that much of the work to date has focused heavily, and quite naturally, on constitutional courts. Valuable as this work has been in laying the groundwork, not much of it has examined how constitutions actually function in a systematic way. There are many other constitutional institutions that use and make law: human rights commissions, corruption commissions, trial judges, ombudsmen, and legislatures, to name only a few. Legal actors outside the courtroom – such as non-governmental organizations, religious groups, police, prosecutors – all have internalized constitutional understandings. These other sites of constitutional legal practice have not been subject to many comparative studies, though surely they ought to be.

We also could use work with more methodological variety. Some scholarship has started to apply large-sample approaches to constitutional law, and case analysis remains the method of choice. But we surely could learn a good deal from constitutional law by utilizing other social science methods, including experiments and surveys (Law 2010). Studies of particular courts and other constitutional institutions can also draw on ethnographic methods which emphasize particular internal understandings over generalization (Scheppele 2004). Pluralistic social science, in other words, can enrich the field even more than it already has, both to inform doctrinal scholarship and to engage in fruitful inquiry for its own sake.

We close with an expression of optimism. It is an exciting time for the field of comparative constitutional law, and we hope that the chapters here convey some of the energy being brought to bear by scholars around the world. We are confident, and heartened, by the knowledge that the contents of this volume only begin to scratch the surface of what the field will look like in the future.

REFERENCES

Barros, Robert (2002), *Constitutionalism and Dictatorship*, New York: Cambridge University Press.

Baun, Michael and Daniel Franklin (1995), *Political Culture and Constitutionalism: A Comparative Approach*, Boston: M.E. Sharpe.

Boralevi, Lea Campos (2002), 'Classical Foundational Myths of European Republicanism: The Jewish Commonwealth', in Martin van Gelderen and Quentin Skinner (eds), *Republicanism: A Shared European Heritage*, New York: Cambridge University Press, pp. 247–61.

Brennan, Geoffrey and Jose Casas Pardo (1991), 'A Reading of the Spanish Constitution (1978)', *Constitutional Political Economy*, 2 (1): 53–79.

Buchanan, James and Gordon Tullock (1961), *The Calculus of Consent*, Ann Arbor: University of Michigan Press.

Bussani, Mauro and Ugo Mattei (2002), *The Common Core of European Private Law*, Boston: Kluwer Law International.

Choudhry, Sujit (2008), *Constitutional Design for Divided Societies: Integration or Accommodation?* New York: Oxford University Press.

Clark, David S. (2001), 'Comparative Law in 1900 and Today', *Tulane Law Review* 75: 871–912.

Clayton, Cornell, and Howard Gillman (1998), *Supreme Court Decision-Making: New Institutionalist Approaches*, Chicago: University of Chicago Press.

Dixon, Rosalind (2008), 'A Democratic Theory of Constitutional Comparison', *American Journal of Comparative Law*, 56: 947–97.

Dixon, Rosalind and Eric Posner (2011), 'The Limits of Constitutional Convergence', *Chicago Journal of International Law*, 11: 399–423.

Elkins, Zachary, Tom Ginsburg and James Melton (2010), *The Endurance of National Constitutions*, New York: Cambridge University Press.

Elster, Jon, Claus Offe and Ulrich Preuss (1998), *Institutional Design in Post-communist Societies: Rebuilding the Ship at Sea*, New York: Cambridge University Press.

Fontana, David (2011), 'The Rise and Fall of Comparative Constitutional Law in the Postwar Era', *Yale Journal of International Law*, 36: 1–53.

Ghai, Yash, (ed) (2001), *Autonomy and Ethnicity: Negotiating Competing Claims in Multiethnic States*, New York: Cambridge University Press.

Holmes, Stephen (1995), *Passions and Constraint: On the Theory of Liberal Democracy*, Chicago: University of Chicago Press.

Horowitz, Donald (1991), *A Democratic South Africa? Constitutional Engineering in a Divided Society*, Berkeley, CA: University of California Press.

Kommers, Donald (2002), *The Constitutional Jurisprudence of the Federal Republic of Germany*, 2nd edition, Durham, NC: Duke University Press.

Law, David (2008), 'Globalization and the Future of Constitutional Rights', *Northwestern University Law Review* 102: 1277–349.

Law, David (2010), 'Constitutions', in Peter Cane and Herbert M. Kritzer (eds), *The Oxford Handbook of Empirical Legal Research*, New York: Oxford University Press, pp. 376–98.

Le Roy, Katy and Cheryl Saunders (eds) (2006), *Legislative, Executive and Judicial Governance in Federal Countries*, Montreal: McGill University Press.

Maine, Henry Sumner (1861) [1986], *Ancient Law*, Tucson: University of Arizona Press.

March, James G. and Johan P. Olsen (1989), *Rediscovering Institutions*, New York: Free Press.

Marcos, Miguel González (2003), 'Comparative Law at the Service of Democracy: A Reading of Arosemena's Constitutional Studies of the Latin American Governments', *Boston University Law Review* 21: 259–324.

North, Douglass (1991), *Institutions, Institutional Change and Economic Performance*, New York: Cambridge University Press.

Persson, T. and G. Tabellini (2003), *The Economic Effects of Constitutions*, Cambridge, MA and London: MIT Press.

Post, Robert (2003), 'Foreword: Fashioning the Legal Constitution: Culture, Courts, and Law, *Harvard Law Review* 117: 4–112.

Powell, Walter and Paul DiMaggio (1991), *The New Institutionalism in Organizational Analysis*, Chicago: University of Chicago Press.

Riles, Annelise (2001), *The Network Inside Out*, Ann Arbor: University of Michigan Press.

Scheppele, Kim Lane (2004), 'Constitutional Ethnography: An Introduction', *Law and Society Review* 38(3): 389–406.

Scheppele, Kim Lane (2006), 'The Migration of Anti-Constitutional Ideas: The Post 9/11 Globalization of Public Law and the International State of Emergency', in Sujit Choudhry, ed., *The Migration of Constitutional Ideas*, New York: Cambridge University Press.

Shapiro, Martin (1993), 'Public Law and Judicial Politics', in Ada W. Finifter, ed., *Political Science: The State of the Discipline*, Washington DC: American Political Science Association, pp. 365–91.

Stone, Alec (1992), *The Birth of Judicial Politics in France*, Oxford: Oxford University Press.

Sunstein, Cass (2001), *What Constitutions Do*, New York: Oxford University Press.

Takii, Kazuhiro (2007), *The Meiji Constitution: The Japanese Experience of the West and the Shaping of the Modern State*, Tokyo: International House of Japan.

Tate, Neal and Thorsten Vallinder (1995), *The Global Expansion of Judicial Power*, New York: NYU Press.

Teitel, Ruti (2002), *Transitional Justice*, New York: Oxford University Press.

Tushnet, Mark (2009), 'The Inevitable Globalization of Constitutional Law', *Virginia Journal of International Law* 49: 985–1005.

Venter, Francois (2000), *Constitutional Comparison: Japan, Germany, Canada, and South Africa as Constitutional States*, The Hague: Kluwer Law International.

Voigt, Stefan (1999), 'Implicit Constitutional Change: Changing the Meaning of the Constitution without Changing the Text', *European Journal of Law and Economics*, 7: 197–224.

Volcansek, Mary (1990), 'Decision-making Italian Style', *West European Politics*, 13: 33–45.

PART I

CONSTITUTIONAL DESIGN AND REDESIGN

2. Drafting, design and gender
Helen Irving

1 INTRODUCTION

The literature on constitution-making is substantial but, until recently, gender as an imperative of design has received little attention, and most analyses have been narrowly framed.[1]
Even giving 'constitutional' its broadest compass – extending beyond the legal instrument, to
institutions of governance and relations between the citizen and the state – we rarely find
gender as a factor of which to take account, let alone as a lens through which to view constitutional design broadly.

Even the conceptualisation of what is at stake may be missing. Neither the Forward, nor
any of the thirteen contributions to a 2009 symposium issue of the *Texas Law Review* 'What,
If Anything Do We Know About Constitutional Design?' identifies gender as an issue for
constitutional design or gender equality as a principle informing design choices. None
acknowledges women as a design constituency (although several consider ethnic, religious,
or cultural minorities as subjects requiring dedicated attention).[2] One chapter alone, out of
fifteen, in a 2008 collection on *Constitutional Design for Divided Societies*, acknowledges
gender as a divider (indeed a 'deep fault line' challenging provisions for constitutional equality (Murray and Simeon 2008: 417)). There are many other examples – monographs,
symposia or collections on constitutional design – where gender as a referent is entirely missing, and where women, if acknowledged at all, are only listed as a sub-set in a taxonomy of
design challenges.[3] In the large body of theoretical writings on constitutional identity, legitimacy, and constituent power – all normatively implicated in constitutional design – gender is
almost entirely overlooked.[4]

This history of neglect or under-recognition should not be taken as confirmation of the non-
relevance of gender to constitutional design. Since we know that gender is relevant in other
comparable fields,[5] there is at least an a priori claim for its relevance to constitutional design.
Furthermore, a significant proportion of the literature on constitutional design concerns principles for redressing power asymmetries or accommodating social cleavages; there is no
reason for gender to be missing from this design kit. Additionally, a small number of individual issues have been 'trialled' in actual constitutional design, and stand as instructive exceptions to the general non-recognition of gender. Women's suffrage is the most obvious and –
these days – the least controversial.[6] Gender equality rights, gender electoral quotas and the
protection of reproductive rights are also readily recognisable as constitutional matters, and
have been incorporated into constitutions in a number of countries. Federalism has been
subject to relatively recent gender analysis, although the practical (as opposed to conceptual)
significance is less immediately evident. The impact of international law on national constitutions has also attracted feminist attention, albeit tangentially to design in most cases.

These examples are useful, but they are fragments or components. They serve to illustrate
the gender-constitutional project, but are not the same as principles or concepts. They are the

foot in the door, rather, which, opened, reveals a whole, hitherto unseen, landscape. It is this perspective – the whole-constitution approach – that has only recently begun to emerge. It is a perspective that subjects the totality (more than the sum of its parts), as well as the concept or *idea* of a constitution, to a full gender audit.

Just as we distinguish the parts from the whole, we must distinguish jurisprudence from design. The two are not unrelated; for example, in framing a constitution, questions arise whether to include express provisions governing interpretation[7] or to leave the courts free to develop an interpretive methodology. In most cases, however, jurisprudential issues arise post-framing, and are meta-design issues, concerned with effectiveness, rather than principles.

In the United States, perhaps because of the antiquity of its Constitution and the privileging of the Constitution's facially indeterminate equality rights, the constitutional moment (real or hypothetical), when design choices are to be made, has been neglected. The idea of gender-constitutional analysis has focused primarily on jurisprudential histories and competing theories of interpretation, seeking to evaluate their impact on outcomes in specific cases.[8] This debate is valuable in identifying a number of matters relevant to design (both with respect to principles governing the drafting of a new constitution, and in auditing an already operating constitution): it draws out equality gaps or silences that need to be filled; ways in which gender equality may be carved out of facially neutral provisions; ways in which concrete provisions may be used as normative platforms or vehicles; and lessons in the unintended consequences of design. However, while many design choices are shaped by jurisprudential predictions or intentions, the overlap should not be confused with the totality. Much design work involves the articulation of structures and processes that will never have a jurisprudential outcome, being non-justiciable or even pre-justiciable (the structural design of the constitutional court, for example, cannot be contemplated as a justiciable matter). In thinking about gender and constitutional design, we must contemplate the words before they go into the constitution, with an eye to, but ahead of, the meanings that a constitutional court (which itself must be designed) will draw from the words once they are there.

In contrast to the scholarship, in *real-world* constitution-making, the need to take account of women's interests, or at least to make space for women's voices in processes prior to the framing of a constitution, has been recognised for some time, both directly and indirectly. While this recognition has often been weak, there are hopeful signs that gender may eventually become a routine, even mandatory item on the constitution drafter's check-list. Constitutional theorists have begun to take notice, although they lag behind the practitioners.

2   THE HISTORY

The recognition of gender in constitutional design is historically recent, but is not without precedent. Although individual women made indirect or passing comments on the gendered implications of constitutions as early as the late eighteenth century,[9] women's structured observations on constitutional design date from the second half of the nineteenth century. In the United States, these developments followed the constitutionalisation of race equality after the Civil War. In the 1870s, American women attempted, unsuccessfully, to have the recently ratified Fourteenth Amendment's protection of the 'privileges and immunities of citizens' extended to women's citizenship rights, including the right to vote, and the right to practise a profession (Morais 1987–8). The ratification of the Nineteenth Amendment in 1920, prohibiting sex-based disqualification from voting, was the final outcome of this early campaign. In the 1890s, in the Australian colonies, women formed or used existing organisations in an attempt to influence the drafting of the Australian Constitution and one South Australian woman stood (unsuccessfully) as a candidate for the elected Federal Convention at which the Australian Constitution was written (Irving 1997: 171–95). Australian women conducted a campaign (unsuccessfully) seeking constitutional entrenchment of universal suffrage. The Australian branch of the Woman's Christian Temperance Union, among others, campaigned (successfully this time) for a provision exempting liquor from a constitutional guarantee of free trade and commerce. In America, the constitutional temperance campaign, again significantly supported by women's organisations, went further, achieving the ratification of the Eighteenth Amendment in 1919. The subsequent campaign for the repeal of national prohibition, which succeeded with the Twenty-First Amendment in 1933, also involved organised women's groups (Irving 2008: 77–9).

It is important to recognise that this promotion of specific norms as constitutional subjects, while narrowly focused, was the strategic expression of a wider and enlarging vision of constitutionalism. Women began to compose a new constitutional epistemology. They sought enfranchisement as a claim upon the concept of constitutional citizenship. They sought constitutional protection from the social and personal abuses they attributed to alcohol consumption, and in doing so, articulated their lived experiences as constitutional subjects. Their campaigns represented evolving, sometimes radically new claims on the duties of constitutional government, indeed on the *idea* of a constitution.

In the immediate wake of the Nineteenth Amendment victory, American women began their campaign for an Equal Rights Amendment. Here we see a further shift. Constitutionalism was now to embody a general and abstract equality principle, to serve as a shield against unspecified gender discrimination in future legislation, rather than a repository of specific and targeted protections. The ERA campaign was to run for fifty-nine years after the proposed amendment was first presented to Congress in 1923. Passed by both Houses in 1972, it was abandoned in 1982, when the (extended) deadline for ratification was reached without success. The constitutional protection of American gender equality evolved in other ways. While the Fourteenth Amendment had resisted such claims in the nineteenth century, by the 1970s, it was interpreted to embrace them. The Supreme Court finally extended the 'equal protection of the laws' to gender equality (albeit without subjecting gender classifications to the same level of scrutiny as race) (*Reed v Reed* 404 US 71 (1971)). As an irony of history, it is almost certain that constitutional amendment would not have been required for the achievement of women's suffrage, had this approach been adopted in 1920.

The lesson from this history for constitutional design is that context frames meanings, meanings evolve, and a high level of uncertainty surrounds the application of constitutional provisions over time. This is also a fundamental design dilemma. How, if at all, can a constitutional meaning or effect be secured? Is there a form or 'model' of drafting that will endure without erosion? Even the plainest and bluntest of language is malleable.[10] Different approaches to interpretation are the issue (or the problem), but how can these be controlled or even anticipated in advance? There is no simple answer.

Nevertheless, where constitutional amendment has been unavailable or its pursuit unrealistic, interpretation has been the historical tool of equality campaigners. In Canada, in the 1920s, a group of women – now celebrated as the 'Famous Five' – campaigned for an interpretation of their country's constitution (the British North America Act, 1867) that would permit the appointment of women to the Canadian Senate. The Supreme Court of Canada rejected their claim, but an appeal to the Judicial Committee of the Privy Council in London was successful (*Edwards v Canada (A-G)* [1930] AC 124). (It also gave rise to the celebrated statement that the constitution was a 'living tree capable of growth and expansion', an observation that has especial application to women's experience, in particular in countries with old constitutions, lacking gender equality provisions.)

Gender equality and women's rights were recognised in a number of constitutions in the inter-war period, including in the Soviet Union and Weimar Germany, but it is unlikely that women played a significant part in constitution-framing prior to the Second World War. Gertrude Bell's role in making drafting suggestions to the British authorities in 1920 about a first constitution for Iraq (Lukitz 2006) was extraordinary, but informal. One Burmese woman took part, albeit as a lone representative, at a British Round Table Conference regarding a proposed Burmese constitution in 1931 (Aung and Williams 2009). From the end of the war, the incremental traces of women's involvement expand. Beate Sirota Gordon served as a member of the Civil Rights Committee of the Constituent Assembly that framed the 1946 Japanese Constitution, and as author of its women's rights provision (Gordon 2001). A small number of women (four out of sixty-five) were directly involved in the framing of the West German Basic Law in 1949 (Markovits 2008). Three women were elected, and four appointed, to the Constituent Assembly established by Britain to prepare a constitution for post-war independent Burma (Aung and Williams 2009).

Such examples notwithstanding, a study of constitution-making between 1787 and 1980 in eight different nations, written by or from the perspective of the constitution makers themselves, records no involvement by women. The editors, noting the proliferation of new constitutions in recent times, comment that '[i]n every part of the world ... there are men (but very few, if any women), still active in public life, who have played a significant role in the writing of the constitution of their own country' (Goldwin and Kaufman 1988: vii). The reference to women is not pursued. The authors express no interest in the significance of women's non-involvement, or in whether women's interests were articulated by non-participants or even considered during the process. Scholarly neglect cannot be confused with factual absence or marginality; it is, however, suggestive of both.

In contrast, in the 'third wave' of constitution-making (Lijphart 2002) – the final decades of the twentieth century – organised feminist voices have been repeatedly raised. We know that women campaigned during the framing of the 1982 Canadian Charter of Rights and Freedoms; the 1991 Colombian Constitution; the 1996 South African Constitution; the 1997 Eritrean; the 2003 Rwandan, and the 2005 Iraqi Constitutions, both informally and as members of the drafting bodies (Kome 1983; Morgan and Buitrago 2004; Seidman 1999; Murray 2001; Selassie 2002; Banks 2008; Arato 2009). There are certain to be others. By the latter part of the 1990s, it could be said with reasonable confidence that women's participation and principles of gender equality were no longer unfamiliar considerations in constitution-drafting. The new constitutions of Afghanistan and Iraq, certain African countries, and the former Soviet bloc countries, all incorporate gender equality provisions. In countries such as Kenya and Nepal, where constitution-making is continuing, or Burma, where it is taking place in exile, women are actively campaigning for the constitutional recognition of gender equality and women's rights (Aung and Williams 2009). Even non-state or transnational constitutions have been subjected to gendered analysis. Charlotte Skeet has argued that, among the factors contributing to the 2005 French and Dutch referendum defeats of the proposed constitution for the European Union, the constitution's unresponsiveness to women's interests was significant (Skeet 2007).

Finally, the need for constituent assemblies to include at least some women members has gained recognition. What has brought this about? Among others, the 'new constitutionalism' has played an important part. Emerging in the heady constitutional politics of the 1990s, new constitutionalism emphasises participation, openness, ongoing conversation, and *belonging* in constitution-making (Hirschl 2004). It challenges the 'old' paradigm of constitution-making as a specialist process, an undertaking between elites, leading to contractual finality. Its logic has been extended at least by some, to take in women's participation. Vivien Hart, for example, notes that a '[p]articipatory constitution is by definition inclusive'. For this reason, she writes, women have been able to take advantage of participatory opportunities; they 'bring attitudes and experience highly appropriate to democratic constitution making and … their increasing participation will give impetus and depth to developing practice' (Hart 2003: 10–11; also Dobrowolsky and Hart 2003).

Constitution makers in this same period have been confronted by organised feminist groups or alliances, as well as international pressure, demanding, and sometimes gaining, representation in the process. In response, women's demands for representation have generated questions about the concrete difference their involvement makes, or requires, including in the details of a constitution's design. In short, the long, slow growth of gender equality constitutionalism, pursued by feminist activists in the margins, has reached a point where, if still far from mainstreamed, it has at least become an acceptable, even necessary, item on the design check-list. It still remains for theoretical attention to catch up.[11]

Equality Rights

The fundamental reason for the scholarly neglect of gender in constitutional design is, no doubt, the failure to recognise that the perspective of women is a legitimate consideration, and that women's constitutional interests cannot be assumed to coincide with men's. It is a failure driven by the false universal: the assumption of a single, gender-neutral perspective, and/or the assumption that the male perspective is that of the totality. Feminists, too, have tended to overlook constitutional design, either focusing on constitutional jurisprudence arising from challenges to gender discriminatory laws, or (I speculate) avoiding the concrete and non-negotiable commitments required in constitutional design, in which conflicting feminist visions or priorities may not be reconcilable (this is discussed below).

Paradoxically, the discourse of constitutional equality rights has also played a role in the relative neglect of a wider gendered perspective on constitutional design. The particular constitutional history of the United States and the service of its Constitution as paradigmatic of the modern constitution, have, I suggest, obscured the relevance of other provisions to women's interests and opportunities. The early and ultimately successful campaign for constitutional recognition of racial equality influenced ideas about constitutional equality principles generally, and focused these on equal rights provisions. In short, America's post-Civil War history in which constitutional rights were inserted as a barrier to racially discriminatory classifications in law appears to have influenced feminist thinking generally, skewing the focus towards gender equality rights as priorities for constitutional amendment. The campaign for an Equal Rights Amendment became emblematic, even paradigmatic, of gender constitutional interventions, distracting from questions of constitutional *design*.

Kathleen Sullivan's 'Constitutionalizing Women's Equality' exemplifies this perspective. Sullivan analogises 'the story of constitutionalizing American women's equality' to writing a 'cookbook ... when there's nothing in the kitchen'. She seeks to identify the choices a 'hypothetical set of feminist drafters' would have to make if they were constitutionalizing women's equality from scratch. The choices, she writes, would be:

(1) Between a general provision favouring equality or a specific provision favouring sex equality, (2) between limiting classifications based on sex or protecting the class of women, (3) between reaching only state discrimination or reaching private discrimination as well, (4) between protecting women from discrimination or also guaranteeing affirmative rights to the material preconditions for equality, and (5) between setting forth only judicially enforceable or also broadly aspirational equality norms. (Sullivan 2002: 747)

Sullivan's paper is admirable, for both its recognition of constitutional design as a feminist issue, and its promotion of a framework approach. It is notable, however, that the choices she identifies are simply different iterations of constitutional equality rights. If one were *really* drafting a constitution *from scratch*, these alternatives would assist, but only in a narrow field. Several constitutional provisions, at most, would be implicated. Untouched and unguided would be design choices governing the distribution and limits of constitutional powers, the processes for choosing representatives, the composition and jurisdiction of the constitutional court, and the means of constitutional amendment, among other matters that are, and must be, routinely included in a written constitution. To push the metaphor further, Sullivan overlooks the need for an oven, sink, preparation space, and so on – in short, for the kitchen itself – before there can be any prospect of cooking what the recipe describes.

In a response to Sullivan, Mary Anne Case challenges the claim that the kitchen is empty. Case identifies a history of American jurisprudence which provides a 'toolkit' for imagining a gender egalitarian constitution. Her subjects are both constitutional principles and statutory forms. Among other things, she expresses a preference for 'hortatory asymmetry', where statutory language appears facially neutral in its conferral of rights or protections, making no reference to gender classifications, but having, in reality, particular relevance to women's disadvantage (Case 2002).[12]

Applying Case's argument specifically to constitutional design (noting that Sullivan's concern was an absence of constitutional provisions, rather than an absence of statutory examples subjected to constitutional scrutiny), what hortatory asymmetry leaves us with is formal equality. In a constitution, this may be qualified with a provision allowing for ameliorative or affirmative substantive departures from formal equality,[13] attached to the hope that courts will 'get it', and will see the hortatory purpose behind the constitutional neutrality. But disparate impacts may be submerged or disguised in gender neutral language, as Case also recognises. A better hortatory alternative might thus be 'recalibrated symmetry'; such as found in the South African Constitution which flips the usual gender alternatives, to give us 'she or he'; and 'woman or man', with the latter expressly attached to positions of authority traditionally dominated by men (Murray 2001). But, as with Sullivan's focus on equality rights, Case's is also limited to the internal details of constitutional provisions – in her case, equality language – and fails also to consider constitutional architecture or structures.

In a chapter in Williams (2009a), I attempt to describe the incompleteness of gender equality provisions as well as the drawbacks of privileging equality rights as the key to constitutional (re)-design, building on the work of feminist writers who have reflected on the experience of equality rights in their own countries' constitutions (Irving 2009; also Lucas 2009). Among others, Judy Fudge argues that the adoption of the 1982 Charter of Rights and Freedoms in Canada has had the effect of requiring the actual experience of inequality to be conceptualised in an abstract, legally constrained manner, sidelining an analysis of social conditions and relations of power and forcing 'the feminist discourse about power' to be 'translated into a discourse of rights' (Fudge 1989: 446).

Relations of power and subordination are, I would add, embedded in many (perhaps all) constitutional provisions, and an awareness of this is a key to understanding the limitations in equality rights as well as their epistemologically distorting effect. Of course, Fudge does not warn against transforming a discourse of power into an analysis of rights in order to see it turned into a *constitutional* discourse. Her argument is about conceptual distortion, where real experiences and the language to describe these become juridified. Her analysis also alerts us to the fact that constitutional provisions, however carefully designed, must not act as proxies for other forms of discourse. Constitutional design principles must also comprehend and make space for what is better *un-constitutionalised*.

Some things are best left to the political sphere (some are best left, *tout court*). The choice whether to constitutionalise or legislate is a complex one, driven by many factors, including whether existing constitutional provisions permit or obstruct particular forms of legislation.[14] The implications for design are at once obvious and obscure. From a feminist perspective, it is obvious, even trite, that a constitution should be designed to permit, indeed encourage, equality-conferring or enhancing legislation. The progressive achievement of equality becomes, then, a matter for progressive legislative initiatives. It is also obvious that a constitution that systematically obstructs legislative equality should be amended. But what remains obscure is the extent to which a constitution, itself, resists, permits, or encourages legislated equality. It is obvious that a constitution is not self-executing (something, however, of which those who contemplate constitutional design may sometimes need reminding), but less obvious why different interpretations are drawn by judges from the same provisions, either contemporaneously or over time. For this reason, it is also unclear whether constitutional provisions provide a higher level of certainty or security than legislation. The choice of constitutional language and the level of precision or transparency in the chosen words may be significant. Very skilful drafting may, perhaps, limit departures from original or intended meaning. But even the finest drafting will not resolve whether constitutional rules or standards are most effective in limiting judicial discretion (Case 2002). It will not resolve, either, whether judges should be bound by original meanings in the first place.

Notwithstanding these shortcomings, the constitutional rights paradigm has become so pervasive and unassailable that the entrenchment of a gender equality provision is, effectively, non-negotiable in designing a new constitution. International norms require it, and modern precedents support these norms. No new constitution could realistically be framed without such a provision while convincingly laying claim to gender inclusiveness. What remains important is to understand that (all) other constitutional provisions, including those concerned with structures, are also inflected with gendered meanings and effects.

3 FEDERALISM

Federalism is perhaps the only structural constitutional design choice to have received significant feminist attention. Its relevance to gender requires a multilevel analysis. This lies in jurisdiction, policy, and impact, and is both normative and practical. In my own work, I draw out these dimensions by asking the following questions: might the choice made by the framers of a constitution to allocate certain regulatory subjects to the federal level of governance and grant or leave others to the states/regions incorporate assumptions about masculine and feminine spheres? Are the parallel institutions of governance and the dual distribution of powers in a federal system advantageous or disadvantageous when considered specifically from the perspective of women's needs and interests? What difference, in practice, does it make to women, whether they are subject to national or uniform laws on a particular subject, or whether there are multiple, diverse, and regionally varying laws on the same subject (Irving 2008: 65–89)?

The American case, *United States v Morrison* 529 US 598 (2000), has served as a lens through which to pose such questions and make the conceptual links concrete. The case concerned the US Violence Against Women Act, a provision of which purported to create a federal civil cause of action against gender motivated violence. Lacking any direct constitutional power, Congress had sought to rely on the Constitution's commerce clause, and in doing so, invoked a long line of cases concerning racial equality laws which, albeit without prima facie a commercial character, had been upheld as valid exercises of this power. However, only a few years earlier, the Supreme Court had signalled a winding back of the scope of the commerce clause (*United States v Lopez* 514 US 549 (1995)). The clause, the Court now reasoned, was limited to the regulation of activities substantially affecting or substantially relating to interstate commerce. No matter how much gender motivated violence might be shown to have an indirect impact on commerce, it lacked the requisite character or nexus. The Constitution, said Chief Justice Rehnquist, 'requires a distinction between what is truly national and what is truly local' (*Morrison*, at 599). Had the Court reasoned only about the limits of 'commerce' from a formal or doctrinal perspective, the conclusion would have been jurisprudentially coherent. But it went further, speculating, *ad terrorum*, that to regard gender motivated violence as a federal matter would lead to the conclusion that *all* family law could be federally regulated. It would, in short, unsettle the very (domestic/national) foundations of the Constitution itself.

This reasoning has been described by Judith Resnik as 'categorical federalism', as assuming that certain constitutional subjects are naturally and permanently assigned to the states and others to the nation (Resnik 2001–02). The reasoning suggests that women's interests are categorically 'local', and that their protection from and redress against violence are not matters of national (or interstate) concern. It implies, further, that the sphere of the family is, and remains, a matter only for local or domestic regulation. This conclusion, Catherine MacKinnon points out, is inaccurate with respect to its own history. Cases concerning interracial marriage, alimony laws, and contraceptive use by married couples, she notes, have been successfully argued as federal matters in the past (MacKinnon 2000–01).

From a comparative perspective, it is noteworthy that, in some relevantly comparable federal countries, marriage and divorce, and laws concerning the custody of children, are constitutionally entrenched as federal legislative subjects. There is, in other words, nothing *truly* or inherently local about such matters; indeed, as early as 1901, in a major commentary on the framing of the Australian Constitution, the most 'conspicuous defect' of the United States Constitution was said to be its lack of congressional powers to pass uniform laws 'on subjects of such vital and *national* importance as marriage and divorce' (Quick and Garran 1901: 610; emphasis added).

Notwithstanding these exceptions, the historical tendency in federal constitutions, as Sally Goldfarb notes, has been 'to regard ... legal matters involving women as domestic relations matters' and therefore as matters for state law (Goldfarb 2002–03: 67). The better test for whether a matter is local or national, she concludes, is whether the federal legislature 'has a rational basis for concluding that federal intervention was justified because the problem being addressed lay beyond the capacity of the states to resolve' (Goldfarb 2002–03: 147). In my work, I have called this 'contextual federalism' – comparable to the *subsidiarity* principle – involving an assessment of whether in a federal system at any particular time, specific needs and interests are best addressed nationally or rather, best regulated at a local level (Irving 2008). From the perspective of design, a range of concrete provisions can be found in existing federal constitutions which lend support to the contextual principle. These include, among others: federal spending powers to make conditional grants to the states; federal powers to incorporate international norms into national legislation on subjects over which states alone would otherwise exercise power; and provision for states to confer upon the federal legislature their powers over legislative subjects which, in reality, lie beyond local capacities and/or require a national approach (Irving 2008: 88). Such provisions permit, indeed encourage, a shift or relaxation in the federal-regional distribution of powers in response to emerging national needs or regional imperatives, without permanently recalibrating the federalism itself. A gendered contextual perspective will factor women's interests into an identification of the national needs or regional imperatives.

Federal relations are contoured by the political landscape. Political cooperation may be as significant as constitutional strategy, either complementary or as an alternative, and it may serve as a means for overcoming constitutional limits. For example, cooperative action and the harmonisation of laws and administrative processes between federal and state governments have been employed in Australia in national strategies and federal-state partnerships on domestic violence (Chappell 2001). Reflective of the political character of federal relations, much federalism scholarship is to be found in political science: the collection, *Federalism, Feminism and Multilevel Governance*, which considers 'the impact of state architecture on women's representation, political opportunities, and policy achievements' in a range of federal systems, is an important recent example (Haussman et al. 2010; see also Vickers 1994, Banazak 2003). Cooperative research networks have been established in recent times, bringing together feminist political scientists and constitutional lawyers. Such initiatives will serve to clarify the political choices in constitutional design, as well as ways through which the effectiveness of choices (such as federal over unitary government) may be measured.

How, if at all, do the constitutional boundaries of federalism assist an understanding of international/national jurisdictional distinctions with respect to gender? Might the national/regional taxonomy found in federal systems provide a counterpart for international/national matters? If so, might the latter, like the older federalism model, incorporate assumptions that the masculine sphere is naturally congruent with enlarged (national) powers, while the feminine sphere remains, *analytically*, 'domestic' or regional? These questions are too large to answer here. I make only a few observations. Feminist international lawyers have drawn attention to the fact that those few international norms that have attained 'the elevated status' of *jus cogens* (peremptory norms that, contrary to the core principle of state sovereignty, create universal jurisdiction) 'indicate that what is regarded as fundamental to international society [is] based on men's experiences' (Charlesworth and Chinkin 2000: 19). Some shifts are beginning to occur, however, with the slow but still very incomplete recognition of women's rights as human rights, deserving of international protection (Irving 2008: 228–30).

But does a shift towards the centre, either nationally or internationally, always signal progress with respect to gender equality? Federalism studies suggest that, all else being equal, it is often – although not always – the case that the national context is the more likely repository of progressive policies (national legislatures have money, resources, expertise, and detachment from sub-cultural constraints that regions often lack). But all things are not equal in the world. International norms cannot always be assumed to be progressive with respect to gender equality; international practice is not in all cases best practice. Is there a way in which this understanding may assist constitutional design? Until we are more confident of international 'mainstreaming' of women's participation and of the recognition of women's interests as core, indeed, uncontroversial, factors in the conceptualisation of the *idea* of international law, constitution drafters may be best advised to lean towards flexibility. Rather than entrenching international law in the constitution (as in South Africa) or even giving international law prevalence over national law (Colombia, Serbia), a constitutional *capacity* to incorporate such international law into national law as is compatible with progressive national standards may be the flexible alternative.

To revert to the federalism analogy, 'supremacy' clauses are typically found in federal constitutions; these are designed to resolve clashes between conflicting but valid laws on the same subject passed by both the federal and the state legislature. Usually (although not always) the clause makes the federal law 'supreme'. A constitutional supremacy clause favouring international law would be injudicious, not so much for the 'blank check' fears expressed by the US Supreme Court in *Morrison*, but because the field of international law is too multifarious, even inchoate, for feminists to be confident of its (enduring) progressive potential, and – importantly – because an understanding of women's constitutional citizenship is insufficiently developed (and, as in national legislatures, women remain seriously underrepresented in international law-making bodies) for feminists, in my view, to want to let go of the national struggle for recognition.

4   GENDER QUOTAS

The structure of a country's legislature, the rules governing candidature and the processes of election are constitutional matters, both in the broad sense and specifically with respect to constitutional design. These matters have attracted significant feminist attention and scholarship in recent years, again much of it in political science. The underrepresentation of women in the vast majority of national legislatures in the world is well-known and well-documented.[15] From a design perspective, the data generate a range of questions about electoral systems, candidature rules, and political party practices, as well as about legislature culture. Gender electoral or legislative quotas have received the greatest attention.

It is well-established that quotas, where these are not defeated by the electoral system, are successful in increasing the raw numbers of women representatives in a country's legislature. But the design choices are numerous and not simple: should quotas be constitutionally entrenched or only statutory? Should there be candidate selection quotas directed at political parties and/or placement mandates governing the order in which women candidates are listed on ballot papers? Should these be aspirational, directive or mandatory? Should reserved seats be specifically allocated to women in the legislature? Should quotas be permanent or transitional? Is the relevant country's electoral system congruent with the design of its gender quotas, and the goals they embody? Can quotas – a form of positive discrimination – surmount constitutional provisions mandating equality generally or prohibiting discrimination?

Drude Dahlrup and Lenita Freidenvall, leading scholars of electoral gender quotas, have examined the introduction of quotas in new or amended constitutions. The constitutional design strategy, they conclude, cannot be isolated from the political process; it depends upon, among other things, the strength of the women's movement, and 'the good faith compliance by political parties' in the relevant country (Dahlrup and Freidenvall 2009: 52). Other feminist writers conclude that, notwithstanding the deeply and multiply controversial character of quotas, the substantive equality for which they aim (and the accompanying democratic ideals they capture) make gender quotas an imperative of feminist constitutional design. Noelle Lenoir treats quotas (as found in the French Constitution) as institutional and structural forms of democracy, comparable to the right to vote and the separation of powers. They are, she writes, 'an operational mechanism' and 'only a minor departure from the principle of universal suffrage' (Lenoir 2001: 219). Susan Williams identifies substantive equality and deliberative democracy as joint principles underlying the need for gender quotas (Williams 2009b). No general conclusions can be reached, however, on whether quotas should be constitutionalised, statutory or merely voluntary. They remain, nevertheless, a non-waivable item for consideration on the constitutional design agenda.

5 REPRODUCTIVE RIGHTS

In many countries, constitutional provisions governing reproductive rights, whether expressly (as in Ireland: Whitty 1993), or by direct implication arising from a 'right to life' provision (as in Costa Rica: Facio et al. 2004) have generated some of the fiercest national political controversies. Constitutional jurisprudence on abortion laws has stirred deep and intractable political conflict. In the United States, since the landmark *Roe v Wade* judgment (410 US 113 (1973)) in which an implied constitutional right to privacy was held to protect a woman's choice to terminate her early-term pregnancy, the issue of reproductive rights has been central to ideas surrounding gender egalitarian constitutional design.

However, in some countries the constitution has little direct relevance to abortion law. In Australia, for example, reproductive rights are not regarded as a constitutional matter. Abortion is regulated at the state level, even though the Constitution includes a provision conferring federal legislative power over medical services, creating at least the potential for indirect constitutionalization of abortion law. There is no evidence that this failure to take the constitutional opportunity means women's reproductive autonomy is more adversely affected there than in countries where constitutional protection extends to abortion rights. Constitutional provisions do not necessarily lead either to protection or to deep political conflict. In India, where the Constitution includes a broad rights framework, and where the Supreme Court, drawing on United States jurisprudence, has identified a right to privacy (in Article 21, which protects 'life and liberty'), '[a]bortion rights have not figured in recent constitutional cases, because abortion is legal and generally uncontroversial' (Nussbaum 2004: 197). In Germany, where even early-term unrestricted abortion has been ruled unconstitutional (as a breach of Articles 1.1 and 2 of the Basic Law, which protect human dignity, right to free development of the person, and right to life, physical integrity and freedom), compromise regulations have governed circumstances where abortions are permitted and have not resulted in a worse outcome for women's choice than in the United States post-*Roe* (Case 2009). A similar outcome has occurred in Israel, which lacks a written constitution but has partly entrenched Basic Laws (extending, among others, to the protection of human dignity and liberty). Abortion, although decriminalized, is surrounded by legal requirements for counselling and prior medical approval. While subjecting women to 'often-intrusive' pre-termination procedures, Ran Hirschl and Ayelet Shachar write, access to a safe, publicly funded abortion is nevertheless guaranteed in Israel. The abortion debate is not highly divisive, and the 'pragmatic arrangement has mitigated much of the intense emotion' that is often found in other countries (Hirschl and Shachar 2004: 218-19).

What, if anything, do these examples tell us with respect to questions of design? Hirschl and Shachar conclude that there are 'general lessons': 'Constitutional rights are never interpreted or implemented in a political or ideological vacuum'; national courts are unlikely 'long [to] hold to norms of justice that are substantially at odds with the surrounding political environment, and the social and economic contexts within which these courts operate' (Hirschl and Shachar 2004: 228).[16] However, despite the 'modest capacity' of constitutions to effect social change, the constitutionalization of formal equality, bodily integrity, and privacy has the potential 'to initiate a real advancement of women's rights' providing these are expressed 'negatively', as freedoms from interference. In contrast, positive constitutional rights – those that mandate progressive steps and require access to 'power, influence, and status' – are much less effective. This inadequacy, they suggest, arises from the fact that positive rights 'often demand[...] that established beneficiaries relinquish their historical advantage', and the courts' 'capacity to promote progressive notions of social justice' is limited (Hirschl and Shachar 2004: 228–9). In addition, I suggest, positive rights are inherently less suited to constitutional protection; the courts' limited capacity arises not only because courts are influenced by the prevailing distribution of power, social standards and norms (and judges are, themselves, members of society), but also because positive rights have resource implications, greater than or unlike those implicated in protecting persons from governmental interference. Courts do not control the resources, public administration or personnel needed to put programs into effect.[17]

Should reproductive rights be expressly protected in a constitution which aims for gender equality? No firm conclusion can be drawn to guide the constitution drafter. Deeply embedded religious values (the United States, Ireland) or histories of shame and oppression (Germany, South Africa) in which the protection of life is implicated, may make a constitutional response unavoidable. Where the conflict between existential norms (current or diachronic) is extreme, settlement at the constitutional level may be the only way of producing a reconciliation of sorts, by appearing to place the question beyond negotiable politics. On the other hand, it may produce the opposite effect, serving to heighten conflict, raising the stakes and rendering a pragmatic response difficult, if not impossible. In the abstract, leaving abortion to the vicissitudes of ordinary politics appears a dangerous strategy for women's reproductive autonomy. In practice, although the picture is far from conclusive, the flexibility permitted by non- or de-constitutionalised legal responses may serve this goal better. Weaving a path through these alternatives, perhaps the best the constitution designer can do – in addition to tailoring the constitution's provisions to the cultural and political temper of the country (albeit without surrendering to its gender oppressive aspects) – is seek to ensure that the constitution does not *obstruct* women's reproductive autonomy. So, for example, a constitutional 'right to life', if included, should be qualified, as in the South African Constitution which also protects the right to 'bodily and psychological integrity which includes the right ... to make decisions concerning reproduction'.

Abortion may dominate, but it is far from the only issue for constitutional design regarding reproductive rights. Reproductive health extends to and requires, among others, provision for affordable and effective ante- and post-natal health services. Reproductive rights claims extend to access to fertility services, including assisted reproductive technologies (Coleman 2002), as well as to contraception. Balancing the protection of pregnant women, the autonomy and liberty of all women, and the protection of the unborn child, remains one of the hardest and most conflicted tasks facing constitution framers once a decision is taken to treat these as constitutional questions.

In these fields, the relationship between formal and substantive equality, universal and targeted protections, and positive and negative rights will be deeply implicated in design choices: for example, prohibitions on discriminatory gender classifications must extend to pregnancy discrimination, and must also accommodate 'discriminatory' exceptions with respect to pregnancy and reproductive health; positive obligations to protect women's reproductive health must be balanced against individual privacy or liberty. The twelve jurisdictions surveyed in Baines and Rubio-Marin (2004) provide many examples, both cautionary and helpful, of different approaches to these imperatives.

6 WHOLE-CONSTITUTION APPROACHES

In addition to the literature on the specific design issues discussed above, a smaller body of literature engages with constitutional design and gender in the whole, or indeed in the *idea* of a constitution. The literature can be divided into several (overlapping) approaches: those that attempt to identify and consider all the relevant fields requiring constitutional provisions; those that approach the question indirectly by addressing a range of constitutional questions and/or surveying the approaches in different jurisdictions; and those that create overarching conceptual or normative frameworks for constitutional deliberation and auditing.

My own *Gender and the Constitution*, while based on a conceptual principle I call 'constitutional opportunity structures', is an example of the first.[18] I take apart the fields and elements of a 'typical' modern constitution, and subject these to a feminist analysis. I trawl through existing constitutions for examples of provisions that have proven either to support or obstruct gender equity and agency in the relevant field. I attempt to construct, in this manner, the 'lenses' or prisms for a complete gender constitutional audit. These identify constitutional provisions governing the choice of language; methodologies of interpretation; federalism; the acquisition, transmission and retention of citizenship; access to and participation in the legislature and government; participation on or before the country's constitutional court; equality and reproductive rights; the recognition (or non-recognition) of international and customary law; and methods of constitutional amendment and compliance.

For the second approach – the accumulation of information and perspectives, both normative and jurisdictional – the edited works of Dobrowolsky and Hart (2003), Baines and Rubio-Marin (2004), and Williams (2009) have been noted. Such works are invaluable in providing comparative perspectives and examples, as well as encouragement, warnings, and transnational 'conversations'. But without more, they do not – at least not directly – assist with trans- or extra-national normative choices, nor do they guide the constitution maker. Introducing their collection, Baines and Rubio-Marin seek thus to draw the matrix of comparative jurisprudence into a feminist constitutional 'agenda'. This, they write, should address '(i) constitutional agency, (ii) constitutional rights, (iii) constitutionally structured diversity, (iv) constitutional equality, with special attention to (v) reproductive rights and sexual autonomy, (vi) women's rights within the family, and (vii) women's socioeconomic development and democratic rights' (Baines and Rubio-Marin 2004: 4). The importance of approaches to interpretation and 'constitutional hermeneutics', they note, should also be recognised. Equality rights remain the primary focus of this agenda but are, nevertheless, supplemented by other agenda items. It is not quite a check-list, but remains an invaluable guide to reading existing constitutions with a feminist eye.

The third approach is conceptually more abstract and challenging. Its application to real-world design choices is less evident (because not only does the overarching analysis bypass the multiple, small design choices that must be made – what, for example, are the gender impacting consequences of setting a particular retirement age for justices of the constitutional court? – it also directs feminist attention to deep constitutional foundations that, for reasons of history and *real politique*, are almost never up for grabs). Paula Monopoli's 'Gender and Constitutional Design' (2006) is, thus, unusually courageous in considering whole models of governance. Monopoli compares presidential and parliamentary systems, with respect to their tendency to favour or obstruct the accession of women to executive office. This is not so much a quantitative test of executive snakes and ladders as an analysis of the forms of authority and agency, and of the epistemological effect embedded in these alternative models. A presidential executive, Monopoli concludes, is built on models of masculine authority, and is 'least likely to result in women's ascending to executive office'. In contrast, the parliamentary executive model is more communal; more likely to attract and facilitate the ascension of women. While limited in its application to design, this form of analysis helps frame an understanding of internal processes and discourses of power, as well as the alternative forms that might be pursued where constitutional choices are not available.

More recently, Vicki Jackson has adopted a wider framework perspective, lengthening the focal distance, and applying Katherine Bartlett's 'woman question'[19] to the (very) idea of a constitution (Jackson 2009). The multiple questions this generates, concerning participation, rights, discrimination, protection and governance, Jackson writes, fall into three issues: entrenchment, jurisdiction, and interpretation. Entrenchment is 'part of the idea of a constitution'; whether an entrenched or a non-entrenched, legislative 'constitution' is preferable with respect to women's equality, demands attention. Jurisdictional issues – whether constitutional power should be allocated federally, and related choices about hierarchy, exclusivity and concurrence of constitutional legislative powers, as well as the part played by the jurisdiction of the international community – also generate feminist choices. So, too, do alternative methodologies of interpretation. Asking the 'woman question' across these conceptual areas, Jackson concludes, will produce 'real pay off'.

In the end, despite the commitment to an overarching perspective, the pay off is illustrated by sub-constitutional examples, specific national responses, cultural particularities and 'multiple sources of law'; in other words, by examples of practice, rather than principles of design. These examples will prove helpful as a menu from which the constitution designer may select. But a reluctance to universalise the interests of women in order to find common standards or forms for their constitutional protection ultimately pervades this framework. Notwithstanding Jackson's invocation of Iris Marion Young's conceptualisation of women as a 'series' (like persons in a queue or line waiting for a bus, sharing particular interests rather than essential or immutable commonalities), there is an underlying anxiety in this over-arching approach about normative imperialism or insensitivity to otherness. Questions are posed, examples are identified, but the analysis stops short of asserting a relevant principle of design or policy. This, I suggest, paradoxically shifts the design project from the practical to the conceptual; it is akin to concluding that the foundational elements of architectural design cannot be applied to the building of whole houses in specific instances, but can only subsist as concepts for the builders to contemplate.

7   THE COMPARATIVIST DILEMMA

A multiplicity of cultural or national forms (and norms) confronts any project of constitu-tional design. Even where the elements or choices are classified and given trans-cultural and translatable names, the risk lies of concluding that no overarching principles can be identified and no foreign examples followed, either in one's own country or in application to others. But, I suggest, common or overlapping principles can be recognised. For constitutional design with respect to gender equality to be meaningful, and for design lessons to be learned and transmitted, the 'family resemblance' needs to be identified, both between constitutional forms, and among women as constitutional subjects (unlike the bus queue, women are not 'dispersed' once the bus arrives). The common or underlying principles need not be complex or multiple. Like all principles of (good) design, they need only capture the core or key elements that create a reliable bridge between interests and the institutions or processes that serve them.

The current literature is not yet sufficiently developed to give us a full 'design manifest' for constitutionalizing gender equality, in part because of the incompleteness of attention to relevant design fields, and also because of the relatively early stage we have reached in observing practice. The scene is, however, far more advanced than even five years ago. Ultimately, as with the now virtually routine recognition of cultural pluralism and attention to design alternatives for giving voice to sub-national cultural communities, the recognition of gender as an element in constitutional design should become a standard part of any constitution-making, or amending, process. Before this is possible, however, feminists will need to bite the bullet and be prepared to go beyond merely posing questions and identifying concepts. They will need to surmount the fear of stereotyping that obscures genuine common-alities.

8   CONCLUSION

The fact that there are many alternative (and sometimes irreconcilable) forms of feminism makes the task of gender egalitarian constitutional design (and even the statement of 'equality' as the goal) extremely difficult, not only – although particularly – where constitutional compar-isons are implicated in national design projects. It is easy to be defeated by the recognition that feminism is a project with multiple forms; by the knowledge that constitutional forms must be shaped to social and cultural contexts; and by arguments against constitutional 'imperialism' (for example, Tully 2007). But the reality is that real-world constitution-making demands real design choices. Words must be put on paper. Constitutional expertise, however culturally inflected and however incomplete, is often sought by those entrusted with the task of writing a constitution 'from scratch'. If gender equality is on the drafters' agenda (as it should be), choices will have to be made and assistance, where sought, provided.

In considering how alternative, and in particular, new, feminisms may be put to the service of gender justice, Rosalind Dixon dismisses the 'strategic essentialism' of older feminisms (in which emphasis is placed on shared feminist concerns, and differences sidelined) as incapable of 'captur[ing] the full range of insights offered by newer feminisms' (Dixon 2008: 305). As an alternative, she identifies three feminist understandings she labels 'disruptive', 'ameliorative', and 'transformative'. These understandings, Dixon writes, connect liberal and newer feminisms, providing a lens through which the approaches or benchmarks of different feminisms may be articulated.

This schema is valuable in conceptual design-work, providing alternative framings or lines-of-sight through which different conceptions of justice may be attached to goals and aspirations. It offers an agnostic toolkit, available not only to different feminisms but also to different national or historical contexts. On the ground, however, while some eclecticism may be viable, ultimately the constitutional parts must fit together; the design must be coherent. Strategic essentialism serves constitutional coherence, but it may also, as Dixon suggests, be blind (or 'tuned out') to the richness offered by new feminisms. As an alternative, an approach one might call 'contextual universalism' works to identify contextual limitations (historical/national/cultural) as well as opportunities for overcoming tractable gender disadvantage in different sites. Principles of constitutional design arise from the attempt to 'marry justice with power', and are 'a way of looking at the world and ... a method of thinking that proceeds from that perspective' (Lutz 2006: 183). Contextual universalism finds feminist commonalities less in the positive claims made by feminist theory than in their identification of different forms of gendered disadvantage. It is conscious of the particularities of gendered cultures, but it does not compromise on the recognition of the *universal* experience of women's subordination or the commitment to its elimination. This is, after all, what feminism is about, and the purpose to which gender egalitarian constitutional design must surely be directed.

NOTES

1. The existing literature focuses almost exclusively on constitutional design and women, treating 'gender' effectively as coterminous with 'women'. John Kang (2009) offers a rare, alternative perspective, applying the concept of 'manliness' to the United States Constitution.
2. (2009) 87 *Texas Law Review* 1265. The absence of any mention of women in the contribution on Iraq's post-Saddam Constitution is particularly striking: Feisal Amin Rasoul al-Istrabadi, 'A Constitution Without Constitutionalism: Reflections on Iraq's Failed Constitutional Process' (cf Arato (2009: 167), which includes a brief but valuable discussion of Iraqi women's constitutional campaigns). The complete absence of women contributors to the Symposium also cannot go without notice. The answer to the Symposium title's question must surely be: *not enough*.
3. While five out of fifteen articles in a 2008 symposium issue of the *William and Mary Law Review* on 'Constitution Drafting in Post-Conflict States' make mention of women, one only – Angela M. Banks, 'Expanding Participation in Constitution Making' – considers the incorporation of women's interest in the

framing of a constitution: (2008) 49 *William & Mary Law Review* 1043. Five out of thirteen contributors to *The Architecture of Democracy: Constitutional Design, Conflict Management, and Democracy*, ed. Andrew Reynolds (2002) mention women, including two, with regard to the processes of constitution-making; however, none of the chapters specifically on constitutional design identifies gender (or women) as referents.

4. See Rosenfeld (1994); Rosenfeld (2010); Loughlin and Walker (2008), among many others. One of the leading legitimacy theorists, Frank Michelman (2003), structures an analysis of constitutional 'respect-worthiness' around the perspective of a 'non-official personage' he calls *Ida*. There is no recognition, however, that her female identity is itself contemplated in 'the moral merit of the [constitutional] system' or the 'normative patterns and principles' Michelman ascribes to her. Michel Rosenfeld's (2010) exploration of constitutional identity briefly considers gender, via a discussion of Carole Pateman's (1988) influential work on the gendered nature of social contract theory. However, his analysis goes no further than an acknowledgement of the historical denial of political rights to women; his exploration of the 'multiple identities' of the constitutional subject lacks recognition of gender, and remains untroubled by this history.

5. As recognised in the large body of political science literature on electoral systems, campaigns and outcomes: for example, Norris (2001); Carroll and Fox (eds) (2005).

6. While gender equality in suffrage laws was achieved in all 'western' countries by the final decades of the twentieth century, questions remain about constitutional design choices implicated in its protection. For example, in Irving (2008), I raise the gendered implications of constitutionalising a guarantee specifically of *citizens'* suffrage.

7. As in the South African Constitution, sections 39(1), 39(2) and 233.

8. For example, despite the 'design' reference in his title, Sunstein's (2001) discussion of gender (Ch. 9: 'Sex Equality versus Religion') is devoted exclusively to discussing the constitutional validity of laws restricting and/or protecting competing equality or liberty claims.

9. Including Olympe de Gouges, *Declaration of the Rights of Woman and the Female Citizen*, 1791; Mary Wollstonecraft, *A Vindication of the Rights of Woman*, 1792.

10. For example, the US Constitution's Fourteenth Amendment states: 'All persons born ... in the United States ... are citizens of the United States...'. The apparently unequivocal language did not prevent the passage and operation of laws in the early decades of the twentieth century stripping citizenship from American-born women who married non-citizens.

11. For example, Donald Lutz's otherwise wide-ranging *Principles of Constitutional Design* (2006) makes no mention of women's interests or campaigns, current or historical.

12. For example, Case notes, in the statutory language of the provision purporting to create a federal civil cause of action for gender-motivated violence in the Violence Against Women Act challenged in *United States v Morrison*. The provision offered remedies to victims regardless of sex, but, it shaped its 'non-sex-respecting rules around problems presently facing many more women than men' (Case 2002: 779).

13. Such as found in section 15 of the Canadian Charter of Rights and Freedoms (1982).

14. It is notable that although constitutional amendment was necessary (or considered necessary) in the United States in order for women to acquire federal voting rights in 1920, female suffrage was achieved by legislation before or around that time in several comparable countries (including Australia and Canada which had written federal Constitutions, but – paradoxically – lacked bills of rights).

15. The Interparliamentary Union keeps a continuously current record: http://www.ipu.org/wmn-e/world.htm.

16. Hirschl and Shacnar refer here to Robert Dahl's 'Decision-Making in a Democracy: The Supreme Court as a National Policy-Maker' (1957) 6 *Journal of Public Law* 279.

17. The much-cited example of the South African Constitution's provision for socio-economic rights is telling; section 26 of the Bill of Rights requires the state to take 'reasonable legislative and other measures, within its available resources, to achieve the progressive realisation' of a range of such rights, including health, housing, and education. The provision acknowledges that governments control resources; as the celebrated *Grootboom* case (*Government of the Republic of South Africa & Ors v Grootboom & Ors* 2000 CCT/11) illustrated, it amounts in practice to an injunction against extreme neglect, rather than a command positively to provide general services.

18. 'Constitutional opportunity structures' – a term I have adapted from political science – are defined as 'rules, institutions, processes, and structures that may ... support or generate expectations [and] ... provide either openings or obstacles to participation or membership in the constitutional community' (Irving 2008: 32).

19. Jackson refers to Katherine T. Bartlett, 'Feminist Legal Methods' (1990) *Harvard Law Review* 103: 829.

REFERENCES

Arato, Andrew (2009), *Constitution-making under Occupation: The Politics of Imposed Revolution in Iraq*, Columbia University Press.

Aung, Thin Thin and Williams, Susan H. (2009), 'Women in the Constitutional Drafting Process in Burma', in Susan Williams (ed.), *Constituting Equality: Gender Equality and Comparative Constitutional Law*, Cambridge University Press.

Bains, Beverley and Rubio-Marin, Ruth (eds) (2004), *The Gender of Constitutional Jurisprudence*, Cambridge University Press.

Banazak, Lee Ann (2003), 'The Women's Movement and the Constraints of State Reconfiguration', in Lee Ann Banazak, Karen Beckwith and Dieter Rucht (eds), *Women's Movements Facing a Reconfigured State*, Cambridge University Press.

Banks, Angela M. (2008), 'Expanding Participation in Constitution Making: Challenges and Opportunities', *William & Mary Law Review* 49: 1043.

Carroll, Susan J. and Fox, Richard L. (eds) (2005), *Gender and Elections: Shaping the Future of American Politics*, Cambridge University Press.

Case, Mary Anne (2002), 'Reflections on Constitutionalizing Women's Equality', *California Law Review* 90: 765.

Case, Mary Anne (2009), 'Perfectionism and Fundamentalism in the Application of the German Abortion Laws,' in Susan Williams (ed.), *Constituting Equality: Gender Equality and Comparative Constitutional Law*, Cambridge University Press.

Chappell, Louise (2001), 'Federalism and Social Policy: The Case of Domestic Violence', *Australian Journal of Public Administration* 60: 59.

Charlesworth, Hilary and Chinkin, Christine (2000), *The Boundaries of International Law: A Feminist Analysis*, Manchester University Press.

Coleman, Carl H. (2002), 'Assisted Reproductive Technologies and the Constitution', *Fordham Urban Law Journal* 30: 57.

Dahlrup, Drude and Freidenvall, Lenita (2009), 'Gender Quotas in Politics – A Constitutional Challenge', in Susan Williams (ed.), *Constituting Equality: Gender Equality and Comparative Constitutional Law*, Cambridge University Press.

Dixon, Rosalind (2008), 'Feminist Disagreement (Comparatively) Recast', *Harvard Journal of Law and Gender* 31: 277.

Dobrowolsky, Alexandra and Hart, Vivien (eds) (2003), *Women Making Constitutions: New Politics and Comparative Perspectives*, Palgrave Macmillan.

Facio, Alda, Sandova, Rodrigo Jimenez and Morgan, Martha I. (2004), 'Gender Equality and International Human Rights in Costa Rican Constitutional Jurisprudence', in Beverley Baines and Ruth Rubio-Marin (eds), *The Gender of Constitutional Jurisprudence*, Cambridge University Press.

Fudge, Judy (1989), 'The Effect of Entrenching a Bill of Rights upon Political Discourse: Feminist Demands and Sexual Violence in Canada', *International Journal of Sociology* 17: 445.

Goldfarb, Sally (2002–03), 'The Supreme Court, the Violence Against Women Act, and the Use and Abuse of Federalism', *Fordham Law Review* 71: 57.

Goldwin, Robert A. and Kaufman, Art (eds) (1988), *Constitution Makers on Constitution Making: The Experience of Eight Nations*, Washington: American Enterprise Institute for Public Policy Research.

Gordon, Beate Sirota (2001), *The Only Woman in the Room: A Memoir*, Kodansha International.

Hart, Vivien (2003), 'Democratic Constitution Making', Special Report 107, United States Institute of Peace.

Haussman, Melissa, Sawer, Marian and Vickers, Jill (eds) (2010), *Federalism, Feminism and Multi-level Governance*, Ashgate.

Hirschl, Ran (2004), 'The Political Origins of the New Constitutionalism', *Indiana Journal of Global Legal Studies* 11: 71.

Hirschl, Ran and Shachar, Ayelet (2004), 'Constitutional Transformation, Gender Equality, and Conflict in Israel', in Beverley Baines and Ruth Rubio-Marin (eds), *The Gender of Constitutional Jurisprudence*, Cambridge University Press.

Irving, Helen (1997), *To Constitute a Nation: A Cultural History of Australia's Constitution*, Cambridge University Press.

Irving, Helen (2008), *Gender and the Constitution: Equity and Agency in Comparative Constitutional Design*, Cambridge University Press.

Irving, Helen (2009), 'More than Rights', in Susan H. Williams (ed.), *Constituting Equality: Gender Equality and Comparative Constitutional Law*, Cambridge University Press.

Jackson, Vicki (2009), 'Conclusion: Gender Equality and the Idea of a Constitution: Entrenchment, Jurisdiction, Interpretation', in Susan H. Williams (ed.), *Constituting Equality: Gender Equality and Comparative Constitutional Law*, Cambridge University Press.

Kang, John M. (2009), 'Manliness and the Constitution', *Harvard Journal of Law and Public Policy* 32: 261.

Kome, Penney (1983), *The Taking of Twenty-Eight: Women Challenge the Constitution*, Toronto: Women's Press.

Lenoir, Noelle (2001), 'The Representation of Women in Politics: From Quotas to Parity in Elections', *International and Comparative Law Quarterly* 50: 217.

Lijphart, Arend (2002), 'The Wave of Power-sharing Democracy', in Andrew Reynolds (ed.), *The Architecture of Democracy: Constitutional Design, Conflict Management, and Democracy*, Oxford University Press.

Loughlin, Martin and Walker, Neil (eds) (2008), *The Paradox of Constitutionalism: Constituent Power and Constitutional Form*, Oxford University Press.

Lucas, Laura (2009), 'Does Gender Specificity in Constitutions Matter?', *Duke Journal of Comparative & International Law* 20: 133.

Lukitz, Liora (2006), *A Quest in the Middle East: Gertrude Bell and the Making of Modern Iraq*, I.B. Tauris.

Lutz, Donald S. (2006), *Principles of Constitutional Design*, Cambridge University Press.

MacKinnon, Catherine (2000–01), 'Disputing Male Sovereignty: On *United States v Morrison*', *Harvard Law Review* 114: 135.

Markovits, Inga (2008), 'Constitution Making after National Catastrophes: Germany in 1949 and 1990', *William & Mary Law Review* 49: 1307.

Michelman, Frank (2003), 'Ida's Way: Constructing the Respect-worthy Governmental System', *Fordham Law Review* 72: 345.

Monopoli, Paula (2006), 'Gender and Constitutional Design', *The Yale Law Journal* 115: 2643.

Morais, Nina (1987-8), 'Sex Discrimination and the Fourteenth Amendment: Lost History', *Yale Law Review* 97: 1153.

Morgan, Martha I. and Buitrago, Monica Maria Alzate (2004), 'Constitution-making in a Time of Cholera: Women and the 1991 Colombian Constitution', in Beverley Baines and Ruth Rubio-Marin (eds), *The Gender of Constitutional Jurisprudence*, Cambridge University Press.

Murray, Christina (2001), 'A Constitutional Beginning: Making South Africa's Final Constitution', *University of Arkansas at Little Rock Law Review* 23: 809.

Murray, Christina and Simeon, Richard (2008), 'Recognition without Empowerment: Minorities in a Democratic South Africa', in Sujit Choudhry (ed.), *Constitutional Design for Divided Societies: Integration or Accommodation?*, Oxford University Press.

Norris, Pippa (2001), 'Gender and Contemporary British Politics', in Colin Hay (ed.), *British Politics Today*, Polity Press.

Nussbaum, Martha (2004), 'India, Sex Equality and Constitutional Law', in Beverley Baines and Ruth Rubio-Mario (eds), *The Gender of Constitutional Jurisprudence*, Cambridge University Press.

Pateman, Carole (1988), *The Sexual Contract*, Polity.

Quick, John and Garran, Robert (1901), *The Annotated Constitution of the Commonwealth of Australia*, Angus and Robertson.

Resnik, Judith (2001–02), 'Categorical Federalism: Jurisdiction, Gender, and the Globe', *Yale Law Review* 111:619.

Rosenfeld, Michel (ed.) (1994), *Constitutionalism, Identity, Difference and Legitimacy*, Duke University Press.

Rosenfeld, Michel (2010), *The Identity of the Constitutional Subject: Selfhood, Citizenship, Culture, and Community*, Routledge.

Seidman, Gay (1999), 'A Gendered Citizenship: South Africa's Democratic Transition and the Construction of a Gendered State', *Gender and Society*, 13: 207.

Selassie, Bereket Habte (2002), in Andrew Reynolds (ed.), *The Architecture of Democracy: Constitutional Design, Conflict Management, and Democracy*, Oxford University Press.

Skeet, Charlotte (2007), 'Gender and "Modern" Constitutionalism: The Treaty Establishing a Constitution for Europe', *Northern Ireland Legal Quarterly* 58: 142.

Sullivan, Kathleen (2002), 'Constitutionalizing Women's Equality', *California Law Review* 90: 735.

Sunstein, Cass R. (2001), *Designing Democracy: What Constitutions Do*, Oxford University Press.

Tully, James (2007), 'The Imperialism of Modern Constitutional Democracy', in Martin Loughlin and Neil Walker (eds), *The Paradox of Constitutionalism*, Oxford University Press.

Vickers, Jill (1994), 'Why *Should* Women Care about Federalism?', in Janet Hiebert (ed.), *Canada: The State of the Federation*, Queen's University School of Public Policy/McGill-Queen's Press.

Whitty, Noel (1993), 'Law and the Regulation of Reproduction: 1922–1992', *University of Toronto Law Journal* 43: 851.

Williams, Susan H. (ed.) (2009a), *Constituting Equality: Gender Equality and Comparative Constitutional Law*, Cambridge University Press.

Williams, Susan H. (2009b), 'Equality, Representation, and Challenge to Hierarchy: Justifying Electoral Quotas for Women', in Susan Williams (ed.), *Constituting Equality: Gender Equality and Comparative Constitutional Law*, Cambridge University Press.

3. Participation in constitutional design
Justin Blount

Ours is an era of constitution-making. Approximately one-quarter of the world's written constitutions have been promulgated since 1974 (Elkins et al., 2009a). The trend over this period has been one of increasing public participation in the constitutional design process. To cite but one example, among currently in-force constitutions specifying their own promulgation procedure, more than 40 percent required public ratification via referendum. The comparable figure for 1950 is approximately 5 percent, even though the proportion of texts specifying any promulgation procedure whatsoever is roughly equivalent (Ginsburg et al., 2009).

The new constitutionalism that has emerged over this period places as much emphasis on process as it does on outcomes (Hart, 2001). In light of this, the formal provision of democratic institutions is no longer sufficient to establish the democratic bona fides of a constitution. Because a constitution is the highest level of lawmaking and provides the ultimate rule of recognition for lawmaking processes (Kelsen, 1945; Hart, 1961), it requires the greatest possible level of legitimation in democratic theory. This need for legitimation dictates that a democratic constitution must be fashioned by democratic means in acknowledgment of the moral claim of a people to the right to participate in the creation of the rules under which they will be governed (Hart, 2001 and 2003; Samuels, 2005).

Participation through input, through ratification and through oversight all differ conceptually, but all are treated as contributing to a process in which the citizen is 'involved' in some sense. Like constitution-making in general, popular constitution-making takes many forms with frequent variation.[1] No single template exists but the most participatory processes combine elements of representation, consultation, popular ratification and oversight in varying degrees.[2]

It must be noted at the outset that the following discussion pertains only to opportunities for popular participation. There is no guarantee that citizens will avail themselves of these; one can, after all, only lead a horse to water.[3] However, experience has demonstrated that states can take affirmative steps to make participation more likely. States can build trust and credibility in the process by being explicit about the stages of the proposed design process and how and when citizens and civil society groups will be involved (Haberfeld, 2006; Benomar, 2004). Ad hoc measures, unpredictability in the rules governing participation and post hoc elite-driven changes to the process can lead to process dissatisfaction and a diminution of participation, both quantitatively and qualitatively.[4]

1 PARTICIPATION IN CONSTITUTIONAL DESIGN

The constitutional design literature is rapidly expanding with a plethora of contributions touting the justifications for mass participation in constitution-making and speculating on its prerequisites, effects and consequences.[5] The present effort touches upon these subjects only tangentially. The primary emphasis of this chapter is simply to sketch the predominant forms of popular participation and how these forms have manifested themselves in a number of contexts. Nevertheless, a quick summary of the various claims, and counterclaims, about public constitutional design will serve as a useful reference point for the discussion to follow as well as illustrating the contradictory nature of a number of hypotheses.

1.1   Justifying Participation

The most frequently cited, and most intuitively plausible, claim for participation is that it enhances constitutional legitimacy (Hart, 2001 and 2003; Samuels, 2006; Voigt, 2004; Karli, 2009). Legitimacy reduces the likelihood of opposition and future renegotiation, imparting stability to a constitutional order (Voigt 2004). Voigt further suggests that even the perception or possibility of participation is sufficient to capture the legitimacy-conferring benefits of inclusive constitution-making.

In addition, participation is theorized to make 'better citizens' through the inculcation of democratic skills, habits and values (Mansbridge, 1995: 1; Barber, 1984). These newly acquired or burnished citizen attributes then provide a foundation for the efficacious functioning of formal democratic institutions enumerated in a new constitution (Barber, 1984; Pateman, 1970). Participation is also educative; it instructs citizens on matters of public import, accelerates the acquisition of political information and equips citizens for more critical evaluations of their government (Mansbridge, 1995; Moehler, 2008). In the constitutional setting, these arguments suggest that participation in, for example, ratification, promotes democratic values in citizens and educates them in the operations of democratic processes as well as the contents of the constitution (Barber, 1984; Finkel, 1987). This may increase the likelihood of the success of democracy at the regime level. Thus participation in the constitutional approval process will carry over to governance under the constitution once adopted.

The preceding arguments dovetail with another in support of mass participation in constitutional design: participation increases a constitution's ability to constrain government. If citizens are to effectively police the actions of government, it must be sufficiently clear what constitutes a violation of the limits of governmental power so that citizens can mobilize to prevent it (Carey, 2000). Constitutions help resolve this coordination problem by generating common knowledge about the scope of acceptable government behavior and by providing a focal point for citizens to coordinate enforcement efforts (Weingast, 1997). To the extent that popular ratification of a constitutional design process serves to construct focal points, it will facilitate the coordination needed to deter potential constitutional violations by government. In the most optimistic scenario, the presence of a focal point in the written text, when coupled with the more robust civil society that emerged as part of a participatory design process, will ensure that the constitution will be enforced and not serve as a mere parchment barrier (Carey, 2000).

Finally, scholars think participatory processes will include more rights provisions and better enforcement mechanisms to protect them, including super-majoritarian institutions, and more public involvement in selecting government agents (Hart, 2001; Samuels, 2006; Ginsburg, 2003; Voigt, 2004).

1.2   Uncertain Benefits

Much of the uncertainty and doubt surrounding the presumed virtues of participatory constitution-making are practical in nature rather than philosophical. Common themes include the
quality of the text, the difficulty of reaching agreement and concerns about the post-adoption
operation and duration of a constitution.

Rather than maximizing the common good by providing a more representative sample of
interests, it has been suggested that participation will produce documents dominated by self-
interest (Scaff, 1975), particularly if it is the case that citizens are motivated more by self-interest than are elites (Cusack, 2003). In this view, participation is largely instrumental, providing
citizens an additional avenue to capture state benefits, protect interests or gain power. Rather
than promoting civil society and building democratic citizens, such self-interested participation
may have the opposite effect (Ghai and Galli, 2006; Scaff, 1975; Salisbury, 1975).

Voigt (2004) voices a practical concern related to the consequences of participatory constitutional design processes for textual coherence. As Horowitz (2002) notes, even under the
best of circumstances, constitutional 'design' – a term he reserves for a cohesive process – is
quite rare, with some process of incremental construction more the norm. Constitution-
making frequently consists of a combination of institutional borrowing, wholesale grafting,
log-rolling and improvization (Horowitz, 2002). As new, and more, actors become involved
in the process, bargaining and negotiation become both more extensive and intensive
(Horowitz, 2002). The constitution that emerges from this process will almost certainly be an
ad hoc creation, rife with internal inconsistencies and institutional mismatches. While the loss
of design consistency may be compensated for by the resultant gains in legitimacy, it may
also render the constitutional scheme unworkable (Horowitz, 2002).

A different line of critique emphasizes the difficulty of reaching agreement itself. More
actors will, *ceteris paribus*, increase the transaction costs of negotiation (Karli, 2009), particularly when participants have veto powers over the adoption of new rules (Tsebelis, 2002). If
the cardinal measure of the success of a design process is the adoption of a new constitution,
then participation-induced procedural inefficiencies that prevent agreement on and the
promulgation of a new text are serious matters (Karli, 2009).

Finally, an older line of theory hypothesizes that mass participation in the design process
has the capacity to destabilize fragile societies either by exacerbating conflicts over resources,
activating latent identities such as ethnicity, or both (Huntington, 1968).[6] Given the large
number of constitutional design episodes occurring in post-conflict or conflict-prone societies, this is not an academic criticism (Widner, 2005b; Reynolds, 2002).[7]

1.3   Deliberation

Democracy theorists agree on the value of participation in constitution-making though
disagreement about methods exists. There is a natural tension between direct or mass democracy and deliberative democracy. This tension is most evident in terms of public oversight
(see Section 5.1 below) but manifests itself in other ways as well. Generally speaking, the
emphasis on popular legitimacy in the mass democracy literature lends itself to particular
modes of participation in constitution-making. Representation, inclusiveness and ratification
via referendum are key to establishing procedural and constitutional legitimacy. The best
practices guidelines of the Commonwealth Human Rights Initiative (1999) urging the adop-

tion of a design process that 'engages the largest majority of the population' (3) are consistent with this view.

Deliberative theorists such as Fishkin (2009) distinguish between institutions of 'refined' and 'raw' opinion. Refined opinion is that 'tested by the consideration of competing arguments and information conscientiously offered by those who hold contrasting views' (14). Raw opinion is untested, generally unsystematic and pervasive in modern democracies. Focus groups, opinion polls and direct democracy instruments like the referendum inhabit the universe of raw opinion. In terms of constitution-making, legitimate popular consultation is an instrument of refined opinion while popular ratification, with its simple yes or no format, is an expression of raw opinion. The Burkean emphasis on representation as a filter rather than a mirror is another difference of import for constitution-making. The purpose of representative institutions is not to ascertain what citizens think but what citizens would think if they were better informed (Fishkin, 2009). Inclusiveness in deliberation then is not justified on equitable grounds but as a means of reaching the 'true' counter-factual of refined opinion.

The tension between deliberative and mass democracy has historical roots. As Fishkin (2009) argues, the arc of democratic development in the United States is one of a transition from more deliberative, filtering political structures to more mass-based, popular ones. Early institutions such as the indirect election of senators, the Electoral College and even the Philadelphia Convention itself were consciously designed to promote measured deliberation. Changes in the conduct of elections, including the candidate-nominating process, and the functional dismissal of the Electoral College have worked to make institutions more reflective of raw public opinion.

2   REPRESENTATION

Popular election of representatives to the body responsible for debating and adopting a constitution is the most straightforward method of engaging the public in the design process. Other selection methods such as appointment by the head of state, the legislature or other corporate bodies like peak associations are used but the trend is toward popular election.[8] Indeed, Widner (2008) reports that since 1987, 65 percent of all processes included elected delegates. From another perspective, one-quarter of new constitutions during this period 'were drafted by bodies that would not be considered representative either in terms of the method of authorization or composition' (1524).

The concept of representative constitution-making involves more than just the identity of those debating and adopting a draft text. It is also a matter of choice about institutional venue. Excluding executive-centered processes as a priori undemocratic and non-participatory, constitutional reformers typically choose between either a legislature-centered reform process or a constituent assembly-centered one. As will be discussed below, it is generally assumed that an elected constituent assembly is more representative and 'other-regarding' than an elected legislature tasked with crafting a new constitution (Ghai, 2004: 9; Elster, 2006; 2009)

2.1   Elections

As noted above, direct election of delegates to the deliberating and/or adopting body is a common means of securing mass participation in the constitution-making process. It is important to note though that elections are simply a means to an end, and not an end in and of themselves. Popular election is simply a mechanism through which to seek full, inclusive representation of citizen interests, preferences and beliefs. It is not a magic bullet and the popular election of delegates is no guarantee of a representative, inclusive body. Election rules, electoral formulas, polling access, citizen information and physical (in-) security of voters can all distort the expression of a people's preferences. To counter this, some countries have allowed social and/or economic groups to select delegates to the deliberating/adopting body in addition to the delegates chosen by the citizenry at large. In contexts in which elections are seen as easily manipulable by political elites, such arrangements may produce a more popularly credible assembly (Widner, 2008). Ideally, this combination of both generalized and specialized constituencies is a way to combine the credibility of elections with the legitimacy conferred by the inclusion of as wide a swath of society as is practicable.

The Ugandan constitutional experience in this regard is illuminating. To begin with, it is likely that public pressure was largely responsible for the ruling National Resistance Council's (NRC) decision to allow a popularly elected constituent assembly to debate and adopt the draft constitution prepared by the Ugandan Constitutional Commission (UCC). There was public skepticism about the initial plan for the NRC to simply transform itself into a constituent assembly to debate and adopt the final draft, as well as a concern that the UCC itself lacked any kind of popular mandate or sanction (Furley and Katalikawe, 1997; Moehler, 2008). Elections were agreed upon in no small part in order to secure legitimacy.

In Uganda, approximately 75 percent of the 284 delegates to the constituent assembly were chosen by direct election.[9] Seats were specifically set aside for women with one woman being elected from each of 39 districts by women leaders within her district. In addition, various groups within Uganda elected delegates to represent their interests. Ten delegates were chosen by the military, two by the National Organization of Trade Unions, one by the National Organization of Disabled People, four youths elected by youth leaders of each region, four elected political leaders and ten presidential appointees (Waliggo, 2001). Despite concerns about the true motivations of the government (see Furley and Katalikawe, 1997) and caveats about individual-level effects of participation, the 1995 constitution enjoys some of the highest levels of public support in Sub-Saharan Africa, surpassing even that of the highly participatory South African process (Moehler, 2006; 2008).

2.2   Exceptional Cases?

There are some notable exceptions to attempts at generating 'popular buy-in' and legitimacy through the election of delegates. Despite their non-participatory origins, the constitutional orders in Eastern Europe, Germany and Japan appear healthy (Elster et al., 1998; Ghai and Galli, 2006; Moore and Robinson, 2002). In the Japanese case, it seems that elite buy-in was accomplished primarily through allowing the Diet to translate the American-written, English language text into Japanese, thereby creating an indigenous, 'Japanese' constitution (Moore and Robinson, 2002).

The product of elite-level round table negotiations, the changes to Hungary's constitution in October 1989 are notable for their almost total absence of popular participation. Hungary's constitutional transition from a socialist system to a constitutionally democratic one was an almost entirely elite affair, accomplished at round table negotiations between the ruling Hungarian Socialist Worker's Party (HSWP) and the opposition. These elite bargains were then sanctioned by the HSWP-dominated parliament, many of whose members had been elected in 1985 under the fast dying regime (Widner, 2005b). The 'Four-Yes' referendum in November 1989 presented some items of constitutional import to voters but as these items were largely moot by the time of the actual vote, the referendum functioned more as an endorsement of prior elite actions (Dezso and Bragyova, 2001). Despite the lack of popular participation in the process and the exercise of constituent power by an unrepresentative parliament (Widner, 2005b), the legitimacy of the Hungarian constitution is largely accepted despite periodic populist complaints (Dezso and Bragyova, 2001).

The Japanese and Hungarian cases illustrate the importance of elite support for new constitutional arrangements.[10] Tushnet (2008) argues that while popular support is important, it is secondary to elite buy-in. Including relevant elite stakeholders minimizes the opportunity for entrepreneurial elites to seek political gain by 'appealing to members of the public who would not have bought in' (1490, 1491). In this perspective, popular participation functions as an additional layer of insurance against attacks on the constitutional order. Ultimately, this is a difference more of degree than of kind as the need to include relevant stakeholders is a frequent constitutional prescription (Benomar, 2004; Hart, 2003), but it does suggest that the potential costs of expanded participation should be more carefully weighed against its supposed benefits.[11]

2.3   Caution: Participation Ahead

A critical assumption underlying the preceding sections has been that representation secured through popular election is an unqualified good. Some cautionary words are perhaps in order. First, elections can remove the veil of ignorance from rival groups or parties. Removing the uncertainty surrounding the 'true' level of support for a group has the capacity to reduce the incentive to compromise. In extreme cases, constitution-making becomes an exercise in majoritarianism, or more cynically, census-taking, rather than consensus. Prominent examples of this include East Timor in 2002 and currently Nepal.

The East Timor assembly was dominated by Freitlin, which won 55 of 88 seats at election. The electoral results so skewed power in the assembly that Freitlin had no need to compromise on its proposals while other groups lacked negotiating leverage (Ghai and Galli, 2006). In addition, the assembly was criticized by Muslim residents as 'unrepresentative since the electoral law prevented many of them from voting' (Widner, 2005b), further attenuating the legitimacy of the process. Freitlin's dominant position within the assembly enabled it to ignore the results of an initial round of public consultation in creating the draft constitution. Ultimately, Freitlin was able to push through a final version of the text following only a seven-day period for public review and comment (Benomar, 2004; Kritz, 2003; Widner, 2005b). It must be noted, however, that despite these procedural concerns, the East Timor constitution has been in operation almost eight years and Freitlin's once-dominant position has eroded.

In the case of Nepal, where the legislature is also doubling as a constituent assembly, the 2008 elections that gave the Unified Communist Party of Nepal – Maoist (UCPN-M) a sizable plurality may have undermined the consensual elements of the 2006 Comprehensive Peace Agreement (International Crisis Group, 2009). The mix of legislative and constituent functions appears to have made an already precarious situation even more fragile. Unable to govern, the Maoists (and others) have pushed constitution-making to the back burner amidst other political crises, making it unlikely that the assembly will meet the May 2010 deadline for a new text.[12] It seems improbable that, in cases marred by breakdowns in elite-level cooperation and deliberation such as these, meaningful mass participation will continue (Benomar, 2004).

Elections, and popular participation more generally, also have the capacity to foment polarization and civil strife.[13] In the Iraqi case, elections contributed to communal polarization and led to the Sunni boycott (Ghai and Galli, 2006); likewise, Chad's participatory process resulted in a heightening of Francophone-Arab tensions (Bannon, 2007; Widner, 2005b). Bannon urges careful consideration of local contexts in designing participatory processes, noting that a single 'participatory model' does not exist. Would-be reformers would likely do well to heed her advice and resist the temptation to understate the potential non-pecuniary costs of participatory constitution-making and be flexible in designing the methods for and rules governing popular input, particularly given the noticeable regional variation in Widner's (2005a) analysis of the relationship between representation and post-ratification violence reduction.

2.4   Deliberations, Where Art Thou?

An additional aspect of representation in popular constitution-making is the choice of reform model (Widner, 2008). The most common approaches are to house such power either in the existing legislature that will assume such a task in addition to its regular legislative functions or in a specially convened assembly with no other purpose than to deliberate upon and/or adopt a proposed constitution. This choice has implications for the extent to which the benefits of a particular method of delegate selection will be realized.

There is a long tradition of debate relating to the legitimacy of the exercise of constituent power. In *The Rights of Man*, Thomas Paine emphasized the need for a distinction between ordinary law and the supreme law of a constitution. Legislative drafting blurs this distinction as legislators may seek to inject policy or partisan concerns into the deliberations or constitutional text itself.[14] This certainly appeared to be the case in the Polish parliament where 'in the course of parliamentary debates, constitutional compromise was increasingly overwhelmed and obscured by political compromise' (Spiewak, 1997: 90). The distinction may likewise be blurry for voters as their constitutional preferences get traded off against other concerns when choosing a representative.

In the same vein, it was frequently noted during the Massachusetts Constitutional Convention of 1779 that the 'body charged with creating the fundamental law could not be the same body that enacts ordinary law' (Breslin, 2009: 19). Gouverneur Morris made this point as well when the Provincial Congress of New York was debating whether it possessed the authority to draft a constitution (Elster, 2009). Similar themes are echoed in the constitutional histories of France and Italy of the late 19th century in which parliaments sought to exercise constituent power with only a vague mandate (Arangio-Ruiz, 1895; Currier, 1893; Saleilles, 1895). Elster's (2006) concern with parliamentary drafting has a long pedigree.

In contrast to the legislature-based reform model, the constituent assembly-based model of constitutional reform is an unequivocal representation of a people's constituent power (Ghai, 2004). Its prima facie legitimacy is unquestioned and largely avoids the conflicts of interest and credibility issues facing legislative drafting. Constituent assemblies are also perceived as more broadly representative (Ghai, 2004). One reason for this is that unlike a legislature where selection rules are typically designed with an eye to governability, and hence majority formation, constituent assemblies seek to include as broad a range of interests as possible (Elster, 2006). Of course, an expansive membership may also complicate the process of agreement and risk deadlock. Secondly, in countries in need of systematic political reform, and thus a new constitution, citizen access to power is likely limited so even if the drafting and deliberation of a new constitution occurs under the auspices of an elected legislature, it is clearly less participatory than an elected constituent assembly. For these reasons, constituent assemblies are hypothesized to enable a more wide-open, reform-minded agenda capable of transformational change than legislatures (Ghai, 2004). Other things being equal, constituent assembly-based models are generally more participatory and representative.

2.5 Focus: Cherokee Nation of Oklahoma

An interesting, and admittedly somewhat unusual, case that illustrates many of the points raised in the preceding sections is that of the constitutional design process used by the Cherokee Nation of Oklahoma (hereinafter the Nation).[15] The case is unusual in that the Nation is not a fully independent, sovereign state that is the typical subject of comparative inquiry. Nevertheless, as an application of various participatory mechanisms, it is an instructive case.

Due to an ongoing political crisis involving all three branches of tribal government that eventually spawned the emergence of dual governments, court systems and police forces, the elite-dominated constitutional commission[16] undertook efforts from the outset to distance itself from existing institutions and establish itself as an independent, credible agent for bringing about constitutional change. The commission believed, probably correctly, that entrusting the deliberation and adoption of the draft constitution to the regular legislature would undermine the legitimacy of the process. In this context, the choice of a constituent assembly reform model, with popular ratification of the adopted text via referendum, was made easily and early.

While committed to a participatory process, the commission explicitly rejected direct elections to the assembly, primarily for logistical and financial reasons as well as for the political difficulties associated with apportioning delegates among districts. Rather, the commission opted to guarantee representation of the major institutional stakeholders by allowing each branch of government to appoint eight convention delegates. To ensure inclusiveness and representation of other interested parties, the commission itself selected 24 delegates from the pool of citizens who had given testimony at public hearings in the months preceding the assembly's opening. To these same ends, 24 delegates were selected, with media in attendance, by lottery from a pool of applicants. Finally, all seven commission members were to be seated as delegates.

These unconventional selection methods ensured representation of all relevant stakeholders and resulted in a diverse set of delegates differing in age, degree of Cherokee blood quantum, educational and occupational background and residence (approximately 25 percent of delegates were part of the Cherokee diaspora). Most had no prior political experience. Lawyers played a limited role and comprised less than 20 percent of the 79 delegates. It is also likely that the commission-appointed and lottery-winning delegates made for a more representative convention than would have been the case had elections been held. In addition, power was so dispersed that no single constituency was strong enough to dominate. Anecdotal evidence of the effect of this wide-ranging representation is found in the specificity of parts of the text, a not unsurprising finding (see Elkins et al., 2009b; Voigt, 2007). In this case, the relatively few lawyers serving as delegates to the assembly as well as tribal administration officials complained that too much specificity and statutory law were being inserted into the text by the citizen drafters. Supporters of this argued that tribal government had been so unresponsive for so long that such language was necessary to force future governments to act.

3   CONSULTATION

In many ways, public consultation has the potential to be the most significant form of popular participation in terms of effects on the content of constitutions and post-constitutional political life. A key determinant in this is not only who participates, but how effective such meetings are in terms of generating real input into the process. The hope is that consultation will provide direct substantive input into the constitutional draft, as opposed to relying exclusively on elites – however selected and however representative – to prepare the document. Still, consultation is a top-down, educative affair, in which elites reveal their deliberations to a larger public in an effort to solicit feedback and corroboration (Samuels, 2006).

3.1   Varieties of Consultation

Haberfeld (2006) explicitly recognizes this potential variation in the quality of consultation by distinguishing between technical and political approaches to constitution-making. The technical approach is characterized by elite drafting followed by public meetings in which elites share their proposals with the populace, provide information and take citizen input. This is typically followed by a ratification referendum. As Banks (2008) terms it, such a process is externally inclusive but internally exclusive, or put another way, 'participation without power' (1045). Citizens have little to no substantive access to or influence upon the drafting process. From a deliberative standpoint this approach is more akin to polling than to consultation (Fishkin, 2009). These processes assume a general congruence of elite and mass opinion and that a technically sound document is what a polity wants or needs.[17]

It is also unclear to what extent citizen input is seriously considered by designers. If consultation is merely educative rather than a sincere effort to solicit feedback and corroboration, then it is less likely that many of the more optimistic claims regarding participation, such as enhanced legitimacy, improved citizen information, post-ratification monitoring of government action and rights promotion will materialize.

In the political approach, consultation is a means of information gathering as well as information dissemination. Citizens and elites alike update their information about one another's expectations, preferences and likely outcomes. Public hearings also become a source of proposed reforms as elites attempt to accommodate citizen preferences. The initial draft emerging from a substantive process of consultation such as this will, to some extent, already represent a negotiated settlement about what participants can and will accept. Consultation during the deliberation and adoption stages of the process can also impact the final product, though it seems unlikely to be as influential as pre-drafting consultation given the possible inertia of the process at that point. Elites, in particular, may be unwilling to re-open for debate once contentious issues that were settled via inter-elite bargains during the drafting stage.

The Rwandan experience in 2002–03 illustrates Banks' (2008) concept of internal exclusion.[18] An elite constitutional commission spent six months holding discussions and informational meetings throughout the country with average attendance in each province of 90,000 (Widner, 2005b). It also developed a 60-question survey based on potentially contentious constitutional issues. To process this input, the commission developed a database to record responses and a grading system to analyze the data. Free telephone lines were made available, as well as email to obtain feedback from the populace. Citizen responses were summarized and published by the commission. Following a two-month drafting period, the commission unveiled its work at a conference which drew 800 people, including international experts invited to attest to the draft's conformity with international standards. A further three months were then allowed for renewed citizen comment and amendment proposal. Subsequently, parliament made several changes which were also then presented to the populace. At referendum, the constitution received 93 percent support on an 89 percent voter turnout (Widner, 2005b).

On its face, the Rwandan process was quite participatory. Though the Transitional National Assembly was unelected, major elite stakeholders were represented in the body and there is evidence that the constitutional commission was sensitive to the results of public feedback, suggesting citizens had some decision-making power in the process (Kritz, 2003). A closer examination, however, gives the impression that participation was controlled and orchestrated by the ruling Rwandese Patriotic Front (RPF). Appointment of members to the constitutional commission was predicated on willingness to play ball with the RPF and adhere to the script it devised. It was further alleged that only RPF members and their sympathizers participated in the commission's hearings and debates, as well as that the unanimity expressed in the referendum was a product of intimidation and ethnic mobilization. It appears then that substantive mass participation was constrained in the Rwandan process. Elites and their popular supporters were given voice and input, but the circle of decision-making power was narrowly drawn. Widner (2005b) notes that of 50,000 surveys administered by the commission, only 7 percent were ever examined; it was primarily a means for the regime to solicit elite opinion. Also, while some changes were apparently made as a result of the consultation process, the commission proved notably inflexible in reducing the executive term from seven years to five, despite popular support for the change and the mobilization of several civil society organizations to that end.

3.2 Decisive Consultation

The challenge for proponents of participatory constitution-making lies in transforming consultation from a purely information-gathering mechanism to a decision-making one, or as Kritz (2003) puts it, synthesizing popular feedback with the draft text. It requires prior planning and elite commitment to genuine participation. Kritz notes that while the Brazilian process of consultation was massive (over 61,000 amendments were proposed by citizens and interest groups (Benomar, 2004)), it was poorly organized, with one individual assigned the task of absorbing the results and attempting to incorporate the proposed amendments into the drafting process. Attempts at public engagement and consultation in South Africa were seemingly more efficiently managed than in Brazil with a civic education campaign and multiple rounds of public meetings bookending the publication of an initial working draft that purported to reflect the results of citizen consultation. Ultimately, the Constituent Assembly received almost 2 million submissions though citizens expressed skepticism throughout the process that their views were wanted or would be taken seriously by the Assembly (Ebrahim, 2001). In contrast to the above examples, the Albanian constitution of 1998 and the afore-mentioned Cherokee Nation constitutional design process of 1999 both managed to unam-biguously incorporate public input to the final draft.

In Albania, an elite parliamentary commission composed of members of the two main political parties and their allies was established to draft a constitution to replace the interim one Albania had been operating under since 1991. The minority Democratic Party (DP) led by former president Berisha largely boycotted the drafting process, despite repeated attempts by the governing coalition urging them to participate, claiming inadequate representation on the commission (Constitution Watch: Albania, 1998b). As the process proceeded without the DP, Berisha embarked on a series of actions designed to short circuit the ongoing process. He called for a round table comprised of all parties to discuss the draft as well as a constituent assembly to replace the existing, established process (Constitution Watch: Albania 1998a). Ironically, the round table was never held due to a coup attempt by Berisha supporters (Constitution Watch: Albania, 1998b).

The lack of participation by a major stakeholder in the process appears not to have adversely affected the legitimacy of the process or the constitution. As Berisha and his faction of the DP continued to define themselves as obstructionist, a number of Albanians, perhaps a majority, began to tire of him and indeed blamed him for much of the turbulence in Albanian political life (Constitution Watch: Albania, 1998a).

Against this backdrop of partisan conflict, the constitutional commission continued its work, preparing a draft with a high degree of public input. A public consultation period was held and organized by a 'special quasi-nongovernmental organization' created for the task and funded by the Albanian and various foreign governments (Widner, 2005b). Upon completion of the initial draft, the commission sought and received the approval of the draft from the Council of Europe's Venice Commission on Law and Democracy. This was consciously done to enhance the legitimacy of the draft and counteract the negative effects of the DP's boycott and Berisha's efforts to discredit the commission (Constitution Watch: Albania, 1998b). The commission also conducted an additional round of public hearings on the completed draft, the result of which were changes to approximately 25 percent of the draft articles (Widner, 2005b). Following parliamentary approval, the draft constitution was approved in a referendum with 90 percent approval on 50 percent turnout despite Berisha's call for a boycott (Constitution Watch: Albania, 1998b; Widner, 2005b). In spite of the polit-ical tensions pervading the country and the open hostility of important elites, the Albanian parliament seems to have overseen a legitimately participatory process that credibly engaged the populace, was generally responsive to citizen preferences and worthy of the international approbation it received for its commitment to a democratic process of constitutional change (Kritz, 2003).

The Albanian design experience of an active, elite-led opposition is strikingly reminiscent of that of South Africa with Buthelezi's Inkatha Freedom Party (IFP) playing the role of Berisha's DP. In South Africa, the IFP walked out of the constituent assembly and was gener-ally obstructionist due to differences concerning regional autonomy and customary law as well as process. The IFP advocated a more non-participatory process relative to the African National Congress and the National Party, at one point denouncing the 'very notion of a democratically-elected constituent assembly *as inherently undemocratic*' (Klug, 2000: 102).

As was to be the case in Albania, South Africa's constitutional designers managed to craft a durable constitution that enjoys considerable popular legitimacy (Moehler, 2006).

4   RATIFICATION

Since the early 20th century, there has been an increasing trend of popular ratification of constitutions (Elkins et al., 2008; Ginsburg et al., 2009). Despite its growing popularity as a mode of public involvement, the referendum is clearly a limited one in that it involves only an up or down vote over a package of provisions.[19] Even under ideal conditions, ratification via referendum probably does not represent a Pareto-efficient outcome though it is certainly to be hoped that it signifies a Pareto improvement over the status quo. Majority support of a sub-optimal text is easily envisaged, if one considers that as voters, citizens may bundle non-constitutional concerns with constitutional ones in deciding how to vote, just as legislative drafters undoubtedly do. A notable example of this is the Democratic Republic of the Congo (DRC), whose voters in 2005 overwhelmingly approved at referendum a constitution they had almost no part in writing. Voters' views on the proposed institutional arrangements were less important than their belief that accepting the constitution would end the war and bring peace (Gathii, 2008).

4.1   Logistical Constraints on Referendum Efficacy

While it is common to think of referenda as primarily a downstream constraint on drafters, it is worth remembering that referenda are not immune to elite manipulation. State control of the logistics of elections can be a substantial upstream constraint, as existing governments or political elites may function as gatekeepers. Even when referenda are allowed to proceed, elites may yet retain significant influence over events. A notable achievement of the Cherokee Nation process was the constitution commission's insistence that its enabling legislation give it the sole authority to call and conduct a ratification referendum (Lemont, 2006a). With the tribal government held in such low regard, this independence enhanced the credibility of the commission and the process.

The timing of referenda can also be manipulated to influence the result. Sufficient time should be devoted to a referendum campaign that allows for public education and debate. Too short a time prevents debate as civil society may not have time to collectively organize, while waiting too long may subsume the constitutional issue into other matters of political import or allow public interest in the process to wane altogether (International IDEA, 2008). The former problem is likely more of a concern in non-democratic contexts as the recent Thailand experience demonstrates. Among the many procedural complaints against the 2007 constitutional design process was the scant 19 days allowed for review of the 300-article draft by the military government (International IDEA, 2008). Other complaints highlight the concerns discussed above. It was suggested that approval of the draft would result in an early return of democratic elections, while its rejection would 'create continuing problems and a chaotic situation' (International IDEA, 2008: 53). Given this, it is difficult to say what proportion of the 57 percent of Thais voting 'yes' did so out of support for the constitution rather than out of a desire for a return to democratic government or simple fear of the unknown.

4.2   Approval Thresholds

An additional consideration in the structure of referenda is the question of a minimum turnout threshold. A number of states impose such thresholds for the adoption of new constitutions or amendments. While a requirement that at least 50 percent of eligible voters must partici-pate for a vote to be valid is normatively appealing on democratic grounds, it can have perverse consequences that can reinforce the status quo and frustrate legitimately popular aims. With a 50 percent threshold, a proposal enjoying unanimous support will be disquali-fied with 49 percent turnout, while a proposal with 26 percent support but 25 percent oppo-sition is a valid result. The incentive for referendum opponents to boycott the process rather than engage in it is obvious and woe to the referendum that fails to be enacted because it did not generate enough opposition (Gallagher, 2001)!

Compulsory voting laws can mitigate this problem but currently only 16 countries both have and enforce such provisions (International IDEA, 2008). Voting in referenda is mandatory in Australia, but like Switzerland, it also imposes a double majority require-ment; referenda must be approved by a majority of the national electorate as well as majori-ties in four of six states (International IDEA, 2008). Since 1924, three referenda items approved by a majority of Australians have failed to reach the territorial threshold, includ-ing one in May 1977 that received 62 percent of the national vote (Australian Electoral Commission, 2007).

4.3   Autocratic Referenda

One feature of the use of referenda in the constitution-making process is its frequent employ-ment by autocrats. Approximately half of all referenda from a sample of 460 constitutional design episodes were used in executive-centered processes (Ginsburg et al., 2009). In these cases, referenda were motivated more by a desire to legitimize the autocrat's control of a polity than to allow the citizens to render a considered verdict on the constitution (Brunner, 2001). The contrast between the early use of ratification referenda in post-Communist Eastern Europe and the later use of ratification as instruments of acclamation in Central Asia makes the point nicely (Brunner, 2001).

Given the advantages of executives in referendum campaigns, such as more control of the process and greater access to state resources including media, one would expect them to be nearly universally successful in their efforts. Indeed, the record looks quite grim. Referenda in Belarus (1996) and Kazakhstan (1995) succeeded in preparing the way for super-presidentialism, while executives in Turkmenistan, Uzbekistan and Kyrgyzstan simi-larly employed referenda to expand power or extend their term of office (Brunner, 2001).

More encouragingly, however, the recent past also provides examples of referenda as binding constraints and not simply rubber stamps. Examples of this include the well-known case of Kenya in 2005, but also Albania in 1994 and Seychelles in 1992. All three cases share a similarity of attempted executive/elite manipulation of established processes. Mid-process changes to drafting and adoption procedures in Kenya undermined the credibility of political elites as good-faith agents of constitutional reform (Cottrell and Ghai, 2007; Bannon, 2007; Whitaker and Giersch, 2009). Likewise, in Albania in 1994, President Berisha attempted an end-run around established constitutional procedures but was thwarted by voters (Brunner, 2001; Widner, 2005b). In Seychelles, efforts by President Rene to ensure himself a legislative majority following the return of multi-party elections were rebuffed in a November 1992 referendum (Hatchard, 1993; Tartter, 1995).

Even the admittedly sporadic success of peoples in blocking executive attempts to manipulate the referendum instrument for their own advancement is an encouraging sign, for it signals that with elite commitment to a democratic process of constitution-making, referenda can function as binding constraints on drafters. Evidence of such a function is the preliminary general support for Samuels' (2006) findings that in non-authoritarian settings, referenda encourage the inclusion of a broader menu of rights provisions and direct democracy devices (Elkins et al., 2008; Ginsburg et al., 2009).

5 PUBLIC OVERSIGHT

The complement to public participation is public oversight of the design process. If it is believed that delegates will behave differently when facing the nation than they will when facing their colleagues, then such oversight can be consequential. However, the case for transparency is not clear cut. A tension exists between transparency and secrecy; finding the right mix between sunlight and shadow can go a long way toward determining the overall success of a design process.

5.1 Transparency, Self-interest and Arguing

While transparency is a general good with regard to the normal operations of a legislature, it is not necessarily the case that this is so with regard to constituent bodies. Constitution-building is a political process as well as a legal one, and a more enduring compact is likely to be established if participants are able to freely deliberate (Arato, 1995; Elster, 1995; Horowitz, 2002; Sunstein, 2001). Certain types of transparency, such as monitoring and/or publishing the speeches and votes of individual delegates, can have a stifling effect on the deliberative process as the human emotions of vanity and fear conspire to reduce the quality of debate (Elster, 2009). Vanity, which prevents people from changing their mind as a result of argument, undermines the fundamental rationale of deliberation (Voigt, 2004). Elster reports James Madison as averring that the secrecy of the Philadelphia Convention allowed each delegate to maintain his position only so long as he was convinced of its truth; in a deliberative setting, consistency is not a virtue. Citing Egret (1950), Elster notes that French delegates in September 1789 'feared for their lives' if they voted for bicameralism or the executive veto (2009: 26).

There is reason to think that transparency will have decisive effects on the manifestations of self-interest. In an ideal world, delegates would be dispassionate judges, calmly deliberating in the interests of the common weal, paying little heed to their own concerns. This will never be the case, but transparency may be able to induce at least its pretense. At best, the 'civilizing force' of this hypocrisy will serve to move the 'most self-serving proposals off the agenda' (Elster, 2009: 27).

In Elster's formulation, secrecy is amenable to hard bargaining, whereas publicity facilitates arguing. Though arguing is preferable to bargaining in his view, thus tending to favor a more transparent process, secret arguing, if it occurs, will be superior to public arguing (Elster, 2009). As a solution to this tension between transparency and secrecy, Elster (2006) employs an hourglass metaphor to describe the optimal role of the public in the process, with participation via public hearings at the upstream stage and some form of ratification possible at the downstream stage. The actual writing and deliberation (the neck of the hourglass) should be shielded from the public eye to avoid the pitfalls described above. The Spanish constitutional design process of 1977–8 mostly achieved this ideal though not entirely by design (Banting and Simeon, 1985; Gunther, 1985).

The initial draft of the post-Franco Spanish constitution was penned by an elite, seven-person drafting subcommittee in the newly elected Congress of Deputies. This draft was negotiated primarily in secret, with one member estimating that the multi-party drafting body managed to reach full agreement on about 80 percent of the text. As public debate began before the Constitutional Committee of the Congress, disagreements arose between Left and Right and a series of close votes in the first few days threatened to undermine the multi-party consensus. Not surprisingly, the tone of the debates became destructive of compromise and moderation.[20] Within several weeks, the decision was made to conduct 'serious negotiations in private, with public speeches in the Cortes functioning mainly to explain or ratify inter-party agreements' (Gunther, 1985: 53). This secretive approach preserved the consensual nature of the process and helped to ensure the continued 'buy-in' of virtually all political elites and groups. Following approval by the Cortes, the new constitution was overwhelmingly approved at referendum.

6   CONCLUSION

As this brief discussion and cursory glance at a handful of cases revealed, there is a fair amount of constrained variation in the constitutional design procedures used by countries. While some forms of public participation are doubtless linked inextricability to their context, others offer up examples and innovations suitable for export. All of them, however, function in varying degrees as a constraint on the adoption of new institutions and rules. Though causal judgments are methodologically difficult to demonstrate, especially given the presence of selection bias in choice of process, participation should be expected to make a difference. Process should matter and there is accumulating evidence that it does – that the counterfactual constitution and subsequent constitutional order with no popular participation would be noticeably different.

NOTES

1. See Ginsburg et al., 2009: 205.
2. Mendez and Triga (2009) conceptualize participation in an analogous manner, comparing constitutional design processes in terms of modes of representation, communicative interaction and legitimation.
3. Citizens may have any number of reasons for non-participation. See Ginsburg (2002) for a public choice perspective. Lemont (2006b) addresses non-participation in the American Indian context.
4. Elite behavior and midstream changes to the rules of the game are partly responsible for the 2005 defeat of the Kenyan constitutional referendum (Cottrell and Ghai, 2007; Bannon, 2007; Whitaker and Giersch, 2009).
5. For a handful of recent examples, see Bannon, 2007; Benomar, 2004; Elkins et al., 2008; Ginsburg et al., 2009; Moehler, 2008; Samuels, 2006; Voigt, 2004; and Widner, 2008.
6. But see Lipset (1959), noting that although intergroup conflict can lead to societal disintegration, social cleavages strengthen democratic institutions.

7. Widner notes more than 150 episodes in the 1975–2003 period, for instance.
8. Widner's (2005b) survey of 194 constitution-writing processes held between 1975 and 2003 in conflict-prone societies indicates that only 15 percent of cases are the exclusive domain of the executive branch. The author's own survey of more than 400 episodes of constitutional design since 1789 found a predominant role for the executive in approximately 20 percent of cases.
9. The elections were legally non-partisan, hampering coordination of would-be opposition groups to the National Resistance Movement. Rallies and demonstrations 'in support of or against any candidate' were prohibited (National Resistance Council, Constituent Assembly Statute No. 6 of 1993).
10. In seven post-Communist Central European countries, including Hungary, the legitimacy of constitutions among political elites is largely independent of process (de Raadt, 2009). Rather, textual ambiguities relating to the formal allocation of powers are more significant predictors of elite constitutional conflict.
11. Exclusion of key stakeholders introduces a downstream constraint on the successful operation of a constitution, as the Ethiopian case, in which opposition groups were excluded from the process, illustrates (Benomar, 2004).
12. A deal extending the term of the constituent assembly-legislature for an additional year was reached on 28 May 2010. The UCPN-M, then in opposition, insisted upon the resignation of the United Communist Party of Nepal – Marxist and Leninist (UML) Prime Minister as a precondition for agreeing to the extension and joining of a national consensus government.
13. See Lipset (1959) and Huntington (1968) about the potentially destabilizing effects of mass participation. Bannon (2007: 1842–9) reiterates some of these arguments in her review of Kenya's constitutional design experience.
14. There is skepticism that legislators will not seek to advantage their own institution at the expense of other branches (Elster, 2006), but see Ginsburg et al. (2009).
15. The details of the Cherokee experience are drawn from Lemont (2006a: 287–322).
16. Each branch of government appointed two members to the commission. The six members selected the chairperson by consensus.
17. Survey data from Nepal following passage of the Comprehensive Peace Agreement, but prior to the legislative elections of 2008, revealed a mass–elite disjunction on the constitution-making process, with citizens viewing the process in terms of peace and development, while political elites saw it through the lens of state reconstruction and the erecting of new political structures (Hachhethu et al., 2008).
18. Unless otherwise noted, the information in this section is derived from Ankut (2005).
19. Interestingly, the 1978 Ecuadorian referendum held by the military government provided for a choice of constitutions. A 'yes' vote indicated support for the newly drafted text, while a 'no' vote indicated support for the previously abrogated 1945 constitution.
20. This would appear to provide some evidence for Stasavage's (2007) game-theoretic justification for limiting transparency – that rather than generating consensus, open deliberation has the potential to lead to mass polarization.

REFERENCES

Ankut, Priscilla Yachat, 'Case Study: Rwanda', in *The Role of Constitution-Building Processes in Democratization* (International IDEA, 2005).
Arangio-Ruiz, G., 'The Amendments to the Italian Constitution', 6 *Annals of the American Academy of Political and Social Science* 31–57 (1895).
Arato, Andrew, 'Forms of Constitution Making and Theories of Democracy', 17 *Cardozo Law Review* 191–231 (1995).
Australian Electoral Commission, Referendum Dates and Results 1906–Present, 2007, available at http://www.aec.gov.au/Elections/referendums/Referendum_Dates_and_Results.htm.
Banks, Angela M., 'Expanding Participation in Constitution-making: Challenges and Opportunities', 49 *William and Mary Law Review* 1043–70 (2008).
Bannon, Alicia L., 'Designing a Constitution-drafting Process: Lessons from Kenya', 116 *Yale Law Journal* 1824–72 (2007).
Banting, Keith G. and Richard Simeon, eds., *Redesigning the State: The Politics of Constitutional Change* (Toronto: University of Toronto Press, 1985).
Barber, Benjamin, *Strong Democracy: Participatory Politics for a New Age* (Berkeley: University of California Press, 1984).
Benomar, Jamal, 'Constitution-making after Conflict: Lessons for Iraq', 15 *Journal of Democracy* 81–109 (2004).
Breslin, Beau, *From Words to Worlds: Exploring Constitutional Functionality* (Baltimore: The Johns Hopkins University Press, 2009).

Brunner, Georg, 'Direct vs. Representative Democracy', in *Direct Democracy: The Eastern and Central European Experience*, edited by A. Auer and M. Butzer (Aldershot: Ashgate, 2001).

Carey, John M., 'Parchment, Equilibria, and Institutions', 33 *Comparative Political Studies* 735–61 (2000).

Constitution Watch: Albania, *East European Constitutional Review* 7 (1) (1998a).

Constitutional Watch: Albania, *East European Constitutional Review* 7 (4) (1998b).

Cottrell, Jill and Yash Ghai, 'Constitution Making and Democratization in Kenya (2000–2005)', 14 *Democratization* 1–25 (2007).

Currier, Charles F.A., 'Supplement: Constitutional and Organic Laws of France', 3 *Annals of the American Academy of Political and Social Science* 51–77 (1893).

Cusack, Thomas, *A National Challenge at the Local Level: Citizens, Elites and Institutions in Reunified Germany* (Aldershot: Ashgate Publishing, 2003).

de Raadt, Jasper, 'Contested Constitutions: Legitimacy of Constitution-making and Constitutional Conflict in Central Europe', 23 *East European Politics and Societies* 315–38 (2009).

Dezso, Marta and Andras Bragyova, 'Hungary', in *Direct Democracy: The Eastern and Central European Experience*, edited by A. Auer and M. Butzer (Aldershot: Ashgate, 2001).

Ebrahim, Hassen, 'The Public Participation Process in South Africa', in *Constitution-making and Democratisation in Africa*, edited by G. Hyden and D. Venter (Pretoria: Africa Institute of South Africa, 2001).

Elkins, Zachary, Tom Ginsburg, and Justin Blount, 'The Citizen as Founder: Public Participation in Constitutional Approval', 81 *Temple Law Review* 361–82 (2008).

Elkins, Zachary, Tom Ginsburg, and James Melton, Comparative Constitutions Project (2009a), available at http://www.comparativeconstitutionsproject.org/index.htm.

Elkins, Zachary, Tom Ginsburg, and James Melton, *The Endurance of National Constitutions* (Cambridge: Cambridge University Press, 2009b).

Elster, Jon, 'Constitution-making in Eastern Europe: Rebuilding the Boat in the Open Sea', 71 *Public Administration* 169–217 (1993).

Elster, Jon, 'Forces and Mechanisms in the Constitution-making Process', 45 *Duke Law Journal* 364–96 (1995).

Elster, Jon, 'Legislatures as Constituent Assemblies', in *The Least Examined Branch: The Role of Legislatures in the Constitutional State*, edited by R. W. Bauman and T. Kahana (Cambridge: Cambridge University Press, 2006).

Elster, Jon, 'The Optimal Design of a Constituent Assembly', Paper read at Conference on Comparative Constitutional Design, 16 October 2009 at University of Chicago.

Elster, Jon, Claus Offe, and Ulrich Preuss, *Institutional Design in Post-Communist Societies: Rebuilding the Ship at Sea* (Cambridge and New York: Cambridge University Press, 1998).

Finkel, Steven E., 'The Effects of Participation on Political Efficacy and Political Support: Evidence from a West German Panel', 49 *The Journal of Politics* 441–64 (1987).

Fishkin, James, *When the People Speak: Deliberative Democracy and Public Consultation* (New York: Oxford University Press, 2009).

Furley, Oliver, and James Katalikawe, 'Constitutional Reform in Uganda: The New Approach', 96 *African Affairs* 243–60 (1997).

Gallagher, Michael, 'Popular Sovereignty and Referendums', in *Direct Democracy: The Eastern and Central European Experience*, edited by A. Auer and M. Butzer (Aldershot: Ashgate, 2001).

Gathii, James Thuo, 'Popular Authorship and Constitution Making: Comparing and Contrasting the DRC and Kenya', 49 *William and Mary Law Review* 1109–38 (2008).

Ghai, Yash, 'The Constitution Reform Process: Comparative Perspectives', Paper read at Toward Inclusive and Participatory Constitution Making, at Kathmandu (2004).

Ghai, Yash and Guido Galli, 'Constitution Building Processes and Democratization', in *Democracy, Conflict, and Human Security: Further Readings* (IDEA, 2006).

Ginsburg, Tom, 'Ways of Criticizing Public Choice: Empiricism and the Use of Theory in Legal Scholarship', *University Law Review* 1139–66 (2002).

Ginsburg, Tom, *Judicial Review in New Democracies: Constitutional Courts in Asian Cases* (Cambridge: Cambridge University Press, 2003).

Ginsburg, Tom, Zachary Elkins, and Justin Blount, 'Does the Process of Constitution-making Matter?', 5 *Annual Review of Law and Social Science* 201–23 (2009).

Gunther, Richard, 'Constitutional Change in Contemporary Spain', in *Redesigning the State: The Politics of Constitutional Change*, edited by K. G. Banting and R. Simeon (Toronto: University of Toronto Press, 1985).

Haberfeld, Steven, 'The Process of Constitutional Reform', in *American Indian Constitutional Reform and the Rebuilding of Native Nations*, edited by E. Lemont (Austin: University of Texas Press, 2006).

Hachhethu, Krishna, Sanjay Kumar, and Jiwan Subedi, *Nepal in Transition: A Study on the State of Democracy* (Stockholm: International IDEA, 2008).

Hart, H.L.A., *The Concept of Law* (Oxford: Oxford University Press, 1961).

Hart, Vivien, 'Constitution-Making and the Transformation of Conflict', 26 *Peace & Change* 153–76 (2001).

Hart, Vivien, 'Democratic Constitution Making', in *Special Report* (United States Institute of Peace, 2003).

Hatchard, John, 'Reestablishing a Multi-party State: Some Constitutional Lessons from the Seychelles', 31 *Journal of Modern African Studies* 601–12 (1993).

Horowitz, Donald L., 'Constitutional Design: Proposals Versus Processes', in *The Architecture of Democracy*, edited by A. Reynolds (Oxford: Oxford University Press, 2002).

Huntington, Samuel, *Political Order in Changing Societies* (New Haven: Yale University Press, 1968).

International Crisis Group, 'Nepal's Future: In Whose Hands?' (2009), available at http://www.crisisgroup.org/home/index.cfm?id=6269&l=1.

International IDEA, *Direct Democracy: The International IDEA Handbook* (Stockholm: International IDEA, 2008).

Karli, Mehmet, 'A Constitutional Convention for Cyprus: Costs, Benefits and Shortcomings', 11 *Journal of Balkan and Near Eastern Studies* 397–411 (2009).

Kelsen, Hans, *General Theory of Law and State*, translated by A. Wedberg (New York: Russell & Russell, 1945 (1961)).

Klug, Heinz, *Constituting Democracy: Law, Globalism and South Africa's Political Reconstruction* (Cambridge: Cambridge University Press, 2000).

Kritz, Neil, 'Constitution Making Processes: Lessons for Iraq', in *Briefings and Congressional Testimony* (Washington, DC: United States Institute of Peace, 2003).

Lemont, Eric, 'Overcoming the Politics of Reform: The Story of the Cherokee Nation of Oklahoma Constitution Convention', in *American Indian Constitutional Reform and the Rebuilding of Native Nations*, edited by E. Lemont (Austin: University of Texas Press, 2006a).

Lemont, Eric, 'Realizing Constitutional Change Through Citizen Participation', in *American Indian Constitutional Reform and the Rebuilding of Native Nations*, edited by E. Lemont (Austin: University of Texas Press, 2006b).

Lipset, Seymour Martin, 'Some Social Requisites of Democracy: Economic Development and Political Legitimacy', 53 *The American Political Science Review* 69–105 (1959).

Mansbridge, Jane, 'Does Participation Make Better Citizens?', 11–12 February 1995, available from http://www.cpn.org/crm/contemporary/participation.html.

Mendez, Fernando, and Vasiliki Triga, 'Constitution-making, Constitutional Conventions and Conflict Resolution: Lesson Drawing for Cyprus', 11 *Journal of Balkan and Near Eastern Studies* 363–80 (2009).

Moehler, Devra, 'Public Participation and Support for the Constitution in Uganda', 44 *Journal of Modern African Studies* 275–308 (2006).

Moehler, Devra, *Distrusting Democrats: Outcomes of Participatory Constitution-making* (Ann Arbor: University of Michigan Press, 2008).

Moore, Ray A., and Donald L. Robinson, *Partners for Democracy: Crafting the New Japanese State under MacArthur* (New York: Oxford University Press, 2002).

Pateman, Carole, *Participation and Democratic Theory* (Cambridge: Cambridge University Press, 1970).

Reynolds, Andrew, ed., *The Architecture of Democracy: Constitutional Design, Conflict Management, and Democracy* (Oxford: Oxford University Press, 2002).

Saleilles, R., 'The Development of the Present Constitution of France', 6 *Annals of the American Academy of Political and Social Science* 1–78 (1895).

Salisbury, Robert H., 'Research on Political Participation', 19 *American Journal of Political Science* 323–41 (1975).

Samuels, Kristi, 'Post-conflict Peace-building and Constitution-making', 6 *Chicago Journal of International Law* 663–82 (2005).

Samuels, Kristi, 'Constitution Building Processes and Democratization: A Discussion of Twelve Case Studies', (International IDEA, 2006).

Scaff, Lawrence A., 'Two Concepts of Political Participation', 28 *The Western Political Quarterly* 447–62 (1975).

Spiewak, Pawel, 'The Battle for a Constitution', 6 *East European Constitutional Review* 2–3 (1997).

Stasavage, David, 'Polarization and Publicity: Rethinking the Benefits of Deliberative Democracy', 69(1) *Journal of Politics* 59–72 (2007).

Sunstein, Cass, 'Deliberative Trouble', in *Designing Democracy* (Oxford: Oxford University Press, 2001).

Tartter, Jean R., 'Seychelles: A Country Study', in *Indian Ocean: Five Island Countries*, edited by H. C. Metz (Washington: GPO for the Library of Congress, 1995).

Tsebelis, George, *Veto Players: How Political Institutions Work* (Princeton, NJ: Princeton University Press, 2002).

Tushnet, Mark, 'Some Skepticism about Normative Constitutional Advice', 49 *William and Mary Law Review* 1473–95 (2008).

Voigt, Stefan, 'The Consequences of Popular Participation in Constitutional Choice – Towards a Comparative Analysis', in *Deliberation and Decision: Economics, Constitutional Theory and Deliberative Democracy*, edited by A. van Aaken, C. List and C. Luetge (Aldershot: Ashgate, 2004).

Voigt, Stefan, 'Explaining Constitutional Garrulity', SSRN eLibrary, 2007.

Waliggo, John, 'The Main Actors in the Constitution Making Process in Uganda', in *Constitution-making and Democratization in Africa*, edited by G. Hyden and D. Venter (Pretoria: Africa Institute of South Africa, 2001).

Weingast, Barry R., 'The Political Foundations of Democracy and the Rule of Law', 91 *American Political Science Review* 245–63 (1997).

Whitaker, Beth Elise, and Jason Giersch, 'Voting on a Constitution: Implications for Democracy in Kenya', 27 *Journal of Contemporary African Studies* 1–20 (2009).
Widner, Jennifer, 'Constitution Writing and Conflict Resolution', 94 *The Round Table* 503–18 (2005a).
Widner, Jennifer, 'Constitution Writing and Conflict Resolution: Data and Summaries' (2005b), available from http://www.princeton.edu/~pcwcr/about/index.html.
Widner, Jennifer, 'Constitution Writing in Post-conflict Settings: An Overview', 49 William and Mary Law Review 1513–41 (2008).

4. Transitional justice and the transformation of constitutionalism

*Ruti Teitel**

This chapter aims at exploring the mutual influence of transitional justice and constitutionalism. Constitutionalism herein is understood broadly, not just as the positive law of written constitutions but as the set of fundamental legal and political norms and practices that are constitutive of the polity, identified by Aristotle as the *politeia*. The chapter proceeds by tracing landmark political and legal developments in various regions in relation to constitutional change, and by looking to relevant transitional justice developments, conceived in terms of the legal responses to the past regime on the road to liberalization (Teitel 2000).

The predominant strands of constitutional theory in the twentieth century, particularly in the Anglo-American world, modeled constitutionalism as a form of pre-commitment and constraint on governmental or state action, usually in the name of individual rights. This form of constitutionalism is also reflected in a vision of separation of powers within the state and sometimes a federal division of powers, checks and balances (Dorsen et al. 2010). Here we can see the significant influence of the US experience, given its contribution of a constitutional structure with restraints internal to the constitution and institutionalized in governmental structure, including judicial review, separation of powers, checks and balances. This model was widely exported often notwithstanding context – political realities on the ground (Tushnet 1999).

The content of contemporary constitutionalism is also being shaped through developments in transitional justice, that is, systematic responses to the wrongs of the prior regime, or which occurred in the course of the political conflict that ultimately was resolved by or resulted in the new regime. Constitutions are created during periods of transition following political repression – indeed the post-World War II period has been characterized as the third wave of constitutionalism. Conversely, the new constitutionalism cannot help but shape our evolving assessment or evaluation of transitional justice itself.

Let us begin with the concept of 'state action', which in the tradition of liberal constitutionalism has been central to defining the ambit of applicability of constitutional norms. As already suggested, twentieth-century constitutionalism at its core was shaped by the demand for limited government as is reflected internally by concepts of separation of powers and judicial review. Increasingly, however, we see in constitutionalism an important concern with *accountability* even for state *inaction*, reflecting an appreciation of the ability of the action of other actors and collectivities to affect underlying constitutional values and interests. Here, constitutionalism is evolving in a subtle relationship with conceptions of state responsibility in international law. Through the globalization of transitional justice, these conceptions have come to bear on understandings of constitutional obligation, further attenuating or nuancing the notion of constitutionalism in terms of the protection of the individual *against* the action of the state. Thirdly, constitutionalism has no longer come to rest on the idea of defining the meaning for the individual of membership in the pre-existing polity, with its claims regarding membership and identity. This is also reflected in the changing nature of rights protection, especially group conceptions of rights that may guide a way to deal meaningfully with the root causes of conflict and provide new parameters by which to identify and respond to political violence.

There is an ever growing demand for *accountability*, captured by the core approaches to judicial guarantees and rights protection. Moreover, accountability appears not to be exhausted or fulfilled either by rights against the state or by democratic self-determination. In modern state constitutionalism, the subject of constitutional law is defined by the state and its aegis, seen in the basis of threshold of state action (Tribe 1986). This is rooted in a distinct political history – the concern for abuses by the sovereign. It also reflects a distinctive view of the public sphere. Here, one might consider the ways that constitutions are informed by an obsession with a repressive past often associated with monarchical abuses and, later, with the legacies of fascism and mass totalitarian politics. To some degree, one can see elements of the essential features of the German Basic Law as responses to the experience of Nazism. Such laws do not merely set constraints on the state, but also reflect anxiety about mass politics and attempts to shape civil society, by putting limits on collective action at the social level.[1] Similarly, the European Convention on Human Rights explicitly prescribes limits on individual rights such as freedom of speech or conscience, wherever these may unduly impact upon other minority rights, or jeopardize democracy.[2] Thus, while Article 10 provides that 'Everyone has the right to freedom of expression . . . (t)he exercise of these freedoms may be subject to such formalities, conditions, restrictions or penalties as are prescribed by law and are necessary in a democratic society'.[3] This view of constitutionalism incorporates or embeds a dynamic understanding of civil society or social order as well as democracy as important values. One can see these provisions as related to historical, postwar experiences where expressive rights were used to incite popular hatred of minorities and mobilize fanatical political prejudice. The more contemporary history in the Balkans and Rwanda has only reinforced a sense of these risks.[4]

Moreover, these historically derived approaches – arguably understood as transitional justice in its constitutional modality – appear to inform contemporary instances of 'militant democracy' which are increasingly visible in Europe. Such instances are particularly apparent in regards to constraints upon exercises of political and religious expression: Burkha bans in several jurisdictions, the protest against the Danish cartoons, the Swiss plebiscite on public symbols of Islam, notably the minaret (Teitel 2008). Indeed, one might perhaps best comprehend these developments in terms of a view of Europe itself in transition, that is, a Union in the midst of regional integration as well as processes of accession (Weiler 1999).

Just what does the state owe its citizens as a constitutional matter? While twentieth-century constitutionalism had the state and its interests at its core, as reflected in the concern for abuse of state action, one can see that transitional constitutionalism in its twenty-first century has more primordial concerns. Here, we can see the vulnerabilities, for example in postwar Europe, in the growing demand for a constitutionalism – beyond the state, notably in contexts involving conflict over religious expression where the state in a sense competes with peoples.[5] This is becoming even clearer with the increase in numbers of weak or failed states, giving rise to a twenty-first-century constitutionalism which addresses both state and non-state actors – with evolving relevant understandings of responsibility beyond the state. This can be seen in the landmark prosecutions of international courts, such as the International

Criminal Tribunal for the Former Yugoslavia (ICTY) and International Criminal Court (ICC), which have often involved non-state actors. Indeed, the landmark first cases in both tribunals fell into this category.

The evolving conception has in one way or another been informed by contemporary developments in transitional justice as well as the growing area of overlaps with international law. This is especially so where international human rights have been informed by precepts of international humanitarian law. Core questions of individual rights and state responsibility, as well as broader understandings of justice, are at issue. One can see the arc beginning earlier, with the postwar human rights covenants, such as the International Covenant on Civil and Political Rights, and the ways these conventions inform constitutional law and the normative commitment states owe their citizens, going to the changing view of individual responsibility in situations of conflict. One might also add the recently expanding jurisdiction of various ad hoc international criminal tribunals aimed at establishing individual responsibility. In *Prosecutor v Tadic*, the first international war crimes trial since World War II, jurisdiction was taken by the ad hoc tribunal although the relevant conflicts were largely internal, informing core obligations to humanity protection even where within the borders of the state, and hence not traditionally within international law understandings of principles of state responsibility. Another illustration is afforded by contemporary case law in the United States Supreme Court, for example, *Hamdan*, expounding upon the normative protections for detainees in US custody under Geneva Common Article III. Indeed, there is an expanding understanding of individual responsibility evidenced by changes in the international conventions, such as the Convention on the Elimination of Discrimination against Women (CEDAW), whose scope reaches beyond the state to the private sphere where core discrimination is at stake.[6] What is now clear is that individual rights protection does not just follow from assertions of individual human rights concerns in the abstract, but rather, is connected to changing concepts of state responsibility. This can be seen in challenges surrounding changing principles of attribution, as in the landmark World Court decision in *Bosnia v Serbia* and other case law at the cusp of individual and state responsibility (Crawford 2002). Lastly, one can see evolution in the substantive norms of accountability in the changing parameters surrounding the protection of non-state actors in interstate affairs, and what duties are owed persons and peoples.

In the remainder of this chapter, drawing upon case law across regions, I aim to identify and discuss sites of contact between transitional and constitutional jurisprudence which I contend reflect normative transformation. From Africa to Eastern Europe to Latin America, developments in transitional justice are now having a significant influence on the evolving conception of constitutionalism, both in the way that judges apply constitutional norms, but also in the way others in the polity understand such norms. Transitional justice expounds a broader understanding of constitutionalism than the traditional account, one that implicates civil society as well as the state.

THE CHANGING CONSTITUTIONAL SELF

In this section, I examine developments regarding the understanding of the self at the heart of two regimes and how these inform and mutually reinforce one another. One might begin with post-cold war transitional justice, and turn to the central example offered by the post-apartheid South African experiment. Here, one can see the evident link between a negotiated political transition and a distinctive perspective upon justice and constitution, in other words, the ways that the transitional legacy might well inform and prefigure constitutional injustice. The analysis might then be useful to understanding of constitutionalism in other transitional contexts.

In South Africa, the interim 1993 constitution set out the basic political bargain that informed the transition to democracy, including provision for amnesties. This provided the backdrop to the Promotion of National Unity and Reconciliation Act and the Truth and Reconciliation Commission (TRC) that it established.[7] As I argued in *Transitional Justice* (Teitel 2000), from the beginning, one can see the close association of the constitution making and transitional justice processes, as the interim constitution is characterized as part of the 'bridge' out of apartheid.[8] Indeed, one can see that it is the parallel commitment to the constitution and its popular ratification processes that also lends the TRC much of its legitimacy. Without this commitment it would be hard to understand amnesties as a form of justice rather than the denial of justice. When the TRC's amnesty provisions were challenged under the permanent South African constitution by victims' groups, but sustained by its Constitutional Court, the decision thereby assimilated the norms governing the transition to constitutionalism as such: 'If the constitution kept alive the prospect of continuous retaliation and revenge, the agreement of those threatened by its implementation might never have been forthcoming, and if it had the bridge itself would have remained wobbly and insecure, threatened by fear from some and anger from others. It was for this reason that those who negotiated the constitution made a deliberate choice, preferring understanding over vengeance, reparation over retaliation, *ubuntu* [Zulu for 'humaneness: or generosity of spirit] over victimization'.[9]

In the South African case, one can see the way the transitional commitment to transformation – and in particular, the central norm of *ubuntu*, the art of humanity – operates as a constitutional value in setting out the parameters of comprehension of perpetrators, victims and the TRC and the constitution (Cornell 2005). Indeed, the clearly asserted humanity value one can see distinguishes the South African approach, even more meaningfully as the first of the new generation of constitutionalism – by its inclusiveness and hence implied consociationalism that aims to cut across past political divisions, across state and non-state actors. This explicit inclusiveness laid the basis that is key to the narrative of parallels put forth in the country's TRC report, which affirmed 'gross violations of human rights were perpetrated or facilitated by all the major role-players in the conflicts of the mandate era'.[10] And, moreover, this dual focus also informed the direction of the constitution, in that the inclusion of outside opposition provided the basis for unity constitutionalism, or consociationalism.[11] The distinctive transitional human rights-based framing, associated with *ubuntu*, has a clear appeal, as here is a norm at once aimed at addressing the wounds of the past, and yet also framed with a commitment to universalizability, as well as having a prospective, outward-looking direction.

Here are the dual optics of justice: the partially backward-looking aims of transitional justice linked to the largely forward-looking constitutional process. From the one side, it seemed plain that the process under way of constitution drafting (going back to the first constitutional negotiations) helped legitimate the Truth and Reconciliation Commission processes. But, the converse also seems evidently true as the very inclusion of social and economic rights would be understood against the backdrop of the country's dire political and economic past and therefore in light of the evident problem of enforceability of such rights.

It follows that their constitutionalization was inevitably predicated upon the transitional normativity (as seen in the draft ANC Bill of Rights), and therefore the ways that rights norms were constructed prefigure the constitution, and build upon the past legacy – namely of confiscation attendant upon state-affirmative duties to repair. One might consider in this regard the Constitution's socio-economic rights, which on the one hand do not set out determinate positive remedies, and yet contemplate state action towards 'progressive realization',[12] rendering the norm in itself explicitly transitional.[13] This must be seen in light of the prior legacy of exploitation and land confiscation and in the commitment to the protection of groups. Consider also the Constitution's protection of language and culture rights both individual and in communal terms.[14] This brings front and center the idea of the constitutional self. More generally, a transitional context itself lends the constitutional project an implicit teleology.

To what extent can truth commission-type processes be exported elsewhere in the absence of a negotiated constitutional transition? On this point, we now have more evidence of the effects of the absence of such full constitutional legitimacy, especially in Latin America. This perspective helps to shed light on the question of just how and why, three decades later, these issues still garner the attention of civil society and have spurred demands for criminal and other justice processes despite the passage of time.

Accountability of actors beyond the state was incorporated expressly into the making of South Africa's transitional constitution. Moreover, going forward, these understandings have continued to shape the normative understanding of constitutional justice in the country. Consider the final South African constitution, which explicitly affirms a social and collective rights approach to these issues, contemplating an explicitly proactive state approach to the realization of these rights (Smiley 2001). In referring to land rights, for example, the constitution expressly contemplates further legislative measures to redress past discrimination. 'A person or community dispossessed of property after 19 June 1913 as a result of past racially discriminatory laws or practices is entitled, ... either to restitution of that property or to equitable redress. No provision ... may impede the state from taking legislative and other measures to achieve land, water and related reform, in order to redress the results of past racial discrimination'.[15] And '(e)veryone has the right to have access to health care services ... food and water ... and social security ... And [t]he state must take reasonable legislative and other measures, within its available resources, to achieve the progressive realisation of each of these rights'.[16]

Contemporary constitutionalism and, in particular, its more universalizable human-rights-based group identity concept, where there is protection of affiliation on the basis of religion or ethnicity and any similar group affiliation, owe a debt to transitional justice developments over recent decades (particularly the South African case). This suggests a backward-looking direction, wherever the relevant categories were framed in terms of past violations and the related group claims for 'restorative justice'.

In *AZAPO*, the South African Constitutional Court upheld the constitutionality of a section of the Truth and Reconciliation Act granting amnesty to a perpetrator of an unlawful act associated with political objectives and committed prior to 6 December 1993.[17] Observing the 'agonizing balancing act between the need for justice to victims of past abuse and the need for reconciliation and rapid transition to a new future',[18] the Court held the Amnesty for civil liability was supported by the epilogue to the Constitution. Moreover, as the *AZAPO* Court's decision suggests, a possible path to legitimacy may well be found in the commonality or overlapping process, the shared agreement at the time on the character of the relevant constitutional self, that is, who is in and who is outside the constitution. These developments elucidate who is the constitutional self, as what became clear early on were the vulnerabilities in the country's transitional constitutionalism, especially regarding the victims, and the extent to which these citizens were largely left outside of the process – in light of the rationale of the transition for unity politics, as the constitutional case law of the time would reflect.[19] Here, one might compare the Brazilian constitutional court amnesty case, *Julia Gomes Lund et al (Guerrilha do Araguaia)*, where the Supreme Federal Court, Brazil's highest court, upheld the country's 1979 law that provided full amnesty to members of the former military for crimes with a political basis committed during Brazil's military dictatorship of 1964–85,[20] which because of the country's popular process lay the basis for its ongoing legitimacy.[21]

It is therefore not surprising that there is now a widely proliferating phenomenon of transitional justice postponed – often decades after the fact, particularly in the African continent, as well as in parts of Latin America. In this transitional justice revisited, it is the victims, and their representatives, that are often the key civil society actors engaged in keeping the question on the table (South Africa's Khulumani support group is one example).[22] In the context of the conceded globalization of judicialization, victims groups have benefited from the proliferation of tribunals by turning to alternative means and fora, including transnational litigation and tort suits under the US Alien Tort Act (for example, *AZAPO*). In Chile, the demand for the extradition of Pinochet via universal jurisdiction in Spain had the effect of reopening transitional justice policy back home. This, of course, would ultimately raise questions for the status of the internal amnesty, as well as for their potential role in transnational lawmaking. Hence, one can see that the claim or stake of universal normativity is always applied in a particular context, and therefore drives a different negotiation even in the local context – via humanity the claim is reconfigured as connected to global society.

In any event, as one can see, wherever transitional justice has not been delivered, there is often a concomitant move away from the state, and its political monopoly, to claim for representation by and on behalf of its constituent peoples. Therefore, not surprisingly, when the *Khulumani* litigation began, the South African government initially raised, then dropped, its opposition – reflecting a changing strategy vis-à-vis transitional justice and state responsibility.[23] This landmark precedent in transitional justice would ultimately guide responses to political violence, inserting itself in the debates about punitive versus restorative justice and individual versus collective responsibility. Yet, often these debates were waged eliding the fuller political context of a connection between Truth and Reconciliation commissions and constitutions, as they both deal with collectivities in such periods. Here, one might compare *Azapo* with *Barrios Altos*, a decision of the Inter-American Court of Human Rights reopening amnesty policies in the Americas rationalized in terms of judicial protection – as it affords, in the context of amnesty, discussion and order of remedies establishing international rights to an investigation and reparation. In the African context, maintaining a dualist view is key to *Azapo*'s ruling of constitutionality, as the high court was called upon to address and distinguish the pertinent international law seen in terms of its relationship to constitutional adjudication, finding it 'relevant only in the interpretation of the Constitution itself' insofar as it can meaningfully guide civil conflict of the sort here.[24] Regarding the amnesty laws, the Court explained, '[T]his incompatibility signifies that those laws are null and void, because they are at odds with the State's international commitments. Therefore, they cannot produce the legal effects inherent in laws promulgated normally and which are compatible with the international and constitutional provisions that engage the State of Peru. The incompatibility determines the invalidity of the act, which signifies that the said act cannot produce legal effects.'[25]

The questions as to the impact on legitimacy of such contestations of domestic constitutionalism relate to a prior point regarding the extent to which prior transitional settlements have been legitimated via their constitutionalization. Hence the evolution of later jurisprudence is relevant to accountability. To what extent might regional rights precedents offer an alternative path to effect norm change within the rule of law – that is, change that might otherwise destabilize domestic constitutional doctrine?

ON THE EVOLUTION OF STATE RESPONSIBILITY IN THE CONTEXT OF TRIBUNALIZATION

The growing tribunalization of judgment concerning conflict-related political violence has constitutional implications, in particular, for changes in the principle of state responsibility. For the last decade has seen the establishment of a permanent court with ongoing jurisdiction over conflict, with a new mandate to supervise the actions by both public and private actors at any echelon of power for grave violations of international humanitarian law, the most serious crimes of international society.[26] Once again, there is potential for significant impact in the generalization or normalization of transitional justice for the transformation of the constitutional subject. This judicialization at the regional level indubitably affects the developments in constitutionalism within the region. The tribunal creates a space for the adjudication of rights at a transnational level. Indeed, its decisions become constitutionalized in the broad sense through their influence on a range of actors, including domestic judiciaries.

To illustrate, consider the commitment to the International Criminal Court and its punitive reach for the contemporary understanding of the constitutional self on the African continent. From the start, since the Court's jurisdiction is premised on 'complementarity', membership reflects a level of normative adherence; not merely mere compliance as a matter of simple cooperation with the tribunal, but rather including steps such as adoption of domestic legislation to facilitate substantive jurisdiction, such as to punish war crimes, analogous to those commitments to domestic measures guaranteed in the other conventions.[27] Beyond this, it would also imply a commitment to implementation at the level of the state. So understood, and scholarly writing to the contrary notwithstanding, the sense in which the ICC forms a part of the raiment of global constitution hardly comports to the zero-sum understanding of political competences and related changes anticipated by scholars regarding the current international/domestic allocation regarding jurisdiction over political violence (Cohen 2005). Indeed, to the contrary, the significance of state cooperation here lies in assuming these added obligations reflexively and in light of other – potentially private – actors. This leads to situations where, so far, there are mostly private, not public, actors on the stand, reflecting the privatization of relevant action and accountability – pointing also to the role of this tribunal in the legitimation of the use of force. It was in the reaction to the convening of ad hoc criminal tribunals, especially the International Tribunal for Rwanda, that the exercise of 'primacy', the assumed priority of international over local prosecution, would inspire opposition, and the critical challenge that any such permanent judicial institution should commence from the start by deferring to the jurisdiction of the state (Alvarez 1999). Yet, by the time the international tribunals become entrenched, it becomes clear that this is too state-centric a view, and that it fails to take in the role of other political actors here that have the potential to shape the constitutional structure, rivaling peoples and their representatives. While, in the mainstream view, the role of international justice tends to be evaluated in state-centric terms,[28] one might compare the effects of the ICTY to the 1990 Milosevic prosecution and its political impact – a legal move credited with affecting an evident political disqualification, with obvious constitutional implications in the region.

Beyond this very prominent instance, one would see in the subsequent proliferation of tribunals that virtually all of the subjects of its supervision are private actors; shedding needed light on exactly where the courts might fit into global governance, important for understanding the judicial implications for maintaining democracy and constitutionalism. So, for example, the first case before the International Criminal Court involves Uganda's taking to court its murderous political opposition, with the rare exception to the ICC docket, via the traditional interstate security framework, as in the Security Council's referral of Bashir for his role in Sudan. The ICC's most recent indictments regarding Kenya and its post-election violence, again, demonstrate the potential of international justice in the attempt to impose constitutionalism and rule of law in the region. This is opening up a space for a new source of legitimation for the successor regime: cooperation with the Court. Here, we can see the court supervising the basic rule of law guiding democratic transition.

EVOLVING UNDERSTANDINGS OF STATE RESPONSIBILITY

'Liberal rights depend essentially on the competent exercise of a certain kind of legitimate public power' according to Stephen Holmes (1997). Yet, it is exactly the absence of such legitimate public power which frames the context for the phenomena discussed here. In particular, the shift in focus both within constitutionalism and transitional justice discourses toward dealing with what are seen as weak, failed or divided states lies at the core of a new global transitional justice. This has clear implications for its relation to and transformative effects on, contemporary constitutionalism (Teitel 2008).

In earlier phases of modern constitutionalism, the focus on state action narrowly understood resulted from time to time in 'tragic choices'. One might recall in this regard a regrettable United States Supreme Court case, *Deshaney v Winnebago*, involving the failure of the state to intervene in a traditionally private area of family life. The case raised the question of what duty was owed children in foster care where, despite allegations of violence, the state did not act and was not held responsible for its omission in the absence of proof to make out state action.[29] Indeed, this norm had been a challenge for transitional justice in the past: how to obtain ruling as to state responsibility in cases of omission? Along with developments, discussed below, regarding the democratic expansion of action attributable to the state, one can see there is another related issue: what is the relation between the state, particularly weak or failed states, and the aim of protection of human beings or human security?

In the Southern Cone, the marked evolution of regional landmark individual rights case law draws in an ongoing way from periods of struggle to deal with the disappearances that pervaded the region for more than a decade. In *Velasquez-Rodriguez*,[30] the Inter-American Court of Human Rights addressed the question of accountability and impunity, directly engaging the nature of the state in the context of a lack of accountability or outright impunity with regard to past acts of political violence. A series of cases coming out of the Inter-American Court, as well as the high courts of states in the region, point to an interesting trend in the concept of state obligation, one that arguably gets beyond the state action limitation as well as the negative rights view, to posit that even where the state has failed to control past political violence, it ought to assume various affirmative obligations that go to the heart of the rule of law.

In *Velasquez-Rodriguez v Honduras*, the Inter-American Commission on Human Rights brought an action in the Inter-American Court of Human Rights regarding the 1981 disappearance of a Honduran student, Angel Manfredo Velasquez Rodriguez.[31] Holding Honduras had violated Articles 4, 5 and 7 of the American Convention on Human Rights, the Court held that, 'under international law a State is responsible for the acts of its agents undertaken in their official capacity and for their omissions, even when those agents act outside the sphere of their authority or violate internal law'.[32] *Velasquez Rodriguez* was a landmark case in the Inter-American Court, and would have effects far beyond the state and even the region in shaping the scope of state responsibility in transitions. Such regional precedents also elucidate the limits of constitutionalism in weak states undergoing transition.

In a context of lawlessness in the region, the question becomes, what is the meaning of state responsibility? Where thousands disappeared to their deaths, what is the state's duty to provide accountability? To what extent is the immediate successor regime responsible, and for what? In this landmark case, the problem at hand was what is the relevance and meaning of state action for purposes of accountability in the transition, in light of the disappearances that had occurred during the prior regime (and indeed as would later be revealed under Operation Condor throughout the region)?[33] For purposes of state responsibility, the Court held that whether the abductors were state actors or not was of no consequence: the disappearance policy implied a presumption.[34] This move allowed the plaintiffs to link up the evidence of systemic harm, even where circumstantial, to establish a pattern of action. Hence, one can see a relaxing of the required nexus or criterion regarding attribution to the state: 'An illegal act which violates human rights and which is initially not directly imputable to a State (for example, because it is the act of a private person)…can lead to international responsibility of the State, not because of the act itself, but because of the lack of due diligence to prevent the violation or to respond to it as required by the Convention'.[35] What might this presumption tell us about the changing view of state responsibility in the context of political violence? For the court: 'the State has a legal duty to take reasonable steps to prevent human rights violations and to use the means at its disposal to carry out a serious investigation of violations committed within its jurisdiction, to identify those responsible, impose the appropriate punishment and to ensure the victim adequate compensation'.[36] Even where a weak state may have failed to prevent, it has added other obligations: where there is violation of rights protected under the convention, the Court has referred to Article 63(1) of the American Convention, which provides that 'the consequences of the breach of the rights be remedied and rule that just compensation be paid' 'the injured party be ensured the enjoyment of his right or freedom'. [37]

After this landmark opinion, the Inter-American Court's elaboration of state responsibility in the context of past human rights violations would influence the conception of state responsibility beyond international law, and would penetrate *within* states to impart their accountability to their own citizens. Accordingly, recent constitutional decisions out of Argentina – which reference the international human rights norms of the *Velasquez*

Rodriguez line of cases – are often misread as being purely about setting limits to state power. They are apparently seen as limiting the political deal-making of the past that had led to amnesties, for example in Chile and Uruguay. But, more importantly, these decisions appear to redraw and newly circumscribe the meaning of the state and its domestic competences, elaborating upon the duties of exercising its powers of judgment and establishing a set of fundamental obligations regarding the state and judicial protection.

In *Barrios Altos*,[38] involving a 1991 politically motivated massacre under the Fujimori regime,[39] the Inter-American Court of Human Rights invalidated the 'self-amnesty', Law No. 26479, which had authorized amnesty to security forces and government officials for any alleged human rights violations. Instead, the Court found state responsibility for violations of core rights under the American Convention, including the right to life in Article 4, the right to a fair trial in Article 8, and rights to judicial guarantees and judicial protection in Article 25.[40] Moreover, the impact of the deprivation of such rights meant that other provisions were violated, such as the obligation to respect rights as well as the obligation in Article 2 to provide for domestic legal effect for the norms of the Convention.

This regional human rights case law is having a clear impact upon the evolution of both transitional justice and constitutionalism in the region and beyond. Of critical importance here is the broader principle by which the regional court linked up the loss of the protection of personal integrity with the ongoing deprivation of meaningful judicial guarantees and protection: 'This court considers that all amnesty provisions, provisions on prescription and the establishment of measures designed to eliminate responsibility are inadmissible, because they are intended to prevent the investigation and punishment of those responsible for serious human rights violations such as torture, extrajudicial, summary or arbitrary execution and forced disappearance, all of them prohibited because they violate non-derogable rights recognized by international human rights law'. Beyond self-amnesty this is significant because the language of the opinion was not itself limited, referring specifically to 'the manifest incompatibility of self-amnesty laws and the American Convention on Human Rights', but also to the measures at issue as inadmissible 'provisions on prescription and the establishment of measures designed to eliminate responsibility' of 'measures aimed at continuing to obstruct the investigation' and referring to 'all amnesty provisions'.

In the Americas, *Velasquez- Rodriguez'* influence would extend beyond its facts, where one can see an instance of its normative effects beyond immediate state compliance. Here, we can see that the norms drawn from this supranational court (albeit signed up to by member states in region) have been picked up within the successor constitutions in the region, often explicitly or via judicial interpretation (Benvenisti 1993; Shany 2006). In particular, in Argentina, there has been an ongoing dynamic regarding the question of what relation transitional justice ought to have with the country's constitutionalism. Here, one might begin by first acknowledging the force of the line of decisions where the human rights provisions which at the time of the most recent transition have previously been introduced through incorporation of international human rights in the Argentine constitution.[41] Consider that the post-authoritarian Argentine constitution explicitly invokes international human rights law (Bohmer 2008); yet, while the first post-successor Argentine constitution had incorporated human rights treaties in the immediate transition, at the time, mere textual inclusion would not turn out to be enough to guarantee meaningful enforcement. Instead, one might best understand the initial policy on trials to have arrived at a rather hasty conclusion, one which now appears to enjoy rather diminished legality or legitimacy, since the demand for transitional justice clearly persists despite the passage of three decades since junta rule.[42] The question has become whether there is any possibility of accountability in this moment. Beyond the state, wherever these questions have been kept alive, it has been largely through civil society and private actors, especially victims' groups and their representatives.

How have these questions, which were associated with the first generation debates on transitional justice, shaped the more contemporary reconceptualization of constitutionalism in the region? One can see the pursuit of transitional justice is under way in the courts now, which is calling the judiciary to a more activist review of transitional precedents, decisions which now are being reconceived in light of human rights developments, regional precedents and rights conventions. These decisions are having a landmark effect in the region, as they have shaped both the course of transitional justice, as well as of constitutional review. Hence, in the landmark case of *Simon, Julio Hector y otros*, involving illegal detention, torture, and disappearances, Argentina's high court wrestled with the critical question of the extent to which the country's amnesty policy was reconcilable with its constitution and binding international law. In the most recent set of precedents,[43] the Court appeared to reverse prior transitional justice policy, in that this Supreme Court decision struck down amnesties, even those that had been politically arrived at and validated within the existing constitutional system (Elias 2008). Amnesties had apparently been accepted within the Argentine constitutional system, despite the legally prevailing context of incorporating human rights treaties into its domestic law (Levit 1999). These parallel developments inevitably had an effect on the legitimacy of domestic constitutionalism, particularly in light of its predecessor record as well as the perceptions of the strength of the country's commitment to international human rights. Indeed, one might see this latter wave of transitional justice as reflexive and responsive to predecessor judicial review and its shortcomings, with consequences for human rights protection in the prior period of repressive rule.

Now, let us turn to the constitutional developments occasioned as a result of the changes in doctrine and normativity discussed above. With the passage of time, non-state actors turned to alternative fora, whether international, or regional, or domestic courts via 'universal jurisdiction', as well as new transitional justice institutions. The ad hoc international criminal tribunals have given new meaning to these treaties. They have been applied and interpreted to vitiate standing amnesties, with implications over the long run for our constitutional balance of powers. Indeed, as we will see, where punishment involves offenses such as the 'crime against humanity', this norm is broad enough to become a placeholder, to evolve over the years with both internal and interstate ramifications, as well as, more broadly, for the course of current foreign affairs discourse.

These developments reflect the evolution of the relevant freedoms at stake – in the direction of the reconceptualization of relevant state power, where the meaning of state action for purposes of transitional justice and constitutionalism is no longer seen as limited or 'negative' as in earlier phases, but, rather, implies the protection of a range of other rights as well. Moreover, these rights weren't conceived purely as limits on state power, but instead, as establishing a basis for action, indeed, presenting obligations for the state and non-state actors. In *Simon*, 2005, the Argentine Supreme Court ruled the Ley de Punto Final and the Ley de Obediencia Debida unconstitutional. Because these crimes fell within the law of the time, that is, Ley de Obediencia Debida, the Court found the legislation 'unconstitutional' largely in terms of international human rights norms, violating the American Convention on Human Rights, the ICCPR, and the Convention against Torture (Bakker 2005). With this case, although close to two decades after the repressive period, the Argentine Supreme Court struck down the laws that had limited prosecutions. In doing so, it drew upon the regional American norms that had evolved in the meantime and were seen as incorporated within the country's constitutionalism.[44]

How should we evaluate this change? One might say that the first transitional and constitutional response in the region was to limit the state. This can be seen in post-authoritarian constitutionalism, with its notion of strong states *with* strong constitutions. For this purpose a form of restoration of the constitutionalism that had preceded the authoritarian rule was enough; but, with the passage of time, it is clear that this is no longer deemed sufficient to establish and convey the rule of law.

To what extent could the change in constitutionalism be effected without a loss of legitimacy? There is a return to a prior normative dimension of transitional justice in constitutional law, as it would be the post-Alfonsin administration that would give human rights treaties constitutional standing when the first successor regime had moved to amend the constitution in 1993.

Simon appears to present a complete overturning of the prior consensus on transitional justice, reflecting an apparent rebalancing of the values of justice of transition, with effects for domestic constitutionalism as well. It reflected a division in the criminal justice power, which would seem to go to the core of enforcement of laws, at least where certain core crimes are no longer completely within domestic jurisdiction. The Argentine Supreme Court held that where crimes against humanity are at stake, there is no temporal limitation on prosecution, despite the three decades and substantial passage of time since the event.[45] The continuity of state responsibility becomes a constitutional principle.

RECONSTITUTING EUROPE: TRANSITIONAL JUSTICE FOR ITS PEOPLES

Lastly, I turn to the ways post-cold war transitional justice is informing understandings of the state and interstate relations, and the conceptualization of the public and the private, of internal and international conflict in the European space. In particular, how do the evolution of current instances of militancy fit into the category? They clearly, for example, share the teleological conception of constitutionalism. Here we can see the context for modern European instances as linked to actual contemporary constitutional transitions in the makeup of European constitutional states.

Once again, we will see the effect of judicialization on the direction of development of conceptions of state responsibility, as well as of the view of its state's relation to other actors as well. Let us begin with the International Tribunal for the former Yugoslavia which, in response to the post-cold war Balkans conflict, reaffirmed Nuremberg's central principle of the subjectivization of responsibility for crimes against humanity and underscored the message of accountability for ethnic persecution, that is, for crimes against peoples. This was a principle of jurisprudence with constitutive dimensions with regard to states and the role of peoples on the continent.

Even more significant for understanding the normativity of constitutionalism, beyond its role in conflict, *strictu sensu*, is where we can see the institutions of punishment offering a basis for the renunciation of military and/or other collective sanctions. Cooperation with judicial processes is seen as evidence of reconciliatory aims and tantamount to a promise to co-operate with other European purposes and institutions. Thus, European Commission President José Manuel Barroso speaking of the arrest of Radovan Karadzic, the war architect of ethnic cleansing: 'This … very positive development … will contribute to bringing justice and lasting reconciliation in the Western Balkans'. Here we can see the EU accession process being made conditional on signs of adoption of transitional justice of a conciliatory nature. And, in so doing, taking what might amount to a stance on just war and demilitarization, plausibly of relevance going forward to integration in the region.

The complexity of the regional transitional justice project would commence with a private actor – a radical transformation in the understanding of state action and responsibility. *Tadic* was the first case before the ICTY and one in which it was confronted with a defendant who was a private, not a state, actor, but where the connection to the state remained an important question. As the tribunal opined, 'It is nevertheless imperative to *specify* what *degree of authority or control* must be wielded by a foreign State over armed forces fighting on its behalf in order to render international an armed conflict which is *prima facie* internal. Indeed, the legal consequences of the characterization of the conflict as either internal or international are extremely important. Should the conflict eventually be classified as international, it would *inter alia* follow that a foreign State may in certain circumstances be held responsible for violations of international law perpetrated by the armed groups acting on its behalf.'[46]

The EU accession process required Serbia to cooperate with the ICTY in a number of ways, including making efforts to apprehend suspects and turning them over to international justice.[47] Whether in regard to constitutionalism within states in the region, or to the European Union as a transnational constitutional order, we can see now the ways that transitional justice operates as a precondition for the EU constitutional project. European Commission President José Manuel Barroso said of the Milosevic trial, 'It proves the determination of the new Serbian government to achieve full cooperation with the ICTY. Observers agree that the EU strategy of conditioning the progress of ex-Yugoslav countries towards joining the union on their cooperation with the International Criminal Tribunal for the former Yugoslavia, ICTY, "has been a key tool in ensuring that perpetrators of war crimes committed during the Nineties Balkans wars face trial and victims see justice." It is also very important for Serbia's European aspirations.' EU foreign policy Chief Javier Solana has said, 'it shows the commitment of the new Serbian government to cooperate with international organizations'. Here, the ICTY – as an institution both transitional and international – operating to reconstitute the relevant community of judgment – offers a rule of law that gestures toward an alternative normative future. Moreover, the Tribunal's purposes reflect the role of politics in rationalizing the broader humanity (human security) bases of these trials.

One can see the ways in which this dimension of transitional justice promotes constitutionalism in Serbia in the broader sense. It shows some willingness to move forward with respect to responsibility, breaking with the previous regime and also addressing the role of non-state actors as to accountability. This approach has now taken off with the RECOM.[48] This would reinforce local justice processes and point in a new direction as to the commitment to protect minorities.

Likewise, we can see in the consideration of other countries, for example, Turkey, respecting EU membership, there has been a need to address a number of unresolved long delayed conflicts. After decades of silence, it is only in the context of EU accession aspirations that Turkey has indicated willingness to engage regarding its past conflicts, involving Armenians and Kurdish peoples. With respect to the Armenians, Turkey has said it has been prepared to acknowledge the past and to address repair, referring the matter to a historical commission.[49] For Prime Minister Erdogan, 'Today is the beginning of a new timeline and a fresh start', saying with regard to its Kurdish population, that it would recognize them and pay compensation: 'fresh start: overhaul would expand use of minority language in a number of settings including national media and politics'. [50] As at the start of the Balkans conflict, the protection of such rights is seen as key to the state's legitimacy in the new union.[51]

Here we can see the assumption regarding these attempts at accountability seems to be that dealing with a state's past grievances reflects on its democratic potential for the future – although dealing with the past may well be easier than showing such capacities exist to deal with conflicts in the here and now. But, more fundamentally, it is predicated on the view that justice is the path to transformation in the treatment of transitional peoples in the region.

CONTEMPORARY CONSTITUTIONALISM AS THE LAW OF PEOPLES

Now let us turn to developments regarding the meaning of self-determination and political equality within the polity. The European Court of Human Rights, in a recent case, *Sejdic and Finci v Bosnia and Herzegovina*, conceded the transitional usefulness of ethnically based representation following the Balkans conflict,

> When the impugned constitutional provisions were put in place a very fragile cease-fire was in effect on the ground. The provisions were designed to end a brutal conflict marked by genocide and 'ethnic cleansing.' The nature of the conflict was such that the approval of the 'constituent peoples' (namely, the Bosniacs, Croats and Serbs) was necessary to ensure peace ... a challenge to the existing power sharing arrangements in Bosnia-Herzogovina on an ethnic 'constituent peoples' basis excluding out representatives other than Bosnian Croats and Serbs, where the Court ruled that such structures were racially and ethnically discriminatory. 'Racial discrimination is a particularly egregious kind of discrimination ... requires from the authorities special vigilance ... the authorities must use all available means to combat racism, thereby reinforcing democracy's vision of a society in which diversity is not perceived as a threat but as a source of enrichment.'[52]

Indeed, by ratifying a Stabilization and Association Agreement with the European Union in 2008, the European Court of Human Rights found that the respondent State had committed itself to 'amend[ing] electoral legislation regarding members of the Bosnia and Herzegovina Presidency and House of Peoples delegates to ensure full compliance with the European Convention on Human Rights and the Council of Europe post-accession commitments' within one to two years.[53]

Here, one can see a growing connection between transitional justice and what Joseph Weiler and others have described as the federal trajectory of Europe (Weiler 1999). Reconciliation processes undertaken in the midst of the accession process, more generally, have resulted in evolution towards protection of indigenous peoples, reflecting new-found capacities for an array of effective judicial and other responses beyond the recognition and protection of individual rights. The state's responsibility in relation to the collective rights of indigenous peoples, a transitional response to 'ethnic cleansing', had already become part of the canon of transitional justice (for example, *Velasquez-Rodriguez*), where affirming these rights implies attendant rights to judicial guarantees such as identification, prosecution and reparations, or other past persecution-oriented rights. In the words of the Court, 'The State has a legal duty to take reasonable steps to prevent human rights violations and to use the means at its disposal to carry out a serious investigation of violations committed within its jurisdiction, to identify those responsible, to impose the appropriate punishment and to ensure the victim adequate compensation'.[54]

Beneath the surface lurks the perennial question about Europe's old divisions, and where exactly the peoples might fit within the modern state, as well as within the new entity of Europe. The element of a persecutory motive[55] uniquely mediates protection of individual and group identities so long as there are systematic mechanisms of state or state-like policy.[56] Indeed, to adjudicate the responsibility for humanity also means reaching the public and the private – whether in its perpetration, going beyond state sponsorship, but also, concern as to the protected person, and the sense of victimhood that goes beyond its relation to the state to the protection of various dimensions of civil society. It also entails protecting and accounting for individuals – as they are – with their affiliations,[57] and related political identities, delineating clear limits on what is, and what is not, legitimate state and parastate action in the twentieth century, and informing a standard of global accountability and governance.

Here, there are at least two lessons, one regarding the impact of transitional justice at the level of the state and the other informing the principles guiding interstate relations. First, and foremost, one can see that such discriminatory tactics can no longer be used to rationalize the state – that a state's constitutional identity can no longer be rationalized or entrenched around the *ethnos* – with implications internally for the conception of the constitution itself. And so for the interstate realm as well: the line of insistence on compliance reflects the clear limits to ethnonationalism being established in suits for corrective justice, such as that brought by Bosnia against Serbia, in the World Court. Laying down strict principles as to the permissibility of 'ethnic cleansing' also offers guidance as to the parameters of legitimate political identity.

This could explain, without necessarily justifying, the absence of representatives of the other communities (such as local Roma and Jewish communities) at the peace negotiations and the participants' preoccupation with effective equality between the 'constituent peoples' in the 'post-conflict society'. However, in this landmark case, the Court went on to set constitutional limits to such exercises of justice, ruling that, even if at an earlier point in the transitions, such political structures might well have a legitimate aim such as peace, at present such measures had to be said to be evaluated in terms of their proportionality:

> ... the maintenance of the system in any event does not satisfy the requirement of proportionality... while the Court agrees with the Government that there is no requirement under the Convention to abandon totally the power-sharing mechanisms peculiar to Bosnia and Herzegovina and that the time may still not be ripe for a political system which would be a simple reflection of majority rule, the Opinions of the Venice Commission ... clearly demonstrate that there exist mechanisms of power-sharing which do not automatically lead to the total exclusion of representatives of the other communities ... it is recalled that the possibility of alternative means achieving the same end is an important factor in this sphere (see Glor v. Switzerland, no. 13444/04, § 94, 30 April 2009).[58]

Given that the *ethnos* is no longer an acceptable basis for state formation, to what extent can its preservation afford a basis for intervention, and if so, in what way? On the question of the direction of state external sovereignty, to some extent one can see that current developments in the conceptualization of state action and state responsibility (for example in the

Bosnia v Serbia case) are explicitly broadening the nexus to the state. This naturally impacts accountability and the view of the state for constitutional purposes. As the World Court held, 'The Court is however of the view that the particular characteristics of genocide do not justify the Court in departing from the criterion elaborated in the Judgment in the case concerning Military and Paramilitary Activities in and against Nicaragua (*Nicaragua v United States of America*). The rules for attributing alleged internationally wrongful conduct to a State do not vary with the nature of the wrongful act in question in the absence of a clearly expressed *lex specialis*. Genocide will be considered as attributable to a State if and to the extent that the physical acts constitutive of genocide that have been committed by organs or persons other than the State's own agents were carried out, wholly or in part, on the instructions or directions of the State, or under its effective control'.[59]

Here, it is interesting to think about the ways the Bosnia case has been influenced and informed both by the ICTY's transitional justice following the world court decision, and to consider other ECHR decisions recognizing the clear limits of ethnonationalism. In the landmark case of *Sejdic and Finci v Bosnia and Herzegovina*, discussed above, the European Court of Human Rights, in supervising the transitional agreement in the region, sharply circumscribed the potential of legislating along ethnic lines, explaining that 'no difference in treatment which is based exclusively or to a decisive extent on a person's ethnic origin is capable of being objectively justified in a contemporary democratic society built on the principles of pluralism and respect for different cultures'.[60]

At the same time, even as it recognized the ways in which this area is now affected by the new post-cold war institutions that seek to identify responsibility of other actors in the system while elaborating a new approach to state responsibility, the World Court has not yet held the state responsible for all of these actions. One might therefore ask why such attribution was rejected in *Bosnia v Serbia*, as the ICJ rejected the notion that the state must pay reparations.[61] It did so despite recent precedents which had an explicit understanding of the significance of collective identity for both the human as individual, and the group as part of humankind, protection in terms of the status of humanity – where normativity always enmeshes the group in its particulars, *as well as* the status of humankind in general.

From the perspective of this justice-oriented case law, we can better understand the site of some of these recurring issues of religion, gender and ethnicity as involving the balancing and reconciliation of the relevant preservation rights of persons and peoples, where group claims can be grounded on part of their traditions. These varying claims help to clarify the reconciliation/accommodation needed at the level of the state.

CONCLUSION: TRANSITIONAL JUSTICE AS TWENTY-FIRST CENTURY CONSTITUTIONALISM

This discussion yields observations as to the relation today of transitional justice and constitutionalism, namely that what we are seeing indubitably amounts to a new constitutionalism – one with distinct subjectivity and rule of law. The evolving normativity is enmeshed with contemporary politics and can tell us something about the conundra that lie at the heart of state politics today.

Principles of state responsibility that cut across the public and the private are being recognized via transitional justice, with implications for the reconceptualization of constitutionalism. There are some interpretations that assert the emergence of a global constitutionalism, representing in Habermas' (2006) words 'the unity of the global legal system'.[62] By contrast, the perspective that informs this chapter emphasizes neither systemic unity nor normative hierarchy, but the dialogic character of interpretation and the mutual influence of diverse legal orders.

The very problem of justice is now being reconceptualized, and it no longer centers on the state. If the classic understanding of the role of the state is to protect its citizens, via its central control of use of force, then these contemporary instances point to instances where there has been a loss of such control.

Rather than the centrality of the state, and the related aim to constitutionalize delimitation of state power, transitional constitutionalism poses a challenge that directly engages non-state actors and their behavior at all levels and entails changing social norms. One can see dimensions of the above paradigm shift reflected in phenomena that address globalizing politics of a transitional nature. In the move away from the immediate post-cold war conflicts that span international to internal conflict, such as in Milosevic's Balkans or Saddam's Iraq, we start out by emphasizing state action, missing relevant transitional justice. We then move to evident weak and failed states, such as Afghanistan or Lebanon, to the paramilitaries in Sudan, where the relevant problem has changed: accounting for the varieties of transitional justice, in light of the growing pursuit of forms of accountability beyond the state. Appreciating fully this shift in perspective helps to explain the rise of international criminal justice, illuminating the role of the institutions of judgment.

The shift will have consequences for the evaluation of transitional justice and its relation to other political questions of conflict and resolution.[63] This chapter's normative take is that better understanding of this recent stage of aims, actors and interests, and associated important changes, will have a significant impact upon the relevant measure for assessment of transitional justice and its relation to constitutionalism in the new century.

As seen above, transitional situations have set the stage for the evolution of constitutionalism such that, in many such situations, it targets rights abuses not committed by official state actors. One can see also the ways group claims have driven the aspiration of transition to a new polity, and, moreover, the reclamation of individual freedom. The task is creation of a legitimate polity in the first place, with transitional justice and constitution building both being about construction/reconstruction of identity building, informing a transformed relationship among collectivities – one which is not simply reflective of the pre-existing structure and identity of society.

NOTES

*   My gratitude to Rob Howse and Nehal Bhuta for very thoughtful comments.
1.   See German Constitution, Article 19; see also Ruti Teitel, 'Militating Democracy: Comparative Constitutional Perspectives', *Michigan Journal of International Law* 29 (2008): 49.
2.   Article 19 of the European Convention on Human Rights provides: 'To ensure the observance of the engagements undertaken by the High Contracting Parties in the present Convention, there shall be set up: 1. A European Commission of Human Rights hereinafter referred to as "the Commission"; 2. A European Court of Human Rights, hereinafter referred to as "the Court".'
3.   Convention for the Protection of Human Rights and Fundamental Freedoms, 4 November 1950, 213 UNTS 221: Article 10.
4.   See *Prosecutor v Ruggui*, Case No. ICTR-97-32-I, Judgment and Sentence (1 June 2000); *Nahimana,*

Barayagwiza, Ngeze v Prosecutor, Case No. ICTR-99-52-A, Appeals Chamber (28 November 2007); *Prosecutor v Kambanda*, Case No. ICTR 97-23-S, Judgment and Sentence (3 September 1998).

5.   Treaty of Lisbon Amending the Treaty on European Union and the Treaty Establishing the European Community, *Lisbon*, 13 December 2007, OJ [2007] C306/1; Bundesvervassungsgericht, Lisbon decision of 30 June 2009, available at http://www.bundesverfassungsgericht.de/entscheidungen/es200906302bve000208en. html.

6.   Convention on the Elimination of All Forms of Discrimination Against Women ('CEDAW'), adopted 18 December 1979, GA Res. 34/180, UN GAOR 34th Sess., Supp. No. 46, UN Doc. A/34/36 (1980) (entered into force 3 September 1981).

7.   See Promotion of National Unity and Reconciliation Act of South Africa, 1995.

8.   See *People's Organization (AZAPO) v The President of the Republic of South Africa*, 1996 (4) SALR 671, para. 19 (South African Constitutional Court) [Hereinafter *AZAPO* case]; see also Teitel (2000).

9.   *AZAPO* case, para. 19.

10. See 'Truth and Reconciliation Commission of South Africa Report', Vol. 5, *Truth and Reconciliation Commission* (29 October 1998), para. 66.

11. For discussion of this form of political arrangement, see Shapiro (1999).

12. See Constitution of the Republic of South Africa (1996), Articles 25–7.

13. See ibid. (in relation to property, housing, health care, food, water, 'the state must take reasonable legislative and other measures, within its available resources, to achieve the progressive realization of these rights'.).

14. See Constitution of the Republic of South Africa (1996), Articles 30, 31.

15. See discussion in Scott and Alston (2000). See *Government of the Republic of South Africa and Others v Grootboom and Others* (CCT11/00) [2000] ZACC 19; 2001 (1) SA 46; 2000 (11) BCLR 1169; (4 October 2000) (holding there is a right to housing); *Minister of Health and Others v Treatment Action Campaign and Others (No 1)* (CCT9/02) [2002] ZACC 16; 2002 (5) SA 703; 2002 (10) BCLR 1075 (5 July 2002) (finding a right to health care and access to HIV/AIDS treatment).

16. South African constitution, Article 26.

17. *AZAPO*, para. 4.

18. *AZAPO*, para. 22.

19. Indeed, the court's conceptualization opposes victimhood. See *AZAPO* case, para. 19 (referring to choice of 'ubuntu. . . humaneness over victimization').

20. 'Brazil Court Upholds Law that Protects Torturers', 30 April 2010, available at http://www.amnesty.org/en/ news-and-updates/brazil-court-upholds-law-protects-torturers-2010-04-30; see also 'Brazil: No Change to Amnesty Law', *New York Times*, 1 May 2010, sec. A5.

21. On 20–21 May 2010, the case was heard at the Inter-American Court of Human Rights. 'Caso Gomes Lund y otros vs. Brasil', Communicado de Prensa, CIDH_CP-08/10 ESPAÑOL, available in Spanish and Portuguese only, at http://www.corteidh.or.cr/.

22. See *Khulumani v Barclay Nat'l Bank Ltd.*, 504 F.3d 254, 258 (2d Cir., 2007), *aff'd Am. Isuzu Motors, Inc. v Ntsebeza*, 128 S. Ct. 2424 (2008).

23. See ibid.

24. See *AZAPO* case, paras 26, 27, 30, 31 citing Geneva Protocol II, Article 6(5).

25. *Barrios Altos Case*, Series C No. 75 [2001] IACHR 5 (14 March 2001), para. 15 (concurring opinion of Judge Ramirez).

26. See *Rome Statute of the International Criminal Court*, Article 28, UN doc. A/Conf. 183/9, (17 July 1998).

27. See American convention, articles 1(1) and 2, whereby states parties are 'obliged to take all measures to ensure no deprivation of judicial protection'. Howse and Teitel (2010).

28. *Prosecutor v Milosevic*, Case No. IT-02-54 (International Criminal Tribunal for the Former Yugoslavia 1999).

29. *Deshaney v Winnebago*, 489 US 189 (1989) ('our cases have recognized that the Due Process Clauses generally confer no affirmative right to governmental aid, even where such aid may be necessary to secure life, liberty, or property interests of which the government itself may not deprive the individual. . . . a State's failure to protect an individual against private violence simply does not constitute a violation of the Due Process Clause.').

30. See *Velasquez Rodríguez v Honduras*, Case 7920, Ser. C., No. 4, IACHR 35, OEA/ser. L/V/III.19 doc. 13 (1988), reprinted in *International Legal Materials* 28 (1989): 291.

31. Ibid.

32. See ibid., para. 170.

33. See ibid., para. 172.

34. See ibid., para. 124 (allowing circumstantial evidence to make out particular disappearance claim).

35. Ibid.

36. See ibid., para. 174.

37. See *Barrios Altos v Peru*, IACHR Ser. C No. 75 (14 March 2001), para. 189.

38. See ibid. Compare para. 41 and para. 44.

39. Ibid., para. 2(j).
40. Ibid., para. 39.
41. See National Constitution of the Argentine Republic (1994), at Section 75(22)–(24) (stating that international treaties are part of the hierarchy of law in Argentina and authorizing Congress to enact laws giving force to international human rights treaties); see Levit (1999: 281).
42. On the course of the transition and prosecution policy, see Nino (1991). On the limits of textual incorporation, see Levit (1999).
43. *Simon, Julio Hector y otros*, 328 Fallos 2056 (2005) (striking unconstitutional Argentine amnesty laws).
44. Corte Suprema de Justicia [CSJN], 22/06/1987, 'Camps, Ramon Juan Alberto y otros / Causa incoada en virtud del decreto 280/84 del Poder Ejecutivo Nacional', Coleccion Oficial de Fallos de la Corte Suprema de Justicia de la Nacion [Fallos] (1987-310-1162) (Arg.).
45. See *Arancibia Clavel, Enrique Lautaro y Otros*, Corte Suprema de Justicia (CSJN), 24/8/2004.
46. *Prosecutor v Tadic*, Case No. IT-94-1, Judgment (International Criminal Tribunal for the Former Yugoslavia, 15 July 1999): para. 97; emphasis in original.
47. The relations between Serbia and the European Union deteriorated in spring 2006 due to the negative assessment of Serbia's cooperation with the International Criminal Tribunal for the former Yugoslavia in The Hague that had insisted on the extradition of Serbian suspected war criminals to the ICTY. Failure of Serbian authorities to locate and arrest remaining fugitives led the European Commission to call off negotiations on the Stabilization and Association Agreement with Serbia and Montenegro on 3 May 2006. See Simon Jennings, 'EU Urged to Boost Balkan Reconciliation Efforts', *Institute for War and Peace Reporting* (May 2009), available at www.iwpr.net; see also Simon Jennings, 'Calls for Bigger EU Role in Balkan Stability Efforts', *Institute for War and Peace Reporting*, 26 May 2009, available at http://www.iwpr.net/report-news/calls-bigger-eu-role-balkan-stability-efforts ('A total of 161 individuals suspected of war crimes have been charged and 60 convicted – is not being followed up with sufficient backing for regional war crimes trials and efforts to counter ethnic divisions still prevalent across the region.').
48. The new civil society project regarding transitional justice in the region; see Humanitarian Law Center website, available at http://www.hlc-rdc.org/.
49. Although regrettably not accepted by Armenia, see 'Turkey in Europe: Breaking the Vicious Circle', second report of the Independent Commission on Turkey (September 2009): 30–31.
50. See Sebnem Arsu, 'Turkey Unveils Plan for Kurdish Rights', *New York Times* (global edition a3, 10 November 2009) (seeking a 'fresh start: overhaul would expand use of minority language in a number of settings including national media and politics').
51. See *Conference on Peace in Yugoslavia, Arbitration Commission*, Opinion No. 1, 11 January 1991, reprinted in 31 ILM 1494 (1992).
52. *Case of Sejdic and Finci v Bosnia and Herzegovina*, Judgment, Application Nos. 27996/06 and 34836/06 (European Court of Human Rights, 22 December 2009): para. 49.
53. *Case of Sejdic and Finci v Bosnia and Herzegovina*, para. 49. The applicants, Mr Dervo Sejdić and Mr Jakob, brought their complaints relating to their ineligibility to stand for election to the House of Peoples and the Presidency of Bosnia and Herzegovina on the ground of their Roma and Jewish origin.
54. *Velasquez Rodriguez Case*, Judgment, (Ser. C) No. 4 (Inter-American Court of Human Rights 1988).
55. See *Convention on the Prevention and Punishment of the Crime of Genocide* (1948) entered into Force, 12 January 1951, 78 UNTS 277 (defining 'genocide' in terms of acts committed 'with intent to destroy, in whole or in part, a national, ethnical, racial or religious group, as such'). Regarding the recognition of crimes against humanity, see Agreement for the Prosecution and Punishment of the Major War Criminals of the European Axis, and Charter of the International Military Tribunal, 82 UNTS 279 (1945): Article 6(c).
56. See *Prosecutor v Kupreskic*, Case No. IT-95-16, Judgment (Trial Chamber, International Criminal Tribunal for the Former Yugoslavia, 14 January 2000): para. 543. In the 1987 prosecution of Klaus Barbie, a Nazi chief in occupied Lyon, France's High Court defined persecution as committed in a systematic manner in the name of '[s]tate practicing a policy of ideological supremacy', *Federation Nationale des Deportes et Internes Resistants et Patriotes and Others v Barbie*, 78 ILR 125, 128 (Criminal Chamber, French Court of Cassation, 1985).
57. On the significance to preservation of identity of such affiliations for persons, see Habermas (2001).
58. *Case of Sejdic and Finci v Bosnia and Herzegovina*, Judgment, Application Nos. 27996/06 and 34836/06 (European Court of Human Rights, 22 December 2009): paras. 46–50.
59. *Case Concerning the Application of the Convention on the Prevention and Punishment of the Crime of Genocide (Bosnia and Herzegovina v Serbia and Montenegro)* 2007 ICJ 91 (2007): para. 401.
60. *Case of Sejdic and Finci v Bosnia and Herzegovina*, Judgment, Application Nos. 27996/06 and 34836/06 (European Court of Human Rights, 22 December 2009): para. 44.
61. Relying on ad hoc international criminal tribunal as to the identification of the targeted group, *Case Concerning the Application of the Convention on the Prevention and Punishment of the Crime of Genocide (Bosnia and Herzegovina v Serbia and Montenegro)* 2007 ICJ 91, 195–201 (2007).
62. Habermas (2006, ch. 8) lays out his view of constitutionalism beyond the state and grounded in international

law. Regarding his view of non-state-based constitutionalization of international law, see Habermas (2008). For an analysis of other pockets of international law characterized as involving the constitutionalization of international law, see Dunoff and Trachtman (2009). Cf. Howse (2008) and Petersmann (2008).

63. *The Rule of Law and Transitional Justice in Conflict and Post-Conflict Societies: Report of the Secretary General*, UN Doc. S/2004/616 (2004).

REFERENCES

Alvarez, Jose (1999), 'Crimes of State, Crimes of Hate, Lessons from Rwanda', *Yale Journal of International Law* 24: 365.

Bakker, Christine A.E. (2005), 'A Full Stop to Amnesty in Argentina: The Simon Case', *Journal of International Criminal Justice* 3(5): 1106.

Benvenisti, Eyal (1993), 'Judicial Misgivings Regarding the Application of International Law: An Analysis of Attitudes of National Courts', *European Journal of International Law* 159.

Bohmer, Martin (2008), 'Hybrid Legal Cultures, Borrowings and Impositions: The Use of Foreign Law as a Strategy to Build Constitution and Democratic Authority', *University of Puerto Rico Law Review* 77: 411.

Cohen, Jean L., ed. (2005), 'Rethinking Sovereignty', Special Issue, *Constellations* 12(2).

Cornell, Drucilla (2005), 'Exploring ubuntu: Tentative Reflections', *African Human Rights Law Journal* 5(2): 195.

Crawford, James (2002), *The International Law Commission's Articles on State Responsibility: Introduction, Text and Commentaries*, Cambridge: Cambridge University Press.

Dorsen, Norman, Michael Rosenfeld, Andras Sajo and Susanne Baer (2010), *Comparative Constitutionalism: Cases and Materials*, 2nd edition, St. Paul, MN: Thomson West.

Dunoff, Jeffrey and Joel Trachtman, eds. (2009), *Ruling the World: Constitutionalism, International Law and Global Governance*, Cambridge: Cambridge University Press.

Elias, Jose Sebastian (2008), 'Constitutional Changes, Transitional Justice and Legitimacy, The Life and Death of Argentina's Amnesty Laws', *Hastings International and Comparative Law Review* 31: 587.

Habermas, Jurgen (2001), *The Postnational Constellation: Political Essays*, Cambridge: Polity Press.

Habermas, Jurgen (2006), *The Divided West*, Cambridge: Polity Press.

Habermas, Jurgen (2008), 'The Constitutionalization of International Law and the Legitimation Problems of a Constitution for World Society', *Constellations* 15(4): 444–5.

Holmes, Stephen (1997), 'What Russia Teaches Us Now: How Weak States Threaten Freedom', *The American Prospect*, 30 June.

Howse, Robert (2008), 'Human Rights, International Economic Law and Constitutional Justice: A Reply', *European Journal of International Law* 19: 945.

Howse, Robert and Ruti Teitel (2010), 'Beyond Compliance: Rethinking Why International Law Really Matters', *New York University Journal of International Law & Politics* 1(2): 127.

Levit, Janet Koven (1999), 'The Constitutionalization of Human Rights in Argentina: Problem or Promise?', *Columbia Journal Transnational Law* 37: 281.

Nino, Carlos S. (1991), 'The Duty to Punish Past Abuses of Human Rights Put into Context: The Case of Argentina', *Yale Law Journal* 100: 2619.

Petersmann, Ernst-Ulrich (2008), 'Human Rights, International Economic Law and Constitutional Justice', *European Journal of International Law* 19: 769.

Scott, Craig M. and Philip Alston (2000), 'Adjudicating Constitutional Priorities in a Transnational Context: A Comment on Soobramoney's Legacy and Grootboom's Promise', *South African Journal of Human Rights* 16(2): 206.

Shany, Yuval (2006), 'How Supreme is the Supreme Law of the Land? A Comparative Analysis of the Influence of International Human Rights Conventions upon the Interpretation of Constitutional Texts by Domestic Courts', *Brooklyn Journal of International Law* 31: 341.

Shapiro, Ian (1999), *Democratic Justice*, New Haven: Yale University Press.

Smiley, Marion (2001), 'Democratic Justice in Transition', *Michigan Law Review* 99: 1332 (reviewing Ian Shapiro, *Democratic Justice*, New Haven: Yale University Press, 1999).

Teitel, Ruti (2000), *Transitional Justice*, Oxford: Oxford University Press.

Teitel, Ruti (2008), 'Militating Democracy: Comparative Constitutional Perspectives', *Michigan Journal of International Law* 29: 49.

Tribe, Larry H. (1986), *Constitutional Choices*, Cambridge, MA: Harvard University Press.

Tushnet, Mark (1999) *Taking the Constitution Away from the Courts*, Princeton: Princeton University Press.

Weiler, Joseph (1999), *The Constitution of Europe: 'Do the New Clothes Have an Emperor?' and Other Essays on European Integration*, Cambridge: Cambridge University Press.

5. Constitutional drafting and external influence
Zaid Al-Ali

1 INTRODUCTION

External influence on a constitution-making process can be exercised actively through the direct intervention of an external actor, or passively through the impact of a series of norms or rules, A wide range of actors can be involved, including multilateral organizations such as the United Nations, the World Bank and the International Monetary Fund, individual states, civil society organizations (including well-established state-funded political organizations such as the German *stiftungen*) and individual scholars or advisers who are commissioned by participants in the constitution-making process itself to provide advice on specific issues. Recent experience indicates that external actors are almost always motivated by a desire to ensure the protection of fundamental rights and adherence to international best practice in the constitution's final draft. Although this necessarily means that they seek to influence the drafting process towards a certain outcome, many observers would probably agree that this type of influence has on the whole been enormously useful in the development of constitutional law in countless countries in recent decades. Importantly, however, recent experience also shows that different categories of external actor behave according to separate standards of behavior, sometimes to the extent that external influence can skew constitution-making processes in favor of undesirable outcomes.

By virtue of the generally accepted principle that nations do not interfere in each other's internal affairs, states tend not to intervene directly in the constitution-making process of other states except under exceptional circumstances, such as in post-conflict situations. Where foreign state actors are involved, however, a number of concerns arise. Recent experience shows that where a specific state actor has an interest – political or economic – in the outcome of a particular drafting process, some of its contributions to the drafting process can be less than benign. Despite the incredible weight and importance that is rightly attributed to the act of drafting a constitution, little to no oversight is exercised on the actions of participating bodies (whether by oversight institutions within the country in question or by oversight institutions in an external actor's home country). As a result, foreign state actors often feel at liberty to place their interests before those of the constitution-making society in question, safe in the knowledge that their actions will almost certainly not be the subject of review by the relevant institutions or bodies back home.[1] The same principle applies to individual actors acting on their own behalf (including individual advisers who have been retained by constitutional committees, particular political parties or even individual drafters) in constitutional drafting exercises, who are typically motivated by a desire to contribute positively but who can also be motivated by self-interest.[2]

In contrast, within multilateral institutions such as the United Nations, the internal convergence of political interests is often such that the institutions as a whole tend to be incapable of pursuing any political aim other than encouraging the constitution-making society in question to satisfy minimum standards in terms of fundamental rights and democratic governance. Also, where multilateral organizations such as the United Nations establish local missions to assist constitution-making societies in the drafting process, the makeup of those missions is often too diverse to permit any national self-interest to impact the advice given.[3] On the other hand, a number of other factors (including institutional weakness, the desire to avoid conflict or even controversy within the international community of actors, amongst others) can also impact the manner in which institutions behave during delicate constitutional negotiations, often forcing them to subordinate their own goals to those of other external actors, in particular state actors.

The particular identity of the external actors that are involved in a constitution-making process is but one of the factors that can determine the type of interaction that will exist between the international community of actors and the constitution-making society in question. Other factors include the identity and legal tradition of the constitution-making society in question, as well as whether the process in question is being organized in a post-conflict situation. Through the study of a number of recent constitution-making processes, this contribution finds that varying circumstances have sometimes led external actors to exercise their considerable influence selectively, sometimes favoring particular areas of intervention over others. At the same time, there is strong evidence that areas of intervention that have been subordinated in favor of specific interests have in many cases resurfaced in later years as being particularly problematic. This contribution ends by arguing in favor of more equal treatment by external actors of areas including fundamental rights and the establishment of an effective system of government, while at the same time making a more concerted effort to prevent national drafters from settling on a set of rules that would threaten to increase the risk of conflict or that would lead to the establishment of ineffective government.

2   CASE STUDIES

It would be natural to expect that external actors would prioritize the protection of fundamental rights in all constitutional processes, and that the framework for governance is an issue that would be carefully studied in all situations with a view to avoiding the establishment of unrepresentative or unresponsive government, or worse to avoid prolonging or instigating a conflict within the country in question. It would also be natural to expect that, where a constitution-drafting process is part of the effort to end a conflict, the priority would be to end the conflict in question by adopting a framework or agreement that would be satisfactory to the warring parties. Iraq, Afghanistan and Bosnia and Herzegovina illustrate the shifting priorities of external actors, and also demonstrate how the international community of actors sometimes contributes to the predicament that many states suffer from today.

2.1   Iraq

During the drafting of the 2006 Constitution in Iraq,[4] the issue of women's rights proved particularly contentious, and provoked a number of interventions on the part of the international community. Despite an early commitment by the Iraqi drafters, apparent from the first drafts that were produced in early July 2005, to the general principle of non-discrimination on the basis of 'gender, race, [sect], origin, colour, religion, creed, belief or opinion' (Article

1, Chapter 2, 20 July draft), a question mark was raised as to whether specific responsibilities would be imposed on women by the constitution, forcing them to conform to a fundamentalist vision of society. Article 6, Chapter 2 of the 20 July draft provides that '[t]he state guarantees the fundamental rights of women and their equality with men, in all fields, according to the provisions of Islamic Sharia, and assists them to reconcile duties towards family and work in society'. Despite the lack of detail, and despite the earlier prohibition against sexual discrimination, the authors of this provision clearly sought to impose their specific vision of Iraqi society on the entire country, which would see women encouraged to become mothers regardless of their own personal choice, to dress modestly and in a way that would not bring disrepute to their male relatives, and to care for their elderly and ill relatives, without necessarily being assisted in any of these tasks by any men, who were not the subject of any specific obligations under the 20 July draft. Article 6, Chapter 2's wording was the source of a great deal of controversy within the Constitutional Committee, and caused consternation amongst women's groups, secular Iraqis and members of the international community, including officials from the United States Embassy and the United Nations. As a result, it was rewritten in practically every draft that was produced over the subsequent weeks, as opposed to other provisions such as the principle of non-discrimination, which remained essentially unchanged until the end of the negotiations. The draft article was eventually replaced by Article 29 of the final version of the Constitution, according to which: 'The State shall guarantee the protection of motherhood, childhood and old age, shall care for children and youth, and shall provide them with the appropriate conditions to develop their talents and abilities.' In the context of Iraqi legal and social traditions, the reference to the protection of motherhood is merely a reference to rights that many Iraqis take for granted today, such as maternity care and free health care in maternity wards. What distinguishes the final version from its original wording is that reference to women's undefined obligations 'towards family and work in society' was replaced by rights that actually conform to Iraqi traditions. The international community's interventions in relation to this issue were therefore successful in ensuring that all internationally recognized fundamental rights remained protected under the 2006 Constitution.

On the other hand, as the negotiations approached their end, a number of concerns were raised by many of the drafters and some internationals on the arrangement for federalism. In particular, by mid-August, the draft provided for a list of exclusive federal powers which many considered to be exceedingly short (to the extent that central government was deprived of the power to raise taxes), and for a mechanism that allowed for the formation of future 'regions' which barely imposed any limitations on the number of governorates that could merge to form a region. That arrangement was controversial for several reasons, including that it had in fact been designed by a minority of parties and incorporated into the draft only after the US Embassy had taken over the administration of the drafting process, over the objections of the majority of Iraqi political forces, who had at that point been excluded from the discussions altogether. In the political climate that was prevalent in Iraq at the time, many argued that the combination of those two provisions would lead to the formation of three large ethno-sectarian regions, and possibly even to the breakup of the country altogether. Many Iraqi drafters were concerned that this arrangement could serve to exacerbate the already intense civil conflict that had been raging in the country for some time.

That fear was shared by many in the international community. Advisers from the United Nations completed an internal 'summary and critical review' of the draft constitution on 15

September 2005, one month before the referendum date. It provided in relevant part that 'the provisions for the conversion of governorates into a region outside Kurdistan create a model for the territorial division of the State which in our view leaves the central government under-powered and possibly under resourced'.[5] Professor Yash Ghai, one of the world's leading constitutional scholars, acted as Process Adviser to the Chairman of the Iraqi Constitutional Committee. In an internal report drafted by Professor Ghai with Jill Cottrell and completed before the referendum date, they explained that the draft constitution 'could sharpen even further the divisions within Iraq and pose a serious threat to the unity and territorial integrity of the country. There are also technical deficiencies in the draft which are to some extent tied to key substantive provisions and will be hard to remedy. We have serious reservations whether the [Draft Constitution] as it stands can be fully and effectively implemented, without grave danger to state and society. Our analysis suggests that Iraqis need to give a great deal more thought to the modalities of its implementation than was possible in the process so far'.[6] That opinion was shared with the Iraqi constitutional committee and some members of the international community at the time but was not made public until much later.

Despite these concerns, the international community as a whole was not moved to intervene in the way that it did to protect fundamental rights and declared that it was satisfied with the Constitution's final text. There was in fact no appetite to debate the issue with the Iraqi constitutional committee given the insistence by the United States that the process should not be extended past the 15 October 2005 deadline, despite the fact that the possibility had been provided for in the interim constitution. The United States was apparently motivated by a desire to meet a certain number of benchmarks in Iraq, particularly with a view to portraying an image of progress for the purposes of domestic US politics. Thus, when the text of the 'summary and critical review' was leaked to the press, the UN Secretary General's Spokesman declared that it did not reflect the UN view and disingenuously added that '[t]he UN view is that the constitution should be judged by the Iraqis. The Secretary-General welcomed the adoption of the draft, the putting forward of the draft for the referendum, and this has always been an Iraqi-owned and Iraqi-led process, and it is up to them to judge the constitution'.[7] Despite this attempt to distance the international community from the constitutional process, the United Nations felt compelled to intervene in relation to Iraq's electoral framework precisely two days later when the Iraqi Transitional National Assembly passed a referendum law that many interpreted as having been designed with a view to disenfranchising a large proportion of the population. On the same day that the law was approved by the National Assembly, the United Nations explained to the press that '[w]e have expressed our position to the national assembly and to the leadership of the government and told them that the decision that was taken was not acceptable and would not meet international standards. Hopefully by tomorrow the situation will be clarified'.[8] Embarrassed into action, the law was amended by the National Assembly the next day in a way that was acceptable to the international community.

2.2   Afghanistan

The Afghan constitutional process bore witness to an almost identical pattern of behaviour.[9] In the period prior to the 2001 war and the introduction of the new constitutional system of government, Afghanistan was characterized by gross human rights violations (including particularly inhuman treatment of women) as well as unaccountable and unstable government (illustrated by frequent conflagrations throughout the country as well as numerous unconstitutional changes in government). As constitutional discussions commenced in the post-2001 period, the international community was heavily involved through the participation of a number of institutions (including the Center on International Cooperation at New York University, the United States Institute of Peace, amongst others), foreign diplomats, and the United Nations (although the latter purportedly sought to leave a light footprint on the discussions in theory to avoid establishing a culture of dependency on the part of the Afghan authorities) (Schoiswohl 2006). Throughout the process, a number of organized interventions were made by external actors to the Afghan Constitutional Commission in the form of position papers in order to suggest certain outcomes, mechanisms or wording in relation to specific issues. In one such intervention, New York University's Professor Barnett R. Rubin sought to encourage the Commission to explore mechanisms that would prevent Afghanistan's future government from being dominated by one faction or from lapsing into the familiar pattern of undemocratic and illegitimate rule. In a presentation to the Constitutional Commission, Professor Rubin advised that 'as drafters of the constitution you can design a presidential system that will reduce these risks. Among the methods for doing so are inclusion of a prime minister, the design of the system for electing the president, and the drafting of the powers of the president, especially in relation to the prime minister, legislature, courts, and provincial or local government'.[10] A number of other interventions were made throughout the Constitutional Commission's tenure in relation to other issues, including the protection of fundamental rights.

As the constitutional negotiations accelerated in late 2003, the dynamics of the discussions transformed. A number of external actors participated in the discussions, and clearly set out the international community's interests and its 'red lines'. In particular, a number of foreign officials made clear to the Afghan drafters that the international community would not countenance an outcome that would subject women's rights to Islamic Sharia and that would not uphold international standards on fundamental rights (Rubin 2004). Despite the efforts of some of the more conservative elements in the Loya Jirga, most of the objectives that had been set by the external actors were achieved. Although the 2004 Constitution provides that '[t]he sacred religion of Islam is the religion of the Islamic Republic of Afghanistan. Followers of other faiths shall be free within the bounds of law in the exercise and performance of their religious rituals' (Article 2) and that '[n]o law shall contravene the tenets and provisions of the holy religion of Islam in Afghanistan' (Article 3), a specific reference was included to international law so as to avoid any ambiguity as to how issues relating to human rights should be decided: 'The state shall observe the United Nations Charter, inter-state agreements, as well as international treaties to which Afghanistan has joined, and the Universal Declaration of Human Rights' (Article 7).

On the other hand, the transition to the Constitutional Loya Jirga phase of the negotiations also saw the introduction for the first time in the draft of a system of government that concentrated significant power in the office of the president. Previous proposals had provided for a semi-presidential system of government that would have subjected the president to greater oversight and control by the legislative branch of government amongst others. The final proposal that took shape in December 2003, however, provided for a powerful directly elected president who was solely responsible for appointing the prime minister as well as other key officials and who was not subject to a vote of no-confidence in the legislature, except for an impeachment process requiring an almost unattainable super-majority (Article

69). Given the state's institutional weakness and the volatility of previous administrations, a number of concerns were raised that the proposed framework could encourage the illegitimate capture of power. Some advisers suggested that collegiate systems of government should be adopted to avoid concentrating too much power in the hands of one individual. None of these concerns was raised by the international community and by those external actors that had established red lines in relation to the role of Islam before the final adoption of the Constitution in January 2004. Some suggestion has been made that the United States and the United Nations had a vested interest in ensuring a strong presidential system centered around the person of Hamid Karzai (Thier 2006).

2.3   Bosnia

In Bosnia and Herzegovina ('BiH'), external actors were equally if not even more involved in the discussions that led to the adoption of the 1995 Constitution, and also spearheaded the effort to reform the constitution a decade later.[11] However, as a result of various circumstances, including a desire to end the country's civil war, the international community pursued a different set of priorities, to the extent that the values that it had established as 'red lines' in both Afghanistan and Iraq were relegated in favor of a number of other concerns. In particular, the BiH Constitution establishes a delicate system of checks and balances, which is designed to provide equal representation to each of BiH's 'constituent peoples' (Bosniacs, Croats and Serbs) in each of the national institutions. Indeed, other than in the Central Bank and the Constitutional Court, each group has a veto power over all essential decision-making. This structure was intended to ensure that ethnic groups would remain equal, but it also gives each ethnic group ultimate decision-making power in relation to any matter that it considers important. In this sense, each group is sovereign. Thus, the three-member Presidency is encouraged to act by consensus. If that fails, two members may adopt a decision, but the dissenting member may then declare that decision 'destructive of a vital interest of the Entity from the territory from which he was elected' in which case the matter is referred to the legislature of the ethnic group from which the dissenting member of the Presidency was elected (Article V(2)(d)). The BiH Constitution also establishes a Parliamentary Assembly, in which each group is granted a veto power. The Assembly is composed of a lower chamber (the House of Representatives) and an upper chamber (the House of Peoples), which is to be composed exclusively of members of the three 'constituent peoples' (Article IV). Both must approve a bill before it can be considered to be law (Article IV(3)(c)). Each of BiH's main ethnic groups enjoys a *de facto* veto by virtue of the quorum requirement, according to which at least three Bosniac, three Croat and three Serb delegates must be present in each of the House of Peoples sessions to be valid (Article IV(3)(d)). The Dayton Accords also established an Office of the High Representative (OHR), which has a responsibility to 'monitor the implementation of the peace settlement' (Article III(I)(a) of Annex 10) which includes overseeing the 'establishment of political and constitutional institutions in Bosnia and Herzegovina' (Article I(1)).[12] The High Representative has since intervened in BiH's governance structure on a number of occasions, including to grant a number of authorities to the state that were not originally provided for by the Constitution.[13]

This clearly discriminatory regime was endorsed by all the external actors that participated in the drafting process, including the United States and the European Union, mainly for the purpose of seeking an accommodation between the three principal warring factions and with a view to ending the conflict. Thus, although the new Constitution and the remainder of the Dayton Peace Accords did successfully achieve that objective, the rights of minorities and fundamental freedoms such as the right to racial and religious equality were subordinated to the Constitution's horizontal distribution of powers, making it impossible for BiH to live up to the commitments it undertook when it joined the Council of Europe.[14] During the following decade, the new state made little progress in resolving its many political, social and economic difficulties. In particular, the two 'entities' failed to cooperate towards a strengthening of the state, with all three 'constituent peoples' entrenching themselves in ethno-sectarian positions, often leading to paralysis within parliament and government. The prospect of acceding to the European Union served as an incentive for some to reform the Constitution, but was ultimately insufficient to cause any real momentum to reform.[15]

An opportunity to amend the Constitution presented itself in 2005 when a number of external actors (including officials from the United States and the European Union) encouraged the eight major political parties that were represented in the Parliamentary Assembly to form a constitutional working group with a view to making a number of amendments. Despite the heavy involvement of external actors (the Secretariat that was tasked with composing a final list of suggested amendments was exclusively staffed by non-BiH officials), the proposal that was eventually put together focused almost exclusively on clarifying governmental procedures with a view to making the state more efficient and creating a path towards European integration, whereas fundamental freedoms such as the right to equality did not register during the discussions. The final proposal that was eventually put together would have increased the number of powers that are attributed to the State (Amendment I), simplified the law-making process by reducing the powers of the House of Peoples (Amendment II), and established new rules relating to the election, mandate, powers and procedures of the Presidency (Amendment III), as well as entirely new provisions relating to the election, mandate, powers and procedures of the Council of Ministers, of the Prime Minister, and even of individual Ministers (Amendment IV).[16] Significantly, however, in their effort to bring BiH closer to European integration, the suggested reforms sought to introduce the following wording into Article III of the BiH Constitution: 'State institutions are responsible for negotiating, developing, adopting and implementing, and the functioning of laws necessary for the fulfillment of European standards, as well as political and economic conditions linked with European integration'. Neither the BiH negotiators and drafters, nor the external actors that were so instrumental in designing the changes, sought to define the term 'European standards', which was somewhat surprising considering how vital this matter was to the negotiations – the proposal therefore sought to solve one difficulty by replacing it with what would inevitably have become an interpretative nightmare for officials and the courts alike. In addition, the proposed changes explicitly sought to maintain the Constitution's discriminatory horizontal distribution of powers between BiH's three 'constituent peoples'. The proposals were eventually put to a vote in the House of Representatives during April 2006, but failed to meet the two-thirds majority required by Article X of the Constitution and therefore did not take effect.[17]

It was eventually left to two private citizens of BiH, one Jewish and one Roma, to bring a claim against the BiH state before the European Court of Human Rights in which they took issue with their ineligibility to stand for election to the House of Peoples and to the Presidency on the basis of their ethnic and religious backgrounds. The court ultimately decided in favour of the complainants, arguing that their 'continued ineligibility to stand for election to the House of Peoples of Bosnia and Herzegovina lacks an objective and reasonable justification'.[18]

3   PATTERNS OF INTERACTION

The above case studies, as well as a number of other recent constitution-making processes, illustrate a number of developments in comparative constitutional practice. Amongst other things, external influence has today extended its reach to all areas of law to the extent that advice is given and pressure is exerted in relation to socio-economic rights, although within each area of law important limitations often work against the exercise of influence (3.1). Our case studies also show that disagreements can arise between external actors and national drafting committees and that the outcome of such a disagreement will often depend on a number of factors, including the type of disagreement that has emerged (3.2).

3.1   The Reach and Limitations of External Influence

Whether by virtue of international conventions, established norms or practices, or the weight of world opinion, external influence can be felt in relation to every area of constitutional law, including fundamental rights, of governance structures, and even macroeconomic policies (Backer 2009). At the same time, however, there are relatively few areas in which a sufficient degree of consensus exists internationally to allow for constitution-making societies to be compelled to adopt a specific outcome. Although most observers would probably welcome the fact that drafters remain free to decide upon whatever options present themselves, past experience nevertheless shows that national drafting committees can sometimes adopt certain arrangements that can lead to or prolong conflict, or that can result in unrepresentative or ineffective government.

On the issue of fundamental rights, a growing number of scholars today agree that there exists a core number of norms that transcend international borders and must be reflected in the constitutional law of any nation that today wishes to be part of the community of nations.[19] These values were greatly influenced by the US Bill of Rights and are easily recognized in many basic texts around the world, including the constitutions of Afghanistan, BiH and Iraq.[20] The consensus on this issue does not enjoy much depth, however, as the agreement only extends to the enumeration of some rights and does not cover a number of issues that are considered fundamental by some and not by others, while the equally important matter of implementation barely registers at the stage of constitutional negotiations (Goldsworthy 2010). The result is that in countries such as Iraq or Ethiopia, which provide for the protection of basic rights in their fundamental texts, life goes on in the courts and in prisons as if those rights did not exist, not necessarily as a result of bad faith or evil intent, but through a number of factors, including a failure in the law-making and regulatory processes. Put another way, in many jurisdictions around the world, constitutional principles in relation to basic rights often remain just that, and are not translated into concrete rules to be followed by state officials, in part as a result of the state in question's failure, but also because of the lack of adequate attention that this issue receives amongst those actors and individuals that focus so much of their efforts on encouraging the inclusion of rights in constitutional texts.

A number of scholars have also maintained that international law has evolved to the point where one can speak of a right to democratic governance (Grant 1999: 102). Although there is some debate as to the existence of such rights or whether there is any means to enforce them in practice (Griffin 2000), there is little question today that the international environment is such that there exists a strong expectation both within and without countries that are involved in a constitution-making exercise that any new framework for governance must include some provisions that limit the exercise of government through any number of practices and norms, including the rule of law, democratic elections, the establishment of supreme audit institutions, amongst others. There was never any question in Afghanistan, BiH and Iraq that these principles and mechanisms would not be provided for in the respective constitutional texts. The difficulty once again is that aside from general principles, there is very little agreement about how democratic governance should function in practice, or even what the constituent elements of notions like the rule of law actually are.[21] From Bosnia to Iraq, judicial independence has been a long-standing constitutional principle, which was applied in both countries in ways that would be unacceptable in the West. As both countries adopted their most recent constitutions, both were bequeathed by US officials judicial councils that were for the first time responsible for managing the judiciary's internal affairs. Since that time, both Iraq and Bosnia have sought to adapt to the new institutional framework, but the notion of independence itself continues to encounter strong resistance in the halls of government, with senior officials wondering how a judge can be considered to be independent if the state pays his or her salary. Similar difficulties have arisen in relation to electoral systems and the relationships between the executive and legislative branches of government. The separation of powers is never challenged as a general principle, but the level of agreement between national actors is as shallow as international consensus on these same issues.

In the period following the collapse of the Soviet Union, as the Washington Consensus of neo-liberal economic policies spread its influence to new geographic areas, so too was its weight felt in the context of modern constitutional negotiations. The threat of being excluded from the international monetary system as well as from debt markets was sufficient in most cases to encourage most constitution-making societies to set aside what are now considered to be outdated economic policies in favor of open market policies. As South Africa began its discussions on the formulation of a final text, subtle influence from the World Bank and the International Monetary Fund helped convince the African National Congress to abandon some of the more left-wing elements of its programme. In Iraq, the drafting process that led to the adoption of the interim constitution in 2004 was heavily influenced by American jurists and officials, many of whom were affiliated to the US Republican Party,[22] which led to Iraq's heavily entrenched welfare system being limited by a sense of neo-liberal realism.[23] Nevertheless, states still retain enough flexibility to decide whether or not to guarantee strong socio-economic rights, as shown by the Iraqi example. During the negotiations that led to the adoption of Iraq's permanent Constitution in 2005, American advisers left a much lighter footprint, particularly in relation to the section on 'Rights and Liberties' (Section Two), therefore allowing enough room for the re-emergence of a number of socio-economic rights that most Iraqis feel automatically entitled to. For example, the 2006 Constitution provides that the state shall guarantee, without limitation, 'social and health security, the basic requirements for living a free and decent life, and shall secure for them suitable income and appropriate housing', 'health care', 'the right to live in safe environmental conditions', and 'free education at all stages' (Articles 30, 31, 33 and 34).

3.2   Categories of Disagreement

Although external actors and national drafting committees do not always see eye to eye, not all disagreements are of the same order of magnitude, in terms of both the legal tenure of the relevant subject matter area, as well as the possible repercussions of the arrangement that the national drafters are proposing to adopt. Three categories of disagreement exist:

(i)   there is first the situation in which the constitution-making society itself is seeking to establish a new constitutional order that would amount to a 'gross violation' of fundamental rights, including basic human and democratic rights;

(ii) the situation in which there is a disagreement between the constitution-making society and external actors in relation to an area that does not concern fundamental rights, but on which there is a consensus on what is commonly referred to as 'international best practice'; and

(iii) the situation in which some elements of the international community, perhaps even a totality of the external actors that are involved in the constitutional process itself, have a 'difference of opinion' in relation to a matter that does not concern fundamental rights and on which there is no established or recognized best practice internationally.

It has been suggested elsewhere that, as a general response to all departures from western liberal constitutional values, the court of world opinion (through 'transnational dialogue') should be used to pressure the constitution-making society in question to amend the relevant wording (Sunder 2005). Although a necessary component of any attempt to encourage constitutional reform within a particular country, world opinion alone is insufficient, particularly in those numerous countries where government is unresponsive to local, let alone world, opinion.[24] In addition, although fundamental rights can often be a source of contention in modern constitution-making processes, the most heated and dangerous disagreements often surround governance-related issues (particularly matters that affect the exercise of power and access to funds), where none of the negotiating parties' positions can easily be identified as more 'liberal' than the others. A more nuanced approach is required, one that will necessarily vary depending on the type of constitutional arrangement that is at issue.

3.2.1   Gross violations

Despite advances in recent decades on the issue of fundamental rights, some constitution-making societies have wavered dangerously close to adopting specific wording that would, if implemented, have led to a violation of a number of fundamental rights. This was the case in Iraq and Afghanistan, where the international community intervened in order to prevent the adoption of wording that, many assumed, would have legitimized gender discrimination as well as other important violations. There is significant agreement between policy makers and scholars alike that some form of direct intervention is permissible or even required in the event fundamental rights are threatened.

In the past, where particular countries have adopted constitutional arrangements that indisputably violate fundamental rights, the international community deployed a number of mechanisms to force a change to the offending wording. The clearest examples are perhaps the international reaction to Southern Rhodesia's unilateral declaration of independence in

1965 and to the establishment of the Apartheid regime in South Africa. Both situations involved the establishment of discriminatory legal regimes that deprived the vast majority of the populations of both countries of basic human and democratic rights on the basis of race. The racism inherent in both systems was so blatant that the international community was prompted into action: in the case of Rhodesia, the United Nations General Assembly called for military intervention, while the Security Council established an economic sanctions regime;[25] the South African state was frequently targeted for condemnation by the United Nations, leading many nations to divest from South African interests altogether.[26] Another possibility that has been raised would be to exclude offending nations from the community of nations through the use of the United Nations' accreditation process, although that option remains theoretical for now as the United Nations is yet to develop any specific criteria that can be applied to reject a request for accreditation (Griffin 2000).

At the same time, however, the evidence also clearly shows that the international community considers that certain interests are of such paramount importance that they trump fundamental rights. This was the case in BiH, where the right to equality was clearly subordinated in favor of the effort to end that country's conflict, despite legitimate complaints that peace could very well have been achieved without such a compromise.

3.2.2 Disagreements on international best practice

Although the term has not been clearly defined, 'international best practice' refers to those areas that are not governed by a binding international treaty or norm, and that do not relate to fundamental rights, but on which scholars, officials and practitioners alike universally accept that specific practices are preferable to others. By way of example, the principle of judicial independence (which is today understood to entail financial independence, self-regulation by the judiciary of its own internal affairs, the absence of political pressure on members of the judiciary, etc.) has been universally accepted by the international community as a vital component of any functional constitutional system.[27] Thus, whereas all past Iraqi constitutions paid lip-service to judicial autonomy while at the same time ensuring that judges would remain under the control of the executive, the 2006 Constitution provides for the first time for the establishment of a 'Higher Judicial Council' that is responsible for managing the judiciary's affairs independently of all other branches of government (Article 90). Other areas in which scholars and practitioners recognize the existence of international best practice include the principle of decentralization (which today entails the right of local communities to choose their own representatives and officials, and for the distribution of powers between central and local government to be firmly established and not left to be modified at will by the central government), as well as the requirement that central government should be provided with the necessary resources to satisfy its constitutional obligations, amongst others.[28] As already mentioned, despite significant progress, the areas in which an established and widely accepted practice has been reached remain relatively limited.[29]

In practice, the difficulty for external actors will be to identify those situations in which, despite their expertise in local affairs, drafters have nevertheless agreed upon a set of rules that, if implemented, would increase the risk of conflict or lead to unresponsive government. Despite the unavoidably difficult working conditions, Afghanistan and Iraq both show that it is possible to identify departures from best practice even in the context of intense pressure to reach an agreement within short deadlines. It was thus that many of the international advisers that were party to the negotiations remarked at the time that Iraq's federal authorities could not fulfill their obligation to 'preserve the unity, integrity, independence, and sovereignty of Iraq' (Article 109) without the power to raise taxes, and that the 2006 Constitution's permissiveness in the formation of new regions was likely to increase ethnosectarian tensions at a time of already intense civil conflict.[30] Similarly, Afghan drafters were warned against establishing an overly powerful office of the president, particularly given their country's long history of institutional weakness, which could potentially serve as an incentive to seize power through illegitimate means.[31] In both cases, however, the international community remained firmly divided on which system of government should be adopted. Despite the warnings of the independent advisers that were involved in the process, the dominant foreign state actor favored the position adopted by one of the negotiating parties over all others, rather than making an objective determination of what arrangement was most likely to lead to effective government. Developments since the respective constitutions entered into force have given truth to the warnings that were made and have dramatically illustrated the dangers that inappropriate constitutional arrangements can create.[32]

3.2.3   Differences of opinion

The third category of disagreement covers areas of law other than fundamental rights and where there is no international best practice, which would include matters such as the type of supreme audit institution that should be established, to which branch of government the audit institution should be answerable, the mechanisms on future constitutional amendment, specific types of social and economic rights, term limits, amongst others. Although it would be natural to expect external actors to concede in favor of national constitutional actors where this type of disagreement arises, there is evidence once again of external actors seeking to skew agreements in favor of particular outcomes and over the objections of national actors. In the delicate negotiations that eventually led to the adoption of the Comprehensive Peace Agreement in Sudan, the interest of US and Norwegian officials was to skew the agreement in favor of the Southern Sudanese, in a way that would have been attractive to the US and Norway's domestic Christian communities. Although they were successful in modifying the draft, the changes were quickly rejected by Khartoum's negotiators, who reacted by downgrading the international community's entire involvement in the drafting process (Dann and Al-Ali 2006).

4   THE IMPACT OF NORMATIVE VALUES ON EXTERNAL INFLUENCE

The behaviour of external actors is guided by several fundamental norms, including state sovereignty, the need to prevent and remove all 'threats to peace', to protect fundamental rights, and to ensure the establishment of stable and effective government. However, in the absence of any oversight, external actors have developed an ad hoc approach to constitutional processes, in which the importance of certain values rises and falls depending on the circumstances. There is a strong argument, however, based on the legal rules already in place and the available evidence, that although external actors should always exercise deference in favor of local rules, traditions and expertise, there are some principles that should always guide the hand of external actors.

4.1 Sovereignty and the Principle of Non-interference

According to the traditional understanding of sovereignty, a state could only be sovereign if it was the sole authority capable of exercising force within specific borders such that it was subject to no authority other than international law. That notion has long served as a means to prevent or discourage external interference or involvement in the internal matters of a particular state. Based on a large body of doctrine and established practice, the United Nations Charter sought to codify that understanding in its Article 2(7), according to which '[n]othing contained in the present Charter shall authorize the United Nations to intervene in matters which are essentially within the domestic jurisdiction of any state or shall require the Members to submit such matters to settlement under the present Charter; but this principle shall not prejudice the application of enforcement measures under Chapter VII'. Although the Charter simultaneously provides that the United Nations has as its objective to prevent and remove all 'threats to the peace' (Article 1), international practice has leaned strongly in favor of a limited interpretation of that term.[33]

That principle has been strained in recent decades under the weight of a large number of doctrinal, legal and political developments. In the first instance, throughout the twentieth century, the majority of the world's states have agreed to curb their own sovereignty through the establishment of multilateral institutions such as the World Trade Organization, which have subjected member states to huge volumes of transnational rules, forcing many to make significant changes to their own domestic legislation in ways that were often unexpected.[34] Also, the network of international court systems has broadened their jurisdiction both substantively and geographically, particularly with the establishment of the International Criminal Court and the increasing number of hybrid courts in operation.[35]

From an institutional perspective, ever more states are turning to international organizations such as the United Nations to participate and sometimes even play a key role in what have traditionally been considered to be sensitive internal processes. For example, the international community participated in the electoral process in both Afghanistan and Iraq, in terms of monitoring and capacity development, but also in administering the electoral process itself. In both countries, the United Nations appointed staff to key positions in national electoral and complaints commissions, and has also participated in the counting process and in announcing official results (while at the same time providing the international community's seal of approval). Similarly, in Bosnia and Herzegovina, the President of the European Court of Human Rights is mandated by the Bosnian Constitution itself to appoint three members to serve full terms in its Constitutional Court. Finally, despite the absence of any international agreements on the matter, the involvement of the international community in the inner workings of national constitution-making processes has become a reality. Indeed, an increasing number of constitutional drafting processes are in and of themselves taking place through some form of international administration, including Iraq (where the 2004 interim constitution was drafted under a recognized international occupation of the country), Sudan (in which the Intergovernmental Authority on Development and a number of western states participated in the mediation process that led to the adoption of the Comprehensive Peace Agreement, and where they continue to play an important role through the Assessment and Evaluation Commission) and East Timor (where the constitutional process was directly administered by the United Nations) (Dann and Al-Ali 2006). Finally, the international community has for 15 years been directly involved in administering BiH's constitutional structure through the OHR.[36]

The pace at which multilateral institutions are being established and the rate at which states are willingly surrendering their own authority in relation to a large number of subject matter areas establishes beyond question that the traditional understanding of sovereignty is evolving in favor of a more integrated legal order. However, a number of scholars and international officials have argued that sovereignty has eroded even further and towards an understanding that imposes on states a number of duties towards the polity that exists under their authority and that such a duty gives rise to enforceable rights, regardless of whether or not the state in question accepts that it is subject to such a duty. Since the end of the Cold War, dozens of hitherto undemocratic states have sought to establish accountable government and to strengthen the protection of fundamental rights within their borders, leading a number of scholars to claim that democratic governance has become an enforceable right.[37] A number of international officials with an interest in the protection of human rights have taken the argument even further, maintaining that a failure on the part of a state to protect its own citizens constitutes a 'threat to the peace' under Article 1 of the United Nations Charter and therefore imposes a duty to intervene on the international community.[38] Meanwhile, developments over the past two decades, including the Balkan wars, September 11 and the invasions of both Afghanistan and Iraq, have encouraged still others to argue in favor of intervention in the case of internal civil conflict in order to promote, preserve or establish democracy or even in the event of passive security threats.[39]

Despite the introduction of democratic and fundamental rights in the debate on sovereignty, the content of those rights remains undefined in the absence of a binding treaty or an international agreement (Griffin 2000). As a result of that, as well as a number of other factors, the suggestion that the international community should have the right to intervene where a particular state has failed to protect its citizens' basic rights has remained particularly controversial. According to Professor Dominik Zaum, '[s]tate practice suggests that human rights, human security, welfare and democracy have become important elements of the beliefs that legitimize authority held in particular by western members of the international community, though not necessarily of all states in the world. [However] even among western states, the notion of sovereignty as responsibility does not seem to have evolved to the extent that all human rights violations, and in particular a right to democratic governance necessarily justify military intervention.'[40] Opinions in the world community tend to reflect that view, particularly given the concern amongst many in the developing world of renewed domination on the part of western nations,[41] and based on the accusation of double standards which saw western nations intervene militarily for the protection of the civilian population in Kosovo, but ignore a much more violent and destructive conflict in Rwanda during the same period.[42]

4.2   'Threats to Peace' and Constitutionalism

While the relationship between state sovereignty and the duty of intervention remains ambiguous today, there is scarcely any debate whatsoever on how the responsibility to prevent and remove all 'threats to the peace' impacts the interaction between external actors and the constitution-making society in question. Most contemporary authors that have addressed this issue tend to focus on individual drafting processes without necessarily discussing the impact of external influence, or limit their deliberations to whether external actors should intervene at all, without entering into how different interests and principles should interact in theory and in practice (Feldman 2005; Sunder 2005). A number of important questions are therefore left open for debate, and are informed by recent experience, including the three case studies discussed earlier in this chapter.

Are 'threats to peace' of such paramount importance that they constitute an overriding factor that forces constitutional processes and external actors to set aside all other concerns? Although a precedent was established in BiH, where some fundamental rights were set aside in favor of the general effort to end the conflict in that country, there is a strong argument against generalizing that practice. Aside from the fact that there are genuine arguments that have yet to be addressed that peace in countries such as BiH can be achieved without compromising basic freedoms, the logical conclusion of the tendency to prioritize the achievement of peace over all other interests leads to bleak scenarios in which the international community can be brought to encourage the suspension of democracy and individual freedoms without limitation where it is considered that 'peace' is at risk. That possibility rings especially true considering that fundamental rights are in fact the only rules that are binding under international law – as discussed earlier, there is as of yet no concrete right to democracy, which leads one to assume that there are less theoretical and legal impediments to suspending democratic governance in the event of a threat to peace. In addition and in any event, external actors in both Iraq and Afghanistan followed a different standard of behavior, working to ensure the protection of all fundamental rights (at least partly in order to respond to the concern that both countries could either lapse or continue in the tradition of Islamic intolerance while under international tutelage), regardless of the increasingly dangerous nature of the conflicts that had already commenced in both countries.

If anything, the result of any analysis of the relationship between the need to eliminate 'threats to peace' and constitutionalism is wholly different. Recent experience clearly shows that external actors have an especially important role to play in the establishment of stable, effective and responsive government (regardless of whether or not international best practice relating to governance is legally enforceable or not under international or national law), given the impact that issues including the distribution of state funds and the horizontal distribution of powers can have in encouraging conflict. External actors should in fact always work on the basis that poor governance represents as important a threat to peace as the failure to guarantee equality or to guarantee other fundamental rights under a constitution. The difficultly in practice will be to develop some form of mechanism which will prevent external actors, particularly foreign state actors, from acting on the basis of what is most politically expedient (as was the case in Iraq, where external actors favored one side in the constitutional discussions merely with a view to forcing an early conclusion of the discussions, and in Afghanistan, where the purpose of their intervention was to ensure that political allies would benefit from the constitutional negotiations) rather than what is most likely to produce a positive outcome for the people of the country in question.

5 CONCLUSION

Recent constitution-making societies illustrate the progress that has been made in comparative practice, but also show that more effort needs to be made to understand the manner in which the international community and national constitution-making bodies should interact in practice. Although one can no longer exist or function without the other in our new globalized world, very little thought has gone into understanding the implications of and the rules that should guide their interaction. External actors clearly have much to contribute to the exercise of drafting a constitution, but there is cause to be concerned about the ramifications of their involvement, particularly in the case of foreign state actors that have a vested interest in the outcome. At the same time, however, significant miscalculations have been made by national drafting bodies themselves, despite their inherent expertise in their own affairs, underlying the importance of involvement by the international community. Moving forward, greater interaction between the two sides is inevitable, but hopefully in an environment in which factors such as the self-interest of external actors will have less of an impact. The challenge moving forward will be to ensure the enforcement of a mechanism that will prevent such factors from playing a role in constitution-making processes in the future.

NOTES

1. Iraq provides an ideal illustration of how this problem can arise in practice. Despite the fact that its own constitutional rules require a two-thirds majority in the Senate for the adoption of an international treaty (see Article II, Section 2, Clause 2 of the United States Constitution), the United States used its more than considerable influence in Baghdad in 2004 to force the requirement under Iraq's interim constitution down to a simple majority of parliament, over the objections of the Iraqi constitutional drafters. US officials were apparently motivated by a desire to negotiate and enter into a long-term status of forces agreement with the Iraqi state, a goal that they presumably felt would be threatened by a high threshold for treaty approval. See Larry Diamond, Squandered Victory: The American Occupation and the Bungled Effort to Bring Democracy to Iraq, New York: Times Books (2005).
2. For example, an individual adviser who played an important role in shaping the Iraqi Constitution had acquired, prior to the constitutional negotiations, a stake in a major oil field in the country and, according to reports, stands to reap very significant financial rewards if the arrangement on natural resources that he helped design is ultimately implemented. See James Glanz and Walter Gibbs, 'US adviser to Kurds Stands to Reap Oil Profits', *New York Times*, 11 November 2009, at <www.nytimes.com/2009/11/12/world/middleeast/12 galbraith.html>, accessed 2 June 2010.
3. In Iraq, the United Nations' Office of Constitutional Support, which was tasked with providing support and advice to the Iraqi Constitutional Committee on a wide range of substantive and procedural issues, was staffed by officers from South Africa, Eritrea, India, Iraq, Sri Lanka, the United Kingdom, New Zealand, Spain, Italy, Egypt, amongst others.
4. The Arabic original of the Iraqi Constitution was published in the Iraqi Official Gazette Issue 4012 (28 December 2005). An official English language translation of the Iraqi constitution has not been published and is not available online. An unofficial translation of the final draft is available here: <www.uniraq.org/documents/iraqi_constitution.pdf>, accessed 12 June 2010. All translations contained in this chapter are the author's own.
5. See Nicholas Haysom, The United Nations' Office of Constitutional Support, Summary and Critical Review of the Draft Constitution Presented to the TNA on 28 August 2005 (15 September 2005), unpublished; a leaked copy of this paper was quoted in Scott Johnson, Babak Dehghanpisheh and Michael Hastings, 'Iraq: Loose Federation or Violent Disintegration?' *Newsweek* (10 October 2005).
6. Yash Ghai and Jill Cottrell, 'A Review of the Draft Constitution of Iraq' (3 October 2005), at <www.law.wisc.edu/gls/arotcoi.pdf>, accessed 15 March 2010.
7. Daily Press Briefing by the Office of the Spokesman for the Secretary-General, 3 October 2005.
8. 'UN Calls for Review of Changes to Referendum Rules in Iraq', the *Guardian*, 5 October 2005, Ewen MacAskill, <www.guardian.co.uk/world/2005/oct/05/iraq.ewenmacaskill>, accessed 1 June 2010.
9. An English language version of the 2004 Afghan Constitution is available at <http://president.gov.af/sroot_eng.aspx?id=68>, accessed 12 June 2010.
10. Barnett R. Rubin, Presentation to Constitutional Commission of Afghanistan, 5 June 2003, available at <www.cic.nyu.edu/peacebuilding/oldpdfs/Presentationto.pdf>, accessed 1 June 2010.
11. The United States and various European states intervened in the Bosnian civil war in part by negotiating and enforcing the General Framework Agreement for Peace in Bosnia and Herzegovina, often referred to as the Dayton Peace Accords, which were entered into in 1995. The General Framework sought to end the conflict by setting fixed boundaries between the two warring factions, namely the Federation of Bosnia and Herzegovina and the Republika Srpska (referred to as the 'entities'). A new constitution for BiH (the 'BiH

Constitution' or the 'Constitution') was set out in Annex 4 to the General Framework. An English language version of the BiH Constitution is available at <www.ohr.int/dpa/default.asp?content_id=372>, accessed 12 June 2010.

12. See <www.ohr.int/dpa/default.asp?content_id=366>, accessed 23 June 2010.

13. See, for example, Venice Commission, *Opinion on the Need for a Judicial Institution at the Level of the State of Bosnia and Herzegovina*, 3 November 1998, <www.venice.coe.int/docs/1998/CDL-INF(1998)017-e.asp>, accessed 23 June 2010; Venice Commission, *Opinion on the Competence of Bosnia and Herzegovina in Electoral Matters*, 19 October 1998, at <www.venice.coe.int/docs/1998/CDL-INF(1998)016-e.asp>, accessed 23 June 2010; and Venice Commission, *Opinion on the scope of responsibilities of Bosnia and Herzegovina in the field of immigration and asylum with particular regard to possible involvement of the Entities*, available at <www.venice.coe.int/docs/1999/CDL-INF(1999)006-e.asp>, accessed 23 June 2010.

14. See International Crisis Group, 'Ensuring Bosnia's Future: A New International Engagement Strategy', 15 February 2007, available at <www.crisisgroup.org/~/media/Files/europe/180_ensuring_bosnias_future.ashx>, accessed 12 June 2010, 9.

15. See Venice Commission, *Opinion on the Constitutional Situation in Bosnia and Herzegovina and the Powers of the High Representative*, 11 March 2005, available at <www.venice.coe.int/docs/2005/CDL-AD(2005)004-e.asp>, accessed 12 June 2010.

16. The text of the April 2006 Proposal is available at <www.coe.ba/pdf/CDL_2006_025-e.doc>, accessed 12 June 2010.

17. See 'Ensuring Bosnia's Future', *supra* note 14, at p. 10.

18. See *Sejdic and Finci v Bosnia and Herzegovina* (2009), available at <www.echr.coe.int/echr/>, accessed 12 June 2010.

19. Thomas M. Franck, 'The Emerging Right to Democratic Governance', 86 *American Journal of International Law* 46 (1992); Gregory H. Fox, 'The Right to Political Participation in International Law', 17 *Yale Journal of International Law* 539 (1992); and Gregory H. Fox and Brad R. Roth (eds), *Democratic Governance and International Law*, Cambridge: Cambridge University Press (2000).

20. Iraq's 2006 Constitution provides for a detailed and very well developed section on fundamental rights, which itself owes much to the South African Constitution. The Constitution of Bosnia and Herzegovina, which contains a section entitled 'Human Rights and Fundamental Freedoms' is completed by a direct reference to 'international standards' according to which '[t]he rights and freedoms set forth in the European Convention for the Protection of Human Rights and Fundamental Freedoms and its Protocols shall apply directly in Bosnia and Herzegovina. These shall have priority over all other law' (Paragraph 2, Article II).

21. For a recent attempt to define the rule of law, see Tom Bingham, *The Rule of Law*, London: Allen Lane (2010).

22. The Law of Administration for the State of Iraq for the Transitional Period, usually referred to as the Transitional Administrative Law or the 'TAL', is available at <www.cpa-iraq.org/government/TAL.html>, accessed 12 June 2010.

23. Article 14 of the TAL provides that: 'The individual has the right to security, education, health care, and social security. The Iraqi State and its governmental units, including the federal government, the regions, governorates, municipalities, and local administrations, *within the limits of their resources and with due regard to other vital needs*, shall strive to provide prosperity and employment opportunities to the people'. Emphasis added.

24. See, for example, Helen Epstein, 'Cruel Ethiopia', *New York Review of Books*, 13 May 2010, <www.nybooks.com/articles/archives/2010/may/13/cruel-ethiopia/>, accessed 12 June 2010 (which describes the manner in which the current Ethiopian government has moved away from multi-party democracy despite significant attention and support from the international community).

25. The General Assembly called on the UK as the administering power to use force to put an end to the illegal racist regime (GA2151 (XXI) 17/11/66). The Security Council resolutions however called only for economic sanctions: voluntary at first, then selective mandatory, and finally comprehensive mandatory sanctions (SCR217, 232, 253). International Commission of Jurists (1976), *Racial Discrimination and Repression in Southern Rhodesia: A Legal Study*, London: Catholic Institute for International Relations, 8–9.

26. For the international effort to ostracize apartheid South Africa, see UNGA, 'First Report of the Credentials Committee', UN Doc. A/9779 (1974), 29th Sess., Annex, Agenda Item 3, at 2; and UNGA Res 3068, 28 UN GAOR Supp. (No. 30) at 75, UN Doc. A/9030 (1973), reprinted in 13 ILM 56 (1974) (entered into force 18 July 1976).

27. On the principle of judicial independence, see Peter H. Russell and David M. O'Brien (eds), *Judicial Independence in the Age of Democracy: Critical Perspectives from Around the World*, Charlottesville: University Press of Virginia (2001).

28. See, for example, Kiichiro Fukasaku and Luiz R. de Mello Jr. (eds), *Fiscal Decentralisation in Emerging Economies: Governance Issues*, Paris: France: Development Centre of the Organisation for Economic Co-operation and Development (1999).

29. See *supra* at IIIA.

30. See *supra* at notes 5 and 6 and corresponding text.
31. See *supra* at note 14 and corresponding text.
32. See, for example, The International Crisis Group, 'Afghanistan: Elections and the Crisis of Governance', Asia Briefing Number 96, 25 November 2009, <www.crisisgroup.org/~/media/Files/asia/south-asia/afghanistan/b96_afghanistan___elections_and_the_crisis_of_governance.ashx>, accessed 13 June 2010; Al-Ali and Fedtke (forthcoming 2011); The International Crisis Group, 'The Next Iraqi War? Sectarianism and Civil Conflict' (27 February 2006), Middle East Report No. 52, 13, <www.crisisgroup.org/en/regions/middle-east-north-africa/iraq-syria-lebanon/iraq/052-the-next-iraqi-war-sectarianism-and-civil-conflict.aspx>, accessed 27 June 2010, 13; and Zaid Al-Ali, 'Iraq's War of Elimination', *Open Democracy* (London, 20 August 2006), <www.opendemocracy.net/conflict-iraq/war_elimination_3839.jsp>, accessed 15 March 2010; Anthony H. Cordesman, *Iraq's Insurgency and the Road to Civil Conflict*, Westport: Connecticut: Praeger Security International (2008), 251. For the opposite view, see Chibli Mallat, 'Reconciliation in Iraq: Taking the Constitution Seriously', *The Daily Star*, 16 July 2009, <www.mallat.com/pdf/Mallat16Jul09.pdf>, accessed 21 June 2010.
33. Article 1 of the United Nations Charter provides that the purposes of the United Nations are '[t]o maintain international peace and security, and to that end: to take effective collective measures for the prevention and removal of threats to the peace, and for the suppression of acts of aggression or other breaches of the peace, and to bring about by peaceful means, and in conformity with the principles of justice and international law, adjustment or settlement of international disputes or situations which might lead to a breach of the peace'.
34. Ulrich Camen and Charles Norchi, 'Challenging Sovereignty: India, TRIPS and the WTO', in *Sovereignty under Challenge: How Governments Respond*, in J. Montgomery and N. Glazer (eds), New Brunswick, NJ: Transaction Publishers (2002), 180–81.
35. Jean Galbraith, 'The Pace of International Criminal Justice', 31 *Michigan Journal of International Law* 79 (2009).
36. See notes 12 and 13 and corresponding text.
37. See Franck, *supra* at note 19.
38. 'The state is now viewed as having an obligation to protect its citizens. When this is not fulfilled there is a growing acceptance that the international community has a right – perhaps even a duty – to step in to fill that gap', Sergio de Mello, quoted in Dominik Zaum, *The Sovereignty Paradox: The Norms and Politics of International Statebuilding*, Oxford: Oxford University Press (2007).
39. Nicholas J. Wheeler, 'The Humanitarian Responsibilities of Sovereignty: Explaining the Development of a New Norm of Military Intervention for Humanitarian Purposes in International Society', in *Humanitarian Intervention and International Relations*, ed. Welsh, Oxford University Press (2006), 32–3; and Douglas Lee Donoho, 'Evolution or Expediency: The United Nations Response to the Disruption of Democracy', 29 *Cornell International Law Journal* 329 (1996).
40. See Zaum, *supra* at note 38, 37. See also Simón Chesterman, *Just War or Just Peace?: Humanitarian Intervention and International Law*, Oxford: Oxford University Press (2002), 45.
41. Donoho, *supra* at note 39, 372–3.
42. Karsten Nowrot and Emily W. Schabacker, 'The Use of Force to Restore Democracy: International Legal Implications of the ECOWAS Intervention in Sierra Leone', 14 *American University International Law Review* 321 (1998).

REFERENCES

Al-Ali, Zaid and Jörg Fedtke (forthcoming 2011) *The Iraqi Constitution: A Contextual Analysis*, Oxford: Hart Publishing.

Backer, Larry Catá (2009), 'From Constitution to Constitutionalism: A Global Framework for Legitimate Public Power Systems', *Pennsylvania State Law Review* 113, 671.

Dann, Philipp and Zaid Al-Ali (2006), 'The Internationalized Pouvoir Constituant – Constitution-making under External Influence in Iraq, Sudan and East Timor', in *Max Planck Yearbook of United Nations Law*, 10, 423 (Armin von Bogdandy and Rüdiger Wolfrum, eds).

Feldman, Noah (2005), 'Imposed Constitutionalism', *Connecticut Law Review* 37, 857.

Goldsworthy, Jeff (2010), 'Questioning the Migration of Constitutional Ideas: Rights, Constitutionalism and the Limits of Convergence', in Sujit Choudhry (ed.), *The Migration of Constitutional Ideas*, New York: Cambridge University Press.

Grant, Thomas D. (1999), *The Recognition of States: Law and Practice in Debate and Evolution*, Santa Barbara, CA: Praeger Publishers.

Griffin, Matthew (2000), 'Accrediting Democracies: Does the Credentials Committee of the United Nations Promote Democracy through its Accreditation Process, and Should It?', *NYU Journal of International Law and Politics* 32, 725.

Rubin, Barnett R. (July 2004), 'Crafting a Constitution for Afghanistan', *Journal of Democracy* 15(3), 13.

Schoiswohl, Michael (2006), 'Linking the International Legal Framework to Building the Formal Foundations of a 'State at Risk': Constitution-making and International Law in Post-conflict Afghanistan', *Vanderbilt Journal of Transnational Law* 39, 819.

Sunder, Madhavi (2005), 'Enlightened Constitutionalism', *Connecticut Law Review* 37, 891.

Thier, J. Alexander (2006), 'The Making of a Constitution in Afghanistan', *New York Law School Law Review* 51, 557.

6. Constitutional amendment rules: a comparative perspective

*Rosalind Dixon**

Formal provision for constitutional amendment is now a near universal feature of national constitutions (see e.g. Lutz 1995; Elkins et al. 2009). However, significant controversy remains over both the function of formal procedures for constitutional amendment and the key determinants of the comparative difficulty of such processes.

An 'amendment' denotes the idea of 'correction/repair or improvement' (*Oxford English Dictionary*) and, for most commentators, constitutional amendment rules are designed to serve exactly these purposes – that is, to allow for the correction of or improvement upon prior constitutional design choices in light of new information, evolving experiences or political understandings (see e.g. Denning and Vile 2002). Another view, which this chapter explores, is that constitutional amendment processes are designed not so much to allow changes to the constitution's original design but rather to allow legislative and popular actors greater scope to influence constitutional courts' evolving interpretation of that design.

Because in each case such processes assume the existence of some prior constitutional instrument as the object of correction or improvement, many constitutional scholars suggest that some forms of constitutional change are too radical or all-encompassing to count as amendments to a prior constitutional instrument (see e.g. Albert 2009; Simeon 2009; Zohar 1995: 318). The distinction may have important legal consequences in some jurisdictions (for instance, in California) because different formal requirements apply to processes of constitutional amendment as opposed to 'revision' (see Constitution of California, Art. XVIII; and discussion in Grodin et al. 1993).

On the other hand, most constitutional scholars agree that not all forms of constitutional change in fact involve processes of constitutional amendment, properly so-called. While there may be no clear line separating amendment from its alternatives (see e.g. Lessig 1993; Levinson 1995; Michelman 1986), most scholars nonetheless agree that constitutional change by way of some processes – such as by judicial interpretation (Lutz 1995; Strauss 1996), shifts in political practice or convention (Young 2007) or more provisional forms of constitutional 'workaround' by the political branches (Tushnet 2009) – does not generally amount to actual constitutional amendment. Rather, constitutional 'amendment' is generally understood to require some kind of formal legal deposit in the text of a written constitution (but see Levinson 1995).

Another view (see Ackerman 1991) is that constitutional amendments denote those forms of constitutional change that originate via certain exceptional or 'higher' forms of law-making, namely: those involving high levels of popular mobilization and inter-branch collaboration, rather than more ordinary forms of legislative, judicial and executive action. On this view, amendments may or may not be reflected in formal changes to the text of a constitution and also be enacted outside, as well as within, formally pre-defined channels for constitutional amendment (Ackerman 1991; Albert 2009).[1] For simplicity, however, this chapter puts to one side this alternative definition of amendments, and instead focuses on the more generally accepted view: that processes of constitutional amendment involve legislative and popular involvement, but also formal change to the text of a written constitution.

Against this background, it considers what existing constitutional experience and scholarship say about (1) the function, danger and difficulty of formal constitutional amendment processes; and (2) what open questions remain, in comparative constitutional scholarship, in this area. Much of the literature and data it draws on in this context are American, in part because of the excellent democratic laboratory American state constitutions provide for testing various hypotheses about constitutional amendment, and also because few countries have amendment rules which have generated the same kind of critical attention as the US (see Griffin 1998; Levinson 1995). However, from a comparative perspective, reference is also made to the constitutional amendment processes in Canada, India, South Africa and Australia; as well as to the findings of large-sample studies of constitutional amendment at a global level. India in particular provides an interesting case-study in this context because of the development by the Supreme Court of India of certain implied limits on the power of constitutional amendment.

1   AMENDMENT FUNCTIONS

In some cases, processes of constitutional amendment will serve much the same function as processes of constitutional enactment or whole-scale revision, namely: to establish (or re-establish) the basic procedural or substantive framework for the process of democratic self-government in a country, or sub-unit of a state. In the US, the leading example of this involves the Reconstruction Amendments (i.e. 13th, 14th and 15th Amendments to the Constitution); and in Canada, the adoption of the Canadian Charter of Rights and Freedoms 1982 (for discussion, see Manfredi). In Australia, there have also been several proposals to amend the Commonwealth Constitution 1901 (so as for example to create an Australia republic) that would have fit this category had they passed (see Winterton 1986; Winterton 2001).

Major constitutional changes such as this can rarely be achieved by formal legal means other than constitutional amendment. In such circumstances, formal constitutional amendment procedures therefore serve not only to promote the chances of large-scale constitutional change, but also to increase the chances that such change will occur (at least more or less) within existing constitutional frameworks, rather than via processes of whole-scale constitutional revision or overthrow (compare Denning and Vile 2002; Griffin 1998; Lutz 1995).[2] This could also be one justification for including in a constitution explicit provision for broad forms of constitutional revision at the initiation of (say) a constitutional convention (see e.g. US Constitution, Art. V, Afghan Constitution, Art. 150).

In a similar but more routine way, constitutional amendment procedures also help constitutional decision-makers alter certain specific aspects of constitutional procedure or structure. Absent amendment, changes to basic constitutional 'rules' such as this, as opposed to more open-ended constitutional standards, will almost always occur informally, rather than through processes of judicial interpretation or explicit legislative 'updating' (on this distinction see, generally, Sullivan 1995, and also more specifically, Murphy 1995: 165; see also Dixon

2010). By creating formal channels for constitutional change of this kind, therefore, constitutional amendment procedures can help promote commitments both to constitutional transparency (see Rawls 1993) and the 'rule of law' (see e.g. Griffin 1998: 42, 52).

Actual constitutional amendments of this kind have also been extremely common in jurisdictions such as Australia, Canada and even the US. In Australia, in more than one hundred years there have been only eight successful referenda under s. 128 of the Commonwealth Constitution and every one of these has approved changes to basic rules of constitutional procedure or structure of this kind.[3] In South Africa, there have been 16 constitutional amendments passed since 1996 and each one has again been directed to clarifying, or altering, the operation of constitutional rules as opposed to standards.[4] In the US, with the important exception of the Reconstruction amendments, it has also been the case that the post-Bill-of-Rights amendments have 'almost exclusively been preoccupied 'with mechanical, textually-explicit revisions governing the election of the President, Vice-President, and members of the Senate, presidential terms and success, and the selection of presidential electors by residents of the District of Columbia – all matters … that have been largely outside the [broadly accepted] interpretive discretion of the judiciary' (see Ferejohn and Sager 2003: 1960).[5]

In other cases, constitutional amendment processes tend to be linked more closely to other mechanisms for constitutional change, such as judicial interpretation. The function of constitutional amendment procedures in such cases will also be distinct: instead of being to allow improvement upon (or correction to) prior constitutional design choices, it will be to help legislatures, and thereby also citizens, to engage in more effective forms of democratic 'dialogue' with courts about the court's interpretation of that design. It may do this in two ways: first, by jump-starting or generating new interpretations of the constitution by courts (see Forbath 2003); and second, by trumping existing judicial interpretations (see Dixon forthcoming; and compare also Denning and Vile 2002 on the 'checking' function of amendments).[6]

For citizens in particular, by generating certain kinds of judicial intervention, amendment procedures can help reduce the agency costs associated with representative forms of government (compare Boudreaux and Pritchard 1993; Levinson 2001: 277, 278). This is one logical explanation for why many states in the US and also some national constitutions (perhaps the most notable example being that of Switzerland) contain distinct provisions allowing citizens to initiate processes of constitutional amendment by popular initiative or petition (see Levinson 1996: 113–15). Another is the influence of theories of popular sovereignty, which, some authors argue, further support an implied right to amendment by plebiscite in certain constitutional contexts (see e.g. Amar 1994 on the US; and Elster 2003 on the French experience of response to constitutional amendment proposals by de Gaulle).

Constitutional amendment procedures can perform these generative and trumping functions in two principal ways: first, by changing the textual basis for subsequent processes of constitutional interpretation by judicial and executive actors; and second, by creating a clearer evidentiary record or source of information about legislative or popular constitutional understandings (compare Levinson 2001 at 273). Changes to the text of a constitution do not only have direct legal consequences. They also, in many cases, serve to create a focal point for additional social movement mobilization for constitutional change (see e.g. Siegel 2006; compare also Denning and Vile 2002: 279). At an evidentiary level, constitutional amendments (and indeed even proposed amendments (Dixon forthcoming)) can also affect courts' willingness to respond to democratic pressures for constitutional change at an evidentiary level, by giving clearer and more principled expression to democratic support for constitutional change.

Good examples of this first effect in the US involve first, the Due Process Clause of the Fourteenth Amendment and the progressive 'incorporation' by the Court of various rights-based guarantees against the states; and second, the role played by the Equal Protection Clause in both generating a substantial body of jurisprudence aimed at eliminating discrimination based on race, nationality and gender and also encouraging the Court formally to over-rule *Dred Scott v Sanford*, 60 US (19 How.) 393 (1857) in the *Slaughterhouse Cases* (Dixon 2010; Vermeule 2006: 236–7).

An example of the second effect involves the 11th Amendment, as a response to the Supreme Court's decision in *Chisolm v Georgia*, 2 US 419 (1793), holding that the plaintiff, as a citizen of South Carolina, could file a suit in the original jurisdiction of the Supreme Court against the state of Georgia, as defendant. In reversing this decision in *Hans v Louisiana*, 134 US 1 (1890), the Court held that one reason that it was free to revisit *Chisolm* was: 'the adoption of the [11th] amendment' (134 US 1, 118–19). However, it also implied that the significance of the amendment in this context was not so much its legal force but rather its connection with the broader 'manner in which *Chisolm* was received by the country' (id).

A similar, if more modest, example in a comparative context of the evidentiary value of formal constitutional amendments, and the generative effect this can have, involves the 1967 amendments to the Australian Commonwealth Constitution 1901, conferring additional powers on the Commonwealth Parliament to make special laws with respect to indigenous Australians. In subsequent cases, such as *Wurridjal v Commonwealth of Australia*, [2009] HCA 2, for example, at least one justice, Justice Kirby, held that '[w]hatever exclusions originally intended by the founders of the Constitution, following the amendments by the 1967 referendum it is clear that the reference in s 51(xxxi) [of the Constitution] to "property" is … not confined to the traditional notions of "property" as originally inherited in Australia from the common and statute law of England [but rather] … incorporate[s] notions of "property" as understood by indigenous Aboriginals, at least so far as such notions are upheld by Australian law' (377–8). The reason for this, Kirby held, was that the effect of the 1967 Amendments was to ensure that the Australian Constitution 'now speaks with equality to [all] Aboriginal Australians' – including those 'observing traditional customs as well as those living in ways indistinguishable from the majority population' – in the same way it does to 'those of other races'.

Further, a clear relationship exists in this context between the aims of particular amendments and their form. For example, amendments designed to generate new constitutional norms seem generally to be framed in broad and open-ended terms, or at least, so as to remove specific restrictions on what are otherwise open-ended standards (see e.g. the text of the 14th Amendment in the US, and the 1967 amendments to ss. 51 and 127 of the Commonwealth Constitution in Australia[7]). On the other hand, amendments designed to trump prior judicial interpretations of a constitution are more frequently framed in concrete, rule-like terms (see e.g. the text of the 11th Amendment).[8]

Despite these examples, some scholars suggest that, in general, formal constitutional amendments will be irrelevant to the ultimate shape of constitutional meaning (see e.g. Eskridge and Ferejohn; Strauss 1996). David Strauss, for example, argues that in the US, because constitutional interpretation tends to be largely common law- rather than text-based, the Supreme Court will generally interpret the Constitution more or less in line with the kinds of changes in circumstances, understandings and even majoritarian demands that can lead to successful constitutional amendments (see Strauss 1996; and compare also Dahl 2003, Friedman 1993). Other scholars, such as Bill Eskridge and John Ferejohn, argue that, even where this is not the case, legislatures will generally fill this gap by the passage of 'super-statutes' designed to generate significant small 'c' constitutional change (Eskridge and Ferejohn 2001).

To a large extent, the degree to which common law-based mechanisms or super-statutes are likely to serve as effective substitutes for formal processes of constitutional amendment will depend on the national constitutional context. As Vicki Jackson and Jamal Greene note elsewhere in this volume, the degree to which national courts adopt an evolving, common-law-based approach to constitutional interpretation, as opposed to a more strictly textual or originalist approach, varies significantly across countries.[9] In some countries, the nature of constitutional federalism will mean that national legislatures have broad scope to enact super-statutes with jurisgenerative effect; whereas in others they will have more limited power to achieve these same ends via legislative means. For example, in Australia the external affairs power in s. 51(xxi) of the Commonwealth Constitution has been held to give the federal parliament broad scope to enact legislation aimed at ending gender-based discrimination (see e.g. *Aldridge v Booth*, (1988) 80 ALR 1); whereas in the US, the commerce clause has been held by the US Supreme Court to impose greater limits on the US Congress in this same context (see e.g. *United States v Morrison*, 529 US 598 (2000)).

In some countries, a number of potential substitute mechanisms are also available to the legislature when it comes to trumping particular judicial decisions. In the US and Australia, Congress and the federal parliament have power to remove certain cases from the appellate jurisdiction of the ultimate court of appeal (see Art. III of the US Constitution; and in Australia, s. 75 of the Commonwealth Constitution). In Canada, s. 33 of the Canadian Charter of Rights and Freedoms 1982 (Charter) gives power both to the federal parliament and to provincial legislatures to override or suspend the application of most rights guarantees under the Charter by ordinary majority vote, on a five-year renewable basis.[10] In Australia, at least one state rights charter, the Victorian Charter of Rights and Responsibilities 2006, contains a nearly identical provision; and other statutory charters (like the UK Human Rights Act 1998) contain a similar implied power to suspend the application of rights by the use of clear statutory language.[11] There is also a similar, if more limited, power to suspend certain rights (and thus courts' interpretation of those rights) under s. 37 of the Constitution of South Africa of 1996. In the US and South Africa in particular, there is also some scope for legislators – and not simply the executive – to influence the direction of judicial appointments in a way that can have an indirect influence on the development of common constitutional meaning.

However, even in those countries where such mechanisms do exist, there remains scope for debate about their effectiveness as substitutes for formal processes of constitutional amendment. The generative and trumping effect of potential amendment substitutes may be less rapid than the effect of formal constitutional amendments (compare Denning and Vile 2002). An example of this in the US involves the attempts by Congress and the President during the New Deal to use non-Article V means in order to reverse the Court's interpretation of the Commerce and Due Process clauses in cases such as *Lochner v New York*, 198 US 45 (1905); *Adkins v Children's Hospital*, 261 US 525 (1923) and *Hammer v Dagenhart*, 247

US 251 (1918): while such efforts ultimately succeeded in cases such as *West Coast Hotel Co. v Parish*, 300 US 379 (1937), *NLRB v Jones Laughlin Steel Corp.*, 301 US 1 (1937) and *United States v Darby Lumber Co.*, 312 US 100 (1941), it seems doubtful that, had the 1924 Child Labor Amendment actually passed, the Court would have waited as long as it did to reverse itself in this way (see Dixon forthcoming; see also Denning and Vile 2002).

The efficacy of amendment substitutes may also be less consistent than that of formal constitutional amendments (see Vermeule 2006). This seems particularly likely to be the case where what is involved is an attempt by a legislature to trump a court's interpretation of a specific constitutional rule, as opposed to standards. In such cases, the interpretive freedom enjoyed by courts is generally understood to be much narrower even in instances involving attempts at dialogue by the legislature (see Balkin 2007; Strauss 1996; Dixon 2010). This may also explain why, in countries such as the US at least, almost every trumping amendment to date (i.e. the 11th and 16th Amendments, as well as the citizenship clause of the 14th Amendment) has focused on the courts' interpretation of specific constitutional rules, as opposed to standards (for discussion of these amendments, see e.g. Stone 1988; Ferejohn and Sager 2003).[12]

Proponents of the amendment irrelevancy thesis argue, however, that (at least in mature democracies) even successful constitutional amendments generally fail to achieve meaningful constitutional change without sustained popular support, in which case constitutional change by a process of judicial interpretation is in any event likely to occur (Strauss 1996).

Here too there is disagreement within the existing constitutional literature. Strauss, for example, argues that the history of amendments such as the 15th and 19th Amendments in the US provides strong support for this aspect of the irrelevancy thesis, but other scholars question the reliability of drawing general lessons from the history of amendments such as the 15th Amendment, given its relatively unique enactment history (Levinson 2006: 161). There is also scope for disagreement over the lessons to be drawn from the history of the 19th Amendment given that the difficulty of amendment under Article V of the US Constitution seems to have contributed to an unwillingness on the part of amendment proponents to publicize their true purposes and objectives, and thereby also to have suppressed the potential evidentiary function of the relevant successful amendment (Marilley 1997).

In a comparative context, there seems quite a clear link between the generative effect of various successful amendments (such as the 1967 race power amendments in Australia) and the more permissive constitutional amendment norms that apply in those countries. In the *Wurridjal* case, Justice Kirby understood the significance of the 1967 Amendments as favoring the recognition of 'traditional' aboriginal people and their *customs*, not simply urban aboriginal people as individuals entitled to formal individual equality. This understanding was also directly supported by the arguments made by various proponents of the 1967 Amendments, such as Bill Groves, a member for the Foundation of Aboriginal Affairs, who argued publicly that the aims of the Amendments were not simply for indigenous Australians to 'be part and parcel of the community' but also to be part of the community on terms that did not involve 'losing [their] identity as Australian Aborigines' (Attwood and Markus 2007 at 124). Had the requirements for successful ratification of an amendment under s. 128 of the Australian Constitution been more demanding, however, and required (say) a two-thirds as opposed to simple majority support from the states, it seems extremely unlikely that activists such as Groves would have been willing to make such arguments. While support for the 1967 Amendments was predicted to be high in urban Australia, opposition was also expected to be strong in many parts of rural Australia, particularly Western Australia and Queensland (where there were certain to be electoral consequences flowing from passage of the Amendments and where there were also still numerous laws formally discriminating against indigenous Australians (Attwood)). Under a two-thirds super-majority requirement, opposition in those two states alone would also have been sufficient to block passage of the proposed amendments.[13]

Without more systematic comparative study of the relationship between formal constitutional amendment rules and the nature of public debate surrounding proposed constitutional amendments, therefore, it seems somewhat premature to conclude that the evidentiary function of formal constitutional processes is necessarily illusory.

2   AMENDMENT CAUTIONS (OR DANGERS)

Whatever the valuable functions played by formal processes of constitutional amendment, such processes also, of course, have the potential to 'render [a] [c]onstitution … too mutable' (Madison, Federalist No. 43).

What reasons do we have to fear excessive constitutional mutability? Existing comparative constitutional scholarship points to two broad reasons why constitutional stability may be valuable: first, its capacity to promote processes of democratic self-government (see e.g. Holmes 1995; Eisgruber 2001; Issacharoff 2003); and second, its capacity to facilitate certain valuable forms of constitutional pre-commitment, particularly those having to do with minority rights and inclusion (see e.g. Elster 2003; Ferejohn and Sager 2003; Sager 2001).

When it comes to processes of democratic self-government, Stephen Holmes likens constitutional amendment rules to rules of grammar in relation to processes of linguistic communication or exchange. 'Far from simply handcuffing people', Holmes suggests, 'linguistic rules allow interlocutors to do many things they would not otherwise have been able to do or even thought of doing', and constitutions perform much the same function (Holmes 1995). As Christopher Eisgruber notes, they 'define pathways for action' in a democracy, without which a polity may be 'unable to formulate policy about foreign affairs, the economy, the environment' and all manner of other critically important issues of social and economic policy (Eisgruber 2001: 13). From this perspective, the danger of overly flexible processes of constitutional amendment is that they may lead to 'a polity [to be] consumed with endless debates about how to structure its basic political institutions' in a way that undermines the ability of a democracy to engage in this kind of collective action (Eisgruber 2001: 13; Elster 2003: 1759). This is particularly so when one considers that, if constitutional amendments are sufficiently frequent, this tends to suggest not only frequent debate about specific constitutional issues, but also a greater likelihood of whole-scale constitutional replacement (see Lutz 1995; Elkins et al. 2009).

For most constitutional scholars, the idea of constitutional democracy also entails some basic level of political competition among political parties, or at least political elites (see Schumpeter 1962), and from this perspective, another danger of overly flexible constitutional amendment processes is that they may allow a temporary political majority to insulate itself against future political competition (Elster 2003: 1776–9). Indeed, for many, '[t]he fixing of the structural rules by which governance occurs, and the assurance that these will not be "gamed" by momentary majorities attempting to lock themselves in power is one of the hallmarks of constitutionalism' (Issacharoff 2003).

A second argument against allowing overly flexible processes of constitutional amendment is that they may undermine the ability of citizens to enter into mutually beneficial forms of constitutional (pre-)commitment. At time 1, citizens may have strong shared 'internal commitments', or understandings or intentions that at time 2 they are nonetheless tempted to sacrifice for reasons of 'partisan interest' or because of 'momentary passions' (Elster 2003: 1758). Knowing this to be the case, others may also be reluctant to make decisions that rely on their honoring those commitments. However, one way in which citizens can respond to this problem at time 1 is to adopt forms of 'external commitment' that make it more difficult for them, at time 2, to dishonor their earlier commitments (see Ferejohn and Sager 2003: 1938); and onerous constitutional amendment rules are generally considered a leading example of such external commitments in a constitutional context (id; Ferejohn 1997: 506).

From this perspective, the principal concern about flexible processes of constitutional amendment is, therefore, that they will undermine the enforcement of various internal constitutional commitments, such as those involving the protection of property or minority rights (see Ferejohn 1997; Ferejohn and Sager 2003). Such an effect seems also especially troubling in the context of minority rights protections, considering that such protections are arguably central to the legitimacy of a democratic system of self-government (see e.g. Rawls 1993), and in many cases to preserving the integrity of an existing liberal democratic order (see e.g. Sullivan 1995; compare also Lessig 1993 on constitutions with 'conservative' and 'transformative' aims). A secondary and somewhat lesser concern is that overly flexibly amendment processes may serve to discourage actions, such as foreign investment or inter-state or international migration (see Ferejohn and Sager 2003: 1929; see also Dixon and Posner forthcoming), which rely on a wide range of internal constitutional commitments being enforced.

These potential downsides to overly flexible constitutional amendment processes may also help explain why various countries have established various distinct tracks for constitutional amendment that vary according to the subject-matter of a proposed amendment.

In India, for example, while most proposals to amend the constitution require the support of only a simple majority of the Parliament present and voting (provided this is also no less than two-thirds of the total number of representatives), amendments to certain fundamental aspects of the 1951 Constitution, such as its provisions governing the representation of the states and the scheduled castes, are subject to the additional hurdle of ratification by a majority of state legislatures (Art. 368).[14] Likewise in South Africa, while most constitutional amendments require the support of only a two-thirds majority of *either* the National Assembly or six (i.e. two-thirds of) provinces in the National Council of Provinces, amendments that affect the provinces are subject to the more demanding requirement of two-thirds support in both houses; and amendments that purport to alter the fundamental constitutional principles found in s. 1 of the 1996 Constitution require the support of three-quarters, as opposed to two-thirds, of the National Assembly (SA Constitution, s. 74(1), (3)).

One of the key premises of such a multi-track approach is that 'by establishing a separate and [more] difficult track for some political issues, the constitution may focus public attention upon those decisions and improve deliberation about them' (Eisgruber 2001: 44). Inducing this kind of increased deliberation about proposed constitutional amendments has, as Jon Elster (2003: 1765) notes, not only the benefit of promoting the role of reason-giving in processes of constitutional self-government (compare also Rawls 1993 on 'public reason'), but also the further benefit of creating the kind of delay in such processes that can 'give passions time to cool down'.

Another explanation for such a multi-track approach is that for legislative proponents of a particular constitutional amendment, higher super-majority requirements will tend to decrease the initial statistical likelihood of there being the necessary threshold level of support for a particular amendment and will also imply higher 'bargaining costs' in order to achieve that threshold (Buchanan and Tullock [1962] 2004). In addition, as Christopher Manfredi notes, the harder it is to pass constitutional amendments on certain questions, the more risk-averse legislators may be about supporting a particular proposed amendment – for fear that, if the amendment turns out to be ill-conceived, it will be extremely difficult to reverse that error by passage of a subsequent amendment (Kelly and Manfredi 2009). (Think, by way of example, of the 19th and 21st Amendments to the US Constitution, or the 15th and 16th Amendments to the South African Constitution.)

In other constitutional contexts, however, constitutional drafters and even judges have been willing to go even further in seeking to counter the danger of amendment to certain aspects of a constitution by imposing absolute limits on the ability of legislative majorities to change the constitution via a process of amendment.

Given the constraints on the amendment of state constitutions imposed by the US Constitution, this is implicitly the model adopted in states in the US that otherwise provide for flexible processes of constitutional amendment (see e.g. *Romer v Evans*, 517 US 620 (1996); Ginsburg and Posner 2010; compare also Choudhry and Hume in this volume and Simeon 2009: 15). It is also the model adopted under the US Constitution in respect of the representation of the states in the Senate (Art. II s. 3 cl. 1), which some scholars have relied on to develop a more extensive theory of implied limits on the power of amendment under Article V of the US Constitution (see e.g. Murphy 1995). In a broader comparative context, precedent for such an approach is further found in numerous foreign constitutions, including, most notably, the German Basic Law of 1949, which adopts a relatively permissive voting rule for most amendments, but also makes 'impermissible' amendments to key constitutional provisions, such as those provisions governing the division of Germany into Länder, and protecting the participation of the Länder in the legislative process, and all of the basic rights 'principles' laid down in Articles 1–20 of the *Basic Law* (see Art. 79(3)) (for discussion in the Eastern European context, see e.g. Holmes and Sunstein 2001).

As noted at the outset of this chapter, a further notable example of such an approach is found in India, where the Supreme Court of India has 'implied' certain limits on the scope of the legislature's power of constitutional amendment under Article 368 of the Indian Constitution (for discussion, see e.g. Neuborne 2003; Jacobsohn 2006). Initially, this involved the Court reading all constitutional amendments as 'laws' subject to the other provisions of the Constitution (see *Golaknath v State of Punjab*, 1967 AIR 1643), but has subsequently involved the Court applying a narrower set of limits that protect only the 'basic structure' of the Constitution from amendment (see *Kesavananda Bharati v The State of Kerala*, AIR 1973 SC 1461 and discussion in Ambwani 2007; Jacobsohn 2006).

3   THE COMPARATIVE DIFFICULTY OF AMENDMENT

Whatever precise balance between constitutional flexibility and rigidity is ultimately judged optimal in a particular constitutional context, existing comparative constitutional scholarship is still at a relatively early stage of development in what it tells us about the actual determinants of the rate or difficulty of constitutional amendment in various jurisdictions.

Even when it comes to various formal hurdles to constitutional amendment, scholars have reached different conclusions as to the influence of such hurdles on the rate or difficulty of constitutional amendment.

Donald Lutz, for example, found that, when he ranked state constitutions in the US according to the hurdles to initiation of a proposed amendment or the degree of majority support required for an amendment to pass either or both houses of the legislature, there was a clear, negative correlation between the difficulty of amendment and the actual rate of amendment, so that, for example, a shift from an ordinary to a 60% majority requirement for passage of a proposed amendment reduced a state's rate of amendment by approximately 26% (Lutz 1995: 256–7; but for criticisms of these conclusions, see Ferejohn 1997). In a cross-national study of 30 national constitutions, Lutz likewise found a clear negative relationship between the presence of super-majority requirements for legislative passage of a proposed amendment, procedural hurdles to the passage of a constitutional amendment by national legislatures (such as double passage by a single house, or passage by two houses), a requirement of state-level approval or ratification of proposed amendments in a federal system and of popular approval of proposed amendments by referendum and the overall rate of constitutional amendment (Lutz 1995: 263). Anecdotal support for several of these findings is also found in the experience of several countries considered in this chapter: in Canada in particular, the most notable recent amendment failures, such as those involving the failure to pass the Meech Lake Accords, resulted from the non-ratification of proposed amendments by only two provinces (see Kelly and Manfredi 2009: 123).

However, John Ferejohn (1997) has raised important questions about the robustness of several of Lutz's findings in this context. For example, when he used a more complex regression technique (rather than a tabular method) to calculate the relationship between various formal hurdles to amendment and amendment rates, relying on Lutz's data, Ferejohn found that states that required a super or double majority for legislative approval of a proposed amendment, or included provision for amendment by popular initiative, did not exhibit any statistically significant difference in their amendment rates, compared to other states (Ferejohn 1997: 524). Moreover, in a global context Ferejohn found no evidence that any form of ratification requirement affected the rate of amendment: the only factors he found to be statistically significant were super- or double-majority requirements for legislative passage of proposed amendment, and legislative bicameralism (Ferejohn 1997: 523).

By contrast, in a subsequent cross-national study of 19 OECD countries, Bjørn Rasch and Roger Congleton found that, according to their estimates, the key determinant of the rate of amendment across countries was whether a constitution required that an amendment be ratified by multiple different bodies, and in particularly by voters at a referendum, rather than whether it required amendments to pass a super-majority of the legislature (2006: 334).

One potential reason for the inconsistency in these findings is that, for many existing studies, the number of independent observations is sufficiently small that there is not enough statistical power to pick up the distinct effect of various hurdles to amendment. In part to address this difficulty, Richard Holden and I have assembled a large, year-by-year dataset for constitutional amendments at a state level in the US, which we have used to re-examine a number of these questions.

Using this dataset, we found that at least within certain ranges, super-majority voting requirements for legislative passage of a constitutional amendment do tend to reduce the rate of constitutional amendment: the move from a majority to two-thirds super-majority requirement (though not a 60% super-majority requirement), we found, had a clear negative and statistically significant effect on the overall rate of constitutional amendment in a state. We also found that the provision in a constitution for amendment by popular initiative had a positive and statistically significant effect on the overall rate of amendment; whereas in the case of a double-passage requirement or single-subject rule for proposed amendments, neither had any statistically significant effect.

Our analysis also confirmed other prior findings by Lutz, Ferejohn and others about the significance of the length and the age of a particular constitution to its probability of amendment (see Lutz 1995: 249, 253; Ferejohn 1997: 524; Elkins et al. 2009). Like others, we found a clear positive and statistically significant correlation between the cumulative age of a constitution and the rate at which it was amended; and also between the length of a constitution and the rate at which it is amended (Dixon and Holden forthcoming). These results seem unsurprising given that, the older a constitution is, the more scope there is for demands for constitutional change to arise in response to changing social circumstances and understandings; and that the length of a constitution is correlated with the degree to which it contains concrete, rule-like constitutional provisions as opposed to more abstract open-ended standards (i.e. it has the 'prolixity of a legal code'), and that, as Section 1 notes, formal processes of amendment will more often be necessary to altering the common law meaning of constitutional rules, than standards.

An additional finding of our study was that a further, potentially under-appreciated, influence on the rate of constitutional amendment in our dataset was the scale of a state's legislature. We found, for example, that a one standard deviation in the number of house members in a state was associated with 0.27 fewer amendments per annum – or 2.7 fewer per decade – or a reduction of 14.6% in the number of amendments, relative to the mean (Dixon and Holden forthcoming).

We also found quite clear evidence of path dependence in the difficulty of amendment. We found, for example, that if a state amended its constitution in a given year, it was 2.8 times more likely than other states to amend it again two years later; and 1.9 times more likely to do so four years later. There was also a strong degree of persistence for this effect; and again, the statistical significance of this finding was high (i.e. significant at the 1% level). One potential explanation for this is simply that there is a close relationship between the rate at which a constitution is amended, and its overall length, and therefore that this finding simply mirrors other findings about the relationship between constitutional length and rates of amendment. Another potential explanation, however, is linked more closely to political attitudes toward the constitution, and the potential for the repeated use of constitutional amendment processes to increase the perceived legitimacy of such processes in the mind of the public, and the infrequent use of such processes to create the opposite result (see Vermeule 2006; and compare also Sullivan 1995 (criticizing apparent changes of this kind in US attitudes in the 1990s)).

What we know thus far in this area, therefore, suggests that formal constitutional amendment procedures do play an important role in determining the likelihood that various actors will use formal amendments as a means of resetting various constitutional rules, engaging in democratic dialogue or reducing agency costs. This also applies, at least within certain bounds, to legislatures and citizens alike, given that both higher legislative super-majority requirements, popular ratification and initiative requirements tend to decrease the rate of amendment across jurisdictions. By influencing popular attitudes toward constitutional change and constitutionalism, such requirements can also indirectly affect the long-term rate of constitutional amendment.

At the same time, the existing empirical literature makes clear that formal constitutional amendment rules are far from an exclusive determinant of the rate of constitutional amendment. Other factors beside formal constitutional procedures, such as a constitution's age, length and a polity's scale, are also important potential determinants of the rate of constitutional amendment in a polity. Substantially more work also remains to be done, both in the US and cross-nationally, in order to understand the precise influence of these, as well as other factors.

Take two factors not addressed by the current empirical literature: the configuration of political parties at a given moment in a particular country; and popular attitudes toward a constitution or constitutionalism. As a logical matter, there seems a significant potential difference between constitutional systems that have only one major or 'dominant' party and those with two major parties (see Choudhry 2007). In the first case, a super-majority voting rule will tend to amount to something like an ordinary majority voting rule; whereas in the second case, it will often require something close to a unanimity or consensus. (Consider the contrast between South Africa and the US in this context: while both countries have a two-thirds super-majority requirement for legislative passage of a proposed amendment, in South Africa, the African National Congress (ANC) has been able to surmount this hurdle almost without any need for support from other parties, whereas in the US this has required virtual bipartisan consensus (see Mansbridge 1986 on ERA)). Only in systems that have multiple small parties, or rather fluid political coalitions does it seem likely that the difficulty of constitutional amendment will tend closely to track the formal super-majority requirements in the text of a constitution.

Popular attitudes toward a constitution also have a clear potential to influence the practical difficulty of constitutional amendment. The more the population is attached to or identifies with the constitution, the greater the burden of persuasion facing those attempting to achieve change via constitutional amendment (Griffin 1998: 53). Similarly, the more the population tends to view the domain of the constitution and constitutional politics as distinct from, or 'above', rather than part of more ordinary political processes, the more difficult it is likely to be, as a political matter, to propose and pass a constitutional amendment (compare Simeon 2009: 5).

At present, however, comparative constitutional scholarship provides almost no guidance in determining the influence of such factors. As Rick Pildes notes elsewhere in this volume, the relationship between political parties and constitutional provisions is a topic which is generally under-developed in comparative constitutional scholarship; and the constitutional amendment literature does no better. When it comes to popular attitudes toward constitutional change, there has been no systematic attempt to compare levels of 'constitutional patriotism' cross-nationally. In part because of this, there has also been little attempt to date to consider the interaction effect between constitutional patriotism and the age and length of a constitution when it comes to rates of constitutional amendment. This is a striking omission when one considers that constitutional patriotism is likely to be both positively correlated with the age of a constitution (compare Madison, Federalist 49 noting the 'veneration … which time bestows' on constitutions) and negatively correlated with a constitution's length.

Even in areas where we do have good evidence about the determinants of constitutional amendment rates, work remains to be done in assessing the degree to which this provides a basis for comparing the difficulty of amendment, across jurisdictions.

Potentially, at least, the rate of constitutional amendment in a jurisdiction may be affected by a number of factors other than the difficulty of constitutional amendment, including: the level of demand for constitutional change in a jurisdiction, and supply-side factors such as the specific aims and language of particular proposed amendments, or the litigation potential they contain (Kelly and Manfredi 2009). The assumption in the constitutional literature to date has been that these factors are sufficiently uncorrelated across jurisdictions that one can treat the actual amendment rate in a jurisdiction as a proxy for the effective difficulty of constitutional amendment. However, in order for us to have greater confidence in this assumption, there is a clear need for further attention to at least three questions: (i) the number of amendments proposed as well as passed in various jurisdictions (see Rasch and Congleton 2006); (ii) the degree to which various constitutional amendments address single as opposed to multiple issues, or enact concrete rule-like versus more open-ended constitutional provisions (for discussion see Rasch and Congleton 2006); and (iii) the relationship between constitutional amendment rates and judicial interpretive norms, such as norms of judicial restraint or originalist interpretation (bearing in mind that such norms may both affect and also be a product of constitutional amendment rates: compare Forbath 2003: 1980). By studying this first question in particular, constitutional scholars could also help address the current gap in our understanding of cross-national patterns of strategic versus sincere legislative voting.

The relevance of all these empirical findings to the design of constitutional amendment rules is also an area which is largely under-developed in existing comparative constitutional scholarship. A key challenge for the next generation of comparative constitutional scholars, therefore, will not only be to deepen our knowledge of the factors that influence the difficulty of constitutional amendment. It will also be to develop new and creative solutions to the potential problems thereby identified.

NOTES

*   I would like to thank Sandy Levinson and Tom Ginsburg for their helpful comments on this chapter.
1.   In the US, an example of the former, according to Ackerman, is the change in constitutional understandings adopted during the New Deal; and an example of the latter the adoption of the Reconstruction Amendments: see Ackerman (1991: 74–82).
2.   The Reconstruction Amendments are, of course, an instance in which Art. V was involved but somewhat modified in application; see discussion in Levinson (2006: 161).
3.   Four referenda approved changes to the Constitution governing the scope of Commonwealth legislative or executive power: so as to expand, or at least clarify, the existence of Commonwealth power to assume prior state debts (1910) or make agreements with the states in respect of state debts (1928); to make laws with respect to 'the provision of maternity allowances, widows' pensions, child endowment, unemployment, pharmaceutical, sickness and hospital benefits, medical and dental services ... and benefits to students and family allowances' (1946); and to make laws with respect to indigenous affairs (1967). One of these (i.e. the 1967 referendum), plus three others, approved changes to various constitutional rules governing the terms of office of senators (1906) and federal judges (1977); the method of counting indigenous voters for the purposes of drawing federal election districts (1977); the rights of territory voters to vote in future constitutional referenda (1977); and the method for filling a Senate vacancy (1977). Only two of these sets of change (i.e. those achieved by the 1946 and 1967 amendments) could arguably have been achieved by other formal processes of legal change, such as judicial interpretation.
4.   One set of amendments sought to alter the operation of various constitutional time-rules, such as those rules defining the period in which amnesty was available under the truth and reconciliation process established by

the original constitution (1st amendment act), the term of municipal councils (2nd amendment act), the time at which elections for the National Assembly or provincial legislatures could be called (4th and 5th amendment acts) and the tenure of constitutional court judges (6th amendment act). A second set of amendments sought to refine constitutional rules governing the eligibility requirements for legislative and executive office holders, including most notably the eligibility requirements for deputy ministers, and the right of local, provincial and national legislators to join or change political parties, while retaining office (the 4th, 6th, 9th, 10th, 11th and 14th amendment acts), and also the designation and swearing in of acting or alternative office-holders, such as an acting president or alternate on the Judicial Services Commission (1st and 2nd amendment acts). A third set of amendments purported to alter the rules governing the drawing of municipal boundaries for those municipalities that crossed provincial boundaries, and also redrew the actual boundary between various provinces (3rd, 12th, 13th, 15th and 16th amendment acts). A fourth class of amendment sought to clarify the method of apportioning membership in the National Council of Provinces (5th and 8th amendment acts). And the fifth and final class of amendments was directed toward changing the name or enumerated power of various public bodies (2nd, 6th, 7th and 11th amendment acts), including the powers and obligations of the National Assembly and its members in respect of 'financial matters' (7th amendment act) and the power of provincial legislatures in respect of local government matters (11th amendment act).

5. The other far less significant exception is, of course, the two prohibition and anti-prohibition amendments (the 19th and 21st Amendments): see Ferejohn and Sager (2003: 1960).
6. Of course, where a legislature's objection to a court's approach is that it is unduly restrained, the two functions may merge into one, but the distinction nonetheless remains useful in other cases. See further note 12 below.
7. The amendments repealed from s. 51(xxvi) the words 'other than the aboriginal race in any State', and repealed entirely the language in s. 127. The consequence of this was to confer certain additional powers on the Commonwealth Parliament to make special laws with respect to indigenous Australians, and to include indigenous Australians in the census, in a way that had some impact on districting practices in Western Australia and Queensland. Another more arguable consequence was to redefine the scope of the Commonwealth's existing powers in respect of racial minorities, so as to ensure that such powers could only be used for the benefit of such minorities.
8. 'The Judicial Power of the United States shall not be construed to extend to any suit in law or equity, commenced or prosecuted against one of the United States by Citizens of another State, or by Citizens or Subjects of any Foreign State', US Constitution, 11th Amendment (1795).
9. Chapter 32, this volume.
10. Other countries that have or have had such a provision include Romania and Poland: see Gardbaum (2010).
11. In the UK, when it comes to at least quasi-constitutional statutory instruments, such as the Human Rights Act 1998, the Westminster parliament also enjoys an explicit power to derogate from protected rights norms.
12. The one possible exception is the 19th Amendment, which is sometimes classified by scholars as a 'trumping' amendment, given its relationship to *Bradwell v State of Illinois*, 83 US 130 (1872): see Ferejohn and Sager (2003: 1960).
13. There are only six states in Australia and hence three states are required to block an amendment under the current 50% rule, and only two states would be required to do so under a two-thirds super-majority rule.
14. Art. 368(2). This requirement is complicated by the fact that a 1971 amendment to the Constitution purported to confer on Parliament, sitting as a Constituent Assembly, plenary power to amend the Constitution: see Art. 368(1), as amended Constitution (Twenty-fourth Amendment) Act, 1971, s. 3.

REFERENCES

Ackerman, Bruce (1991), *We the People: Foundations*, Cambridge, MA: The Belknap Press of Harvard University Press.
Albert, Richard (2009), 'Nonconstitutional Amendments', *Canadian Journal of Law and Jurisprudence* 22: 5–47.
Amar, Akhil Reed (1994), 'The Consent of the Governed: Constitutional Amendment Outside Art V', *Columbia Law Review* 94: 457–511.
Amar, Vikram David (2000), 'People Made Me Do It: Can the People of the States Instruct and Coerce their State Legislatures in the Article V Constitutional Amendment Process', *William & Mary Law Review* 41: 1037–92.
Ambwani, Justice Sunil (2007), 'I.R. Coelho (dead) by L.Rs. Vs. State of Tamil Nadu & Others: A Case Study', Lecture Delivered at the Advocates Association organized by SAMVAAD.
Attwood, Bain and Andrew Markus (2007), *The 1967 Referendum: Race, Power, and the Australian Constitution*, 2nd edition, Canberra: Aboriginal Studies Press.
Balkin, Jack M. (2007), 'Original Meaning and Constitutional Redemption', *Constitutional Commentary* 24: 427–532.

Boudreaux, Donald J. and A.C. Prichard (1993), 'Rewriting the Constitution: An Economic Analysis of the Constitutional Amendment Process', *Fordham Law Review* 62: 111–62.

Buchanan, James M, and Gordon Tullock [1962] (2004), *The Calculus of Consent: Logical Foundations of Constitutional Democracy*, vol. 2, Indianapolis: Liberty Fund, Inc.

Choudhry, Sujit (2007), 'Rethinking Comparative Constitutional Law: Multinational Democracies, Constitutional Amendment, and Secession', Paper presented at the annual meeting of the Law and Society Association.

Choudhry, Sujit (2010), '"I Have a Mandate": The South African Constitutional Court and the African National Congress in a Dominant Party Democracy', Working Paper.

Dahl, Robert A. (2003), *How Democratic is the American Constitution?*, 2nd edition, New Haven: Yale University Press.

Denning, Brannon P. and John R. Vile (2002), 'The Relevance of Constitutional Amendments: A Response to David Strauss', *Tulane Law Review* 77: 247–82.

Dixon, Rosalind (2010), 'Updating Rules', *Supreme Court Review* 2009: 319–46.

Dixon, Rosalind (forthcoming), 'Partial Constitutional Amendments', *University of Pennsylvania Journal of Constitutional Law* 7.

Dixon, Rosalind and Richard Holden (forthcoming), 'Constitutional Amendment Rules: The Denominator Problem', in *Comparative Constitutional Design*, edited by Tom Ginsburg, New York: Cambridge University Press.

Dixon, Rosalind and Eric Posner (forthcoming), 'The Limits of Constitutional Convergence', *University of Chicago Journal of International Law*.

Eisgruber, Christopher L. (2001), *Constitutional Self-Government*, Cambridge, MA: Harvard University Press.

Elkins, Zachary, Tom Ginsburg and James Melton (2009), *The Endurance of National Constitutions*, Cambridge: Cambridge University Press.

Elster, John (2003), 'Don't Burn Your Bridges Before You Come to It: Some Ambiguities and Complexities of Precommitment', *University of Texas Law Review* 81: 1751–88.

Eskridge, William Jr. and John Ferejohn (2001), 'Super-Statutes', *Duke Law Journal* 50: 1215–76.

Ferejohn, John (1997), 'The Politics of Imperfection: The Amendment of Constitutions', *Law and Social Inquiry* 22: 501–30.

Ferejohn, John and Lawrence Sager (2003), 'Commitment and Constitutionalism', *University of Texas Law Review* 81: 1929–63.

Forbath, William E. (2003), 'The Politics of Constitutional Design: Obduracy and Amendability? A Comment on Ferejohn and Sager', *University of Texas Law Review* 81: 1965–84.

Friedman, Barry (1993), 'Dialogue and Judicial Review', *Michigan Law Review* 91: 577–682.

Gardbaum, Stephen (2010), 'Reassessing the New Commonwealth Model of Constitutionalism', *International Journal of Constitutional Law* 8: 167–206.

Ginsburg, Tom and Eric Posner (2010), 'Subconstitutionalism', *Stanford Law Review* 62: 1583–628.

Griffin, Stephen M. (1998), 'The Nominee is . . . Article V', in *Constitutional Stupidities, Constitutional Tragedies*, edited by William N. Eskridge and Sanford Levinson, New York: New York University Press, pp. 51–3.

Grodin, Joseph R., Calvin R. Massey and Richard B. Cunningham (1993), *The California State Constitution: A Reference Guide*, Santa Barbara, CA: Greenwood Press.

Holmes, Stephen (1995), *Passions and Constraint: On the Theory of Liberal Democracy*, Chicago: University of Chicago Press.

Holmes, Stephen and Cass Sunstein (1995), 'The Politics of Constitutional Revision in Eastern Europe', in *Responding to Imperfection: The Theory and Practice of Constitutional Amendment*, edited by Sanford Levinson, Princeton: Princeton University Press, pp. 275–306.

Issacharoff, Samuel (2003), 'The Enabling Role of Democratic Constitutionalism: Fixed Rules and Some Implications for Contested Presidential Elections', *University of Texas Law Review* 81: 1985–2012.

Jacobsohn, Gary (2006), 'An Unconstitutional Constitution? A Constitutional Perspective', *International Journal of Constitutional Law* 4: 460–87.

Kelly, James B. and Christopher P. Manfredi, eds. (2009), *Contested Constitutionalism: Reflections on the Canadian Charter of Rights and Freedoms*, Vancouver: University of British Columbia Press.

Lessig, Lawrence (1993), 'Fidelity in Translation', *University of Texas Law Review* 71: 1165–268.

Levinson, Sanford (1995), 'How Many Times Has the United States Constitution Been Amended? (A) < 26; (B) 26; (C) 27; (D) > 27: Accounting for Constitutional Change', in *Responding to Imperfection: The Theory and Practice of Constitutional Amendment*, edited by Sanford Levinson, Princeton: Princeton University Press, pp. 13–36.

Levinson, Sanford (1996), 'The Political Implications of Amending Clauses', *Constitutional Commentary* 13: 107–24.

Levinson, Sanford (2001), 'Designing an Amendment Process', in *Constitutional Culture and Democratic Rule*, edited by John Ferejohn, Jack M. Rakove and Jonathan Riley, Cambridge: Cambridge University Press, pp. 271–87.

Levinson, Sanford (2006), *Our Undemocratic Constitution*, New York: Oxford University Press.

Lutz, Donald S. (1995), 'Toward a Theory of Constitutional Amendment', in *Responding to Imperfection: The Theory and Practice of Constitutional Amendment*, edited by Sanford Levinson, Princeton: Princeton University Press, pp. 237–74.

Mansbridge, Jane J. (1986), *Why We Lost the ERA*, Chicago: University of Chicago Press.

Marilley, Suzanne M. (1997), *Woman Suffrage and the Origins of Liberal Feminism in the United States, 1820–1920*, Cambridge, MA: Harvard University Press.

Michelman, Frank L. (1986) 'The Supreme Court 1985 Term, Foreword: Traces of Self-government', Harvard Law Review 100: 4–77.

Murphy, Walter F. (1995), 'Merlin's Memory: The Past and Future Imperfect of the Once and Future Polity', in *Responding to Imperfection: The Theory and Practice of Constitutional Amendment*, edited by Sanford Levinson, Princeton: Princeton University Press, pp. 163–90.

Neuborne, Bert (2003), 'The Supreme Court of India', *International Journal of Constitutional Law* 1: 476–510.

Rasch, Bjørn Erik and Roger D. Congleton (2006), 'Amendment Procedures and Constitutional Stability', in *Democratic Constitutional Design and Public Policy: Analysis and Evidence*, edited by Roger D. Congleton and Birgitt Swedenborg, Cambridge, MA: MIT University Press, pp. 319–42.

Rawls, John (1993), *Political Liberalism*, New York: Columbia University Press.

Sager, Lawrence (2001), 'The Birth Logic of a Democratic Constitution', in *Constitutional Culture and Democratic Rule*, edited by John Ferejohn, Jack M. Rakove and Jonathan Riley, Cambridge: Cambridge University Press, pp. 110–46.

Schumpeter, Joseph (1962), *Capitalism, Socialism, and Democracy*, New York: Harper & Row.

Siegel, Reva (2006), '2005–2006 Brennan Center Symposium Lecture: Constitutional Culture, Social Movement Conflict and Constitutional Change', *University of California Law Review* 94: 1323–420.

Simeon, Richard (2009), 'Constitutional Design and Change in Federal Systems: Issues and Questions', *Publius: The Journal of Federalism* 39: 241–61.

Stone, Geoffrey R. (1988), 'Precedent, the Amendment Process, and the Evolution of Constitutional Doctrine', *Harvard Journal of Law and Public Policy* 11: 67–74.

Strauss, David (1996), 'Common Law Constitutional Interpretation', *University of Chicago Law Review* 63: 877–936.

Sullivan, Kathleen M. (1995), 'Constitutional Amendmentitis', *The American Prospect*, September 21.

Tushnet, Mark (2009), 'Constitutional Workarounds', *Texas Law Review* 87: 1499–516.

Vermeule, Adrian (2006), 'Constitutional Amendments and Common Law', in *The Least Examined Branch: The Role of Legislatures in the Constitutional State*, edited by Richard W. Bauman and Tsvi Kahana, Cambridge: Cambridge University Press, pp. 229–73.

Winterton, George (1994), *Monarchy to Republic: Australian Republican Government*, Oxford: Oxford University Press.

Winterton, George (2001), 'The Resurrection of the Republic', Law and Policy Paper 15, Centre for International and Public Law, ANU.

Young, Ernest (2007), 'The Constitution Outside the Constitution', *Yale Law Journal* 117: 408–73.

Zohar, Noam (1995), 'Midrash: Amendment through the Molding of Meaning', in *Responding to Imperfection: The Theory and Practice of Constitutional Amendment*, edited by Sanford Levinson, Princeton: Princeton University Press, pp. 307–18.

7. Constitutional endurance
Tom Ginsburg

Constitutions, by their nature, operate in time, seeking to regulate the future on behalf of the past. By providing a relatively enduring basis for politics, constitutions facilitate the operation of government, while at the same time setting out limits on government action. Constitutions also exist in a world of change, and so must adjust to changing conditions. Much constitutional theory wrestles with these dualisms of past and future, empowerment and constraint, change and stability.

This chapter focuses on the issue of constitutional endurance. Most drafters of constitutions act as if their handiwork should last a long time (Kay 2000: 33), and constitutional scholars since Aristotle have generally assumed that endurance is valuable. Indeed, it is safe to say that virtually every normative constitutional theory presumes that constitutions survive over a relatively extended period of time. Without endurance, constitutions cannot provide a stable basis of politics and cannot constitute a people out of diverse elements. The assumption of endurance is thus built into the very idea of a constitution (Raz 1998: 153).[1]

In the real world, however, it turns out that most written constitutions are relatively short-lived. In a recent contribution, Zachary Elkins, James Melton and I explored constitutional endurance in some depth (Elkins et al. 2009). We found that the predicted lifespan for constitutions for all countries is 19 years; the observed median is even lower.[2] For some regions of the world, the life expectancy is quite low indeed: the average constitution will last a mere eight years in Latin America and Eastern Europe (see also Negretto 2008 on Latin America).

The fact of constitutional fragility raises a number of positive and normative questions. First, does constitutional durability really matter? If so, what are the determinants of endurance? Should we care about the survival of a bundle of provisions called the 'constitution' or rather the stability of individual norms, which may or may not be instantiated in the text? This chapter reviews the literature on constitutional endurance, focusing on both the normative and positive questions.

Endurance is closely related to core normative issues involving constitutional amendment (see Chapter 6 by Dixon in this volume.) This chapter does not consider amendment per se, but may be read in conjunction with others to provide a complete analysis.

1 WHY SHOULD CONSTITUTIONS ENDURE?

In attempting to control the future, constitution-makers are engaged in an act of 'temporal imperialism' (Norton 1988: 460) and so have long been subject to critique from those in favor of more radical and continuous notions of democracy. As Noah Webster, a contemporary of the American founders, put it, 'The very attempt to make perpetual constitutions is the assumption of a right to control the opinions of future generations; and to legislate for those over whom we have as little authority as we have over a nation in Asia'. Thomas Jefferson engaged in the most extensive of these critiques, arguing that the dead had no right to govern the living. Jefferson famously calculated the precise period after which a current majority would be replaced by a new one, and argued for constitutional replacement every 19 years so that each generation could determine its own fundamental rules. Jefferson's view is that periodic reconsideration of fundamental principles will keep them fresh and keep the citizenry engaged in the process of self-governance.

The critiques of Webster and Jefferson emphasized the importance of social and environmental change. As societies and their underlying conditions change over time, institutions must adjust with them to be effective. The position that the entire constitution ought to be reconsidered implicitly assumes that normal mechanisms of constitutional amendment will be insufficient to produce optimal tailoring of rules to society. Ordinary amendment processes may be too difficult, and their incremental character may lead citizens to be insufficiently global in their consideration of alternative institutional arrangements. It was thus important to encourage citizens to recast their eyes to more global arrangements. One institutional legacy of this approach is found at the level of American states, a number of which require periodic consideration of constitutional conventions.

On the other hand, there are some good normative reasons to support at least moderate stability in law. Aristotle's *Politics* is the touchstone in this regard. For Aristotle, the strength of law lies in citizens' habits of obedience, which are the only force that gives law power. Instability in law, he argued, can weaken the notion of law itself (Schwartzburg 2007: 62). Aristotle recognized, to be sure, the need for ongoing interpretation in the context of application of law, a feature demanded by the general character of law itself. But frequent change in the primary rules would seem to undercut the ability of law to inculcate habits of obedience.

Another reason to support the endurance of fundamental rules is that it allows the development of collateral institutions that are not directly created by the constitution but are necessary to make it function effectively. For example, political parties are not directly created by constitutional rules, yet many consider them to have a constitutional character in the sense of being crucial intermediaries for democratic governance. The media and civil society may develop a quality of fitting their particular constitutional environment, so that change in fundamental rules would disrupt their effective functioning. These institutions exhibit what we might call constitution-specificity, a quality of being organically related to the constitutional schemes they inhabit.

Constitution-specific institutions will tend to reinforce existing political arrangements. As collateral institutions develop, they develop constituencies that invest in their processes and structures, and will resist efforts to overturn or modify basic structures too drastically. These constituencies may also have a crucial stake in enforcing the constitution, potentially restricting sovereign power. Periodic changes in the fundamental rules, on the other hand, might encourage opportunistic elites to engineer institutions for their short-term benefit. Furthermore, frequent change makes monitoring by citizens more difficult, and may exacerbate general collective action problems of investment in monitoring.

We thus have reason to think that constitutional endurance can help underpin social and political stability, encouraging gradualist and organic processes of change. Furthermore, the prospect of an enduring constitution can itself resolve political differences among those who are negotiating and drafting the constitution. Van den Hauwe (2000: 632) points out that stability is a distinct dimension of constitutional choice that can improve bargaining incentives. As time horizons lengthen, each drafter's ability to predict the position she will hold in subsequent arrangements, and so the negotiation takes on the quality of a veil of ignorance. This might itself produce fairer or more impartial rules. In addition, if drafters are concerned with stability, they might recognize the need to produce political benefits for groups besides themselves: the concern for stability and endurance of the rules can partially mitigate the effects of self-interest at the constitutional level.

Van den Hauwe's story is one in which normative concerns about constitutional quality are aligned with concern for constitutional endurance. One can, however, imagine cases when these factors cut against each other. A constitution that focuses on the public interest may generate insufficient political support at the level of ordinary politics to withstand interest group pressures for modification. Excessive concern for endurance, it might be argued, can lead drafters to ignore the short-term payoffs necessary to adopt a constitution. The focus on endurance implies that a certain amount of redistribution and rent-seeking may be tolerable and even valuable to the extent that it gives interest groups a stake in enforcement of the bargain down the road.

2   CONSEQUENCES OF ENDURANCE

One might think these myriad theoretical arguments about the costs and benefits of endurance would be subject to rigorous testing, but there is little literature on the consequences of endurance. We thus cannot state for certain that constitutions that endure are good ones in a normative sense. Elkins et al. (2009) focus on written constitutions of independent nation-states, and demonstrate significant associations between long-lived constitutions and various social and political goods including rights protection, democracy, wealth and political stability. Countries with enduring constitutions are richer and more democratic. But efforts to determine a causal relationship are plagued by concerns about missing variables and endogeneity. It might be, for example, that countries that have a stable underlying social structure are more inclined to enjoy both constitutional endurance and democracy, in which case one cannot assume a direct association between the latter two phenomena. It also seems possible, indeed likely, that constitutional endurance and these other goods have feedback effects. For example, economic growth probably helps to reinforce constitutional stability by reducing pressure for renegotiation; in turn stability underpins further economic growth, leading to positive feedback effects. The relationship between endurance and other goods is thus likely to be complex and multi-channeled.

Furthermore, it is not always the case that a single written document called a constitution is the important unit of analysis. Many provisions of such documents may not be constitutional in character or function, so that their replacement or amendment is of little practical or theoretical consequence. It may be that the benefits of constitutional endurance inhere at the level of individual norms that play a constitutional function, rather than bundles of norms instantiated into a single written text. Certainly the older notion of the term 'constitution', in which the term is understood as the set of norms about government that are relatively enduring, implies that the important thing is institutions rather than documents.

The literature on presidentialism and parliamentarism is somewhat relevant here. Even if formal constitutional turnover is frequent, the 'real' constitution will be stable if fundamental features of the political system such as regime type and governmental system remain constant. This is the position taken by scholars such as Hayo and Voigt (2010) and Persson and Tabellini (2003) who treat the presidential/parliamentary choice as the key constitutional design dimension for political systems.

Focusing on the consequences of this fundamental choice of political system, participants in debates over regime type have focused in part on endurance as a dimension as a metric to evaluate governmental systems. Stepan and Skach (1993) found that, of non-OECD countries, none of the 36 new countries that emerged after World War II that adopted presidentialism were continuously democratic between 1980 and 1989, while 14 of 41 of such countries that adopted parliamentary systems were democratic during that period. Cheibub and Limongi (2002) note that one out of every 23 presidential regimes died between 1946 and 1999, whereas only one in every 58 parliamentary regimes died. Boix (2005) provides further support for the proposition that parliamentary systems are better for democratic survival (Boix 2005). The logic of the argument is that presidential systems tend to lead to minority executives and government gridlock; this in turn can encourage actors to take extra-constitutional steps to gain power, leading to political instability and eventually the death of democracy. Cheibub (2007), however, shows that this instability is not caused by the choice of regime, but rather reflects selection effects. Unstable countries tend to choose presidential constitutions. But this finding is somewhat orthogonal to understanding the consequences of constitutional endurance.

In short, the claims for the value of endurance are largely theoretical rather than empirical in character. Tricky methodological issues are largely responsible for this. The suggestive evidence is strong, however: Elkins et al. (2009) point out that no rich democratic country has had high levels of constitutional turnover, while nine of the ten longest currently living constitutions belong to OECD members (see Table 7.1).

Table 7.1   *Most enduring constitutions as of 2010*

Rank	Country	Years	Lifespan
1	United States of America	1789–	221
2	Norway	1814–	196
3	Belgium	1831–	179
4	Sweden	1809–1974	165
5	Netherlands	1848–	162
6	New Zealand	1852–	158
7	Canada	1867–	143
8	Luxembourg	1868–	142
9	Liberia	1847–1980	133
10	Switzerland	1874–2000	125
11	Australia	1901–	109
12	Colombia	1886–1991	105
13	Mexico	1917–	93
14	Chile	1833–1921	92

It is also worth noting that claims about the value of endurance are now ones for which there is a good deal of theoretical agreement, at least since the decline of the Jeffersonian position. Even critics who argue for the replacement of particular enduring constitutional texts such as the American one (Levinson 2006; Dahl 2001; Sabato 2007) do not claim that endurance per se is a bad thing.

3   THEORIES OF ENDURANCE

What might make constitutions endure? There is a small amount of theory in a rational choice vein addressing this question. The dominant current view draws on the literature on self-enforcing institutions. Constitutions, as Hardin (1989), Niskanen (1990), Przeworski (1991) and Ordeshook (1992) pointed out, do not have an external enforcer who can ensure that the terms of the constitution are enforced. While courts purport to enforce the constitution through the power of judicial review, one must still develop an account as to why powerful actors obey the courts. Constitutions must therefore be self-enforcing, meaning that it is in the interest of all powerful factions to abide by the provisions of the constitution. A constitution will endure so long as parties believe they are better off within the bargain than in risking new constitutional negotiations. A well-designed constitution becomes an equilibrium, so that no one with the power to defect has an interest in doing so.

Weingast (1997) generalizes this idea to explain that constitutions represent coordination devices that allow citizens and elites to develop shared understanding of the limits of government, and to enforce those limits. In democracies, enforcement of these constitutional limitations ultimately relies on citizens. If they can coordinate, citizens can prevent the government from imposing costs on them and violating the political bargain. If they cannot coordinate, democracy may not be stable, as the government will continuously adjust the bargain in its favor with political acquiescence. The coordination problem is that citizens, having disparate interests, will be unlikely to reach agreement on their own as to what is considered to be a violation of the constitution, and on when and how to enforce the bargain. A willingness to stand against the government requires a belief that others will join the citizen; otherwise the potential protestor will fear ending up in jail while oppression continues. When all citizens coordinate their expectations that others will join in the protest, however, the expectations become self-fulfilling and government will refrain from violating the bargain. Written constitutions may be useful instruments to help citizens overcome the coordination problem, because texts define violations and thus increase the probability of coordination (Carey 2000). We might also expect that constitutions adopted with widespread participation would be more widely known and hence more likely to be self-enforcing (see Blount chapter in this volume).

If endurance results from self-enforcement, we still cannot have confidence that enduring constitutions are always good constitutions. It may be the case that political payoffs to interest groups are required to keep the bargain stable. Sutter (2003) derives conditions under which durability will facilitate the general interest rather than rent-seeking. He argues that constitutions that make rents transferable and that require rent-seekers to turn over periodically can dis-incentivize interest groups from rent-seeking. Because any rents acquired early on will be potentially taken away in later stages by new coalitions, such constitutions reduce the value of rents. Sutter suggests that democracy, by requiring periodic turnover, approximates the second condition. On the other hand, if interest groups have already secured advantage in the current system, autocracy might provide a mechanism for breaking through rent-seeking equilibria.

Sutter's argument builds on other work by scholars who are skeptical about constitutional provisions that are too detailed. As stated by Przeworski (1991: 36): 'Constitutions that are observed and last for a long time are those that . . . define the scope of government and establish rules of competition, leaving substantive outcomes open to the political interplay'. This position is echoed in the literature on constitutional political economy, which has developed normative arguments in favor of endurance and opposed to special interest provisions in constitutions (e.g. Wagner 1987). The literature has tended to assume that these two things go together.

Elkins et al. (2009) build on self-enforcement theory to argue for three specific design features that will help constitutions to endure. They follow the conventional approach of conceiving of constitutions as bargains among major groups that must remain supportive of the constitution for it to endure. They argue that the primary threat to bargains among these groups lies in 'shocks' that affects costs and benefits flowing from the constitution. Such change can be exogenous or endogenous: it might consist of a global financial crisis, or a change in the relative power of the groups produced by constitutional terms. Either way, a shock will put pressure on a constitutional bargain and render it less likely to survive. They argue that flexible constitutions that are easy to amend will be able to adjust when new social and political circumstances arise. They also argue that inclusion – greater public involvement in the creation of the constitution – will render it more likely to be enforced. Inclusion refers to the involvement of important groups in society – broadly speaking, the more groups with a stake in the constitution, the more likely it is to endure. Finally, they argue that more specific constitutions are likely to survive in that they will represent greater levels of investment on the part of the drafters.

4   OBSERVED PATTERNS

This section summarizes the empirical literature on constitutional endurance, which is of relatively recent vintage. As Table 7.1 shows, only 12 historical constitutions have managed to last more than a century. Of these, several are of anomalous form in that they involve collections of documents rather than a single text (New Zealand, Sweden, Canada). In such countries, major changes such as the adoption of a bill of rights might be considered to mark the adoption of a new constitution. For most countries, however, constitutional replacement is a relatively clear concept, as it involves the adoption of a single discrete document entitled the constitution.

Employing a hazard model to analyze such formal texts, Elkins et al. (2009) find that constitutions are becoming increasingly brittle over time. Constitutions in the 19th century were more enduring than in the 20th. The interwar period was particularly hazardous for constitutions (Elkins et al. 2009:135), a fact likely explained by the effect of war on many countries. But constitutions adopted after World War II seem to be somewhat less enduring than those in the 19th century. This might be explained by the tripling in the number of states after World War II (Alesina and Spolaore 2003). Since the creation of each new state involves, in some sense, a failure of an old constitutional bargain, it is not surprising that an expansion in states has corresponded with constitutional death. In addition, a more benevolent international environment has reduced the costs of small state size. Both the postwar security system, which legally protects the integrity of states, and the open trade regime have reduced the dis-utility of being small (Lake and O'Mahoney 2004). This environmental factor might lower the stakes of constitutional dissolution and replacement.

Elkins et al. (2009) also find regional effects. Constitutions in Latin America and Eastern Europe are particularly short-lived, with constitutions in Africa and East Asia also enjoying shorter life expectancy than those in Western Europe or Oceania (see also Negretto 2008 on Latin America). Yet it is not the case that long-lasting constitutions are exclusively a phenomenon of the industrialized west. Mexico, for example, has a constitution that is almost a hundred years old and has provided for stable rule under both authoritarian and democratic regimes. India's constitution has endured through episodes of authoritarian challenge, and helped to integrate a centrifugal society. Furthermore, national patterns of endurance are internally diverse for countries with multiple constitutions. A typical pattern is to observe constitutions of a shorter duration early in a state's existence, with longer constitutional durations as the state ages. This is consistent with the idea that new states must search for institutions that fit the society, and also the notion that governance becomes easier once populations develop agreement about the fundamental bases for society.

In terms of the determinants of endurance, Elkins et al. (2009) find that environmental shocks such as wars and coups have some association, though most of these effects are not statistically significant. Older states and those with a history of enduring constitutions tend to have longer-lived texts. This suggests that citizens who are able to overcome the collective action problem of enforcement may inculcate a culture of constitutional adherence. And there appear to be 'diffusion' effects, such that the probability of drafting a new text is increased when neighbors do so.

They also find support for their argument that there are certain design features that will be associated with enduring constitutions. Not surprisingly, they find that flexibility in the amendment rule is associated with constitutional endurance, so that the bargain can adjust over time, but they also find that the effect is not linear. Highly malleable and highly rigid constitutions will both be subject to early death. They find that India's fairly flexible rule (see also Dixon and Jacobsohn in this volume) is about optimal. They further find that participatory institutions are associated with constitutional endurance, supporting the notion that the constitution is best enforced when citizens are aware of its contents. Finally, and somewhat counter-intuitively, they find that more detailed constitutions are more enduring. This finding conflicts with a common popular and scholarly supposition described above that more loosely drafted 'framework' constitutions are more enduring.

The finding about detail is consistent with the findings of Hammons (1999). Hammons analyzed all constitutions of American states to evaluate the conjecture that detail leads to early death (see e.g. Friedman 1988: 36). He characterized constitutional language as either broadly about the institutions of government or more detailed 'public policy' language that might conventionally be found in statutes. He found a good deal of the latter content in constitutions, but also found that more detailed language and longer texts were associated with greater constitutional endurance, controlling for time and region. His result thus parallels Elkins et al. (2009).[3]

Another analysis of state constitutions in the US is that of Berkowitz and Clay (2005).

Exploiting historical variation in the history of US states, they focus on the colonial origin of constitutions as being either civil law or common law. They argue that weaker property rights associated with the civil law will lead to more constitutional and political instability, controlling for other factors such as geography and economic performance. Their results support the analysis that the civil law is associated with more constitutional instability.

To be sure, it is not clear that the state-level constitutions are performing the same functions as those of nation-states. Ginsburg and Posner (2010) use an agency cost framework to argue that constitutions of subnational units ought to be less enduring than those for nation- states. This is because the stakes of constitutional change are lower. A constitution provides a framework for the polity to hire government to carry out certain tasks. Limits on government power provided by the constitution help to ensure that the agents do not deviate from their assigned tasks, and the constitution provides a framework to monitor the performance of those agents. If the constitution can be easily amended or replaced, it will be less able to limit agency costs of government. One of the features of constitutions of subnational units such as states in a federation is that the super-state carries out some of the monitoring and disciplining of government agents. For example in the United States, the federal guarantee of a republican form of government means that there is limited damage a wayward state government can accomplish. The limits provided in state constitutions, therefore, are of less importance than those in a nation-state, and hence can be changed more frequently.

Some evidence for this can be found in US states, some 14 of which have constitutional requirements that the people be consulted on a regular basis by the legislature as to whether to call a constitutional convention (Martineau 1970; Williams 2000). Two national constitutions with similar provisions are those of Fiji (1990, Art. 161), which required review every ten years, but was replaced before a decade elapsed, and Micronesia's Constitution of 1990, which was highly influenced by US constitutional practice. US state constitutions are amended quite frequently, and replaced fairly often: the average state has had three constitutions in the course of its existence, and the average lifespan of a state constitution is 45 years, far shorter than the national constitution (Hammons 2001: 1339; but see Hammons 1999: 839 (70 years)).

By focusing on the written constitution, this literature shifts the emphasis away from the endurance of particular institutions across the written texts, or of institutions not found in the constitution. It can be argued that French constitutional instability, which was endemic before 1870 and again from World War II through 1958, has had less severe consequences than it might otherwise have had because of the stability of other French institutions. For example, the enduring nature of the French Civil Code of 1804 has provided great stability for private legal relations, and played a 'constitutional' function of providing previously disenfranchised groups with formal legal equality. The Conseil d'Etat, which plays the function of an administrative court and helps ensure the autonomy of the state bureaucracy, has also been enduring. Arguably, formal constitutional endurance becomes less important in a country with other forms of institutional stability.

Hayo and Voigt (2010) focus on the presidential-parliamentary choice as the key constitutional dimension for analysis. They employ a hazard model to examine switches from one form of government to another across time and space. Their general results are that country conditions matter, with regional effects (Africa and the Middle East) and colonial legacy (all but the British and French) predicting switches in governmental form.

Notwithstanding the general finding in the literature that parliamentary systems are associated with democratic survival (Stepan and Skach 1993), they find that presidential systems are more enduring in the sense of being less likely to be replaced with a parliamentary system. This combination of results is not surprising given that dictators who replace a democratic president may be perfectly comfortable keeping the form of government, while democrats may have more heterogeneous preferences about government type. This interpretation is consistent with the argument of Cheibub (2007).

The Hayo and Voigt approach of looking at particular constitutional institutions rather than constitutional texts as a whole is a promising one. One might imagine further studies looking at the survival of various rights or enforcement institutions that survive the demise of a formal text to have impact down the road (Ginsburg 2009). In conjunction with studies of formal change, such work would allow us to better understand the consequences of constitutional replacement.

At the same time, it would not be advisable to reduce the study of constitutional endurance to the study of regime endurance, meaning the persistence of dictatorship or democracy. Notwithstanding claims to the contrary (Russell 1993:16) democratic countries periodically modify their constitutional texts without a regime change, or even without a profound shock to the system.[4] Dictatorships vary in terms of their use of constitutions to legitimate their rule, from systems like Chile under Pinochet which took constitutions somewhat seriously (Barros 2002) to those like the former Soviet Union in which the Constitutions provided at best a symbolic document (Solomon 1996). So constitutional change is a discrete phenomenon from regime change, though in many cases they may be linked.

Further, a shift of analytic focus to non-constitutional institutions leads to two methodological concerns. The first is to define in a rigorous way all institutions that are 'constitutional' but not found in the formal constitution. Different scholars have offered different examples of statutes, political statements, court decisions and unwritten norms that might be considered to play a constitutional function. While these sources of norms are quite properly considered constitutional for many purposes, it is tricky to come up with a precise definition that works across geographic and temporal contexts. Thus shifting to the informal constitution makes it difficult to be comparative even as it increases one's understanding of what is 'constitutional'.

The second methodological issue is that, by shifting to informal institutions, analysts sometimes make an implicit assumption that formal institutions are less important. This move raises a puzzle. If the written constitution is of relatively low stakes, why do states spend so much energy in drafting written texts and negotiating institutional choices embodied in them? And why do others resist attempts at formal constitutional change through amendment or redrafting processes? The puzzle suggests that writing does matter, though we are only beginning to rigorously theorize the ways that it does (Breslin 2009).

5   CASES

Beyond large-sample studies, there are some examinations of constitutional change that help to illuminate the phenomenon of endurance. Weingast (2006b) traces the history of the American constitution from the perspective of constitutional self-enforcement. He argues that the founders formed a bargain between states that turned out to be largely self-enforcing. In part this was because of particular supermajority rules that gave each side of the slavery divide a veto, and the inclusion of the Senate as a guarantee of small state interests. The North-South balance was maintained with the adoption of the Missouri Compromise and other pacts in the early 19th century. These bargains were stable because neither side had an incentive to leave the constitutional order, and neither could dominate the other, even as the country expanded to the west. The rule ensuring that states entered the union in pairs ensured that the sectional balance would be maintained. When slavery reached its natural limit in the American southwest, however, the bargain broke down, leading ultimately to the civil war. We thus have an account of both constitutional maintenance and breakdown from the perspective of self-enforcement theory.

Another long-lived constitution is that of Sweden, which might be considered a case of super-longevity like the United States. Like the United Kingdom, Sweden has a long history of constitutionalism dating back to arrangements between monarchy and nobles around public finance. Swedes trace their constitutional history to 1319 when the King signed the Letter of Privilege binding him to govern using the rule of law and consult before imposing taxes (Congleton 2003). After many centuries of evolution, including the passage of several important statutes, the modern constitution was formed with the passage of the Instrument of Government in 1809 and the subsequent revision of several other key acts (Verney 1957).[5]

Aside from the King and his Council, there was a legislature composed of four Estates – the Nobles, Clerics, Burghers, and Farmers. A majority of three of the four Estates and the King both had to approve legislation, although there were some areas the King was granted exclusive jurisdiction to decide and the Estates were granted exclusive jurisdiction to levy taxes. Constitutional amendments required approval of all four Estates in two separate sittings as well as the approval of the King (Verney 1957; Congleton 2003). These devices can be seen as providing a mutual veto among the major groups in society, similar to Weingast's account of the self-enforcing Missouri compromise.

Over the next century and a half, there were gradual movements for expanding the franchise and other liberal reforms. A bicameral legislature was established, property restrictions on the franchise gradually reduced, and eventually universal suffrage was adopted. But high thresholds of amendment meant that the process was gradual in character. Gradualism resulted in Sweden's postponement of enfranchisement of the general population until 1921 and retention of formal powers of the King until 1974, while both of these events occurred much sooner throughout the rest of Europe. Gradualism was facilitated by a de facto change in the amendment rule. Although the formal rule remained in place, the elimination of the Estates and their replacement with a bicameral parliament in 1866 meant that amendment actually became relatively easy in Sweden.

The next major changes to the constitutional structure of Sweden did not take place for 50 years. This was a period of political stability under the rule of the Social Democrats, leading non-socialist parties to begin to argue for a more proportional, unicameral Parliament in the 1950s (Congleton 2003). In 1969, Parliament voted to amend the Riksdag Act of 1866, transforming the legislature from a bicameral to a unicameral entity and creating a more proportional system (Immergut 2002). This led to a new constitution clarifying the government structure in 1974.

Sweden illustrates how formal continuity can exist with massive change. Sweden is also exceptional in that it appears to have experienced constitutional change without prerequisites, namely without significant shocks. No doubt the patterns of compromise and cooperation that were established in the long evolution of Sweden's constitution have meant that pressures build up more incrementally. It seems to be an example of constitutional change triggered only by the accumulation of small pressures, leading to, at some point, a tipping effect toward constitutional revision. At this writing, a new movement seems to be brewing for constitutional reform (Bull 2005), but if history is any guide, amendment rather than revision will be the modality.

Another case of constitutional endurance, perhaps more surprising than the others given the centrifugal nature of the underlying society, is that of India. A constitution had been a central demand of the Congress Party since well before independence, and its drafting was the first major act of state, carried out by a large and inclusive constituent assembly. The document that emerged from this process was long and detailed, containing both general goals to integrate a diverse nation as well as detailed principles to guide governance. Constitutional politics early on focused on attempts to take land for redistribution to the poor, with the judiciary providing some limits to the process and thus upsetting the Congress government. The government responded with the first of many amendments in 1951 (Austin 1999). The first amendment set up a schedule of topics immune from judicial review, and initiated a long process of dialogue between court and legislature that has continued to this day.

In the 1970s the Constitution came under severe threat from the government of Indira Gandhi. Supreme Court made a historical ruling in the *Golak Nath* case.[6] In this case, the court asserted that Parliament's power to amend the constitution was limited in cases when fundamental rights were at issue. The case provoked a backlash from parliament, which amended the constitution to over-rule it, but the Court responded with *Kesavananda*.[7] (See discussion in Jacobsohn, Chapter 8.)

Frustrated with the courts, facing removal from office for election fraud, and responding to an increasingly vigorous opposition, Gandhi declared a state of emergency in 1975, passing another set of amendments to remove oversight of states of emergency and election cases from the judiciary. The judiciary upheld many of the provisions of these amendments, while asserting that the *Kesavananda* principle still stood. Gandhi responded again with the 42nd amendment curbing judicial jurisdiction and raising the threshold to declare laws unconstitutional. But shortly thereafter, she lost an election and the Janata Dal party set about undoing her excesses.

The constitution suffered its gravest threats during this well-known series of events. But it did not break, notwithstanding suggestions to Gandhi that she replace the document. Perhaps the symbolic association with her father and with Congress was part of the reason she felt restrained, but the ease of amendment certainly played a role as well. With a large majority in the National Assembly, Congress could amend the Constitution at will, and has done so nearly 100 times since the founding of the Constitution. In the course of its history, the Indian Constitution has become the embodiment of independence and the 'cornerstone of the nation' (Austin 1966).

These brief case studies illustrate the importance of flexibility for endurance, but flexibility is not a sufficient condition. It certainly helps when a constitution becomes the embodiment of a regime, as is that of the United States or India; but the Swedish case illustrates that occasionally countries will change constitutions even when the regime is stable.

6   CONCLUSION

Constitutions are generally intended to endure, but frequently do not do so in reality. While scholars are beginning to make some headway on the determinants of endurance, there are many unanswered questions about the positive and normative consequences of this fact. We conclude with some suggestions for future work.

More thorough comparative study of constitutional breakdown and endurance would be helpful. Latin America is a promising region in this regard, as its countries exhibit great diversity in constitutional endurance. Some countries, such as Uruguay, have experienced long periods of stability, only to be followed by breakdown and a series of short-lived constitutions. Others, such as Mexico, go through a period of experimentation early in the national history, but eventually find a stable set of institutions. A small number of countries, including the Dominican Republic and Haiti, rewrite constitutions with great frequency and never seem to find a stable system. Longitudinal studies of these diverse environments would elaborate on the relationship between constitutional and institutional instability.

As mentioned above, studying the consequences of endurance raises tricky methodological issues. Perhaps instrumental variables can be identified to isolate the effect of constitutional stability, but it is likely that more progress will be made in identifying determinants of endurance than its consequences. Further work connecting the circumstances of constitutional drafting with endurance would be welcome. It is particularly important to identify substantive and procedural factors that are within the control of institutional designers. The stakes are high, especially in an era in which constitution-making has become a central element of state-building and conflict resolution.

NOTES

1. Raz (1998: 153) places endurance among the central features that define a constitution: 'it is, and is meant to be, of long duration'.
2. We use the predicted mean rather than the observed mean as the central analytical measure in our work. Focusing only on observed deaths has the problem of excluding all constitutions currently alive, which as we know includes the United States Constitution of 1789 and several other enduring texts. This is the problem of right-censored data: excluding such cases might lead to an inordinately low estimate of constitutional endurance.
3. Hammons finds no effect for historical era of adoption, though he does find regional effects: constitutions from New England tend to be more enduring (and shorter), while those in the Lower South are less enduring.
4. Russell asserts: 'No liberal democratic state has accomplished comprehensive constitutional change outside the context of some cataclysmic situation such as a revolution, world war, the withdrawal of empire, civil, war, or the threat of imminent breakup'.
5. Scholars identify several other statues as having constitutional character, including the Riksdag Act, regulating the procedures and policies of the parliament, first passed in 1617; the Act of Succession, whose antecedents go back to 1544, stating the rules of the hereditary monarchy; and the Freedom of the Press Act, originally passed in 1776. Holmstrom (1994).
6. *I.C. Golak Nath and Ors. v State of Punjab and Anrs.* (AIR 1967 SC 1643).
7. *His Holiness Kesavananda v The State of Kerala and Others* (AIR 1973 SC 1461).

REFERENCES

Alesina, Alberto and Enrico Spolaore (2003), *The Size of Nations*, Cambridge, MA: MIT Press.
Austin, Granville (1966), *The Indian Constitution: Cornerstone of a Nation*, London: Oxford University Press.

Austin, Granville (1999), *Working a Democratic Constitution*, New Delhi: Oxford University Press.

Barros, Robert (2002), *Constitutionalism and Dictatorship*, New York: Cambridge University Press.

Berkowitz, Daniel and Karen Clay, (2005), 'American Civil-law Origins: Implications for State Constitutions', *American Law and Economics Review* 7(1): 62–84.

Boix, Carles (2005), 'Constitutions and Democratic Breakdowns', paper presented at Comparative Law and Economics Forum, Chicago, IL, October 2005.

Breslin, Beau (2009), *From Words to Worlds: Exploring Constitutional Functionality*, Baltimore, MD: Johns Hopkins University Press.

Bull, Thomas (2005), 'Constitutional Changes and the Limits of Law', *European Public Law* 11: 187–95.

Carey, John (2000), 'Parchment, Equilibria, and Institutions', *Comparative Political Studies* 33: 735–61.

Cheibub, José Antonio (2007), *Presidentialism, Parliamentarism and Democracy*, New York: Cambridge University Press.

Cheibub, José Antonio and Fernando Limongi (2002), 'Democratic Institutions and Regime Survival: Parliamentary and Presidential Democracies Reconsidered', *Annual Review of Political Science* 5(1), 151–79.

Dahl, Robert (2001), *How Democratic is the American Constitution*, New Haven: Yale University Press.

Elkins, Zachary, Tom Ginsburg and James Melton (2009), *The Endurance of National Constitutions*, New York: Cambridge University Press.

Friedman, Lawrence M. (1988), 'State Constitutions in Historical Perspective', *Annals of the American Academy of Political and Social Science* 496 (March): 33–42.

Ginsburg, Tom (2009), 'Constitutional Afterlife: The Continuing Impact of Thailand's Post-Political Constitution', *International Journal of Constitutional Law* 7(1): 83–105.

Ginsburg, Tom and Eric Posner (2010) 'Subconstitutionalism', *Stanford Law Review* 62: 1583–628.

Hammons, Christopher (1999), 'Was James Madison Wrong? Rethinking the American Preference for Short, Framework-Oriented Constitutions', *American Political Science Review* 93(4): 837–49.

Hammons, Christopher W. (2001), 'State Constitutional Reform: Is it Necessary?', *Albany Law Review* 64: 1327–47.

Hardin, Russell (1989) 'Why a Constitution?', in Bernard Grofman and Donald Wittman, eds., *The Federalist Papers and the New Institutionalism*, New York: Agathon Press, pp. 100–20.

Hayo, Bernd and Stefan Voigt (2010), 'Determinants of Constitutional Change: When and Why do Countries Change their Form of Government?' (March). Available at SSRN: http://ssrn.com/abstract=1562553.

Holmstrom, Barry (1994), 'The Judicialization of Politics in Sweden', *International Political Science Review* 15: 153–64.

Immergut, Ellen M. (2002), 'The Swedish Constitution and Social Democratic Power: Measuring the Mechanical Effect of a Political Institution', *Scandinavian Political Studies* 25: 231–57.

Kay, Richard (2000), 'Constitutional Chronomony', *Ratio Juris* 13(1): 31–48.

Lake, David and Angela O'Mahoney (2004), 'The Incredible Shrinking State: Explaining the Territorial Size of Countries', *Journal of Conflict Resolution* 48: 699–722.

Levinson, Sanford (2006), *Our Undemocratic Constitution*, New York: Oxford University Press.

Martineau, Robert J. (1970), 'The Mandatory Referendum on Calling a State Constitutional Convention: Enforcing the People's Right to Reform their Government', *Ohio State Law Journal* 31: 421–55.

Negretto, Gabriel (2008), 'The Durability of Constitutions in Changing Environments: Explaining Constitutional Replacements in Latin America', Kellogg Institute, Working Paper No. 350.

Niskanen, William (1990), 'Conditions Affecting the Survival of Constitutional Rules', *Constitutional Political Economy* 1(2): 53–62.

Norton, Ann (1988), 'Transubstantiation. The Dialectic of Constitutional Authority', *University of Chicago Law Review* 55: 458–72.

Ordeshook, Peter C. (1992), 'Constitutional Stability', *Constitutional Political Economy* 3(2): 137–75.

Persson, Thorsten and Guido Tabellini (2003), *The Economic Effects of Constitutions*, Cambridge, MA and London: MIT Press.

Przeworski, Adam (1991), *Democracy and the Market*, Cambridge, UK: Cambridge University Press.

Raz, Joseph. (1998) 'On the Authority and Interpretation of Constitutions: Some Preliminaries', in *Constitutionalism: Philosophical Foundations*, edited by Larry Alexander, New York: Cambridge University Press, pp. 152–93.

Russell, Peter (1993), *Constitutional Odyssey: Can Canadians Become a Sovereign People?*, Toronto: University of Toronto Press.

Sabato, Larry (2007), *A More Perfect Constitution: Why the Constitution Must be Revised?*, New York: Walker and Company.

Schwartzburg, Melissa. (2007), *Democracy and Legal Change*, New York: Cambridge University Press.

Solomon, Peter (1996), *Soviet Criminal Justice under Stalin*, New York: Cambridge University Press.

Stepan, Albert and Cindy Skach (1993), 'Constitutional Frameworks and Democratic Consolidation: Parliamentarism versus Presidentialism', *World Politics* 46(1), 1–22.

Sutter, Daniel (2003), 'Durable Constitutional Rules and Rent Seeking', *Public Finance Review* 31(4): 413–28.

Van den Hauwe, Ludwig (2000), 'Public Choice, Constitutional Political Economy and Law and Economics', in Boudewijn Bouckaert and Gerrit De Geest (eds), *Encyclopedia of Law and Economics, Volume 1: The History and Methodology of Law and Economics*, Cheltenham, UK and Northampton, MA, USA: Edward Elgar, pp. 603–59.

Verney, Douglas V. (1957), *Parliamentary Reform in Sweden 1866–1921*, London: Oxford University Press.

Wagner, Richard E. (1987), 'Parchment, Guns, and the Maintenance of Constitutional Contract', in *Democracy and Public Choice: Essays in Honor of Gordon Tullock*, edited by Charles K. Rowley. New York: Basil Blackwell, pp. 105–21.

Weingast, Barry (1997), 'The Political Foundations of Democracy and the Rule of Law', *American Political Science Review* 91: 245–63.

Weingast, Barry (2006a), 'Designing Constitutional Stability', in *Democratic Constitutional Design and Public Policy*, edited by Roger Congleton and Birgitta Swedborg, Cambridge, MA: MIT Press.

Weingast, Barry (2006b), 'Self-enforcing Constitutions: With an Application to Democratic Stability in America's First Century', Stanford, CA: Hoover Institution, Working Paper.

Williams, Robert F. (2000), 'Is Constitutional Revision Success Worth its Popular Sovereignty Price?', *Florida Law Review* 52: 249–73.

PART II

CONSTITUTIONAL IDENTITY

8. The formation of constitutional identities
Gary J. Jacobsohn

1 THE CONCEPT OF CONSTITUTIONAL IDENTITY

Constitutional theorists have had relatively little to say about the identity of what they study. There are, however, attributes of a constitution that allow us to identify it as such, and there is a dialogical process of identity formation that enables us to determine the specific identity of any given constitution. Representing a mix of aspirations and commitments expressive of a nation's past, constitutional identity also evolves in ongoing political and interpretive activities occurring in courts, legislatures, and other public and private domains.

Understandably, some constitutional theorists have been skeptical that identity can be anything more than a tendentiously applied label used to advance a politically and constitutionally desirable result. Laurence Tribe's (1983: 440) view is doubtless reflective of a not uncommon attitude: '[T]he very identity of "the Constitution" – the body of textual and historical materials from which [fundamental constitutional] norms are to be extracted and by which their application is to be guided – is ... a matter that cannot be objectively deduced or passively discerned in a viewpoint-free way'. Much as a term like 'identity theft' may have relevance to credit cards and other aspects of our digitally filled lives, the concept's bearing on matters of constitutional salience is arguably obscure. Yet, if the philosopher Joseph Raz (1998: 152) is correct in maintaining that constitutional theories 'are [only] valid, if at all, against the background of the political and constitutional arrangements of one country or another', then pursuing the question of constitutional identity surely warrants serious consideration.

The texts of many constitutions point explicitly, if generally, to their identity. For example, the Guaranty Clause of the American Constitution (Article IV, Section 4) in effect says that a republican form of government must prevail throughout the federal system, that failure to secure such a form would strike at the very nature of what the constitutional polity is all about. Similarly, a number of constitutions – for example, Turkey's in its commitment to secularism; the French document, in its express prohibition of any change that would destroy the republican form of government – are protective of basic, regime-defining characteristics that provide general definitional content to constitutional identity. In theory, these textual barriers to certain kinds of constitutional change are designed to preserve a pre-existing identity by obstructing the removal of those attributes without which the object in question would become something very different. When those who frame a constitution act to prevent future actors from changing certain elements of their handiwork, they are in effect establishing an insurance policy in favor of a present identity against an imagined future identity that is deemed unacceptable. This is the underlying logic of constitutional entrenchment.

A constitution acquires an identity through experience; this identity exists neither as a discrete object of invention, nor as a heavily encrusted essence embedded in a society's culture, requiring only to be discovered. Rather, identity emerges *dialogically* and represents a mix of political aspirations and commitments that are expressive of a nation's past, as well as the determination of those within the society who seek in some ways to transcend that past.[1] It is changeable but resistant to its own destruction, and it may manifest itself differently in different settings. As Beau Breslin (2008: 30) notes, '[T]he question of *how* a regime alters its collective identity through the process of constitutional transformation depends on the specifics of a polity's particular historical narrative: no two transformations are exactly alike'. Such a sentiment is echoed in an early and important case from the new South African Supreme Court: 'Viewed in context, textually and historically the fundamental rights and freedoms have a poignancy and depth of meaning not echoed in any other national constitution I have seen ... [O]ur Constitution is unique in its origins, concepts and aspirations.'[2] In other words, the South African Constitution has an identity of its own reflective of its particular circumstances.

Important as the country-specific circumstances are, so too are the cross-national similarities discernible in the formative patterns of constitutional identities. The fundamental dynamics of identity are less the result of any specific set of background cultural or historical factors than the expression of a developmental process endemic to the phenomenon of constitutionalism. How is the South African constitutional identity to be known? By its beginning ('origins'), its middle ('concepts'), and its end ('aspirations'), 'viewed in context ... historically'. With important differences in political, cultural, and institutional arrangements, there will obviously be great comparative variation in the specific ways in which the process unfolds, but comparative inquiry would do well to pursue the question of constitutional identity in light of conceptual categories reflective of the constitutional condition more generally.

Perhaps the most important of these concepts is constitutional disharmony. A vital component of the disharmony of the constitutional condition consists of identifiable continuities of meaning within which dissonance and contradiction play out in the development of constitutional identity. The forging of constitutional identity is thus not a preordained process in which one comes to recognize in the distinctive features that mark a constitution as one thing rather than another the ineluctable extension of some core essence that at its root is unchangeable. The disharmonies of constitutional law and politics ensure that a nation's constitution – a term that incorporates more than the specific document itself – may come to mean quite different things, even as these alternative possibilities retain identifiable characteristics enabling us to perceive fundamental continuities persisting through any given regime transformation. In Hanna Pitkin's (1987: 167) instructive formulation, '[T]o understand what a constitution is, one must look not to some crystalline core or essence of unambiguous meaning but precisely *at* the ambiguities, the specific oppositions that this specific concept helps us to hold in tension'.

There are two dimensions along which disharmony fuels the development of constitutional identity: the first is internal to the document (assuming one exists) and includes alternative visions or aspirations that may embody different strands within a common historical tradition; the second entails a confrontational relationship between the constitution and the social order within which it operates. Most constitutions are fundamentally acquiescent in the sense that their framing is not likely to culminate in a document antagonistic to the very societal structures of stability that provide ballast for the constitutional enterprise. These constitutions, too – the American being a good example – may take on a militancy at some point in their history, as the tensions within the first dimension create a dynamic of change that proves ultimately transformative in the evolution of the nation's constitutional identity.

But even when a constitution is militant vis-à-vis the social order of which it is a part, the relative intractability of a nation's socio-cultural experience to legally inspired re-shaping means that the relationship between the way identity is inscribed constitutionally and the way of life of the people to whom it is intended to apply – its behavioral identity – will be one of negotiation rather than incorporation. The 'document called the Constitution', Michael Perry (1998: 99) reminds us, may not be identical with 'the norms that constitute the "supreme Law" '. Many constitutions, of course, do not seek behavioral transformation; what is set out in their provisions is intended to conform to the general configuration of the society. Here too, however, one needs to anticipate and consider the changes inevitably occurring in the mores and practices of a social order and their likely impact on the substance of constitutional identity.

2 IDENTITY AND DISHARMONY

2.1 A Constitutional Text as Point of Departure

As Andras Sajo (2005: 243) argues, 'The text itself has only limited potential for forging identity. A legally binding document is but a first step on the long and winding road from a political design for collective identity to a socially embedded institution that actually fosters such identity'. Some independent empirical demonstration that the text is in fact mainly consistent with constitutional experience will be required. This suggests the need to withhold judgments about identity until after confirming that the codified rules and principles of the document actually resonate in the practices and culture of the body politic. A constitution's language may indicate a commitment on the part of its authors and subsequent interpreters to establish a constitutional identity, but until confirmed in the accumulated practice of a constitutional community, the goal, however noble, will remain unfulfilled. Who would say, for example, that the constitutional identity of the former Soviet Union was discernible within the folds of its governing charter?

Of course, to establish the identity of a constitution, it obviously makes sense to scrutinize carefully the text itself. This provides us with a documentary transcript of how a particular group of framers provided for the governance of their polity, and it often includes their aspirations for its subsequent development. These aspirations may co-exist harmoniously within the four corners of the document, or their articulation may reveal, explicitly or implicitly, a certain dissonance that will need to be addressed through the constitutional politics that commences with the adoption of the document. Still, a perfectly harmonious constitution is an illusion, as will be evident once we agree that the object of our interest is only partly incorporated in any given written charter.

Again, Hanna Pitkin (1987: 169) is illuminating: '[H]ow we are able to constitute ourselves is profoundly tied to how we are already constituted by our own distinctive history'. We need not adopt the specific Burkean formulation of the prescriptive constitution, 'whose sole authority is, that it has existed time out of mind', to understand that submission to the authority of constitutional rule is bound up in the narrative of a people's prior experiences, that the constitution is 'less something we *have* than something we *are*' (Pitkin 1987: 167). But who we are is also entwined in the conflicts of the past, which do not dissipate with the inception of a new constitutional experiment, even one that culminates in a seemingly coherent document. There will be common historical reference points; for example in nations descended from imperial England, an extended resistance to a colonial empire that established a political ethos as the backdrop to, and perhaps the backbone of, the new constitutional transition. Invariably, however, these shared memories will be recalled from different places on the political spectrum – in India, by Muslims, Hindu nationalists, and reform-minded Hindus; in the United States, by abolitionists and slaveholders; in Israel, by Zionists of varied persuasions; in Ireland, by conservative ecclesiastically oriented Catholics and affiliates more imbued with the social gospel – and these too will become part of the broader constitutional tradition that will shape and drive the dynamics of constitutional identity. Only by distinguishing the constitutional text from the constitutional order will this process become clear to us.

Still, ' "who we are" is often – perhaps always – contestable and actively contested'.[3] The dilemma is particularly acute for the 'expressivist', who views constitutions as instruments through which 'a nation goes about defining itself'.[4] Mark Tushnet (2006) rightly points out that for the expressivist, preambles to constitutions are exceptionally informative in conveying the underlying meaning of the collective enterprise that is the constitution. For example, the first words of the Turkish Preamble read: 'In line with the concept of nationalism and the reforms and principles introduced by the founder of the Republic of Turkey, Atatürk ...'. By contrast, the corresponding opening in the Irish document invokes 'the Most Holy Trinity, from Whom is all authority and to Whom, as our final end, all actions both of men and States must be referred ...'.

To the extent that expressivism finds in these emphatic proclamations the essence of Turkish and Irish identity, it asks that language bear more weight than it should or can. It also invests the words with a declarative meaning, asserting that this is what these identities are – Turkey is defined according to the (extreme secular) principles of its founder and Ireland in accordance with the precepts of Christian theology. This in turn tends to yield a static view of constitutional identity, fixing its content in the codified affirmations of a specific time and place, whereas a more modest understanding of the constitution's expressive function is what is called for. To this end, a more fluid concept of identity may be required, in which constitutional assertions of self-definition are part of an ongoing process entailing adaptation and adjustment as circumstances dictate. It is not fluidity without boundaries, however, and textual commitments such as are embodied in preambles often set the topography upon which the mapping of constitutional identity occurs.

2.2   Bounded Fluidity

The future of constitutional identity is inscribed in its past. In a landmark Indian case that reaffirmed that country's jurisprudential commitment to the idea that constitutional amendments may be declared unconstitutional by the Supreme Court, one of its justices wrote: '*[T]he Constitution is a precious heritage*; therefore you cannot destroy its identity'.[5] For others, of course, the constitution need not be viewed in this way at all. To them it is the constitution's *deplorable* heritage that stands out, in which case its identity perhaps *should* be destroyed and reconstituted. Radical abolitionists in the United States, for example, could be said to have reached such a conclusion. Or, as is likely the case for most people, the constitution's heritage is, in the cold light of political and social transformation, a mixed blessing, leaving open the question of how and whether its identity might be changed.

As to the prescriptive component of identity, there is great diversity among constitutions regarding the degree of continuity that prevails over time. Formal constitutions display vary-ing measures of defiance and compliance towards the legacies bequeathed to the founding generation. While a defiant or confrontational constitution – for example, South Africa's – may proclaim its transformational document as a 'birth certificate of a nation', its emerging identity cannot fully escape the past, including some of those aspects that persist as searing memories in the recollections of its new citizens. Even when a nation experiences a great rupture in its constitutional development, 'Some core of shared belief, constitutive of alle-giance to the tradition, has to survive every rupture' (MacIntyre 1988: 356; see also Meierhenrich 2008). And so, along with the fresh commitment to a regime of universalist aspirations, the South African Constitution includes communitarian obligations that, while arguably designed with the best of intentions, carry with them the burdens of a complicated and troubled past.

Much of the mutability of constitutional identity is traceable to the disharmony within the constitution, but the strands that constitute the tension in this disharmony also set limits on the nature of the change engendered. Consider in this regard Eamon de Valera, the principal author of the Irish Constitution, who was at once the embodiment of a democratic vision for his country, but also, as Bill Kissane (2007: 211) notes, the 'symbol of the intensely conser-vative society he presided over for so long'. The democratic ethos of the 1922 Constitution was retained and expanded in the 1937 incarnation and conjoined with a religious commit-ment that, while absent in the text of the earlier document, had long been at the core of the nation's prescriptive constitution. Just as the 1922 Constitution had not entrenched a consti-tutional identity within its text, neither had the 1937 version; but it did establish the broad parameters within which that identity would evolve. Moreover, both the democratic and Catholic traditions were themselves fractured traditions, which, much like the analogous developments in India and elsewhere, provided additional impetus for the dialogical engage-ments that propelled Irish constitutional identity. As problematic as the idea of an immutable or static identity is, so too is the belief that the modifications of it are unconstrained by the traditions that carried it to its transformative moment.

2.3   The Dynamics of Dissonance

A dialogical engagement between the core commitment(s) in a constitution and its external environment is crucial to the formation and evolution of a constitutive identity. In this sense the identity of any constitution presumes that, as Robert C. Post (2003: 8) notes, '[C]onstitu-tional law and culture are locked in a dialectical relationship, so that constitutional law both arises from and in turn regulates culture'.

This relationship is an essential element in understanding the ways in which constitutional disharmony drives the process of identity development and clarification. 'Those who consti-tute themselves in writing', Anne Norton acutely observes, 'too often remain willfully uncon-scious of the unending dialectic of constitution. They prefer to see the writing of the Constitution as the perfect expression of an ideal identity' (1988: 467). In Turkey, for exam-ple, the core of the constitution reflected the secular republican vision of its founder, but the actual constitutional identity of the polity was not irrevocably fixed in the inscribed details of the document's provisions.

Thus, the protracted struggle in that country over the right of women to wear headscarves in institutions of higher learning vividly revealed the interactive dynamics of identity formation.

Since the time of Ataturk and his attack on the fez and other items of traditional Muslim attire, garments had become an important symbolic focus for the effort to re-constitute Turkish national identity. Constitutional amendments adopted in 2008 were a response to an earlier judgment by the Constitutional Court annulling headscarf-friendly legislation. Passed overwhelmingly, these amendments reflected the improved political environment for a relaxation of the more demanding of the regime's secular requirements, with polls showing overwhelming support for allowing university students to wear the headscarf. But for the defenders of the divergent Kemalist understanding, the two amendments clearly contradicted the very foundations of the secular state.

With a decisive 9-2 vote the Constitutional Court agreed, concluding that the amendments did indeed undermine secularism, 'the basic principle of the Republic', and therefore they were in express violation of the mandate of the Constitution. Subsequent events, however, beginning with the intense reaction to the Court's extraordinary action – featuring the claim that the judiciary had become an impediment to achieving a necessary convergence between constitutional law and the changing realities of Turkish society – established that this episode was a single development in an ongoing dialogical process in the evolution of the nation's constitutional identity. The rejoinder to the charge that the amendments represented a frontal assault on the Constitution's very identity was that identity must be viewed as an evolving phenomenon, the meaning and vitality of which could only be preserved if its content reflected significant shifts in societal mores and behavior.

The ruling by the Court did not end the legislative/judicial struggle over identity, as was made clear by the Court's later decision not to use its specific power under Articles 68 and 69 to ban the country's governing party from doing things like generating unconstitutional amendments allegedly challenging the secular foundations of the state. The episodic and untidy process of constitutional definition, with its thrusting and counter-thrusting in and out of courtrooms, has proceeded in tandem with the increasingly evident disharmony between rules and behavior, and with no obvious or definitive end in sight. That disharmony, whether manifest in the incongruities lodged within a constitution, or, as in the Turkey case, in the gap between inscribed commitments and external realities, is the main impulse behind the shaping of constitutional identity.

> The written text, which exists beyond the moment of its composition, speaks to the people and their posterity of their identity and aspirations. It claims to speak to them not as artifacts of the past, but as present Law. No text, however transcendent, is unmarked by its time. No text, however abstract, speaks to all circumstances. For all these reasons there will be disjunctions between what is said to be and what is, between a people and its Constitution. (Norton 1988: 169)

To the extent, then, that the commitment to secularism was constitutive of the Turkish regime, its specific content would vary over time, tethered to the text, but only loosely, so as to accommodate the dialogical interactions between codified foundational aspirations and the evolving mores of the Turkish people. '[C]onstitutional law will be as dynamic as the cultural values and beliefs that inevitably form part of the substance of constitutional law' (Post 2003: 10).

Of course, the balance of political forces at any given time is always a key variable in how this all plays out, with the judiciary, as Ran Hirschl (2004a: ch. 6) points out, often serving as the vehicle through which questions of 'foundational collective identity' are addressed. Whether in Turkey, where secular and non-secular (or at least less-secular) parties compete for recognition as the authentic voice of traditional values; in India, where a dominant, inclusive nationalist outlook has regularly been challenged by an alternative view with strong ethnic aspirations; in Israel, where a persistent and fragile political equilibrium is traceable to the dual commitments of the nation's founding; the course of constitutional identity is impelled by the discord of ordinary politics within limits established by commitments from the past.

For example, a satisfactory account of Israeli constitutional identity must address how the competing strands in the political tradition of that society contest against the backdrop of intersecting historical narratives involving two peoples and an international community very much implicated in the country's domestic tribulations. Upholding 'the values of Israel as a Jewish and democratic state', as is required under the Basic Laws, entails multiple dialogic interactions, with the Supreme Court serving as the main (but not exclusive) recipient 'of core collective identity questions' (Hirschl 2004b: 1858). What these values mean will reflect the particularities of the Israeli experience, but they also will incorporate universalist aspirations that, while addressing the needs of specific interests and elites within the society, will also become a part of the polity's evolving constitutional identity.

The disharmony internal to a constitutional text will ordinarily not be as prominent as it is in Israel. Indeed, in many polities it will be deftly obscured in the mists of compromise language authored by determined constitution-makers. But for the comparative constitutional theorist, Israel's evolving formal constitution only renders more transparent than elsewhere a process that is unusual in that nation mainly for the quality of its translucence. The same dynamic, however, is in place – if in less bold relief – wherever competing commitments or aspirations internal to a constitution engage each other while concurrently being deployed in a dialectical relationship with energized forces in the larger social order. This is, in fact, likely to be the case wherever we look, with the development of constitutional identity varying to the extent that internal and external disharmonies are weighted differently as we travel from country to country.

The uniqueness of the Israeli situation may mean that the various disharmonies that make up the constitutional reality of the state play out in exceptional ways, but polities constituted very differently will experience versions involving comparable developmental patterns. Whether it is Canadian judges seeking to clarify their Constitution's Section 1 standard of a 'free and democratic society' by engaging with what other societies have concluded in reference to these terms; or Irish judges (and legislators) pursuing strategies for navigating the turbulent waters of the secular/sectarian divide over the constitutionally sacrosanct protections for the family, all the while anticipating the inevitable encounters with European family and privacy law jurisprudence; the quest for a compelling unity will be the common preoccupation of all who are concerned with the problem of constitutional identity.

Either by design or by accident, the dissonance in a polity's formal constitution functions as a provocation to change. Much of what derives from the discord will have an interpretive aspect to it – '[i[nterpretation ... lives in dialectical tension' (Raz 1998: 180) – although we would be remiss if this led us to a narrow focus on the activity of courts. The judiciary is of course a principal actor in the shaping of constitutional identity, but it is rarely a unilateral actor. As Keith Whittington (2007: 291) explains, 'The constitutional choices made with the drafting and ratification of the text only partially covers the field. ... A great deal has to be worked out in subsequent practice, most familiarly through judicial interpretation of the Constitution but routinely and importantly through political action that construes, implements, and extends the constitutional text' (Whittington 2007: 291). Viewed from a comparative perspective, Abraham Lincoln's response to the American Supreme Court's decision in the *Dred Scott* case, in which he summoned non-robed political actors to rectify the errors of the Court by addressing the most constitutive of all issues facing the nation, seems less remarkable than it sometimes does in the United States. Although the political incentives for passing the buck on a regime's 'meta-narrative' from the more transparently political institutions to the courts has been well documented (Hirschl 2008), a pattern of interactive institutional involvement in such questions is nevertheless ubiquitous. The contesting strands in a nation's constitutional tradition will find their alternative visions embodied in competing power centers, leading to activity that may serve to clarify the uncertainties surrounding constitutional identity or expand its meaning in a particular direction.

The disharmonic invitation may also extend beyond the nation's borders. Consider again the Turkish example. At the time of the Turkish Republic's proclamation, there was great uncertainty regarding the retention of the Caliphate, which had been a fixture for centuries in the governance of the Islamic world. Ataturk wasted little time in abolishing it, but before doing so, 'The question of the Caliphate aroused interest far beyond the borders of Turkey, and brought anxious inquiries, especially from India, about the intentions of the republican regime' (Lewis 2002: 262). Similar anxieties are present in the contemporary scene, with Turkey's admission into the European Union dependent in large part upon its ability to persuade the existing members of that body of nations that its internal constitutional policies were compatible with the professed values of the European Community. The two sides in the headscarf controversy, for example, were acutely mindful of these distant sensibilities, and their interpretations of the basic principles of Secularism and Republicanism were developed to appeal to both foreign and domestic audiences. Indeed, from the American Declaration of Independence's gesture to 'a decent Respect to the Opinions of Mankind', to the Israeli Declaration's embrace of a set of principles that would gain 'them title to rank with the peoples who founded the United Nations', to the framers of the South African Constitution who provided explicit instructions for aligning their law with the standards of the international community, the process of shaping a constitutional identity has entailed dialogical engagement in several dimensions, including the transnational.

The external aspect occurs as a stage in the adjudicative process, in which one side of a divided constitutional legacy seeks to benefit from an expansion in the scope of conflict by having its cause adopted by an extra-territorial body with authority to intervene in a domestic dispute, as famously happened in Ireland with regard to the abortion issue. For the larger question of identity, this should not, however, be viewed as a simple transference of decision-making to an external source of authority, so much as it is a step in a multi-pronged constitutional give-and-take stimulated by the imperfections naturally revealed in disharmony. '[T]hese imperfections' are at once 'the source of our troubles [and] … the source of our greatness' (Norton 2008: 469). They may exist as contradictions embodied in a constitutional text or as the inevitable disjunction between the actual and the ideal provided for in a constitutional document. Constitutional borrowing, the judicial practice of seeking guidance from foreign sources, offers appealing prospects for overcoming imperfection, but there is, at least in the United States, fierce opposition to the activity. Often expressed as a warning about the loss of identity, this fear is not entirely misplaced, although it is not so much a loss of identity that is at stake as much as it is the direction in which constitutional identity might evolve through engagement with foreign law. Like all invitations, however, this one can be declined, and we should be as interested in the non-acceptances as we are with the acceptances. In both cases, they will illuminate the jurisprudence of the local court, and through it, the constitutional identity of the larger constitutional order.

2.4   The Balance of Internal and External Disharmonies

Much of the aspirational content of a nation's specific constitutional identity consists of goals and principles that are shared by other nations and that are indeed part of a common stock of aspirations we have come to associate more generally with the enterprise of constitutionalism. These aspirations may be described collectively as 'the inner morality of law' (Fuller 1964) or the requirements of 'generic constitutionalism' (Kahn 2003: 2702) or the 'universal norms' (Katz 1999) implicit in a nation's discourse of justice. Such norms need to be reconciled with the particularistic commitments of local traditions and practices; the contours of constitutional identity will to a large extent reflect how these disharmonies get resolved. As Heinz Klug (2002: 3) notes in his study of South African constitutional framing, '[T]he challenge is to understand the specifics of [a globalizing constitutionalism's] incorporation into particular national legal systems as well as to understand the potentially multiple roles that constitutionalism is playing in the reconstruction of different polities'.

   The South African case's 'interaction of local participation, context and history with international influences and conditionalities' (Klug 2002: 3) provides a textbook example of dialogic constitution making. The reasons for the international engagement can be characterized in various ways, including of course explanations that emphasize the economic advantages to elites within South Africa inhering in the reintegration of the state into the world community. Nothing in this explanation is inconsistent with alternative accounts that stress the gain in legitimacy to be anticipated from the clear break from the past that would be symbolized in an auspicious debut on the world stage. But as the deliberative process that culminated in a new constitution made abundantly clear, separating from the past is not so easily accomplished, whatever the benefits associated with it. Incorporating international standards – for example, equal treatment of individuals under law – within the set of newly mandated constitutional aspirations would still require reconciliation with a quite different aspirational legacy that was as intractable as the historical narrative from whence it derived.

   A very different angle on the challenge to constitutional design posed by the tension between universalistic and particularistic demands appears in the effort to adopt a constitution for Europe. The issue here is also focused on the question of identity, not so much how extra-national precepts and principles are to be integrated into the jurisprudence of nations possessing unique histories and ways of doing things, but how – or whether – the distinctive political and legal cultures of a diverse group of nations can be incorporated within an overarching framework of international governance such as to create a constitutional identity for the new entity as a whole. So far the effort has been more encouraging for constitutional theorists than for politicians.[6]

   By way of contrast, consider India, where the formation of constitutional identity has advanced quite far in the constitutional jurisprudence of that country. The Indian Supreme Court has been unusually self-conscious in its use of the concept of constitutional identity. The Court has done so mainly through elaboration of the controversial doctrine of 'Basic Structure', in which it has designated a number of constitutional features to be of such importance that it would be prepared to challenge any action, including an amendment to the

Constitution, perceived as a threat to their existence. Moreover, in the spirit of the multilateralism that serious engagement with the problem would seem to require, it has upheld extraordinary actions by other institutions that were arguably motivated by a proper regard for constitutional identity.

Understandably, much of the debate in India over judicial enforcement of the basic structure doctrine has concerned its application to the issue of secularism. The Indian Constitution was adopted against a backdrop of sectarian violence that was only the latest chapter in a complex centuries-old story of Hindu–Muslim relations on the Asian sub-continent. Much of that history had been marked by peaceful co-existence; nevertheless the bloodbath that accompanied Partition reflected ancient contestations and insured that the goal of communal harmony would be a priority in the constitution-making process. But it was not the only priority. If not as urgent, then certainly as important, was the goal of social reconstruction, which could not be addressed without constitutional recognition of the state's interest in the 'essentials of religion' (Jacobsohn 2003). So deep was religion's penetration into the fabric of Indian life, and so historically entwined was it in the configuration of a social structure that was by any reasonable standard grossly unjust, that the framers' hopes for a democratic polity meant that state intervention in the spiritual domain could not be constitutionally foreclosed. The design for secularism in India required a creative balance between socio-economic reform that could limit religious options and political toleration of diverse religious practices and communal development. Taken together, the ameliorative and communal provisions evince a constitutional purpose to address the social conditions of people long burdened by the inequities of religiously inspired hierarchies.

Over the years this constitutional equilibrium has come under repeated assault from different locations on the political spectrum, with the greatest challenge issuing from the Hindu right. The Supreme Court's main response has been to declare secularism a 'part of the basic structure of the Constitution and also the soul of the Constitution'.[7] Describing the commitment to secularism in this dramatic way added a notable rhetorical flourish to a landmark decision in Indian jurisprudence, but it also suggested that the same concern with constitutional identity that lay behind the Court's earlier rulings on unconstitutional amendments generated the outcome in the secularism case. To be sure, there is no reason to think that a judicial reference to the 'soul of the Constitution' was used with any awareness of debates in the 17th and 18th centuries (or indeed as far back as Plato) over the significance and place of the soul in determining personal identity, but there is every reason to suppose that its usage was intended to mark secularism as critical to Indian constitutional identity.

Indian secularism, however, poses an interesting challenge for a theory of identity. We might call it the 'presumption in favor of settled practice' problem. We want to retain the idea of prescription without having to embrace a correspondence logic that requires us to extend the legitimacy of the constitution to the society of which it is a part. But when reviewing the debates about religion and politics at the Constituent Assembly and the various judicial pronouncements on the subject over the years, one sees very clearly that a principal purpose behind the Indian commitment to secularism was to challenge an entrenched way of life and to modify it in the direction of a democratic way of life rooted in equality. In a very real sense the constitutional 'soul' was intended to be ornery, projecting an identity that was at once confrontational and emblematic of the document's abiding commitments. The concept of identity is often associated with the idea of continuity rather than transformation. How then are we to explain the expansive ambitions of the soulful concept at the core of Indian constitutional design?

There are two points to be made in response. First, constitutional identity can accommodate an aspirational aspect that is at odds with the prevailing condition of the society within which it functions. The prescriptive constitution might suggest that what is must be (identity as pure discovery), but a strictly positivistic inference need not be drawn from the principle of inheritance. In the case of India's constitutional framers, the prevailing social structure, while deeply rooted in centuries of religious and cultural practice, was contestable in accordance with sources from within the Indian tradition that are also a part of the prescriptive constitution. As H. Patrick Glenn (2000: 17) observes, 'Opposition to a tradition may be ... conducted within the tradition itself, using both its language and its resources (the struggle from within)'.

History revealed disharmony within established traditions and between the dominant strand and the society. 'One of the remarkable developments of the present age', wrote Nehru (1997: 515) shortly before independence, 'has been the rediscovery of the past and of the nation'. Nehru was one of several delegates at the Constituent Assembly to invoke the name of Ashoka, the third king of the Mauryan dynasty in the third century BC, and a legendary figure whose famous edicts have endured as a source of moral and ethical reflection for more than a millennium. Used both as an emulative model for behavior towards society's destitute and as a basis for criticizing the Hindu nationalist rejection of Indian nationhood as rooted in a composite culture, the Ashokan example shows how continuity in the construction of a constitutional identity can draw upon alternative (and even dissenting) sources within one tradition, and then re-constitute them to serve at times as a reproach to other strands (and their societal manifestations) within the same tradition.

A defense of secularism as a central feature of the Indian Constitution's basic structure inevitably finds people differing in the meanings they assign to this consensus fundamental commitment. For example, the Hindu right has often assured Indians that it accepts the constitutional centrality of secularism, which it embraces as a version of the strict separationist model endorsed by many in the United States, and which it contrasts with the 'pseudo-secularism' championed by its political opponents. The latter include the justices on the Supreme Court, most of whom have incorporated the differing perspectives of Gandhi, Nehru, Ambedkar and others to articulate a uniquely Indian understanding that has been aptly described by Rajeev Bhargava as 'contextual secularism'. At the core of this position is the strategy of 'principled distance', which, according to Bhargava (1998: 515) means that '[T]he State intervenes or refrains from interfering, depending on which of the two better promotes religious liberty and equality of citizenship'. Thus, the specific forms that secular states take should reflect the particular constitutive features of their respective polities. In India this means (as is so enshrined in the Constitution) that for certain purposes – for example, establishing separate sectarian electorates – the state cannot recognize religion, but for others – for example, establishing a limited regime of personal laws – it may do so. The state need not relate to all religions in the same way; the bottom line, however, is that public policy regarding intervention, non-interference, or equidistance be guided by the same non-sectarian principle of equal dignity for all.

The process by which this concept of secularism emerged as a mark of constitutional identity, then to be extended protected status under the Court's basic structure jurisprudence, is roughly analogous to the dialogical formation of personal identity. Much as a self evolves interactively within the specific contours of its environment, India's constitutional identity, as refracted through the determinative lens of secularism, is the product of historically conditioned circumstances in which choices are limited by the dual realities of complex communalism and religiously inspired societal inequality. The nation as an 'idea of continuity', in which, as Burke said, a constitution discloses itself 'only in a long space of time', can go far to explain how the main outlines of a secular identity are discoverable as a contingent part of the political and moral order. But within these broad outlines is considerable space for inventive statesmanship, as is illustrated not only in the work of the Constituent Assembly, but also in the earlier efforts of the Indian National Congress culminating in such documents as the Nehru Constitutional Draft of 1928 and the Karachi Resolution of 1931.[8]

Secularism's designation as a basic structure makes it, in the words of a former Indian Chief Justice, 'immutable in relation to the power of Parliament to change the Constitution'.[9] The constitutional theorist, Jed Rubenfeld (2005: 9), has described '[r]adical interpretation … [as] a new interpretation of the basic principles or purposes behind a constitutional provision'. In relation to Indian constitutional secularism, a radical move is one that seeks to replace the commitment underlying this basic structure with something fundamentally different. The Chief Justice's comment in 2000 was made in response to an initiative of the BJP-led government to establish a National Commission to review the Constitution and to make recommendations for change within the constraints of basic structure. For those who suspected the intentions of the Hindu nationalists in power, the concern was not that the Commission would consign secularism to oblivion, but that the commitment would in effect become a victim of identity theft. If, for example, it were denuded of its ameliorative content, or rendered incompatible with public policies protective of religious minorities, then there would be reason to worry about a fundamental transformation in the concept's essential meaning. Were secularism to be redefined to implement the principle of non-cognizance of religion (in other words, strict separation), this development would mark a substantial change in constitutional identity.

3 CONCLUSION

If constitutions are distinguishable according to the degree to which their internal disharmonies are deeply inscribed, so too are they diversely situated commensurate with their relationship to the surrounding social order. For example, the constitutional texts in polities such as India, South Africa, and Turkey display an aggressive stance toward entrenched societal structures, whose existence became suspect under the provisions and ethos of the document adopted in those polities. To be sure, in each of these places status quo interests were not left bereft of constitutionally sanctioned recourse to defend their interests, but the balance between internal and external disharmonies was weighted more heavily towards the latter, such that the earliest constitutional identity in the three countries possessed a fairly unambiguous confrontational character. As the course of constitutional politics unfolded, the dissonance within the document (a reflection of divisions within the society) served to mitigate or restrain the movement toward an unalloyed realization of the identity embodied in the dominant official ethos of constitutional militancy.

Finally, consider the American Constitution. On its face, the 1787 document can scarcely be called confrontational with respect to the institution of slavery; indeed, there is language that is clearly complacent towards its existence. But even that language – requiring, for example, the end of the slave trade in 20 years – indicates a level of internal disharmony that is at least consistent with the many contentious debates surrounding that issue during the framing of the Constitution. Once, however, the constitutional order is widened to include a philosophical tradition that incorporates the nation's founding document, American constitutional identity assumes an aspirational dimension incompatible with the holding of human beings as property. This was the view held by Abraham Lincoln and eventually Frederick Douglass, both of whom in effect emphasized the profound discordance between constitution and social order.

One need not adopt their aspirational perspective – and many progressives in their time as well as prominent scholars in ours have not – to recognize the dynamic through which an anti-discrimination principle became a fundamental component of American constitutional identity. In contrast with India and Turkey, over the years the American document (if not always its interpretation) took on a more aggressive stance towards entrenched interests, at least those implicated in the most egregious of the society's inequalities. The Civil War and the amendments that followed in its wake either radically reconstituted the American polity or enabled it in time to make due on its inaugural promise. Yet the dialogical interaction of internal and external constitutional disharmonies is discernible regardless of one's interpretive preference. Thus, codification by the post-war amendments of the principle of equal treatment was a signal moment in the development of American constitutional identity, marking the official ascendance of the universalist strand in the nation's conflicted constitutional tradition. But the system's highly fragmented distribution of political power guaranteed that the other more particularistic strand in that tradition would not lack for institutional muscle as its advocates fought to undermine the constitutive significance of the changes wrought through the amendment process. The constitutional identity of the text may have changed, but the constitutional identity of the American people (citizens and public officials) was only beginning its transformation. Ultimately, stability in the identity of the constitutional order depended on convergence of the two.

The uniqueness of the American and Indian stories should not obscure the fact that the dynamic through which a constitutional identity emerged through the challenges of political and legal contestation is remarkably similar to what has and is occurring in polities very different from the United States and India. A high priority for comparative constitutional scholarship in the years ahead is to examine the validity and limitations of this claim in a multitude of constitutional settings.

NOTES

1. I use the word 'commitments' in the sense employed by Jed Rubenfeld (2005: 112), who distinguishes it from 'intentions', the latter term lacking the temporally extended dimension that creates constitutional obligations.
2. *DuPlessis v DeKlerk*, 1996 (3) SA 850.
3. Or as Sanford Levinson (1988: 124) observes, '[T]he Constitution can be said to be a model instance of what the philosopher W.B. Gallie has labeled an "essentially contested concept"'.
4. Ibid. 79.
5. *Minerva Mills, Ltd. v Union of India*, AIR 1980 SC 1789, 1798; emphasis added.
6. See, for example, the entries in the special issue on the proposed European Constitution published in the *International Journal of Constitutional Law* in May 2005.
7. *S.R. Bommai v Union of India*, at 143. This is the leading Indian case on secularism. In it the Court upheld the authority of the Central Government to dismiss the elected governments in three states because of the alleged failures of their administrations in implementing and respecting the constitutional commitment to secularism. By upholding the deployment of emergency powers under Article 356, the Court agreed that these governments had not acted 'in accordance with the provisions of the Constitution'. Article 356 had been modeled after the

American Guaranty Clause (Article IV, Section 4), but the willingness of the Indian Court to confront the question of identity contrasts sharply with the American Supreme Court's reluctance to engage it.

8. These documents addressed in particular the rights of minorities to their own culture and religion. But the prescriptive constitution is not inscribed only in official documents. A constitutional identity expresses as well important – and continuous – developments in the private sphere that are integral to the dialogical process of identity formation. In India this includes the very long tradition of reform movements within the various Hindu communities that helped shape the Constitution's commitment to socio-economic reconstruction. See in this regard Heimsath (1964).

9. M.N. Venkatachaliah, 'There are Some Things of Eternal Verity', Interview in *Frontline*, 17, February 19, 2000.

REFERENCES

Bhargava, Rajeev (1998), 'What is Secularism for?', in Rajeev Bhargava, ed., *Secularism and its Critics*, Oxford: Oxford University Press.

Breslin, Beau (2008), *From Words to Worlds: Exploring Constitutional Functionality*, Baltimore: Johns Hopkins University Press.

Fuller, Lon (1964), *The Morality of Law*, New Haven: Yale University Press.

Glenn, H. Patrick (2000), *Legal Traditions of the World*, Oxford: Oxford University Press.

Heimsath, Charles H. (1964), *Indian Nationalism and Hindu Social Reform*, Princeton: Princeton University Press.

Hirschl, Ran (2004a), *Toward Juristocracy*, Cambridge, MA: Harvard Univerrsity Press.

Hirschl, Ran (2004b), 'Constitutional Courts vs. Religious Fundamentalism: Three Middle Eastern Tales', *Texas Law Review* 82: 1819–60.

Hirschl, Ran (2008), 'The Judicialization of Mega-politics and the Rise of Political Courts', *Annual Review of Political Science* 11: 93–118.

Jacobsohn, Gary Jeffrey (2003), The Wheel of Law: India's Secularism in Comparative Constitutional Context, Princeton: Princeton University Press.

Kahn, Paul W. (2003), 'Comparative Constitutionalism in a New Key', *Yale Law Journal* 101(8): 2677–705.

Katz, Stanley (1999), 'Constitutionalism in East Central Europe: Some Negative Lessons from the American Experience', in Vicki C. Jackson and Mark Tushnet, eds., *Comparative Constitutional Law*, New York: Foundation Press.

Kissane, Bill (2007), 'Eamon de Valera and the Survival of Democracy in Inter-war Ireland', *Journal of Contemporary History* 42(2): 213–26.

Klug, Heinz (2002), *Constituting Democracy*, New York: Cambridge University Press.

Levinson, Sanford (1988), *Constitutional Faith*, Princeton: Princeton University Press.

Lewis, Bernard (2002), *The Emergence of Modern Turkey*, Oxford: Oxford University Press, 2002.

MacIntyre, Alasdair (1988) *Whose Justice? Which Rationality?*, South Bend: University of Notre Dame Press.

Meierhenrich, Jens (2008), *The Legacies of Law: Long-run Consequences of Legal Development in South Africa, 1652–2000*, Cambridge: Cambridge University Press.

Nehru, Jawaharlal (1997), *The Discovery of India*, Oxford: Oxford University Press.

Norton, Anne (1988), 'Transubstantiation: The Dialectic of Constitutional Authority', *University of Chicago Law Review* 55: 467–72.

Perry, Michael J. (1998), 'What is "The Constitution"? (and Other Fundamental Questions)', in Larry Alexander, ed., *Constitutionalism: Philosophical Foundations*, Cambridge: Cambridge University Press, 99–150.

Pitkin, Hanna Fenichel (1987), 'The Idea of a Constitution', *Journal of Legal Education* 37: 167–71.

Post, Robert C. (2003), 'The Supreme Court, 2002 Term – Forward: Fashioning the Legal Constitution: Culture, Courts, and Law', *Harvard Law Review* 117: 4–112.

Raz, Joseph (1998), 'On the Authority and Interpretation of Constitutions: Some Preliminaries', in Larry Alexander, ed., *Constitutionalism: Philosophical Foundations*, Cambridge: Cambridge University Press.

Rubenfeld, Jed (2005), *Revolution by Judiciary: The Structure of American Constitutional Law*, Cambridge, MA: Harvard University Press.

Sajo, Andras (2005) 'Constitution without the Constitutional Moment: A View from the New Member States', *International Journal of Constitutional Law*, 2: 243–61.

Tribe, Laurence (1983), 'A Constitution We are Amending: In Defense of a Restrained Judicial Role', *Harvard Law Review* 97: 433–45.

Tushnet, Mark (2006), 'Some Reflections on Method in Comparative Constitutional Law', in Sujit Choudhry, ed., *The Migration of Constitutional Ideas*, New York: Oxford University Press.

Whittington, Keith E. (2007), *Political Foundations of Judicial Supremacy: The Presidency, the Supreme Court, and Constitutional Leadership in U.S. History*, Princeton: Princeton University Press.

9. Citizenship and the boundaries of the constitution
Kim Rubenstein and Niamh Lenagh-Maguire

1   INTRODUCTION

Citizenship is a prime site for comparisons between different constitutional systems, for the idea of citizenship, and the ideals it is taken to represent, go to the heart of how states are constituted and defined. Who is governed by the constitution? What are the boundaries of the constitution? The definition of the class of 'citizens' of a state and the identification of their rights, privileges and responsibilities is one way to answer these questions, and is a core function of national constitutions and a central concern of public law. In this chapter, we consider several written constitutions and attempt to convey some of the diversity in constitutional approaches to this fundamental and universal project for nation states.

It is tempting to suggest a thematic approach in this chapter by providing labels to the different constitutional models we discuss that are not country-specific. These could be 'constitutional', 'quasi-constitutional' and 'statutory models' of citizenship but, as the case studies we examine illustrate, complexities arise in asserting such categories. Instead, the goals of the chapter are fairly modest: the aim is to present, briefly, a selection of constitutional approaches and to examine how those different systems have dealt with similar issues. We then make some preliminary suggestions about what these examples reveal about constitutional citizenship, and about the process of comparing constitutions.

Given this chapter is not a comprehensive survey, we have chosen a small number of countries that meet two criteria. The comparator nations, Australia, Canada, the United States of America and Israel all have written constitutions (in some form) and they each have a history of extensive managed migration, which has made citizenship an evolving and contested concept.[1] Drastic changes in the composition of national communities has led to prolonged re-examination of what it means to be a 'citizen' in a diverse, multicultural society, both in terms of the liberal democratic challenges described influentially by Will Kymlicka,[2] and in the narrower sense of citizenship as a legal status that needs to adapt to the changing needs of those who hold it.[3] They are also nations sharing a British legal ancestry, yet have each diverged markedly, and in different ways, from that common heritage. Three of these comparator nations are federations, adding a further level of complexity to constitutional citizenship, since citizenship in federal nations can also denote multiple levels of legal and political membership.[4] There may be lessons in these multivalenced forms of citizenship for constitutional ideas of membership more broadly; as Vicki Jackson has suggested, federalism may provide 'structures for contesting visions of citizenship over time, as well as for a positive model of the possibility of multiple but compatible citizenships'.[5]

2   CITIZENSHIP AND THE TEXT OF NATIONAL CONSTITUTIONS

We begin by examining the place of citizenship in the text of national constitutions, and other key structural aspects of constitutions that bear on what it means, in constitutional terms, to be a citizen. While the text of the constitution is a convenient place to begin, in all of the juris-dictions considered there is considerably more to the constitutional concept of citizenship than is evident from the text alone. This is one reason why 'constitutional citizenship' is not necessarily a neat descriptor in itself.

Australia is a suitable place to begin because it is the constitutional context with which we are most familiar. Familiarity and acculturation within a particular constitutional system affect the way in which 'comparativists' approach other systems, so presenting the Australian Constitution first is one way of making our perspective more visible.

2.1   Australia

The Australian Constitution does not refer to the status of 'citizen' in relation to native-born or naturalized people of the Commonwealth. The 'people' are referred to in several places. Elsewhere the people who are entitled to vote are described as 'electors'. In harmony with the notions of the time, the Constitution refers to the national status of Australians as that of 'a subject of the Queen'.[6]

The Australian Constitution does not define Australian 'citizenship', nor does it classify the people to whom it applies in terms of their status as Australian citizens.[7] Rather, the Constitution refers to a number of other status-based categories – 'subjects of the Queen' (reflecting Australia's position in the British Empire);[8] 'residents of a state' (reflecting the federal structure of the Commonwealth of Australia)[9] and 'aliens'.[10] Significantly, the word 'citizen' appears only once in the Australian Constitution, in a provision dealing with the disqualification of a 'citizen of a foreign power' from being elected to the Federal Parliament.[11] (This rule is discussed in more detail below.) However, the Constitution clearly contemplates there will be distinctions between people in Australia based on their status as 'aliens' and 'non-aliens'.[12] The Federal Parliament is given the power to make laws with respect to 'naturalisation and aliens' (the aliens power), which it has relied upon to legislate first for the naturalization of British subjects in Australia and, since 1948, for a statutory form of Australian citizenship,[13] as well as enacting laws dealing with the terms on which 'non-citizens' may enter and remain in Australia and the removal of 'unlawful non-citizens'.[14]

Despite the apparent silence of the Australian Constitution on the topic, Australian citizenship has a constitutional dimension. The High Court appears to have accepted, without deciding expressly, that the Parliament's power to make laws with respect to naturalization and aliens is broad enough to support the creation of a statutory form of Australian citizenship.[15] The Court has also stressed that the legal status of Australian citizenship is purely statutory. However, as Justice Gaudron observed in *Chu Kheng Lim v Minister for Immigration, Local Government and Ethnic Affairs*, the statutory concept of citizenship is both constitutionally unnecessary and constitutionally useful:

> Citizenship, so far as this country is concerned, is a concept which is entirely statutory, originating as recently as 1948. It is a concept which is and can be pressed into service for a number of consti-tutional purposes. But it is not a concept which is constitutionally necessary, which is immutable or which has some immutable core element ensuring its lasting relevance for constitutional purposes.[16]

This reference to the 'pressing into service' of citizenship for constitutional purposes is apt. Both statutory citizenship and concepts of constitutional nationality or 'membership' have been central to the High Court's development of constitutional doctrine, particularly with respect to the limits of the Parliament's power to treat particular classes of person as 'aliens',[17] the Executive's power to do the same,[18] and the constitutional rights implications of a person's status as a 'citizen' or member of the Australian community.[19] Therefore, there is a constitutional citizenship in Australia even though the word citizen does not appear, and so to this extent it is 'quasi constitutional', yet in other ways it reflects a 'statutory model' as most of the practical consequences of citizenship are legislative.

2.2 Canada

Canada too reflects a mix of a 'quasi constitutional' and 'statutory model' of citizenship. Canada's Constitution, like Australia's, does not define Canadian citizenship. The boundaries of citizenship are left largely to the legislature to define – the Canadian Federal Parliament is given power to make laws with respect to 'naturalization and aliens', and in the mid-20th century legislated in reliance on that power to create a purely statutory form of Canadian citizenship.[20]

Unlike the United States, whose Constitution reflects its revolutionary origins and the clear separation of the new federation from its colonial past, Canada's path to constitutional independence was a much longer, more incremental one.[21] The political and legal imperatives that made it desirable to include a definition of citizenship in the United States Constitution (see discussion below) do not have clear equivalents in the Canadian constitutional experience. Like some of the discussion at the Australian Federation Conventions, the Canadian Confederation debates reveal the clear wish of the prospective members of the Confederation to retain their allegiance to the British Crown. As the Hon. Sir Etienne-Pascal Tache is recorded as having told the Confederation Debates, Confederation was imperative if Canadians 'desired to remain British and monarchical, and … desired to pass to our children these advantages'.[22]

While the Canadian Constitution does not create a constitutional form of citizenship, it has played an important role in shaping the substantive legal content of Canadian citizenship, and the British-subject status that preceded the creation of a statutory form of citizenship. Within fifty years of the enactment of the British North America Act, cases concerning the rights of persons of Chinese descent who had been naturalized as British subjects in Canada were heard. In a case concerning a British Columbia statute that prevented people of Chinese descent being employed in mines, the Privy Council held that it was exclusively within the power of the Federal Parliament to make laws with respect to 'naturalization and aliens', and that power should be interpreted broadly to include the power to make laws about 'the rights and privileges pertaining to residents in Canada after they have been naturalized'.[23]

More recently, the adoption of the Canadian Charter of Rights and Freedoms has given additional meaning and depth to the statutory concept of citizenship in Canada. First, the Charter guarantees that 'citizens' enjoy certain rights. (We consider the relationship between citizenship and the Charter in more detail below.) Secondly, and less certainly, there may be a constitutional concept of citizenship based in the Canadian Charter. The Federal Court of Appeal ruled in 2000 that although the Canadian Charter refers to 'citizens', that concept has no meaning apart from that created by statute.[24] Taken at face value, this decision suggests that the Charter protects the rights of a class of people defined by statute and is capable of legislative redefinition. On that reasoning, the legislature is given the power to determine the extent of the constitutional protection of individual rights, by widening or narrowing the definition of the class of 'citizens'. There is a risk that if the legislature could redefine those who are the beneficiaries of Charter rights, one would think that, analogously, it could also redefine 'Government' and thereby immunize itself from Charter obligations.[25]

Galloway and others have argued that such an interpretation is untenable, and that 'citizen' in the context of the Charter must have some constitutional meaning independent of the statutory framework established by the legislature.[26] Indeed there may be similarities here with the High Court of Australia's elucidation of a constitutional concept of 'membership' of the Australian community that is distinct from, but may control, the statutory status of citizenship.[27]

2.3   United States of America

Citizenship in the United States is given an explicit constitutional dimension by the Fourteenth Amendment to the US Constitution, and is the only country which has a 'constitutional citizenship' as it provides, at § 1:

> All persons born or naturalized in the United States, and subject to the jurisdiction thereof, are citizens of the United States and of the State wherein they reside. No State shall make or enforce any law which shall abridge the privileges or immunities of citizens of the United States.

Prior to the insertion of the Fourteenth Amendment, as Lawrence Tribe has noted, the US Constitution maintained a 'tactful silence' on the topic of citizenship.[28] That silence became untenable following the US Supreme Court's holding in *Dred Scott v Sandford* that former slaves, and their descendants, were not citizens of a state or of the United States.[29] The Fourteenth Amendment was intended to implement civil rights reform by preventing it from being overturned by the Supreme Court or Congress, and to render unconstitutional other attempts to deprive African Americans of the rights that they enjoyed by virtue of their citizenship[30] and is understood principally as a constitutional response to the Supreme Court's decision in *Dred Scott v Sandford*. Justice Taney, delivering the opinion of the Court, held that, as a result:

> no State can, by any act or law of its own, passed since the adoption of the Constitution, introduce a new member into the political community created by the Constitution of the United States.[31]

We examine the reasons for including a constitutional definition of citizenship in the United States Constitution, and their impact on the constitutional meaning of citizenship, in our discussion of different models of citizenship definition, further below.

The Court has accordingly explored the meaning of the amendment by reference to the legal principles that applied prior to its commencement. On this basis, a person born in the United States is clearly a citizen by virtue of Article 1, notwithstanding the citizenship of their parents or their parents' eligibility to be naturalized.[32] However, the phrase 'subject to the jurisdiction thereof' has been held to limit the constitutional conferral of citizenship to people capable of coming within United States jurisdiction, and to thereby exclude the children of diplomats and of enemy aliens in hostile occupation,[33] as well as members of Indian tribes who remained subject to tribal law.[34]

Reading the Fourteenth Amendment in the context of the fairly limited goals of its drafters has had significant consequences for the scope of the protection afforded to the 'privileges or immunities' of US citizenship. In a group of consolidated test cases (the *Slaughterhouse Cases*[35]), the Supreme Court held, by majority, that while nothing in the Fourteenth Amendment displaced the distinction between federal and state citizenship,[36] the Amendment had clearly been intended to invert the rule in *Dred Scott*.[37]

It is quite clear that there is a citizenship of the United States, and a citizenship of a state, which are distinct from each other, and which depend upon different characteristics or circumstances in the individual.[38]

Citizenship of a state became dependent on federal citizenship. As a result of the Fourteenth Amendment, citizenship of the United States became, at least formally, 'paramount and dominant instead of being subordinate and derivative'.[39] However, because Article 1 of the Fourteenth Amendment refers to 'the privileges or immunities of citizens of the United States', a majority held that the protection offered by the clause was limited to privileges or immunities 'which owe their existence to the Federal Government, its National character, its Constitution, or its laws' and not to the privileges and immunities of state citizens.[40] The privileges or immunities of federal citizenship are limited,[41] in contrast to the robust interpretation afforded the due process clause of the Fourteenth Amendment (which does not depend on the status of citizenship). While the US Constitution is the strongest example of a 'constitutional citizenship' in the sense of referring specifically to it in the text of the constitution, it is in fact the due process clause that does most of the work in this area. (We develop our discussion of US citizenship and rights below.)

2.4   Israel

Israel has not adopted a unitary, freestanding constitutional document. However, over the course of Israeli statehood a collection of instruments have come to be accorded constitutional status and can be categorized as 'quasi constitutional'. In 1948, the Knesset decided that rather than drafting a constitution for the new state of Israel immediately, it would task the parliament's Constitution, Law and Justice Committee with preparing a constitution piece by piece (the Harari decision). The Knesset began to enact Basic Laws with respect to the organization of national government and, latterly, personal rights. While the Basic Laws are, in effect, applied by courts as though they were parts of a national constitution,[42] there remains no formal basis on which those laws take precedence over other legislation passed by the Knesset,[43] nor have the Basic Laws yet been consolidated into one complete document. Accordingly, we examine the role of citizenship as a political ideal in Israel, and the relationship between citizenship laws and the Basic Laws, rather than examining constitutional rules that directly control Israeli citizenship.

Given that citizenship is one of the constitutive ideas in any nation state, issues of nationality and citizenship take on a particular significance and complexity in Israel, given the unique cultural, historical and religious context in which the state was formed. Israel was founded as a place to which members of the Jewish Diaspora would be welcome to return. It was always contemplated that 'the renewal of the Jewish State in the Land of Israel ... would open wide the gates of the homeland to every Jew',[44] that people who identified as Jewish would want to become members of the Israeli community and that identity would give them the right to enter and remain there. As Ayelet Shachar notes, 'immigration also serves as an important strategy in the project of nation building, and a means to affect the demographic balance between Jews and non-Jews occupying the land'.[45]

A Jewish person's right to return to Israel is legally separate from their right to Israeli citizenship. The Law of Return establishes the 'right of aliyah' (right of return).[46] The Law of Return also provides:

> Every Jew who has immigrated into this country before the coming into force of this Law, and every Jew who was born in this country, whether before or after the coming into force of this Law, shall be deemed to be a person who has come to this country as an oleh under this Law.[47]

The Nationality Law deals with the acquisition of the status of an Israeli national, whether by return, by residence in Israel, by birth or by naturalization.[48]

Citizenship in Israel has, since the formation of the state, played a key role in nation-building, by both defining the boundaries of the nation state and encouraging a sense that the citizens of Israel were engaged in a common Zionist venture. The Law of Return has been regarded as one of the fundamental laws, which may also be considered in some senses as quasi-constitutional, expressing the raison d'etre of Israel as a Jewish State.[49] As Suzi Navot argues:

> From the national perspective, the conditions prescribed for obtaining citizenship are determinative for the character of the state, and important also from a demographic perspective. The preservation of a Jewish majority among Israeli citizens is largely dependent upon a policy of granting citizenship that expresses clear preferences for Jews.[50]

3   DIVERGENT CONSTITUTIONAL APPROACHES TO CONTEMPORARY ISSUES IN CITIZENSHIP LAW

Having examined and briefly compared the constitutional rules and principles governing citizenship in a range of immigration-receiving countries, with 'constitutional', 'quasi-constitutional' and 'statutory' forms of citizenship, we now consider how those constitutions have shaped and controlled legal responses to a range of challenging citizenship issues and the extent to which their different forms necessitate certain outcomes for questions like: who is governed by the constitution, and what are the boundaries of the constitution?

3.1   Defining Citizenship

It will be apparent from our brief examination of the text of the Australian, Canadian, United States and Israeli constitutions that, in most cases, citizenship is conspicuous in its absence. The express definition of citizenship in the Constitution of the United States stands out as an example of a relatively rare constitutional choice.

There is a range of legal and historical factors that might lead some nations to entrench definitions of citizenship at a constitutional level, while others leave the bare legal meaning of citizenship to be determined, and re-determined, via sub-constitutional laws. Constitutional definitions of citizenship might be associated with a traumatic social, political or constitutional event; such definitions might be seen as protective against particular kinds of feared abuse. For example, the United States Supreme Court has accepted that s 1 of the Fourteenth

Amendment was intended to remedy a specific issue – the constitutional vulnerability of black citizens.[51] However, defining citizenship in a constitution is not the only, or necessarily the most effective, way of ensuring that citizenship is a protected, and protective, status. There are myriad examples of more recently drafted constitutions, which have also grappled with radical reconceptions of the nation after colonialism, crisis or civil war, but have still devolved some choice about the meaning of citizenship to the legislature, while dealing in more detail with the particular constitutional rights that will be associated with citizenship. See, for example, s 20 of the Constitution of the Republic of South Africa,[52] or Section II of the Constitution of the Republic of Kazakhstan.[53]

Arguably, the absence of a narrowly defined, constitutionally entrenched definition of citizenship facilitates much-needed flexibility, particularly for countries such as those we have focused on in this chapter, with high levels of immigration. Australia and Canada have been able to manage the transition from British subjecthood to independent citizenship without constitutional amendment, although, at least in Australia's case, not without constitutional upheaval.

Until Australia's Federal Parliament exercised its legislative power to create a statutory form of Australian citizenship in 1948, Australians' citizenship or nationality status was 'British subject'. At common law, British subject status depended on a person's allegiance to the Crown,[54] with birth within the dominion of the Crown being generally determinative of such allegiance.[55] In addition to the common law principles governing subjecthood (codified to some extent under British law by the turn of the 20th century[56]), Australia had some capacity to control the conferral and recognition of British subject status, and in particular to discriminate against certain British subjects on the basis of their race.[57] The Australian Naturalization Act 1903 (Cth) was predominantly intended to provide a mechanism for selectively naturalizing people in Australia based on their ethnic origin.[58] As Helen Irving has observed, the capacity to deny access to Australian citizenship based on colour remained a central concern of both sides of the Federal Parliament when, in 1948, it passed the Australian Citizenship and Nationality Act 1948 (Cth):

> While British subject status was intended to be a wide and generous embrace, an attribute of birth, a common fellowship of allegiance, a matter of good character and sportsmanship, it had always been a matter of race for Australians.[59]

The statutory concept of Australian citizenship has endured since 1948, although the rules governing the status have been subject to extensive modification.[60] The racially motivated imperative to limit the conferral of citizenship has been replaced by other normative judgements about what makes a person suitable to be an Australian.[61] In this respect, the Constitution has afforded the Parliament considerable scope to adapt Australia's citizenship regime to suit prevailing political ideals, in part because the Constitution does not impose any express restriction on how Australian nationality should be regulated.

Similarly, Canada's constitutional instruments do not define citizenship, but statutory concepts of citizenship and nationality played an important role in shaping Canadian nationhood post-Confederation. In this context, the constitutional similarities between Canada and Australia were echoed in their similar parallel legislative approaches to citizenship and naturalization. Both countries enacted immigration-restricting laws early in the 20th century designed to restrict membership of their respective communities to white British subjects.[62] Both countries enacted legislation based on the cooperative nationalization scheme established under the British Nationality and Status of Aliens Act 1914,[63] but did not extend recognition and reciprocal nationality rights to British nationals from Commonwealth countries other than those from the United Kingdom.[64] Later, after the Second World War, the Canadian government proposed a bill to create a statutory form of Canadian citizenship.[65] The Canadian Bill was, in effect, a catalyst for reform of nationality laws in a range of countries throughout the British Empire, including Australia. Following a conference of legal experts from various parts of the Commonwealth in London in 1947, the Australian Government followed Canada's lead, introducing the Nationality and Citizenship Act 1948 (Cth).[66]

Donald Galloway has argued that the Canadian response to attempts by the British Parliament to 'imperialise' British nationality should be seen in the context of efforts by a number of Dominions to 'assert their developing status as independent countries rather than colonies', at a time in which 'authority over the political status of Canadians was seen as a vital toehold in the climb towards independence'.[67] In Galloway's analysis, the Immigration Act 1910 and the Canadian Nationals Act 1921, in which the existing rules governing British nationality were essentially re-enacted in a modified Canadian-specific form, were attempts to derive strategic and political benefits by being seen to exert control over Canadian nationality, within the confines of the Parliament's constitutional legislative power, and to strengthen Canada's claim to independence from colonial rule.[68] Legislating to create a specifically Canadian form of citizenship enabled Canada to nominate a 'Canadian national' to the International Court of Justice – an instance in which 'the concept of citizenship is invoked not to express a relationship between the individual and the state or amongst members of a political community, but to accord to Canada a benefit accorded to other autonomous and independent countries'.[69]

3.2 Birthright Citizenship

In the creation of any legal status, the rules governing eligibility and inclusion are crucially important, for apart from their most obvious gate-keeping function – determining who is in and who is out – these rules affect the substantive and normative qualities of the status itself. When the eligibility criteria for citizenship are perceived as under- or over-inclusive, the normative content of citizenship may be affected. As Peter Spiro has written, 'inclusion waters down the strength of national identity';[70] under-inclusiveness, however, can also be perceived as socially divisive and unjust.[71] *Jus soli* citizenship rules, for example, mean that a person born within a state's territory becomes part of the privileged class of citizen-insiders irrespective of their subsequent relationship with the state, whereas a person who has a stronger connection with a nation (for example, through long-term residence) but happens to have been born outside its territory does not have the same legal status.[72] Similarly, *jus sanguinis* rules allow the transmission of valuable membership titles to persons born outside a national community, in circumstances where inheritance of that membership title may be the strongest link between the citizen and the state, whereas people who are in other respects members of that community lack formal membership rights and, crucially, lack the capacity to transmit membership rights to their children.[73]

In terms of eligibility for citizenship, states have historically had a limited range of rule-bases to choose from. Citizenship is generally attained either by birthright or by naturalization. The distinction between recognition of nationality on the basis of the *jus soli* or the *jus sanguinis* has been translated into constitutions and citizenship laws worldwide.[74] Both involve the recognition of citizenship by attribution based on the circumstances of a person's birth and their connection at birth with the nation – either by virtue of having been born within its boundaries or being the descendant of a citizen. However, clearly whether a state adopts a *jus sanguinis* or *jus soli* conception of birthright citizenship has significant consequences for individuals and for national communities.

The United States is the only country of those considered in this chapter that constitutionally entrenches birthright citizenship. Of itself, this is significant in terms of comparative citizenship law; it is even more so given that the form of birthright citizenship that the US Constitution entrenches is based on *jus soli*. As explained above, the Fourteenth Amendment provides that '[a]ll persons born or naturalized in the United States, and subject to the jurisdiction thereof, are citizens of the United States and of the State wherein they reside'.[75] Subject to the limited exceptions derived from the scope of the United States' 'jurisdiction' for the purposes of this clause,[76] a person born on United States soil is a citizen, irrespective of their parentage. As Ayelet Shachar argues, 'the arbitrary fact of birthplace is elevated to an *absolute norm*: if the accident of birth occurs within the territory, then that child is one of us; if not, she is a total stranger, an outsider, a non-citizen'.[77]

The citizenship status of children born to US citizen parents outside US territory is more problematic. 'Are they "natural born citizens," eligible for the presidency? Or do they fall into a constitutional twilight zone, neither "natural born" nor "naturalized," but nonetheless citizens.'[78] This question is significant not just for a person's access to citizenship by birthright, but because it also determines the ultimate extent of their participation in federal politics, as we will see below. In *Wong Kim Ark*, the Court considered that as the Fourteenth Amendment does not deal with the citizenship status of children born to US citizen parents outside US territory, that is a matter left 'to be regulated, as it had always been, by Congress in the exercise of the power conferred by the Constitution to establish an uniform rule of naturalization'.[79] The Court has upheld Congress' power to confer such citizenship subject to conditions, provided that those conditions are 'not unreasonable, arbitrary or unlawful'.[80]

Statutory rules are used to ameliorate some of the under-inclusiveness of this rule,[81] but nothing can easily be done to remedy its perceived over-inclusiveness. While many other countries have long since abandoned or at least significantly curtailed their recognition of birthright citizenship based on a person's place of birth, *jus soli* citizenship survives in the United States because it is constitutionally protected. Amendment of the constitutional rule has been proposed frequently, but the necessary legislative steps have never been seriously attempted.

In the absence of explicit constitutional conferral of birthright citizenship, it is clearly a much more malleable and uncertain entitlement. In Australia and Canada, where citizenship is largely constructed and controlled by statute, national constitutions have been held to offer only very limited protections for, or entitlements to, birthright citizenship. In Australia, where statutory citizenship has, since 1986, been based largely on a *jus sanguinis* model (with a limited form of birthright citizenship for children born in Australia to non-citizen parents who reside in Australia for the first ten years of their life), the High Court has held that the Constitution does not recognize a form of citizenship or nationality on the basis of birth in Australia.[82] Likewise, birth to an Australian parent does not confer constitutional citizenship rights.[83] The absence of any constitutionally guaranteed form of birthright citizenship has had significant consequences for particular sections of the Australian community – including children born in Australia to unlawful non-citizens,[84] persons at risk of statelessness[85] and people born in the former Australian territory of Papua whose claim to Australian citizenship was effectively quashed when Papua New Guinea (PNG) attained independence in 1975.[86]

The statutory rules governing birthright citizenship in Canada differ quite markedly from Australia's. There may also be important differences between the constitutional position regarding birthright citizenship in both countries. In Canada, the Citizenship Act makes any person born in Canada a Canadian citizen,[87] as well as a person born outside Canada if, at the time of the person's birth, one of their parents was a Canadian citizen.[88] *Jus soli* birthright citizenship is controversial in Canada, as it is in the United States; however, in contrast to the situation in the United States, prima facie there is no absolute constitutional guarantee of birthright citizenship on the basis of the *jus soli* that would prevent the Canadian legislature from determining new citizenship rules.

However, as Sarah Buhler has argued, the Canadian Charter may limit the possibility of repealing statutory birthright citizenship rules.[89] The equality rights guaranteed under Article 15 of the Charter may prevent legislative measures that effectively treat the children of non-citizens in Canada unequally, based on their parents' nationality status.[90] There may be precedents in Canadian Charter jurisprudence to support an argument that discriminating against children on the basis of a characteristic of their parents may infringe Article 15:

> The possibility that the Charter might require birthright citizenship to be conferred on an 'equal' basis to persons born in Canada, if birthright citizenship is to be conferred at all, demonstrates one of the clearest points of difference between constitutional citizenship jurisprudence in Canada and Australia, despite the facial similarity of their respective 'naturalization and aliens' clauses.[91]

In the Israeli context, the concept of 'citizenship by return' reflects a fundamental commitment to the prospective membership of every Jewish person in the Israeli national community. As we discuss above, there is a distinct category of eligibility for Israeli citizenship for those who enter Israel as *olim* under the Law of Return. The Law of Return, while based on descent, captures a broader concept of 'birthright' than the traditional *jus sanguinis* model. A person can be born to Jewish parents, who are not Israeli citizens themselves, and by virtue of their parentage be entitled to conferral of an Oleh's certificate if they return to Israel.[92] However, citizenship via return requires a more significant level of commitment to the Israeli state than other forms of *jus sanguinis* nationality, given that it is based on a person having made the decision to move to Israel. While it does not purport to confer 'citizenship', the Law of Return establishes a certain base-level protection for citizenship-like rights to enter and remain in Israel based on birthright. In addition to citizenship by return, the Nationality Law confers citizenship on people born in Israel to an Israeli-citizen parent, or outside Israel to an Israeli-citizen parent who is themselves a citizen by return, residence in Israel, naturalization, birth in Israel or adoption.[93] Effectively, the latter *jus sanguinis* ground limits birthright citizenship for those born outside Israel to one generation of descent.

3.3   Dual Nationality

The idea that a person may hold citizenship of more than one country concurrently has only relatively recently gained any significant degree of acceptance around the world. Hansen and Weill attribute the growing acceptance of dual nationality to the increase in migration worldwide, and the equalization of men and women's legal rights in liberal democracies. They argue that 'emigration and immigration result in an intermingling of laws, leading to the expansion of dual citizenship'.[94] The children of migrant parents may acquire citizenship both in the country of their birth and in the countries of their parents' citizenship. This trend is accelerated once women are able, independently, to confer citizenship on their children:

> Whereas women in the prewar period lost their citizenship when marrying a non-citizen, generally acquiring his citizenship, a trend towards equalisation has touched all liberal democracies. Today, men and women have the same right to maintain their nationality and marriage and to pass it on to their children.[95]

To some extent, states cannot opt out entirely of an increasingly globalized legal order, in which national citizenship laws frequently overlap. Because dual citizenship involves the intersection of domestic, foreign and international law, national constitutional rules are not the sole, or even dominant, determinant of a state's approach.[96] As states have no control over the way in which other states regulate their citizenship, they cannot easily enforce comprehensive rules against dual citizenship. For example, until 2002 Australian law provided that Australians who obtained another nationality lost their Australian citizenship;[97] however, if Australia nationalized a person as a citizen who held citizenship in another country, Australia could not legally strip the naturalized person of their other nationalities. There was, therefore, a class of Australian citizens who held dual nationality, despite the Australian government's policy preferences. In this way, as Hansen and Weill argue, dual nationality is a reality to which national legislatures may be challenged to respond, rather than something that can be effectively resisted.[98] Because dual citizenship involves the intersection of domestic, foreign and international law, national constitutional rules are not the sole, or even dominant, determinant of a state's approach. However, constitutional principles that affect how states confer and withdraw citizenship may shape the state's response to the challenges presented by dual nationality.

The evolution of Australia's laws on dual citizenship has been circular and constitutionally unclear.[99] As discussed above, in Australia citizenship is a statutory construction and, at least in theory, can be legislatively conferred, modified and withdrawn. Although recent changes to legislative citizenship rules in Australia have, as we note above, allowed Australians to hold dual citizenship, there are inconsistencies or anomalies between the statutory provisions that allow dual citizenship and the constitutional consequences for those who hold it.

In recent decisions involving the Federal Parliament's power to make laws with respect to 'aliens', the High Court appears to have developed a constitutional concept of 'membership' of the Australian community, which has influenced its decisions in cases involving citizenship rights, and which may have particular application to dual citizens. If a person does not possess 'full membership' of the Australian community, the Court has held that their statutory status as a citizen does not necessarily prevent them from being constitutionally 'alien', and subject to the legislative and executive powers of the Commonwealth on that basis. The High Court has upheld the whole-scale expatriation of a whole class of Australian citizens – people born in the former Australian-administered territory of Papua – on the basis that Papuans' 'membership' of the Australian polity was of a lesser quality than that of citizens resident in the Australian States and internal Territories. In *Re Minister for Immigration, Multiculturalism and Indigenous Affairs; ex parte Ame*, the Court held that Papuans were constitutionally 'aliens' despite possessing statutory Australian citizenship.[100] Interestingly, the majority in *Ame* was influenced by the fact that the Constitution of PNG prevented Papuans from holding dual citizenship – a departure from the idea advanced by Weill (above) that nations cannot control and are not bound by the way in which other nations deal with dual citizenship.

Ame has significant implications for the constitutional position of Australian dual nationals. Read in conjunction with the Court's subsequent decision in *Singh* that an alien is a person who owes permanent allegiance to a foreign power,[101] *Ame* may suggest that an Australian who possesses a second nationality (and thereby owes allegiance to a foreign power) remains an 'alien' for constitutional purposes and so could face legislative expatriation.

The judges in *Ame* were clearly concerned to limit the precedent value of their decision by suggesting that there might be a constitutional impediment to revoking the citizenship of people who were members of 'the people of the Commonwealth' referred to throughout the Constitution.[102] However, given that the Court has recently narrowed its understanding of 'the people of the Commonwealth', excluding an entire class of British citizens resident in Australia who previously had been treated as non-citizen, non-aliens,[103] the protection conferred by membership of this constitutional class may be uncertain. The consequences of the decisions in *Ame* and *Singh* for non-citizens have not been tested. It may be, as Peter Prince has suggested, that Mr Ame's situation is readily distinguishable from that of Australians who are dual nationals. These people have 'real' Australian citizenship with the right to freely enter the country, vote in elections and work in the public service etc. Arguably they receive protection against deprivation of citizenship by their membership of the 'people of the Commonwealth' referred to in the Constitution.[104]

However, the idea that possessing a dual nationality might call into question an Australian citizen's membership of the Australian community in constitutional terms, and may bring them within the scope of the Commonwealth's wide-ranging and coercive powers with respect to aliens, would almost certainly be a matter of surprise and disquiet for many dual citizens.

In the United States, although the Constitution is silent as to whether or not United States citizens may hold multiple citizenships, Fourteenth Amendment doctrine has a significant impact on the law of dual citizenship. The Supreme Court held, in one of its early citizenship decisions, that a person who had been born in the United States to Chinese parents could not be treated as an alien, but was a United States citizen by virtue of the Fourteenth Amendment irrespective of his Chinese nationality.[105] While that decision made it clear that a foreign allegiance did not nullify a person's status as a natural-born United States citizen, it did not provide a comprehensive constitutional endorsement of the right of a US citizen to hold dual nationalities.

Subsequent Supreme Court decisions have established the boundaries of US citizens' right to hold multiple nationalities. The Court has held that Congress may legislate to deem some dual citizens to have relinquished their US citizenship if they fail to renew their relationship with the nation within a prescribed period of time.[106] The Fourteenth Amendment prevents Congress from legislating so as to institute different deemed expatriation rules for persons 'born or naturalized in the United States';[107] however, it does not prevent the application of differentiated rules for those who obtain their US citizenship by descent via their US-citizen parent.[108]

The more modern approach to expatriation is to deem a person to have relinquished their US citizenship if they engage in certain conduct. The leading case in this area, *Afroyim v Rusk*,[109] established that Congress cannot legislate so as to deprive a person of their constitutionally conferred citizenship without the person's consent. The majority held that:

> the Fourteenth Amendment was designed to, and does, protect every citizen of this Nation against a congressional forcible destruction of his citizenship, whatever his creed, color, or race. Our holding does no more than to give to this citizen that which is his own, a constitutional right to remain a citizen in a free country unless he voluntarily relinquishes that citizenship.[110]

A citizen could not be deemed to have relinquished their citizenship because they voted in a foreign election, or if they swore allegiance to a foreign country or served in foreign armies, unless the citizen intended to abandon their US citizenship.[111] Later, in *Vance v Terrazas*,[112] the Court confirmed that the intention to give up US citizenship can be inferred from a person's actions, but that the proof of a certain action cannot be used to deem that person to have had the requisite intention.[113] However, Congress can stipulate that the citizen bears the onus of proving that they did not undertake prescribed actions voluntarily.[114] This is the model adopted under the *Immigration and Nationality Act*.[115]

In Canada, as in Australia, there is no constitutional prohibition on holding dual citizenship. Canadian law no longer requires that persons being naturalized as Canadian citizens renounce their foreign allegiances: however, the repeal of this requirement followed a finding that it was ultra vires the applicable statute, rather than the requirement being beyond the power of the legislature to impose.[116] There appears to have been no suggestion that because a Canadian citizen is also a citizen of another country, they are somehow constitutionally less Canadian, or could be treated at law though they were not a Canadian national by virtue of their competing foreign allegiance. Perhaps this reflects a general acceptance that Canadian citizenship is antonymic to constitutional alienage, even though the Australian experience of applying very similar constitutional provisions shows that this is not necessarily the only available interpretation. A comparative understanding of the ways in which Canada and Australia have historically 'absorbed' migrants into their social and political communities may also provide some explanation for the development of a much more complex and contested constitutional doctrine in Australia. Much of the difficulty in reconciling statutory citizenship and constitutional alienage in Australia has stemmed from the unique package of citizenship-like rights Australia has extended to non-citizen British subject residents. They were not statutory citizens, but the High Court struggled over several decades to determine whether or not they were aliens. That struggle is now reflected in the constitutional doctrine concerning citizenship, which as we discuss above may now have serious implications for the constitutional rights of dual nationals in Australia. In contrast, once Canada adopted a statutory form of Canadian citizenship, a clearer distinction emerged between Canadian citizens and constitutional aliens. (As we discuss below, the relevance of this distinction in terms of constitutional rights has been more contested.)

Finally, dual citizenship is dealt with differently under Israeli law, depending on the basis upon which a person obtains Israeli citizenship. The Nationality Law does not prohibit dual citizenship, or provide for loss of Israeli nationality upon acquiring an additional citizenship. As described above, a Jewish person who returns to Israel as an oleh has a virtually automatic entitlement to Israeli citizenship, which is unqualified by any requirement that they relinquish their other nationalities. However, a person who is not an oleh and who seeks naturalization as an Israeli is required to relinquish their previous allegiances.

This distinction is another reflection of the deeply entrenched ethnocultural conception of Israeli citizenship and immigration policy. It likely assumes that a 'feeling of solidarity and loyalty to the political community can be presumed only of those persons who by way of common interests or shared historical experience' are already part of the nation, whereas those who are not by religion, ancestry or family affinity related to the Jewish people, must assert their loyalty to the Israeli state by severing their citizenship ties to a former political community.[117]

This differential treatment of Jewish Israelis and other citizens, on the basis of a presumed loyalty or felt identity, has some parallels in the automatic or semi-automatic ascription of citizenship on the basis of birthright, which can also be seen as based on a set of assumptions about the way in which a person born in a country, or to citizen parents, will identify.

3.4   Differential Rights for Dual Nationals

Other constitutional provisions have particular application to dual nationals. For example, the Australian Constitution expressly restricts the capacity of a dual national to participate fully in federal politics. Section 44 of the Australian Constitution prevents a dual citizen from being elected to the Federal Parliament:

> Any person who –
> (i.) Is under any acknowledgement of allegiance, obedience, or adherence to a foreign power, or is a subject or a citizen or entitled to the rights or privileges of a subject or citizen of a foreign power … shall be incapable of being chosen or of sitting as a senator or a member of the House of Representatives.

Effectively, this means that a dual citizen is ineligible to stand for election, even if they have not taken any positive action to acquire an additional citizenship or have no subjective connection with the country to which they owe a putative allegiance. For a period, naturalized Australian citizens were required to take an oath in which they renounced their former allegiances;[118] those oaths have been held not to amount to an effective renunciation of other citizenships for the purposes of s 44, as foreign citizenship is essentially a matter of foreign law.[119]

The Israeli Basic Law: Knesset contains a fairly similar provision to s 44 of the Australian Constitution. Amendment 10 to s 6 of the Basic Law, passed in 1987, inserts a new clause (b) providing:

> Where an Israeli national is a national also of another state, and the law of that state enables his release from its nationality, he shall not be a candidate for the Knesset unless, by the time of the submission of the candidates' list including his name and to the satisfaction of the chairman of the Knesset Central Elections Committee, he has done everything required on his part to be released therefrom. For this purpose, a person shall not be regarded as a national of another state unless, at any time, he had a passport of that state or another document attesting to his being a national of that state.[120]

The application of this provision is narrower than s 44, in that it deems a person to be a national of a particular state if the person holds a passport or other document attesting their citizenship. However, in effect it operates as a prohibition on most dual nationals standing for election to the Knesset, even though dual citizenship is otherwise permitted under the Israeli Nationality Law.

In contrast, dual citizens of the United States are eligible to stand for election to the federal legislature, provided that they satisfy the applicable age and residency criteria. (Many dual citizens would, however, be ineligible for the offices of President or Vice-President of the United States, which are reserved for native-born US citizens.[121]) Similarly, any citizen of Canada is eligible to vote in federal elections and to stand for election to the federal Parliament.[122] Interestingly, in neither case have the kinds of conflicts of interest or contests of allegiance that are cited frequently as justifications for the constitutional prohibitions imposed in Australia and Israel manifested themselves as significant problems for the United States and Canadian legislatures.

3.5   Special Categories of Non-citizen

A comparison of the constitutional treatment of citizens has an obvious corollary in the constitutional status of non-citizens, or constitutional 'aliens'. While space precludes a sustained comparison of the constitutional consequences of outsider status, and the development of what Virginie Guiraudon has termed 'citizenship rights for non-citizens',[123] it is interesting to note that, even in the limited sample selected for this chapter, there is considerable variation.

In Australia, Canada and Israel, there are, or have been 'special categories' of non-citizen, whose constitutional status differs from that of other aliens. In Australia, the incremental development of constitutional principles governing citizenship and nationality in Australia led to the recognition, for a period, of a category of 'non-citizen, non-aliens' – essentially, the class of British subjects who live in Australia and in many respects share in the rights and privileges of Australian citizenship without holding that legal status.[124] These cases also demonstrate the extent to which Australian constitutional citizenship jurisprudence has been shaped by shifts in Australia's position in relation to the international community, and its relationship with the United Kingdom in particular.[125] Similarly in Canada, the federal franchise was extended to British subjects even after the creation of a statutory form of Canadian citizenship, until 1975.[126]

The concept of a 'special category' of non-citizens manifests itself in a different way in the Israeli context. Israel is in the fairly unique position of extending its notion of citizenship outside its own borders, and actively soliciting people to migrate to Israel and take up an offer of full citizenship. Whereas many immigration-receiving countries maintain a distinction, in constitutional and legislative terms, between native-born or naturalized citizens and recently arrived migrants, the Law of Return and Nationality Law do not. Olim are entitled to become citizens upon their arrival in Israel (or upon the grant of an oleh's certificate) without being required to serve out a period of qualification or demonstrate a further connection with the state.[127] Every Jew who migrated to Israel before the Law of Return commenced, and every Jew born in Israel before or since, is taken to be a person who 'returns' under the Law.[128] As Gouldman points out, this approach reverses the approach taken in other immigration-receiving states:

> In the eyes of the law, it is not the new immigrant who is considered as though he were a native-born Israeli; rather are the Jew born in Israel and the veteran who settled here before the enactment of the Law of Return deemed to be immigrant.[129]

It has been argued that this reflects an ethnocultural concept of membership, in which a form of citizenship is distinguished on the basis of ethnic and religious identity. In Shachar's description:

> as with other family-related perceptions of ethnocultural membership, Israeli citizenship law views persons eligible for return as *already* belonging to the constitutive community; that is, they are considered to have a status equal to Israeli-born citizens.[130]

In contrast, those who migrate to Israel other than as olim are not granted citizenship as of right, but must reside in Israel for a prescribed period, demonstrate their commitment to permanent residence in Israel, and renounce other allegiances before being eligible for citizenship.[131]

The United States maintains a much clearer distinction between constitutional insiders and outsiders, at least in relation to the distinction between citizens and aliens. A person who is not a citizen or a national of the United States is an alien.[132] As is the case in migration-receiving countries, there are pervasive controversies about the legal rights afforded to 'aliens', particularly those who are in the country unlawfully.[133] However, in terms of constitutional categorization, the position is not clouded by the special categories based on history, ethno-cultural imperatives or political concessions that have complicated the constitutional idea of citizenship in other nations.

3.6   Citizenship and Rights

The final thematic comparison in this chapter concerns the relationship between national constitutions, citizenship and individual rights in each of our comparator states. Citizenship has been described as 'the right to have rights';[134] however, rarely is the constitutional position of citizens so straightforward. The status of citizen can, but does not necessarily, bring with it a number of entrenched entitlements that are not afforded to non-citizens. However, in countries that do not constitutionally entrench rights, or that do not distinguish between the rights of citizens and the rights of other members of a national community, the relationship between citizenship and rights is more complex.

Unlike some of the other constitutions considered in this chapter, the Australian Constitution does not contain a list of constitutionally entrenched rights. As a result, some of the constitutional consequences that flow from citizenship of Canada or the United States are unparalleled in the Australian context. A citizen of Canada or the United States enjoys certain constitutionally protected rights by virtue of their status as 'citizen'. The Australian Constitution, while it does contain certain, limited, rights protections (some implied, and some expressed as limits on legislative power) generally allocates these rights on the basis of other constitutional statuses (for example, residents of a state are protected from discrimination on the basis of that state residence,[135] and persons who hold property are protected against its acquisition pursuant to Commonwealth law without the payment of just terms compensation[136]). There is also a range of common law rights recognized under Australian law; however, these are not reserved for Australian citizens.[137]

There are, arguably, constitutional rights that flow from the status of 'non-alien', in the sense that if a person is not an 'alien' within the meaning of s 51(xxiv) of the Constitution then it is not within the competence of the Federal Parliament or the Executive to treat them as such. However, to the extent that the status of 'non-alien' confers constitutional rights, they are more in the nature of negative rights arising from limits on legislative power, rather than positive entitlements. In any case, it is not clear that the status of 'non-alien' is consonant with constitutional 'citizenship'.[138]

As Helen Irving has argued, seeking to define a constitutional form of citizenship by reference to the rights that citizens in Australia enjoy is problematic. For example, although many citizens in Australia enjoy the right to vote, the federal franchise is not limited to statutory Australian citizens, nor does it include all of them.[139] While some British residents in Australia, who the High Court has confirmed are not citizens, may vote in Australian elections,[140] an Australian citizen serving a prison sentence of three years or more is disqualified from voting.[141] Similarly, not all citizens may stand for election to the Federal Parliament[142] or be granted an Australian passport.[143]

Turning to Canada, the Canadian Charter of Rights and Freedoms forms part of the national Constitution and is binding throughout all of the Provinces (subject to derogation under s 33 of the Charter). The rights protected by the Charter may be loosely categorized as those rights belonging to 'everyone' and those rights belonging to 'every citizen of Canada'.[144] In addition to the rights enjoyed by 'everyone' (which generally reflect those contained in the International Covenant on Civil and Political Rights[145]), citizens enjoy additional, specific rights. These are the right to vote in elections for, and be a member of, the House of Commons or a legislative assembly;[146] the right to enter, remain in and leave Canada;[147] the right to live and work in any Province (a right also extended to permanent residents of Canada);[148] and rights relating to the minority language education of citizens' children.[149]

This relationship between citizenship and Charter rights may have particular salience in Canada's federal constitutional system. As Alan Cairns argues, '[f]or its Anglophone supporters, the Charter fosters a conception of citizenship that defines Canadians as equal bearers of rights independent of provincial location. This legitimates a citizen concern for the treatment of fellow Canadians by other than one's own provincial government.'[150] (In this sense, Cairns argues that these citizenship rights are in tension with traditional conceptions of federalism which, he argues, 'presuppose[s] high fences and uninquisitive neighbours'.[151]) In Cairns' analysis, the kind of 'roving normative Canadianism' created by the Charter is in tension with proposals to afford special recognition to Quebec as a 'unique society', and is one reason that proposals such as those mooted at Meech Lake in 1989 were unsuccessful.[152]

Just as under the Canadian Charter some rights are conferred at large on any person who is subject to the Constitution, and others are reserved for Canadian citizens, so too does the US Constitution make distinctions based on the constitutional status of 'citizen'. These range from rights of political participation – eligibility for election to the House of Representatives and the Senate is contingent on the duration of a person's citizenship,[153] and eligibility to be elected President is reserved for 'natural born citizens'[154] to protection against discrimination on the basis of State citizenship.[155] These enhance the bundle of rights that citizens enjoy by virtue of their presence in the United States (that is, rights that are not reserved exclusively for citizens) and together with those rights add substantive content to the constitutional concept of citizenship.

Article IV of the United States Constitution provides, at s 2, 'the Citizens of each State shall be entitled to all Privileges and Immunities of Citizens in the several States'. In *Paul v Virginia*, the Supreme Court held that the object of the 'privileges and immunities' clause was to 'place the citizens of each State upon the same footing with citizens of other States, so far as the advantages resulting from citizenship in those States are concerned'.[156] Importantly, the clause is concerned with the rights of citizens of one State as against other States.[157] Indeed, there has been a resurgence of interest in the United States in the last two decades in the extent of rights (such as the right to travel) under the privileges and immunities clause under Article IV as evidenced in *Saenz v Roe*.[158]

Moreover, the complexity of these issues in the US is, as stated at the beginning of the chapter, also complicated by the fact that in a federal system the power to define the rights of citizens against non-citizens may be much broader at a national as compared to the sub-national level.[159] The US Supreme Court in the *Slaughterhouse Cases* recognized that United States citizens hold two distinct forms of citizenship – at the federal and state levels – and suggested that there were rights that flowed from both kinds of citizenship. Justice Miller's leading opinion in the *Slaughterhouse Cases* neatly avoided any need to catalogue all the rights that might derive from citizenship of the United States by concluding that the labour rights in question in those cases were clearly reserved for the States' control. However, His Honour did suggest that there were a limited number of rights associated with citizenship of the United States.

The government's response to the threat of terrorism following the 11 September attacks on New York and Washington has tested the scope of some of the constitutional protections that citizens of the United States enjoy.[160] The landmark decision of the US Supreme Court in *Hamdi v Rumsfeld*,[161] overruling the refusal by the Court of Appeals for the Fourth Circuit of a grant of habeas corpus, confirmed that citizen-detainees cannot be indefinitely detained by Executive order without being afforded basic rights of procedural due process in order to challenge their detention.[162] It is not clear to what extent those rights of procedural fairness are required to be extended to non-citizens or to citizens in the custody of the United States outside United States territory. On the basis of the Court's accompanying decision in *Rasul v Bush*,[163] together with the decision of the plurality in *Hamdi*, it at least appears that rights of habeas corpus should be afforded to citizens and non-citizens alike, irrespective of whether or not they are detained on United States soil.

Finally, in relation to the United States, it should be noted that the United States Constitution entrenches rules concerning the acquisition of citizenship, but does not confer an unqualified constitutional right to retain citizenship. As our examination of the law concerning dual citizenship demonstrates, the constitutional status of citizenship has not always been held securely, as federal law provided for the mandatory loss of citizenship on the basis of various forms of expatriating conduct.

Israel's rapid development from a frontier society to a contemporary liberal democracy has added additional constitutional and political dimensions to Israeli citizenship. Israel's Declaration of Independence establishes that in addition to being open for Jewish immigration, the State of Israel will:

> foster the development of the country for the benefit of all its inhabitants ... it will ensure complete equality of social and political rights to all its inhabitants irrespective of religion, race or sex; it will guarantee freedom of religion, conscience, language, education and culture.[164]

The Declaration reflects a liberal conception of citizenship, with its emphasis on equal enjoyment and protection of rights and freedoms. In turn, these values are reflected in the Basic Laws, and to that extent form part of the constitutional framework of Israeli citizenship.

Israel has adopted a wide range of explicit rights protections as part of its quasi-constitutional Basic Law. Civil and political rights are protected irrespective of a person's nationality; the Basic Law: Human Dignity and Liberty enshrines rights to the preservation of life, body and dignity, protection of property, protection of life, body and dignity, personal liberty, freedom to depart Israel and rights of personal privacy.[165] In addition, the Basic Law: Freedom of Occupation, guarantees: 'Every Israel national or resident has the right to engage in any occupation, profession or trade; there shall be no limitation on this right except by a Law enacted for a proper purpose and on grounds of the general welfare'.[166] Other Basic Laws provide that certain rights – notably the right to enter Israel, to vote in national elections and to hold office in the Knesset or national judiciary, are reserved for Israeli nationals.[167]

Recognition and protection of human rights under Israeli law is not limited to, or by, the Basic Laws. As David Kretzmer has observed, prior to the enactment of the Basic Law: Human Dignity and Freedom, the Supreme Court had held that 'basic civil rights, as accepted in other democratic countries, are an integral part of the Israeli legal system'.[168] However, as Kretzmer notes, these rights constitute a form of 'soft law'; government authorities may not infringe them without statutory authorization, but they do not constrain the legislative power of the Knesset, or form a basis for judicial review of legislation,[169] whereas it is clear that the Supreme Court will engage in judicial review regarding the Basic Laws. However, the enactment of the Basic Laws has not completely codified human rights protection in Israel. In *Adalah v Minister of Interior*,[170] the President of the High Court of Justice, Judge Aharon Barak, accepted that the right to personal dignity enshrined in the Basic Law: Human Dignity and Freedom encompasses a range of 'derivative' rights in addition to those enumerated in the Basic Law.[171]

Israel's quasi-constitutional human rights guarantees do not necessarily sit comfortably with the distinctions that Israeli law maintains between different categories of citizens. In particular, there remains constitutional controversy as to whether the Citizenship and Entry into Israel Law (the Citizenship Law) is consistent with the Basic Law: Human Dignity and Liberty. The Citizenship Law has the effect of denying Israeli citizenship or rights of permanent residence in Israel to occupants of the Gaza Strip and the West Bank, subject to limited exceptions. The Citizenship Law was amended in 2007 to extend its coverage to a number of states engaged in hostile activities against Israel.[172] Originally enacted on a temporary basis, the operation of the Citizenship Law has been extended several times and remains in force. The law primarily affects the spouses and families of Israeli nationals, who had previously been able to take advantage of family reunion provisions in the Nationality Law and obtain Israeli citizenship. As Daphne Barak-Erez writes,

> Formally, the amendment was enacted as a provisional measure to address the special security situation and, as such, was designed to be of limited duration. In practice, it had a significant effect on Israel's Arab population because it affected mainly the naturalization of Palestinians who had married Israelis.[173]

In 2006, by a narrow majority, the Israeli High Court of Justice upheld the validity of the Citizenship Law against a claim that it was inconsistent with the Basic Law.[174] The petitioners in *Adalah et al. v Minister of Interior* argued the Citizenship Law infringed constitutionally protected rights to family life and equality and was thereby inconsistent with the limitations clause in s 8 of the Basic Law, which provides: 'There shall be no violation of rights under this Basic Law except by a law befitting the values of the State of Israel, enacted for a proper purpose, and to an extent no greater than is required'.

While the Court accepted that the right to human dignity protected by the Basic Law connotes a right to family life and equality,[175] a majority did not agree that Citizenship Law violates that right to a disproportionate extent. Some members of the majority, like Justice Cheshlin, did not accept that the Citizenship Law infringed the rights of Arab Israelis, who do not have a right to have foreign members of their family immigrate to Israel,[176] while others in the majority acknowledged that the law violates constitutionally protected rights, but held that those rights must be balanced against the superordinate rights of all Israelis to personal security.[177] The minority accepted the legitimacy of the security goals that underpin the Citizenship Law, but would have struck down the law largely on the basis that it permitted no consideration of the relative risks involved in individual cases.[178] The High Court's decision in *Adalah* both confirms the liberal rights-conferring dimensions of Israeli citizenship and reveals the scope for differential protection of the rights of different classes of citizen. As Professor Ruth Gavison has written, '[th]e justice of the amendment to the Citizenship Law is anchored in maintaining the Jewish People's right to self-determination'.[179]

In March 2009, the Supreme Court conducted a hearing into further petitions challenging the validity of the Citizenship Law.[180] At the time of writing, the case is still before the Supreme Court.[181]

In keeping with the republican ideal of citizenship that has shaped nationality in Israel, the rights associated with citizenship are accompanied by obligations. Most clearly, the duty of virtually all citizens to perform military service exemplifies the strength of the duties that citizens owe to the State.[182] Performing military service has long been associated with citizenship in a wide range of countries, and continues to be one of the 'opportunities' to demonstrate membership of a national community that distinguishes citizens from other occupants of a nation. As Susanne Baer writes, in the context of the relationship between citizenship and gender, 'a particularly long-lasting vision of citizenship was based on the conjunction of citizenship and the defense of one's mother country. The formula of citizenship and participation was fight and vote.'[183] However, Israel is relatively rare among contemporary liberal democracies in continuing to impose a compulsory military service obligation on its citizens.[184]

4   CHALLENGES FOR COMPARATIVE APPROACHES TO CONSTITUTIONAL LAW

There is a range of reasons to consider taking a comparative approach to constitutional citizenship law. Comparison may yield insights into citizenship: what it means to be a citizen, the sorts of relationships between the individual and the state that citizenship connotes, and the challenges of sustaining any general functionalist assumptions about what citizenship does for individuals, nations and the international legal order.[185] Does it mean the same thing, even in 'strictly' legal terms, to be a citizen of the United States as to be a citizen of Australia? Is there a core constitutional function that citizenship performs, or should there be?[186] As Phillip Cole has suggested recently, there are important links between the ideal of citizenship as a status and the ideal of citizenship as a practice (echoing, but questioning, Kymlicka and

Norman's distinctions between citizenship-as-legal-status and citizenship-as-desired-activity[187]). The distinction between theories of 'citizenship-as-political-activity' and 'citizenship-as-legal-status' may, at least for some purposes, be illusory.[188] In addition, comparing citizenships might tell us something about the comparability of constitutions, and the methodological and conceptual challenges associated with this field of comparative study.[189]

The preliminary comparisons presented in this chapter suggest that the text and structure of a constitution are likely to have some impact, perhaps a very significant impact, on the nature of 'citizenship' in that constitutional system. However, the nature of that relationship is unclear. What does it mean, for example, to have a constitutional concept of 'citizenship' in the absence of an express reference to 'citizenship' in the text of a constitution? Does that make citizenship less stable (as might be suggested by the protracted upheaval in Australia concerning what it means to be an 'alien') or does it leave a conceptual space in which citizenship can evolve or adjust to take account of fundamental changes in the nature of national communities? Conversely, does entrenching a definition of citizenship in a constitution create problems of over- or under-inclusion, so that citizenship does not mean what, in contemporary circumstances, a national community might want it to mean?

Another way of approaching a comparison between different constitutional citizenship laws might be to evaluate citizenships in terms of rights. Perhaps what matters is not whether a constitution defines citizenship, but rather whether or not citizens have rights, and whether those rights set citizens apart from non-citizens. Perhaps the real similarity between citizenship in the United States and Canada is that rights are constitutionally protected (albeit by quite distinct constitutional means) and so citizens have a different relationship with the state, and with each other, than would be the case in a country where rights are not constitutionally entrenched. However, we might query whether the same similarity exists between Canada, the United States and Israel. The Israeli experience of trying to meld a liberal conception of citizens as equal, rights-bearing individuals with a republican, ethnocentric idealization of a particular kind of citizen might complicate that account of the relationship between citizenship and rights.

Ultimately, the select comparisons presented in this chapter do not provide a conclusive basis on which to draw firm conclusions about any of these questions or any clear consequences of having a 'constitutional', 'quasi-constitutional' or 'statutory model' of citizenship. The material in this chapter does demonstrate the need for ever-more detailed, more nuanced understandings of constitutional law before meaningful comparison is possible. Further comparisons might also assist, including the ways in which newer national constitutions have dealt with citizenship, or the place of the citizen in supranational constitutions.

5   CONCLUSION

We began this chapter claiming that the relationship between constitutions and citizenship is a prime site for comparisons between different constitutional systems, for the idea of citizenship, and the ideals that it is taken to represent, go to the heart of how states are constituted and defined.

Given constitutions are foundational to a community's legal order and structure, assessing the limits of membership and the parameters of community within the nation state through citizenship assists us in understanding the boundaries of constitutions. Each of the examples in the four jurisdictions covered in this chapter illustrate that what is and isn't in the text of the constitution is significant in determining the manner in which membership of the community is determined, and the consequences of that status for those with and without that status. It leaves open for further in-depth inquiry other avenues of research and analysis of the ever-changing social and political influences that will continue to impact upon citizenship in nation states' constitutions in an increasingly connected international environment.

NOTES

1. See generally Will Kymlicka and Wayne Norman (eds), *Citizenship in Diverse Societies* (Oxford University Press, 2002); Douglas B. Klusmeyer and Thomas Alexander Aleinikoff, *From Migrants to Citizens: Membership in a Changing World* (Carnegie Endowment for International Peace, 2000); Douglas B. Klusmeyer and Thomas Alexander Aleinikoff, *Citizenship Policies for an Age of Migration* (Carnegie Endowment for International Peace, 2002); Linda Bosniak, *The Citizen and the Alien: Dilemmas of Contemporary Membership* (Princeton University Press, 2008).
2. Will Kymlicka, *Multicultural Citizenship: A Liberal Theory of Minority Rights* (Clarendon Press, 1995).
3. See for example Peter Spiro's work on citizenship in the context of global movement: Peter Spiro, 'Dual Citizenship as Human Right' (2010) 8 *International Journal of Constitutional Law* 111; Peter Spiro, 'Embracing Dual Nationality', in Randall Hansen and Patrick Weill (eds), *Dual Nationality, Social Rights and Federal Citizenship in the US and Europe: The Reinvention of Citizenship* (Berghahn, 2001).
4. See Peter Schuck, 'Citizenship in a Federal System' (2000) 48 *American Journal of Comparative Law* 195; Vicki C. Jackson, 'Citizenship and Federalism', in T. Alexander Aleinikoff and Douglass B. Klusmeyer (eds), *Citizenship Today: Global Perspectives and Practices* (Carnegie Endowment for International Peace, 2001) 127.
5. Jackson, 'Citizenship and Federalism', above n 42, 131.
6. *DJL v Central Authority* (2000) 201 CLR 226, 277 (per Kirby J).
7. The omission of a definition of citizenship from the Australian Constitution was a considered choice by the Constitution's drafters: see further Kim Rubenstein, *Australian Citizenship Law in Context* (Federation Press, 2002) Ch 2, Kim Rubenstein, 'Citizenship and the Constitutional Convention Debates: A Mere Legal Inference' (1997) 25 *Federal Law Review* 295, Helen Irving, *To Constitute a Nation: A Cultural History of Australia's Constitution* (Cambridge University Press, 1997) Ch 9.
8. Australian Constitution, ss 34, 117.
9. Australian Constitution, ss 25, 75, 117.
10. Australian Constitution, s 51(xix).
11. Australian Constitution, s 44.
12. Australian Constitution, s 51(xix).
13. See Naturalisation Act 1903–1920 (Cth); Nationality Act 1920 (Cth); Australian Citizenship Act 1948 (Cth); Australian Citizenship Act 2007 (Cth).
14. For an overview of migration legislation in Australia post-Federation, see Mary Crock, *Immigration and Refugee Law in Australia* (Federation Press, 1998); John Vrachnas, Kim Boyd and Mirko Bagaric, *Migration and Refugee Law: Principles and Practice in Australia*, 2nd edition (Cambridge University Press, 2008) Ch 2.
15. There remains some uncertainty about the scope of s 51(xix) with respect to citizenship laws: see Constitutional Commission, *Final Report of the Constitutional Commission* (1988, vol 1) 160; Rubenstein, *Australian Citizenship Law in Context*, above n 7, 71–2.
16. (1992) 176 CLR 1, 54.
17. *Pochi v Macphee* (1982) 151 CLR 101; *Nolan v Minister for Immigration and Ethnic Affairs* (1988) 165 CLR 178; *Re Patterson; Ex parte Taylor* (2001) 207 CLR 291; *Shaw v Minister for Immigration and Multicultural Affairs* (2003) 281 CLR 28 ('*Shaw*'); *Re Minister for Immigration and Multicultural and Indigenous Affairs; Ex parte Ame* ('*Ame*') (2005) 222 CLR 439; *Singh v Commonwealth* (2004) 222 CLR 322 ('*Singh*').
18. *Ruddock v Taylor* (2005) 222 CLR 612.
19. *Sue v Hill* (1999) 199 CLR 462; *Street v Queensland Bar Association* (1989) 168 CLR 461 ('*Street*').
20. Canadian Citizenship Act 1946.
21. Janet Ajzenstat, Paul Romney, Ian Gentles and William D. Gairdner (eds), *Canada's Founding Debates* (Stoddart, 1999); Joel Bakan, John Borrows and Soujit Choudhry, *Canadian Constitutional Law*, 3rd edition

(Edmond Montgomery Publications Ltd, 2003), Ch 3; Peter Hogg, *The Constitutional Law of Canada* (Carswell, 2003).

22. Parliamentary Debates on the Subject of the Confederation of the British North American Provinces (Legislative Council, 3 February 1865) 7.
23. *Union Colliery Co v Bryden* [1899] AC 580.
24. *Solis v Canada (Minister for Citizenship and Immigration)* (2000) 186 DLR (4th) 512.
25. Donald Galloway, 'The Dilemmas of Canadian Citizenship Law' (1999) 13 *Georgetown Immigration Law Journal* 201, 203.
26. Galloway, ibid; Sarah Buhler, 'Babies as Bargaining Chips: In Defence of Birthright Citizenship in Canada' (2002) 17 *Journal of Law and Social Policy* 87.
27. For discussion of the constitutional idea of membership of the Australian community, see *Street* (1989) 168 CLR 461, 485 (Mason J) and 521–5 (Deane J); see also *Shaw* (2003) 281 CLR 28; *Ame* (2005) 222 CLR 439; *Singh* (2004) 222 CLR 322.
28. Lawrence Tribe, *American Constitutional Law*, 2nd edition (The Foundation Press, 1988) 356.
29. 60 US 393 (1857). See further Bickel, 'Citizenship in the American Constitution' (1973) 15 *Arizona Law Review* 369.
30. Following the end of the Civil War, legislatures in States which had hitherto permitted slavery enacted laws designed to limit the 'citizenship' rights of emancipated slaves (including, in some States, the creation of inferior courts to adjudicate the rights of black citizens). These 'Black Codes' had the effect of limiting the gains made by former slaves after the Civil War. See Christopher Waldrep, 'Substituting Law for the Lash: Emancipation and Legal Formalism in a Mississippi County Court' (1996) 82(4) *Journal of American History* 1425.
31. Ibid, 406 (Taney J).
32. This reflects the legal position as it was understood at common law prior to the adoption of the Fourteenth Amendment. See *Wong Kim Ark* 169 US 649, 682 (1898).
33. Ibid, 689.
34. See *Elk v Wilkins*, 112 US 94 (1884).
35. (1873) 83 US (16 Wall.) 36, 71, 77–9.
36. Ibid, 77–9 (Miller J).
37. Ibid, 73–4 (Miller J).
38. Ibid, 74 (Miller J).
39. *Arver v United States*, 245 US 366, 389 (1918).
40. *Slaughterhouse Cases*, 83 US 36, 78–9 (1873).
41. See *Edwards v California*, 314 US 160, 183 (1941).
42. The limitations clauses in Article 4 of the Basic Law: Freedom of Occupation (1994) and Article 8 of the Basic Law: Human Dignity and Liberty (1992) have been used to derive a basis for a form of judicial review: see *United Mizrahi Bank Ltd. v Migdal Village* C.A. 6821/93, 49 (4) P.D. 221 (1995) (Supreme Court of Israel). (We have relied on the edited version in English translation in Norman Dorsen, Michael Rosenfeld, Andras Sajo and Susanne Baer, *Comparative Constitutionalism: Cases and Materials* (West, 2003), 103–10.)
43. Daphne Barak-Erez, 'From an Unwritten to a Written Constitution: The Israeli Challenge in American Perspective' (1995) 26 *Columbia Human Rights Law Review* 309.
44. Declaration of the Establishment of the State of Israel (14 May 1948).
45. Ayelet Shachar, 'Whose Republic? Citizenship and Membership in the Israeli Polity' (1999) 13 *Georgetown Immigration Law Journal* 233.
46. Law of Return, 5710–1950, s 1. Available in English translation at http://www.mfa.gov.il/MFA/MFAArchive/1950_1959/Law%20of%20Return%205710-1950.
47. Ibid, s 4.
48. Nationality Law 5712–1952.
49. David Kretzmer, *The Legal Status of the Arabs in Israel* (Westview Press, 1990) 36.
50. Suzi Navot, *Constitutional Law of Israel* (Kluwer, 2007) 187.
51. *Slaughterhouse Cases* (1873) 83 US (16 Wall.) 36, 71, 77–9. See also *United States v Wong Kim Ark* 169 US 649, 688–9 (1898) ('*Wong Kim Ark*').
52. See further Jonathan Klaaren, 'Constitutional Citizenship in South Africa' (2010) 8 *International Journal of Constitutional Law* 94.
53. For a revealing explanation of the contemporary constitutional history of Kazakhstan, see C Tilly, 'Why Worry about Citizenship?', in M Hanigan and C Tilly (eds), *Extending Citizenship, Reconfiguring States* (Rowman & Littlefield Publishers, 1999) 247.
54. *Nolan v Minister of State for Immigration and Ethnic Affairs* (1988) 165 CLR 178, 189 (Gaudron J); Michael Pryles, *Australian Citizenship Law* (1981) Ch 2.
55. Pryles, above n 54, 14; *Sue v Hill* (1999) 199 CLR 462, 527 at n 228.
56. British Naturalization Act 1948 (UK), British Nationality and Status of Aliens Act 1914 (UK).

57. The British Naturalization Act 1870 gave a British colony the capacity to naturalize people within the colony as British subjects on terms determined by the colonial government, but provided that recognition of that subject-status was limited to the colony in which it had been conferred.

58. See Australian Naturalization Act 1903 (Cth), s 5.

59. Helen Irving, 'Citizenship and Subject-Hood in 20th Century Australia', in Pierre Boyer, Linda Cardinal and David Headon (eds), *From Subjects to Citizens: A Hundred Years of Citizenship in Australia and Canada* (University of Ottawa Press, 1999) 13. For an interesting comparative piece of scholarship looking at race in Commonwealth countries, see Marilyn Lake and Henry Reynolds, *Drawing the Global Colour Line: White Men's Countries and the Question of Racial Equality* (Melbourne University Publishing, 2008).

60. See, for example, the recent re-enactment of the *Australian Citizenship Act 1948* (Cth) as the *Australian Citizenship Act 2007* (Cth). More generally, see Rubenstein, *Australian Citizenship Law in Context*, above n 7, Ch 4.

61. In 2007, the rules governing conferral of Australian citizenship were changed so as to require prospective citizens to have lived in Australia for a longer period of time (generally four years rather than two) and to require them to successfully undertaken a citizenship test: *Australian Citizenship Act 2007* (Cth), ss 22, 23A.

62. In Canada, the *Immigration Act 1910* allowed a person to be denied entry into Canada on the basis of their 'probable inability to become readily assimilated or to assume the duties and responsibilities of Canadian citizenship.' As Sarah Buhler notes, 'even before there was legal citizenship in Canada, "citizenship" terminology was used as a rhetorical tool to contrast those deemed worthy of membership in Canadian society (white, British people) from those who were constructed as "aliens".' (Buhler, above n 26, 95.)

63. A framework allowing for ' "imperial" rather than merely local naturalization, with the proviso that it have effect in other Dominions only if they too adopted a parallel measure.' Galloway, above n 25, 211.

64. See Nationality Act 1920 (Cth); Canadian Nationals Act 1921 (Can).

65. Citizenship Act 1946 (Can).

66. As Rubenstein notes, the then Minister for Immigration, Arthur Calwell, had proposed creating a statutory form of Australian citizenship several years earlier, but had decided to defer introduction of the law pending the passage of the Canadian Act in 1946, and the outcome of the conference of Commonwealth nationality experts in 1947: see Rubenstein, *Australian Citizenship Law in Context*, above n 7, 63–4.

67. Galloway, above n 25, 211.

68. Ibid, 211–14.

69. Ibid, 211–12.

70. Peter Spiro, 'The Citizenship Dilemma' (1999) 51 *Stanford Law Review* 597, 599.

71. See Ayelet Shachar, *The Birthright Lottery: Citizenship and Global Inequality* (Harvard University Press, 2009) 26.

72. Ibid, 116–20.

73. Ibid, 120–3.

74. See, for example, Patrick Weill, 'National Policies in Comparative Perspective: Access to Citizenship: A Comparison of Twenty-five Nationality Laws', in T. Alexander Aleinikoff and Douglas Klusmeyer, *Citizenship Today: Global Perspectives and Practices* (Carnegie Endowment for International Peace, 2001).

75. Constitution of the United States of America, Fourteenth Amendment, § 1.

76. *Wong Kim Ark,* 169 US 649, 682.

77. Ayelet Shachar, 'Children of a Lesser State: Sustaining Global Inequality through Citizenship Laws' (Jean Monnet Working Paper 2/03, 2003) 10; emphasis in original. See further Shachar, *The Birthright Lottery,* above n 71.

78. Lawrence Solum, 'Originalism and the Natural Born Citizens Clause' (Illinois Public Law and Legal Theory Research Papers Series No. 08-17, 5 September 2008) 1.

79. *Wong Kim Ark,* 169 US 649, 688-9.

80. See, for example, *Rogers v Bellei* (1971) 401 US 815, 831 (Blackmun J).

81. The Immigration and Naturalization Act widens the scope of United States citizenship, so as to include, for example, a person born to a US citizen parent overseas, or a child adopted by US citizen parents: 8 USC 1401, 1431 (see also 8 USC 1101 in relation to adopted children).

82. *Singh* (2004) 222 CLR 322.

83. *Minister for Immigration and Multicultural and Indigenous Affairs v Walsh* (2002) 125 FCR 31; *Ame* (2005) 222 CLR 439.

84. *Singh* (2004) 222 CLR 322.

85. *Koroitamana v Commonwealth* (2006) 227 CLR 31 ('*Koroitamana*').

86. *Walsh* (2002) 125 FCR 31; *Ame* (2005) 222 CLR 439. See also Kim Rubenstein, 'The Lottery of Citizenship: The Changing Significance of Birthplace, Territory and Residence to the Australian Membership Prize' 22(2) *Law in Context* 25.

87. Citizenship Act 1985 (Can) s 3(1)(a).

88. Ibid, s 3(1)(b).

89. Buhler, above n 26, 110.
90. *Benner v Canada (Secretary of State)* [1997] 1 SCR 358.
91. In Australia, statutory provisions for birthright citizenship were repealed essentially in order to ensure that legal rights did not accrue to the non-citizen parents of children born in Australia. See *Kioa v West* (1985) 150 CLR 550 and Rubenstein, *Citizenship Law in Context*, above n 7, 93.
92. On the contested notion of Jewishness, see M.D. Gouldman, *Israeli Nationality Law* (Institute for Legislative Research and Comparative Law, 1970), 23.
93. Nationality Law, 5712–1952, 3(a)–3(b).
94. Randall Hansen and Patrick Weill, 'Introduction', in Randall Hansen and Patrick Weill (eds), *Dual Nationality, Social Rights and Federal Citizenship in the US and Europe: The Reinvention of Citizenship* (Berghahn, 2001) 2.
95. Ibid, 2–3.
96. Although the national constitutions considered in this chapter do not expressly prohibit citizens from holding more than one nationality, there are examples of constitutions which contain such rules. See, for example, the Constitution of the Independent State of Papua New Guinea, s 64. In this chapter, we discuss the implications of this constitutional rule for the dual citizenship of people born in the former Australian-administered territory of Papua, now part of Papua New Guinea.
97. Australian Citizenship Act 1948 (Cth), s 17 (repealed 4 April 2002).
98. Hansen and Weill, above n 94. See also Spiro, 'Embracing Dual Nationality', above n 3.
99. See K. Rubenstein, 'From Supranational to Dual to Alien Citizen: Australia's Ambivalent Journey' in S. Bronitt and K. Rubenstein, *Citizenship in a Post-National World* (Centre for International and Public Law, Law and Policy Paper 29, Federation Press, 2008), 38.
100. *Ame* (2005) 222 CLR 439.
101. *Singh* (2004) 222 CLR 322.
102. See *Ame* (2005) 222 CLR 439, 457 (Gleeson CJ, McHugh, Gummow, Hayne, Callinan and Heydon JJ), 79 (Kirby J).
103. *Shaw* (2003) 281 CLR 28; *Sue v Hill* (1999) 199 CLR 462.
104. Peter Prince, 'Mate!: Citizens, Aliens and "Real Australians": The High Court and the Case of Amos Ame' (Research Brief 2005-06 no. 4, Australian Department of Parliamentary Services, Parliamentary Library, 2005) 11.
105. *Wong Kim Ark*, 169 US 649 (1898).
106. *Perkins v Elg*, 307 US 325 (1939).
107. *Schneider v Rusk*, 377 US 163 (1964).
108. *Rogers v Bellei*, 401 US 815 (1971).
109. 387 US 253 (1967). See, earlier, *Trop v Dulles*, 356 US 86 (1958).
110. Ibid, 268 (Black J).
111. Ibid, 267 (Black J).
112. 444 US 252 (1980).
113. Ibid, 258–63.
114. Ibid, 262–3.
115. Immigration and Nationality Act, 8 USC 1481.
116. *Ulin v The Queen*, 35 DLR(3d) 738.
117. Shachar, 'Whose Republic', above n 45, 254.
118. Rubenstein, *Australian Citizenship Law in Context*, above n 7, 78–9; 136–7.
119. *Sykes v Cleary* (1992) 176 CLR 77.
120. See unofficial translation at http://www.knesset.gov.il/laws/special/eng/basic2_eng.htm.
121. Constitution of the United States of America, Article 2 § 1.
122. Constitution Act, RSC 1982, s 3. See also Constitution Act, RSC 1867, s 41 and Canada Elections Act, RSC 1985; Parliament of Canada Act, RSC 1985.
123. V. Guiraudon, 'Citizenship Rights for Non-citizens: France, Germany, and The Netherlands', in C. Joppke (ed.), *Challenge to the Nation State* (Oxford University Press, 1998) 272.
124. Rubenstein, above n 99, 40.
125. The replacement of 'British subject' status with a statutory form of Australian citizenship marked an important step towards legal independence, with British subjects henceforth being deemed to owe allegiance to a 'foreign power': see *Sue v Hill* (1999) 199 CLR 462, 527-8. See also Rubenstein, above n 99, 38.
126. Galloway, above n 25, 215; see also Dominion Elections Act 1920 (Can) and Canada Elections Act 1960 (Can).
127. Nationality Law 5712–1952.
128. Law of Return 5710–1950, s 4.
129. Gouldman, above n 98, 21.
130. Shachar, 'Whose Republic', above n 45, 236; emphasis in original.

131. Nationality Law 5712–1952, s 5.
132. 12 USC § 1101(3).
133. See, generally, C. Joppke, 'The Evolution of Alien Rights in the United States, Germany and the European Union', in T. Alexander Aleinikoff and Douglass B. Klusmeyer, eds, *Citizenship Today: Global Perspectives and Practices* (Carnegie Endowment for International Peace, 2001) 36.
134. *Trop v Dulles* 356 US 86, 102 [1958], per Warren CJ (influenced, presumably, by Hannah Arendt).
135. Australian Constitution, s 117.
136. Australian Constitution, s 51(xxxi).
137. See, for example, *Re Bolton; Ex parte Beane* (1987) 162 CLR 514, in which Justice Brennan held that 'the laws of this country secure the freedom of every lawful resident, whether citizen or alien, from arrest and surrender into the custody of foreign authorities on a mere executive warrant' (at 521). See further discussion in Rubenstein, *Australian Citizenship Law in Context*, above n 7, 273–6.
138. See further Kim Rubenstein and Niamh Lenagh-Maguire, 'Citizenship', in Ian Freckleton and Hugh Selby (eds), *Appealing to the Future: Michael Kirby and His Legacy* (Lawbook Co., 2009) 105.
139. Helen Irving, 'Still Call Australia Home: The Constitution and the Citizen's Right of Abode' (2008) 30 *Sydney Law Review* 133.
140. Commonwealth Electoral Act 1918 (Cth) s 93(1)(b)(ii).
141. *Roach v Electoral Commissioner* (2007) 233 CLR 162.
142. *Sykes v Cleary* (1992) 176 CLR 77; *Sue v Hill* (1999) 199 CLR 462.
143. Australian Passports Act 2005 (Cth) ss 11–17.
144. 'Everyone' has been held to include 'every human being who is physically present in Canada and by virtue of such presence amenable to Canadian law', *Singh v Minister of Employment and Immigration* [1985] 1 SCR 177, 202.
145. 999 UNTS 171, entered into force 23 March 1976.
146. Canadian Charter of Rights and Freedoms, Article 3.
147. Canadian Charter of Rights and Freedoms, Article 6(1).
148. Canadian Charter of Rights and Freedoms, Article 6(2).
149. Canadian Charter of Rights and Freedoms, Article 23.
150. Alan Cairns (Douglas Williams, ed), *Reconfigurations: Canadian Citizenship and Constitutional Change: Selected Essays* (McLelland & Stewart, 1995) 218.
151. Ibid.
152. Ibid, 219.
153. Constitution of the United States of America, Article 1 § 2, 3.
154. Constitution of the United States of America, Article 2 § 1.
155. Constitution of the United States of America, Article 4 § 1.
156. 75 US (8 Wall) 168 (1869).
157. *United Building & Construction Trades Council v Mayor and Council of Camden*, 465 US 208 (1984).
158. 526 US 489 (1999).
159. See *Mathews v Diaz*, 426 US 76 (1976); cf *Graham v Richardson*, 403 US 365 (1971).
160. There is also another whole discussion about the relationship between post 9/11 security issues and general waves of pro- and anti-immigration sentiment which may lead to changing approaches to defining citizens/non-citizens and rights/non-rights holders in the various jurisdictions. See Catharine Dauvergne, 'Citizenship with a Vengeance' (2007) 8(2) *Theoretical Inquiries in Law* 489–507.
161. 542 US 507 (2004).
162. Ibid, 26–8 (O'Connor J).
163. 542 US 466 (2004).
164. Declaration of the Establishment of the State of Israel (14 May 1948).
165. Basic Law: Human Dignity and Freedom (1992), ss 2–7. Available in English translation at http://www.knesset.gov.il/laws/special/eng/basic3_eng.htm.
166. Basic Law: Freedom of Occupation (1994), s 1. Available in English translation at http://www.knesset.gov.il/laws/special/eng/basic4_eng.htm.
167. Basic Law: The Knesset; Basic Law: Judiciary (1984). Available in English translation at http://www.knesset.gov.il/laws/special/eng/basic8_eng.htm.
168. David Kretzmer, 'The New Basic Laws on Human Rights: A Mini-Revolution in Israeli Constitutional Law' (1992) 26 *Israeli Law Review* 238, 239. See, for example, *Kol Ha'am v Minister of Interior* (1953) 7 PD 871.
169. Ibid, 239–40.
170. HCJ 7052/03 (14 May 2006) '*Adalah*'. Judgment available in English at: http://elyon1.court.gov.il/files_eng/03/520/070/a47/03070520.a47.pdf.
171. *Adalah* HCJ 7052/03 (14 May 2006), 46–8. See also Daphne Barak-Erez, 'Israel: Citizenship and Immigration Law in the Vise of Security, Nationality and Human Rights' (2008) 6 *International Journal of Constitutional Law* 184.

172. The Citizenship and Entry into Israel Law (Temporary Provision) (Amendment no. 2) 5767–2007.
173. Daphne Barak-Erez, 'Israel: Citizenship and Immigration Law in the Vise of Security, Nationality and Human Rights', above n 171, 186. As Barak-Erez notes, some critics of the law suggest that its demographic implications represent more than a collateral impact. See, for example, the arguments advanced (unsuccessfully) by the petitioners in *Adalah* HCJ 7052/03 (14 May 2006), 99–101. In an article in the *Jerusalem Post*, Haim Shapiro cited the Israeli Interior Minister Eli Yishai as explaining that the Citizenship Law is 'motivated by demography, security and economics in equal measure ...': 'Yishai Freezes Arab Naturalization Requests' (*Jerusalem Post*, 13 May 2002, 1).
174. *Adalah* HCJ 7052/03 (14 May 2006). As well as being Israel's ultimate appellate court, the Supreme Court, sitting as the High Court of Justice, exercises jurisdiction at first instance in 'matters in which it deems it necessary to grant relief for the sake of justice and which are not within the jurisdiction of another court ...' (Basic Law: The Judiciary, s 15.)
175. *Adalah* HCJ 7052/03 (14 May 2006), 36–42 (Barack P); 153–4 (Cheshlin VP); 227–9 (Beinisch J); 333–8 (Joubran J); p 252 (Hayut J); 254 (Procaccia J); 274–6 (Grunis J); 284–5 (Naor J); 299 (Adiel J); 308–10 (Rivlin J); 324 (Levy J).
176. Cheshin VP, Grunis and Naor JJ.
177. Adiel, Rivlin and Levy JJ.
178. Barak, P, Beinisch, Joubran, Hayut and Procaccia JJ.
179. The full text of the newspaper article 'Family Unification in Two States', Prof. Ruth Gavison, Yediot Ahronot, 5 August 2003, p. B11 (Translated by The Israel Government Press Office) is available online at http://www.ngo-monitor.org/article.php?id=925.
180. Adalah Centre for Arab Minority Rights in Israel, 'Supreme Court to Decide Soon on Whether the Citizenship Law, which Discriminates on the Basis of Nationality and Violates the Right to Family Life, is Compatible with Israel's Basic Laws' (Media release, 16 March 2009), available at http://www.adalah.org/eng/press releases/pr.php?file=09_03_16 (accessed 10 November 2009).
181. Adalah Centre for Arab Minority Rights in Israel, 'Eleven Justice Panel of Israeli Supreme Court Holds Hearing on Citizenship Law Case; Court Orders State to Provide New Data on Why the Law is Needed for Security Reasons', available at http://www.adalah.org/eng/pressreleases/pr.php?file=14_3_10.
182. Defence Service Law 1986 (Consolidated Version). See further, Shachar, 'Whose Republic?', above n 45, 258–64.
183. Susanne Baer, 'Citizenship in Europe and the Construction of Gender by Law in the European Charter of Fundamental Rights', in Karen Knop (ed.), *Gender and Human Rights* (Oxford University Press, 2004) 83, 84.
184. Interestingly, the Israeli Defence Service Law is also a relative rarity in that it imposes broadly similar service obligations on women and men, although as Daphne Barack-Erez has shown, not without more subtle gender-based distinctions: 'The Feminist Battle for Citizenship: Between Combat Duties and Conscientious Objection' (2007) 13 *Cardozo Journal of Law and Gender* 531.
185. See generally Bosniak, *The Citizen and the Alien*, above n 1; Michel Rosenfeld, *The Identity of the Constitutional Subject* (Taylor & Francis, 2008); Douglas Klusmeyer, *Between Consent and Descent: Conceptions of Democratic Citizenship* (International Migration Policy Program, 1995).
186. As to the possibility of 'sameness' between laws, and the implications for comparative studies in law, see Pierre Legrand, 'The Same and the Different', in Pierre Legrand and Roderick Munday (eds), *Comparative Legal Studies: Traditions and Transitions* (Cambridge University Press, 203) 240.
187. Kymlicka and Norman, above n 1, 353.
188. Phillip Cole, 'Introduction', in G Calder, Phillip Cole and Jonathan Seglow (eds), *Citizenship Acquisition and National Belonging: Migration, Membership and the Liberal Democratic State* (Palgrave, 2010) 3.
189. As to which, see Vicki C. Jackson, *Constitutional Engagement in a Transnational Era* (Oxford University Press, 2010); Vicki C. Jackson and Mark Tushnet (eds), *Defining the Field of Comparative Constitutional Law* (Praeger, 2002), David S. Law. 'Generic Constitutional Law' (2005) 89 *Minnesota Law Review* 652.

10. Comparative constitutional law and Indigenous peoples: Canada, New Zealand and the USA

Claire Charters

1 INTRODUCTION

In formerly colonial states, such as Canada, New Zealand and the USA, almost all state law relevant to Indigenous peoples is constitutional in nature in that it is inextricably linked to the state's historical and ongoing constitutive processes. Assumptions of the legitimacy of colonial assertions of sovereignty are inherent in state attempts to exercise authority over Indigenous peoples. Consequently, the amount of law, and topics, potentially caught within an analysis of comparative constitutional law and Indigenous peoples is huge.

In this chapter, I provide an overview of comparative constitutional law as it relates to Indigenous peoples in Canada, New Zealand and the USA, also commenting on relevant comparative legal scholarship. It is limited, for reasons of size, to the most fundamental of constitutional issues, with a focus on: the demographic, historical, political, social and cultural influences on constitutional law relevant to Indigenous peoples; the foundations of state constitutional law relating to Indigenous peoples; the constitutional and legal significance of treaties with Indigenous peoples as parties; land rights; the relationship between human rights and Indigenous peoples' rights; and projections about the potential significance of evolving international law on Indigenous peoples on constitutional law in Canada, New Zealand and the USA. It finishes with some brief comments on the contemporary direction of constitutional law as it relates to Indigenous peoples in the three jurisdictions.

2 CONTEXT

2.1 Demographic, Historical, Political, Social and Cultural Influences on Constitutional Law and Indigenous Peoples

Canadian, New Zealand and USA constitutional law relevant to Indigenous peoples shares its historical genesis in the assumption of sovereignty over Indigenous peoples and their territories by, in the main and in the finish, the English, although what is now the USA and Canada were also subject to other European colonial forces, especially French. English constitutional and legal doctrine continues to be applied in and informs all three jurisdictions, albeit to different degrees, with the New Zealand legal system most resembling, and being dogmatically wedded to, that of the English today. Canada, New Zealand and the USA also share a

---

* This chapter reflects the views of the author and are not necessarily those of the United Nations.

strong recent history of Western, liberal and democratic rule, which has been contentious for Indigenous peoples, who are neither necessarily liberal in outlook nor democratic in governance, in the sense of electing authorities through one person, one vote elections.

Each American Indian, First Nation, Hawaiian, Inuit, Maori and Metis group has its own unique history, pre- and post-colonisation, and has suffered, and changed, as a result of colonisation in different ways. However, they share experiences of extreme disenfranchisement, including loss of land, culture, sovereignty and political and legal influence, the effects of which are still very much felt today, and reflected in ongoing comparatively poor social, economic and cultural conditions. Moreover, they constitute minorities within the democracies that were established on their territories, translating into little, albeit of varying degrees, political influence and visibility, negatively impacting on their ability to effectively agitate for protection of their rights in the political domain. While written of the American Indian, this famous Cohen quote applies equally to other Indigenous groups in Canada, New Zealand and the USA (Cohen, 1953, 390):

> Like the miner's canary, the Indian marks the shifts from fresh air to poison gas in our political atmosphere; and our treatment of Indians, even more than our treatment of other minorities, reflects the rise and fall in our democratic faith.

What must not be forgotten in any comparative constitutional legal analysis of Indigenous peoples is this: many Indigenous peoples continue to live in post-colonial-legal worlds in that they are subject to constitutional legal systems that are not their own, and are not premised on, nor necessarily consistent with, their own cultural legal values (McHugh, 2004). Thus, Indigenous peoples are systemically disadvantaged under the state constitutions applicable to them, which can be confounded by the bias inherent in democracies against persistent minorities (Kymlicka, 1995).

In each jurisdiction, the size and power of settler populations relative to the size and power of Indigenous populations heavily influenced the development of law. Indeed, the relative power of Indigenous peoples explains many of the early ebbs and flows in recognition of Indigenous peoples' rights in each jurisdiction. For example, European states historically recognised Indigenous peoples' authority over their peoples and territories in areas now known as Canada, New Zealand and the USA while settlers were politically and physically non-dominant or it was politically expedient to secure the allegiance of Indigenous groups in inter-European-state conflict. As soon as colonial physical dominance was assured, colonial policy became more assimilationist and assertive. More contemporaneously, New Zealand's respect, and disrespect, for Indigenous peoples' rights, is partly explained by the political force that Maori, making up approximately 15% of the population, bring to bear, which can be compared with the roughly 2–4% Indigenous population in the USA and Canada respectively.

Generally, constitutional developments relevant to Indigenous peoples have been reactive to the broader political, social, economic and cultural contexts, highlighting the vulnerability of the rule of law in the face of colonial impulses, and increasing the desirability of positive and enforceable laws to insulate Indigenous interests against political whim. The timing of particular juridical events, such as the bringing of cases that would establish foundational constitutional principles, indelibly contoured the evolution of constitutional doctrine. Generally, during times of relative state respect for Indigenous peoples, or more pluralistic understandings of law and sovereignty (McHugh, 2004), norms more cognisant and respectful of Indigenous peoples' autonomy and own legal systems resulted, even if still ultimately premised on paternalistic assumptions (Walters, 2009, 24). Conversely, constitutional principles formed during times of assumed social, economic and/or cultural state superiority, or colonial understandings of sovereignty as a unitary state power, were generally assimilationist in nature.

The foundational constitutional structure, and constitutional instruments, of each jurisdiction also have a very real impact on the method and extent of constitutional protection of Indigenous peoples' interests. One of the main sources of difference in approach in Canada, New Zealand and the USA, explored in more detail below, is the extent to which Indigenous legal and political issues are ultimately determined in the judicial and/or the political domains.

New Zealand's Constitution is not set out in a primary written document and can be amended relatively easily through, for example, legislation and the evolution of new constitutional convention. Also, New Zealand courts lack the express authority to strike down legislation for non-compliance with the Constitution; in Tushnet's description (Chapter 18 in this volume), it has weak-form judicial review. Its Bill of Rights Act 1990, the principal law to protect human rights, is even expressly subordinate to other legislation that conflicts with it. The upshot of New Zealand's constitutional structure is that respect for Maori interests is often achieved through political lobbying and voting – influencing the Executive and Parliament – rather than through litigation, even though Maori are a minority. This is not to say that the courts are unimportant players – New Zealand courts have shaped much important constitutional law as it applies to Maori, especially as it relates to land and non-territorial rights – just that the Legislature and Executive have higher ultimate authority to determine constitutional law relevant to Maori. That much constitutional activity occurs in the political domain in New Zealand, and the Constitution is flexible, means it can be difficult to get an accurate picture of constitutional developments: newspapers can be a better source of information about the Constitution than the law reports. In contrast, in the USA and Canada, the authority vested in courts to overturn legislation inconsistent with the Constitution and constitutional doctrine means that the courts are at least as important a venue as the legislature and the executive in defending and giving meaning to Indigenous interests.

2.2   State Acquisitions of Sovereignty

Questions remain about the legality of colonial assertions of power in Canada, New Zealand and the USA. Broadly, international law provided the overall, albeit contested (Anghie, 2004), regulatory structure to legalise colonial acquisitions of sovereignty over territories inhabited by Indigenous peoples, including the doctrines of discovery and settlement, conquest and cession. The self-serving nature of these doctrines, emanating as they do from Europe, to authorise the extension of European power undermine their authority to legitimise, on any initial or even ongoing basis, assertions of colonial control over Indigenous peoples.

Moreover, and equally problematically, it is questionable whether international legal doctrines regulating sovereignty transfer were adequately complied with in the Canadian, New Zealand and USA contexts. Thus, the legal acquisition of sovereignty remains contestable, despite the political and legal reality that much Indigenous peoples' sovereign power has transferred to the state (Brookfield, 2007).

The doctrine of discovery is largely cited as the source for the assumption of the USA's sovereignty over its territories.[1] The same is true also in Canada,[2] where, as in the USA, treaties between Indigenous peoples and colonial powers generally did not purport to cede sovereignty; indeed, in early encounters treaties supported Indigenous peoples' sovereignty and control of their lands, territories and resources. In New Zealand, claims that the Treaty of Waitangi of 1840 between various Maori iwi, hapu and individuals and the British Crown ceded sovereignty to the British are undermined by the at least equally and possibly more authoritative Maori text, which guarantees Maori the retention of their tino rangatiratanga (or chieftainship). Alternative claims to sovereignty based on discovery are undermined by official English recognition of Maori sovereignty prior to English assumptions of sovereignty and the very clear appreciation of Maori occupancy of their territories, even in the lower South Island where English claims to sovereignty based on discovery are loudest. The incorrect application of the discovery doctrine – its inability to legitimately found colonial sovereignty where territories were occupied by Indigenous peoples – has been exposed in decisions such as *Mabo and Others v Queensland*.[3] However, alternative legal justifications for assumptions of sovereignty are also contestable. With some exceptions, conquest poorly explains the transfer of sovereignty in Canada, New Zealand or the USA, unless conquest is interpreted to include the gradual and ongoing suppression of Indigenous peoples not only through warfare but also the decimation of Indigenous populations through introduced illness, the sheer zealousness with which colonial law was applied and the eventual outnumbering of Indigenous individuals by citizens of the colonising state.

The international legal source of claims to a legal transfer of sovereignty impacts on the continuing constitutional status of Indigenous law under state legal systems. In cases of conquest and cession, Indigenous law applies until changed by the new sovereign authority,[4] meaning that all Indigenous law remains applicable except where it has been explicitly overridden by the colonial sovereign power. Only in cases of discovery and settlement – where the territories are deemed 'terra nullius' – does the colonial law flow in with the colonising power, there being, theoretically, no pre-existing law to 'displace'. Given Canada, New Zealand and the USA were inhabited by Indigenous peoples on contact and discovery is an inaccurate description of the transfer of sovereignty in those states, in theory, Indigenous law continues to apply to the extent that it has not been trumped by state law. However, the doctrine of the residual application of Indigenous law has been poorly applied, if at all, in Canada, New Zealand and the USA, with the exception of on Indian reservations in the USA, discussed below. Especially in Canada and New Zealand, most perceive that, in practice, state law has fully replaced Indigenous law.

3   FUNDAMENTAL CONSTITUTIONAL COMPARISONS

Consistently with broader similarities between Canada, New Zealand and the USA, constitutional developments have loosely mirrored one another in the jurisdictions, even if fundamental differences remain. As mentioned, in all three, early contact between colonial forces and Indigenous peoples was marked by official respect for Indigenous peoples' sovereignty and control of their lands, seen in treaties between European powers and Indigenous peoples. However, the full inconvenience of legal instruments and doctrines requiring respect and protection of Indigenous interests were later avoided by the evolution of newer doctrines to weaken the state's enforceable obligations to Indigenous peoples. Examples include the

Canadian Indian Act 1876, the development of USA Congressional plenary power over American Indians and the description of the Treaty of Waitangi as a 'simple nullity'. They were also coupled with policy and law that had the practical impact of depriving Indigenous peoples of their territories, be it through land legislation such as the USA Allotment Act and Maori land legislation. Much later, post the rights movements of the 1960s and 1970s, which included much Indigenous agitation, the political and legal language of Indigenous and state relations moved towards concepts of self-government, especially in Canada, self-determination, especially in the USA, and partnership, especially in New Zealand. Constitutional and legal changes followed, most profoundly in Canada. Less optimistically and more contemporaneously, there appears to be a political and legal backlash against recognition of Indigenous peoples and their rights in all three states, best reflected in that they were the last states in the UN to express their support for it.

3.1   Canada

Early and constitutionally-significant instruments applicable in Canada made by the British, post their assertion of authority over the region and defeat of the French, recognised Indian land rights. The Royal Proclamation of 1763 and the bill drafted a year later to regulate Indian relations reflected that the British did not have, nor assert, control over Indians at that point. As Walters writes (2009, 25),

> [t]here was no talk of claims based on discovery here, no references to a Hobbesian state of nature or absolute Crown sovereignty. Rather the assumption seems to have been that indigenous inhabitants had polities and laws that were acknowledged and accommodated within territories over which the Crown asserted exclusive rights vis a vis other European states.

However, with the passage of the Constitution Act 1867, the ground was set for the assumption of absolute Canadian sovereignty over Indigenous peoples. It provided for the federal Parliament's exclusive control over Indians and lands reserved for them under section 91(24). In 1876, the Canadian Parliament utilised this power with the first version of the Indian Act, still in force today. The Indian Act is controversial. It was, and remains to some extent, paternalistic but is also a mechanism by which many First Nations have retained some land – on reserves – and self-government powers, although the latter, in contrast to the USA, have been conceptualised as a delegated rather than inherent power. The Indian Act has also often been significantly repealed and amended as policy has changed, and in major ways. For example, it was amended in 1951 to provide that provincial laws of general application apply on Indian reserves, unless inconsistent with federal law or a treaty.

Of the three jurisdictions discussed here, it is Canada that has had the most profound constitutional moment during the more recent rights-recognition policy phase common also to New Zealand and the USA. In 1982 Canada passed its Constitution Act, which included, as a result of a long and robust lobby by Indigenous groups, section 35. It states that 'the existing Aboriginal and treaty rights of the Aboriginal peoples of Canada are hereby recognized and affirmed'. Section 35 applies to all Indian, Inuit and Metis peoples of Canada and, also, treaties expressly include contemporary land claims agreements, such as those reached post 1982. Of note, and despite the efforts of Indigenous groups, section 35 did not expressly recognise and affirm Indigenous self-government.

Located in part 2 of the Canadian Constitution Act 1982, section 35 is distinct from the part 1 Charter of Rights and Freedoms, thus separating Indigenous rights from human rights. This positioning also 'immunises' Aboriginal and treaty rights from the section 1 provision enabling the state to impose justified limitations on part 1 rights and freedoms. In addition, section 25 states that the human rights and freedoms expressed in part 1 'shall not be construed so as to abrogate or derogate from any aboriginal, treaty or other rights or freedoms that pertain to the aboriginal peoples of Canada'. Some extra provisions were included, however, to require equality under the Constitution Act for Indigenous men and women: sections 28 and 35(4) in effect guarantee all Aboriginal and treaty rights to women and men equally.

Section 35 means that Canadian legislation is now subordinate to Aboriginal and treaty rights. Comparatively, New Zealand does not include such formal constitutional protections of Maori rights and, as discussed below, the constitutional position of Indigenous peoples in the USA is largely determined by extra-Constitutional doctrine, with the written Constitution largely silent on Indian, Inuit and Hawaiian issues.

The impact of section 35 on jurisprudence in Canada has been profound, including an increasing judicialisation of Indigenous legal issues. Aboriginal title has been recognised,[5] as well as non-territorial Aboriginal rights. Both historical and contemporary treaties have been enforced.[6] However, the strong protection of rights has also precipitated the development and concretisation of tests to be met before the courts will recognise rights, some of which function to make it difficult for some Indigenous groups to prove their Aboriginal and treaty rights. For example, to prove section 35 Aboriginal title, an Indigenous group must show exclusive possession of territories at the time of the transfer of sovereignty to the Crown, requiring elaborate, and often difficult to establish, evidence.[7] Recognition of broad self-government powers as an Aboriginal right has been undermined by tests requiring proof that each specific activity was integral to the culture.[8] However, there remains some scope for further judicial consideration of Indigenous self-government rights in Canada given, in the context of a case involving a contemporary settlement recognising First Nations' self-government, the British Columbia Supreme Court acknowledged residual Indigenous self-government powers. Certain regulations restricting section 35 rights are permitted on the proviso that they comply with certain tests, such as the Crown's fiduciary obligations to the Indigenous group in question.[9]

The 'bite' in Canada's enforcement of treaties is in its more restrictive interpretation of treaty obligations when compared to, for example, the approach taken by the USA Supreme Court and the 'principles' approach to New Zealand's Treaty of Waitangi, both discussed below. In *R v Marshall*; *R v Bernard*, the Supreme Court rejected Indigenous individuals' claims based on a 1760s treaty between the Mi'kmaq and the British to cut and commercially trade timber from Crown lands. Under the relevant treaty clause, the British were to provide the Mi'kmaq, who had largely supported the French prior to their defeat, with trading posts where Mi'kmaq agreed to trade exclusively. Having already previously determined that the trade clause would only ever entitle the Mi'kmaq to a moderate livelihood from trade in the products of traditional activities, the Supreme Court determined that trade in wood products did not constitute a logical evolution of Mi'kmaq trading activity in the 1760s, and thus was not section 35 protected.

Related to section 35 jurisprudence is the development of the 'honour of the Crown' doctrine in Canadian law, under which Crown obligations to consult with First Nations and accommodate their interests, and fiduciary duties fall.[10] In practice, this doctrine can be significant in providing First Nations with the opportunity to participate in governance decisions that impact on them.

During the 1990s in particular, there was considerable political activity in the Canadian context for greater recognition of Indigenous peoples' autonomy and governance powers. The Charlottetown Accord of 1992 proposed an amendment of the Constitution Act 1982 to include recognition of Indigenous self-government, but was defeated at referendum, believed to be more because of the inclusion of provisions to recognise greater Quebecois independence. With 'grand mega constitutional reconciliation off the Canadian agenda' (Russell, 2005, 178), Canada moved robustly forward politically, recognising Aboriginal peoples' self-government under section 35 of the Constitution Act as a matter of policy and in line with Royal Commission reports. One of the principal means of achieving this recognition is through agreements with Indigenous peoples, of which there are literally hundreds, which include the vesting of considerable power in Indigenous governance structures. The negotiation of Aboriginal self-government and its express prescription in agreements undermines the sense that Canada is moving towards broad recognition of Aboriginal inherent sovereignty, even if agreements recognise Aboriginal self-government as inherent. As discussed later, this reflects perhaps, as in New Zealand, that the negotiation process is inspired by a sense of the need to reconcile Indigenous with non-Indigenous interests rather than fully realising the legitimate claims of those groups wrongly denied sovereignty and territory in the past.

The forward-looking nature of Canada's political approach to Indigenous peoples' claims is highlighted when its contemporary treaty-making process is compared to New Zealand's ongoing treaty settlement process and the USA's previous Indian Claims Commission. The latter two are focused on providing redress for historical wrongs, to 'fully and finally' settle Indigenous peoples' claims. The former, the Canadian approach, is more concentrated on realising Indigenous self-government into the future. Perhaps, in this way, Canada shows its leadership in reconciling Indigenous difference and equality in a pluralistic and multicultural way.

Membership in tribal groups is a contested issue for some Indigenous peoples and individuals in Canada, seen in challenges to both state and Band membership regulations, especially where they discriminate against Indigenous women.[11] They have also raised broader questions, as in the United States, as to the role the state should have in determining such a crucial issue, going as it does directly to Indigenous group and individual identity. If self-government is to be realised, it must include the power to determine who constitutes the self. Moreover, as in New Zealand, questions about legitimate types of governance entities continue.

3.2   New Zealand

The Constitution of Aotearoa/New Zealand differs significantly from that of Canada and the USA. It does not include, as mentioned, a formal written Constitution. Instead, New Zealand's constitutional norms are comprised of a collection of instruments including constitutional convention and ordinary statutes, such as the Constitution Act 1986 setting out the branches of government and the Bill of Rights Act 1990. Constitutional norms can change relatively readily in response to the evolution of new ways of doing things (Palmer, 2007). Parliament reigns supreme: courts cannot overturn legislation for incompatibility with constitutional rights, although the possibility of New Zealand courts making a declaration that legislation is inconsistent with the Bill of Rights Act 1990 exists (Geiringer, 2009).

In contrast to Canada and the USA, New Zealand's popular and contemporary constitutional narrative is built on the above-mentioned Treaty of Waitangi, between the British Crown and some Maori representatives, of 1840. The ongoing relevance of the Treaty of Waitangi illustrates that Maori and state relations are central to New Zealand's understanding of itself, its national psyche and its Constitution. When comparing the Constitution of New Zealand to that of Canada and the United States, there is less of a sense that Canada and United States are constitutionally built on the encounter between Indigenous peoples and colonial power.

However, the rhetorical significance of the Treaty of Waitangi is somewhat misplaced when it is compared to the Treaty of Waitangi's shifting legal status over the decades as well as its inherent ambiguities. As mentioned, it was the original basis on which the English asserted sovereignty over Maori territories in 1840 and despite inconsistencies between Maori and English texts. Then, a short 37 years later, it was described by the Chief Justice of the time, in the *Wi Parata* case, as 'a simple nullity' in so far as it purported to cede sovereignty on the grounds that '[n]o body politic existed capable of making cession of sovereignty'.[12] Today, the *Wi Parata* decision has been discredited.[13] Nonetheless, the legal position that the Treaty of Waitangi cannot be enforced unless incorporated into statute undermines its position as a 'constitutional' document, although this must be viewed in the context of New Zealand's overall comfort with non-legally binding constitutional doctrine (Palmer, 2008). Still, Cabinet is required to sign off on bills' compliance with the Treaty and, importantly, the principles of the Treaty of Waitangi have been incorporated into a number of statutes, and have been given force by the courts.[14]

An upshot of New Zealand's constitutional culture is its malleability and susceptibility to changing political whim. In a rather unconstrained democracy, where the majority has the purported power to enact any law it pleases, political sentiment can quickly be translated into legal, and even constitutional, principle, leaving the rights of minorities, including those of Maori, vulnerable (Charters, 2006). This was seen most acutely with the passage of the Foreshore and Seabed Act 2004, which legislatively extinguished all Maori land title in the foreshore and seabed without any guarantee of redress. It was the, now generally accepted as mistaken, response to a misaligned and misinformed public fear that recognition of Maori land interests in the foreshore would result in the denial of New Zealanders' access to New Zealand beaches. Of late, the perception that state recognition of Maori rights, such as their property interests, constitutes racial discrimination against non-Maori has filtered its way into the legal and constitutional fields, impairing attempts to realise legitimate Maori claims (Charters, 2009).

Perhaps the most significant facet of New Zealand's constitutional structure, comparatively viewed, is the guaranteed Maori seats in Parliament, elected by voters registered, voluntarily, on the Maori as opposed to the general electoral roll. The proportion of seats assigned to Maori is determined by the number of Maori who register on the Maori roll, and currently stands at seven out of approximately 120 seats in total. In conjunction with the establishment of the Maori Party in 2004, partly a reaction against the enactment of the Foreshore and Seabed Act 2004, and New Zealand's mixed member proportional voting system, making it highly unlikely that any one political party will acquire the votes to rule alone, the Maori seats function to guarantee at least some Maori voice in Parliament. That mainstream parties are required, or deem it politically expedient, to enter into coalition agreements with the Maori Party has translated into some leverage for the better realisation of Maori interests, such as a review of the Foreshore and Seabed Act 2004.

Today, the constitutional rights of Maori are protected, or not, through an array of various instruments, including above-mentioned references to the principles of the Treaty of Waitangi in some legislation. Section 20 of the Bill of Rights Act, the right to culture, has been little utilised by Maori, perhaps because it is expressed as a right belonging to individuals rather than groups, like iwi (tribal groups), and is not an effective tool where Parliament enacts legislation clearly inconsistent with it. Some legislative initiatives have empowered some Maori groups, such as the Resource Management Act 1990, with its requirement, in some circumstances, for consultation with Maori and provision for Maori interests.

The common law doctrine of Aboriginal rights, including the recognition of title and non-territorial rights, applies in New Zealand, as it does in Canada, although it does not have the constitutional status that it does under section 35 of the Canadian Constitution Act 1982. However, partly due to New Zealand's early decision to legislatively regulate Maori land, dating back to the 1860s, there has been little scope, in practice, for the application of Aboriginal title doctrine, leaving the jurisprudence underdeveloped. Regrettably, New Zealand Maori land legislation, like the USA Allotment Act of 1887, also facilitated the loss by Maori of much of their land, in part responsible for the sad statistic that Maori own less than 5% of the total land in New Zealand today. Similarly, judicial recognition of extant Aboriginal rights, such as fishing rights,[15] is commonly superseded by legislation, ousting the courts' jurisdiction to determine Maori rights.

As mentioned, New Zealand has a now relatively long-standing Treaty of Waitangi settlements process, which involves direct negotiations between representatives of the Crown and Maori groups, coupled with, on settlement, legislation implementing the settlement. Settlements are directed at responding to historical grievances and redress generally includes financial redress, cultural redress and also an apology or acknowledgement. Increasingly, the settlement process is coming under fire, especially from Maori groups. The process, and policy behind it, is determined by the Executive, and cannot be challenged in the courts. There are shortcomings in that the Crown will not consider claims based on self-determination or to natural resources such as oil and gas, has excluded smaller groups from the negotiation process and has settled on more favourable terms with some iwi than with others.

The Waitangi Tribunal, which was established in 1975, has, since 1985, had the jurisdiction to inquire into any alleged breach of the Treaty of Waitangi since 1840 and make recommendations to the Crown. Its reports are often voluminous and constitute a remarkable history of Maori and state relations. Unfortunately, however, its recommendations are not binding – on the Crown or courts – and its interpretations of the Treaty of Waitangi, while influential, are not authoritative outside of the legislation under which it is authorised to function. In more recent years, the Crown has refused to follow the recommendations of the Waitangi Tribunal in a number of high profile instances, including in relation to the above-mentioned foreshore and seabed issue.

In contrast to state and Indigenous approaches to membership in some Indigenous groups in Canada and the USA, Maori cultural approaches to membership are inclusive; if a person's whakapapa, or genealogy, includes a certain tribe, the person is generally included in the tribe. Moreover, the state has not attempted, historically at least, to define who is or isn't Maori, even for the purposes of determining who can legally sign up to the Maori electoral roll. However, there are increasing pressures for the state to authorise the groups to be recognised as tribes and the entities that represent the tribes, such as for the purposes of determining to whom to distribute the assets from settlements. Additionally, as some Maori tribal groupings acquire more resources, such as in relation to the lucrative fishing industry, the personal incentive to activate one's membership in a tribe increases, putting pressures on the group. In the light of these stimuli, it is expected that the politics around state recognition of Maori groups on the one hand and membership in Maori groups on the other will intensify in the near future.

3.3   USA

The constitutional position of American Indians, Hawaiians and Indigenous peoples in Alaska is different, reflective of the differences between their history of contact with colonial forces and the dominant policy of the colonial or USA governments at the time of constitutionally-significant events.

The constitutional situation of the American Indian is unique in that some residual American Indian sovereignty has always been recognised under the USA constitutional structure. Indeed, the USA has shared sovereignty and jurisdiction with American Indians throughout, even if not to the extent demanded or expected by some American Indian peoples. Especially on their land, often on reservations, American Indians have had the inherent authority to regulate some matters in accordance with their own laws and norms, although some argue tribal norms often emulate the law and norms of the neighbouring state/s or the USA federal government (Barsh, 1999).

The legal foundation of American Indians' ongoing residual sovereignty comes not directly from the USA Constitution but from judicially-developed constitutional doctrine from the early 1830s. In *Cherokee Nation v State of Georgia* and *Worcester v Georgia*, Chief Justice Marshall held that while the Cherokee Nation was not a foreign state under the Constitution, it was correctly denominated as a 'domestic dependent nation' with its own boundaries.[16] State laws have no force.[17] The Supreme Court's decisions in these cases must be seen as emanations of their time, and especially the social and political context of the early 1830s. Political arms of the USA had until that time treated American Indians mainly as sovereign entities, for example entering into treaties with them and legislating to regulate trade and intercourse with them in ways that respected their status as separate nations. Both of these facts were significant to Chief Justice Marshall. The broader significance of the Marshall doctrines of the 1830s include that American Indian peoples are outside the US Constitution; American Indian law is not subject to the USA Constitution.

However, the impact of residual sovereignty doctrine was curtailed by the judicial development of the doctrine of Congressional plenary power in the late 19th and early 20th centuries, by which time the American Indian had become physically dominated. In essence, Congressional plenary power authorises Congress to pass legislation applicable in Indian territories, which, if the legislation so provides, can be enforced in federal courts and takes precedence over Indian laws. It was initially described as a 'political' power little constrained by treaties between American Indians and the USA and not subject to judicial oversight.[18]

Suspicions from the academy and the judiciary about the legality of the Congress' plenary power doctrine pervade American Indian federal law and American Indian legal scholarship (Newton, 1984). Thomas J, in 2004, highlighted the tension between the 'incompatible and doubtful' assumptions of Congress' plenary power and tribes' residual sovereignty.[19] As he noted, Congress' plenary power is not sourced in the written US Constitution, which determines the scope of the powers of the arms of the USA government.

Instead, the initial justifications for Congress' plenary power included that the American Indian was, by 1886, within the geographical limits of the USA, under the political control of the United States government and the national government had exclusive sovereignty over the USA. The latter justification warrants particular circumspection given that it undermined the previous (and contemporary) understanding of the continuation of Indian residual sovereignty as the source of their ongoing law-making authority, as recognised for example in *Worcester v Georgia*. Other justifications, based on the fact of USA physical power, included that Indian tribes were 'wards' and 'dependent on the United States', including for the daily food.[20] As was stated, '[f]rom their very weakness and helplessness, so largely due to the course of dealing with the Federal Government with them and the treaties with which it has promised there arises a duty of protection, and with it the power'. Again, such a paternalistic rationale, and turning miserable facts into the basis for undermining Indian sovereignty, continue to upset American Indians. As Clinton, Goldberg and Tsosie have pointed out, it was part of a broader 'American will to empire and its growing reliance on colonial rule in place of notions of consent of the governed' at the time (2007).

Perhaps in the light of concerns about the legality, and justice, behind Congress' plenary power, it has been somewhat limited by the need for it to be express before it will oust Indian tribal jurisdiction.[21] Nonetheless, tense and often judicially-policed jurisdictional boundaries between federal, state and tribal law continue with questions over tribal jurisdiction over non-Indians and non-members being particularly fraught and contested.[22] Similarly, the extent of limitations on Congress' plenary power under fiduciary duties to Indian nations is contested.

Outside of basic questions about the extent of tribal sovereignty, federal Indian law has, as in Canada and New Zealand, oscillated considerably over the decades and centuries. Policy and law have gone from periods of assimilation through to the individualisation of Indian land title around the 1880s, to recognition of tribal authority under the Indian Reorganisation Act 1934, to the practice of terminating federal recognition of tribes and extending state jurisdiction over tribes in the 1950s to the rights-era of the 1960s and onwards. Today, the upshot of continued tribal sovereignty includes the general recognition of Indian jurisdiction and control over resources on tribal reservations, albeit subject to a checkerboard of Congressional legislation, some supportive of tribal authority and some less so.

The status of treaties between American Indians and the USA under constitutional law is different again from that of the legal status of treaties under Canadian or New Zealand constitutional law. They do not have the same 'higher' constitutional status as treaties between Indigenous groups and the state in Canada, but are not unenforceable unless incorporated into legislation as they are in New Zealand. Indian treaties, like any international treaty, have the constitutional status of 'the supreme law of the land', meaning they are akin, constitutionally, to federal legislation. The significance of this status was apparent in the controversial *Washington v Washington State Commercial Passenger Fishing Vessel Association* decision,[23] where the Supreme Court upheld the Yakima off-reservation fishing right, guaranteed under Treaty, interpreting the Treaty as it would have been understood by the Indians and as superior to conflicting state law. Only explicit statutory language in federal legislation could override a treaty right.

As in Canada, particularly pressing ongoing legal issues include rules regulating federal recognition of Indian groups as tribes and, also, tribal and state regulation of membership of Indian tribes (Gover, 2009). Federal recognition of a group of American Indians as a tribe is crucial for the tribe to receive continuing federal support, and well over 500 tribes are currently federally recognised. The rules regulating both inclusion on the register and the decisions made on their application are, and will continue to be, contentious.

In contrast to the USA, as mentioned, Canada and New Zealand have rarely, if ever, constitutionally acknowledged any ongoing Indigenous peoples' inherent sovereignty, although Canada's position has been changing over the last two decades. As described above, the concept that there may be more than one sovereign within a state – competing with the authority of Parliament – is an anathema to New Zealand's constitutional ethos and structure. In Canada, as mentioned, any law-making power exercised by First Nations under, say, the Indian Act, has been mostly perceived to be a power delegated from the state rather than inherent, maintaining the myth of unitary sovereignty. It may be that the USA's relative comfort with ongoing legal pluralism is influenced by its adherence to the constitutional principle, and belief in the advantages, of the separation of powers compared to the ongoing influence of the British doctrine of consolidation of ultimate sovereignty in one entity in Canada and New Zealand.

The constitutional situation of Hawaiians is somewhat more akin to that of Maori in that the USA annexation of Hawaii included the colonial assumption of absolute sovereignty over the islands, with no space for shared sovereignty with Indigenous Hawaiians. In a piecemeal transfer of power, which occurred over 11 years, first led by US citizens and then followed by eventual support from the US President and government, Hawaii was finally annexed by the USA in 1899, at which point the federal government assumed legislative jurisdiction over Hawaii. Hawaiian land loss was facilitated through US legislation, such as the Hawaiian Homes Commission Act 1921.

With the primary exception of specific legislation relating to Hawaiian ongoing interests in land, operated through the Office of Hawaiian Affairs, Hawaiians have been treated as, along with and equal to other inhabitants of the Hawaiian Islands, citizens of the state of Hawaii and the USA. Unlike American Indian tribes, their residual sovereignty has never been recognised and they exercise no separate jurisdiction over publicly regulated matters. Indeed, the Supreme Court has ruled that, unlike American Indians, Hawaiians are a racial grouping, meaning that distinct legal entitlements for native Hawaiians conflict with USA constitutional protections against discrimination.[24] A comparable case dealing with American Indians conceives of them as members of political groups, not racial groups, and thus unique legal entitlements do not discriminate contrary to the Constitution.[25]

Over the last two decades, moves have been made to address the legal wrongs suffered by Indigenous Hawaiians. For example, Congress officially apologised in 1993 for the role played by the USA in the overthrow of the Kingdom of Hawaii in 1893, albeit without assuming any corresponding legal responsibility. Since 2000, attempts have been made to pass legislation establishing a process for native Hawaiian groups to acquire federal recognition like that of Indian tribes. Native Hawaiians have taken different positions on its desirability, some rejecting it for not recognising full Hawaiian sovereignty, while others see it as an opportunity to assume some autonomous authority, albeit within the USA's constitutional structure.

Constitutional doctrine dealing with Alaskan Indigenous peoples differs again, and substantially, from that relating to American Indians and Hawaiians. The USA's claim to

Alaska comes from its purchase of Russian interests in Alaska in 1867, although the ability of Russia to pass on interests in the territory, inhabited by different Indigenous groups at the time, is questionable.

After World War II, the USA included Alaska on the United Nations list of non-self-governing territories entitled to decolonise, reflecting the extent to which Alaska was perceived to be a territorial entity jurisdictionally separate from the USA. However, in 1959 the USA removed Alaska from the non-self-governing list on the basis that it was to become a state, in accordance with the expressed wishes of the Alaskan population expressed in a referendum. Ongoing complaints against the referendum include that all those living in Alaska at the time were entitled to vote when Indigenous views should have taken precedence and that Alaskans who could not read or write, many of whom were indigenous, were excluded.

A short 12 years after Alaska attained statehood, and galvanised by the discovery of oil and gas in Alaska, the Alaska Native Claims Settlement Act was passed in 1971. It extinguished Indigenous Alaskan Aboriginal title in Alaska in return for shares in title to a smaller selection of state lands, amounting to approximately one-ninth of the state, and compensation. It also established a new regime of village and regional corporations to manage Indigenous Alaskan interests in their lands and resources, undermining traditional governance structures.

4   COMPARISONS IN CONSTITUTIONAL LAW RELEVANT TO INDIGENOUS PEOPLES: THE EXAMPLE OF THE APPLICATION OF HUMAN RIGHTS NORMS TO INDIGENOUS GOVERNANCE

Perhaps the most enlightening differences between constitutional law and Indigenous peoples in Canada, New Zealand and the USA can be seen when contrasting the outcome of legal action by an individual to seek Indigenous governance structures' compliance with constitutional human rights norms. Such a situation might, and does, arise where, say, an Indigenous governing body denies a woman tribal membership but not a man with similar qualifications for membership.

The application of state human rights norms to Indigenous governance squarely pitches Indigenous peoples' sovereignty, self-determination and cultural rights against some of the most highly prized values in Western liberal democracies like Canada, New Zealand and the USA, such as individual liberty and autonomy. It also touches on the debate between cultural relativism and universalism, the ideal hierarchy of individual and collective rights and is an area of significant contemporary contention in all three states. Concerns about Indigenous peoples' alleged and relative lack of attachment to individuals' rights are often raised as reasons why Canada, New Zealand and the USA philosophically struggle to accommodate Indigenous peoples' collective rights, including to governance (Kymlicka, 1995).

In Canada, if the exercise of tribal governance is an expression of an Aboriginal or treaty right protected by section 35 of the Constitution Act, it expressly takes precedence over human rights in the Canadian Charter of Rights and Freedoms under section 25. The only exception relates to discrimination between the sexes given that section 35(4) requires the application of Aboriginal and treaty rights to male and female persons equally. The problem from the tribal perspective, as we have seen, is that First Nations first have to prove they have an Aboriginal right to self-government,[26] which the Supreme Court has made difficult through the development of restrictive tests. The issue remains unresolved, however, as the

British Columbia Supreme Court decision of *Campbell* suggests some judicial recognition of residual First Nations governance might be possible in the future.[27]

If an Indigenous people practises governance power under legislation, such as membership determination powers under the Indian Act,[28] or in accordance with a contemporary agreement, which generally requires compliance with the Canadian Charter of Rights and Freedoms, Indigenous government will be required to comply with constitutional human rights guarantees.

In New Zealand, the situation is quite different given that the state does not recognise any ongoing Maori legal or governing authority other than that emanating from, or delegated from, the state. Accepted legal wisdom is that Maori customary law has no authority in the public domain unless it has been sanctioned by legislation, which is rare. Thus, the Bill of Rights Act, which only applies to the arms of state government and entities undertaking public functions, does not apply to, say, the application of custom in private settings.

However, a number of Maori organisations are potentially caught by the Bill of Rights Act 1990 as they take on public functions and acquire legislatively-delegated powers (Charters, 2003). Where Maori organisations attempt to exercise delegated power consistently with customary law, and it raises questions about their compliance with human rights, there is little scope within the structure and application of the Bill of Rights Act 1990 for nuanced analysis, especially the balancing of the philosophical premises behind Maori customary norms and human rights. Instead, questions about Maori compliance with human rights play out in the public domain, where Maori voice is in the minority.

In the USA, the basic position is that tribal law exercised in accordance with inherent residual tribal authority is not required to comply with the USA Constitution, including constitutional rights and freedoms. Yet, in 1968, Congress exercised its plenary power by passing the Indian Civil Rights Act (ICRA) and imposing a number of constitutional rights guarantees on tribal governments. The potential impact of the ICRA on tribal sovereignty has been mitigated, in the interests of respecting tribal sovereignty, by the Supreme Court's decision in *Santa Clara Pueblo v Martinez*.[29] The Court held that as the ICRA only expressly permits access to the federal courts to seek a remedy in relation to the writ of habeas corpus, complainants cannot seek federal enforcement of the other ICRA rights against the tribal governments: such remedies must be sought under the Indian legal system.

5 COMPARATIVE CONSTITUTIONAL LAW, INDIGENOUS PEOPLES, AND INTERNATIONAL LAW

Aboriginal peoples from Australia, American Indians, First Nations, Hawaiians, Maori, Metis, native Alaskans, Inuit and Metis have all brought attention to their circumstances, and called for recognition of their rights, in international fora, from the UN human rights institutions to the World Trade Organization (WTO) to the World Bank. In doing so they have profoundly influenced and in some cases even led the development of new and oftentimes strong norms to protect and respect the rights of Indigenous peoples at the international level. Similarly, Indigenous peoples have also created and exploited international spaces to question state authority over them, bringing debates about constitutional law relevant to indigenous peoples to external venues, which, in turn, influence domestic constitutional developments.

As mentioned, Canada, New Zealand and the USA have taken a similar stance to international Indigenous peoples' rights. None has ratified the ILO Convention 169 on Indigenous and Tribal Peoples and they initially opposed the UN Declaration on the Rights of Indigenous Peoples. Despite this, looking into the future, Canadian, New Zealand and the USA constitutional evolution will continue to be affected by evolving international jurisprudence on Indigenous peoples and particularly, in the case of Canada and the USA, that of the Inter-American Court and Inter-American Commission of Human Rights on Indigenous peoples' rights. This is true, even though, having not ratified the American Convention on Human Rights, Canada and the USA are not subject to the Court's jurisdiction. Inter-American jurisprudence strongly recognises Indigenous peoples' communal and collective property rights as well as rights to their natural resources, and reflects the growing trend in international jurisprudence more widely to give teeth to Indigenous peoples' territorial claims.[30] While there is no equivalent regional human rights system in the Pacific, New Zealand, like Canada and the USA, is constantly being questioned by international human rights bodies on its compliance with Indigenous peoples' norms, which was possibly influential in its decision to review and repeal the Foreshore and Seabed Act 2004.

6   CONTEMPORARY CONSTITUTIONAL TRENDS, LOOKING INTO THE FUTURE

Many scholars have commented on a relational approach to Indigenous peoples and state interaction in Canada, New Zealand and the USA, and elsewhere, that developed from the late 1970s, through the 1980s and into the 1990s (McHugh, 1998). Largely a result of Indigenous peoples' agitation and resistance, mentioned above, there are examples of the Canadian, New Zealand and USA governments responding with, for example, greater official recognition of Indigenous peoples' self-government and self-determination, especially in Canada and the USA respectively (McHugh, 2004). Concepts of partnership began to filter into official dialogue in all three (McHugh, 2004). Underlying a relational approach to Indigenous and state interaction, based on equality, is the idea that a political process based on partnership is better than one based on assimilation or one propelled by litigation. It also constitutes belated state-building in that it is an after-the-event attempt to legitimise state authority over its territories.

The shift to a more relational approach to Indigenous issues has been reflected in many ways. In Canada, it partly explains federal policy to recognise self-government as protected by section 35 and ongoing settlements that include the recognition of Indigenous law-making powers. In New Zealand, the establishment of the Waitangi Tribunal, the negotiation of settlements to provide some redress for historical grievances, the inclusion of Treaty of Waitangi principles in legislation, and so on, all realise, to some extent, the goal of working in partnership with iwi and hapu. In the USA, policies and laws recognising and facilitating greater American Indian governance achieve the same.

While it would be unfair to say that state law and policy have regressed to the paternalistic and assimilationist patterns common prior to the 1970s, and for the century prior to that, it is clear that there have been pressures on the relational approach to state and Indigenous peoples' interaction over the last decade. The most vivid illustration of this is, of course, Canada, New Zealand and the USA's initial approach to the UN Declaration and statements that recognition of Indigenous peoples' rights must not come at the expense of non-Indigenous peoples' rights.[31] In Canada, ongoing agitation around, for example, continuing exploitation of Lubicon Lake Band territories for oil and gas exploitation and violence against Indigenous women highlights gaps in Canadian Indigenous policy. In New Zealand, the Executive and Parliament joined forces to pass legislation extinguishing land rights and the Executive has rejected a number of Waitangi Tribunal decisions, suggesting a broader political fatigue with Maori issues and renaissance. Concerns about the fairness and, consequentially, the longevity of settlements between iwi and the Crown are being voiced vociferously. In the USA, failures to adequately protect Indigenous peoples' lands and address Indigenous Alaskan and Hawaiian claims attract human rights censure.[32] For Indigenous peoples, this means that renewed and constant vigilancy is necessary to ensure continued and greater respect and protection of their rights into the future. For constitutional law as it relates to Indigenous peoples in Canada, New Zealand and the USA, it means that it is likely that the legal landscape will continue to oscillate in response to changing political, social, cultural and demographic dynamics.

7   COMPARATIVE CONSTITUTIONAL SCHOLARSHIP ON INDIGENOUS PEOPLES IN CANADA, NEW ZEALAND, AND THE USA

Both similarities and differences between the constitutional approach to Indigenous peoples in Canada, New Zealand and the USA inform and complicate comparative constitutional scholarship on Indigenous peoples. Overall, there is a greater difference between the constitutional approaches to Indigenous peoples in New Zealand and the USA than between those of Canada and New Zealand or those of Canada and the USA, perhaps explaining the relative dearth of comparative scholarship focused on comparing New Zealand and the USA (exceptions include Miller and Ruru, 2009). Moreover, there is generally more comparative scholarship, certainly in the form of edited collections (for example, Havemann, 1999), comparing Australia, Canada and New Zealand, and excluding the USA, perhaps reflecting the closer proximity those states' constitutions retain to that of the United Kingdom. Until Canada moved to a strong-form judicial review model to protect rights in 1982, Australia, Canada and New Zealand had weak-form judicial review models for rights, like the United Kingdom. In contrast, the USA has had a famously long-standing strong-form model of judicial review of rights.

Further, with some exceptions (Getches et al., 2005), scholarship in the USA, and from scholars based in the USA, on Indigenous legal issues appears to be less comparative in nature than, say, scholarship from Australia, Canada and New Zealand, where a number of collaborative research projects have been undertaken. In the USA, scholars appear to be more focused on issues arising within the USA jurisdiction, and international developments, than on other jurisdictions. Indeed, there are a number of cases where contributions on comparative constitutional law and Indigenous peoples from a USA perspective are written by scholars based outside and not from the USA (Richardson, 2009; McHugh, 2004; Russell, 2005). Generally, experience indicates that there is greater academic traffic between Australia, Canada and New Zealand on the law and Indigenous peoples.

Particular areas of law lend themselves to greater comparative analysis. Where similarities in constitutional and legal doctrine are common, such as in the development of the doctrine of Aboriginal title, often called original title in the US context, abound, nuances between the jurisdictions can be isolated. In areas of law marked with greater difference, such as the legal approach to treaties between Indigenous peoples and states, more general, less definitive, comparisons can be drawn. The difference between constitutional approaches to Indigenous peoples makes drawing analogies difficult, like comparing apples and pears. However, comparisons between types of constitutional structure coupled with an assessment of the degree of protection of respective types of Indigenous peoples' rights, for example land rights, are illuminating. They suggest, albeit baldly, that certain types of constitutional structure and method may be systemically better, or worse, in realising Indigenous interests.

Overall, comparative constitutional law scholarship related to Indigenous peoples is often revealing and instructive, and incorporates much history and politics also, as is appropriate (McHugh, 2004). Examples of good and bad practices in one state can, and do, inform law reform and policy shifts in another. Equally, especially Australian, Canadian and New Zealand courts have taken cognisance of one another's jurisprudence, for example and notably in relation to Aboriginal title, and drawn on US judicially-developed principles.

Comparative constitutional scholarship and dialogue on Indigenous issues are robust, alive, critical and challenging. One weakness is perhaps that much work, as Ruru has pointed out, consists in edited books, which, 'while instrumental, consist of chapters that are mostly written with one country in mind, albeit united under certain themes' (2007, 428). However, the work of scholars such as McHugh (2004), Russell (2005) and Scholtz (2006), which expertly examine Indigenous peoples and the law in Australia, Canada, New Zealand and the USA together, make up for much of the singular jurisdictional focus found in collaborative books.

NOTES

1. *Johnson v McIntosh* 21 US (8 Wheart.) 543 (1823).
2. *Rex v Syliboy* [1929] 1 DLR 307 (NS Co Ct) 313.
3. (1992) 175 CLR 1.
4. *Campbell v Hall* (1774) Loft 655.
5. *Delgamuukw v British Columbia* [1997] 3 SCR 1010.
6. *R v Marshall* [1999] 3 SCR 1075.
7. *Delgamuukw v British Columbia* [1997] 3 SCR 1010.
8. *R v Pamajewon* [1996] 2 SCR 221.
9. *R v Sparrow* [1990] 1 SCR 1075.
10. *Haida Nation v British Columbia (Minister of Forests)*, [2004] 3 SCR 511.
11. See, for example, *McIvor v Canada (Registrar of Indian and Northern Affairs)* (2009) BCCA 153 and *Scrimbett v Sakimay Band Council* (2000) 1 CNLR 205 (FCC T Div).
12. *Wi Parata v The Bishop of Wellington* (1877) 3 NZJur 72 (SC).
13. *Ngati Apa v AG* [2003] 3 NZLR 643.
14. *New Zealand Maori Council v Attorney General* [1987] 1 NZLR 641.
15. *Te Weehi v Regional Fisheries Officer* [1986] 1 NZLR 680 (HC).
16. *Cherokee Nation v Georgia* (1831) 30 US 1; and *Worcester v Georgia* (1832) 31 US (6 Pet) 515.
17. 31 US (6 Pet) 515 (1832).
18. *Lone Wolf v Hitchcock* 187 US 533 (1903).
19. *US v Lara* 541 US 193 (2004).
20. *US v Kagama* 118 US 375 (1886).
21. *Santa Clara Pueblo v Martinez* 436 US 49 (1977).

22. See, for example, questions of civil and criminal jurisdiction over non-Indians in *Oliphant v Squamish Indian Tribe* 435 US 191 (1978); *Duro v Reina* 495 US 676 (1990); and *Nevada v Hicks* 533 US 353 (2001).
23. 443 US 658 (1979).
24. *Rice v Cayetano, Governor of Hawaii* (2000) 528 US 495.
25. *Morton v Mancari* (1974) 417 US 535.
26. *Scrimbett v Sakimay Band Council* [2000] 1 CNLR 205.
27. *Campbell v British Columbia (Attorney General)* (2000) DLR (4th) 333 (BCSC).
28. *McIvor v Canada (Registrar of Indian and Northern Affairs)* (2009) BCCA 153.
29. 436 US 49 (1977).
30. *Saramaka People v Suriname* (Preliminary Objections, Merits, Reparations, and Costs). I/A Court H.R., Judgment of 28 November 2007. Series C No. 172.
31. UN General Assembly Department of Public Information, *General Assembly Adopts Declaration on the Rights of Indigenous Peoples* (New York, 13 September 2007), available at http://www.un.org/News/Press/docs/2007/ga10612.doc.htm (last accessed 1 April 2010).
32. UN Human Rights Committee, *Concluding Observations of the Human Rights Committee: United States of America* UN Doc CCPR/C/USA/CO/3/Rev.1 (18 December 2006).

REFERENCES

Books

Anghie, Antony, *Imperialism, Sovereignty and the Making of International Law* (Cambridge University Press, Cambridge, 2004).
Brookfield, F.M., *Waitangi and Indigenous Rights: Revolution, Law and Legitimation*, 2nd edition (Auckland University Press, Auckland, 2007).
Clinton, Robert N., Carol E. Goldberg and Rebecca Tsosie, *American Indian Law: Native Nations and the Federal System: Cases and Materials*, 5th edition (LexisNexis, New Providence, NJ, 2007).
Getches, David H., Charles F. Wilkinson and Robert A. Williams, *Cases and Materials on Federal Indian Law,* 5th edition (Thomson West, St Paul, MN, 2005).
Kymlicka, Will, *The Rights of Minority Cultures* (Oxford University Press, New York, 1995).
McHugh, P.G., *Aboriginal Rights and the Common Law: A History of Sovereignty, Status and Law* (Oxford University Press, Oxford, 2004).
Palmer, Matthew, *The Treaty of Waitangi and New Zealand's Law and Constitution* (VUW Press, Victoria University of Wellington, 2008).
Russell, Peter H., *Recognizing Aboriginal Title: The Mabo Case and Indigenous Resistance to English-Settler Colonialism* (Toronto University Press, Toronto, 2005).
Scholtz, Christa, *Negotiating Claims: The Emergence of Indigenous Land Claim Negotiation Policies in Australia, Canada, New Zealand and the United States* (Routledge, New York, 2006).

Edited Books

Havemann, Paul (ed.), *Indigenous Peoples' Rights in Australia, Canada and New Zealand* (Oxford University Press, Auckland, 1999).
Richardson, Benjamin J., Shin Imai and Kent McNeil (eds), *Indigenous Peoples and the Law: Comparative and Critical Perspectives* (Osgoode Readers, Hart Publishing, Oxford, 2009).

Journal Articles

Barsh, Russel, 'Putting the Tribe in Tribal Courts: Possible? Desirable?' (1999) 8 *Kansas Journal of Law and Public Policy* 74.
Charters, Claire, 'Maori, Beware the Bill of Rights Act!' [2003] *New Zealand Law Review* 401.
Charters, Claire, 'BORA and Maori: Fundamental Issues' [2003] *New Zealand Law Review* 459.
Charters, Claire, 'Responding to Waldron's Defence of Legislatures: Why New Zealand's Parliament Does Not Protect Rights in Hard Cases' [2006] *New Zealand Law Review* 621.
Charters, Claire, 'Do Maori Rights Discriminate Against Non-Maori?' (2009) 40(3) *Victoria University of Wellington Law Review* 649.

Cohen, Felix S., 'The Erosion of Indian Rights, 1950–1953: A Case Study in Bureaucracy' (1953) 62 *Yale Law Journal* 348.
Geiringer, Claudia, 'On a Road to Nowhere: Implied Declaration of Inconsistency and the New Zealand Bill of Rights Act' (2009) 40(3) *Victoria University of Wellington Law Review* 613.
Gover, Kirsty, 'Genealogy as Continuity: Explaining the Growing Preference for Descent Rules in United States Tribal Membership Governance' (2009) 33(1) *American Indian Law Review*.
Miller, Robert J. and Jacinta Ruru, 'An Indigenous Lens into Comparative Law: The Doctrine of Discovery in the United States and New Zealand' (2009) 111 *West Virginia Law Review* 849.
Newton, Nell Jessup, 'Federal Power over Indians: Its Sources, Scope, and Limitations' (1984) 132 *University of Pennsylvania Law Review* 195.
Palmer, Matthew, 'New Zealand Constitutional Culture' (2007) 22 *New Zealand Universities Law Review* 567.

Book Chapters

McHugh, P.G., 'Aboriginal Identity and Relations in North America and Australasia', in Ken S. Coates and P.G. McHugh, *Living Relationships – Kokiri Ngatahi: The Treaty of Waitangi in the New Millennium* (Victoria University Press, Wellington, 1998) 107.
McNeil, Kent, 'Legal Rights and Legislative Wrongs: Maori Claims to the Foreshore and Seabed', in Claire Charters and Andrew Erueti (eds), *Maori Property Rights and the Foreshore and Seabed: The Law Frontier* (Victoria University of Wellington Press, Wellington, 2007).
Richardson, Benjamin J., 'The Dyadic Character of US Indian Law', in Benjamin J. Richardson, Shin Imai and Kent McNeil (eds), *Indigenous Peoples and the Law: Comparative and Critical Perspectives* (Osgoode Readers, Hart Publishing, Oxford, 2009) 51.
Russell, Peter H., 'Indigenous Self-determination: Is Canada as Good as it Gets?', in Barbara Hocking (ed.), *Unfinished Constitutional Business? Rethinking Indigenous Self-Determination* (Aboriginal Studies Press, Canberra, 2005) 170.
Walters, Mark D., 'Promise and Paradox: The Emergence of Indigenous Rights in Canadian Law', in Benjamin J. Richardson, Shin Imai and Kent McNeil (eds), *Indigenous Peoples and the Law: Comparative and Critical Perspectives* (Osgoode Readers, Hart Publishing, Oxford, 2009) 21.

Book Reviews

Jacinta, Ruru, 'Book Review: *Recognizing Aboriginal Title: The Mabo Case and Indigenous Resistance to English-Settler Colonialism* by Peter H. Russell (Toronto: Toronto University Press, 2005)' (2007) 45(2) *Osgoode Hall Law Journal* 425.

11. A new global constitutional order?
*David Schneiderman**

Accompanying the rise of new transnational legal rules and institutions intended to promote global economic integration are questions about the linkages between transnational legality and constitutional law. In what ways does transnational economic law mimic features of national constitutional law? Does transnational law complement in some ways or supersede in other ways what we typically describe as constitutional law? To these questions we can now add the following: are transnational rules and institutions a proper subject of study for comparative constitutionalists? This chapter makes a case for the incorporation of forms of transnational legality into comparative constitutional studies.[1] Taking as my focus the regime of international investment law, I argue that an appreciation of the constitutional functions of transnational legality deepens understandings of how constitutional law develops within, across and beyond national systems of law. More specifically, elements of transnational legality can help to explain the phenomenon of convergence and divergence in constitutional law. This expansion of the comparativist's toolkit of resources, though challenging conventional understandings of constitutional law as grounded exclusively in states, better captures current developments.

Comparative constitutionalists traditionally have been preoccupied with the identification of difference and similarity between families of national constitutional systems (see e.g. Finer 1979). Today, the dominant trend among comparative constitutionalists is to seek out not just differences and similarities but convergence. With a focus on judicial branches operating within national constitutional systems, proportionality review typically is singled out as evidence of an emerging worldwide consensus in constitutional matters (Beatty 2004; Kumm 2009). For those states not participating in this global convergence on standards of review – the United States usually is singled out for this exceptionalism, though this is not an entirely accurate representation (Gardbaum 2008) – they simply will have missed out on the manna of the post-war rights model (Weinrib 2002). That this convergence has occurred at the very same time as global economic integration has proceeded at a breathtaking pace plays little role in these analyses. Instead, there is a strange separation between global political economy and rights (Schneiderman 2002). The constitutionalization of property rights, to be sure, has been the subject of some important comparative work (Alexander 2006; Allen 2000; Van der Walt 1999) but, even here, the scholarship mostly is divorced from the simultaneous movement toward greater economic integration. Outside of work on the World Trade Organization (WTO) and the European Union (EU) – which invite such linkages (Fligstein and Stone Sweet 2002; Joerges and Neyer 2006) – this is the case with very few exceptions.[2]

In the text that follows, I contrast scholarly approaches by distinguishing between 'constitutionalism as project' and 'constitutionalism as critique',[3] roughly tracking the distinction between those who submerge the simultaneous spread of rights discourse and global economic relations and those who noisily take note of it. In the first, ascribing constitutional features to aspects of transnational legality is undertaken not only to uncover as yet unrecognized features of this new legal order but as part of a normative project of stabilization and legitimation (Kennedy 2009: 40). Global constitutionalism as 'project' has as its object the improvement of institutions for 'global governance'. Constitutionalism becomes a resource for entrenching global best practices around limited government and market reforms (Rittich 2006). Constitutionalism as critique, by contrast, brings power and political economy back into the folds of transnational legality, reconnecting the spread of rights discourse to the end game of removing barriers to trade, persons and capital.[4] Critical constitutionalism is an approach that best captures, I argue below, recent trends driving toward global constitutional engagement, even convergence.[5] Though some scholarship bridges these divides,[6] it is fair to conclude that project constitutionalism is the dominant mode of inquiry today. By contrast, I advance a critical mode of inquiry by taking up the case of international investment law. Irrespective of which account is favoured, I hope to show how transnational legal norms and forms associated with economic globalization should be considered part of comparative constitutional law's frame of inquiry.

The discussion proceeds as follows. First, I turn to the problem of stretching the constitutional analogy beyond the borders of national states and, in so doing, contrast project- and critique-constitutionalist approaches. I then take up the investment rules regime in some detail as a form of transnational constitutional law, examining its dominant features and linkages to national constitutional law. Lastly, I turn to contending non-constitutional interpretations of international investment law and suggest that, whatever the explanatory power of each of the counter-claims, they are best understood as part of a larger debate about which features of the new global legal order are deserving of the moniker 'constitutional'.[7]

1   CONSTITUTIONALIST PROJECTS

In the face of emergent transnational legal orders whose implications are only beginning to be understood, it comes as little surprise that analysts will look to tools readily at hand (Tushnet 1999: 1286) and assimilate these orders under the rubric of constitutionalism. In the many domains in which transnational law dominates, constitutional ideas have migrated (Choudhry 2006) in order to make sense of what is partially coming into view. John Jackson, for instance, describes the Uruguay Round World Trade Organization (WTO) system as a constitution for international trade relations (1997: 339). By this, he means to describe both the structure of rules that constitute the international trading system and the constraints they impose on governments. Jackson is not naïve about the linkages between national constitutional systems and the emergent trade constitution: both inform each other, he observes (1997: 340). McGinnis and Movsevian (2000) push the analogy even further, arguing the WTO institutionalizes Madisonian checking functions so as to deter factionalism in the international economic system by establishing a 'world trade constitution'. Petersmann (2000) goes so far as to promote a fully constitutionalized trade and human rights system at the global level through the WTO. These descriptive and normative accounts of the WTO have been subject to critiques by Cass who finds that the WTO falls well short of the typical markers of a 'fully constitutionalized entity' (2005: 19; Walker 2001: 50; Walker 2002: 355) while Howse and Nicolaïdis (2001) claim that conceiving of the WTO as constitutionalized is a counterproductive response to the WTO's legitimacy crisis (also Dunoff 2006). Rather than raising WTO dispute settlement to a 'higher law' that is above the fray, what is needed is more politics, not less (Howse and Nicolaïdis 2001: 229).

Moving beyond the multilateral trading system, theorists have been inspired by Kant's sketch of a 'perpetual peace' based on a federation of republican states (1795). Habermas (2006) suggests that a global constitutional law can be managed not by a new global state but, following Kant, by intermediary federated institutions such as those of a reformed United Nations. Koskenniemi (2007) looks to constitutionalism in international law as a way of endowing human suffering with normative meaning through the constitutional norms of equality, autonomy and human dignity, while Kumm (2009) discerns a new cosmopolitan law, drawing on the European Court of Human Rights experience, premised on a framework of proportionality and subsidiarity. National constitutional law is legitimate for Kumm only to the extent that it is conceived as part of a new cosmopolitan paradigm.

How well do these constitutionalist accounts translate to newly operative global legal regimes (Walker 2003)? The answer turns, in part, on whether one conceives of constitutionalism as thin or thick. In its thin conception, constitutionalism refers to laws that establish and regulate groups and associations (Raz 1998: 153). Teubner, drawing on Luhmann's systems theory (2004),[8] describes the turn to global constitutionalism as reflecting a 'multiplicity of civil constitutions' emerging outside of states initiated by various actors operating in autonomous global sectors – whether they be transnational corporations, federated trade unions or human rights networks (Teubner 2004: 8). These turn out to be specialized centers of law production that are 'independent global villages' or sub-constitutions of a world society (Teubner 2004: 14). Teubner's account turns out to be a legal pluralist one (Berman 2007), resembling early twentieth-century British political pluralist formulations (Hirst 1989). Thinner versions, it would appear to be the case, translate relatively well to the global level. Thicker versions refer to constitutional features such as the separation of powers, fundamental rights or judicial supremacy (Raz 1998: 153) and seemingly appear more difficult to translate. Walker (2002), for instance, wishes to distinguish between societal constitutionalism or legal pluralism per se (resembling the thin version) and constitutional pluralism (akin to the thicker one). In the European context, this means moving beyond the inter-state paradigm of constitutional monism in the direction of a heterarchical pluralism in which the European order 'makes its own independent constitutional claims . . . [which] exist alongside the continuing claims of states' (Walker 2002: 337). Stone Sweet similarly observes that certain treaty regimes, like the European one, are constitutional as they are 'built on a normative foundation that is very similar to higher-law constitutions' and so are overlaid onto existing national constitutional spaces (Stone Sweet 2009; Stone Sweet 1994).

A number of objections immediately arise. At base, these regimes appear to lack the basic element of a liberal constitutional order: a constituent authority or *demos*. A common rejoinder is to say that, at least in the EU case, this is an example of a quasi-constitutional legal order that is only beginning to work out fully its idea of constitutionalism (Weiler 1999: 8; Joerges and Neyer 2006). Alternatively, one might say that these are instances (in the long history of the subject) of constitutionalism without a *demos* (Newton 2006: 330). Others object on the basis that it is inappropriate or simply beyond credulity to stretch constitutionalism beyond the state (Walker 2008: 520–22). One might reply by saying that, at a functional level, transnational legal regimes exhibit constitution-like features and employ techniques and discourses familiar to national constitutional law (Dunoff and Trachtman 2009a: 9). To this end, constitutionalism is 'a prism through which one can observe a landscape' and isolate certain of its features (Weiler and Trachtman 1996–7: 359). At a normative level, if one understands constitutionalism as an open-ended project under construction rather than a fully realized accomplishment – as an 'ethical discourse under a constant process of re-imagining and reconstruction' (Walker 2008: 525) – then postnational constitutionalism becomes not only a possibility but, for some, an imperative. Here arises one common animating concern among much meta-level constitutional theorizing. Almost all of these accounts have the object of positively identifying nascent or extant transnational constitutionalism for the purpose of pursuing 'constitutionalism as a project' (Kennedy 2009: 40). By way of contrast, I turn next to a mode of constitutional analysis that has as its object not legitimation but critique. It is this critical edge that helps to make this mode of transnational analysis advantageous to comparative constitutionalists.

2   CONSTITUTIONAL CRITIQUES

I have in mind a critical discourse that brings power, history and political economy back into view. It is an approach that best captures the rise of a 'new constitutionalism' – a term coined by Stephen Gill (2003) to describe the worldwide political project to shrink political authority over markets and to replicate mythical paths to development of wealthy, capital-exporting states. If constitutional design concerns itself, in part, with the proper relationship between politics and markets – about regulating the amount of politics to let into markets – then the model of development associated with the 'Washington consensus' has been preoccupied with placing constitution-like limits on exercises of political power (Rittich 2006: 221; Dezalay and Garth 2002: c. 10). New constitutionalist proposals, writes Gill, are 'intended to "lock in" commitments to liberal forms of development, frameworks of accumulation and of dispossession so that global governance is premised on the primacy of the world market' (Gill 2008: 254; 2003: 132). There are a number of features that this work shares with other critical approaches to globalization (Mittelman 2004: 224–5): it is reflexive about the interests served by the rules and institutions of globalization (Bourdieu 2000: 70); it is attentive to the historical and national contexts out of which emerge these rules and institutions (Santos 2002: 179); it does not presume to defend the vested interests of powerful economic actors and resists being preoccupied exclusively with 'northern theory' (Connell 2006); and, methodologically, insists upon interdisciplinarity as the most appropriate means of understanding the phenomenon associated with globalization (Rosamond 2006). The literature collectively aims to locate openings whereby law, politics and economy can be reconnected, whether inside or outside of the national state.

A few scholars have taken up the new constitutionalist research agenda, principally examining developments internal to national constitutional systems. Hirschl, for instance, describes the advent of judicial review under new constitutions in Canada, Israel, New Zealand and South Africa as generated principally by self-interested elites seeking to insulate their hegemonic rule from democratic impulse (2004: 99). Kelsey takes up the case of the Supreme Court of the Philippines which approved ascension to the WTO by effectively reading out of the Philippines constitution its strong economic nationalist discourse (1999: 515). Teivainen explores new constitutionalist strategies deployed by Peruvian President Fujimori in the 1990s to freeze and then de-regulate state mechanisms for steering markets (2002: 164).[9]

Gill described a new constitutionalism operating at both local and global scales (1995: 81–6), and so had in mind not only macro-institutional reform within national states but disparate international legal formations that promote privatization and free trade, such as the International Monetary Fund (IMF) and the WTO, or regional arrangements such as the EU and the North American Free Trade Agreement (NAFTA). I have attended to the transnational dimension of the new constitutionalism by focusing on the legal regime to promote and protect foreign investment (Schneiderman 2008).[10] A regime made up of some 2,700 bilateral investment treaties (BITs), together with a small number of regional trade and investment treaties (UNCTAD 2009a: 32), it exhibits, at a functional level, constitution-like features and, at a normative level, is intended to spread 'market-friendly human rights' worldwide for investors and citizens alike (Baxi 2006). I have described the regime's ensemble of rules and institutions as a form of precommitment strategy (following Elster 1984) that binds future generations to certain forms and substantive norms by which politics is practised. Like constitutions, they are difficult to amend, include binding enforcement mechanisms, and oftentimes draw on the language and experience of national constitution systems (Schneiderman 2008: 4). These limits on state action are enforceable not only by states party to these agreements but by foreign investors themselves – the great innovation of this form of transnational legality (Lauterpacht 1997).

Investment treaties guarantee a variety of substantive rights to investors that are analogous to those found in national constitutional systems, among them non-discrimination rights (or national treatment) and prohibitions against takings (nationalization and expropriation or equivalent measures) (Been and Beauvais 2003). A 'fair and equitable treatment' standard has been interpreted in ways analogous to a due process clause (ibid.) and to clauses guaranteeing the enforceability of contracts. Each of these standards of protection has their counterpart in the national constitutional systems of capital-exporting states, principally norms associated with rights to property and to contract. The promotion of the takings rule in the Fifth and Fourteenth Amendments to the US constitution, for instance, is emblematic of efforts to have local law ascend to the plane of the universal (Schneiderman 2008: c. 2). It is this desire – what has been called a 'Fourteenth Amendment psychology' (Wild 1939: 10) – that undoubtedly has animated both US and western European attitudes toward the protection of property and contract under international law (Williams 1928: 24). Some will deny that investment rules pedigrees are traceable back to the constitutional norms of economically powerful states (e.g. Ratner 2008). Whatever their precise origins, it turns out that investment rules, in practice, impose harsher restraints than even these national constitutional systems would permit. This helps to explain the response of the US Congress to expansive interpretations of the takings rule by international investment tribunals, discussed further below. Latitudinal interpretations precipitated reform to US model treaty text, as mandated by the Trade Promotion Authority Act of 2002, so that treaty practice fell back into line with domestic constitutional practice.

As mentioned, enforcement mechanisms (dispute resolution procedures) are available not only to states party to these investment treaties. Investors are entitled to seek damages for regulatory initiatives that may run afoul of these laconic entitlements. Investors need not exhaust local remedies (*Lanco International* 2001) nor need their connection to the home state be any more tangible than the place of incorporation (*Aguas del Tunari* 2004). For these and related reasons, the regime has been described as the 'most effectively enforceable in the international system' (Alvarez 2009: 565). Typically, resolution of investment disputes is sought before arbitration tribunals hosted by facilities such as the International Centre for the Settlement of Investment Disputes (ICSID) located at the World Bank or under rules promulgated by the

United Nations Commission on International Trade Law (UNCITRAL). Awards usually are then enforceable within the defaulting state's national system of courts. Van Harten likens international investment arbitration to adjudication of public law matters in national high courts, entitling investors to seek review of 'governmental choices regarding the regulatory relationship between individuals and the state' (2007: 10). For these reasons, this form of transnational legality has the potential to subject a myriad of national law-making and law-administering authority to investment law disciplines that mimic constitutional strictures.

That international investment law has attributes making it remarkably similar to national constitutional law was admitted by arbitrator Bryan Schwartz in the case of *S.D. Myers* (2001). Because trade and investment agreements like NAFTA, he wrote in a separate opinion, 'have an enormous impact on public affairs in many countries', Schwartz likened these agreements to 'a country's constitution' as they 'restrict the ways in which governments can act and they are very hard to change'. While governments usually have the right to withdraw with notice, Schwartz admits that this 'is often practically impossible to do'. 'Pulling out of a trade agreement may create too much risk of reverting to trade wars, and may upset the settled expectations of many participants in the economy', he observes. Amendment is made no easier, he writes, 'just as it is usually very hard to change a provision of a domestic constitution' (*S.D. Myers* 2001 [separate opinion]: paras 33–4). This is no argument, then, that transnational legal forms supersede (in a technical sense) national constitutional formations. Nor is this to claim that it is impossible to terminate these agreements – Ecuador in 2009 terminated nine BITs that it considered oppressive and with little impact on attracting new inward investment (UNCTAD 2009b). Though rescission can be done unilaterally, investments established under the auspices of these treaties continue to benefit from their protections, typically, for a period of ten to fifteen years. The point, instead, is that they resemble national constitutional texts in important respects and, because of the resilience of constitutional discourse, together with the surveillance of international actors and financial institutions, render investment rules difficult to escape. Tully's suggestive formulation of an 'informal paramountcy', likely drawing on Canadian constitutional doctrine,[11] captures this sort of relationship. Transnational law is paramount (or supreme) only in an informal, rather than in a formal and positivistic, way (Tully 2008: 260).

For critical constitutionalists, analogizing to constitutionalism reveals real problems with the investment rules regime and this gives rise to legitimacy problems that project constitutionalists aim to resolve. First, the regime purports to determine the appropriate balance between states and markets – a subject that remains one of the most significant aspects of statecraft and constitutional design. That this problem is resolved in ways that structurally tilt regulatory solutions to public problems away from states and in favour of markets is a contestable and often crude formulation. Rather than enabling state-market relations to be more fluid and open to change and innovation – one of the great virtues of democratic practice (Tocqueville 2000: 202) – the regime embraces a constitution-like rigidity (see Bryce 1901). Second, there is virtue in endowing states with the capacity to change course – to have what Weiss calls 'transformational capacity' (1998: 5) – in response to changing international economic environments.[12] This is a capacity that corresponds well to the competitive environment in which states find themselves. States should be equipped, then, to respond to the multitude of risks and challenges they currently confront (Rodrik 2007: 176). Third, diversified responses to current socio-economic challenges facilitate development strategies better suited to complement the needs of specific political communities at differing stages of development (North 2005: 164). Rather than mimic mythical paths to development promoted by wealthy states (Chang 2002; Schneiderman 2008), developing states should have the capacity – belied by any new global constitutional order – not only to change course but to experiment and innovate in unorthodox ways (Rodrik 2002: 9).

3 THE INVESTMENT RULES REGIME

It follows from both the project- and critical-constitutionalist accounts that international investment arbitration is generating a corpus of constitutional law that should be of interest to comparative constitutionalists. Consider the *Metalclad* case (2001), concerning the shuttering of a hazardous waste facility site in Guadalcazar, Mexico. The site, previously closed down by the Mexican federal government for having leeched waste into local water supplies, was purchased by Metalclad Corporation of Newport Beach California in 1993. As the site was being expanded and remediated, *campesinos* expressed opposition to its reopening by blocking access to the site while municipal authorities refused to grant necessary construction permits (it was alleged that Mexican federal authorities misled the investor into thinking such permits were unnecessary) (Schneiderman 2008: 82–6). Ultimately, the governor of the state effectively terminated Metalclad's operations by declaring the site part of an ecological reserve for the protection of rare cactus. An international investment tribunal concluded that there was a compensable expropriation under NAFTA and that its takings rule caught not only the outright seizure of property by the host state but also 'covert or incidental interference with the use of property which has the effect of depriving the owner, in whole or in significant part, of the use or reasonably-to be-expected[13] economic benefit of property even if not necessarily to the obvious benefit of the host State' (*Metalclad* 2001: para. 103).[14] Resembling the per se rule in takings doctrine under US constitutional law (*Lucas* 1992; Dana and Merrill 2002: 94 ff),[15] the ruling went significantly further than even US Fifth Amendment doctrine would have allowed in the circumstances, observe Been and Beauvais (2003: 128). Indeed, it is pretty clear that the high standards implied by the investment regime's takings rule would never be tolerated within operative national constitutional systems (Dolzer 1981: 575). More startling was the tribunal's finding that there was a denial of 'fair and equitable treatment' under NAFTA by reason of the 'improper' denial of the permit by the municipality 'for any reason other than those related to the physical construction or defects in the site' (*Metalclad* 2001: para. 86). The municipality, the tribunal concluded, had acted beyond its constitutional capacity in denying Metalclad its construction permit despite Mexico's constitutional submissions to the contrary (*Metalclad* 2001: para. 81). Mysteriously, the tribunal preferred the investor's interpretation that federal authority resided within the jurisdiction of the federal government and that the city had no authority to take into account environmental concerns in the issuance of municipal construction permits. What the tribunal accomplished, observe Frug and Barron, was to incorporate the functional equivalent of a rule of US municipal law into international investment law (2006: 44),[16] Dillon's Rule, a late-nineteenth-century canon regulating constitutional relations between state and local government and intended to preserve private property from local government action,[17] 'empowers the central government to determine the legitimacy of a city's attempt to subject private actors to novel regulations of their conduct' (Frug and Barron 2006: 4343). The tribunal's ruling in *Metalclad* mimics this antipathy to local authority in circumstances where the central government has not condoned intrusions into the private sphere. The point is not that the tribunal uncontroversially held national authority responsible under the treaty for the misconduct of sub-national authority. Rather, the problem is that the tribunal purported to settle a matter of constitutional interpretation over the objections of the presumably more authoritative national government, in which case, Mexico's objections either were made in bad faith (of which the tribunal made no finding) or simply wrong and that international investment lawyers knew better.

From another angle, one might consider the case of *CMS* (2005), one of a surfeit of disputes filed against Argentina arising out of measures taken to abate the financial meltdown of 2001 (generally, Alvarez and Khamsi 2009). Having lured investors to take over public utilities at certain fixed rates, Argentina unilaterally modified the terms and conditions of licenses and framework legislation in order to abate the economic crisis. As tariffs were no longer being converted into US dollars, Michigan-based CMS filed a claim for damages under a US-Argentina BIT. CMS insisted that the government had guaranteed a rate of return on its investment regardless of financial hardship to the state and its citizens (*CMS* 2005: para. 66). The investment tribunal agreed that profits were to be guaranteed irrespective of the financial situation on the ground, finding that the promise of conversion to US dollars amounted to a denial of 'fair and equitable treatment'. There could be little doubt that, the tribunal unanimously wrote, 'a stable legal and business environment is an essential element of fair and equitable treatment' (*CMS* 2005: paras 274, 284). The operative legal framework, together with the operating license, was in the nature of a 'guarantee' that these undertakings would bind the state far into the future (*CMS* 2005: para. 161).[18] The harsh rigidity underlying these rulings matches, even exceeds, early interpretations of the US Constitution's prohibition on states 'impairing the obligation of contracts'[19] (see *Dartmouth College* 1819).[20] It also resembles late nineteenth-century prejudice against class- or special-interest legislation that disrupts the seeming neutrality of the *status quo ante* (Sunstein 1993: 41; Gillman 1993).

Not only is a nascent constitutional order observable from outside the borders of national states, renovation is occurring within states as well. This is not merely to take note of the myriad ways in which international law gets incorporated into the domestic law of national states via established constitutional mechanisms (Ginsburg 2006: 716).[21] What I have in mind are constitutional adjustments undertaken within states – via constitutional reform or judicial interpretation – that facilitates the open-armed embrace of the contemporary global economic order. Consider amendments taken up by Mexico in the process leading to the accession of NAFTA in 1994. In addition to sweeping reforms made to ordinary Mexican law, over thirty constitutional changes were mandated, principally concerning Article 27 of the Mexican Constitution (Sandrino 1994). Considered one of the most significant achievements of the 1910 Revolution, Article 27 provided, among other things, for the redistribution of rural lands (*ejidos*) for use by indigenous *campesinos*. The communal property provisions were altered to permit for more 'efficient' use of the *ejidos*, including individual property holding, relaxing limits on individual acres held, and enabling commercial or industrial joint ventures with third parties (Vargas 1994: 21). It is no coincidence that the Zapatista National Liberation Army (EZLN) launched its rebellion in Chiapas province on New Year's Day 1994, the same day NAFTA entered into force. The EZLN demanded that Article 27 amendments be repealed and that the 'right to land … once again be part of our constitution' (Vargas 1994: 75). It is noteworthy that the other NAFTA partners (the United States and Canada) did not have to undertake sweeping constitutional reform (Alvarez 1996: 305). This is because aspects of transnational legality are experienced unevenly and depend on the state's place within the hierarchy of the global power order. This is suggested by the Philippines Supreme Court ruling in *Tanada* (1994). Despite explicitly nationalist commitments in the Philippines constitution, the Supreme Court read the constitution in ways that ensured that there would be no discrepancy between the text and ascension by the Philippines to the World Trade Organization (Kelsey 1999: 515). Otherwise, wrote Justice Panganiban for the Court, there would be 'isolation, stagnation, if not economic self-destruction' (*Tanada* 1994: 26).

This unevenness in legal experiences is explained, argues Santos, by the fact that globalization is not the product of interstate bargaining and negotiation between equal parties but of interstate competition in which certain local phenomena achieve supremacy and thereby become successfully globalized ('globalized localism'). Local conditions correspondingly are restructured in light of these transnational hegemonic practices ('localized globalism') (Santos 2002: 179). To claim otherwise is to promote a false universality, recalling Bourdieu's notion that we be attentive to the repressed economic and social conditions that channel access to the universal (Bourdieu 2000: 65). A handful of scholars have been attentive to this phenomenon. Dezalay and Garth (1996), in an important book inspired by Bourdieu's work, describe a transnational struggle over commercial arbitration practice, centered in the international arbitration centres of New York, London, Paris and Geneva, and driven principally by global law firms. It is a struggle between a flexible, case-by-case determination in accordance with the traditional law merchant (*lex mercatoria*) and a rigid, more predictable, rule-bound approach favored by Anglo-American trade lawyers. The US rule-of-law side, Dezalay and Garth report, is winning (1996: c. 4).

Nevertheless, international lawyers continue to describe investment rules as non-national law that is geographically neutral as to its origins (McLachlan 2008: 377). Ratner, for instance, addressing the fragmented legal production of international law concerning regulatory takings, identifies a consensus among scholars and decision makers over the following proposition: that 'decision makers should not mechanically transcribe national notions of noncompensable takings law to the international arena ... [as such] reliance is inappropriate as a means of creating rules of international law generally' (2008: 483). Yet, municipal practice has long been an important source for the development of international law (Lauterpacht 1929: 85; Wild 1939: 10). Moreover, warn project constitutionalists Weiler and Trachtman, 'it is irresponsible and defeatist to think that no cross-fertilization among legal systems is possible' (1996–7: 355). Consider 2002 debates concerning trade promotion authority being granted to then President G.W. Bush to negotiate a hemispheric free trade agreement together with a number of bilateral trade and investment treaties. In the course of these debates, Congressional leaders made clear that it was the American standard for the protection of private property, as found in the Fifth and Fourteenth Amendments to the US Constitution, which was being promoted globally. Senator Gramm traced the origins of investment protections agreements, taking note of the forty-five bilateral investment treaties which the US had then signed to date. These protections, the Senator noted, 'were modeled on familiar concepts of American law, [and they] became the standard for protection of private property and investment around the world' (S4595). In the resulting Trade Promotion Authority Act of 2002, foreign investors 'are not [to be] accorded greater substantive rights with respect to investment protections than US investors in the US and [that] investors' rights [be] comparable to those that would be available under US legal principles and practice' (s. 2102[b][3]). To this end, the 2004 US model treaty identifies criteria to aid in determining whether an 'indirect' taking has occurred – loosely mirroring factors identified by the leading US Supreme Court case on regulatory takings in *Penn Central* (1977). Taking note of these Congressional developments, Poirier admits that investment protection going forward 'will be American indeed' (2003: 898).[22] Ratner, nonetheless, denies that there is any national competition in the struggle over defining international law in the area of regulatory takings and, if there are similarities, it is mere coincidence. He acknowledges in a footnote that it is 'worth noting the significant similarity' between the three factors making up the customary international law of regulatory takings (around which there is a Rawlsian 'overlapping consensus') and those adopted by the US Supreme Court in *Penn Central* (1977). He draws no further implications from this otherwise noteworthy observation (Ratner 2008: 483).

What, then, are the advantages of 'constitutionalism as critique' over 'constitutionalism as project' for comparative constitutionalists? In contrast to the project approach, which is primarily about building consensus and legitimacy around particular global legal projects, a critical approach hones in on the sources of global constitutionalism and the resulting unevenness of its operation at meta-levels and internally at national levels. It highlights both constitutional difference and similarity and reveals the circuits by which constitutional experiences flow transnationally. The critical approach also is reflexive and so calls upon those involved in scholarly production to reflect on their relationship to particular constitutional traditions – they are called upon to beware, in Frankenburg's words, of the 'hegemonic self' (Frankenburg 1997: 263; Frankenburg 1985: 443). Though the two approaches overlap considerably in the scholarly literature, they provide a heuristic for understanding the merits of critique and, moreover, the political stakes in preferring one approach over the other.

4   ALTERNATIVE READINGS

Some scholars take issue with a constitutionalist interpretation of the investment rules regime either as project or as critique. Rather than emphasizing its constitution-like features, these scholars have proposed that the investment rules regime is better conceptualized as related to other sub-fields within the law. Having already anticipated some of these objections, I turn briefly to a discussion of each.[23]

In the first reading, the regime of rules for the protection of foreign investment are better understood as advancing a private law model of commercial arbitration. This is a model intended to resolve disputes rather limited in scope, *in camera* and *ad hoc*, with little or no national judicial oversight. This is an understanding of the investment law dispute resolution process as serving largely commercial objectives (Douglas 2009: 32). A constitutional model, by contrast, covers a wider range of actionable conduct, draws on precedent and constitutional practice, together with oversight by a permanent judicial body with the requisite independence. This kind of oversight, Alvarez notes, requires a 'meaningful, long-term political commitment involving substantial resources and extensive efforts to provide transparency that … is not now apparent' in this field (2003: 412). For reasons already mentioned, this is not a very convincing objection. Investment law disputes typically concern matters that are 'deeply political' (Stone Sweet 2010: 49), namely, the permissible scope of government regulation concerning a wide array of policy subjects (Van Harten 2007). Government action is tested against vague and abstract standards, often drawn from national constitutional discourse, interpreted and enforced by tribunals exercising skills likened to judicial decision making (Lalonde quoted in Melnitzer 2004: 21; Petersmann 2009: 527). Even if some claims arise out of contractual disputes, they do not all do so and this will often make little difference in the result (*CMS* [2005] and *LG&E* [2006]). The private law objection, it safely can be said, elides the overarching public law features of international investment law.

A second reading of the investment rules regime considers general international law as a better place to locate international investment law (not merely as a special sub-species of international law).[24] In its first iteration, a number of the rules found in BITs associated with international investment law amount to the codification of customary international law (Wälde and Kolo 2001: 846; Fachiri 1925: 169). The argument presupposes a pre-existing international consensus, developed over the last one hundred years or so, which provides the legal scaffolding for the modern investment treaty regime. In a second iteration, if not previously a customary rule of international law, the specific content of, for instance, the takings rule (including a prohibition on regulatory takings) or the fair and equitable treatment standard has risen to the level of customary law by virtue of the 2,500 bilateral investment treaties signed over the past two decades (Hindelang 2004; McLachlan 2008: 394). Either iteration is difficult to reconcile with the claim that investment treaty proliferation is explained by states seeking an advantage in the competition for scarce foreign investment (Guzman 1998: 686; Stopford and Strange 1991: 120) and with qualified publicists who prescribe great caution when identifying new customary international law emerging out of treaty practice (Shaw 1997: 92). Yet others take issue with the conclusion that customary international law reveals a consensus concerning many issues raised by investment rules (Guzman 1998; Sornarajah 2010), including those concerning regulatory takings (Dolzer 1986; Dolzer 2002). This gives rise to a third iteration, that of looking to 'general principles of law recognized by civilized nations' as providing a safer harbour for investment rules.[25] The intention behind 'general principles' is to inform the development of international law with doctrine developed out of local 'jurisprudence, in particular of private law, in so far as they are applicable to relations of States' (Lauterpacht 1929). This approach bears a relationship to an earlier 'minimum standard treatment' demanded by the rules of civilized justice. According to one of its early proponents, the minimum standard 'was compounded of general principles recognized by the domestic law of practically every civilized country' rather than a reflection of 'the crudest municipal practice' (presumably of the uncivilized) (Borchard 1939: 61). The minimum standard is 'nothing more nor less', writes another, 'than the ideas which are conceived to be essential to a continuation of the existing social and economic order of European capitalistic civilization' (Dunn 1928: 175; cf. Williams 1928: 18). The notion of minimum standard, underscoring the transference of local law to the international plane, perhaps better captures the process that international lawyers aim to describe. Capital-exporting states, after all, long have attempted to claim as international law idealized versions of their own domestic legal arrangements (Lipson 1985: 20). Dolzer recommends, to this end, that arbitrators survey 'typical liberal' constitutions (the US, UK, French and German national legal systems) in order to fill out the meaning of an international takings rule. Such an exercise will reveal 'identical positions' in regard to permissible state restrictions on the use of private property. Among the problems generated by this exercise in transnational justice is that it conveniently reflects the position of only capital-exporting states. By declining to consider alternative constitutional arrangements for the protection of property (Schneiderman 2008: c. 2), Dolzer outlines a constitutional order that perpetuates unequal access to the norm-generating mechanisms of transnational legality (Sornarajah 1997).

A third reading looks to the 'embryonic' field of global administrative law as a preferred home for international investment law. Associated with the objective of promoting substantive and procedural norms worldwide, global administrative law aims to lay down standards regarding 'transparency, participation, reasoned decision, and legality ... by providing effective review of ... rules and decisions' (Kingsbury et al. 2005: 17). Leading authors in the field warn that direct analogies between national and transnational administrative law 'must be viewed with great caution' though it is likely that this emergent field will 'fulfill functions at least somewhat comparable to those administrative law fulfills domestically' (ibid.: 28). Building on this scholarly architecture, Van Harten and Loughlin describe investment treaty arbitration as perhaps the '*only* case of global administrative law in the world today' (2006: 149). Performing functions similar to domestic administrative law, international investment law concerns the review of government action in the exercise of public authority. Arbitrators typically 'rule on the legality of state conduct, evaluate the fairness of government decision-making, determine the appropriate scope and content of property rights and allocate risks and costs between business and society'. This, they write, 'is the stuff of administrative law' (2006: 147; emphasis in original) – one might add, as Van Harten does subsequently, that this is also the stuff of constitutional law (2007: 71). In the most comprehensive treatment of the subject to date, Kingsbury and Schill (2009) aim to inject elements of good governance, represented by principles associated with global administrative law, into international investment law. Given the far-reaching implications for public administration arising from investment treaty arbitration, bringing the system into line with the theory and practice of global administrative law, they surmise, is a means of bringing legitimacy and credibility to the investment law enterprise (2009: 4, 50, 52). They prescribe, to this end, the 'rapid adoption' of proportionality review – as occurring within national constitutional systems and in the European Court of Human Rights – as a 'coherent, practical means of responding to these basic legitimacy questions' (2009: 40; also Stone Sweet 2009; Wälde and Kolo 2001).[26] They recommend, more precisely, that the elements making up the standard of 'fair and equitable treatment' be made more robust by undertaking 'a comparative analysis of the major legal systems, and of major approaches in international law and institutions, in order to grasp common features those legal systems establish for the exercise of public power' (Kingsbury and Schell 2009: 19). Their prescription appears little different from the law-of-civilized-nations approach to the development of international law, mentioned above. It is noteworthy that in their earlier programmatic statement, Kingsbury, Krisch and Stewart warn that global administrative law might 'privilege and reinforce the dominance of Northern and Western concepts of sound law and governance' (2005: 27). We should be attentive to their recommendation that strategies be developed to resist this condemnable result.

One might conclude that any distinction between approaches rooted in administrative law on the one hand and in constitutional law on the other merely is one of degree. Overlapping considerably in both common law and civilian jurisdictions, 'disentangling' the two, Krisch acknowledges, is often practically difficult to do (2010: 259). Yet another approach is to split the difference – to admit that there are both administrative and constitutional elements present in the investment rules regime and other realms of transnational legality (Burke-White and von Staden 2009: 9). Whatever the case, we might agree with Anderson (2005) that debates over how best to characterize forms of transnational legality ultimately are political ones.

How we describe aspects of our legal world not only sharpens the prescriptive choices available but also determines the preferred next steps (Anderson 2005: 106). It follows that the successful embrace of any analogous sub-field of law will help shape the future direction of transnational legality's domains. In the realm of investment rules, for instance, an administrative law analogy could have the effect of curbing the substantive reach of investment rules by focusing on process concerns (though this is by no means certain) (Krisch 2010); constitutionalism as project would seek the further convergence of investment rules with constitutional norms; while constitutionalism as critique would beat a retreat from constitutional standards to less rigid models of policy-making accountability (Rose-Ackerman 2005: 5). One can expect these sorts of questions, however, to be resolved not within the legal sub-field making a claim to ownership, but by the circuits of power relations (both state and non-state) operating within and across national borders.

5 CONCLUSION

This chapter makes a case for the significance of transnational legality for comparative constitutionalists. It has been contended that particular national legal experiences inform the domains of transnational law and help to determine its content. One can go so far as to say that what often is labelled as 'transnational', 'universal,' or 'global' is the outcome of national legal systems vying for legal supremacy. We should comprehend legal developments in transnational domains, then, as having a direct relationship to national constitutional experiences and producing what is, in effect, a new constitutional law. Furthermore, legal developments at this meta-level likely will have transformative impacts within national constitutional systems. In which case, comparative constitutionalists also should be on the lookout for reforms precipitated by transnational legal exigencies.

By undertaking a detailed examination of the investment rules regime, I have sought to exemplify the ways in which elements of constitutional law play a determinative role within the transnational legal regime but also influence national constitutional developments elsewhere. The investment rules regime is experiencing a legitimacy crisis, in part, because of this interface with national constitutional law. There are those – 'project' constitutionalists – who wish to shore up legitimacy concerns by linking the regime more expressly to the strong discourse of constitutional law. 'Critique' constitutionalists, by contrast, aim to destabilize the regime by emphasizing these particularistic constitutional analogues. It might be thought that a way of defusing the crisis somewhat will be found by having project constitutionalists link arms with those promoting alternative readings of the investment rules regime that emphasize its non-constitutional features. This would only temporarily delay rather than forestall, constitutional critics warn, the inevitable repoliticization of these transnational legal domains.

NOTES

* I am grateful to Rosalind Dixon, Tom Ginsburg, Vicki Jackson and Gus Van Harten for helpful comments.
1. This is a derivation of Beck's term 'translegality' (Beck 2005: 71 ff.) though I follow here Zumbansen (2006), who describes 'transnational law' as reconnecting the domestic to the international plane and public to private law domains (at 741–2).
2. Law (2008) and Anderson (2005) may be the few exceptions to this rule.

3. For the purposes of this chapter, I do not distinguish between notions of 'constitutional law', 'constitutionalism' and 'constitutionalization'. For a parsing of these terms, see Peters (2009).
4. I say reconnecting because, some argue, this is a longstanding connection. Elkin, for instance, views both Aristotle and Madison as telling us that 'in thinking about a political constitution we must also think about an economic constitution' (2006: 4).
5. Engagement assumes that foreign or international law should be taken into account, though not necessarily followed, by national constitutional systems. According to Jackson, this is the dominant mode by which constitutional texts direct and national high courts consider foreign sources of law. Convergence, associated with cosmopolitanism, is a far less common posture and so is less accurately descriptive of how constitutions function (Jackson 2009: 8–9). Note that Weiler and Trachtman predict the convergence of European Community law (which they liken to constitutional law) and public international law (Weiler and Trachtman 1996–7: 360).
6. Consider, for instance, Van Harten (2007), who generates a convincing constitutionalist critique of international investment law but then recommends judicial-like reforms, including appellate review, which, if adopted, would generate legitimacy for the system. But see Van Harten et al. (2010, para. 14), recommending that states withdraw from or renegotiate their investment treaties and 'take steps to replace or curtail the use of investment treaty arbitration'.
7. On the politics associated with calling something constitutional see Anderson (2005: 107). I discuss this further in section 4, below.
8. Together with Sciulli's theory of societal constitutionalism (1992).
9. Teivainen also maintains that the new constitutionalism cannot fully account for events in Peru. Fujimori, after all, exercised presidential power in unconstitutional ways. There is also the potential for constitutionalism in its human rights guise to re-democratize politics in Peru, he maintains.
10. Wälde and Kolo describe the regime as a 'proto-constitutional order of the global economy' (2001: 814).
11. In Canadian constitutional law, 'paramountcy' refers to rule of interpretation that renders federal (national) law paramount to provincial (sub-national) law in the case of conflict (see Hogg 2008: 421 ff). It was an overriding principle in the British imperial system of governance in colonial India (see Keith 1936).
12. 'State capacity', writes Weiss, 'in this context refers to the ability of policy-making authorities to pursue domestic adjustment strategies that, in cooperation with organized economic groups, upgrade or transform the industrial economy' (1998: 5). A similar observation has been made by Elkins, Ginsburg and Melton (2009) in regard to constitutional design. Flexibility 'allows the constitution to adjust to the emergence of new social and political forces' and so enables the constitution to endure over time, though the optimal balance between flexibility and rigidity, they write, is 'not obvious *a priori*' (2009: 82).
13. Little mention was made of the troubles giving rise to the local populace's opposition to a revived hazardous waste site and that this local opposition was entirely foreseeable.
14. An application for judicial review to the British Columbia Supreme Court resulted in the quashing of numerous elements of the tribunal's ruling. This finding, regarding the scope of NAFTA's takings rule, was not vacated, though Justice Tysoe cautioned that the tribunal's interpretation 'is sufficiently broad ... to include legitimate rezoning of property by a municipality or other rezoning authority' (*United Mexican States* 2001: para. 99).
15. These are categorical rules automatically requiring the provision of just compensation under the US Constitution, namely, the government exercise of eminent domain, permanent physical occupations or the complete loss of economic value (Dana and Merrill 2002: 94).
16. One could also look to the nineteenth-century common law rule of *ultra vires*, which performed similar functions in limiting municipal (and even federal) power in Canadian constitutional law. See Schneiderman (1998: 520–22).
17. In his 1872 treatise, Dillon proposed that municipal authority be limited to 'public' purposes, i.e. taxation and circumscribed nineteenth-century police power regulations. The performance of private purposes, such as 'build[ing] markets', was 'better left to private enterprise' (see Dillon 1872: 22–3). Dillon principally feared, as he put it, 'the despotism of the many' (quoted in Fine 1964: 134). Fischel describes the 'original problem that Dillon wanted to address was local majoritarianism, which had opportunities to exploit immobilized wealth' (1995: 277). Frug however, interprets Dillon as forerunner to the Progressive tradition, protecting 'private property not only against abuse by democracy but also against abuse by private economic power' (1999: 46).
18. It mattered little that the CMS claim was based on a license or contract as a subsequent tribunal ruled against Argentina for similar reasons in circumstances where the investor relied only on the legal framework in operation at the time of the investment (*LG&E* 2006: para. 125).
19. United States Constitution, Article 1, clause 10.
20. It certainly does not mirror the more relaxed constitutional standard as it developed through the nineteenth and then into the twentieth centuries (see Tribe 1988: 618).
21. In the United States, for instance, Article VI renders self-executing treaties the 'supreme law of the land', which then can be superseded by ordinary legislative enactment.

22. In August 2009, the US State Department's Subcommittee on Investment of the Advisory Committee on International Economic Policy Regarding the Model Bilateral Investment Treaty issued a divided report but rallied around the idea that any new model US investment treaty should mirror property protections in the US Constitution. They disagreed, however, on whether the US takings clause was expansive or more narrowly confined (2009: para. 18).
23. The following two paragraphs draw on Schneiderman (2006).
24. The International Law Commission (2006: 254) describes general international law as referring, at the least, to 'general customary international law as well as "general principles of law recognized by civilized nations" '.
25. A source of law according to the Statute of the International Court of Justice, Article 38(1)(c).
26. The instances of proportionality review in investment arbitration are, to date, feeble and episodic. See Schneiderman (2010).

REFERENCES

Alexander, Gregory S. (2006), *The Global Debate over Constitutional Property: Lessons for American Takings Jurisprudence*, Chicago: The University of Chicago Press.
Allen, Tom (2000), *The Right to Property in Commonwealth Constitutions,* Cambridge: Cambridge University Press.
Alvarez, José E. (1996), 'Critical Theory and the North American Free Trade Agreement's Chapter Eleven', *Inter-American Law Review*, 28 (2), 303–12.
Alvarez, José E. (2003), 'The New Dispute Settlers: (Half) Truths and Consequences', *Texas International Law Journal*, 38, 405–44.
Alvarez, José E. (2009), 'The Internationalization of US Law', *Columbia Journal of Transnational Law*, 47 (3), 537–75.
Alvarez, José and Kathryn Khamsi (2009), 'The Argentine Crisis and Foreign Investors: A Glimpse into the Heart of the Investment Regime', in Karl P. Sauvant (ed.), *Yearbook on International Investment Law and Policy*, Oxford: Oxford University Press, pp. 379–478.
Anderson, Gavin W. (2005), *Constitutional Rights after Globalization*, Oxford: Hart Publishing.
Baxi, Upendra (2006), *The Future of Human Rights*, 2nd edition, New Delhi: Oxford University Press.
Beatty, David M. (2004), *The Ultimate Rule of Law*, Oxford: Oxford University Press.
Beck, Ulrich (2005), *Power in the Global Age*, trans. Kathleen Cross, Cambridge: Polity Press.
Been, Vicki and Joel C. Beauvais (2003), 'The Global Fifth Amendment: NAFTA's Investment Protections and the Misguided Quest for an International "Regulatory Takings" Doctrine', *New York University Law Review*, 78, 30–143.
Berman, Paul Schiff (2007), ''Global Legal Pluralism', *Southern California Law Review*, 80, 1155–237.
Borchard, Edwin (1939), 'The 'Minimum Standard' of the Treatment of Aliens', *American Society of International Law Proceedings*, 33, 51–63.
Bourdieu, Pierre (2000), *Pascalian Meditations*, Stanford, CA: Stanford University Press.
Bryce, James (1901), 'Flexible and Rigid Constitutions', in James Bryce, *Studies in History and Jurisprudence*, Oxford: Oxford University Press, pp. 124–213.
Burke-White, William W. and Andreas von Staden (2009), 'Private Litigation in a Public Law Sphere: The Standard of Review in Investor-State Arbitrations', *Yale Journal of International Law*, 35, 283–346.
Cass, Deborah Z. (2005), *The Constitutionalization of the World Trade Organization*, Oxford: Oxford University Press.
Chang, Ha-Joon (2002), *Kicking Away the Ladder: Development Strategy in Historical Perspective*, London: Anthem Press.
Choudhry, Sujit, (ed) (2006), *The Migration of Constitutional Ideas*, Cambridge: Cambridge University Press.
Connell, Raewyn (2006), 'Northern Theory: The Political Geography of General Social Theory', *Theory and Society*, 35, 237–64.
Dana, David A. and Thomas W. Merrill (2002), *Property: Takings*, New York: Foundation Press.
Dezalay, Yves and Bryant G. Garth (1996), *Dealing in Virtue: International Commercial Arbitration and the Construction of a Transnational Legal Order*, Chicago: University of Chicago Press.
Dezalay, Yves and Bryant G. Garth (2002), *The Internationalization of the Palace Wars: Lawyers, Economists, and the Contest to Transform Latin American States*, Chicago: Chicago University Press.
Dillon, John F. (1872), *Treatise on the Law of Municipal Corporations*, Chicago: James Cockcroft & Co.
Dolzer, Rudolf (1981), 'New Foundations of the Law of Expropriations of Alien Property', *American Journal of International Law*, 75, 553–89.
Dolzer, Rudolf (1985), 'New Foundations of the Law of Expropriation of Alien Property', *American Journal of International Law*, 75, 553–89.

Dolzer, Rudolf (1986), 'Indirect Expropriation of Alien Property', ICSID Review, *Foreign Investment Law Journal*, 1, 41–65 (1986).

Dolzer, Rudolf (2002), 'Indirect Expropriations: New Developments?', *New York University Environmental Law Journal*, 11, 64–93.

Douglas, Zachary (2009), *The International Law of Investment Claims*, Cambridge: Cambridge University Press.

Dunn, Frederick Sherwood (1928), 'International Law and Private Property Rights', *Columbia Law Review*, 28, 166–80.

Dunoff, Jeffrey (2006), 'Constitutional Conceits: The WTO's "Constitution" and the Discipline of International Law', *European Journal of International Law*, 17, 647–75.

Dunoff, Jeffrey L. and Joel P. Trachtman (2009a), 'A Functional Approach to International Constitutionalization', in Jeffrey L. Dunoff and Joel P. Trachtman (eds), *Ruling the World? Constitutionalism, International Law and Global Governing*, pp. 3–35.

Dunoff, Jeffrey L. and Joel P. Trachtman (eds) (2009b), *Ruling the World? Constitutionalism, International Law and Global Governance*, Cambridge: Cambridge University Press.

Elkin, Stephen L. (2006), *Reconstructing the Commercial Republic: Constitutional Design after Madison*, Chicago: Chicago University Press.

Elkins, Zachary, Tom Ginsburg and James Melton (2009), *The Endurance of National Constitutions*, Cambridge: Cambridge University Press.

Elster, Jon (1984), *Ulysses and the Sirens: Studies in Rationality and Irrationality*, Cambridge: Cambridge University Press.

Fachiri, Alexander P. (1925), 'Expropriation and International Law', *British Yearbook of International Law*, 6, 159–71.

Fine, Sidney (1964), *Laissez Faire and the General Welfare State: A Study of Conflict in American Thought, 1865–1901*, Ann Arbor: The University of Michigan Press.

Finer, S.E. (ed.) (1979), *Five Constitutions: Contrasts and Comparisons*, Harmondsworth: Penguin Books.

Fischel, William A. (1995), *Regulatory Takings: Law, Economics, and Politics*, Cambridge, MA: Harvard University Press.

Fligstein, Neil and Alec Stone Sweet (2002), 'Constructing Politics and Markets: An Institutionalist Account of European Integration', *American Journal of Sociology*, 107, 1206–43.

Frankenburg, Günter (1985), 'Critical Comparisons: Re-thinking Comparative Law', *Harvard International Law Journal*, 26, 411–55.

Frankenburg, Günter (1997), 'Stranger than Paradise: Identity & Politics in Comparative Law', *1997 Utah Law Review*, 259–74.

Frug, Gerald E. (1999), *City Making: Building Communities without Building Walls*, Princeton: Princeton University Press.

Frug, Gerald E. and David J. Barron (2006), 'International Local Government Law', *The Urban Lawyer*, 38, 1–62.

Gardbaum, Stephen (2008), 'The Myth and the Reality of American Constitutionalism Exceptionalism', *Michigan Law Review*, 107, 391–466.

Gill, Stephen (1995), 'Globalisation, Market Civilisation, and Disciplinary Neoliberalism', *Millennium: Journal of International Studies*, 24, 399–423.

Gill, Stephen (2003), *Power and Resistance in the New World Order*, Basingstoke: Palgrave Macmillan.

Gill, Stephen (2008), *Power and Resistance in the New World Order*, 2nd edition, Basingstoke: Palgrave Macmillan.

Gillman, Howard (1993), *The Constitution Beseiged: The Rise and Decline of Lochner Era Police Powers Jurisprudence*, Durham, NC: Duke University Press.

Ginsburg, Tom (2006), 'Locking in Democracy: Constitutions, Commitment, and International Law', *New York University Journal of Law and Politics*, 38, 707–59.

Guzman, Andrew T. (1998), 'Why LDCs Sign Treaties that Hurt Them: Explaining the Popularity of Bilateral Investment Treaties', *Virginia Journal of International Law*, 38, 639–88.

Habermas, Jürgen (2006), 'Does the Constitutionalization of International Law Still Have a Chance?', in Jürgen Habermas, *The Divided West*, Cambridge: Polity, pp. 113–93.

Hindelang, Steffen (2004), 'Bilateral Investment Treaties, Custom and a Healthy Investment Climate: The Question of Whether BITs Influence Customary International Law Revisited', *Journal of World Investment and Trade*, 5, 789–809.

Hirschl, Ran (2004), *Towards Juristocracy: The Origins and Consequences of the New Constitutionalism*, Cambridge, MA: Harvard University Press.

Hirst, Paul Q. (ed.) (1989), *The Pluralist Theory of the State: Selected Writings of G.D.H. Cole, J.N. Figgis, and H.J. Laski*, London and New York: Routledge.

Hogg, Peter W. (2008), *Constitutional Law of Canada*, student edition, Scarborough: Thomson Canada.

Howse, Robert and Kalypso Nicolaïdis (2001), 'Legitimacy and Global Governance: Why Constitutionalizing the WTO is a Step too Far', in Roger P. Porter, Pierre Sauvé, Arvind Subramanian and Americo Beviglia Zampetti (eds), *Efficiency, Equity, Legitimacy: The Multilateral Trading System at the Millennium*, Washington: Brookings Institution Press, pp. 227–52.

International Law Commission (2006), 'Fragmentation of International Law: Difficulties Arising from the Diversification and Expansion of International Law, Report of the Study Group of the International Law Commission', UN Doc. A/CN.4/L682 (13 April), online at http://dacess-dds-ny.un.org/doc/UNDOC/LTD/G06/610/77/PDF/GU661077.pdf?OpenElement.

Jackson, John H. (1997), *The World Trading System: Law and Policy of International Economic Relations*, 2nd edition, Cambridge, MA: The MIT Press.

Jackson, Vicki (2009), *Constitutional Engagement in a Transnational Era*, New York: Oxford University Press.

Joerges, Christian and Jürgen Neyer (2006), 'Deliberative Supranationaliism Revisited', EU Working Papers Law No. 2006/20, online at http://cadmus.eui.eu/bitstream/handle/1814/6251/LAW-2006-20.pdf?sequence=1.

Kant, Immanuel (1991), 'Perpetual Peace: A Philosophical Sketch', in *Political Writings*, trans. H. Nesbit, Cambridge: Cambridge University Press, pp. 93–130.

Keith, Arthur Berriedale (1936), *A Constitutional History of India*, London: Methuen & Co.

Kelsey, Jane (1999), 'Global Economic Policy-Making: A New Constitutionalism?', *Otago Law Review*, 9, 535–55.

Kennedy, David (2009), 'The Mystery of Global Governance', in Jeffrey L. Dunhoff and Joel P. Trachtman (eds), *Ruling the World? Constitutionalism, International Law and Global Governance*, Cambridge: Cambridge University Press, pp. 37–68.

Kingsbury, Benedict, Nico Krisch and Richard B. Stewart (2005), 'The Emergence of Global Administrative Law', *Law & Contemporary Problems*, 68, 15–61.

Kingsbury, Benedict and Stephan Schill (2009), 'Investor-State Arbitration as Governance: Fair and Equitable Treatment, Proportionality and the Emerging Global Administrative Law', IILJ Working Paper 2009/6 (Global Administrative Law Series) (2009), online at http://ssrn.com.

Koskenniemi, Martti (2007), 'Constitutionalism as Mindset: Reflections on Kantian Themes about International Law and Globalization', *Theoretical Inquiries in Law*, 8(1), 9–36.

Krisch, Nico (2010), 'Global Administrative Law and the Constitutional Ambition', in Petra Dobner and Martin Loughlin (eds), *The Twilight of Constitutionalism?*, Oxford: Oxford University Press, pp. 245–66.

Kumm, Mattias (2009). 'The Cosmopolitan Turn in Constitutionalism: On the Relationship between Constitutionalism in and Beyond the State', in Jeffrey L. Dunoff and Joel P. Trachtman (eds), *Ruling the World? Constitutionalism, International Law and Global Governance*, Cambridge: Cambridge University Press, pp. 258–324.

Lauterpacht, Elihu (1997), 'International Law and Private Foreign Investment', *Indiana Journal of Global Legal Studies*, 4, 259–76.

Lauterpacht, H. (1929), 'Decisions of Municipal Courts as a Source of International Law', *British Yearbook of International Law* 10, 65.

Law, David (2008), 'Globalization and the Future of Constitutional Rights', *Northwestern University Law Review*, 102, 1277–350.

Lipson, Charles (1985), *Standing Guard: Protecting Foreign Capital in the Nineteenth and Twentieth Centuries*, Berkeley: University of California Press.

Luhmann, Niklas (2004), *Law as a Social System*, trans. Klaus A. Ziegert, Oxford: Oxford University Press.

McGinnis, John P. and Mark L. Movsevian (2000), 'The World Trade Constitution', *Harvard Law Review*, 114, 511–605.

McLachlan, Campbell (2008), 'Investment Treaties and General International Law', *International and Comparative Law Quarterly*, 57, 361–401.

Melnitzer, Julius (2004). 'The New Peacekeepers', *Canadian Lawyer*, August, 18–21.

Mittelman, James H. (2004), 'What is Critical Globalization Studies?', *International Studies Perspectives*, 5, 219–30.

Newton, Scott (2006), 'Constitutionalism and Imperialism Sub Specie Spiniozae', *Law Critique*, 17, 325–55.

North, Douglass C. (2005), *Understanding The Process of Economic Change*, Princeton: Princeton University Press.

Peters, Ann (2009), 'The Merits of Global Constitutionalism', *Indiana Journal of Global Legal Studies*, 16(2), 397–411.

Petersmann, Ernst-Ulrich (2000),'The WTO Constitution and Human Rights', *Journal of International Economic Law*, 3(1), 19–25.

Petersmann, Ernst-Ulrich (2009),'International Rule of Law and Constitutional Justice in International Investment Law and Arbitration', *Indiana Journal of Global Legal Studies*, 16(2), 513–33.

Poirier, Marc R. (2003), 'The NAFTA Chapter 11 Expropriation Debate through the Eyes of a Property Theorist', *Environmental Law*, 33, 851–928.

Ratner, Steven R. (2008), 'Regulatory Takings in Institutional Context. Beyond the Fear of Fragmented International Law', *The American Journal of International Law*, 102, 475–528.

Raz, Joseph (1998). 'On the Authority and Interpretation of Constitutions: Some Preliminaries', in Larry Alexander (ed.), *Constitutionalism: Philosophical Foundations*, Cambridge: Cambridge University Press, pp. 152–93.

Rittich, Kerry (2006), 'The Future of Law and Development: Second-generation Reforms and the Incorporation of the Social', in David M. Trubek and Alvaro Santos (eds), *The New Law and Economic Development: A Critical Appraisal*, Cambridge: Cambridge University Press.

Rodrik, Dani (2002), 'Feasible Globalizations', mimeo, pp. 203–52.
Rodrik, Dani (2007), *One Economics, Many Recipes: Globalization, Institutions, and Economic Growth*, Princeton: Princeton University Press.
Rosamond, Ben (2006), 'Disciplinarity and the Political Economy of Transformation: The Epistemological Politics of Globalization Studies', *Review of International Political Economy*, 13, 516–32.
Rose-Ackerman, Susan (2005), *From Elections to Democracy: Building Accountable Government in Hungary and Poland*, Cambridge: Cambridge University Press.
Sandrino, Gloria (1994), 'The NAFTA Investment Chapter and Foreign Direct Investment in Mexico: A Third World Perspective', *Vanderbilt Journal of Transnational Law*, 27, 259–327.
Santos, Boaventura de Sousa (2002), *Toward a New Legal Common Sense: Law, Globalization and Emancipation*, 2nd edition, New York: Routledge.
Schneiderman, David (1998), 'A.V. Dicey, Lord Watson and the Law of the Canadian Constitution in the Late Nineteenth Century', *Law and History Review*, 16, 495–526.
Schneiderman, David (2002), 'Comparative Constitutional Law in an Age of Globalization', in Vicki C. Jackson and Mark V. Tushnet (eds), *Comparative Constitutional Law: Defining the Field*, Westport: Greenwood Press, pp. 237–59.
Schneiderman, David (2006), 'Constitution or Model Treaty? Struggling over the Interpretive Authority of NAFTA', in Sujit Choudhry (ed.), *The Migration of Constitutional Ideas*, Cambridge: Cambridge University Press, pp. 294–315.
Schneiderman, David (2008), *Constitutionalizing Economic Globalization: Investment Rules and Democracy's Promise*, Cambridge: Cambridge University Press.
Schneiderman, David (2010), 'Judicial Politics and International Investment Arbitration: Seeking an Explanation for Conflicting Outcomes', *Northwestern Journal of International Law & Business*, 30, 383–416.
Sciulli, David (1992), *Theory of Societal Constitutionalism: Foundations of a Non-Marxist Critical Theory*, Cambridge: Cambridge University Press.
Shaw, Malcolm (1997), *International Law*, 5th edition, Cambridge: Cambridge University Press.
Sornarajah, M. (1997), 'Power and Justice in Foreign Investment Arbitration', *Journal of International Arbitration*, 14, 103–40.
Sornarajah, M. (2010), *The International Law on Foreign Investment*, 3rd edition, Cambridge: Cambridge University Press.
Stone Sweet, Alec (1994), 'What is a Supranational Constitution? An Essay in International Relations Theory', *The Review of Politics*, 56, 441–74.
Stone Sweet, Alec (2009), 'Constitutionalism, Legal Pluralism and International Regimes', *Indiana Journal of Global Legal Studies*, 16, 621–45.
Stone Sweet, Alec (2010), 'Investor-state Arbitration: Proportionality's New Frontier', *Law and Ethics of Human Rights*, 4, 47–76.
Stopford, John and Susan Strange (1991), *Rival States, Rival Firms: Competition for World Market Shares*, Cambridge: Cambridge University Press.
Sunstein, Cass R. (1993), *The Partial Constitution*, Cambridge, MA: Harvard University Press.
Teivainen, Teivo (2002), *Enter Economism, Exit Politics: Economic Policy and the Damage to Democracy*, London: Zed Books.
Teubner, Gunther (2004), 'Societal Constitutionalism: Alternatives to State-centred Constitutional Theory?', in Christian Joerges, Inger Johanne Sand and Gunther Teubner (eds), *Transnational Governance and Constitutionalism*, Oxford: Hart Publishing, pp. 3–28.
Tocqueville, Alexis de (2000), *Democracy in America*, trans. Harvey C. Mansfield and Delba Winthrop, Chicago: The University of Chicago Press.
Tribe, Lawrence (1988), *American Constitutional Law*, 2nd edition, Mineola, NY: The Foundation Press.
Tully, James (2008), *Public Philosophy in a New Key, Volume II: Imperialism and Civic Freedom*, Cambridge: Cambridge University Press.
Tushnet, Mark (1999), 'Foreword: The New Constitutional Order and the Chastening of Constitutional Analysis', *Harvard Law Review*, 113, 26–109.
United Nations Conference on Trade and Development (2009a), *World Investment Report 2009: Transnational Corporations, Agricultural Production and Development*, New York and Geneva: United Nations.
United Nations Conference on Trade and Development (2009b), 'Recent Developments in International Investment Agreements (2008–June 2009)' IIA Monitor No. 3 (2009), online at http://www.unctad.org/en/docs/webdiaeia20098_en.pdf.
Van der Walt, A.J. (1999), *Constitutional Property Clauses*, Cambridge, MA: Kluwer Law International.
Van Harten, Gus (2007), *Investment Treaty Arbitration and Public Law*, Oxford: Oxford University Press.
Van Harten, Gus, et al. (2010), 'Public Statement on the International Investment Regime' (31 August), available online at http://www.osgoode.yorku.ca/public_statement/.
Van Harten, Gus and Martin Loughlin (2006), 'Investment Treaty Arbitration as a Species of Global Administrative Law', *The European Journal of International Law*, 17, 121–50.

Vargas, Jorge A (1994), 'NAFTA, the Chiapas Rebellion, and the Emergence of Mexican Ethnic Law', *California Western International Law Journal*, 25, 1–79.

Wälde, Thomas and Abba Kolo (2001), 'Environmental Regulation, Investment Protection and "Regulatory Taking" in International Law', *International and Comparative Law Quarterly*, 50, 811–48.

Walker, Neil (2001), 'The EU and the WTO: Constitutionalism in a New Key', in Gráinne de Búrca and Joanne Scott (eds), *The EU and the WTO: Legal and Constitutional Issues*, Oxford: Hart Publishing, pp. 31–57.

Walker, Neil (2002), 'The Idea of Constitutional Pluralism', *Modern Law Review*, 65, 317–59.

Walker, Neil (2003), 'Postnational Constitutionalism and the Problem of Translation', in J.H.H. Weiler and Marlene Wind (eds), *European Constitutionalism beyond the State*, Cambridge: Cambridge University Press, pp. 27–54.

Walker, Neil (2008), 'Taking Constitutionalism beyond the State', *Political Studies*, 56, 519–34.

Weiler, J.H.H. (1999), *The Constitution of Europe: 'Do the Clothes Have an Emperor?' and Other Essays on European Integration*, Cambridge: Cambridge University Press.

Weiler, J.H.H and Joel P. Trachtman (1996–7), 'European Constitutionalism and its Discontents', *Northwestern Journal of International Law and Business*, 17, 354–97.

Weiler, J.H.H. and Marlene Wind (2008), 'Taking Constitutionalism beyond the State', *Political Studies*, 56, 519–43.

Weinrib, Lorraine (2002), 'Constitutional Conceptions and Constitutional Comparativism' in Vicki C. Jackson and Mark Tushnet (eds), *Defining the Field of Comparative Constitutional Law*, Westport: Praeger Publishers, pp. 3–34.

Weiss, Linda (1998), *The Myth of the Powerless State*, Ithaca, NY: Cornell University Press.

Wild, Payson S., Jr. (1939), 'International Law and Mexican Oil', *The Quarterly Journal of Inter-American Relations*, 1, 5–21.

Williams, Sir John Fischer (1928), 'International Law and the Property of Aliens', *British Yearbook of International Law*, 9, 1–30.

Zumbansen, Peer (2006), 'Transnational Law', in Jan Smits (ed.) *Encyclopedia of Comparative Law*, Cheltenham, UK and Northampton, MA, US: Edward Elgar, pp. 738–54.

Cases

Aguas del Tunari, SA v Republic of Bolivia (2005) (Decision on Respondent's Objections to Jurisdiction) ICSID Case No. ARB/03/3 (21 October).

Charles River Bridge v Warren Bridge, 36 US (11 Pet.) 420 (1837).

CMS Gas Transmission Company v Républica Argentina (2005) (Award) ICSID Case No. ARB/01/08, International Legal Materials 44, 1205–63 (12 May 2005).

Dartmouth College (Trustees of) v Woodward, 17 US (4 Wheat.) 517 (1819).

Lanco International Inc. v Argentina (2004) (Decision on Jurisdiction) International Legal Materials (2001), ICSID Case No. ARB/97/6, 40: 457–73 (8 December 1998).

LG&E Energy Corp. v Argentine Republic (2006) (Decision on Liability) ICSID Case No. ARB/02/01 (3 October), ICSID Reports 11, 414.

Lucas v South Carolina Coastal Council, 112 S.Ct. 2886 (1992).

Metalclad Corporation and the United Mexican States (2001), World Trade and Arbitration Materials 13, 47–80 (30 August 2000).

Penn Central Transportation Co. v New York City, 438 US 104 (1977).

S.D. Myers, Inc. v Government of Canada (2001) (Partial Award) (UNCITRAL) International Legal Materials 40, 1408–92 (13 November 2000).

Tanada v Angara (1997) 272 SCRA 18 (Philippines Supreme Court).

United Mexican States v Metalclad, 2001 BCSC 664 (BCSC).

PART III

CONSTITUTIONAL STRUCTURE

12. Legislative-executive relations

José Antonio Cheibub and Fernando Limongi

1 INTRODUCTION

Legislative-executive relations refers to the institutions that govern and the processes that characterize the interactions between two of the three conventional branches of a democratic political system (the third being, of course, the judiciary). This entails a consideration of the legal (constitutional and statutory) provisions that regulate the formation of the government, the rules for electing the legislative assembly, the way the formation of each of these branches affects the performance of the others, the rules for producing legislation, and the behavior (strategic or otherwise) of the actors that make up the 'executive' (the head of government and the ministers) and the 'legislative' (individual legislators and political parties). This is a large area of research, which could reasonably encompass everything that would traditionally go under the heading of 'comparative government'. A thorough treatment of all these topics here is impossible for reasons of space, and so we offer a selective treatment of the issues based on our particular perspective of how studies of legislative-executive relations have evolved.

In order to simplify the analysis we divide the vast and heterogeneous literature that concerns us here into two, which we call the 'earlier' and the 'later' generations of studies of legislative-executive relations. The distinctive feature of the earlier studies is that they analyze inter-branch relations as being essentially shaped by the way the chief executive and the legislators obtain their mandates. The independence or the dependence of the executive's mandate with respect to the legislature is the key factor determining whether the relationship between the two powers will likely be characterized by conflict or cooperation, and whether it will remain within the bounds prescribed by the constitution. In these studies executives and legislatures tend to be conceived as unified actors who compete for influence over policy outcomes. The institutional framework shapes the nature of the interaction between the two branches, determining which one, if any, will dominate the policy process. The institutional embodiment of this distinction is, of course, represented by the contrast between parliamentary and presidential systems. Whereas the former represents a system of mutual dependence between the government and the legislature, the latter represents a system of independence of the two (Stepan and Skach 1993). The best example of this approach can be found in the comparative studies of parliamentary and presidential systems, which we review below.

It is only more recently that inter-branch conflict has begun to give way to more complex models, in which executive-legislative relations are conceived not necessarily as the interaction between two branches of the government, but as the relationship between the government, political parties and groups of legislators, all of whom must cooperate with one another in order to govern, and yet must also compete to gain votes in periodic elections. From this perspective, the question is not so much what triggers conflict or cooperation between the executive and the legislature, but about the institutions and the strategies that allow governments to obtain the support of a majority in the legislature to implement policy change. These more recent studies are quite heterogeneous; what allows us to group them together is the recognition, first, that relevant actors seek multiple goals that may be in conflict with one another, and, second, that factors internal to the legislative process itself are crucial for understanding how a majority organizes itself in the two branches and is effective in the pursuit of its policy objectives.

In what follows we seek to characterize both the earlier and the later studies of legislative-executive relations. Section 2 deals with the former, focusing on parliamentary (Section 2.1) and presidential (Section 2.2) systems. We also discuss studies of semi-presidential systems (Section 2.3). Chronologically, these are more recent due, in part, to the fact that the number of democracies with such systems increased significantly only after the end of the Cold War. Yet, as we will show, the research questions guiding studies of semi-presidentialism have been informed primarily by the questions raised by the earlier paradigm contrasting parliamentary and presidential systems. In Section 3 we turn to the later studies of legislative-executive relations, highlighting three substantive areas that helped re-define the field. Section 4 concludes the chapter.

2   EARLIER STUDIES

Early studies of legislative-executive relations were primarily concerned with understanding how governments are formed, based on the assumption that politicians are primarily office-seekers. In this perspective, the analysis of inter-branch relations was reduced to the identification of the incentives office-seeking politicians might have to cooperate in governing a country. In spite of the common preoccupation with government formation and the common assumption about politicians' goals, the early literature was bifurcated; it evolved into two separate and independent bodies of work, with very little exchange between the two. One literature focused on parliamentary systems and the other on presidential systems.

2.1   Parliamentary Democracies

The literature on parliamentarism focused on the process of government formation. Government formation is crucial because, it was believed, it is the moment in which the government's ability to act throughout its existence is determined.

In the most basic view, the very nature of parliamentarism is such that parties operate under a majoritarian imperative; that is, the requirement that governments must be composed by parties that together command more than 50% of legislative seats. In this view, governments are formed as parties exchange cabinet positions for legislative support: a party is considered to be in government if it controls one or more cabinets; when in government, a party's members of parliament are expected to vote in support of government measures.

If a party alone commands more than 50% of the seats in the legislature, it forms a single-party government; it keeps to itself all the benefits of being in the government as it does not need the support of other parties to remain in power. If no party controls more than 50% of the legislative seats, then parties must form a coalition government by sharing cabinet positions. Given the fact that in the majority of parliamentary democracies no party commands more than 50% of the seats, one of the central research questions in the early studies of executive-legislative relations is which parties will come together into the government and how they will share the limited number of portfolios.

There is a vast literature that deals with coalition formation and termination, and here is not the place to review it in detail.[1] For our purposes, it is sufficient to say that formation and termination are directly associated in most accounts, implying that the operation of the government between these two moments does not require attention or explanation. The primary function of parliaments is to make or break governments (Laver 2006: 122). Regarding coalition formation specifically, the most popular and influential theory assumes purely office-seeking politicians and predicts the formation of minimum-winning coalitions (Riker 1962). Parties try to form the smallest possible coalition and to keep as much as possible of the spoils of government, subject to the constraint that these coalitions have to be majoritarian. As Laver and Schofield (1998) note, the failure of the minimum-winning coalition theory to predict actual outcomes led scholars to revise some of Riker's assumptions and broaden their search for the criteria that would guide the coalition formation process. In so doing they did not entirely do away with the office-seeking postulate. This is the case of the minimal connected winning coalition theory proposed by Axelrod (1970), in which the ideological proximity is introduced not as policy concern per se, but as a way of reducing the coalition internal conflict. As Laver and Schofield (1998: 110) argue, even De Swaan's (1973) attempt to place policy concerns at the center of the coalition formation process 'retains an implicit concern with office-seeking motivations'.

In most theories of coalition formation (always in parliamentary regimes) one constraint that parties always face, regardless of their motivation, is the majoritarian one. In this sense, minority governments – governments formed by one or more parties that together control less than 50% of legislative seats – necessarily represent a failure of the government formation process. They result from crises that are induced by high levels of political fragmentation and polarization. Minority governments, therefore, cannot be explained except as anomalies induced by a dysfunctional political system.

The type of government that emerges from the formation process matters for its duration. Because minority governments are the product of an underlying situation characterized by fragmentation and polarization, they are the most unstable and ungovernable. Single-party majority governments, on the other hand, are at the opposite end, tending to last long and implement important policy programs. Coalition governments are the true interesting political phenomena. After all, they rest on a precarious bargain among parties over how to divide the spoils of government and set major policies. They are fragile in the sense that a coalition may break over major and minor issues. Thus, coalition governments are vulnerable to (parties' anticipation of) even small shifts in voters' preferences, as well as to the idiosyncrasies of each coalition member.

Although it is hard to come up with a consensual list of factors that affect government survival, it is safe to say that the literature has identified economic, ideological and institutional factors as being of relevance for the duration of a parliamentary government. Thus, the position of parties in the left-right policy space interacts with the economic conditions governments face and the institutions under which they operate to affect how long parliamentary governments will survive (Warwick 1994).

The coalition formation and termination literature took on a life of its own.[2] The relevant points to retain from the perspective of executive-legislative relations is that it privileges office-seeking considerations when it comes to politicians' motivations and concentrates on the two extreme moments in the existence of any government: its formation and its termination. The actual operation of the government, the way executive-legislative relations are structured and unfolded during the ordinary life of the government, was not an object of scrutiny.

2.2   Presidential Democracies

The preoccupation of those who have studied presidentialism has been different. The fact that the head of government's mandate originates in popular elections leads to a totally different world where coalitions and government' duration are irrelevant. The president and the legislature have a fixed term in office and government duration, therefore, becomes a moot question. The fact that the president does not need to generate majority support in the legislature in order to remain in office, in turn, makes coalition governments unnecessary.

Comparative studies of presidential systems started much later than those of parliamentary ones. There is, of course, a large literature on the United States. But this literature is not comparative in any significant way as it is concerned primarily with accounting for the rather unique features of the overall US political system, and not with analyzing it as one among many presidential democracies. Moreover, as presidential and legislative studies have developed as independent subfields, and given the more qualitative and anecdotal approach that dominates the former,[3] executive-legislative relations has not been a central lens through which to view the functioning of the US system.

The dearth of early comparative studies of presidential systems was partly due to the scarcity of available cases for analysis. Most presidential democracies outside of the United States, at least until the re-democratization of Latin America in the 1980s, experienced at least one regime breakdown. Scholarly attention, therefore, was redirected to the study of the dictatorships that replaced them or the conditions that produced their demise. Given the prevalence of structural-functionalism and Marxism, the constitutional structure and the details of institutional design regulating executive-legislative relations did not figure prominently, if at all, in these studies.

It is not until the 1980s that presidentialim as an institutional form became the object of systematic analysis. Here the work of Juan Linz is absolutely central. In calling attention to the role of incentives generated by a system of separation of powers in the crises that led to democratic breakdowns in Latin America, Linz set out the agenda and the tone for comparative studies of executive-legislative relations under presidentialism.[4]

Linz's argument is well known. Here we provide only a brief sketch of the Linzian view to highlight the steps that connect the separation of powers that defines presidentialism to the eventual breakdown of democratic regimes. According to this view, presidential constitutions, contrary to parliamentary ones, provide few or no incentives for coalition formation. There are three reasons for this: (1) because the president's survival in office does not depend on any kind of legislative support, a president need not seek the cooperation of political parties other than his or her own; (2) because presidents are independent from the legislature when it comes to survival, and are elected in nationwide contests that provide widespread popular support, they have an inflated sense of power and overestimate their ability to govern alone; (3) finally, presidential politics is a zero-sum winner-takes-all affair, which is hardly conducive to cooperation or coalition formation. For these reasons, coalitions are difficult to form and do form 'only exceptionally' (Linz 1994: 19) under presidentialism (Mainwaring

1990; Stepan and Skach 1993: 20; Linz and Stepan 1996: 181). As Niño (1996: 169) puts it, presidentialism 'operates against the formation of coalitions'; for this reason, according to Huang (1997: 138), 'the very notion of majority government is problematic in presidential systems without a majority party'.

In the Linzian framework, therefore, while parliamentary regimes are supposed to foster cooperation, presidential regimes encourage independence. Under parliamentarism, political parties have an incentive to cooperate with one another. Parties in government will support the executive, and parties out of government will refrain from escalating any conflict because they may, at any time, become part of the government; individual members of parliament, in turn, will align themselves with their parties. The consequence is that parliamentary governments are supported by a majority composed of highly disciplined parties that are prone to cooperate with one another. Presidentialism, on the other hand, is characterized by the absence of such incentives and hence is likely to generate either minority governments or governments that are only nominally majority governments. In fact, given that legislators do not depend on the president to obtain and retain their seats, and given that they cultivate their own ties with voters, they have few, if any, incentives to support the president and to pay attention to national issues.

The lack of incentives for coalition formation and the resulting high incidence of minority governments under presidentialism, particularly multiparty presidentialism (Mainwaring 1993), implies conflict between the executive and the legislature as well as governments that are legislatively ineffective. As Jones (1995: 38) states, 'when an executive lacks a majority in the parliamentary systems the norm tends to be what Lijphart terms "consensual government" (i.e., government by coalition). In presidential systems, when the executive lacks a majority (or close to it) in the legislature, the norm is conflictual government.' The higher likelihood of executive-legislative conflict and deadlock in presidential democracies is thus the product of the system's defining feature. It 'stems primarily from the separate election of the two branches of government and is exacerbated by the fixed term of office' (Mainwaring 1993: 209).

Presidents who do not have legislative support will try to bypass congress in order to implement their programs. They will, for instance, make increasing use of their decree powers and, in the process, undermine democratic legitimacy. As Valenzuela (2004: 14) states, 'by resorting to decree powers presidents may become stronger, but the presidential system becomes weaker and more brittle, encouraging confrontation rather than accommodation'. Hence they undermine democratic institutions as they try 'to shore up their weaknesses as presidents'. Under these circumstances, democracy is delegative rather than liberal (O'Donnell 1994), meaning that it relies on the plebiscitary link between voters and the president at the expense of 'horizontal' links of accountability.

In sum, because there are no incentives for inter-branch cooperation, presidentialism is characterized by frequent minority governments as well as conflict and deadlocks between the government and the legislature. Because these regimes lack a constitutional principle that can be invoked to resolve conflicts between the executive and the legislature, such as the vote of no confidence in parliamentary regimes, minority presidents and deadlock provide incentives for actors to search for extra-constitutional means of resolving their differences. As a consequence, presidential democracies become more prone to instability and eventual death.

The Linzian view, as we said, is widely held.[5] In it, presidential institutions are simply not conducive to governments capable of handling the explosive issues that populate the political agenda in many countries, particularly new democracies in the developing world. These issues make governing difficult under any circumstances. Governing becomes almost impossible when the institutional setup is likely to generate governments with weak legislative support as well as parties and politicians whose dominant strategy is to act independently. Given the lack of constitutional solutions to the crises that are likely to erupt, political actors have no choice beyond appealing to those with guns to intervene and put an end to their misery.

This broad view has at least three important implications. First, the notion that presidentialism is detrimental to democratic consolidation because of the very nature of the system, the sense that there is something inherently problematic about presidential institutions, something that needs to be neutralized for the system to operate properly and generate positive outcomes, is a legacy of the Linzian framework that is hard to dispel.

Second, in the Linzian view, politicians are strictly office-seeking and the pitfalls of presidentialism follow at least partially from this assumption. Yet, once one assumes that politicians also care about policies, it becomes apparent that presidents do have an incentive to seek support in the Legislature, even if their survival in office does not depend on a majority in the legislature. Thus, as Cheibub, Przeworski and Saiegh (2004) argue, the undeniable institutional differences between presidential and parliamentary systems are not sufficient to make coalition governments rare under the former.

Finally, the model of executive-legislative relations that underlies the Linzian view is one of potential conflict. The conflict may lead to deadlock, presidential or congressional domination. Under this view, deadlock, as we have seen, is democracy's kiss of death as there is no constitutional solution to it. Presidents will dominate when they have strong constitutional powers. Constitutionally strong presidents will be able to impose their views over the legislature and will, eventually, usurp powers from it. It is only when the president is weak, institutionally incapable of dominating the legislative process, that presidential democracies stand a chance of functioning in a satisfactory way. Consequently, the primary focus of institutional design should be balancing presidential powers so as to prevent them from overwhelming the political process.

This view was clearly spelled out by Shugart and Carey (1992), who, while calling our attention to the fact that presidential regimes are not all alike, remain within the Linzian framework insofar as their work presupposes an inherently conflictive relationship between the executive and the legislature in presidential regimes. It is this view that leads them to believe that regimes whose constitutions endow presidents with considerable legislative powers have a greater probability of breaking down. Strong presidents, they argue, have the institutional means to impose their will on congress and, for this reason, will have fewer incentives to negotiate with the legislature; paralysis and crisis become more likely. Weak presidents, in turn, know that they have no alternative but to negotiate with congress. Thus, inter-branch conflict dominates cooperation and the possibility is not considered that presidents with strong legislative powers may operate, much like prime ministers in parliamentary systems, as organizers (and not antagonists) of the majority.

2.3   Semi-presidential Democracies

Systems that combine a government dependent on the confidence of a legislative assembly and a popularly elected president have become very popular in the past two decades or so.

These are semi-presidential or mixed systems and countries with such a system today represent about 25% of the democracies in the world (Cheibub 2007: 43). Naturally, the number of scholarly works seeking to evaluate their performance has grown in tandem with the increase in the number of countries that adopted them.

The vast majority of the work on semi-presidential systems has focused on the presidency, seeking to identify the combination of presidential powers that would mitigate what are considered to be the intrinsic difficulties of a semi-presidential form of government. These difficulties are related to the dual nature of the executive, the fact that both the president and the prime minister may claim to be the effective executive leader as both are the product of the democratic process. Problems arise as competencies are not well defined and/or one of the actors seeks to impinge on the domains that the constitution reserves to the other. The potential for conflict increases considerably in situations of 'co-habitation', namely the situations in which a president faces a legislative majority – and consequently a prime minister – from a different (or opposition) party. These are the cases in which the system faces the highest threat to its operation, and the ones that have attracted most attention from scholars. Presidents with strong constitutional powers only make matters worse as they will feel more compelled to play an active role in the political process.

Thus, semi-presidential systems are supposed to be inherently problematic, prone to conflicts between presidents and prime ministers and to legislative paralysis, particularly under 'co-habitation' and/or when presidents have strong constitutional powers; crises will be frequent, which will be detrimental to the country's democratic standing.

It is fair to say that this perspective represents a mere extension to the study of semi-presidentialism of the usual thinking about pure presidentialism. In a similar vein, extending the concern of those who study parliamentary democracies, considerable effort has been dedicated to understanding the duration of governments in semi-presidential regimes (Roper 2002; Elgie 2004; Nikolenyi 2004; Cheibub and Chernykh 2009). Thus, the same points we raised above concerning studies of parliamentary and presidential systems apply to semi-presidential ones.

This is not to say that semi-presidential systems do not raise interesting issues of their own. Here we want to call attention to two main ones, which have been too little studied: the apparent disjuncture between constitutional precepts and practice in semi-presidential systems and the importance of focusing on the powers of the government – as opposed to the powers of the president – when studying semi-presidential democracies.

Regarding the first point, consider the following. Presidential democracies are different in many respects, some of them as crucial and important as the method of election and the existence of constitutional term limits. But, in all presidential democracies, the president, once chosen, is the head of the government, which, once formed, cannot be dismissed by the assembly. Similarly, not all parliamentary systems are alike, and the differences may be as consequential as the formal process of governmental investiture and dismissal. However, in all parliamentary democracies, the government is subject to the confidence of a legislative majority, which, if lost, implies the dismissal of the government as a whole.

Semi-presidential systems do not share such a common feature. Although all semi-presidential systems have constitutions that combine a directly elected president, who is constitutionally allowed to influence the existence of the government, with a government that needs the confidence of the parliament in order to exist, not all of them have presidents who effectively participate in the political process and share governing responsibilities with the prime minister.

On the one hand, we have systems like France, where the president is an effective power in the process of government formation and dismissal, actively participates in governing, and is regarded as being at least partially responsible for policies; the presidency is a desirable post, and increasingly so, as attested by the competitiveness of presidential elections in that country. On the other hand, we have systems such as Iceland, where presidential elections are often uncontested and the directly elected president is commonly perceived as 'a figurehead and symbol of unity rather than a political leader' (Kristinsson 1999: 87), and Finland, where even before the 2000 constitution that codified a more ceremonial role for the president, the system had functioned like a parliamentary democracy (Raunio 2004). Thus, identifying a democratic constitution as semi-presidential does not really convey the way the system actually operates. We need more information to know if it is a system in which the president really matters or if the president plays a more ceremonial, symbolic role. The president matters if the government is effectively dependent on the president in order to exist and this cannot be known from the constitutional text alone.

To pursue the point a little further, constitutions that allow for equally strong presidents may have very different patterns of interaction between the head of state and the head of government. Consider the constitutions of Iceland (1944), Germany (1919) and France (1958). Regarding government formation and assembly dissolution, the German and French constitutions read, in many ways, very much like the Icelandic constitution. Yet, Iceland's political system is considered to function like a parliamentary democracy, Weimar is considered to be the epitome of presidential-parliamentary systems, which are characterized not only by the government's assembly responsibility but also by the primacy of the president (Shugart and Carey 1992:24), and France is considered to be the prototypical mixed, semi-presidential, or premier-parliamentary system (Duverger 1980; Shugart and Carey 1992; Sartori 1994). Thus, according to the Weimar constitution, the prime minister is appointed and dismissed by the president (article 53); the same is true, however, of the prime minister in France (article 8) and in Iceland (article 15). In Iceland, article 24 allows the president to dissolve the assembly with no limitations on this power; in France, according to article 12, the president must consult the prime minister and the presidents of the assemblies before dissolving the assembly, and must wait a year in order to be able to do it again; in Weimar, article 25 allowed the president to dissolve the assembly, but only once for the same reason.

So, the constitutional allocation of powers between the president and the other components of the executive is not sufficient to distinguish semi-presidential systems in which the president 'really' matters from those in which the president plays no significant role in politics. It is intriguing why similarly designed constitutions entail practices that are as divergent as the ones we observe in countries such as Iceland, Austria, Cape Verde, Central African Republic, France, Iceland, Madagascar, Russia and the Ukraine.

Part of the issue may be merely definitional, that is to say, some semi-presidential regimes are no more than parliamentary regimes with an elected president. It is possible to argue that what distinguishes contemporary forms of democratic governments is whether they have assembly confidence or not. Given assembly confidence, whether the president is directly elected may be of little relevance. In all likelihood, the adoption of semi-presidential constitutions in most recent democracies was not driven by the explicit goal of carefully dividing authority between a directly elected president and a government responsible to the parliament. It is more likely that the choice was to create an assembly confidence system and, at the same time, to institute a head of state which, by virtue of its independence from the parliamentary majority, would somehow guarantee the continuity of the state. That this head of state was to be elected by popular vote is almost the default option, given the lack of legitimacy of the alternatives.

Thus, the exclusive focus on the powers of the president when studying semi-presidential systems may be misleading. It is quite possible that governance in assembly confidence systems is guaranteed not by the way the president is elected, or the amount of powers he has, but by other institutional features that strengthen the government, that is, that component of the political structure that needs to obtain the confidence of the legislature: mechanisms that allow the government to shape the legislative agenda, to organize a legislative majority and to keep it reasonably together in the face of the multiplicity of often contradictory interests legislators must reconcile in the course of their careers.

France, the prototypical case of a semi-presidential regime of the more workable variety, provides a good example of how relatively unimportant the role of the president may be in accounting for the system's overall performance. There is general agreement that France under the semi-presidential Fifth Republic became a more stable and governable system than it was under the parliamentary Fourth Republic. One of the most notable features of the new constitution was the introduction of a strong presidency, shaped, it is often said, to fit the personality of the man who was the force behind it.[6] Yet, to say that France became governable as it moved from the Fourth to the Fifth Republics *because* of the constitutional provisions regarding the presidency is to disregard other, probably more significant constitutional changes also introduced with the 1958 constitution. Two of these changes were the package vote (article 44.3), which allows the government to close debate on a bill and force an up or down vote on a proposal that only contains the amendments accepted by the government, and the confidence vote procedure (article 49.3), which, when invoked by the government, stops debate on a bill and, if no motion of censure is introduced and adopted, implies approval of the bill shaped by the government.

We will return to this point in Section 3. Here it is sufficient to note that provisions such as the ones found in the French 1958 constitution are not rare among existing semi-presidential ones. Cheibub and Chernykh (2009) show that 59% of the constitutions in place since 1919 allow the government to request a confidence vote on specific legislation; 48% grant the government control over the budget process; 35% place restrictions on the assembly's ability to pass a vote of no confidence in the government; 37% forbid legislators from serving in the government; and 23% contain provisions that allow the government to request urgency in the treatment of legislative proposals. It is remarkable that while a lot of effort has been spent in trying to identify the effects of the constitutional powers of the president in semi-presidential systems, powers which, as we suggested above, are not really descriptive of the way the system actually works, virtually no work has been done on the effect of the powers of the government on the performance of these systems. We attribute this oversight to the fact that much of the literature on semi-presidentialism has been informed by the concerns of the earlier generation of studies of both parliametarism (as expressed in the preoccupation with the duration of cabinets) and presidentialism (as expressed in the virtual obsession with the powers of the president). Newer studies, however, suggest that we look at legislative-executive relations differently. It is to them that we now turn.

3   MORE RECENT STUDIES

What distinguishes the studies we discuss in this section from the previous ones is that they do not assume that the mode of government formation completely shapes 'governability' or the legislative process. According to the more traditional view reviewed above, interests generated in the electoral arena ultimately define relations between the two branches. On this view, governments under parliamentarism have a built-in mechanism to overcome inter-branch conflict, namely, the threat to dissolve the assembly and provoke early elections. It is the incentive to avoid new elections that leads the rank-and-file members of parliament to subject to partisan directives and support the governments of which their parties are members. Presidents, in turn, cannot count on the dissolution threat and, for this reason, are deprived of consistent support in the legislature. In this view, politicians are primarily office-seekers and the possibility of losing office is what drives their behavior. The legislative arena proper, that is, the locus of the interaction between the executive and the legislature over policy, is completely irrelevant. It is this arena that is stressed by what we are calling the new generation of studies of executive-legislative relations. As a matter of fact, it is the emphasis on the way legislatures organize their business and define who holds the power to control the agenda that allows us to speak of the otherwise widely heterogeneous studies we will discuss below as belonging to a common generation.

There are two other features of the new studies of legislative-executive relations, which follow from their common emphasis on the legislative arena. First, the expected pattern of interaction between the two branches becomes one of coordination rather than conflict. Inter-branch relations are modeled as a coordination or bargaining game rather than as a zero-sum game where the gains of the executive happen at the expense of the legislature. Second, there is a marked shift in the assumptions regarding politicians' motivations. Just as office seeking is associated with the conflict view, the supposition that politicians *also* care about policy is associated with the coordination view of legislative-executive relations. And given that policies cannot be enacted unilaterally by one of the branches, it is only through the continuous existence of a majority that controls both the executive and the legislature that the policies preferred by both will become reality. In this sense, the incentive to coordinate rather than confront is inherent in the democratic political framework, regardless of the way these bodies are formed.

Finally, these studies recognize the importance of electoral competition among parties, even those who coordinate to support a government. Legislative coordination must be achieved with an eye to the fact that, at elections, parties will fiercely compete for votes. Communication with voters about the party's or the legislator's positions is an essential part of this competition. As will become clear in the discussion below, this fact offers a new perspective on legislative behavior and certain types of governments that, at first sight, appear to be the outcome of irreconcilable conflict among political actors and between the legislative and the executive branches.

We will organize our discussion in terms of three main themes, stressing the empirical regularities associated with them and their implications for the study of executive-legislative relations in democratic regimes. The first is the discovery that minority governments in parliamentary regimes are neither infrequent nor ephemeral; the second is the acknowledgment that coalition governments are neither rare nor uniquely unstable in presidential systems; and the third is the recognition that the executive's use of restrictive legislative tools does not necessarily imply that it is unilaterally imposing its will on the legislature. Each one of these 'discoveries' contributed to reducing the divide between presidential and parliamentary forms of government. By employing knowledge generated in the study of one of these systems to understand the other, these studies have demonstrated that the radical distinction that exists between the two systems when it comes to formation and survival does not necessarily extend to their operation.

3.1 Minority Governments in Parliamentary Democracies

Minority governments are hard to explain under the traditional view of parliamentary democracies. Given office-seeking politicians and the 'majoritarian imperative' created by the confidence mechanism, minority governments should never exist. If they do, they must have resulted from some kind of system malfunction and would disappear as soon as these problems were 'solved'.[7] It was not until Strom's seminal book (1990) that this view was radically changed, with consequences for how we think about both parliamentary and presidential systems in general, and legislative-executive relations in particular.

Strom's contribution is both empirical and theoretical. Empirically, he shows that minority governments are not infrequent in European parliamentary democracies and that they do not do worse when compared to majority coalition governments. Theoretically, Strom's contribution is to show that minority governments emerge out of party leaders' calculus about the costs and benefits of participating in government. Assuming that politicians care about office and policy (as well as votes), Strom argues that there are conditions under which rational parties will *prefer* to remain out of the government. The decision to refrain from joining a government is affected by the degree of policy influence parties can exert from the outside, as well as by their expectation regarding electoral returns (positive or negative) of joining the government. Out-of-government policy influence, in turn, depends essentially on the organization of parliament, that is, factors such as the existence of standing committees, their degree of specialization, their scope of action, and the way they are allocated. Electoral consequences depend on the decisiveness and competitiveness of the electoral process. When parties can affect policies even if they are not in the government, and the electoral costs of incumbency are perceived to be high, parties will rationally choose to stay out of the government. The emergence of minority governments, therefore, has nothing to do with political systems that are dysfunctional.

From the perspective of this review, what is relevant is the fact that Strom's analysis accounts for variation within parliamentary democracies by highlighting factors related to the internal organization of the legislature. Legislative organization had either been neglected in analyses of parliamentarism or, more commonly, had been assumed to be constant within each form of democratic regime. Thus, discussions of legislative organization were organized around the two paradigmatic cases of England and the United States: a centralized and a decentralized legislature, respectively, and, as we know, a parliamentary and a presidential democracy. Arguments about decision making in democracies tended to contrast these two systems and assume, often implicitly, that all legislatures and, for that matter, the decision-making process, are centralized under parliamentarism and decentralized under presidentialism.

Strom's analysis suggests that legislative organization varies significantly under parliamentary regimes, at least sufficiently to affect how political parties calculate the value of formally joining a government. In close affinity to models developed to account for the operation of the US Congress, which emphasize the role of standing committees in providing opportunities for all parties to influence policy (Shepsle 1979; Shepsle and Weingast 1987), he shows that minority governments in parliamentary democracies will be more frequent when the parliament is organized in such a way as to offer 'structural opportunities for oppositional influence' (Strom 1990: 72). It follows from this that the way the legislature is organized can explain the variation in legislative-executive relations *across* types of democratic regime.

The recognition that minority governments may be functional in parliamentary systems has a direct bearing on the discussions about the perils of presidentialism stimulated by Linz. As we indicated above, minority presidents were considered to be ineffective and, consequently, would have strong incentives to find ways to circumvent or to altogether ignore the legislature. But minority presidents may be as effective as minority prime ministers if opposition parties care about similar things in both systems (office, policy and votes) and go through the same calculus about supporting a government. Since there are no good reasons to believe that parties have different goals in parliamentary and presidential systems, it is easy to see that, even though they all aspire to capture the presidency at the next election, opposition parties may cooperate with the incumbent president on policy grounds. Moreover, since presidents may also form coalition governments, something we discuss next, minority presidents do not imply minority governments.[8]

3.2 Coalition Government

At the root of the view that presidentialism causes democratic instability is the idea that presidential institutions provide no incentive for coalition formation. This fact, as we have seen, would have disastrous consequences: minority presidents would be unable to obtain the support of a majority of legislators, deadlock would ensue as legislative activity is brought to a halt and, given the impossibility of constitutionally removing the government from office, actors would have an incentive to invoke extra-constitutional solutions.

That government coalitions do exist in presidential democracies has been recognized and served as the premise of several analyses at least since the 1980s. Abranches (1988) is probably the earliest author to refer to a type of presidential system that is characterized by the occurrence of coalition governments: '*presidencialismo de coalizão*', a label that is now part of the vernacular of academics and other analysts in Brazil and elsewhere. In his wake, several case studies were conducted, including, for example, Altman (2000) about Uruguay, Mejía Acosta (2009) about Ecuador, among others. There are also earlier comparative studies that take the occurrence of coalition governments as given and analyze secondary issues directly related to coalitions. For example, Deheza (1997) is primarily concerned with the relationship between electoral and governmental coalitions; Amorin Neto (1998) focuses on the way presidents manage existing coalitions and the impact different styles of management have on government performance; Zelaznik (2001) is concerned with the different strategies presidents adopt to form a coalition government.

Important as these studies are, they simply asserted that coalition governments existed under presidentialism and proceeded to analyze them. By ignoring the issue of the incentives for coalition formation, they remained open to the charge that observed coalitions in presidential democracies are flimsy, short-lived and devoid of any meaning. They may form but do not last and do not imply any policy commitment on the part of the coalition members.

Cheibub, Przeworski and Saiegh (2004; see also Cheibub 2007) directly addressed the incentive issue. They argued that while there is no doubt that presidential and parliamentary systems characterize distinct forms of democratic governments, what matters is whether the differences between these two systems are sufficient to generate opposite incentives for coalition formation. We proceed now to summarize their analysis.

Parliamentary and presidential systems are indeed different when it comes to the institutional features relevant for coalition formation. Cheibub et al. (2004) identified two main ones. First, in presidential democracies the president is always the government *formateur*, while in parliamentary democracies any party is a potential *formateur*. Thus, not only is the number of *possible* government coalitions smaller in presidential than in parliamentary systems, the party of the president, regardless of its size, will always be in the government. Second, failure to form a coalition government leads to different outcomes in each system. In parliamentary democracies, with few exceptions, it is the occurrence of new elections: voters are given the chance to return a new distribution of seats, hopefully one that will allow for the formation of a viable government. In presidential systems, failure to form a coalition implies that the party of the president is the only one to hold government portfolios, while policies may or may not continue the status quo.

But do these differences imply that parties in one system will want to join together to form a coalition government, whereas in the other they will want to pursue their goals independently and exclusively strive to achieve the presidency? Borrowing from existing models of coalition formation in parliamentary democracies, where parties care about both office and policy, Cheibub et al. show that there are conditions under which presidents will invite and parties will accept offers to join the government in coalition. Specifically, whether a coalition government will emerge depends on the distance between the party of the president and the next party in the policy space. When presidents do not dominate the legislative process and parties have dispersed policy preferences, presidents will offer, and non-presidential parties will accept, portfolios in the government in exchange for policy cooperation and a coalition government will be formed. If parties have policy positions that are close to each other, then presidents will keep all portfolios for their party, will allow policy to be set by a non-presidential party, and a minority single-party government will emerge.

Of great relevance here is the fact that, given a lack of presidential dominance over the legislative process, the conditions under which a coalition government will emerge are identical in presidential and parliamentary systems. This is not so when presidents dominate the legislative process, in which case the outcome will depend on the location of the status quo. If the status quo is situated between the ideal policies of two non-presidential parties, then, as before, the outcome – coalition or minority governments – will depend on how close the parties' policy positions are to one another. If the status quo is situated between the ideal policy of the president and that of a non-presidential party, then the Linzian scenario may emerge: there will be no combination of policy and portfolio that can convince a non-presidential party into participating in the government; yet, since the president dominates the legislative process, the non-presidential parties cannot ally in the legislature and set policies that they prefer over those proposed by the president. Thus, while confirming that under presidentialism, but not under parliamentarism, a minority portfolio government may face a hostile legislative majority, the results of this analysis show that coalition governments are far from being an abnormality in presidential democracies.

There are several implications of this analysis that directly challenge the traditional view of executive-legislative relations. To begin with, as stated above, it shows that under some circumstances coalition and minority governments will emerge for exactly the same reasons in both presidential and parliamentary systems. Moreover, it follows from this analysis that the absence of coalition governments does not automatically imply a lack of cooperation among political parties. The crucial distinction here, already explicit in Strom (1990), is that between *government* (or portfolio) and *legislative* coalitions, which do not always coincide: there will be governments composed of one single party that are nonetheless supported by a legislative coalition. Thus, given that no party holds more than 50% of legislative seats, some minority governments occur under presidentialism for the same reason that they emerge under parliamentarism: no legislative majority wants to replace them because enough parties get policies they like. They are, in this sense, supported minority governments that will be at least as effective legislatively as coalition governments.

Thus, according to Cheibub et al. (2004), the structure of presidential systems is not sufficient to make coalition governments atypical. These governments may be more frequent under parliamentarism than under presidentialism, but they form in the latter in response to the same incentives that lead parties to coalesce in the former: a desire to balance their simultaneous objectives of being in office and seeing the policies they like being enacted. Those who see presidential institutions providing no incentives for coalition formation have placed excessive emphasis on the first goal – offices – to the detriment of the other goal – policies. It is only by seeing politicians as actors who care about both goals that we can understand that presidents, in spite of the fact that they do not need to share office in order to survive, may want to do so in order to govern.

3.3   Agenda Power and the Decision-Making Process

In the traditional model of legislative-executive relations, a strong government, that is, one endowed with a large array of legislative powers, will use these powers against the legislature. The greater the conflict between the two branches of government, the greater the incentives the executive will have to use these powers in order to see its will prevail over the recalcitrant legislature.

This view has been challenged and the seminal work in the field is Huber's (1996) study of policy making under the 1958 French constitution. Specifically, in his book Huber focuses on the role of the package vote and the confidence vote procedure – two features of the 1958 constitution that strengthen the government's legislative powers[9] – in shaping how the executive and the legislature interact.

Using an adapted version of the classical agenda-setter model (Romer and Rosenthal 1978) and drawing heavily upon models developed to understand the relations between the floor and committees in the US Congress, Huber accomplishes a series of tasks that re-direct the way one should think about the use of restrictive legislative procedures by the executive. In the first place, he demonstrates theoretically and empirically that, contrary to the prevailing perception of students of French politics, the use of restrictive procedures is not related to the degree of policy conflict between the government and the parliament. In other words, the government does not use restrictive procedures as a way to guarantee that its preferences prevail when these preferences are at odds with those of the legislature.[10]

Second, Huber shows that not all restrictive procedures are the same. He demonstrates that the package vote is a mechanism used by the government to protect the outcome of bargaining in a multidimensional policy space among parties within the governing coalition, or between the government and the opposition. By halting legislative debate and forcing an up-or-down vote on a bill that contains only the amendments the government chooses to retain, the package vote compels legislators to choose between a specific policy package and the status quo. Since the legislature is the last one to act – it has the last word – it will approve the bill only if it is preferred to the status quo. In this sense, the government does not impose its will; rather it forces a choice between the status quo and a policy change.

Finally, Huber shows that the confidence vote plays a different role than the package vote in the legislative process. While it can also serve as a mechanism for protecting policy bargains in multidimensional spaces – it allows coalition members to implement a given policy while criticizing it in the parliament – its primary role is to allow parties in the majority to compete for votes at the same time that they cooperate to pass legislation. Thus, members of the majority can make sincere, position-taking proposals in the legislature in order to communicate their policy positions to their voters, force the government to use the confidence vote and, given that now the vote is no longer on the policy issue alone but on the very survival of the government, refrain from supporting the censure motion and allow the policy to be enacted. This policy, however, as with the package vote, is not unrelated to the preferences of the majority. Although the prime minister will explore the first mover advantage of proposing a specific policy, her choice will be constrained by the preferences of the majority. That is to say, the PM will propose a policy that is closest to her ideal point within the set of policies the majority prefers over the status quo. In this sense, while they give some leeway to the government to pick a policy it likes, neither the vote of confidence nor the package vote can be used *against* the majority.

The implications of this analysis are profound when it comes to analyzing executive-legislative relations. To begin with, the analytical focus shifts from outside forces – the way legislators and governments get and retain their mandates – to the specific rules regulating executive-legislative relations. As with Strom, and perhaps even more forcefully than he, the relevant variables for understanding policy making are located inside rather than outside the legislature. Second, not all parliaments are rationalized in the sense used by Huber (see also Lauvaux 1988), that is, not all parliaments contain provisions that allow the government to control the flow of legislation. In this sense, government control over the legislative agenda is neither intrinsic to nor follows from the principle that defines parliamentarism. That is to say, the strong cabinet control of the legislative process and the near irrelevance of individual members of parliament in this process, which characterizes England, are not inherent in parliamentary governments, as illustrated by the cases of Italy after 1945 and France in the Third and Fourth Republics. In both cases, the government had no control over the definition of the legislative agenda, committees had considerable power, and the rights of individual legislators were not 'expropriated'.[11] Similarly, and by extension, there is nothing in presidentialism that requires that a well-functioning system be one in which a weak president faces a strong congress. Although this describes the allocation of powers across branches in the US system and the US is the only presidential democracy that has lasted for a long time, it does not follow that the success of the US system can be attributed to the specific way powers are allocated across the presidential and the legislative branches.[12]

This characterization sheds new light on the mechanisms that produce party discipline. The threat of dissolution and early elections is not a sufficient condition to hold party members in line, as the frequent fall of the French and Italian governments demonstrates. And it is not a necessary condition either, since it does occur under presidentialism. Nor, it should be noted, can it be inferred from characteristics of the electoral laws since disciplined parties are observed in countries that adopt candidate-centered rules, such as Finland, Brazil, and Chile among others. Discipline is rather a function of restrictive procedures, of denying the rank-and-file members the space for opportunistic behavior. In other words, party discipline is less a product of punishing free riders than of pre-empting the opportunities for free-riding. The expropriation of the rank-and-file legislative rights implied by the concentration of agenda powers in the hands of the executive renders the individual and independent action of legislators futile. For these legislators, the rational course of action when it comes to voting in the assembly is to follow their parties' directives. This is the only way they will be able to influence public policies and send signals to voters (see Limongi and Figueiredo 1998).

If Huber's analysis is correct, and we believe it is, a legislatively strong government, be it under parliamentarism or under presidentialism, does not imply a powerless legislative majority. Given the near obsession of the comparative literature on presidentialism with the risks resulting from strong presidents, this point needs to be examined in further detail.

3.3.1   Strong presidents and decree power

Almost all presidential constitutions give some legislative powers to the presidency. The most important powers include veto, decree, and urgency powers, as well as the government's exclusive power to introduce legislation in specified areas.[13] All these features of presidential agenda powers are rather consequential, and they combine into institutionally weaker or stronger presidencies. Although there are many who believe that strong presidents are problematic in that they will clash with congress and eventually generate government and even regime crises, there are those who argue that strong presidents are not necessarily bad for the operation of presidential constitutions. For instance, the strong presidential agenda powers established by the post-authoritarian constitutions of countries such as Brazil and Chile are considered to be largely responsible for the high level of legislative success of their governments (Figueiredo and Limongi 2000a and 2000b; Siavelis 2000; Jones and Hwang 2005; and Amorin Neto et al. 2003; Londregan 2000).

The case of Brazil seems to be highly relevant here given the large number of centrifugal elements built into the system, which in combination with presidentialism would suggest high volatility and ungovernability: a federally structured country with economically diverse regions, political parties with weak popular penetration, the adoption of an open-list proportional representation system with low barriers to entry, and features that make state governors influential over party decisions. Yet, legislative behavior in the Brazilian Congress has exhibited remarkably high levels of partisanship, with presidents capable of relying on stable coalitions that supported them on most of their legislative agenda. This unexpected pattern, in turn, is a function of the president's legislative powers granted by the 1988 constitution, which include all of the powers discussed above: partial-veto power, decree power, the power to request urgency in the consideration of specific legislation, and the exclusive power to initiate budget legislation. The concentration of legislative powers in the executive's hand, coupled with a highly centralized decision-making structure in the legislative chambers, explains the high degree of legislative success of Brazilian presidents – a success that is not much different from that obtained in parliamentary democracies (Figueiredo and Limongi 2000a, 2000b and 2007).

The operation of this mechanism, of course, raises a number of interesting questions. Most prominent is the issue of whether the president, in his capacity as the head of government, is imposing his preferences rather than those of the legislative majority. Despite some divergences, to which we will turn below, the vast majority of the analyses that address this issue adopt a model of conflict between the two branches. The possibility that these instruments – in a way similar to the restrictive procedures analyzed by Huber – can be used as tools for the coordination of a governing majority is not even considered. This can be clearly observed in the scholarly debate about the use of decree power by Brazilian presidents. Although a series of high-quality and sophisticated studies have been recently produced on this theme, they primarily see the interaction between the government and congress as if it were zero-sum.

In order to provide some context, here are some of the basic facts about decrees since the 1988 constitution came into force in September 1989: every president who governed since 1989 has liberally used their decree powers. On average, 3.9 decrees were issued between September 1989 and September 2001.[14] Sarney (who governed under the 1988 constitution from September 1989 to February 1990) issued 7.1 decrees per month; Collor (March 1990–October 1992) 2.8 per month; Itamar Franco (November 1992–December 1993) 5.4 per month, and Cardoso (January 1994–December 2001) 3.3. Collor is the only president who, in spite of forming coalition governments, did not reach majority status. He is also the president with the lowest rate of success in transforming his decrees into laws: 77.6%, as opposed to well above 80% for all the other presidents.

There are two broad types of explanations for the variation in the use of decrees by recent Brazilian presidents, the political-conditional and the institutional. The first sees decrees as one among alternative options in a menu of instruments available to presidents seeking to implement their legislative agenda. The choice between these instruments is seen as a function of the political context within which presidents must interact with the legislature, and of circumstantial factors, such as the president's popularity, the occurrence of elections, or the existence of pressures for speedy executive action.

The political-conditional view of presidential decree usage, in fact, sustains two competing positions, which Pereira, Power and Rennó (2006) call 'unilateral action' and 'delegation' theories. In the former, presidents use their decree powers when they do not have the necessary support to get ordinary legislation approved in Congress. In this perspective, the use of decrees constitutes a way for the president to bypass an unfriendly congress. Thus, the share of decrees in the president's overall legislative strategy will increase when he cannot count on the reliable and steady support of a legislative majority. The share of seats controlled by the parties also holding cabinet positions often indicates this support. Delegation theory, in turn, sees presidential decrees as a convenient means at the disposal of the legislative majority, which may prefer to transfer some of its powers to the executive for a variety of reasons. These may include partisan support for individual governments, collective action problems within the legislature, or electoral incentives of individual legislators (Carey and Shugart 1998).

Both unilateral-action and delegation theories predict that the reliance on decrees by presidents is a function of the political conditions they face; the only difference is that they predict opposite effects. According to unilateral-action theory, the use of decrees will increase when the president faces unfavorable political conditions; according to delegation theory, the use of decrees will increase when the president faces favorable political conditions. The balance of the evidence provided by the literature is mixed: Pereira et al. (2006) found that the results are highly dependent upon the particular starting conditions, but they do show, in some instances, that the evidence supports delegation theory. On the other hand, Amorin Neto, Cox and McCubbins (2003) suggest that the data best conform to the unilateral-action theory.

In spite of their differences, both unilateral action and delegation theories see the usage of decrees as a decision taken by the executive that does not involve the legislature. Yet, inspired by analyses such as Huber's, we can formulate a more institutional hypothesis that does not postulate any kind of necessary antagonism between the two branches. According to this hypothesis, the post-1988 institutional structure that was built in Brazil facilitated the shaping and sustaining of a legislative majority by the government. Presidential decree power represents one of the main instruments for doing this – it is a mechanism whereby through negotiation and bargaining the executive can lead the process of shaping a legislative majority in support of the policies it wishes to implement. Although he leads, the president does not mandate: the majority in the legislature has the last word and any decree that the president issues that is not preferred by the majority to the *status quo ante* can be rejected. And, as Amorin Neto et al. (2003: 571) show, this is precisely what happened during Collor de Mello's presidency (1990–92): led by the pivotal Partido do Movimento Democrático Brasileiro (PMDB), the opposition was able to counter Collor's decree powers by rejecting important decrees and forcing him to form a new coalition in order to be able to govern (see also Figueiredo and Limongi 1999). This shows how there is no way the president can circumvent the legislature. Unilateral action as a way of governing and setting policies contrary to preferences of the majority is simply not feasible. In this sense, the use of decrees by the executive is neither an act of delegation by the legislature nor unilateral power grabbing by the executive; attempting to adjudicate among these two perspectives is, we believe, probably futile.

Decrees are, by design, instruments that allow the executive to set the legislative agenda; through this action, however, the government is able to bring together a legislative majority, a necessary step if it wants the policies implemented through decrees to become law. Thus, the matter is not whether congress delegates or the president usurps legislative powers. The question is: how does the president use decrees to shape the legislative agenda and to bring about a legislative majority?

According to the institutional hypothesis, decrees are used both as convenient means to address routine issues and as regular instruments in the negotiations and bargaining that characterize the legislative process. Since they are neither usurpation nor delegation, they do not vary systematically with political factors such as the legislative strength of the president, his ability to manage his coalition, or his popularity. Some circumstantial factors, such as macroeconomic pressures leading to the implementation of emergency stabilization plans, matter, but they do so simply because it is only through decrees that presidents can act with the speed, secrecy and surprise that are sometimes considered to be essential for the policy's success. Even in these cases, however, presidents can and often do succeed in transforming their decrees into regular legislation.

Although we have dealt at some length with the Brazilian case, it is worth reinforcing that this is far from being a unique case. Most presidents are endowed with decree power by their respective constitutions. Indeed, recent scholarly work has shown that in some countries where this power is denied to them, presidents have been able to force their way and get some sort of de facto decree power. Argentina from 1983 to 1995 and the United States are two prominent examples. As Rubio and Goretti (1998) have shown, both

Alfonsin and Menén relied on some old precedents to issue 'decrees of necessity and urgency' (DNU). Although primarily aimed at curbing hyperinflation, DNUs were also used to regulate more mundane affairs. The doubtful constitutional basis of this presidential prerogative was resolved with the 1995 constitutional reform, which introduced presidential decree powers that are similar to those granted by the 1988 Brazilian constitution.

In the US, the constitutional provision stipulating that the president 'shall take care that the Laws be faithfully executed' led to the unilateral issuing of executive orders, which have been interpreted by the Supreme Court as having the same status as a law passed by Congress. Executive orders have been issued to deal with important matters, including nationalizations, internment of Japanese-Americans during World War II, desegregation of the military, creation of the Peace Corps and the Environmental Protection Agency, federalization of the national guard, multiple health care initiatives, affirmative action policies, and the creation of special military tribunals to try non-US citizens accused of terrorism (Howell 2003: 1–6). Thus, even in the absence of any formal decree power, US presidents can still influence policy in a way similar to the 'strong' presidents designed by the Brazilian and Chilean constitutions.

What is important to retain from this discussion, though, is that institutionally strong presidents are not necessarily detrimental to the functioning of presidential democracies. Attempts to weaken them on the ground that they usurp the power that should rest with the assembly must, therefore, be re-evaluated and considered in light of the benefits they bring about in terms of government performance (Croissant 2003; Londregan 2000).

4   CONCLUSION

As we said at the beginning, this is necessarily an incomplete review of a large literature. Our goal was to establish a contrast between what we called a 'traditional' and a 'recent' set of works that, in spite of their heterogeneity, have in common a conception of the way the executive and the legislative interact in a democratic system. 'Traditional' works adopt a perspective of conflict between the two powers, which derives from the emphasis they give to the way governments and legislatures are formed, and from a narrow view of politicians' motivations as being purely office-oriented. 'Recent' works, in contrast, expand their purview to include the legislative process per se, that is, the moment of proposing and supporting policies. They also adopt a broader view of politicians' motivations, who, in addition to office, also care about policies and must compete for votes.

One broad consequence of this shift in perspective is a blurring of the distinction between presidential and parliamentary forms of government. Of course this does not mean that presidentialism and parliamentarism are identical; they clearly are not and actors in each system may have available to them strategies that are not feasible in the other. The point is that once we accept that politicians across systems have similar motivations, and that legislative institutions are not dependent on the form of government, it is possible to see that the democratic process of passing laws, which necessarily involves both the executive and the legislature, is in fact quite similar across different types of political systems.

NOTES

1. See Laver and Schofield (1998) for the best analysis of the different theories of coalition formation.
2. See Grofman and Van Roozendaal (1997) and Laver (2003) for reviews.
3. Reviews of presidential studies usually lament their lack of scientific depth and general backwardness when compared to the rest of the discipline. For an example, see Edwards III et al. (1993). For a more optimistic and recent review see Moe (2009).
4. The initial argument appeared in Linz (1978) and was developed in a paper that was widely circulated before it was published in (1994). See also Linz (1990a and 1990b).
5. See, for a few examples, Mainwaring and Scully (1995: 33), Gonzalez and Gillespie (1994: 172), Riggs (1988), Ackerman (2000: 645), Stepan and Skach (1993: 17), Valenzuela (2004: 16).
6. Direct presidential elections were not introduced until 1962.
7. Also troubling for the traditional view are oversized coalitions, which should also not exist. Yet, they do exist. According to Laver and Schofield (1998: 70), 25% of the cabinets that existed in 12 European democracies between 1945 and 1987 were surplus majority coalitions.
8. The only exception is, of course, in a two-party presidential system, where, save for national fronts, which emerge in extraordinary circumstances, a minority president will imply a divided government. Note, however, that presidential two-party systems are infrequent and exist primarily in Costa Rica and the United States. The frequency with which, in the latter country, they have emerged in the post-World War II period has led to the emergence of an enormous literature, which we will not address here. For our purposes here, suffice it to say that much of this literature revolves around the seminal book by Mayhew (1991), which reports no difference in the policy effectiveness of divided and unified governments and proposes an explanation for this similarity that is compatible with Strom's explanation of minority governments.
9. The package vote (article 44.3) allows the government to close debate on a bill and force an up-or-down vote on a proposal containing only the amendments proposed or accepted by the government; the confidence vote procedure (article 49.3), when invoked by the government, stops debate on a bill and, if no motion of censure is introduced and adopted, implies approval of the bill shaped by the government.
10. Huber's argument is analogous to the one developed by Shepsle (1979), Shepsle and Weingast (1987) and Shepsle and Weingast in their discussion with Krehbiel (Krehbiel et al. 1987) to the effect that congressional committees in the US cannot legislate against the will of the floor.
11. In France, until 1911, it was the Chamber presidents who defined the legislative agenda. As Andrews (1978: 471) reports, despite several incremental reforms, the government did not have firm control over the definition of the legislative agenda and it was easy to introduce no-confidence votes, leading to the fall of the government. Moreover, committees could veto policy, since a report from the committee was necessary for consideration of a bill by the floor. The government could expedite the committee report but could not avoid it. Therefore, committees could respond to government pressure with an unsatisfactory report. Besides, according to Andrews (1978), the Third and Fourth Republics placed few restrictions on the ability of private members to propose initiatives that would increase expenditures and reduce revenues. In the Italian parliament, the presidents of each house, and not the government, define the legislative agenda. Bills introduced by the government have no special calendar or precedence over private members' bills. Article 72 of the Italian constitution grants standing committees the authority to pass laws. As for individual members of parliament, until the 1988 reform, roll calls were secret and could be easily requested at any stage of the law-making process (Cotta 1990: 77). Hence, the government fell prey to the action of the *franco attiratori*. In other words, members of the majority could not be sanctioned, either by the government or their parties.
12. But see below for a different account of the institutional power of US presidents.
13. See Cheibub (2009) for a brief description of each of these powers.
14. This is when the constitution was amended to change the rules governing presidential decrees. Aimed at curbing the number of decrees, it attempted to clarify the conditions under which they could be issued, it limited the number of times a decree could be re-issued, and it forced the Congress to take action on a decree rather than simply allow it to expire. For reasons that are too extensive for us to address here, the number of decrees actually increased following the 2001 constitutional amendment (Figueiredo and Limongi 2007). The numbers in the paragraph reflect only new decrees, and not the reissuing of old decrees. If the latter are considered, the averages change significantly, reaching, for example, hundreds a month during Cardoso's government.

REFERENCES

Abranches, Sérgio (1988), 'Presidencialismo de Coalizão: O Dilema Institucional Brasileiro', *Dados*, 31 (1), 5–33.
Ackerman, Bruce (2000) 'The New Separation of Powers', *Harvard Law Review*, 113 (3), 642–727.

Altman, David (2000), 'The Politics of Coalition Formation and Survival in Multiparty Presidential Democracies: The Case of Uruguay (1989–1999)', *Party Politics*, 6 (3), 259–83.

Amorin Neto, Octávio (1998), 'Of Presidents, Parties, and Ministers: Cabinet Formation and Legislative Decision-Making under Separation of Powers', Ph.D. Dissertation, University of California, San Diego.

Amorin Neto, Octávio, Gary Cox and Mathew D. McCubbins (2003). 'Agenda Power in Brazil's Camara dos Deputados, 1989–98', *World Politics*, 55 (4), 550–78.

Andrews, William. G. (1978), 'The Constitutional Prescription of Parliamentary Procedures in Gaullist France', *Legislative Studies Quarterly*, 3 (3), 465–506.

Axelrod, Robert (1970), *Conflict of Interest: A Theory of Divergent Goals with Applications to Politics*, Chicago: Markham.

Carey, John M. and Mathew Shugart (1998), 'Calling out the Tanks or Just Filling Out the Forms?', in John M. Carey and Mathew Shugart (eds), *Executive Decree Authority*, New York: Cambridge University Press, pp. 1–32.

Cheibub, José Antonio (2007), *Presidentialism, Parliamentarism and Democracy*, New York: Cambridge University Press.

Cheibub, José Antonio (2009), 'Making Presidential and Semi-Presidential Constitutions Work', *Texas Law Review*, 88 (7), 1375–408.

Cheibub, José Antonio and Svitlana Chernykh (2009), 'Are Semi-presidential Constitutions Bad for Democracy?', *Constitutional Political Economy*, 20 (3–4), 202–29.

Cheibub, José Antonio, Adam Przeworski, and Sebastian Saiegh (2004), 'Government Coalitions and Legislative Success under Parliamentarism and Presidentialism', *British Journal of Political Science*, 34 (4), 565–87.

Cotta, Maurizio (1990). 'The Centrality of Parliament in a Protracted Democratic Consolidation: The Italian Case', in U. Liebert and M. Cotta (eds), *Parliament and Democratic Consolidation in Southern Europe*, London: Pinter Publishers, pp. 55–91.

Croissant, Aurel (2003), 'Legislative Powers, Veto Players, and the Emergence of Delegative Democracy: A Comparison of Presidentialism in the Philippines and South Korea', *Democratization*, 10 (3), 68–98.

Deheza, Grace Ivana (1997). 'Gobiernos de Coalición en el Sistema Presidencial: América del Sur', Ph. D. Dissertation, European University Institute, Florence, Italy.

De Swaan, Abram (1973). *Coalition Theories and Cabinet Formations*, Amsterdam: Elsevier.

Duverger, Maurice (1980), 'A New Political System Model: Semi-Presidential Government', *European Journal of Political Research*, 8 (2), 166–87.

Edwards, George C. III, John Howard Kessel and Bert A. Rockman (1993), 'Introduction', in George C. Edwards III, John Howard Kessel and Bert A. Rockman (eds), *Researching the Presidency: Vital Questions, New Approaches*, Pittsburgh: University of Pittsburgh Press, pp. 3–22.

Elgie, Robert (2004). 'Semi-presidentialism: Concepts, Consequences, and Contested Explanations', *Political Studies Review*, 2, 313–30.

Figueiredo, Argelina and Fernando Limongi (1999), *Executivo e Legislativo na Nova Ordem Constitucional*, Rio de Janeiro: Editora FGV.

Figueiredo, Argelina and Fernando Limongi (2000a), 'Constitutional Change, Legislative Performance, and Institutional Consolidation', *Brazilian Review of Social Sciences*, 1, special issue, October, 1–22.

Figueiredo, Argelina and Fernando Limongi (2000b), 'Presidential Power, Legislative Organization and Party Behavior in the Legislature', *Comparative Politics*, 32 (2), 151–70.

Figueiredo, Argelina and Fernando Limongi (2007), 'Instituciones Políticas y Governabilidad: Desempeno del Gobierno y Apoyo Legislativo en la Democracia Brasileña', in Carlos Ranulfo de Melo and Manuel Alcãntara Sáez (eds), *La Democracia Brasilena: Ballance y Perspectivas para el Siglo XXI*, Salamanca: Ediciones Universidad Salamanca, pp. 117–55.

González, Luis Eduardo and Charles Guy Gillespie (1994), 'Presidentialism and Democratic Stability in Uruguay', in J. Linz and A. Valenzuela (eds), *The Failure of Presidential Democracy: The Case of Latin America, Vol. 2*, Baltimore: Johns Hopkins University Press, pp. 151–78.

Grofman, Bernard and Peter Van Roozendaal (1997), 'Review Article: Modelling Cabinet Durability and Termination', *British Journal of Political Science*, 27, 419–51.

Howell, William G. (2003), *Power without Persuasion: The Politics of Direct Presidential Action*, Princeton: Princeton University Press.

Huang, The-fu (1997), 'Party Systems in Taiwan and South Korea', in Larry Diamond, Marc F. Plattner, Yun-han Chu and Hung-mao Tien (eds), *Consolidating the Third Wave Democracies: Themes and Perspectives*, Baltimore: Johns Hopkins University Press, pp. 135–59.

Huber, John D. (1996), *Rationalizing Parliament*, New York: Cambridge University Press.

Humphreys, Macartan (2008), 'Coalitions', *Annual Review of Political Science*, 11, 351–86.

Jones, Mark P. (1995), *Electoral Laws and the Survival of Presidential Democracies*, Notre Dame: Notre Dame University Press.

Jones, Mark. P. and Wonjae Hwang (2005), 'Party Government in Presidential Democracies: Extending Cartel Theory beyond the U.S. Congress', *American Journal of Political Science*, 49 (2), 267–82.

Krehbiel, Keith (1987), 'Sophisticated Committees and Structure-induced Equilibria in Congress', in Mathew McCubbins and Terry Sullivan (eds), *Congress: Structure and Policy*, Cambridge: Cambridge University Press, pp. 376–402.

Krehbiel, Keith, Kenneth A. Shepsle and Barry R. Weingast (1987), 'Why are Congressional Committees Powerful?', *American Political Science Review*, 81 (3), 929–35.

Kristinsson, Gunnar Helgi (1999), 'Iceland', in Robert Elgie (ed.), *Semi-Presidentialism in Europe*, Oxford: Oxford University Press, pp. 86–103.

Lauvaux, Philippe (1988), *Parlementarisme Rationalisé et Stabilité du Pouvoir Exécutif*, Brussels: Bruylant.

Laver, Michael (2003), 'Government Termination', *Annual Review of Political Science*, 6, 23–40.

Laver, Michael (2006), 'Legislatures and Parliaments in Comparative Context', in Barry R. Weingast and Donald A. Wittman (eds), *The Oxford Handbook of Political Economy*, Oxford: Oxford University Press, pp. 121–40.

Laver, Michael, and Norman Schofield (1998), *Multiparty Government: The Politics of Coalition in Europe*, Ann Arbor, MI: University of Michigan Press.

Limongi, Fernando and Argelina Figueiredo (1998), 'As Bases Institucionais do Presidencialismo de Coalizão', *Lua Nova*, 44, 81–106.

Linz, Juan J. (1978), *The Breakdown of Democratic Regimes: Crisis, Breakdown, and Reequilibration*, Baltimore: Johns Hopkins University Press.

Linz, Juan J. (1990a), 'The Perils of Presidentialism', *Journal of Democracy*, 1 (1), 51–69.

Linz, Juan J. (1990b), 'The Virtues of Parliamentarism', *Journal of Democracy*, 1 (4) , 84–91.

Linz, Juan J. (1994), 'Presidential or Parliamentary Democracy: Does it Make a Difference?', in Juan Linz and Arturo Valenzuela (eds), *The Failure of Presidential Democracy: The Case of Latin America*, Baltimore: The Johns Hopkins University Press, pp. 3–87.

Linz, Juan J. and Alfred Stepan (1996), *Problems of Democratic Transition and Consolidation: Southern Europe, South America, and Post-Communist Europe*, Baltimore: Johns Hopkins University Press.

Londregan, John (2000), *Legislative Institutions and Ideology in Chile*, New York: Cambridge University Press.

Mainwaring, Scott (1990), 'Presidentialism in Latin America', *Latin American Research Review*, 25 (1) 157–79.

Mainwaring, Scott (1993), 'Presidentialism, Multipartism, and Democracy: The Difficult Combination', *Comparative Political Studies*, 26 (2), 198–228.

Mainwaring, Scott and Timothy R. Scully (1995), 'Introduction: Party Systems in Latin America', in Scott Mainwaring and Timothy R. Scully (eds), *Building Democratic Institutions: Party Systems in Latin America*, Stanford, CA: Stanford University Press, pp. 1–34.

Mayhew, David R. (1991), *Divided We Govern: Party Control, Lawmaking, and Investigations, 1946–1990*, New Haven: Yale University Press.

Mejía Acosta, Andrés (2009), 'The Politics of Coalition Formation and Survival in Multiparty Presidential Democracies: The Case of Uruguay (1989–1999)', *Party Politics*, 6 (3), 259–83.

Moe, Terry M. (2009), 'The Revolution in Presidential Studies', *Presidential Studies Quarterly*, 39 (4), 701–24.

Nikolenyi, Csaba (2004), 'Cabinet Stability in Post-Communist Central Europe', *Party Politics*, 10 (2), 123–50.

Niño, Carlos Santiago (1996), 'Hyperpresidentialism and Constitutional Reforms in Argentina', in Arend Lijphart and Carlos H. Waisman (eds), *Institutional Design in New Democracies: Eastern Europe and Latin America*, Boulder, CO: Westview Press, pp. 161–73.

O'Donnell, Guillermo (1994), 'Delegative Democracy', *Journal of Democracy*, 5, 55–69.

Pereira, Carlos, Timothy J. Power and Lucio Rennó (2006), 'Under What Conditions Do Presidents Resort to Decree Power? Theory and Evidence from the Brazilian Case', *Journal of Politics*, 67 (1), 178–200.

Raunio, Tapio (2004), 'The Changing Finnish Democracy: Stronger Parliamentary Accountability, Coalescing Political Parties and Weaker External Constraints', *Scandinavia Political Studies*, 27 (2), 133–52.

Riggs, Fred W. (1988), 'The Survival of Presidentialism in America: Para-constitutional Practices', *International Political Science Review*, 9 (4), 247–78.

Riker, William H. (1962), *The Theory of Political Coalitions*, New Haven: Yale University Press.

Romer, Thomas and Howard Rosenthal (1978), 'Political Resource Allocation, Controlled Agendas, and the Status Quo', *Public Choice*, 33, Winter, 27–43.

Roper, Steven D. (2002), 'Are All Semipresidential Regimes the Same? A Comparison of Premier-presidential Regimes', *Comparative Politics*, 34 (3), 253–72.

Rubio, Delia Ferreira and Matteo Goretti (1998), 'When the Presidents Govern Alone: The Decreatazo in Argentina, 1989–93', in John M. Carey and Mathew Shugart (eds), *Executive Decree Authority*, New York: Cambridge University Press, pp. 33–61.

Sartori, Giovanni (1994), *Comparative Constitutional Engineering: An Inquiry into Structures, Incentives and Outcomes*, New York: New York University Press.

Shepsle, Kenneth A. (1979), 'Institutional Arrangements and Equilibrium in Multidimensional Voting Models', *American Journal of Political Science*, 23, 27–60.

Shepsle, Kenneth A. and Barry Weingast (1987), 'The Institutional Foundations of Committee Power', *American Political Science Review*, 80, 85–104.

Shugart, Matthew and John M. Carey (1992), *Presidents and Assemblies: Constitutional Design and Electoral Dynamics*, Cambridge: Cambridge University Press.

Siavelis, Peter M. (2000), 'Executive-legislative Relations in Post-Pinochet Chile: A Preliminary Assessment', in Scott Mainwaring and Mathew Shugart (eds), *Presidentialism and Democracy in Latin America*, New York: Cambridge University Press, pp. 321–65.

Stepan, Alfred, and Cindy Skach (1993), 'Constitutional Frameworks and Democratic Consolidation', *World Politics*, 46 (1), 1–22.

Strom, Kaare (1990), *Minority Government and Majority Rule*, Cambridge: Cambridge University Press.

Valenzuela, Arturo (1994), 'Party Politics and the Crisis of Presidentialism in Chile: A Proposal for a Parliamentary Form of Government', in J.J. Linz and A. Valenzuela (eds), *The Failure of Presidential Democracy: The Case of Latin America, vol 2*, Baltimore: Johns Hopkins University Press, pp. 91–150.

Valenzuela, Arturo (2004), 'Latin American Presidencies Interrupted', *Journal of Democracy*, 15 (4), 5–19.

Warwick, Paul. V. (1994), *Government Survival in Parliamentary Democracies*, Cambridge: Cambridge University Press.

Zelaznik, Javier (2001), 'The Building of Coalitions in the Presidential Systems of Latin America: An Inquiry into the Political Conditions of Governability', Ph.D. dissertation, University of Essex, England.

13. The separation of legislative and executive powers

Ronald J. Krotoszynski, Jr.

From a global perspective, separating and dividing legislative and executive power constitutes a very low structural priority. Parliamentary systems of government, which predominate across the globe (Ackerman 2000, pp. 645–6), invariably unite legislative and executive authority in the same hands. Professor Sartori counts only thirty nations that have adopted a presidential, as opposed to parliamentary, system of government (Sartori 1994, p. 107).

The performance of parliamentary systems of government, although far from perfect, generally has been considerably better than presidential and semi-presidential systems featuring divided executive and legislative authority (Sartori 1994). Presidential systems are 'mostly concentrated in Latin America' and 'the record of presidentially governed countries is – aside from the United States – quite dismal' (id.; see Ackerman 2000, pp. 645–6 ('There are about thirty countries, mostly in Latin America, that have adopted American-style systems. *All* of them, without exception, have succumbed to the Linzian nightmare [the collapse of constitutional government in favor of direct presidential or military control of the government] at one time or another, often repeatedly.')). Far more nations have adopted and maintain a parliamentary system of government, which lacks the separation of legislative and executive powers.

Most political scientists and political theorists favor the parliamentary system because of its obvious efficiency advantages and its tendency to promote stable government (at least when contrasted with presidential forms of government) (Ackerman 2000). Thus, if dividing and separating legislative and executive power really represents an essential attribute of a well-ordered government, most national governments in the larger world come up short; on the other hand, as Professor Ackerman wryly asks, 'Given the British success in avoiding the inexorable slide into tyranny predicted by Madison and Montesquieu, perhaps we should give up on the separation of powers [in the United States]?' (Ackerman 2000, p. 640).

A related, but distinct, question involves whether judges should actively superintend legislative/executive branch relations. In other words, even if a constitution initially attempts to separate legislative and executive authority, if at some later point in time incumbent officers of each branch decide to enact statutes that blend these powers, should a reviewing court disallow a de facto reallocation of powers, particularly if the structural arrangement was necessary to secure passage of the legislation in the first place? An obvious example might be contingent authority to reorganize an executive department. For example, Congress might agree to grant contingent power to a president or attorney general to reorganize the Department of Justice, but only if Congress has an opportunity to superintend the exercise of this delegated power. Faced with the choice of an unconstrained delegation or no delegation, Congress might well elect the 'no delegation' option.

The point is a relatively simple one: achieving practical results efficiently might well lead perfectly rational legislative and executive branch officers to blend in practice powers that, at a constitutional level, are structurally separate and distinct (Albert 2009, pp. 531–4, 541–8).

This raises the question of the appropriate judicial response: should judges actively referee reallocations of power between a legislature and a chief executive? In the United States, the federal courts have generally enforced the constitutional separation of powers strictly with respect to statutory power-sharing arrangements between Congress and the President (Redish and Cisar 1991, pp. 450–51). Although this is one answer to the problem, as Justice White's dissent in *Chadha* suggests, it plainly is not the only possible answer.

In Latin American countries that have adopted presidential systems modeled on the US Constitution, such as Argentina and Honduras, judicial officials also have found themselves called to referee disputes between the legislative and executive branches of government. The Argentine federal courts having to decide whether President Cristina Kirchner could lawfully seize control of the Central Bank of Argentina's foreign currency reserves over the Central Bank President's objections or, alternatively, remove the bank's president and then take control of reserves provides a contemporary example (Moffett 2010; Moffett and Cowley 2009).

In response to a suit filed by opposition party members of Congress, a federal trial judge, Maria Jose Sarmiento, ruled against President Kirchner on both questions, holding that the president could neither place Argentina's foreign currency reserves under direct presidential control nor fire central bank President Martín Redrado without the approval of Congress (Moffett and Cowley 2009). The Court of Federal Administrative Disputes subsequently affirmed Judge Sarmiento's decision on appeal (Barrionuevo 2010, p. A11). Daniel Kerner, a senior political analyst for the Eurasia Group, a political risk consulting firm, noted that ' "[t]his is the beginning of what will probably be a long and complicated battle between the government [led by President Kirchner] and Congress [currently controlled by an opposition party], and, potentially, the Supreme Court" ' (Barrionuevo 2010, p. A8). Although President Kirchner ultimately succeeded in removing central bank President Redrado and replacing him with Mercedes Marcó de Pont in February 2009 (Grady 2010; Barrionuevo 2010, p. A11), the Supreme Court of Argentina is likely to provide the ultimate resolution of these crucially important questions.[1]

The June 2009 presidential succession crisis in Honduras provides yet another example of the successful assertion of judicial supervision of the separation of powers in a Latin American nation with a presidential system of government. President Manuel Zelaya, wishing to succeed himself in violation of a strict one-term limit in the Honduran Constitution (see Constitution of the Republic of Honduras 1982, tit. II, ch. 6, art. 239), planned to hold an 'informational plebiscite' to determine whether the Constitution should be amended to permit his re-election during the national elections to be held on 29 November 2009 (Booth 2009; Estrada 2009). The Honduran Constitution permits amendments only with a two-thirds vote of the Congress, in two successive regular annual sessions (see Constitution of the Republic of Honduras 1982, tit. VII, ch. 1, art. 373), but expressly forbids any amendment that would either extend the four-year term of the president or permit presidential re-election (Constitution of the Republic of Honduras 1982, tit. VII, ch. 1, art. 374). Thus, President Zelaya's informational plebiscite seemed to be on a collision course with the plain text of the Honduran Constitution; the President essentially was attempting to exercise a power (the power to amend the Constitution) that the Constitution of Honduras expressly reserved to the National Congress and, moreover, to use this usurped power in a fashion that the Constitution itself prohibited even to the National Congress.

The Attorney General, with the support of a majority of the National Congress, brought an action in the Supreme Court of Honduras, seeking to block the referendum (Estrada 2009).

The Supreme Court declared the proposed referendum unlawful and issued an injunction requiring the military to prevent the vote from taking place (Estrada 2009; Renderos and Wilkinson 2009, p. A1). The head of the Honduran Joint Chiefs of Staff, General Romeo Vasquez, complied with the Supreme Court's order and seized the ballots, which had been imported from Venezuela, and refused to release them either to President Zelaya or to his supporters.

On 24 June 2009, President Zelaya attempted to fire General Vasquez and regain control of the ballots, but the Supreme Court once again intervened and ordered General Vasquez reinstated to his post (Renderos and Wilkinson 2009, p. A1). After President Zelaya refused to comply with this order, the Supreme Court ordered him removed from office; on June 28, 2009, the Congress also voted, by a margin of 122 to 6, to remove Zelaya from office (Booth 2009; Estrada 2009; Renderos and Wilkinson 2009, p. A1). Consistent with the Supreme Court's order and the Congress's impeachment vote, the military removed President Zelaya from office and, going beyond the letter of the Supreme Court's order, also expelled him from Honduras. Roberto Micheletti, President of the National Congress, and next in the line of presidential succession because the Honduran Vice-President, Elvin Santos, previously had resigned his office in order to run for President, immediately took office as interim president on the same day (Booth 2009; Estrada 2009; Renderos and Wilkinson 2009, p. A1).

The scheduled presidential election took place without incident on 29 November 2009 and Porfirio 'Pepe' Lobo, the conservative National Party candidate, defeated Elvin Santos, of Zelaya's Liberal Party, by a wide margin (Ellingwood and Renderos 2010; Renderos and Wilkinson 2009, p. A4). Even so, the Supreme Court's involvement in this constitutional crisis between the legislative and executive branches of government was not finished; in early January 2010, the Attorney General asked the Supreme Court to consider criminal charges against General Vasquez and five other military commanders for their decision to involuntarily deport President Zelaya from Honduras after his removal from office, an action that the Attorney General argued was illegal. The Supreme Court agreed to take the case, but rejected the Attorney General's argument, ruling instead that General Vasquez and the other military officers had acted in good faith and, accordingly, had not acted unlawfully or otherwise breached their constitutional duties (Ellingwood and Renderos 2010).

Just as the judiciary has undertaken a key role in resolving the crisis between Argentina's executive and legislative branches of government over control of Argentina's central bank and national foreign currency reserves, the Supreme Court of Honduras played a key role throughout the presidential crisis and consistently found itself having to mediate competing and conflicting claims of legitimacy advanced by the executive and legislative branches of government. Thus, as these examples demonstrate, it would be quite mistaken to suppose that judicial enforcement of the separation of legislative and executive powers constitutes a public law concern only in the United States.

Even though the separation of legislative and executive powers is a central defining characteristic of most presidential systems of government, as noted earlier, viewed from a global perspective, this approach to structuring the operation of government remains very much a minority approach. Moreover, the rejection of legislative/executive separation of powers concerns completely bridges the common law and civil law world; both common law and civil law jurisdictions feature parliamentary systems of government in which the highest executive officers also serve as sitting members of the national legislature (Jackson and

Tushnet 1999, pp. 36–63, 710–11). Indeed, these arrangements do not seem particularly bothersome to persons, including lawyers and legal academics, living in these nations.

1   THE US MODEL: STRICT SEPARATION

In the United States, a strong commitment to separating and dividing legislative and executive power exists at the federal level (it exists in most state constitutions as well). This separation of powers commitment appears front and center in recent opinions of the Supreme Court; it reflects concerns appearing in bold relief in the legislative history of the Constitution; and, perhaps most importantly, the text of the Constitution itself commands a strong form of legislative/executive separation of powers.

1.1   The Supreme Court of the United States and Legislative/Executive Separation of Powers.

The Supreme Court of the United States has rigorously enforced the separation of powers, disallowing a number of novel institutional innovations that the Congress and the President adopted in order to facilitate good governance (Edley 1990, pp. 172–5, 213–15, 221–34). As Justice Powell observed in *Buckley*, '[t]he principle of separation of powers was not simply an abstract generalization in the minds of the Framers: it was woven into the document that they drafted in Philadelphia in the summer of 1787' (*Buckley v Valeo*, 424 US 1, 124 (1976)). Accordingly, '[t]he Framers regarded the checks and balances that they had built into the tripartite Federal Government as a self-executing safeguard against the encroachment or aggrandizement of one branch at the expense of the other' (id. at p. 123). Thus, as Professor Martin H. Redish and Elizabeth J. Cisar have perceptively noted, '[a]lthough one may of course debate the scope or meaning of particular constitutional provisions, it would be difficult to deny that in establishing their complex structure, the Framers were virtually obsessed with a fear – bordering on what some might uncharitably describe as paranoia – of the concentration of political power' (Redish and Cisar 1991, p. 451).

The consistency of the Supreme Court's efforts at enforcing separation of powers principles is open to criticism, however. As Redish and Cisar note, '[i]n the separation of powers area, however, the modern Court has evinced something of a split personality, seemingly wavering from resort to judicial enforcement with a formalistic vengeance to use of a so-called "functional" approach that appears to be designed to do little more than rationalize incursions by one branch of the federal government into the domain of another' (Redish and Cisar 1991, p. 450). That said, in the area of policing the blending of legislative and executive functions, the Supreme Court has been relatively strict in enforcing separation of powers limits, disallowing both encroachments on one branch by the other and attempts by one branch to aggrandize itself at the expense of the other.

In *Chadha*, for example, the Supreme Court invalidated the use of so-called legislative vetoes, a procedure whereby Congress delegates authority to the President, but reserves for itself, via a single house or a committee of a single house, the power to oversee, and even to disallow, the President's use of this delegated authority (*INS v Chadha*, 462 US 919, 944–54 (1983)). Writing for the *Chadha* Court, Chief Justice Burger explained that in order to modify a law, a bill must be enacted by both houses of Congress and presented to the President for signature or veto; as the Court put the matter, '[t]hese provisions of Article I are integral parts of the constitutional design for the separation of powers' (*Chadha*, 462 US at 946). Because Congress cannot execute laws and because bicameral action and presentment are necessary to modify an existing law (for example, to disallow the President's use of previously delegated authority), a one house or one committee 'legislative veto' represents an unconstitutional aggrandizement of Congress at the expense of the President (id. at 945–57).[2]

Similarly, in *Bowsher v Synar* (478 US 714 (1986)), the Supreme Court invalidated the Balanced Budget and Emergency Deficit Control Act of 1985, also known as the Gramm-Rudman-Hollings Act, because it vested execution of the law with the Comptroller General, a government officer only nominally appointed by the President (from a list devised by Congress) and an officer subject to removal by Congress without resort to impeachment. The Court explained that '[t]o permit an officer controlled by Congress to execute the laws would be, in essence, to permit a congressional veto' (*Bowsher*, 478 US at 726). Because '[t]he structure of the Constitution does not permit Congress to execute the laws', Chief Justice Burger concluded that 'it follows that Congress cannot grant to an officer under its control what it does not possess' (id.).

Other major US Supreme Court decisions involve strong efforts to enforce the structural separation of legislative and executive powers, including cases such as *Buckley v Valeo* (424 US 1 (1976) (holding that Congress may not appoint members of a commission charged with enforcing the Federal Election Campaign Act of 1971, as amended, because legislative appointment to an executive office does not comport with the Appointments Clause of Article II, § 2, cl. 2)) and *Clinton v City of New York* (524 US 417 (1998) (invalidating the Line Item Veto Act, a statutory effort to vest the President with the power to cancel 'any dollar amount of discretionary budget authority', 'any new item of direct spending' or 'any limited tax benefit' after having signed the law authorizing the appropriation or creating the limited tax benefit because only Congress can repeal a statute once a statute has been enacted and by the exercise of a line item veto '[i]n both legal and practical effect, the President has amended two Acts of Congress by repealing a portion of each')). Thus, the Supreme Court has repeatedly rejected efforts to blend legislative and executive powers in novel ways, even if Congress and the President mutually agreed to such power sharing, and even if concrete benefits might be associated with the novel power sharing arrangements (Krotoszynski 1997, pp. 475–81).

One should be careful, of course, not to overstate the point; contrary evidence and trends exist, and one must acknowledge them. For example, the Supreme Court has largely abandoned efforts to enforce the non-delegation doctrine (Krotoszynski 2005, pp. 264–7), which purportedly limits the scope of delegated authority that Congress may grant to the executive branch (Krotoszynski 2005, pp. 260–68). In theory, unless Congress provides an 'intelligible principle' that limits the scope of delegated authority, the delegation violates the separation of powers by vesting the President with core legislative powers; in practice, however, virtually any statutory mandate that Congress enacts meets the 'intelligible principle' standard (Krotoszynski 2005, pp. 265–8). In this area, US separation of powers *practice*, if not *theory*, seems remarkably consistent with the approach taken to these questions in parliamentary democracies, such as Canada and Australia.

Were the Supreme Court to enforce the separation of powers doctrine as aggressively in this context as in the legislative veto and appointments cases, far more federal laws would be invalidated for violating the non-delegation doctrine. Thus, the Supreme Court's efforts to enforce the separation of legislative and executive powers are not all-encompassing or unyielding. Even with this caveat, however, the fact remains that the Supreme Court has not simply left Congress and the President free to referee the appropriate metes and bounds of their respective institutional authority (Redish and Cisar 1991, pp. 450–51).

1.2 The Original Understanding and Legislative/Executive Separation of Powers

It would be easy to assume that the contemporary commitment to formalism in enforcing the separation of powers in the US is a modern innovation; such an assumption would not be warranted. To be sure, the structural separation of legislative, executive and judicial powers into three distinct branches does not, of its own force, preclude the voluntary redistribution of such powers among and between the branches going forward (as seems to have happened, for example, in Australia). However, the *Federalist Papers* confirm the view that the initial allocation of powers between the three branches was meant to be more than simply an initial starting point.

In Federalist No. 47, James Madison emphasized the importance of establishing and maintaining the separation of powers:

> The reasons on which Montesquieu grounds his maxim are a further demonstration of his meaning. 'When the legislative and executive powers are united in the same person or body,' says he, 'there can be no liberty, because apprehensions may arise lest *the same* monarch or senate should *enact* tyrannical laws to *execute* them in a tyrannical manner.' Again: 'Were the power of judging joined with the legislative, the life and liberty of the subject would be exposed to arbitrary control, for *the judge* would then be *the legislator*. Were it joined to the executive power, *the judge* might behave with all the violence of *an oppressor*.' Some of these reasons are more fully explained in other passages; but briefly stated as they are here, they sufficiently establish the meaning which we have put on this celebrated maxim of this celebrated author (Federalist No. 47, at 300, 303 (James Madison) (Hamilton et al. 1961) (emphasis in the original)).

Thus, for Madison, the division of legislative and executive power represented an essential bulwark against tyranny. And, in turn, the Framers carefully separated and divided legislative and executive power, placing legislative power in the hands of Congress and executive power squarely in the hands of the President (see *Buckley v Valeo*, 424 US 1, 120 (1976) (noting that 'the Constitution was nonetheless true to Montesquieu's well-known maxim that the legislative, executive, and judicial departments ought to be separate and distinct')).

Madison's concerns with the risk of tyranny did not cease with ratification of the Constitution in 1788. Although largely forgotten, one of Madison's proposed amendments to the Constitution, included in the package of proposed amendments that later became the Bill of Rights, was a proposed amendment that would have reiterated the irrevocable nature of the separation of powers:

> The powers delegated by this constitution are appropriated to the departments to which they are respectively distributed: so that the legislative department shall never exercise powers vested in the executive or judicial, nor the executive exercise powers vested in the legislative or judicial, nor the judicial exercise the powers vested in the legislative or executive branch (Gales and Seaton, 1834, pp. 435–6) (8 June 1789)).

Had this amendment been adopted, this new provision would have been largely redundant with the existing vesting clauses in Artice I, § 1, which vests 'all legislative Powers herein granted' in the Congress, Article II, § 1, which vests '[t]he executive Power' in the President, and Article III, § 1, which vests '[t]he judicial Power of the United States' in the Supreme Court and the inferior federal courts (should Congress create lower federal courts). Madison defended the amendment as necessary in order to ensure that the powers of the federal government would remain 'separate and distinct' and argued that the vesting clauses were an insufficient safeguard (id. at 760).

Thus, even though the Framers, including Madison himself, had carefully and expressly made the vesting of clearly separated legislative, executive, and judicial power the very first provision of each article constituting a particular branch of the federal government, Madison nevertheless feared the reunification of these powers through voluntary, or perhaps even involuntary, transfers of power among the branches of the federal government. Accordingly, Madison sought to establish a textual prohibition against any branch, through whatever means, exercising the powers vested in the other two branches of the federal government. The House of Representatives actually adopted the proposed amendment by the requisite two-thirds vote, but the Senate, for reasons lost to history, declined to adopt this amendment (2 Schwartz 1971, p. 1150).[3]

For many of the Framers, including James Madison, the aim was to divide power, in hopes of better controlling it. In particular, the Framers believed that rather than relying on a perpet-ual supply of virtuous and wise rulers (a commodity that the Framers knew to be in very short supply and which history suggested could be something of a null set), the better course was to create a carefully calibrated system of government that would create strong institutional incentives to resist encroachments against one branch by the other branches of the federal government (Federalist No. 51, at 320, 320–22 (James Madison) (Hamilton et al. 1961); see also Redish and Cisar 1991, p. 505). 'We see [this principle] particularly displayed in all the subordinate distributions of power, where the constant aim is to divide and arrange the several offices in such a manner as that each may be a check on the other – that the private interest of every individual may be a sentinel over the public rights' (Federalist No. 51, at 322 (James Madison) (Hamilton et al. 1961)).

The Framers' thinking on these questions was undoubtedly influenced significantly by the writings of Enlightenment political philosophers who strongly advocated the separation of legislative, executive and judicial powers, such as John Locke and Montesquieu. As Madison himself noted, in Federalist No. 47, '[t]he oracle who is always consulted and cited on this subject [the separation of powers] is the celebrated Montesquieu' (Federalist No. 47, at 301 (James Madison) (Hamilton et al. 1961)). Thus, even if existing British constitutional arrangements did not incorporate the separation of powers (Hyre 2004, pp. 430–35; Skold 2007, pp. 2154–5),[4] the Framers certainly would have been familiar with the concept and the arguments in favor of struc-turing government institutions to incorporate it. The Framers' innovation was not so much the creation or articulation of the concept, but rather a strong commitment to implementing the prin-ciple in the Constitution of 1787 (Vile 1967, pp. 58–61; see Redish and Cisar 1991, pp. 456–5).

1.3   The Constitutional Text and Legislative/Executive Separation of Powers

The Supreme Court has not developed its concern with the separation of legislative and exec-utive powers based solely on its own fears or those of the Framers. Instead, the text of the

Constitution itself contains a strong wall of separation between the Legislative and Executive Branches: the Incompatibility Clause. The Incompatibility Clause provides that:

> No Senator or Representative shall, during the Time for which he was elected, be appointed to any civil Office under the Authority of the United States, which shall have been created, or the Emoluments whereof shall have been encreased during such time; and *no Person holding any Office under the United States, shall be a Member of either House during his Continuance in Office* (US Constitution, art. I, § 6, cl. 2 (emphasis added)).

The Incompatibility Clause effectively prevents a sitting member of the House or Senate from serving as a cabinet secretary without resigning her seat in Congress (*Freytag v Comm'r*, 501 US 868, 904 (1991) (Scalia, J, concurring). Of course, members of Congress have served – and do serve – in the Executive Branch after resigning from Congress before receiving a formal appointment to an Executive Branch office (Calabresi and Larsen 1994, pp. 1078–86).

James Madison, one of the principal architects of the Constitution, firmly believed that legislative service in the executive branch was not merely a prescription for legislative featherbedding, but also an affirmatively dangerous practice. Writing on the subject to Thomas Jefferson, Madison observed that:

> The power of the Legislature to appoint any other than their own officers departs too far from the Theory which requires a separation of the great Departments of Government. One of the best securities against the creation of unnecessary offices or tyrannical powers is an exclusion of the authors from all share in filling the one, or influence in the execution of the other (6 Boyd 1952, pp. 308, 311).

Thus, the rationales for the Incompatibility and Ineligibility Clauses are both highly practical (in the absence of such a clause the legislature will create unnecessary sinecures for its members at the public's expense) and highly theoretical (merger of the legislative and executive powers is conducive to 'tyranny', even if bad results do not actually occur).[5]

The Constitution itself thus prevents the adoption of the common practice in parliamentary democracies of staffing senior executive branch posts with sitting legislators (Jackson and Tushnet 1999, pp. 361–2, 710–11); the Framers designed and 'We the People' ratified a document that squarely rejects a very common institutional design that marries legislative expertise with responsibility for oversight over an executive department.[6] In the United States, those drafting the Constitution perceived the division of legislative and executive power to be an essential component of a just government, an imperative no less pressing than a written constitution, the creation of an independent judiciary with the power of judicial review, and the retention of states as a kind of vertical federalism check on possible overreaching by the central government.

Moreover, one also should note that the Framers were very much aware of the fact that the Incompatibility and Ineligibility Clauses represented a stark break with existing separation of powers practices in other nations, including Great Britain. At the Federal Convention in Philadelphia, Nathaniel Gorham, of Massachusetts, strongly supported weakening the Ineligibility Clause because without such amendment 'we go further than has been done in any of the States, or indeed any other Country' (Madison, 1965, p. 572) (3 September 1787). Significantly, however, no delegate argued in favor of permitting a sitting member of the House or Senate also to serve in an executive or judicial office; the debate focused solely on how broadly to write the proscription against appointment of incumbent members of Congress to newly created federal offices or to existing offices with recent salary enhancements.

Given the strength of the Framers' concerns about the danger of mixing executive and legislative functions, and the salience of these concerns up to the present day, at least in the pages of the *US Reports*, one would think that the concern would have found some measure of traction in other nations. To state the matter simply, if merging legislative and executive functions is conducive to tyranny (Redish and Cisar 1991, pp. 476–8, 505–06), one would predict that persons drafting new constitutions would assiduously avoid merging legislative and executive powers. This has not, however, proven to be the case.

2   PARLIAMENTARY SYSTEMS IN THE COMMON LAW WORLD (THE WESTMINSTER MODEL)

Consideration of the parliamentary, or Westminster, model of government, the model from which the Framers of the US Constitution of 1787 intentionally broke, will shed further light on the question of the necessity, and desirability, of separating legislative and executive government powers. In such systems, control of both the legislative and executive branches of government rests in the same hands. The executive branch of government remains theoretically accountable to the legislative branch of government, which retains the formal power to remove executive branch officers from office. However, the dual role of a prime minister as head of the executive branch and concurrently leader of the majority party in the legislature gives the executive branch, in practice, much more freedom of action than a president usually enjoys in a presidential system of government.

Thus, in the United Kingdom, Canada, and Australia, all common law jurisdictions, the majority party in the national parliament also selects the principal executive officers, usually drawn from within its own ranks (Jackson and Tushnet 1999, pp. 360–64). These officers, in turn, form the 'cabinet', an executive leadership corps that usually enjoys complete control over the legislative agenda and decides not only whether a particular measure will receive a floor vote, but also whether a particular amendment will receive a vote (Atiyah and Summers 1987, pp. 301–04). Cabinet-level ministers are invariably incumbent members of the legislature drawn from the majority party. To be sure, an independent 'executive branch' exists that features lower-level bureaucrats who work entirely independently of the national legislature. Accordingly, even in parliamentary democracies using the common law, a weak form of separation of powers exists below the highest offices within the ministries (Currie 1994, p. 173). The fact remains, however, that persons with substantial responsibility for writing and revising the laws also enjoy principal responsibility for enforcing the laws as well (1 Hogg 2007, §§ 9.1–9.5, pp. 9-1 to 9-22).

It would be nonsensical, of course, to attempt a discussion of judicial supervision of the separation of legislative and executive powers in the context of a parliamentary system that intentionally vests these powers in the same hands. In other words, in the absence of a structural separation of legislative and executive powers, a reviewing court would have no cause to object to a parliamentarian undertaking an executive task, or vice versa. This practical limit on the role of judges arises independently of the effect of the doctrine of parliamentary supremacy that remains a dominant feature of British constitutional law; simply put, a properly enacted act of Parliament is valid and the British courts have an absolute duty to enforce a properly enacted statute (Atiyah and Summers 1987, pp. 227–9, 267–70). As Atiyah and Summers (1987, p. 55) emphatically state the proposition, '[s]tatutes are of paramount authority, and any conflict between a statute and a judicial decision must be decided in favour of the statute'.

One might object that international obligations to entities such as the European Union and the Council of Europe effectively limit the scope of Parliament's legislative powers (Atiyah and Summers 1987, pp. 54–5; see Slaughter 2000, p. 1106 (arguing that the British courts have 'overturned the sacrosanct doctrine of parliamentary sovereignty' in order to ensure that the United Kingdom does not breach obligations owed to the European Union); but compare Atiyah and Summers 1987, pp. 54–5 (arguing that European Union treaty obligations do not affect or limit Parliament's formal domestic legislative authority)). To be sure, it is highly unlikely that Parliament would intentionally place the United Kingdom in breach of duties owed to the European Union or the Council of Europe. But this is a matter of practical politics, not a judicially enforceable limit on the scope of Parliament's legislative powers. It remains the case today that the British judiciary lacks the power of judicial review, and the decisions of both the European Court of Justice (an EU entity) and the European Court of Human Rights (a Council of Europe entity) are not self-enforcing under the domestic law of the United Kingdom, and instead require Parliament to enact implementing legislation.

Of course, judicial enforcement of the separation of executive and legislative powers still exists, at least at the margins, in the United Kingdom. British courts exercise a supervisory jurisdiction over administrative regulations adopted by government agencies; when hearing a petition for review, the British courts, applying *Wednesbury* review principles, determine whether a reasonable regulator could reasonably have adopted the particular regulation (*Associated Provincial Picture Houses Ltd. v Wednesbury Corp.*, 1 KB 223, 230 (1948) (holding that an administrative regulation may not stand if it is 'so unreasonable that no reasonable authority could ever have come to it'); see Wade 1988, pp. 388–462). It is a forgiving standard of review, to be sure, and the House of Lords (whose judicial functions now reside in the Supreme Court of the United Kingdom) emphasizes that its authority is not 'appellate' (or de novo), but rather merely 'supervisory' (i.e., limited to ensuring that the agency has not grossly overstepped the bounds of the agency's delegated authority) (*Regina v Secretary of State for the Home Department, Ex Parte Brind*, [1991] 1 App. Cas. 696, 748–9).

If the British courts were to play absolutely no role in policing the boundaries of legislative and executive action, if the two spheres of government power were really unified in both theory and in practice, then the notion of enforcing limits, even very broad limits, on the scope of administrative power would make no sense: if the executive and legislative departments were truly one in the same, it would be nonsensical to ask whether the left hand properly implemented the mandate from the right hand. Clearly, then, the very fact of judicial review of agency work product in the United Kingdom, even under a double-barreled 'reasonableness' standard that courts apply with great deference, suggests that courts, at least at the margins, police the boundary between executive authority (delegated from Parliament; limited in its scope) and legislative authority (plenary).

However superficially attractive this argument might be, however, another narrative exists that can better explain judicial review of administrative action in Great Britain. Although the leader of the majority party in the House of Commons serves as Prime Minister, and as Prime Minister, names the heads of the executive departments and agencies (Atiyah and Summers 1987, pp. 299–304), these ministerial officials, and the agencies themselves, do act as the agents of the collective, Parliament. One could conceive of judicial review of agency action not as an effort to police the boundaries of legislative and executive power, but rather as a necessary means of enforcing parliamentary supremacy.

Whatever authority an executive agency enjoys, it enjoys only because Parliament has delegated that authority in the first place and designated the department or agency as the recipient. Both the precise scope of the delegated authority and the terms of its use are questions that Parliament answers, and answers definitively. *Wednesbury* review of agency regulations simply constitutes a means of ensuring that an agency does not transgress (at least badly) the scope or terms of delegated power. Thus, courts reviewing administrative regulations (commonly called 'secondary legislation' in the United Kingdom) really serve more as an auditor than as an enforcer of constitutional boundary lines. Moreover, if Parliament wished to abolish judicial review of agency regulations, it would be free to do so; the very existence of this judicial review power continues only at the sufferance of Parliament. Thus, the judiciary plays this role because Parliament wishes it to do so, not because the British Constitution limits the scope of power that Parliament may transfer to executive branch entities.

Unlike Congress in the United States, Parliament would be quite free to adopt unusual governmental structures that condition delegations to the executive branch on the approval of a standing committee of the House of Commons or of the House of Commons itself. Of course, it would be almost unimaginable that Parliament would adopt a legislative veto provision, precisely because the highest executive officer and head of government, the Prime Minister, also serves as the leader of the majority party in the House of Commons. In the absence of the possibility of divided government, and in the absence of a structural separation of legislative and executive power, the concept of a legislative veto makes very little sense. Why should Parliament reserve for itself a veto over the work product of its own members serving as ministers?[7]

Canada presents a similar case; like the United Kingdom, the federal Parliament in Ottawa selects from its own ranks the principal officers of the executive branch and the Prime Minister is invariably the leader of the majority party in the House of Commons (1 Hogg 2007, § 9.4, pp. 9-8 to 9-15). As Professor Peter W. Hogg (1 2007, § 9.4(a), p. 9-9), the leading Canadian constitutionalist, succinctly states the matter, '[i]t is basic to the system of responsible [parliamentary] government that the Prime Minister and all other ministers be members of Parliament'.

In fact, if the Prime Minister appoints a minister who is not a member of the federal Parliament, she 'must quickly be elected to the House of Commons or appointed to the Senate', and '[i]f the minister fails to win election, and is not appointed to the Senate, then he or she must resign (or be dismissed) from the ministry' (1 Hogg 2007, § 9.4(a), p. 9-9). As in the United Kingdom, professional civil servants also work in the executive departments, with the highest-ranking civil servants holding the rank of 'deputy minister' (1 Hogg 2007, § 9.4(a), p. 9-9 n.20; § 9.4(d), p. 9-13).

As in the United Kingdom, the ministers collectively constitute the 'cabinet' and '[t]he cabinet formulates and carries out all executive policies, and it is responsible for all of the departments of government' (1 Hogg 2007, § 9.4(b), pp. 9-10 to 9-11). As Professor Hogg (1

2007, § 9.5(e), p. 9-20) observes, '[i]t will now be obvious that in a system of responsible [parliamentary] government there is no "separation of powers" between the executive and legislative branches of government'. The cabinet, selected from members of the legislature, exercises effective control over the Parliament itself. Moreover, '[t]he control of the legislature by the executive is not normally something that the courts are concerned with' (1 Hogg 2007, § 9.5, p. 9-21).

Thus, '[t]here is no general "separation of powers" in the [Canadian] Constitution Act, 1867', and '[t]he Act does not separate the legislative, executive, and judicial functions and insist that each branch of government exercise only "its own" functions' (1 Hogg 2007, § 7.3(a), p. 7-37). Indeed, '[a]s between the legislative and executive branches, any separation of powers would make little sense in a system of responsible government' (1 Hogg 2007, § 7.3(a), p. 7-37).

The Canadian courts, unlike their counterparts in the United Kingdom, do enjoy the power of judicial review and may invalidate both federal and provincial legislation that transgresses Charter rights. Since 1982, this power of judicial review has been express (Hogg 1982, pp. 64–6, 104–06; Russell 1992, pp. 33–4). Prior to 1982, however, the Supreme Court of Canada possessed a more limited power of judicial review to determine whether a particular legislative matter belonged to the federal government or to the provincial governments (Hogg 1977, pp. 197–8).

Since 1982, judicial review has rested on a firmer constitutional footing, with two provisions of the Charter expressly authorizing courts to review both legislative and executive actions for consistency with Charter values, and empowering them to invalidate any government act that violates a provision of the Charter. This has empowered the Canadian courts to more directly protect fundamental human rights from government encroachment; it has not, however, involved the Canadian courts in supervising the division of legislative and executive authority. The Charter did nothing to alter the parliamentary system of government that existed at both the national and provincial levels and this system of government did not – and does not – provide for structural separation of legislative and executive powers.

One finds in Canada, as in Britain, that federal courts enjoy a power to review agency action and to disallow 'ultra vires' agency decisions (1 Hogg 2007, § 1.8, pp. 1-16 to 1-17; 2 Hogg 2007, § 34.2, pp. 34-2 to 34-6). Review involves a two-step process, with the reviewing court engaging in de novo review of an administrative tribunal's construction of the scope of its jurisdiction (*Canadian Broadcasting Corp. v Canada*, [1995] 1 SCR 157 (Can.); *Pezim v Superintendent of Brokers*, [1994] 2 SCR 557 (Can.); *UES, Local 298 v Bibeault*, [1988] 2 SCR 1048, 1088 (Can.)), but engaging in a much more circumscribed review of an agency's use of policymaking authority clearly within the scope of its jurisdiction. As Chief Justice Dickson stated the matter, a reviewing court must determine whether an administrative agency has:

> so misinterpreted the provisions of the Act as to embark on an inquiry or answer a question not remitted to it? Put another way, was the Board's interpretation so patently unreasonable that its construction cannot be rationally supported by the relevant legislation and demands intervention by the court upon review? (*Canadian Union of Public Employees, Local 93 v New Brunswick Liquor Corp.*, [1979] 2 SCR 227, 237 (Can.); see Allars 1994).

Thus, as one commentator has stated the point, 'judicial review of administrative action in Canada has become a two-part merit review' (Weiler 1995, p. 91 n.39). At step one, '[i]f the court really disagrees with the body's decision, it will classify it as jurisdictional' and invalidate it (Weiler 1995, p. 91 n.39; Allars 1994, pp. 193–4). On the other hand, if a reviewing court 'only disagrees mildly, it can either find the decision patently unreasonable or let it stand' (Weiler 1995, p. 91 n.39). Accordingly, as in the United Kingdom, a legally incorrect agency decision that is not 'patently unreasonable' should survive judicial review.

As Professor Hogg explains (2 Hogg 2007, § 34.2, p. 34-6), in Canada 'courts have confined the scope of official discretion by holding that power conferred in broad terms may not be "abused" by exercise in bad faith or for an improper purpose or upon irrelevant considerations'. Even so, he notes (2 Hogg 2007, § 34.2, p. 34-6) that the Canadian courts have developed and applied these rules cabining executive discretion 'without any denial of parliamentary sovereignty, and without the aid of a bill of rights …'. Instead the common law tradition itself presumes 'the availability of remedies to citizens injured by illegal official action' (2 Hogg 2007, § 34.2, p. 34-5).

One also should note that Canada's federal Parliament cannot escape constitutional limitations through the expedient of delegating authority to an administrative tribunal to engage in an unconstitutional course of conduct and then seek to block judicial review of the agency's (presumably unconstitutional) actions through a 'privative clause' that purports to withdraw the availability of judicial review over the agency's use of the delegated authority. 'There can be no quarrel with the proposition that a legislative body should not be able to insulate its statutes or its administrative tribunals from judicial review on constitutional grounds' (1 Hogg 2007, § 7.3(f), p. 7-55).

The larger point remains that judicial review of agency action in Canada, whether on constitutional or statutory grounds, has much to do with enforcing the Charter and common law notions of rational governance, and nothing to do with attempting to police the boundary between the legislative and executive branches of government. As Professor Hogg puts it (1 Hogg 2007, § 14.2(a), p. 14-5), '[t]he difference between the Canadian and American systems resides not only in the different language of the two constitutional instruments, but in Canada's retention of the British system of responsible government'. Moreover, '[t]he close link between the executive and legislative branches which is entailed by the British system is utterly inconsistent with any separation of executive and legislative function' (1 Hogg 2007, § 14.2(a), p. 14-5).

Thus, in a parliamentary, or 'responsible', system of government, the addition of a written Bill of Rights and the vesting of judicial review powers in the national courts does not alter the structural fact that legislative and executive powers are held by the same people. As Professor Currie (1994, p. 172) explains, '[a] parliamentary system, which Germany shares with most other successful democracies, necessarily entails a sacrifice of separation to better coordination of official policy and more effective safeguards against the abuse of executive authority'.[8]

Even in common law countries, featuring a parliamentary system of government, that maintain written constitutions that facially incorporate a structural separation of powers, courts are not much inclined to attempt to enforce any structural separation of powers between the legislative and executive branches. For example, courts in Australia, forced to reconcile a constitution that, unlike Canada's constitution, enumerates and separates legislative, executive, and judicial powers, have concluded that the constitutional text *does not* impose or legitimate any court-enforced limits on delegations from the Parliament to the executive branch, even if the scope of a particular delegation is such that one might plausibly claim that Parliament has transferred core legislative powers to the executive branch (*Victorian Stevedoring and Gen. Contracting Co. Pty. v Dignan*, (1931) 46 CLR 73 (Austl.); *Roche v Kronheimer*, (1921) 29 CLR 329 (Austl.); see Aronson and Dyer 1996, p. 204). In Australia, the tradition of unified control of legislative and executive powers in a parliamentary system effectively overrides any structural implication that might otherwise be drawn from the constitutional text.[9] (Australian courts do, however, conduct jurisdictional error-based review similar to the Canadian Supreme Court.)

3   PARLIAMENTARY SYSTEMS IN THE CIVIL LAW WORLD

Turning to parliamentary nations outside the common law orbit, one will not find any greater concern with separating legislative and executive powers – much less any interest in deploying judges to enforce such a separation. Civil law nations, such as France, Germany, and Japan, also feature constitutional arrangements that tend to blend, rather than strictly separate, legislative and executive power. France is instructive in this regard because the President enjoys some measure of lawmaking authority – in this sense, then, the Executive Branch enjoys the power to legislate, at least with respect to certain subject matter. But, even in France, the Prime Minister, selected from the majority party in the legislature,[10] retains significant responsibility for the implementation of government policies and difficulties can arise when a President of one party is forced to work with a Prime Minister drawn from the opposition party's ranks (periods of so-called *cohabitation*).

The French system's blending of lawmaking power in both the Parliament and the President, however, creates both the possibility for and the necessity of judicial review of the Parliament's exercise of its legislative powers; if the Parliament promulgates a law (*loi*) that the President believes to be beyond the scope of its authority, the President may seek and obtain review of the question before the Conseil Constitutionnel. This, of course, is a kind of mirror image of judicial enforcement of the separation of legislative and judicial power in the United States; because the French Constitution vests certain lawmaking powers in the President, the question can arise whether the Parliament has overstepped the bounds of its legislative authority and transgressed Presidential policymaking powers through the issuance of regulations (*réglements*). Determining where the President's unilateral power to act ends and Parliament's power to legislate – or not – begins plainly constitutes a kind of judicial enforcement of the separation of powers.[11]

Ironically, perhaps, the drafters of the Constitution of the Fifth French Republic created the Conseil Constitutionnel with the express purpose of having the body serve to defend presidential prerogatives; given the long history of parliamentary supremacy in France, they feared that absent a check on the National Assembly and Senate, the legislature might encroach on presidential authority to issue regulations with the force and effect of law (Bell 1992, pp. 14–33, 78, 87–111; Brown and Bell 1998, pp. 9–24; Stone 1992, pp. 57, 60–61). Indeed, François Mitterand dismissed the Conseil Constitutionnel in 1964 as an entity whose 'sole utility is to serve as an errand boy for General de Gaulle' and whose function in the early years of the Fifth Republic François Luchaire uncharitably described as serving as 'a cannon aimed at Parliament' (Stone 1992, pp. 59–60). In other words, the Conseil Constitutionnel came into existence precisely for the purpose of enforcing newly established limits on the scope of the Parliament's legislative powers, limits intended to give the President of the

French Republic some measure of autonomous policymaking through the issuance of regulations.

Thus, in France we see a system intentionally designed to enforce the blending, rather than the separation, of legislative responsibilities between the Legislative Branch and the Executive Branch, a kind of mirror image of *Chadha*. Instead of lending some empirical support to the US system of separation of powers, however, the French example tends to reconfirm the oddity of the US approach, at least if viewed in a broader comparative law perspective.

4   CONCLUSION: THE US AS OUTLIER

Even though concerns over the constitutional separation of powers are widely shared in other democratic republics, the specific US concern with the conflation of legislative and executive power, and the concomitant commitment of enforcement of this separation of powers by the federal judiciary, has failed to gain much traction, not only in places like France or Germany, but also in neighboring common law jurisdictions like Canada.

In the United States, a rich literature exists not so much on the existence of the legislative/executive separation of powers under the original US Constitution, or with regard to the Framers' obsessive concern with the concept, but rather with regard to the proper role of the federal courts in actually enforcing the Framers' separation of legislative and executive powers (Strauss 1987; Tushnet 1992; see Flaherty 1996, pp. 1755–807). By contrast, in parliamentary systems, one would look in vain for scholarship addressing these same points. For nations that have adopted the Westminster model, the question of whether to abandon – or even to question – the cabinet's control of the apparatus of government, including both the executive and legislative branches, simply does not arise. The related question, the role of courts in enforcing a non-existent separation of powers between the executive and legislative branches, also simply does not occur to law professors or political scientists studying the operation of parliamentary systems of government. Neither question has any relevance in a system that intentionally promotes efficiency over abstract concerns with a threat of tyranny.

For me, a more interesting question than the causes and effects of the lack of transnational scholarly interest in the US separation of powers obsession, indeed, a question that demands to be asked and answered is: Why do other nations find the conflation of legislative and executive policymaking power to be entirely unproblematic? As explained earlier in Section 2, the Framers of the US Constitution, and contemporary federal judges, appear to view the merging of legislative and executive powers as creating a potentially dangerous concentration of power. From the perspective of the rest of the world, such dual roles provoke yawns, rather than dire predictions of 'tyranny' (Redish and Cisar 1991, pp. 463–5, 476–8).

Diagnosing the root causes of this phenomenon lies beyond the scope of this chapter. That said, I can offer a few preliminary observations about why legislative/executive separation of powers, a concern with such salience in the United States, represents a kind of 'shot (not) heard 'round the world'.

The US, to this day, features a skepticism towards government and governmental institutions that is not widely shared in other nations.[12] As Professor Michael Asimow has stated the proposition, '[a] generalized distrust of government officials and government power is a recurrent strain in American history' (Asimow 2007, p. 662). To a remarkable degree,

Americans tend to be hostile toward government and its motives (Asimow 2007, pp. 662–3 ('A substantial number of Americans suspect government officials and agencies of meddle-someness, incompetence, or corruption.')).

Both before and after the Great Depression, and certainly in the modern era since the election of Ronald Reagan as President in 1980, the rhetoric of US politics has reflected a shared assumption that government is the problem, not the solution (Asimow 2007, pp. 663 and 663 n.45). Recall that President Bill Clinton famously declared that 'the era of big government is over' (Clinton 1996, p. 90) and worked assiduously to unravel the social safety net through legislation like the 1996 Welfare Reform Act (Personal Responsibility and Work Opportunity Reconciliation Act of 1996, Pub. L. No. 104-193, 110 Stat. 2105 (1996); 42 USC §§ 601–79 (codifying material provisions of the Welfare Reform Act of 1996)).

In a similar vein, President Barack Obama ran on a platform of reforming the federal government, not celebrating its accomplishments or the benefits of massively expanding its reach except as necessary to address the current financial and economic crises. To the extent that the contemporary economic crisis has opened the door to more ambitious government intervention in private markets, the Obama Administration, like the Bush Administration before it, tends to style these efforts to combat the financial crisis as a necessary evil, rather than a positive or desirable permanent state of affairs.

To a remarkable degree, US citizens mistrust government and seek to minimize its ability to impact their daily lives. The unwieldy design of the federal government, replicated in all of the states save Nebraska, which has a unicameral legislature (Nebraska Constitution art. III, §§ 1, 7), incorporates the notion that slowing down the ability of government to act is a good, not bad, idea.[13] For reasons having to do with an idiosyncratic political culture, 'government' in the contemporary United States is almost an epithet. I do not wish to essentialize the attitudes of citizens of Canada, France, Germany or Japan, but my strong impression is that citizens in these nations do not view government with the same level of skepticism, if not outright hostility, that US citizens often manifest toward their own governing institutions (Hacker 1997, p. 86; Westin 1983, p. 31; but compare L'Heureux-Dube 2001, p. 18 ('Whereas Americans have always distrusted government, Canadians seem to have inherited from Great Britain a certain faith in both the role and the nature of the state.')).

The US obsession with impeding the ability of government to act is entirely rational if one views government as a problem, rather than as the provider of solutions. And, a more efficient, streamlined model of governance, one that empowers rather than impedes the ability of government to act, makes perfect sense in a polity where citizens repose faith in the ability of the government to make wise decisions on a predictable basis (L'Heureux-Dube 2001, pp. 16–19; see Currie 1994, p. 172). One still needs to inquire into the source of US hostility toward government and its institutions.

My own view is that US hostility toward government is a feature of the pluralistic nature of the United States; the US was, in large measure, a nation built not on ties of religion, ethnic kinship, or even geography, but rather on immigration (Wills 1999, p. 17). In such a cultural jambalaya, is it at all surprising to find that members of one ethnic group might view with suspicion and hostility the motives and actions of government officials who happen to be members of another ethnic group (Perea 1992)?

The division lines are hardly limited to those based on ethnicity or race. Religious differences, for better or worse, have played a major role in US politics. There are other cleavages – cultural, regional and urban-rural – that also make the country particularly diverse.

Going back to the time of the framing of the US Constitution, strong factions, whether defined by race, ethnicity, religion, region or urbanization, have been a persistent feature of domestic politics (The Federalist No. 10, at 78–9, 81–4 (James Madison) (Hamilton et al. 1961); see Sunstein 1985). These divisions create suspicion of those drawn from outsider groups and, ultimately, of government itself because members of outsider groups might well enjoy a majority in the city council, the state legislature, or the Congress.

In a nation sharing a common ethnic, religious and cultural heritage, trust in government might well come more naturally, and be held more readily, than in a nation built of immigrants that still features significant divisions based on race, ethnicity, religion, region, urbanization and culture (Cross 2005, pp. 1532–43; see L'Heureux-Dube 2001, pp. 28–9). Thus, that the citizens of the United Kingdom or Canada do not fear 'tyranny' from a central government in which members of the national legislature also head the major executive departments of the government should not be particularly surprising. When government features people drawn from a common national culture, who share longstanding ties of language, religion and kinship, it is not at all surprising that citizens would repose more trust, more reflexively, than when institutions of government are staffed by persons viewed in important respects as outsiders.

NOTES

1. Argentina's constitutional crisis over control of the Central Bank of Argentina and the nation's foreign currency reserves actually involves Congress asserting that *blended* control, rather than unilateral presidential control, governs the central bank, which is an independent executive agency. Argentina's Congress has claimed that the President cannot either fire the incumbent bank president or take control of the nation's foreign currency reserves without the Congress's consent; thus, it is asserting some measure of legislative control over both questions. In the United States, whether the President could unilaterally fire an executive branch officer appointed by the President with the advice and consent of the Senate, without first securing the Senate's approval to the discharge, remained an open, and hotly disputed, question of separation of powers law until the Supreme Court of the United States issued its landmark decision in *Myers v United States*, 272 US 52 (1926), holding that the President could lawfully remove an executive branch officer without first seeking the Senate's consent. Indeed, this very question provided the predicate for Congress's unsuccessful attempt to impeach President Andrew Johnson in 1868 (*Myers v United States*, 272 US 52, 114–15, 166–7, 175–7 (1926)).
2. Of course, Congress could delegate power to the President, with a duty to report on how he exercises it, and provide for accelerated consideration of legislation disallowing the President's action – but such legislation would have to be enacted by both houses of Congress and presented to the President for a probable veto. Moreover, Congress could require the President to wait for a prescribed period of time before implementing his plan. Thus, so-called 'report and wait' provisions do not fall afoul of *Chadha*'s rule against legislative vetoes (*Chadha*, 462 US at 935 n.9; see also *Alaska Airlines v Brock*, 480 US 678, 690 (1987); Koplow 1992, p. 1061 (noting that report and wait provisions do not raise the same constitutional problems as legislative veto provisions)). Since 1996, all 'major' regulations have been subject to mandatory 'report and wait' periods (5 USC §§ 801–08 (2006); see Rubin 2003, pp. 133–4 (advocating increased congressional oversight of federal agencies and suggesting that the generic comprehensive report and wait obligation for all major regulations provides a means of accomplishing this objective)).
3. For a concise history of the legislative debate of Madison's proposal in the House of Representatives, see Schwartz 1990, pp. 589–91.
4. The United Kingdom, then and now, maintains a 'balance of powers' rather than a 'separation of powers' (Hyre 2004, pp. 430–35; see Skold 2007, pp. 2154–5 ('In contrast to the American system based on a clear separation of powers and effective checks and balances, the British system traditionally has fused the three branches of government together, creating more of a balance of powers than a separation.')).
5. Interestingly, no formal bar exists on judicial personnel serving in the Executive Branch and, from time to time, federal judges have served in the Executive Branch concurrently with their Article III judicial service (*Mistretta v United States*, 488 US 361, 397–8 (1989); see Calabresi and Larsen 1994, pp. 1131–46 (canvassing historical examples of joint service, as well as refusals by Article III judges to undertake extra-judicial duties within

the Executive Branch)). Even so, a de facto constitutional custom against such joint service has developed. As Professors Calabresi and Larsen (1994, p. 1139) state the proposition, 'it is fair to say that a tradition has evolved that very nearly replicates the situation that would exist if [the Constitution contained] a judicial-executive incompatibility clause'. On the other hand, neither the Constitution nor the contemporary practices of the Framers establish any prohibition on joint federal/state officeholding; a member of Congress is free to serve in a state government post concurrently with her federal service (*Metropolitan Washington Airports Auth. v Citizens for the Abatement of Aircraft Noise*, 501 US 252, 282–3 (1991) (White, J, dissenting)). That said, a strong – and largely unbroken – tradition of 'one person, one office' exists in this context as well (Calabresi and Larsen 1994, pp. 1146–56). Thus, '[t]oday, it seems almost unimaginable for one individual to hold salaried, full-time federal and state offices' (Calabresi and Larsen 1994, p. 1151).

6. For a sympathetic treatment of such institutional arrangements, see Ackerman 2000, pp. 642–56, 688–90.

7. Perhaps, however, the idea is not as entirely nonsensical as I have suggested. If we imagine that an idiosyncratic member of Parliament comes to serve in a cabinet post, it might be conceivable that her policies would not necessarily reflect those of the party caucus in all cases. But, in the British system, the Prime Minister would be able to remove a renegade minister from office at will; the majority also could simply disallow the regulations through a direct legislative veto. In the absence of a meaningful bicameral system (the House of Lords can only delay the enactment of most legislation, not prevent it) and a President with a veto power, the problem of a disagreement between the executive and legislative branches of government simply cannot arise. In a very real sense, then, a case like *Chadha* is simply unthinkable in the United Kingdom, primarily because Parliament would never need to have recourse to a legislative veto, but also because the Prime Minister, unlike the President, lacks a wholly independent role in the legislative process.

8. With respect to the latter point – avoiding abuse of executive authority – the matter could be framed in favor of separation of powers, i.e., an independent legislative branch would seem to have more power, and more incentive, to ferret out wrongdoing than a majority party would possess in embarrassing the party's leader (viz., the prime minister or chancellor).

9. It should go without saying that courts in the United Kingdom and Canada also do not attempt to enforce any limits on the scope of delegated authority from the legislative branch to the executive branch. With respect to Canada, '[t]here is no requirement that "legislative" and "executive" powers be exercised by separate and independent bodies' and 'a delegation cannot be attacked on the ground that it confers "legislative" power on the executive branch of government' (1 Hogg 2007, § 14.2(a), p. 14-4 to 14-5). And, in the United Kingdom, '[a]ny House of Lords decision with serious political implications is open to subsequent modification or reversal by Parliament, sometimes even with retrospective effect' (Atiyah and Summers 1987, p. 269). Moreover, 'in the British political system, this is no mere ritual phrase on the lips of judges anxious to disclaim ultimate responsibility for the long-term state of the law', but instead 'a reflection of political reality' (Atiyah and Summers 1987, p. 269).

10. Interestingly, however, the French Constitution contains an incompatibility clause, Article 23, which provides that 'The functions of members of the Government are incompatible with the exercise of any parliamentary mandate, any role of representing a profession at the national level, and any public employment or professional activity' (Constitution of the Fifth French Republic, art. 23; see Bell 1992, p. 17 ('Article 23 creates an incompatibility between being a minister and being a member of Parliament, with the result that ministers need have no parliamentary experience.')).

11. Strictly speaking, the Conseil Constitutionnel lacks jurisdiction to determine whether a regulation exceeds the scope of Article 37 and trenches on a matter reserved to Parliament under Article 34. That said, Parliament, if controlled by the opposition, could attempt to protect its legislative prerogatives by enacting a statute that overrides the presidential regulation. The President would then likely challenge the constitutionality of the statute before the Conseil Constitutionnel and seek a declaration that the subject matter fell within Article 37, rather than Article 34 (Bell 1992, pp. 86–91). This process of disallowing laws that go beyond the scope of Parliament's authority under Article 34 is called 'declassification' (Bell 1992, pp. 86–91; see also Constitution of the Fifth French Republic, art. 37(2)).

12. This proposition is perhaps too obvious to require support, but the academic literature is rife with works that establish the truth of this assertion (see Blendon et al., 1997; Kingdon 1999, pp. 23–56; Wills 1999, pp. 15–22, 297–320). As Professors Atiyah and Summers (1987, p. 40) put it, juxtaposing the US and British legal systems:

> For whereas the English legal and political machine is a well integrated machine in which the various constituent parts operate with a high degree of trust for each other's functions and role, the American legal and political machine is to a large extent based on a contrary principle, a principle of *distrust* for other constituent parts. . . . It could, indeed, be said that the American system of government has even institutionalized its distrust to a considerable degree. The people distrust all government, so the powers of government are limited, divided, checked, and balanced (emphasis in the original).

13. As Professor Gary Wills (1999, p. 319) sarcastically states the proposition, '[i]nefficiency is to be our safeguard against despotism'. Even though Wills (id.) identifies this as part of the prevailing national political ethos, he flatly rejects the proposition, noting that '[i]nefficient governments are often the most despotic' and asks rhetorically, '[i]n your own observation of life around you, has inefficiency been a protection against the arbitrariness of an employer, the random vindictiveness of a teacher, the insecure bluster of a physician?' We nevertheless embrace inefficiency in the United States because of a general belief 'that a government unable to do much of anything will be unable to oppress us' (id.).

REFERENCES

Ackerman, Bruce, 'The New Separation of Powers', *Harvard Law Review* 113 (2000): 634, 640, 645–6.
Albert, Richard, 'The Fusion of Presidentialism and Parliamentarianism', *American Journal of Comparative Law* 57 (2009): 531.
Allars, Margaret, 'On Deference to Tribunals: With Deference to Dworkin', *Queen's Law Journal* 20 (1994): 163–4.
Aronson, Mark and Bruce Dyer, *Judicial Review of Administrative Action*, Law Book Company of Australia, 1996.
Asimow, Michael, 'Access to Justice: Law and Popular Culture', *Loyola Law Review* 40 (2007): 653.
Atiyah, P.S. and Robert S. Summers, *Form and Substance in Anglo-American Law: A Comparative Study of Legal Reasoning, Legal Theory, and Legal Institutions*, New York: Clarendon Press, 1987.
Barrionuevo, Alexei, 'Argentine Bank President is Formally Dismissed', *New York Times* 4 February 2010: A11.
Barrionuevo, Alexei, 'Argentine Banking Dispute Goes to Congress', *New York Times* 26 January 2010: A10.
Barrionuevo, Alexei, 'Debt Plan in Argentina Sets Bank against the President', *New York Times* 11 January 2010: A8.
Bell, John, *French Constitutional Law*, New York: Oxford University Press, 1992.
Blendon, Robert J. et al., *Why People Don't Trust Government*, Cambridge, MA: Harvard University Press, 1997.
Booth, William, 'Two Hondurans Headed for Clash', *Washington Post* 1 July 2009: A8.
Boyd, Julian P., ed., 'Madison's Observations on Jefferson's Draft of a Constitution for Virginia', *Papers of Thomas Jefferson*, Princeton, NJ: Princeton University Press, 1952, 308.
Brown, L. Neville and John S. Bell, *French Administrative Law*, 5th edition, New York: Oxford University Press, 1998.
Calabresi, Steven G. and Joan L. Larsen, 'One Person, One Office: Separation of Powers or Separation of Personnel?', *Cornell Law Review* 79 (1994): 1045.
Clinton, William J., 'Address before a Joint Session of the Congress on the State of the Union', *Weekly Compilation of Presidential Documents* 32 (January 1996): 90.
Cross, Frank B., 'Law and Trust', *Georgetown Law Journal* 93 (2005): 1457.
Currie, David P., *The Constitution of the Federal Republic of Germany*, Chicago: University of Chicago Press, 1994.
Edley, Christopher J., *Administrative Law: Rethinking Judicial Control of Bureaucracy*, New Haven: Yale University Press, 1990.
Ellingwood, Ken and Alex Renderos, 'One Sworn In, Another Flies Out', *Los Angeles Times* 28 January 2010: A17.
Estrada, Miguel A., 'When a Coup Isn't; Under Honduras' Constitution, the Ouster of President Manuel Zelaya was Legal', *Los Angeles Times* 10 July 2009: A29.
Flaherty, Martin S., 'The Most Dangerous Branch', *Yale Law Journal* 105 (1996): 1725.
Gales, Joseph A. and W.W. Seaton, eds., *The Debates and Proceedings of the Congress of the United States*, volume 1, New York: New American Library, 1834.
Grady, Mary Anastasia, 'Argentina Seizes the Central Bank', *Wall Street Journal* 9 February 2010: A19.
Hacker, Jacob, *The Road to Nowhere*, Princeton, NJ: Princeton University Press, 1997.
Hamilton, Alexander, James Madison and John Jay, *The Federalist Papers*, ed. Clinton Rossiter, New York: New American Library, 1961.
Hogg, Peter W., *Constitutional Law of Canada*, 1st edition, Toronto: The Carswell Company, 1977.
Hogg, Peter W., *Canada Act 1982 Annotated*, Toronto: The Carswell Company Limited, 1982.
Hogg, Peter W., *1 & 2 Constitutional Law of Canada*, 5th edition, Scarborough, Ont.: Thomson Carswell, 2007.
Hyre, James, 'Comment, The United Kingdom's Declaration of Judicial Independence: Creating a Supreme Court to Secure Individual Rights under the Human Rights Act of 1998', *Fordham Law Review* 73 (2004): 423.
Jackson, Vicki C. and Mark Tushnet, *Comparative Constitutional Law*, 1st edition, New York: Foundation Press, 1999.
Kingdon, John W., *America the Unusual*, 1st edition, Bedford and St. Martins: Worth Publishers, Inc., 1999.
Koplow, David A., 'When is an Amendment Not an Amendment?: Modifications of Arms Control Agreements without the Senate', *University of Chicago Law Review* 59 (1992): 981.
Krotoszynski, Ronald J. Jr., 'On the Danger of Wearing Two Hats: *Mistretta* and *Morrison* Revisited', *William and Mary Law Review* 38 (1997): 417.

Krotoszynski, Ronald J. Jr., 'Reconsidering the Nondelegation Doctrine: Universal Service, the Power to Tax, and the Ratification Doctrine', *Indiana Law Journal* 80 (2005): 239.

L'Heureux-Dube, Claire, 'Outsiders on the Bench: The Continuing Struggle for Equality', *Wisconsin Women's Law Journal* 16 (2001): 15.

Locke, John, *Two Treatises on Government, The Second Treatise of Government*, 3rd edition, Cambridge: Cambridge University Press, 1698, ed. Peter Laslett. 1988.

Madison, James, *Notes of Debates in the Federal Convention*, ed. Adrienne Koch, Athens, OH: Ohio University Press, 1965.

Moffett, Matt, 'Meanwhile, A Standoff in Buenos Aires', *Wall Street Journal* 25 January 2010: A1+.

Moffett, Matt and Matthew Cowley, 'Argentine Opposition Takes on President in Court', *Wall Street Journal* 30 December 2009: A11.

Montesquieu, Charles de Secondat, *The Spirit of the Laws*, 1748, ed. J.V. Pritchard, trans. Thomas Nugent, Littleton, CO: Rothman & Co., 1991.

Perea, Juan, 'Demography and Distrust: An Essay on American Languages, Cultural Pluralism, and Official English', *Minnesota Law Review* 77 (1992): 269.

Redish, Martin H. and Elizabeth J. Cisar, '"If Angels Were to Govern": The Need for Pragmatic Formalism in Separation of Powers Theory', *Duke Law Journal* 41 (1991): 449.

Renderos, Alex and Tracy Wilkinson, 'Coup Sparks Violent Protest', *Los Angeles Times* 30 June 2009: A1.

Renderos, Alex and Tracy Wilkinson, 'Hondurans Back Opposition Leader', *Boston Globe* 30 November 2009: A4.

Rubin, Ed, 'It's Time to Make the Administrative Procedure Act Administrative', *Cornell Law Review* 89 (2003): 89.

Russell, Peter H, 'The Growth of Canadian Judicial Review and the Commonwealth and American Experiences', *Comparative Judicial Review and Public Policy*, ed. Donald W. Jackson and C. Neal Tate (1992), 29.

Sartori, Giovanni (1994), 'Neither Presidentialism Nor Parliamentarianism', *The Failure of Presidential Democracy*, ed. Julian J. Linz and Arturo Valenzuela, 1994, 106.

Schwartz, Bernard, ed., *The Bill of Rights: A Documentary History*, New York: Chelsea House Publishers, 1971.

Schwartz, Bernard, 'Curiouser and Curiouser: The Supreme Court's Separation of Powers Wonderland', *Notre Dame Law Review* 65 (1990): 587.

Skold, Michael, 'The Reform Act's Supreme Court: A Missed Opportunity for Judicial Review in the United Kingdom?', *Connecticut Law Review* 39 (2007): 2149.

Slaughter, Anne-Marie, 'Judicial Globalization', *Virginia Journal of International Law,* 40 (2000): 1103.

Stone, Alec, *The Birth of Judicial Politics in France: The Constitutional Council in Comparative Perspective,* New York: Oxford University Press, 1992.

Strauss, Peter L., 'Formal and Functional Approaches to Separation-of-powers Questions – A Foolish Inconsistency?', *Cornell Law Review* 72 (1987): 488.

Sunstein, Cass R., 'Interest Groups in American Public Law', *Stanford Law Review* 38 (1985): 29.

Tushnet, Mark V., 'The Sentencing Commission and Constitutional Theory: Bowls and Plateaus in Separation of Powers Theory', *Southern California Law Review* 66 (1992): 581.

Vile, M.J.C., *Constitutionalism and the Separation of Powers*, Oxford: Clarendon Press, 1967.

Wade, William, *Administrative Law*, 6th ed., New York: Oxford University Press, 1988.

Weiler, Todd J., 'Curial Deference and NAFTA Chapter 19 Panels: Is What is Good for the Goose, Good for the Gander?', *Journal of International Legal Studies* 1 (1995): 83.

Westin, Alan F. (1983), 'The United States Bill of Rights and the Canadian Charter: A Socio-Political Analysis', *The U.S. Bill of Rights and the Canadian Charter of Rights and Freedoms*, ed. William R. McKercher, Toronto: Ontario Economic Council, 1983, 31.

Wills, Gary, *A Necessary Evil: A History of American Distrust of Government*, New York: Simon & Schuster, 1999.

14. Political parties and constitutionalism
Richard H. Pildes

1   INTRODUCTION

Constitutions and judicial review are often thought of, particularly in more recent decades, as devices for ensuring the protection of individual rights and, through equality provisions, the rights of potentially vulnerable minority groups. Within this conception, constitutional law is viewed as a means of restraining potentially oppressive majorities from running roughshod over personal liberties or the interests of minority groups. This rights-equality conception tends to emphasize what might be called 'negative constitutionalism': constitutions as shields against majoritarian excesses.

But constitutions also serve to constitute political power. In constitutional democracies, constitutions empower democracy: they create the institutional structures, offices of government and framework for decisionmaking that organize the diffuse preferences of a mass society into recognizable, meaningful and legitimate political outcomes. The study of how constitutions create positive political power, and how constitutional law sustains (or fails to sustain) this power, might be called 'positive constitutionalism'.[1] Though most modern constitutional scholarship focuses on the role of constitutions as checks on political power, the role of constitutions as creators of political power is at least as important, both historically, in terms of why constitutions were created originally, and in terms of the practice of governance today. For example, the American Constitution, the oldest constitution, was created to realize this kind of positive constitutionalism: its central purpose was to create a powerful, effective system for governance at the national level. Only after that Constitution was created was the Bill of Rights, the provisions designed to check the national government, then grafted on. In general, the *raison d'être* of constitutions is to create power, albeit power that is checked and channeled appropriately.

That means creating the institutions, structures, organizations and legal framework that enable democratic government (at least in constitutional democracies). And in any modern state, one of the most essential elements in democratic self-government is the political party. Although the romantic vision of the individual citizen as the vehicle of democratic self-governance still has powerful emotional and symbolic resonance, the reality is that in any large state, the most enduring and powerful vehicle for organizing citizens into effective participants in politics is the political party. Parties are central to defining political agendas, organizing coalitions of voters, amplifying the voices of diffuse groups and keeping officeholders accountable. In recognition of this fact, Germany's Federal Constitutional Court (*Bundesverfassungsgericht*), has described the post-World War II German Constitution as having created a 'party state'; the meaning of this idea is that democracy is only secured and made meaningful to the extent that free and vibrant political parties are permitted to compete for political power. But political parties in control of the powers of government can also use that power to seek to entrench themselves and reduce competitive pressures from other parties. Thus, constitutional regimes must both protect the role of political parties in democratic processes and protect democracy from partisan attempts to manipulate the rules of political engagement. This chapter explores how constitutional texts and court decisions have engaged the now well-recognized centrality of political parties to making democratic self-government meaningful.

2   CONSTITUTIONAL TEXTS

A great deal of variance exists as to whether constitutions refer to political parties at all and, if so, what kinds of protections are provided. To some extent, this variance is a function of when a constitution was adopted: more recent constitutions tend to reference political parties, while older ones do not. Thus, fewer than 10% of the constitutions in force in 1875 mentioned parties, while over 80% of those in force in 2006 do so.[2] Similarly, before 1950 the right to form political parties was virtually non-existent; since then, this right has become much more common, with 60% of the constitutions in effect in 2000 guaranteeing such a right.[3] These differences reflect transformations over time in the understanding of what the practice of democracy means in large societies.

The difference between the American and German constitutions is emblematic of this history. The oldest constitution, the American one, does not mention political parties at all; not only did the American Framers fail to anticipate the rise of modern political parties and their centrality to democracy, the American Constitution was actually conceived in hostility to parties.[4] Political parties were one quintessential form of the 'factions' that James Madison, in defending the American constitutional design, decried.[5] In trying to design a constitutional system that would preclude the rise of parties, the American Framers were simply reflecting a deeper, more longstanding tradition in Europe of 'antipartyism' – the view that political parties, because they are sectarian and partisan, are divisive elements that corrode the capacity of democratic government to pursue the common good.[6]

In contrast, constitutions formed in the direct aftermath of 20th century totalitarian regimes, or in the knowledge of how such regimes functioned, reflected awareness of the fact that one of the first things such regimes did was to eliminate party competition and consolidate one-party rule. Thus, the post-World War II German Constitution, in its well-known Article 21 provision, provides express protection of the right to form political parties – while also requiring, in reaction to the Nazi era, that parties internally be structured along democratic lines:

> Political parties participate in the formation of the political will of the people. They may be freely established. Their internal organization must conform to democratic principles. They must publicly account for their assets and for the sources and the use of their funds.[7]

In the eyes of the German Constitutional Court, Article 21 has 'raised [political parties] to the rank of constitutional institutions' and recognizes that parties are 'constitutionally integral of government'.[8] Further reflecting the ways historical context has shaped the place of political parties in constitutional texts, there is substantial regional variation. Almost every constitution in place in 2000 in Eastern Europe and the post-Soviet countries, as well as Latin America, East Asia and sub-Saharan Africa makes reference to political parties; only about

60% of the constitutions in effect in 2000 in Europe, the United States and Canada do so, while about 40% of those in Oceania (Australia, New Zealand and other Pacific islands) do so.[9] A listing of representative provisions is provided below.[10]

3   CONSTITUTIONAL LAW

Broadly speaking, three different forms of constitutional issues concerning political parties can be identified in the decisions of courts across different systems. The first are 'competition-protecting' decisions; these are decisions that seek to ensure the vitality of the democratic process by ensuring that a vibrant system of competitive parties remains in place. The second category are decisions, perhaps unique to the American context, that provide strong protection to the autonomy of political parties. Finally, the third form of issue that courts have confronted involves attempts to ban various political parties, often on the grounds that the party at issue is itself a threat to the continuation of democracy, because the party is 'anti-democratic'.

3.1   Ensuring Political Competition

3.1.1   Ballot access and campaign financing[11]
The most robust jurisprudence seeking to protect democratic competition through protecting the rights and interests of political parties is probably that of the German Constitutional Court. That court has recognized consistently, in various ways, that existing political power-holders will be tempted to use their power over election laws to stifle political competition. In response, the German Court has been aggressive in striking down regulations that limit a political party's access to the ballot. Thus, in the Ballot Admission Case, the German Court invalidated a stringent signature requirement that applied only to the candidate of a party not already represented in the national or state legislatures, while existing parties needed the approval only of the relevant state party executive committee.[12] Despite the increased risk of political instability from multiparty competition, the German Court found that the 500-signature requirement for new parties interfered with open and fair political competition. The German Court has been even more concerned with ballot access restrictions in local elections. For example, it held unconstitutional one state's requirement that a candidate nominated by local voters' groups secure a minimum number of signatures to appear on the ballot, while political parties did not face a similar obligation.[13] The German Constitutional Court reasoned that '[i]n the field of election law the legislature enjoys only a narrow range of options. Differentiations in the field always require a particularly compelling justification.'

Similarly, in the area of election financing, the German Court has been extraordinarily attentive to the possible partisan manipulation of financing regulations by dominant parties. Indeed, the Court has essentially defined the rules that govern public funding of political parties. In one striking venture into this area, the German Court in 1958 struck down provisions making donations to political parties tax deductible.[14] The Court reasoned that since progressive taxation meant that income tax rates increased as income increased, such a system of financing disproportionately benefitted wealthy (and corporate) taxpayers. Thus, the Court concluded, because tax-deductible party contributions favored certain political parties – those wealthy donors were inclined to support – this policy violated the constitutional principle of equality of opportunity for political parties. In this line of cases, the Court suggested that in order to ensure effective competition and diminish special-interest influence, the government could provide public financing to parties. The Court was careful to stress that such financing could not increase existing de facto inequalities between parties.

When the German government began public financing, the laws distributed funds based on the proportion of parliamentary seats each party won.[15] Parties that did not win seats could not receive public financing, leading parties that had actively campaigned but lost to challenge these limitations.[16] The German Court struck these provisions down as unconstitutional infringements on the rights of minor parties: 'It is inconsistent with the principle of equal opportunity for [the legislature] to provide these funds only to parties already represented in parliament or to those which ... win seats in parliament'. At the same time, the Court recognized that public reimbursement would encourage new parties and that the legislature could act against the formation of 'splinter' parties by making reimbursement contingent upon a new party obtaining a certain percentage of votes.

After the Bundestag responded by imposing a 2% threshold, the Court struck this down as well, on the ground that it violated general equality principles and constitutional provisions mandating universal and equal suffrage.[17] As a matter of constitutional law, the Court then specified that any party capturing 0.5% of the vote 'manifests its seriousness as an election campaign competitor' and should receive a portion of public funds. Later, in a separate case, the Court held that independent candidates were also eligible for public funding under certain circumstances.[18] The German Court thus has been quite active in drawing the constitutional boundary between political parties and the state – a difficult task complicated by public financing. For many years, the Court struggled to distinguish between public funding designed to defray legitimate campaign costs and public funding designed for the general support of parties. Eventually the Court abandoned that distinction as unworkable and instead held that the total of state funding could not exceed the total amount the parties themselves raised.[19] The Court established this rule to ensure that the parties remained tied to their voters and did not become too entrenched. The Court has also attentively monitored tax deductions for party contributions and has banned tax deductions for corporate contributions to parties and for individual contributions so large that they raised concerns about equality between parties.

The Canadian Supreme Court has similarly invoked that country's constitution to protect the constitutional rights of regional or smaller political parties in the context of campaign-finance laws. In the important *Figueroa* case,[20] the Canadian Supreme Court confronted election laws that required a political party to nominate candidates in at least 50 election districts in order to be an officially registered party. Among the benefits of registered party status at issue in the case were the right of registered parties to issue tax receipts for donations the parties received outside the official election period, the right of candidates to transfer unspent election funds to the party (rather than to the government), and the right of the party's candidates to list their party affiliation on the ballot. The purpose of these provisions, according to the government, was to ensure that only parties representing large coalitions, with some geographic breadth of appeal, would receive the benefits of party status. Thus, the provisions aimed to reduce the fragmentation and splintering of parties.

In a decision unanimous in outcome but split in reasoning, the Court held that these provisions violated the Canadian Charter of Rights and Freedoms, Canada's constitutional text. The majority applied more of an individual rights analysis and concluded that these provisions unjustifiably infringed upon a constitutional right of each citizen to play a meaningful role in the electoral process; voters who supported smaller parties would be unduly burdened by the 50-district requirement for party status. A minority group of Justices was more willing to permit government to subordinate individual interests to various structural or systemic aims in the design of electoral institutions. Thus, this group of Justices thought electoral institutions could be designed for the aim of creating and sustaining more centrist, 'accommodative' parties. These Justices pointed to the Canadian Court's handling of gerrymandering claims, in which the Canadian Court had not applied a strict rule of population equality across all election districts, but had instead permitted government to design districts to overrepresent rural areas in order to create more of a sense of inclusion and fair representation. But even though this group of Justices was willing to permit government to treat major and minor parties differently for certain, justifiable ends of democracy itself – such as encouraging parties that represent a national perspective – these Justices nonetheless also concluded, as the majority did, that the 50-district requirement for party status was unconstitutional. In large provinces, a regional party could mount 50 candidacies, while parties in small provinces could not; thus, the law was not tailored to ensuring only broad, national parties and effectively did not treat different regions of Canada or different provinces equally – and for that reason, violated the Charter. Thus, for quite different reasons, both groups of Justices concluded that dominant political actors had used their power over election laws to diminish, unconstitutionally, the role of smaller parties.

3.1.2   Internal parliamentary rights of minor parties and independent officeholders

To ensure that dominant parties do not capture politics in yet other ways, the German Court has also been willing to review the internal distributions of policymaking influence within the legislature itself. In particular, the German Court has held that opposition parties have a participatory interest that the ruling coalition cannot suppress through parliamentary procedures.[21] For example, the constitution of one German state allowed one-fourth of the members of parliament to request a committee to investigate problems with government. In one instance, after a minority party had established an investigative committee, the majority party sought to add additional charges to the committee's mandate, including a counter-corruption charge against the leader of the minority party. The minority sued, and the Court upheld the minority's constitutional power to define the terms of its own investigation. In an insightful passage, which recognized that competition between parties was a main mechanism through which government could be held accountable, the Court noted:

> The constitutional meaning of the rights of the minority lies in the safeguarding of this control [over defining the terms of its own investigations] ... The original tension between parliament and government – as it existed during the constitutional monarchy – has changed. In a parliamentary democracy the majority [party] normally dominates the government. Today, this relationship is characterized by the political tension between the government and the parliamentary factions supporting it, on the one hand, and the opposition [party or parties], on the other hand. In a parliamentary system of government [therefore] the majority does not primarily watch over the government. This is rather the task of the opposition, and thus, as a rule, of the minority [party] ... If the right of the minority – and thus the parliamentary right to control – is not to be weakened unduly, then the minority must not be left at the mercy of the majority.[22]

In other litigation, a member of the Bundestag (the German Parliament) who had first been elected as a representative of the Green Party resigned from that party and became an independent representative. He sued after he was stripped of all committee positions, and the Court held that a representative without a party affiliation could not be excluded from committees merely because he was not a member of any party (although he could be denied the right to vote in committee).[23] As the Court put it, the 'constitutional protection of parliamentary minorities – a right following from the principle of democracy – also applies to independent representatives'. In general, the Court has taken the position that 'parties must be represented on committees in proportion to their strength'.[24] Finally, in a case not involving interparty competition, but one in which the Court was aware of the possibilities for partisan manipulation, the Court held that when a successful candidate on a party's list withdraws or resigns after election, the party cannot simply name a substitute, nor can it shift the order of the candidates on its list. To respect the preferences of voters, the candidate who is next in line on the list elected must be given the seat.[25] This line of cases explores the structure of relationships between parties and their candidates, and between parties within the legislative process, and reveals the extent to which the German Court has taken an active role in protecting the political process from manipulation by partisan majorities.

3.1.3 Electoral thresholds

A recurring constitutional issue across democracies that rest on proportional representation has been the constitutionality of various thresholds of representation. These thresholds have been challenged by minor parties as being inconsistent with constitutional commitments to democracy. Courts have responded by embracing the legitimacy of judicial oversight over these thresholds, rather than treating them as political choices to which courts should be highly deferential. On the merits, courts have sought to find a balance between the need for thresholds at some level – a response to the failed parliamentary systems between the wars, which were thought to be paralyzed in part because representation was highly fragmented among numerous parties, including small ones – and the fact that high thresholds could be a means by which dominant political parties suppress political challenge.

Thus, the German Court has rejected numerous challenges to that system's 5% threshold by accepting a weighty governmental interest in effective governance institutions, which in that Court's view justified measures to avoid party splintering 'which would make it more difficult or even impossible to form a majority'.[26] In similar fashion, the constitutional courts of the Czech Republic and Romania have upheld challenges to their systems' 5% threshold for representation.[27] At the same time, the German court struck down 5% thresholds in the immediate aftermath of reunification, on the basis that such a threshold would suppress competition and representation from the former East Germany, in light of the lack of electoral experience and hence the ability to forge effective aggregate actors, such as parties, in the first steps of East Germany's transition to democracy.[28]

3.2 Bans on Political Parties

The cases above can all be categorized as ones in which courts seek to maintain the conditions of robust democratic political competition by ensuring that the electoral ground rules do not inappropriately constrict the opportunities of political parties – typically, minority parties – to challenge more dominant parties for power. A second major categorization of cases that engage the role of political parties in constitutional regimes can be conceptualized all the way at an opposite pole: whether states can shut certain political parties out of the process of democratic competition altogether by banning or otherwise regulating those parties. This question has bedeviled the high courts of countries as diverse as Germany, Spain, India, Turkey and Israel, along with the quasi-constitutional European Court of Human Rights.

The types of political parties subject to various modes of state prohibition, or extreme regulatory restriction, include parties deemed to be 'antidemocratic', those considered to be separatist and ethnic parties.[29] These bans or regulatory restrictions are justified in Europe under the post-World War II rubric of 'militant democracy', or the need for democratic states to be vigilant and aggressive in defending themselves against antidemocratic threats from within – particularly the threat posed in the electoral arena by antidemocratic parties using democratic elections to assume power. Parties that states have viewed as antidemocratic include, for example, neo-Nazi and Communist parties in Germany. In Turkey, religiously based parties (Islamic parties) have also been treated as antidemocratic because they depart from the Turkish constitutional vision of Turkey as a democratic, secular state. Separatist parties include those that seek to fragment an existing state by the demand for territorial independence; Kurdish parties in Turkey, for example, have been banned under this rationale. Ethnic party bans can be found in many constitutions in Asia, sub-Saharan Africa, post-communist Eastern Europe and the fledgling constitutions of Afghanistan and Iraq.[30] Many of these party bans and regulatory restrictions have been challenged as violating the constitutions of the relevant states.

The form of the restriction on impermissible parties ranges in different countries from outright bans on certain parties to less comprehensive measures. India, for example, does not ban parties, but its electoral code regulates 'corrupt practices', which include appeals to vote for or against candidates on the ground of religion, race, caste, community or language or the use of, or appeal, to religious symbols.[31] The Indian High Court has permitted state electoral authorities to overturn election results when winning candidates have been found to violate these prohibitions.[32] In Israel, as a result of interplay between the Israeli Supreme Court and the parliament, the state denies 'antidemocratic' parties the right to seek elective office but does not ban them more broadly.[33]

For the most part, constitutional courts have upheld these party bans or related measures, though not without concern for the tension that banning any political party poses for democratic systems. Surely it was no surprise that the German Constitutional Court in 1952 upheld a ban on the Socialist Reich Party, a clear vestige of the Nazi party, on the basis of the party's aim to overthrow democratic government in Germany.[34] And while the German court in the 1950s upheld a ban on the Communist Party, it is noteworthy that when another Communist Party was formed in 1968, the German government took no steps to ban it, perhaps because the strength of the post-World War II German democratic order was perceived as sufficiently secure to tolerate previously banned parties.[35]

Perhaps the most interesting in the line of cases involving party bans is a series of cases from Turkey dealing with the Refah Partisi (Welfare Party), a mass-based Islamic organization with wide enough popular support to have made it at one time the largest single party in the Turkish parliament. Nonetheless, the Turkish Constitutional Court ordered the dissolution of the party, the surrender of its assets to the state and the removal of four Refah members from Parliament, while also banning the party's leaders from elective office for five years.[36] The Court did so on the ground that the party was 'antidemocratic' because it violated the Turkish constitutional commitment to a democratic and secular state. The Welfare Party case is noteworthy not only because the party was a major force in Turkey, not a fringe party, but also because the Welfare Party was able to appeal to a supranational human rights tribunal, the European Court of Human Rights (ECHR).[37] Thus, the case tested Europe-wide principles concerning the boundaries, if any, of political party participation in constitutional democracy. The ECHR upheld the decision of the Turkish courts on the ground that 'a State cannot be required to wait, before intervening, until a political party has seized power and begun to take concrete steps to implement a policy incompatible with the standards of the Convention and democracy, even though the danger of that policy for democracy is sufficiently established and imminent'. Thus, this line of cases across many countries, and their endorsement in the Turkish cases by the ECHR, reveals that the constitutional orders in many countries permit restraints on 'extremist parties' that would clearly be unconstitutional within the First Amendment tradition of the United States. To some extent, that is not surprising; the United States has long tolerated extremist speech in general that other democracies proscribe. But it is one thing to regulate even the speech of an individual. The stakes are even higher when the issue becomes the constitutionality in democratic states of regulating, and even banning, entire political parties.

3.2.1   Party rights to autonomy?

Beyond the context of ensuring that minor parties continue to be able to put competitive pressure on major parties and the context of 'extremist parties', constitutions and courts vary greatly as to whether parties should enjoy a broad, general constitutional right to autonomy. The German system expressly rejects this view, in the sense that the German Constitution specifically regulates the internal structure and organization of parties; as a reflection of the Nazi experience, Article 21 of the German Constitution requires that parties be internally organized to be democratic. The German Court has taken this provision to mean that a political party 'must be structured from the bottom up, that is, that the members must not be excluded from decision-making processes, and that the basic equality of members as well as freedom to join or to leave must be guaranteed'.[38]

American constitutional doctrine lies all the way at the other end of the spectrum. The American Supreme Court has held unconstitutional legislative attempts to control the internal organization of political parties.[39] Even more dramatically, most American states have long required political parties to choose their nominees through a primary election, rather than having party leaders or some other internal party process select candidates. Yet the Supreme Court has held unconstitutional efforts by the state to expand the electorate entitled to participate in those primaries. Thus, the Supreme Court has held that it violates the American Constitution for legislatures to require political parties to permit non-members to participate in these primary elections.[40] This is so even when legislatures seek to regulate the major political parties to increase participation in their primary elections. Although the American Constitution contains no express provision recognizing parties, or granting them any rights against the state, the Supreme Court has concluded that the First Amendment protects the right of free political association, and through that, the rights of political parties. This approach has, in turn, generated the strongest constitutional right of political party autonomy to be found in any major system.

The full scope of this emerging right to party autonomy is still in the process of development in the United States. Whether such a right should be constitutionally recognized is also a matter of much dispute within the American Supreme Court and academic literature. To the extent such a right erects barriers to legislative attempts to enhance the democratic process or the democratic character of political parties, as the right of party autonomy appears to do in the United States, questions have been raised as to whether constitutional rights to party autonomy further or undermine the democratic system.[41]

4   CONCLUSION

In the aftermath of World War II, if not long before, vibrant political parties have come to be recognized as essential to democratic politics. Indeed, democracy has come to be defined as multiparty competition for political power. Modern constitutions reflect this view by granting constitutional status to political parties and enshrining various protections for parties.

In all democratic systems, those who occupy political office will be tempted to use their temporary power to adopt rules that make it more difficult for their potential challengers to succeed. Because rival political parties are the most potent form through which such challenges are likely to be mobilized and organized, all democratic systems face the risk that those in power will seek to adopt rules that weaken rival parties. A central task for modern constitutionalism, therefore, is to seek to preserve and sustain ground rules of political competition that enable parties to compete for political power on fair and appropriate terms. The German Constitutional Court has probably developed the leading jurisprudence thus far on these issues.

At the same time that parties are the principal carriers of democratic participation, they also can pose risks to the democratic system. Courts in many countries in different religious, geographical and historical contexts have struggled with the issue of whether the constitutional order should permit states to ban, or otherwise restrict, political parties that are considered 'extremist' and hence threatening to the maintenance of democracy itself. Precisely how to draw the boundary between protecting parties as vital sources of competition and constraining extreme parties as threats to democracy remains a profound and difficult question that bears future study, particularly as religiously based parties appear to be on the march in many countries.

NOTES

1. I borrow this phrase from my colleague, Stephen Holmes.
2. See Elkins, Ginsburg and Melton (2009) at 19.
3. ConstitutionMaking.Org (2008) at 3.
4. See Hofstadter (1970).
5. The Federalist No. 10.
6. On this tradition of antipartyism, see Rosenblum (2008) at 25–165.
7. Constitution of the German Federal Republic, Article 21.
8. Kommers (1997) at 200, 209.
9. ConstitutionMaking.Org (2008) at 1.
10. 'The freedom of association includes the right to establish and join political associations and parties and, through them, to work jointly and democratically to give expression to the will of the people and to the organization of political power' (Portugal 2004, Article 51)

    'In the Republic of Hungary political parties may be established and may function freely, provided they respect the Constitution and laws established in accordance with the Constitution' (Hungary 2003, Article 3.1)

    'A person shall enjoy the liberty to unite and form a political party for the purpose of making [the] political will of the people and carrying out political activities in fulfillment of such will along [with] the democratic regime of government with the King as Head of the State as provided in this Constitution' (Thailand 1997, Article 47)

'The rights of a citizen include the right to form and join political parties, to take part in political campaigns, and to vote and to be a candidate in free and fair elections of members of the House of Representatives held by secret ballot and ultimately on the basis of equal suffrage' (Fiji 1998, Article 6.fE)

'Political parties or groups take part in the elections and the political, economic and social life. They form and conduct their activities freely' (Central African Republic 2004, Article 20)

'Political parties express the democratic pluralism, assist in the formulation and manifestation of the popular will and are a basic instrument for political participation. Their creation and the exercise of their activity are free within the observance of the Constitution and the law. Their internal structure and functioning must be democratic' (Spain 1992, Article 6)

'The Republic of Poland safeguards the freedom for the creation and the functioning of political parties. Political parties shall be founded on the principle of voluntariness and the equality of Polish citizens, with the goal of influencing the formulation of the policy of the State by democratic means' (Poland 1997, Article 11.1)

'Creation, merger, incorporation, and dissolution of political parties is free, with due regard for national sovereignty, the democratic regime, multiplicity of political parties and fundamental human rights, observing the following precepts ...' (Brazil 2005, Article 17).

11. The material here and in the next few pages is drawn from Issacharoff and Pildes (1998).
12. 3 BVerfGE 19 (1953).
13. *Stoevesandt Case*, 12 BVerfGE 10, 25 (1960).
14. *Party Finance Case II*, 8 BVerfGE 51 (1958).
15. Party Finance Act of 1959.
16. *Party Finance Case III*, 20 BVerfGE 56 (1966).
17. *Party Finance Case IV*, 24 BVerfGE 300 (1968).
18. *Daniels Case*, 41 BVerfGE 399 (1976).
19. *Party Finance Case VII*, 85 BVerfGE 264 (1992).
20. *Figueroa v Canada* (Attorney General) [2003] 1 SCR 912.
21. *Schleswig-Holstein Investigative Committee Case*, 49 BVerfGE 70 (1978).
22. *Id.*
23. *Wüppesahl Case*, 80 BVerfGE 188 (1989).
24. Currie (1994) at 110.
25. See *id.* at 106–07.
26. Kommers (1997) at 187.
27. See generally Sadurski (2005) at 154–5.
28. *National Unity Election Case*, 82 BVerfGE 322 (1990).
29. Issacharoff (2007); Basedau (2007).
30. Basedau (2007).
31. Representation of the People Act, No. 43 of 1951, § 123(3).
32. See, e.g., *Prabhoo v Shri Prabhakar Kasinath Kunte et al*, 1995 SCALE 1 (upholding invalidation of the election of the mayor of Bombay).
33. See Basic Law: The Knesset § 7A (excluding antidemocratic parties from elections).
34. *Socialist Reich Party Case*, 2 BVerfGE 1 (1952).
35. Issacharoff (2007) at 1435.
36. Turkish Constitutional Court, Decision no. 1998/1 (1/16/1998).
37. *Refah Partisi (The Welfare Party) and Others v Turkey, Grand Chamber Judgment*, Strasbourg, 13 February 2003.
38. *Socialist Reich Party Case*, 2 BVerfGE 1 (1952).
39. *Eu v San Francisco County Democratic Central Committee*, 489 US 214 (1989).
40. *Cal. Democratic Party v Jones*, 530 US 567 (2000).
41. See Pildes (2004) at 101–30.

REFERENCES

Basedau, Matthias (2007), 'Ethnic Party Bans in Africa: A Research Agenda', *German Law Journal*, 8, 617–34.
ConstitutionMaking.Org, Option Report – Political Parties (2008) (available at www.constitutionmaking.org/files/political_parties.pdf).
Currie, David P. (1994), *The Constitution of the Federal Republic of Germany*, Chicago: University of Chicago Press.
Elkins, Zachary, Tom Ginsburg and James Melton (2009), *The Endurance of National Constitutions*, Cambridge: Cambridge University Press.

Fox, Gregory H. and Georg Nolte (1995), 'Intolerant Democracies', *Harvard International Law Journal*, 36, 1–70.

Hofstadter, Richard (1970), *The Idea of a Party System*, Berkeley, CA: University of California Press.

Issacharoff, Samuel (2007), 'Fragile Democracies', *Harvard Law Review*, 120, 1405–67.

Issacharoff, Samuel and Richard Pildes (1998), 'Politics as Markets', *Stanford Law Review*, 50, 643–717.

Kommers, Donald P. (1997), *The Constitutional Jurisprudence of the Federal Republic of Germany*, 2nd edition, Durham, NC: Duke University Press.

Pildes, Richard (2004), 'Foreword: The Constitutionalization of Democratic Politics', *Harvard Law Review*, 118, 29–154.

Rosenblum, Nancy L. (2008), *On the Side of the Angels: An Appreciation of Parties and Partisanship*, Princeton, NJ: Princeton University Press.

Sadurski, Wojciech (2005), *Rights before Courts: A Study of Constitutional Courts in Postcommunist States of Central and Eastern Europe*, Dordrecht: Springer.

15. The rise of specialized constitutional courts
Víctor Ferreres Comella

1 WHAT ARE SPECIALIZED CONSTITUTIONAL COURTS? SOME CONCEPTUAL CLARIFICATIONS

An increasing number of countries have decided to establish special courts to deal with constitutional matters. They are often called 'constitutional courts' (or 'constitutional tribunals'). This expression, however, can be used in different ways.

Strictly speaking, 'constitutional courts' are special institutions that are separate from the rest of the judiciary. This is the standard way of using the expression in the literature (Fromont, 1996; Rousseau, 1998; Stone Sweet, 2000; Schwartz, 2000; Olivetti and Groppi, 2003; Sadurski, 2002, 2005; Ginsburg, 2003; Ferreres Comella, 2009). Constitutional courts, so conceived, are especially widespread in Europe. Out of the 27 states that make up the European Union, for example, 18 have created such bodies (Austria, Belgium, Bulgaria, Czech Republic, France, Germany, Hungary, Italy, Latvia, Lithuania, Luxembourg, Malta, Poland, Portugal, Romania, Slovakia, Slovenia and Spain). Post-communist Europe is strongly associated with constitutional courts too. We also find them in other regions in the world – in Latin America, Africa and Asia (for a comprehensive view, see Ramos, 2006).

It is possible, however, to use this expression in a broader sense, to also encompass institutions that are specialized in constitutional law even if they are not organically detached from the rest of the judiciary. In some Latin American countries (Costa Rica, El Salvador, Honduras, Nicaragua, Paraguay, Venezuela), for example, a special chamber within the regular supreme court has been set up to deal with constitutional issues (Frosini and Pegoraro, 2009; Brewer-Carías, 2009). In a broad sense, these chambers can be regarded as 'constitutional courts' since they perform very similar tasks to those that are assigned to constitutional courts in the strict sense.

We could go further and employ the expression in a looser way, to refer to any court that devotes a substantial part of its time to deciding constitutional cases. The Supreme Court of the United States, for instance, is sometimes taken to be a 'constitutional tribunal' in many respects, given the significant percentage of constitutional cases that it decides every year (Rogowski and Gawron, 2002).

In order to shape the conceptual contours of the discussion here, I will use the expression in the strict sense, which is the most common in the literature. As I hope to show, constitutional courts, so conceived, give rise to a specific set of questions and problems that have generated an interesting agenda for research.

2   IS SPECIALIZATION IN CONSTITUTIONAL LAW POSSIBLE?

A first foundational question to confront is this: in what sense is it possible for a court to specialize in constitutional law? How do we define the boundaries of the field such a court is supposed to focus on?

Traditionally, the law has been classified in different departments (civil law, criminal law, administrative law, labor law, tax law, commercial law, etc…), each dealing with a specific dimension of social reality. In many countries, moreover, the judicial branch has been internally divided, at least in part, in light of that classification. It might seem that a further move towards specialization in constitutional law should be relatively unproblematic. But this is not so, for the question arises: what is constitutional law supposed to regulate?

The answer was relatively easy in the past, when most constitutions were merely of a structural nature, in that they confined themselves to establishing and regulating the main governmental bodies. Consequently, if a judicial institution were specialized in constitutional law, it would be issues concerning the organization of the state that would define its jurisdiction. In the German tradition, for example, the first courts that were created during the nineteenth century to address constitutional matters focused on conflicts between various institutions within the political organization of the state (Cruz Villalón, 1987; Kommers, 1997). Nowadays, however, constitutions all over the world tend to be more ambitious, for they seek to protect certain principles of fundamental justice. In an increasing number of countries, moreover, such principles are taken to bind, not only governmental institutions, but private individuals too, whether directly or indirectly. As a result, the Constitution can penetrate all areas of the law (Tushnet, 2003; Sajó and Uitz, 2005; Kumm, 2006; Gardbaum, 2008). What the Constitution says about freedom of speech and privacy, or about workers' rights, or about the rights of the accused, has an obvious impact on private law, labor law and criminal law, for example. From this perspective, constitutional law is not a new legal field to be added to the traditional ones. Rather, it provides new lenses through which the traditional branches of the law have to be critically viewed. Lawyers and judges working in any area of the law have to play the constitutional game now.

If constitutional law permeates the business of all courts in this way, then, what are specialized constitutional tribunals supposed to focus on? Is it really possible to carve out a specific jurisdictional domain for such tribunals? Indeed, as Frank Michelman has persuasively argued ('The Interplay of Constitutional and Ordinary Jurisdiction', in this volume), the idea of a specialized constitutional court is in deep tension with the prevailing theory in many countries that takes the Constitution to embody transformative principles that are supposed to affect all spheres of social life. An 'acoustic separation' between constitutional law and ordinary law can only be maintained in a stable manner if the Constitution has a more limited scope – if it is merely a charter for the government.

Several arguments, however, have traditionally been given to justify the establishment of a constitutional court.

3   THE CENTRALITY OF LEGISLATIVE REVIEW

Historically, the emergence of constitutional tribunals is linked to the salience of legislative review as part of constitutional adjudication. In many European countries, for example, the starting point for the creation of such bodies has been the intuition that checking the validity of statutes under the Constitution is not an ordinary task. Even though the Constitution must be taken into account by all judges when deciding cases, a special institution should intervene when it comes to declaring that a parliamentary enactment is unconstitutional. It is not surprising that comparative scholars have paid particular attention to the relationships between constitutional courts and legislatures (Landfried, 1988; Stone Sweet, 2000; Volcansek, 2000).

This does not mean, however, that legislative review is the only task assigned to constitutional courts. This is sometimes the case (as in Belgium and Luxemburg, for instance), but most countries have preferred to entrust such courts with some additional responsibilities, such as supervising the regularity of elections and referenda, or verifying the legality of political parties, or enforcing the criminal law against high governmental authorities, or protecting fundamental rights against administrative and judicial decisions, or resolving conflicts among state authorities, etc.... There are many variations in this respect from country to country.

Variations also emerge concerning the question of who has access to the court. It is typical for political institutions (such as the government, a qualified minority of Parliament, the Ombudsman, etc...) to be entitled to challenge statutes in the abstract. Private individuals are also granted standing in some countries. In others, they have to convince the ordinary judge deciding their case to petition the constitutional court to review the validity of the applicable statute (Fromont, 1996; Rousseau, 1998; Olivetti and Groppi, 2003). These are all important variations, which give rise to important differences within the centralized model.

In Europe, for example, we can distinguish two polar systems, the French and the German, and an intermediate system, the Italian (Ferejohn and Pasquino, 2004). Under the French system, only political institutions have traditionally been entitled to challenge statutes. In practice, most challenges have been brought by the parliamentary opposition (60 deputies of the National Assembly or 60 senators). These procedures of abstract review take place before the law in question is promulgated by the President of the Republic. This institutional arrangement, however, has been deeply transformed as a result of a constitutional reform of July 2008, which has introduced for the first time in France the possibility for ordinary judges to certify questions to the Constitutional Court if they conclude that the applicable statute may violate constitutionally guaranteed rights and liberties. The question posed by ordinary judges, however, needs to pass the filter of the relevant supreme court (the Court of Cassation or the Council of State, depending on the area of the law).

Germany represents the other pole in Europe. Abstract review initiated by political institutions is only a small part of the Constitutional Court's docket. Most decisions by the Court deal with 'constitutional complaints' brought by individuals who claim that their fundamental rights have been infringed upon by public authorities. Normally, the individual must first try to seek redress from the ordinary courts. There is thus a strong link between the Constitutional Court and the ordinary judiciary, since the former can quash the decisions rendered by the latter. In the context of the complaints procedure, the Court can also examine the validity of the relevant piece of legislation. Obviously, legislative review does not take place in the abstract in such instances, for there is a particular case the constitutional issue is linked to. In addition, ordinary judges in Germany can directly certify questions to the Court whenever they regard a statute as unconstitutional.

Italy somehow represents a middle ground position. Individuals have no access to the

Court, for there is no complaints procedure. Ordinary judges, however, can petition the Court whenever they entertain doubts about the constitutional validity of the applicable statute, and they do so quite often. Abstract review brought by political institutions is also available, but it is very limited in scope, for it only operates in the field of regionalism.

So there are many variations within the centralized model. The principal theme, however, is the same: constitutional review of legislation is a special task – one that cannot be ascribed to ordinary judges.

Now, what's so special about legislative review? Why should a court be granted a monopoly in this field? Three important arguments have been offered to answer this question. They are linked to legal certainty, expertise and democracy, respectively.

3.1   Legal Certainty

First of all, it has been argued that statutes are so central to any modern legal system that it is very important for citizens and governmental officials to be clear as to whether any given statute is constitutional or not. Under a decentralized system of judicial review, the risk exists that different courts will come up with different conclusions regarding the constitutional validity of a law. Only gradually, as the highest courts establish the pertinent precedents, will some measure of uniformity be achieved. Under a centralized model, in contrast, since the constitutional court is the only institution that can pass judgment on the validity of statutes, no judicial disagreement among courts will arise in this connection. To the extent, moreover, that such a court can be accessed directly in many instances, without the plaintiff having to work his way through the ordinary judicial pyramid, issues concerning the validity of statutes can be settled rather quickly.

This argument from legal certainty has been advanced with particular emphasis when applied to countries that belong to the civil law tradition (Kelsen 1928, 1942; Cappelletti, 1971; Eisenmann, 1986). A decentralized system, it has been claimed, can work fine in common law jurisdictions that adhere to the doctrine of stare decisis. The disagreements among courts as to the constitutionality of a given statute can be settled by the supreme court, whose decisions lay down binding precedents. In the civil law world, in contrast, it is harder for the supreme court to impose its views on lower courts, since the latter are technically free to deviate from them.

Scholars have quarrelled, however, over the strength of this argument. From a comparative perspective, it has been objected that the civil law is not particularly unfriendly to the decentralized model of the constitutional review of legislation (Brewer-Carías, 1989). Even if the supreme courts in civil law countries are not officially authorized to lay down binding precedents, their interpretive judgments about the law tend to be accepted and followed by lower courts as a matter of fact. If so, their judgments regarding the constitutional validity of legislation would also be respected by lower courts, if a decentralized system of constitutional review were introduced.

Actually, the argument from legal certainty is built on unstable ground, for there is a tension underlying its premises. The centralized model that is being defended is based on a sharp distinction: whereas questions regarding the constitutional validity of statutes are ascribed to the constitutional court exclusively, questions regarding the interpretation of those statutes are left to all judges, working under the doctrines established by the pertinent supreme court. Does this distinction make sense, however? Why is centralization believed to be necessary when it comes to questions of validity, while decentralization is thought to be fine when it comes to questions of interpretation? If the supreme court can do a good job at settling interpretive controversies among lower courts, why should we believe that it cannot do a similarly good job at settling controversies over the constitutional validity of statutes? Conversely, if we believe that the supreme court cannot generate sufficient uniformity with respect to issues of constitutional validity, why should we think that its performance will be successful in terms of bringing judicial convergence in interpretive matters? This tension deserves further theorizing when the argument from legal certainty is advanced to highlight the shortcomings of the decentralized model.

The argument from legal certainty, moreover, points to the advantages of centralizing constitutional review in a single institution, but it does not tell us why a special constitutional court should be created. The advantages of centralization can also be obtained if only the existing supreme court is authorized to control statutes for their conformity with the Constitution, or if a special chamber is created for these purposes within the supreme court. Why should a separate institution, detached from the ordinary judiciary, be set up?

3.2   Expertise

Given some of the limitations of the argument from legal certainty, other reasons have been supplied in the literature to strengthen the case in favour of constitutional courts. One of them relates to expertise. Interpreting the Constitution for purposes of legislative review is a partic- ularly difficult task. It involves the interpretation of a text (the Constitution) that is often very open-ended and expresses basic moral principles that are of foundational importance to the political community. What is at stake, moreover, is whether a law enacted by a popularly elected assembly deserves to be struck down. Judges in charge of this delicate task should be specially qualified. They should be mature jurists who have had long and prestigious careers.

A diversity of professional backgrounds, moreover, should be brought to the task of legislative review. University professors, former governmental officials and politicians, for example, should take part in it, in addition to ordinary judges, lawyers and prosecutors. To the extent that this sort of diversity is to be celebrated, an argument can be made in favor of constitutional courts as separate institutions. This is especially so in civil law countries, where the judiciary tends to be organized according to the so-called 'bureaucratic model'. The lower courts are often run by very young judges, who are appointed soon after they graduate from law school. Those judges start a career that will slowly bring them to occupy the highest courts. In such countries, the supreme court tends to be composed of individuals whose views of the constitutional world are too 'judicial', given their past professional experience. Constitutional courts, in contrast, can be more internally diverse in terms of professional backgrounds, thus bringing a fresh perspective from outside the regular judiciary.

This thesis, as applied to civil law countries, seems plausible, but it would be interesting to research this topic more systematically. It would also be illuminating, in this connection, to test whether the constitutional chambers within the supreme court that have been created in some Latin American countries are more 'judicial' in their composition than separate constitutional courts.

Like the argument from legal certainty, the argument from expertise relies on a sharp distinction between legislative review and the other instances of adjudication. It may be objected, however, that constitutional principles have nowadays entered all areas of the law, and that ordinary judges are expected to take those principles seriously when adjudicating cases. Even if the task of legislative review is assigned to the constitutional court exclusively, many difficult legal questions of a constitutional nature are now asked of ordinary judges. If so, it seems that we should be worried about the qualifications, expertise and diversity of those judges too. Focusing so much on who the members of the constitutional court are may be a simplistic strategy.

3.3   Democracy

A third way to justify the preference for constitutional courts involves democratic principles. The idea here is that democracy is conceptually linked to the existence of a political procedure that gives all citizens an equal right to vote. Given the advantages of the division of labor in modern societies, direct democracy is not the best option, however. It is better for laws to be enacted by a parliamentary assembly. Such laws have nevertheless a special value because of their democratic source. This being so, the argument goes, constitutional review should be entrusted to a body whose members have the requisite democratic credentials. Even if constitutional review may be justified on instrumental grounds (to the extent, for example, that constitutional principles may be better protected), it is still necessary to enhance its democratic legitimacy. To this effect, judges in charge of constitutional review should be selected through procedures that are particularly democratic (such as parliamentary procedures), and their tenure should not be too long.

This is the intuition that led many European countries to prefer constitutional courts (Cruz Villalón, 1987). There is always a 'democratic objection' to the institution of judicial review of legislation, and the arguments that are usually offered to answer the objection are not conclusive (Troper, 2003). In the United States, the practice of judicial review has always provoked controversies concerning its legitimacy. In recent decades, a rich academic literature has been generated to deal with the so-called 'counter-majoritarian difficulty' (Bickel, 1962; Friedman, 2002). Given all this, it seems advisable to link constitutional judges to the democratic process. Thus, members of constitutional courts in Europe are typically selected through more politicized procedures than those generally followed to pick ordinary judges. In most countries, moreover, the tenure of constitutional judges is limited to a specific period of time (nine years in France, Italy, Portugal and Spain, for example; 12 years in Germany). In this way, the jurisprudence of the constitutional court is expected not to deviate too much from the basic moral and political beliefs held by a majority of the people and their representatives.

The democratic argument has special force in the context of post-authoritarian regimes (Ferejohn and Pasquino, 2002, 2004). If the ordinary judges who enforced the laws under the past dictatorship are not removed from their positions of authority when the new democratic era begins, it seems better to create a new institution to carry out legislative review: the constitutional judges can be selected in more democratic ways than ordinary judges are, and their legal attitudes are likely to be more sensitive to the liberal and transformative spirit of the new Constitution. As a matter of fact, the correlation between constitutional courts and post-authoritarian scenarios is quite strong, not only in Europe but in other regions of the world too (Ginsburg, 2003). It should be noted, however, that in some countries, the transition to democracy did cause the supreme court to be renewed in its composition. In Poland, for example, all the judges of the supreme court were appointed anew after the regime change of 1989 (Sadurski, 2005).

The democratic argument has considerable weight. Like the two other arguments we have examined before, however, it relies heavily on a categorical distinction: for purposes of striking down statutes under the Constitution, we need to rely on judges that have a special democratic pedigree; for purposes of interpreting those statutes, in contrast, no such pedigree is necessary. To a certain extent, this is a reasonable contrast to draw, for the democratic branches are in a more difficult position when a statute is invalidated than when a statute is interpreted. In the former case they have to amend the Constitution to override the judicial decision they disagree with, while in the latter case they can simply modify the statute through the ordinary parliamentary procedure. In practice, however, this difference is not as large as it is sometimes believed to be. Judges have ample room to maneuver when they interpret legislation, which is increasingly unclear, and Parliament's capacity to respond to them through a new law is sometimes limited, given the many items that burden the political agenda. It is not surprising, therefore, that a vibrant debate has developed in many countries about the right way to appoint ordinary judges in a democratic system, given their enormous power (Guarnieri and Pederzoli, 2002). Constitutional courts are not the only courts whose democratic legitimacy may have to be enhanced.

It is also important to note that this argument in favor of constitutional courts addresses the problem of democratic legitimacy in an indirect way. It tries to strengthen the connections between the judges who exercise legislative review and the democratic political processes. It assumes, however, that judicial review is of the 'strong form': it is impossible for an ordinary legislative majority to override the court's judgments; a more burdensome process of constitutional amendment needs to be followed. But this is not the only way to articulate the institution of judicial review. In more recent times, 'weak forms' of judicial review have been implemented in various countries (such as Canada, Great Britain and New Zealand), where judicial determinations as to the constitutional validity of a statute can be overturned through an ordinary legislative procedure (See Tushnet, 'The Rise of Weak-form Judicial Review', in this volume). The democratic objection loses most of its force in those countries. It would be interesting to explore, in this regard, the potential advantages and disadvantages of combining a specialized constitutional court with a weak form of review – a combination that no country seems to have experimented with yet.

4   THE ACTIVISM OF CONSTITUTIONAL COURTS

An important issue that should be more fully researched refers to the conditions under which constitutional courts tend to be relatively activist when exercising legislative review. Activism has two aspects.

First, a court is activist when it does not refuse to deal with the constitutional issues that a statute poses. The claim has been made that constitutional courts have some in-built tendency towards this form of activism (Ferreres Comella, 2009). The argument is this: since, under a centralized model, constitutional courts are the only courts that can engage in legislative review, it is hard for them to keep clear from constitutional issues. If a law is challenged by an institution or individual that has standing, the constitutional court has to pronounce its judgment. Also, to the extent that the court centers its task on constitutional law, it is not easy for it to resort to ordinary legal arguments to escape from the constitutional questions that are posed to it. Under a decentralized model, in contrast, the supreme court can take some time before it reviews the validity of a particular statute, since lower courts are meanwhile exercising their powers of review. It is relatively easy for all courts, moreover, to focus on ordinary legal arguments in order to avoid the more delicate constitutional issues that a case can give rise to (on the use of these 'passive' devices in the United States, for example, see Bickel, 1962).

Activism has a second aspect to it: a court is activist when it is eager to enforce a reading of the Constitution that differs from the constitutional reading that the legislature has implicitly relied upon in the course of enacting a particular statute. One way to measure how large a gap there is between the court's jurisprudence and parliamentary choices is to calculate the percentage of laws that are struck down by the court (or corrected by the court through 'interpretive' or 'reconstructive' decisions), out of the total number of laws that are challenged. This 'ratio of unconstitutionality', however, is but an imperfect way to measure judicial activism. To begin with, some laws are more important than others. A court would not be really activist, for example, if it never deviated from the parliament with respect to the key issues, even if it overturned lots of legal provisions of marginal importance. (Interestingly, the very fact that a constitutional court cannot easily abstain from deciding all the constitutional challenges that are placed on its doorstep makes it possible for the court to concentrate its aggressiveness on the politically less important statutes. From a qualitative point of view, such a strategy would not be activist.) In addition, it may very well happen that a parliamentary majority abstains from enacting a particular law out of fear that the court will invalidate it. A strong judiciary may cause this sort of 'chilling effect' on the legislature.

In spite of these difficulties when it comes to measuring judicial activism, we should ask ourselves whether constitutional courts tend to be less timid when they exercise legislative review than are regular courts working under a decentralized model – other things being equal. Constitutional courts, it has been argued (Ferreres Comella, 2009) cannot be very deferential towards the legislature. Since their principal mission is to check laws for their constitutionality, it would be surprising if they rarely found a statute to be invalid. The decision by the constitutional framers to establish such special tribunals rests, to a significant extent, on their expectation that a sufficiently large number of statutory provisions will be constitutionally problematic in the future. Only under that assumption does it make sense to set up specific institutions in charge of striking down statutes on constitutional grounds. The tendency towards some degree of judicial activism is stronger, moreover, when the constitutional court is relatively 'pure' – that is, when legislative review is the only task (or by far the most important task) that the court is entrusted with.

Some evidence has been marshalled to support this thesis, but more research needs to be done. Apart from any structural pressure towards activism, moreover, constitutional courts may be more or less deferential depending on other variables. Thus, the more 'veto points' the legislative process contains (in the form of bicameralism and executive veto, for example), the more moderate the legislative changes are likely to be and, consequently, the disagreements between the legislature and the judiciary in the constitutional field will be less significant (Stone Sweet, 2000). On the other hand, it has been argued that courts will feel more secure against majoritarian retaliations when the political process is fragmented than when it is greatly concentrated. The more diffuse politics are, the more space courts have in which to operate (Ginsburg, 2003). It would be interesting to study, in this connection, whether courts whose members are appointed through democratic political procedures, and who sit for limited terms, are likely to be more deferential than courts whose members are appointed through less politicized procedures and who serve for life (or until retirement age). The degree of visibility of the constitutional court is another consideration to bear in mind. It has been argued that the more visible the court's decisions are, the more likely it is that it will be protected against political reactions (provided that it enjoys sufficient public support). The higher the court's public visibility, then, the more aggressive its performance is likely to be (Vanberg, 2005).

5 THE BATTLES BETWEEN SPECIAL CONSTITUTIONAL COURTS AND ORDINARY COURTS

When a country establishes a constitutional tribunal, it runs a risk: tensions may arise between the new institution and ordinary courts. The risk exists, in particular, that the constitutional tribunal will clash with the supreme court. Actually, if the distinction between 'constitutional law' and 'ordinary law' is ultimately hard to maintain, the division of labor between those two courts will be very unstable in practice, leading to collisions that may have to be resolved through some kind of self-restraint on the part of the constitutional court, as Michelman has illustrated using the German and the South African cases (Michelman, 'The Interplay of Constitutional and Ordinary Jurisdiction', in this volume). This does not mean, however, that it is advisable for constitutional courts to avoid all confrontations with the supreme court. To the extent that the criteria to define the underlying division of labor need to be developed and refined, it may be necessary for constitutional courts to sometimes enter institutional battles, so that the jurisdictional issues are frankly dealt with. As in other institutional contexts, it is sometimes better not to suppress conflicts: a solution needs to be worked out that can serve as a precedent for the future (Posner and Vermeule, 2008).

The available literature gives us examples of judicial tensions (see, for instance, Garlicki, 2007). It would be interesting to use national case studies as a basis for a more general theory that would seek to identify the factors that tend to make the conflict more or less likely. It would be useful, for example, to come up with some generalizations as to whether the conflict is more likely to occur when the constitutional court has the power to quash decisions rendered by ordinary courts (including the supreme courts). It would also be interesting to study the potential impact of the composition of constitutional courts in this regard. Is the tension likely to increase, for example, the more people are appointed to the constitutional court whose background is not judicial? Similarly, it would be fruitful to be provided with a systematic study of the consequences of creating a special constitutional chamber within the supreme court, as an alternative to a separate constitutional tribunal. Is such an option better, in terms of reducing potential conflicts?

'Mixed models' of constitutional review can be particularly interesting to explore in this connection. Under such models, the constitutional court can strike down statutes, but ordinary judges are also entitled to set them aside on their own authority. (Portugal and Colombia are examples of such a mixed regime.) Are ordinary judges more likely to adhere to the constitutional court when no monopoly is granted to the latter?

There is a particular topic that scholars have studied with considerable detail when dealing with judicial conflicts: how should the constitutional court interpret the statutes whose validity it is asked to assess? Should it read them in light of the case law generated by the supreme court, or should it read them independently? The supreme courts in various countries have sometimes been critical of constitutional courts that have neglected the existing statutory case law. Their criticism seems justified. It does not make much sense for a constitutional court to examine the validity of a statute in light of a statutory interpretation that differs from the one that the supreme court has established, and which lower courts actually follow. The statute whose validity we want the constitutional tribunal to control is the statute that is applied in real life (Zagrebelsky, 1988).

A connected issue is this: suppose the constitutional court concludes that the statute it has reviewed is indeed unconstitutional, but there is a way to read the statute that would save it from the constitutional fire. Is the court entitled to issue an 'interpretive decision', which holds the statute constitutional, provided it is interpreted in a particular manner? From a theoretical point of view, this type of decision is easy to defend. If, for example, the statute being examined could be interpreted in different ways (to mean A or to mean B), and the constitutional court concludes that only a specific interpretation (A) would make the statute constitutionally valid, it is reasonable for the court to declare that, from now onwards, the statute must be read to mean A. The ordinary judges are to be bound by such a declaration, for if they deviated from it, they would be applying an unconstitutional norm (the norm that emerges if the statute is read to mean B).

In practice, however, things have proven to be more complex in some countries. In Italy, for example, the ability of the constitutional court to impose its 'interpretive decisions' on ordinary judges has encountered an obstacle: according to Italian law, only decisions that declare statutes unconstitutional are binding. Since, technically, an 'interpretive decision' upholds the challenged statute, its authority vis-à-vis ordinary courts is more questionable (Zagrebelsky, 1988).

Quite apart from these technical complications, the tensions between constitutional tribunals and supreme courts can have an ideological component. In some countries, constitutional tribunals have been born with the mission to give concrete meaning to a new Constitution, which entails a break with the past. Many constitutional courts have been set up in a post-authoritarian context, as was already mentioned (Ferejohn and Pasquino, 2002, 2004; Ginsburg, 2003). Their jurisprudence is thus likely to be more progressive than that generated by traditional supreme courts working under the old laws. In such countries, a constitutional court that did not provoke some level of tension vis-à-vis the ordinary judiciary would not be enforcing the Constitution to its fullest extent. Too smooth a relationship with the supreme court might mean that the aspirations expressed in the new Constitution were not being given concrete and operational meaning. Institutional collisions are sometimes a price worth paying.

6   SPECIAL CONSTITUTIONAL COURTS AND THE SUPRANATIONAL SPHERE

A final set of questions concerns the impact of supranational developments. There are two aspects to consider.

6.1   Constitutional Specialization at the Supranational Level

The first issue is whether or not some form of constitutional specialization has developed in the supranational field. Interestingly, we do not find constitutional courts (properly so called) at that level.

In the European context, for example, the European Court of Human Rights sitting in Strasbourg is a specialized court whose jurisdiction is exclusively tied to human rights issues. Its task is to interpret and enforce the European Convention on Human Rights of 1950 (and its protocols) against the ratifying states. Since the protection of human rights is one of the core functions of domestic constitutions, we can say that the European Court of Human Rights is specialized in (an important part of) constitutional law. We cannot consider it to be a constitutional court in the strict sense, however, for legislative review is not its raison d'être.

The European Court's job is to decide whether states (which are brought to it as subjects of international law) have violated the rights guaranteed by the Convention. Only rarely does the Court have to hold, incidentally, that the national statute that is applicable to the case breaches the Convention. Nor does the Court have any monopoly in the field of legislative review: in many countries national courts are entitled to disregard national legislation that offends the Convention (Keller and Stone Sweet, 2008). There are important institutional differences, therefore, between the European Court of Human Rights and domestic constitutional courts. The same is true of the Inter-American Court of Human Rights, based in San José, Costa Rica, in charge of enforcing the American Convention on Human Rights of 1969.

In spite of these differences, however, the question arises whether constitutional courts and human rights international courts exhibit similar attitudes. Given their specific mandate to protect individual rights, are they 'biased' in favor of rights when the latter clash with governmental interests? Would non-specialized courts be more 'objective'? Is it plausible to argue, however, that fundamental rights are so important and fragile that it is advisable to create courts that are likely to be especially attentive to the individuals who invoke them?

A different kind of court, based on a completely different logic, emerges when a supranational organization is created to enact common policies, and the need arises to make the member states play by the rules. The European Union (EU) is the prime example of this phenomenon. Its workability depends on the existence of a court – the European Court of Justice (ECJ) sitting in Luxembourg – that acts as the supreme interpreter of EU law.

Interestingly, this court is non-specialized, when compared to national courts. Within the area of EU law, the ECJ performs diverse functions: it acts as an 'ordinary' supreme court that lays down the interpretation of EU law for lower courts to follow. It also acts as an 'administrative' court that checks the decisions of the supranational executive branch. And it serves as a 'constitutional court' that controls the validity of EU legislation. At the domestic level in many European countries, in contrast, these three functions have been allotted to different judicial branches. Proposals have been made to introduce some degree of constitutional specialization within the judicial architecture of the EU, but they have not been followed (Weiler, 1999; Alonso García, 2005). It would be interesting to explore the possible differences between the domestic and the supranational spheres in this regard. Is the impulse toward constitutional specialization less attractive when extended to the supranational domain?

6.2 The Erosion of Constitutional Courts as a Result of Supranationalism

The other question to consider is whether constitutional courts have lost their prominence as a result of supranationalism. Their monopoly over legislative review, in particular, has actually been eroded in several ways. Most obviously, the move towards supranational structures leads to the creation of courts of a higher level, with powers to check the actions of member states. It would make no practical sense for a group of states to set up an ambitious organization of a supranational kind, if they did not include a court with the power to interpret the common rules and enforce them against member states. For the organization to be workable, national statutes must be made subject to some kind of judicial review by a supranational court. As a result, legislative review is no longer the exclusive province of domestic constitutional tribunals.

Less obviously, supranationalism can also undermine the centrality of domestic constitutional courts from another angle. In the context of the European Union, for example, the ECJ has held that ordinary judges deciding concrete controversies at the domestic level are required to set aside any piece of national legislation that is at odds with EU law. The constitutional courts, therefore, have lost the monopoly they used to have: they are no longer the only courts at the domestic level that can engage in legislative review (Slaughter et al., 1998; Alter, 2001). If, in the future, EU law includes more and more fundamental rights norms, the erosion that constitutional courts will suffer in a core area of their jurisdiction will be more serious. The collisions between the ECJ and constitutional courts, moreover, may become more frequent, if they offer different interpretations of the underlying fundamental rights that ordinary judges have to adjudicate in specific cases. Some principles to accommodate these tensions need to be worked out (Kumm, 2005; Torres Pérez, 2009).

REFERENCES

Alonso García, Ricardo (2005), 'El juez nacional como juez europeo a la luz del tratado constitucional', in Marta Cartabria, Bruno de Witte and Pablo Pérez Tremps (eds.), *Constitución europea y Constituciones nacionales*, Valencia: Tirant lo blanch, pp. 639–92.

Alter, Karen (2001), *Establishing the Supremacy of European Law: The Making of an International Rule of Law in Europe*, Oxford: Oxford University Press.

Bickel, Alexander (1962), *The Least Dangerous Branch*, New Haven: Yale University Press.

Brewer-Carías, Allan-Randolph (1989), *Judicial Review in Comparative Law*, Cambridge: Cambridge University Press.

Brewer-Carías, Allan-Randolph (2009), *Constitutional Protection of Human Rights in Latin America: A Comparative Study of the Amparo Proceedings*, Cambridge: Cambridge University Press.

Cappelletti, Mauro (1971), *Judicial Review in the Contemporary World*, Indianapolis: Bobbs-Merrill.

Cruz Villalón, Pedro (1987), *La formación del sistema europeo de control de constitucionalidad (1918–1939)*, Madrid: Centro de Estudios Constitucionales.

Eisenmann, Charles (1986), *La justice constitutionnelle et la Haut cour constitutionnelle d'Austriche*, Paris: Economica; Aix-en-Provence: Presses Universitaires d'Aix-Marseille.

Ferejohn, John and Pasquale Pasquino (2002), 'Constitutional Courts and Deliberative Institutions: Towards an Institutional Theory of Constitutional Justice', in Wojciech Sadurski (ed.) *Constitutional Justice: East and West,* The Hague: Kluwer Law International, pp. 21–36.

Ferejohn, John and Pasquale Pasquino (2004), 'Constitutional Adjudication: Lessons from Europe', *University of Texas Law Review*, 82, 1671–704.

Ferreres Comella, Víctor (2009), *Constitutional Courts and Democratic Values: A European Perspective*, New Haven and London: Yale University Press.

Friedman, Barry (2002), 'The Birth of an Academic Obsession: The History of the Countermajoritarian Difficulty, Part Five', *Yale Law Journal*, 112, 153–259.

Fromont, Michel (1996), *La justice constitutionnelle dans le monde*, Paris: Dalloz.

Frosini, Justin and Lucio Pegoraro (2009), 'Constitutional Courts in Latin America: A Testing Ground for New Parameters of Classification?', in Andrew Harding and Peter Leyland (eds.), *Constitutional Courts: A Comparative Study*, London: Wildy, Simmonds & Hill Publishing, 345–76.

Gardbaum, Stephen (2008), 'The Myth and the Reality of American Constitutional Exceptionalism', *Michigan Law Review*, 107, 391–466.

Garlicki, Lech (2007), 'Constitutional Courts versus Supreme Courts', *International Journal of Constitutional Law*, 5 (1), 44–68.

Ginsburg, Tom (2003), *Judicial Review in New Democracies: Constitutional Courts in Asian Cases*, Cambridge: Cambridge University Press.

Guarnieri, Carlo and Patrizia Pederzoli (2002), *The Power of Judges: A Comparative Study of Courts and Democracy*, Oxford: Oxford University Press.

Keller, Helen and Alec Stone Sweet (eds.) (2008), *A Europe of Rights: The Impact of the ECHR on National Legal Systems*, Oxford: Oxford University Press.

Kelsen, Hans (1928), 'La garantie jurisdictionnelle de la Constitution (La justice constitutionnelle)', *Revue du droit public et de la science politique en France et à l'etranger*, 46, 197–257.

Kelsen, Hans (1942), 'Judicial Review of Legislation: A Comparative Study of the Austrian and the American Constitution', *Journal of Politics*, 4, 183–200.

Kommers, Donald (1997), *The Constitutional Jurisprudence of the Federal Republic of Germany*, Durham, NC and London: Duke University Press.

Kumm, Mattias (2005), 'The Jurisprudence of Constitutional Conflict: Constitutional Supremacy in Europe Before and After the Constitutional Treaty', *European Law Journal*, 11, 262–307.

Kumm, Mattias (2006), 'Who is Afraid of the Total Constitution? Constitutional Rights as Principles and the Constitutionalization of Private Law', *German Law Journal*, 7, 341–70.

Landfried, Christine (ed.) (1988), *Constitutional Review and Legislation: An International Comparison*, Baden-Baden: Nomos Verlagsgesellschaft.

Olivetti, Marco and Tania Groppi (eds.) (2003), *La giustizia costituzionale in Europa*, Milan: Giuffrè.

Posner, Eric and Adrian Vermeule (2008), 'Constitutional Showdowns', *University of Pennsylvania Law Review*, 156, 991–1048.

Ramos, Francisco (2006), 'The Establishment of Constitutional Courts: A Study of 128 Democratic Constitutions', *Review of Law & Economics*, 2, 103–35.

Rogowski, Ralf and Thomas Gawron (2002), *Constitutional Courts in Comparison: The U.S. Supreme Court and the German Federal Constitutional Court*, New York and Oxford: Berghahn Books.

Rousseau, Dominique (1998), *La justice constitutionnelle en Europe*, Paris: Montchrestien.

Sadurski, Wojciech (ed.) (2002), *Constitutional Justice, East and West: Democratic Legitimacy and Constitutional Courts in Post-Communist Europe. A Comparative Perspective*, The Hague: Kluwer Law International.

Sadurski, Wojciech (2005), *Rights before Courts: A Study of Constitutional Courts in Postcommunist States of Central and Eastern Europe*, Dordrecht: Springer.

Sajó, András and Renáta Uitz (eds.) (2005), *The Constitution in Private Relations*, Utrecht: Eleven International Publishing.

Schwartz, Herman (2000), *The Struggle for Constitutional Justice in Post-communist Europe*, Chicago: University of Chicago Press.

Slaughter, Anne-Marie, Alec Stone Sweet and Joseph Weiler (eds.) (1998), *The European Court and National Courts: Doctrine and Jurisprudence*, Oxford: Hart Publishing.

Stone Sweet, Alec (2000), *Governing with Judges: Constitutional Politics in Europe*, Oxford: Oxford University Press.

Torres Pérez, Aida (2009), *Conflicts of Rights in the European Union: A Theory of Supranational Adjudication*, Oxford: Oxford University Press.

Troper, Michel (2003), 'The Logic of Justification of Judicial Review', *International Journal of Constitutional Law*, 1 (1), 99–121.

Tushnet, Mark (2003), 'The Issue of State Action/Horizontal Effect in Comparative Constitutional Law', *International Journal of Constitutional Law*, 1 (1), 79–98.

Vanberg, Georg (2005), *The Politics of Constitutional Review in Germany*, Cambridge: Cambridge University Press.

Volcansek, Mary (2000), *Constitutional Politics in Italy: The Constitutional Court*, New York: St. Martin's Press.

Weiler, Joseph (1999), *The Constitution of Europe*, Cambridge: Cambridge University Press.

Zagrebelsky, Gustavo (1988), *La giustizia costituzionale*, Bologna: il Mulino.

16. The interplay of constitutional and ordinary jurisdiction

Frank I. Michelman

I   INTRODUCTION

'Constitutional' jurisdiction is the power of a court (or similar body) to pronounce on the compatibility of questioned laws and acts with constitutional requirements, with some measure of decisive effect on legal outcomes. 'Ordinary' jurisdiction, by contrast, is the usual power of a court to construe and apply non-constitutional law. Countries vary in forms and degrees of commitment (if any) to the institutional segregation of constitutional from ordinary jurisdiction. These variations have been widely discussed and ably treated, in Chapter 15 of this volume and elsewhere (including Cappelletti 1989, at 132–49; Favoreu 1990a; Favoreu 1990b; Ferreres Comella 2009; Stone Sweet 2000, at 32–8; Tushnet 2006; and, for the views of the celebrated inventor of the 'European' model of separated jurisdictions, Kelsen 1942). The special mission of this chapter is to consider jurisdictional division in relation to what may seem a distinct question of constitutional design, that of the scope of application of substantive constitutional guarantees.

We recall some basic terminology. 'Ordinary law' is law that is not of constitutional stature and hence may be subject to control by constitutional law. 'Ordinary courts' are those courts that are generally empowered to interpret, apply, and (with regard to common and perhaps customary law) develop ordinary law. A system of ordinary courts may be unified, with all cases entering the system potentially subject to review by a single top court (Canada, for example), or it may be multi-peaked, with separate divisions for (say) civil, criminal, and administrative matters, each headed by its own court of last resort (Germany, for example).

Powers of constitutional control may or may not be distributed widely and generally to ordinary courts. If they are, the system is one of 'diffused' or 'decentralized' review power. If constitutional jurisdiction is reserved to a single court, the system is one of 'concentrated' or 'centralized' review power. In theory, the single empowered court in a centralized system might also serve as a part of the ordinary, 'generalist' judiciary whose competence extends to the resolution of questions of ordinary law (as if, for example, in Canada, constitutional jurisdiction had been restricted to the Supreme Court of Canada, which also heads up Canada's ordinary judiciary). However, for reasons we shall soon be recalling, courts holding sole powers of constitutional review are typically conceived as non-ordinary, specialist 'constitutional' courts, sitting 'outside of', rather than 'on top of', the 'regular judicial apparatus' (Favoreu 1990a, at 111–12).

Here, we must immediately take care not to confuse two questions that are best held distinct. Where powers of constitutional review are widely dispersed to ordinary courts, we may expect also to find that some single, pinnacle court, reachable through readily available channels of review, is assigned to serve as that system's tribunal of last resort on constitutional questions arising in the course of concrete case adjudications.[1] We may call that court the system's 'constitutional supreme tribunal' ('CST'). Now, we find that a CST in a system of diffused review powers may quite possibly be a part of the ordinary, generalist judiciary (the Supreme Court of Canada) and it may also quite possibly be created as a specialized, non-ordinary 'constitutional' court (the Constitutional Court of South Africa).

We see, then, that constitutional designers, contemplating powers of constitutional control in at least one court, face two, intersecting axes of choice regarding the organization of such powers. They must decide how far to concentrate these powers in specially entrusted tribunals, and they must decide whether the system's court of last (perhaps sole) resort on constitutional matters (its CST) is to be a specialist/non-ordinary or a generalist/ordinary tribunal.

Consider, now, how these choices regarding judicial institutional arrangement may be conditioned by constitutional choices on a quite different level. Constitutions vary widely in the manner in which they address themselves (if they do at all) to matters of substantive justice and rights. One dimension of this variance is the expected scope of application of substantive guarantees. Some guarantees may be conceived strictly with regard to the conduct of government operations, others with a wider regard to the conduct of private (civil-society) relationships. These scope-of-application decisions may carry implications for decisions regarding the centralization and specialization of judicial powers of constitutional review, and vice versa (Uitz 2005, at 12; Kumm and Ferreres Comella 2005, at 243–4; Tushnet 2003). At first glance, it seems that a choice for strict concentration and specialization of constitutional review powers does not mesh well with a choice for a society-blanketing, pervasive influence for substantive constitutional norms. In the recent experience of South Africa, for example (Section 5.2, below), we see the Constitution's original, express commitment to jurisdictional separation failing under pressure from another promise detected in the Constitution: to bring and keep the country's entire legal order in line with the 'objective normative value system' for which the Constitution speaks (*Carmichele*, paras 33, 54; Lewis 2005, at 513–19; Michelman 2005, at 6–11). The cause of this embarrassment is plain to see. If no application of law can ever be held exempt from inspection for compatibility with the Constitution's substantive norms, then no adjudicative issues lie securely beyond reach of a nominally contained, 'constitutional' jurisdiction. The resulting potential for friction and confusion between 'constitutional' and 'ordinary' jurisdictions is apparent (Garlicki 2007, at 63, 65; Taylor 2002, at 214). But behind these simple-seeming observations lies a thick tangle of complexities, which it is the business of this chapter to unravel.

2. THE IDEAL AND ALLURE OF ACOUSTIC SEPARATION

2.1 The Ideal, Perfect and Imperfect

We can imagine constitutional designers aiming at a complete 'acoustic separation' between exercises of ordinary and constitutional jurisdiction in their country's system of courts.[2] Not only would the judiciary be bifurcated into 'constitutional' and 'ordinary' branches, separately staffed and organized, but each branch would be barred from ever referring at all to the work or the business of the other. Ordinary courts would apply ordinary law, and only ordinary law, to the resolution of disputes brought before them, while constitutional courts would apply only constitutional law. Taken to such an extreme, this separationist vision may strike us as both pointless and unworkable. Certainly, a pursuit of *perfect* separation can make little sense to designers who envisage a future legal order reflecting the sustained, effective influence of a set of substantive values and aims (as distinguished from the bare mechanics of government) that the designers associate specially with the provisions of their Constitution. Our point for now, though, is that demands for *imperfect* acoustic separation between constitutional and ordinary jurisdiction have occupied national constitutional reform efforts over the past century, in places around the world. The evidence seems consistent with a view of designers yielding on *perfect* separation, but only because and insofar as they perceive that their substantive aims require them to do so. Now, the possible forms of compromise turn out to be many and various. And in order to understand how designers might come to prefer some of these forms over others, we first need to recall the attractions of jurisdictional division.

2.2   The Standard Case for Separation

Notionally, we can describe approaches to acoustic separation of constitutional and ordinary jurisdictions in three, ordered steps.[3] First comes the choice to locate the system's CST outside the established formation of ordinary courts. Next comes the choice to make that 'outsider' tribunal a strict concentrator in constitutional law, confining sharply its competence in matters of ordinary law. Finally comes the choice to restrict constitutional jurisdiction more or less exclusively to the specialist, non-ordinary constitutional tribunal.

Driving these choices are considerations of various types, having to do with (i) perceptions of functional and methodological differentia between constitutional and ordinary law; (ii) related perceptions of needs for differing sorts of talents and skills in the respective judicial ministries of the two types of law; (iii) concerns about the achievement of doctrinal control and coordination, especially on the constitutional side; (iv) concerns about political resistance from an ordinary-courts constituency fearing encroachments on their turf by an outsider body; and (v) concerns about the continuing, doctrinal autonomy and integrity of the established body (or bodies) of ordinary law. The first four types of consideration are familiar to the literature, and we next present them in a brief summation. The fifth type of concern, about threats to the doctrinal autonomy of the corpus of ordinary law, may be less familiar, and we reserve it for separate treatment in Section 4.2.

Quite typically, it seems, twentieth-century – particularly European – constitutional designers have ascribed deeply different characteristics to what they have perceived as the two distinct bodies of substantive-constitutional and ordinary, civil law. These can take shape as any or all of differences in historical provenance and source of authorship, in aim and function, in modes of expression, and in ideological valence. Different methods and styles of interpretation and application, designers have often thought, are respectively best suited to these two different bodies of law: for ordinary law, a formal-exegetical style that is bureaucratically restrained and subservient to the words of the statute, and for constitutional law, a more openly 'teleological' style, aimed at optimal achievement of the animating values of the constitution in the changing conditions of social life (Cappelletti 1989, at 137–8; Grimm 1994, at 272–4; Kühn 2004, at 532–8). Respectively corresponding to these differing adjudicative styles would be differing conceptions of judicial-institutional role and role-morality. Entrenched modes of training, recruitment, and professionalization of ordinary judicial personnel – presumably designed to select for, instill, and fortify the requisite skills and motivations for ordinary adjudicative work – are not so well suited (the thought has often run) to the new and different project of giving real effect to *constitutional* principles in the day-to-day conduct of the country's legal affairs (Cappelletti 1989, at 143, 145; Kühn 2005, at 237–8).

Sometimes, designers have doubted that a pre-constitutional judicial bureaucracy enjoys sufficient public stature to deliver legitimacy in the politically delicate and controversial work of constitutional oversight of parliamentary lawmaking (Favoreu 1990a, at 109; Ginsburg 2002, at 58).[4] Designers may mistrust the commitment of an old-order judiciary to newly codified constitutional principles (Favoreu 1990a, at 110; Sadurski 2009, at 3). They may worry that the country's received idea of the separation of powers, having always conceived the judiciary as a second-rate, subservient agent of one or both of the executive and the legislative branches, allows no conceptual space for a *Marbury*-like, independent, third source of legal policy direction to contend on an equal footing with the other two (Sadurski 2005, at 44; Stone Sweet 2000, at 32–3; Favoreu 1990b, at 55–6). Accordingly, designers may conclude that an effective *constitutional* judiciary had better take shape as a unique and exceptional tribunal, one that decidedly is *not* a part of the familiar, humdrum judicial furniture but rather is specially fitted to the newly conceived status of 'a power above [all] others', charged to 'assure respect of the Constitution in all areas' (Favoreu 1990a, at 111–12; compare Stone Sweet 2003, at 2770, suggesting that European-style constitutional courts have been designed to occupy a distinctive 'constitutional space', one that is neither 'judicial' nor 'political').[5] Designers have further, sometimes, believed that, by placing the guardianship of the constitution in a new and specially dedicated tribunal, they appropriately cement into visible, institutional arrangements a long-term commitment to the redemptive values of the new constitutional order (Ferreres Comella 2004b, at 1711). For some combination of these reasons, European constitutional designers over the past century have typically opted for creation of a non-ordinary, outsider tribunal to serve as the system's CST, to be staffed by personnel drawn from different career sectors, selected through different channels and by different means, on different terms of tenure of office, than those that will continue to replenish the ordinary judiciary (Ferreres Comella 2004a, at 468–70).[6]

But then it may seem natural to go a small step further. The reasons pointing to establishment of an outside-the-ordinary tribunal to preside over constitutional adjudication may seem to argue, also, for focusing that tribunal's energies on the important business for which its members have been specially chosen, leaving the daily run of ordinary adjudication to others specifically trained and selected for that work (Lewis 2005). Accordingly, the designers may lean toward making their new-model CST a specialist-not-generalist tribunal, confined to constitutional matters. Then diplomacy may be heard chiming on the same note: fencing the new judiciary off the accustomed turf of the old caters nicely for anxieties of the old over loss of business or status to the new, which might otherwise rouse resistance to the constitutional reform effort.

To this point in the thought of our constitutional designers, reasons of effectiveness and coordination, along with considerations of political feasibility and diplomacy, have been arguing in favor of a new and specialized tribunal to serve as the system's CST, its judicial tribunal of last resort for constitutional questions. But these same or allied considerations can carry constitutional designers one more, quite large step further, to making this new tribunal the system's sole and exclusive judicial constitutional reviewer. Designers may decide that it is wiser to restrict to one uniquely elevated bench the privilege of intrusion on accustomed executive and parliamentary dignities, than to leave those dignities exposed to insult by rank-and-file judges (Sadurski 2005, at 44; Stone Sweet 2000, at 40). And if the country's legal tradition should happen to be one that shuns the doctrine of precedent ('stare decisis') in favor of the freedom and responsibility of each judge, each time, to decide in accordance with the law as that judge then and there finds the law to be, a felt need for a consistently ordered body of constitutional-legal doctrine may itself become a decisive argument in favor of strict concentration of constitutional-adjudicative powers in a single, specialized constitutional court (Cappelletti 1989, at 138; Ferreres Comella 2004, at 1705; Ferreres Comella 2004a, at 465–7; Kühn 2004, at 559–61; Sadurski 2005, at 21–3, 44–5).

3   THE COMPETING DEMAND FOR SUBSTANTIVE CONSTITUTIONAL EFFECT

3.1   What Kind of Constitution Is It?

We have now reviewed what might be called the standard case for a specialized, concentrated constitutional jurisdiction. The general cogency of this case, and its fittingness to actual conditions in one or another country, are matters for debate (Sadurski 2005, at 40–51). Let us, however, suppose that the case has been found, on the whole, compelling by a group of constitutional designers: pending possible further considerations not yet in view, they would opt for a both-ways exclusive jurisdictional boundary, so that whatever falls within the competence of one judicial branch falls outside the competence of the other – perfect acoustic separation. What else of possible value to them might they have to sacrifice in order to achieve such a goal?

The answer could be nothing at all, if the constitution they want should happen to be one that will concern itself only with the formalities of elections and legislation, governmental structures and procedures, and the like, and will not otherwise present itself as a code of substantive rights or political-moral values and principles (Garlicki 2007, at 47). The 'constitutional' court can then be confined to decision of constitution-based claims of institutional or procedural error on the part of legislative and executive bodies conducting votes, appointing officers, making and enforcing laws, and so on; substantive pleas, regarding applications of procedurally unimpeachable laws and decrees, will find no hearing in that court. In return, the ordinary courts can refer all constitution-based claims, of the structural/procedural sort, to the constitutional court for resolution. Uncertainties and complications may crop up around the edges, but none beyond the normal abilities of smart lawyers to work out. Approximately the same could hold if the constitution does contain some substantive guarantees, *if* the designers are prepared to insulate whole large fields of law – such as 'background' private law, commercial law, or family law – from the reach of those guarantees. Again we must expect uncertainties and disputes around the edges, but perhaps, again, none that cannot be worked out by legally adept judges who honestly aim to respect the jurisdictional divide.[7]

Designers, however, may choose precisely *against* the insulation of any part or particle of their country's law from influence by substantive constitutional norms. They will have strong reason to do so, insofar as they intend their constitution to serve as an engine of general societal and legal transformation or renewal. Quite arguably, after all, it is the general background law – the civil, private, or common law that governs daily commercial and civil-society relationships – whose reform or reconception holds the key to success in a social-transformative project (Davis and Klare forthcoming; Tushnet 2008, at 168). Accordingly, a constitution's framers may see fit to deny refuge for any sector of the country's law from exposure to constitutional scrutiny, or at least to move some distance in that direction. As we are about to see, the further out they move on this axis of constitutional choice, the more they will have to yield on the point of acoustic separation of constitutional and ordinary jurisdictions.

3.2   Concrete Effectuation of Substantive Constitutional Norms

When constitutional designers take up questions of the organization of their country's courts and court-like tribunals, and of the distribution of competencies among these bodies, the designers presumably act with a view to ensuring that their constitution's substantive, prescriptive content will become and remain a truly effective force in the future conduct of their country's political and social affairs (Ginsburg 2002, at 56). A typical constitutional supremacy clause contains an apparent demand for such real effect (as we may call it) for substantive constitutional norms.[8] Such a demand does not, however, settle the *meanings*, the *extensions*, of a constitution's substantive guarantees. More specifically, it does not settle whether the guarantees reach so-called 'horizontal' disputes between non-governmental parties relying on rules of 'private', 'civil', 'general', or 'background' law. If a constitutional guarantee against (say) race-based discrimination is non-controversially understood to target only cases of active discrimination by state functionaries, giving real effect to that guarantee means ensuring its proper application to that class of cases; it does not mean extending it to cases of private-on-private discrimination.

Nor does 'real effect' mean that applicable constitutional law necessarily topples or displaces statute law, common law, or customary law that otherwise would be decisive for the case at hand – such as (say) the tort, contract, or regulatory law that might govern a complaint of race-based discrimination by some arm of the state when acting in the employment or housing market or running an educational institution. Most weakly and generally described, a demand for real effect is a demand upon adjudicators that they not cede unquestioned decisive force to otherwise applicable, ordinary law, insofar as that law arguably runs too hard against the grain of the constitution's applicable, substantive guarantees. Thus, when judges find that a proposed application of ordinary law to a pending case will fail to give due heed to the pertinent constitutional norms, they will be expected, at the very least, to consider possibilities of alternative, constitutionally compatible interpretations of the material in question. Of course, the demand may go beyond that relatively weak one, perhaps to the point of requiring judges to discard from consideration in the case at hand any ordinary legal material that they find intractably resistant to any interpretation leading to a constitutionally tolerable application to that case.

Such a power in an adjudicating court – to refuse effect to some piece of ordinary law as it would work in a pending case, on grounds of 'incidental' incompatibility with substantive norms of the constitution – has been found distinguishable, in concept, from a judicial power to nullify laws found unconstitutional.[9] How much really rides, in practice, on this distinction is a matter of debate. The answer may vary from country to country, depending on contingencies of juridical culture.[10] What we, here, can safely say – and all we need to say, for the moment – is that enlistment of a country's judiciary in the system-wide realization of substantive constitutional values requires that (at least) one court hold (at least) the power to weed out constitutionally repugnant, incidental applications of ordinary legal material (Garlicki 2007, at 267).

3.3   A First Breach in the Acoustic Wall

But will one court be enough? Plainly, a choice to confine constitutional control to a single tribunal sits in some tension with a goal of reliable, system-wide effectuation of the constitution's substantive norms. Empowerment of one tribunal only to decide the limits of the constitutional tolerability of proposed applications of ordinary laws cannot possibly satisfy such an aim, unless that tribunal is empowered to take over, on referral from other courts (if not for complete resolution then for resolution of the constitutional question), all adjudications in which an arguable constitutional incompatibility of a potentially decisive piece of ordinary law turns up. And, indeed such arrangements are typical of European-style models of centralized review (Ferreres Comella 2004a, at 465 n. 14; Ferreres Comella 2004b, at 1709 n. 13; Sadurski 2005, at 5, 19, 65). We may regard them as a first, most modest form of compromise of the total-separation ideal, brought on by pursuit of effective, pervasive implementation of substantive constitutional norms. To call upon ordinary judges to decide when a proposed application of ordinary law will be constitutionally questionable is already, after all, to pierce the acoustic barrier.

4   ACOUSTIC SEPARATION UNDER FULL-SCALE TRANSFORMATIVE CONSTITUTIONALISM

4.1   The Dilemma Presented

Acting on some combination of the reasons reviewed in Section 2.2, constitutional designers – let us suppose – decide that their system's 'constitutional' court is to act only on constitutional questions, leaving ordinary-law decisions to the ordinary courts, and vice versa. But suppose, now (on the recent example of South Africa), that our designers are further deeply committed to the idea that the country's entire legal order is to undergo refurbishing – perhaps even transformation – under firm and persistent guidance from a set of emancipatory values and principles they are writing into substantive constitutional law (Klare 1998; Van der Walt 2001; Michelman 2005, at 40–44). If, having made such a choice, they also try to make their 'constitutional' court the sole tribunal for matters implicating the constitution, they will, in effect, have made that court the country's sole tribunal, period, for all points of law arising in cases that enter the judicial system.

Let us back up a step or two. A constitution's substantive guarantees may or may not be written or construed so as to demand notice on every single occasion when someone is expected to decide or to act in accordance with law. The values and principles represented by these guarantees may or may not be meant to go everywhere the law goes – to 'radiate' (as it is sometimes said) to every nook and cranny of the law, infusing themselves into common law development and statutory interpretation, in every legal field, every step of the way. Whether or not a given constitution's guarantees are correctly so construed is itself a point of constitutional law, presumably to be resolved (in case of any doubt) by a judicial act of constitutional interpretation. But then consider what follows if the country's CST reads the constitution to settle that question in the affirmative – as have, for examples, the CSTs in South Africa (Michelman 2005, at 18–23), and Germany (Zeidler 1987, at 506). Every particular application made by any judge, in any case, of any piece of ordinary law, over the opposition of any litigant, is potentially laid open to review for constitutional acceptability. But such contextualized judgments of constitutional compatibility are constitutional matters, the grist of concrete constitutional review. The result is that no legal issue arising in any case that comes to court falls outside the nominally restricted 'constitutional' jurisdiction of a specialized constitutional court. If perfect acoustic separation prevails – if whatever falls within that court's competence *ipso facto* falls outside the competence of any other court – the ordinary judiciary is out of business.

Of course the designers do not intend any such bizarre result. The question is how they are to avert it. How are they to secure an all-pervasive influence for the norms of their designedly transformative constitution, while also paying dues to whatever considerations – of efficiency, effectiveness, or practical politics – drew them in the first place to the idea of acoustic separation between the two jurisdictions, constitutional and ordinary?

We canvass some possibilities.

4.2   Parallel Legal Systems and Private-law Integrity

The designers could specify that the constitution's substantive guarantees place no demands at all on ordinary law or ordinary adjudication; rather, they compose their own, freestanding code of regulation for the conduct of members of society in relation to each other, wholly aside from anything ordinary law may have to say. In the terms of a standard, academic terminology, the constitution's code of substantive guarantees will be 'horizontally' applied, but only 'directly' to a defending party's conduct, and never 'indirectly', that is, by forcing reconsideration of ordinary law on which a litigating party relies for her claim or defense (Tushnet 2008, at 197; Gardbaum, Chapter 21, this volume). What would then give the constitutional code its potentially pervasive influence on society would be the sheer range and variety of types of transactions and relations that its broadly drafted clauses may be taken to reach. ('No one shall be subjected to unfair discrimination, or to denial or invasion, without sufficient justification in terms of the principles of this constitution, of the rights to personal security, dignity, property, privacy, freedom of expression, religion, thought, or conscience, freedom of trade and occupation [and so on]').

Those wishing to complain legally of others' conduct would choose between resort to the body of ordinary-law demands on conduct and the body of constitutional demands on conduct, but never the twain would meet. Does *A* seek legal relief against *B* for *B*'s unauthorized publication of embarrassing facts about *A*, or for *B*'s apparent deviation from the terms of an employment contract? *A* can sue for violation of whatever articles of ordinary private or regulatory law he believes may address this matter. Alternatively, *A* can sue for violation of whatever constitutional provisions he believes may address it. In the first instance, the case goes to an ordinary court for decision according to the ordinary *corpus juris*. In the second instance, the case goes to a specialized constitutional tribunal for decision according to that court's readings of the constitutional guarantees and whatever doctrine accumulates around such readings.

Under such an arrangement, perfect acoustic separation prevails. It does so in a way that highlights an additional reason, beyond those so far considered, why the maximum achievable separation may count as a goal of great importance to some fraction, at least, of a country's legal community. In some countries – not all – we find jurists who place a high value on the internal coherence and autonomy of private (or common) law *as such*. They conceive of private law as a self-contained assemblage of trans-political, distinctively *legal* learning, insight, method, and craft; and they see this normative assemblage, furthermore, as socially beneficent, as moving on a curve of progressively informed and refined accounting for the human rights and interests at stake in typical social conflicts. To those who do thus apprehend the nature and merit of the private law corpus, a move to expose this corpus relentlessly to 'improvement' under pressure from acolytes of a politically engineered constitutional instrument has not at all times and places seemed an unmixed blessing. Worries arise about the mutilation of a time-tested, evolving, private-law wisdom by an openly teleological, openly politicized form of 'constitutional' argument that always, inevitably, comes down to some judge's or lawmaker's trade-off among clashing interests and claims of rights. Some private lawyers will call that, unhappily, a 'constitutional colonization' of the private law (Van der Merwe 2000; Michelman 2003, at 431–6; Taylor 2002, at 193, 209).

Ideas of this kind are not everywhere confined to a special band of intensely dedicated private lawyers. In more or less moderated form, such views may be quite widespread across a country's juristic community – reaching even (as we shall see in Section 5) into the dispositions of the constitutional judiciary itself. With them come attraction to an acoustic separation between constitutional and ordinary jurisdiction, most radically represented by our imagined, strict scheme of parallel legal systems. Where constitutional law and private law can never come into contact, fears of a ruinous invasion or corruption of private law by the more openly politicized, discursive methods ascribed to constitutional lawyers are held at bay.

Despite this possible attraction, the parallel-systems model, in its pristine form, is insupportable. Assuming such an arrangement could make sense in other ways, it must fall to one, crushing objection, common to schemes of substantively overlapping, parallel jurisdictions: forum-shopping. (Compare Scolnicov 2006, discussing overlap of secular and religious jurisdictions in Israel.) In each case that is brought to court, one party or the other must have the last word (else the system won't be operable) as to which judicial house will finally receive the case. Either the plaintiff's initial choice governs, or the defendant's choice to remove to the other house governs, or some more complicated rule leaves one or the other party with the upper hand to make the choice that finally governs. So where there is detectable variance between the expected outcomes under the two bodies of law, which party prevails will depend on which has that upper hand. Such a prospect would perhaps strike most constitutional designers as morally and politically intolerable. What is more to our point, though, is that such an arrangement blatantly fails to carry out the project of a pervasive, transformative influence for the constitution's substantive guarantees.

South Africa provides a clear example. In a series of cases, South Africa's Supreme Court of Appeal (SCA), the head court of that country's ordinary judiciary, chose to base its judgments strictly on ordinary law, expressly disclaiming any sort of reference to or influence from substantive constitutional law, even when constitutional law would have supported identical case outcomes. The SCA apparently expected that its judgments, thus based and explained, would be final, proof against review by a Constitutional Court whose jurisdiction is restricted to constitutional matters (Michelman 2005, at 16–23). The Constitutional Court emphatically disagreed. 'There are not two systems of law,' declared that court in response, 'each operating in its own field with its own highest court. There is only one system of law. It is shaped by the Constitution which is the supreme law, and all law . . . is subject to constitutional control.' (*Pharmaceutical Manufacturers Association*, para 44; compare Scolnicov 2006, at 734–5.)

Plainly enough, the Constitutional Court was determined to ensure that all law in South Africa, potentially in all applications, is exposed to sustained, reformist pressure from the Constitution's substantive principles and values. That is why the Court rejected the nascent scheme of parallel legal systems envisaged by the SCA. Constitutional designers might try to satisfy the Constitutional Court's concern (and fix the forum-shopping problem) by including a stipulation that a case goes to the constitutional system whenever any party so chooses. Such a cure, however, would only start up other grave objections. On one side of the divide, resentment and resistance from the ordinary judiciary would be certain. (Compare Scolnicov 2006, at 740.) On the other side, the constitutional judiciary would be thrust into the position of creating, on the basis of necessarily vaguely worded constitutional clauses, what would have to be, for all intents and purposes, a comprehensive body of ordinary and private law (Barak 2001, at 30–31). But that is work for which, by the standard argument in support of a specialized CST, those chosen for service on the constitutional tribunal will not necessarily be well suited and prepared, and for which at any rate they lack the requisite time and energy.

Is there some other way to accommodate pursuit of transformative constitutionalism with a worthwhile measure of acoustic separation between constitutional and ordinary jurisdiction?

4.3   Semi-concretized Detached Review

Constitutional designers, intent on maintaining separation between constitutional and ordinary jurisdictions, might decide to equip a single, constitutional court with the sole power to conduct detached ('abstract') reviews of statutes, or portions of statutes whose constitutionality is doubted by any applicant to the court or *sua sponte* by the court itself. (A 'detached' review is a review disconnected from any pending case.) Judgments of incompatibility issued by the court would stand as statutes ('*erga omnes*') to ordinary adjudicators. With a view to ensuring proper effectuation of constitutional values throughout the law and all its applications, claims and judgments of incompatibility might be framed as concretely as an applicant or the court might choose. ('Sections abc and xyz of the Civil Code are constitutionally unacceptable insofar as they may be read, separately or in combination, to permit eviction of any person from immovable property occupied by that person as his or her home, as the means of collecting or satisfying any unsecured indebtedness.') In this way, even common law may be brought under detached review. (For 'sections abc and xyz of the Civil Code', substitute 'the common law governing evictions, contracts, debt-collection, and execution of judgments'.)

Such schemes – of semi-concretized, detached review – are not unknown in practice. (Sadurski 2005, at 6–8, 11–12, describes such a use of detached review in some countries of central and eastern Europe.) They may take the form of a pronouncement of 'partial nullity' of a statute, owing to the omission of some reservation or limitation that would have barred a certain, constitutionally intolerable 'particular application' of an otherwise acceptable law (Zeidler 1987, at 509). Or the constitutional court, acting 'abstractly', outside of any pending adjudication, may be authorized to hand down binding interpretations of statutes (Sadurski 2005, at 11–12), achieving a similar effect.[11]

Authorization of semi-concretized, detached review appears to bestow upon the constitutional court what is to all intents and purposes a share of the country's legislative power, and may meet resistance on that ground (Sadurski 2005, at 8–10). This practice does, however, go some distance toward achievement of acoustic separation. Judicial judgments regarding constitutionality emanate only from specialists in the field, working at it full time, chosen with a view to whatever sorts of political or value-oriented skills, sensibilities, and commitments – and whatever sorts of public eminence or distinction – are deemed requisite for constitutional as opposed to ordinary adjudicators. No mere ordinary court is invited to rule on constitutional questions or impose its authority on the parliament or the executive. No strange skills and habits of judicial precedent-following are imposed on ordinary judges unaccustomed to them (beyond the requirement to heed the constitutional court's abstract rulings just as if they were statutes), but neither does there arise any clutter of conflicting constitutional rulings from sundry, headstrong courts.

It seems, then, that adoption of semi-concretized, detached review allows for some worthwhile approach to acoustic separation, while at the same time responding to demands for insinuation throughout the law of the constitution's transformative constitutional principles, leaving no particle of ordinary law exempt from a kind of constitutional muster. This system faces, however, a serious objection: it is, in effect, a crippled form of incidental (live-case), concrete review. The questions to be decided are more or less concretized, as applicants or the court may propose on the basis of their own, novelistic efforts of social imagination: such-and-such a fact configuration is thought to be sufficiently frequent, likely, and/or constitutionally salient as to merit a ruling. But why rely solely on such exercises of armchair speculation to set the agenda for the authorized constitutional interpreter? Why not let social life itself – or, in other words, the cases as they really come along – help set the agenda? Of course, letting the cases set the agenda means enlisting the ordinary, trial-level judges in the work of constitutional review (and to that extent relaxing separation), at least to the point of relying on them to decide when applications of ordinary law demanded in pending cases are sufficiently constitutionally questionable to require clearance from the constitutional tribunal.

The modified, detached-review scheme thus turns out to be in no respect better, and in obvious respects worse, than a scheme of concrete review by the constitutional tribunal, upon referral of questions of constitutional compatibility as they incidentally present themselves to ordinary courts in active litigation contexts. But a choice to move, then, to a referral scheme involves its own instability. Such a choice must presuppose both the ability and the readiness of the ordinary courts to play their part in making referrals as occasion requires. (Ferreres Comella 2004a, at 470–71, reports doubts about satisfaction of this condition in some European countries.) But once given the assumption of capable and cooperative ordinary courts, there seems little reason to stop short of authorizing those courts to deal fully, themselves, with incidentally arising questions of constitutional compatibility – subject, of course, to available review and correction by the system's CST.

Such an arrangement totally solves the problem of how to radiate the constitution everywhere without sidelining the ordinary judiciary. It may have further advantages. Such a scheme might meet less resistance from the ordinary judiciary than would a scheme for a CST monopoly on constitutional review powers. (Kühn 2004, at 553–8, and Sadurski 2005, at 20–25, 43, describe hostility of ordinary courts in central and eastern Europe to monopolization of constitutional review by the specialized constitutional tribunal.) By handing ordinary judges a share of active responsibility for furtherance of the constitutional project, it might help recruit them away from ingrained, oppositionist dispositions and habits of mind (Stone Sweet 2007, at 89; Kühn 2005, at 228).[12] Most simply and obviously, allowance of dispersed review under a specialist CST averts interruptions of ordinary-court litigation whenever colorable questions of constitutional compatibility crop up. Error-correction and doctrinal oversight are obtained, instead, through the smoother-running, less administratively awkward process of constitutional-compliance review, by the specialist CST, of complete case judgments by ordinary courts. (An obvious, attendant stipulation would be that no lower court's finding of unconstitutional action by the national executive or parliament becomes final or takes effect unless and until approved by the specialist CST.[13])

Ferreres Comella (2004a, at 471–4) describes in similar terms an 'internal pressure' in centralized review systems for movement toward decentralization of constitutional review powers. Inexorably, it seems, the logic of a commitment to pervasive, systemic influence for substantive constitutional norms moves against strict concentration of constitutional jurisdiction in the CST. Does it move as strongly against restriction of the CST's jurisdiction to constitutional matters, so that ordinary-law adjudication lies beyond its reach?

5 DEEPLY COMPROMISED REGIMES

5.1 Germany: The Model of Sustained Tension

In countries where a clear prescription for jurisdictional separation meets up with a prescription for system-wide influence for distinctly 'constitutional' value-orderings, courts face the challenge of upholding the tension between the prescriptions, so that each receives its due. No country's experience better typifies and represents to the world a response to this challenge than that of Germany and its Federal Constitutional Court (FCC).

Germany's 'dualist' judicial organization reserves to ordinary courts the selection of the applicable legal norms, and the determination of their proper application, in cases in civil litigation (Ferreres Comella 2004, at 1717; Grimm 1994, at 292). The FCC exists, within that structure, as a strictly specialized tribunal in the Kelsen tradition, confined to decision on questions arising under the Basic Law (Zeidler 1987, at 504; Currie 1994, at 27). The problem for the FCC comes in honoring this restriction of its competence, in the wake of that Court's determination – in its most widely noted, single decision – of the Basic Law's enactment of a value-ordering to govern the general, civil law, giving rise to the doctrine of 'indirect third party effect' (*mittelbare drittwirkung*) for the 'rights' guarantees of the Basic Law (Taylor 2002, at 202, 214).

In *Lüth* (1958, at 4–7), the FCC determined that the Basic Law's rights guarantees have a double aspect. As specifically worded guarantees ('subjective rights'), they obligate only the state and its officials. These clauses also, however, speak – as a 'fundamental constitutional decision' of the German people – for a set of underlying values and principles, an 'objective value system' for the whole of German civic life. The Basic Law's value-orderings must, accordingly, 'influence the civil law' throughout, obligating ordinary judges to construe and apply the background-law provisions of the Civil Code always 'in its spirit' and never 'in contradiction with' it. Correspondingly, it becomes the duty of the FCC, as guardian of the Basic Law, authorized to hear 'constitutional complaints' against any and all official failures to observe its requirements, to 'check whether [an ordinary court's disposition of a civil case] has rightly assessed the scope and effect of the fundamental rights in the sphere of civil law'. As a result, even as every dispute in litigation between private individuals remains at all times 'substantively and procedurally a civil legal dispute' governed by civil (ordinary) law, every resolution of a civil case by an ordinary court is potentially 'subject to constitutional review' by the FCC (Grimm 1994, at 277). The resulting dilemma for the FCC – which, as a Kelsenian specialized constitutional tribunal, is not supposed to displace the ordinary judiciary as adjudicator of ordinary civil cases, or as final authority regarding the meaning and application of the civil laws – is evident (Grimm 1994, at 277–8, Rinken 2002, at 276–7).

The FCC quite visibly strives to avoid presenting itself as a 'super [ordinary] court' (Zeidler 1987, at 524), even as it also must oversee constitutional observance by the ordinary courts construing and applying ordinary, background law. Thus, the FCC focuses on so-called 'general clauses' in the Civil Code – those places where the Code resorts to open-ended standards such as 'good faith' and 'good morals' to decide legal consequences in private disputes – as the preferred entry-ways for constitutional value-orderings into the civil law (*Lüth* at 5, 9–10; Eberle 2002, at 300). Where a constitutionally satisfactory solution is unobtainable under some plausible judicial gloss on a general clause or other Civil Code provision, the Court suspends judicial proceedings, pending legislative remedies (Taylor 2002, at 206–07). The Court disclaims any power to impose what it finds to be the all-things-considered best or correct interpretation of disputed civil-law provisions, ruling only on whether a specifically challenged application is subject to insuperable, constitutional objection (Zeidler 1987, at 511). And even there, the Court avowedly refrains from imposing debatable constitutional limits on ordinary adjudication, restricting itself to decision on whether a challenged civil-law application by an ordinary court is in apparent, complete defiance of the Basic Law values – shows a 'fundamentally incorrect opinion' or a 'complete misunderstanding' of the Basic Law's possible bearing on the case (Zeidler 1987, at 524; Grimm 1994, at 292–3).

Such postures of relative deference toward ordinary-law construction by ordinary courts, in ordinary civil litigation – straining to leave the ordinary judiciary with 'the last word' (Eberle 2002, at 30) – are described as typical of European, Kelsenian 'constitutional' tribunals (Ferreres Comella 2004b, at 1717–20). Observers appear to disagree about how far, in the German case, the FCC's efforts toward compliance with jurisdictional separation have any final effect on the judicial division of labor. In the eyes of some, the *Lüth* commitment to indirect third-party effect of constitutional guarantees, enforceable against allegedly aberrant ordinary judges by the procedure of constitutional complaint to the FCC, results, inevitably, in a 'radical departure' from acoustic separation and a thorough 'constitutionalization' of civil law (Garlicki 2007, at 46–51). For others, the FCC's express and sustained attention to jurisdictional boundaries, girded by the evident practical impossibility of comprehensive supervision of civil-law development by the FCC, and also the FCC's need to maintain harmonious relations with the ordinary judiciary, results in an over all credible practice of self-restriction by the FCC to a form of 'reasonableness review' of the outside constitutional acceptability of ordinary adjudications (Tushnet 2008, at 222–4; Tushnet 2003, at 86–7).

5.2 South Africa: A Different Path to the Compromised Model

The FCC's deployment of the constitutional complaint device in Germany represents (in our depiction) a judicial workaround of the problem posed by simultaneous, colliding commitments to (i) a system-pervading influence for the objective order of values represented by the

Basic Law's provisions on fundamental rights, and (ii) the institutional forms of jurisdictional acoustic separation, implying exclusion of the constitutional judiciary from ordinary-law domains (Taylor 2002, at 202). In South Africa, a like experience of collision has been met, in part, by express relaxation of a set of initial, textual prescriptions for strong acoustic separation.

The Interim Constitution, in force from 1994 to 1996, not only restricted the Constitutional Court's adjudicative competence to 'matters relating to the interpretation, protection and enforcement of the provisions of this Constitution' (Constitution of South Africa, 1993, s 98(2)), it reciprocally excluded the Appellate Division of the Supreme Court ('AD') – as the head tribunal of the ordinary judiciary was then named – from adjudication of 'any matter within the jurisdiction of the Constitutional Court' (s 101(5)). Almost certainly, that exclusion spoke for mistrust, on the part of some drafters, of the old-order judiciary's commitment to the values of the new Constitution (Lewis 2005, at 510). Interestingly, for our purposes, the exclusion has also been explained, in somewhat opposite terms, as a concession to the AD – a device for securing the AD's continuing status as a top-ranking court of final instance, the thought being that a court that would never deal with constitutional questions could never be overruled or outflanked by a Constitutional Court dealing only with such questions (Spitz 2000, at 194).

Looking back, we can see that any such aim for an acoustic separation of the two jurisdictions was headed from the start toward instability. The Interim Constitution – surely under influence from the German example – expressly codified a commitment to a system-wide infiltration, through indirect horizontal application, of the objective value-orderings represented by its bill of rights (*Du Plessis*; *Carmichele*). By command of section 35(3), 'in the interpretation of any law and the application and development of the common law and customary law, a court shall have due regard to the spirit, purport and objects of [the Bill of Rights]'. Since any challenge to the adequacy of lower-court compliance with that express, constitutional directive, in any given case, would obviously qualify as a 'matter relating to the interpretation . . . and enforcement of [the] Constitution', all such challenges would evidently fall within the jurisdiction of the Constitutional Court – and, hence, by force of section 101(5), would fall outside the competence of the AD. And since there could be no case in which such a challenge might not possibly be presented to the Constitutional Court, by appeal or on referral (Interim Constitution s 102), there loomed the possibility of an AD more or less totally stripped of jurisdiction. The Constitutional Court (*Du Plessis*) found a way out of the box: the AD surely fell within the class of courts ('any court') commanded by section 35(3) to exercise due regard for the Bill of Rights in all interpretations and applications of law, and that command to the AD must, therefore, qualify the apparent exclusion of the AD from constitutional jurisdiction by section 101(5).

The lesson of this contretemps was not lost on the drafters of the 'final' Constitution of 1996. They took care to correct the design error of 1993, by providing (s 168(3)) that 'the Supreme Court of Appeal (SCA) [as the old AD is now renamed] may decide appeals in any matter' and 'is the highest court of appeal except in constitutional matters'. And while the Constitutional Court is still nominally confined to 'constitutional matters' (s 1673(b)), the inclusion (s 39(2)) of a virtual repetition of the indirect-horizontality command of Interim Constitution section 35(3) – along with a new clause (s 173) expressly confirming in the Constitutional Court, along with other courts, the inherent power to develop the common law – makes clear that there is now no case over which the Constitutional Court is formally barred from assuming final control, with a view to ensuring that all the applications of law in that case comport with the 'spirit, purport, and objects' of the Bill of Rights (Michelman 2008, at 18–21). Thus, as a practical matter – if not, strictly speaking, as a formal one – the walls of acoustic separation etched into the initial constitutional blueprint have come down under pressure from the idea of a socially transformative, constitutional bill of rights.

Informed participants in South African juridical affairs quite well understand that such is the case (Lewis 2005, at 513–19). It is not the whole story, though. At least equally striking is the manner in which the Constitutional Court, although in reality free to take up any appeal it may choose, has internalized the attractions of jurisdictional specialization and *sua sponte* implements them.

Granted, says the Court, it is a constitutional requirement that both the application and the development of South African general background law – its common law – be brought and kept in harmony with constitutional value-orderings; yet common law development ought also to be 'appropriate for the common law within its own paradigm'. Common law doctrines, the Court observes, tend to be composed of multiple moving parts – such as duty, wrongfulness, intentionality, privilege, justification, remedy. Often, when the pre-constitutional common law's treatment of a problem is found to require an update, a trained common lawyer will be able to perceive the possibility of several different doctrinal entry points for making the needed adjustment, any one of which might satisfy the Constitution and so preserve the unity (in that sense) of the entire law of South Africa (compare Taylor 2002, at 213–14, describing German views). In these cases, the Constitution – as some might say – runs out before all the available legal-doctrinal options are resolved. And the choice, then, among constitutionally satisfactory common-law resolutions, ought to be shaped by considerations having to do with which choice would be most 'beneficial for the common law' when regarded as an identifiable, bounded component of South African law, organized internally by its own logic or 'paradigm' (*Carmichele*, paras 55–6).

Deciding among such constitutionally acceptable choices is, therefore, normally and properly business in which the SCA, not the Constitutional Court, should take the lead. The Constitutional Court implements this view through discretionary exercise of its powers of docket control – typically, by refusing leave for direct access, or for direct appeal from trial-level decisions, before litigants have exhausted their remedies (so to speak) in the ordinary judiciary, including the SCA (Michelman 2003, at 440–41; Michelman 2005, at 6 n. 2). Judges whose decisional writ cannot outrun the Constitution see fit, in such cases, to hand the laboring oar to others to whom the Constitution has ostensibly assigned a broader jurisdictional competence. Thus does the Constitutional Court construct for itself a way to pay its respects to the Constitution's express directive to confine itself within a less-than-plenary, 'constitutional' jurisdiction. The eventual result, in practice, may be a close approximation of the German regime of CST oversight of indirect horizontal application of constitutional principles by the ordinary judiciary.

5.3   Canada: A Counter-instance?

Germany and South Africa have been serving, for us, as instances of constitutional designers playing with institutional forms, with an eye to the accommodation of colliding commitments to pervasive, substantive constitutionalism, on the one hand, and to separation of constitutional and ordinary jurisdictions, on the other. (In both instances, our 'designers' have included judges engaged in constitutional-legal construction, within leeways charted by constitutional texts.) We have found, in these two instances, a broad convergence of solutions, worked out of entirely distinct formal/textual dispensations.

Now, it hardly seems that Canada can possibly present a comparable case. Utterly non-controversially, Charter jurisdiction accrues widely to Canada's ordinary courts. Conversely, Canada's CST – the Supreme Court of Canada (SCC) – is a generalist court. There is, simply, no Canadian constitutional commitment to acoustic separation, to be played off against any commitment the courts might find to a pervasive, 'horizontal' effect for Charter values (Taylor 2002, at 214). Our interest in the Canadian instance arises from precisely this absence of any ostensible concern about acoustic separation, on the part of constitutional authors. We look briefly to see whether separationist ideas have, nevertheless, seeped into the jurisprudence, as if such ideas were a force of nature.

In Canada, Charter guarantees are construed to impose their obligations on 'state' actors only; they do not speak directly to controversies between private parties, in which no 'act of government' is involved (*Dolphin Delivery*, para. 39; *Local 558*, para. 19).[14] But, of course, courts in common law systems are responsible, on a continuing basis, for interpreting and developing the common law in response to changes in 'social conditions and values' (*Hill*, para. 91). And because the Charter undoubtedly figures as a major statement of 'the fundamental values which guide and shape [Canadian] society', courts engaged in common law adjudication not only 'ought', they 'must', conduct this work 'in a manner consistent with the fundamental values enshrined in' the Charter (*Dolphin Delivery*, para. 39; *Hill*, para. 20; *Local 558*, para. 91). The ostensible result is a virtual Canadian reproduction of the German doctrine of 'radiating effect' – with the subtle difference that, in Canada, the effect comes through the ordinary judicial duty to keep the common law attuned to societal values (of which the Charter is deemed a definitive voice), whereas, in Germany, the effect comes via positive mandate from the Basic Law.

Just as, in Germany, the enforcer of the radiating effect is the FCC, so, in Canada, the enforcer is the SCC. But there we meet a difference. As a 'specialist' court confined to decision on constitutional matters, the FCC is under pressure to maintain and respect a division between constitutional and ordinary jurisdiction, and hence between constitutional and ordinary (private) law. On some accounts, at least, the FCC's mode of compliance has been to treat the private law corpus as a relatively autonomous body of doctrine, upon which the Basic Law, a distinct body of doctrine, imposes a set of abstractly conceived values that strike the private law corpus around the edges, so to speak, but otherwise leave it unmolested – demanding only that private-law solutions reflect some 'reasonable understanding of abstractly stated constitutional norms' (Tushnet 2008, at 222–3).

In Canada, the generalist SCC comes under no comparable pressure to differentiate a private law value-system or 'paradigm' from that of the Charter. Might we, nevertheless, detect in that Court's judgments – as we do in those of the South African Constitutional Court – some sign of a glance in that direction? Considering whether the common law of libel required refurbishing in the light of the Charter's free-expression principle, the SCC described Canadian libel law as 'a carefully crafted regime which has functioned fairly for the media and complainants for many years' (*Hill*, para. 138, internal quotation marks omitted). The SCC has written, more generally, of 'a host of legitimate interests' protected by the common law but 'not engaged by the *Charter*', and of a resulting need to 'weigh' Charter values 'against' the 'principles which underlie the common law' (*Local 558*, para. 21; *Hill*, para. 97). At least as pronounced in the judgments, however, has been a contrary idea: that courts, when choosing among plausible, alternative common law solutions, must seek out the one that 'best balances the interests at stake in a way that conforms to the fundamental values reflected in the *Charter*' (*Local 558*, paras. 37, 65).

The SCC thus speaks for the unity of Canadian law, under strong guidance from Charter values. Granted, the Court's judgments warn repeatedly against Charter-instigated common law modifications that are excessively drastic or 'major', or that overturn doctrines that have long been considered settled (*Local 558*, para. 16). They do so, however, out of an expressed concern for 'the ... balance between judicial and legislative action' (*Hill*, para, 85), not for a 'balance' between distinct and colliding sets of constitutional and private-law values. Comparing the Canadian with the German and South African instances, we might infer (on slight evidence) that private-law autonomy – the impulse to insulate private or background law from the full blast of constitutional values – is in some degree a product of a country's choices regarding judicial organizational structure; or we might (on evidence no stronger) infer the converse.

NOTES

1. There is no conceptual necessity that this be so. We can easily conceive of provision for dispersed review in a multi-peaked system of ordinary courts, in which the buck stops at any of the respective top courts of the various divisions of the ordinary judiciary, depending on which division received the case at initial entry. The obvious practical objection to such a scheme is that these multiple supreme courts 'are not well placed to generate a consistent [constitutional] case law that resolves the interpretive conflicts that lower courts create' (Ferreres Comella 2004a, at 466; Favoreu 1990a, at 109; Favoreu 1990b, at 45).
2. For the original use of the idea of acoustic separation in legal studies (somewhat distant from our use of it here), see Dan-Cohen 1984.
3. Of course, this notional reconstruction does not describe with full accuracy the reasons behind any concrete, historical instance of choice for the 'Kelsenian' model. In some cases, as recently in central and eastern Europe, the choice may hardly have been considered in these terms at all (Sadurski 2009, at 1–4).
4. Contingencies of local constitutional culture might swing that argument the other way. 'Political'-looking constitutional courts may lack access to 'moral capital that ordinary courts may have accumulated as impartial interpreters and observers of the law' (Ferreres Comella 2004b, at 1728).
5. A special 'constitutional' court, sitting distinctly outside the institutional subsystem of ordinary courts, need not be strictly confined to application of that specific body of law called 'the constitution'. The 'constitutional' tribunal may, for example, have exclusive powers to supervise elections under applicable statutes, or to handle criminal prosecutions of high state officials (Ferreres Comella 2004b, at 1707).
6. Where the going system of ordinary courts should happen to be multi-peaked, it may further be the case that no extant ordinary court can qualify as the obvious candidate for CST status (Cappelletti 1989, at 143).
7. The widely questioned use in the United States of a 'state action' rule to limit the horizontal effect of constitutional guarantees is frequently explained (if not necessarily approved) as a judicially developed anti-poaching device, where legislative competence in the fields of family and background-private law is understood to be reserved to the legislatures and common-law judiciaries of the several states, away from central-government authorities (barring significant interstate or transnational entanglements) (Kumm and Ferreres Comella 2005, at 270–71, 273–6; Tushnet 2008, at 198; id. at 183 n. 59, 184–5, presenting and questioning this account).
8. See, e.g., Constitution of South Africa s 2 ('This Constitution is the supreme law of the Republic; law or conduct inconsistent with it is invalid, and the obligations imposed by it must be fulfilled.').
9. The distinction has assumed some salience in debates over the distribution of constitutional jurisdiction. Garlicki (2007, at 58–9, 65–6) describes conflicts between constitutional and ordinary courts, in Poland and elsewhere, over possession and exercise of the refusal-to-apply power, where the constitutional tribunal concededly holds the sole authority to nullify statutes. Sadurski (2005, at 7; 2009, at 12) reports dissatisfaction with systems in Poland and Hungary that limit constitutional-review tribunals to passing on the validity of the law or the rule 'itself', leaving no recourse against a constitutionally objectionable application of a law. The distinction is invoked in sundry other contexts as well. Stone Sweet (2003, at 257–8), recalls use of it by 20th-century French theorists to reconcile US-style judicial review with French separation-of-powers theory.

Jackson and Tushnet (2006, at 466), use it to describe so-called 'hybrid' systems of judicial review, characteristically Latin American, in which ordinary courts have the refuse-to-apply power but only one court has the invalidation power.

10. When strong *stare decisis* effects are accorded to a pinnacle court's case-by-case findings that pieces of ordinary law are incidentally incapable of application without unacceptable setback to constitutional requirements, the results may be hard to distinguish from those that would flow from judicial judgments of total or partial nullification issued by that court (Kelsen 1942, at 189; Stone Sweet and Shapiro 2002, at 370–72; Sadurski 2005, at 46, 50).

11. National systems appear to differ with regard to the authority of constitutional courts, when acting on referrals from ordinary courts, to issue so-called 'interpretive rulings', in which 'a decision on the constitutionality of law is taken not in absolute terms but in relation to a particular interpretation [or application] of the provision at issue'. Exercises of the latter sort of power are contentious in some places. Garlicki (2007, at 54–7, 59, 65–6), reports disputes in Italy and Poland over whether 'interpretative' (i.e., contextualized) rulings of the Constitutional Court have a binding – as opposed to a merely persuasive – effect for the ordinary courts.

12. It has been suggested that the likelihood of such a benign effect may depend on whether ordinary superior judges are recruited from the ranks of the career-bureaucratic judiciary or from among legal academics and practitioners. See Kühn (2005, at 237–8) contrasting, in this regard, Poland with the Czech Republic and Slovakia.

13. See, for example, Constitution of South Africa s 172(2)(a).

14. Application of the reservation for cases involving 'acts of government' gives rise to a complex and puzzling body of doctrine (Tushnet 2008, at 201–13), which need not concern us here.

REFERENCES

Books and Articles

Barak, Aharon (2001), 'Constitutional Rights in Private Law', in Daniel Friedmann and Daphne Barak-Erez (eds), *Human Rights in Private Law,* Oxford and Portland, OR: Hart Publishing, pp. 1–42.

Cappelletti, Mauro (1989), *The Judicial Process in Comparative Perspective,* Oxford: Oxford University Press.

Currie, David P. (1994), *The Constitution of the Federal Republic of Germany,* Chicago: University of Chicago Press.

Dan-Cohen, Meir (1984), 'Decision Rules and Conduct Rules: On Acoustic Separation in Criminal Law', *Harvard Law Review,* 97(2): 625–77.

Davis, Dennis M. and Karl Klare (forthcoming), 'The Common and Customary Law in Transformative Constitutionalism', *South African Journal on Human Rights.*

Eberle, Edward (2002), *Dignity and Liberty: Constitutional Visions in Germany and the United States,* Westport, CT: Praeger Publishers.

Favoreu, Louis (1990a), 'American and European Models of Constitutional Justice', in David Clark (ed.), *Comparative and Private International Law: Essays in Honor of John Henry Merriman,* Derlin: Dunckler & Humblot, pp. 105–20.

Favoreu, Louis (1990b), 'Constitutional Review in Europe', in Louis Henkin and Albert J. Rosenthal (eds), *Constitutionalism and Rights: The Influence of the United States Constitution Abroad,* New York: Columbia University Press, p. 38.

Ferreres Comella, Victor (2004a), 'The European Model of Constitutional Review of Legislation: Toward Decentralization?', *International Journal of Constitutional Law,* 2(3), 461–91.

Ferreres Comella, Victor (2004b), 'The Consequences of Centralizing Constitutional Review in a Special Court: Some Thoughts on Judicial Activism', *Texas Law Review,* 82 (7), 1705–36.

Ferreras Comella, Victor (2009), *Constitutional Courts and Democratic Values: A European Perspective,* New Haven: Yale University Press.

Garlicki, Lech (2007), 'Constitutional Courts Versus Supreme Courts', *International Journal of Constitutional Law,* 5 (1), 44–68.

Ginsburg, Tom (2002), 'Economic Analysis and the Design of Constitutional Courts', *Theoretical Inquiries in Law* 3 (1), 49–84

Grimm, Dieter (1994), 'Human Rights and Judicial Review in Germany', in David M. Beatty (ed.), *Human Rights and Judicial Review: A Comprehensive Perspective,* Dordrecht: Kluwer/Martinus Nijhoff, pp. 268–95.

Jackson, Vicki C. and Mark Tushnet (2006), *Comparative Constitutional Law,* 2nd edition, New York: Foundation Press.

Kelsen, Hans (1942), 'Judicial Review of Legislation: A Comparative Study of the Austrian and American Constitution', *Journal of Politics,* 4 (2), 183–200.

Klare, Karl (1998), 'Legal Culture & Transformative Constitutionalism', *South African Journal on Human Rights*, 14 (1), 146–88.

Kühn, Zdeněk (2004), 'Worlds Apart: Western and Central European Judicial Culture at the Onset of the European Enlargement', *American Journal of Comparative Law*, 52 (3), 531–67.

Kühn, Zdeněk (2005), 'Making Constitutionalism Horizontal: Three Different Central European Strategies', in András Sajó and Renáta Uitz (eds), *The Constitution in Private Relations: Expanding Constitutionalism*, Utrecht: Eleven International Publishing, pp. 217–40.

Kumm, Mattias and Victor Ferreres Comella (2005), 'What is so Special about Constitutional Rights in Private Litigation?', in András Sajó and Renáta Uitz (eds), *The Constitution in Private Relations: Expanding Constitutionalism*, Utrecht: Eleven International Publishing, pp. 241–86.

Lewis, Carole (2005), 'Reaching the Pinnacle: Principles, Policies, and People for a Single Apex Court in South Africa', *South African Journal on Human Rights*, 21 (4), 509–24.

Michelman, Frank I. (2003), 'The Bill of Rights, the Common Law, and the Freedom-friendly State', *Miami Law Review* 58 (1), 401–48.

Michelman, Frank I. (2005), 'Constitutional Supremacy and the Rule of Law', in Stuart Woolman, Theunis Roux and Michael Bishop (eds), *Constitutional Law of South Africa*, 2nd edition, vol. I, Johannesburg: Juta, ch. 11 (chapters separately paginated).

Michelman, Frank I. (2008), 'On the Uses of Interpretive Charity: Some Notes on Application, Avoidance, Equality and Objective Unconstitutionality from the 2007 Term of the Constitutional Court of South Africa', *Constitutional Court Review*, 1, 1–61.

Rinken, Alfred (2002), 'The Federal Constitutional Court and the German Political System', in Ralph Rogowski and Thomas Gawron (eds), *Constitutional Courts in Comparison: The U.S. Supreme Court and the German Federal Constitutional Court*, Oxford and New York: Berghahn Books.

Sadurski,Wojciech (2005), *Rights before Courts*, Dordrecht: Springer.

Sadurski,Wojciech (2009), 'Twenty Years after the Transition: Constitutional Review in Central and Eastern Europe', Legal Studies Research Paper No. 09/69, Sydney Law School, University of Sydney, available at http://papers.ssrn.com/sol3/papers.cfm?abstract_id=1437843.

Scolnicov, Anat (2006), 'Religious Law, Religious Courts and Human Rights within Israeli Constitutional Structure', *International Journal of Constitutional Law*, 4 (4), 732–40.

Spitz, Richard (2000), *The Politics of Transition: A Hidden History of South Africa's Negotiated Settlement*, Oxford, Hart Publishing.

Stone Sweet, Alec (2000), *Governing with Judges: Constitutional Politics in Europe*, Oxford: Oxford University Press.

Stone Sweet, Alec (2003), 'Why Europe Rejected American Judicial Review: And Why it may Not Matter', *Michigan Law Review*, 101 (8), 2744–80.

Stone Sweet, Alec (2007), 'The Politics of Constitutional Review in France and Europe', *International Journal of Constitutional Law*, 5, 69–92.

Stone Sweet, Alec and Martin Shapiro (2002), *On Law, Politics, and Judicialization*, Oxford: Oxford University Press.

Taylor, Greg (2002), 'The Horizontal Effect of Human Rights Provisions, the German Model and its Applicability to Common-Law Jurisdictions', *Kings College Law Journal*, 13 (2), 187–218.

Tushnet, Mark (2003), 'The Issue of State Action/Horizontal Effect in Comparative Constitutional Law', *International Journal of Constitutional Law*, 1 (1), 79–98.

Tushnet, Mark (2005), 'The Relationship between Judicial Review of Legislation and the Interpretation of Non-constitutional Law, with Reference to Third Party Effect', in András Sajó and Renáta Uitz (eds), *The Constitution in Private Relations: Expanding Constitutionalism*, Utrecht: Eleven International Publishing, pp. 168–81.

Tushnet, Mark (2006), 'Comparative Constitutional Law', in Mathias Reimann and Reinhard Zimmermann (eds), *The Oxford Handbook of Comparative Law*, Oxford: Oxford University Press, pp. 1226–57.

Tushnet, Mark (2008), *Weak Courts, Strong Rights: Judicial Review and Social Welfare Rights in Comparative Constitutional Law*, Princeton: Princeton University Press.

Uitz, Renáta (2005), 'Introduction', in András Sajó and Renáta Uitz (eds), *The Constitution in Private Relations: Expanding Constitutionalism*, Utrecht: Eleven International Publishing, pp. 1–20.

Van der Merwe, Derek (2000), 'Constitutional Colonisation of the Common Law: A Problem of Institutional Integrity', *Journal of South African Law*, 2000 (1): 12–32.

Van der Walt, A. J. (2001), 'Dancing With Codes: Protecting, Developing and Deconstructing Property Rights in a Constitutional State', *South African Law Journal*, 118 (2): 258–311.

Zeidler, Wolfgang (1987), 'The Federal Constitutional Court of the Federal Republic of Germany: Decisions on the Constitutionality of Legal Norms', *Notre Dame Law Review*, 62 (4), 504–25.

Judicial Decisions

Germany (Federal Constitutional Court)
Lüth Case (1958), BVerfGE 7, 198, 1 BvR 400/51, English translation in (1998) *Decisions of the Bundesverfassungsgericht – Federal Constitutional Court – Federal Republic of Germany*, vol. 2/Part 1, Baden-Baden: Nomos Verlagsggesellschaft.

Canada (Supreme Court)
Hill v Church of Scientology of Toronto, [1995] 2 SCR 1130.
RWDSU v Dolphin Delivery Ltd, [1986] 2 SCR 573.
RWDSU, Local 558 v Pepsi-Cola Canada Beverages (West) Ltd, [2002] 1 SCR 156, 2002 SCC 8.

South Africa (Constitutional Court)
Carmichele v Minister of Public Safety, 2001 (10) BCLR 995 (CC).
Du Plessis v De Klerk, 1996 (5) BCLR 658 (CC).
In re Pharmaceutical Manufacturers Association of South Africa, 2000 (3) BCLR (CC).

17. Constitutional experimentation: rethinking how a bill of rights functions
Janet L. Hiebert

Legal and political scholars are curious about how recently adopted bills of rights in Canada, New Zealand, the United Kingdom, the Australian Capital Territory (ACT) and the Australian state of Victoria conceive of the project of rights protection. In choosing to adopt a bill of rights, these Westminster parliamentary systems have set aside constitutional orthodoxy, which presumed the necessity of having to make a stark choice between parliamentary supremacy and granting courts authority to determine the validity of legislation where rights are implicated.[1] They have charted a new path that neither emulates the European post-war reliance on constitutional courts based on the German model, nor accepts judicial monism associated with American-style judicial review, despite its being said to have provided 'the inspiration for the rights-protecting constitutions of liberal democracies throughout the world' (Weinrib 2006, 84).

Like more conventional approaches, these new bills of rights codify rights that are used to assess legislation and executive actions, and authorize judicial review to evaluate whether state actions are consistent with protected rights. Yet, at the same time, they distinguish the concept of judicial review from the idea that courts have final authority to determine the legitimacy of state actions where rights are implicated. In so doing, they accept the legitimacy of legislative dissent from judicial rulings, which is possible by conceiving of the scope of judicial power as more limited than in the United States (where American courts consider themselves, and are considered by most, as the ultimate authority on constitutionality).[2] With the exception of Canada, these new bills of rights require that the determination of remedies for rights violations occurs in the political rather than judicial arena (and in Canada, although courts have power to grant remedies that include the invalidation of legislation, most judicial decisions can be set aside on a temporary but renewable basis, through ordinary legislation). These bills of rights also conceive of rights protection as being a more complex project than reliance on judicial review, and envisage rights-based scrutiny of proposed legislation by public and political officials. Consequently, judicial review constitutes neither the first nor the last stage when assessing whether legislation is consistent with rights, but instead represents a later and penultimate stage.

These bills of rights contradict three core premises of the United States Bill of Rights as it has evolved: that courts have exclusive responsibility for interpreting rights and determining whether the actions of public and political officials contravene what is permitted by a bill of rights; that judgment about rights has the force of a constitutional or extraordinary law in that it cannot be altered through ordinary legislative means;[3] and that a bill of rights requires judicial power to grant remedies that can include setting aside inconsistent legislation. These differences have led scholars to characterize these bills of rights as constituting an alternative approach, referred to as the Commonwealth model (Gardbaum 2001), hybrid approach

(Rishworth 1995, 4; Goldsworthy 2003, 483), weak-form model (Tushnet 2008), or parliamentary rights model (Hiebert 2004, 1963).

One way to understand variations in this model is to situate each jurisdiction on a continuum distinguishing what has long been considered as constituting two rival poles: at one end, parliamentary supremacy, where parliament's judgment on matters involving rights is final, and at the other end, the American practice of judicial supremacy, where courts' judgment on constitutional rights is paramount (Gardbaum 2001, 710).[4] On this conceptual continuum, New Zealand would occupy a spot closer to the end of the parliamentary supremacy pole and Canada a spot fairly close to the judicial supremacy pole associated with the United States. Australia would be situated reasonably close to New Zealand and the United Kingdom somewhere between Australia and Canada.

But scholarly interest goes well beyond how to characterize these bills of rights. One obvious question is why would political leaders in these parliamentary systems support such a radical reorientation of governing principles, particularly given that these reforms represent possible constraints on their own powers?[5] A second question, which tends to attract country-specific assessments, is what jurisprudence is emerging? A third question is: do these bills of rights actually carve out a unique space that resembles neither parliamentary supremacy nor judicial supremacy? Another way to frame this question is: how stable is this model (Tushnet, 2008)?

This chapter asks a different question: how does this new model conceive of the function of a bill of rights? This question is explored through recurring debates about the nature of judicial power and the institutional relationships these bills of rights are said to foster. First, authorizing a weaker form of judicial review and recognizing that remedies for negative judicial rulings can be delayed or are not forthcoming at all, has encouraged scholars to reassess the relationship between judicial review and the broader rights project these bills of rights represent. Second, the ideas that legislative decision-making processes should involve judgment about rights and that judges are not the only actors responsible for interpreting rights, have challenged scholars to reassess the role of legislatures in terms of rights protection. Third, the possibility for legislation to prevail in the face of a negative judicial ruling has generated questions about the balance this model strikes between political and judicial responsibility, and how the resolution of inter-institutional disagreements is conceived. These debates will be examined in Section 2. First, a brief discussion is warranted of the genesis of this alternative model for a bill of rights, which from hereon will be referred to as the Parliamentary Rights Model.

1 EMERGENCE OF THE PARLIAMENTARY RIGHTS MODEL

In all of the above jurisdictions, public, political and scholarly debates reflect strong scepticism about the quality of how Westminster-based parliamentary systems have been functioning. The dominance of executive governance has challenged traditional assumptions about parliament's rights-protecting capacity. The traditional British understanding of how rights were protected assumed that a bill of rights was not necessary (and, in any event, inconsistent with the constitutional principle of parliamentary supremacy). Freedom did not require a fundamental statement of principles operating in the form of higher law, but was thought to be protected by an independent parliament that could hold the government to account and restrain its illiberal intentions and, also, by the common law, where the judiciary protected the idea that citizens are free to do as they wish, unless the activity in question is expressly prohibited by law (Bradley and Ewing 2003, 404–05). But these assumptions were based on 19th century practices; a period considered 'the high-water mark of an independent Parliament acting as a watchdog of the executive' when Parliament 'was a body which chose the government, maintained it and could reject it' and 'operated as an intermediary between the electorate and the executive'. No longer do these assumptions characterize how modern parliaments function, in large part because the 'inexorable growth of the party system and its attendant discipline has seen the executive increasingly gain control of the House of Commons'.[6]

Yet, despite this scepticism about how parliament functions, and the attendant concern for rights, democratic considerations have outweighed interest in an American-style bill of rights, where judicial review is conceived of as encompassing the remedial power of allowing the judiciary to effectively veto inconsistent legislation.

An important turning point in reconciling Westminster-based parliamentary systems to the possibility of a bill of rights was an innovative idea instrumental in overcoming political opposition to the then proposed Canadian Charter of Rights. This was the idea embodied in the notwithstanding clause, which now constitutes s. 33 of the Charter. Although Canadian judicial power closely resembles the strong form associated with the United States in the sense that Canadian courts have remedial power that can include setting aside offending legislation, what is different about Canada is that provincial and federal legislatures have the power to dissent from judicial rulings and set aside their effects (on a temporary but renewable basis) by passing ordinary legislation.[7] This capacity arises from the inclusion in the Charter of the notwithstanding clause, a late concession to provincial premiers who, for ideological and democratic reasons, opposed the idea of assigning courts new power to constrain parliament, and hoped to mitigate the constraints judicial review might otherwise have on legislation (Hiebert, 2009).

Beyond its significance in brokering political agreement for the Charter, to other parliamentary systems, the notwithstanding clause introduced the possibility of bridging what had earlier been thought of as competing and mutually exclusive constitutional paradigms.[8] Conceptually, this clause allowed a critical distinction to be made between the practice of judicial review and the idea that judges' decisions necessarily displace political decisions where rights are implicated. This argument about the conceptual importance of the notwithstanding clause is not meant to suggest that this Canadian innovation precipitated mobilization by political leaders in other parliamentary systems to adopt a bill of rights. These decisions were in response to domestic and international pressures (see, for example, Palmer 1979; Klug 2000; Rishworth 1995; Erdos 2009). Nevertheless, the logic of the notwithstanding clause helped fuel the imagination of a new middle ground, previously assumed not possible (Hiebert 2009, 119–20). This new middle ground was a blend of British and American constitutional principles, so as to introduce judicial review but in a weaker or penultimate form, and thereby preserve the principle of parliamentary supremacy (Gardbaum 2001; Tushnet 2003; Perry 2003; Goldsworthy 2003).

Yet, despite the subsequent adaptation of the idea of limited judicial review, the 'genius' of the notwithstanding clause was not immediately apparent, whether in Canada or elsewhere. The clause quickly drew disdain from Canadian commentators, and many Canadian constitutional scholars continue to regard this mechanism as being the product of an unfortunate compromise, or as a pragmatic and instrumental device borne out of a stalemate, but lacking any intrinsic merit (Cameron 2004, 141). Some scholars who approve of the notwithstanding clause also disapprove of the idea of a bill of rights. The notwithstanding clause helps mitigate the effects of the Charter, but they consider a bill of rights as an inappropriate way of conceiving of institutional checks and balances.[9] Relatively few scholars who accept the merits of the Charter also believe the notwithstanding clause has inherent virtue (see, for example, Weiler 1984; Russell 1991; Hiebert 2002; Albert 2008). Support for the notwithstanding clause also comes from scholars who embrace the metaphor of dialogue when analysing Charter developments (Hogg and Bushell 1997; Roach 2001), but their court-centric assumptions might tempt them to revisit their approval of the notwithstanding clause if Canadian legislatures were to invoke this power more regularly.[10]

A majority of Canadian scholars, politicians and public officials consider the notwithstanding clause inconsistent with a new constitutional order that privileges legal adjudication over political judgment where rights are implicated (Whyte 1990, 350–51). This scepticism is influenced by American ideas of constitutionalism and legalism. The idea that a notwithstanding clause is inconsistent with a bill of rights was made explicit in an address by then Justice Brennan of the United States Supreme Court to a British audience, when he advised that the virtue of a bill of rights is to stand as a 'constant guardian of individual liberty' and warned against repeating Canada's error by including a notwithstanding power (Brennan 1989, 437).

Yet, ironically, while the notwithstanding clause remains unpopular within Canada,[11] support can be found in American scholarship for the idea that a bill of rights can validly authorize legislative dissent from judicial rulings (Tushnet 2000; Kramer 2004; Fisher 1991; Fisher 1998). Support for this idea can also be inferred from those who lament constitutional development away from a coordinate approach (Agresto 1984, 119).

The notwithstanding clause has also drawn more interest on the international stage. It is difficult to pinpoint when this idea gained more currency. Unlike the Canadian Charter debate, where political participants struggled with the question of how to temper the impact of judicial authority within the compressed and intensely political terrain of a late spurt of ongoing constitutional negotiations, and without a comparable model to draw upon, reform-minded politicians and scholars elsewhere have had the luxury of time and the Charter's example when considering the appropriate scope of judicial power. For those who were interested in a bill of rights, and yet reluctant to displace parliamentary supremacy with judicial supremacy, the notwithstanding clause represented the possibility of limiting the scope of judicial power under a bill of rights, so as to constitute what Mark Tushnet has characterized as weak-form judicial review (distinguished from strong-form judicial review where judicial interpretations of the bill of rights are final and unrevisable through ordinary legislative means) (Tushnet 2008, 18–42). The decisions of other parliamentary systems to conceive of judicial power in more limited terms than in Canada negated the need for an explicit mechanism to reverse the effect of a judicial ruling. Thus, the influence of the notwithstanding clause was at this level of an idea – allowing for legislative dissent from judicial review – rather than as a specific power to be copied or adapted elsewhere.

New Zealand was the first jurisdiction after Canada to introduce a bill of rights, which it did in 1990. Although the Canadian Charter of Rights is said to have inspired the New Zealand Bill of Rights Act,[12] legal scholarship does not suggest that the notwithstanding clause influenced the design of the NZBORA.[13] In New Zealand, the notwithstanding clause was considered to represent a minor setback in Canada's attempt to develop a full-fledged constitutional bill of rights and, as such, reflected the particularities of the Canadian political debate rather than a distinct component of a new model.[14] Once it became clear there was insufficient support in New Zealand for a strong bill of rights that would authorize courts to invalidate inconsistent legislation, a mechanism such as the notwithstanding clause was considered inadequate. The New Zealand rights debate considered the Canadian Charter, even with its notwithstanding clause, as too closely resembling the strong form of judicial power associated with the United States Bill of Rights to be worthy of emulating.[15] The New Zealand Bill of Rights Act authorizes constrained judicial power. Judges are instructed that wherever an enactment can be given a meaning that is consistent with the rights and freedoms contained in the bill of rights, this 'meaning shall be preferred to any other meaning'. But judges are not formally empowered to rule that other enactments have been impliedly repealed or revoked or to decline to apply any provision considered to be inconsistent with any provision in the Bill of Rights.

By the time of the next 'rights revolution',[16] the United Kingdom's introduction of the Human Rights Act, which came into effect in 2000, the notwithstanding clause had become a more explicit part of constitutional considerations. Political reluctance to formally relinquish the principle of parliamentary supremacy had long represented a serious sticking point for those in the United Kingdom proposing a bill of rights, whether as a home-grown project or one taking the HRA's form and incorporating the European Convention of Human Rights into domestic law. A 1993 Labour policy contemplated use of a notwithstanding mechanism based on Canada's notwithstanding power. But as discussion about a bill of rights evolved, this proposal subsequently disappeared (Wadham 1997, 141–2). The political architects of the HRA became increasingly aware of how political attitudes to the notwithstanding clause were evolving in Canada, and concern set in that if the Canadian approach were emulated, reluctance to use the notwithstanding clause would contradict the spirit of constrained judicial power.[17] But at the same time, those developing the HRA also thought it necessary to diverge from the New Zealand approach, where courts lack the authority to make an explicit declaration of inconsistency when unable to interpret legislation in a manner that is consistent with the Bill of Rights Act.[18] Under the HRA, judges are obliged to interpret legislation 'so far as possible so as to be compatible with Convention rights' and where such interpretations are not possible, the HRA empowers a superior court to make a 'declaration of incompatibility' if primary legislation cannot be interpreted in a manner that is consistent with Convention rights. United Kingdom judges cannot invalidate inconsistent legislation, as can Canadian judges.

Australian political and scholarly discussion of a bill of rights has been significantly influenced by awareness of the experiences and debates in Canada, New Zealand and the United Kingdom. Australian scholars associate the notwithstanding clause with the idea of constrained or weak judicial power, considered by many as a desirable way of conceiving of the judicial role under a bill of rights, and also as a practical way to overcome political and popular opposition to a bill of rights (Williams 2000; Byrnes et al. 2009). Two Australian jurisdictions (Australian Capital Territory and Victoria) have statutory bills of rights. As in the United Kingdom, the conception of judicial power is in limited terms, without a remedial capacity to declare inconsistent legislation invalid. Consequently, there is no need for a notwithstanding clause to explicitly reverse a judicial ruling of inconsistency. As in the United Kingdom, the trigger mechanism for disagreeing with a judicial ruling is different than in Canada. Whereas Canadian parliaments have to act assertively to disagree with a court ruling of inconsistency, by enacting legislation that includes the notwithstanding clause, United Kingdom and Australian legislatures have to act assertively to give effect to a judicial ruling, and introduce remedial measures. But the Victoria Charter of Human Rights includes a notwithstanding clause as a pre-emptive mechanism, described as a way to simplify judicial interpretation. If the legislature invokes the clause, this signals to courts that the Charter does not apply to the legislation in question and therefore should not be subject to a judicial declaration of inconsistency (Evans and Evans 2008, 69–70).

2   REVISITING THE FUNCTION OF A BILL OF RIGHTS

The remainder of the chapter focuses on how the parliamentary rights model envisages the function of a bill of rights and explores recurring debates about the nature of judicial power and the institutional relationships these bills of rights are expected to promote. First, authorizing a more constrained form of judicial review and allowing for the possibility that remedies for negative judicial rulings can be delayed or not forthcoming at all, has encouraged scholars to reassess the relationship between judicial review and the broader rights project these bills of rights represent. Second, these bills of rights conceive of rights protection as proactive and not simply reactive, and envisage rights-based scrutiny not only by judges but also by bureaucratic, governmental and parliamentary actors. But this idea of shared responsibility has challenged scholars to reassess the role of legislatures in terms of judgment about rights. Third, the possibility for legislation to prevail in the face of a negative judicial ruling has generated questions about the balance this model strikes between political and judicial responsibility, and how the resolution of inter-institutional disagreements is conceived.

2.1   Reconsidering the Function of a Bill of Rights

As has been discussed, parliamentary bills of rights conceive of the scope of judicial power in weaker or more constrained terms than in the United States Bill of Rights. Judicial review in the former is penultimate rather than final,[19] does not encompass the power to declare legislation invalid (Canada is an exception), and bills of rights allow parliaments to lawfully persist with legislation after courts have declared it is inconsistent with rights.[20]

But many are sceptical about conceiving of judicial review in limited or constrained terms, particularly if they consider that the principal function of a bill of rights is to 'invoke the machinery of the courts to set binding constraints on political decision making'.[21] Questions asked about this model include: how are rights protected if courts lack remedial power to veto rights-offending legislation? And what is the purpose of having a bill of rights, if courts cannot 'guarantee' that rights will be protected?[22] For those whose preferences are for strong rights protection,[23] parliamentary bills of rights are looked upon as inadequate. Others might also suggest that they risk jeopardizing the authoritative character of law because of the capacity for non-judicial actors to influence the scope of rights (Alexander and Schauer 1997). Such questions are understandable from an orientation that assumes that the principal function of a bill of rights is to allow one institution (the judiciary) to correct the mistakes of the other governing institutions (the executive and legislature) and to impose binding remedies when executive or legislative decisions restrict rights.

But the parliamentary rights model treats the function of a bill of rights differently than does the more conventional model. It conceives of judgment about rights as being proactive, more fluid, and involving more state actors than reliance exclusively or primarily on judges. Judicial review, in other words, is but one component of a more complex rights project (Stanhope 2003).

The parliamentary rights model reflects a philosophy about rights protection that is both more modest and yet more ambitious than a more conventional model. The modesty is with respect to claims for remedies. All jurisdictions allow for legislative dissent from judicial rulings by either pre-empting or setting aside the effects of a judicial ruling (Canada) or by not formally obliging legislatures to give effect to a judicial ruling (all remaining jurisdictions). Thus there is no promise for corrective remedies for rights violations. In New Zealand, the United Kingdom and Australia, courts are not authorized to grant remedies apart from those that arise via judges' interpretive powers when reviewing legislation. So unless judges can reinterpret the scope or effects of legislation to ensure compliance with rights, remedial measures are dependent on political will and action. However, it is necessary to qualify this statement of modesty when considering Canada. The Canadian judiciary's remedial powers are considerably stronger than in the other parliamentary bills of rights and, in practice, their scope and effects on legislation are almost indistinguishable from those of American courts. As mentioned above, Canada is situated far closer to the American end of the continuum distinguishing weak from strong-form judicial review. This position is due in large part to the constitutional authority of courts to grant strong-form remedies that include declaring legislation invalid, and the willingness of the Canadian judiciary to interpret its role in a robust manner. But this position is also explained by the emergence of a political culture of legal compliance, in which governments regularly accept the authority of judicial rulings and rarely invoke the notwithstanding clause (the federal government has never used this power) or refuse to revise legislation to satisfy judicial objections. Thus, Canadian political practices and assumptions greatly undermine the significance of having adopted the notwithstanding clause as a way of tempering judicial power.

But if the parliamentary model must claim modesty in terms of remedies (Canada, being the exception), in another sense it is far more ambitious than a more traditional, court-centric approach. Instead of relying on courts to remedy rights violations that have already arisen, parliamentary bills of rights reflect the optimistic ambition that new incentives and procedures will encourage public and political officials to consider rights explicitly in their deliberations about what constitutes good public policy decisions, and reduce the likelihood of passing legislation that violates rights, whether done so unknowingly or knowingly. This attention to rights is expected to accrue from having to fulfil the ministerial requirement to report to parliament if legislative bills are inconsistent with rights (discussed below) and also from a strong political incentive to avoid parliamentary and political criticism, expected to follow upon a decision to introduce rights-offending legislation (Driedger 1977). Some have characterized this approach as a 'ground up' rights culture as distinct from the 'top-down' version associated with judicial supremacy (Huscroft and Rishworth 2009). If successful, this proactive idea suggests a far more comprehensive and systematic approach to rights protection than a reactive one where protection is limited principally to the infrequent occurrences of successful constitutional litigation.

In summary, conflicting views about the prudence or desirability of a weak-form model reflect a debate about how a bill of rights functions, and how judicial review relates to the rights project. The more established version is that a bill of rights functions principally as an instrument to ensure that judicial answers to rights conflicts prevail over political judgment, and to correct rights problems that have occurred (while also recognizing, implicitly, that judicial decisions will provide guidelines for future legislative decisions, but without necessarily being mindful of whether this occurs). The parliamentary rights version differs. It is less inclined to equate judicial rulings with the definitive authority on the legitimacy of legislation. Instead of relying exclusively on courts to resolve contested issues, more emphasis is placed on the idea of facilitating awareness of how state actions implicate rights at the time legislative initiatives are considered, framed and evaluated. In short, it places less emphasis on the idea of correcting rights infringements and more emphasis on how to improve the quality of legislative decision-making.

2.2 Reassessing the Role of Legislatures in Judgment about Rights

Constitutional commentators have long lamented the institutional division of labour that bills of rights encourage; specifically, the tendency to look to courts rather than parliament to resolve contentious issues that implicate rights and divide society. James Bradley Thayer discussed this danger for the United States more than a century ago (Thayer 1893) and Peter Russell echoed this concern 90 years later in the Canadian context, warning that the Charter could transform social and political conflicts into technical-legal questions, for which citizens and politicians look to courts for answers (Russell 1983, 49).

But another perceived problem with American-style judicial review is not unlike the problem many associated with Westminster-systems before they adopted bills of rights: the lack of assurance that public and political officials are sufficiently attentive to rights when developing and evaluating legislation. The concern with the American approach arises from its heavy reliance on judicial review to resolve conflicting views of constitutional norms, resulting not only in the concerns Thayer addressed, but also in dependence on a 'constrained' body that can offer, at best, partial and delayed remedies (Rosenberg 1991). Only a fraction of legislation will actually be litigated and thus if legislatures pass rights-offending legislation, very little of this will result in explicit judicial censure. In short, reliance only on judicial review would not change the fact that the majority of legislation is unchecked in terms of its consistency with rights. Many American scholars have argued for more political and popular engagement with rights to address perceived problems with a court-centric (and for some overly formalistic) interpretation of rights. For example, Mark Tushnet argues for a more 'populist constitutional law' that leaves 'a wide range open for resolution through principled political discussions' rather than equating judicial rulings with strict constitutional requirements (Tushnet 2000, 185); Larry Kramer calls for an earlier tradition of popular constitutionalism to recognize 'the democratic pedigree and superior evaluative capabilities of the political branches' (Kramer 2004, 220), and Cornelia Pillard argues that the executive branch should refrain from casting judicial constitutional doctrines as 'exhaustive of the Constitution's normative scope'.[24]

Parliamentary bills of rights respond to the concern for political engagement with constitutional principles by making it difficult for government to pass legislation without consideration for or awareness of its implication for rights. A key consideration for many reform-minded politicians and constitutional scholars in Westminster systems has been whether and how a bill of rights can improve rights sensitivity in legislative decision-making.[25] Unease with both rival approaches, and the realization that a blend of Westminster and American constitutional principles is indeed possible, encouraged broaching a bill of rights as an exercise in constitutional engineering: an attempt to construct a rights project to change political and bureaucratic behaviour.

This way of looking at constitutional reform was evident in early Canadian debates about a bill of rights, when a statutory bill of rights was viewed as a good way to augment parliament's rights-protecting capacity.[26] However, a different set of political incentives drove the Charter debate two decades later, and emphasized nation-building objectives instead.[27] But in subsequent developments, explicit consideration that a bill of rights could improve legislative processes became a more important part of bill of rights debates. In New Zealand, support for a bill of rights grew out of concerns about checking executive dominance (Rishworth 1995) and former opponents of a bill of rights began to argue in favour of this radical reform (Palmer 1992, 51–70). When it became apparent that an entrenched bill of rights was not a viable option, then Prime Minister Geoffrey Palmer decided to adapt the Canadian practice of having the executive review bills in terms of their consistency with protected rights and report to parliament, which he saw as serving two useful functions: 'First, to ensure that the internal mechanisms of government addressed the issues seriously and with full legal analysis and second, that the political consequences of breaching the standards were brought to the fore'.[28] The idea of using a bill of rights to improve legislative decision-making in this way was also important in rights debates in the United Kingdom.[29] United Kingdom politicians have claimed the benefits of political rights review in no less profound terms than the potential to transform political culture. As Lord Falconer stated in 2004, 'we didn't bring in the Human Rights Act to get a litigation culture. We brought it in to get a human rights culture' (Falconer 2004). This idea was also prominent in Australian bill of rights debates,[30] where proponents have optimistically touted the potential of a bill of rights to prevent 'human rights problems arising in the first place' by 'improving the work of government and Parliament in the making and application of laws and policies' (Williams 2006, 893).

All of the parliamentary jurisdictions discussed here have adopted a requirement that parliament be apprised if the relevant minister is unable to report the bill is compatible with rights (some jurisdictions require compatibility reports as well). This precipitates regular assessments of legislative initiatives by the government's policy and legal advisors.[31] Proponents envisaged this practice of political rights review would enhance bureaucratic and political awareness about how legislation implicates rights; encourage political ministers to think long and hard about the merits of introducing rights-offending legislation (largely because of anticipated criticism of the introduction of rights-offending legislation); and increase parliament's attention to the rights dimension of legislation and augment its willingness to hold government to account for decisions affecting rights (Hiebert 2004; 2006). This reporting obligation differs slightly between jurisdictions, and obliges the Minister of Justice (Canada), Attorney General (New Zealand and ACT), relevant cabinet minister (United Kingdom), or the member introducing a bill (Victoria) to report to parliament on whether legislation is compatible with the bill of rights.[32]

Although some question the claimed significance of political rights review as a distinct characteristic of the parliamentary rights model (see, for example, Gardbaum, 2009), important differences exist between Westminster systems and separated systems such as the United States in terms of the nature and regularity of political rights review, when in the legislative process it occurs, and the incentives driving it.

In Westminster systems, political rights review has become a regular and systematic part of the policy process and occurs before legislation is introduced to parliament.[33] Specific guidelines and processes have been developed in all of the jurisdictions discussed here, not only to apprise relevant policy and political officials of how proposed legislation implicates rights, but also to consider changes to mitigate potential rights problems when they are considered excessive or inappropriate. One motivation for these new processes and guidelines is the new ministerial reporting obligation on compatibility, which in some jurisdictions has inspired a strong political presumption against introducing legislation that requires acknowledging it is inconsistent with rights. Judgment about consistency is influenced significantly by relevant case law. But in some jurisdictions (in particular, Canada and the United Kingdom), the more compelling motivation has been to anticipate and minimize the likelihood that courts will rule that legislation is invalid or incompatible with protected rights.[34] The Canadian and United Kingdom bills of rights have created new concerns for governments about the stability or longer-term viability of legislation and, in response, public and political officials have integrated judicial perspectives on rights and proportionality (derived from case law) when assessing and refining legislative initiatives. This is done both to gauge the level of risk associated with proposed legislation and to derive ways to reduce that risk. This practice occurs despite limits on judicial power because political dissent is not always possible (for political reasons in Canada and because of the presumption of treaty compliance in the United Kingdom). Although governments do not always adopt risk-averse measures, what is important to realize is the significance of how the Westminster systems operate; the executive dominates, strict party discipline prevails, and legislation is introduced at an advanced stage to a weak parliament. Thus, should government decide to incorporate judicial norms when deciding the scope of proposed legislation or the means used to pursue the policy objective, its hegemony over the legislative process ensures it generally encounters weak resistance from parliament (Hiebert 2011).[35]

In contrast, although rights talk takes place in the United States Congress, it occurs in a less formal and more political way. Parallel surveys conducted over a 20-year interval reveal that a majority of Congressional respondents believe Congress should exercise its own judgment on constitutional questions (Peabody 2005). However, this perception does not appear to have radically skewed how Congress operates. For the most part, constitutional issues are not treated as priority concerns for Congress where decision-making is dominated by political and policy considerations (Pickerill 2004). Moreover, even if a political interest or institutional mechanism existed that compelled members to assess whether proposed legislation is consistent with rights, the separation of powers ensures Congress has far greater institutional capacity to amend or derail proposed legislation. Thus it would be unlikely that even if proposed legislation consciously started out as being consistent with rights, it would necessarily remain so upon its passage.

Differences in pre-legislative review are not as significant when comparing Westminster systems with European political systems. Alec Stone Sweet's analysis of political behaviour under constitutional courts in France, Germany, Italy and Spain suggests similar practices as occur in Westminster systems (particularly Canada and the United Kingdom) in terms of the use of case law to minimize the possibility of judicial censure.[36] As Stone Sweet argues, legislators regularly express their policy differences in the vocabulary of constitutional judges; so much so that debates about the merits of policy have been largely displaced by debates about constitutional compliance. Thus, as Stone Sweet states, 'governing with judges means governing like judges' (Stone Sweet 2000, 204).

Little published research compares the effects of political rights review in parliamentary jurisdictions and whether and how it affects outcomes. Four large questions come to mind when considering political rights review. First, is parliamentary behaviour changing so as to exert more pressure on government to account for its judgment where questions arise about whether proposed legislation is compatible with rights? And if so, are some issues more likely than others to result in parliament playing a robust role in this regard? Second, do all parliamentary jurisdictions operate in the same way? Where differences exist, what accounts for these? Specifically, does the scope of judicial power matter or whether a bill of rights is constitutional or statutory? Third, how is compatibility determined? Is compatibility determined on the basis of assessments of similar issues in existing case law and/or predictions about how courts will likely rule? Or does political judgment about compatibility reflect political actors' independent assessments (particularly on issues of proportionality around which the majority of questions of compatibility arise)? Fourth, does the existence of a specialized parliamentary committee enhance parliament's capacity to engage in robust rights-based scrutiny?

With respect to the first question, preliminary research on Canada, New Zealand and the United Kingdom does not suggest that parliament has been overly active when evaluating governmental claims that legislation is compatible with rights (in Canada, the government's claim of compatibility must be inferred from the absence of a report that a bill is incompatible). Commentators suggest that the absence of reports in Canada and the lack of explanation for the government's assumptions behind its implicit claims of compatibility have discouraged parliamentary attention to the issue (Hiebert 2002; Kelly 2005; Kelly 2009). Moreover, James Kelly argues that unless a change is made at the federal level of government in Canada to separate the Office of the Minister of Justice from the Office of the Attorney-General, it is unlikely that assessments of compatibility can escape partisan perspectives (Kelly 2009, 98–103). In New Zealand, some scholars argue that the problem is that too many bills are subject to reports of incompatibility (even in cases where reasonable claims can be made that the 'offending' bill is consistent with proportionality criteria), which undermines parliament's willingness to pay attention to these (Hiebert 2005; Huscroft 2003, 214–16). Others criticize the New Zealand process for being incomplete for not evaluating amended legislation in terms of compatibility and also for not subjecting the Attorney-General's claims of compatibility to scrutiny by a dedicated parliamentary committee (Butler and Butler 2005).

The relatively weak role played by Westminster parliaments in challenging legislation on rights-based terms appears to be inconsistent with what occurs in Europe. European opposition parties utilize constitutional strategies more vigorously to change legislative outcomes; in particular, by taking advantage of the practice of abstract review by constitutional courts. As Alec Stone Sweet argues, abstract review is a popular and relatively cost-free way for opposition politicians to pursue their own policy objectives, by creating the possibility for judicial decisions that bind the legislative majority without the possibility for appeal. This possibility, and the frequency with which it is employed, has resulted in substantial judicial influence over legislation (Stone Sweet 2000, 74–5). In contrast, Westminster systems do not have abstract review[37] and, consequently, opposition parties lack this extra-parliamentary opportunity afforded European opposition parties to veto or alter legislative outcomes. Thus, the extent to which Westminster governments incorporate judicial norms into decision-making is largely determined by a government's calculations of the likely judicial and political consequences associated with either pursuing risky legislation or constraining the scope or effects of a legislative initiative in an attempt to minimize the risk of a negative judicial ruling (Hiebert 2011).

But whatever strategies government employs, strong reasons exist for scepticism that a bill of rights will empower parliament vis-a-vis the executive, despite optimistic claims to the contrary. Evidence does not indicate that these bills of rights have significantly increased parliament's willingness or capacity to regularly or frequently force the government to amend bills that have adverse implications for rights. Notwithstanding the new statutory reporting obligation on whether bills are compatible with protected rights, the very idea that legislative debates focus on consistency with a bill of rights represents a significant departure from the behaviour and practices of Westminster parliamentary systems. Westminster parliaments operate in a manner where debate amongst highly disciplined and adversarial political parties is oriented to emphasize two viewpoints – in favour or opposed of the government's actions. Not only is this approach not conducive to a principled debate on the justification of legislation from a rights perspective, but since government generally dominates parliament, it is often able to exercise its hegemony over the legislative process to resist amendments that would delay or alter bills. If government finds itself in the position of having to regularly accept proposed amendments, this will be interpreted, politically, as a sign of weakness. This concern is intensified by the peremptory character of rights-based criticisms. Although all parties expect and confront disagreement on the basis of ideology or the policy differences that distinguish political parties, for a government to be criticized for violating rights can seem uncomfortably close to being viewed as morally suspect. For these reasons, a government is extremely reluctant to encourage a form or language of parliamentary debate where rights-based claims can be used to alter, delay or veto government bills (Hiebert 2011).

As for the second question, preliminary research suggests that the degree to which a bill of rights alters or constrains legislation in Westminster-based parliamentary systems is influenced significantly by whether governments perceive there are substantial political and legal consequences for failing to comply with rights. Canada has the highest costs associated with passing inconsistent legislation, not only because courts can invalidate legislation, but also because a political culture of legal compliance has emerged, which discourages government from enacting the s. 33 notwithstanding clause to set aside the effect of a negative judicial ruling. But the United Kingdom also incurs significant costs for passing inconsistent legislation because of the treaty character of the European Convention of Human Rights, which operates to foster a presumptive expectation of compliance. Thus, governments in Canada and the United Kingdom must regularly make difficult political calculations about whether they are willing to incur the political costs and consequences associated with passing legislation that will likely incur judicial censure. New Zealand and Australia do not have the same impetus for legal compliance with court rulings and the principal consideration for government when determining whether or not to comply with judicial rulings is largely political: how will defiance or compliance affect the government's claim of competence; how does compliance affect policy objectives to which the government is strongly committed; and what are the political and electoral consequences of compliance or defiance of judicial opinions? (Hiebert 2011).

With respect to the third question, preliminary research suggests that the policy advice given to ministers is heavily influenced by relevant case law.[38] However, in terms of parliamentary behaviour, bicameralism might be a variable influencing whether parliament challenges or accepts judicial perspectives on compatibility, at least in the context of the United Kingdom. Danny Nicol (2004) reveals that sharp differences occur between the rights culture in the Commons and the Lords. In the Commons, considerable controversy has arisen about whether and how rights should frame political debates, and whether judicial interpretations of rights should constrain parliament's will when deciding how best to reconcile social policy concerns with Convention rights (particularly on matters of order and security). However, responses differ significantly in the House of Lords, where a culture of compliance is more discernible, and where peers 'fall over themselves to raise Convention points in order to dissuade government' from legislating in ways that may be inconsistent with judicial interpretations of Convention rights.[39] In Canada, although a strong political culture of legal compliance generally exists, in rare cases parliament has exerted independent judgment about the scope of rights. The best example occurred in the context of judicial rules in sexual assault criminal proceedings, where parliament passed legislation that made explicit its views that the Supreme Court had reached an inappropriate judgment about the resolution of conflicting rights (Hiebert 2002, 91–117). In New Zealand, despite a large number of Attorney-General reports that bills are inconsistent with the Bill of Rights, these have seldom led to parliamentary challenges of their assumptions or pressure for amendments (Hiebert 2005, 77–89).

With respect to the fourth question, scholars have argued for the creation of specialized parliamentary committees to scrutinize ministerial claims that bills are compatible with rights and to focus attention on whether bills are justified in light of their implications for rights (Hiebert 2002; Kelly 2005; Butler and Butler 2005). The United Kingdom was the first jurisdiction to adopt a specialized committee (the Joint Committee on Human Rights) and both Australian jurisdictions have parliamentary committees to examine issues of compatibility (Evans and Evans 2008). Research is required to address the question of whether the creation of a specialized committee can overcome the institutional constraints that currently undermine parliament's capacity or willingness to hold government to account for its interpretation and judgment about rights. Some of the relevant questions are: does the size of parliament matter in terms of finding members willing to resist party discipline or the sanctions imposed by party leaders? Does it make a difference if parliament is unicameral or bicameral, or if the committee is jointly constituted? Is the committee chaired by a member of government or the opposition? Do government members constitute a numerical majority on the committee? How much influence does the legal advisor exert? How early or late in the process does the committee report? Does the government respond to the committee's questions and, if so, does this occur at a stage when amendments can be made?

In the absence of more research on whether and how reporting obligations influence parliament's behaviour, or what impact parliamentary rights committees have, many remain sceptical about claims made that bills of rights and/or procedures for political rights review will fundamentally alter parliamentary behaviour. The very idea that these reporting mechanisms would increase parliament's capacity in this way reflects a basic paradox; parliamentary bills of rights are simultaneously defended because parliament is considered too weak to force government to ensure that legislation is consistent with rights, and yet are celebrated because of the hope that parliament will play a strong rights-protecting role. But these ministerial reporting requirements have not augmented parliament's formal powers in any way. For these reasons, Keith Ewing warns that parliamentary control 'can only be as effective as parliament is powerful' (Ewing 2007, 316), while John Uhr similarly cautions that parliament (or more accurately a parliamentary committee) 'is only as powerful as its relationship to the house from which its members come and to which it reports' (Uhr 2006, 53). James Kelly argues that rather than enhance parliament's role, the process of evaluating proposed legislation for its consistency with rights has actually weakened parliament, at least in Canada, because rights vetting 'complicates an essential role of parliamentarians – the political and constitutional scrutiny of the Cabinet's legislative agenda' (Kelly 2009, 94). Others question the logic of having those who restrict rights also judge whether these restrictions are appropriate. Thus, Cécile Fabre argues that if individuals 'have rights against the legislature, the latter should not be judge in conflicts it has with rights-bearers' (Fabre 2002, 89).

2.3   Questioning the Relationship between Legislative and Judicial Judgment

A third issue that provokes scholarly debate is the relationship between legislative and judicial judgment. Scholars dispute the balance this model strikes between political and judicial responsibility, and how the resolution of inter-institutional disagreements is conceived.

Michael Perry believes this possibility for parliamentary dissent from a judicial ruling is valuable in addressing the longstanding concern attributed to Thayer, that a bill of rights could otherwise condition government and the people to renege on their responsibility to work through difficult issues that implicate rights, and rely instead on courts to resolve the issues (Perry 2003, 693). But even if scholars accept the virtue of conceiving of judicial review in a penultimate rather than final form, many are sceptical about the balance this model will achieve between political and judicial judgment. At a general level, scepticism is directed at the very stability of the parliamentary rights model itself. Mark Tushnet argues that instability could occur at both ends of the continuum distinguishing weak- from strong-form systems. At one end of the continuum, constrained court models could relapse into parliamentary sovereignty if governments refuse to reassess legislation after courts identify rights problems, or if the courts capitulate to political decisions where strong institutional disagreements arise. At the other end of the continuum, these systems could evolve to resemble the judicial dominance associated with the US model, particularly if there is judicial insistence on increasingly precise requirements to ensure legislation is compliant with protected rights. It might also evolve in this way if there are high political costs associated with relying on constitutionally accepted forms of political disagreement (Tushnet 2003, 827–37). In support of this view is Tom Campbell's argument that political behaviour could be highly susceptible to judicial perspectives because of the perception that only judges are competent to decide what constitutes a right or an appropriate restriction on a right. As he argues, the equation of rights with law is difficult to resist, no matter whether a bill of rights allows for explicit disagreements with judicial perspectives (Campbell 2001, 87).

Another factor that could undermine stability is if judges regularly interpret legislation in a way that alters its scope or effects. Should they do so, these judgments might escape political notice because they do not involve the publicly visible act of declaring that legislation is incompatible, or require jurisdictions to act assertively to restore the earlier legislative intention. As Danny Nicol argues in the context of the United Kingdom, if courts do not feel compelled to respect legislative intentions or language, their power to effectively 'rewrite' legislation represents a potent yet 'relatively invisible means of changing the law in contrast to headline-grabbing declarations of incompatibility' (Nicol 2004, 468).

Related to this scepticism about the stability of the parliamentary rights model, are questions about the effectiveness of limits on judicial power. Tom Campbell argues that the 'scope and power of the interpretive techniques that are licensed by the United Kingdom's HRA will make judges the determinate body with respect to a wide range of policy issues which have hitherto been fully within the sphere of parliamentary responsibility' (Campbell 2001, 80). Similarly, Alison Young argues that the judiciary's interpretive role will impose a more dramatic constraint on parliament than might have been anticipated, suggesting that the wording of the judiciary's responsibilities gives it 'carte blanche to determine when it is impossible to interpret statutes in a manner compatible with Convention rights' because the limits imposed on judicial power are so malleable as to have little meaning (Young 2002, 64–5). Even in New Zealand where judicial power is extremely weak, sceptics like James Allan argue that judicial interpretative techniques undermine the claim that weak-form judicial review represents a substantive alternative to strong form judicial review (Allan 2001, 390).

Many scholars also challenge a central claim of the model; as managing to introduce judicial rights review and yet preserve parliament's capacity to have the final word. In Canada, it is difficult to argue persuasively that parliament has any more than a temporary ability to delay a judicial ruling. Not only is the notwithstanding clause rarely used (and does not apply to all rights in the Charter), it does not operate to change constitutional meaning. Courts have the final authority on the interpretation of the Charter, and on what constitutes appropriate remedies for rights violations, as stipulated in s. 52 of the Constitution Act 1982.[40] In the United Kingdom, although political proponents have been adamant that the HRA does not compromise the principle of parliamentary supremacy,[41] many suggest this claim is hollow. Mark Elliott argues that even prior to the introduction of the HRA, claims of parliamentary sovereignty did not accurately describe the reality of the legislature's constitutional position because of British membership in the European Union, where the European Court of Justice has ruled that EU law takes priority over the laws of individual states (Elliott 2004).

Another purported benefit of this model is its claimed potential to encourage intra- and inter-institutional reflection on the justification of legislation that implicates rights. Several features of this model facilitate this: the ministerial reporting obligation on compatibility (discussed above); the creation in some jurisdictions of a specific parliamentary committee to review legislation that implicates rights (United Kingdom, ACT and Victoria); and recognition that legislative dissent from judicial rulings is constitutionally permissible. This idea of inter-institutional reflection is often portrayed in dialogic terms. Although the metaphor of dialogue is also used in the United States, its use differs in parliamentary models. Constitutional dialogue in the American context has more to do with theories of separation of powers[42] or the broad influence judicial rulings have on societal or legislative perceptions about controversial legislation.[43] But those using this metaphor in Westminster systems tend to think of it in terms of a specific reaction to judicial review. This idea that judicial rulings will (and should) influence legislation is extremely prevalent in Canada (Hogg and Bushell 1997; Roach 2001). This understanding of dialogue has also been pervasive in the United Kingdom,[44] where despite political criticism of the Human Rights Act and judicial review of it, a strong expectation prevails that the UK parliament should pass remedial legislation when courts make a declaration of incompatibility.[45] Consistent with this expectation, the HRA incorporates an expedited procedure for passing remedial legislation. References to dialogue are even more prominent in Australian rights debates[46] and both bills of rights have institutional mechanisms intended to encourage political responses to negative judicial rulings.[47]

But scholars are divided on the virtues of conceiving of institutional relationships in dialogic terms. The claim most associated with the dialogue metaphor in Westminster systems is that by permitting legislative dissent, this model allows for judicial influence on legislation in ways that mitigate democratic objections to a bill of rights. This is because judicial rulings do not prevent legislative revision to address rights-offending elements of legislation, and this possibility for a legislative response thwarts democratic objections to judicial review (Hogg and Bushell 1997; Hogg et al. 2007).

Yet many are sceptical about whether dialogue is a useful metaphor for assessing institutional relationships under a bill of rights. Some criticize this concept of dialogue because of its presumption that other branches of government should be bound to act in accordance with the judiciary's interpretation of the Charter rather than challenge it if they think the Court has erred (Huscroft 2007, 101) and for the assumption of those invoking this metaphor that legislative outcomes that differ from a judicial ruling are exceptions to rights, rather than alternative interpretations of their appropriate scope (Manfredi 2001, 188–95). These concerns have led to the suggestion that the more appropriate metaphor is 'monologue' (Morton 2001) or 'ventriloquism' (Manfredi and Kelly 1999, 521). However, a more recent formulation of dialogue theory for Canada addresses this concern, in part, by arguing that the Supreme Court should defer to the legislature's interpretation of the Charter in 'second look cases' where 'deference is reasonable when judged by reference to certain minimal criteria' (Dixon 2009, 240).

Others criticize the metaphor of dialogue as masking the problem of having unelected courts influence social policy and political priorities, particularly when contested values are involved (Petter 2007). A different criticism of the debate, at least the Canadian version, is that the judicial contribution to dialogue does not occur around the clash in philosophical opinions about the meaning of rights or the importance of particular rights claims versus the public importance of a legislative goal. It arises instead over the more technical, policy-laden issues about the quality of government's chosen means for pursuing a particular legislative goal. But this is precisely the terrain for which courts are at a disadvantage, relative to the resources available to government (Hiebert 2002, 50–51). Finally, some commentators have criticized the Canadian version of this debate for being preoccupied with stages of the judicial inquiry, rather than addressing the broader notion that shared responsibility for constitutional interpretation presumes there will be occasions when parliaments and courts disagree (Gardbaum 2009).

3   CONCLUSIONS

The parliamentary rights model charts a new path that differs significantly from the constitutional foundations from which it arose and from those that inspired change. It challenges earlier practices in Westminster systems, where rights did not function as discrete standards against which parliamentary actions would be judged, and where courts had no explicit role to pronounce on the merits of duly-enacted legislation from a rights perspective. It also challenges the more conventional model of a bill of rights that gives courts final authority to interpret the meaning of rights and determine the appropriate remedies where rights are infringed.

Yet despite conceiving of judicial review in limited or more constrained terms, in an important sense, the parliamentary rights model has a similar objective to more conventional bills of rights: to elevate rights as critical standards from which to evaluate the legitimacy of state actions. But this objective is pursued by reimagining how a bill of rights functions. All bills of rights can stimulate public debate about the meaning of a polity's public norms and values. But more conventional bills of rights emphasize the institutionalization of this debate as occurring more at the judicial than at the political level. Political debates in Congress might engage rights, but the way the United States Bill of Rights has evolved does not assume that political judgment about what makes for good policy will consciously confront the question of whether this policy is consistent with protected rights. Judgment about compatibility with rights norms is considered almost entirely the province of courts.

This is where the parliamentary rights model differs, at least at the level of its vision. It conceives of the function of a bill of rights more in terms of stimulating reflection about rights amongst all who exercise power, rather than being principally the occupation of courts. Rights considerations are expected to consciously guide and constrain legislative actions at the time these decisions are proposed and evaluated. And, leaving aside Canada, if legislation is challenged and courts subsequently disagree that legislation is compatible with rights, these rulings serve to prompt renewed legislative assessments, rather than revoke the earlier legislative decision. In Canada, judicial rulings can set aside legislation, but legislatures can lawfully disagree and set aside the effects of the ruling. Thus, the parliamentary rights model rejects the central assumption associated with conventional views about a bill of rights – that concern for rights is principally a reactive exercise, conducted almost exclusively by courts, which have final authority when interpreting the meaning of rights and determining appropriate remedies where rights are infringed. Explained in terms of how a bill of rights functions, in the American model, it operates principally to correct errant legislation; in the parliamentary model it operates to ratchet up the quality of rights-reflection at all stages of the political process.

Yet despite these significant differences in conceiving the function of these bills of rights, whether the parliamentary rights model will lead to different outcomes has not been determined, and requires qualitative and comparative research. Relevant questions include: does the design of the bill of rights in each jurisdiction affect how policy processes respond to a bill of rights or what legislative outcomes emerge? Does it matter if a bill of rights is statutory or constitutional in terms of how it affects political behaviour or policy assumptions? Is the scope of judicial power relevant to how government behaves? Does the nature of the legislature (unicameral vs. bicameral or size) or the kind of electoral system in place (single member plurality or proportional representation) affect parliament's capacity to engage in robust rights scrutiny? Is parliament willing and able to compel government to revise legislative initiatives where rights are being restricted and, if so, under what circumstances? What explains decisions by government to abide by rights-based constraints that prevent or alter legislative objectives to which it is strongly committed, particularly when bills of rights allow for disagreement with judicial decisions? Conversely, what explains government decisions to knowingly introduce legislation that has a high risk of being declared inconsistent with rights? These questions provide legal scholars and political scientists with a rich research agenda in the coming years.

NOTES

*   I would like to acknowledge financial assistance in the form of a grant from the Social Science and Humanities Research Council of Canada.
1.   Conventional wisdom considered the ideas of parliamentary supremacy and an effective bill of rights as being mutually exclusive, and that no middle ground was possible. The incompatibility arose from the presumption that a bill of rights establishes lawful constraints on parliament's powers; the scope of which are determined not by parliament but by the judiciary, which is authorized to grant remedies for infringements that can include the invalidation of inconsistent legislation. Thus, to grant the judiciary authority to limit parliament's power in these ways contradicts the parliament's capacity to have the final word on what constitutes constitutionally permissible state action.
2.   See, for example, *City of Boerne v Flores*, 521 US at 519. For discussion, see Tushnet (2003), 818.
3.   This point must be qualified for Canada. The Canadian Charter is a constitutional bill of rights that gives courts final authority on issues of compatibility. Although provincial legislatures or the federal parliament can set aside the effects of a judicial ruling under the Charter, these decisions, while renewable, are still temporary and do not alter the court's interpretation of constitutional requirements.
4.   Conceptually, the idea of a continuum could be problematic because, as Mark Tushnet argues, a single political system can have tendencies towards both polls. Tushnet (2008), 43–76.
5.   This question is not unique to the reasons for adopting parliamentary bills of rights, but has been considered in a much broader context. See, for example, Ginsburg (2003), Hirschl (2004), Finkel (2008), and Erdos (2008).
6.   Bradley and Ewing (2003), 404–05, quoting from J.P. Mackintosh, *The Government and Politics of Britain*, 7th edition (1988).
7.   The majority of but not all Charter rights are subject to the notwithstanding clause. Exceptions include voting rights, the requirement that legislative assemblies meet and regular elections be held, mobility rights, and minority education language rights.
8.   The notwithstanding clause also represents the Charter's most obvious concession to federalism, because by allowing provincial (as well as federal) legislatures to dissent from judicial decisions, or pre-empt judicial review altogether, it allows for the accommodation of territorial-based diversity. But this federal feature has little impact on constitutional developments elsewhere, as the only parliamentary federal jurisdiction to adopt a bill of rights (Australia) has done so only at the sub-national level.
9.   This can be inferred from Rainer Knopff's and F.L. Morton's criticism of the Charter and their preference for political rather than judicial checks on power. See Knopff and Morton (1992) and Morton and Knopff (2000).
10.   For an assessment of the uses of the notwithstanding clause, see Kahana (2001).
11.   In the early days of the Charter, it was not uncommon for Canadian constitutional scholars to encounter gentle gibes from American colleagues about the half-hearted or imitation bill of rights the Charter purportedly represented, because of its inclusion of the notwithstanding clause.
12.   Paul Rishworth writes that the Canadian Charter provided inspiration for the White Paper draft proposed a bill of rights. The Charter was also influential in that its text provided a useful precedent for a New Zealand Bill of rights, and also because early Charter experience gave New Zealand 'clues' as to what these rights might mean. Rishworth (1995), 13.
13.   Although proponents of or commentators on a New Zealand Bill of Rights do not consider the notwithstanding clause to have influenced the choice or design of the Bill of Rights, it is important to remember that its original genesis in the 1960 statutory Canadian Bill of Rights conveyed the presumption that courts were to interpret legislation as intending to respect rights unless faced with an explicit indication to the contrary. This same presumption underlies the authority conferred on courts in the New Zealand Bill of Rights Act.
14.   Information obtained from email conversation between the author and Paul Rishworth, 15 September 2009.
15.   Email conversation with Paul Rishworth, 15 September 2009.
16.   This term is borrowed from Charles Epp (1998).
17.   Some supporters of a bill of rights had the opposite concern with the idea of a notwithstanding clause – that it would be invoked too often. Lord Lester (1997), 128–9.
18.   Interview with Francesca Klug, May 18 2004, London.
19.   Canada is an exception here because judicial review represents the authoritative interpretation of the Canadian Charter of Rights and Freedoms. For this reason, I quibble with the characterization of Canada as a weak-form system. See Hiebert (2006), 10–12.
20.   In Canada, this requires use of the notwithstanding clause of s. 33 of the Charter. In New Zealand, the scope of the judicial power does not allow courts to formally declare legislation inconsistent.
21.   Sujit Choudhry uses this conception in his discussion of the nation-building function of a bill of rights. Choudhry (2009), 239.
22.   This question is posed frequently by students who puzzle over the significance of a model that does not give courts the remedial powers to 'fix' the problem. That these students are Canadian reinforces the fact that

Canada does not fit as comfortably within this new paradigm or hybrid approach to rights protection as might be assumed from the Charter's purported 'hybrid' character.

23. I am borrowing here from a conversation with Michael Tolley who, in discussing this new model, quipped that he preferred a 'strong rights model' in the sense of stronger remedial powers to correct rights-offending legislation. Meeting of the Research Committee on Comparative Judicial Studies (International Political Studies Association, Group No. 9), Montréal, 25–6 June 2008.

24. Cornelia Pillard identifies numerous opportunities for executive constitutional judgment, as a result of inherent gaps in what courts can review, ambiguity in what previous rulings mean for new or novel issues, the possibility of shaping judicial reviews during litigation, judicial avoidance, and judicial deference, particularly on national security, military or immigration issues. Pillard (2005), 9, 44.

25. Tom Campbell has suggested an alternative form of rights protection: a Rights Council that would have institutional mechanisms to hold the government to account for decisions that harm rights. Campbell (2006), 319–41.

26. In 1960, then Prime Minister John Diefenbaker introduced the Canadian Bill of Rights; a statutory bill of rights that applied only to the federal level of government. Diefenbaker differed from conventional views about the role and function of a bill of rights. Rather than rely exclusively on judicial review, he thought it possible and desirable to improve the working of Parliament so as to strengthen its role as custodian of civil liberties. For a good discussion of the origins of the Canadian Bill of Rights, see MacLennan (2003), 148.

27. Constitutional negotiations reflected conflicting nation-building projects, one reflecting a pan-Canadian version of nationalism (complicated by differing views on the appropriate balance of powers between the provincial and federal governments), and a very different nation-building project, emphasizing Quebec nationalism and seeking economic and political autonomy. A constitutional bill of rights was a core element of then Prime Minister Pierre Trudeau's pan-Canadian project, but was extremely contentious, particularly at the political level. Trudeau's desire for a constitutional bill of rights with emphasis on individual rights, which he hoped would transcend provincial and, in particular, Quebec identities, was strongly opposed by the Quebec premier and a majority of the other provincial premiers, who perceived it as an abrupt rupture to, rather than refinement of, Canadian constitutional principles. For a good discussion of the constitutional debates around the Charter, see Russell (2004).

28. Palmer (1992), 59–60.

29. As Jack Straw, then Home Secretary, said of the role of the HRA: 'We didn't incorporate the Convention principles and norms as playthings for the lawyers. They have a much wider and more important social utility. The point here is that the Human Rights Act makes the Convention principles and norms all-pervasive. Ministers and all public authorities will need to be ready to show that they have had them constantly in mind in making decisions affecting people's civil and political rights …' Straw (1999). See also Francesca Klug (2000).

30. The Report of the Victoria Human Rights Consultation Committee concluded that one of the strongest arguments for adopting a bill of rights is to improve governance, and recommended a specialist unit be established in the Department of Justice to assist the government in identifying and considering human rights. *Rights, Responsibilities and Respect: The Report of the Human Rights Consultation Committee* (Victoria) (2005), 108–11. See also George Williams (2006).

31. James Kelly and I have interviewed more than 150 public officials in these various jurisdictions to examine how bills are evaluated. In all jurisdictions, there is heavy reliance on case law when determining whether or not bills are consistent with rights. Advice is provided to relevant ministers, often in the form of a risk assessment of the likelihood of a negative judicial ruling. This research is as yet unpublished and has been undertaken for a comparative book project on whether and how these parliamentary bills of rights are influencing legislative outcomes.

32. In Canada, s. 4.1 of the Department of Justice Act requires the Minister of Justice in Canada (who also serves as Attorney-General) to alert parliament where bills are inconsistent with the Charter. Section 7 of the New Zealand Bill of Rights Act requires that the Attorney-General advise parliament when bills are not consistent with its provisions. In the United Kingdom, s. 19 of the HRA requires the sponsoring minister of a bill to report either that it is compatible with Convention rights or that he or she is unable to make a report of compatibility. This report must be made to both houses of parliament (Canada requires a report only to the House of Commons while New Zealand is a unicameral system). What this means in the UK is that when a bill passes from one house to the other, a second statement will be required, which must take into account earlier amendments made. The respective statements will be made by whichever minister has been given responsibility in the particular house. In the Australian Capital Territory, ss. 37(1) and (2) oblige the Attorney-General to make a compatibility statement about every bill presented to the Assembly by a minister. In Victoria, s. 28(2) of the Victoria Charter of Human Rights and Responsibilities Act requires that a member of Parliament who introduces a Bill into a House of Parliament must 'cause' a statement of compatibility to be prepared and presented before the House of Parliament into which the bill is introduced before his or her second reading speech on the bill.

33. See Kelly (2005); Hiebert (2002), 3–19. Comparative research undertaken by both authors (as yet unpublished) indicates that a similar practice occurs in all of the parliamentary jurisdictions discussed here.

34. Although this reporting obligation was originally intended to improve parliament's rights-protecting role, now that courts have been granted remedial powers that can include setting aside inconsistent legislation, governments' principal focus when evaluating bills is the risk of possible judicial invalidation. No report of incompatibility has ever been made to parliament. This does not mean that Charter considerations have not influenced bills. In fact, new procedures have been introduced requiring that proposed bills be certified as being consistent with the Charter, before proceeding as legislative bills before Parliament. However, there is no transparency and parliament is left unable to ascertain the level of risk that a bill will be ruled inconsistent with the Charter. For criticism of the way this reporting approach has evolved, see Kelly (2009); Hiebert (2005).

35. In New Zealand, it is more difficult for pre-legislative rights review to impact legislation because the electoral system of Mixed Member Proportional (MMP) provides parliament with greater power vis-à-vis the executive, resulting in frequent amendments to bill.

36. Alec Stone Sweet's discussion of the incentives for what he refers to as autolimitation bears a strong resemblance to the kind of pre-emptive judgment made in Canada. Stone Sweet (2000, 75–9).

37. Canada has a procedure for government to place a reference case before the Court for advisory review, but this is not an option for opposition parties.

38. This interpretation is based on research conducted by Kelly and Hiebert.

39. Nicol focused on four important debates in the Commons and Lords spanning six years, including the debate leading up to the Human Rights Act, the Terrorism Bill 1999–2000, the Anti-Terrorism, Crime and Security Bill 2001 and the Nationality, Immigration and Asylum Bill 2002. Nicol (2004), 454–74.

40. S. 52 of the Constitution Act 1982 proclaims: 'The Constitution of Canada is the supreme law of Canada, and any law that is inconsistent with the provisions of the Constitution is, to the extent of the inconsistency, of no force or effect'.

41. This view is well reflected in the Labour government's White Paper that, upon the adoption of human rights legislation, courts should not replace parliament in having the final say on important matters of public policy. A similar claim was made in parliamentary debates about adopting the HRA. White Paper (1997), para. 2.13. See also Jack Straw, House of Commons, 21 October 1998, vol. 317, col. 1357.

42. Louis Fisher (1988).

43. See, for example, Alexander Bickel who equated a judicial ruling with interaction 'with other institutions, with whom it is engaged in an endlessly renewed education conversation'. Bickel (1975), 111. See also Friedman (1993) and Bateup (2007).

44. Jack Straw, HC Deb. [UK] vol. 314, col. 1141 (June 1998).

45. This is suggested by the statement of Lord Irvine, then Lord Chancellor, when he indicated that in the event of a judicial declaration of incompatibility, 'Parliament may, not must, and generally will, legislate. If a Minister's prior assessment of compatibility … is subsequently found … by the courts to have been mistaken, it is hard to see how a Minister could withhold remedial action'. HL Deb. vol. 582, col. 1227–8 (3 November 1997).

46. In speaking of the dialogic potential of the Human Rights Act, Jon Stanhope, Chief Minister, argued before the legislative assembly that the HRA would 'promote a dialogue about human rights within the parliament, between the parliament and the judiciary, and, most importantly, within the Canberra community'. Stanhope (2003), 4250.

47. They instruct the judiciary that an interpretation of legislation that is consistent with rights is preferred, but if the Court concludes that a law is not consistent with rights, it may declare this incompatibility (ACT) or inconsistency (Victoria). Both jurisdictions require that when such judicial declarations of inconsistency are made, the Attorney-General must notify the legislative assembly of this declaration (in ACT within six sitting days of receiving the declaration and in Victoria as soon as reasonably possible) and, within six months, prepare and present to the legislative assembly a written response to the declaration of incompatibility. Part 5 of the Australian Capital Territory Human Rights Act requires the Attorney-General to prepare a written statement of compatibility for the Legislative Assembly, which must state either that the bill is consistent with human rights or if it is not consistent, how it is not consistent. The Charter of Human Rights and Responsibilities Act in Victoria requires in Part 3 (Division 8) that any member of parliament who proposes to introduce a bill into a House of Parliament 'must cause a statement of compatibility to be prepared in respect of that Bill' and must indicate either that the Bill is compatible with rights and, if so, how it is compatible, or that it is incompatible with human rights, and the nature and extent of the incompatibility.

REFERENCES

Agresto, John (1984), *The Supreme Court and Constitutional Democracy*, Ithaca, NY; Cornell University Press.
Albert, Richard (2008), 'Advisory Review: The Reincarnation of the Notwithstanding Clause', *Alberta Law Review*, 45 (4), 1037–69.

Alexander, Larry and Frederick Schauer (1997), 'On Extrajudicial Constitutional Interpretation', *Harvard Law Review*, 110, 1359–87.

Allan, James (2001), 'The Effect of a Statutory Bill of Rights where Parliament is Sovereign: The Lesson from New Zealand', in Tom Campbell, Keith Ewing and Adam Tomkins (eds), *Skeptical Essays on Human Rights*, New York: Oxford University Press.

Bateup, Christine (2007), 'Expanding the Conversation: American and Canadian Experiences of Constitutional Dialogue in Comparative Perspective', *Temple International & Comparative Law Journal*, 21 (2), 1–57.

Bickel, Alexander (1975), *The Morality of Consent*, New Haven: Yale University Press.

Bradley, A.W. and K.D. Ewing (2003), *Constitutional and Administrative Law*, 13th edition, Harlow, Essex: Pearson Education Limited.

Brennan, William, Jr. (1989), 'Why have a Bill of Rights?', *Oxford Journal of Legal Studies*, 9, 425–40.

Butler, Andrew and Petra Butler (2005), *The New Zealand Bill of Rights Act: A Commentary*, Wellington, Lexis Nexis.

Byrnes, Andrew, Hilary Charlesworth and Gabrielle McKinnon (2009), *Bills of Rights in Australia: History, Politics and Law*, Sydney: University of New South Wales Press.

Cameron, Jamie (2004), 'The Charter's Legislative Override: Feat or Figment of the Constitutional Imagination', in Grant Huscroft and Ian Brodie (eds), *Constitutionalism in the Charter Era*, Toronto: LexisNexis, Butterworths, pp. 135–167.

Campbell, Tom (2001), 'Incorporation through Interpretation', in Tom Campbell, Keith Ewing and Adam Tomkins (eds), *Skeptical Essays on Human Rights*, New York: Oxford University Press.

Campbell, Tom (2006), 'Human Rights Strategies: An Australian Alternative', in Tom Campbell, Jeffrey Goldsworthy and Adrienne Stone (eds), *Protecting Rights without a Bill of Rights*, Aldershot: Ashgate Publishing Limited.

Choudhry, Sujit (2009), 'Blls of Rights as Instruments of Nation Building in Multinational States: The Canadian Charter and Quebec Nationalism', in James B. Kelly and Christopher P. Manfredi (eds), *Contested Constitutionalism. Reflections on the Canadian Charter of Rights and Freedoms*, Vancouver: UBC Press.

Dixon, Rosalind (2009), 'The Supreme Court of Canada, *Charter* Dialogue, and Deference', *Osgoode Hall Law Journal*, 47, 235–86.

Driedger, Elmer A (1977), 'The Meaning and Effect of the Canadian *Bill of Rights*: A Draftsman's Viewpoint', *Ottawa Law Review*, 9, 303–20.

Elliott, Mark (2004), 'United Kingdom: Parliamentary Sovereignty under Pressure', *International Journal of Constitutional Law*, 2 (3), 545–627.

Epp, Charles (1998), *The Rights Revolution: Lawyers, Activists, and Supreme Courts in Comparative Perspective*, Chicago: University of Chicago Press.

Erdos, David (2008), 'Elite Supply "Blockages" and the Failure of National Bill of Rights Initiatives in Australia: A Comparative Westminster Analysis', *Commonwealth & Comparative Politics*, 46 (3), 341–64.

Erdos, David, (2009), 'Ideology, Power Orientation and Policy Drag: Explaining the Elite Politics of Britain's Bill of Rights Debate', *Government and Opposition*, 44 (1), 20–41.

Evans, Carolyn Maree and Simon Evans (2008), *Australian Bills of Rights: The Law of the Victorian Charter and ACT Human Rights Act*, Chatswood, NSW: LexisNexis, Butterworths.

Ewing, Keith (2007), 'The Political Constitution of Emergency Powers: A Comment', *International Journal of Law in Context*, 3 (4), 313–18.

Fabre, Cécile (2002), 'A Philosophical Argument for a Bill of Rights', *British Journal of Political Science*, 30, 77–98.

Falconer, Lord (2004), 'Speech to the Law Society and Human Rights Lawyers' Association', London, 17 February, available at www.hrla.org.uk/.../human%20rights%20and%20constitutional%20reform.doc (checked 15 January 2010).

Finkel, Jodi S. (2008), *Judicial Reform as Political Insurance: Argentina, Peru, and Mexico in the 1990s*, Notre Dame, IN: University of Notre Dame Press.

Fisher, Louis (1991), 'The Curious Belief in Judicial Supremacy', *Suffolk University Law Review*, 25 (1), 85–116.

Fisher, Louis (1998), *Constitutional Dialogues: Interpretation as Political Process*, Princeton, NJ: Princeton University Press.

Friedman, Barry (1993), 'Dialogue and Judicial Review,' *Michigan Law Review*, 91, 571–682.

Gardbaum, Stephen (2001), 'The New Commonwealth Model of Constitutionalism', *American Journal of Comparative Law*, 49, 707–61.

Gardbaum, Stephen (2009), 'Reassessing the New Commonwealth Model of Constitutionalism', Paper presented at the University of Toronto Constitutional Roundtable on 2 December.

Ginsburg, Tom (2003), *Judicial Review in New Democracies: Constitutional Courts in Asian Cases*, New York: Cambridge University Press.

Goldsworthy, Jeffrey (2003), 'Homogenizing Constitutions', *Oxford Journal of Legal Studies*, 23 (3), 482–505.

Hiebert, Janet L. (2002), *Charter Conflicts: What is Parliament's Role?*, Montreal: McGill-Queen's University Press.

Hiebert, Janet L. (2004), 'New Constitutional Ideas: Can New Parliamentary Models Resist Judicial Dominance When Interpreting Rights?', *Texas Law Review*, 82, 1963–87.

Hiebert, Janet L. (2005), 'Rights-vetting in New Zealand and Canada: Similar Idea, Different Outcomes', *New Zealand Journal of Public and International Law*, 3 (1), 63–103.

Hiebert, Janet L. (2006), 'Parliamentary Bills of Rights: An Alternative Model?', *Modern Law Review*, 69 (1), 7–28.

Hiebert, Janet L. (2009), 'Compromise and the Notwithstanding Clause: Why the Dominant Narrative Distorts our Understanding', in James B. Kelly and Christopher Manfredi (eds), *The Charter at 25*, Vancouver: UBC Press, pp. 107–25.

Hiebert, Janet L. (2011), 'Governing like Judges', in Tom Campbell, K.D. Ewing and Adam Tomkins (eds), *The Legal Protection of Human Rights: Sceptical Essays*, Oxford: Oxford University Press.

Hirschl, Ran (2004), *Towards Juristocracy: The Origins and Consequences of the New Constitutionalism*, Cambridge, MA: Harvard University Press.

Hogg, Peter W. and Allison Bushell (1997), 'The Charter Dialogue between Courts and Legislatures (Or Perhaps the Charter of Rights isn't Such a Bad Thing After All)', *Osgoode Hall Law Journal*, 35, 75–124.

Hogg, Peter W., Allison A. Bushell-Thornton and Wade K. Wright (2007), 'Charter Dialogue Revisited – Or Much Ado about Metaphors', *Osgoode Hall Law Journal*, 45 (1), 1–65.

Huscroft, Grant (2003), 'The Attorney-General's Reporting Duty', in Huscroft, Grant and Paul Rishworth (eds), *Rights and Freedoms: The New Zealand Bill of Rights Act 1990 and the Human Rights Act*, Wellington: Brookers.

Huscroft, Grant (2007), 'Constitutionalism from the Top Down', *Osgoode Hall Law Journal*, 45 (1), 91–104.

Huscroft, Grant and Paul Rishworth (2009), 'You Say You Want a Revolution: Bills of Rights in the Age of Human Rights', available at http://papers.ssrn.com/sol3/papers.cfm?abstract_id=1299903 (checked, 14 January 2010).

Kahana, Tsvi (2001), 'The Notwithstanding Mechanism and Public Discussion: Lessons from the Ignored Practice of Section 33 of the Charter', *Canadian Public Administration*, 44 (3), 255–91.

Kelly, James B. (2005), *Governing with the Charter: Legislative and Judicial Activism and Framers' Intent*, Vancouver: UBC Press.

Kelly, James B. (2009), 'Legislative Activism and Parliamentary Bills of Rights', in James B. Kelly and Christopher Manfredi (eds), *Contested Constitutionalism: Reflections on the Charter of Rights and Freedoms*, Vancouver: UBC Press, pp. 86–106.

Klug, Francesca (2000), *Values for a Godless Age: The Story of the United Kingdom's New Bill of Rights*, London: Penguin Books.

Knopff, Rainer and F.L. Morton (1992), *Charter Politics*, Scarborough, Ontario: Nelson Canada.

Kramer, Larry (2004), *The People Themselves: Popular Constitutionalism and Judicial Review*, New York: Oxford University Press.

Lester, Lord (1997), 'First Steps Towards a Constitutional Bill of Rights', *European Human Rights Law Review*, 2 (2), 124–31.

MacLennan, Christopher (2003), *Toward the Charter*, Montreal: McGill-Queen's University Press.

Manfredi, Christopher P. (2001), *Judicial Power and the Charter: Canada and the Paradox of Liberal Constitutionalism*, 2nd edition, Don Mills, Ontario: Oxford University Press.

Manfredi, Christopher P. and James Kelly (1999), 'Six Degrees of Dialogue: A Response to Hogg and Bushell', *Osgoode Hall Law Journal*, 37 (3), 513–27.

Morton, F.L. (2001), 'Dialogue or Monologue?', in Paul Howe and Peter H. Russell (eds), *Judicial Power and Canadian Democracy*, Montreal: McGill-Queen's University Press.

Morton, F.L. and Rainer Knopff (2000), *The Charter Revolution and the Court Party*, Peterborough, Ontario: Broadview Press Limited.

Nicol, Danny (2004), 'The Human Rights Act and the Politicians', *Legal Studies*, 24, 451–79.

Palmer, Geoffrey (1979), *Unbridled Power? An Interpretation of New Zealand's Constitution and Government*, Wellington: Oxford University Press.

Palmer, Geoffrey (1992), *New Zealand's Constitution in Crisis*, Dunedin, New Zealand, John McIndoe.

Peabody, Bruce G. (2005), 'Congressional Attitudes toward Constitutional Interpretation', in Neil Devins and Keith Whittington (eds), *Congress and the Constitution*, Durham, NC: Duke University Press.

Perry, Michael J. (2003), 'Protecting Human Rights in a Democracy: What Role for the Courts?', *Wake Forest Law Review*, 38, 635–95.

Petter, Andrew (2007), 'Taking Dialogue Theory Much Too Seriously (or Perhaps Charter Dialogue isn't Such a Good Thing After All)', *Osgoode Hall Law Journal*, 15, 147–67.

Pickerill, J. Mitchell (2004), *Constitutional Deliberation in Congress: The Impact of Judicial Review in a Separated System*, Durham, NC: Duke University Press.

Pillard, Cornelia T.L. (2005), 'The Unfulfilled Promise of the Constitution in Executive Hands', *Michigan Law Review*, 103, 676–758.

Rights, Responsibilities and Respect: The Report of the Human Rights Consultation Committee (2005), Melbourne, Australia.

Rishworth, Paul (1995), 'The Birth and Rebirth of the Bill of Rights', in Grant Huscroft and Paul Rishworth (eds), *Rights and Freedoms: The New Zealand Bill of Rights Act 1990 and the Human Rights Act*, Wellington: Brookers.

Roach, Kent (2001), *The Supreme Court on Trial: Judicial Activism or Democratic Dialogue?*, Toronto: Irwin Law.

Rosenberg, Gerald N. (1991), *The Hollow Hope: Can Courts Bring About Social Change?*, Chicago, IL: University of Chicago Press.

Russell, Peter H. (1983), 'Political Purposes of the Canadian Charter of Rights and Freedoms', *Canadian Bar Review*, 61, 30–64.

Russell, Peter H. (1991), 'Standing Up for Notwithstanding', *Alberta Law Review*, 29 (2), 293–309.

Russell, Peter H. (2004), *Constitutional Odyssey: Can Canadians Become a Sovereign People?*, 3rd edition, Toronto: University of Toronto Press.

Stanhope, Jon (2003), Australian Capital Territory, Debates of the Legislative Assembly, 18 November 2003, 4250.

Stone Sweet, Alec (2000), *Governing with Judges: Constitutional Politics in Europe*, Oxford: Oxford University Press.

Straw, Jack (1999), 'Building a Human Rights Culture', Address to Civil Service College Seminar, 19 December 1999, available at http://www.nationalarchives.gov.uk/ERORecords/HO/415/1/hract/cscspe.htm (checked 22 April 2008).

Thayer, James Bradley (1893), *The Origin and Scope of the American Doctrine of Constitutional Law*, Boston: Little, Brown and Company.

Tushnet, Mark (2000), *Taking the Constitution Away from the Courts*, Princeton, NJ: Princeton University Press.

Tushnet, Mark (2003), 'New Forms of Judicial Review', *Wake Forest Law Review*, 38, 813–38.

Tushnet, Mark (2008), *Weak Courts, Strong Rights: Judicial Review and Social Welfare Rights in Comparative Constitutional Law*, Princeton, NJ: Princeton University Press.

Uhr, John (2006), 'The Performance of Australian Legislatures in Protecting Rights', in Tom Campbell, Jeffrey Goldsworthy and Adrienne Stone (eds), *Protecting Rights without a Bill of Rights*, Aldershot: Ashgate Publishing Company, pp. 41–59.

Wadham, John (1997), 'Bringing Rights Half-way Home', *European Human Rights Law Review*, 2, 141–54.

Weiler, Paul (1984), 'Rights and Justice in a Democracy: A New Canadian Version', *University of Michigan Journal of Law Reform*, 18, 51–92.

Weinrib, Lorraine E. (2006),'The Postwar Paradigm and American Exceptionalism', in Sujit Choudhry (ed.), *The Migration of Constitutional Ideas*, Cambridge: Cambridge University Press, pp. 84–111.

White Paper, (1997), *Rights Brought Home: The Human Rights Bill* (CM 7382).

Whyte, John D. (1990), 'On Not Standing for Notwithstanding', *Alberta Law Review*, 28 (2), 347–57.

Williams, George (2000), *A Bill of Rights for Australia*, Sydney: UNSW Press.

Williams, George (2006), 'The Victoria *Charter of Human Rights and Responsibilities*: Origins and Scope', *Melbourne University Law Review*, 30, 880–905.

Young, Alison L. (2002), 'Judicial Sovereignty and the Human Rights Act 1998', *Cambridge Law Journal*, 61 (1), 53–65.

18. The rise of weak-form judicial review
Mark Tushnet

1 INTRODUCTION

Constitutional review, known in the United States as 'judicial review', originated in the United States. It took the form of a practice in which upon finding a statute inconsistent with constitutional norms a court gave the statute no legal effect in the case at hand and, because of the operation of rules of *stare decisis* in US law, other courts subordinate to the deciding court would similarly give the statute no legal effect in cases coming before them.[1] For more than a century this form of review, to which I have given the label 'strong-form', provided the only model for constitutional review. As parliaments increasingly rested on majoritarian theories of democracy and as constitutionalism spread, the tensions between the two were alleviated by accounts of parliamentary supremacy that stressed legislative responsibility for adherence to constitutional norms. That responsibility could be 'enforced' by political norms regulating legislators' actions or more effectively by legislators' electoral responsiveness to constituents who themselves cared about adherence to constitutional norms.

Proponents of strong-form constitutional review sometimes contend that that practice is either compelled or strongly supported by the existence of a written constitution. Yet even written constitutions can accommodate pure legislative responsibility for adherence to constitutional norms, either in the large or with respect to specific provisions. The constitution of the Netherlands specifically states that none of its provisions is judicially enforceable, although the impact of that limitation is qualified by another provision requiring judicial enforcement of international treaties to which the Netherlands is a party. The Irish constitution of 1937 contains a set of 'directive principles of public policy', which are expressly committed solely to the care of the legislature and unenforceable by the courts.[2] The Swedish constitution, which provides for what appears to be strong-form review, constrains the courts through a limitation that allows them to declare a statute unconstitutional only if the inconsistency between the statute and constitutional norms is (in one translation) manifest. Even in the United States, the home of strong-form review, the 'political question' doctrine is best understood as identifying constitutional norms whose enforcement is left in the hands of elected representatives.[3]

Systems of complete parliamentary supremacy took strong, sometimes debilitating blows during the twentieth century, when experience was thought to show that purely political constraints on legislatures were insufficient to avoid a descent into totalitarianism or more modest but still troubling forms of authoritarian rule. Sometimes urged by US advisers as in Germany and Japan and sometimes emulating the German model for designing a constitutional court, constitution designers gravitated toward the only available model of constitutional review, the US-style strong-form system, as a remedy.[4] Defenders of parliamentary supremacy and constitutionalism argued that strong-form review raised persistent questions about the relation between on the one hand the right of the sovereign people to govern themselves, proximately through legislation adopted by their representatives or by direct legislation the people themselves enacted and ultimately through their constitution, and on the other the power of constitutional courts to refuse to treat as legally effective statutes they determined were inconsistent with the constitution's higher norms. Constitution designers came up with a number of mechanisms to address these questions and at least weaken their sting, including the creation of specialized constitutional courts selected by mechanisms different from those used to select 'ordinary' judges and restrictions on the preclusive effect of determinations of unconstitutionality.

In the late twentieth century, constitution designers developed another response, which I have called weak-form constitutional review.[5] Weak-form review combines some sort of power in courts to find legislation inconsistent with constitutional norms with some mechanism whereby the enacting legislature can respond to a court decision to that effect. Weak-form systems vary with respect to both the nature of the judicial power, which can be merely declaratory or provisionally suspensive, and the form of legislative response, which can be re-enactment or slight modification of the impugned legislation. After describing several of the weak-form's design features, this chapter examines the development of weak-form constitutional review in Canada, New Zealand and Great Britain. It concludes with some speculations about the future of weak-form constitutional review.

2   CONSTITUTIONAL REVIEW, REASONABLE DISAGREEMENT AND THE AMENDMENT PROCESS

Two features of modern constitutions lie at the foundation of the development of weak-form constitutional review. Every constitution's terms are subject to reasonable disagreement among interpreters and specifically between legislators and constitutional court judges. Weak-form review is a mechanism for dealing with such disagreement in a way that preserves parliamentary supremacy to as large an extent as possible. In addition, every constitution has some provision for its own amendment. The ease or difficulty of amending a constitution should affect the choice between strong-form and weak-form constitutional review.

Put most generally, constitutionalism requires some limitations on parliamentary/legislative sovereignty. Those limitations can be enforced culturally and politically. A culture of legality among political elites might induce legislators to deliberate seriously about whether their preferred policy proposals are consistent with constitutional limitations on their power. A culture of legality in the public might lead voters to remove from office legislators who in the voters' judgment have failed to comply with constitutional limitations.

The US model of constitutionalism seeks institutional mechanisms for enforcing constitutional limitations on parliamentary sovereignty, and the judgment that such mechanisms are a desirable feature of constitutional design has now become nearly universal. These mechanisms typically involve some determination by an institution independent of the legislature on the question of a proposal's consistency with constitutional limitations. The institution might be a body that screens proposals before they are submitted for legislative consideration. Sweden and Japan have such institutions, and some observers contend that the near absence in those nations of judicial determinations that statutes are unconstitutional results from the effectiveness of the screening process in those institutions.[6] A screening body might have the power to prevent legislative consideration. More typically, these 'rights-vetting' institutions offer their views as advice.[7]

Strong-form constitutional review places the power to determine the consistency of legislation with constitutional norms in a court authorized to deny legal effect to statutes it concludes are inconsistent with those norms. The phrase 'it concludes' is crucial to understanding the persistent nervousness in constitutional theory in the United States and elsewhere about strong-form constitutional review. At least occasionally, and to many observers rather often, there can be reasonable disagreement over the proposition that a statute is inconsistent with constitutional norms.[8] It is hardly clear that constitutionalism requires that the reasonable views of the courts or other reviewing institution prevail over the reasonable views of the enacting legislature.

Mechanisms of weak-form constitutional review address the nervousness about giving reviewing courts the final and unrevisable word on such questions. In their most general form, such systems continue to authorize independent courts to analyze and express their judgments about legislation's consistency with constitutional norms, but allow legislatures to respond if legislators conclude that the legislation is consistent with constitutional norms reasonably understood. Of course even strong-form systems of constitutional review provide at least one mechanism for responding to what seem to some mistaken decisions to deny legal effect to a statute. That mechanism is the process for amending the nation's constitution. Faced with a strong-form court's decision that a statute is inconsistent with constitutional norms, a nation's people can revise those norms.[9] The easier it is to amend the constitution, the smaller the distinction between strong-form and weak-form review. Put differently, strong-form review raises questions about the relation between courts and parliaments only in systems where constitutional amendment is significantly more difficult than is the enactment of ordinary legislation.[10]

3   TYPES OF WEAK-FORM CONSTITUTIONAL REVIEW

Weak-form review is a relatively recent development. It seems likely that the design possibilities extend beyond those already in force. Enumerating some mechanisms of weak-form review may nonetheless bring to the fore several important characteristics of these mechanisms.

(1) The weakest form of weak-form review may perhaps not deserve the name of constitutional review at all. It is the pure interpretive mandate, which can best be understood against the background of purely statutory bills of rights. In a statutory bill of rights, a legislature enacts a list of rights as ordinary legislation. That bill of rights is not entrenched against repeal or subject to any special rules regarding its later amendment. How should courts treat the statutory bill of rights? The answer is relatively straightforward with respect to laws on the books at the time the statutory bill of rights is enacted. Courts should treat the statutory bill of rights as amending all existing legislation, which thereafter should be interpreted to be consistent with the statutory bill of rights. The situation with respect to later-enacted laws is more complex because there are two equally plausible approaches to interpreting them. A court might assume that subsequent legislatures wish to comply with the statutory bill of rights and therefore interpret later-enacted statutes to be consistent with it. Alternatively, a court might treat later-enacted statutes as raising the possibility that they are *pro tanto*

subject-specific amendments to the statutory bill of rights, which would lead to interpreting them without giving any special regard to their relation to the statutory bill of rights.

The pure interpretive mandate is a legislative directive that courts should where fairly possible interpret legislation, both existing and later-enacted, to be consistent with some list of protected rights. The interpretive mandate purports to rule out the choice of the second approach to statutory bills of rights. The primary question that arises in connection with interpretive mandates is their relation to ordinary principles of statutory interpretation. Does the direction to interpret a statute to be consistent with the protected rights operate merely as a tie-breaker? If so, a court would use the ordinary rules of statutory interpretation to determine the statute's meaning and invoke the protected rights only if the court was genuinely uncertain after doing so what the statute meant. Proponents of interpretive mandates typically argue that the mandate must do more than that, largely because situations of genuine uncertainty are rare. They argue that courts should use the list of protected rights as a new 'canon' of statutory interpretation. The fact that a statute interpreted in the ordinary way has some adverse effect on a protected right is in their view a reason for interpreting the statute otherwise. At the extreme, this approach to statutory interpretation can give the protected rights overriding weight, displacing even the plain meaning of a statute's words.[11]

Defenders of parliamentary sovereignty reject such an aggressive use of an interpretive mandate. For them, the fundamental questions go not to how courts should respond to interpretive mandates but to their implications for subsequent legislatures. An interpretive mandate purports to place some burden of special clarity on later legislatures that seek to enact statutes that can be challenged as rights-violating. But as a matter of constitutional theory, the power of one legislature so to bind a later one by ordinary legislation is quite unclear.

(2) Less weak is a form of review in which a court is empowered to declare a statute incompatible with fundamental rights, typically after determining that it is unable to interpret the statute so that it does not infringe such rights. The circumstances under which such a declaration will make a difference might be limited to situations in which the rights-violation was inadvertent. It might be that a legislature simply did not understand that its legislation would have an adverse impact on rights, perhaps because the impact was buried in the details of a complex statutory scheme. Ordinarily, courts should be able to deal with such difficulties by applying the interpretive mandate, but occasionally they will be unable to escape a statute's clear wording. The more likely scenario is one in which the statutory language is both clear and obvious. Here the purported rights-violation may well have been precisely what the legislature intended. Again, the existence of reasonable disagreement about whether rights are violated matters. To oversimplify somewhat, either the legislature intended to violate rights or it held a view of rights under which the statute did not actually violate rights. In either case, the legislature is unlikely to do anything in response to the judicial declaration.

This conclusion should be qualified to take account of the informational effect of a judicial declaration of incompatibility. That effect may make no difference where there is strong party government because almost necessarily the party leadership knew what it was doing when it promoted the impugned legislation. Where party discipline is weaker, some members of the majority party understood as a coalition may have harbored reservations about the legislation that they subordinated to party loyalty but to which they would give effect once informed that their reservations were well founded. A public informed by a declaration of incompatibility may respond at the next election, and the anticipation of such a response might induce the leadership even in a strong party system to alter its legislation.

(3) The strongest of the weak-form mechanisms gives the court power to suspend the legal effect of a statute pending a legislative response through ordinary legislation rather than constitutional amendment. Canada's so-called 'notwithstanding clause', Section 33 of the Charter of Rights, is the primary example of such a mechanism. (Another description of the provision is that it allows a legislature to override constitutional provisions.) The clause authorizes the national legislature or a provincial one with respect to legislation within their respective jurisdictions to make a statute legally effective notwithstanding enumerated constitutional provisions dealing with individual rights.[12] Statutes protected by a notwithstanding declaration expire after five years, but the declaration is renewable. The five-year 'sunset' period ensures that an election intervene between initial enactment and renewal, thereby increasing the likelihood that legislative responsibility will be enforced through political accountability.

The presence of a 'notwithstanding' or similar clause in a constitution presents some important interpretive questions. When a legislature invokes such a clause, must it identify precisely those constitutional provisions with which the statute might be inconsistent, or may it invoke the clause in general terms, such as 'notwithstanding any provision of this constitution'? May a legislature invoke such a clause prior to any judicial suspension of an enactment's legal effect, or may it do so only after a court has found a statute inconsistent with constitutional norms? These questions are not entirely unrelated. After a court finds a statute inconsistent with a specific constitutional norm, the legislature can make its statute legally effective by referring to that constitutional norm in its override.[13]

These questions help bring out some general features of weak-form constitutional review.[14] Proponents of weak-form review note that legislators may simply overlook constitutional questions implicated in their policy proposals. A statute might not in fact embody a reasoned legislative determination that the statute is consistent with constitutional norms. Weak-form review offers the legislature an opportunity to focus on that question without necessarily precluding the legislature from re-enacting the impugned statute. In addition and perhaps related, legislators are not specialists in constitutional law. Weak-form review in contrast is performed by such specialists. Weak-form review may provide legislators with information that they lacked at the enactment stage. Specialization can of course distort as well as inform judgment. Distracted by their attention to nuances of constitutional law, constitutional court judges might undervalue the contributions a statute makes to overall social wellbeing. Again weak-form review has the advantage of allowing legislatures to take these and similar distortions into account as they respond to the court's decision. These processes have been described through the metaphor that weak-form review creates a 'dialogue' between courts and legislatures.[15]

Requiring an override to be cast in specific terms substantially reduces the possibility that the legislature's action in adversely affecting constitutional rights, at least in the eyes of some, is inadvertent, and may increase the possibility that voters will be sufficiently informed as to hold legislators responsible for their decision. Anticipatory and specific overrides, that is, those made before a court finds a statute inconsistent with constitutional norms identified in the overriding legislation itself, run the risk that the legislature will identify only one constitutional problem with its enactment, while others are severe enough to lead the courts to invalidate the legislation anyway. Anticipatory overrides also cannot capitalize on the information that would be provided by a judicial invalidation, although the relevant information may be widely enough available, for example by inferences from prior court decisions, to reduce the severity of this concern. In addition, anticipatory overrides cannot contribute to a dialogue between courts and legislatures on questions of constitutional interpretation.

4   WEAK-FORM REVIEW AND THE IDEA OF JUDICIAL-LEGISLATIVE DIALOGUE

Weak-form review can be quite weak, as the examples of the pure interpretive mandate and the declaratory form of review show. What benefits might there be from such an institution in a world where courts and legislatures can reasonably disagree on the question of a statute's consistency with constitutional norms? As noted above, one benefit is dialogue between courts and legislatures. The tension between strong-form constitutional review and parliamentary sovereignty is strongest when fully informed legislatures simply but reasonably disagree with the interpretation a court gives to a constitutional limitation on legislative power. Dialogue allows courts to inform a legislature of the courts' understanding of the constitutional provision, while allowing the legislature to respond and take conclusive action based on its own understanding.

Two episodes in Canadian law illustrate different forms of dialogue. (1) In *R v O'Connor* ([1995] 4 SCR 411), a sharply divided Supreme Court developed the common law in light of the Charter to allow relatively generous opportunities for defense counsel to gain access to the medical and counseling records of a complainant in a prosecution for sexual assault. Parliament responded with a statute that essentially adopted the dissenters' views on when such access should be granted. The Supreme Court then upheld the statute against constitutional challenge, observing that it did not 'hold a monopoly' on Charter interpretation (*R v Mills*, [1999] 3 SCR 668). (2) In 1989 Parliament adopted a comprehensive and rather strict system regulating advertising of tobacco products. The Supreme Court found that the system violated constitutional guarantees of free expression because each component of the system failed under one or more of the tests for proportionality (*RJR-MacDonald Inc v Canada (Attorney General)*, [1995] 3 SCR 199). Its proportionality analysis delineated the outlines of constitutionally permissible legislation, and Parliament responded by enacting a statute that conformed to those outlines.

Responses can take several forms depending on the precise contours of the weak-form mechanism. Consider first a weak-form mechanism authorizing courts to do no more than declare a statute incompatible with constitutional norms, the declaration having no immediate legal consequences. A legislature need do nothing to make its statute legally effective after such a declaration. It may of course face political pressure or social expectations that it do something in response, but the simple declaration of incompatibility puts the legislature in no different legal position than it was in before the declaration. Next consider a weak-form mechanism that suspends a statute's legal effectiveness subject to later legislative action. Importantly, one possible response is doing nothing because the legislature informed by the court's decision concludes that constitutional norms do indeed preclude it from accomplishing its policy goal. A legislature that on reflection wishes to make its statute legally effective does have to respond. Depending on the design of the weak-form mechanism, it can do so by re-enacting the statute either by the ordinary process of legislation or under some modestly enhanced procedural requirements, such as a qualified majority rule requiring a majority of the legislature as a whole rather than simply a majority of legislators present and voting, or a modest supermajority requirement.[16]

The responses described so far reflect a legislature's judgment that its own reasonable view that the statute is consistent with constitutional norms should prevail over the reviewing court's view. The Canadian experience illustrated by the 'dialogue' on tobacco advertising suggests that the most common legislative response will be tinkering with the statute to ensure that it conforms to the reviewing court's view. This response has two notable characteristics. It is one in which the legislature accepts rather than rejects the reviewing court's constitutional interpretation, perhaps because the legislature initially overlooked constitutional concerns or perhaps because the legislature's reflective reconsideration led to a change in a majority's views about constitutionality. In addition, the tinkering will almost certainly come at some cost to the legislature's initial non-constitutional policy goals. Modest adjustments in procedures will increase implementation costs, which in turn will reduce the number of occasions on which the statute will be invoked. Tinkering as a response may reflect a legislative judgment that the reduction in the statute's effectiveness is not large enough to justify incurring the political costs of directly disagreeing with the courts.

5 THE DEVELOPMENT OF WEAK-FORM CONSTITUTIONAL REVIEW

By the late twentieth century, parliamentary supremacy was the reigning constitutional theory in only a handful of nations, mostly in the British Commonwealth. Their legal elites came to believe that some mechanism for overseeing legislative compliance with constitutional norms was desirable.[17] Canada adopted the strongest of the weak-form systems, followed by New Zealand's choice of the weakest, and then the United Kingdom's choice of the intermediate variant.[18]

(1) After beginning his career as a constitutional lawyer, Canada's minister of justice and prime minister Pierre Trudeau came to the view that Canada's persistent division between Quebec and the rest of Canada over national identity could be solved by patriating the Canadian constitution. Doing so, Trudeau believed, would provide a basis for reconfiguring national identity around the constitution as a charter of rights and around multiculturalism rather than bilingualism. A 1981 advisory opinion from the Canadian Supreme Court held that patriation required extensive consultation with the provinces and substantial agreement among them over the constitution's terms. Meetings with the provinces' first ministers produced agreement on many terms, but division persisted over the creation of an enforceable charter of rights, with leaders of social democratic parties skeptical about US-style constitutional review because of experience in the 1930s in the United States and Canada when courts obstructed economic recovery programs. Trudeau was committed to such a charter as an essential component of constitutional reform. The ministers compromised by inserting two provisions in the proposed constitution, and the Canadian constitution was patriated in 1982 with an accompanying Charter of Rights enforceable in the courts.

The first provision affecting constitutional review was the notwithstanding clause, a real innovation in constitutional design.[19] It authorized legislative responses to judicial invalidation in the form of straightforward re-enactment of the impugned legislation. Quebec's political leadership had not accepted patriation, and immediately after the constitution became effective, invoked the notwithstanding clause to protect all of the province's statutes against constitutional challenge. The most controversial of those statutes was a bill requiring that all commercial signage in Quebec be in French. Several businesses challenged the sign law as a violation of their Charter rights and the use of the notwithstanding clause as improper. The Canadian Supreme Court held that it could examine only whether Quebec's use of the notwithstanding clause was formally valid (*Ford v Quebec (Attorney General)*, [1988] 2 SCR 712).[20] Despite or perhaps because of this holding, the notwithstanding clause has not been used since 1988 to insulate any significant legislation against constitutional challenge.

The second provision was a general limitations clause applicable to the rights enumerated in the charter. Modeled on language in existing international human rights documents, where the terms were used to identify permissible limitations on particular rights, the clause provides that all the rights are 'subject only to such reasonable limits prescribed by law as can be demonstrably justified in a free and democratic society'. The general limitations clause invited a different type of legislative response. As Canadian constitutional doctrine has evolved, courts make two determinations. They ask first whether the challenged legislation infringes on a constitutional right. The standard for determining whether a right is infringed is in general easy to satisfy. Once it is, the second, more consequential, determination must be made. The court asks whether the infringement is demonstrably justified. Constitutional doctrine has converted this into a multi-stage proportionality test.

The language of the general limitations clause suggests one form that challenges to legislation can take. Litigants might argue that the statute limits a constitutional right, and that the limitation is not demonstrably justified. If the courts agree, the legislature can respond by providing a stronger justification than it had earlier, for example by compiling a more complete legislative record of the statute's effectiveness at addressing a social evil and the relative ineffectiveness of alternatives. The proportionality doctrine has components that invite cognate responses. To satisfy the proportionality requirement, legislation must 'impair "as little as possible" the right', and 'there must be a proportionality between the effects of the measures ... and the objective' of the statute (*R v Oakes*, [1986] 1 SCR 103). Legislation that fails the proportionality test in either of these ways might be re-enacted with a demonstration that no alternatives achieve the legislation's goals with a smaller effect on rights. More commonly, the legislature responds with slight alterations in the legislation to reduce the adverse effect on rights while preserving the statute's main features.

(2) In New Zealand as in Canada, a law professor politician was the moving force behind the adoption of a bill of rights and, as in Canada, questions about national identity played a role. Having received a law degree and taught at law schools in the United States, Geoffrey Palmer had a principled commitment to a fully enforceable bill of rights, and worked for its adoption as minister of justice and then prime minister. He saw such a bill of rights as part of a package of constitutional reforms, which included proportional representation and the recognition of constitutional status for the Treaty of Waitangi (1840) between New Zealand's indigenous Maori people and its British settlers. Palmer's advocacy of an entrenched bill of rights failed in the face of strong assertions of a national commitment to parliamentary supremacy. Shortly before the Labour Party led by Palmer lost its majority in 1990, the New Zealand parliament adopted a statutory Bill of Rights, listing protected rights and containing an interpretive mandate.

New Zealand's courts have been rather cautious but not completely inactive in their use of the interpretive mandate. Some judges have invoked theoretical concerns about the ability of an earlier legislature to bind a later one to justify their caution. Yet in one notable case, the nation's high court held that the Bill of Rights Act authorized the courts to remedy some violations with a damages remedy despite the fact that they have no authority even to declare legislation incompatible with the Act (*Baigent's Case*, [1994] 3 NZLR 667). More recently, the court overturned the conviction of a schoolteacher and political activist for 'dishonouring' the nation's flag by burning it in a political protest, invoking the interpretive mandate as requiring that the word 'dishonour' be given as narrow an interpretation as possible to ensure that the statute not infringe free speech rights (*Hopkinson v Police*, [2004] 3 NZLR 704).

(3) The British Human Rights Act 1998 was the culmination of a campaign by the Labour Party to 'bring rights home', as one of the Party's documents put it. Historically, the Labour Party had been quite hostile to the judiciary. The *Taff Vale* decision (1901), which imposed monetary liability on a labor union for actions taken in a strike that was held to violate common law rules against interference with contractual relations, held an iconic and notorious place in Labourites' understanding of courts and the law. Labour leaders believed that judges as members of the ruling class and typically of upper-class origins themselves were inevitably biased against the working class, which cautioned strongly against developing policies that required judicial support to be effective. The US experience in the first decades of the twentieth century with the enforcement of notions of due process to limit social welfare legislation was taken as exemplary. Further, the Labour Party was committed to parliamentary sovereignty with widespread public participation in elections and a strong party system, which its leaders believed would eventually guarantee their program's long-term success.

The Labour Party's position changed after Margaret Thatcher became prime minister in 1979. Leading a strong and cohesive Conservative Party government, Thatcher was able, as Labour leaders saw it, to force through legislation inconsistent with long-standing British traditions, which they believed would have been blocked by courts empowered to enforce human rights. Other developments contributed to changing attitudes within the Labour Party about judicial protection of rights. The democratization of the legal profession promised to transform the judiciary, at least in the long run. Constitutional changes occurred in other components of the British system of parliamentary supremacy, weakening the case against constitutional review. Practices of ministerial and cabinet responsibility changed dramatically, for example.[21] The United Kingdom's accession to the European Community and to the human rights regime of the European Convention on Human Rights had theoretical and practical effects as well. Constitutional theorists struggled to reconcile the doctrine of parliamentary supremacy with the doctrine that European Community law had direct effect within the United Kingdom. No solution was entirely satisfactory, but one promising route was a modification of the doctrine that no earlier parliament could bind a later one. That modification would provide support for the adoption of an entrenched bill of rights. Perhaps more important, British politicians were embarrassed by the rate at which the European Court of Human Rights found that the United Kingdom had violated rights protected by the Convention.

Labour Party leader John Smith put together a package of constitutional reforms to incorporate in the Party's platform, including devolution of power to Scotland and Wales, and his successor Tony Blair implemented many of the reforms. One was the Human Rights Act 1998. The HRA made most of the rights protected by the European Convention enforceable as domestic law through an interpretive mandate, coupled with a power in higher courts to declare primary legislation incompatible with the enumerated rights.[22] Such a declaration would have no immediate legal effect. The Labour government stated its expectation that declarations of incompatibility would promptly produce the introduction of legislation to eliminate the incompatibility. In addition, the HRA authorized fast-track procedures for such remedial legislation, and even authorized the minister with jurisdiction over the matter to modify the impugned statute by executive order pending prompt submission to parliament of remedial legislation.

The House of Lords has been reasonably aggressive in its use of the interpretive mandate, with some decisions appearing to invoke human rights concerns to override the plain meaning of statutory language. An anti-terrorism case known as the *Belmarsh* decision is the most celebrated and controversial use of the declaration of incompatibility (*A v Secretary of State*, [2004] UKHL 56). Several persons suspected of terrorism offenses were detained at Belmarsh Prison without charge, for an indefinite period. Justifiably concerned that indefinite detention might be held to violate the detainees' rights under the European Convention, the government filed a derogation from the Convention with respect to the detentions. The House of Lords held that the derogation was legally ineffective and declared that the detentions were incompatible with the HRA because the standards for detention improperly discriminated between citizens and non-citizens equally suspected of terrorism-related offenses, and because indefinite detention was a disproportionate response to the threat the detainees posed.[23] Subsequent decisions have upheld many provisions of terrorism-related legislation, to the point where some of those who strongly supported the adoption of the HRA have expressed disappointment with its impact.

6   SPECULATIONS ON THE FUTURE OF WEAK-FORM CONSTITUTIONAL REVIEW

Strong-form review has existed for two hundred years in the United States and for many years in other jurisdictions, providing a rich empirical basis for evaluating it. The much shorter experience with weak-form review means that evaluating it empirically requires a great deal of speculation. The primary empirical question about weak-form review is whether the mechanism in any of its forms is likely to be stable over time. Instability might occur in both directions. Review might be so weak that the system 'degenerates' into parliamentary supremacy. Alternatively, review might 'degenerate' into strong-form review if legislatures never take a stand against judicial invalidations. Whether the latter should be regarded as 'degeneration' is unclear. Suppose courts regularly declare statutes unconstitutional and legislatures regularly fail to respond by overriding the courts' decisions, or respond by enacting new statutes that conform to the courts' requirements. That course of conduct might reflect a considered judgment by the legislature that strong-form review is in practice better than weak-form review, and that it can embed a strong-form system simply by regularly complying with judicial declarations. Another way of putting what amounts to the same point is that legislatures might regularly find that the political costs of overriding judicial decisions exceed the policy and political benefits of doing so.

What limited experience there is suggests that sustaining a weak-form mechanism is difficult. The notwithstanding clause in Canada has fallen into desuetude, largely discredited by its use to insulate French-language-favoring legislation in Quebec from review under the national Charter of Rights and by occasional threats, never effectively carried out, to use the clause to protect legislation discriminating against gays and lesbians. The clause remains an important symbol of parliamentary supremacy as the governing theory of Canadian constitutionalism: a party leader's suggestion that the clause be eliminated to 'perfect' Canadian constitutionalism met a strong and highly critical response. The general-limitations clause in Canada has become the textual basis for testing all legislation against a requirement of proportionality, inviting 'tinkering' responses that accept the courts' supremacy in constitutional interpretation. Evaluations of the vitality of the judicial-legislative dialogue reach mixed conclusions, depending on whether modifying a statute to conform to judicial requirements is treated as an example of productive dialogue or as an example of judicial supremacy.

In Great Britain, the Labour government routinely modified legislation in response to declarations of incompatibility. Most such declarations involved provisions that were probably inadvertent rights-violations even from the government's point of view, but the most prominent decisions involved aspects of anti-terrorism legislation and crime control laws. The Labour government grudgingly accepted those decisions. It responded by developing a discussion paper on 'rights and responsibilities', which asserted that the government was 'proud that it introduced the Human Rights Act and it will not resile from it nor repeal it'.[24] Yet uneasiness with expansive interpretations of the protected rights continues in Great Britain. Conservative Party leaders have been uncomfortable with those interpretations, and at this writing it is unclear whether the Human Rights Act will retain its current form. Interpretation of statutes to ensure conformity with the Human Rights Act placed some strain on traditional theories of statutory interpretation, although not to breaking point.

In New Zealand too, occasional expansive uses of the interpretive mandate have generated concern that the mandate will create a system of strong-form review. More commonly, observers assert that the government pays too little attention to human rights issues when it introduces legislation, citing the rather large number of instances in which the Attorney General, an official with a fair amount of independence from the government, has reported that government legislation is inconsistent with the bill of rights.

Weak-form constitutional review is one of only a handful of inventions in designing constitutional courts to occur over the past two centuries. Whatever its ultimate fate, its mechanism for reducing the tension between parliamentary supremacy and constitutional limitations on that supremacy provides the ground for serious reflection on fundamental features of constitutional design in modern democracies.

NOTES

1. This formulation captures the strong-form character of constitutional review in the United States, the focus of this chapter. For a discussion of other features in the design of constitutional review, see Victor Ferreres Comella, 'The Rise of Specialized Constitutional Courts', Chapter 15 in this volume.
2. The Indian constitution of 1950 contains a similar section, modeled on the Irish one. The Indian Supreme Court has referred to the directive principles in its interpretations of constitutional provisions that are judicially enforceable. The Irish Supreme Court has gestured in that direction as well, but has resisted the temptation more successfully.
3. In *Luther v Borden*, 48 US (7 How) 1 (1848), the Supreme Court held that whether a state's system of government satisfied the constitutional requirement that the United States guarantee that each state have a republican form of government was a political question, meaning that it was to be determined by the legislative and executive branches.
4. This chapter deals only with weak- and strong-form constitutional review, and not with questions about whether review is dispersed among a number of courts or centralized in a single one (either a specialized constitutional court or a generalist court). Nor does it consider the suggestion made to me by Vicki Jackson that constitutional courts whose members serve for short terms might come to resemble weak-form courts, with quick replacement of judges who render decisions politicians disagree with.

5. The first scholar to identify weak-form constitutional review as a distinctive and general feature of constitutional design was Gardbaum (2001). For my contribution, see Tushnet (2007).
6. On Japan, see Law (2009). Law addresses but rejects the argument that Japan's screening mechanism accounts for the low level of judicial invalidations.
7. For a discussion of these institutions, see Janet L. Hiebert, 'Constitutional Experimentation: Rethinking How a Bill of Rights Functions', Chapter 17, this volume.
8. Jeremy Waldron has been the legal theorist most insistent on this claim and its implications for constitutional review. For his most careful formulation, see Waldron (2006).
9. Subject to whatever limitations the system places on the ability of a people to amend their constitution. For a survey of the issue of unamendable constitutional provisions, see Gözler (2008).
10. I think it important to note here that those who think about constitution design should not assume that the enactment of ordinary legislation is a simple majoritarian process. It might be, as it tends to be in pure parliamentary systems with strong political parties, but it need not be. Enactment is not a simple majoritarian process in separation of powers systems or even in parliamentary systems with weak party discipline.
11. The issue has been mooted in a number of British cases, with some judges defending this approach in principle though never actually applying it.
12. The clause does not apply to voting and language rights.
13. Subject to the possibility that the court ruled on only one constitutional challenge in a situation where others might remain available.
14. For a discussion bearing on these responses, see Dixon (2008).
15. The metaphor was introduced in Hogg and Bushell (1995), and has spread widely.
16. The only limitation on these procedural enhancements is that they cannot be as stringent as those required for constitutional amendment.
17. The major hold-out among nations committed to parliamentary supremacy was France, where the Constitutional Council created in 1957 was initially understood as a mechanism to adjudicate disagreements over the allocation of law-making authority between the president and the parliament and only gradually became a mechanism for general constitutional review. The last step appears to have been taken with a constitutional amendment adopted in 2008 that authorizes the Constitutional Council to determine the constitutionality of statutes after enactment, although that recent development has not taken effect as of this writing and its impact therefore cannot be determined.
18. Designers of constitutional courts in central and eastern Europe in the 1990s chose strong-form review, almost certainly under the influence of the German model and so probably independent of their views on the relation between parliamentary supremacy and constitutionalism.
19. There is some dispute over who first devised this solution.
20. For complex reasons, the court was able to find that the sign law violated Quebec's provincial bill of rights, and the broader sign law was replaced by one requiring that signage be predominantly but not exclusively in French.
21. For a discussion of these and other constitutional changes, see Oliver (2003). For a survey of changes in their incipiency, see Jowell and Oliver (1985).
22. The Convention right to effective remedies for rights violations was excepted from the list, out of concern that incorporating such a right would be inconsistent with the limited declaratory remedy created by the HRA.
23. The government responded by creating a system of fairly stringent house arrest rather than detention in a prison-like facility.
24. Ministry of Justice, Rights and Responsibilities: developing our constitutional framework (March 2009).

REFERENCES

Dixon, Rosalind (2008), 'A Democratic Theory of Constitutional Comparison', *American Journal of Comparative Law*, 46, 947–97.
Gardbaum, Stephen (2001), 'The New Commonwealth Model of Constitutionalism', *American Journal of Comparative Law*, 49, 707–60.
Gözler, Kemal (2008), *Judicial Review of Constitutional Amendments: A Comparative Study*, Bursa: Ekin Press.
Hogg, Peter and Allison Bushell (1995), 'The Charter Dialogue between Courts and Legislatures', *Osgoode Hall Law Journal*, 35, 75–124.
Jowell, Jeffrey and Dawn Oliver (eds.) (1985), *The Changing Constitution*, Oxford: Oxford University Press.
Law, David S. (2009), 'The Anatomy of a Conservative Court: Judicial Review in Japan', *Texas Law Review*, 87, 1545–93.

Oliver, Dawn (2003), *Constitutional Reform in the United Kingdom*, Oxford: Oxford University Press.
Tushnet, Mark (2007), *Weak Courts, Strong Rights: Judicial Review and Social Welfare Rights in Comparative Constitutional Law*, Princeton: Princeton University Press.
Waldron, Jeremy (2006), 'The Core of the Case Against Judicial Review', *Yale Law Journal*, 115, 1346–406.

19. Constitutions and emergency regimes

Oren Gross

1 INTRODUCTION

A tension of 'tragic dimensions' exists between democratic values and responses to violent emergencies.[1] The existence of restrictions and limitations on governmental powers is a fundamental attribute of democratic regimes. The ideals of democracy, individual rights, legitimacy, accountability, and the rule of law suggest that even in times of acute danger, government is limited, both formally and substantively, in the range of activities that it may pursue and powers that it may exercise to protect the state. Yet, constitutional arrangements ought also to ensure sufficient powers to government so that it may meet any type of future exigency. The question, therefore, is how to allow government sufficient discretion, flexibility, and powers to meet crises, while maintaining limitations and control over governmental actions so as to prevent or at least minimize the danger that such powers would be abused.

While states differ in their constitutional and legal approaches to this basic conundrum, the discourse concerning emergency regimes in democratic societies has almost invariably been governed by 'models of accommodation'.[2] These models recognize that when a nation is faced with emergencies, its legal, and even constitutional, structures may be somewhat relaxed (and even suspended in parts). This compromise, it is suggested, enables continued adherence to the rule of law and faithfulness to fundamental democratic values, while providing the state with adequate measures to withstand the storm wrought by the crisis.

Section 2 of this chapter outlines the contours of the Roman dictatorship, a constitutional arrangement whose traces are still reflected in modern-day constitutions. Section 3 follows with a detailed comparative analysis of the main features of constitutional emergency provisions. Section 4 closely examines the most common method of adapting constitutional language to concrete exigencies, i.e., through legislative modifications that are incorporated into the existing ordinary legal terrain. It goes on to analyze critically a recent proposal for the regulation of emergency powers via institutional mechanisms. Section 5 discusses briefly the role of courts in interpreting constitutional and statutory provisions against the background of emergency. Finally, Section 6 concludes with a discussion of the main arguments in support of, and opposition to, the models of accommodation.

2 THE ROMAN DICTATORSHIP

The institution of the Roman dictatorship is the prototype for most modern forms of models of accommodation.[3] The Romans introduced a system in which an emergency institution was a recognized and regular instrument of government built into a constitutional framework. The main thrust of the dictatorship was its constitutional nature. Operating within the republican constitutional framework, the dictator was vested with extraordinary yet constitutional powers. However, the institution of the dictatorship was alien to the basic governmental structure of the republic that was based on the principles of collegiality, equal power, and limited, non-renewable, term of office. Hence, although giving the dictator all the powers needed to defend the republic against its enemies, well-defined constitutional restrictions were laid down to prevent abuse of the powers of the dictator. Many of these restrictions can be found today in modern constitutional arrangements.

The most significant limitations pertained to the exceptional nature of the circumstances that would warrant the appointment of a dictator and to the temporal duration of that extraordinary appointment. Traditionally, the dictator was supposed to carry out military functions that would be necessary to defend the republic against external threats. The dictator's term of office was limited to six months or to the end of the term of the consuls who appointed him, whichever came first, and could not be renewed.[4] Moreover, according to constitutional custom, the dictator was expected to step down and relinquish his powers once he overcame the particular crisis that led to his appointment in the first place.

The dictator was expected to restore order and safety to the republic in the face of a particular threat. He could not embark, of his own initiative, on an aggressive war against an external enemy. His was a defensive role. Similarly, the dictator was called to maintain and protect the existing constitutional order. He could not use his powers to change the basic character of the state or its institutional framework.[5] Nor could he promulgate new legislation. Although the appointment of a dictator was a radical constitutional move undertaken in exceptional times of crisis, the regular institutions of the state – the consulship, the tribunes, the Senate, and all other office holders – continued to fulfill their normal functions and retained their full authority. The result was that 'the Senate, the consuls, the tribunes, remaining in their authority, came to be like a guard on [the dictator] to make him not depart from the right way'.[6]

Another set of critical checks related to the process and procedures for the appointment of a dictator. Most significantly, the appointment of a dictator by the consuls, coupled with the provision that no consul might appoint himself as dictator, ensured that the dictatorship would be invoked by officers other than the dictator himself, separating those who decided that an emergency existed and those who exercised the most awesome emergency measures.[7] In addition, although the appointment of the dictator was a matter for the full discretion of the consuls, the practice that developed was that it could not be made without the Senate's recommendation, and the imperium of the dictator had to be confirmed by a law passed by the Curiate Assembly.

These salient features of the dictatorship – temporary character, recognition of the exceptional nature of emergencies, appointment of a dictator according to specific constitutional forms that separated, among other things, those who declared an emergency from those who exercised dictatorial powers on such occasions, the appointment of dictators for well-defined and limited purposes, and the ultimate goal of upholding the constitutional order rather than changing or replacing it – are often regarded as setting the basic guidelines for modern-day constitutional emergency regimes.

3   EMERGENCY PROVISIONS IN CONSTITUTIONAL DOCUMENTS

His analysis of the Roman dictatorship led Machiavelli to conclude that the ideal republic ought to provide for emergency institutions ex ante and to structure those around the contours of the Roman dictatorship: 'republics should have a like mode [to the dictatorship] among their orders … a republic will never be perfect unless it has provided for everything with its laws and has established a remedy for every accident and given the mode to govern it'.[8]

Modern constitutional systems differ greatly in their treatment of emergency powers. However, following the example of the Roman republic, many constitutions contain explicit, frequently detailed, emergency provisions. Yet, while explicit constitutional reference to emergencies is common, it is by no means universal. The constitutions of the United States, Japan, and Belgium, for example, are almost entirely devoid of references to states of emergency and to emergency powers.[9] The American constitution only refers indirectly to emergencies in article I, section 8, clause 15, which vests the power in Congress 'To provide for calling forth the Militia to execute the Laws of the Union, suppress Insurrections and repel Invasions', and article I, section 9, clause 2, which provides that 'The Privilege of the Writ of Habeas Corpus shall not be suspended, unless when in Cases of Rebellion or Invasion the public Safety may require it'. Although certain other clauses mention terms such as 'war', or 'time of war', none attaches special powers to any branch of government in the event of such exigencies. However, this omission of emergency provisions is limited to the federal level. Unlike the Federal constitution, many State constitutions contain explicit emergency provisions.

3.1 Defining Emergencies

Some national constitutions, while providing for a special type of emergency regime in the case of war, do not specify constitutional emergency arrangements for events that fall short of war. Indeed, defining a state of emergency in advance is no easy task. Emergency is an elastic concept.[10] Alexander Hamilton captured the difficulty of defining the term in advance, arguing that '[i]t is impossible to foresee or to define the extent and variety of national exigencies, and the correspondent extent and variety of the means which may be necessary to satisfy them. The circumstances that endanger the safety of nations are infinite, and for this reason no constitutional shackles can wisely be imposed on the power to which the care of it is committed'.[11]

How, then, do drafters of national constitutions respond to this difficulty? Many constitutional documents differentiate among several types of emergencies. Distinctions are drawn based on the factual circumstances under which a declaration of emergency may be constitutionally permissible. Such classifications affect not only the methods by which a particular emergency may be declared and the duration for which such proclamation may hold valid, but also matters such as the nature, extent and scope of governmental emergency powers, and the possibility of derogating from constitutional rights and safeguards.

Some constitutions establish a dual structure of emergency powers. Under the constitutions of The Netherlands and Portugal, for example, there are two possible types of emergencies. The Dutch constitution authorizes the declaration of a 'state of war' and a 'state of emergency'. The constitution of Portugal distinguishes between a 'state of emergency' and a 'state of siege'. Similar dual structures can also be found in the constitutions of many former Communist countries.[12]

Latin and South American constitutions often draw distinctions among a multiplicity of states of exception (*estado de excepción*), allocating different emergency powers to government according to the particular type of exigency at hand. Not less than nine different states of exception can be thus identified.[13] It is common to find several distinct states of exception in the same constitutional document.[14] The mechanism used to distinguish among the various situations is based on general descriptions of factual circumstances that may lead to invoking each particular state of exception. Such factual circumstances include external war, breach of the peace and the public order, economic exigencies, natural disasters, and threats of disturbances.[15] In addition, each constitution lists the legal results arising out of the declaration of each state of exception by way of suspension of individual rights (*suspensión de garantias*) and the vesting of extraordinary powers in the executive branch of government.

Multilevel constitutional arrangements can also be found in the constitutions of Western countries such as Canada, Germany, and Spain, as well as some former Communist countries. The preamble to section 91 of the Canadian Constitution Act of 1867, confers on the federal parliament the power to make laws 'for the peace, order and good government of Canada'. That residuary power, which the federal parliament can exercise only with respect to matters 'not coming within the classes of subjects ... assigned exclusively to the Legislatures of the provinces', has been interpreted as authorizing the federal parliament to enact emergency legislation.[16] Based on this constitutional authorization, in August 1914, parliament enacted the War Measures Act ('WMA'). WMA was applied during the two world wars and in response to the October 1970 FLQ crisis,[17] before it was replaced by the Emergencies Act of 1988. The Emergencies Act authorizes the federal government to declare four different types of emergencies.[18] 'Public welfare emergency' may be declared in circumstances of natural disasters; 'public order emergency' may be invoked when serious threats to the security of Canada emerge; 'international emergency' deals with situations involving acts of intimidation towards Canada or other countries; finally, 'war emergency' may be proclaimed in case of real or imminent armed conflict involving Canada or any of its allies.[19] Under the Act, the initial duration of each proclaimed emergency varies (from 30 days in the case of 'public order' up to 120 days when 'war emergency' is concerned) and so does the nature and scope of permissible emergency powers granted to the federal government.

The question whether to incorporate emergency provisions into national constitutions was subject to heated debates in Europe and particularly in Germany after World War II. Responding to the lessons derived from the inability of the Weimar republic to defend itself and to the realities of the Cold War, some countries adopted the notion of 'militant democracy' – a term coined by Karl Loewenstein – and made it part of their national constitutions. Writing just shortly before World War II broke out, Loewenstein argued that the enemies of democracy would abuse the democratic guarantees of the rule of law and hide behind the protection of basic individual rights to promote their cause.[20] Arguing that liberal-democratic order was designed for normal times, he advocated the abandonment of the 'exaggerated formalism of the rule of law' in time of crisis.[21] Rigid democratic fundamentalism ought to give way to militant democracy that is founded on 'the will and the spirit of both the government and the people in democracies to survive'.[22] In that respect, '[t]he statute-book is only a subsidiary expedient of the militant will for self-preservation'.[23] Democracy must not fall into the trap of 'legalistic self-complacency and suicidal lethargy'.[24] Rather, it should allow for 'the application of disciplined authority, by liberal-minded men, for the ultimate ends of liberal government: human dignity and freedom'.[25]

The concept of 'militant democracy' (*Streitbare Demokratie*) became one of the cornerstones of the post-war constitutional order of the Federal Republic of Germany, standing for the defense of the core values of the German polity and of its 'free democratic basic order'.[26]

Responding directly to the lessons learned from the collapse of the Weimar republic, article 18 of the German Basic Law provides for the forfeiture of rights of persons who abuse them to combat the free democratic basic order, and article 21(2) allows any political party that has similar goals to be declared unconstitutional. Under article 21(2), the German Federal Constitutional Court declared unconstitutional two parties, the Socialist Reich Party and the Communist Party.[27] Similar concepts appeared also in the jurisprudence of other national[28] and regional courts.[29]

Another constitutional mechanism connected to emergency powers more generally was added to the German Basic Law in May 1968. Constitutional amendment that ushered in the 'emergency constitution'[30] distinguished between 'Internal Emergency' (*Innerer Notstand*), a 'State of Tension' (*Spannungsfall*), and a 'State of Defense' (*Verteidigungsfall*).[31] Under these provisions, an Internal Emergency occurs in situations when it is necessary 'to avert an imminent danger to the existence or free democratic basic order of the Federation or of a Land'. A State of Defense may be declared when 'the federal territory is under attack by armed force or imminently threatened by such an attack'. The circumstances that may give rise to a State of Tension are not defined in the Basic Law.

The Spanish constitution identifies three distinct scenarios involving a 'state of alarm' (*estado de alarma*), 'state of emergency' (*estado de excepción*), and 'state of siege' (*estado de sitio*). Article 116 of the Constitution deals with the authority to declare each of the three types of emergency regimes, outlines general procedures for such declaration and prescribes the initial duration for which a declaration may apply. In addition, article 86 provides for governmental 'provisional legislative decisions' in the form of decree-laws in case of 'extraordinary and urgent necessity'. The constitution does not define the three classes of emergencies but rather leaves it for an organic law to regulate them as well as the corresponding powers and limitations thereon. Pursuant to this provision, Organic Law 4/1981 defines the different circumstances under which each type of emergency regime may be exercised.[32]

The pattern of separating several types of emergency regimes is not universally followed. The constitution of South Africa recognizes only one type of emergency regime, following a declaration of a state of emergency. However, such a state of emergency may be invoked in a range of cases when 'the life of the nation is threatened by war, invasion, general insurrection, disorder, natural disaster or other public emergency'.[33] Similarly, the Israeli Basic Law: the Government recognizes only the possibility of declaring a 'state of emergency'. However, the Basic Law neither defines the term, nor describes the circumstances that may give rise legitimately to such a declaration. It recognizes the possibility of declaring a state of emergency without setting out substantive guidelines as to when such a declaration may be appropriate.

The main purpose behind multilevel constitutional classifications is to tailor and, at the same time, limit the powers made available to government in connection with particular types of emergencies. Natural disasters presumably call for the exercise of governmental powers that are distinct from those that may be necessary to face a foreign invasion. Both situations may, in turn, be distinguishable from economic crises. Moreover, when a constitution recognizes only one type of emergency regime, the government may invoke that regime in the face of foreign aggression – when a proclamation of a state of emergency may be considered legitimate by a majority of the population – and then use the same mechanism in other, less drastic situations, while not abandoning any of its expansive war-related powers. A war-driven emergency will be put in the same constitutional category as natural disasters, economic crises, and internal riots. Once the public and its leaders get used to the fact that 'emergency' entails certain governmental powers, that may continue to hold true also for future emergencies, albeit of a different and 'lesser' nature. Classifications may also be seen to reflect a hierarchical order of possible proclamations of emergencies. While each proclamation can be made in the context of a broad panoply of dangers and threats, the powers made available to the executive increase and the protection of individual rights and civil liberties diminishes in scope as we step up the emergency ladder.

However, classifying and categorizing emergencies is not without its problems. Review of the existing classifications of states of emergency reveals a substantial (perhaps inevitable) degree of vagueness, ambiguity, and overlap among the different categories. Some of the key terms, such as 'danger' and 'imminent threat', are broad enough to make the choice among the possible categories mostly a political one. Creating a sliding scale of emergency regimes may encourage a government to resort to some type of emergency regime that may be considered not as serious as, for example, a state of war. A declaration of such a 'low-level' state of emergency may be more readily accepted by legislatures, courts, and the general public. Considering certain types of emergencies to be 'not-so-serious' may undermine the basic notion that emergencies correspond to exceptional situations, relating especially to the exceptional nature of the threat to the community. This can condition the public to live with some type of emergency as part of the normal way of life. It would then be easier for government to 'upgrade' to a higher-level emergency regime. In contradistinction, when any state of emergency potentially makes available to government the full panoply of permissible emergency powers, including the most draconian ones, the public may be more cautious in accepting as valid a declaration of emergency in suspect circumstances. The pronounced effect of 'crossing the threshold' may be absent when a scale of emergencies is offered.

3.2 The Authority to Declare an Emergency

Different constitutional arrangements exist with respect to the organ or organs that are authorized to declare an emergency. Under most constitutional schemes, the authority to invoke an emergency regime is shared by the executive and legislative branches of government. However, the exact point of equilibrium varies with the specific type of emergency involved and with the general constitutional culture of any given jurisdiction. Institutional power sharing is designed to prevent a situation in which the organ that is to exercise emergency powers is also the one authorized to declare the emergency in the first place and activate its own powers. At the same time, it is aimed at ensuring that the branch of government most capable of acting rapidly and effectively to counter a crisis is not paralyzed.

Modern constitutions frequently vest the primary authority for declaring a state of emergency in the legislature. At times such power to declare an emergency is coupled with the provision that parliament will act upon the request or proposal of the government.[34] However, it is also common to find provisions allowing the government or the president (where relevant) to declare a state of emergency when circumstances are such that parliament cannot convene or act in time against the exigency. Such circumstances may also pave the way for the exercise of provisional legislative emergency powers by the executive. Executive declaration of an emergency and acts of a legislative nature are then subject to a subsequent prompt ratification by parliament if they are to remain in force.[35]

Other constitutional provisions vest the primary responsibility and authority to declare a state of emergency in the executive. Thus, for example, constitutions of Latin and South

American countries (and of several former Communist countries) tend to vest the authority to declare a state of exception in the president, reflecting the strong position traditionally enjoyed by the executive in those countries. Of the constitutions that focus on the executive for declaring a state of emergency, some require prior authorization or subsequent ratification to be given by the legislative branch.[36] Where it is the president who has the constitutional power to declare an emergency, a counter-signature by certain ministers or an approval by the government may be required for the declaration to be valid.[37] However, in societies with a strong presidency culture, a mere consultation with government prior to declaring a state of emergency may be sufficient.[38] Several constitutional arrangements merely require the government to notify the parliament of the proclamation of a state of emergency without giving an additional role to parliament.[39] Finally, under some constitutional schemes, certain types of emergency regimes are declared by the executive while others are declared by the legislature. Thus, for example, article 116(2) of the Spanish constitution vests the power to declare a state of alarm in the government, while requiring notification to the House of Representatives. Article 116(3) gives the power to declare the next level – state of emergency – to the government, conditional on prior approval by the House. Article 116(4), dealing with a state of siege – the most wide-ranging of the three emergency regimes – grants the power to declare such a state of exception to the House, based on a governmental proposal.[40]

Various constitutional arrangements can also be found concerning the required majority in parliament that must approve or ratify an executive declaration of emergency or proclaim an emergency when the power to so declare is vested in the legislature. Existing arrangements range from demanding a simple majority to requiring a qualified majority.[41] In addition, some constitutional arrangements require what Bruce Ackerman calls a 'supermajoritarian escalator' (see infra).[42] Article 37(2)(b) of the South African constitution provides that the first renewal of a declaration of a state of emergency requires the supporting vote of a majority of members of the Assembly, whereas further renewals require support of at least 60 percent of those members.[43]

Different arrangements exist also with respect to the duration for which an initial declaration of a state of emergency may be in force and to the possibility of further renewals of that declaration. The principle of temporal duration, so intrinsically linked to the fundamental understanding of the concept of emergency, requires that states of emergency be short-lived. This principle is reflected in using one or both of the following constitutional techniques: (1) setting temporal limitations on a declared state of emergency; and (2) setting strict procedures concerning the extension of a declared state of emergency. Some constitutions set limits on the number of permissible extensions to the initial declaration of emergency or on the number of emergencies that may be declared in any given period (usually one calendar year).[44]

3.3   The Effects of Declaring a State of Emergency

To what extent may a constitution be suspended, in whole or in part, in times of emergency? May individual rights, otherwise protected by the constitution, be suspended or derogated from under such circumstances? To what extent may emergency measures change the institutional features of the constitutional order? And to what extent may the constitution be modified, amended, changed or even repealed in such conditions?

Many constitutions provide that a declaration of emergency may lead to the suspension of certain individual rights and freedoms. For the most part, those constitutions follow one of two approaches: (1) enlisting those rights and freedoms that may be suspended during a declared state of emergency (a positive list approach),[45] or (2) enumerating those rights and freedoms that may not be restricted or in any way violated even in times of acute exigency (a negative list approach).[46] Other constitutions take a mixed approach, using a negative list in the context of, for example, a declared state of emergency, while invoking a positive list with respect to a state of natural disaster.[47] Some constitutional arrangements adopt by reference the limitations prescribed in international human rights treaties on derogation from otherwise protected rights.[48] Of course, states that are parties to any of these conventions are legally constrained by their dictates and run the risk of violating their own international obligations if they choose to disregard the treaty rules.

Augmented extraordinary powers conferred upon the executive branch are another likely constitutional outcome of a declaration of a state of emergency. Emergencies lead to expansion of (national) government powers and concentration of such powers in the hands of the executive branch of government. 'Crisis government is primarily and often exclusively the business of presidents and prime ministers.'[49] One important aspect of such expansion and concentration of powers concerns the ability of the executive to engage in the process of law-making. Law-making powers may be granted to the government by an explicit constitutional provision or by way of delegation of some legislative power from the legislature by means of specific and temporary legislation, broad delegation of powers from the legislature, an enabling act, or permanent legislation with an 'emergency flavor'. The force of such emergency executive decrees may depend on a subsequent ratification by the legislative organ. Alternatively such executive legislation may be valid so long as not repealed by either the executive or the legislature.[50] Legislative-type emergency powers can take the form of authorizing the executive to issue decree-laws and regulations that may have the power to amend or even suspend parliamentary legislation, or even derogate from constitutional provisions.[51] The power to issue provisional legislation may also be conferred upon the executive in situations such as the German 'Legislative Emergency' (*Gesetzgebungsnotstand*) when the president may, at the request of the federal government and with the authorization of the Bundesrat and when the Bundestag was to be dissolved following a successful no-confidence vote but has not yet been so dissolved, 'declare a state of legislative emergency with respect to a bill which is rejected by the Bundestag although declared urgent by the Federal government'.[52] Such emergency legislation needs to be approved by parliament once the causes for the legislative emergency have expired.

Several other effects of a declared state of emergency should be noted. First, in federal states, one of the first 'victims' of exigencies and crises is the principle of federalism. This is explicit not only in various constitutional provisions found in the constitutions of, for example, Germany, India, and Russia,[53] but is also the constitutional practice in the United States[54] and Canada.[55] Second, in order to prevent repetition of the mistakes that led to the destruction of the Weimar constitutional experiment, modern constitutional provisions often proscribe any change to, or modification of, the constitution itself during an emergency, or at least any change to, or modification of, the nature of the regime and its core constitutional norms.[56] Similarly, it is frequently provided that the legislature may not be dissolved during an emergency.[57] In fact, some constitutions provide that the term of office of the legislature is automatically extended during a state of emergency.[58]

However, certain constitutional doctrines seem to leave the door open for broad suspension of constitutional provisions in time of exigency. Thus, for example, under the doctrine of *régime des pleins pouvoirs*, the Swiss federal government may act in a way that would otherwise be considered unconstitutional, if deemed necessary to safeguard the state's security, its independence and neutrality as well as its economic interests. This emergency regime may be invoked by the federal government when parliament cannot meet or when the legislative process can no longer function. This emergency regime, which has so far been invoked only during the two world wars, offers practically no constitutional limitations on its employment. The only limitation is derived from Switzerland's accession to the European Convention on Human Rights.

Article 28.3.2° of the Irish constitution provides that 'In the case of actual invasion ... the Government may take whatever steps they may consider necessary for the protection of the State'. Article 28.3.3° then immunizes from any constitutional challenge not only parliamentary-enacted legislation but also acts done, 'or purporting to be done', in time of violent crises in pursuance of such legislation. As one of the judges of the Irish Supreme Court suggested, 'The Constitution here envisages a crisis during which the normal rule of law is, at least to a considerable extent, superseded by the Rule of the Executive in the domain of emergency law ... subject only to the control of the Legislature'.[59] The result is 'to provide a means of freeing the Oireachtas [National Parliament] from the limits imposed upon it by the Constitution ... So long as the statute is expressed to be for the purpose specified, nothing whatever in the Constitution may be invoked to invalidate it ... In theory [the Oireachtas] could, by invoking the Article 28.3.3° formula and keeping the emergency in being, re-write the Constitution.'[60] While the Irish constitution puts certain fundamental rights outside the reach of any legislative act, the effect of Article 28.3.3° is that even such rights may be derogated from, or in fact suspended and revoked, in times of emergency.[61]

3.4   Checks and Balances

Some constitutional provisions provide explicitly for judicial review not only of particular emergency measures employed by the government but also of the declaration of emergency.[62] Few others limit explicitly, or outright prevent, judicial review over the declaration of a state of emergency or of legislative emergency measures.[63] Most constitutions are silent on this matter. However, practice shows that domestic courts tend to support the government's position either by invoking judicial tools such as the political question and standing doctrines to avoid having to decide the case on the merits or, when deciding a case on its merits, accepting the government's position.[64] That judicial attitude becomes even more pronounced when the courts are called upon to deal with cases *durante bello* as opposed to deciding them when the crisis is over.[65]

No less problematic are the checks by the legislative branch in times of emergency. Most constitutional arrangements provide for such checks through parliamentary involvement in the processes of declaring and terminating an emergency and the need for parliamentary approval of executive emergency legislative acts. These are added to the ordinary methods by which parliament exercises control and supervision over the government, such as approving appropriations, parliamentary inquiries, hearings and questioning, special parliamentary committees, and no-confidence votes. Yet in practice legislators tend to abdicate responsibility in times of emergency. Several reasons may account for that. First is the 'rally round the flag' effect: 'a short, low-cost military measure to repel an attack ... is almost invariably popular at least at its inception. So too are many other kinds of assertive action or speech in foreign policy.'[66] A government's emergency measures are likely to draw significant domestic support, at least initially. Periods of emergency are characterized by an absence of conflict. James Madison already noted that constitutions originated in the midst of great danger that led, among other things, to 'an enthusiastic confidence of the people in their patriotic leaders, which stifled the ordinary diversity of opinions on great national questions'.[67] It is likely that the emotional effects of emergencies and the desire to appear patriotic to voters will lead legislators to support vesting in the government broad and expansive authorizations and powers and to do so without delay.

The executive branch of government has traditionally been considered to be in the best position with respect to the conduct of foreign and national security policies. Perceived advantages such as secrecy, dispatch, and access to broad sources of information are often mentioned in this regard. One result of this structural advantage is that the executive is often the first to act in the face of emergency and, in any event, its actions are most visible since '[i]n drama, magnitude and finality his decisions so far overshadow any others that almost alone he fills the public eye and ear'.[68] When added to the consensus-generating quality of emergencies, that means that the executive will dictate and dominate the agenda, including the legislative agenda. Such domination is facilitated further by the realities of party politics. In parliamentary systems, government is supported by a majority in parliament. While in presidential systems such control of the legislature is not guaranteed, in countries such as the United States the realities of the modern political party system have extended the president's effective control into branches of government other than his own, allowing him often to 'win, as a political leader, what he cannot command under the Constitution'.[69] The fact that in periods of emergency conflicts that seem to be mere partisan politics are set aside (leading, almost inevitably, to the adoption of policies advocated by the executive) ensures that presidents need not be overly envious of prime ministers.

Finally, the targets of counter-emergency measures are frequently perceived as outsiders, frequently foreign nationals or members of minority groups. Targeting outsiders means that while the benefits (perceived or real) of fighting terrorism and violence accrue to all members of a society, the costs of such actions seem, on the face of it, to be borne by a distinct, smaller, and ostensibly well-defined group of people. Under such circumstances, the danger is that the politically accountable branches of government will tend to strike a balance disproportionately in favor of security and impose too much of a cost on the target group, without facing much resistance (and, in fact, receiving strong support) from the general public.[70]

3.5 Inherent Emergency Powers

President Lincoln's actions during the Civil War, especially in the first 12 weeks between the bombardment of Fort Sumter, on April 12, 1861, and the convening of Congress on July 4, 1861, have been the subject of much study and debate. During this period Lincoln demonstrated perhaps the most awesome display of executive power in American history. Whereas some of these measures could be construed as falling within the constitutional or statutorily delegated presidential powers, others were questionable. The president's unilateral enlargement of the armed forces violated an express constitutional provision vesting in Congress the power to raise and support Armies and to provide and maintain a Navy. Similarly, the power to suspend the writ of habeas corpus was generally thought at the time to belong exclusively to Congress. The Emancipation Proclamation, which '[w]ith the stroke of a pen (backed, admittedly, by Union guns) ... wiped out property rights worth many millions of dollars', was also deemed unconstitutional when made.[71]

One possible legal explanation of Lincoln's actions considers such actions to be within the boundaries of the Constitution under the doctrine of the 'war powers' of the federal government. At one point Lincoln himself argued: 'It became necessary for me to choose whether, using only the existing means, agencies, and processes which Congress had provided, I should let the Government fall at once into ruin or whether, availing myself of the broader powers conferred by the Constitution in cases of insurrection, I would make an effort to save it, with all its blessings, for the present age and for posterity.'[72]

Lincoln's wartime presidency ushered in a theory of crisis government based on the concept of inherent presidential powers. Since then, arguments put forward in support of the executive's resort to emergency powers have revolved around the claim that the president enjoys a wide range of constitutionally inherent powers, including emergency powers. Arguments invoking presidential inherent powers have been heard mostly, albeit not exclusively, in the context of foreign affairs and national security, separating those from ordinary, domestic matters. Such arguments focus on the benefits of flexibility in the face of unpredictability. If it is impossible to cover all contingencies by a priori, general, fixed legal norms and rules, there is a need for discretion and flexibility. Since the executive branch of government may be suited best to deal with emergencies, it follows that it should be the one to exercise such flexibility. However, inherent powers invoke the specter of abuse and the concern about the ability to limit governmental powers in times of emergency. If it is the president, for example, who decides when the need arises for the use of such powers and the extent to which such powers ought to be used in any given case, then he enjoys truly unlimited powers. He may decide, at his unfettered discretion, to apply those awesome powers to any situation and be accountable to none. Thus, Justice Jackson rejected forcefully the Truman administration's assertions of unlimited executive power in times of emergency: '[Inherent] power either has no beginning or it has no end. If it exists, it need submit to no legal restraint. I am not alarmed that it would plunge us straightway into dictatorship, but it is at least a step in that wrong direction.'[73] Justice Jackson then stated that the Constitution did not reflect the scope of the president's real power and identified 'vast accretions' of federal power and concentration of such powers in the executive, leading him to conclude that 'I cannot be brought to believe that this country will suffer if the Court refuses further to aggrandize the presidential office, already so potent and so relatively immune from judicial review'.[74]

The test for inherent executive emergency powers must be that of factual necessity. But if that is the case, and if the necessity is extreme and grave, it may well be that what is necessary is for the executive to disregard constitutional obligations and act against explicit constitutional dictates and statutory norms in order to save the nation. But if that is so, why would any constitutional provision setting limitations on inherent powers be able to withstand such actions? If necessity is so grave, should not the executive be able to disregard all constitutional and statutory provisions whatever they are? The logical outcome of this is President Nixon's claim of unbridled authority under the Constitution: '[W]hen the President does it, that means that it is not illegal'.[75] Under this reading, inherent powers must amount to, as Justice Jackson suggested, an unlimited power, constrained neither by any legal norms nor by principles and rules of the constitutional order.

4   LEGISLATING FOR EMERGENCIES

Drafters of constitutions can neither anticipate all future exigencies nor can they provide detailed and explicit arrangements for all such occasions. Thus, constitutional emergency provisions must use broad and flexible language that sets general frameworks for emergency rule. The most common method of adapting the constitutional language to concrete exigencies is through legislative amendments and modifications that are incorporated into the existing ordinary legal terrain. Such modifications may be introduced into ordinary legislation and become part of the ordinary legal system. Alternatively, rather than attempt to modify existing legal norms, replacement or supplementary emergency laws are enacted and regulations adopted. Such emergency legislation may, but need not, take the format of stand-alone legislation, as when emergency provisions are included in specific 'emergency' legislation. Such provisions may also be incorporated into an ordinary piece of legislation while retaining their specific emergency features. Indeed, modern practice across jurisdictions shows that when the executive branch of government exercises emergency powers, the source of such powers is much more likely to be found in legislative means than emanate directly from the constitutional document itself.[76]

However, violent emergencies tend to bring about a rush to legislate reminding one of the observation by the Athenian of Plato's *The Laws* that 'no man ever legislates at all. Accidents and calamities occur in a thousand different ways, and it is they that are the universal legislators of the world.'[77] The prevailing belief may be that if new offenses are added to the criminal code and the scope of existing offenses broadened, and if the arsenal of law enforcement agencies is enhanced by putting at their disposal more sweeping powers to search and seize, to eavesdrop, to interrogate, to detain without trial, and to deport, the country will be more secure and better able to face the emergency.[78] It is often easier to pass new legislation than to examine why existing legislation, and the powers granted under it to government and its agencies, was insufficient. By permitting the government to claim that the pre-existing legal infrastructure was somehow deficient and forestalled efficient responses to the threats, adding new legislation may result in the piling up of legislative measures into a complex state of emergency.[79] The unpredictability of threats and their changing nature, coupled with the need for rapid counter-response, ensure that the legislative branch will suffer from the 'red queen effect', i.e., it would take all the legislative running it can do in order to keep in the same place. The rush to legislate also means that when emergency legislation is initially introduced, often no meaningful debates over it take place. The passage of new legislation allows government, in turn, to demonstrate that it is doing something against the dangers facing the nation rather than sitting idly. As Justice Robert Jackson noted: 'fear and anxiety create public demands for greater assurance which may not be justified by necessity but which any popular government finds irresistible'.[80]

Reassuring the public that its government is acting forcefully against terrorists is a worthy goal.[81] A successful terrorist campaign met by a hesitant governmental counteraction may eliminate inhibitions against using force and violence to accomplish political, social, and economic goals by other committed groups and individuals within the community.[82] A sense that the government is not doing enough to protect the nation and the life of its citizens may lead to disintegration of political, social, and institutional structures and to their replacement by others, perhaps less democratic alternatives. It may also lead to loss of popular confidence in existing constitutional institutions and mechanisms and, perhaps, to a general disrespect for the law. If the state is expected to guarantee the 'liberty' of its citizens, surely it is supposed to protect and guarantee their 'life'.[83] However, the problem emerges when the reassurance function becomes the sole, or even the primary, justification for legislation or other counter-emergency measures. Certain measures that may have an apparently high reassuring value may prove of little practical effect in making the nation safer against future attacks and, in fact, may even make the nation less safe.[84] Moreover, reassurance in and of itself does not present any meaningful substantive limitations on the powers exercised by government in particular situations.[85] Nor does it inform us of the content of the powers to be vested in the executive by a declaration of emergency.[86]

Bruce Ackerman puts forward the constitutional mechanism of 'escalating cascade of supermajorities' ('ECS') as the lynchpin for his proposed constitutional overhaul 'of the emergency power provisions currently found in many of the world's constitutions'.[87] While vesting in the executive broad emergency powers Ackerman posits ECS as a curb on the rush to use – and abuse – emergency powers.[88] Based on the constitutional framework introduced in article 37 of the constitution of South Africa, Ackerman's ECS seeks also to reduce the possibility of emergency powers becoming entrenched and 'normalized' by insisting on the temporary nature of such measures and making extensions thereof increasingly harder. He proposes that a (simple) majority vote by the legislature would be required for the emergency to continue for the first two months, and that each additional two months extension of the emergency would require increasing the majority vote up to 80 percent vote that would be required for any extension beyond the initial six months.

Ackerman's proposal is problematic. The combination of the consensus-generating nature of crises, the 'first-mover' advantage enjoyed by the executive, and the 'threat' of the actual success of proposals such as ECS to curb and restrain the executive's responses to crises, may push the executive branch to capitalize on the early broad support that it is likely to receive and to aggregate as many broad powers as possible at that point. The government may reasonably conclude that such powers and measures will no longer be available to it at a later point in time in light of the need to ensure increasing legislative supermajorities.[89] At the same time, the requirements of ECS, combined with the phenomenon of early rallying around the flag, may also encourage individual legislators to not oppose initial executive measures on the assumption that such measures are going to be temporary and expire shortly (if only due to the executive's inability to garner the requisite supermajority).[90] This may give further incentive to the executive to push for (overly) broad emergency powers and authorization of sweeping initial measures which may not only be unnecessary, but, once granted and accepted, become entrenched.

The perception that a robust ECS may hamper the executive's ability to fight future crises successfully may encourage the legislature to accept the need for exceptions to be carved out of the 'normal' procedural requirements of the escalating cascade of supermajorities. Indeed, this is a recognized feature of many constitutional arrangements around the world: a constitution may mandate, for example, that a 'normal' declaration of emergency be made by parliament, while recognizing special circumstances when the authority to so declare is vested in the president. In addition, ECS is also likely to come under severe pressures in precisely those situations that it is designed to forestall, i.e., cases of prolonged states of emergency. For if, contrary to the design of ECS, a particular state of emergency is not short-lived, ECS would mean that, 'twenty-one percent of the nation's representatives could disband emergency powers even when seventy-nine percent agree that emergency conditions continue'.[91] At the same time, Ackerman's proposal of an emergency constitution, which would substitute the 'normal' constitution in states of emergency, assumes that periods of emergency and normalcy could be clearly demarcated and kept separate.[92] For if that is not the case, the risk is that the emergency constitution will become the constitution for all times, whether times of emergency and war or times of peace. As I argue below, such separation is illusory. Institutional proposals such as ECS come with a clear, yet unrealistic, vision of emergency regulation. ECS also seeks to reduce the possibility of emergency powers becoming entrenched and 'normalized' by insisting on the temporary nature of such measures and making extensions thereof increasingly harder. But how would ECS achieve that goal if one considers, for example, the possibilities of legislative accommodation through the modification of ordinary laws or the various forms of interpretive accommodation, i.e., forms of accommodating for emergency powers without, necessarily, invoking the need for an 'official' proclamation of emergency or for special emergency legislation? Many counter-terrorism measures do not necessarily take the form of 'emergency' powers and legislation. Thus, for example, the Bush administration was able to engage in a campaign of preventive detention without invoking special emergency powers – such as section 412 of the USA Patriot Act – by relying on pre-existing immigration and criminal law provisions.[93] These forms of 'dispersed emergency regulation'[94] are not easily, if at all, amenable to mechanisms such as ECS.

5   INTERPRETING EMERGENCY PROVISIONS

Judges, like the general public and its political leaders, 'like[] to win wars'[95] and are sensitive to the criticism that they impede the war effort. In states of emergency, courts assume a highly deferential attitude when called upon to review governmental actions and decisions. Judges may invoke judicial mechanisms such as the political question doctrine and proclaim issues pertaining to emergency powers to be nonjusticiable, or, when deciding cases on their merits, they are likely to uphold the national government's position.

When dealing with 'emergency' cases, courts may interpret existing constitutional and legal rules in a way that is emergency-sensitive, accommodating the need for additional governmental powers to fend off a dangerous threat by exercising 'the elastic power of interpretation'[96] to give an expansive, emergency-minded interpretative spin to existing norms, transforming various components of the ordinary legal system into counter-emergency facilitating norms.[97] While the law on the books does not change in times of crisis, the law in action reveals substantial changes that are introduced into the legal system. Richard Posner argues, for example, that '[i]f the Constitution is not to be treated as a suicide pact, why should military exigencies not influence the scope of the constitutional rights that the Supreme Court has manufactured from the Constitution's vague provisions?'[98] In other words, '[t]he point is not that law is suspended in times of emergency ... The point rather is that law is usually flexible enough to allow judges to give controlling weight to the immediate consequences of decision if those consequences are sufficiently grave.'[99] In times of crisis, we can expect expansive judicial interpretations of the scope of police powers, with a concomitant contraction of individual rights. As Harold Lasswell wrote, referring to the constitutional protection against unreasonable searches and seizures: 'what seems unreasonable in reasonable times may look reasonable in unreasonable times'.[100]

6   CHALLENGES

The various models of accommodation offer the benefit of constitutional and legal flexibility in the face of crisis and emergency. Legal principles and rules, as well as legal structures and institutions, may be adjusted, relaxed, or perhaps even suspended in part, in order to meet the needs of answering violent threats successfully. Recognizing that extraordinary powers are, in fact, going to be used in times of great peril, the legal system retains enough flexibility to allow such use within legal confines rather than outside them.

Resorting to models of accommodation may actually result in less draconian emergency measures being implemented. In the absence of legal permission to employ special emergency powers or in the event that the legally available powers are insufficient, government may be reluctant to take emergency measures extra-legally. This hesitation may force the government to respond to the emergency only at a later stage, when the crisis has further developed and the danger escalated, and when more extreme actions are required to overcome it. If emergency powers are part of the government's legal arsenal, it may be able to use them to nip the emergency in the bud. At the same time, allowing government to act responsibly, within a legal framework, against threats and dangers means that mechanisms of control and supervision against abuse and misuse of powers – such as judicial review and parliamentary oversight over the actions of the executive branch of government – are available and functioning.

However, it is precisely the fear of such abuse and misuse of powers that presents the major challenge to the models. Accommodation, it may be argued, is unprincipled, apologetic and open to abuse. The models enable the authorities to mold and shape the legal system, including the constitutional edifice, under the pretense of fighting off an emergency. Moreover, constitutional or legal modifications may tempt the authorities to test their limits and expand their powers. The very existence of such system of emergency rules and regulations may result in greater and more frequent use of emergency powers by officials, making extraordinary powers part of the ordinary discourse of government: '[E]mergency powers would tend to kindle emergencies'.[101] Once created and put into place, such constitutional and legal emergency modifications will be similar to Justice Jackson's famous 'loaded weapon ready for the hand of any authority that can bring forward a plausible claim of an urgent need'.[102]

The most troubling example of such abuse and misuse is the role played by article 48 of the Weimar constitution in bringing down the Weimar republic. Under article 48, the president could, when in his opinion public safety and order were seriously disturbed or endangered, take measures necessary for the restoration of public safety and order and could temporarily suspend several of the fundamental rights guaranteed by the constitution. While the use of article 48 was supposed to be subject to certain limitations, in practice none of these limitations proved an obstacle to the exercise of unfettered dictatorial powers. Between 1919 and 1932, article 48 was invoked more than 250 times. It became a constitutional source for the promulgation of an extensive array of executive decrees, most frequently in the context of economic disturbances. Towards the end of the life of the Weimar republic, article 48 had been used as practically the exclusive legal source for governmental action, with the ordinary legislative and administrative processes virtually suspended. When Hitler became the chancellor in 1933, article 48 was used by the Nazis to finish off the republic.[103]

Perhaps even more significantly, the models of accommodation are based on an unrealistic assumption. The assumption of separation is defined by the belief in our ability to separate emergencies and crises from normalcy, counter-terrorism measures from ordinary legal rules and norms. Emergencies are conceptualized in terms of a dichotomized dialectic. The term 'emergency' connotes a sudden, urgent, usually unforeseen event or situation that requires immediate action, often without time for reflection and consideration. The notion of 'emergency' is inherently linked to the concept of 'normalcy' in the sense that the former is considered to be outside the ordinary course of events or anticipated actions. In order to be able to talk about normalcy and emergency in any meaningful way, the concept of emergency is informed by notions of temporal duration and exceptional danger. Traditional discourse on emergency powers posits normalcy and crisis as two separate phenomena and assumes that emergency is the exception. Its basic paradigm is that of 'normalcy–rule, emergency–exception', which is based on a clear separation of the normal and exceptional cases.[104]

However, such bright-line distinctions between normalcy and emergency are frequently untenable.[105] Fashioning legal tools to respond to emergencies on the belief that the assumption of separation will serve as a firewall that protects human rights, civil liberties, and the normal legal system as a whole may be misguided. The belief in our ability to separate emergency from normalcy focuses our attention on the immediate effects of emergency measures and powers, while hiding from view their long-term costs and the danger that emergency-specific accommodation will become an integral part of the regular legal system.

NOTES

1. Pnina Lahav, 'A Barrel Without Hoops: The Impact of Counterterrorism on Israel's Legal Culture' (1988) 10 *Cardozo Law Review* 529 at 531.
2. Oren Gross and Fionnuala Ní Aoláin, *Law in Times of Crisis: Emergency Powers in Theory and Practice* (2006) 17–85. This chapter focuses exclusively on the models of accommodation. For discussion of alternative models see ibid., pp. 86–170.
3. Clinton L. Rossiter, *Constitutional Dictatorship: Crisis Government in Modern Democracies* (1948), p. 15. See also Gross and Ní Aoláin, *Law in Times of Crisis*, pp. 17–26.
4. The period of six months was chosen to comport with the army's 'working year' and thus with the maximum duration of a military campaign.
5. Niccolo Machiavelli, *Discourses on Livy* (Harvey C. Mansfield and Nathan Tarcov trans., 1996), p. 74.
6. Ibid., p. 76.
7. Ibid., p. 74.
8. Ibid., pp. 74–5.
9. The Democratic Constitution of Japan, which is based on the American constitutional model and the Charter of the United Nations, does not contain emergency provisions or any provisions dealing with acts of war or martial law. However, article 71 of the Japanese Police Law authorizes the Prime Minister to declare a state of 'national emergency' and assume direct control over Japan's police. While the Coordinated Constitution of Belgium is silent on the issue of emergency, it does provide that 'The Constitution may not be wholly or partially suspended' (article 187) as well as state that no constitutional revision may be undertaken or pursued 'during times of war or when the Houses are prevented from meeting freely on federal territory'. Article 196.
10. See, e.g., The International Law Association Paris Report 59 (1984).
11. 'The Federalist No. 23', at 153 (Alexander Hamilton) (Clinton Rossiter ed., 1961).
12. Venelin I. Ganev, 'Emergency Powers and the New East European Constitutions', 45 *American Journal of Comparative Law* 585 (1997).
13. These include, among others, the state of siege (*estado de sitio*), state of emergency (*estado de emergencia*), state of alarm (*estado de alarma*), state of prevention (*estado de prevención*), state of defense, and state of war (*estado de guerra*). See, e.g., article 111 of the Constitution of Bolivia; article 137 of the Constitution of Peru; article 23 of the Argentine Constitution; article 37(8) of the Constitution of the Dominican Republic; articles 47 and 51 of the Constitution of Panama; article 139 of the Constitution of Guatemala; article 238(7) of the Constitution of Paraguay; article 136 of the Constitution of Brazil. See also Diego Valadés, *La*

Dictadura Constitucional en América Latina (Mexico: UNAM, Instituto de Investigaciones Jurídicas, 1974); Brian Loveman, *The Constitution of Tyranny* (Pittsburgh, PA: University of Pittsburg Press, 1993).

14. See also articles 21(V), 84(ix) and (x), and 136–9 of the Brazilian Constitution; articles 40 and 41 of the Constitution of Chile; articles 212, 213 and 215 of the Constitution of Colombia.

15. See, e.g., article 40(1) of the Constitution of Chile; article 138 of the Constitution of Guatemala; article 185 of the Constitution of Nicaragua; articles 37(7) and 55(7) of the Constitution of the Dominican Republic; articles 136 and 137 of the Brazilian Constitution; article 202(13) of the Constitution of Paraguay.

16. Peter W. Hogg, *Constitutional Law of Canada* (5th ed., 2008), Ch. 17, pp. 19–32.

17. On the application of WMA and emergency powers in Canada during the two world wars see, e.g., Note, 'Civil Liberties in Great Britain and Canada During War', 55 *Harvard Law Review* 1006 (1942); Herbert Marx, 'The Emergency Power and Civil Liberties in Canada', 16 *McGill Law Journal* 39, 71–88 (1970); Patricia Peppin, 'Emergency Legislation and Rights in Canada: The War Measures Act and Civil Liberties', 18 *Queen's Law Journal* 129 (1993). In October 1970 the Canadian Government invoked the WMA for the first time ever in peacetime. The immediate cause for this was the kidnapping of a British diplomat and a Quebec Cabinet Minister by the Front de Liberation du Québec ('FLQ'). WMA was activated by the Trudeau government after the kidnapped minister, Pierre Laporte, had been found dead. In the early hours of October 16, shortly after the government brought WMA into force by proclaiming a state of 'apprehended insurrection', hundreds of Canadians were arrested in accordance with regulations promulgated by the government under WMA which made it a criminal offence to be a member of the FLQ. The regulations were issued by the government at 4 a.m. and put into action within minutes thereafter before any publication was made of their issuance. In addition, under the Regulations, attendance at an FLQ meeting was made prima facie evidence of membership in that organization, even if the attendance took place before the issuance of the Regulations. On the use of emergency powers during the 'October crisis' see Herbert Marx, 'The "Apprehended Insurrection" of October 1970 and the Judicial Function', 7 *University of British Columbia Law Review* 55 (1972); Douglas A. Schmeiser, 'Control of Apprehended Insurrection: Emergency Measures v. The Criminal Code', 4 *Manitoba Law Journal* 359 (1971). See also Dan G. Loomis, *Not Much Glory: Quelling the F.L.Q.* (Toronto: Deneau, 1984); Ron Haggart and Aubrey E. Golden, *Rumours of War* (Toronto: J. Lorimer, 1979); Fernand Dumont, *The Vigil of Quebec* (Tornoto: University of Toronto Press, 1974); Gerard Pelletier, *The October Crisis* (Toronto: McClelland and Stewart, Joyce Marshall trans., 1971).

18. See, e.g., Eliot Tenofsky, 'The War Measures and Emergency Acts', 19 *American Review of Canadian Studies* 293 (1989); Peter Rosenthal, 'The New Emergencies Act: Four Times the War Measures Act', 20 *Manitoba Law Journal* 563, 593–8 (1991).

19. Sections 5, 16, 27 and 37 of the Emergencies Act, respectively.

20. Karl Loewenstein, 'Militant Democracy and Fundamental Rights' (1937) 31 *American Political Science Review* 417 and 638 at 424, 426–31, 638–56; Karl Loewenstein, 'Legislative Control of Political Extremism in European Democracies' (1938) 38 *Columbia Law Review* 591 and 725.

21. Ibid., p. 432.

22. Loewenstein, 'Legislative Control', 774.

23. Loewenstein, 'Militant Democracy', 657.

24. Ibid., p. 431.

25. Ibid., p. 658; Loewenstein, 'Legislative Control', 774.

26. Donald P. Kommers, *The Constitutional Jurisprudence of the Federal Republic of Germany* (2nd ed., 1997), pp. 37–8; David P. Currie, *The Constitution of the Federal Republic of Germany* (1994), p. 213.

27. The Socialist Reich Party Case, 2 BVerGE 1 (1952); The Communist Party Case, 5 BVerGE 85 (1956). Ronald J. Krotoszynski, Jr., 'A Comparative Perspective on the First Amendment: Free Speech, Militant Democracy, and the Primacy of Dignity as a Preferred Constitutional Value in Germany' 78 *Tulane Law Review* 1549 (2004).

28. See, e.g., for Israel: E.A. 1/65, *Yardor v Chairman of Central Elections Comm. for Sixth Knesset*, 19(3) P.D. 365; E.A. 2/84, *Neiman v Chairman of Central Elections Comm. for Eleventh Knesset*, 39(2) P.D. 225; E.A. 2/88, *Ben Shalom v Central Election Committee for the Twelfth Knesset*, 43(4) P.D. 221; E.A. 2600/99, *Erlich v Chairman of the Central Elections Commission*, 53(3) P.D 38; E.B. 50/30, *Bishara v Central Election Commission*, 57(4) P.D. 1. Ariel Bendor, 'The Right of Parties to Participate in Elections to the Knesset' (1988) 18 *Mishpatim* 269. See also Gregory H. Fox and Georg Nolte, 'Intolerant Democracies' (1995) 36 *Harvard International Law Journal* 1 and the responses to it in volume 37.

29. See, e.g., Paul Harvey, 'Militant Democracy and the European Convention on Human Rights' (2004) 29 *European Law Review* 407.

30. John E. Finn, *Constitutions in Crisis – Political Violence and the Rule of Law* (1991), pp. 196–200.

31. Article 91 of the German Basic Law tackles the issue of Internal Emergency, article 80a refers to the State of Tension and Chapter Xa (Article 115a–115l) deals with the state of defense. In addition, articles 35(2)–(3) of the Basic Law deal with natural disasters. Note, 'Recent Emergency Legislation in West Germany', 82 *Harvard Law Review* 1704 (1969).

32. Ley Orgánica 4/1981 de los Estados de Alarma, Excepción y Sitio (June 1, 1981).
33. Article 37(1)(a) of the Constitution of South Africa. See Nicole Fritz, 'States of Emergency', in Stuart Woolman (ed.), *Constitutional Law of South Africa*, 2nd edition (Cape Town: Juta, 2008), Ch. 61. For similar examples see articles 180–82 of the Constitution of Ecuador; article 29 of the Constitution of Mexico.
34. See, e.g., article 48(1) of the Greek Constitution; articles 78 and 87 of the Italian Constitution; article 115a of the German Basic Law; article 34(1) of the Constitution of South Africa; article 37(7) and (8) of the Constitution of the Dominican Republic; article 92 of the Slovenian Constitution; article 38(a) of Israel's Basic Law: The Government; article 19(3)(i) of the Constitution of Hungary.
35. See, e.g., article 38(c) of the Israeli Basic Law: The Government; article 48(2) of the Greek Constitution; article 18(3) of the Austrian Constitution; article 23 of the Constitution of Denmark.
36. See, e.g., articles 137(d) and 141 of the Constitution of Portugal; article 111 of the Constitution of Bolivia; articles 2(II) and (V), 49(II) and (IV), 84 (IX) and (X), 136 and 137 of the Brazilian Constitution; article 121(6) of the Constitution of Costa Rica; article 51 of the Constitution of Panama; article 238(7) of the Constitution of Paraguay.
37. See, e.g., article 143 of the Constitution of Portugal; article 111 of the Constitution of Bolivia; article 190(11) of the Constitution of Venezuela; article 99 of the Constitution of Romania; article 352 of the Constitution of India.
38. See, e.g., articles 16(1) and 19 of the French Constitution.
39. See, e.g., article 137 of the Constitution of Peru; article 190(6) of the Constitution of Venezuela; article 16 of the French Constitution; article 78(n) of the Constitution of Ecuador; article 150(9) of the Constitution of Nicaragua.
40. See also articles 16 and 36 of the French Constitution; article 288 of the Constitution of Paraguay.
41. See, e.g., article 48 of the Greek Constitution; articles 80a and 115a of the German Basic Law; article 352(6) of the Constitution of India.
42. Bruce Ackerman, 'The Emergency Constitution' (2004) 113 *Yale Law Journal* 1029, 1037.
43. Ibid., pp. 1047–9.
44. See, e.g., article 111 of the Constitution of Bolivia.
45. See, e.g., article 121(7) of the Constitution of Costa Rica; article 55 of the Spanish Constitution; article 48 of the Greek Constitution; article 139 of the Brazilian Constitution; article 138 of the Constitution of Guatemala; article 103(2) of the Dutch Constitution; article 183(2) of the Constitution of Cyprus.
46. See, e.g., article 186 of the Constitution of Nicaragua; article 19(6) of the Portuguese Constitution; article 37 of the South African Constitution; article 56(3) of the Constitution of Russia; article 200 of the Constitution of Peru; article 241 of the Constitution of Venezuela; article 45 of the Armenian Constitution; article 63(2) of the Constitution of Belarus; article 57(3) of the Constitution of Bulgaria; article 17(3) of the Croatian Constitution; article 130 of the Constitution of Estonia; article 8(4) of the Hungarian Constitution; article 115(8) of the Constitution of Nepal.
47. See, e.g., article 175 of the Constitution of Albania; article 233 of the Polish Constitution; article 16 of the Slovenian Constitution.
48. See, e.g., article 23 of the Constitution of Finland; article 37(4)(b)(i) of the Constitution of South Africa. On the derogation regime under the major human rights conventions, see, e.g., Oren Gross, '"Once More unto the Breach": The Systemic Failure of Applying the European Convention on Human Rights to Entrenched Emergencies' (1998) 23 *Yale Journal of International Law* 437.
49. Rossiter, *Constitutional Dictatorship*, pp. 12, 288–90. See also Arthur S. Miller, 'Crisis Government becomes the Norm' (1978) 39 *Ohio State Law Journal* 736 at 738–41; Harold H. Koh, *The National Security Constitution* (1990) 117–49; Edward S. Corwin, *Total War and the Constitution* (1947), pp. 172–9.
50. See, e.g., article 112 of the Constitution of Bolivia; article 62 of the Brazilian Constitution; article 23 of the Constitution of Denmark; article 24 of the Irish Constitution; article 18(3) of the Austrian Constitution; article 86 of the Spanish Constitution; article 357 of the Constitution of India.
51. See, e.g., article 39(c) of the Israeli Basic Law: The Government; article 115k of the German Basic Law; article 48(5) of the Greek Constitution.
52. Article 81(1) of the German Basic Law.
53. Article 53(a)(2) of the German Basic Law; articles 353, 356, and 360 of the Constitution of India; article 88 of the Russian Constitution. See also Durga Das Basu, *Introduction to the Constitution of India*, 9th edition (New Delhi: Prentice-Hall of India, 1982), pp. 302–16.
54. Corwin, *Total War*, pp. 35–77.
55. Marx, 'Emergency Power', at 57–61; Donald G. Creighton, *Dominion of the North: A History of Canada* (Boston: Houghton Mifflin, 1944), p. 439; Rosenthal, 'The New Emergencies Act', pp. 576–80.
56. See, e.g., articles 187 and 196 of the Constitution of Belgium; articles 170(5) and 177(2) of the Constitution of Albania; article 60(1) of the Constitution of Brazil; article 133 of the Constitution of Cambodia; article 89(4) of the French Constitution; article 113 of the Constitution of Luxembourg; article 148 of the Romanian Constitution; Chapter 13, article 5(2) of the Swedish Constitution; article 18(5) of the Austrian Constitution.

57. See, e.g., articles 16 and 89 of the French Constitution; article 289 of the Constitution of Portugal; articles 169 and 116(5) of the Spanish Constitution; article 101 of the Constitution of Croatia; article 28A of the Constitution of Hungary; article 128 of the Constitution of Macedonia; article 288(9) of the Constitution of Paraguay.

58. See, e.g., article 115h of the German Basic Law; article 53 of the Constitution of Greece; article 228 of the Polish Constitution. See also Rossiter, *Constitutional Dictatorship*, p. 192.

59. *State (Walsh) v Lennon* [1941] I.R. 112, 120 (per G. Duffy J.). See also *Re McGrath and Harte* [1941] I.R. 68.

60. James Casey, *Constitutional Law in Ireland* (2000), p. 150.

61. D.M. Clark, 'Emergency Legislation, Fundamental Rights, and Article 28.3.3 of the Irish Constitution' (1977) 12 *The Irish Jurist* 283. See also *In re Art. 26 and the Emergency Powers Bill*, 1976 [1977] I.R. 159.

62. See, e.g., article VII(18) of the Constitution of the Philippines; article 37(3) of the Constitution of South Africa.

63. See, e.g., article 150(8) of the Malaysian Constitution; article 219 of the Constitution of Thailand; articles 26 and 28.3.3 of the Irish Constitution.

64. See, e.g., Christina E. Wells, 'Questioning Deference' (2004) 69 *Missouri Law Review* 903; Thomas M. Franck, *Political Questions/Judicial Answers: Does the Rule of Law Apply to Foreign Affairs?* (1992), pp. 10–30, 116–25; Lee Epstein et al., 'The Supreme Court during Crisis: How War Affects only Non-War Cases' (2005) 80 *New York University Law Review* 1; Koh, *The National Security Constitution*, pp. 134–49; John Hart Ely, *War and Responsibility: Constitutional Lessons of Vietnam and its Aftermath* (1993), pp. 54–60; Laurence Lustgarten and Ian Leigh, *In from the Cold: National Security and Parliamentary Democracy* (1994), pp. 320–59; George J. Alexander, 'The Illusory Protection of Human Rights by National Courts during Periods of Emergency' (1984) 5 *Human Rights Law Journal* 1 at 15–27. But see John C. Yoo, 'Judicial Review and the War on Terrorism' (2003) 72 *George Washington Law Review* 427.

65. But see David Cole, 'Judging the Next Emergency: Judicial Review and Individual Rights in Times of Crisis' 101 *Michigan Law Review* 2565 (2003) (courts play a significant role in the long run, in limiting what can be done in 'the next emergency'). See also William H. Rehnquist, *All the Laws but One* (1998), pp. 219–21; Jack Goldsmith and Cass R. Sunstein, 'Military Tribunals and Legal Culture: What a Difference Sixty Years Makes' 19 *Constitutional Commentary* 261, 284–9 (2002).

66. Bruce Russett, *Controlling the Sword: The Democratic Governance of National Security* (1990), pp. 34–8; Gad Barzilai, *A Democracy in Wartime: Conflict and Consensus in Israel* (1992), pp. 247–60.

67. Clinton Rossiter (ed.), *The Federalist Papers* (1961), No. 49, p. 315 (James Madison); Karl R. Popper, *The Open Society and its Enemies* (5th ed., 1971), vol. 1, pp. 43, 198.

68. *Youngstown Sheet & Tube Co. v Sawyer*, 343 US 579 at 653 (1952) (Jackson, J., concurring).

69. *Youngstown*, 343 US 579 at 654 (1952) (Jackson, J., concurring); Mark Tushnet, 'Controlling Executive Power in the War on Terrorism' (2005) 118 *Harvard Law Review* 2673, 2678–9.

70. Gross and Ni Aolain, *Law in Times of Crisis*, pp. 220–28; Juan E. Méndez, 'Human Rights Policy in the Age of Terrorism' (2002) 46 *Saint Louis University Law Journal* 377, 383; William J. Stuntz, 'Local Policing After the Terror' (2002) 111 *Yale Law Journal* 2137, 2165.

71. Daniel A. Farber, *Lincoln's Constitution* (2003), pp. 171–6. See also Sanford Levinson, 'Was the Emancipation Proclamation Constitutional? Do We/Should We Care What the Answer Is?' (2001) *University of Illinois Law Review* 1135.

72. James D. Richardson, *A Compilation of the Messages and Papers of the Presidents* (1896–9), vol. 6, p. 78 (emphasis added).

73. *Youngstown*, 343 US 579 at 652–3 (1952) (Jackson, J., concurring).

74. Ibid., p. 654.

75. 'Excerpts from Interview with Nixon about Domestic Effects of Indochina War', *New York Times*, May 20, 1977, p. A16.

76. John Ferejohn and Pasquale Pasquino, 'The Law of the Exception: A Typology of Emergency Powers' (2004) 2 *International Journal of Constitutional Law* 210, 216–17.

77. Plato, *The Laws* (Trevor J. Saunders trans., 1970), p. 164.

78. Kent Roach, 'The Dangers of a Charter-proof and Crime-based Response to Terrorism' in Ronald J. Daniels, Patrick Macklem and Kent Roach (eds.), *The Security of Freedom: Essays on Canada's Antiterrorism Bill* (2001), p. 131 at 138–42.

79. 'Study of the Implications for Human Rights of Recent Developments Concerning Situations Known as States of Siege or Emergency', UN Commission on Human Rights, 35th Sess., Agenda Item 10, UN Doc. E/CN.4/Sub.2/1982/15 (1982), p. 29.

80. Robert H. Jackson, 'Wartime Security and Liberty under Law' (1951) 1 *Buffalo Law Review* 103 at 107.

81. Ackerman, 'The Emergency Constitution', p. 1037.

82. Philip B. Heymann, *Terrorism and America: A Commonsense Strategy for a Democratic Society* (1998) 16.

83. Irwin Cotler, 'Thinking Outside the Box: Foundational Principles for a Counter-Terrorism Law and Policy'

in Ronald J. Daniels, Patrick Macklem, and Kent Roach (eds.), *The Security of Freedom: Essays on Canada's Antiterrorism Bill* (2001), p. 111.

84. David Cole, *Enemy Aliens: Double Standards and Constitutional Freedoms in the War on Terrorism* (New York: New Press, 2003) 47–56.

85. See, e.g., David Cole, 'The Priority of Morality: The Emergency Constitution's Blind Spot' 113 *Yale Law Journal* (2004) 1753, 1795–9.

86. Laurence H. Tribe and Patrick O. Gudridge, 'The Anti-Emergency Constitution' (2004) 113 *Yale Law Journal* 1801, 1803.

87. Ackerman, 'The Emergency Constitution'.

88. Ibid., pp. 1047–9.

89. Eric A. Posner and Adrian Vermeule, *Terror in the Balance: Security, Liberty, and the Courts* (2007), p. 168.

90. Posner and Vermeule, *Terror in the Balance*, p. 168.

91. Cole, 'The Priority of Morality', p. 1774.

92. Ackerman, 'The Emergency Constitution', p. 1076.

93. Cole, 'The Priority of Morality', pp. 1775–80. On prolonged states of emergency see Gross and Ní Aoláin, *Law in Times of Crisis*, pp. 175–80.

94. Nasser Hussain, 'Beyond Norm and Exception: Guantánamo' (2007) 33 *Critical Inquiry* 734, 751.

95. Clinton Rossiter and Richard P. Longaker, *The Supreme Court and the Commander in Chief* (expanded edition, 1976), p. 91.

96. Richard A. Posner, *Law, Pragmatism, and Democracy* (2003), p. 295.

97. Gross and Ní Aoláin, *Law in Times of Crisis*, pp. 72–9.

98. Posner, *Law, Pragmatism, and Democracy*, p. 294.

99. Ibid., p. 295.

100. Harold D. Lasswell, *National Security and Individual Freedom* (1950), p. 141.

101. *Youngstown*, 343 U.S. 579, 650 (1952) (Jackson, J., concurring). See also Mark Tushnet, 'Defending Korematsu?: Reflections on Civil Liberties in Wartime' (2003) *Wisconsin Law Review* 273 at 303–04.

102. *Korematsu v United States*, 323 U.S. 214, 246 (1944) (Jackson, J., dissenting); Ackerman, 'The Emergency Constitution', p. 1041.

103. *Youngstown*, 343 U.S. 579, 650–51 (1952) (Jackson, J., concurring).

104. Gross, '"Once More unto the Breach"', p. 440; Fionnuala Ní Aoláin, 'The Emergence of Diversity: Differences in Human Rights Jurisprudence' (1995) 19 *Fordham International Law Journal* 101.

105. Gross and Ní Aoláin, *Law in Times of Crisis*, pp. 171–243.

REFERENCES

Ackerman, Bruce (2004), 'The Emergency Constitution', *Yale Law Journal*, 113, 1029.

Alexander, George J. (1984), 'The Illusory Protection of Human Rights by National Courts during Periods of Emergency', *Human Rights Law Journal*, 5 (1), 1.

Barzilai, Gad (1992), *A Democracy in Wartime: Conflict and Consensus in Israel*, Tel-Aviv: Sifriat Polaim.

Bendor, Ariel (1988), 'The Right of Parties to Participate in Elections to the Knesset', *Mishpatim*, 18, 269.

Casey, James (2000), *Constitutional Law in Ireland*, Dublin: Round Hall.

Clark, D.M. (1977), 'Emergency Legislation, Fundamental Rights, and Article 28.3.3 of the Irish Constitution', *The Irish Jurist*, 12, 283.

Cole, David (2003a), *Enemy Aliens: Double Standards and Constitutional Freedoms in the War on Terrorism*, New York: New Press.

Cole, David (2003b), 'Judging the Next Emergency: Judicial Review and Individual Rights in Times of Crisis', *Michigan Law Review*, 101, 2565.

Cole, David (2004), 'The Priority of Morality: The Emergency Constitution's Blind Spot', *Yale Law Journal*, 113, 1753.

Corwin, Edwin S. (1947), *Total War and the Constitution*, New York: Knopf.

Cotler, Irwin (2001), 'Thinking Outside the Box: Foundational Principles for a Counter-Terrorism Law and Policy', in Ronald J. Daniels, Patrick Macklem and Kent Roach (eds.), *The Security of Freedom: Essays on Canada's Antiterrorism Bill*, Toronto: University of Toronto Press.

Creighton, Donald G. (1944), *Dominion of the North: A History of Canada*, Boston: Houghton Mifflin.

Currie, David P. (1994), *The Constitution of the Federal Republic of Germany*, Chicago: The University of Chicago Press.

Ely, John Hart (1993), *War and Responsibility: Constitutional Lessons of Vietnam and its Aftermath*, Princeton: Princeton University Press.

Epstein, Lee, Daniel E. Ho, Gary King and Jeffry A. Segal (2005), 'The Supreme Court during Crisis: How War Affects only Non-war Cases', *New York University Law Review* 80, 1.

Farber, Daniel A. (1991), *Lincoln's Constitution*, Chicago: The University of Chicago Press.

Ferejohn, John and Pasquale Pasquino (2004), 'The Law of the Exception: A Typology of Emergency Powers', *International Journal of Constitutional Law*, 2, 210.

Finn, John E. (1991), *Constitutions in Crisis: Political Violence and the Rule of Law*, Oxford: Oxford University Press.

Fox, Gregory H. and Georg Nolte (1995), 'Intolerant Democracies', *Harvard International Law Journal*, 36, 1.

Franck, Thomas M. (1992), *Political Questions/Judicial Answers: Does the Rule of Law Apply to Foreign Affairs?*, Princeton, NJ: Princeton University Press.

Fritz, Nicole (2008), 'States of Emergency', in Stuart Woolman (ed.), *Constitutional Law of South Africa*, 2nd edition, Cape Town: Juta.

Ganev, Venelin I. (1997), 'Emergency Powers and the New East European Constitutions', *American Journal of Comparative Law*, 45, 585.

Goldsmith, Jack and Cass R. Sunstein (2002), 'Military Tribunals and Legal Culture: What a Difference Sixty Years Makes', *Constitutional Commentary*, 19, 261.

Gross, Oren (1998), ' "Once More unto the Breach": The Systemic Failure of Applying the European Convention on Human Rights to Entrenched Emergencies', *Yale Journal of International Law*, 23, 437.

Gross, Oren and Fionnuala Ní Aoláin (2006), *Law in Times of Crisis: Emergency Powers in Theory and Practice*, Cambridge: Cambridge University Press.

Hamilton, Alexander (1787), 'The Federalist No. 23', reprinted in Clinton Rossiter (ed.) (1961), *The Federalist Papers*, New York: The Penguin Group.

Harvey, Paul (2004), 'Militant Democracy and the European Convention on Human Rights', *European Law Review*, 29, 407.

Heymann, Philip B. (1998), *Terrorism and America: A Commonsense Strategy for a Democratic Society*, Cambridge, MA: MIT Press.

Hogg, Peter W. (2008), *Constitutional Law of Canada*, 5th edition, Toronto: The Carswell Company.

Hussain, Nasser (2007), 'Beyond Norm and Exception: Guantánamo', *Critical Inquiry*, 33, 734.

Jackson, Robert H. (1951), 'Wartime Security and Liberty under Law', *Buffalo Law Review*, 1, 103.

Koh, Harold H. (1990), *The National Security Constitution: Sharing Power after the Iran-Contra Affair*, New Haven: Yale University Press.

Kommers, Donald P. (1997), *The Constitutional Jurisprudence of the Federal Republic of Germany*, 2nd edition, Durham, NC: Duke University Press.

Krotoszynski, Jr., Ronald J. (2004), 'A Comparative Perspective on the First Amendment: Free Speech, Militant Democracy, and the Primacy of Dignity as a Preferred Constitutional Value in Germany', *Tulane Law Review*, 78, 1549.

Lahav, Pnina (1988), 'A Barrel without Hoops: The Impact of Counterterrorism on Israel's Legal Culture', *Cardozo Law Review*, 10, 529.

Lasswell, Harold D. (1950), *National Security and Individual Freedom*, Chicago: McGraw-Hill.

Levinson, Sanford (2001), 'Was the Emancipation Proclamation Constitutional? Do We/Should We Care What the Answer Is?', *University of Illinois Law Review*, 1135.

Loewenstein, Karl (1937), 'Militant Democracy and Fundamental Rights', *American Political Science Review*, 31, 417.

Loewenstein, Karl (1938), 'Legislative Control of Political Extremism in European Democracies', *Columbia Law Review*, 38, 591.

Loveman, Brian (1993), *The Constitution of Tyranny*, Pittsburgh: University of Pittsburgh Press.

Lustgarten, Laurence and Ian Leigh (1994), *In from the Cold: National Security and Parliamentary Democracy*, Oxford: Clarendon Press.

Machiavelli, Niccolo (1513), *Discourses on Livy*, reprinted in Harvey C. Mansfield and Nathan Tarcov (eds.) (1996), Chicago: University of Chicago Press.

Madison, James (1787), 'Federalis No. 49', reprinted in Clinton Rossiter (ed.) (1961), *The Federalist Papers*, New York: The Penguin Group.

Marx, Herbert (1970), 'The Emergency Power and Civil Liberties in Canada', *McGill Law Journal*, 16, 39.

Marx, Herbert (1972), 'The "Apprehended Insurrection" of October 1970 and the Judicial Function', *University of British Columbia Law Review*, 7, 55.

Méndez, Juan E. (2002), 'Human Rights Policy in the Age of Terrorism', *Saint Louis University Law Journal*, 46, 377.

Miller, Arthur S. (1978), 'Crisis Government becomes the Norm', *Ohio State Law Journal*, 39, 736.

Ní Aoláin, Fionnuala (1995), 'The Emergence of Diversity: Differences in Human Rights Jurisprudence', *Fordham International Law Journal*, 19, 101.

Note (1942), 'Civil Liberties in Great Britain and Canada During War', *Harvard Law Review*, 55, 1006.

Note (1969), 'Recent Emergency Legislation in West Germany', *Harvard Law Review*, 82, 1704.
Peppin, Patricia (1993), 'Emergency Legislation and Rights in Canada: The War Measures Act and Civil Liberties', *Queen's Law Journal*, 18, 129.
Plato (360, BCE), *The Laws*, reprinted in Trevor J. Saunders (ed.) (1970), New York: The Penguin Group.
Popper, Karl R. (1971), *The Open Society and its Enemies*, 5th edition, New York: Routledge.
Posner, Eric A. and Adrian Vermeule (2007), *Terror in the Balance: Security, Liberty, and the Courts*, Oxford: Oxford University Press.
Posner, Richard A. (2003), *Law, Pragmatism, and Democracy*, Cambridge, MA: Harvard University Press.
Rehnquist, William H. (1998), *All the Laws but One: Civil Liberties in War Time*, New York: Knopf.
Richardson, James D. (1896–9), *A Compilation of the Messages and Papers of the Presidents*, Washington, DC: Government Printing Office.
Roach, Kent (2001), 'The Dangers of a Charter-proof and Crime-based Response to Terrorism', in Ronald J. Daniels, Patrick Macklem and Kent Roach (eds.), *The Security of Freedom: Essays on Canada's Antiterrorism Bill*, Toronto: University of Toronto Press.
Rosenthal, Peter (1991), 'The New Emergencies Act: Four Times the War Measures Act', *Manitoba Law Journal*, 20, 563.
Rossiter, Clinton L. (1948), *Constitutional Dictatorship: Crisis Government in Modern Democracies*, Princeton, NJ: Princeton University Press.
Rossiter, Clinton and Richard P. Longaker (1976), *The Supreme Court and the Commander in Chief*, expanded edition, Ithaca, NY: Cornell University Press.
Russett, Bruce (1990), *Controlling the Sword: The Democratic Governance of National Security*, Cambridge, MA: Harvard University Press.
Stuntz, William J (2002), 'Local Policing After the Terror', *Yale Law Journal*, 111, 2137.
Tenofsky, Eliot (1989), 'The War Measures and Emergency Acts', *American Review of Canadian Studies*, 19, 293.
Tribe, Laurence H. and Patrick O. Gudridge (2004), 'The Anti-Emergency Constitution', *Yale Law Journal*, 113, 1801.
Tushnet, Mark (2003), 'Defending Korematsu?: Reflections on Civil Liberties in Wartime', *Wisconsin Law Review*, 273.
Tushnet, Mark (2005), 'Controlling Executive Power in the War on Terrorism', *Harvard Law Review*, 118, 2673.
Valadés, Diego (1974), *La Dictadura Constitucional en América Latina* (UNAM, Instituto de Investigaciones Jurídicas, 1974).
Wells, Christina E. (2004), 'Questioning Deference', *Missouri Law Review*, 69, 903.
Yoo, John C. (2003), 'Judicial Review and the War on Terrorism', *George Washington Law Review*, 72, 427.

20. Federalism, devolution and secession: from classical to post-conflict federalism

Sujit Choudhry and Nathan Hume

1 INTRODUCTION

Federalism has long been a topic of study for comparative constitutional law. However, the scholarly literature on federalism is in a process of transition. For most of the twentieth century, the study of federalism was oriented around a standard set of cases in the developed world: Australia, Canada, Switzerland and the United States of America. These cases provided the raw material for certain fundamental questions: what is federalism? Why should federations be adopted? What role is there for courts? For the most part, these questions appear to have been answered, often with the aid of comparative analysis. To be sure, important debates persist. For example, scholars disagree over the relative priority to be given to the different goals served by federalism and how those goals should shape the allocation of jurisdiction. In the area of environmental policy, for example, new opportunities for democratic self-government and policy experimentation argue for greater regional authority but also generate inter-jurisdictional externalities, which argue against it. This debate relies on an implicit understanding of its terms and range, and participants in such discussions of federalism often draw on the same standard set of jurisdictions as illustrations of models to be followed and dangers to be avoided.

Recent developments in the practice of constitutional design have challenged this consensus. Many states in the developing world, such as Ethiopia, Iraq, Nigeria and Sudan, have adopted federal solutions to manage ethnic conflict, often as part of a broader package of post-conflict constitutional reforms. In these federations, internal boundaries are drawn to ensure that territorially concentrated national minorities constitute regional majorities. The difference between the standard and emerging cases is not just geographic. Rather, the very mission of federalism is different. Its principal goals are not to combat majority tyranny or to provide incentives for states to adopt policies that match their citizens' preferences, but rather to avoid civil war or secession. Federalism promotes not public accountability or state efficiency but rather peace and territorial integrity. Post-conflict federalism pursues different goals than classical federalism and thus provides an opportunity to revisit the basic assumptions underlying the field.

Advocacy of federalism as a tool for managing ethnic conflict continues to grow, with respect to a diverse set of cases that spans the globe from South and East Asia to Eastern Europe. However, its purported benefits have been challenged by those who argue that federalism exacerbates, instead of mitigates, ethnic conflict. This academic debate about the merits of post-conflict federalism has reached an impasse, largely as a consequence of methodology. Proponents and opponents of drawing boundaries to empower national minorities point to different cases of federal success and failure. But recent scholarship in comparative politics that combines large-sample quantitative analysis with small-sample qualitative case studies promises a way forward. It shows how we might test these competing claims about the ability of federalism to control ethnic conflict across a variety of cases and begin to identify the factors that explain when post-conflict federalism succeeds and when it does not.

2 CLASSICAL FEDERALISM

Three questions dominate the classical literature on comparative federalism. What is federalism? Why should we adopt it? What role is there for courts? These questions and the standard answers to them are drawn from the experiences of a few canonical federal states and the dominant academic accounts of those experiences. The model we call 'classical federalism' emerges from these analyses.

2.1 What is Federalism?

What is federalism? In his seminal *Federal Government*, K.C. Wheare provided this influential definition of the 'federal principle': for a state to be federal, 'the general and regional governments must be coordinate and independent in their respective spheres' (Wheare 1964: 4–5). The constitutional implications of this federal principle included a written constitution expressly conferring powers on the central and regional governments, a system of direct elections for both levels of government, the power of each level of government to act (or not act) independently of the other, and the existence of an independent high court to serve as the 'umpire' of federalism. This definition has informed many investigations into the political, social and institutional conditions required for different orders of government to preserve their independence while coordinating their actions (Elazar 1987). It also has inspired scholars to propose other definitions. For example, William Riker criticized Wheare for fostering a legalistic approach to federalism and offered an alternative formula: federalism is 'a political organization in which the activities of government are divided between regional governments and a central government in such a way that each kind of government has some activities on which it makes final decisions' (Riker 1975: 101). While Riker's definition does not emphasize the use of constitutions to create and entrench federal arrangements, it is identical in substance (Riker 1964: 11). Ronald Watts, by contrast, elaborated Wheare's constitutional model. He added the formal distribution of legislative and executive authority, the allocation of sufficient revenues to ensure the autonomy of each order of government, the representation of regional views in the central legislature (e.g. through an upper chamber), a constitutional amendment procedure requiring a substantial degree of regional consent, and an enforcement mechanism that included courts, referendums or a special role for the upper chamber (Watts 1966).

Wheare developed his definition from a set of standard cases that embodied the federal principle to varying degrees: Australia, Canada, Switzerland and the United States. To be sure, Watts extended the field to the new federations then emerging from the British Empire (i.e. India, Pakistan, Malaysia, Nigeria, Rhodesia and the West Indies) and firmly demonstrated that federalism was not confined to Wheare's four original cases. But those classical federal constitutions set the intellectual agenda for the study of federalism, and they continue to serve as the focus, or at least the point of departure, for orthodox engagements in comparative federalism. As the initial and most prominent modern example of federalism, the United States is often considered first among equals. Although Daniel Elazar attributed a biblical pedigree to his preferred definition ('shared rule plus self rule'), he identified American federalism as the prototype for modern federalism and used it to orient his explorations in the field (Elazar 1987: 12 and 144–6). Riker also used his model of American federalism to make sense of federal experiments elsewhere (Riker 1964; Stepan 2001). With its rich history and widespread influence, American federalism remains a valuable foil for contemporary developments elsewhere, including the European Union (see, e.g., Nicolaidis and Howse eds. 2001). This narrow focus has facilitated comparative investigation, but it also has limited the relevance of the literature. The four central cases are relatively stable, prosperous and democratic. They have rarely faced domestic threats to their very existence. The theories and models that have resulted from elaborating their conditions may illuminate aspects of their experience but, at the same time, obscure distinctive developments elsewhere. Many legal scholars interested in comparative federalism have followed the lead of these political scientists by examining the same classical cases and seeking to elaborate or complement their arguments (see e.g. Aroney 2006).

The question of what is federalism has raised two derivative questions. First, what is *not* federalism? Historically, scholars were preoccupied with distinguishing federations from confederations on the basis of the mechanism for choosing political office-holders in central institutions. In federations, citizens elect central governments directly, whereas in confederations, delegates of regional governments run central institutions (Watts 1998). More recently, scholars have emphasized the distinction between devolution and decentralization, on the one hand, and federalism, on the other (Cross 2002; Feeley and Rubin 2008). Devolution and decentralization have the same political dynamic and legal form. They both involve the redistribution of authority and capacity from the central government to smaller, subordinate units of government. Consistent with this dynamic, attempts to devolve and decentralize power typically take the form of laws or regulations adopted unilaterally by the central government, in contrast to federal constitutions, which are often understood as compacts among the constituent regions. Although similar in many ways, devolution is thought to entail larger and more powerful sub-units than decentralization: comparable to provinces and municipalities, respectively (Grindle 2009). In contemporary discussions, devolution is regularly identified with the United Kingdom, while decentralization is observed in a large number of jurisdictions. However, the lack of standard definitions for devolution and decentralization make generalizations of this sort unhelpful. Following Wheare's definition, the key difference between federalism and these other forms of government is that the autonomy of the regions that comprise a federation is guaranteed by a constitution that the central government may not alter unilaterally, whereas the institutions that exercise delegated powers in a decentralized or devolved political system may have their powers modified or revoked by the central government, often through the ordinary legislative process.

Second, which constitutions that appear to be federal truly deserve that label? Even if the central and regional governments derive their powers from a constitution, on closer look that constitution may fall short of federal status. Wheare himself originally described India and even Canada as 'quasi-federal' due to their centralizing tendencies. In Canada, he was concerned with the power of the federal government to prevent provincial laws from coming into force (disallowance) or to set aside provincial legislation (reservation); in India, he was bothered by the power of Parliament to unilaterally create new states and change state boundaries, as well as the power of the central government to assume the direct rule of states in an emergency (President's rule) (Wheare 1964). The difficulties raised by the standard definition prompted Elazar to pursue a more ambitious project, in which he sought to catalogue the many institutional manifestations ('species' or 'expressions') of the federal principle, from confederations and federacies to leagues and condominiums (Elazar 1987: 38–59). Such conceptual and categorical refinements may help to resolve certain descriptive or theoretical controversies. From the standpoint of public policy, their value is more ambiguous. On the one hand, they serve to catalogue the variety of constitutional forms through which states can respect the federal principle. In short, they indicate the broad scope for constitutional choice. On the other hand, they may draw political actors into debates over categorization (e.g. whether a proposed constitutional design is federal or confederal) that divert attention from the concrete political problems to which federalism is a response. Such debates might lead political actors to conclude that the constitutional forms discussed exhaust the institutional possibilities of federalism, when they are better understood as variations on a theme that remains open to a great deal of adaptation and experimentation.

Some scholars working within the traditional paradigm have responded to these concerns by performing empirical surveys of existing federal systems (see e.g. Kincaid and Tarr eds. 2005; Griffiths ed. 2005; Majeed et al. eds. 2006; Watts 2008; Halberstam and Reimann forthcoming). These surveys extend far beyond the four core cases of Australia, Canada, Switzerland and the United States. However, the current literature suffers from shortcomings. Although these studies amass a large amount of material on federalism and its many forms, they are rarely analytical and generally do not seek to explain the commonalities and diversity that exist in the design and operation of federal systems. Moreover, there has been little attempt to evaluate the success of the design choices made by different federations. The flight from prescription is fuelled by the methodology of these studies, which employ a minimal or ecumenical definition of federalism and aim to identify its various manifestations. This line of research should therefore be understood as an important first step that provides the raw material for more analytical and prescriptive work.

2.2 Why Federalism?

Classical federalism presupposes a shared account of how federations come into being. Federations form from pre-existing political units that are politically independent from each other. They may be sovereign states or colonies in an imperial order that lack full statehood but enjoy extensive rights of self-government. These political units are the actors that decide to form a new political community, which entails the pooling and surrendering of some of their sovereignty to a central government while retaining an important degree of autonomy. The central government's authority is derived from this political agreement. The federal constitution is a pact, compact or bargain among the regions; this agreement constitutes the central government, creates its institutions and allocates powers to them. Riker built his theory of federalism on this account, which Al Stepan aptly terms 'coming-together federalism' (Stepan 2001: 320).

Set against this backdrop, 'why federalism?' becomes a two-part question. First, 'why should existing political units combine in any form?' Scholars of classical federalism tend to invoke either collective security or economic prosperity (Riker 1964; Wheare 1964). A federation can be understood as a mutual defence alliance against external military threats. Whether the threat comes from a former colonial ruler or another state seeking to expand its territory, the members of a federation can provide a more effective deterrent together than alone. A federation also can be understood as a common market that is larger and more efficient than one in which international borders impede the flow of goods, services and capital.

Since political units that desire such military and economic benefits could choose to pursue them by pooling their sovereignty in a new unitary state, the second part of 'why federalism?' is 'why federalism and not unitary rule?' As a preliminary matter, federalism may reduce the burden of coming together and thus make union more likely and more durable than if previously independent units sought to form a single unitary state. Federalism allows groups that have a history of self-government or a distinct culture or economy to preserve some measure of autonomy (Wheare 1964; Watts 1966). By definition, it offers the benefits of unity without the costs of imposing uniformity on a diverse population.

Once formed, a classical federal system is believed to offer numerous advantages over a unitary state. For example, it is thought to bolster democracy by guaranteeing the existence of a tier of regional governments. It not only ensures another set of offices to elect and contest and thus increases the number of opportunities for political participation; it also improves the quality of political participation by empowering relatively small political communities, in which citizens are more likely to have more in common, individual votes and voices are likely to have more influence, and representatives are likely to be more responsive to their concerns (see e.g. Merritt 1988; Friedman 1997). Classical federalism also is said to enhance efficiency in various ways. The existence of two tiers of government allows a diverse society to allocate responsibilities and assign liabilities in a manner that improves the quantity and quality of public goods by engineering a closer fit between those who benefit from them and those who bear the cost. Those goods, like military defence, that the regions might fail to produce adequately can be assigned to the central government, while those that depend on local knowledge and preferences, like education and perhaps some aspects of environmental regulation, can be left to the regions (Esty 1996; Revesz 1996). In addition, federalism makes it easier for citizens to move from one region to another, which means they can sort themselves into like-minded communities and, through the enduring threat of exit, impel their governments to satisfy their diverse policy preferences as well as or better than another regional government might (Tiebout 1956). Finally, federalism is believed to protect liberty by reinforcing limited government. By dividing power between the two levels of government, it gives politicians at each level the incentives and the means to prevent their counterparts from abusing their constitutional authority (Federalist No. 51 (Madison); Merritt 1988; Amar 1991). By engineering a competition among regional governments for mobile people, resources and money, it also ensures that those governments face economic and political pressure to refrain from infringing upon property rights and markets: a result that just so happens to enhance economic efficiency across the federal system (Weingast 1995).

These arguments prompt an array of critical responses. Some concern the manner in which federalism has been implemented: actual regions are too big, centralized and heterogeneous to deliver the democratic dividends associated with small political units (Briffault 1994; Cross 2002); they are too few and too similar (and the practical constraints on the mobility of individuals and ideas remain too severe) to sustain meaningful inter-jurisdictional competition and thus do not enhance efficiency or promote innovation as promised (Daniels 1991; Feeley and Rubin 2008); they have not, in practice, served as reliable bulwarks against encroachments on individual and group liberties, whether by central governments or other regions (Shapiro 1995); their boundaries are too rigid and arbitrary to capture the myriad externalities their policies produce (e.g. positive and negative, economic and environmental), and agreements to redistribute those burdens and benefits efficiently are too difficult to negotiate and enforce, so they are not likely to supply an optimal bundle of public goods, regulatory or otherwise (Levy 2007). Other criticisms concern inherent characteristics of federalism. Most importantly, federalism has democratic costs that must be weighed against its contested democratic benefits. While it empowers discrete provincial majorities to make certain decisions, it compromises the ability of the national majority to set policies for the entire country. Indeed, by setting constitutional limits on the concentration and exercise of government authority, federalism may frustrate attempts to address our most pressing moral and practical problems (Riker 1964; Stepan 2001).

The arguments for and against federalism are well known. Many of them are drawn from American experience, and together they constitute the intellectual framework for contemporary analytical work on federalism within the classical mold. Although debates about federalism remain vigorous, the classical framework within which they occur is fairly stable. These criteria do not themselves require comparative analysis, and there is a vast body of country-specific work that relies on them without reference to foreign federal examples. Although the bulk of this work is done in economics and political science, legal scholars contribute to and draw upon this literature. In the American legal academy, for example, there has been an extensive debate on environmental policy and federalism. Participants dispute not only the optimal allocation of responsibility for environmental regulation among the federal and state governments but also the proper basis on which to make such decisions (see e.g. Stewart 1977; Revesz 2001).

In addition, there have been a smaller number of comparative studies that draw upon this intellectual framework in specific substantive areas. The work is both analytical and prescriptive. Comparative models offer both negative and positive guidance. Barry Weingast has collaborated with other scholars to elaborate and apply his conception of market-preserving federalism in countries from England and the United States to India and Russia (Parikh and Weingast 1997; Figueirido et al. 2007). Similar projects have considered topics that range from environmental regulation (Kimber 1995; Farber 1997) and the evolution of corporate law (Stith 1991; McCahery and Vermeulen 2005; Deakin 2006) to the fight against cyber-crime (Mendez 2005). The arguments may be familiar but, perhaps for that very reason, 'why federalism?' remains a rich and relevant question.

2.3 What Role for Courts?

Comparative legal analyses of the judicial role in federations present a puzzle. Scholars and statesmen alike have long recognized that courts are an important, if not an integral, component of federal government because of the need for a mechanism to resolve jurisdictional disputes (Federalist No. 78 (Hamilton); Wheare 1964; Watts 1966). Not surprisingly, constitutional judicial review first developed in three of the classical federations: the United States, Canada and Australia. As federalism spread to Latin America in the nineteenth century, judicial review came along with it. Indeed, the rise and spread of judicial federalism occurred more than a century before the global diffusion of judicial power associated with the 'Rights Revolution' and the third wave of democratization. However, whereas this more recent phenomenon has inspired an explosion of comparative literature, judicial federalism has attracted less comparative attention.

In part, this may be a function of the different roles played by courts of final appeal in maintaining different federal systems. In India, debates over state boundaries and the imposition of President's Rule eclipse questions about the role of courts in the federal system. Likewise Ethiopia, where disputes between the ethnic groups that comprise the federation are resolved not by judges but by the upper house of Parliament (Baylis 2004). By contrast, the United States Supreme Court has been actively engaged in the adjudication of federalism disputes during various periods of American history. This discrepancy, coupled with the passionate American debate over judicial review, may explain why the bulk of the comparative work on judicial federalism is American in origin. But even in the United States, it has been suggested that the primary determinants of the federal balance lie in the political process, and that courts play the role of enforcing constitutional baselines, such as subsidiarity, the right to free movement, the institutional integrity of the federal and state governments, the prohibition on state discrimination against persons, goods and services originating in other states, and the various burdens of justification for government action (Halberstam 2008).

The literature on courts and comparative federalism emphasizes both substance and method. The former involves the constitutional concepts, rules and doctrines appropriate or even necessary for a court operating within a federal system. These include democratic ideals, conflict-of-laws rules, tests for territorial jurisdiction and, more controversially, an anti-commandeering principle (see e.g. Halberstam 2001). Such tools enable courts to maintain and even tinker with the federal structures of their constitutions as circumstances and endeavors evolve. For example, the Supreme Court of Canada has selectively invoked American constitutional text and doctrine to support the introduction of unwritten constitutional principles of order, fairness and efficiency that reconcile elements of Canadian private international law and thus the Canadian federal system to what it perceives as contemporary economic imperatives (Hume 2006).

The latter concerns the risks, benefits and legitimacy of judicial references to foreign law when dealing with federal aspects of the constitution. Some theorists encourage such references because knowledge about foreign arrangements can illuminate new domestic possibilities and clarify existing practices. For example, Halberstam suggests that German constitutional practice could serve as a model for American courts to shift the political morality underlying American federalism jurisprudence from one that emphasizes the entitlements of different orders of government to decide whether to act in a cooperative or competitive manner to a fidelity approach that imposes duties to cooperate and act responsibly in the interest of the entire system (Halberstam 2004). Others are more equivocal about the relevance of foreign federal experiments for domestic judges, since federal constitutions are package deals defined by contextual compromises. More a product of pragmatism than of principle, their lessons often require intimate knowledge of their history and operation, which judges from other countries rarely possess. Nonetheless, Vicki Jackson concedes that judges might profit from studying foreign experience when deciding issues of federal structure and constitutional principle on which the relevant text is silent (Jackson 2004).

These debates are important, but their importance is limited to those countries in which courts play a major part in the federal system. Such issues are unlikely to resonate in federal states where the constitution is viewed predominantly as a contested, contingent political compromise rather than as a settled legal framework for the resolution of political controversies. More generally, arguments that deduce the nature and implications of federalism from a small and increasingly unrepresentative sample of states risk error and irrelevance when applied beyond that narrow realm.

3   POST-CONFLICT FEDERALISM

3.1   Setting the Stage

Scholars who contribute to the literature of classical federalism disagree on many important issues: the goals served by federalism, their relative priority, the weight of any countervailing considerations and the manner in which the design of a federal system should reflect these calculations. However, this literature also tends to rely on a shared yet generally tacit set of basic assumptions. These assumptions include the following: once pre-existing political units have come together in a federal state, they shall remain members of a single political community bound in a common constitutional order; this new political community is a nation that inhabits the entire territory of the state and possesses the right to self-government; and debates over the design of the federal system are debates about how this nation should organize itself internally and thus do not raise the prior question of whether the nation should continue to exist.

That existential question is precisely what lies at the heart of constitutional politics in what Choudhry has termed a divided society (Choudhry 2008). As a category of political and constitutional analysis, a divided society is not merely a society that is ethnically, linguistically, religiously or culturally diverse. The age of the ethnoculturally homogeneous state, if there ever was one, is long over. What marks a divided society is that these differences are politically salient. That is, they are persistent markers of political identity and bases for political mobilization. In a divided society, ethnocultural diversity translates into political fragmentation: political claims are refracted through the lens of ethnic identity, and political conflict is synonymous with conflict among ethnocultural groups.

Scholars of ethnic politics have long drawn distinctions among different types of ethnic groups. There are many dimensions on which to do so: the relationship they assert between ethnicity and territory, the manner in which they have been incorporated into their respective states, their relative economic and political status, the terms in which they frame their constitutional arguments and the substance of their constitutional claims. One such type is what Will Kymlicka has termed a national minority (Kymlicka 1995). National minorities are regionally concentrated ethnic groups who once enjoyed political autonomy and have become part of states in which they constitute an ethnic minority through conquest, colonization or voluntary incorporation. Other terms for this type of ethnic group include 'ethnonationalists' (Gurr 1993: 18–20). They mobilize politically around assertions of national identity and self-determination. The goal of such mobilization is to recover the extensive self-government they claim to have enjoyed historically. The degree of self-government they seek ranges from autonomy to independent statehood, which would entail secession. National minorities accept the premise that states are the means by which nations exercise their right to self-determination over their territory, but they use this premise to challenge particular combinations of state, nation and territory. National minorities argue that the state in which they live contains more than one nation, that each of those nations possesses an inherent and identical right to self-determination, and that they are therefore entitled to their own separate state.

Why do national minorities mobilize, and why do they anchor their specific policy goals around the right to self-determination? The 'grievance' or 'relative deprivation' school of civil war studies, which focuses on the question of how ethnic conflict becomes violent, offers a leading answer to these questions. On this account, ethnic difference per se is not the spark for the rise of ethnic politics. Rather, ethnic groups mobilize politically in response to their experience of economic and political disadvantage. Political disadvantage entails the systematic limitation of access to political office or basic political rights; economic disadvantage involves the systematic denial of economic goods and opportunities. The different dimensions of disadvantage are often mutually reinforcing: political disadvantage insulates politics from attempts to address economic disadvantage, and economic disadvantage undermines an ethnic group's ability to exercise political influence. Ethnic groups vary in their response to disadvantage. Some groups may demand the reform of those state institutions in which they are consistently outvoted. National minorities entertain secession because they desire the additional protection that comes from forming a political majority in an independent state. Most ethnic groups demand voice; national minorities emphasize exit.

Some states resist political mobilization by national minorities because the very existence of such groups threatens the equation of nation, state and territory on which those states base their claims to political legitimacy. A state that perceives its territory as indivisible and integral to its identity may be more likely to react in that manner (Toft 2003). In such cases, there is a clash between competing nationalisms with parallel logics: a minority nationalism that is confined to one region and seeks to realign nations, states and territories; and a statewide nationalism that asserts the exclusive existence of a single nation throughout the territory of the state and thus denies the need for realignment. Gurr argues that the conflict between competing nationalisms typically escalates in stages: from non-violent protest to violent protest and finally to rebellion. This escalation occurs through a pattern of demands and responses: non-violent protest is met with a lack of political responsiveness, which in turn leads to violent protest, which is met with a violent reaction, and which then leads to rebellion and an armed conflict (i.e. civil war). Indeed, the evidence suggests that self-determination disputes are the most common variety of civil war and are more resistant to settlement than other kinds of disputes, especially when states face more than one potential separatist claim (Walter 2009).

3.2   Theoretical Debate

This diagnosis suggests that minority nationalism may lead to civil war and secession. The question is whether federalism, either on its own or as part of a larger package of constitutional reforms, is an effective response that diminishes these risks and serves peace and territorial integrity. This question has sparked a vigorous academic debate (Hale 2008). Scholars fall into one of two diametrically opposed camps. One school holds that federalism can dampen secessionist sentiment; the other holds that federalism will in fact fuel it. In other words, federalism is either a solution or a catalyst for ethnic violence. Thus framed, these two positions are mutually exclusive.

Classical federalism cannot answer this question because it focuses on polities in which the existence of the nation is not the crux of constitutional politics. For example, although Wheare and Watts observe how federal systems can accommodate racial, religious and linguistic differences, these concerns are peripheral to their work. By contrast, this is the central question for post-conflict federalism and it is the subject of vigorous and ongoing debate. The core design feature of post-conflict federalism is the drawing of internal borders to ensure that a national minority constitutes a majority in a region. The allocation of jurisdiction between different levels of government ensures that the national minority is not outvoted by the majority and has sufficient powers to protect itself from economic and political disadvantage. These arrangements are constitutionally entrenched and enforced by independent courts. This approach has been variously termed multinational federalism, plurinational federalism, ethnic federalism or ethnofederalism. It even shares some features and sympathies with what Stefan Wolff has labeled 'complex power sharing' (Wolff 2009). Here, we refer to 'post-conflict federalism' because we want to focus on how federalism in particular can help to contain and perhaps quell ethnic conflict. Although some of the societies that have adopted the arrangements we discuss have not yet suffered secession, ethnic violence or civil war, the term 'post-conflict' is still appropriate, since federalism is designed to prevent such conflict from occurring, and those societies are often deployed as positive constitutional models in post-conflict contexts.

The stakes in these debates are very high. Many states in the developing world, such as Ethiopia, Iraq, Nigeria and Sudan, have adopted federal solutions to control ethnic conflict, often as part of a package of post-conflict constitutional design. Moreover, the advocacy of federalism as a tool for managing ethnic conflict continues to gather momentum around the globe. In South Asia, federalism has been advocated as a solution for ethnonational conflict in Nepal, Pakistan and Sri Lanka. Federalism has also been proposed as a remedy to the frozen conflicts of the former Soviet Union: Armenia, Azerbaijan, Georgia, Abkhazia, South Ossetia, and Nagorno Karabach. In the world of post-conflict constitutional design, it has been 'marketed as a palliative to secessionist conflict' (Erk and Anderson 2009: 191). However, while Philip Roeder seems to suggest that post-conflict federalism has emerged as the presumptive policy prescription to manage ethnonationalist conflict, Will Kymlicka has the better view. He carefully charts how, in Eastern and Central Europe, international institutions have taken a much more ambivalent and complex stance to post-conflict federalism, firmly rejecting it as part of the emerging international legal framework regarding the rights of national minorities, while accepting it on a case-by-case basis in order to diffuse violent conflict (Roeder 2009; Kymlicka 2007). But even with that caveat, if federalism exacerbates rather than mitigates conflict, then the most recent wave of constitutional design proceeds from dangerously erroneous premises. It is vitally important to determine how federalism actually performs in such difficult circumstances.

The centre of gravity in this academic debate is firmly anchored in political science. Ethnonationalism and secession have been studied by scholars working from a variety of subfields within that discipline: political sociology, comparative politics, international relations and political theory. Although their debates, questions, motivations, frameworks and methodologies may differ, these scholars share a reliance on qualitative research methods that focus on a relatively small number of cases to explain the complex relationship between constitutional design and political behaviour in states with politically mobilized national minorities.

On the one hand, there are those who argue that federalism dampens secessionist sentiment. Kymlicka, a political theorist, is representative of this position (Kymlicka 1998). He proceeds from the starting point that ethnic conflict in states with politically mobilized national minorities is, at root, a conflict between competing nationalisms. This is a zero-sum conflict in which one side will necessarily lose. If secession occurs, a statewide nationalism will lose territory that belongs to the nation as a whole. If secession does not occur, minority nationalists will argue that state and nation must still be brought into alignment. Kymlicka's case for multinational federalism responds by challenging the premise that there must be a one-to-one correspondence between nation and state. Post-conflict federalism acknowledges that the state contains more than one constituent nation and structures its institutions in such a way as to recognize and empower each of them. Post-conflict federalism halts the clamor for secession without dismembering the state because it satisfies the demand for self-determination with powers of self-government that fall short of independent statehood. Although they differ in some respects, many scholars have in essence taken this position: Nancy Bermeo, Rogers Brubaker, Ted Gurr, Yash Ghai, Arend Lijphart, Al Stepan, and John McGarry and Brendan O'Leary (Bermeo 2002; Brubaker 1996; Gurr 2000; Ghai 2000; Lijphart 1977; Stepan 1999; McGarry and O'Leary 2009).

At first blush, post-conflict federalism may superficially resemble Riker's 'coming-together' federalism because each bases the legitimacy of federal arrangements on the consent of the constituent units, which create and empower a central entity as part of a constitutional bargain. But upon closer examination, both the process of creating a post-conflict federation and the premises on which it relies are quite different. In most cases, a post-conflict federation is created from a state that already exists, and the constitutional imperative is not to make a new state but to reconstitute the existing one along federal lines in order to prevent it from coming apart. The process of reconstituting an existing state as a post-conflict federation is suitably described as 'holding together' an existing political entity for which the alternative to reconstitution is secession or perhaps even dissolution (Stepan 1999). For Riker, federalism is just one, often unsatisfactory, way for a nation to exercise its right to self-government. The existence of a single political community, which governs itself through the institutions and procedures created by the constitution, is not in question. For post-conflict federalism, this is the fundamental question. To transform a unitary, devolved or classical federal state into a post-conflict federation entails more than changes to its constitutional structure. It requires a new understanding of the state as the institutional compromise required to preserve a composite or layered political community in which the basic question of constitutional politics is what the terms of political association should be among the constituent nations (Simeon and Conway 2001).

This brief, abstract account of post-conflict federalism contains a number of ambiguities on precise questions of constitutional design that require further research. Consider the causal mechanism whereby federalism dampens the demand for secession. In the world of post-conflict federalism, secession is a defensive response to the policies of the central government. For federalism to be a substitute for secession, it must remedy the disadvantages these policies cause by providing a constitutional self-defence mechanism for the aggrieved minority nation. But scholars differ on the character of the disadvantages against which federalism is a defence. The design of an effective post-conflict federalism will accordingly vary depending on the nature of the harms to which it is a response. Kymlicka (2001) and Brubaker (1996) emphasize culture. They use the concept of nation-building to describe a set of policies that aim to create a shared national identity across a state by promoting a common language and shared historical narrative. For them, regional jurisdiction over education and the language of the public and private sectors will be of paramount importance. Scholars who highlight the failure by central governments to ensure that national minorities receive adequate benefits from the extraction of natural resources in their territories will prioritize regional or local ownership, management and revenue-sharing. Gurr dwells on instances of political discrimination, such as the exclusion of national minorities from political power and public sector employment. On this account, any federal arrangements would multiply the opportunities to wield political power.

Set against those who promote post-conflict federalism as a tool to manage and prevent ethnonationalist conflict, there are scholars who argue that it not only will fail to stem secession but will have precisely the opposite effect and intensify the conflict it purports to manage. Philip Roeder has offered the most recent and extended argument of this position. He claims that post-conflict federalism is inherently unstable and is characterized by a constant struggle between the two extremes of centralization and secession: 'a recurring crisis of politics' that is oriented around 'competing nation-state projects that pit homeland governments against the common-state government' (Roeder 2009: 209). This political pattern is the product of four purportedly unavoidable consequences of post-conflict federalism.

First, post-conflict federalism shapes the development of political identities, in particular, regional political identities. The creation of an ethnically defined region has the effect of institutionally privileging a conception of regional political identity in which the region is imagined as the property and homeland of an ethnic group. Post-conflict federalism also provides regions with the political and economic resources to develop these distinct identities through jurisdiction over education, the adoption of official language policies and cultural policy instruments such as public holidays and monuments. These regional identities will compete with statewide political identities as a source of citizen identification and belonging. They will become political resources for regional political elites to mobilize support during conflicts with central authorities. Second, the multiplication of national identities within post-conflict federations transforms the character of political conflict between the centre and the regions. Moments of high constitutional politics that raise constitutive questions regarding the status and the powers of the national minority and the relationship between the two nation-building projects crowd out ordinary policy disputes; the latter are reframed as raising fundamental questions regarding the right to self-determination. National identity becomes the principal political cleavage. As a consequence, political debate runs the constant risk of escalating from the demand for greater powers toward the existential constitutional question of secession, which would be the logical culmination of the nation-building project of the national minority. Third, post-conflict federalism endows regional governments with coercive policy instruments that national minorities can use as institutional weapons against central authorities, whether by engaging in competitive nation-building or by pushing for enhanced powers and greater autonomy. Such instruments may include the power to interfere with statewide electoral processes and revenue collection. Finally, the constitutional empowerment of the regions entails not just autonomy but also an institutionalized voice in common institutions, up to and including vetoes. These vetoes can weaken the decision-making ability of central authorities and hobble their ability to exercise their authority and thwart minority nationalism. Roeder's views are shared by other scholars (Bunce 1999; Leff 1999; Crawford 1998).

Roeder presents these four features as flowing from the logic of post-conflict federalism and, by implication, as absent from mononational federations. But this is not entirely true. The political resources he identifies – the ability to interfere with the operation of central authorities through coercive means and regional vetoes in central institutions – are contingent features of constitutional design that do not inhere in the very nature of post-conflict federations. To be sure, these were features of the constitution of the Soviet Union, and Roeder generalizes from the failure of the Soviet Union to argue that multinational federalism will fail more generally. But it is legitimate to ask whether the same patterns will hold in post-conflict federations that lack these institutional elements. Roeder himself states that '[t]inkering with the institutional details of different forms of ethnofederalism or autonomy is unlikely to exorcise the demons, for the devil is to be found in ethnofederalism and autonomy arrangements themselves' (2009: 207), which suggests that post-conflict federalism will collapse regardless of their adoption. However, the logic of his account suggests they are necessary for post-conflict federalism to fail. Moreover, if the presence of these features is necessary for federal failure, it is not sufficient, because they are also present in some enduring mononational federations. So Roeder's critique really turns not on the presence of these political resources but on the impact of political agendas on their use. At the root of the political dynamics that he describes are the new political agendas nurtured by post-conflict federalism: in particular, the institutionalization of minority nationalism through the designation of a region as a national minority's homeland. Since this new political orientation is precisely the point of post-conflict federalism, his critique strikes at its very heart.

3.3   Evidence

Both academic camps – those who advocate the use of post-conflict federalism to manage ethnonational conflict, and those who oppose doing so – support their arguments by reference to examples of federal success and federal failure. This debate was sparked by the collapse of the former communist dictatorships of Eastern and Central Europe (ECE) in the early 1990s (Choudhry 2007). Students of ECE were confronted with a jarring contrast. Three of the former ECE communist dictatorships – Yugoslavia, the Soviet Union and Czechoslovakia – had been post-conflict federations prior to the transition to democracy. All three began to disintegrate within 18 months after embracing democracy. By contrast, unitary states, including several with large national minorities (e.g. Poland, Hungary) and some in which nationalism served as the axis of internal political conflict, did not fall apart. If the ambition of post-conflict federalism is to manage competing nation-building projects within a single state, federalism may in fact have failed to meet its basic objective. Yet the problem went deeper still. Since only the post-conflict federations broke up, and all of them did, the suspicion was that federalism had fuelled secession, whereas unitary state structures prevented it. So in ECE, post-conflict federalism had fuelled precisely those political forces it was designed to suppress. ECE has been central to the case against post-conflict federalism. Indeed, scholars who argue that post-conflict federalism inflames ethnonational conflict have tended to be specialists on ECE who have extended their arguments to indict post-conflict federalism more generally.

The best way to respond to the anti-models of Yugoslavia, Czechoslovakia and the Soviet Union was to identify models where post-conflict federalism had actually worked. In the literature, the leading counter-examples are Canada, India and Spain. The founding of the Canadian federation in 1867 and the creation of Quebec was a direct response to the failure of the United Province of Canada, a British colony that existed from 1840 to 1867 and that had two wings: one with a French-speaking majority and one with an English-speaking majority. Each wing elected equal numbers of representatives to a legislative assembly, although the largely French-speaking citizens of the former outnumbered the largely English-speaking citizens of the latter. The goal behind the merger and the departure from representation by population was linguistic assimilation. The English-speaking wing eventually became more populous and demanded greater representation in the joint legislature, a request that was resisted by the French-speaking wing, which feared it would be outvoted on matters important to its linguistic identity. The result was political paralysis. Federalism was the solution: a compromise that provided representation by population at the federal level, but also created a Quebec with jurisdiction over those matters crucial to the survival of a French-speaking society in that province. Had Quebec not been created, it is likely that the French-speaking parts of Canada would have eventually seceded.

A similar story can be told about India (Choudhry 2009). At independence, India was organized as a federation. The question that generated intense controversy at the time was whether provincial boundaries would coincide with linguistic boundaries. India has a dozen regional languages, spoken in fairly compact linguistic regions. States could easily have been drawn on linguistic lines. But the Constituent Assembly decided against drawing inter-state boundaries to coincide with linguistic boundaries, out of a fear that they would fuel secessionist mobilization in India's border states and doom the country to disintegration. However, debates over the choice of official language – especially the language of public sector employment – thrust this issue back onto the constitutional agenda. This process began in the south, with the creation of Telegu-speaking Andhra Pradesh and Tamil-speaking Tamil Nadu. Once that precedent was established, it sparked further demands for linguistic states, to which the central government responded by creating the States Reorganization Commission. The Commission proposed the redrawing of state boundaries along linguistic lines, and the process took place during the 1950s and 1960s. The accepted view is that, had this not been done, India would have come apart. The failure to address a similar dynamic in Pakistan and Sri Lanka has been a major cause of constitutional failure in those two countries (DeVotta 2004; Ayres 2009).

This academic debate has reached an impasse, largely as a consequence of methodology. As Dawn Brancati has argued, the use of qualitative case studies are at best 'useful for generating interesting ideas about decentralization' but 'do not provide strong evidence of their claims' (Brancati 2006: 653). The reason is that scholars tend to select cases on the basis of the dependent variable, with critics studying the failed communist-era federations of ECE, and advocates analysing the more successful examples. But recent scholarship in comparative politics that employs large-sample quantitative studies holds the potential to advance our understanding of federalism's capacity to manage ethnic conflict. Such studies can test competing empirical claims across a broad variety of cases and identify the factors that explain when post-conflict federalism succeeds and when it does not.

Three studies warrant discussion.

First, Roeder recently constructed a global database around the notion of the 'segmented state', which he defines as a state that 'divides its territory and population into separate jurisdictions, and gives the population that purportedly is indigenous to each jurisdiction a distinct political status' (Roeder 2007: 12). In such states, there is a 'common state' that possesses jurisdiction over the entire population and territory, as well as separate 'segment-states' that have jurisdiction over a portion of that territory and people. A segment-state is not merely a territorial subdivision; it contains 'peoples who purportedly have special claim to that jurisdiction as a homeland' (12–13). Roeder observes that, in the twentieth century, 86% of new states had been segment-states prior to independence, from which he concludes that segmented states are far more likely to experience secession than are states that are not segmented. Although Roeder does not use the language of post-conflict federalism, it clearly overlaps with his definition of a segmented state. The interesting question Roeder poses is under what conditions is secession from the segmented state (or post-conflict federation) more likely. Roeder answers this question by reference to a global data set of segmented states created before 1990, with annual observations. The independent variables were (a) the constitutional relationship between the common-state and segment-state, on a spectrum ranging from fully exclusive common-state autocracy to fully inclusive common-state democracy, and (b) whether the segment-state was self-governing or not. His key finding is that, in anocracies and democracies that excluded the population of segment-states from central governance, self-government in a segment-state increased the likelihood of secession. Since self-governing regions are core elements of post-conflict federalism and are designed to prevent secession, Roeder concludes that the evidence does not support this policy prescription and in fact counsels against it.

But Roeder's conclusion does not follow from his results. One of his most striking findings is that the most stable form of post-conflict federalism is a fully inclusive democracy in which the regions enjoy extensive forms of self-government. Two comparisons drawn from his data are important here: (1) inclusive democracies are much more stable than other regimes when their regions are not self-governing; and (2) unlike exclusionary democracies and anocracies, inclusive democracies do not suffer an increased risk of secession when their regions *are* self-governing. What this suggests is that the rise of secessionist politics might instead be a function of the structure of politics at the centre. Roeder's data do not offer an explanation as to why, but it is possible to speculate. The finding that exclusionary democracies are less stable than inclusive democracies is consistent with theories of minority nationalism that explain the rise of minority nationalism as a defensive response to the policies of the central state, whether characterized as nation-building or as economic, political or cultural discrimination. It may be that common states have a freer hand to pursue these policies when they exclude the populations of segment-states from central governance. At a prescriptive level, this suggests that proponents of post-conflict federalism should not neglect the design of central institutions. This points to the need for further research on the link between federalism and central power-sharing, as discussed below.

Second, a more recent study by Lars-Erik Cederman and his colleagues supports the conclusion that federalism can reduce the likelihood of secession (Cederman et al. 2010). They work from the grievance school of civil war studies. Ethnic political mobilization can take a variety of forms. One hypothesis they test is that the probability of ethnonationalist conflict increases with the degree of exclusion from central executive power. To test the relationship between political exclusion and violent conflict, Cederman et al. constructed the Ethnic Power Relations data set (EPR), which identified all politically mobilized ethnic groups and measured their access to state power on an annual basis from 1946 to 2005. They draw an important set of distinctions between those groups that are excluded from central power: 'regional autonomy' (elites wield local authority within the state, e.g. through federal arrangements), 'separatist autonomy' (elites wield local authority coupled with declaration of independence), 'powerless' (elites excluded from central and local authority without explicit discrimination) and 'discrimination' (elites excluded from central and local authority as a consequence of deliberate discrimination). Violent conflict is linked to any ethnic group in whose name an armed group instigated conflict.

As anticipated, excluded groups are more likely to instigate violent conflict than those that are not excluded. But if one disaggregates excluded groups, those that enjoy regional autonomy are much less likely to instigate violent conflict than those that experience other forms of political exclusion. Even more striking is that groups that are excluded from central power but enjoy regional autonomy are *less* likely than those groups who are *included* in power – either as senior or junior partners – to instigate violent conflict. Although these observations are based on descriptive statistics and they change somewhat with regression analysis, with junior partners less likely to rebel than excluded groups that enjoy regional autonomy, the latter are still less likely to rebel than those that experience more severe forms of political exclusion, such as the powerless and the targets of discrimination. These results support the claims of those who argue that post-conflict federalism may operate as a conflict-management technique.

A third study takes the literature in a different direction. Federal arrangements may stem secession in some contexts but fuel it in others. The outcome may be a function of the central government's commitment to democratic inclusion but, as Brancati points out, federalism may fuel secession even in democratic states (Brancati 2009). The question is what additional factors explain the uneven effects of post-conflict federalism. The answer is to be found in the electoral strength of regional political parties. If they are strong, they can gain power and deploy the institutional resources provided by a federal constitutional structure to foster regional identity and mobilize a national minority around this identity to pursue secession; if they are weak, this is much less likely to happen. Regression analysis demonstrates that federalism reduces ethnic conflict and secession while controlling for the strength of regional parties, but that ethnic conflict increases with regional party electoral strength.

Critics of post-conflict federalism would counter that this constitutional arrangement itself fuels the rise of regional parties. But the evidence is more complex. While post-conflict federalism creates the opportunity for the rise of strong regional parties, they do not emerge in every post-conflict federation. The question is which other features of constitutional design, if any, determine whether that potential is realized. Brancati's principal findings are that regional parties are stronger (a) where there are more regional legislatures, because they provide more opportunities for regional parties to wield power; (b) where regional legislatures select the upper house of the central legislature, which increases the impact of regional parties in central institutions and creates additional incentives to form such parties; and (c) when national and regional elections occur at different times, which offsets the coat-tails effect pursuant to which elections to higher office influence the results in concurrent elections to lower offices.

Taken together, Brancati suggests that, in order to harness the benefits of federalism for managing ethnic conflict while mitigating its dangers, the focus should not be on federal design but on regional political parties. This leads to two sets of policy proposals. One focuses on the rules governing political parties and electoral competition. For example, it suggests that parties that run in national elections should be required to field candidates in more than one region in order to win seats. Additional research is required to untangle the relationship between the electoral system and the rise of regional parties. But the other set of proposals shifts the focus to the centre, in particular the interaction of central institutions with regional political processes. Here, the prescriptions appear to point in opposite directions. Requiring direct elections for the upper chamber would appear to disentangle the central and regional governments, whereas coordinating the timing of central and regional elections would politically connect the two levels of government. However, if adopted as a package, the two measures should be understood as promoting the autonomy and priority of central political processes at the expense of the electoral strength of regional parties.

3.4   Future Directions for Research

We highlight and briefly discuss four areas for future research under the aegis of post-conflict federalism: (1) regional borders; (2) the relationship between federalism and the organization of central authority; (3) the status and role of local government; and (4) natural resources.

3.4.1   Regional borders
Every state that opts for a federal constitution must decide the number and shape of its regional governments. This is a topic that has been inadequately researched, but which is of the highest practical importance. Iraq's failure to resolve the boundaries of the Kurdistan region demonstrates how difficult these decisions can be, especially when the memory of ethnic strife is fresh and valuable resources are at stake (Galbraith 2008; O'Leary 2009).

Donald Horowitz has devoted the most attention to the question of regional boundaries, and his particular proposals flow from his broader views on constitutional design in ethnically divided societies (Horowitz 2000). For Horowitz, the political pathology to which constitutional design must respond is the rise of ethnicity as the principal basis of political cleavage. In polities defined by their ethnic divisions, political competition occurs among ethnic parties and within ethnic groups, who outbid each other and push politics toward extremism. Horowitz's overarching goal is to design constitutions to create incentives for inter-ethnic cooperation, by empowering ethnic moderates over ethnic radicals. The key is to 'make moderation pay' (Horowitz 1990). His principal focus has been the electoral system. The mechanism for rewarding moderation is the transfer of votes across ethnic lines, which Horowitz refers to as 'vote pooling' and for which the key mechanism is the alternative vote. The alternative vote makes moderation pay because it rewards ethnic parties that appeal across ethnic lines and should offset electoral losses from intra-ethnic competition on the extremes.

For Horowitz, regional boundaries should be drawn with the same goals in mind. The leading case around which he constructs his account is Nigeria, which offers a natural experiment. Nigeria's First Republic was a failure; its Second Republic was a success. Horowitz argues that this difference was a function of the poor design of federalism under the former and good design under the latter. The First Republic divided Nigeria into three regions, which tracked the country's major ethnic divides. Politics within each region was intra-ethnic; politics at the centre was inter-ethnic. The problem is that the largest ethnic group, the Hausa-Fulani, used the province in which it constituted the largest group as a base to capture the centre and dominate Nigeria, which ultimately led to civil war and attempted secession. For Horowitz, the Second Republic solved this problem through a combination of strategies. There were in fact three key goals: fragmenting the power of the largest group; creating cross-cutting cleavages through federal design, in order to promote non-ethnic bases for political competition; and reducing the stakes of losing the battle for power at the centre. The Second Republic pursued all three goals simultaneously. First, it divided the Hausa-Fulani into multiple states, which diminished their capacity to capture the centre and created cross-cutting cleavages (e.g. on the basis of natural resource endowments) that generated new forms of intra-ethnic political competition. Second, it created ethnically heterogeneous states. The new internal boundaries made allies out of ethnic groups who otherwise would have been competitors. For example, members of different ethnic groups would unite around their shared material interest as residents of the same state and then compete economically against people who shared their ethnicity but happened to live in other states. Third, it created many states in order to multiply the opportunities to wield political power and dispense patronage, which in turn reduced the relative importance of controlling the centre.

Horowitz's analysis raises two questions for further research. The first question is whether his second strategy – the creation of heterogeneous regions that divide and recombine ethnic groups – coheres with post-conflict federalism. At first glance, they would appear to be inconsistent because post-conflict federalism is premised on the belief that relatively homogeneous regions, in which one ethnic group constitutes a majority, are required to satisfy demands for self-determination and to relieve the risk of secession. Moreover, comparative experience suggests that heterogeneous regions may produce political conflict. The leading counter-example to Nigeria is India, which contained many linguistically heterogeneous states after independence. These units proved to be very unstable because ethnic groups could not agree on the choice of official language. The reorganization of Indian states was a direct response to this political conflict, and resulted in the creation of states that were linguistically homogeneous and relatively stable, at least along linguistic fault lines.

The difference between the Nigerian and Indian cases raises a question for further research. One hypothesis is that different markers of ethnic identity might interact differently with the demarcation of regions. For example, compare religion and language, two possible bases of ethnic identification. While a regional government can in principle be neutral with respect to religion (i.e. not adopt an official religion), it must choose one or a few official languages in which to conduct legislative affairs, deliver public services, provide education and administer justice. So if language is the basis for minority nationalism, then the Nigerian solution might be ill-advised. The emerging large-sample studies are ill-equipped to answer this question, since they do not appear to differentiate among the different dimensions of ethnic identification.

The second question raised by Horowitz's work concerns the design of regions that contain the ethnic group, if any, that forms a national majority. To date, the scholarship on post-conflict federalism has largely focused on the design of regions that contain national minorities and has given relatively minimal attention to the manner in which internal boundaries should deal with a dominant ethnic group. Indeed, given its preoccupation with satisfying the demand for self-determination by national minorities, post-conflict federalism might appear indifferent to the constitutional structure of the rest of the state. The remainder could be federal or it could be unitary, in which case the post-conflict federation would be a federacy. However, Henry Hale has demonstrated that this indifference would be a mistake (Hale 2004). Hale observes that post-conflict federations with a dominant ethnic group that is concentrated in a single region (which he terms a 'core ethnic region') are much less stable than those where that national majority is fractured among different regions. Thus, while Nigeria (the First Republic), the Soviet Union, Pakistan, Yugoslavia, Czechoslovakia and Serbia and Montenegro collapsed (some violently), Canada, Switzerland, Spain, the Russian Federation, Ethiopia and Nigeria (the Second and Third Republics) have or did not.

For Hale, core ethnic regions undermine the stability of post-conflict federations because: (1) they lead to 'dual power' situations where leaders of the core ethnic region have the political resources to challenge the legitimacy and authority of the central state to represent the interests of the dominant ethnic group and thus may threaten the existence of the central government by mobilizing members of the ethnic majority to shift their primary political loyalty from the central government to the core ethnic region; and (2) they fuel the rise of secession as a defensive response because they diminish the capacity of the centre to make credible commitments to national minorities, in part because the centre is more likely to exploit those minorities in an attempt to retain the support of the dominant ethnic group. Conversely, when a core region is absent, 'the core group faces high hurdles to collective action that is aimed at realizing core-group goals within the union state and that can threaten union collapse for the reasons outlined above' (Hale 2004: 176). For Hale, this explains the contrasting experiences of the USSR (which had a core ethnic region and collapsed) and Russia (which lacks a core ethnic region and has not).

Hale complicates standard accounts of the failure of post-conflict federations. Most critics of post-conflict federations (e.g. Roeder) blame political mobilization by national minorities for secession. Although advocates of post-conflict federalism generally do not try to explain situations of federal failure, if they did they would also likely place great emphasis on the role of regional governments in mobilizing minority nations. They would likely argue that federal failure is the consequence of (a) the failure of the centre to respond to the demands of national minorities for constitutional self-defence with sufficient legislative and fiscal autonomy or (b) the failure to reduce the demand for secession by inhibiting the rise of regional parties through electoral engineering. Hale suggests that we ignore the design of the remainder of the state at our peril. Although it is accepted that central government policies may fuel secessionist mobilization, little thought has been given to how constitutional design may increase or reduce that risk. Likewise, the link between constitutional design and the ability of the centre to address and overcome secessionist mobilization once the latter has commenced has not been sufficiently explored. Finally, the risk that the ethnic majority could abandon the central state is a new problem for constitutional design. In sum, we should shift our attention to the impact of the design of regions containing the dominant ethnic group on the ability of the federal structure to integrate the dominant ethnic group, discriminate against and otherwise aggravate national minorities, and accommodate those minorities.

3.4.2   Federalism and power-sharing at the centre

There is a long-standing debate over the design of political institutions in ethnically divided societies. There are two main contending positions, offered by Arend Lijphart and Donald Horowitz. Lijphart is virtually synonymous with the approach known as consociationalism (Lijphart 1977; Lijphart 2008). According to consociational theory, the constituent groups of a divided society can attain a democratic peace by striking a 'grand bargain'. This bargain consists of two essential guarantees for each constituent group: (1) power-sharing, which consists of guaranteed participation in political decision-making; and (2) segmental autonomy over matters that affect its distinct identity, such as culture and education. The classic form of power-sharing institution is a grand coalition cabinet encompassing representatives of the major ethnic segments. Segmental autonomy may consist of federalism (where territorial boundaries follow ethnic boundaries) or non-territorial federalism (where they do not). These two core elements can be supplemented by two supporting elements: (3) proportionality (in legislative representation, representation in cabinets, civil service, police, military and public expenditure) and (4) mutual vetoes on vital interests. Elements of the consociational 'grand bargain' can be found in a number of post-conflict constitutions, such as Bosnia and Herzegovina, Ethiopia and Iraq. The second position is Horowitz's incentives-based approach, introduced above. In addition to the use of the alternative vote for legislative elections to encourage inter-ethnic political appeals and a federal system based on heterogeneous units, Horowitz advocates a strong executive president who would serve a unifying role that transcends ethnic divides. The procedures for presidential elections should be designed to ensure support across different ethnic groups. In a state with geographically concentrated ethnic groups, the solution would be to require a minimum level of support from each group (as was the case under the Nigerian Second Republic).

This debate is vigorous and we need not repeat it here (for a detailed account, see Choudhry 2008). What interests us is how Lijphart and Horowitz define the nature of the problem. Both write against the backdrop of pluralists who ask why political actors who lose within democratic processes do not respond by turning on the system. This behaviour is produced by cross-cutting cleavages, a conclusion that supports a competitive model of democratic politics in which coalitions and majorities shift, political parties compete for median voters at the ideological centre, and electoral jockeying creates pressures towards moderation. Parties cycle in and out of power, and no segment of society is permanently excluded from it. In ethnically divided societies, however, cleavages are mutually reinforcing and political divisions map onto ethnic divisions. These tendencies lead political parties to organize themselves along ethnic lines. Political competition does not exist across ethnic divides. The danger is that national minorities will become perpetual political losers and will eventually reject the political system instead of continuing to participate in it.

Lijphart and Horowitz are not focused on the specific problems of secession, threats to territorial integrity and the risk of civil war. This is in part a function of timing: the Lijphart/Horowitz debate originated a decade before the developments in ECE during the 1990s that prompted this explosion of scholarly interest in minority nationalism. The question is whether this long-standing debate should change in light of what we have since learned about secessionist conflict. Future research should address two issues.

First, post-conflict federalism is a way to create incentives for national minorities to participate within the constitutional order, as opposed to repudiating that order and attempting to secede. It appears to map most closely onto the consociational model. This suggests that central institutions should be designed to reap the virtues of power-sharing, proportionality and mutual vetoes. The reason to share power at the centre is to reduce the risk that the central state will engage in economic, political or cultural discrimination, which in turn will trigger minority nationalism as a defensive response. Roeder's finding that, within the set of segmented states, exclusionary democracies are less stable than inclusive democracies supports this view. The question that requires further research is how exactly to design the centre, given the range of possibilities, in order to limit its offensive capacity.

A useful starting point would be the vast literature on the choice between presidential, semi-presidential and parliamentary forms of government (see e.g. Linz 1990a; Linz 1990b; Stepan and Skach 1993; Norris 2008). This literature has not yet addressed this basic constitutional choice within post-conflict federations. Moreover, these decisions must be studied across a large enough number of cases to permit some generalizations. At first blush, a proponent of consociationalism would likely argue for proportional representation and a parliamentary model. If drafters opt for a parliamentary system, they will have to decide whether and how to regulate the allocation of cabinet positions, including that of the Prime Minister, among the regions and other salient social groups. But the apparent conceptual fit between parliamentary democracy and post-conflict federalism needs to be tested against the alternatives. Recent and emergent post-conflict federations have opted for other arrangements. For example, in Bosnia and Herzegovina, there is a collective presidency shared by the regional governments (Banks 2005). At the time of writing, Nepal is on the verge of adopting a strong version of presidential government, alongside a federal structure designed in part to manage ethnic conflict. The scope for choice within presidential systems is broad. If the drafters of the constitution opt for a presidential system, they must decide whether the president will be chosen by election or by appointment. If the former, they must determine whether a simple majority will suffice or whether some additional indication of broad regional support will also be required. If the president is to be appointed, the drafters will need to decide whether (and, if so, how) the position should rotate among ethnic groups or regional governments. In each case, they also will need to choose between a single-person presidency and a multi-person office, as in Bosnia and Herzegovina.

A similar set of questions arises with respect to the design of constitutional courts, which has been largely ignored in the literature on post-conflict federalism. Literature on classical federalism amply demonstrates their central role in federal states. The extent to which a constitution is a credible commitment to thwart exploitation by the centre will turn on the structure of courts. In particular, the following questions will be important: membership (e.g. minority nation representation), appointment mechanism (e.g. involvement of regions), panel composition with respect to federalism disputes, jurisdiction (e.g. direct access by regional governments) and decision-rules (e.g. majority vs. super-majority vs. minority vetoes).

Second, this line of analysis presupposes that the central problem faced by post-conflict federalism is the accommodation of national minorities. However, the basic goal of post-conflict federalism is in fact to reconcile competing nationalisms within the same state. A significant amount of energy has been devoted to the study of the constitutional arrangements that would satisfy calls for self-determination by national minorities and dampen demands for secession. As argued above, this must be supplemented by further study on the design of the centre. In contrast, relatively little thought has been given to the constitutional arrangements that would disrupt the development of a statewide nationalism and accordingly diminish the incentives to centralize authority and transform a federation into a unitary state. This issue is key to ensuring a stable allocation of authority between the central and regional governments. Scholars have not yet approached the design of central institutions in post-conflict federations with this problem in mind.

Hale seems to suggest that this problem may arise only where a core ethnic region provides the institutional resources to the dominant ethnic group to launch a statewide nation-building project. Thus, the answer may be to reduce rather than accommodate demands from the ethnic majority for more influence. However, since his dependent variable is state collapse, he fails to measure the existence of political conflict between competing nationalisms that does not reach the level of existential constitutional crisis. Post-conflict federations must integrate both minorities and majorities. The centre must have sufficient scope for action. That is, the central government must have adequate authority to mollify incipient statewide nationalism and the decision-rules for exercising that authority must not frustrate it. The research question is how to reconcile this constitutional agenda with a counter-agenda that prioritizes the need to protect national minorities from an overreaching central state.

3.4.3 Local government in post-conflict settings

Local government is incidental to classical federalism. Whether explicitly or by default, the four classical federal constitutions leave the details of local government to the discretion of regional governments. Their drafters did not foresee the rapid population growth, technological innovations and social transformations that concentrated political and economic power in cities during the twentieth century (Hirschl 2009). In contrast, contemporary scholars of comparative constitutional law and politics seem increasingly interested in local government (see e.g. Steytler ed. 2009). However, comparative studies of its role in post-conflict environments remain scarce (Jackson and Scott 2007). The studies that do exist rely on anecdotal evidence and assumptions, such as the vital importance of local government in delivering basic public goods and services (e.g. water, roads and sewers) that demonstrate state capacity and build state legitimacy, but may have little basis in experience.

Framers of post-conflict constitutions face a knot of procedural, formal and substantive questions about local government. They must decide whether, and if so how, to include local governments in the processes by which the constitution is drafted, ratified and implemented. They must decide whether, and if so how, to recognize those governments in the resulting document: as a third order of government equivalent to the central and regional governments, as a matter left to the discretion of the regional governments or as some sort of hybrid, as in India where the states are obligated to establish local governments with specific structures but allowed to choose which powers to devolve in order to facilitate self-government (Mathew and Hooja 2009). They must decide which level of government is responsible for demarcating the boundaries of local governments, whether to entrench any rules regarding their finances, how to assuage the strategic concerns of regional governments and the manner, if any, in which local governments will be represented at the centre. This list of issues is only a partial one, but the challenge is clear.

In general, we need more empirical evidence of the nature and operation of local government across various post-conflict environments. But, since the two issues traditionally associated with local government are democracy and development, we especially need to know more about how local government can best serve these goals in such circumstances. Since local governments are usually tasked with routine matters, they may seem to promise a departure from divisive ethnic politics in favour of a pragmatic, non-partisan approach that focuses on solving common local problems (Steytler 2007). However, a recent qualitative survey of 12 federal states, some of which are ethnically divided and some of which are not, suggests that national parties tend to dominate local politics (Steytler 2009). As noted above, Brancati has observed a connection between the strength of regional parties and the risk of a post-conflict federation succumbing to secession. It may be worthwhile to examine the relationships between institutional design, party affiliation and political outcomes at each of the central, regional and local levels in order to identify the conditions under which local governments might serve not only as effective providers of public goods but also as counterweights to secessionist tendencies in regional governments. For example, a comparative analysis of the local elements of comprehensive power-sharing arrangements and their ability to defuse ethnic tensions in an urban setting would complement the available case studies and perhaps provide valuable guidance (see e.g. Bieber 2005).

An alternative would be to consider which political practices and legal mechanisms might make constitutional commitments to local governments more credible. The responsibilities of local governments regularly exceed their fiscal resources, especially in societies that are both divided and developing. They depend on financial transfers from the other levels of governments in order to even attempt to fulfil their obligations. But in post-conflict states, government revenues are often depleted by violence and diverted by ongoing ethnic competition for political and economic rents. In Nigeria, for example, the financial transfers envisioned by the constitution are diverted by opaque accounting practices, corruption and other pathologies (Galadima 2009). If local governments in such states lack a reliable resource base, they may be unable to meet the basic needs of their constituents. This failure to meet even minimal expectations may generate resentment towards a particular party or level of government or perhaps even undermine support for the entire post-conflict constitutional settlement (Manning 2003; *Harvard Law Review* Note 2008). Thus, development is linked with democracy, at least at the local level. Studies, whether qualitative or quantitative, that examine the institutional aspects of this relationship may make a significant contribution to post-conflict federalism.

3.4.4   Natural resources and post-conflict settings

In recent years, natural resources have provided a rich seam for scholars of civil war, who have explored a range of issues relevant to post-conflict constitutional design. They have used comprehensive data sets to distinguish not only different resources, such as oil, diamonds and drugs, but also different forms of the same resource, such as offshore and onshore oil or mined and alluvial diamonds, and different types of conflict, from ethnic groups seeking regional autonomy to military factions seeking control of the central state (Ross 2006; Buhaug 2006). They have developed sophisticated statistical models to isolate the effects of these resources on the initiation, duration and severity of such conflicts (Ross 2004; Lajala 2009). They also have tested multiple causal mechanisms by which these resources may spark and sustain conflict: some propose that the exploitation and degradation of traditional territory exacerbates grievances among a national minority; others suggest that a state weakened by its dependence on resource revenues presents an easy and valuable target; others still posit that lootable resources entice and enable rebel groups to extend their campaigns against the state (e.g. Ross 2004; Collier and Hoeffler 2004; Fearon 2005). As these scholars have paid relatively little attention to the institutional structure of those states that experience and avoid such conflicts, both fields could gain from being brought together (see e.g. Aspinall 2007).

The primary task of a post-conflict constitution is to contain violent conflict. Natural resources complicate this task. Although they often fuel conflict, they can also be used to finance peace. The more that constitutional scholars and framers know about the physical, historical and institutional circumstances under which certain resources are likely to inflame certain conflicts, the more effective and viable their constitutional designs will become. The new civil war scholarship could help them to diagnose the particular challenges they face, since oil reserves in the remote traditional territory of a large ethnic minority pose a different set of problems and possibilities than do contraband crops that thrive across an accessible and ethnically heterogeneous region (Lajala 2009). The former promise more substantial and legitimate revenues but require much larger investments to extract and export. However, scholars disagree on whether (and, if so, how, why and the extent to which) such deposits increase the likelihood, length and intensity of violent conflict, secessionist or otherwise (e.g. Walter 2006; Ross 2006; Lajala 2009). Similar debates surround drugs, diamonds and other resources that are relatively easy to collect. While post-conflict constitutional design might benefit from greater attention to civil war scholarship, any such benefit will depend on the scope and quality of consensus those scholars ultimately obtain.

In the meantime, we can try to learn from those post-conflict federal systems that have managed, however scarcely or briefly, to turn natural resources from an obstacle into a platform for peace. To have any chance of success, a post-conflict constitution must define a peace that the parties find both plausible and more desirable than war. When natural resources are involved, the appeal of a constitutional settlement is likely to depend on whether they perceive it as more profitable than conflict (Wimmer 2004; Wennmann 2009). The value of any such settlement, including a federal one, depends on its content and its credibility.

For example, many post-conflict federal constitutions distinguish between the ownership of a natural resource, the management of that resource and the collection and distribution of revenues from it. By assigning these various facets of natural resources to different actors in the new constitutional order, parties in divided societies like Iraq and Sudan have been able to isolate contentious political issues (e.g. ownership of oil deposits) from relatively uncontroversial technical matters that are more relevant to attracting investment, expanding production and generating wealth (e.g. management and revenue collection). If successful, this approach enables post-conflict federal states to increase the total amount of resource revenues extracted and to share those revenues in a manner that reinforces the former combatants' commitment to the new constitution (Hayson and Kane 2009).

Success may begin with creative constitutional text, but poor implementation will derail even the most ingenious legal compromise. For example, under the Nigerian Constitution, the federal government is responsible for collecting and pooling all oil revenues for distribution among federal, state and local governments. The constitution mandates a minimum 13% share for the oil-bearing states, which are largely concentrated in the Niger Delta and populated by relatively small ethnic groups, but otherwise leaves the distribution formula to be determined by a federal statute (Suberu 2009). This approach is not only subverted by poor governance, as noted above; it is also considered inadequate by many residents of the Delta states, some of whom have engaged in organized violence and sabotage against both the government and the oil industry. The Iraqi Constitution provides a newer and perhaps less familiar example. It grants the federal, regional and governorate governments concurrent authority to manage the country's oil reserves but does not specify the procedures by which they will make these decisions (Hayson and Kane 2009). In light of such cases, it might be useful to look past the relevant constitutional language and research the legislative, political and administrative steps taken to make these provisions work. By comparing such measures and their results, we might learn more about the circumstances in which different provisions do (or do not) produce the intended effects.

Another feature of post-conflict federal constitutions that relates to natural resources and warrants further inquiry is the use of scheduled referendums on regional autonomy. Although these mechanisms take different forms and promise different degrees of autonomy, they perform a similar function: they encourage national minorities whose traditional territory contains valuable oil deposits to support the federal project by increasing their control over the terms on which they participate. The 2005 Iraqi Constitution, for example, obligates the federal government to conduct a referendum in the city of Kirkuk and other disputed territories to determine whether they should join the Kurdistan Region (McGarry and O'Leary 2008). The deadline for this vote was 31 December 2007, but just as the government failed to fulfil its constitutional obligations to resettle residents of those territories displaced by the prior regime, compensate them where appropriate and conduct a census in the area, it has failed to meet this deadline and numerous negotiated extensions. In contrast, the

Comprehensive Peace Agreement that preserves the tense relationship between the governments of north and south Sudan promises the latter, which sits atop most of the country's oil reserves, a referendum on independence by the end of January 2011. Given the uncertain political situation in Sudan, doubts persist as to whether this vote will be held, whether it will be free and fair, and whether, if successful, the north will allow the south to secede without a fight (Wennmann 2009).

Such arrangements may be understood as attempts to increase the credibility of their respective constitutional packages. National minorities that control territory endowed with valuable natural resources may have reason to distrust, and thus to reject, agreements with a central government. In theory, the central government likely will face severe economic and political pressure to renege on any promise of autonomy and assert greater influence over those resources, especially if members of other ethnic groups also reside in the contested region (Fearon 2004; Ross 2004). By granting such regions the option to exit (or, in the case of Kirkuk, to join the region of Iraq most capable of demanding additional concessions and eventually obtaining independence) at a specified date in the near future, these provisions may reduce the cost of committing to such an agreement and thus make peace more probable. In turn, and again in theory, the constitutional option to exit or form a larger and more self-sufficient region may create incentives for the central government and other ethnic groups to refrain from exploiting or otherwise antagonizing these national minorities. However, if central governments do face such strong pressures to renege on promises made to resource-rich minorities, it is unclear why vulnerable minorities would trust the promise to hold and respect a referendum on secession or amalgamation more than the initial promise of autonomy. Without additional research, it is unclear whether, and if so how, such provisions make a post-conflict federal constitution more credible. As a result, it might be worthwhile to compare the origins and outcomes of these provisions to determine why they appeal to national minorities and the conditions, if any, under which they can be implemented effectively.

4   CONCLUSION

We hope that the idea of post-conflict federalism will promote critical constitutional scholarship. The familiar conception of classical federalism has fuelled important debates about essential elements of the most stable and successful federal systems. But lessons drawn from states like Australia and the USA often do not apply to more volatile conditions, such as those facing states seeking to recover from ethnic conflict. Post-conflict states must solve a very different set of constitutional problems, and in deciding whether and how to implement federalism they must respond to a very different set of challenges. At the very least, such analyses will remind us that even the most common ideas and institutions have a particular provenance, so they may be less relevant or useful in other contexts. On a more abstract level, by positing that the experiences of post-conflict federal states can support a coherent conception of federalism distinct from that fostered by the experiences of the first wave of federal states, post-conflict federalism offers a new perspective on basic questions like 'what is federalism?' and even 'what is a constitution?'. Finally, this brief sketch of post-conflict federalism suggests yet another promising avenue for inquiry. Many of the issues central to classical federalism, such as the division of powers, the role of courts and the development of a common market, receive little or no attention in scholarship about post-conflict federalism. Even if these issues prove less relevant in post-conflict environments, it will be helpful to know how and why.

REFERENCES

Amar, Akhil Reed (1991), 'Some New World Lessons for the Old World', *University of Chicago Law Review*, 58: 483–510.

Aroney, Nicholas (2006), 'Formation, Representation and Amendment in Federal Constitutions', *American Journal of Comparative Law*, 54: 277–336.

Aspinall, Edward (2007), 'The Construction of Grievance: Natural Resources and Identity in a Separatist Conflict', *Journal of Conflict Resolution*, 51: 950–72.

Ayres, Alyssa (2009), *Speaking like a State: Language and Nationalism in Pakistan*, Cambridge: Cambridge University Press.

Banks, Angela M. (2005), 'Moderating Politics in Post-conflict States: An Examination of Bosnia and Herzegovina', *UCLA Journal of International Law and Foreign Affairs*, 10: 1–65.

Baylis, Elena A. (2004), 'Beyond Rights: Legal Process and Ethnic Conflicts', *Michigan Journal of International Law*, 25: 529–604.

Bermeo, Nancy (2002), 'The Import of Institutions', *Journal of Democracy*, 13: 96–110.

Bieber, Florian (2005), 'Local Institutional Engineering: A Tale of Two Cities, Mostar and Brčko', *International Peacekeeping*, 12: 420–33.

Brancati, Dawn (2006), 'Decentralization Fueling the Fire or Dampening the Flames of Ethnic Conflict and Secessionism', *International Organization*, 60: 651–85.

Brancati, Dawn (2009), *Peace by Design: Managing Intrastate Conflict through Decentralization*, Oxford: Oxford University Press.

Briffault, Richard (1994), ' "What about the 'ism'?" Normative and Formal Concerns in Contemporary Federalism', *Vanderbilt Law Review*, 47: 1303–53.

Brubaker, Rogers (1996), *Nationalism Reframed: Nationhood and the National Question in the New Europe*, Cambridge: Cambridge University Press.

Buhaug, Halvard (2006), 'Relative Capability and Rebel Objective in Civil War', *Journal of Peace Research*, 46: 691–708.

Bunce, Valerie (1999), *Subversive Institutions: The Design and the Destruction of Socialism and the State*, Cambridge: Cambridge University Press.

Cederman, Lars-Erik, Andreas Wimmer and Brian Min (2010), 'Why Do Ethnic Groups Rebel? New Data and Analysis', *World Politics*, 62: 87–119.

Choudhry, Sujit (2007), 'Does the World Need More Canada? The Politics of the Canadian Model in Constitutional Politics and Political Theory', *International Journal of Constitutional Law*, 5: 606–38.

Choudhry, Sujit (2008), 'Bridging Comparative Politics and Comparative Constitutional Law: Constitutional Design in Divided Societies', in Sujit Choudhry (ed.), *Constitutional Design for Divided Societies: Integration or Accommodation?*, Oxford: Oxford University Press, pp. 3–40.

Choudhry, Sujit (2009), 'Managing Linguistic Nationalism through Constitutional Design: Lessons from South Asia', *International Journal of Constitutional Law*, 7: 553–76.

Collier, Paul and Anke Hoeffler (2004), 'Greed and Grievance in Civil War', *Oxford Economic Papers*, 56: 563–95.

Crawford, Beverly (1998), 'Explaining Cultural Conflict in Ex-Yugoslavia: Institutional Weakness, Economic Crisis, and Identity Politics', in Beverly Crawford and Ronnie D. Lipschutz (eds.), *The Myth of Ethnic Conflict*, Berkeley: International and Area Studies, pp. 3–43.

Cross, Frank B. (2002), 'The Folly of Federalism', *Cardozo Law Review*, 24: 1–59.

Daniels, Ronald J. (1991), 'Should Provinces Compete? The Case for a Competitive Corporate Law Market', *McGill Law Journal*, 36: 130–90.

Deakin, Simon (2006), 'Legal Diversity and Regulatory Competition: Which Model for Europe?', *European Law Journal*, 12: 440–54.

DeVotta, Neil (2004), *Blowback: Linguistic Nationalism, Institutional Decay, and Ethnic Conflict in Sri Lanka*, Stanford, CA: Stanford University Press.

Elazar, Daniel (1987), *Exploring Federalism*, Tuscaloosa: The University of Alabama Press.

Erk, Jan and Lawrence Anderson (2009), 'The Paradox of Federalism: Does Self-rule Accommodate or Exacerbate Ethnic Divisions?', *Regional & Federal Studies*, 19: 191–202.

Esty, Daniel C. (1996), 'Revitalizing Environmental Federalism', *Michigan Law Review*, 95: 570–653.

Farber, Daniel A. (1997), 'Environmental Federalism in a Global Economy', *Virginia Law Review*, 83: 1283–319.

Fearon, James D. (2004), 'Why Do Some Civil Wars Last so Much Longer than Others?', *Journal of Peace Research*, 41: 275–301.

Fearon, James D. (2005), 'Primary Commodity Exports and Civil War', *The Journal of Conflict Resolution*, 49: 483–507.

Feeley, Malcolm M. and Edward Rubin (2008), *Federalism*, Ann Arbor: The University of Michigan Press.

Figueiredo Jr., Rui J.P. de, Michael McFaul and Barry R. Weingast (2007), 'Constructing Self-Enforcing Federalism in the Early United States and Modern Russia', *Publius*, 37: 160–89.

Friedman, Barry (1997), 'Valuing Federalism', *Minnesota Law Review*, 82: 317–412.

Galadima, Habu (2009), 'Federal Republic of Nigeria', in Nico Steytler (ed.), *Local Government and Metropolitan Regions in Federal Systems, A Global Dialogue on Federalism: Volume 6*, Montreal: McGill-Queen's University Press, pp. 234–66.

Galbraith, Peter W. (2008), *Unintended Consequences: How War in Iraq Strengthened America's Enemies*, New York: Simon & Schuster.

Ghai, Yash (2000), 'Ethnicity and Autonomy: A Framework for Analysis', in Yash Ghai (ed.), *Autonomy and Ethnicity: Negotiating Competing Claims in Multi-Ethnic States*, Cambridge: Cambridge University Press, pp. 1–26.

Griffiths, Ann L. (ed.) (2005), *Handbook of Federal Countries*, Montreal: McGill-Queen's University Press.

Grindle, Merilee S. (2009), *Going Local: Decentralization, Democratization, and the Promise of Good Governance*, Princeton: Princeton University Press.

Gurr, Ted Robert (1993), *Minorities at Risk: A Global View of Ethnopolitical Conflicts*, Washington: United States Institute of Peace Press.

Gurr, Ted Robert (2000), *Peoples versus States: Minorities at Risk in the New Century*, Washington: United States Institute of Peace Press.

Halberstam, Daniel (2001), 'Comparative Federalism and the Issue of Commandeering', in Kalypso Nicolaidis and Robert Howse (eds.), *The Federal Vision: Legitimacy and Levels of Governance in the United States and the European Union*, Oxford: Oxford University Press, pp. 213–51.

Halberstam, Daniel (2004), 'Of Power and Responsibility: The Political Morality of Federal Systems', *Virginia Law Review*, 90: 731–834.

Halberstam, Daniel (2008), 'Comparative Federalism and the Role of the Judiciary', in Keith E. Whittington, R. Daniel Keleman and Gregory A. Caldeira (eds.), *The Oxford Handbook of Law and Politics*, Oxford: Oxford University Press, pp. 142–64.

Halberstam, Daniel and Mathias Reimann (forthcoming), 'Federalism and Legal Unification: A Comparative Empirical Examination of 20 Systems'.

Hale, Henry (2004), 'Divided we Stand: Institutional Sources of Ethnofederal State Survival and Collapse', *World Politics*, 56: 165–93.

Hale, Henry E. (2008), 'The Double-edged Sword of Ethnofederalism: Ukraine and the USSR in Comparative Perspective', *Comparative Politics*, 40: 293–312.

Harvard Law Review Note (2008), 'Counterinsurgency and Constitutional Design', *Harvard Law Review*, 121: 1622–43.

Hayson, Nicholas and Sean Kane (2009), 'Negotiating Natural Resources for Peace: Ownership, Control and Wealth-Sharing', Center for Humanitarian Briefing Paper, available at: http://www.hdcentre.org/files/Negotiating%20natural%20resources%20for%20peace.pdf.

Hirschl, Ran (2009), 'The "Design Sciences" and Constitutional "Success" ', *Texas Law Review*, 87: 1339–74.

Horowitz, Donald (1990), 'Making Moderation Pay: The Comparative Politics of Ethnic Conflict Management', in Joseph V. Montville (ed.), *Conflict and Peacemaking in Multiethnic Societies*, Lexington: Lexington Books, pp. 451–75.

Horowitz, Donald L. (2000), *Ethnic Groups in Conflict*, 2nd edition, Berkeley: University of California Press.

Hume, Nathan (2006), 'Four Flaws: Reflections on the Canadian Approach to Private International Law', *Canadian Yearbook of International Law*, 44: 161–248.

Jackson, Paul and Zoe Scott (2007), 'Local Government in Post-conflict Environments', United Nations Development Programme Commissioned Paper, available at: http://www.undp.org/oslocentre/docs08/oslo1107/Annex_4_%20PaperGovernment_in_Post_Conflict.pdf.

Jackson, Vicki C. (2004), 'Comparative Constitutional Federalism and Transnational Judicial Discourse', *International Journal of Constitutional Law*, 2: 91–138.

Kimber, Clíona J. M. (1995), 'A Comparison of Environmental Federalism in the United States and the European Union', *Maryland Law Review*, 54: 1658–90.

Kincaid, John and G. Alan Tarr (eds.) (2005), *Constitutional Origins, Structure and Change in Federal Countries*, Montreal: McGill-Queen's University Press.

Kymlicka, Will (1995), *Multicultural Citizenship: A Liberal Theory of Minority Rights*, Oxford: Clarendon Press.

Kymlicka, Will (1998), 'Is Federalism a Viable Alternative to Secession?', in Percy Blanchemains Lehning (ed.), *Theories of Secession*, London: Routledge, pp. 111–50.

Kymlicka, Will (2001), *Politics in the Vernacular: Nationalism, Multiculturalism, and Citizenship*, Oxford: Oxford University Press.

Kymlicka, Will (2007), *Multicultural Odysseys: Navigating the New International Politics of Diversity*, Oxford: Oxford University Press.

Lajala, Paivi (2009), 'Deadly Combat over Natural Resources: Gems, Petroleum, Drugs, and the Severity of Armed Civil Conflict', *Journal of Conflict Resolution*, 53: 50–71.

Leff, Carol Skalnik (1999), 'Democratization and Disintegration in Multinational States: The Breakup of the Communist Federations', *World Politics*, 51: 205–35.

Levy, Jacob T. (2007), 'Federalism, Liberalism, and the Separation of Loyalties', *American Political Science Review*, 101: 459–77.

Lijphart, Arend (1977), *Democracy in Plural Societies: A Comparative Exploration*, New Haven: Yale University Press.

Lijphart, Arend (2008), *Thinking about Democracy: Power Sharing and Majority Rule in Theory and Practice*, New York: Routledge.

Linz, Juan J. (1990a), 'The Perils of Presidentialism', *Journal of Democracy*, 1: 51–69.

Linz, Juan J. (1990b), 'The Virtues of Parliamentarism', *Journal of Democracy*, 1: 84–91.

Madison, James, Alexander Hamilton and John Jay (1788/1987) *The Federalist Papers*, London: Penguin.

Majeed, Akhtar, Ronald L. Watts and Douglas M. Brown (eds.) (2006), *Distribution of Powers and Responsibilities in Federal Countries*, Montreal: McGill-Queen's University Press.

Manning, Carrie (2003), 'Local Level Challenges to Post-conflict Peacebuilding', *International Peacekeeping*, 10: 25–43.

Mathew, George and Rakesh Hooja (2009), 'Republic of India', in Nico Steytler (ed.), *Local Government and Metropolitan Regions in Federal Systems: A Global Dialogue on Federalism: Volume 6*, Montreal: McGill-Queen's University Press, pp. 166–99.

McCahery, Joseph A. and Erik P. M. Vermeulen (2005), 'Does the European Company Prevent the "Delaware Effect"?', *European Law Journal*, 11: 785–801.

McGarry, John and Brendan O'Leary (2008), 'Iraq's Constitution of 2005: Liberal Consociation as Liberal Prescription', in Sujit Choudhry (ed.), *Constitutional Design for Divided Societies: Integration or Accommodation?*, Oxford: Oxford University Press, pp. 342–68.

McGarry, John and Brendan O'Leary (2009), 'Must Pluri-national Federations Fail?', *Ethnopolitics*, 8: 5–25.

Mendez, Fernando (2005), 'The European Union and Cybercrime: Insights from Comparative Federalism', *Journal of European Public Policy*, 12: 509–27.

Merritt, Deborah Jones (1988), 'The Guarantee Clause and State Autonomy: Federalism for a Third Century', *Columbia Law Review*, 88: 1–78.

Nicolaidis, Kalypso and Robert Howse (eds.) (2001), *The Federal Vision: Legitimacy and Levels of Governance in the United States and the European Union*, Oxford: Oxford University Press.

Norris, Pippa (2008), *Driving Democracy: Do Power-Sharing Institutions Work?*, Cambridge: Cambridge University Press.

O'Leary, Brendan (2009), *How to Get Out of Iraq with Integrity*, Philadelphia: University of Pennsylvania Press.

Parikh, Sunita and Barry R. Weingast (1997), 'A Comparative Theory of Federalism: India', *Virginia Law Review*, 83: 1593–615.

Revesz, Richard L. (1996), 'Federalism and Interstate Environmental Externalities', *University of Pennsylvania Law Review*, 144: 2341–416.

Revesz, Richard L. (2001), 'Federalism and Environmental Regulation: A Public Choice Analysis', *Harvard Law Review*, 115: 553–641.

Riker, William (1964), *Federalism: Origin, Operation, Significance*, Boston: Little, Brown.

Riker, William (1975), 'Federalism', in Fred I. Greenstein and Nelson W. Polsby (eds.), *Handbook of Political Science: Governmental Institutions and Processes*, Reading: Addison-Wesley, pp. 93–172.

Roeder, Philip G. (2007), *Where Nation-states Come from: Institutional Change in the Age of Nationalism*, Princeton: Princeton University Press.

Roeder, Philip G. (2009), 'Ethnofederalism and the Mismanagement of Conflicting Nationalisms', *Regional & Federal Studies*, 19: 203–19.

Ross, Michael (2004), 'How Do Natural Resources Influence Civil War? Evidence from Thirteen Cases', *International Organization*, 58: 35–67.

Ross, Michael (2006), 'A Closer Look at Oil, Diamonds, and Civil War', *Annual Review of Political Science*, 9: 265–300.

Shapiro, David L. (1995), *Federalism: A Dialogue*, Evanston: Northwestern University Press.

Simeon, Richard and Daniel-Patrick Conway (2001), 'Federalism and the Management of Conflict in Multinational Societies', in Alain-G. Gagnon and James Tully (eds.), *Multinational Democracies*, Cambridge: Cambridge University Press, pp. 338–65.

Stepan, Alfred (1999), 'Federalism and Democracy: Beyond the US Model', *Journal of Democracy*, 10: 19–34.

Stepan, Alfred (2001), *Arguing Comparative Politics*, Oxford: Oxford University Press.
Stepan, Alfred and Cindy Skach (1993), 'Constitutional Frameworks and Democratic Consolidation: Parliamentarism versus Presidentialism', *World Politics*, 46: 1–22.
Stewart, Richard (1977), 'Pyramids of Sacrifice? Problems of Federalism in Mandating State Implementation of National Environmental Policy', *Yale Law Journal*, 86: 1196–272.
Steytler, Nico (2007), 'Comparative Reflections on Local Government and Metropolitan Regions in Federal Systems', in Raoul Blindenbacher and Chandra Pasma (eds.), *Dialogues on Local Government and Metropolitan Regions in Federal Countries*, Montreal: McGill-Queen's University Press, pp. 3–8.
Steytler, Nico (2009), 'Comparative Conclusions', in Nico Steytler (ed.), *Local Government and Metropolitan Regions in Federal Systems: A Global Dialogue on Federalism: Volume 6*, Montreal: McGill-Queen's University Press, pp. 393–436.
Steytler, Nico (ed.) (2009), *Local Government and Metropolitan Regions in Federal Systems: A Global Dialogue on Federalism: Volume 6*, Montreal: McGill-Queen's University Press.
Stith, Clark D. (1991), 'Federalism and Company Law: A "Race to the Bottom" in the European Community', *Georgetown Law Journal*, 79: 1581–618.
Suberu, Rotimi (2009), 'Federalism in Africa: The Nigerian Experience in Comparative Perspective', *Ethnopolitics*, 8: 67–86.
Tiebout, Charles M. (1956), 'A Pure Theory of Local Expenditures', *The Journal of Political Economy*, 64: 416–24.
Toft, Monica Duffy (2003), *The Geography of Ethnic Violence: Identity, Interests and the Indivisibility of Territory*, Princeton: Princeton University Press.
Walter, Barbara F. (2006), 'Information, Uncertainty, and the Decision to Secede', *International Organization*, 60: 105–35.
Walter, Barbara F. (2009), *Reputation and Civil Wars: Why Separatist Conflicts are so Violent*, Cambridge: Cambridge University Press.
Watts, Ronald L. (1966), *New Federations: Experiments in the Commonwealth*, Oxford: Clarendon Press.
Watts, Ronald L. (1998), 'Federalism, Federal Political Systems and Federations', *Annual Review of Political Science*, 1: 117–37.
Watts, Ronald L. (2008), *Comparing Federal Systems*, 3rd edition, Montreal: McGill-Queen's University Press.
Weingast, Barry (1995), 'The Economic Role of Political Institutions: Market-preserving Federalism and Economic Development', *The Journal of Law, Economics, & Organization*, 11: 1–31.
Wennmann, Achim (2009), 'Wealth Sharing beyond 2011: Economic Issues in Sudan's North-South Peace Process', Centre of Conflict, Development and Peacebuilding, available at: http://graduateinstitute.ch/webdav/site/ccdp/shared/5925/CCDP-Working-Paper-1-Sudan.pdf.
Wheare, K.C. (1964), *Federal Government*, 4th edition, New York: Oxford University Press.
Wimmer, Andreas (2004), 'Toward a New Realism', in Andreas Wimmer, Richard J. Goldstone, Donald L. Horowitz, Ulrike Joras and Conrad Schetter (eds.), *Facing Ethnic Conflicts: Toward a New Realism*, Lanham: Rowman & Littlefield, pp. 333–59.
Wolff, Stefan (2009), 'Complex Power-sharing and the Centrality of Territorial Self-governance in Contemporary Conflict Settlements', *Ethnopolitics*, 8: 27–45.

PART IV

INDIVIDUAL RIGHTS AND
STATE DUTIES

21. The structure and scope of constitutional rights

*Stephen Gardbaum**

The title and subject of this chapter is the structure and scope of constitutional rights. Because this is not (yet) a generally or widely recognized sub-field of comparative constitutional law, it is quite possible that some readers will find themselves scratching their heads wondering what exactly these words refer to. Indeed, the very term 'the structure of constitutional rights' might appear to be something of a contradiction for, as the organization and table of contents of this volume well illustrate, issues of 'constitutional structure' (Part III) are generally understood to be distinct and separate from issues of 'individual rights' (Part IV). The former cover such matters of institutional and inter-institutional design as separation of powers, federalism and judicial review, whereas the latter concern the direct constitutional relationship between the state and the individual. Even if, in Madisonian vein, we acknowledge that traditional issues of constitutional structure have important effects on this relationship, such as limiting the concentration of political power, these effects are indirect and distinct from the impact of rights.

So let me begin by doing what probably no other contributor to this book will need to do: explain the chapter title. The structure of constitutional rights may usefully be distinguished from their substance. The latter concerns the content and parameters of particular rights that exist in a given constitutional system. By contrast, the structure is the underlying framework – set of concepts, principles, doctrines and institutions – that applies to, organizes and characterizes constitutional rights analysis as a whole within that system (Gardbaum, 2008). Specifically, this chapter will discuss the following three major comparative structural issues concerning rights. First, is there a common general conception both of a constitutional right – what you have in virtue of having a right (Kumm, 2007) – and of limits on those rights among contemporary systems of constitutional law? Second, what is the comparative scope of constitutional rights? What types of law are governed by and subordinated to constitutional rights, and which governmental and non-governmental actors do they bind? Third, how and to what extent do contemporary constitutional systems recognize positive constitutional rights of various types as well as negative ones?

Although each of these three issues has been separately acknowledged and addressed to a greater or lesser degree in practice and scholarship, their commonality and connectedness as forming a distinct sub-field of constitutional rights jurisprudence has generally not. As a subject, the comparative structure of constitutional rights, of course, looks at these issues comparatively: to what extent do different constitutional systems converge on or share a similar or common framework for analyzing and adjudicating rights, whatever may be the individual differences in content. This chapter will conclude with a plea for recognizing the topic as a distinct sub-field within comparative constitutional rights jurisprudence.

Positive rights
- police protection
- right to food, housing, education

387

negitive rights
- freedom of speech
- life, private property
- freedom from violent crimes (etc)

1   CONCEPTIONS OF CONSTITUTIONAL RIGHTS AND THEIR LIMITS

For practical (if not necessarily for philosophical) purposes, the dominant general conception of a constitutional right among contemporary constitutional systems around the world – what an individual has by virtue of being able to claim protection of a constitutional right – is an important prima facie legal claim against (mostly) government infringement that can, nonetheless, be limited or overridden by certain conflicting public policy objectives. At least as it applies in the United States, this general conception has been referred to as constitutional rights as 'shields' (Schauer, 1993) in contrast to the peremptory or absolute conception of constitutional rights as 'trumps'. It also contrasts, although less starkly, with a third conception of constitutional rights as specifying exclusionary reasons for government action (Pildes, 1994, 1998).

Within this general conception, the weight of the presumption in favor of the constitutional rights claim varies somewhat from country to country and from right to right. It is sometimes claimed, for example, that the United States has a more 'categorical' conception of rights in this sense, not because rights are necessarily trumps but because of a greater general presumptive weight in favor of a constitutional right (Kumm and Ferreres Comella, 2005). This claim has, however, not gone undisputed (Gardbaum, 2008).

This general conception of a constitutional right is typically operationalized and adjudicated through a two-step process. The first step determines whether a constitutional right is implicated and has been infringed; that is, whether the prima facie claim has been established. The second step determines whether the infringement is nonetheless a justified one; that is, whether the government has rebutted this prima facie case by satisfying the constitutional criteria for limiting or overriding the right. This first step concerns the definition and scope – the interpretation – of a constitutional right; by contrast, the second step involves considering the strength and relevance of the government's conflicting public policy objective.

These two near-universal steps of constitutional rights analysis respectively employ two different types of limits on constitutional rights: internal and external limits. Internal limits on rights concern the definitional scope of a constitutional right and are part of the first-step process of determining whether a constitutional right is implicated in a given situation in the first place. Thus, for example, does the constitutional right to liberty, autonomy or free development of personality include the freedom to choose an abortion? Does freedom of expression include the right to expend money on political campaigns, to engage in 'hate speech' or defame public or private individuals? External limits, by contrast, are constitutionally permissible restrictions on rights that are implicated and do apply in a given situation. That is, they are part of the second-step process of specifying the circumstances in which the government can pursue a public policy objective even though doing so conflicts with and infringes a constitutional right. So, for example, where the constitutional right to liberty, autonomy or free development of personality is interpreted to include the right to choose abortion, the external limit issue is when, if ever, may conflicting public policy objectives asserted by the government limit or override that right? If freedom of expression is interpreted to include 'hate speech', when, if ever, may the government limit or override that right to protect its victims (Gardbaum, 2007)?

Although constitutional scholars have generally viewed these two types of limits as mutually exclusive conceptualizations and debated their respective merits – the internal versus external theory of limits (Alexy, 2002), definitional versus ad hoc balancing (Nimmer, 1968; Butler, 2002) – the actual practice of constitutional rights jurisprudence tends not to treat them as alternatives by choosing one or the other but to employ both, to a greater or lesser degree, one in each of the two steps of analysis.

It is sometimes claimed that, exceptionally, the United States engages only in the first step of constitutional rights analysis and not the second; that is, courts in the United States treat constitutional rights claims exclusively – or almost exclusively – as issues of definition and scope and not also as issues of balancing rights against conflicting public policy objectives (see the South African Constitutional Court decision in *S v Makwanyane* (1995), at 435; Kumm and Ferreres Comella, 2005). This claim is a second and distinct version of the 'more categorical' conception of rights claim that we saw above and is made in large part because, unusually by comparative standards, the US Constitution contains very few express limits of either type on the constitutional rights it proclaims, but particularly few – if any – express *external* limits. Again, this claim has not gone undisputed, on the basis that such limits have long been judicially implied in the United States (Butler, 2002; Webber, 2003; Gardbaum, 2007, 2008; Dixon, 2009).

As just suggested, both types of limits – internal and external – may be express or implied. Article 9(2) of the German Basic Law provides an example of an express internal limit on the right to freedom of association: 'Associations whose purpose or activities conflict with criminal statutes or that are directed against the constitutional order or the concept of international understanding are prohibited'. Article 13(2) of the Basic Law is an example of an express external limit (here on the right to inviolability of the home): 'Intrusions and restrictions [on the right] may otherwise [than specified in Article 13(2)] be made only to avert a public danger or a mortal danger to individuals, or, pursuant to statute, to prevent substantial danger to public safety and order, in particular to relieve a housing shortage, to combat the danger of epidemics or to protect juveniles who are exposed to a moral danger.' The First Amendment to the US Constitution is an example of a constitutional right with both implied internal and external limits. Thus, neither what types of expression lie outside the right to 'free speech' in the first place nor the circumstances if any in which the government may justifiably limit what is within the right are expressed in the text, but the US Supreme Court has implied both. So it has generally held (1) that obscenity, 'fighting words' and expressions that amount to 'clear and present danger of imminent harm' are not protected at all and (2) that protected 'free speech' may be restricted where necessary for a compelling government interest.

Express external limits are of two types: either a single general statement of the external limits that apply to all constitutional rights (a general limitations clause) or different customized external limits that attach to specific rights, as in the example of Article 13(2) of the Basic Law above. Section 1 of the Canadian Charter of Rights and Freedoms contains a well-known general limitations clause that states: 'The Canadian Charter of Rights and Freedoms guarantees the rights and freedoms set out in it subject only to such reasonable limits prescribed by law as can be demonstrably justified in a free and democratic society'. Section 36(1) of the South African Constitution contains the following general limitations clause:

> The rights in the Bill of Rights may be limited only in terms of law of general application to the extent that the limitation is reasonable and justifiable in an open and democratic society based on human dignity, equality and freedom, taking into account all relevant factors, including –

> the nature of the right;
> the importance of the purpose of the limitation;
> the nature and extent of the limitation;
> the relation between the limitation and the purpose;
> less restrictive means to achieve the purpose.

The second step of constitutional rights analysis and adjudication is typically and increasingly operationalized by application of the principle of proportionality. Having its origins in German administrative law, the proportionality principle began to be applied by the Federal Constitutional Court (FCC) a few years after it came into being, in the late 1950s, and has spread over the succeeding decades at rapid speed to many countries and constitutional regimes around the world, including Canada, Israel, South Africa, most European countries and the European Convention on Human Rights (Stone Sweet and Mathews, 2008).

The proportionality principle is nowhere expressly contained or referenced in the text of a constitution – section 36 of the South African Constitution and section 8 of Israel's Basic Law: Human Dignity and Liberty come the closest – but has been implied by courts as the proper methodology for applying textual limitations clauses. Strictly speaking, the proportionality principle determines whether the means employed by the government to promote its conflicting public policy objective are justified but – at least where they are not specified in relevant limitations clause (as, for example, in Article 13(2) of the Basic Law quoted above) – most countries also apply a prior or threshold test to this objective itself. That is, the justification of a rights limitation under second-step analysis typically involves both means and ends requirements. Thus, under its famous *Oakes* test, the Supreme Court of Canada (SCC) first asks whether the government objective in question is 'of sufficient importance to warrant overriding a constitutionally protected right or freedom' and that 'it is necessary, at a minimum, that an objective relate to concerns which are pressing and substantial in a free and democratic society before it can be characterized as sufficiently important'.

The proportionality principle is operationalized through a common three-prong test: (1) that the means used are suitable or rationally related to this objective; (2) that they are necessary or minimally impair the right; and (3) that the means used are proportionate; that is, they do not impose disproportionate burdens on the right relative to the objective. This last prong is often referred to as 'proportionality *stricto sensu*', and requires balancing the relative weight of the right and the limitation in the particular circumstances (Alexy, 2002). In this way, even though this same verbal test applies to limitations of all constitutional rights within a system, it does not necessarily involve a single presumption or presumptive weight attaching to all rights equally as the third prong may take into account the relative importance of different constitutional rights.

Although this three-prong content of the proportionality test is fairly uniform, there are at least two variations in how it is applied by courts in different countries. The first is that the courts of certain countries, such as Canada and Germany, employ a more formalized version in which the three prongs of the test are considered separately and in order; only if the previous prong is satisfied does the court move on to the next. By contrast, the South African Constitutional Court (SACC) and the European Court of Human Rights (ECtHR) tend to employ a more gestalt, or all-things-considered, version without breaking down the test into its component parts. The second variation is that the practice of several common law countries in particular reflects a certain unease with the third prong, sometimes by treating the necessity/minimal impairment as the final stage of proportionality review, by formally omitting it from statements of the test, by conflating it with the necessity test or by rarely relying on it in practice (Rivers, 2006).

As is well known, the United States does not employ the proportionality test for its second-step analysis of determining whether limits on constitutional rights are justified. Rather, it employs the doctrinal framework of fixed tiers of review in which each right is protected by one of a handful of different standards of review – strict scrutiny, intermediate scrutiny, rational basis scrutiny, undue burden standard – imposing greater or lesser burdens of justification on the government. It is widely acknowledged, however, that this second-step methodology still requires US courts to 'balance' rights against conflicting government interests; indeed, the so-called 'anti-balancing critique' is far from limited to countries applying the proportionality principle (Habermas, 1996), but is well represented in US scholarly and judicial writings (Aleinikoff, 1987; Pildes, 1994; Rubenfeld, 2001; Scalia J., e.g. *Crawford v Washington*, 2004). Although it is thus uncontested that the United States employs neither the label nor the precise content of the proportionality test in constitutional rights adjudication, several scholars have argued that the differences between the two second-step methodologies are far smaller and less significant than often assumed or claimed (Jackson, 1999; Beatty, 2004; Law, 2005; Fallon, 2007) and, more generally, do not justify – along with other claimed differences mentioned above – ascribing to it an exceptional conceptualization of constitutional rights (Gardbaum, 2007, 2008).

As part of a sub-field of comparative constitutional law that largely doesn't yet exist, it is not surprising to find that the scholarship in this area is sporadic rather than comprehensive. Two areas in particular seem to be worthy of more attention in the future. First, the focus of study should expand beyond the core group of countries most commonly discussed and compared, not so much to discover different conceptions of rights but a wider range of applications in practice. Second, with a few recent exceptions (Beatty, 2004; Kumm, 2007; Gardbaum, 2007, 2010; Tsakyrakis, 2009; Webber, 2009), there is a relative absence of normative scholarship on proportionality and constitutional balancing, despite a large and growing literature on the conceptual (Alexy, 2002; Fallon, 1993), doctrinal (Emiliou, 1996), historical (Porat and Cohen-Eliya, 2010) and positive dimensions (Stone Sweet and Mathews, 2008) of the topic.

2   THE SCOPE OF CONSTITUTIONAL RIGHTS: VERTICAL AND HORIZONTAL EFFECT

A second fundamental structural issue concerning constitutional rights is their scope of application. Once we know who the subjects – or beneficiaries – of constitutional rights are in any given jurisdiction (typically either all citizens or all persons within it), an equally important but far more complex question arises about their objects: who and what is burdened or constrained by constitutional rights? Which individuals and what types of law do they bind? In particular, what is their reach into the 'private' sphere? Within comparative constitutional law this issue is generally known under the rubric of 'vertical' and 'horizontal effect'. These alternatives standardly refer to whether constitutional rights regulate only the conduct of governmental actors in their dealings with private individuals (vertical) or also relations among private individuals (horizontal).

The traditional animating idea informing the vertical approach is the perceived desirability of a public-private division in the scope of constitutional rights, leaving civil society and the private sphere free from the uniform and compulsory regime of constitutional regulation. The well-known justifications for this division lie in the values of liberty, autonomy, privacy and market efficiency. A constitution's most critical and distinctive function, according to this general view, is to provide law for the lawmaker not for the citizen, thereby filling what would otherwise be a serious gap in the rule of law (Kay, 1993).

The arguments for adopting the opposite, horizontal approach express an almost equally well-known critique of the 'liberal' vertical position. First, to the extent the function of a constitution is seen as expressing a society's most fundamental and important values, they should be understood to apply to all its members. Second, at least in the contemporary context, constitutional rights and values may be threatened at least as much by extremely powerful private actors and institutions as by governmental ones, and the vertical approach automatically privileges the autonomy and privacy of such citizen-threateners over those of their victims. In this way, the autonomy of racists, sexists and hate-speakers is categorically preferred to that of those harmed or excluded by their actions, without any obvious justification in terms of an overall assessment of net gains and losses in autonomy. Moreover, since the vertical position does not *ipso facto* prevent private actors from being regulated by non-constitutional law, it is unclear why autonomy is especially or distinctively threatened by constitutional regulation (Chemerinsky, 1985; Fiss, 1986).

The analytical and practical complexity of the general issue of the scope of constitutional rights is, however, belied by this seemingly straightforward and simple bifurcation between vertical and horizontal effect. For, as only a little scratching beneath the surface soon reveals, the fact that under the vertical approach (where it applies) private individuals are not bound by constitutional rights in no way entails that constitutional rights do not govern their legal relations with one another (Horowitz, 1955), and thereby determine what they can lawfully be authorized to do and which of their interests, choices and actions may be protected by law. Rather, the traditional vertical position merely forecloses the most direct way in which a constitution might regulate private individuals, by imposing constitutional duties on them (Gardbaum, 2003).

Accordingly, in order to attain a richer understanding of the scope of constitutional rights in any given system and to appreciate the range of answers that exist in practice, it is necessary to supplement the most basic question of vertical or horizontal effect (are individuals as well as governmental actors bound by constitutional rights?) with the following three additional ones. First, even with respect to governmental actors, do constitutional rights bind all such actors or only some; and, if only some, which? In particular, do they bind the legislature and the courts? Second, do constitutional rights apply to private law (and, in common law jurisdictions, to common law) as well as public law? Third, do constitutional rights apply to litigation between private individuals?

There is a fairly wide array of answers to these supplementary questions in practice, with the consequence that the broader question of horizontal effect – the impact of constitutional rights on private individuals – is not a simple yes or no issue but rather a matter of degree. Even with respect to the basic question, those countries that adopt the direct horizontal position by subjecting private individuals to constitutional rights do so to differing degrees and in different ways. So, for example, in Ireland, the 'constitutional tort action' has been implied by the courts from a general textual duty on the state to protect and enforce the rights of individuals. By contrast, in South Africa, which has been a major focus of scholarly attention as an important case study in horizontal effect, direct horizontality is the express, if partial and complex, mandate of sections 8(2), 8(3) and 9(4) of the constitution (Michelman, 2008).[1]

Even though both the German Basic Law and the Canadian Charter have been determined not to impose constitutional duties on private individuals, in answer to the first supplementary question the SCC has held that Charter Rights do not bind the countries' courts (because section 32, the application clause, refers only to legislatures and 'government', with the latter meaning the executive branch only).[2] By contrast, the FCC has held that the rights in the Basic Law do bind the courts; indeed, the vast majority of successful constitutional complaints in Germany are against the lower courts. Under the *statutory* bills of rights enacted in the United Kingdom and both the Australian Capital Territory and state of Victoria, the rights are expressly stated not to bind the legislature, so as to maintain the essential core of parliamentary sovereignty – although the one enacted in New Zealand does – and in the United Kingdom and New Zealand, but not in the two Australian bills of rights, the rights also bind the courts.

On the second supplementary question, the issue of whether private law (and especially the Civil Code) is subject to the Basic Law and its constitutional rights in Germany was the cause of a major and prolonged debate before the FCC fixed its position in the landmark and influential *Lüth* decision of 1958.[3] The common law was held to be subject to Charter rights by the SCC in the case of *Dolphin Delivery* but, as we will see shortly, not as fully or equally as private statute law. In South Africa, the common law is subject to both 'direct' (under section 8) and 'indirect' (under section 39) application of the Bill of Rights (Michelman, 2008). Both Australian jurisdictions have excluded the common law from being subject to their statutory bills of rights, and this issue has not yet been definitively resolved in the UK.

Finally, on the third question, because the Charter applies neither to private individuals nor to the courts, the SCC also held in *Dolphin Delivery* that Charter rights do not apply to common law litigation between private individuals where the only official action is a court order.[4] By contrast, the major argument in the United Kingdom that the Human Rights Act does apply to such litigation stems from the inclusion of the courts among the 'public authorities' bound to act consistently with Convention rights. In South Africa, the Bill of Rights can apply directly to such suits, although it can also apply indirectly – by developing the common law in line with its 'spirit, purport and objects' (Michelman, 2008).

Again, these different answers to the supplementary questions reflect different degrees of horizontality or practical burden of constitutional rights on private individuals even among countries that share the basic vertical position of imposing constitutional rights duties only on governmental actors. Some of the typical legal areas in which these practical burdens play out are defamation, invasion of privacy suits and employer-employee law.

The issue of horizontal effect has sparked great interest among comparative constitutional law scholars in recent years. The reasons are, I think, twofold. First, it has become of enormous practical importance in the wake of the spectacular burst of constitution-making that has taken place around the world since 1989. Along with such other basic choices concerning the structure of constitutional rights as whether to include positive as well as negative rights, constitution drafters have had to decide whether, how and to what extent private individuals are to be subject to new constitutional rights provisions. Second, the very range of situations with which these new constitutions have been designed to deal – from post-apartheid to post-communism – has challenged and stimulated scholars to think anew about

the nature and functions of constitutions. Are they merely law for the lawmakers or normative charters for reborn societies? Hobbesian social contracts between rulers and ruled, or
Lockean ones among equal citizens? In this context, the issue of horizontal effect has been a
central one, provoking fresh consideration of how constitutional law differs from other types
and sources of law.

One of the major contributions that comparative constitutional law scholars have
attempted to make to these real-world transformations has been to clarify the somewhat
complex and confusing conceptual framework of the issue of horizontal effect and to develop
a coherent and user-friendly menu of options so that informed choices can be made. This
became necessary because, for the reasons suggested above, the original and straightforward
bipolar distinction between vertical and horizontal effect proved too crude to explain the
different ways in which constitutional rights can have an impact on private actors or to
capture the most common types of current constitutional practices.

The principal scholarly achievement in this area has been the creation and refinement of a
concept that describes an intermediate third position in between the polar positions of vertical and horizontal effect. Originating in the FCC's landmark *Lüth* decision, this concept is
known in German as '*mittelbare Drittwirkung*' and more generally as 'indirect horizontal
effect', as distinct from the 'direct' horizontal effect of the second polar position. In essence,
this intermediate position is that although constitutional rights apply directly only to the
government, they nonetheless have some degree of indirect application to private actors.
More precisely, the distinction between direct and indirect horizontal effect is that between
subjecting private *actors* to constitutional rights on the one hand (direct), and subjecting
private *laws* to constitutional rights on the other (indirect) (Gardbaum, 2003; Tushnet, 2003;
Cheadle, 2005). In other words, there are two different ways in which constitutional rights
might regulate private actors, that is, have horizontal effect: (1) directly, by governing their
conduct; or (2) indirectly, by governing the private laws that structure their legal relations
with each other. This second, indirect method of regulation limits what private actors may
lawfully be empowered to do and which of their interests, preferences and actions can be
protected by law.

This distinction should put to rest a certain lingering confusion in the literature about what
is 'indirect' in the concept of indirect horizontal effect. For it is sometimes assumed that indirect horizontal effect requires the indirect subjection of private law to constitutional rights in
order to distinguish this position from direct horizontal effect. This assumption is incorrect.
What is indirect is the effect of constitutional rights on private actors. Unlike the direct effect
of constitutional rights resulting from the imposition of constitutional duties in the fully horizontal position, indirect horizontal effect is achieved via the impact of constitutional rights on
the private law that individuals rely on and/or invoke in civil disputes. Now this impact on
private law can, in turn, be either direct (where constitutional rights apply to it fully, equally
and specifically) or indirect (where courts are required or empowered to take constitutional
values into account in interpreting and developing its provisions). To distinguish these two,
the former has been termed 'strong indirect horizontal effect' and the latter 'weak indirect
horizontal effect' (Phillipson, 1999, Gardbaum 2003). But whichever of these two methods
is used, it is the indirectness of the effect on private actors, not on private law, that defines
the general position.

If there are two ways in which a constitution might regulate private actors – directly and
indirectly – there is only one way to ensure that it will not regulate them at all, that is, have

no horizontal effect. This is to limit the scope of application of constitutional rights to public law, the law regulating the relations between individuals and the state. Once the concept of indirect horizontal effect enters the picture, it is insufficient to characterize verticality as subjecting only government to constitutional rights provisions – or as regulating laws and state conduct alone. While this characterization remains useful in anchoring and distinguishing the polar horizontal position, it does not distinguish a truly vertical position from indirect horizontal effect. This is because indirect horizontal effect is quite consistent with this restriction – only government has constitutional duties – yet it still permits significant impact on private individuals by subjecting private laws to constitutional rights scrutiny. For example, Canada and Germany each generally adhere to the traditional vertical approach that constitutional rights bind only the government and yet, in both countries, such rights have significant (indirect) impact on private actors. This traditional approach to verticality, in other words, radically undetermines the true scope of constitutional rights. It is too blunt – that is, consistent with too many relevantly distinct positions on the scope of constitutional rights – to be useful without further refinement. Hence, a better conception of the vertical position is one that distinguishes it from indirect horizontal effect by not permitting any horizontal effect at all. This conception – which might be termed 'strong vertical effect' – is that the scope of constitutional rights is limited to public law only (Gardbaum, 2003; Sommeregger, 2005).

The net result is that the generally understood spectrum of positions has been enlarged to add indirect horizontal effect as a new third position in between the traditional polar ones. In line with the suggestion in the previous paragraph, it has also been proposed that the spectrum of general positions can and should be further refined so that it is understood in the following fourfold way: (1) no horizontal effect at all (strong verticality), (2) weak indirect horizontal effect, (3) strong indirect horizontal effect and (4) direct horizontal effect (Gardbaum, 2003, 2006). Of course, for countries at the direct horizontal end of the spectrum, these are not necessarily mutually exclusive choices as they typically also adopt some form of indirect horizontal effect, as, for example, in Argentina.

A second strength of the comparative scholarship has been exploration of the connections between the structural issue of the scope of constitutional rights and the substantive issue of their content. Of course, the general argument that the structure of constitutional rights should be recognized as a distinct sub-field does not turn on a claim of being hermetically sealed and having no interaction with substance; to the contrary, part of its remit would be to explore the connections in both directions. Given that, as we have seen, indirect horizontal effect subjects (all or most) private law to constitutional rights scrutiny, in any country adopting this position – or, of course, direct horizontal effect – the actual or concrete consequences for private individuals turn wholly on the substance of those rights. So, for example, very broad substantive constitutional equality or free speech norms (such as incorporating disparate impact or incidental burdens on speech) would result in much traditional contract, property and tort law being unconstitutional or significantly altered to cohere with constitutional norms, and so have greater impact on individuals; narrower substantive norms (such as prohibiting only intentional government discrimination or content-specific speech regulation) would not (Tushnet, 2003; Gardbaum, 2003). Indeed, this connection has led Tushnet to argue that the threshold 'state action' issue is conceptually equivalent to the issue of constitutional social and economic rights: the more extensive a commitment to social and economic rights, the more easily courts will lower barriers of scope; the greater the resistance to such substantive rights, the more courts will employ verticality as a threshold defense technique (Tushnet,

2003). Similarly, scholars have explored the subtle connections between jurisdictional, institutional and procedural differences among certain highest courts – whether they are specialist constitutional or generalist courts, whether they have jurisdiction to interpret and apply private, common or state/provincial law – and the operation of indirect horizontal effect in those countries (Tushnet, 2003; Kumm and Ferreres Comella, 2005; Michelman, 2008).

One specific issue about which there has been a fair amount of disagreement – or at least somewhat contradictory understandings – in comparative constitutional scholarship is the actual position of the United States on horizontal effect. So, on the one hand, probably the dominant view is that the US's well-known 'state action doctrine' results in it rejecting or limiting indirect horizontal effect and so being closer to the vertical end of the spectrum than many other contemporary constitutional systems, including Germany and Canada (Hunt, 1998; Tushnet, 2003; Kumm and Ferreres Comella, 2005; Halmai, 2005). On the other hand, it has been claimed specifically that Canadian courts and the courts of other common law countries have taken a 'more cautious' approach than the US Supreme Court on the issue (Uitz, 2005; Saunders, 2005) and, more generally, that far from rejecting or limiting indirect horizontal effect, the US adheres to it in its *strong* form: that is, all law – including private law statutes and court-made common law at issue in private litigation – is fully, equally and directly subject to constitutional rights scrutiny (Gardbaum, 2003, 2006).

Despite this recent flowering of interesting and high quality comparative constitutional scholarship on the topic, which often compares favorably with purely domestic scholarship in the area, much remains to be done. Perhaps the two most important gaps to be filled are these. First, almost inevitably and like much other work in these still fairly early days of the revival of the discipline as a whole, the scholarship tends to be focused on a fairly small cluster of countries – here, mostly Germany, Canada, the US and South Africa. To some extent this is justified because, as with the case of the proportionality principle discussed in Section 1, the German approach has been enormously influential and adopted with or without modification in many other countries. And developments in South Africa, in this area and others, have been important in rethinking the functions and possibilities of constitutional law. Nonetheless, on this topic, apart from the standard or general concerns of skewed data points and representativeness, there is the more specific one that comparative scholarship has mostly ignored fascinating and original developments on direct horizontal effect in recent years in several Latin American countries – including Colombia, Argentina and the US territory of Puerto Rico – under the writs of *amparo* and *tutela* (Rivera-Perez, forthcoming). Indeed, these countries provide the best case studies of a position that has largely been treated as a theoretical option only in the literature. The second major gap is a comparative empirical assessment of the total impact of constitutional rights – or, more likely, of particular ones – on private actors resulting from a combination of all the relevant structural and substantive issues. These are: (1) which position on the refined vertical-horizontal spectrum a country takes; (2) the jurisdiction of its constitutional court or courts; (3) the content of its constitutional rights provisions; and (4) the existence of positive constitutional rights (for the explanation, see the next section).

3   NEGATIVE AND POSITIVE CONSTITUTIONAL RIGHTS

A third important topic concerning the comparative structure of constitutional rights is the distinction between negative and positive constitutional rights that is manifested and institutionalized within and among different contemporary constitutions. Thus, some contain no or very few positive rights, others include both negative and positive constitutional rights and some constitutional courts give positive interpretations to certain seemingly negatively phrased rights but not others.

The basic conceptual distinction between negative and positive constitutional rights is well-known and straightforward. Negative constitutional rights – or what are commonly known as defensive rights (*Abwehrrechte*) in Germany – are rights not to have certain things done to you, typically (but not necessarily) by the government. In this sense, negative constitutional rights impose limits or duties of forbearance on (mostly) government action, on what governments can lawfully do. Thus, classic negative rights include the right not to be deprived of liberty or private property and not to be subject to cruel or inhumane punishment. By contrast, positive constitutional rights are rights to certain states of affairs; that is, they are constitutional entitlements. They impose affirmative obligations – rather than limits – or duties of action on (mostly) government actors. Classic positive rights include the right to vote, to protection from violence, to education and healthcare. Although, of course, this distinction does concern the content of constitutional rights, it also raises more general issues that are appropriately thought of as structural.

Analytically, this issue of negative and positive rights is distinct from that of horizontal effect considered in the previous section because it concerns the nature or type of the duties that constitutional rights impose on *whomever* they bind. Usually, as we have seen, this is only government actors (even under indirect horizontal effect), but where and to the extent that constitutional rights also bind private actors, they may, at least in theory, impose affirmative obligations on them (for example, to protect their neighbors from theft or violence). Despite this analytical distinction, in practice positive rights are an important source of indirect horizontal effect. This is because to the extent that constitutional rights require government to regulate private actors, private actors are indirectly affected by and subject to them (Gardbaum, 2003, 2006). Mark Tushnet has, in addition, argued that substantively the two are connected insofar as 'the more extensive a nation's commitment to social welfare values in its legislation, the readier that nation's courts will be to utilize an expansive doctrine of state action/indirect horizontal effect. The reason is simple. The state action doctrine is, at bottom, *about* social and economic rights' (Tushnet, 2003, 2008; emphasis in original).

Modern constitutions contain two main types of positive constitutional rights. The first is social and economic rights – or constitutional welfare rights – as, for example, the rights to education, healthcare, housing, minimum standard of living and work. The second is protective rights: constitutional rights to protection or security from the state against certain types of action by fellow-citizens, such as violence and theft. Constitutions may and do contain (1) both types of positive rights, (2) one type but not the other or (3) neither. This distinction between the two main types of positive rights serves as a reminder that not all positive rights are social and economic in nature and also that the converse is true: not all social and economic rights are positive rights. For example, such significant social and economic rights as the right to choose an occupation and the right to educate one's child privately – where recognized in a constitution – may (but need not) be exclusively negative in scope, requiring only governmental forbearance from prohibiting business entry and banning private schools. These examples also make clear that the positive or negative nature of a constitutional right cannot automatically be inferred from its general formulation as a right 'to' or 'not to be'.

There are many examples of positive social and economic rights in modern constitutions, although the number and extent of such rights varies enormously from region to region and also from country to country. Both this fact and the gap in truly comprehensive comparative scholarship on the issue make generalizations perilous and, often, over-broad. Nonetheless, two can be stated with a high degree of confidence. First, as 'second generation' rights, constitutional social and economic rights are primarily the product of one of the two great modern bursts of constitution-making, the first after 1945 and the second after 1989. Accordingly, the existence of at least express constitutional welfare rights is highly correlated with constitutions written (or amended) during one of these periods. The 1947 Italian and the 1996 South African constitutions are perhaps paradigmatic in this regard. Second, and notwithstanding this first point, overall the constitutions of the newly liberated countries of central and eastern Europe and South Africa, as well as other developing and formerly colonized nations, more consistently contain significant numbers of social and economic rights than other countries, including those in Western Europe (Gardbaum, 2008). The most common examples of positive social and economic constitutional rights are the rights to public education, to healthcare and to social security.

Whereas where granted, positive social and economic rights are typically expressly contained in a constitutional text, constitutional rights to protection are a little more evenly divided between text and judicial implication. So, for example, the constitutions of South Africa, Greece, Switzerland and Ireland contain express rights to state protection.[5] Elsewhere, protective duties have been implied by the judiciary from certain textual rights that seem on their face negative. Thus, the best-known and most important protective duties (*Schutzpflichten*) in Germany concern the right to life and freedom of expression. The FCC famously interpreted the former in the First Abortion Case to require the state to protect the lives of fetuses against such private actors as their mothers, presumptively through the criminal law.[6] The right to freedom of broadcasting was also interpreted by the FCC to require state regulation to ensure the protection of citizens' access to the full range of political opinions necessary for them to make informed decisions at elections.[7] Although admittedly an international court, the ECtHR has been particularly active in inferring protective duties from the seemingly negatively phrased civil and political rights contained in the European Convention. In a series of cases, it has ruled that both the right not to be subject to 'inhuman or degrading treatment' under Article 3 and the 'right to respect for … private and family life' under Article 8 require states to enact laws effectively protecting children from sexual and other physical abuse by adults. It has also held that freedom of assembly under Article 11 requires positive action, including effective police protection, to ensure the right may be exercised.[8]

Unlike the case generally with negative constitutional rights, the practical impact of both types of positive constitutional rights is sometimes significantly reduced either by express statements in the constitution that some or all such rights are not judicially enforceable or by judicial practice to similar effect. Starting with social and economic rights, the constitutions of Ireland, India and Spain (in the latter case, apart from the right to education) expressly distinguish between rights proper and 'directive' or 'guiding principles' of social and economic policy that are intended to guide the legislature but are not cognizable by any court. Similarly, apart from the rights to primary education and to 'aid in distress', the Swiss Constitution contains a set of 'social goals' that is expressly declared to be non-justiciable. The Netherlands Constitution declares that '[i]t shall be the concern of the authorities' to promote or secure certain social and economic *goals*, such as 'sufficient employment', 'the health of the population' and 'sufficient living accommodation', but it specifically grants '*rights*' only to a 'free choice of work' and to 'aid from the authorities for those unable to provide for themselves'. Moreover, Article 120 of the constitution expressly denies Dutch courts the power of judicial review at all, which prevents these two rights from being enforced against the legislature.

Even where judicially enforceable, constitutional courts have generally been cautious about the scope of their review of social and economic rights and have tended to grant legislatures wide discretion as to the means of fulfilling their affirmative obligation. Accordingly, a reasonableness test has been the norm. In South Africa, this reasonableness standard – relative to available resources – is actually contained in the text as defining the positive obligations of the state with respect to most of its social and economic rights, and the constitutional court has as a result rejected the proposition that such rights entitle individuals to be provided with 'a minimum core'. As is well known, however, in the important cases of *Grootboom* and *Treatment Action Campaign*, the SACC held that government policies in the areas of housing for the desperately needy and combating mother-to-child transmission of HIV were unreasonable and thus unconstitutional. Moreover, in the latter case, the SACC ordered the government to change its restrictive policy on access to the drug Nevirapine. Both the Japanese and Korean supreme courts have subjected textual rights to minimum living standards to highly deferential reasonableness tests under which government programs were upheld, although both acknowledged that government failure to act at all to promote the constitutional objective would amount to an unconstitutional abuse of discretion. The Italian Constitutional Court has also generally interpreted the many social and economic rights contained in the 1947 Constitution as imposing a reasonableness test on government policy in the relevant areas (Llorente, 1998). These differences have led Tushnet to classify social and economic rights into three types: (1) merely declaratory; (2) weak substantive rights and (3) strong substantive rights (Tushnet, 2008).

Similarly, the level of judicial scrutiny to which constitutional rights to protection are subject is typically lower – more deferential – than that afforded to negative rights within the same constitution. Accordingly, protective rights generally grant to governments greater discretion in doing what they must do than negative ones grant in what they cannot. As we saw in Section 1, constitutional rights are typically protected by a proportionality test under which the intensity of scrutiny varies, among other things, with the importance of the right in question. Even the relatively less important rights, though, are subject to the second, minimal impairment prong that provides additional protection above and beyond the first, rationality prong. Protective rights, however, are generally subject only to a form of reasonableness test, rather than the usual proportionality test. That is, courts typically ask only whether the state has reasonably fulfilled its positive duty, a usually lenient and deferential test that rarely results in findings of failure. The reasons for this more lenient test are the standard reasons for wariness about including positive rights in constitutions that we will briefly canvass in the next subsection: that in telling the elected branches of government what they must do, the judiciary lacks institutional expertise and assumes control of the public purse. In Germany, the FCC has not held that the government violated its protective duty with respect to the right to life and health in any case other than the two concerning abortion (Neuman, 1995).

Apart from descriptive work on particular countries, and here South Africa and the former Soviet-bloc nations have been the major subjects, more general or structural scholarship on negative and positive constitutional rights has mostly focused on the following two issues. First, certain scholars have called into question the conceptual distinction between negative and positive rights, and others, while accepting the distinction in theory, have argued that the difference between them in practice is far smaller than assumed. Second, there has been a robust debate on whether constitutions should contain positive rights and to what extent, if any, socio-economic rights guarantees in particular make much difference in practice. A third, perhaps slightly more parochial, issue and one that is generally less the occasion for argument than assumption is the following: how distinctive is the United States Constitution on this topic?

Although not the first to do so, Cass Sunstein has cast doubt on the general distinction between negative and positive constitutional rights by arguing (1) that 'most of the so-called negative rights require government assistance, not governmental abstinence', giving the examples of the creation and dependence of private property, freedom of contract and criminal procedure rights on law and courts, and (2) that '[a]ll constitutional rights [and not only positive ones] have budgetary implications; all constitutional rights cost money' (Sunstein, 2005). To the extent this is intended as an argument about the conceptual rather than the practical difference between the two, I think Sunstein succeeds in showing that it is possible for property and contract rights to mandate governmental assistance *as a matter of constitutional law* – by, for example, requiring the state to create and protect property and enforce contracts against private infringements; that is, the right to a system of private property – but I'm not sure he shows that it is inherent or necessary. A purely negative constitutional right to property is surely conceivable and might include only a right against government takings of private property (where it exists) without just compensation or government deprivation of property without due process, and freedom of contract only against arbitrary government regulation. That is, there are or may be distinct negative and positive constitutional rights concerning property and contract. Whether or not the United States or any other country has such extensive constitutional (as distinct from legislative or common law) rights to property and contract as to incorporate the positive side, the basic conceptual distinction between negative and positive constitutional rights appears to survive the challenge (Gardbaum, 2008).

This debate, of course, overlaps with the one in the international human rights arena concerning the concept of the 'generations' of rights, which includes – but is certainly not limited to – the issue of whether there is a valid distinction or inherent difference between the so-called 'first generation' of human rights (civil and political rights) and the 'second generation' (economic, social and cultural rights) (Alston, 2001; Daintith, 2004).

More specifically on practical differences between negative and positive rights, David Currie pointed out that the effect of common general constitutional anti-discrimination provisions, such as the US's equal protection clause, is to create 'conditional affirmative' duties of protection and provision of government services. '[I]f government undertakes to help A, it may have to help B as well.' Moreover, given the practical impossibility of abandoning certain protective laws (such as the criminalization of murder and theft) and government welfare programs, the effect of such anti-discrimination provisions will often be the same as if there were an absolute affirmative constitutional duty to enact the laws or program (Currie, 1986). Currie's point explains, for example, why in the United States, even absent a constitutional duty to protect the right to life of a fetus as exists in Germany, a finding that a fetus is a 'person' for constitutional purposes would probably entail in practice that the state must protect its life along with the other persons it chooses to protect. Failure to do so would likely amount to unconstitutional discrimination.

A second area that has attracted a good deal of scholarly attention is the issue of whether or not constitutions in general – and particularly the new constitutions of countries seeking to make the transition from centralized to market economies in central and eastern Europe – should include social and economic rights. Most of the arguments, for and against, have focused on pragmatic or instrumental concerns rather than theoretical, moral or intrinsic ones. Arguments against such rights include that they either become meaningless promises and thereby threaten to undermine negative rights and the rule of law or are ruinously expensive for poorer countries (Sajó, 1996), and that they unduly interfere with the attempt to create market economies and hobble the creation of civil society (Sunstein, 1993). More generally, it has been argued that pragmatic understanding of the operation of government and particularly the judicial system dooms any hopes that the recognition of positive rights will improve the lives of the intended beneficiaries (Cross, 2001). One argument for such rights is that court decisions on social rights can bolster elected politicians' ability to stand up to international financial institutions preaching 'market fundamentalism' and thereby enhance public support for democracy (Scheppele, 2004). Another is that failure to include such rights would be viewed by the people as an attempt by the ruling elite to deprive citizens of their acquired rights and fatally undermine popular support for the new regime (Osiatynski, 1996).

Whether and how positive rights in general and social and economic rights in particular are justiciable and enforceable has always been a major part of this issue (Craven, 1999; Scheinin, 2001). Two developments in the past decade have enriched this aspect of the scholarly debate. First, the fact that the SACC first declared the final constitution's social and economic rights to be judicially enforceable and then the manner in which it enforced two of them in the *Grootboom* and *Treatment Action Campaign* cases mentioned above had a substantial impact on this issue, even persuading some academic commentators to partially change their minds (Sunstein, 2001). It has also provided fresh evidence and insights on the questions of whether and how social and economic constitutional rights make any real difference to the lives of the poor (Davis, 2008). Second, the recent establishment and growth of what has variously been termed 'weak-form judicial review' (Tushnet, 2002) and 'the new Commonwealth model of constitutionalism' (Gardbaum, 2001) has provided a new form of judicial review – in which the legislature has the legal power of the final word – that may be particularly appropriate for social and economic rights (Tushnet, 2004; Dixon, 2007).

A third issue is the distinctiveness of the United States on this issue. Is it distinctive, to what extent and in what precise regard? And if so, what is the explanation? The starting point is the observation, encapsulated in a well-known phrase from a lower court opinion, that the US Constitution is a 'charter of negative rather than positive liberties'. And the common implication is that this makes the United States exceptional by contemporary standards. Thus, it has occasionally been argued – but more often simply stated or assumed – that the US Constitution is highly exceptional in not creating any social and economic rights (Sunstein, 2005). Although undoubtedly reflecting the broad scholarly consensus within comparative constitutional law, this claim about the extent or degree of US exceptionalism has not, however, gone entirely unchallenged. Gardbaum has argued that (1) US constitutional culture cannot be assessed only from the federal perspective because many state constitutions in the United States contain some social and economic rights; (2) few other common law jurisdictions contain social and economic rights in their constitutions or bills of rights; and (3) even among continental West European constitutions, the extent to which they contain such rights can and is easily exaggerated. In short, the US is not unique on this issue and, especially when compared to its 'peer' group of developed countries, not really that distinctive. Perhaps most importantly, the extent and existence of modern welfare states do not appear to be correlated in any obvious way to the presence, absence or scope of constitutional social and economic rights. Welfare states are overwhelmingly the products of ordinary legislative processes rather than constitutional mandates. Even with respect to protective duties, he argues that the US is less exceptional than often thought (Gardbaum, 2008).

Regardless of how distinctive its position really is, the standard explanations for the absence of constitutional social and economic rights in the United States are the age of its constitution, the relative difficulty of amending it, the traditional focus on 'hard', judicially enforceable rights and broader political/cultural exceptionalism that includes the near-unique absence of a strong socialist movement. Sunstein has recently shown the limitations of these conventional explanations and proposed a more plausible and original 'realist' one, focusing on the contingency of presidential election results and consequent judicial nominations at the critical moments when US courts might otherwise have done what was done elsewhere and reinterpreted existing constitutional provisions to include social and economic rights (Sunstein, 2005).

In terms of gaps or weaknesses in the scholarly literature in this area, the major one is perhaps the insufficient amount of truly comparative work on positive rights – as distinct from (1) either more abstract or heavily contextualized arguments for and against recognizing them, and (2) a focus on specific individual rights or countries. Fortunately, of course, there are exceptions (e.g. Daintith, 2004). But in the general absence of such work, this tends to be an area in which assumptions and overgeneralizations are too often repeated rather than analyzed or questioned.

4   CONCLUSION

The fact that this chapter has discussed three important, general structural issues concerning constitutional rights with only very limited reference to their substance or content illustrates that the two topics are – though hardly entirely unconnected – distinct, and strongly suggests they should be recognized as forming a unified and separate sub-field within comparative constitutional rights jurisprudence. For one thing, this will permit more focused study on the interactions between the two.

Another reason is the sheer importance of constitutional rights in modern constitutionalism. Of course, it is possible to have both constitutionalism without a codified constitution and a constitution without having constitutional rights – as the original body of the US Constitution and the existing Australian Constitution mostly illustrate. However, protection of fundamental or human rights has been the central driving force behind the tremendous growth of constitutionalism and judicial review around the world since the end of World War II, so that the greater analytical and scholarly tools that would come from sub-dividing comparative constitutional rights jurisprudence into its two components of structure and content would appear to be a promising prospect.

As part of this greater refinement, it will also encourage (1) examination of the extent to which structural positions operate as axiomatic, foundational or threshold principles shaping and constraining the substance of rights and (2) independent consideration of the extent to which structure and substance may be more or less similar or different among constitutional systems. If, for example, it turns out that the structure of constitutional rights tends to be more similar than their content across constitutional systems, this will be an interesting and important finding calling for explanation and resulting in a deepening of our understanding of constitutional rights as a whole.

Indeed, the two parts of constitutional rights jurisprudence may well be subject to somewhat different influences. Thus, structural similarities or convergences among constitutional systems may perhaps be best explained as a form of practical near-necessity within the dominant form of liberal-democratic constitutionalism that embraces constitutionalized rights (as distinct, that is, from the increasingly marginal form that does not). So, for example, once rights have been constitutionalized, the claims of conflicting public policy objectives create strong pressures to affirm a general conception of rights as shields rather than trumps with a two-stage process of analysis. Once a constitution – including a bill of rights – is granted supreme law status and so uniquely provides law for the lawmaker, there is a certain force to the claim that it should govern all law, private as well as public, but not otherwise directly regulate individual citizens. And once a bill of rights is being framed or subsequently interpreted, there are pragmatic reasons for focusing on more traditional civil and political rights and leaving the existence or extent of positive social and economic rights to legislative decision. After all, unlike conventional tyranny-of-the majority reasons for endorsing the former, those who benefit from social and economic entitlements typically form the electoral majority so that there is no prima facie reason to distrust the democratic process in this area.

By contrast, substantive differences in constitutional rights within the general parameters set by these structural principles may be best explained by a combination of contextual factors, including differences in political and legal culture, expressive values and the age and content of constitutional text. That is, these factors of divergence may tend to play out here rather than at the level of structure.

In sum, greater focus on the structure of constitutional rights and greater recognition of the division between structure and substance promise to open up exciting and important new possibilities within comparative constitutional scholarship, and from here to practice.

NOTES

*   I would like to thank the co-editors, Rosalind Dixon and Tom Ginsburg, for extremely helpful comments on a previous draft.
1.   Irish Constitution, Art. 40.3.1 (1937); see e.g. *Meskell v Coras Iompair Eireann*, [1973] IR 121. 'A provision of the Bill of Rights binds a natural or juristic person if, and to the extent that, it is applicable, taking account of the nature of the right and the nature of any duty imposed by the right'. South African Constitution, section 8(2). Section 9(4) imposes a duty on private individuals not to discriminate against others on the same comprehensive set of grounds applicable to the state.
2.   *Retail, Wholesale & Dep't Store Union v Dolphin Delivery Ltd.*, [1986] 2 SCR 573.
3.   BVerfGE 7, 198 (1958).
4.   At the same time, the SCC stated in *Dolphin Delivery* that Charter rights are not entirely irrelevant to such private litigation. Rather, 'the judiciary ought to apply and develop the principles of the common law in a manner consistent with the fundamental values enshrined in the Constitution' [1986] 2 SCR, at 605. The distinction between the direct application of Charter *rights* and the general influence of Charter *values* in private, common law litigation has been maintained by the SCC ever since, and it elaborated on the practical significance of the distinction in *Hill v Toronto*, [1995] 2 SCR 1130. Arguably, however, more recent cases in which courts have modified the common law in line with Charter values, such as *Grant v Torstar Corp.*, [2009] SCC 61 (creating new defence in common law defamation actions of 'reasonable communication on matters of public interest'), have rendered the distinction a very fine one in practice.

5.   See e.g. South African Constitution, section 12(1): 'Everyone has the right to freedom and security of the person, which includes the right ... to be free from all forms of violence from either public or private sources'.
6.   BVerfGE 39, 1 (1975).
7.   BVerfGE 12, 205 (1961).
8.   *X and Y v The Netherlands*, 91 ECtHR (ser. A) (1985); *Plattform 'Ärtze für das Leben'*, 139 ECtHR (ser. A) (1988).

REFERENCES

Aleinikoff, Alexander (1987), 'Constitutional Law in the Age of Balancing', *Yale Law Journal*, 96, 943.
Alexy, Robert (2002), *A Theory of Constitutional Rights*, Oxford: Oxford University Press.
Alston, Philip (2001), in Philip Alston (ed.), *Peoples' Rights*, Oxford: Oxford University Press.
Beatty, David M. (2004), *The Ultimate Rule of Law*, Oxford: Oxford University Press.
Butler, Andrew S. (2002), 'Limiting Rights', *Victoria University Wellington Law Review*, 33, 113.
Cheadle, Halton (2005), 'Third Party Effect in the South African Constitution', in András Sajó and Renáta Uitz (eds.), *The Constitution in Private Relations: Expanding Constitutionalism*, Utrecht: Eleven International Publishing.
Chemerinsky, Erwin (1985), 'Rethinking State Action', *Northwestern University Law Review*, 80, 503.
Craven, Matthew (1999), 'The Justiciability of Economic, Social and Cultural Rights', in Richard Burchill, D.J. Harris and A. Owers (eds.), *Economic, Social and Cultural Rights: Their Implementation in United Kingdom Law*, Leiden: Martinus Nijhoff.
Cross, Frank B. (2001), 'The Error of Positive Rights', *UCLA Law Review*, 48, 857.
Currie, David P. (1986), 'Positive and Negative Constitutional Rights', *University of Chicago Law Review*, 53, 864.
Daintith, Terence (2004), 'The Constitutional Protection of Economic Rights', *International Journal of Constitutional Law*, 2, 56.
Davis, Dennis M. (2008), 'Socioeconomic Rights: Do they Deliver the Goods?', *International Journal of Constitutional Law*, 6, 687.
Dixon, Rosalind (2007), 'Creating Dialogue about Socio-economic Rights: Strong versus Weak-form Judicial Review Revisited', *International Journal of Constitutional Law*, 5, 391.
Dixon, Rosalind (2009), 'The Supreme Court of Canada, Charter Dialogue and Deference', *Osgoode Hall Law Review*, 47, 235.
Emiliou, Nicholas (1996), *The Principle of Proportionality in European Law: A Comparative Study*, London: Kluwer Law International.
Fallon, Richard H. (1993), 'Individual Rights and the Powers of Government', *Georgia Law Review*, 27, 343.
Fallon, Richard H. (2007), 'Strict Judicial Scrutiny', *UCLA Law Review*, 54, 1267.
Fiss, Owen M. (1986), 'Free Speech and Social Structure', *Iowa Law Review*, 71, 1405.
Gardbaum, Stephen (2001), 'The New Commonwealth Model of Constitutionalism', *American Journal of Comparative Law*, 49, 707.
Gardbaum, Stephen (2003), 'The "Horizontal Effect" of Constitutional Rights', *Michigan Law Review*, 102, 387.
Gardbaum, Stephen (2006), 'Where the (State) Action Is', *International Journal of Constitutional Law*, 4, 760.
Gardbaum, Stephen (2007), 'Limiting Constitutional Rights', *UCLA Law Review*, 54, 789.
Gardbaum, Stephen (2008), 'The Myth and the Reality of American Constitutional Exceptionalism', *Michigan Law Review*, 107, 391.
Gardbaum, Stephen (2010), 'A Democratic Defense of Constitutional Balancing', *Law & Ethics of Human Rights*, 4, 78.
Habermas, Jürgen (1996), *Between Facts and Norms: Contributions to a Discourse Theory of Law and Democracy*, Cambridge, MA: MIT Press.
Halmai, Gábor (2005), 'The Third Party Effect in Hungarian Constitutional Adjudication', in András Sajó and Renáta Uitz (eds.), *The Constitution in Private Relations: Expanding Constitutionalism*, Utrecht: Eleven International Publishing.
Horowitz, Harold W. (1955), 'The Misleading Search for "State Action" under the Fourteenth Amendment', *Southern California Law Review*, 30, 208.
Hunt, Murray (1998), 'The "Horizontal Effect" of the Human Rights Act', *Public Law*, 423.
Jackson, Vicki C. (1999), 'Ambivalent Resistance and Comparative Constitutionalism: Opening up the Conversation on "Proportionality", Rights and Federalism', *University of Pennsylvania Journal of Constitutional Law*, 1, 583.
Kay, Richard S. (1993), 'The State Action Doctrine, the Public-Private Distinction, and the Independence of Constitutional Law', *Constitutional Commentary*, 10, 329.
Kumm, Mattias (2007), 'Political Liberalism and the Structure of Rights: On the Place and Limits of the Proportionality Requirement', in George Pavlakos (ed.), *Law, Rights and Discourse: The Legal Philosophy of Robert Alexy*, Oxford: Hart Publishing.

Kumm, Mattias and Victor Ferreres Comella (2005), 'What is So Special about Constitutional Rights in Private Litigation? A Comparative Analysis of the Function of State Action Requirements and Indirect Horizontal Effect', in András Sajó and Renáta Uitz (eds.), *The Constitution in Private Relations: Expanding Constitutionalism*, Utrecht: Eleven International Publishing.

Law, David (2005), 'Generic Constitutional Law', *Minnesota Law Review*, 89, 652.

Llorente, Francisco Rubio (1998), 'Constitutionalism in the "Integrated" States of Europe', NYU School of Law, Jean Monnet Center, Working Paper No. 5/98.

Michelman, Frank (2008), 'On the Uses of Interpretive "Charity": Some Notes on Application, Avoidance, Equality and Objective Unconstitutionality from the 2007 Term of the Constitutional Court of South Africa', *Constitutional Court Review*, 1, 1.

Neuman, Gerald L. (1995), 'Casey in the Mirror: Abortion, Abuse and the Right to Protection in the United States and Germany', *American Journal of Comparative Law*, 43, 273.

Nimmer, Melville B. (1968), 'The Right to Speak from *Times* to Time: First Amendment Theory Applied to Libel and Misapplied to Privacy', *California Law Review*, 56, 935.

Osiatynski, Wiktor (1996), 'Social and Economic Rights in a New Constitution for Poland', in András Sajó (ed.), *Western Rights?: Post-communist Application,* The Hague: Kluwer Law International.

Phillipson, Gavin (1999), 'The Human Rights Act, "Horizontal Effect" and the Common Law: A Bang or a Whimper?', *Modern Law Review*, 62, 824.

Pildes, Richard H. (1994), 'Avoiding Balancing: The Role of Exclusionary Reasons in Constitutional Law', *Hastings Law Journal*, 45, 711.

Pildes, Richard H. (1998), 'Why Rights are not Trumps: Social Meanings, Expressive Harms, and Constitutionalism', *Journal of Legal Studies*, 27, 725.

Porat, Iddo and Moshe Cohen-Eliya (2010), 'American Balancing and German Proportionality: The Historical Origins', *International Journal of Constitutional Law*, 8, 263.

Rivera-Perez, Willmai (forthcoming), 'International Human Rights and the Doctrine of Horizontal Effect in Latin America', SJD dissertation at UCLA School of Law on file with author.

Rivers, Julian (2006), 'Proportionality and Variable Intensity of Review', *Cambridge Law Journal*, 65, 174.

Rubenfeld, Jed (2001), 'The First Amendment's Purpose', *Stanford Law Review*, 53, 767.

Sajó, András (1996), 'How the Rule of Law Killed Hungarian Welfare Reform', *East European Constitutional Review*, 5, 31.

Saunders, Cheryl (2005), 'Constitutional Rights and the Common Law', in András Sajó and Renáta Uitz (eds.), *The Constitution in Private Relations: Expanding Constitutionalism*, Utrecht: Eleven International Publishing.

Schauer, Frederick (1993), 'A Comment on the Structure of Rights', *Georgia Law Review*, 27, 415.

Scheinin, Martin (2001), 'Economic and Social Rights as Legal Rights', in Asbjorn Eide, Catarina Krause and Allan Rosas (eds.), *Economic, Social and Cultural Rights: A Textbook*, Leiden: Martinus Nijhoff.

Scheppele, Kim Lane (2004) 'Constitutional Courts in the Field of Power Politics: A Realpolitik Defense of Social Rights', *Texas Law Review*, 82, 338.

Sommeregger, Georg (2005), 'The Horizontalization of Equality: The German Attempt to Promote Non-discrimination in the Private Sphere via Legislation', in András Sajó and Renáta Uitz (eds.), *The Constitution in Private Relations: Expanding Constitutionalism*, Utrecht: Eleven International Publishing.

Stone Sweet, Alec and Jud Mathews (2008), 'Proportionality, Balancing and Global Constitutionalism', *Columbia Journal of Transnational Law*, 47, 72.

Sunstein, Cass R. (1993), 'Against Positive Rights', *Eastern European Constitutional Review*, 2, 35.

Sunstein, Cass R. (2001), 'Social and Economic Rights? Lessons From South Africa', in *Designing Democracy: What Constitutions Do*, Oxford: Oxford University Press.

Sunstein, Cass R. (2005), 'Why Does the American Constitution Lack Social and Economic Guarantees', in Michael Ignatieff (ed.), *American Exceptionalism and Human Rights,* Princeton: Princeton University Press.

Tsakyrakis, Stavros (2009), 'Proportionality: An Assault on Human Rights?', *International Journal of Constitutional Law*, 7, 468.

Tushnet, Mark (2002), 'State Action, Social Welfare Rights, and the Judicial Role: Some Comparative Observations', *Chicago Journal of International Law*, 3, 435.

Tushnet, Mark (2003), 'The Issue of State Action/Horizontal Effect in Comparative Constitutional Law', *International Journal of Constitutional Law*, 1, 79

Tushnet, Mark (2004), 'Social Welfare Rights and the Forms of Judicial Review', *Texas Law Review*, 82, 1895.

Tushnet, Mark (2008), *Weak Courts, Strong Rights*, Princeton: Princeton University Press.

Uitz, Renáta (2005), 'Yet Another Revival of Horizontal Effect of Constitutional Rights: Why? And Why Now?', in András Sajó and Renáta Uitz (eds.), *The Constitution in Private Relations: Expanding Constitutionalism*, Utrecht: Eleven International Publishing.

Webber, Jeremy (2003). 'Institutional Dialogue between Courts and Legislatures in the Definition of Fundamental Rights: Lessons from Canada (and elsewhere)', *Australian Journal of Human Rights*, 9 (1), 9.

Webber, Gregoire (2009), *The Negotiable Constitution: On the Limitation of Rights*, Cambridge: Cambridge University Press.

22. The comparative constitutional law of freedom of expression

Adrienne Stone

Freedom of expression is among the most widely protected of constitutional rights. Rights of freedom of expression can be found in constitutions drawn from all continents: throughout western Europe as well as in the constitutions of the new democracies of Eastern Europe, in constitutions in Asia, South America, Africa and Australasia (Barendt 2005; Krotoszynski 2006; Rishworth et al. 2003; Currie and de Waal 2005; Stone 2005).

Even in those few democracies without comprehensive constitutional protection of rights, freedom of expression finds constitutional protection in other ways. It can plausibly be argued that parliamentary systems like the United Kingdom and New Zealand – even in the era before the adoption of charters of rights – recognized a constitutional principle of freedom of expression that, though not enforceable by judicial review, was understood as a fundamental value that informed the reading of statutes and the common law (Barendt 2005, p. 40; Rishworth et al. 2003, p. 308). In addition, there are some legal systems that recognize a judicially enforceable principle of freedom of expression despite the absence of a written constitutional right. The Australian Constitution contains no textual provision that protects freedom of expression but the Australian courts have recognized an unwritten principle of freedom of 'political communication' as a necessary incident of the establishment of democratic government (Stone 2005). A somewhat similar development has occurred in Israel where the Supreme Court has derived a principle of freedom of expression from the rather textually sparse provisions of Israel's Basic Law (Navot 2007, p. 234).

1 FUNDAMENTAL ELEMENTS OF FREEDOM OF EXPRESSION RIGHTS

1.1 Constitutional Text

There is some variation among the constitutions of the world in the nomination of 'speech', 'expression' and 'communication' as the subjects of constitutional protection. The Canadian Charter of Rights and Freedoms (Article 2(b)), like the Constitution of the Republic of South Africa (Article 16), refers to 'expression'; the Constitution of India protects 'freedom of speech and expression' (Article 19(a)); the Bill of Rights Ordinance of Hong Kong refers to 'freedom of opinion and expression'; and the Constitution of Japan (in the translation provided by the Ministry of Justice) refers to 'speech, press and all other forms of expression'.

There are other textual variations as well. Most commonly, these provisions are expressed as a declaration that everybody holds a certain right. For instance, the International Covenant on Civil and Political Rights provides that 'everyone shall have the right to freedom of expression'. The form of the First Amendment to the Constitution of the United States, which is expressed as a limitation on government ('Congress shall make no law ... abridging the freedom of speech') is much less common.

Freedom of expression guarantees are often accompanied by related guarantees, though these too vary somewhat. The United States' First Amendment also protects freedom of religion (in its non-establishment and free exercise clauses), freedom of the press and rights of assembly and petition. The Canadian Charter's protection of expression is found in the second paragraph of Article 2 which, in other paragraphs, protects freedom of conscience and religion; freedom of thought, belief, opinion and expression, including freedom of the press and other media of communication; freedom of peaceful assembly; and freedom of association. Other constitutions (including the South African Constitution in Section 16(c) and the German Basic Law in Article 5(1)) explicitly protect artistic and academic freedom.

These textual details are no doubt important in some contexts, but as will become apparent, there are more significant points of convergence and divergence among rights of freedom of expression and the law derived from them. Therefore this chapter will focus, first, on the conceptual structure of rights of freedom of expression and, second, upon the substantive conceptions of 'freedom of expression'.

1.2 The Structure of a Freedom of Expression Principle

1.2.1 Coverage and protection

A guarantee of freedom of expression, like other rights, has two conceptually distinct elements: 'coverage', which refers to the acts or things to which the principle applies, and 'protection', which refers to the weight of the principle or the level of protection that the right covers on those acts or things (Schauer 1982, p. 91).

The concept of 'speech' or 'expression'   Determining the 'coverage' of a right of freedom of expression requires a conception of 'expression' or 'speech'. It is fairly obvious that a right of freedom of expression extends to speaking and writing, and freedom of expression rights, including those framed as rights of 'freedom of speech', routinely apply to non-linguistic means of communication as well. In addition, some non-linguistic communication is commonly recognized as the functional equivalent of 'speech' or 'expression'. Thus, there is little doubt that communication through Morse code, Braille or sign language constitutes expression for these purposes (Schauer 1982, p. 96; Greenawalt 1989, p. 52). It is also well accepted that artistic expression, even where it does not involve linguistic utterances, should be covered by a principle of freedom of expression (Greenawalt 1989, p. 55. For prominent cases treating art as 'expression' or 'speech' see *Vereinigung Bildender Kunstler v Austria* (68354/01) (25 January 2007) (European Court of Human Rights); *National Endowment for the Arts v Finley* 534 US 569 (1998) (United States Supreme Court)).

Further, it is generally recognized that much 'ordinary' conduct is expressive and therefore covered by freedom of expression principles. The United States Supreme Court has led the way, extending the coverage of the First Amendment to activities such as burning a draft card (*United States v O'Brien* 391 US 367 (1968)), flag burning (*Texas v Johnson* 491 US 397 (1989); *United States v Eichman* 496 US 310 (1990)), the wearing of a black armband (*Tinker v Des Moines School District* 393 US 503 (1969)) and the display of a swastika (*Skokie v National Socialist Party of America*, 373 NE 2d 21 (1978)). The United States

Supreme Court has also recognized that sexually explicit conduct, such as nude dancing, may be expressive conduct within the coverage of the First Amendment (*Barnes v Glen Theatres* 501 US 560 (1991)).

The proposition that expressive conduct is covered by constitutional principles of freedom of expression is widely accepted in other countries. Flag desecration is recognized as expression in Germany (see *Flag Desecration Case* (1990) 81 BVerfGE 278 (Federal Constitutional Court of Germany); Hong Kong (*HKSAR v Ng Kung Siu* [2001] 1 HKC 117 (Hong Kong Court of Final Appeal)); New Zealand (*Hopkinson v Police* [2004] 3 NZLR704 (High Court of New Zealand); *The Queen v Iti* [2007] NZCA 119 (New Zealand Court of Appeal)) and the United Kingdom (*Percy v DPP* [2002] Crim LR 835).

A New Zealand court has also recognized the display of a swastika as expression within the New Zealand Bill of Rights (*Zdrahal v Wellington City Council* [1995] 1 NZLR 700); the Canadian Supreme Court has extended the coverage of Section 2(b) of the Charter to picketing (*RWDSU v Dolphin Delivery Ltd.*, [1986] 2 SCR 573); and the Australian High Court has extended the coverage of constitutionally protected communication to a public demonstration involving holding up dead ducks in front of television cameras to protest against duck hunting (*Levy v Victoria* (1997) 189 CLR 579).

Moreover, some constitutional provisions provide specific guidance as to the kinds of expression covered by a right of freedom of expression. Section 16 of the South African Constitution protects freedom of expression in its first subsection and in Section 16(2) explicitly excludes from its coverage 'propaganda for war', 'incitement of imminent violence' and 'advocacy of hatred that is based on race, ethnicity, gender or religion, and that constitutes incitement to cause harm'. A provision of this nature can be read simply as a 'carve-out', creating exceptions to the coverage without indicating anything about the nature of freedom of expression covered by the first part of the section. Alternatively, the nature of the 'carve-out' may be taken as informing the values underlying freedom of expression generally and thus may inform the freedom of expression provision as a whole. Section 16(2) appears to have been read in the latter way. These forms of expression are excluded because they threaten 'the dignity of others' and thus their exclusion gives effect to the principle of 'dignity, equal worth and freedom' on which the Constitution of South Africa is founded (*Islamic Unity Convention v Independent Broadcasting Authority* (2002) 4 SA 294 (Constitutional Court of South Africa) para. 10).

At its edges, however, determining the coverage of freedom of expression poses some difficulties. Virtually all conduct can convey a message and even if coverage is limited to activity *intended* to convey a message, the concept is still so broad that it risks merging the principle of freedom of expression with a general principle of liberty (Schauer 1982, pp. 92–4). For this reason, Frederick Schauer argues that the coverage of a principle of freedom of expression is best determined by reference to the underlying rationales for the principle (Schauer 1989, p 91. On rationales for freedom of expression see Section 2 of this chapter). This analysis explains why some undoubtedly communicative activity – violent terrorism for instance or political assassination – is unlikely to be considered expression within the coverage of a constitutional principle of freedom of expression (Barendt 2005, pp. 79–80) and non-violent expression within the context of criminal activity – the expression involved in the committing of conspiracy or fraud for instance – may be excluded as well (as appears to be the case under the First Amendment (Greenawalt 1995, p. 19)).

However, the place of criminal activity within a system of freedom of expression is not entirely clear (see the extensive treatment in Greenawalt 1989). Even in the United States, with its long history of constitutional protection of speech, the courts have not fully and explicitly addressed the question, though it appears that courts work on the assumption that much ordinary criminal activity is excluded from the coverage of the First Amendment (Greenawalt 1995, p. 19; and on the related question of 'crime facilitating speech', Volokh 2005). The Canadian Supreme Court, by contrast, has extended the coverage of Section 2(b) of the Charter to *all non-violent action intended to convey meaning* including, somewhat controversially (see Greenawalt 1995, p. 19) illegal solicitation (*Reference re ss. 193 and 195.1(1)(C) of the Criminal Code (Man.),* [1990] 1 SCR 1123).

Limitations on expression   Determining 'coverage' is only the first step in resolving a question about the application of a right of freedom of expression. Expression that is covered by a right can nonetheless be limited in the name of competing rights or interests. So while flag desecration is recognized as 'expression' or 'speech' in the United States, Germany and Hong Kong, courts in those countries have reached quite different conclusions on the permissibility of flag desecration laws. In the United States, the challenged flag desecration laws have been ruled invalid, while in Hong Kong flag desecration laws were upheld as a protection of the public order. In Germany, though the Constitutional Court ruled invalid the law challenged in the *Flag Desecration Case*, it seems clear that the Constitutional Court recognizes a state interest in preventing flag desecration and might be prepared to accept a flag desecration law in some circumstances (Quint 1992; Barendt 2005, p. 85).

Often a constitution's text explicitly limits freedom of expression. Qualifications sometimes appear in the same provision that protects the right. For instance, Article 5 of Germany's Basic Law provides in its second paragraph that 'These rights find their limits in the rules of the general law, the statutory provisions for the protection of youth and the right to personal honor'. Article 10 of the European Convention on Human Rights, which is incorporated by the Human Rights Act 1998 (UK), provides in its second paragraph that:

> The exercise of these freedoms, since it carries with it duties and responsibilities, may be subject to such formalities, conditions, restrictions or penalties as are prescribed by law and are necessary in a democratic society, in the interests of national security, territorial integrity or public safety, for the prevention of disorder or crime, for the protection of health or morals, for the protection of the reputation or rights of others, for preventing the disclosure of information received in confidence, or for maintaining the authority and impartiality of the judiciary.

Alternatively, some constitutions include a general limitation applicable to all, or most, rights in a constitution. Section 1 of the Canadian Charter provides that the rights it protects are 'subject only to such reasonable limits prescribed by law as can be demonstrably justified in a free and democratic society'. This section provided the principal model for Section 36 of the Constitution of South Africa (Currie and de Waal 2005, p. 165).

But, significantly, courts treat freedom of expression rights as limited even where limitations are not expressed in the text. The unwritten constitutional principles found in Australian and Israeli constitutional law are subject to limitation (Stone 1999; Navot 2007, p. 234). Even the United States' First Amendment, despite confusion created by its apparently absolute terms, is subject to judicially developed limitations. A truly 'absolutist' interpretation of the First Amendment's protection of expression pursuant to which 'speech' is immune from all regulation has never been advanced by a member of the Supreme Court. (Despite Justice

Hugo Black's well-known declaration that 'I believe that the First Amendment's unequivo-cal command that there shall be no abridgment of the rights of free speech and assembly', *Konigsberg*, 366 US 36, 61 (1961), he in fact held that view only in relation to a class of free speech cases (see Kalven 1967, pp. 442–3).) Indeed, constitutional rights of freedom of expression are universally limited and thus all constitutional systems must address the ques-tion of how, and in what circumstances, freedom of expression can be restricted.

1.3   Doctrinal Structure: Categories and Balancing

Although all constitutions limit freedom of expression rights, there are some significant methodological differences as to how these limitations are drawn. One point frequently made in the comparative literature on freedom of expression is that the American doctrine of the First Amendment is characterized by a 'conceptual' or 'categorical' approach, according to which freedom of expression law is dominated by relatively inflexible rules, each with appli-cation to a defined category of circumstances.

The dominant alternative approach – found in various forms throughout European juris-dictions, Canada and South Africa – is to use a 'proportionality' test which requires an exam-ination of the 'end' pursued by the law and the 'means' used to pursue it, and which explicitly authorizes 'balancing' (Schauer 2005a; Stone 1999; Grimm 2007; Jackson 1999). The Canadian formulation of the test requires that a law infringing upon freedom of expression (or any other Charter right) may nonetheless be valid provided that it serves a 'pressing and substantial objective' and uses means that are 'reasonably and demonstrably justified'. The second requirement in turn requires that the law be 'rationally connected' to that objective; 'minimally impair' the protected right; and that there be 'a proportionality' between the restrictions imposed and the objective pursued (*R v Oakes* [1986] 1 SCR 103).

There is a large literature debating the competing merits of these two approaches. Early encounters in this debate occurred among scholars of the First Amendment, as over the course of the second part of the 20th century, the Supreme Court of the United States replaced a rela-tively flexible test which allowed for a measure of balancing competing rights and interests in the context of the case of itself with the categorical approach that now dominates American law (Frantz 1963). More recent literature has returned to the debate in the context of compar-ative constitutional law (Stone 1999; Schauer 2005a; Mount 2003).

To summarize a complex literature, proportionality tests are valued for their capacity to structure judicial inquiry and to provide a transparent account of judicial reasoning. In addi-tion, the advantage of proportionality tests is said to lie in their flexibility, which allows courts more latitude to respond to the circumstances of individual cases and to unforeseen complexities. Where a court adopts a relatively determinate rule, that rule might prove to be highly inconvenient, or even erroneous, in later cases, which may provide a significant prob-lem, especially where rules are enforced by lower courts. The intellectual modesty of the flex-ible approach might be thought to be especially valuable given the complexity of free speech questions (Stone 1999).

By the same token, the advantages of the categorical approach are said to lie in the formu-lation of rules that give judges comparatively little flexibility but correspondingly more certainty in their application. This approach thus responds to a conception of the rule of law that values an identifiable set of rules on which citizens can rely to guide their behavior (Stone 1999). In addition, a doctrine consisting of defined and relatively inflexible rules is said to insulate the judge in any particular instance from political pressures relating to that case. A judge can appeal to a pre-determined rule rather than justify, in its own terms, the decision to protect expression over a competing right or interest – a matter thought especially significant in relation to freedom of expression (Nimmer 1968, p. 945; Ely 1980, pp. 109–116).

For the moment First Amendment law (which is dominated by categories and rules) is highly unusual in comparative terms (Gardbaum 2008, pp. 422–3; Schauer 2005a). Frederick Schauer has argued, however, that this aspect of the First Amendment's 'exceptionalism' may be temporary. The categorization of First Amendment law at least partly reflects the age of the American constitutional tradition of freedom of expression and he expects that constitutional courts outside the United States will 'develop the encrustations of doctrines, rules, caveats, qualifications, maxims, principles, exceptions, and presumptions that any mature set of legal or constitutional rights will over time develop' (Schauer 2005a, p. 56).

While a degree of convergence may be a feature of the relationship between (comparatively flexible) legal standards like proportionality and (comparatively inflexible) legal rules (Schauer 2003), there are reasons to question whether the difference in these approaches will entirely disappear. The preference of First Amendment law for defined rules reflects the high value placed on freedom of expression in American constitutional law (Nimmer 1968; Ely 1980). Other systems – which may accord different weight to freedom of expression – may be correspondingly less inclined towards the 'rulification' of doctrine and may value the flexibility of this approach for its own sake. There is some evidence of this in Canadian law. For instance, the Supreme Court of Canada has said:

> The analysis under s. 1 of the Charter must be undertaken with close attention to context. This is inevitable as the test devised in *R. v Oakes* [1986] 1 S.C.R. 103, requires a court to establish the objective of the impugned provision, which can only be accomplished by canvassing the nature of the social problem it addresses. Similarly, the proportionality of the means used to fulfil the pressing and substantial objective can only be evaluated through a close attention to detail and factual setting. In essence, *context is the indispensable handmaiden* to the proper characterization of the objective of the impugned provision, to determining whether that objective is justified, and to weighing whether the means used are sufficiently closely related to the valid objective so as to justify an infringement of a Charter right. (*Thomson Newspapers Co. v Canada (AG)* [1998] 1 SCR 877 at para. 87 (emphasis added). For similar statements see *R v Sharpe* [2001] 1 SCR 45, McLachlin CJ, paras 32, 155).

If, as these cases suggest, the flexibility of the proportionality test is valued for its own sake rather than as a staging point in the development of a more rulified approach, some resistance to 'rulification' may be expected (see Choudhry 2006).[1]

1.4 The Application of Freedom of Expression Guarantees

Positive and negative application A final set of structural considerations relates to the application, or scope, of a right of freedom of expression. Conceptually, like other rights, rights of freedom of expression might be 'positive', entitling the rights holder to demand that enjoyment of right be ensured, or 'negative', protecting the rights holder only from interference. Although the drawing of this distinction is much criticized (Sunstein 2006, p. 207), it remains significant in the constitutional law of freedom of expression. In the United States and other countries of the common law world, constitutional rights are thought to have an exclusively negative cast. So, for instance, the High Court of Australia was quickly able to dismiss a claim that the Australian constitutional right to freedom of political communication entitled a candidate in a national election to media coverage (*McClure v Australian Electoral Commission* [1999] HCA 31).

Scholars of constitutional law in these countries have not been blind to the argument that, under a negative conception of rights, meaningful enjoyment of that right might be frustrated by inadequacies or inequality in the private distribution of resources. The insight that the capacity of citizens to engage in political discourse depends upon the private allocation of resources and thus can easily be dominated by those whose wealth allows them access to the means of communication is the foundation of arguments for the regulation of political campaigning. However, the argument, as it is usually put, is that the problem of private inequity provides a reason to consider campaign finance laws to be consistent with a right of freedom of expression, rather than that a right of freedom of expression founds a positive right of access to effective means of expression (Sunstein 1995, pp. 93–101; Fiss 1996, pp. 15–26).

In many countries, however, there is no general reticence about positive constitutional rights and some constitutions guarantee 'duties of protection' explicitly, while in other cases courts have developed them. In the freedom of expression context, the German doctrine is especially notable. An important early case recognized that Article 5 of the Basic Law imposed a duty on the state to ensure that broadcasters maintain 'balance, objectivity and reciprocal respect' in programming (*Television I Case* (1961) 12 BVerfGE 205; Kommers 1997, pp. 404–06) and this case is now seen as an important stage in the development of a more general duty to protect which gives the civil and political rights of the German Basic Law a positive cast (Grimm 2005, pp. 144–6).

Horizontal and vertical application   The scope of constitutional rights of freedom of expression is also affected by their classification along another axis. Like other constitutional rights, they can be classified as 'vertical' rights (rights against the state) or 'horizontal' rights (rights that apply to private actors). The verticalist position to constitutional rights is usually taken to be exemplified by the United States, while an overtly horizontal position is adopted in Ireland pursuant to the Irish Constitution (Gardbaum 2003). In addition, a third model of the relation between constitutional rights and private action is found in slightly different forms in Canada, Germany and Australia, which have adopted a conception of 'indirect horizontal application' of the constitution to private actors. On this conception, a constitution enters the private sphere by affecting the development of the private law.

Freedom of expression cases have figured especially prominently in the development of this third position. In a foundational case in German constitutional law (*Lüth* (1958) 7 BVerfGE 198; Kommers 1997, pp. 361–8), the Federal Constitutional Court overturned an injunction against the boycott of a film on free speech grounds, finding that the lower court failed to apply the German civil code with sufficient regard for the 'influence' of the constitutional law on private law.

The position in Australia is, in effect, similar, though the question in that jurisdiction has been how the Constitution affects the judge-made common law (rather than, as in Germany, a private civil code). When considering the relationship between the Australian constitutional right of 'freedom of political communication' and the common law of defamation (*Lange v Australian Broadcasting Corporation* (1997) 189 CLR 520), the Australian High Court's approach was to develop the common law so that it conformed to the constitutional protection of political communication.

A similar result was reached in Canada. The Canadian Supreme Court first addressed the relationship between the common law and its *Charter* in *RWDSU v Dolphin Delivery Ltd.*, [1986] 2 SCR 573 in which, in a decision that predates the Australian case law on this question, it recognized that those manning a picket line were protected from the private law of trespass by virtue of the operation of Section 2(b) of the Charter. As in Australia, the Canadian position (recently confirmed in *Grant v Torstar Corporation* 2009 SCC 61 and *Cusson v Quan* 2009 SCC 62), is that the constitutional rights inform the development of the common law of Canada. But, in an apparently distinctive twist, the Canadian position is that the common law must be consistent with 'Charter values' rather than the Charter itself.

Although these systems apparently adopt a different conception of the relationship between constitutional rights and private law from the 'verticalist' position adopted under the United States Constitution, in practice these positions may be functionally equivalent. A robust state action doctrine – which recognizes for instance that 'state action' is present where private law is invoked in a dispute between private parties – can achieve much the same result as a doctrine of indirect horizontal effect (Tushnet 2003). Thus, despite its 'vertical' conception of the First Amendment, the Supreme Court of the United States had no difficulty in finding that the common law of defamation was subject to the First Amendment free speech clause (*New York Times v Sullivan* 376 US 254 (1964)).

Indeed, Stephen Gardbaum argues that the German and United States' approaches to the relationship between constitutional rights and the private law is in substance identical: in both countries, all law, public and private, is subject to the Constitution (Gardbaum 2003, p. 421). The Australian law seems much the same on this point: although the Australian Constitution applies indirectly to private individuals (in the sense that it does not grant entitlements or impose obligations upon them), the Constitution's effect on the common law is strong and direct. The common law must conform to the Constitution and those developments are immune from subsequent legislative alternation (Stone 2002).

For these reasons, Stephen Gardbaum has concluded that while the direct horizontal application of constitutional rights remains a conceptually distinct approach to the scope of constitutional rights, the 'opposing' positions are better conceived as points along a spectrum of possible positions on the scope of constitutional rights (Gardbaum 2003, pp. 434–5).

2   COMPARATIVE CONCEPTIONS OF FREEDOM OF EXPRESSION

These structural issues arise when considering freedom of expression as a question of law. But structural questions – as much as any other question about freedom of expression – reflect underlying substantive values about freedom of expression and rights in general. Indeed, the philosophy of freedom of expression lies just beneath the surface of the constitutional law of freedom of expression.

2.1   Philosophical Foundations of Freedom of Expression

In an extensive philosophical literature on freedom of expression, three especially prominent lines of argument have emerged: the first values freedom of expression for its capacity to promote the search for 'truth'; the second values freedom of expression for its relationship to human autonomy and the third values freedom of expression for its capacity to promote democratic government or 'self-government' (Schauer 1982, pp. 15–72).

The argument from truth finds its most important statement in liberal political theory in J.S. Mill's *On Liberty*. Mill's argument for freedom of expression is founded on a belief in the fallibility of human judgement. Freedom of expression, by subjecting received wisdom to contradiction, exposes falsehoods and produces a proper understanding of the truth. Another important statement of the idea is found in United States Supreme Court Justice Oliver Wendell Holmes' famous dissent in *Abrams v United States* ('the best test of truth is the power of the thought to get itself accepted in the competition of the market': 250 US 616 (1919)).

The argument from autonomy values freedom of expression on the grounds that freedom of expression protects (or is integral to) individual autonomy because it allows individuals to form their own opinions about their beliefs and actions (Scanlon 1972). Relatedly, freedom of expression might be protected because it is integral to 'self-realization' – a version of the argument which values the relationship between freedom of expression and self-development (Emerson 1963; Redish 1982) – or because by respecting freedom of expression, we treat an individual with the equal concern and respect due to independent moral actors (Dworkin 1996, pp. 200–1).

Thirdly, the argument from democracy, perhaps the most widely adopted in modern legal systems, proceeds from the basic proposition that the capacity for citizens to hold their governments to account and to effectively exercise the power to choose their governments depends upon a free flow of information about government (Ely 1980). One influential form of this argument, advanced by Alexander Meiklejohn, draws an analogy between public discourse and the traditional New England 'town hall meeting', an analogy that allows for some regulation of expression to ensure the fair and orderly conduct of public debate.

This last argument gives rise to the problematic task of defining a category of 'political expression' (see discussion in Bork 1971; BeVier 1982; Stone 2002), but some forms of the argument from democracy seek to provide a justification for a right of freedom of expression which is not so limited. Alexander Meiklejohn focused upon the role of freedom of expression in developing 'the intelligence, integrity, sensitivity, and generous devotion to the general welfare that, in theory, casting a ballot is assumed to express' and thus cast the net of 'political expression' very widely (Meiklejohn 1961, p. 255).

These ideas are only the main lines of thought that can be found in a large and varied literature. There are also important arguments for freedom of expression that turn on a mistrust of government, either because government is thought to be inherently self-interested or even corrupt or because of a belief that the fallibility of government officials provides a reason to mistrust government's capacity to regulate expression even when acting in good faith (Schauer 1989). Alongside these run more general arguments about the utility of suppression of expression which in some cases at least is thought to be ineffective or even counterproductive (think of the publicity given to films or books subject to censorship or to the holocaust denier who becomes a 'free speech martyr' when prosecuted) (Schauer 1982, pp. 75–7). Intimately related to the question 'why protect freedom of the expression?' is the question 'why and to what extent can freedom of expression be limited?' The Millian idea that freedom of expression can be limited only where it caused 'harm' to others is central to liberal political theory of freedom of expression (Mill 1978, p. 9), but it has opened a large debate about the nature of the harms that expression can cause.

2.2 Freedom of Expression Values in Constitutional Systems

Many of these philosophical debates have taken place with a keen awareness of, and are sometimes explicitly conducted in terms of, constitutional disputes about freedom of expression. In the United States, legal theories of freedom of expression have often been developed in the course of analyses of the law of the First Amendment. These include arguments that the First Amendment in particular, and freedom of expression in general, promotes or builds the capacity for 'tolerance' (Bollinger 1988); that it prevents state 'paternalism' and promotes 'civic courage' (Blasi 1988b); that it nurtures healthy challenges to the status quo (Shiffrin 1990); that it exposes abuse of power and corruption (Blasi 1988a) and that it provides a 'safety valve' by preventing the inflexibility and stultification associated with suppression while at the same time encouraging those who lose in the political process to accept decisions that go against them (Emerson 1969, p. 7).

Courts have also been influenced by the philosophical literature, sometimes explicitly. The Supreme Court of Canada, for instance, has acknowledged the three principal arguments for freedom of expression (the arguments from truth, autonomy and democratic self-government) ground the Canadian Charter's protection of freedom of expression (*Irwin Toy v Quebec* (1989) 1 SCR 927, 976). Indeed, as a general matter, freedom of expression has proved a fertile ground for cross-fertilization between the disciplines of law and political philosophy (Campbell 1995, pp. 207–09).

The ideas that emerge from this philosophical literature have been important in comparative analysis as well. In addition to the large literature examining freedom of expression in any given system, there is a small but growing comparative literature, much of which focuses upon distilling differences in value or motivating commitments as between constitutional systems. This literature includes some 'whole country' comparative studies which compare the law of freedom of expression in one country with others (Greenawalt 1995; Krotoszynski 2006; Barendt 2005; Cram 2006). For instance, in a significant study of freedom of expression in major democracies, Ronald Krotoszynski traces distinctive features of the constitutional law of freedom of expression, noting that the distinctive American commitment to a 'market' philosophy of freedom of expression and a strong distrust of government provides expression with especially strong protection against government regulation. He contrasts this approach with the dominance of 'dignity' as the preferred constitutional value in Germany, the Canadian emphasis on equality and multiculturalism and, in Japan, the dominance of a 'Meiklejohnian' conception of democratic self-government, each of which allows for considerably more regulation of expression (Krotozynski 2006). In addition, there are many comparative analyses that focus upon one or two controversies that have confronted courts in a number of countries: flag burning (Quint 1992), hate speech (Rosenfeld 2003), the regulation of political campaigns and advertising (Dawood 2006) and the law of defamation (Stone and Williams 2000).

Supplementing (and no doubt encouraging) the scholarly interest in comparative analysis of freedom of expression is comparative analysis by judges. Although the United States Supreme Court has generally been uninterested in foreign law on freedom of expression (Alford 2008, p. 4), there is considerable international judicial dialogue among other countries, at least in common law countries and related constitutional systems. The Israeli Supreme Court's important freedom of expression decision in *Bakri v Film Censorship Board* [2003] HCJ 314/03, for instance, cites cases from Australia and the United Kingdom as well as key First Amendment decisions.

A particularly vivid illustration of international judicial dialogue is provided by the widespread consideration of the United States Supreme Court's decision in *New York Times v Sullivan* (1964) 376 US 254 by courts in the common law world. Courts in Australia, Canada, India, Israel, New Zealand, South Africa and the United Kingdom have all considered *New York Times v Sullivan* in the course of determining their own rules regarding freedom of expression and the law of defamation (Stone and Williams 2000; Barak 1988, p. 243). (Indeed, neatly making Vicki Jackson's point that comparativism need not be 'convergent' (Jackson 2005), these courts have to varying degrees rejected or at least modified the *New York Times v Sullivan* rules.) Over time, the judicial conversation has broadened to include other common law countries so that in the Canadian Supreme Court's most recent decision on the issue, it considered decisions of courts from Australia, New Zealand and the United Kingdom, as well as *New York Times v Sullivan* and other American cases (*Grant v Torstar Corporation* (2009) SCC 61).

However, as with any comparison across constitutional systems, the task of comparing freedom of expression principles is fraught with the dangers of misunderstanding.

To begin with, identifying the value or set of values underlying any single constitutional system of freedom of expression is likely to be difficult. At the most fundamental level, the philosophy of freedom of expression itself is complex and contested. Indeed, the relationship between even the main strands of argument just stated is subject to multiple interpretation. Frederick Schauer casts Justice Holmes' 'market' of ideas argument, often advanced as an argument from truth, as an argument from democratic government: freedom of expression reflects a distrust of government, and while government neutrality as between ideas might not produce the ideal outcome of freedom of expression questions, it is better than the distortion produced by government self-interest, bias or incompetence (Schauer 1982, pp. 33–4). Robert Post has recast arguments from autonomy in a similar way. His argument is that freedom of expression gives individuals a sense of participation in the processes of government and a sense of legitimacy and identification with the government, which he takes to be an element of the 'internal logic of self-government' (Post 1993). Philosophers of freedom of expression also differ greatly as to how their fundamental commitments resolve specific problems. Ronald Dworkin, from the liberal premise that individuals are worthy of equal concern and respect, makes an argument against censorship of pornography, while Rae Langton derives the opposite conclusion from the same starting point (Dworkin 1985; Langton 1993).

Further, the sheer complexity of the problems posed by a guarantee of freedom of expression makes it unlikely that a single 'theory' or 'set of values' might be appropriate for the entire range of freedom of expression problems (Schauer 1982; Greenawalt 1989, pp. 13–15; Shiffrin 1983, pp. 1197–8). Any body of law derived from a guarantee of freedom of expression is, therefore, grounded in an amalgam of ideas and any given system of freedom of expression might be fully explained only by reference to a series of ideas or sets of values running in conjunction. In the light of all these features, and because of inevitable disagreement about the meaning of rights (Waldron 2000, pp. 227–8), there will almost certainly be disagreement about the meaning of freedom of expression within any given tradition.

Moreover, the task of divining how these arguments are reflected in the constitutional law of even one system is complicated by the nature of judicial decision-making. At least in the systems reviewed in this chapter, the constitutional law of freedom of expression is produced in the distinctive institutional context of courts engaged in the practical task of judging. The obvious constraints on courts (which include limited time, the need to produce agreement in a multi-member institution and changes in personnel over time) make it unlikely that a court will, or will want to, produce a clear, comprehensive statement of underlying philosophy or motivating values. Nor are judicial decisions themselves likely to acknowledge that there are competing understandings of freedom of expression. On the contrary, the institutional practice of courts is to present an interpretation of a right of freedom of expression as a *correct* interpretation rather than as a choice between contested visions.

Distilling the underlying philosophy or motivating commitments of any body of law on freedom of expression of law thus has inherent difficulties. Comparative analysis complicates the task further. As with other aspects of constitutional law, freedom of expression principles are deeply affected by the cultural, legal and political context of the constitutional system in which they arise. So for instance, the place of 'dignity' within the German constitutional system (overtly declared by the Federal Constitutional Court as the pre-eminent value within an 'objective order of values' established by the Basic Law) is traced to a cultural emphasis on personal 'honor' (Whitman 2000). The special sensitivity of German law toward holocaust denial and more generally toward expression aimed at undermining democracy is readily traceable to the history of the Third Reich (Grimm 2009).

The Canadian approach to pornography and hate speech which, at least compared to the United States, is considerably more restrictive of expression, is often explained as demonstrating a distinctive commitment to equal democratic participation and multiculturalism (Mahoney 1992; Hogg 2004, pp. 954, 962; Weinrib 1991, pp. 1429–30). The Canadian commitment to these values equally responds to some important features of Canadian constitutionalism. Canada has faced the challenges of cultural diversity in an especially stark manner and thus the Canadian Charter reveals a strong commitment to their resolution through the recognition of group language and education rights.

Precisely because the conception of freedom of expression is deeply embedded in the surrounding legal and political culture, it is not easily accessible to a foreign lawyer. Moreover, for the institutional reasons already discussed, judicial decisions will usually be couched primarily in legal terms: as a discussion of the constitutional text, previous cases and other legal principles. The salient structural, cultural and political influences on the decision are likely to be unmentioned and may even be unacknowledged. It is easy therefore for comparativists to overlook important differences as between constitutional systems or to overlook the extent to which ideas about freedom of expression are contested within a given system.

For instance, the common casting of Canadian free speech law as showing a distinctive commitment to equality is often made by way of a comparison with First Amendment law, which is cast as exhibiting a preference for liberty over equality (Mahoney 1992). But simply stated, the comparison overlooks the extent to which the relationship between freedom of expression and equality is contested (Weinstein 1999). Some defend First Amendment approaches to hate speech on the basis that a highly protective free speech principle actually serves the equality interests of minorities (Weinstein 1999, p. 118). Put in general terms, the argument is that equality requires strong limitations on governmental powers of censorship to protect the most vulnerable (Strossen 1996; Amar 1992, pp. 154–5). It has also been argued that a strong free speech principle like the First Amendment can promote the tolerance required for effective multiculturalism (Bollinger 1988; Post 1997).

There are, of course, difficult questions as to which of these accounts are right. To many, the First Amendment faith that equality and cultural diversity will fare best in an open contest of ideas seems nothing like as strong as the Canadian commitment to limiting speech in the interest of these values. The point here is not to enter into that debate but to show how the simple invocation of equality and multicultural diversity as an explanation of the difference fails to capture the whole story.

The difficulties posed by comparativism are especially acute when it is courts engaging in the comparative analysis. Courts have special limitations. They will often lack the time and institutional resources to engage in the deep comparative study required to locate foreign law of freedom of expression in its full context and to canvass critical analyses and alternative positions. But at the same time, the stakes of comparative analysis in the courts are especially high. Though courts may not necessarily seek to bring their own systems into line with others, courts will typically refer to foreign law as a source of guidance. There is a risk therefore that a superficial comparativism may lead to some hasty adoption of foreign law without a full appreciation of alternatives. (For an argument that some of the High Court of Australia's early decisions displayed uncritical over-enthusiasm for the law of the First Amendment, see Stone 1999.)

3   CONCLUSION: COMPARATIVISM AND FREEDOM OF EXPRESSION

These difficulties have led some scholars to question whether comparing free speech principles across constitutional systems is practical or useful for courts interpreting or applying constitutional principles of freedom of expression (Alford 2008). This critique is an instance of a wider critique of comparativism in the courts. The complexity of (and disagreement about) underlying philosophical commitments, the opacity of judicial decision-making, and cultural specificity of any particular body of law, though formidable problems for the comparativists, are raised as squarely by other constitutional rights and indeed by the structural elements of a constitution as well (Stone 2008).

And, to sound a by now familiar note, the case for comparativism may differ from context to context. It is strongest in relation to a constitution that explicitly signals the membership of a state in some broader community of states or a commitment to internationally shared values (such as the Constitution of South Africa, which requires courts to consider international law and explicitly authorizes the consideration of foreign law, or the New Zealand Bill of Rights, which 'affirms' a commitment to the International Covenant on Civil and Political Rights), as between constitutions that bear a historical relationship to each other (Choudhry 1999) and in relation to new constitutions, or new guarantees of freedom of expression, where courts are facing freedom of expression cases without many legal resources. The case for comparativism may be weaker in relation to constitutional principles that have developed their own rich set of resources and a distinctive conception of freedom of expression.

This latter description fits the First Amendment most neatly – it is the oldest judicially interpreted free speech provision and has produced a rich and substantively distinctive body of case law (Gardbaum 2008; Schauer 2005b) – and may partly explain the United States Supreme Court's resistance to comparativism. Moreover, this attitude is not entirely unique to that Court. It is notable, for instance, that the Federal Constitutional Court of Germany has not been much influenced by foreign law (Jackson 2010, pp. 34–5). But, outside of such contexts, the case for comparativism is much stronger. It is not surprising, then, that constitutional comparativism in freedom of expression cases, as well as in other areas, is certainly very widespread (Jackson 2010, pp. 40–41, 43–5, 73–7).

In any event, this critique goes only to one use of comparative analysis in constitutional law: the use of foreign law as an interpretive resource. There remain of course many other circumstances in which comparative inquiry may be useful. Constitutional design is one obvious instance. Comparative inquiry will also be required in cases that do not involve the straightforward application of freedom of expression principles. For instance, courts may consider foreign law on freedom of expression under choice of law rules where expression originating in one jurisdiction causes or is alleged to cause harm in other jurisdictions or when questions arise as to the enforceability of foreign judgments. (Issues of this nature were raised in *Dow Jones v Gutnick*[2] and in litigation between Yahoo! Inc and the French organization La Ligue Contre Le Racism et L'Antisemitism.[3]) Cases of this kind are likely to become more common as interactions across national borders increase (Jackson 2010, pp. 278–9). In the context of freedom of expression, the increasing ease of trans-jurisdictional communication enabled by the internet seems especially significant.

Comparativism in one context or another is, therefore, an almost inevitable element of constitutional analysis in all legal systems. This fact poses a challenge for constitutionalists to which scholars are well placed to respond. Successful comparativism within the field of freedom of expression, as elsewhere, requires a rather deep and critical engagement with foreign law that encompasses critical legal and philosophical literature on freedom of expression as well as case law. There is thus an increasing need for a research 'infrastructure' of informed, critical and widely comparative studies of freedom of expression that can support this task.

NOTES

1. Thanks are due to Simon Evans for helping me develop this argument.
2. *Dow Jones v Gutnick* (2001) 210 CLR 575 (High Court of Australia) (considering whether Australian law or American law governed a defamation action brought by an Australian resident against a United States corporation in relation to material which could be downloaded in Australia but uploaded onto the World Wide Web in the United States).
3. 169 F. Supp 2d 1181 (ND Cal 2001) (refusing to enforce a French court's decision because to do so would be inconsistent with the First Amendment); rev'd 379 F. 3d 1120 (9th Cir. 2004); re-heard *en banc* 433 F. 3d 1199 (9th Cir. 2006) (the members of the Court disagreed as to whether the French court's decision was inconsistent with the First Amendment and dismissed the action for other reasons).

REFERENCES

Alford, Roger P. (2008), 'Free Speech and the Case for Constitutional Exceptionalism', *Michigan Law Review*, 106, 1071.

Amar, A. (1992), 'The Case of the Missing Amendments: *R.A.V. v St Paul*', *Harvard Law Review*, 106, 124.

Barak, Aharon (1988), 'Freedom of Speech in Israel: The Impact of the American Constitution', Tel Aviv University Studies in Law, 8, 241.

Barendt, Eric (2005), *Freedom of Speech*, 2nd edition, Oxford: Oxford University Press.

BeVier, Lillian (1978), 'The First Amendment and Political Speech: An Inquiry into the Substance and Limits of Principle', *Stanford Law Review*, 30, 299.

Blasi, Vincent (1988a), 'The Checking Value in First Amendment Theory', *American Bar Foundation Research Journal*, 3, 521.

Blasi, Vincent (1988b), 'The First Amendment and the Ideal of Civic Courage: The Brandeis Opinion in Whitney v California', *William and Mary Law Review*, 29, 653.

Bollinger, Lee (1988), *The Tolerant Society*, Oxford: Oxford University Press.

Bork, Robert (1971), 'Neutral Principles and Some First Amendment Problems', *Indiana Law Journal*, 47, 1.

Campbell, Tom D. (1995), 'The Contribution of Legal Studies', in Robert E. Goodwin and Phillip Pettit (eds.), *A Companion to Contemporary Political Philosophy*, Cambridge: Blackwell, 183–211.

Choudhry, Sujit (1999), 'Globalization in Search of Justification: Toward a Theory of Comparative Constitutional Interpretation', *Indiana Law Journal*, 74, 819.

Choudhry, Sujit (2006), 'So What is the Real Legacy of Oakes? Two Decades of Proportionality Analysis under the Canadian Charter's Section 1', *Supreme Court Law Review*, 34 (2), 501.

Cram, Ian (2006), *Contested Words: Legal Restrictions on Freedom of Speech in Liberal Democracies*, Aldershot: Ashgate Publishing.

Currie, Iain and Johan de Waal (2005), *The Bill of Rights Handbook*, 5th edition, Lansdowne: Juta and Co. Ltd.

Dawood, Yasmin (2006), 'Democracy, Power and the Supreme Court: Campaign Finance Reform in Comparative Context', *International Journal of Constitutional Law*, 4 (2), 269–93.

Dworkin, Ronald (1985), *A Matter of Principle*, Cambridge, MA: Harvard University Press.

Dworkin, Ronald (1996), *Freedom's Law*, Cambridge, MA: Harvard University Press.

Ely, John Hart (1980), *Democracy and Distrust*, Cambridge, MA: Harvard University Press.

Emerson, Thomas I (1969), *The System of Freedom of Expression*, New York: Vintage Books.

Fiss, Owen (1996), *The Irony of Free Speech*, Cambridge, MA: Harvard University Press.

Frantz, Laurent B (1963), 'Is the First Amendment Law? – A Reply to Professor Mendelson', *California Law Review*, 51, 729.

Gardbaum, Stephen (2003), 'The "Horizontal Effect" of Constitutional Rights', *Michigan Law Review*, 102, 388–459.

Gardbaum, Stephen (2008), 'The Myth and Reality of American Constitutional Exceptionalism', *Michigan Law Review*, 107, 391–466.

Greenawalt, Kent (1989), *Speech, Crime and the Uses of Language*, Oxford: Oxford University Press.

Greenawalt, Kent (1995), *Fighting Words: Individuals, Communities and Liberties of Speech*, Princeton: Princeton University Press.

Grimm, Dieter (2005), 'The Protective Function of the State', in Georg Nolte (ed.), *European and US Constitutionalism*, Cambridge: Cambridge University Press.

Grimm, Dieter (2007), 'Proportionality in Canadian and German Constitutional Jurisprudence', *University of Toronto Law Journal*, 57, 383.

Grimm, Dieter (2009), 'The Holocaust Denial Decision of the Federal Constitutional Court of Germany', in Ivan Hare and James Weinstein, *Extreme Speech and Democracy*, Oxford: Oxford University Press, 557.

Hogg, P.W. (2004), *Constitutional Law of Canada*, Carswell: Ontario.

Jackson, Vicki C. (1999), 'Ambivalent Resistance and Comparative Constitutionalism: Opening up the Conversation on "Proportionality," Rights And Federalism', *University of Pennsylvania Journal of Constitutional Law*, 1, 583.

Jackson, Vicki C. (2005), 'Constitutional Comparisons: Convergence, Resistance, Engagement', *Harvard Law Review*, 119, 109–28.

Jackson, Vicki C. (2010), *Constitutional Engagement in a Transnational Era*, New York: Oxford University Press.

Kalven, Harry Jr. (1967), 'Upon Rereading Mr. Justice Black on the First Amendment', *University of California, Los Angeles Law Review*, 14, 428–53.

Kommers, Donald P. (1997), *The Constitutional Jurisprudence of the Federal Republic of Germany*, 2nd edition, Durham, NC and London: Duke University Press.

Krotoszynski, Ronald J., Jr. (2006), *The First Amendment in Cross-Cultural Perspective*, New York: New York University Press.

Langton, Rae (1993), 'Whose Right? Ronald Dworkin, Women and Pornographers', *Philosophy and Public Affairs*, 19, 311.

Mahoney, Kathleen (1992), 'R v Keegstra: A Rationale for Regulating Pornography', *McGill Law Journal*, 37, 242.

Meiklejohn, Alexander (1961) 'The First Amendment is an Absolute', *Supreme Court Review*, 245.

Mill, J.S. (1978), *On Liberty*, Elizabeth Rapaport, ed., Indianapolis: Hackett Publishing Company (1st edition, 1859).

Mount, Simon (2003), 'R v Shaheed: the Prima Facie Exclusion Rule Reexamined', *New Zealand Law Review*, 1, 45.

Navot, Suzie (2007), *The Constitutional Law of Israel*, Dordrecht: Kluwer Law International.

Nimmer, Melville, B. (1968), 'The Right to Speak from *Times* to *Time*: First Amendment Theory Applied to Libel and Misapplied to Privacy', *California Law Review*, 56, 935.

Post, Robert (1993), 'Meiklejohn's Mistake: Individual Autonomy and the Reform of Public Discourse', *University of Colorado Law Review*, 1109.

Post, R. (1997), 'Community and the First Amendment', *Arizona State Law Journal*, 29, 473.

Quint, Peter (1992), 'The Comparative Law of Flag Desecration', *Hastings International and Comparative Law Review*, 15, 613.

Redish, Martin (1982), 'The Value of Free Speech', *University of Pennsylvania Law Review*, 130, 591.
Rishworth, P., Grant Huscroft, Scott Optician and Richard Mahoney (2003), *The New Zealand Bill of Rights*, Oxford: Oxford University Press.
Rosenfeld, Michael (2003), 'Hate Speech in Constitutional Jurisprudence: A Comparative Analysis', *Cardozo Law Review*, 24, 1523.
Scanlon, T.M. (1972), 'A Theory of Freedom of Expression', *Philosophy and Public Affairs*, 1, 204.
Schauer, Frederick (1982), *Free Speech: A Philosophical Enquiry*, New York: Cambridge University Press.
Schauer, Frederick (1989), 'The Second Best First Amendment', *William & Mary Law Review*, 31, 1.
Schauer, Frederick (2003), 'The Convergence of Rules and Standards', *New Zealand Law Review*, 303.
Schauer, Frederick (2005a), 'Freedom of Expression Adjudication in Europe and the United States: A Case Study in Comparative Constitutional Architecture', in George Nolte (ed.), *European and US Constitutionalism*, Cambridge: Cambridge University Press.
Schauer, Frederick (2005b), 'The Exceptional First Amendment', in Michael Ignatieff (ed.), *American Exceptionalism and Human Rights*, Princeton: Princeton University Press, 29–56.
Shiffrin, Steven (1983), 'Liberalism Radicalism and Legal Scholarship', *University of California, Los Angeles Law Review*, 30, 1103.
Shiffrin, Steven (1990), *The First Amendment Democracy and Romance*, Cambridge, MA: Harvard University Press.
Stone, Adrienne (1999), 'The Limits of Constitutional Text and Structure', *Melbourne University Law Review*, 23, 668–708.
Stone, Adrienne (2002), The Common Law and the Constitution: A Reply', *Melbourne University Law Review*, 26, 646–65.
Stone, Adrienne (2005), 'Australia's Constitutional Rights and the Problem of Interpretive Disagreement', *Sydney Law Review*, 27, 29–48.
Stone, Adrienne (2008), 'Judicial Review without Rights', *Oxford Journal of Legal Studies*, 28, 1–32.
Stone, Adrienne and George Williams (2000), 'Freedom of Speech and Defamation in the Common Law World', *Monash University Law Review*, 26, 36–378.
Strossen, N. (1996), 'Hate Speech and Pornography: Do We Have to Choose between Freedom of Speech and Equality?', *Case Western Reserve Law Review*, 46, 449.
Sunstein, Cass (1995), *Democracy and the Problem of Free Speech*, New York: Free Press.
Sunstein, Cass (2006), 'A New Progressivism', *Stanford Law and Policy Review*, 197.
Tushnet, Mark V. (2003), 'The Issue of State Action/Horizontal Effect in Comparative Constitutional Law', *International Journal of Constitutional Law*, 1, 79–98.
Volokh, Eugene (2005), 'Crime-Facilitating Speech', *Stanford Law Review*, 57, 1095.
Waldron, Jeremy (2000), *Law and Disagreement*, Oxford: Clarendon Press.
Weinrib, Lorraine E. (1991), 'Hate Promotion in a Free and Democratic Society: R v Keegstra', *McGill Law Journal*, 36, 1416.
Weinstein, James (1999), *Hate Speech, Pornography and the Radical Attack on Free Speech Doctrine*, Colorado: Westview Press.
Whitman, James Q. (2000), 'Enforcing Civility and Respect: Three Societies', *Yale Law Journal*, 109, 1279–398.

23. Comparative constitutional law and religion

Ran Hirschl

1 INTRODUCTION

The rule of law and the rule of God – two of the most powerful ideas of all time, an 'odd couple' of sorts, diametrically opposed in many respects, yet at the same time sharing strikingly similar characteristics, each with its own sacred texts, interpretive practices, and communities of reference – seem destined to collide. Their charged encounters are further accentuated by the intersection of two broad trends: the return of religion to the forefront of world politics and global convergence to constitutionalism. Religion and the belief in God have made a major comeback. From the fundamentalist turn in predominantly Islamic polities to the spread of Catholicism and Pentecostalism in the global south, and from the increase in religiously devout immigrants in Europe to the rise of the Christian right in the United States, it is hard to overstate the significance of the religious revival in late twentieth and early twenty-first century politics. At the same time, the world has witnessed the rapid spread of constitutionalism and judicial review. Constitutional supremacy – a concept that has long been a major pillar of the American political order – is now shared, in one form or another, by over 150 countries and several supra-national entities across the globe.

   In this chapter, I delineate two key aspects of the tense intersection of constitutional law and religion worldwide: (i) the range of constitutional models – from atheism or strict separation to full enshrinement – for arranging 'religion and state' relations; and (ii) the main types of religion and state constitutional controversies as they have manifested themselves under each of these models over the last few decades. Because the constitutional status of religion varies considerably across constitutional models, there appears to be more cross-country divergence in the comparative constitutional jurisprudence of religious freedom than with respect to most other freedoms. In the following pages, I identify the main existing constitutional models for arranging the relationship between state and religion, and, where applicable, illustrate each model's unique features by reference to landmark court rulings that define the rules of engagement between state and religion in each setting.

2 EIGHT MODELS OF STATE AND RELIGION RELATIONS

A taxonomy of contemporary approaches to govern religion and state relations suggests eight archetypical models may be identified, ranging from atheism or strict separation to weak establishment, and from models of jurisdictional enclaves to strong establishment or parallel governance of constitutionalism and religion.

2.1 The Atheist State

At least at the declarative level, communist regimes stand at the most anti-religious end of the contemporary continuum of models of state and religion. Following Marx's famous maxim, communist regimes view religion as the 'opiate to the masses', and hold an atheist position that associates religion in both the public and the private spheres with backwardness, colonialism, and false consciousness. The establishment of the People's Republic of China in 1949, for example, was accompanied by a campaign to eradicate religion from Chinese life and culture. China's attitude toward religion was relaxed considerably in the late 1970s, with the 1978 Constitution's formal guarantee of freedom of religion. In Ethiopia, the Ethiopian Orthodox Church was disestablished as the state church in 1974, and its Patriarch was executed by the Marxist Derg military junta in 1979. The introduction of strict anti-religious laws followed a military junta's ferocious overthrow of Emperor Haile Selassie, a sacred figure for the Rastafarian movement in Jamaica, believed to be the descendant of King Solomon and Queen Sheba who negotiated the autonomous status of the Ethiopian Orthodox Church. A move in the opposite direction may be seen in the Russian state of the post-communist era, which unlike the days of the Soviet Union, is no longer anti-religious and has become passively secularist, effectively resulting in the Orthodox Church's return to prominence (see Kuru 2009, 11). At any rate, because the communist-atheist vision of state and religion includes a concentrated effort by the state to eradicate religion, there is virtually no meaningful constitutional jurisprudence in communist states pertaining to religion per se.

2.2 Assertive Secularism

This model establishes a form of assertive, even militant, secularism that goes beyond neutrality towards religion or a declared a-religiosity, to advance an explicitly secular civic religion that resents manifestations of religion in public life and views secularism as a core element of the modern nation and its members' collective identity. The longstanding French policy of *laïcité* is arguably the clearest manifestation of such a desire to restrict clerical and religious influence over the state and to establish a uniform, religion-free citizenship and nationhood (Ahdar and Leigh 2005, 73). Pertinent French jurisprudence reflects that notion. A recent example is the *Faiza M.* case. Faiza Silmi ('Mme M') was born in Morocco. She married a French citizen of Moroccan origin and in 2000 moved to France, where she had three French-born children. In 2004, she applied for French citizenship, as French law allowed for non-citizen spouses of French citizens to apply for citizenship after two years of marriage. In May 2005, the French government denied her application, reasoning that her religious beliefs were 'incompatible with the fundamental values of the French community, and particularly with the principle of equality of the sexes'. She appealed. The Conseil d'État, France's highest court for matters of administrative law, confirmed that the government's apprehension of the incompatibility of an applicant's religious beliefs and insufficient assimilation into French society was a legitimate basis for rejecting her application for citizenship. The Conseil d'État relied on reasons provided by the government according to which Silmi only began wearing the niq'ab (a veil worn by some Muslim women that covers the face) when she arrived in France, refused to remove her headscarf and niq'ab in public, rarely left her home without her husband, and had been living in 'submission' to men. The government viewed this interpretation of the facts as indicative of Silmi's insufficient assimilation into French society.

Turkey provides another example of such assertive secularism. Following the demise of the Ottoman Empire, the Kemalist secular-nationalist elite rejected Islamic culture and laws in favor of secularism and modernism. Accordingly, the words 'the religion of the Turkish State is Islam' were removed from the constitution in 1928. In 1937, the words 'republican, popular, atheist, secular, and reformist' were inserted into the constitution to better reflect modern Turkey's adherence to a strict separation of state and religion. Both the 1961 and the 1982 constitutions established an official state policy of secularism.

This official policy has become a linchpin of Turkish constitutional identity, but has been challenged repeatedly over the last two decades by the rise of political Islam in Turkey. In response to these challenges, the Turkish Constitutional Court (TCC) has become a main guardian of secularist interests. On several occasions it disbanded Islamist political parties, most notably the Welfare (*Refah*) Party (1998) and the Virtue (*Fazilet*) Party (2001). In half a dozen landmark rulings, the TCC disallowed wearing of religious attire, most notably the Islamic headscarf, in the public education system. Arguably, one of the pinnacles of this line of jurisprudence is the TCC's ruling in 2008 that declared unconstitutional an amendment introduced by the moderately religious Justice and Development Party (AKP)-led government that effectively lifted the ban on wearing the Islamic headscarf in the public education system. The Court viewed strict secularism as a basic norm of Turkish constitutionalism that may not be overridden even by a properly adopted constitutional amendment. In two important decisions over the last few years the European Court of Human Rights (ECtHR) sided with the TCC's avid protection of secularism in that country at the expense of individual and political freedoms. In 2003, the ECtHR dismissed an appeal against the TCC's ruling in the *Refah* dissolution case and concurred with the TCC's view of Shari'a norms as incompatible with core principles of democracy. In the *Leyla Sahin v Turkey* case (2005), the ECtHR deferred to Turkish authorities' discretion, thereby approving a decision to deny enrollment in Istanbul University from a female medical student who wore an Islamic headscarf while attending school. The AKP-led government held a national referendum in 2010 on a package of constitutional amendments; it was approved by a majority of approximately 58% of those casting ballots. Among the new provisions are changes to party closure procedures, judicial appointment processes and to the composition of and access to the Constitutional Court (a long-time stronghold of statist-secularist views). It remains to be seen what will be the effect of the amendments on the notion of assertive secularism in Turkish constitutional law.

2.3   Separation as State Neutrality toward Religion

Arguably the most common model among separationist states is the separation-as-neutrality mode. It emphasizes the state's impartial, neutral stance toward religious creeds rather than active advancement of secularism per se. Whereas religion has always been a core element of American society and culture, the First Amendment to the US Constitution provides that: 'Congress shall make no law respecting an establishment of religion, or prohibiting the free exercise thereof'. The 'Establishment Clause' prohibits the state from adopting, preferring or endorsing a religion as well as from preferring religion over non-religion (the 'non-establishment' principle); the 'Free Exercise Clause' enjoins the state from interfering with the religious freedom of its citizens (the freedom of religious expression principle). There is a 'natural antagonism between a command not to establish religion and a command not to inhibit its practice' (Rotunda and Nowak 2008, § 21.1(a)). There is, however, at least one commonality to both clauses: each advances neutrality toward religion by preventing the government from singling out specific religious sects for special benefits or burdens unless the action is necessary to promote a compelling interest (*id.*).

Whereas neutrality toward religion is the motto here, this model is often accompanied by an 'assimilationist' or 'melting pot' approach to national identity. At the same time, comparative polls often suggest that Americans are among the most likely in the West to refer to God or draw upon religious morality or principles in their everyday lives. 'In God We Trust' is on all American currency; each Supreme Court session begins with the invocation 'God save the United States and this Honorable Court' (see Kuru 2009). Given such a disharmony, to borrow Gary Jacobsohn's (2010) phrase, it is hardly surprising that over its many years of existence, the US Supreme Court has issued hundreds of landmark rulings on the scope and nature of each of the two clauses, as well as on their intersection with each other, and with other constitutional provisions.[1]

With respect to the non-establishment principle – the essence of the state neutrality concept in the United States – the commonly accepted view is that the Establishment Clause prohibits the sponsorship of any religion, as well as the preference for religion over non-religion (Rotunda and Nowak, 2008, § 21.3(a)). According to the so-called 'Lemon test' (introduced by the US Supreme Court in *Lemon v Kurtzman*, 1971), the prohibition on the establishment of religion requires that statutes have a secular purpose, a principal or primary effect that does not advance or inhibit religion, and does not promote excessive entanglement between government and religion. In 1997 (*Agostini v Felton*; see also *Zelman v Simmons-Harris*, 2002), the Court modified this analysis, holding that the question of 'excessive entanglement' was really part of the inquiry into whether the impugned legislation or activity aided or inhibited religion. The Court further listed three factors for evaluating whether a law that aids religious organizations has a non-religious primary effect: (1) whether the aid was used in or resulted in governmental 'indoctrination', (2) whether the aid program defined recipients by some reference to religion, and (3) whether there was an excessive entanglement between government and religion as a result of the aid program. Any denominational preference granted by legislation will obviate the need for the three-part *Lemon* test as the government will automatically have the burden of showing that the law is necessary to promote a compelling interest.

One of the hotly contested issues with respect to the Establishment Clause has been the place of religion in the public education system. In principle, mandatory prayers may not be part of the curriculum in public schools. In *Lee v Weisman* (1992), the Court held (5:4) that a policy permitting invocation and benediction prayers at a public middle school graduation ceremony violated the Establishment Clause. Similarly, in *Santa Fe Independent School District v Doe* (2000), the Court struck down a policy that allowed for a 'non-sectarian, non-proselytizing prayer' before football games.

More challenging questions arise in relation to the funding of religious schools. In *Board of Education of Kiryas Joel Village School District v Grumet* (1994), the US Supreme Court invalidated a law that created a separate school district for a village populated exclusively by Jewish Satmar Hasidim. The goal of the law was to provide accommodation for Satmar children with special needs. The majority of the Court struck down the law on the basis that it violated the neutrality principle. Three judges (Scalia, Rehnquist and Thomas JJ) dissented, holding that the Court's precedent of prohibiting religious accommodation was improper. Later, in *Agostini v Felton* (1997), the Court held that a public school board could provide educational assistance (e.g. providing staff to run remedial programs) to students of a religious school. The Court found the purpose of such a program was to aid all students in a jurisdiction rather than to give preference to students at the religious school. Similarly, the Supreme Court has also held that allowing a religious organization to use a public forum for religiously oriented speech does not violate the Establishment Clause provided that no religious groups are given preferential treatment. Accordingly, a school board could not deny a religious organization the right to conduct a meeting in the school building after hours when the same right had been granted to non-religious organizations (*Lamb's Chapel v Center Moriches Union Free School District*, 1993; *Good News Club v Milford Central School*, 2001).

With respect to the free religious exercise principle, the Court has held that a law passed for the main purpose of burdening or providing a benefit to a group on the basis of its members' substantive religious beliefs is unconstitutional. Thus, in *Church of Lukumi Babalu Aye, Inc. v Hialeah* (1993), a city ordinance that prohibited animal slaughter as part of a sacramental practice was held unconstitutional as the Court unanimously found that the law was passed in order to encourage a religious sect to leave the city. In the same vein, the Supreme Court struck down a state constitutional provision that required a declaration of a belief in God before a person could assume public office (*Torasco v Watkins*, 1961).

The Court's jurisprudence is mixed in cases involving Free Exercise Clause-based claims for exemption from government laws. The Court has held that some laws of general application require exemptions for religious reasons. In a landmark 'expansive accommodation' ruling in *Wisconsin v Yoder* (1972), the Court held that the state could not compel members of the Amish church to send their children to school beyond the eighth grade. Members of the Old Amish community who reached the age of fourteen were thus exempted from two additional years of schooling that would have otherwise been mandated by the state's compulsory education law.

At the same time, a religion-based free-exercise claim seldom exempts a person from the application of a religiously neutral criminal law. In *Employment Division, Dept. of Human Resources v Smith* (1990), the Supreme Court held that a law banning the use of peyote was constitutional, despite a claim that the Native American Church used peyote for sacramental purposes. The political backlash against this ruling was significant. In 1993, Congress adopted the Religious Freedom Restoration Act (commonly known as RFRA), in an attempt to reinstate the supremacy of the Free Exercise Clause and prevent laws from substantially burdening free exercise of religion. However, in 1997, the Supreme Court struck down parts of RFRA as it overstepped Congress' power to enforce the Fourteenth Amendment (*City of Boerne v Flores*, 1997). However, parts of RFRA continue to stand. In 2006 (*Gonzales v O Centro Espirita Beneficente Uniao do Vegetal*), the Supreme Court invoked the free exercise clause to dismiss charges against a church that during a religious ceremony it used a sacramental tea that included an otherwise (federally) illegal substance. The Court decisively stated that the federal government must show a compelling state interest in restricting religious freedom. The Court also disagreed with the government's central argument that the uniform application of the Controlled Substances Act does not allow for exceptions.

The struggle over free exercise-based exemptions extends to other areas, such as military service or tax exemptions. In *United States v Seeger* (1965), for example, the Supreme Court evaluated a law that granted an exemption from conscription to persons who by 'religious training and belief in relation to a Supreme Being' were opposed to war in any form. The law also stated that the objection could not be based on 'essentially political, sociological or philosophical views or a merely personal moral code'. The Court interpreted this exemption as applying to persons whose non-theistic beliefs occupied the place of religion in their lives (Rotunda and Nowak 2008, § 21.9(a)). In response to the ruling, the Military Service Act of 1967 was rephrased to remove the reference to the Supreme Being. This Act was challenged in *Gillette v United States* (1971) on the basis that some religiously based views are opposed to unjust wars, not all wars. The majority of the Court upheld the Act, holding that it had a secular purpose in creating a fair and uncomplicated exemption. And in *Goldman v Weinberger* (1986), the Court held that the free exercise clause did not require the Air Force to allow a serviceman to wear a *yarmulke* while on duty and in uniform. The Air Force's regulations prohibited personnel from wearing non-regulation clothing; the Court held that the free exercise clause neither invalidated the regulation nor mandated an exemption.

With respect to tax exemptions, the Court held in *Swaggart Ministries v Board of Equalization* (1990) that religious organizations cannot refuse to pay sales and use taxes that apply to all tangible personal property. Because it was facially neutral, the tax was not subject to the compelling interest test. In *Bob Jones University v United States* (1983), the Court upheld the decision of the Internal Revenue Service to deny a tax exemption to Bob Jones University. The university had a racially discriminatory admissions policy that it said stemmed from religious doctrine. The Court held that while the denial of tax benefits would affect the school, it would not prevent the school from observing its religious tenets. Further, the Court held that the government had an overriding interest in eradicating racial discrimination. At the same time, Title VII of the Civil Rights Act of 1964 exempts religious organizations from the prohibition against religious discrimination in employment. The Supreme Court upheld the validity of this exemption in *Corporation of the Presiding Bishop of the Church of Jesus Christ of Latter-Day Saints v Amos* (1987), where an employee of an organization affiliated with the Church was fired because he was not a member of the Church. The Court unanimously found that the employee could not seek the benefit of the Civil Rights Act because of the exemption, which was deemed constitutional because it was related to a legitimate interest.

The United States' constitutional experience of the last two centuries provides an interesting illustration of how a constitutional order itself can acquire a near-pious status. As Sanford Levinson astutely observes, the American Constitution is the nation's most revered text, and has evolved into a pillar of American 'civil religion' (Levinson 1988). In fact, 'for the past two hundred years', notes another incisive observer, 'the Constitution has been as central to American political culture as the New Testament was to medieval Europe. Just as Milton believed that "all wisdom is enfolded" within the pages of the Bible, all good Americans, from the National Rifle Association to the ACLU, have believed no less of this singular document' (Lazare 1988, 21). And noted scholar of Christian thought Jaroslav Pelikan suggests that 'with the reduction in the private authority of the Christian Scripture, and especially in its public authority, American Scripture has been called upon to fill some of the gap' (Pelikan 2004).

2.4   Weak Religious Establishment

Here there is a formal, mainly ceremonial, designation of a certain religion as 'state religion', but this designation has few or no implications for public life. Several European countries illustrate this model. A case in point is the designation of the Evangelical Lutheran Church as the 'state church' in Norway, Denmark, Finland and Iceland – arguably some of Europe's most liberal and progressive polities. Norway's head of state, for example, is also the leader of the church. Article 2 of the Norwegian Constitution guarantees freedom of religion, but also states that Evangelical Lutheranism is the official state religion. Article 12 requires more than half of the members of the Norwegian Council of State to be members of the state church. Similarly, Greece and Cyprus formally designate the Greek Orthodox Church as their state church. In England, the monarch is 'Supreme Governor' of the Church of England and 'Defender of the Faith'. The Crown has a role in senior ecclesiastical matters and, by the same token, the church is involved in the coronation of a new monarch, and senior bishops are represented in the House of Lords. A diluted version of this model is at work in Germany, where the institutional apparati of the Evangelical, Catholic and Jewish religious communities are designated as public corporations and therefore qualify for state support pursuant to the German church tax.

While the institutional features of the weak religious establishment accommodation differ from the state neutrality model, the constitutional jurisprudence of religion under the two models is quite similar. In the landmark *Classroom Crucifix* case (1995), the German Federal Constitutional Court ruled that the placing of a cross or crucifix in the classrooms of a State (in this case Bavaria) school that is formally designated as non-denominational infringes Article 4(1) of the German Basic Law (*Grundgesetz*). Section I of that Article states that 'Freedom of faith and conscience, and freedom of religious or ideological creed, are inviolable'. Section II adds that 'The undisturbed practice of religion is guaranteed'. Though these guarantees appear absolute, the Constitutional Court held in the *Classroom Crucifix* case that limits on these religious freedoms that flow from the Basic Law and are constitutionally grounded may be justified. The Court stated that: 'The basic right to religious freedom is guaranteed without reservation. This does not however mean that it might not be subject to some sort of restrictions. These would, however, have to follow from the constitution itself. The setting up of limits not already laid out in the constitution is not something the legislature can do. Constitutional grounds that might have justified intervention are not however present here.' 'To this day', added the Court, 'the presence of a cross in a home or room is understood as an expression of the dwellers' Christian faith ... because of the significance Christianity attributes to the cross, non-Christians and atheists perceive it to be the symbolic expression of certain faith convictions and a symbol of missionary zeal. To see the cross as nothing more than a cultural artifact of the Western tradition without any particular religious meaning would amount to profanation contrary to the self-understanding of Christians and the Christian church' (*id.*, cited in Kommers 1997, 475). So the classroom crucifixes had to be removed from non-denominational schools in Bavaria.

More recently, the question of crucifixes in the European classroom reached the ECtHR. In 2009, a seven-judge Chamber decided unanimously in *Lautsi v Italy* that the presence of crucifixes in Italian classrooms contravenes Article 9 (freedom of thought, conscience and religion) of the European Convention of Human Rights, as well as Protocol 1, Article 2, which provides that 'the State shall respect the right of parents to ensure such education and teaching in conformity with their own religious and philosophical convictions'. A request by a Finnish-born, atheist Italian mother whose children attended an Italian school to remove the crucifixes from her children's classrooms was dismissed by Italy's *Consiglio di Stato*, on the ground that the cross had become one of the secular values of the Italian Constitution and represented the values of civil life. In accepting the mother's appeal, the ECtHR advanced a clear 'neutrality' or 'disestablishment' reasoning. In 2011, upon appeal by Italy (and following intervention by eight other European countries), the Grand Chamber of the ECtHR reversed the decision and upheld, 15:2 the right of Italy to display the crucifix in public school classrooms. It ruled that 'the decision whether crucifixes should be present in State-school classrooms is, in principle, a matter falling within the margin of appreciation of the respondent State' (para. 69–70). The Court went on to suggest that the fact that there is no European consensus on the question of the presence of religious symbols in State schools speaks in favour of such a deferential approach. The Grand Chamber ruling also engages in a discussion of the crucifix in the classroom as a 'passive' (and thus supposedly less intrusive) religious symbol, as opposed to active speech or mandatory curricular religious teachings.

A related issue is the limits on wearing religious attire by teachers. Fereshta Ludin, a German citizen born in Afghanistan, applied to teach at a state school in the state of Baden-Württemberg in southwestern Germany. When she informed the school board that she would wear a headscarf while teaching, the board rejected her application. Ludin protested, saying that the wearing of the veil was both a personal and a religious expression, and that she did not wear it as a symbol or to provoke or influence any students. The school board argued that it was not merely a private symbol but an explicitly political symbol that subjected students to undue religious influence. State authorities backed the school board by arguing that wearing the headscarf under the circumstances of the case could not be squared with the constitutional requirement of state neutrality in questions of religion. Ludin appealed the school board's decision, and her case eventually proceeded to Germany's Federal Constitutional Court.

Ludin argued that her freedom of religion, protected by Article 4, Sections I and II of the Basic Law, had been violated by the ban on the headscarf in the classroom. Following the ruling in the *Classroom Crucifix* case, the core legal question in Ludin became whether limits on freedom of religion in this context flow from or may be justified under the German constitution. In a 3:2 decision (2003), the Federal Constitutional Court allowed Ludin's appeal. However, this was based on the primarily technical grounds that the laws of the state of Baden-Württemberg (where the school board in question was based) did not, at the time, include an explicit ban on wearing the headscarf in the public school system. Had such a law been in effect, the board's decision to reject Ludin's application would have withstood judicial scrutiny. The State was held to have a legitimate interest in protecting religious and ideological neutrality in the classroom to ensure separation of church and state and the encouragement of pluralism and diversity (*Ludin*, 2003, para. 43). Parents of the children in school were also held to have a natural right, guaranteed by Article 6 of the Basic Law, to educate and bring up their child free from religious influences that did not accord with the parents' wishes. The students also had a right to be free from the exercise of freedom of religion by others where they might be held captive to the influence of one person's religion. In other words, there were several constitutional grounds for upholding limits to religious expression in this context.

The Court also refused to reject the idea that the scarf was a 'danger'. It maintained that the abstract danger posed by the scarf could only justify the school board's rejection of Ludin's application if the board had been authorized by statute to employ such a policy against religious dress. States were free, according to the Federal Constitutional Court, to enact statutes identifying the appropriate level of religious dress to be displayed in classrooms after taking into account local context and religious and cultural rights. The court held it was conceivable that a legislature could require strict secularism and neutrality in some contexts in order to address an increasingly diverse religious community. Because no such statute existed in Ludin's case, there was no justification for the school board's decision.

The minority opinion held that because freedom of religion is an explicitly individual or private matter, one's freedom of religion is not engaged when one seeks employment in the public sector. Rights guaranteed by the Basic Law are held against the state, and where someone has sought employment as a state official they cannot assert those rights against the body of which they are a part, except in very limited circumstances. These government employees are differently situated than the students at the school and their parents, who retain legitimate interests protected under the Basic Law. Further, the majority's apprehension of an 'abstract danger' was held by the minority to constitute reason enough for the school board to reject Ludin's application. The mere possibility of the creation of tension or undue influence should be enough to justify the school board's decision, and the minority held that this danger would not have to materialize into real damage before it could be prevented by the board. In the larger European context, this ruling was relatively favorable to the headscarf claim. Nonetheless, and consistently with the Court's ruling, a majority of German states have passed laws prohibiting teachers from wearing certain religious attire. The state of Baden-Württemberg itself passed such a law in 2004.

Deference to local authorities is also evident in several other landmark European court rulings on religious attire in the classroom. A notable illustration is the *Shabina Begum* case (2006), where the British House of Lords upheld a school's decision not to allow a student to wear a jilbab (a traditional dress which was said to conceal to a greater extent the contours of the female body), mainly on the grounds that the school had consulted with local religious authorities and took advice from community leaders regarding the conformity of its dress code with Islamic dress requirements. The House of Lords also noted that as there were other schools that permitted the jilbab that Ms Begum could have attended, there was no interference with Begum's right to manifest her belief in practice or observance. One of the Law Lords wrote that ' "freedom to manifest one's religion" does not mean that one has the right to manifest one's religion at any time and in any place and in any manner that accords with one's beliefs'.[2]

2.5   Formal Separation with *De Facto* Pre-eminence of One Denomination

This model is featured in countries where formal separation of church and state and religious freedoms more generally are constitutionally guaranteed, but where longstanding patterns of politically systematized church hegemony and church-centric morality continue to loom large over the constitutional arena. Many Latin American countries, where the vast majority of the population is Roman Catholic and where the history of Catholic Church dominance dates back to the pre-independence era, fall in this category. Despite the considerable variance in the legacy of Church pre-eminence among these countries, there is a strong echo of such Catholic morality in the constitutional jurisprudence of all of these countries, as well as in that of other predominantly Catholic polities such as the Philippines, Poland or Ireland, and to a lesser degree in Spain or Italy. The special status of Catholicism was removed from the Irish Constitution in 1973. But Article 41 of the Constitution 'recognises the Family as the natural primary and fundamental unit group of Society, and as a moral institution possessing inalienable and imprescriptible rights, antecedent and superior to all positive law'. Prior to the fifteenth amendment (1995) that provided for the dissolution of marriage in certain specified circumstances, the Constitution essentially banned divorce and remarriage, and in effect subjected Irish Catholics to concurrent jurisdiction of the Church and the State in such matters. Article 44, which continues to be in effect today, reads 'The State acknowledges that the homage of public worship is due to Almighty God. It shall hold His Name in reverence, and shall respect and honour religion.' And the influence of Catholic morality, formal separation of church and state notwithstanding, does not end there. The Eighth amendment (1983) – the 'Pro-Life Amendment' passed by referendum – asserts that the fetus has an explicit right to life equal to that of the pregnant woman, and that the Irish State guarantees to vindicate that right. However, exceptions are made in cases where there is a threat to the life of the mother, and it may not be used to limit the right to travel to other countries to procure an abortion (see *AG v X*, 1992).

Several other predominantly Catholic countries in Europe, most notably Malta and Poland, and to a considerably lesser degree Slovakia, Spain and Italy, continue to grapple with similar tensions. The gradual convergence toward judicial review, constitutional rights and liberties, gender equality amid a history of church dominance and legalized religion-centered morality, have characterized the constitutional jurisprudence of many predominantly Catholic countries in the global 'south'. Courts in the Philippines, Chile and Ecuador, to pick three examples, have been quite adamant in their refusal to liberalize various aspects of women's reproductive freedoms. The Chilean Constitutional Court – long known for its deference to the government and conservative standing – ruled in a recent 5:4 decision that the free distribution by the government of the so-called 'morning-after pill' amounted to abortive medicine. In other countries – Colombia, Mexico or Argentina, for example – constitutional courts have been notably more receptive to challenges against systematized religion-centric morality. In 2008, the Colombian high court held that emergency contraception is not abortive and does not infringe the right to life. Colombia's Constitutional Court ruled in the same year that conscientious objection to providing certain medical services is a human right, not an institutional right. As a matter of principle, conscientious objection cannot be invoked by institutions such as hospitals with the effect of violating women's fundamental rights to lawful healthcare.

2.6 Separation Alongside Multicultural Accommodation

This model combines formal separation of religion and state with an 'accomodationist' approach to diversity and religious difference. This model, quite common in 'immigrant' societies, most notably Canada, reflects a true commitment to multiculturalism and diversity – a 'mosaic' or 'accomodationist' approach to difference rather than 'melting pot' or 'assimilationist' approach. State and religion are separated, but the conception of citizenship is not tied to strict secularism or neutrality. The true sense of citizenship in this model, indeed of liberalism more generally, is respecting the common aspects of statehood and nationality while celebrating the difference in citizens' cultural and religious traditions. Section 2(a) of the Canadian Charter of Rights and Freedoms protects freedom of religion; Sections 16–23 of the Charter establish the constitutional status of (French/English) bilingualism in Canada; Section 27 of the Charter complements these principles by enshrining multiculturalism and diversity as one of the linchpins of Canadian constitutional identity (Ryder 2008; Kymlicka 1995).

Over the years, the Supreme Court of Canada has developed a rich jurisprudence in support of state-endorsed multiculturalism and generous accommodation of cultural and religious difference in the public sphere. It issued landmark free exercise rulings concerning Sunday closing (e.g. *R v Big M Drug Mart*, 1985; *R v Edwards Books and Art Ltd.*, 1986), alongside controversial rulings concerning continuation of public funding for Roman Catholic schools in Ontario (e.g. *Adler v Ontario*, 1996). In two rulings over the last few years, for example, the Court went out of its way to generously address faith-based claims falling squarely within the parameters of multicultural citizenship as advancing a vision of 'diversity as inclusion'. In *Syndicat Northcrest v Amselem* (2004) – a case involving Orthodox Montreal Jews who erected *sukkahs* on their balconies in a residential condominium partly in contravention of a boilerplate tenancy contract – the majority advocated tolerating a practice where the individual sincerely believes it is connected to religion, regardless of whether the practice is required by a religious authority. In *Multani v Commission scolaire Marguerite-Bourgeoys* (2006), the Court drew on a proportionality test (so-called 'Section 1' analysis) to overturn a Quebec school board decision not to allow a Sikh student to carry the *kirpan* (a ceremonial dagger) due to potential safety hazards and an apparent conflict with the school's prohibition on weapons and dangerous objects. Indeed, the very categorization of the *kirpan* – as either a prohibited weapon in a schoolyard (as the school board claimed) or as an important religious symbol (the position of the student, his parents and the interveners on behalf of the Sikh community) – was at the heart of this legal dispute. A decision to universally ban the *kirpan*, the Court ruled, was not the least drastic means to address the rather limited harm potential, especially when weighing the sincerity of the student's religious beliefs and the fact that the interference (the ban on the *kirpan*) was not trivial. The Court thus held in favor of Multani, providing a resounding statement of the 'diversity-as-inclusion' theme of differentiated citizenship: 'The argument that the wearing of kirpans should be prohibited because the kirpan is a symbol of violence and because it sends the message that using force is necessary to assert rights and resolve conflict must fail. Not only is this assertion contradicted by the evidence regarding the symbolic nature of the kirpan, it is also disrespectful to believers in the Sikh religion and does not take into account Canadian values based on multiculturalism' (*ibid.*, para. 71).

But even Canada's multicultural policy, arguably one of the most accommodating constitutional regime presently on offer (South Africa, described as the 'rainbow nation', may also be classified in this category), has been obliged to set its boundaries. When it comes to clashes of religion and culture, arguments that move beyond requests for accommodation (or specific exemption from general laws) to attempts to advance alternative, extrajudicial moral or adjudicative orders appear to fall beyond the limits of tolerance (Hirschl and Shachar 2009). This is the dividing line where 'diversity as inclusion' ends and 'non-state law as competition' emerges, the latter often bringing with it the wrath of the state. Unlike the many diversity-as-inclusion cases requesting reasonable accommodation under the rule of law (as these terms are interpreted by the courts or legislatures of the secular state), arguments that pursue the claim that faith-based sources of authority and obligation are, or ought to be, completely unregulated and parallel or superior to the general rule of law are typically answered with ironclad resistance. This is evident in several Supreme Court of Canada's rulings such as *R v Jones* (1986) or *Bruker v Marcovitz* (2007), as well as in the Province of Ontario's decision, following an acrimonious public controversy, not to allow autonomous religious arbitration in matters of personal status law in the province.

2.7 Religious Jurisdictional Enclaves

This model is based on the selective accommodation of religion in certain areas of the law. The general law is secular, yet a degree of jurisdictional autonomy is granted to religious communities, primarily in matters of personal status and education. Core features of this arrangement originated from the Ottoman *millet* system of semi-autonomous jurisdictional enclaves for religious minorities. The concept was later adjusted to local circumstances by colonial empires, and then inherited by the post-colonial world. It is now prevalent in dozens of countries in Africa and Asia. Countries such as Kenya, India and Israel grant recognized religious or customary communities the jurisdictional autonomy to pursue their own traditions in several areas of law, most notably family law. Kenya, for example, has enacted a set of statutes to recognize the diversity of personal laws pertaining to different groups of citizens. India has long been entangled in a bitter debate concerning the scope and status of Muslim and Hindu religious personal laws, versus the individual rights and liberties protected by the Indian Constitution. Each religious community in Israel, including the Jewish community, has autonomous religious courts that hold jurisdiction over its respective members' marriage and divorce affairs. Religious affiliation, conversion and the provision of religious services are controlled by statutory religious bodies, whose decisions must comply with general principles of administrative and constitutional law.

The *religious jurisdictional enclaves* model may be based on spatial/regional boundaries (e.g. federalism), as is the case in Nigeria. The Constitution of Nigeria (1999) establishes it as a secular state with constitutionally enshrined freedom of religion. At the same time, the constitution allows sub-national units to grant additional jurisdiction to their local courts. This has been drawn upon by twelve predominantly Muslim northern states to expand the substantive jurisdictional boundaries of their Shari'a tribunals. Unlike their counterparts in the liberal-democratic world that tend to deal with matters of free expression or establishment of religion, constitutional courts operating under this model (e.g. the Supreme Court of India, the Supreme Court of Israel or Malaysia's Federal Court) are often preoccupied with determining the scope of substantive jurisdictional autonomy granted to religious tribunals. One of the perennial bones of contention in the Indian context, to pick one example, is the struggle between advocates of universal secularism (and by extension, the adoption of a uniform civil code) and proponents of the status quo, in which religious minorities, most notably Muslims, enjoy certain jurisdictional autonomy in matters of personal status, primarily marriage and divorce. Section 44 of the Indian constitution states that, 'The State shall endeavour to secure for the citizens a uniform civil code throughout the territory of India'. However, for a host of political reasons, not least the pressure to preserve the status quo of religious jurisdictional enclaves, little has been done in practice to enact such a uniform law. At the more abstract level, the tension between these competing visions of secularism has taken the form of a clash between group rights and the individual rights of potentially vulnerable group members, for example, women.

The *Shah Bano* saga is a good illustration. It involved an elderly Muslim woman who was divorced by her husband of forty-three years through the Muslim practice of *talaq*, which allows a husband to effect a unilateral, immediate divorce. However, lacking the resources to support herself and her five children, Shah Bano sought maintenance payments in the courts. Under Muslim personal law, Shah Bano's ex-husband was only obligated to pay her a small sum of maintenance money during the three months after the divorce, known as the period of *iddat*. Section 125 of the Code of Criminal Procedure stipulates that a husband may be ordered to pay maintenance to his wife or ex-wife if she is unable to maintain herself. However, according to Section 127 of the same law, these maintenance payments are to be reassessed by the court where the woman has received the sum due to her under the personal law.

In its famous ruling in *Mohammed Ahmad Khan v Shah Bano Begum*, the Supreme Court of India held that the state-defined statutory right of a neglected wife to maintenance stood regardless of the personal law applicable to the parties. In other words, individual rights and gender equality norms are more fundamental than India's longstanding practice of Muslim self-jurisdiction in personal status matters. The Court held that the right to maintenance under Section 125 was a secular legal right that could be 'exercised irrespective of the personal law of the parties', and that 'section 125 overrides the personal law, if there is any conflict between the two'. It also rejected the husband's argument that Section 127 was automatically satisfied by his payment of a dowry (*mahr*).

Traditionalist representatives of the Muslim community considered this to be proof of Hindu homogenizing trends that threatened to weaken Muslim identity. India's Parliament, led by Rajiv Gandhi's Congress Party, bowed to massive political pressure by conservative Muslims and overruled the Indian Supreme Court's decision in *Shah Bano* by passing the Muslim Women's (Protection of Rights of Divorce) Act. Despite its reassuring title, this new bill undid the court's ruling by removing the rights of Muslim women to appeal to state courts for post-divorce maintenance payments. It also exempted Muslim ex-husbands from other post-divorce obligations. So harsh was the Muslim reaction to *Shah Bano* that notable commentators see it as one of the reasons for the subsequent ascent of right-wing Hindu politicians. The Muslim Women's Act served to agitate many Hindus and galvanize support for the Hindu right-wing, which accused the Congress Party of compromising the principles of secularism in order to appease Islamic fundamentalists and get Muslim votes (Sathe 2003, 192). Some commentators also tie the ruling to the volatile public atmosphere that led to the notorious destruction of the historic Babri mosque by Hindu militants at a disputed religious site in the city of Ayodhya in 1992, and the spate of sectarian violence that followed (see Jacobsohn 2003, 106). Thus, whereas the Court has been effective at stoking significant public controversy concerning personal laws, its secularist jurisprudence on the matter has been quite counterproductive in achieving its declared goals of a uniform civil code and national integration.

In 2001, the court returned to the issue of personal status laws in *Danial Latifi v Union of India*. Here, the abovementioned Muslim Women's Act was challenged on various constitutional grounds, including the violation of Article 14 (equality) and Article 15 (non-discrimination) of the Constitution, as well as violating the basic constitutional feature of secularism. The court upheld the constitutionality of the Act, but did so through a broad, liberal construction of the Act's requirement that the husband make a 'reasonable and fair provision and maintenance within the period of iddat'. The Court commented that if the statute only authorized maintenance for three months, this would appear to violate the constitutional rights provisions on equality and discrimination. However, applying the constitutional avoidance canon (an interpretive device of reading legislation such that it complies with the Constitution), the Court construed the statute to authorize maintenance orders for 'reasonable and fair' sums that may provide support for the divorced wife for much longer than just the three-month period of *iddat*, so long as the payment itself is made during the period of *iddat*.

This ruling, although contrary to the common understanding of the Act's purpose, followed the actions of lower courts at the state level, which had already been interpreting the statute in this fashion and awarding relatively generous lump-sum maintenance payments to divorced Muslim women. Thus, the *Latifi* ruling used creative statutory interpretation to dodge constitutional controversy, while still preserving judicial discretion in determining the size of maintenance awards based on the facts of each case. This strategy suggests that the Court understood the not-so-subtle message sent by the public outcry and legislative response in the wake of *Shah Bano*. Its ruling in *Danial Latifi* was less ambitious and notably more moderate and diplomatic than its original ruling in *Shah Bano*.

Similar tensions between a quest for uniformity, equality and modernization on the one hand, and accommodation of group-based religious difference and jurisdictional autonomy on the other, is evident in virtually all countries where the religious jurisdictional enclaves model is in place. In Israel, to pick another example, no unified civil law applies to all citizens in matters of marriage and divorce. Instead, for various political and historical reasons (the roots of contemporary Israeli family law go back as far as the Ottoman Empire's pre-modern *millet* system), the courts of the different religious communities hold exclusive jurisdiction over marriage, divorce and directly associated personal status matters (see generally Scolnicov 2006). A number of other personal status matters may be adjudicated through the rabbinical court system (controlled by Orthodox Judaism), if the involved parties consent to such extended jurisdiction. Muslim, Christian and Druze courts also have exclusive jurisdiction over the personal status affairs of their respective communities.

Since the mid-1990s, the Supreme Court of Israel has gradually been attempting to limit the authority exercised by religious courts. The most important judgment regarding these matters was rendered in 1995 in the *Bavli* case. In this ruling, the Supreme Court held that *all* religious tribunals, including the Great Rabbinical Court, are statutory bodies established by law and funded by the state; in principle, their judgments are thus subject to review by the Supreme Court. While the Court recognized the special jurisdictional mandate awarded to Jewish, Muslim, Christian and Druze courts by the legislature, it nevertheless asserted its power to impose constitutional norms upon their exercise of authority. Rabbinical court officials have responded by publicly asserting their resistance to the idea that the Supreme Court, as a secular entity, possesses the authority to review their adjudication, which rests on religious law. Some have gone so far as to declare their intention to ignore the Court's ruling in *Bavli*, which they perceive as an illegitimate intrusion into their exclusive jurisdictional sphere. The Supreme Court was not impressed. Based on its landmark decision in *Bavli*, the Court went on to overturn at least two dozen other Rabbinical Court and Shari'a Court rulings for not conforming with general principles of Israel's constitutional and administrative law, including gender equality, reasonableness, proportionality, natural justice and procedural fairness.[3]

2.8 Strong Establishment – Religion as a Constitutionally Enshrined Source of Legislation

Here, the entire legal and constitutional system is based on an inherently dual commitment to religious fundamentals and constitutional principles, or a bi-polar system of constitutional *and* sacred texts and authority. This model comes close to what I have termed elsewhere *constitutional theocracy* (Hirschl 2010). The 'ideal' version of this model can be summarized by outlining four main cumulative elements: (1) the presence of a single religion or religious denomination that is formally endorsed by the state, akin to a 'state religion'; (2) the constitutional enshrining of the religion, its texts, directives and interpretations as *a* or *the* main source of legislation and judicial interpretation of laws – essentially, laws may not infringe upon injunctions of the state-endorsed religion; (3) a nexus of religious bodies and tribunals that often not only carry tremendous symbolic weight, but are also granted official jurisdictional status on either regional or substantive bases, and which operate in lieu of, or in an uneasy tandem with, a civil court system; and (4) adherence to some or all core elements of modern constitutionalism, including the formal distinction between political authority and religious authority, qualified protection of religious freedoms for minorities, and the existence of some form of active judicial review. Most importantly, their jurisdictional autonomy notwithstanding, some key aspects of religious tribunals' jurisprudence are subject to constitutional review by apex courts, often state-created and staffed.

The 1979 Islamic revolution in Iran established a paradigmatic example of constitutional theocracy. The preamble of the 1979 Islamic Republic of Iran's Constitution enshrines the Shari'a as the supreme law – superior even to the Constitution itself. Articles 2 and 3 declare that authority for sovereignty and legislation has a divine provenance (from the Shari'a) and that the leadership of the clergy is a principle of faith. According to Article 6, the administration of the state is to be conducted by the wider population: the general public participates in the election of the President, the Majlis representatives (members of parliament) and municipality councils. Article 8 further entrenches principles of popular participation in deciding political, economic and social issues. Most notably, Iran has seen the emergence of the Guardian Council – a *de facto* constitutional court armed with mandatory constitutional preview powers and composed of six mullahs appointed by the Supreme Leader – and six jurists proposed by the head of the judicial system of Iran and voted in by the Majlis. The Supreme Leader has the power to dismiss the religious members of the Guardian Council, but not its jurist members (Article 91). At the same time, Iran's constitutional regime combines religious supremacy, pragmatist institutional innovations (e.g. Ayatollah Khomeini's 1989 introduction of the Regime's Discernment Expediency Council to serve as the final arbiter between the generally more progressive Consultative Assembly and the distinctly more conservative Guardian Council), alongside carried-over legacies of the 1906 Imperial Constitution, primarily with respect to the notion of popular sovereignty, elected parliament and some separation of powers principles.

While Iran features what is arguably one of the strictest manifestations of strong establishment, several softer versions of this model have emerged, primarily in the Islamic world. From the early 1970s to 2000 alone, at least two dozen predominantly Muslim countries, from Egypt to Pakistan, declared the Shari'a 'a' or 'the' source of legislation (Arjomand 2007, 123). These countries evince to principles of human rights, constitutional law and popular sovereignty. The more recent constitutions of Afghanistan (2004) and Iraq (2005) reflect this softer version of the *strong establishment* model. In Egypt, for example, the criminal penal code is largely non-religious, as are numerous economic, property and investment rules. The 1971 constitution preserved Egypt's socialist legacy and, at the same time, stated that Shari'a was *a* primary source of legislation in Egypt. Judicial review was introduced in 1979. In 1980, Article 2 of the Egyptian Constitution was amended so as to establish principles of Islamic jurisprudence (the Shari'a) as *the* (not *a*) primary source of legislation in Egypt. For nearly thirty years now, the Egyptian political and constitutional order, and consequently Egypt's courts, most notably Egypt's Supreme Constitutional Court, have been grappling with the contested status and role of Shari'a as a potentially determinative source of authority in an otherwise 'strong state' with a historically power-ful executive branch. To address this question in a moderate way, the Court developed a complex, innovative interpretive matrix of religious directives – the first of its kind by a non-religious tribunal. It departed from the ancient traditions of the *fiqh* (Islamic jurispru-dence or the cumulative knowledge/science of studying the Shari'a) schools, and has instead developed a flexible, modernist approach to interpretation that distinguishes between 'unalterable and universally binding principles, and malleable applications of those principles' (see Brown 1999). Legislation that contravenes a strict, unalterable prin-ciple recognized as such by all interpretive schools is declared unconstitutional and void, while at the same time, *ijtihad* (contemplation or external interpretation) is permitted in cases of textual lacunae, where the pertinent rules are vague, open-ended, or where no consensus exists even within religious jurisprudence. Furthermore, the government has been given broad legislative discretion in policy areas where the Shari'a is found to provide unclear or multiple answers, provided that the legislative outcome does not contravene the general spirit of the Shari'a (Brown 1999).

Another variation on the *strong establishment model* is essentially a mirror image of the religious jurisdictional enclaves discussed earlier. Here, most of the law is religious; however, certain areas of the law, such as economic law or certain aspects of gender equal-ity, are 'carved out' and insulated from influence by religious law. An interesting case in point is Saudi Arabia, arguably one of the countries whose legal system comes the closest to being fully based on *fiqh* (Islamic jurisprudence). Article 1 of the Saudi Basic Law (1993) reads: 'The Kingdom of Saudi Arabia is a sovereign Arab Islamic state with Islam as its religion; God's Book and the Sunnah of His Prophet, God's prayers and peace be upon him, are its constitution'. Article 23 establishes the state's duty to advance Islam: 'The state protects Islam; it implements its Shari'a; it orders people to do right and shun evil; it fulfills the duty regarding God's call'. At the same time, Chapter 4 of the Basic Law (titled: Economic Principles) protects private property, provides a guarantee against the confiscation of assets, and suggests that 'economic and social development is to be achieved according to a just and scientific plan'. Moreover, whereas Saudi courts apply Shari'a in all matters of civil, criminal or personal status, Article 232 of a 1965 Royal Decree provides for the establishment of a commission for the settlement of all commer-cial disputes. Although judges of the ordinary courts are usually appointed by the Ministry of Justice from among graduates of recognized Shari'a law colleges, members of the commission for the settlement of disputes are appointed by the Ministry of Trade. In other words, Saudi Arabia has effectively exempted the entire finance, banking and corporate capital sectors from application of Shari'a rules. Softer examples of this model are common in the Islamic world, from Qatar or the United Arab Emirates to exotic destinations such as the Maldives or Comoros in the Indian Ocean. In short, religion has made a major come-back over the last few decades, and is now a *de facto* and often *de jure* pillar of collective identity, national meta-narratives and constitutional law in numerous predominantly Muslim countries in Asia, Africa and the Middle East. The strong establishment model is back in vogue in these places, albeit subject to various constitutional and jurisprudential ingenuity aimed at mitigating the tensions between religious directives and modern-life necessities, worldviews and interests.

3   CONCLUSION

Expanding our horizons comparatively reveals more diversity than often meets the eye with respect to constitutional models for arranging religion and state relations worldwide. The dichotomous view of separation in the West versus entanglement of religion and state elsewhere is rather unrefined. In reality, several prototypical models exist, ranging from atheism or assertive forms of secularism to constitutional enshrinement of religion as a state religion and as a main source of legislation. Even within the separationist model – arguably the most common worldwide – considerable variance exists between secularism as a form of state 'religion' (e.g. France), state neutrality toward religion (e.g. the United States), weak establishment (e.g. Germany), and accommodation, or even celebration, of religious difference (e.g. Canada or South Africa). In other settings, the relationship between state and religion is even more complex, with constitutional jurisprudence dealing with either a legacy of religion-infused morality (e.g. Ireland), enclaves of religion-based jurisdictional autonomy (e.g. India, Israel) or strong establishment of religion (e.g. so-called 'Islamic constitutionalism').

Obviously, there is considerable variance within, let alone among, these prototypical or 'ideal' models; each comes in different shapes, forms and sizes, with local nuances and idiosyncrasies abounding. This variance is often rooted in distinctive political legacies, differences in constitutional structures and aspirations, dissimilarities in historical inheritances and formative experiences, as well as non-trivial differences in value systems and foundational national meta-narratives. These differences often feed and shape the specific ways in which the tension between religion and constitutional governance manifests itself. But these differences notwithstanding, a common motif in today's post-secularist age seems to be the increasing reliance worldwide on constitutional law and courts to contain, tame and limit the spread and impact of religion-induced policies. Consequently, constitutional courts operating under each and all of these models have become key mediators between the calls of faith and the interests of the modern state.

Unlike the conventional image of a 'clash of civilizations' or the 'west' and the 'rest', there is actually a strong echo of religion in each and all of these models. In fact, all constitutions, every single one of them – from France to Iran and anywhere in between – address the issue of religion head on. Some constitutions despise it, others embrace or even defer to it, and yet others are agnostic but are willing to accommodate certain aspects of it. But not a single constitution abstains, overlooks or remains otherwise silent with respect to religion. With the exception of the concrete organizing principles and prerogatives of the polity's governing institutions, the only substantive domain addressed by all modern constitutions is religion. What could be a more telling illustration of religion's omnipresence in today's world, or a stronger testament to constitutionalism's existential fear of religion?

NOTES

1. Comprehensive and resourceful analyses of these cases is provided in Kent Greenawalt (2009a; 2009b).
2. Para. 86.
3. A similar logic served as a basis for the newly established UKSC's ruling in *R (E) v Governing Body of JFS School* [2009] UKSC 15 [UK].

REFERENCES

Ahdar, Rex and Ian Leigh (2005), *Religious Freedom in the Liberal State*, Oxford University Press.
Arjomand, Said A. (2007), 'Islamic Constitutionalism', *Annual Review of Law and Society*, 3, 115–40.
Brown, Nathan J. (1999), 'Islamic Constitutionalism in Theory and Practice', in Eugene Cortan and Adel Omar Sherif (eds.), *Democracy, the Rule of Law and Islam*, Kluwer Law International.
Greenawalt, Kent (2009a), *Religion and the Constitution: Volume I: Free Exercise and Fairness*, Princeton University Press.
Greenawalt, Kent (2009b), *Religion and the Constitution: Volume II: Establishment and Fairness*, Princeton University Press.
Hirschl, Ran (2010), *Constitutional Theocracy*, Harvard University Press.
Hirschl, Ran and Ayelet Shachar (2009), 'The New Wall of Separation: Permitting Diversity, Restricting Competition', *Cardozo Law Review*, 30, 2535–60.
Jacobsohn, Gary J. (2003), *The Wheel of Law: India's Secularism in Comparative Constitutional Context*, Princeton University Press.
Jacobsohn, Gary J. (2010), 'The Disharmonic Constitution', in Stephen Macedo and Jeffrey Tulis (eds.), *The Limits of Constitutional Democracy*, Princeton University Press.
Kommers, Donald (1997), *The Constitutional Jurisprudence of the Federal Republic of Germany*, Duke University Press.
Kuru, Ahmet T. (2009), *Secularism and State Policies toward Religion: The United States, France, and Turkey*, Cambridge University Press.
Kymlicka, Will (1995), *Multicultural Citizenship: A Liberal Theory of Minority Rights*, Oxford University Press.
Lazare, Daniel (1998), 'America the Undemocratic', *New Left Review*, 232, 3–40.
Levinson, Sanford (1988), *Constitutional Faith*, Princeton University Press.
Pelikan, Jaroslav (2004), *Interpreting the Bible & the Constitution*, Yale University Press.
Rotunda, Ronald D. and John E. Nowak (2008), *Treatise on Constitutional Law: Substance and Procedure*, 4th edition, Vol. 5, West Group.
Ryder, Bruce (2008), 'The Canadian Conception of Equal Religious Citizenship', in Richard Moon (ed.), *Law and Religious Pluralism in Canada*, UBC Press.
Sathe, S.P. (2003), *Judicial Activism in India: Transgressing Borders and Enforcing Limits*, Oxford University Press.
Scolnicov, Anat (2006), 'Religious Law, Religious Courts and Human Rights within Israeli Constitutional Structure', *International Journal of Constitutional Law*, 4, 732–40.

Cases

AG v X (1992) IESC 1; (1992) 1 IR 1 (March 5, 1992) (commonly known as the 'X Case') [Ireland].
Adler v Ontario [1996] 3 SCR 609 [Canada].
Agostini v Felton, 521 US 203 (1997).
Bavli v The Grand Rabbinical Court, HCJ 1000/92, 48(2) PD 6 (1996) [Israel].
Board of Education of Kiryas Joel Village School District v Grumet, 512 US 687 (1994).
Bob Jones University v United States, 461 US 574 (1983).
Bruker v Marcovitz [2007] 3 SCR 607 [Canada].
Church of Lukumi Babalu Aye, Inc. v Hialeah, 508 US 520 (1993).
City of Boerne v Flores, 521 US 507 (1997).
Classroom Crucifix Case, BVerfGE 93, 1 1 BvR 1087/91 (1995) [Germany].
Corporation of the Presiding Bishop of the Church of Jesus Christ of Latter-Day Saints v Amos, 483 US 327 (1987).
Danial Latifi v Union of India, AIR 2001 SC 3958 [India].
Décision du Conseil D'Etat No. 286798 (*Faiza M.* case; 2008) [France].
Employment Division, Dept. of Human Resources v Smith (Smith II), 494 US 872 (1990).
Gillette v United States, 401 US 437 (1971).
Goldman v Weinberger, 475 US 503 (1986).
Gonzales v O Centro Espirita Beneficente Uniao do Vegetal, 546 US 418 (2006).
Good News Club v Milford Central School, 533 US 98 (2001).
Lamb's Chapel v Center Moriches Union Free School District, 508 US 384 (1993).
Lautsi v Italy, ECtHR, 18 March 2011, Application No. 30814/06.
Lee v Weisman, 505 US 577 (1992).
Lemon v Kurtzman, 403 US 602 (1971).
Leyla Sahin v Turkey, ECtHR, 10 November 2005, Application No. 44774/98.

Ludin Case, BverfG, 2 BvR 1436/02 (2003) [Germany].
Mohammed Ahmed Khan v Shah Bano Begum, AIR 1985 SC 985 [India].
Multani v Commission scolaire Marguerite-Bourgeoys [2006] 1 SCR 256 [Canada].
R. v Big M Drug Mart Ltd. [1985] 1 SCR 295 [Canada].
R. v Edwards Books and Art Ltd. [1986] 2 SCR 713 [Canada].
R. v Jones [1986] 2 SCR 284 [Canada].
R (Begum) v Headteacher and Governors of Denbigh High School [2006] UKHL 15 (*Shabina Begum* case) [UK].
R (E) v Governing Body of JFS School [2009] UKSC 15 [UK]
Refah Partisi (The Welfare Party) and Others v Turkey, 13 February, 2003, Application No. 00041340/98; 00041342/98; 00041343/98; 00041344/98 [ECtHR].
Santa Fe Independent School District v Doe, 530 US 290 (2000).
Swaggart Ministries v Board of Equalization, 493 US 378 (1990).
Syndicat Northcrest v Amselem [2004] 2 SCR 551 [Canada].
TCC Decision 1/1998 (Welfare [Refah] Party Dissolution case), 16 January 1998 [Turkey].
TCC Decision 57/2001 (Virtue [Fazilet] Party Dissolution case), 21 June 2001 [Turkey].
Torasco v Watkins, 367 US 488 (1961).
United States v Seeger, 380 US 163 (1965).
Wisconsin v Yoder, 406 US 205 (1963).
Zelman v Simmons-Harris, 536 US 639 (2002).

24. Autonomy, dignity and abortion

Donald P. Kommers*

I INTRODUCTION

Autonomy and dignity are associated concepts variously invoked to justify a woman's decision to procure an abortion as well as to support legal measures to protect unborn life. Both values are deeply rooted in constitutional democracies devoted to the protection of individual liberty and the promotion of justice. Indeed, as the rights of speech, privacy and association demonstrate, they are multi-faceted concepts that overlap and collide in the fundamental rights jurisprudence of modern constitutional courts. Especially is this so on abortion. In the following comparative analysis of abortion law in Ireland, Germany and the United States, we shall find that each country has defined these values differently. Depending on how a society – or law – views unborn life, the two values often clash. As the constitutional jurisprudence of the United States, Germany and Ireland show, autonomy and dignity spar with one another when a woman's 'right' to reproductive freedom clashes with the 'right' to life of the unborn.[1] In this chapter, I examine how three constitutional democracies have sought to balance and define the values of dignity and autonomy in settling or reconciling the competing claims of pro-choice and pro-life interests. Accordingly, the analysis below is mainly descriptive, although its normative implications will merit some attention in the concluding section of this chapter.

Why have I chosen to focus on Ireland, Germany and the United States? Economy is one reason. Limiting this chapter to three representative jurisdictions allows for a more careful examination of the factual and normative assumptions on which alternative abortion policies are based. Another reason is their widely differing abortion policies. Among contemporary liberal democracies, Ireland and the United States represent respectively the most restrictive and permissive states, while Germany falls roughly between these polarities. Each country's written constitution, structure of basic rights, scope of judicial review and cultural, religious and political history have doubtlessly influenced its abortion regulations. Yet each country is a secular democracy rooted in the principle of popular sovereignty, each subscribes to the rule of law, each has an independent judiciary, each recognizes the universality of human dignity and each belongs to the family of nations seeking to anchor common or shared values in its basic laws. Why similar constitutional democracies produce widely different abortion policies is a question the comparative enterprise seeks to answer. In addition, and fortuitously, in all three countries, we are also dealing with contemporaneous bodies of law authored by judges fully aware of each other's judicial work-product. Finally, each country has experienced accelerated social change, for each has been faced with similar pressures to repeal, modify or retain its traditional abortion laws.

This chapter is divided into five sections. Sections 2, 3 and 4 are devoted respectively to the constitutional abortion policies of the three countries. These sections focus on specified articles and clauses in the three constitutional charters, along with the abortion jurisprudence arising out of these provisions. At a deeper level, I try to relate the abortion policies of the three countries to the central values – or conceptions of the polity – underlying their separate constitutional orders. For the United States, Germany and Ireland, these central values or conceptions may be described roughly as liberal individualism, communal liberalism and integral communalism. Each projects a different vision of the relationship between dignity and autonomy. These public value systems are not fixed or unchangeable categories. They are more of the order of predispositions, and each system is potentially open to the influence of the other. As these sections show, the legal status of abortion in the three countries remains fluid, just as their constitutional texts remain susceptible to differing interpretations of autonomy and dignity. Section 5, finally, attempts to assess the abortion policies of the three democracies in the light of each other and to explore the possibility of bridging their existing differences.

2   IRELAND

Abortion in Ireland is prohibited by law except when necessary to avoid a 'real and substantial risk' to the life of the mother. The 'substantial risk' exception to Ireland's total ban on abortion resulted from the highly publicized and controversial *X Case* of 1992.[2] The Supreme Court decided the *X Case* under the Irish Constitution of 1937, the charter that eliminated all traces of allegiance to Great Britain and affirmed Ireland's status as a modern constitutional democracy. It should be noted that the Constitution is unabashedly Catholic-Christian in several of its provisions. The Preamble, for instance, creates a constitutional polity in 'the name of the most Holy Trinity' and acknowledges its 'obligations to our Divine Lord, Jesus Christ', just as a related provision on religious freedom recognizes the 'homage of public worship [that] is due to Almighty God' (Article 44.1). Although in its most recent version the Constitution declines to privilege any particular religious denomination and prohibits discrimination on religious grounds, it acknowledges God as the ultimate source of all authority (Article 6.1).[3]

Other provisions equally reflect the tradition of Catholic social thought. These include the fundamental rights articles on marriage and the family,[4] frequent references to the state as 'guardian of the common good', and related clauses calling for a political and social order based on 'prudence, justice, and charity'.[5] Relatedly, the state is obligated constitutionally to safeguard 'with especial care the weaker sections of the community' so that, in the words of the Preamble, 'the dignity and freedom of the individual may be assured'.[6] Altogether, these provisions come close to identifying the public good with the promotion of a virtuous citizenry, just as they envision the polity as an integrated moral community undergirded by a constitutionalism of integral communalism.[7]

When originally adopted, Ireland's Constitution contained no reference to unborn life, although Article 40.3.2 obliged the state 'as far as practicable … to respect … and vindicate the life [and] person … of every citizen'. In addition, in 1953, Ireland signed on to the European Convention on Human Rights which committed member States to enact laws for the protection of '[e]veryone's right to life' (Article 2) and to defend and respect the right to 'private and family life' (Article 8). The Convention permitted limitations on private and family life but only when prescribed by law, justified as a democratic necessity and enacted, *inter alia*, 'for the protection of health or morals'.[8] These and related provisions of the Irish

Constitution were construed to protect unborn life. In 1983, however, pro-life groups secured the adoption, in a referendum, of an anti-abortion amendment to the Constitution.[9] This, the Eighth Amendment, prevailed against the backdrop of abortion rulings in the United States (1973) and Germany (1975). *Roe v Wade* in particular triggered fears in Ireland that the Supreme Court might interpret the Constitution as including a right to abortion.

Accordingly, the Eighth Amendment (Article 40.3.3) declares: 'The State acknowledges the right to life of the unborn and, with due regard to the equal right of the mother, guarantees in its laws to respect, and, as far as practicable, by its laws to defend and vindicate that right'.[10] But even these clauses were rife with ambiguity; they could be construed to ban abortion altogether or, like the policies of most other countries, to permit abortion in the presence of specified conditions or to provide for term solutions by allowing elective abortions early on but punishing them after a specified period.[11] In addition, the Amendment fails to specify when unborn life begins. Many years later, in 2009, in a landmark case involving whether a frozen embryo constituted 'unborn life' within the meaning of Article 40.3.3, the Court held that it applied only to unborn life within the womb but that it was up to the legislature to specify when life begins.[12] We need to be reminded, finally, that the Amendment creates no new right; it simply acknowledges a pre-existing one.

The Eighth Amendment touched off a second round of legal developments centering on a sweeping injunction restraining the dissemination of information to pregnant women concerning abortion facilities abroad. The constitutional reasoning of the Supreme Court in support of the injunction helped to fortify the Constitution's integral communalism. By imposing upon the state the duty 'to defend and vindicate' by its laws 'the right to life of the unborn', Article 40.3.3 seems to have sanctioned the view that speech and travel employed to promote the right to abortion should be limited by law, especially when seen in tandem with the Preamble's principle of *human* dignity. In short, as Germany's Federal Constitutional Court would say of the Basic Law, the Constitution is a unified whole; one core value cannot be interpreted to diminish the importance of another. Similarly, if the state's task is to promote dignity and safeguard the *commons* – particularly respect for the dignity of life and family – a person's autonomy will be correspondingly limited.[13] From this perspective, dignity is not inextricably linked, as in the United States, to a liberal-individualist conception of the human person or a minimalist conception of the state's responsibility.

In 1992, the European Court of Human Rights (ECHR) held that the injunction against abortion counseling was an unjustified interference with the free speech provisions of the European Convention on Human Rights.[14] Observing that Irish law imposed no express limits on any discussion of abortion or on the right of women to travel abroad to obtain one, the ECHR declared that the measure nevertheless constituted a disproportionate means to achieve an otherwise legitimate end.[15] The ECHR carefully avoided saying whether the ban on abortion as such would implicate a woman's right to privacy or an unborn child's right to life. In any event, Ireland's reaction to the decision was the passage of the Thirteenth and Fourteenth Amendments guaranteeing respectively the right to *travel* abroad and to obtain *information* 'relating to services lawfully available in another state'.[16] In 1995, finally, pursuant to these amendments, the Oireachtas passed the Pregnancy Services Act (PSA) authorizing doctors and other counselors to inform pregnant women of abortion services available abroad.[17]

Speaking of the ECHR, and before moving on to Ireland's abortion case law, it should be noted that in November 2009 the ECHR accepted a case posing a direct challenge to Ireland's abortion law. The case was filed by three women (A, B and C) who sought abortions abroad and whose pregnancies allegedly threatened their health and well-being. The *X Case*, as noted, allowed abortion only where the mother's life was at risk, but the state has not laid down guidelines for the general rule's implementation. Yet 683 abortions were carried out legally in Ireland in 2008. (The reported figures for 2007 and 2006 were 628 and 543.)[18] It would be difficult at this writing to predict the case's outcome, but the likely result is a narrowly framed decision requiring the state to enshrine its abortion policy in precise – and unpopular – legislation.

The Irish Supreme Court's abortion jurisprudence arose out of a social context highly regulative of marriage and procreation. The applicable case law begins with the *Ryan* and *McGee Cases* of 1965 and 1973 respectively.[19] *Ryan* is important for the Supreme Court's acceptance of the High Court's view that the 'personal rights' protected by the Constitution's Article 40.3.1 include implied rights; indeed, and to wit, all those rights 'which flow from the Christian and democratic character of the State'.[20] No less than the Papal Encyclical *Pacem in Terris* was cited in defense of the proposition that 'every man has the right to life ... and to the means ... necessary ... for the proper development of life'. In *McGee*, the Supreme Court added marital privacy to its list of unspecified rights antecedent to positive law, unanimously holding that marital privacy covers the right to *use* contraceptives within the marital relationship.[21] Abortion, however, was another matter. Bristling with the language of natural rights and the common good – important elements of Ireland's integral communalism – *McGee's* lead opinion leaves no doubt that the right to life is a natural right and that any action by a married couple or the state to limit family size 'by endangering or destroying human life [is] an offense against the common good [and] the guaranteed personal rights of the human life in question'.[22]

In Ireland, *G v An Bord Uchtala* (1980) constituted the prelude to the Supreme Court's defense of unborn life, much as *Griswold v Connecticut* (1965) in the United States provided a contrasting overture to *Roe v Wade*. Three years prior to the 'Unborn Life' amendment, *An Bord* declared that the state's duty under Article 40.3.2 to 'vindicate the life ... of every citizen' includes 'the right to be guarded against all threats directed to its existence *before* and after birth' (emphasis added). Indeed, said the Court, 'the child's natural right to life and all that flows from that right are independent of any right of the parent as such'.[23] The image of the human family that emerges from these remarks – and the Court's jurisprudence generally – is once again that of a moral community united by the 'cardinal' virtues of justice, prudence and charity. These virtues, along with the related principles of dignity and autonomy, inhabit Ireland's domain of *common good* reasoning whose core ingredient resides in its recognition of human sociality and connectedness. *McGee* draws on no less than 'Aristotle and the Christian philosophers' to support the proposition that 'justice, prudence, and charity' must be invoked to moderate the rigors of positive law, a perspective advanced in the famous *X Case* of 1992.

In seeking to reconcile the right of the unborn child with the right to life of the mother in the *X Case*, the balance, the Court felt – with due regard to justice, prudence and charity – had to come down on the mother's side. As mentioned earlier, the *X Case* held that a pregnant woman is entitled to have an abortion in Ireland or abroad if her pregnancy presents 'a real and substantial risk' to her life. The constitutionally sanctioned virtues of 'prudence, justice, and charity' were invoked still again, this time to 'harmonize' the principles of dignity and autonomy implicit in the two main clauses of the Eighth Amendment, the first and second of which respectively acknowledge 'the right to life of the unborn' and 'due regard to the equal right to life of the mother'. Accordingly, wrote Chief Justice Finlay, 'the Court must … concern itself with the position of the mother within the family, with persons on whom she is dependent, [with persons] who are dependent on her and her interaction with other citizens and members of society in areas in which her activities occur'. Hence, the life of the unborn child can be terminated if necessary to avoid an 'immediate risk to the life of the mother'.

Since the *X Case*, abortion adjudication in Ireland has dealt largely with the counseling of abortion services outside of Ireland. Initially, the Supreme Court held that giving such information to pregnant women amounted to 'assistance in the destruction of the life of the unborn' in violation of the Eighth Amendment.[24] As noted earlier, this situation changed with the ratification of the Thirteenth and Fourteenth Amendments, together with the subsequent passage of the PSA which President Robinson, pursuant to Article 26, referred to the Supreme Court for a decision on its constitutionality. *In re Article 26* sustained the statute, but the decision is also important because for the first time the Court rejected its earlier view that the Constitution was founded on natural law. The Court insisted that when it identifies rights 'superior and antecedent to positive law', it is engaged less in natural law reasoning than in an interpretative process rooted in the express constitutional values of justice, prudence and charity. In short, the Court advanced an Irish version of a 'living Constitution'.

Yet the Chief Justice once again repeated the oft-stated view that the right to life of the unborn was – and is – an implied personal right long before the Eighth Amendment gave it explicit protection. But he also noted that the 'travel' and 'information' rights protected by the Thirteenth and Fourteenth Amendments stand on their own bottom and do not *as such* undermine the right to unborn life. Accordingly, the Court upheld all the provisions of the PSA while rejecting arguments that its limits on the nature of the counseling offended the Constitution. The conditions imposed on the dissemination of abortion information, ruled the Court, 'does not constitute an unjust attack on the rights of the pregnant woman', any more than other aspects of the statute impinge on the rights of parents, husbands or other persons. The Court found that these limits 'represent a fair and reasonable balancing of the rights involved' and are fully consonant with *constitutional* justice.[25]

3   UNITED STATES

In the United States abortion policy is largely a matter of local or state law, whereas in Germany and Ireland the policy is laid down in national law. The statutory and constitutional provisions at issue in the American abortion controversy can be quickly summarized. The Texas statute nullified in *Roe v Wade* was typical of most state laws. The state's penal code made abortion a crime except for one 'procured or attempted by medical advice for the purpose of saving the life of the mother'. Georgia's statute, struck down in *Doe v Bolton* – companion case to *Roe* – was more permissive in that it contained provisions legalizing abortion if in the best clinical judgment of a licensed physician, an abortion is necessary to preserve a mother's health, to avoid the birth of a genetically defective fetus, or to stop a pregnancy resulting from forcible or statutory rape.[26] Also worth mentioning is the American Law Institute's Model Penal Code which distinguished between *unjustified* and *justifiable* abortion. An abortion was unjustified – and punishable – if purposely carried out to prevent a live birth before the 26th week of pregnancy. But like Georgia's statute, a justifiable abortion could be carried out by a licensed physician in the presence of serious medical, genetic or criminal indications. Any such procedure, however, would have to be performed in a licensed hospital and only after two physicians have certified in writing that they believe circumstances justify the abortion.[27]

In striking the Texas and Georgia statutes, the Supreme Court declared that the term *liberty* within the meaning of the Fourteenth Amendment – '[No state shall] deprive any person of life, liberty, or property without due process of law' – includes the right to privacy, an implied right the Court had seen fit to protect in a series of pre-1973 cases related to marital relations, procreation, family relations and child rearing.[28] Armed with these precedents, the Court declared in *Roe v Wade* that '[t]his right of privacy ... is broad enough to encompass a woman's decision whether or not to terminate her pregnancy'. The key precedent was *Griswold v Connecticut* (1965) in which the Court endorsed the *institutional* right of married persons to use contraceptives. But in 1972 the Court severed this right from its institutional base in marriage. 'If the right to privacy means anything,' said the Court, 'it is the right of the individual, married or single, to be free from unwarranted governmental intrusion into matters so fundamentally affecting a person as the decision whether to bear or beget a child.'[29] Although the *Roe* Court distinguished *Griswold* by noting that abortion 'is inherently different from marital intimacy' and that '[t]he pregnant woman cannot be isolated in her privacy', Justice Blackmun for the Court discovered in the due process liberty clause a *personal* interest in privacy that appeared to trump any countervailing social or common good claim.[30]

Roe was especially noteworthy for its division of pregnancy into trimesters with separate constitutional rules attached to each. In the first trimester, no compelling state interest could be constitutionally advanced to block a woman's decision to procure an abortion; in the second, the abortion *procedure* could be regulated to protect a woman's health but not to limit her freedom to choose; in the last three months, finally, and subsequent to viability, the state could lawfully proscribe abortion altogether, *if it wished*, in the interest of protecting *potential* human life except when necessary to preserve the pregnant woman's health. *Doe v Bolton*, however, advanced a capacious definition of 'health' that essentially overrode the nuances of *Roe's* trimester framework. *Doe* elevated the role of the physician by characterizing the abortion decision as a 'medical judgment' in furtherance of the woman's reproductive autonomy – virtually at any stage of pregnancy. In combination, *Roe* and *Doe* left little doubt that a woman's interest in procuring an abortion is an *individual* right of the highest order, one whose *fundamentality* under the Constitution could no longer be questioned.

The *fundamental* nature of the abortion right became indisputably clear in the years following *Roe* when the Court invalidated numerous abortion regulations whose constitutionality was yet to be assessed.[31] The laws invalided even included state-imposed standards of care on physicians when directed toward requiring them to preserve the life and health of a viable fetus.[32] If *Roe* itself left any doubt as to exactly how far the abortion liberty would extend, it became increasingly clear that it was evolving into an ideology of free choice cut off from any marital or other social context. Rejecting the Irish view of marriage and family as integrated moral units, the Court chiseled into the Constitution the near-absolute personal nature of the woman's right to choose. In short, government would be barred from any attempt to influence that choice. Unlike the integral communalism of Ireland's right-to-life jurisprudence, *Roe* and its immediate progeny endorsed the principle of choice maximization and the theory of liberal individualism that infuses so much of the Supreme Court's modern work-product in the field of personal rights and liberties. The Court spoke in the language of individual autonomy. The concept of dignity, which would play a central role in Germany's abortion jurisprudence, appeared to have little purchase in the American context.

Yet, as early as 1981, an increasingly fractured Court began to question several of *Roe* and *Doe's* assumptions, even noting – in a decision upholding a federal statute banning the use of Medicaid funds for non-therapeutic abortions – that there is a 'significant state interest' in protecting potential life 'throughout the course of a woman's pregnancy'.[33] For the first time too, the Court acknowledged that an attending physician may be ill-equipped to render certain kinds of advice on abortion.[34] *Doe's* image of the attending physician as a benevolent 'Dr. Welby' making a medical judgment 'in the light of all factors – physical, emotional, psychological, [and] familial' – was beginning to crumble in the Court's jurisprudence.[35] (As noted later on, Germany's Federal Constitutional Court would similarly reject the notion that a physician, particularly one with a financial interest in performing an abortion, could be an objective counselor.) In addition, the Supreme Court would eventually uphold several of the regulations it struck down in the years following *Roe*.[36]

Two watershed abortion cases handed down respectively in 1989 and 1992 constituted further modifications of the abortion liberty. Both cases were decided against the backdrop of strong pressures on and off the bench to overrule *Roe v Wade*.[37] In the benchmark case of *Webster v Reproductive Health Services*, the Court upheld statutory provisions it would have overturned earlier – among them a provision requiring doctors to conduct a viability test before performing an abortion – and ruled, *inter alia*, that the states may prefer childbirth over abortion in their public policies.[38] Three years later, in *Planned Parenthood of Southeastern Pennsylvania v Casey,* the Supreme Court was faced directly with whether *Roe* should be overruled, as the US government was urging. But in the famous joint opinion of Justices O'Connor, Kennedy and Souter, the Court reaffirmed *Roe's* 'essential holding', even as it recognized its 'basic flaws', one of which, the opinion noted, 'undervalues the State's interest in potential life'. *Casey* not only rejected *Roe's* trimester analytical framework, but also ruled that a state was now free to adopt measures to further its 'profound interest in potential life' *throughout* pregnancy so long as their purpose is not to place an 'undue burden' in the path of a woman seeking an abortion before her fetus attains viability. Accordingly, once again reversing earlier holdings, the Court upheld a parental consent requirement, a 24-hour waiting period, and measures to ensure that a woman's choice is informed by truthful information about the nature of the health risks attending abortion and childbirth.[39]

Casey, however, did strike down a spousal consent requirement. This regulation, said the Court, 'imposes an undue burden on the woman's ability to [choose]' and thus 'reaches into the heart of the liberty protected by the Due Process Clause'. The upshot of *Casey* is that no third party can be vested with control over the woman's decision. Her interest in procuring an abortion before viability remains a fundamental liberty and no less than a choice, under the joint opinion, 'central to personal dignity and autonomy' (clearly, in this case, 'dignity' construed as autonomy). In this respect too, *Casey* represents a major shift from *Roe's* foundation in privacy to an exclusive focus on liberty defined as autonomy. The opinion was emphatic about this, declaring that '[t]he controlling word in the case before us is "liberty" '.[40] A similar shift had taken place in the academic literature; several commentators, including the future Justice Ginsburg, insisted that equality is a more solid foundation than privacy on which to build a woman's liberty interest in procuring an abortion.[41]

A short detour is necessary here to note that *Casey's* approval of state bans on post-viability abortions did not prevent the Court from striking down, in *Stenberg v Carhart*

(2000), a state statute prohibiting 'partial birth abortions' unless necessary to save the mother's life.[42] The law was voided because it failed to include a 'health' exception, underscoring once again *Doe's* broad definition of health. Several years later, *Stenberg* was called into question by *Gonzales v Carhart* in which the Court sustained a similar *federal* statute.[43] The majority in *Gonzales*, however, seemed less interested in upholding the state's interest in banning partial-birth abortions than in preventing certain *moral* harms such as undermining respect for unborn life, damaging the integrity of the medical profession and coarsening society's moral sense. It is also of interest that Justice Kennedy, who co-authored *Casey's* joint opinion, defected to the majority in *Gonzales*. The two cases together – *Stenberg* and *Gonzales* – underscore a unique feature of American abortion jurisprudence: 'they illustrate the importance of the abortion issue to the process of nominating and confirming Supreme Court justices, and, by extension, the election of US presidents'.[44]

Finally, as the dissenting opinions in *Casey* explain, there is nothing axiomatic or inevitable about the joint opinion's definition of liberty. Yet a plausible textual basis exists for the opinion's focus on liberty construed as autonomy. Unlike Ireland's Constitution and Germany's Basic Law, the US Constitution does not proclaim human dignity as the foundation of the political order. It creates neither a *communal* democracy, as in Ireland, nor, as we shall see, a *social* democracy as in Germany. Rather, it creates a *liberal* democracy in which choice maximization disengages liberty from the morality of duty implicit in Irish constitutional values such as prudence, justice, and charity or, for that matter, the social discipline implicit in an older concept of *ordered* liberty (along with its communitarian overtones) that once prevailed in the Supreme Court's jurisprudence.[45] (The difference between liberty and *ordered* liberty is like the difference between activity and *ordered* activity.) But as Laurence M. Friedman argues in his incisive overview of American legal history, the United States has evolved – certainly since *Roe v Wade* – into a 'republic of choice' in which autonomous or anti-statist individualism prevails.[46]

4   GERMANY

Abortion reform in postwar Germany has passed through two stages, the first beginning with the rules laid down by the Federal Constitutional Court in 1975, the second with Germany's reunification in 1990. The Court's 1975 decision invalidated a recent West Germany statute legalizing abortion in the first 12 weeks of pregnancy, but only after the pregnant woman had conferred with a physician or registered counseling center. In East Germany, by contrast, abortion was permitted on demand in early pregnancy but regulated thereafter, as in West Germany. When Germany reunified, the Unification Treaty called for a revision of abortion policy to 'ensure better protection of unborn life and provide a better solution in conformity with the Constitution of conflict situations faced by pregnant women ... than is the case in either part of Germany at present'.[47] The treaty called for fresh legislation to be passed by 31 December 1992. The new all-German parliament worked long and hard to reconcile West Germany's more restrictive abortion policies with East Germany's more permissive one. The law emerging from this no less than grueling deliberative process was the subject of further constitutional litigation in 1993, one year after the US Supreme Court reconsidered aspects of American abortion policy set forth in *Roe v Wade*. In the German case too, the Constitutional Court would reconsider aspects of its 1975 ruling.

The punishment of abortion in Germany traces its origin to the Prussian Penal Code of 1851 and later appeared as the famous – or infamous – § 218 of Germany's Penal Code of 1871. The punishment was draconian. A pregnant woman who intentionally aborted her fetus could be sentenced to five years in a penitentiary, a provision that applied equally to any accessory to an abortion. In spite of numerous efforts after 1871, especially during the Weimar Republic, to reform and even to abolish § 218, abortion continued to be punished as a matter of principle unless the pregnancy resulted from an assault or was necessary to preserve the life or health of the mother. This is where the law stood before the passage of the Abortion Reform Act of 18 June 1974.[48] The reform of § 218, the result of a decade-long parliamentary struggle to moderate its penalties, was Germany's first major attempt substantially to liberalize the criminal law of abortion without at the same time abandoning protection of the unborn child. It took months of legislative give and take in early 1974 to win majority support for the reform measure. Supported by a coalition of Social and Free Democrats, the Abortion Reform Act legalized abortion in the first trimester of pregnancy if performed by a licensed physician after compulsory counseling and a short waiting period. Criminal penalties, however, would continue to apply beyond this stage except in the verifiable presence of serious moral, medical or genetic indications. A bill rejected by parliament would have included 'social hardship' among the indications warranting an early abortion. An abortion later than the third month of pregnancy was punishable by a fine or up to three years' imprisonment.

The ink on the new statute had barely dried when five *Länder* under Christian Democratic rule, together with 193 Christian Democratic members of the national parliament (*Bundestag*), challenged the Act's validity in an abstract judicial review proceeding before the Federal Constitutional Court. Germany's structure of judicial review is important for understanding the Court's decision. Under abstract review – one of several of the Court's jurisdictional categories – a *Land* government or a specified number of parliamentary members can challenge the constitutionality of a statute before it enters into force. No American-like case or controversy is required. The function of the Court on abstract review is not to vindicate the subjective or negative right of an individual complainant but rather 'objectively' to rule on the validity or invalidity of a statute's general provisions and thus to enforce the 'value decisions' of the constitutional order as a whole. The Basic Law incorporates what the Constitutional Court has often described as an 'objective order of values' crowned by the principle of human dignity. In the German theory of rights, every subjective right is informed by its objective value. A subjective right can be vindicated in a constitutional complaint against the state; an objective value, by contrast, imposes on the state a positive obligation to see that the value in question becomes an integral part of the general legal order.[49] This constitutionalism of positive obligation is a main line of division between German and American constitutional thinking.

Several provisions of the Basic Law (Germany's Constitution) were implicated in the first abortion case (*Abortion I*). The most important was the concept of human dignity, the crowning value, as just noted, that 'all state authority' under the Basic Law is bound 'to respect and protect' (Article 1 [1]). As the Constitution's highest objective value, dignity informs the meaning of all guaranteed rights, two of which came into play in the Court's holding, namely, the 'right to life and bodily integrity' and the right of 'every person' to 'the free development of his [or her] personality insofar as he [or she] does not violate the rights of others or offend against the constitutional order or the moral code' (Article 2). More indeterminate than the explicit protection of unborn life under the Irish Constitution, the Basic Law's provisions on dignity, life, bodily integrity and personality could easily be construed to authorize, as the dissenting opinion noted, the balance of subjective rights and objective values parliament sought to realize in the Abortion Reform Act. The reference to balancing implicates the related interpretive principle of 'concordance' (*Kondordanz*), which essentially means that competing rights and values are to be accommodated. In the integrated constitutional order created by the Basic Law, an objective value cannot fully negate another objective value. Instead, because both are constituent and objective components of the constitutional order, each must be reconciled or, to use the Court's terminology, 'optimized' to the extent possible, as the first abortion case exemplifies.

In its 6:2 opinion, the Constitutional Court invalidated the bulk of the reform statute. *Abortion I* contrasts sharply with *Roe v Wade*. It may be summarized as follows: first, the human dignity and right to life clauses of the Basic Law protect not only life developing within the womb; they also impose on the state a 'solemn obligation to protect and foster this life', one that has, according to the Court, 'an independent legal value' under the Basic Law. Second, and within the hierarchy of objective values the Court has ascribed to the Basic Law, the state's duty to protect unborn life outranks the mother's wishes as a matter of principle throughout the duration of pregnancy. Important in this connection are the subjective and objective aspects of dignity. The first implicates the dignity of the individual and his or her subjective rights, the second the dignity attached to life itself – its objectivity within the general system of bioethics – and the responsibility of the community to advance and protect unborn as well as post-natal life. In Germany's system of objective constitutional values, unborn life is an integral part of humanity, just as the human person is integrally relational by nature. As the Court has often remarked, the human person is not 'an isolated, sovereign individual'. Human beings are relational and thus dependent on the community's protection *before* and after birth, a communal orientation that understands a woman's 'choice' as conditioned by all sorts of social factors, including social responsibilities.

Third, and acknowledging the legislature's primary responsibility for protecting unborn life, the Court noted that parliament may select means other than punishment so long as the 'totality of measures' adopted to preserve unborn life 'corresponds to the importance of the legal value (namely life) to be guaranteed'. (In the absence of such measures, said the Court, criminal penalties must be restored.) Fourth, law must make unmistakably clear that abortion is a legal wrong. On this matter, the state cannot be neutral. (The Second Senate described abortion as 'an act of killing'.) Finally, out of regard for the principle of self-determination guaranteed to every person under the 'personality' clause of Article 2 and the moral autonomy it implies, the Court sanctioned the termination of a pregnancy without punishment in the face of a grave social reason that would force a woman to bear an extraordinary burden well beyond the normal stresses of childbirth. The Court thus saw fit to restore the 'social hardship' indication voted down by parliament.

Unlike the US Supreme Court, the German tribunal did not hesitate to define when life begins. Its reasoning was juridical. 'Life in the sense of the historical existence of a human individual', declared the Court, 'exists according to definite biological-physiological knowledge ... from the 14th day after conception'. Unsurprisingly, and unlike *Roe v Wade*, the Court made no reference to the relevancy of religion. In addition, the Second Senate described fetal growth as a continuous process of development incapable of any breakdown into 'stages of [unborn] life'. In one of the opinion's most notable features, and yet again in contrast to *Roe*, the Court declared that the state has a positive duty to protect unborn life from any and all persons who would interfere with it. For this reason, among others, the state must require pro-life counseling as a prerequisite to obtaining any abortion when and where permissible. As with its other rulings, the Court explained by reference to the Basic Law's 'life' and 'dignity' clauses: 'Human life', declared the Court, 'represents within the order of the Basic Law an ultimate value' and no less than 'the living foundation of human dignity and the prerequisite for all other fundamental rights'. In the Court's view, as in that of Ireland's Supreme Court, a woman's right to the 'free [autonomous] development' of her personality pales by comparison to the supreme value human dignity attaches to both pre- and post-natal human life.

Germany's constitutional abortion policy was destined to change, however, in the face of the country's reunification. The Unity Treaty required the change. It charged, as noted, the new all-German parliament to pass regulations to provide better protection for both pregnant woman and unborn life than currently in East or West Germany. Such regulations, according to the treaty, would include 'legally guaranteed entitlements for women', along with advice and support. The result was the Pregnancy and Family Assistance Act (PFAA) of 1992 permitting abortion within the first 12 weeks of pregnancy but only if performed by a licensed physician with the woman's consent after required counseling, certification, and a three-day waiting period.[50] The new change in the penal code simply declared that the interruption of pregnancy within this time frame is 'not illegal' (*nicht rechtswidrig*).[51] Modeled on the Abortion Reform Act invalidated by the Constitutional Court in *Abortion I*, PFAA was a hard-won compromise painfully worked out in the parliamentary trenches and against the backdrop of strong pressures from religious, feminist and eleemosynary groups. The new all-German law – a counseling model that incorporated pro-life inducements but left the ultimate choice to the woman – appeared to split the difference between the 'indications' model laid down in *Abortion I* and East Germany's policy of allowing a woman to procure an abortion on demand at any time and for any reason within the first trimester of pregnancy.

Like the 1974 statute, PFAA was straightaway challenged in an abstract judicial review proceeding. Once again, in *Abortion II*, the Court struck the statute, this time by finding the Act's 'not illegal' language fatally flawed. The Court reiterated its earlier view that an abortion can never be justified and must in principle be defined as 'illegal' at every stage of pregnancy. But the Senate went on to say that an illegal act need not be punished if extenuating circumstances of a severe nature diminish an actor's guilt (*Schuld*). Accordingly, abortion need not be punished within the first trimester if parliament adopts a regulatory scheme that on the whole 'effectively and efficiently' seeks to preserve unborn life. Such a scheme, instructed the Court, would require compulsory pro-life – but non-intimidating – counseling backed up with generous public support, including guarantees that women and mothers would not be disadvantaged in the job market or undergo serious financial hardship following pregnancy or childbirth. Such measures would be designed to encourage women to carry their pregnancies to term. But if after counseling the woman still insists that she wants an abortion, a certificate to that effect must be provided so long as the physician-counselor is not the person who actually performs the abortion. Much of the Court's opinion was taken up with suggestions for a plan of social assistance for 'women in distress' that would satisfy constitutional standards. Like the Supreme Court in *Planned Parenthood v Casey* (1992), the Constitutional Court in *Abortion II* (1993), although modifying its earlier reasoning, upheld the 'essential core' of its abortion jurisprudence.

5   COMPARATIVE ASSESSMENT

This chapter has sought to relate the varying abortion policies of the United States, Germany and Ireland to their respective regime values of liberal individualism, communal liberalism and integral communalism. These contrasting models of constitutionalism also represent corresponding variants of democracy. The United States may be described as a *liberal* democracy, Germany as a *social* democracy and Ireland as a *fraternal* democracy. Yet these are not mutually exclusive categories. Liberalism, sociality and fraternity are overlapping concepts, and the meaning of each cannot be fully explored without reference to the influence of the others. Similarly, each of these constitutional democracies celebrates the values of dignity and autonomy but each calibrates them in different ways. How dignity and autonomy are defined, related or applied in the abortion context depends on the text of each country's constitutional charter, as we have seen, along with its structure of rights and liberties and system of judicial review. Each of these factors helps to explain the variation in the abortion policies of the three democracies; and while the policies are similar in several respects, the different images they project of the relationship between dignity and autonomy is more than a matter of emphasis.

Despite their genealogical affinity, the three constitutional orders project different images of state, society and human personhood – and thus of the relationship between dignity and autonomy. Ireland's integral (or *fraternal*) democracy associates dignity and freedom with human flourishing within a social order overseen by the state as guardian of the common good, one additionally leavened by the cardinal virtues – and constitutional values – of justice, prudence and charity. These values or virtues blend into what may be regarded juristically as an integrated moral order. Other elements of this moral order are the Constitution's veneration of the family, its elevation of a 'common good' principle that idealizes women as mothers and homemakers, and its instantiation of a 'social order in which justice and charity shall inform all the institutions of national life' (Article 45.1). The Constitution's express protection of unborn life, a provision inspired originally by the Supreme Court's natural law jurisprudence, fits snugly into this constitutional order of values. Yet the same provision recognizes 'the equal right to the life of the mother'. And so, although abortion is banned in Ireland unless a pregnancy threatens the life of the mother, the Constitution permits women – presumably (in the Irish view) owing to the Christian values of prudence, justice and charity – to seek and obtain abortion services outside the country. Indeed, as already noted, nearly 2,000 legal abortions took place in Ireland between 2006 and 2009.

Germany's communal liberalism, on the other hand, rests on the more secular foundation of social democracy. But like Ireland, society is seen as inherently relational and the state as a facilitator of solidarity and human dignity. In addition, each negative right under the Basic Law is linked to a positive obligation. As with Ireland, and unlike the United States, this linkage of negative rights and objective values performs an integrative role in the sense of viewing the human person not as a freestanding individual but as a *person* embedded in *communio* and whose freedom is therefore bound up with corresponding responsibilities to family, spouse, lover, children, neighbor and the wider community in which he or she lives. For this reason, the Basic Law's protection of the 'right to life' carries with it, in the words of the Constitutional Court, an affirmative duty to safeguard 'developing life within the womb'. This jurisprudential view stems from the notion that dignity attaches to the human species of which 'developing life within the womb' is an integral part. Similarly, human persons are not isolated individuals; as the Constitutional Court has frequently noted, 'the Basic Law favors a relationship between individual and community in the sense of a person's dependence on and commitment to the community, without infringing upon a person's individual value'. One similarity with Ireland is the special protection the state is obliged to confer on the institutions of marriage and the family, both foundational components of their respective constitutional orders. Ireland's integral communalism, however, flows from the Constitution's foundation in Catholic social theory, whereas Germany's communal liberalism derives from the more secular – and distinctively German – tradition of the *social* state (*Sozialstaat*) based on the rule of law.[52]

Under the Basic Law's 'social state' clause (Article 20 [1]), society is more than an aggregation of individuals driven by self-interest. The court's vigilant defense of personal freedom is exercised in the context of the polity's common life. Dignity resides not only in individuality but in sociality as well, and in this way German constitutionalism seeks to harmonize, however imperfectly, the values of autonomy and dignity. Dignity, to be sure, requires the protection of a person's 'right to the development of his [or her] personality', but this right is limited by 'the rights of others' (including 'developing life'), the 'moral law', and the 'constitutional order' (Article 2 [2]), of which the 'social state' is an essential component. Relatedly, as the Court has repeatedly declared in its general liberty jurisprudence, dignity also defends – and promotes – the social goods of relationality, participation, communication and civility. As often noted, the Basic Law also speaks in the language of rights and duties, the meaning of which, it is important to reiterate, the master value of human dignity informs. As the highest objective value of the Basic Law, dignity also underscores both the negativity *and* positivity of basic rights. Needless to say, the constitutionalism of duty derived from the Basic Law's positivity is conspicuous by its absence in the US constitution, at least as interpreted by *Roe v Wade* and its progeny.

At the risk of overdrawing the comparison, the US Constitution may be said to incorporate a vision of personhood that is entirely self-regarding, whereas the Basic Law incorporates a vision that is both personalist and communal. As the abortion cases demonstrate, the US Constitution extols the ethic of individualism, expressing a profound distrust of governmental power. The Basic Law, by contrast, while it surely vindicates the quest for personal self-fulfillment, sees the individual in terms of his or her social attachments and commitments. In sum, one vision of personhood is partial to the city perceived as a private realm in which the individual is alone, isolated, and in competition with his fellows, while the other vision is partial to the city perceived as a public realm where individual and community are bound together in reciprocity. Thus the authority of the community, as represented by the state, to define the liberty interests of mothers and unborn life finds a more congenial abode in German than in American constitutional law.

Where the line should be drawn between these liberty interests in the three countries has also been influenced by the scope or intensity of judicial review. In both Germany and Ireland, unlike the United States, the highest courts of judicial review have regarded abortion largely as a policy matter committed to the legislature even as constitutional values control the perimeter of these policies. In Ireland, the Constitution itself authorizes the state to vindicate 'by its laws' the 'right to life of the unborn' and the 'equal right to life of the mother'. Like the Supreme Court in *Roe v Wade*, Ireland's Supreme Court declined to say when unborn life begins. But in contrast to the former, the latter has consigned this decision to the Irish parliament.[53] Although Germany's Constitutional Court took up this challenge for itself, it has had a running dialogue with parliament over the adequacy of measures required to balance the interests of mother and unborn life. Judges and legislators in Germany, far more than in the United States, even in the aftermath of *Casey* and *Gonzales*, are largely in agreement over the need for the protection of unborn life. The main contestants in the German abortion debate, both on and off the Court, have not questioned the state's duty to protect fetal life at all stages of pregnancy. On this question, broad political agreement prevails; the debate centers on whether the Constitutional Court has exceeded the limits of judicial power in the rulings handed down in *Abortion I* and *II*.[54]

Apart from the foregoing effort to *explain* variations in the abortion policies of the constitutional democracies under study, what benefits can we expect from an exercise such as this in comparative constitutional analysis? I take it to be one of the purposes of comparative analysis to see if some kind of transnational consensus is possible given the critical importance of human dignity and individual autonomy in modern constitutional democracies. There seems to be a transnational consensus that unborn life (at some stage) and personal self-determination are both worthy of constitutional protection. What is more, the American and German abortion policies appear to have tilted toward convergence as a result of *Casey* and *Abortion II*. To be sure, unborn life prior to viability receives greater protection in Germany, yet ironically first trimester abortions are more easily and readily available in Germany than in the United States. Still, in the post-*Casey-Gonzales* world, the decision to bear a child ranks higher on the scale of current American constitutional values than the right to abort, although in Germany pre-viability abortions in the second trimester of pregnancy are forbidden except in the presence of specified indications.

A broader range of countries than represented here would have unveiled a greater diversity of abortion policies. Mary Ann Glendon's comparative overview of abortion regulation in 20 western democracies reveals the extent of the variation. In her survey, as in this study, Ireland and the United States represented respectively the most restrictive and most permissive nations. Five countries allowed elective abortion in early pregnancy – a 'term limit' rule – but strictly regulated it thereafter. Several others permitted abortion only for cause – an 'indications' rule – some on 'hard' and others on 'soft' grounds, while in still other countries abortion was allowed after early pregnancy but only in the presence of criminal, genetic or medical indications.[55] By 2008, 20 years later, most of the countries in Glendon's survey had retained their existing policies. Some countries, however, had moved in a more libertarian direction, shifting generally from 'abortion for cause' to 'elective abortions' in early pregnancy. Germany, as we have seen, would be included in the shift toward greater permissiveness. A shift has even occurred in Ireland, with the abandonment of natural law reasoning by the Supreme Court and its endorsement of recent legislation supportive of the 'equal right to life of the mother'. The movement cannot be unrelated to constitutional developments in Ireland and Germany.

No one solution to the problem of unwanted pregnancies yet commands universal acceptance among constitutional democracies, even though each of them recognizes the universality of human dignity and the rights of personhood rooted in conscience and reason. Similarly, no one set of abortion regulations has been hailed as morally superior to another. As with regulations of speech, a variety of approaches seems compatible with the idea of liberal democracy. Yet, in this age of globalization and legal harmonization, as justices of the world's most important constitutional courts continue communicating with one another, comparative constitutional law has come to play a central role in domestic constitutional adjudication. Especially is this so in complex areas of life and law where constitutional courts are looking to receive guidance from one another.

One function of the comparative enterprise, as I see it, is to identify points of convergence in the constitutional law of advanced democracies. After all, we live in a globalized human community. And if morally 'right' answers are to be found in constitutional law, they might be located at the point where the laws or jurisprudence of advanced democracies converge. We have seen that Germany and the United States have been moving toward convergence and that Ireland too is moving away, however slightly, from its 'hard grounds' approach to abortion. Still, the United States remains an outlier among nations with respect to its failure steadfastly to protect unborn life even in the late stages of pregnancy. Nearly every advanced constitutional democracy invokes constitutional values in its effort to achieve a workable balance between the right to life of the unborn and a woman's right to self-determination – or autonomy. Unlike Germany's Basic Law, however, the United States Constitution has never been interpreted to include objective values along with subjective rights, but in the interest of cross-national harmonization or convergence, there may be good reasons why American courts should begin to *permit* what the Federal Constitutional Court *requires* – that is, policies ranging from pro-life counseling to mandated information about fetal development. Such a policy would reflect the balance between dignity and autonomy that appears to prevail in other advanced – and secular – democracies.

NOTES

*   I would like to thank Michael Chambliss, Yvonne McDermott and the Irish Center for Human Rights for their research assistance, particularly on Ireland. For their helpful comments on the manuscript, I'm also grateful to Carter Snead, V. Bradley Lewis, Paolo Carozza, John Coughlin, Donald Stelluto, Vicki Jackson and Richard Garnett.

1. The tension between the values of dignity and autonomy is also a dominant theme in the vast literature on the competing rights at stake in the abortion context. A small sample of this literature would include Feldman, David. 'Human Dignity as a Legal Value', *Public Law* 682–702 (1999); Ullrich, Dierk. 'Concurring Visions: Human Dignity in the Canadian Charter of Rights and Freedoms and the Basic Law of the Federal Republic of Germany', 3 *Global Jurist Frontiers* 1–103 (2003); Kommers, Donald P. 'Liberty and Community in Constitutional Law: The Abortion Cases in Comparative Perspective', *Brigham Young University Law Review* 371–409 (1985); Morris, D.G. 'Abortion and Liberalism: A Comparison Between the Abortion Decisions of the United States and the Constitutional Court of West Germany', 11 *Hastings International and Comparative Law Review* 159–245 (1988); McAllister, M. 'Human Dignity and Individual Liberty in Germany and the United States as Examined through Each Country's Leading Abortion Cases', *Tulsa Journal of Comparative Law* 491–520 (2004); Neuman, G. L. 'Casey in the Mirror: Abortion, Abuse, and the Right to Protection in the United States and Germany', 43 *American Journal of Comparative Law* 273–314 (1995); Tribe, Laurence H. *Abortion: The Clash of Absolutes* (New York: Norton, 1990); Dworkin, Ronald. *Life's Dominion* (New York: Alfred A. Knopf, 1993); and Henkin, Louis. 'Privacy and Autonomy', 74 *Columbia Law Review* 1410 (1974).

2. The *X Case* wrote the exception into Ireland's 1979 Health (Family Planning) Act, the statute that continued and affirmed England's Offenses Against the Person Act of 1861. The case itself involved the rape of a 14-year-old girl that resulted in pregnancy. She threatened to commit suicide if not permitted to abort her fetus. Ireland's High Court issues an injunction prohibiting the girl from traveling abroad for an abortion. On appeal, the Supreme Court reversed, holding that a pregnancy could be terminated in Ireland or abroad if it presents 'a real and substantial risk to the life of the mother'. The Court found that this standard was met by the risk of suicide. *Attorney General v X and Others*, [1992] 1 IR 1 (5 March 1992), 53–4.

3. In its original version, Article 44.1.2 recognized the special position of the Catholic Church but in 1972 the provision was removed from the document in a popular referendum.

4. Article 41.1.1 exalts the family 'as a moral institution possessing inalienable and imprescriptable rights, antecedent and superior to all positive law'. Equally pivotal is the elevated status the Constitution confers on women and motherhood. According to Article 41.2.1, 'the State recognizes that by her life within the home,

woman gives to the State support without which the common good cannot be achieved'. Thus women – mothers in particular – 'shall not be obliged by economic necessity to engage in labor to the neglect of their duties in the home'. That the Constitution would therefore require the state 'to guard with special care the institution of marriage, on which the Family is founded' is unsurprising.

5. Prudence and justice are cardinal virtues in Catholic social thought, while charity, along with faith and hope, is a supernatural virtue. On the meaning of the common good in Catholic thought, see 'Common Good', *The New Dictionary of Catholic Social Thought* (Collegeville, MN: The Liturgical Press, 1994), 192–7.

6. Accordingly, Ireland has adopted a generous social welfare system (analogous to Germany's) that grants payments of various kinds to families, including payments to one-parent families and early child care supplements for children under 5 years of age. See http://www.citizensinformation.ie/categories/social-welfare-payments-to-families-and-children/one_parent_family_payment.

7. This vision is roughly comparable to the political theory embedded in Catholic philosopher Jacques Maritain's idea of integral humanism. See *Integral Humanism* (Notre Dame: University of Notre Dame Press, 1973).

8. European Convention, Article 8 (1). In 1992, Ireland became a Party to the Maastricht Treaty, which identified the Convention as a source of fundamental rights in the European Union. Protocol 17, however, stated that Ireland's constitutional abortion regulations would not be affected by the treaty or any other treaty of the Euoropean Communities. See Treaty on European Union and Final Act, 7 February 1992, 31 ILM 247, 362.

9. The Eighth Amendment was adopted with 66.90% of the electorate voting 'yes' and 33.10% voting 'no'.

10. Constitution of Ireland, Article 40.3.3 (1983).

11. Owing to an important intervening case (a controversial High Court decision (known as the *C Case*) holding that a 13-year-old girl who was raped, and whose pregnancy caused suicidal tendencies, could be taken abroad for an abortion over the objection of her parents (see *A. & B. v E. Health Bd., Judge Mary Fahy & C. & the Attorney Gen.*, [1998] 1 ILRM 460 (IrHCt), the Irish government proposed the Twenty-Fifth Amendment to the Constitution, which would have followed the language of the Eighth Amendment but included neither a rape nor a 'risk of suicide' exception and required that any change in an abortion law would have to be submitted to a referendum. The proposed amendment was narrowly rejected by a vote of 50.42% to 49.58%.

12. *Roche v Roche* [2009] IESC 82 (15 December 2009).

13. See discussion of Casey in Section 3.

14. A year earlier the European Court of Justice ruled that these information services were a protected economic right under the European Economic Community Treaty. See *Society for the Protection of Unborn Children v Grogan*, Case C-159/90, [1991] 2 CEC 539 (September 1991). See also Hilbert, Anne M. 'The Irish Abortion Debate: Substantive Rights and Affecting Commerce Models', 26 *Vanderbilt Journal of Transnational Law* 1117, 1143–7 (1994).

15. See, respectivly, *SPUC v Open Door Counselling Limited and Dublin Wellwoman Centre Limited*, [1988] IR 593 (IrHCt), *SPUC v Grogan*, [1989] 4 IR 753 (IrHCt), aff'd in part, rev'd in part, [1989] 4 IR 760 (IrSC), and *Open Door Counselling Well Woman v Ireland*, 15 EHRR 244 (1992).

16. Constitution of Ireland, Article 40.3.3 (1992). The proposed Twelfth Amendment, which would have modified the holding in the *X Case*, did not pass. It would have read: 'It shall be unlawful to terminate the life of an unborn unless such termination is necessary to save the life, as distinct from the health, of the mother where there is an illness or disorder of the mother giving rise to a real and substantial risk to her life, not being a risk of self-destruction'.

17. The PSA applies only to agencies which choose not to disseminate such information and bars persons or agencies from doing so if they have any financial interest in an actual abortion service outside the country. See Regulation of Information (Services Outside the State for Termination of Pregnancies) Act, No. 5 (1995).

18. *Irish Times*, 13 January 2010, http://irishtimes.com/newsppaer/ireland/2010/0106/122426173.

19. *Ryan v Attorney General*, [1965] IR 294 (IrSC) and *McGee v Attorney General*, [1974] IR 284 (IrSC).

20. Ryan unsuccessfully challenged the fluoridation of a public water supply as violative of the 'personal rights' protected by Article 40.3.

21. Two of the Court's members, however, found that the ban on the sale and importation of contraceptive devices and drugs did not violate the marital right of privacy. But they emphatically agreed that the Constitution includes natural and human rights over which the state has no authority.

22. [1974] IR 284, 298 (IrSC). The personal right to the mother's life was also a central claim in *McGee*. The court took this claim to heart, for the woman involved in the case had a heart condition that might have endangered her life had she become pregnant.

23. *An Bord*, [1980] IR 32, 69 (IrSC). The plaintiff in *An Bord* was a 21-year-old unmarried woman who sought to reclaim the daughter she had given up for adoption several months earlier. The Court sided with the plaintiff because a mother has a 'natural right to the custody of her child' unless the state as the guardian of the common good intervenes in the child's best interests. It was in this context that the Court postulated the right to life of all children, legitimate or illegitimate, and that threats to life before and after birth must be guarded against at all times.

24. [1988] IR 619, 625 (IrSC).

25. The Court's emphasis on constitutional justice reaffirmed once again its reluctance to rely on natural law reasoning, a reluctance again manifested in the recent *Frozen Embryo Case* where the Supreme Court ruled that 'unborn life' within the meaning of Article 40.3.3 applies only to an embryo in the womb. A woman had requested a Dublin clinic to release frozen embryos to her so that she might become pregnant. The clinic refused after her estranged husband objected. The Court rejected the woman's constitutional argument based on the right to unborn life under Article 40.3.3. See supra note 12.

26. The law also required the physician to reduce his judgment to writing with which two other licensed physicians would have to concur. In addition, a hospital committee of no fewer than three members, excluding the physician proposing the procedure, was required to approve the abortion by majority vote. 410 US 179 (1973).

27. See § 230.2, paragraphs 2 and 3.

28. Some constitutional scholars have suggested that abortion regulations would be more appropriately reviewed under the Fourteenth Amendment's equal protection clause – 'nor [shall any state] deny to any person within its jurisdiction the equal protection of the laws' – rather than under the concept of 'due process liberty'. See Ginsburg, Ruth Bader. 'Some Thoughts on Autonomy and Equality in Relation to Roe v Wade', 63 *North Carolina Law Review* 375 (1985). Up to now the equal protection clause has come into play only when the state treats some abortions differently than others or discriminates between abortion and other child-bearing decisions. One prominent example is *Maher v Roe*, 432 U. S. 464 (1977), holding that there is no violation of the Equal Protection Clause where states subsidize therapeutic but not elective abortions.

29. *Eisenstadt v Baird*, 405 US 438, 453.

30. *Roe v Wade*, 410 US 113 (1973).

31. These regulations included requirements such as spousal consent, parental notification, waiting periods, pre-abortion counseling, fetal burial requirements, second physician approval, and compulsory disclosure of information on fetal development. See, for example, *Planned Parenthood of Central Missouri v Danforth*, 428 US 52 (1976), *Akron v Akron Center for Reproductive Health, Inc.*, 462 US 416 (1983), and *Thornburgh v American College of Obstetricians and Gynecologists*, 476 US 747 (1986).

32. *Colautti v Franklin*, 439 US 379 (1979).

33. *Beal v Doe*, 432 US 438, 446 (1977). This was a major reinterpretation of Roe which held that the state had no compelling interest in limiting a woman's right to choose until fetal viability in the third trimester.

34. See *H.L. v Matheson*, 450 US 409 in which the Court by a 6:3 vote sustained a state statute requiring the physician to notify, if possible, the parents of a minor upon whom an abortion is being performed. Parental consultation, the Court suggested, is often desirable and in the best interest of the minor. The justices were of course referring not to medical advice but to social and moral considerations presumably outside the competence of the medical profession.

35. 410 US 179, 192. *Marcus Welby, M.D.* was a popular ABC-TV show featuring a kind and generous family doctor with a bedside manner. (The medical drama aired from 1969 to 1976.) Whether attending physicians – abortion doctors in particular – have the best interests of their patients in mind is a neglected issue in the literature. An exception is Appleton, Susan F. 'Doctor, Patients and the Constitution: A Theoretical Analysis of the Physician's Role in "Private" Reproductive Decisions', 63 *Washington University Law Quarterly* 183 (1985).

36. See respectively *Beal v Doe*, 432 US 490 (1989), *Maher v Roe*, 432 US 464 (1977), and *Poelker v Doe*, 432 US 519 (1977). See also *Hodgson v Minnesota*, 497 US 417 (1990, upholding a 48-hour waiting period between notifying parents of a minor's intent to obtain an abortion and its performance).

37. One such effort came from the US Department of Justice whose lawyers argued on behalf of the United States (in an amicus curiae brief) for the overruling of *Roe v Wade*, the effect of which would have returned the abortion issues back to the states.

38. 492 US 490.

39. 505 US 833 (1992).

40. The joint opinion solemnly explained: 'At the heart of liberty is the right to define one's own concept of existence, of meaning, of the universe, and of the mystery of human life. Beliefs about these matters could not define the attributes of personhood were they formed under the compulsion of the State' (mocked by some as the so-called 'mystery' passage). 505 US 833, 851.

41. See, for example, Ginsburg, supra note 28; MacKinnon, Catherine. 'Reflections of Sex Equality under Law', 100 *Yale Law Journal* 1281 (1991); and Siegel, Reva. 'Reasoning from the Body: A Historical Perspective on Abortion Regulation and Questions of Equal Protection', 44 *Stanford Law Review* 261 (1992); and Law, Sylvia A. 'Rethinking Sexuality and the Constitution', 132 *University of Pennsylvania Law Review* 955 (1984), and Colker, Ruth. 'Anti-Subordination Above All: Sex, Race, and Equal Protection', 61 *New York Law Review* 1003 (1986). For a strong defense of abortion as a right to privacy, see Reubenfeld, Jed. 'The Right of Privacy', 102 *Harvard Law Review* 737 (1989).

42. 530 US 914.

43. *Gonzales v Carhart*, 550 US (2007).

44. From Orlando Carter Snead in his letter to the author of 5 December 2009.

45. See Kommers, Donald P. 'Liberty and Community in American Constitutional Law: Continuing Tensions',

Bicentennial of the U.S. Constitution Lecture Series (Bloomington, IN: The Poynter Center, Indiana University, 1986).

46. *The Republic of Choice: Law, Authority, and Culture* (Cambridge, MA: Harvard University Press, 1990).

47. Treaty of 31 August 1990 Between the Federal Republic of Germany and the German Democratic Republic (Unification Treaty), Article 31 (4). The abortion policies referred to were West Germany's Federal Constitutional Court decision of 1975, upholding the unborn child's right to life at all stages of pregnancy, and East Germany's policy of abortion on demand in the first trimester of pregnancy.

48. Abortion Reform Act, 1974 Bundesgesetzblatt [BGBl] I, 1297. An account of abortion reform efforts prior to 1974 is included in the German *Abortion Case I* at 39 BVerfGE 3–18 (1975). A full translation of the case appears in 9 *The John Marshall Journal of Practice and Procedure* 605–84 (1976).

49. See Kommers, Donald P. 'Germany: Balancing Rights and Duties', in *Interpreting Constitutions: A Comparative Study*, edited by Jeffrey Goldsworthy (Oxford: Oxford University Press, 2006), 179–81.

50. To this end, counselors were obliged to supply women with detailed medical, social, and legal advice, including the availability of 'practical assistance' designed to mitigate the distress of both mother and child. The counseling bureau was required to keep a record of each session, but in the interest of privacy and at the woman's request her identity would not be revealed.

51. See Schwangeren- und Familienhilfegesetz of 27 June 1992, BGBL. I 1398. Strafgesetzbuchreform [St.GBR], Article 13 of the Pregnancy and Family Assistance Act, amended §§ 218 and 219 of the German Penal Code.

52. It should be noted, however, that in Germany's post-war constitutional convention (Der parlamentarische Rat) Christian democratic natural law thought combined with secular, social democratic interests to constitutionalize the Sozialstaat.

53. *Roche v Roche*, supra note 12.

54. At the same time there is a sense in which judicial review may have been exercised more strongly in Germany than in the United States. In Germany, judicial review extended to national laws under an abstract review procedure and thus prior to their enforcement. In the United States, by contrast, review has extended to a variety of state laws. In addition, the laws struck down in *Roe* and related cases had been on the books for generations and were kept there through legislative inertia without regard to intervening social change. In Germany, the Court reviewed new laws that had been hammered out laboriously on the anvil of serious discussion and debate, laws which in turn reflected honest efforts to recognize the legitimate interests of both mother and unborn child.

55. *Abortion and Divorce in Western Law* (Cambridge, MA: Harvard University Press, 1987), 13–24. The so-called hard grounds typically involved serious danger to the pregnant woman's health, whereas the so-called soft grounds typically permitted abortion under a variety of circumstances, including those which pose exceptional hardship for the pregnant woman. Canada, incidentally, was not included in Glendon's study. In 1986, in *R v Morgentaler*, the Supreme Court struck down Canada's abortion 'for cause' statute, but mainly on procedural grounds. No parliamentary majority, however, has emerged to impose substantive restrictions on the abortion liberty that the Supreme Court may have allowed.

25. Human dignity in constitutional adjudication
Paolo G. Carozza[1]

Since the mid-twentieth century, the idea of human dignity has emerged as the single most widely recognized and invoked basis for grounding the idea of human rights generally, and simultaneously as an exceptionally widespread tool in judicial discourse concerning the content and scope of specific rights. It has become a pervasive part of the fabric of constitutional law worldwide.[2] From South Africa, where judges concluded that dignity requires the government to implement 'a comprehensive and coordinated programme progressively to realize the right of access to adequate housing' (*South Africa v Grootboom* 2001, para. 23); to Israel, where the Supreme Court banned corporal punishment for violating the dignity of children (*Plonit v Israel* 2000; see Ezer 2003), to the decision of the Supreme Court of the United States finding criminal sodomy laws to be unconstitutional (*Lawrence v Texas* 2003), courts have assumed responsibility for identifying and guaranteeing the basic requirements of human dignity. Their decisions not only discuss human dignity but rely on the concept to explain, justify and determine case outcomes. As the South African Constitutional Court has put it, 'dignity is not only a value fundamental to our constitution, it is a justiciable and enforceable right that must be respected and protected' (*Khosa v Minister of Social Development* 2004, para. 41). The same can be said of a number of other constitutional systems. For these reasons human dignity has been appropriately described as the 'ur-principle' of the protection of the human person in the contemporary era (Henkin et al. 1999, 80).

While many scholars have applauded judicial reliance on human dignity, even to the extent of urging their own national courts to regularly employ the value (Bracey 2005, 719; Moon 2006), other commentators have been less enthusiastic. Critics see it as a vacuous term that has no stable meaning and that can be given any content (Bagaric and Allan 2006; Bates 2005). The alleged absence of meaning in turn raises concerns about the degree of discretion that invocation of human dignity provides to judges and about the degree of ideological manipulation to which the concept is subject (Bates 2005, 165; cf. Harris 1998, 31; Carozza 2007). Some judges of the European Court of Human Rights have even suggested that human dignity is therefore a 'dangerous concept' (*Vereinigung Bildender Künstler v Austria* 2007, Spielman, J. and Jebens, J., dissenting §9).[3]

Two broad questions thus arise out of a comparative analysis of the widespread constitutional tendency to appeal to human dignity in adjudication. First, does the concept itself have any sufficiently common or determinable meaning across different constitutional systems? A second question, not unrelated to the first problem of substantive content, is a more functional one: for what purposes do courts deploy the idea and the rhetoric of human dignity in constitutional adjudication?

1   THE MULTIPLE MEANINGS OF HUMAN DIGNITY

At its broadest level, the invocation of human dignity denotes two interrelated ideas: (a) an ontological claim that all human beings have an equal and intrinsic moral worth; and (b) a normative principle that all human beings are entitled to have this status of equal worth respected by others and also have a duty to respect it in all others. The latter responsibility includes within it the obligations of the state to respect human dignity in its law and policy as well (McCrudden 2008; Carozza 2008; Lee and George 2008). Based on this core common meaning of human dignity, there is broad consensus across legal systems that certain ways of treating other human beings ought always to be prohibited by law. The prohibitions on genocide, slavery, torture, disappearance, and systematic racial discrimination, for instance, represent some important (but not exclusive) examples of universal acceptance of the implications of the status and basic principle of human dignity. It is not surprising that many of these clearest instantiations of the requirements of human dignity also coincide with the strongest and exceptionless norms of international law, found for example in the definitions of crimes against humanity or *jus cogens*.

The difficulties and controversies that arise in constitutional adjudication rarely if ever go to that hard minimal core of the meaning of human dignity. Rather, they arise where the requirements of human dignity are more contested and uncertain, and where the broad universal principle needs to be specified concretely in a given social, political, and cultural context. In those cases, the commonality of understanding across jurisdictions quickly dissipates and the meaning of dignity becomes 'elusive' and 'amorphous' (Rao 2008), even to the point of being arguably just an 'empty shell' (McCrudden 2008).

For example, while dignity is frequently used to support autonomy, as in a German Constitutional Court decision which held that human dignity required a Muslim schoolteacher to be allowed to observe her religion by wearing a headscarf in the classroom (Bundesverfassungsgericht 1436/02, 2003),[4] in other cases, however, dignity is invoked instead to limit free choice in order to protect some independent value considered essential to the respect for persons' equal moral worth. In a well-known French decision, dwarf-tossing was prohibited as demeaning to human dignity (against the protests of the dwarves who made their living from the sport) (Conseil D'Etat, 27 October 1995, Commune de Morsang-sur-Orge).[5] In Canada, in contrast to both the autonomy-limiting and autonomy-protecting strands of human dignity analysis, the principle is almost exclusively mentioned in the context of equality jurisprudence (Fyfe 2007, 18; Moon 2006, 697–705; *Law v Canada* 1999). Even within the same national court, varying usage can make it difficult to determine consistently what judges mean by dignity. Notwithstanding the headscarf case, 'dignity' in other cases in Germany often appears to mean little more than 'privacy' (Bundesverfassungsgericht 2378/98, 2004) (although arguably this represents a very distinct sense of privacy when compared with that which dominates US law (Whitman 2004)).[6] The Hungarian Constitutional Court upheld a law preventing citizens from displaying swastikas, explaining that dignity required a tempering of free expression (Alkotmánybíróság 14/2000, V. 12); months later, the same court explained in a welfare case that all living people have the same amount of human dignity regardless of their lives' circumstances, so nothing could harm dignity, save death (Alkotmánybíróság 42/2000, XI. 8). Shortly thereafter, the court shifted perspectives once again, striking down legislation that limited citizens' ability to change their names, in order to ensure human dignity through self-determination (Alkotmánybíróság 58/2001, XII. 7).[7]

Even when dealing with strongly similar situations, different courts, and indeed different judges within the same court, can rely on human dignity to come to two entirely different conclusions. In France, the Conseil Constitutionnel in 2001 advised the legislature that a proposed law which would change the legal period for abortion from the first 10 weeks of gestation to the first 12 was unconstitutional because of the importance of safeguarding the dignity of the fetus after 10 weeks. In addition to the general dignity in the right to develop into a human being, the decision also notes that because the gender and basic features of a child can usually be determined starting in the tenth week, there might also be dignity concerns arising from the increased use of abortion for eugenic reasons or sex selection. In Germany, similarly, the Constitutional Court first held that a law permitting abortion is unconstitutional under certain circumstances because of the need to protect the dignity (and the life) of the unborn fetus (Bundesverfassungsgericht 39, 1, 1975; McAllister 2004, 511). Later, however, the same court permitted a substantially more liberalized abortion law and recognized that dignity concerns also exist not only on behalf of the unborn fetus but also on the side of the pregnant woman, whose autonomy and personal development are strongly implicated in the decision to terminate the pregnancy. In Hungary, where the constitution is largely modeled on German law and centered on human dignity, courts determined that there is no bar on abortion (Dupré 2003, 116). In the United States, dignity is also mentioned in abortion cases, but it is typically the dignity and autonomy of the mother that is stressed in justifying why abortion must remain legal (*Planned Parenthood v Casey* 1992). Scholarly literature on abortion and human dignity, even when arguing that the weight of the principle should favor one side in the dispute, acknowledges the presence of potentially valid dignity-based arguments on both (Dixon and Nussbaum 2011).

Similarly, human dignity has been invoked by those on both sides of the assisted suicide debate (*Pretty v United Kingdom* 2002; Bates 2005, 167). Not only is dignity implicated in the right (or absence of a right) to live, but also in the right to die. In one of the few British cases to address human dignity, the High Court ruled that a dying man's right to dignity meant he should be guaranteed the medical treatment that would keep him alive for as long as possible (*R (Burke) v General Medical Council* 2004). On appeal, the House of Lords focused instead on the negative impact on the dignity of an incompetent patient who might be kept alive for an extended period of time, despite great pain, because of an advanced direc- tive (*R (Burke) v General Medical Council* 2005). Multiple perspectives on the relationship between dignity and assisted suicide can be found even in a single decision, such as the Hungarian Constitutional Court's treatment of the issue. After surveying the laws of several European countries and the several states of the United States as well as Australia, the Hungarian Court determined that laws forbidding assisted suicide were not in violation of patients' right to dignity (Alkotmánybíróság 22/2003, IV. 28). Although the Court asserted that all people, whether terminally ill or not, have the right to die when they choose because of the right to self-determination implied in the right to dignity, the majority of the Court concluded that the importance of the right to life justifies limiting the right to die to instances where the individual is terminally ill and competently refuses life-saving treatments. Each of the multiple dissents in the case adds different perspectives on the right to die with dignity, turning on whether dignity is best understood as a conglomeration of lesser rights, another name for the right to life itself, or a supreme right that trumps all others.

In significant part, the multiple and sometimes mutually contradictory uses of human dignity in constitutional adjudication stem from the multivalent sources of the idea.[8] The word's roots are Latin, but ancient Romans primarily used it in a context that referred to the respect due to those who were of elevated social status – for example, senators had *dignitas* but women, slaves and common men did not. It was a term that drew status distinctions between people, rather than suggesting universal moral equality. In contrast, the Judeo-Christian notion of human dignity, deriving from the traditional belief that man is made in the image of God, identifies an inherent worth in every individual. Kantian philosophy is often closely associated with discussions of human dignity as well, particularly those contemporary understandings of dignity that place a heavy emphasis on individual autonomy, and on not treating anyone merely as a means to other ends.[9] Still other Enlightenment philosophers, such as Rousseau, have bequeathed a slightly different emphasis to the idea of dignity, associating it with more communitarian and republican ideals. Outside of European traditions, human dignity has been linked to other concepts, like *ubuntu* or *dharma*, that belong to distinctive philosophical, religious and cultural traditions and yet that may arguably serve in their particular contexts as functional analogues to the idea of human dignity. The point here is not to catalogue all the possible sources of the idea of dignity, and even less to enter into their details or merits. Rather, it is simply to highlight that dignity's roots are not just highly diverse but emerge from traditions of thought that represent deeply divergent ideas about why human persons have any inherent value that demands the respect of others (the status of dignity), and what it entails to respect the moral worth of another (the principle of dignity).[10] One should therefore expect to find very significant variations in the use of human dignity across different constitutional courts, especially as the very broad and abstract principle of dignity is given concrete application and more determinate meaning in specific cases.

Despite its indeterminacy and the variations in its application, the idea of human dignity as applied in the jurisprudence of different constitutional systems does allow a certain degree of categorization or at least groupings of cases to be made, even if the groups are not necessarily conceptually tightly knit and even if there is often substantial overlap between one group and others.

The most widespread and evident use of dignity in adjudication can be found in cases dealing with the protection of life itself and the integrity (physical or mental) of human persons. Cases are legion where inhuman and degrading treatment is found to violate the inherent dignity of the victims. Prison conditions, the treatment of detainees, and the administration of criminal punishments are obvious contexts giving rise to discussion and judicial protection of human dignity.[11] References to the requirements of human dignity pervade the case law of the European Court of Human Rights under Article 3 of the European Convention on Human Rights, for example (*Yankov v Bulgaria* 2003; *Price v the United Kingdom* 2001). Even in the United States, where the language of human dignity typically plays a less prominent role in constitutional discourse than it does in many other jurisdictions,[12] the Supreme Court has emphasized that it is the basic principle undergirding the Eighth Amendment's prohibition of cruel and unusual punishments. For instance, in *Hope v Pelzer* (2002), involving a prison inmate who was tied to a hitching post in the sun for seven hours with little water, Justice Stevens explained that the treatment was antithetical to human dignity and thus cruel and unusual within the meaning of the Eighth Amendment (730).[13] Dignity-based limitations on punishment across different systems range from prohibitions on corporal punishment in nations like Israel and South Africa (*Christian Education South Africa v Minister of Education* 2000; *Plonit v Israel* 2000; see Ezer 2003), to the impermissibility of a sentence of life in prison without parole, in Germany (Bundesverfassungsgericht 45, 187, 1977).

Similarly, in many different constitutional courts, dignity features prominently in judicial discussions of the legitimacy of the death penalty (Carozza 2003). In short, in the constitutional protection of human life and physical and mental integrity, one finds the most widely accepted recognition and application of the status and principle of human dignity.

In a second and entirely different set of decisions, courts discuss dignity as a value central to the definition and protection of individuals' social status and social roles. This formulation is especially prominent in several Hungarian cases, for instance, which focus on individuals' dignity and self-determination in shaping their identities (Alkotmánybíróság 45/2005, XII. 14; 58/2001, XII. 7). Similarly, the German and South African Constitutional Courts have fined or even banned books because, though presented as works of fiction, they shared too many details about a particular individual's private life (Bundesverfassungsgericht 1783/05, 2007; *NM v State* 2007). French courts frequently require newspapers to pay damages after they publish stories or photographs about individuals without respect for their dignity.[14] One case decided by the European Court of Human Rights concerned an obscene painting, which included a depiction of an Austrian political figure (*Vereinigung Bildender Künstler v Austria* 2007). The Austrian courts, as well as several judges in the ECHR, found in favor of the politician and his harmed dignity, even at the expense of the artist's freedom of expression.[15] This conception of dignity is primarily employed within European courts, and seems to be closely related to European conceptions of privacy. Furthermore, many of these cases almost convey a sense of the privileged social status of the victim of the indignity, whether they feature the Austrian party leaders included in the shocking painting, princesses who wish to keep photographs of their private lives out of the tabloids (*Von Hannover v Germany* 2004), or supermodels who are unhappy about published stories about their involvement in drug rehabilitation (*Campbell v Mirror Group Newspapers* 2004). In these cases, the Roman conception of senatorial *dignitas* does not seem so far removed (cf. Whitman 2004), even if it is sometimes extended to 'common' people.[16]

In contrast, a third distinct group of cases shows that dignity can go far beyond the private details of a person's life, and can be employed to address the sweeping conditions that shape the lives of entire communities living in poverty and extreme vulnerability. In South Africa, the Constitutional Court heard a case brought by hundreds of impoverished families living in tents pitched on a crowded field, while they waited for more government subsidized housing to be built (*South Africa v Grootboom* 2001). The court concluded that these citizens' dignity required that the government devote substantial resources to developing and carrying out a plan to progressively realize the right to adequate housing. In India, the Supreme Court came to a similar conclusion when it reviewed the conditions of young children living with their convicted mothers in state jails (*R.D. Upadhyay v State of A.P.* 2006). The dignity of these infants and toddlers, the court declared, required that they be provided with appropriate food, clothing and educational opportunities, as well as frequent outings to experience the world outside the prison walls. The Indian court has also required that laws be instituted to limit noise pollution, because a life of dignity is one where the right to quiet and peaceful enjoyment is respected (*In Re: Noise Pollution* 2005). In a comparable vein, the Israeli Supreme Court has also held that the protection of human dignity by the government means that laws must not deprive people of money that is necessary for minimal subsistence and that a man living on the streets, starving, deprived of access to basic medical treatment, or compelled to live in humiliating material conditions is a man whose human dignity has been impaired.[17]

Such situations involving the dignity of excluded groups are closely related to the use of human dignity in a fourth set of cases: those invoking equality as necessary to the respect for human dignity. Based on the proposition that all people are inherently and equally entitled to human dignity, this view is especially developed in Canadian jurisprudence,[18] has become common in South Africa (Grant 2007), and can be found in other jurisdictions as well.[19] This is in an important sense the antithesis of the Roman idea of *dignitas*; rather than drawing distinctions between the privileged and everyone else, dignity in the equality context demands that such differentiations be set aside. While the use of dignity in the realm of equality has been criticized (O'Connell 2008), it would appear to be a growing category. In this vein, for example, many jurisdictions, including Canada, the United States and South Africa, have invoked human dignity in a central way in judicial discussions of the rights of gays and lesbians.[20] Similarly, in several jurisdictions, including Canada, India and Israel, judges rely on dignity as justification for enforcing laws against sexual harassment in the workplace.[21] The connection between dignity as requiring guarantees of equality and dignity as leading to the protection of the social and economic conditions of vulnerable populations can be seen very clearly in a South African case requiring the extension of state-funded educational benefits to certain non-citizens (*Khosa v Minister of Social Development* 2004). Justice Mokgoro of the South African Constitutional Court noted pointedly that 'the exclusion of permanent residents from the scheme is likely to have a severe impact on the dignity of the persons concerned, who, unable to sustain themselves, have to turn to others to enable them to meet the necessities of life and are thus cast in the role of supplicants' (para. 80).

The distinction between the dignity of prominent individuals and the broader human dignity invoked to guarantee the material needs and the equality of marginalized populations is not the only dichotomy at work in the judicial interpretation and application of the concept. As mentioned above, and as explored in much of the scholarly literature on dignity, cases on human dignity are also split between understandings of dignity as liberty-reinforcing and dignity as requiring constraints on unfettered individual choice (Capps 2009, 108; Fyfe 2007, 2). From one perspective, human dignity clearly demands autonomy. A government that does not respect people's choices to shape their identities violates their dignity, at least in the eyes of the Hungarian Constitutional Court (Alkotmánybíróság 58/2001, XII. 7). In discussing laws restricting legal names, the court held that dignity includes an inalienable right to bear a name reflecting one's self-identity. Similarly, in affirming the right of transsexuals to present themselves to society as they choose (*I v the United Kingdom* 2002), the European Court of Human Rights observed in that decision that 'society may be reasonably expected to tolerate a certain inconvenience to enable individuals to live in dignity and worth in accordance to the sexual identity chosen by them at great personal cost' (para. 71). Dignity's role in guaranteeing personal autonomy can also extend beyond central questions of shaping one's identity. For instance, the Indian Supreme Court struck down a law limiting donations of land to charitable organizations, on the grounds that treating people with dignity requires allowing them to will their land to whomever they choose (*John Vallamattom and Anr. v Union of India* 2003). Many jurisdictions, including France, ground the autonomy of patients to make free and informed choices about their medical care in human dignity.[22]

In contrast to this use of dignity, which empowers people to make free choices, dignity also plays a role in empowering government to limit the freedom of their citizens. Probably the most famous example of this case was decided by a French court when it determined that the sport of dwarf-throwing was an affront to human dignity, even when it was done with the full consent of all parties involved (Conseil D'Etat, 27 October 1995, Commune de Morsang-sur-Orge). More recent examples confirm that the sentiment this case expresses is not obsolete.[23] Furthermore, dignity-as-constraint is not limited to French law. The Hungarian Constitutional Court, for example, rejected a petitioner's argument that the right of self-determination, implicit in dignity, should give people the right to use narcotic substances, citing the importance of protecting people, especially children, from the indignity of substance addiction (Alkotmánybíróság 54/2004, XII. 13).[24] The same court upheld mandatory vaccination requirements as consistent with the requirements of dignity (Alkotmánybíróság 39/2007, VI. 20). In Germany, a prohibition on peep shows has been found to be a valid protection of the human dignity of the (consenting) women being exhibited (1981 BVerwGE 64, 274), while the South African Constitutional Court upheld a ban on prostitution because the commodification of one's body necessarily diminished the human dignity of the prostitutes (*Jordan v State* 2002).

At times, the dualistic nature of the relationship between dignity and autonomy manifests itself dramatically. In the Hungarian case dealing with name restrictions, for instance, the court did not invalidate all of the naming laws, even though it found an inalienable right to shape one's self-identity (Alkotmánybíróság 58/2001, XII. 7). Obscene names and puns could not be used, the court said, because allowing them would violate the dignity of children who might be saddled with such names. Furthermore, the dignity of other living individuals made it necessary to prevent people from assuming different family names if there was potential for confusion or deception. The dignity of having free choices is always tempered by restrictions placed on those choices, necessary to safeguard the dignity of others. As these examples imply, in most instances when the conflict between dignity-as-liberty and dignity-as-constraint appears, the issue is not actually two competing definitions of dignity, but rather the competing dignities of two different people whose interests may collide. This explains cases like the Hungarian naming decision, and helps unravel the otherwise puzzling ability of courts to rely on dignity in support of either side of the abortion divide. Similarly, in Canada women have been prohibited from arbitrarily denying men parental rights, because of the need to protect the dignity of the fathers (*Trocuik v British Columbia* 2003) – another example of competing claims of dignity within the context of a single dispute over rights.

Sometimes, however, a court must actually prioritize irreconcilable values, rather than merely choose between the dignity of two people. A vivid illustration of such a case is *Indiana v Edwards*, decided by the United States Supreme Court in 2007 (*Indiana v Edwards* 2007). The decision features a heated debate between the majority and the dissent on whether the real affront to human dignity was to deny a mentally challenged defendant the right to be 'master of his own fate' and represent himself in court (J. Scalia and Thomas dissenting, 2393), or to allow him to embarrass himself and the legal system by giving him the opportunity to do so (majority opinion, 2387).[25]

In sum, this array of different approaches to human dignity reflects not only the variety of intellectual and moral traditions in which the concept has its roots, but also differences in the specific political, social and cultural contexts in which the very broad principle needs to be instantiated. The process of specifying the meaning and application of the general and abstract concept in concrete circumstances is a classic example of the *determinatio* of moral principles through the positive law (Carozza 2003; Carozza 2008, 933).

2   THE MULTIPLE USES OF HUMAN DIGNITY

The highly variable and context-specific substantive content of the principle of human dignity in constitutional adjudication provokes a further set of questions about the way that the principle functions in practice. If the meaning of dignity is so amorphous, especially as one moves farther away from the (relatively) non-disputed use of the idea to protect the central core of an individual's physical and psychological integrity, why is it so frequently invoked, for what uses and to what effect? Christopher McCrudden has argued for shifting the discussion of human dignity in constitutional adjudication away from the substantive content of the principle and instead for examining the functional and institutional uses of the principle (McCrudden 2008).

One important role that human dignity plays is to provide an overarching and integrating constitutional value. In that pre-eminent position, the language of dignity is the currency for mediating between other more specific and distinct rights and principles, even ones that may otherwise be incommensurable. For example, the abortion cases discussed earlier present particularly vexing clashes of fundamental values. In its attempt to justify a balancing between the right to life of the unborn child and the right to autonomy and the development of personality of the woman, the German Constitutional Court has framed both in terms of dignity as the overarching constitutional value (Mahlmann 2010). Similar appeals to dignity serve as the framework for judicial resolution of the conflicts between (certain forms of) privacy and freedom of expression described above.

Yet dignity does more than merely mediate between and unify the existing pieces of the constitutional protection of rights. In many cases, courts appeal to the idea of human dignity to expand the scope of fundamental rights, either by finding that human dignity requires a substantially extended understanding of a recognized right or by justifying the recognition of a new constitutional right by reference to the requirements of dignity. Such uses of dignity range across a broad spectrum of constitutional rights. They include, for example, finding that dignity inherently includes the protection of the family in South Africa (*Dawood v Minister of Home Affairs* 2000), the right to education in India (*Islamic Academy of Education v State of Karnataka* 2003), minority language rights in Israel (*Adalah v The Municipality of Tel-Aviv-Jaffa* 2002),[26] and the freedom to seek sterilization for contraceptive purposes in Hungary (Alkotmánybíróság 43/2005, XI. 14). In many instances, the rhetorical grounding of such new or expanded rights in human dignity appears even more prominent and pronounced when the subject is one of sharp social controversy. In such cases, human dignity seems to be offered as a way of justifying the court's intervention and resolution of the question in ways that may not reflect prevailing popular sentiment, such as in the several court decisions mandating same-sex marriage, for example.

The rights-expanding role that human dignity plays is all the more notable insofar as it is used by courts even in the absence of an explicit constitutional text referring to dignity.[27] This practice leads to the identification of a third broad category of functions that human dignity plays: it is invoked by courts to justify their reliance on legal sources that do not have an authoritative pedigree in the positive law. Appealing to human dignity indirectly authorizes constitutional courts to reach beyond the strictures of the formal hierarchy of sources. Some of the clearest examples can be found in decisions relying on or otherwise incorporating foreign court decisions. Most constitutional courts typically lack an explicit textual warrant for their use of foreign or comparative law.[28] By linking the relevant foreign law to a common commitment to the protection of human dignity, however, courts can seek to overcome the risk to interpretive legitimacy that foreign law represents. Numerous examples of this practice can be found across a range of rights, but in no area is the transnational link forged by reference to human dignity more clear than with regard to the rights to life and physical integrity, including in particular the death penalty (Carozza 2003).

It is notable that this link of the constitutional order of fundamental values to the transnational is sometimes especially strong in constitutional systems that have recently emerged from periods of totalitarian rule, like Hungary, or criminally systematic oppression, like South Africa. It has been argued persuasively that this reflects the ability of dignity to signal and symbolize the transition to a new constitutional order that respects the human person, and to mark the definitive rejection of former regimes (Dupré 2003).

Whether in conveying a new set of fundamental constitutional values, authorizing new sources of law or constructing expanded understandings of rights, the problem of the institutional legitimacy of the judiciary often lies very close to the surface in such cases. What makes the exercise of judicial authority justified, relative to the political lawmaking branches (or the constitutive assembly through the constitutional text itself) is exactly the courts' reliance on a higher principle, human dignity. That claims for itself an objective status not reducible merely to judicial preference or arbitrariness. Where the basic human rights claim in question can result in enormous public expenditures and the mobilization of broad public policies, or where it brings the courts into especially sharp conflict with elected bodies, the reliance on dignity as an institutional legitimation technique can be especially important. It can be seen in this sense as one important method for mitigating the bite of constitutional courts' countermajoritarian roles (McCrudden 2008).

Those cases of institutional competence that implicate the allocation of responsibilities for guaranteeing rights and the common good in a constitutional system illustrate particularly clearly the structural function that human dignity plays in adjudication. Nevertheless one can observe that in fact all of the typical uses of the idea of dignity in constitutional adjudication depend at least implicitly on the premise that dignity provides some sort of supra-positive value to which the details of constitutional law ought to be held accountable (Carozza 2008).[29]

3 CONCLUSION

There is at least a certain paradox, and sometimes outright contradiction, between the substantive meaning of human dignity across the constitutional jurisprudence of different systems, on the one hand, and the functional role that human dignity plays in fortifying judicial legitimacy, on the other. To the extent that the content of dignity is vacuous, or at least significantly indeterminate and accordingly subject to the discretionary interpretation of judges, it is likely to be less capable of serving as a justification for the strong judicial roles that it is called upon to sustain. It is for this reason that even scholars who have commented positively in general terms on the use of dignity in constitutional adjudication also have identified the risk of over-use or abuse of the idea (Carozza 2008; Rao 2008; Feldman 2000). Others warn of at least the potential for the invocation of human dignity by courts to be no more than an insincere 'sham' or a 'cover' for decisions based on other ideological grounds (McCrudden 2008). It would therefore appear that the legitimating functions of human dignity in constitutional adjudication are strongest in those domains where there is a clear core consensus about its meaning – for instance, in cases involving unambiguous violations of the physical and mental integrity of persons – and more tenuous as the content and requirements of human dignity become more sharply contested. Much more development both of the law across a widely diverse set of traditions and of the scholarly literature on dignity will be needed before the substantive and the functional dimensions of human dignity will be able to reinforce each other more fully.

NOTES

1. I am grateful to LaShel Shaw for her excellent research assistance.
2. Much of this development is related to the growth and influence of international human rights law as well, which consistently incorporates references to human dignity as a foundational value throughout its network of treaties, declarations and other instruments. Although this chapter will focus on the comparative constitutional aspects of the idea of human dignity rather than on its role in international law, these two dimensions are often difficult to separate and inevitably bleed into each other, as will be apparent in the subsequent discussion. The European Court of Human Rights (ECHR), as an international tribunal that plays a significant constitutional function within the states of the Council of Europe, lies at the crossroads of that relationship, and accordingly this discussion will also include various references to the ECHR.
3. Cf. The Supreme Court of India in *Rameshwar Prasad and Ors. v Union of India and Anr. – 24/01/2006 –* which questions moral realism's presumption that there are discoverable standards to judge whether public policies infringe on human dignity.
4. Available in English at http://www.bverfg.de/entscheidungen/rs20030924_2bvr143602en.html.
5. Available in French at http://www.rajf.org/article.php3?id_article=245.
6. Available in English at http://www.utexas.edu/law/academics/centers/transnational/work_new/german/case.php?id=658.
7. Many of the Hungarian Constitutional Court decisions cited in this essay can be found in English translation in Holló and Erdei 2005.
8. The varied historical roots of the idea are amply elaborated in Kretzmer and Klein 2002, which also represents the single most broad-ranging and useful survey of the use and development of the idea of human dignity in comparative and international law.
9. One of the most interesting illustrations of the dignity-based imperative to treat persons as ends and not means can be found in the German Constitutional Court's decision to strike down anti-terrorism laws that allowed the air force to shoot down aircraft that had been hijacked, because the importance of the dignity of other passengers and crew members required that they not be objectified and have their lives sacrificed for the greater good. Bundesverfassungsgericht [BVerfG] [Federal Constitutional Court] 357/05, 2 February 2006. http://www.bundesverfassungsgericht.de/entscheidungen/rs20060215_1bvr035705.html. Matthias Mahlmann contends that this Kantian version of human dignity is the most representative of the German constitutional tradition (Mahlmann 2010).
10. See the very interesting discussion by the Supreme Court of India in *M. Nagaraj & Others v Union of India & Others – 9/10/2006*, philosophizing at length about the relationship between Indian conceptions of human dignity and the German understanding of dignity, and the extent to which German ideals thus inform their decision.
11. See e.g. HC 5100/94 *Public Committee against Torture v Government of Israel* [1999], available in English at elyon1.court.gov.il/files_eng/94/000/051/a09/94051000.a09.pdf [6I]; *Napier v The Scottish Ministers* [2004] SLT 555 (UK) [3A].
12. Some scholars have nevertheless argued that human dignity plays an important role as a background value in US constitutional jurisprudence despite the limited explicit invocations of the term (Goodman 2005).
13. See also *Atkins v Virginia*, 536 US 304 (2002) (explaining that human dignity undergirds Eighth Amendment, in finding the application of the death penalty to a mentally retarded defendant to be unconstitutional).
14. See e.g. *F P+B, F. c/ Sté Hachette Filipacchi associés*, Cour de Cassation première chambre civile [Cass. 1re. civ.] 7 March 2006; *SNC Hachette Filipacchi associés c/ Épx G.*, Cour de Cassation deuxiéme chambre civile [Cass. 2e civ.] 4 November 2004; *SNC Prisma Presse et a. c/ Saada, dit Sarde*, Cour de Cassation première chambre civile [Cass. 1re. civ.] 12 July 2001.
15. *Id.*, see especially (Spielman, J. and Jebens, J., dissenting). The case was decided 4:3, with the majority finding a violation of Article 10's Freedom of Expression in the Austrian court's decision.

16. Cf. the French Cour de Cassation in Cass. crim., 12 November 2008, no. 07-83.398, *F PF, v c/ Assoc. Act Up Paris et al.* The decision upholds limits on freedom of expression in the form of fines imposed on a man for publishing an article contending that homosexuals are morally inferior and dangerous to humanity. The Court determined that the punishment was justified because his words were offensive and contrary to human dignity.

17. *Gamzu v Yeshaiahu (alternatively, Yesayahu).* RCA 4905/98 [2001] 55(3) PD 360. Good descriptions of the case can be found in Rabin and Shaney (2003–2004) and in Barak-Erez and Gross (2007). The case itself can be found online, in Hebrew, at http://elyon1.court.gov.il/files/98/050/049/A11/98049050.a11.pdf.

18. The judicial test for equality established by the Canadian Supreme Court in *Law v Canada* ([1999] 1 SCR 497) has two parts. First, the court must determine if the law or government policy distinguishes between different classes of people, whether facially or through its effects. If the law does have such a distinction, *and* the resulting discrimination harms human dignity, then the law is unconstitutional under section 15 of the Canadian Charter.

19. In Israel, for instance, Justice Barak's dissent in *Adalah v Minister of the Interior* HCJ 7052/03 [2006] (upholding temporary Israeli laws that limited Arab family reunification for security reasons) explains that equality is a fundamental part of dignity and offers an explanation of the importance of family to human dignity, complete with an extensive look at jurisprudence from countries around the world. The case has been translated into English by the Israeli court, and can be found at http://elyon1.court.gov.il/files_eng/ 03/520/070/a47/03070520.a47.pdf.

20. See e.g. *M v H* [1999] 2 SCR 3 (Can.) (giving same-sex couples the same legal rights as opposite-sex couples in common law marriages); *National Coalition for Gay and Lesbian Equality v Minister of Justice* 1999 (1) SA 6 (S. Afr.) (banning laws against sodomy as unconstitutional); *National Coalition for Gay and Lesbian Equality v Minister of Home Affairs* 2000 (2) SA 1 (S. Afr.) (removing legal distinctions between same-sex couples and opposite-sex couples in the context of immigration laws) [4I]; *Du Toit v Minister of Welfare and Population Development* 2003 (2) SA 198 (CC) (S. Afr.) (mandating that otherwise qualified same-sex couples be permitted to adopt children); *Minister of Home Affairs v Fourie* 2006 (1) SA 524 (CC) (S. Afr.) (finding that same-sex couples had the constitutional right to marry); *Lawrence v Texas*, 539 US 588 (2003) (striking down state laws prohibiting consensual sodomy).

21. See e.g. *Vriend v Alberta* [1998] 1 SCR 493; *Apparel Export Promotion Council v A.K. Chopra* 1999 (1) SCR 117 (Ind.); HCJ 1284/99 *Jane Doe [Plonit] v IDF Commander [Galili/Brigadier General]* [1999] (Isr.). Note, however, that the Israeli use of dignity rather than equality to address sexual harassment cases has been sharply criticized (Rimalt 2008).

22. E.g. Cass. 1re. civ., 9 October 2001; *A. C. c/ C. et a* [arrêt no. 1511 P+B+R] [Juris-Data no. 011237]. For commentary on the case see Cachard (2002).

23. A recent French article, for instance, urged that weight requirements and physical inspections be imposed on all fashion models, in order to ensure that fashion shows do not become spectacles exploiting those suffering from anorexia. See Le Roy (2008).

24. Note that the Hungarian Court does nevertheless invalidate the majority of the narcotic drug law because the language was unclear and contradictory, which could lead to arbitrary enforcement, and which would therefore offend human dignity. The court also stresses the importance of allowing rehabilitation programs instead of/alongside punishment, for the sake of dignity. Cf. also *Jordan v State* 2002 (6) SA 642 (CC); (11) BCLR 1117 (CC). Though principally about the gender inequality of a law that punished prostitutes but not their consumers, the South African court explains that prostitution, unlike sodomy, can be regulated because there is not the same kind of dignity in buying and selling sex as there is in expressing love as part of a relationship.

25. Cf. *Quebec v Sydicat national des employes de l'hopital St-Ferdinand* [1996] 3 SCR 211, which lays out the philosophical origins of dignity in Canadian jurisprudence and grapples with the question of whether nudity is an affront to dignity if the person is so severely handicapped that he is not aware of his naked condition.

26. Discussed in Saban (2004).

27. In some systems, of course, the constitution itself refers to the foundational value of dignity, as in Germany and South Africa. Grundgesetz für die Bundesrepublik Deutschland [Constitution], Article 1; Constitution of the Republic of South Africa, chapter 2, § 10. Similarly, in Israel, the Basic Law on Human Dignity and Liberty has since the mid-1990s codified the fundamental value of dignity.

28. Again, the South African system provides an exception, including in its constitutional text an explicit requirement to take foreign and international law into account in its interpretation of the constitution. Constitution of the Republic of South Africa, chapter 2, § 39 ('When interpreting the Bill of Rights, a court, tribunal or forum (a) must promote the values that underlie an open and democratic society based on human dignity, equality and freedom; (b) must consider international law; and (c) may consider foreign law').

29. On the idea of human rights as supra-positive values more generally, see Neuman (2003).

REFERENCES

Bagaric, Mirko, and Allan, James (2006), 'The Vacuous Concept of Dignity', *Journal of Human Rights*, 5: 257–70.
Barak-Erez, Daphne and Aeyal M. Gross (2007), 'Social Citizenship: The Neglected Aspect of Israeli Constitutional Law', in Daphne Barak-Erez and Aeyal M. Gross (eds), *Exploring Social Rights*, Oxford: Hart Publishing, 243–61.
Bates, Justin (2005), 'Human Dignity – An Empty Phrase in Search of Meaning?', *Judicial Review*, 10: 165–68.
Bracey, Christopher A. (2005), 'Dignity in Race Jurisprudence', *University of Pennsylvania Journal of Constitutional Law*, 7: 669–720.
Cachard, Olivier (2002), 'La Contagion Rétroactive de l'Obligation Médicale d'Information [The Retroactive Application of the Medical Duty to Inform]', *La semaine juridique*, édition générale, 12, 551–4.
Capps, Patrick (2009), *Human Dignity and the Foundations of International Law*, Oxford: Hart Publishing.
Carozza, Paolo G. (2003), 'My Friend is a Stranger: The Death Penalty and the Global *Ius Commune* of Human Rights', *Texas Law Review*, 81: 1032–89.
Carozza, Paolo G. (2007), 'Il Traffico dei Diritti Umani nell'Età Post-Moderna [Trafficking in Human Rights in the Post-Modern Age]', in Luca Antonini (ed.), *Il Traffico dei Diritti Insaziabili* [Trafficking in Insatiable Rights], Soveria Manelli, Italy: Rubbettino, 81–105.
Carozza, Paolo G. (2008), 'Human Dignity and Judicial Interpretation of Human Rights: A Reply', *European Journal of International Law*, 19: 931–44.
Dixon, Rosalind and Martha Nussbaum (2011), 'Abortion, Dignity and a Capabilities Approach', in Beverly Baines, Daphne Barak-Erez and Tsvi Kahana (eds), *Feminist Constitutionalism*, Cambridge: Cambridge University Press.
Dupré, Catherine (2003), *Importing the Law in Post-Communist Transitions*, Oxford: Hart Publishing.
Ezer, Tamar (2003), 'Children's Rights in Israel: An End to Corporal Punishment?', *Oregon Review of International Law*, 5: 139–214.
Feldman, David (2000), 'Human Dignity as a Legal Value – Part II', *Public Law*, 2000: 61–76.
Fyfe, R. James (2007), 'Dignity as Theory: Competing Conceptions of Human Dignity at the Supreme Court of Canada', *Saskatchewan Law Review*, 70: 1–26.
Gimeno-Cabrera, Véronique (2004), *Le Traitement Jurisprudentiel du Principe de Dignité de la Personne Humaine*, Paris: Librairie Générale de Droit et de Jurisprudence.
Goodman, Maxine D. (2005), 'Human Dignity in Supreme Court Constitutional Jurisprudence', *Nebraska Law Review*, 84: 740–94.
Grant, Evadné (2007), 'Dignity and Equality', *Human Rights Law Review*, 7: 299–329.
Harris, John (1998), *Clones, Genes, and Immorality*, Oxford: Oxford University Press.
Henkin, Louis, Gerald L. Neuman, Diane F. Orentlicher and David W. Leebron (1999), *Human Rights*, New York: Foundation Press.
Holló, András and Árpád Erdei (eds) (2005), *Selected Decisions of the Constitutional Court of Hungary (1998–2001)*, Budapest: Akadémiai Kiadó.
Kretzmer, David and Eckart Klein (eds) (2002), *The Concept of Human Dignity in Human Rights Discourse*, The Hague: Kluwer Law International.
Lee, Patrick and Robert P. George (2008), 'The Nature and Basis of Human Dignity', *Ratio Juris*, 21: 173–93.
Le Roy, Mark (2008), 'Le Maire, le Mannequin, et la Protection de la Dignite de la Personne Humaine [The Mayor, the Mannequin, and the Protection of the Dignity of the Human Person]', *Actualité Juridique Edition Droit Administratif*, 80, http://www.psychanalyse-en-mouvement.net/anorexie:voix.off/index.php.
Mahlmann, Matthias (2010), 'The Basic Law at 60 – Human Dignity and the Culture of Republicanism', *German Law Journal*, 11: 9–32.
McAllister, Marc Chase (2004), 'Human Dignity and Individual Liberty in Germany and the United States as Examined Through Each Country's Abortion Jurisprudence', *Tulsa Journal of Comparative and International Law*, 11: 491–520.
McCrudden, Christopher (2008), 'Human Dignity and Judicial Interpretation of Human Rights', *European Journal of International Law*, 19: 655–724.
Moon, Gay (2006), 'From Equal Treatment to Appropriate Treatment: What Lessons from Canadian Equality Law on Dignity and on Reasonable Accommodation Teach the United Kingdom?', *European Human Rights Law Review*, 6: 695–921.
Neuman, Gerald (2003), 'Human Rights and Constitutional Rights: Harmony and Dissonance', *Stanford Law Review*, 55: 1863–900.
O'Connell, Rory (2008), 'The Role of Dignity in Equality Law: Lessons from Canada and South Africa', *International Journal of Constitutional Law*, 6: 267–86.
Rabin, Yoram and Yuval Shaney (2003–2004), 'The Israeli Unfinished Constitutional Revolution: Has the Time Come for Protecting Economic and Social Rights?', *Israel Law Review*, 37: 299–345.
Rao, Neomi (2008), 'On the Use and Abuse of Dignity in Constitutional Law', *Columbia Journal of European Law*,

14: 201–56.

Rimalt, Noya (2008), 'Stereotyping Women, Individualizing Harassment: The Dignitary Paradigm of Sexual Harassment Law between the Limits of Law and the Limits of Feminism', *Yale Journal of Law and Feminism*, 19: 391–447.

Saban, Ilan (2004), 'Minority Rights in Deeply Divided Societies: A Framework Analysis and the Case of the Arab-Palestinian Minority in Israel', available at http://elyon1.court.gov.il/files/99/120/041/A10/99041120.a10.pdf.

Whitman, James Q. (2004), 'The Two Western Cultures of Privacy: Dignity Versus Liberty', *Yale Law Journal*, 113: 1151–221.

Cases

Adalah Legal Centre for Arab Minority Rights in Israel v Minister of Interior, HCJ [Israeli High Court of Justice] 7052/03 [2006] (1) IsrLR 443.

Adalah Legal Centre for Arab Minority Rights in Israel v Tel-Aviv-Jaffa Municipality, HCJ [Israeli High Court of Justice] 4112/99, PD 56(5) 393 (2002).

Alkotmánybíróság [AB] [Hungarian Constitutional Court] 14/2000 (V. 12).

Alkotmánybíróság [AB] [Hungarian Constitutional Court] 42/2000 (XI. 8).

Alkotmánybíróság [AB] [Hungarian Constitutional Court] 58/2001 (XII. 7).

Alkotmánybíróság [AB] [Hungarian Constitutional Court] 22/2003 (IV. 28).

Alkotmánybíróság [AB] [Hungarian Constitutional Court] 54/2004 (XII. 13).

Alkotmánybíróság [AB] [Hungarian Constitutional Court] 43/2005 (XI. 14).

Alkotmánybíróság [AB] [Hungarian Constitutional Court] 45/2005 (XII. 14).

Alkotmánybíróság [AB] [Hungarian Constitutional Court] 39/2007 (VI. 20).

Atkins v Virginia, 536 US 304 (2002).

Apparel Export Promotion Council v A.K. Chopra, 1999 (1) SCR [Supreme Court of India] 117.

Bundesverfassungsgericht [BVerfG] [Federal Constitutional Court] 39, 1, 1975.

Bundesverfassungsgericht [BVerfG] [Federal Constitutional Court] 45, 187, 1977.

Bundesverfassungsgericht [BVerfG] [Federal Constitutional Court] 1436/02, 24 September 2003, available in English at http://www.bverfg.de/entscheidungen/rs20030924_2bvr143602en.html.

Bundesverfassungsgericht [BVerfG] [Federal Constitutional Court] 2378/98, 3 March 2004, available in English at http://www.utexas.edu/law/academics/centers/transnational/work_new/german/case.php?id=658.

Bundesverfassungsgericht [BVerfG] [Federal Constitutional Court] 357/05, 2 February 2006.

Bundesverfassungsgericht [BVerfG] [Federal Constitutional Court] 1783/05, 13 June 2007.

1981 BVerwGE 64, 274 (Federal Administrative Court).

Campbell v Mirror Group Newspapers [2004] 2 AC (House of Lords) 457.

Christian Education South Africa v Minister of Education 2000 (10) BCLR [Constitutional Court of South Africa] 1051 (CC).

Conseil D'Etat [CE] [Highest Administrative Court, France], 27 October 1995, Commune de Morsang-sur-Orge.

Cour de Cassation [Appellate Court, France] in Cass. crim. [Criminal Appeal], 12 November 2008, no. 07-83.398, F PF, *v c/* Assoc. Act Up Paris et al.

Cour de Cassation [Appellate Court, France] première chambre civile [Cass. 1re. civ.], 12 July 2001, SNC Prisma Presse et al. c/ Saada, dit Sarde.

Cour de Cassation [Appellate Court, France] première chambre civile [Cass. 1re. civ.], 9 October 2001; A. C. c/ C. et al. [arrêt no. 1511 P+B+R] [Juris-Data no. 011237].

Cour de Cassation [Appellate Court, France] deuxième chambre civile [Cass. 2e civ.], 4 November 2004, SNC Hachette Filipacchi associés c/ Épx G.

Cour de Cassation [Appellate Court, France] première chambre civile [Cass. 1re. civ.], 7 March 2006, F P+B, F. c/ Sté Hachette Filipacchi associés.

Dawood, Shalabi and Thomas v Minister of Home Affairs 2000 (3) SA [Constitutional Court of South Africa] 936 (CC).

Du Toit v Minister of Welfare and Population Development 2003 (2) SA [Constitutional Court of South Africa] 198 (CC) (S. Afr.).

Gamzu v Yeshaiahu (alternatively, Yesayahu), RCA 4905/98 (2001) 55 (3) PD 360.

Hope v Pelzer, 536 US 730 (2002).

I v The United Kingdom, no. 25680/94, ECHR [European Court of Human Rights] 2002.

In Re: Noise Pollution, 2005 (1) Supp. SCR [Supreme Court of India] 624.

Indiana v. Edwards, 554 US 208 (2008).

Islamic Academy of Education v State of Karnataka, 2003 (6) SCC [Supreme Court of India] 697.

Jane Doe [Plonit] v IDF Commander [Galili/Brigadier General] (1999), HCJ [Israeli High Court of Justice] 1284/99.

John Vallamattom and Anr. v Union of India, 2003 (1) Supp. SCR [Supreme Court of India] 638.
Jordan v State 2002 (6) SA [Constitutional Court of South Africa] 642 (CC); (11) BCLR 1117 (CC).
Khosa v Minister of Social Development, 2004 (6) SA [Constitutional Court of South Africa] 505 (CC).
Law v Canada (Minister of Employment and Immigration), [1999] 1 SCR [Canadian Supreme Court] 497.
Lawrence v Texas, 539 US 558, 574 (2003).
M v H [1999] 2 SCR [Canadian Supreme Court] 3.
M. Nagraj v Union of India, 2006 (8) SCC [Supreme Court of India] 212.
Minister of Home Affairs v Fourie 2006 (1) SA [Constitutional Court of South Africa] 524 (CC) (S. Afr).
Napier v The Scottish Ministers [2004] SLT 555 (UK) [3A].
National Coalition for Gay and Lesbian Equality v Minister of Home Affairs 2000 (2) SA [Constitutional Court of South Africa] 1.
National Coalition for Gay and Lesbian Equality v Minister of Justice 1999 (1) SA [Constitutional Court of South Africa] 6.
NM v State 2007 (5) SA [Constitutional Court of South Africa] 250 (CC) (S. Afr.).
Planned Parenthood v Casey, 505 US 833, 916 (1992).
Plonit v Israel, CrimA [Israeli Criminal Appeals Court] 4596/98 (2000), IsrSC 54(1) 145.
Pretty v United Kingdom, no. 2346/02, ECHR [European Court of Human Rights] 2002-III.
Price v the United Kingdom, no. 33394/96, ECHR [European Court of Human Rights] 2001-VII.
Public Committee against Torture v Government of Israel, HCJ [Israeli High Court of Justice] 5100/94 (1999). Available in English at http://elyon1.court.gov.il/files_eng/94/000/051/a09/94051000.a09.pdf.
Quebec v Sydicat national des employes de l'hopital St-Ferdinand [1996] 3 SCR [Canadian Supreme Court] 211.
R (Burke) v General Medical Council, [2004] EWHC Admin (UK) 1897.
R (Burke) v General Medical Council [2005] EWCA Civ (UK) 1003.
R.D. Upadhyay v State of A.P. 2006 (3) SCR [Supreme Court of India] 1132.
Rameshwar Prasad (VI) v Union of India, 2006 (2) SCC [Supreme Court of India] 1.
South Africa v Grootboom 2001 SA [Constitutional Court of South Africa] 46 (CC).
Trocuik v British Columbia [2003] 1 SCR [Canadian Supreme Court] 835.
Vereinigung Bildender Künstler v Austria, no. 68354/01, ECHR [European Court of Human Rights] 2007-II.
Von Hannover v Germany, no. 59320/00, ECHR [European Court of Human Rights] 2004-VI.
Vriend v Alberta [1998] 1 SCR [Canadian Supreme Court] 493.
Yankov v Bulgaria, no. 39084/97, ECHR [European Court of Human Rights] 2003-XII.

26. Equality

Kate O'Regan and Nick Friedman

Equality is not only the Leviathan of Rights; it is also a Tantalus. It promises more than it can ever deliver. (Chief Justice of Canada, Beverley McLachlin (McLachlin 2001, at 20))

The right to equality is found in nearly all modern democratic constitutions. Yet the interpretation and application of this right present acutely difficult questions for lawyers and courts. These difficulties arise from the conception of equality itself. In this brief chapter we shall identify some of the difficult questions that arise in developing an equality jurisprudence and then consider how different legal systems (Canada, the United Kingdom and South Africa), have approached these questions.[1]

At the outset, we should acknowledge that the right to equality presents particular challenges for comparative constitutional analysis as each jurisdiction's response to equality is in significant ways dependent on the constitutional text in question (and the legislative framework) as well as each jurisdiction's social and political history. Understanding the equality jurisprudence of any jurisdiction will generally require some understanding of the social and economic circumstances of that society, unfortunately a matter beyond our scope in this brief chapter. This does not mean that comparative analysis is futile, but just that it should be approached with circumspection (see the useful discussions in Kahn-Freund 1974; Watson 1976; and Watson 1978).

We should also note here that in many jurisdictions the right to equality is not only a constitutional guarantee, but is protected in legislation as well. The consequence of this dual protection often produces complexity within national legal systems, a matter we shall consider in the individual jurisdictions we discuss.

1   THE CONCEPTION OF EQUALITY

The idea of equality as an enforceable right is modern (Fredman 2002, at 4), but as a philosophical principle it is ancient, stretching back to Aristotle's principle that 'persons who are equal should have assigned to them equal things' (Barker 1946, at ch XII §1). Although equality has been entrenched in constitutions since the eighteenth century, direct reliance on equality as the basis of a justiciable legal claim only developed widespread currency in the twentieth century.

The Aristotelian concept implies that like should be treated alike. This definition focuses on treatment as the core of equality. Before turning to the well-known critiques of the principle of equal treatment, we should acknowledge that the principle is full of promise in societies which routinely exclude certain people from a range of benefits. For Black South Africans under apartheid, Roma people throughout Europe, Jewish people in Nazi Germany or women in patriarchal societies all over the world, the principle of equal treatment – that they may not be treated differentially because of their race, ethnicity or sex – is a deeply affirming principle (see the similar remarks by Wintemute 2004, at 1180).

There are at least three problems, however, with the equal treatment approach to equality. First, societies and legal regulation are built on differentiation. The age at which you may vote, the classes of people entitled to social benefits and rates of taxation are all based on necessary differentiation between different people. How does an equal treatment approach determine which of these differentiations is justifiable and which not? The principle of equal treatment, which simply requires like to be treated alike, cannot on its own establish when it is permissible not to treat people the same (for a full discussion, see Westen 1982; and Hogg 2005, at 40). Indeed, Aristotle's own writing recognized this difficulty: 'But here arises a question which must not be overlooked. Equals and unequals – yes; but equals and unequals in what?' (Barker 1946, ch XII §2).

The second problem with the principle of equal treatment is that at times treating people equally can serve to entrench their inequality. Anatole France's ironic remark about the 'majestic equality of the law, which forbids the rich as well as the poor to sleep under bridges, to beg in the streets and to steal bread' (Fredman 2002, at 1) illustrates the fact that a facially neutral law may impact more harshly on some than others. At times too, patterns of deep social inequality may require special treatment for those who are disadvantaged in order to give them real access to opportunities.

A third problem with equal treatment lies in the fact that it tends to focus on individuals rather than on groups. And because it focuses on like treatment, it tends to overlook or eradicate difference. But human beings are constituted by the social networks within which they live and membership of a particular group, whether cultural or religious, for example, is often of deep importance to that individual. The celebration of difference, at times, might require different, rather than similar treatment. The principle of equal treatment cannot easily accommodate such claims.

The shortcomings of an approach based on equal treatment resulted in the development of other approaches. Perhaps the earliest example is to be found in *Griggs v Duke Power Company*,[2] a case brought under Title VII of the Civil Rights Act, in which the United States Supreme Court held that a law that on its face does not appear discriminatory may in its impact have a discriminatory effect. The principle established in *Griggs* applies only to Title VII, and not to the Fourteenth Amendment, which remains focused on unequal treatment disclosing a discriminatory purpose (see *Washington v Davis*; *McCleskey v Kemp*). The shift from focusing on treatment to impact is fundamental. It places the disadvantaged group at the centre of the enquiry, and has become the starting point for what has been referred to as a jurisprudence of substantive equality, rather than formal equality.

The more divided a society, the deeper the consequences of a discriminatory impact jurisprudence, as Justice White observed in *Washington v Davis* (at 248):

> A rule that a statute designed to serve neutral ends is nevertheless invalid, absent compelling justification, if in practice it benefits or burdens one race more than another would be far reaching and would raise serious questions about and perhaps invalidate, a whole range of tax, welfare, public service, regulatory and licensing statutes that may be more burdensome to the poor and to the average black than to the average white.

There can be no doubt that often there is a tension between an equal treatment approach to equality and a disparate impact approach (see the extended discussion of this in Collins

2003). This tension is ordinarily best illustrated by the manner in which the two approaches view the lawfulness of remedial action or affirmative action programmes. Recently, it was vividly illustrated in a slightly different context. In *Ricci et al v DeStefano et al* the United States Supreme Court was faced with a case which became famous during the confirmation hearings of the Associate Justice of the United States Supreme Court, Judge Sotomayor.

The case arose from human resources practices in the fire-fighting department of the City of New Haven. Tests set to determine who would be eligible for promotion resulted in no African-American candidates and only two Hispanic candidates proving eligible, in a City whose Hispanic and African-American residents jointly constitute nearly 60% of the population. New Haven was threatened with legal action in terms of Title VII of the Civil Rights Act on the grounds that, on a disparate impact analysis, the test was discriminatory. New Haven withdrew the test and the results and planned to find a different way to determine promotion questions. The withdrawal was challenged by an association of white fire-fighters on the grounds that the withdrawal ran foul of the equal treatment requirement of the Civil Rights Act, as the City was refusing to promote the white fire-fighters who had passed the tests 'because of their race'. The trial court and then a bench of the Second Circuit (of which Sotomayor was a member) upheld the City's right to withdraw the test. On appeal to the Supreme Court, a majority disagreed, holding that the City could only succeed if it could show a 'strong basis in evidence' that it would have lost a disparate impact challenge. Scalia J wrote a separate concurrence in which he said:

> I ... write separately to observe that [the Court's] resolution of this dispute merely postpones the evil day on which the Court will have to confront the question: Whether, or to what extent, are the disparate-impact provisions of Title VII of the Civil Rights Act of 1964 consistent with the Constitution's guarantee of equal protection? ... But the war between disparate impact and equal protection will be waged sooner or later, and it behooves us to begin thinking about how – and on what terms – to make peace between them.

Drawing on the idea that equality should focus on impact rather than treatment, the Canadian Supreme Court (as we shall describe in greater detail later) has developed an equality jurisprudence based on section 15 of the Canadian Charter of Rights and Freedoms which recognises that equal treatment is not the central idea of unfair discrimination. The Court held that discrimination is 'a distinction, whether intentional or not but based on grounds relating to personal characteristics of the individual or group, which has the effect of imposing burdens, obligations or disadvantages on such individual or group not imposed on others' (*Law Society of British Columbia v Andrews*, at para 19).

Adopting an approach which accepts that the purpose of an equality guarantee is to seek to remedy patterns of group disadvantage in a society requires the courts to answer the question – what is inequality? There are many answers to this question (Fredman 2002, at 11–23; Westen 1982; Young 1990; Minow 1990; Dworkin 2000). Should we define inequality by reference to material inequality? Or should we consider inequality to arise when human beings are treated as less worthy of respect because of their membership of a particular group? Or should we consider inequality to exist where social groups are excluded from important social, political and economic institutions? Courts in both Canada and South Africa have grappled with these questions as the more detailed discussion below will illustrate.

An approach to equality that focuses on effect or impact rather than treatment or discriminatory intent will ordinarily accept that establishing programmes to benefit those who have been disadvantaged by patterns of discrimination in the past is not inconsistent with equality, if such programmes will contribute to the eradication of disadvantage in the future. Both section 15(2) of the Canadian Charter of Human Rights and Freedoms and section 9(2) of the South African Constitution expressly permit such programmes within the constitutional provision protecting equality.

We can see from the above that different conceptions of equality will have a material impact on the jurisprudence of a particular jurisdiction. In considering the specific jurisdictions below, some of the questions that have arisen from this very brief introduction should be borne in mind. They are the following:

(1)   Does the jurisdiction consider that an equality guarantee (or prohibition on discrimination) is primarily aimed at preventing unequal treatment or at preventing unequal impact?
(2)   If the jurisdiction starts from the premise that unequal impact should be prevented, what does it consider to be the defining characteristic of inequality (if this question is considered at all)? Material inequality? Failure to treat people as of equal worth?
(3)   Does the jurisdiction permit remedial action (or affirmative action) to be taken to remedy the consequences of past discrimination? If so, what are the legal principles that govern such action?

We now turn to a consideration of the first of three jurisdictions, Canada.

2   CANADA

Canada's guarantee of equality is contained in section 15 of the Charter of Rights and Freedoms. That section provides:

> (1) Every individual is equal before and under the law and has the right to the equal protection and benefit of the law without discrimination and, in particular, without discrimination based on race, national or ethnic origin, colour, religion, sex, age or mental or physical disability.
> (2) Subsection 1 does not preclude any law, program or activity that has as its object the amelioration of conditions of disadvantaged individuals or groups including those that are disadvantaged because of race, national or ethnic origin, colour, religion, sex, age or mental or physical disability.

The section binds not only the federal government, but every provincial government in Canada. It should be noted that all the provinces, both territories and the federal parliament have enacted human rights codes which prohibit unfair discrimination by private individuals and associations and provide remedies for the breach of this prohibition (Tarnopolsky 1985, at para 2.3).[3] In most provinces,[4] Human Rights Commissions have been established to administer the human rights legislation. The Commissions receive complaints and then investigate and seek to settle them (Tarnopolsky 1985, at para 14.60.6). If a Commission considers it warranted after investigation, the complaint may be referred to the relevant Human Rights Tribunal to adjudicate the claim. The jurisprudence developed by the Supreme Court of Canada in respect of section 15 is of importance to the determination of discrimination complaints lodged under the various Human Rights Codes (Tarnopolsky 1985, at para 16.2.1). Perhaps the most famous case illustrating the relationship between section 15 of the

Charter and the human rights codes is *Vriend v Alberta*, in which the Supreme Court of Canada held that the Individual's Rights Protection Act of Alberta was in conflict with section 15 of the Charter because it failed to prohibit discrimination on the ground of sexual orientation.

Section 15 was first interpreted by the Supreme Court of Canada in *Law Society of British Columbia v Andrews*. That decision makes the following clear: first, the Court interprets section 15 so as to promote a substantive, not merely formal, understanding of the equality guarantee, specifically focusing on the impact of a legislative distinction on a claimant. Second, section 15 is a provision that prohibits discrimination on any of the enumerated grounds or on a ground analogous to the enumerated grounds. The enumerated grounds are race, national or ethnic origin, colour, religion, sex, age and mental or physical disability. At least three analogous grounds have been identified by the Canadian Supreme Court: citizenship (which was recognized as an analogous ground in *Andrews* itself);[5] marital status;[6] and sexual orientation.[7] Third, legislation which violates section 15 may nevertheless be justified in terms of section 1 of the Charter. Two of the six judges[8] who participated in the decision in *Andrews* held the legislative provision to be justified under section 1 of the Charter.[9]

In a pair of cases dealing with section 15 handed down on the same day (25 May 1995),[10] *Egan v Canada* and *Miron v Trudel*, the judges of the Supreme Court of Canada diverged on the correct test for discrimination in terms of section 15. The first approach (followed by Lamer CJ and La Forest J, Gonthier J and Major J) adopted an 'internal relevance' test, holding that there will be no violation of section 15 if the distinction drawn by legislation is relevant to the functional values underlying the legislation. Thus, if the underlying purpose of the legislation is to protect the traditional institution of marriage (as in heterosexual marriage), then it is permissible to distinguish between heterosexual and homosexual couples in pursuit of that protection (see the judgment of La Forest in *Egan*, at para 13).

McLachlin J, Cory J, Iacobucci J and Sopinka J followed approaches that were similar to one another, although not identical. They all rejected the 'internal relevance' test and considered that distinctions based on enumerated or analogous grounds will almost always violate section 15 and require justification under section 1 of the Charter. Thus, in *Egan*, they all held that the distinction between heterosexual and homosexual couples constituted a violation of section 15, but although the other three judges considered the legislative distinction to be unjustified under section 1, Sopinka J held the distinction to be justified. L'Heureux-Dubé J adopted a different approach to the determination of what constitutes discrimination in the two cases. In *Egan,* she held that:

> A person or group of persons has been discriminated against within the meaning of section 15 of the Charter when members of that group have been made to feel, by virtue of the impugned legislative distinction, that they are less capable, or less worthy of recognition or value as human beings or as members of Canadian society, equally deserving of concern, respect and consideration. (At para 40)

These different approaches persisted for some years, although during that time there were several cases in which the Court held that whatever approach was adopted, the outcome would be the same (see, for example, *Eldridge v British Columbia (Attorney-General)*; and *Benner v Canada (Secretary of State)*). The differences were resolved in the case *Law v Canada*,[11] which became the leading case on the proper approach to section 15 for nearly a decade (see, for example, *Hislop v Canada*). In terms of *Law,* a court called upon to determine a section 15 claim must undertake three broad inquiries (at para 39):

1. Does the impugned law (a) draw a formal distinction between the claimant and others on the basis of one or more personal characteristics, or (b) fail to take account of the claimant's already disadvantaged position in society resulting in substantively different treatment on the basis of one or more personal characteristics? If so, there is differential treatment for the purposes of section 15(1).
2. Was the claimant subject to differential treatment on the basis of one or more of the enumerated/analogous grounds?
3. Does the differential treatment discriminate in a substantive sense, bringing into play the purpose of section 15(1) in remedying ills such as prejudice, stereotyping and historical disadvantage?

In considering, in relation to the third leg of the test, whether a particular legislative provision discriminates in a substantive sense, Iacobucci J summarized the purpose of section 15 as follows:

> It may be said that the purpose of section 15(1) is to prevent the violation of essential human dignity and freedom through the imposition of disadvantage, stereotyping, or political or social prejudice, and to promote a society in which all persons enjoy equal recognition at law as human beings or as members of Canadian society, equally capable and equally deserving of concern, respect and consideration. (*Law*, at para 51)

This reasoning placed human dignity at the centre of Canadian equality law, and established four factors relevant to the determination of whether human dignity has been impaired, although the Court expressly stated that this was not a closed list (*Law*, at para 62). These factors are: (i) pre-existing disadvantage; (ii) the relationship between the grounds of distinction and the claimant's circumstances; (iii) the ameliorative purposes or effects of the impugned legislation; and (iv) the nature and scope of the interests affected (*Law*, at paras 63–75).

The reasoning in *Law* and, in particular, its employment of the value of human dignity attracted some support (see, for example, Mendes 2000, at 19–23; Reaume 2003), but also criticism (Gretschner 2002, at 302; Brodsky 2003; Martin 2001; Sheppard 2004; Hogg 2005, at 55). The three primary concerns were the following: First, it was said that *Law* provided for considerations more relevant to the section 1 limitations analysis, which were to be considered in determining whether discrimination had taken place for the purposes of the section 15 analysis (see, for example, Hogg 2005, at 58–9; Hogg 2007, at 55.9). Second, it was said that the test focuses too closely on the purpose of the legislation (Brodsky 2003, at 207ff). It was argued that a narrow construction of those purposes leads to a non-substantive approach to equality. Third, the centralization of dignity within equality is vague and incapable of providing reliable predictive certainty as to which legislative distinctions will fall foul of section 15 (see, for example, Fudge 2007, at 237). Some commentators also noted that the human dignity requirement has, on an analysis of section 15 cases, proved a formidable hurdle for claimants (Ruder et al 2004, at 116).

In a recent case, *R v Kapp*, the Supreme Court of Canada has reconsidered the role of human dignity in the section 15 jurisprudence. The case concerned the grant of communal fishing licences to three aboriginal bands to fish for salmon at the mouth of the Fraser River in British Columbia for a period of 24 hours during August 1998. The appellants, who were engaged in commercial fishing on the same river, and who were not members of the aboriginal community, argued that the grant of these fishing rights discriminated against them on the grounds of race. The Crown argued that the purpose of the communal fishing licences was ameliorative within the meaning of section 15(2) of the Charter. This argument was upheld, with the result that the appellant's claim that they had been subjected to discrimination under section 15(1) failed. In the course of their joint judgment, McLachlin CJ and Abella J (with the support of all the other members of the Court)[12] acknowledged that the *Law* test which incorporated human dignity had created difficulties. They wrote:

> But as critics have pointed out, human dignity is an abstract and subjective notion that, even with the guidance of the four contextual factors, cannot only become confusing and difficult to apply; it has also proven to be an additional burden on equality claimants, rather than the philosophical enhancement it was intended to be. Criticism has also accrued for the way *Law* has allowed the formalism of some of the Court's post-*Andrews* jurisprudence to resurface in the form of an artificial comparator analysis focussed on treating likes alike. (*Kapp*, at para 22)

McLachlin CJ and Abella J went on to confirm the four factors identified in *Law* as being relevant to the discrimination analysis. They noted that the four factors are based on the principle of 'the perpetuation of disadvantage and stereotyping as the primary indicators of discrimination' (*Kapp*, at para 23).

It is clear from the foregoing that adopting a conception of equality based on substantive inequality is not a straightforward exercise. It gives rise to difficult questions relating to the conception of equality underlying section 15; and to complex methodological issues as to how to establish a workable test.

Another issue that illustrates the challenges arising from a commitment to employing a substantive conception of equality is the question of appropriate comparators. Equality is normally understood as a comparative concept requiring a complainant to point to some person who has been better treated in order to ground a claim and this has been the general approach in the Canadian jurisprudence.[13] There is no doubt that a conception of equality based on equal treatment does indeed presuppose a comparator group. Is the same true of a conception of equality focused on impact and with the purpose of preventing 'the violation of essential human dignity and freedom through the imposition of disadvantage, stereotyping, or political or social prejudice'?

There are two issues to be considered here: the first is that the deeper the existing disadvantage with the consequence that a disadvantaged group or individual is differently placed to others, the more difficult it may be to find a comparator who is similarly situated for the purposes of comparison. The second is that if the focus of substantive equality is to prevent disadvantage or social or political exclusion, it may not be necessary to establish that a comparator exists at all, if it can be shown that the effect of a provision is socially disadvantageous on a prohibited ground or political exclusionary on the same ground (see, for a discussion, Moreau 2006). This is a question a full consideration of which is beyond the scope of this chapter, but it is interesting to note that the identification of the appropriate comparator has caused difficulties in Canadian jurisprudence. Indeed it has been described by one judge as 'an important battleground in much of the section 15(1) jurisprudence' (Binnie J in *Hodge v Canada*, at para 18).

In *Hodge v Canada,* the appellant was seeking a survivor's pension in terms of the Canada Pension Plan as the survivor of a man with whom she had had a common law heterosexual partnership spanning eleven years. Before he died, the partnership had permanently ended, according to the applicant, because of the physical and verbal abuse she had suffered from the man. The Pension Plan made provision for married spouses who were separated to claim as survivors, but not for divorcees or partners where the partnership was permanently ended. The appellant argued that the rules of the Plan were discriminatory on the ground of marital status because they permitted married spouses who were separated to receive a pension, but not a partner in her circumstances. The Supreme Court of Canada emphasized that the selection of a comparator in a section 15 claim is of importance at every step of the section 15 analysis (*Hodge v Canada*, at para 17).

The appellant had identified the appropriate comparator group as the group of separated married spouses but Binnie J, for a unanimous court, held that this was not the correct comparator. He reasoned that as the appellant no longer considered herself to be a spouse in any sense of the term, even on the extended 'common law' definition, the proper comparator was not separated married spouses, but former married spouses (that is, divorcees), who also could not claim under the Plan (*Hodge v Canada*, at para 2). As a result, her claim failed.

From *Hodge*, we can see that the selection of the comparator can determine the outcome of the case. This was sharply illustrated in another case heard in the same term by the Supreme Court of Canada, *Auton (Guardian, ad litem of) v British Columbia (Attorney General)*.[14] A group of autistic children and their parents challenged the province of British Columbia's failure to provide for a form of behavioural therapy for pre-school autistic children in the provincial health plan.[15] The therapy was expensive, costing between Can $45 000 and $60 000 per year per child. The appellants argued that the appropriate comparator group was non-disabled children and their parents or adult persons with mental illness. McLachlin CJ on behalf of a unanimous court rejected these groups, following the reasoning in *Hodge*: 'the comparator group should mirror the characteristics of the claimant or claimant group relevant to the benefit or advantage sought, except for the personal characteristic related to the enumerated or analogous ground raised as the basis for discrimination' (*Auton*, at para 53).

Applying the criteria, the Court held that the appropriate comparator group was 'a non-disabled person or a person suffering a disability other than a mental disability (here autism) seeking or receiving funding for a non-core therapy important for his or her present and future health, which is emergent and only recently becoming recognized as medically required' (*Auton*, at para 55). The Court held that there was no evidence that there was such a comparator group that had received access to a non-core therapy and the claim therefore failed. Two concerns arise from this approach.

First, the Court, by characterizing the appropriate comparator group in this way on appeal and differently to the comparator groups identified by the claimants, rendered it impossible for the appellants to adduce evidence on whether such a group existed, and if it did, whether it had been benefited in a manner that the group represented by the claimants had not. Second, the considerations that animate the characterization of the comparator group are considerations that might best be considered in the section 1 analysis. They raise the question of whether a provincial health plan may be justified when it fails to provide non-core treatment for a therapy which is only just emerging as a recognized and recommended medical intervention. An important issue in *Auton* is the fact that the Court is dealing with a social healthcare plan. The costs of upholding the equality claim would have been significant, as appears from the above, and would inevitably have impacted in some way on the allocation of the health budget in British Columbia. Of course, the adjudication of any human rights claims may often have this consequence. However, equality claims with their distributive focus may often bring a court close to issues that inform the separation of powers, with the result that courts need to develop principles which will inform the manner in which the separation of powers will be considered in such cases.

A case which illustrates some of the sharp questions posed by the issues relating to the separation of powers in equality cases is *Newfoundland (Treasury Board) v Newfoundland Association of Public Employees (NAPE)*. The case arose out of a pay equity agreement signed by the government of the province of Newfoundland with five public sector trade unions, the purpose of which was to ensure that the principle of 'equal pay for work of equal value' applied to women employed by the provincial government. The agreement was signed in 1988 and provided for annual wage adjustments to achieve pay equity to start in April 1988 and end in 1992. The process of determining the adjustments to achieve pay equity took longer than expected and was only completed in March 1991, at which stage the provincial government estimated that immediate (and retroactive) implementation of the pay equity scheme would cost the health sector Can $24 million. At the time, however, the provincial government was experiencing an unprecedented financial crisis and it enacted a Public Sector Restraint Act freezing wage scales. Section 9 of that Act rendered void any obligation to implement pay equity adjustments retrospectively. The effect of the Act, thus, was to erase the provincial government's immediate Can $24 million pay equity obligation. It was agreed between the union and the province that the pay equity adjustments would be made by a series of future annual adjustments, not exceeding 2% of individual salaries per year, until pay equity was achieved (*Newfoundland*, at para 10).

Grievances were filed by union members in relation to the non-payment of the agreed retroactive pay equity adjustments. When the matter came before the Newfoundland Court of Appeal, the Court of Appeal in a celebrated remark commented that the tests for determining whether the limitation of a right is justified in terms of section 1 of the Charter that had been set in *R v Oakes* might need revisiting 'to oil their hinges to assure they swing in harmony with the Separation of Powers' (*Newfoundland*, at para 25) and dismissed the discrimination claim. On appeal, the Supreme Court of Canada found that section 9 did give rise to a breach of section 15 but held that it was justified under section 1 of the Charter. The Court did not find it necessary to adjust the *Oakes* test.

The government evidence in support of its justification argument under section 1 of the Charter was that, in addition to the wage freeze imposed on public sector employees (including Cabinet Ministers, members of the provincial legislature and others), it had closed 360 acute care hospital beds, frozen per capita student grants and grants to school boards, laid off 1300 permanent workers, as well as 350 part-time and 350 seasonal workers and terminated Medicare coverage for items such as routine dental surgery and basic optometry treatments (*Newfoundland*, at para 61). Binnie J, on behalf of a unanimous court, held that the severity of these measures indicated the depth of the financial crisis experienced by the provincial government. He found that the postponement of the achievement of pay equity was in the circumstances justified and dismissed the discrimination claim.

The judgment has been criticized for failing to protect the right to equality and as evidence of the limited capacity to effect redistribution through equality claims (Fudge 2007, at 251). It seems to us that the question raised in this case is similar to the question raised in *Auton*: what is the proper role for courts when an equality claim raises questions of budgeting and affordability, and should the doctrinal approach to equality vary in such circumstances?

3   THE UNITED KINGDOM

The United Kingdom does not have a written Constitution. It is different, therefore, from other countries that have written Constitutions, many of them with bills of rights entrenching the right to equality. This might lead some to query its place in this chapter. The fact that the United Kingdom does not have a single, written document entitled 'The Constitution' does not mean that it has no constitution. It does have a constitution (much of it written) which is an amalgam of statutes, rules and conventions which govern the way in which Britain is governed and the relationship between the government and the people (Turpin and Tomkins 2007, at 139).

Equality law in the United Kingdom is governed by the intersection of three strands of law, at least the first two of which might be described as part of the constitutional architecture of the United Kingdom: the European Convention on Human Rights, which became directly enforceable in the United Kingdom in 2000 as a result of the enactment of the Human Rights Act 1998, and European Union legislation. The third strand of law is domestic legislation prohibiting discrimination. Space does not permit a full analysis of all three sources of law. Instead, we shall deal briefly with the latter two before focusing on the jurisprudence emerging under article 14 of the European Convention.

The European Union grew out of the European Economic Community which was established by six founding member states through the Treaty of Rome in 1957 (also known as 'The Treaty on the functioning of the European Union'). The United Kingdom joined the Community in 1972.[16] The European Economic Community is now known as the European Community and is one of the three pillars of the European Union, which now has 27 member states. The Treaty of Rome has been considerably supplemented with further treaties. Significant supplementing treaties include the Treaty of Maastricht (also known as 'The Treaty on European Union', which came into force in 1993, and shifted the scope of the European Union to include political union and monetary union) and the Treaty of Lisbon (which came into force in late 2009, and significantly amended both the Treaty of Rome and the Treaty of Maastricht).

The original focus of the European Union was economic union, which was built on four key principles: the free movement of goods (article 28 of the Treaty of Rome, as amended by the Treaty of Lisbon); the free movement of persons (article 45, as amended); the free movement of services (article 56, as amended) and the free movement of capital (article 63, as amended). The treaty provisions regulating the economic aspect of the Union are directly binding on member states and enforceable in the European Court of Justice. In relation to discrimination law, a key provision is article 157 of the Treaty of Rome (originally article 141) which provides that '[e]ach member state shall ensure that the principle of equal pay for male and female workers for equal work or work of equal value is applied'. The interpretation of this provision by the European Court of Justice has produced an influential equality jurisprudence (see, for example, *Bilka-Kaufhaus GmbH v Weber von Hartz*; *Enderby v Frenchay*; *Kowalska v Freie und Hansestadt Hamburg*).

The commitment to the non-discrimination principle is to be found in other provisions in the Treaty of Rome as well, such as article 45 (as amended) which prohibits discrimination in employment on the grounds of nationality. The commitment to non-discrimination has increasingly animated a range of important European Union directives as well. Early directives were confined to workplace equality between men and women: the Equal Pay Directive 1975,[17] the Equal Treatment Directive 1976 and the Pregnant Workers Directive 1992.

More recent directives, enacted under a power conferred by the Treaty of Amsterdam (1997) to permit the European Union to legislate against discrimination on a wider range of grounds, have included the Race Directive which came into force in July 2000 (see Lester 2000) and the Framework Directive on Equal Opportunities in Employment (October 2000). The latter requires member states to take steps to prohibit discrimination on the grounds of age, disability, religion and sexual orientation. The former requires member states to prohibit discrimination on grounds of race not only in employment and social security (to which earlier Directives were confined), but also in relation to education and the access to supply of goods and services, including housing. A further Directive in 2004 extended the prohibition of discrimination in relation to goods and services to all grounds of discrimination (Equal Treatment in Goods and Services Directive 2004). Directives are a form of law-making in the European Union and 'shall be binding, as to the result to be achieved, upon each member State' (Treaty of Rome, article 288, as amended).

Many of the developments in the domestic anti-discrimination law in the United Kingdom have been spurred by the need to comply with these directives. Until recently, the overall effect in the United Kingdom was a patchwork of legislation and regulations with different grounds of discrimination attracting different levels of protection. There were a range of statutes prohibiting discrimination, including the Race Relations Act 1976, the Sex Discrimination Act 1975, the Equal Pay Act 1970, the Disability Discrimination Act 1995 and the Equality Act 2006. In addition, numerous regulations have been passed (often to comply with European Union directives) to extend anti-discrimination provisions to new grounds, such as sexual orientation, religion and age (see, for example, the Employment Equality (Sexual Orientation) Regulations 2003; the Sexual Orientation (Goods and Services) Regulations 2007; the Employment Equality (Religion or Belief) Regulations 2003; and the Employment Equality (Age) Regulations 2006). In an attempt to make the existing equality law simpler and more coherent, the United Kingdom Parliament passed the Equality Act 2010 (most provisions of which entered into force on 1 October 2010) replacing nine major pieces of legislation and around 100 other measures with a single Act.

4 ARTICLE 14 OF THE EUROPEAN CONVENTION ON HUMAN RIGHTS AND THE HUMAN RIGHTS ACT 1998

The European Convention on Human Rights is an international treaty drafted in the aftermath of the horrors of the Second World War under the auspices of the Council of Europe. The United Kingdom was its first signatory in March 1951. The United Kingdom has a dualist approach to international law (Brownlie 1979, at 49ff) so the European Convention was not incorporated into its domestic law immediately although, on the international plane, the United Kingdom was bound by its provisions. After the adoption of the Human Rights Act 1998, however, the Convention became directly enforceable in the United Kingdom in October 2000.

The Council of Europe now has 47 member states. It is based in Strasbourg, France, as is the European Court of Human Rights which is responsible for the enforcement of the Convention. There is one judge on the Court for each member state.[18] The Court receives an enormous number of claims each year, many of which are found not to be admissible.[19] If a claim proceeds, it is forwarded to a chamber of seven judges who consider both the admissibility and merits of the claim. At times, a claim may be referred to a Grand Chamber of 17 judges if it is concerned with a difficult question of interpretation or requires reconsideration of existing case-law.

Article 14 of the Convention is the provision directly concerned with equality. It provides, '[t]he enjoyment of the rights and freedoms set forth in this Convention shall be secured without discrimination on any ground such as sex, race, colour, language, religion, political or other opinion, national or social origin, association with a national minority, property, birth or other status'.

Article 14 prohibits discrimination in respect of 'the enjoyment of the rights and freedoms' in the Convention. For this reason the article has been described as a 'derivative' equality provision (Fredman 2002, at 85) in that a claimant must establish that the discrimination of which he or she complains relates to one of the other Convention rights.[20] It is not necessary, however, for the claimant to show that the other Convention right has been infringed (see, for example, *Abdulaziz, Cabales and Balkandali v United Kingdom*; and *Case relating to certain aspects on the use of languages in education in Belgium*). It is merely necessary that the discriminatory provision or conduct 'falls within the ambit' of another Convention right (*Abdulaziz, Cabales and Balkandali v United Kingdom*, at 259; *Rasmussen v Denmark*, at para 29; and *Botta v Italy*, at 259) and not necessary for a claimant to allege a breach of another Convention right (*Inze v Austria*). We shall return in a moment to this issue.

The Committee of Ministers of the Council of Europe has adopted a Protocol to the Convention, Protocol 12, which establishes a general prohibition of discrimination. Article 2 of the Protocol provides that: 'No one shall be discriminated against by any public authority on any ground such as those mentioned in' article 14. The United Kingdom has not ratified this Protocol apparently because, amongst other things, the text is 'too general and too open-ended' (see 617 House of Lords Official Report, cited in Lester et al 2009, at 4.14.2). Seventeen member states of the Council of Europe have ratified the Protocol, however, and it entered into force in ratifying states on 1 April 2005.[21]

Article 14 is narrowly framed and does not have the reach of section 15 of the Canadian Charter, or of section 9 of the South African Constitution. The effect of article 14 has arguably been most profound in relation to article 8 of the Convention which provides that everyone has 'the right to respect for his private and family life, his home and his correspondence' (Livingstone 1997, at 27) and in relation to social security benefits which are understood to fall within the ambit of article 1 to the First Protocol of the Convention, which concerns the peaceful enjoyment of possessions (*Stec and Others v United Kingdom*, at paras 54–5).

Between 1951 and 2000, the provisions of the European Convention of Human Rights, including article 14, were not directly enforceable within the United Kingdom. That changed with the adoption of the Human Rights Act which marked a radical departure for the United Kingdom in relation to the entrenchment and protection of human rights. In many senses, the Convention now operates as a Bill of Rights within the United Kingdom, though without giving the courts the power to declare legislation invalid (Klug 2007, at 712; Lester et al 2009, at 2.05).

The Act carefully stipulates the powers of courts in relation to the direct enforcement of the Convention. It provides that domestic courts 'must take into account' the jurisprudence of the European Court on Human Rights (section 2 of the Act).[22] The Act contains an interpretive obligation requiring courts to read and give effect to primary and subordinate legislation 'so far as it is possible to do so' in a way which is compatible with the Convention rights (section 3(1) of the Act).[23] The Act then provides that if the court concerned with the matter is a superior court[24] and the court is satisfied that a provision of primary legislation is incompatible with a Convention right, it may make a declaration of incompatibility which will not affect the validity of the provision (section 4(6)(a) of the Act). The making of such an order is considered to be a measure of last resort (*R v A (No 2)*, at para 44; *Ghaidan v Godin-Mendoza*, at para 39). Finally, section 6 of the Act makes it unlawful for a public authority (which includes a court or tribunal) to act in a way which is incompatible with Convention rights. This provision makes it plain that the Convention rights impose obligations upon public authorities, but not directly on private individuals or associations.

Given the provision of section 2, which requires courts in the United Kingdom to 'take into account' the jurisprudence of the European Court of Human Rights, it will be useful to set out briefly the approach of that Court to article 14. The approach taken by the European Court of Human Rights to determine whether discrimination exists was set out in one of the early cases, *Case relating to certain aspects on the use of languages in education in Belgium*, and, by and large, it has been followed consistently by the European Court since. The Court held that the article will not be violated if the differential treatment has a legitimate government purpose and there is a 'reasonable relationship of proportionality between the means employed and the ends sought to be realised' (*Belgian Language Case*, at 284; see also Wildhaber 2002, at 74). A complainant need not establish discriminatory intent (*Abdulaziz, Cabales and Balkandali v United Kingdom*, at paras 84–85) and the list of prohibited grounds of discrimination is not closed, although it is limited. Remedial action or positive discrimination will be subject to the same test: is it in furtherance of a legitimate government aim and is there a reasonable proportionality between the aim and the means employed? (See *Belgian Language Case*, at para 10: 'certain legal inequalities tend only to correct factual inequalities'.)

The question whether article 14 was applicable to disparate impact discrimination was considered in a recent and important Grand Chamber decision, *D.H. and Others v Czech Republic*.[25] The Court had to decide whether a race-neutral policy, shown statistically to have a disparate impact on a racial group, was discriminatory within the meaning of article 14. The case concerned Roma children in the Czech Republic and the evidence showed that Roma children were vastly over-represented in 'special schools' and under-represented in ordinary primary schools (*D.H. and Others*, at paras 192–3). This the Court held was sufficient to establish a prima facie case of indirect discrimination and to require the Government of the Czech Republic to show that the differential impact of the legislation was a result of objective factors unrelated to ethnic origin (*D.H. and Others*, at para 195). The Court found that the government had not shown a reasonable or justifiable basis for the differential impact and concluded that a breach of article 14 had been established (*Marckx v Belgium*, at 346).

One of the first questions faced by the courts in the United Kingdom was whether it should follow the test established by the European Court of Human Rights for determining whether a breach of article 14 had been established. In an early case concerning article 14, *Wandsworth London Borough Council v Michalak*, Brooke LJ in the Court of Appeal adopted a test (drawing on the European Court of Human Rights jurisprudence) formulated by a leading textbook (namely, Grosz et al 2000, at C14-08). That test was the following:

(i) Do the facts fall within the ambit of one or more of the substantive Convention provisions?
(ii) If so, was there different treatment as respects that right between the complainant on the one hand and other person put forward for comparison ('the chosen comparators') on the other?
(iii) Were the chosen comparators in an analogous situation to the complainant's situation?
(iv) If so, did the difference in treatment have an objective and reasonable justification: in other words, did it pursue a legitimate aim and did the differential treatment bear a reasonable relationship of proportionality to the aim sought to be achieved?

Brooke LJ noted that if the answer to any of these questions is no, then the claim will fail. He also noted that the questions constituted 'only a framework' and that there is potential for overlap between the last two and possibly the last three questions. Subsequently, a fifth question was suggested by Stanley Burnton J in the court of first instance *R (Carson) v Secretary of State for Work and Pensions,* namely whether the discrimination was on one of the specified grounds.

Later judgments, however, have eschewed the step-by-step approach followed in *Michalak.* Several of the judges in the House of Lords in *Carson* questioned whether the framework was really helpful; and pointed to the overlapping nature of several of the questions (particularly the third and fourth questions) (*Carson*, House of Lords judgment, at paras 2–3, 28–33, 61–4, 97; *Ghaidan v Godin-Mendoza,* at para 134).[26] Since then, the framework approach adopted in *Michalak* has generally not been used. The first question remains in one form or another: does the discriminatory act or rule in question fall within the ambit of one of the rights? (We return to this in a moment.)

There are then, broadly speaking, two remaining enquiries. The first is what has been called the 'comparability test' (Van Dijk and Van Hoof 1998, at 722; Feldman 2002, at 144; *Carson*, at para 69) and the other 'the justification test'. The former test, of course, is concerned with comparator groups and whether they are similarly or analogously situated to the complainant. The latter test focuses on the reason for the distinction and whether the reason is in pursuance of a legitimate government purpose and whether its effect is reasonably proportionate to that purpose (this is the test set in the *Belgian Language Case,* discussed above). Current article 14 jurisprudence in the United Kingdom focuses on the second leg of the test rather than on the first, in accordance with the approach taken in Strasbourg.

In the recent case of *AL (Serbia) v Home Secretary,* Baroness Hale of Richmond observed that under the Convention jurisprudence the focus is whether there is *different treatment,* whereas domestic discrimination legislation in the United Kingdom tends to focus on whether there is *less favourable treatment.* She noted, 'the classic Strasbourg statements of the law do not place any emphasis on the identification of an exact comparator. They ask whether "differences in otherwise similar situations justify a different treatment" ' (at para 24).

She concludes that it is better to focus not on the question whether the comparator is appropriate, but 'on the reasons for the difference in treatment and whether they amount to an objective and reasonable justification' (*AL (Serbia)*, at para 25). As we have seen in the discussion relating to Canada, extensive focus on the appropriate comparator can cause difficulty. The focus on justification, carrying with it the flexible proportionality standard, may help to avoid these difficulties and require courts to consider simply whether the difference in treatment pursues a legitimate government objective that is proportional to the purpose sought to be achieved.[27]

In some cases justifying the differential treatment will be particularly difficult, as Baroness Hale also acknowledged:

What does matter is whether this condition falls within the class for which 'very weighty reasons' are required if a difference in treatment is to be justified. Thus, for example, Strasbourg has said that where 'a difference of treatment is based on race, colour or ethnic origin, the notion of objective and reasonable justification must be interpreted as strictly as possible.' (*DH v Czech Republic* (Application No 57325/00) (unreported) 13 November 2007, para 196), while 'very convincing and weighty' reasons are required to justify a difference in treatment based on sex (eg *Abdulaziz, Cabales and Balkandali v United Kingdom* 7 EHRR 471, para 78) or sexual orientation (eg *EB v France* (Application No 43546/02) (unreported) 22 January 2008, para 91) or birth or adopted status (eg *Inez v Austria* (1987) 10 EHRR 394, para 41; *Pla v Andorra* (2004) 42 EHRR 522, para 61) or nationality (eg *Gaygusuz v Austria* (1996) 23 EHRR 364, para 42). (*AL (Serbia)*, at 29)

Baroness Hale then pointed to the differences between this jurisprudence under article 14 of the European Convention and the Fourteenth Amendment of the United States Constitution. She noted that not all differential treatment will fall within the scope of article 14 (*AL (Serbia)*, at para 30); moreover, the grounds which require 'very weighty reasons' are not the same grounds that attract strict scrutiny under the Fourteenth Amendment (*AL (Serbia)*, at para 30);[28] and finally, the test for justification under the European Convention is proportionality, regardless of the ground for the differentiation. The rational explanation test has not been adopted in Europe (*AL (Serbia)*, at para 30).

Two last questions arise for consideration: how have the United Kingdom courts determined whether alleged discriminatory rules or conduct fall within the ambit of one of the other rights? And how do they determine what grounds of discrimination fall within the scope of article 14?

The question of how the European Court addresses the question whether the discriminatory conduct falls within the 'ambit of' convention rights has been briefly considered above. The House of Lords has followed a similar approach. The suggestion in a textbook that 'even the most tenuous link with another provision in the Convention will suffice' has been rejected (Grosz et al, at C14-10; *R (on the application of RJM) v Secretary of State for Work and Pensions*, at para 60). In an important decision, *R (on the application of RJM)*, Lord Bingham proposed a core-penumbra test: the closer the issues in the case to the core of a convention right, the more likely article 14 will be engaged; the more penumbral the issues to the convention right, the less likely it will be (*R (on the application of RJM)*, at para 4). This test requires a purposive approach to the Convention right in question and an analysis of the core of the protection afforded by it.

In a more recent case, *R (on the application of Clift) v Secretary of State for the Home Department*, Lord Bingham again considered the approach and explained it further as follows:

Plainly expressions such as 'ambit', 'scope' and 'linked' used in the Strasbourg jurisprudence are not precise and exact in their meaning. They denote a situation in which a substantive Convention right is not violated, but in which a personal interest close to the core of such a right is infringed. This calls, as Lord Nicholls said in M, at para 14, for a value judgment. The court is required to consider, in respect of the Convention right relied on, what value that substantive right exists to protect. (At para 13)

It is worth concluding by noting that where the government operates a social security scheme, it will fall within the ambit of the First Protocol to the Convention which protects the right to the peaceful enjoyment of possessions (*R (on the application of RJM)*, at paras 31–4, relying on *Stec*, at paras 54–5). The scope of article 14 thus includes social security schemes.

As in Canada, when the question of non-discrimination arises in relation to social security schemes, the courts have been reluctant to engage in 'second-guessing' the legislative choices made. The decision in *R (on the application of RJM)* provides a recent and illuminating example of this approach. The case concerned an applicant who had been receiving a disability grant on account of his mental health problems. The scheme regulating the payment of disability grants provided that the disability grant would cease if the person receiving it became homeless. The House of Lords, relying on the European Court of Human Rights decision in *Stec*, found that the claim fell within the ambit of article 1 of the First Protocol (*R (on the application of RJM)*, at para 34). The Court also held that the rule in the scheme did discriminate against homeless people and that 'homelessness' was a prohibited ground within the meaning of article 14 (*R (on the application of RJM)*, at para 46).

The Court then had to consider whether the discrimination was justified. Lord Neuberger of Abbotsbury noted that the government had proffered two reasons to justify the discrimination: the first was that the provision was an attempt to encourage the disabled homeless to seek shelter and therefore help. The government noted that 90% of those without accommodation in the United Kingdom have problems connected with substance abuse and about 45% have mental health problems. The second reason provided by government was that those who have no accommodation are less likely to need the disability grant than those who have, because 'claimants in accommodation have a range of expenses and financial pressures ... that claimants without accommodation do not have' (*R (on the application of RJM)*, at para 51). In considering whether the discrimination was justified in these circumstances, Lord Neuberger reasoned as follows:

> However, policy concerned with social welfare payments must inevitably be something of a blunt instrument, and social policy is an area where a wide measure of appreciation is accorded by the European Court of Human Rights to the state ... As Lord Bingham said about a rather different statute, '(a) general rule means that a line must be drawn, and it is for Parliament to decide where', and this 'inevitably means that hard cases will arise falling on the wrong side of it, but that should not be held to invalidate the rule if, judged in the round, it is beneficial': *R (Animal Defenders International v Secretary of State for Culture, Media and Sport* [2008] AC 1312 para 33.
> ... In my view, the discrimination in the present case was justified, in the sense that the Government was entitled to adopt and apply the policy at issue. This is an area where the court should be very slow to substitute its view for that of the executive, especially as the discrimination is not on one of the express, or primary grounds.... (*R (on the application of RJM)*, at paras 54–6).[29]

This case illustrates the reluctance of courts in discrimination cases to second-guess the manner in which social security schemes have been designed out of respect for the democratic arms of government. The approach of the courts in matters such as these has often been criticized as too deferential (see, for example, Laurie 2009; Kavanagh 2004; Edwards 2002; Fredman 2006; and Allan 2006). Yet most commentators do accept that courts' power to intervene in matters such as these should be limited (Laurie 2009, at 411; Fredman 2006, at 55–7). Determining the proper role for courts in such cases is one of the most contested questions in modern democracies. We have seen that similar concerns arise in Canada, and when we turn to South Africa, we shall see that the question is pertinent there as well.

We turn now to the final question in this section of the chapter. As indicated above, article 14 prohibits discrimination on the grounds of sex, race, colour, language, religion, political or other opinion, national or social origin, association with a national minority, property, birth or other status. It is clear that this is not a closed list and the question arises how to determine what other bases for discrimination will fall within the phrase 'or other status'. It is now established in the United Kingdom that it also includes, amongst others, sexual orientation (*Dudgeon v United Kingdom*; *Fretté v France*; and *Ghaidan v Godin-Mendoza*), marital status (*Re P (A Child)*) and homelessness (*R (on the application of M)*). In the leading judgment on this question, the European Court of Human Rights explained that 'Article 14 prohibits, within the ambit of the rights and freedoms guaranteed, discriminatory treatment having as its basis or reason a personal characteristic ("status") by which persons or groups of persons are distinguishable from each other' (*Kjeldsen, Busk Madsen and Pedersen v Denmark*, at para 56). The House of Lords has emphasised that the test of 'personal characteristic' requires one to 'concentrate on what somebody is, rather than what he is doing or what is being done to him' (*R (on the application of RJM)*).[30]

The determination of what is included within the scope of 'or other status' is similar to the questions raised in Canada as to determining what are 'analogous' grounds falling within the prohibition of discrimination in article 15(1) of the Charter; and as we shall see, to the similar questions asked in South Africa. All three jurisdictions have adopted different, though not unrelated tests.

5   SOUTH AFRICA

Equality law in South Africa is governed by section 9 of the 1996 Constitution, which provides as follows:

1. Everyone is equal before the law and has the right to equal protection and benefit of the law.
2. Equality includes the full and equal enjoyment of all rights and freedoms. To promote the achievement of equality, legislative and other measures designed to protect or advance persons, or categories of persons, disadvantaged by unfair discrimination may be taken.
3. The state may not unfairly discriminate directly or indirectly against anyone on one or more grounds, including race, gender, sex, pregnancy, marital status, ethnic or social origin, colour, sexual orientation, age, disability, religion, conscience, belief, culture, language and birth.
4. No person may unfairly discriminate directly or indirectly against anyone on one or more grounds in terms of subsection (3). National legislation must be enacted to prevent or prohibit unfair discrimination.
5. Discrimination on one or more of the grounds listed in subsection (3) is unfair unless it is established that the discrimination is fair.

The equality provision displays a profound commitment to substantive equality. This commitment is visible most notably in section 9(2), which, in the first place, states that the focus of equality must be the 'full and equal *enjoyment* of all rights and freedoms', rather than equal access or equal treatment.[31] Second, section 9(2) permits government to undertake positive steps to alleviate material disadvantage – thus, the equality provision seeks to respond (similarly to section 15(2) of the Canadian Charter of Rights) to the harsh socio-economic inequalities left in the wake of apartheid. In this sense, the Constitution's equality guarantee includes a commitment to what might be called restitutional equality in that it seeks to remedy the inequalities that have arisen as a result of discriminatory policies in the past. That section 9 protects substantive equality is also evident from subsections (3) and (4), which prohibit not only direct discrimination, but also indirect discrimination, thus ensuring that equality is not undermined by facially neutral laws which in fact have an unequal impact.

It is no surprise that the South African Constitution focuses so strongly on substantive equality. As was described at the beginning of this chapter, one of the primary difficulties with formal equality is that, in focusing on equal treatment, it assumes that all persons are already equal to one another in important respects (specifically, though not exclusively, in respect of their socio-economic backgrounds). Therefore, requiring that two individuals be subjected to the same treatment may have the effect, given the social and economic equalities so deeply entrenched in South African society, that patterns of social and economic equality are maintained or even deepened. The protection of equality in South Africa necessarily takes place against this background, and thus suggests a substantive approach to equality, since a focus on merely formal equality might well perpetuate existing inequality along racial lines.

Beyond the commitment to substantive equality, section 9 is an unusually broad equality guarantee in two important respects. First, section 9(1) provides protection against any arbitrary or irrational differentiation in legislation, whether or not that differentiation is based on the grounds of discrimination listed in section 9(3) or an analogous ground. The government is obliged to establish that a challenged differentiation is rationally connected to a legitimate government purpose (*Prinsloo*, at para 25).[32]

Second, section 9(4) expressly provides that the prohibition of unfair discrimination imposes obligations upon private citizens and associations as well as upon the state. Section 9(4) also enjoins Parliament to pass legislation to prevent unfair discrimination. This is the only provision of the Bill of Rights which in so many words is expressly made binding on private individuals and institutions. In so doing, section 9 recognizes the need, given South Africa's discriminatory past, to eliminate discrimination in the private as well as the public sphere. It is true that section 8(2) of the Bill of Rights provides that constitutional rights will bind natural and juristic persons 'if, and to the extent that, it is applicable, taking into account the nature of the right and the nature of any duty imposed by the right', but section 9(4) renders it unnecessary to apply this test to the equality clause.

In 2000, the legislation required by section 9(4) was enacted – the Promotion of Equality and Prevention of Unfair Discrimination Act. The short title to the Act states that it is 'to give effect to section 9 … so as to prevent and prohibit unfair discrimination and harassment; to promote equality'. Like section 9, it prohibits unfair discrimination on the grounds listed in the Constitution (section 6 read with the definition of 'prohibited grounds' in section 1 of the Act). Like the Constitution, the list of prohibited grounds is open-ended. The definition of 'prohibited ground' lists all the prohibited grounds to be found in section 9(3) of the Constitution and continues –

> or (b) any other ground where discrimination based on that ground –
>   (i) causes or perpetuates systemic disadvantage;
>   (ii) undermines human dignity; or
>   (iii) adversely affects the equal enjoyment of a person's rights and freedoms in a serious manner that is comparable to discrimination [on one of the constitutionally prohibited grounds].

In respect of either the constitutionally prohibited grounds or analogous grounds, the Act requires that a complainant establish a prima facie case of discrimination, at which point the respondent will bear an onus to show that the discrimination in question was not unfair (section 13 of the Act). The Act also prohibits hate speech (section 10)[33] and harassment. The Act does not cover, generally speaking, discrimination complaints arising out of employment which are covered by the Employment Equity Act (see section 5(3) of the Equality Act; Employment Equity Act 55 of 1998).

The Act provides for equality courts and empowers those courts to hear proceedings instituted in terms of the Act.[34] It also places a wide range of remedies at the disposal of these courts, including the award of damages, an order restraining discriminatory conduct or harassment or hate speech, an order that an unconditional apology be made and an order directing the reasonable accommodation of a group or class of persons (section 21 of the Act). Finally, another interesting provision of the Act is the provision in a schedule of an 'illustrative list of unfair practices in certain sectors'. For example in relation to education the list reads:

(a) Unfairly excluding learners from educational institutions, including learners with special needs.
(b) Unfairly withholding scholarships, bursaries or any other form of assistance from learners of particular groups identified by the prohibited grounds.
(c) The failure to reasonably and practicably accommodate diversity in education.

Although section 9 of the Constitution provides the overarching principles of the equality guarantee, and all legislation is subordinate to the constitutional guarantee, complaints of unfair discrimination must ordinarily be instituted in terms of the Act. The Constitutional Court has held that where Parliament has enacted legislation to give effect to a constitutional right, complaints based on the alleged infringement of rights must be pursued through the legislative mechanisms provided, unless it is alleged that the legislative mechanisms themselves are inconsistent with the Constitution (*Bato Star* (in the context of the Promotion of Administrative Justice Act, 3 of 2000 which gives effect to the constitutional right to administrative justice in section 33 of the Constitution); *Pillay*, at para 40 (in the context of section 9 and the Equality Act); and *South African National Defence Union*, at para 52 (in the context of labour legislation and the labour rights protected in section 23 of the Constitution)). This principle has come to be known as the principle of constitutional subsidiarity (for academic commentary on the principle, see Van der Walt 2008 and Klare 2008). The principle does not mean, however, that the jurisprudence concerning section 9 of the Constitution is irrelevant. That jurisprudence will be of direct relevance to the interpretation and application of the Equality Act. Indeed, the Equality Act contains many concepts and principles first developed by the courts in their section 9 jurisprudence.

The Constitutional Court's early equality jurisprudence was developed in relation to section 8 of the interim Constitution,[35] the Constitution which regulated the transitional period between April 1994 when the first democratic elections were held, and February 1997, when the 1996 Constitution drafted by the Constitutional Assembly came into force. The text of section 8 of the interim Constitution was similar though not identical to the text of section 9. The Constitutional Court has held that given the similarities between the two sections, the jurisprudence that had developed relating to section 8 of the interim Constitution was generally applicable to section 9 of the 1996 Constitution (*National Coalition*, at para 15). Indeed, since the Court mapped out its framework for dealing with equality claims in *Harksen v Lane* (decided in terms of section 8 of the interim Constitution), the Court has followed that framework (for some examples from the recent jurisprudence, see *Geldenhuys*; *Hassam*; *Bhe*; *Gumede*; *Shilubana*; *Daniels*; and *Pillay*).

Right from the start, the Constitutional Court recognized that the equality guarantee was not merely aimed at ensuring equal treatment. In the first equality case considered by the Constitutional Court, *Brink v Kitshoff*, the court held that the equality clause was:

... adopted then in the recognition that discrimination against people who are members of disfavoured groups can lead to patterns of group disadvantage and harm. Such discrimination is unfair: it builds and entrenches inequality amongst different groups in our society. The drafters realised that it was necessary both to proscribe such forms of discrimination and to permit positive steps to redress the effects of such discrimination. (*Brink*, at para 42)

Almost without exception, this has been the approach of the Court since. For example, in *Hoffmann v South African Airways*, the Court reasoned as follows:

At the heart of the prohibition of unfair discrimination is the recognition that under our Constitution all human beings, regardless of their position in society, must be accorded equal dignity. That dignity is impaired when a person is unfairly discriminated against. The determining factor regarding the unfairness of the discrimination is its impact on the person discriminated against. (At para 27)

In *Brink,* as well, after a brief analysis of the approach to equality in several other constitutional democracies, the Court concluded that constitutional equality guarantees are worded differently and that their interpretation and application is at least in part dependent on the specific historical circumstances of different jurisdictions as well as on the conception of equality that informs their interpretation. The Court concluded that '[p]erhaps more than any of the other provisions in chapter 3 [the Bill of Rights], its interpretation must be based on the specific language of section 8, as well as our own constitutional context. Our history is of particular relevance to the concept of equality' (*Brink*, at para 40). Despite this, the jurisprudence of the Supreme Court of Canada was considered and cited in some early decisions of the Constitutional Court (see, for example, *Harksen,* at paras 50 and 92). Perhaps this is not surprising given the similarity between section 15 of the Canadian Charter and the South African equality guarantee.

The precise manner in which the equality guarantee should be approached was set out in *Harksen,* where the Court developed a comprehensive test. The Court held that the inquiry into a violation of the right to equality entailed the following progressive stages:

(a) Does the provision differentiate between people or categories of people? If so, does the differentiation bear a rational connection to a legitimate government purpose? If it does not then there is a violation of section 8(1) [now section 9(1) of the 1996 Constitution]. Even if it does bear a rational connection, it might nevertheless amount to discrimination.

(b) Does the differentiation amount to unfair discrimination? This requires a two stage analysis:
    (i) Firstly, does the differentiation amount to 'discrimination'? If it is on a specified ground, then discrimination will have been established. If it is not on a specified ground, then whether or not there is discrimination will depend upon whether, objectively, the ground is based on attributes and characteristics which have the potential to impair the fundamental human dignity of persons as human beings or to affect them adversely in a comparably serious manner.
    (ii) If the differentiation amounts to 'discrimination', does it amount to 'unfair discrimination'? If it has been found to have been on a specified ground, then unfairness will be presumed. If on an unspecified ground, unfairness will have to be established by the complainant.
    If, at the end of this stage of the enquiry, the differentiation is found not to be unfair, then there will be no violation of section 8(2).

(c) If the discrimination is found to be unfair then a determination will have to be made as to whether the provision can be justified under the limitations clause. (*Harksen*, at para 54)

The question of unfairness (para b(ii) above) centres on an analysis of the following three factors: (i) the position of the complainant in society and whether they have suffered in the past from disadvantage arising from discrimination; (ii) the nature or purpose of the impugned provision, including whether it is directed at furthering the goal of equality for all; and (iii) the extent to which the discrimination has affected the rights or interests of complainants and whether it has led to an impairment of their fundamental human dignity or affected them adversely in a comparably serious manner.

The first leg of the test, where the constitutional challenge is directed at a legislative provision, thus addresses the rationality question: is the differentiation rationally connected to a legitimate government purpose?[36] The requirement of a rational connection does not involve a deep level of scrutiny. If the legislative provision is held to be rational, the Court then turns to consider whether the differentiation in question constitutes unfair discrimination (the section 9(3) question). Implicit in this order is that it may well be that a legislative provision which is rational may nevertheless be unfairly discriminatory. In a later case, *Hoffmann,* the Court held that the first leg of the test need not be applied where the case concerns discrimination on a listed or analogous ground (*Hoffmann,* at para 26).

Where the case concerns discrimination on a prohibited ground, the next question will be whether it is unfair discrimination. There is a rebuttable presumption that the discrimination will be unfair if it is based on a listed ground (section 9(5) of the Constitution). The unfairness analysis focuses on the effect of the discrimination on the complainant and will take into account the position of the complainant in society and whether he or she has suffered in the past from disadvantage arising from discrimination as well as the extent to which the discrimination has affected the rights of interests of the complainant. Finally, the court will also consider the nature or purpose of the impugned provision, including whether it is directed at furthering the goal of equality. This last consideration introduces a proportionality analysis. It can be seen that the approach to unfairness introduces an element of asymmetry: a complainant who has suffered disadvantage in the past will find it easier to establish that further discrimination is unfair; whereas a complainant who has not will find it more difficult to establish.

One of the most difficult questions that must be addressed arises where the discrimination is not on a listed ground. This is a problem that also arises under section 15 of the Canadian Charter and article 14 of the European Convention. In seeking to provide an answer as to when other grounds would fall within the section 9(3) prohibition, the Court considered the purpose of the equality guarantee and what the prohibited grounds listed in section 9(3) had in common. The Court reasoned as follows:

> What the specified grounds have in common is that they have been used (or misused) in the past (both in South Africa and elsewhere) to categorise, marginalise and often oppress persons who have had, or who have been associated with, these attributes or characteristics. These grounds have the potential, when manipulated, to demean persons in their inherent humanity and dignity. There is often a complex relationship between these grounds. In some cases they relate to immutable biological attributes or characteristics, in some to the associational life of humans, in some to the intellectual, expressive and religious dimensions of humanity and in some cases to a combination of one or more of these features. The temptation to force them into neatly self-contained categories should be resisted. (*Harksen,* at para 49)

From this the Court concluded that grounds analogous to those listed should have the potential to have the harmful impact the specified grounds might or could have. This test is similar to the test for unfairness; that test having been developed on the basis of the same purposive analysis. Once a complainant has established that the ground in question is an analogous ground, then the complainant will also have to show that the discrimination is unfair (the shift of the burden of proof which occurs as a result of section 9(5) does not apply to analogous grounds). Perhaps the most notable example of an analogous ground of discrimination that has been accepted by the Court relates to people living with HIV/AIDS (*Hoffmann*, at para 40).

Once the discrimination is established to be unfair, then the final question will arise as to whether the unfair discrimination is nevertheless justifiable within the contemplation of section 36 of the Constitution.[37] Academic commentators have remarked that given the proportionality analysis inherent in determining whether discrimination is unfair, it seems unnecessary to have a further proportionality analysis under section 36 (Albertyn and Goldblatt 1998, at 269–72; Goldblatt 2001, at 29). Another concern raised by academic commentators relates to the role of human dignity in the equality analysis (Albertyn and Goldblatt 1998, at 257; Davis 1999; Fagan 1998), although some commentators have supported the approach (Liebenberg and O'Sullivan 2001, at 84; Cowen 2001). Human dignity is relevant in two ways: first, by the fact that dignity is at the centre of the inquiry to determine analogous grounds and second, because dignity is an important factor in the determination of whether discrimination is unfair.

The approach established in *Harksen* applies regardless of the ground of discrimination alleged. It will have been noted that the list of prohibited grounds in section 9(3) is broader than that under either section 15 of the Canadian Charter or article 14 of the European Convention. It includes, for example, discrimination on the grounds of sexual orientation.

This provision has led to a significant jurisprudence in the Constitutional Court. One of the first cases concerned a challenge to the common-law crime of sodomy which, amongst other things, rendered criminal anal sexual intercourse between consenting males. The Court held the common law crime to be inconsistent with the Constitution and declared it invalid (*National Coalition*). Thereafter, the Court had to consider a challenge to the pension rules for judges that afforded benefits to spouses but not to permanent same-sex life partners. The challenge was upheld (*Satchwell*). A further challenge to the adoption legislation which provided that only married couples could adopt was also upheld. The Court held that not only did the provisions infringe the right to equality, but also the principle that a child's best interests should be paramount in matters concerning them (see *Du Toit*; and *J and Another*, where the Court held that a rule that permitted married couples to become joint parents of a child borne out of artificial insemination was unconstitutional in not affording the same benefit to same-sex partners). In *Fourie*, the Court held that the common-law definition of marriage was inconsistent with section 9(3) of the Constitution because it only permitted heterosexual couples to marry. Parliament was given a year to enact legislation to remedy this constitutional inconsistency. Parliament enacted the Civil Union Act which provided for civil unions to be entered into by either heterosexual or homosexual couples.[38]

Two other areas have been of particular importance in relation to section 9. The first has been family law. South Africa is a diverse society and family relationships are constituted under a range of different legal rules. African customary or indigenous law still regulates the marriages of many South Africans of indigenous African descent. The Constitution recognizes the importance of indigenous law in South Africa. Like other laws in South Africa, the validity of customary law rules is also dependent on constitutional compliance.[39] In *Bhe,* the

Court had to consider whether the principle of male primogeniture upon which the indigenous law rules governing intestate succession are based was consistent with the Constitution. The Court ruled unanimously that the principle as applied in relation to intestate succession was in conflict with section 211(3) and 10[40] of the Constitution but divided on the appropriate remedy.[41]

In a subsequent case (*Shilubana*), the Court had to consider whether the appointment of a female chief by customary institutions was consistent with the Constitution. The male descendant who had not been appointed challenged the appointment on the grounds that it was not consistent with customary law. The Court held that section 211(2)[42] of the Constitution permits those responsible for the application of indigenous law to develop it in line with the Constitution. The challenge was therefore dismissed. The Court has also had to deal with cases relating to marriages entered into in terms of Muslim personal law. Such marriages have historically not been recognized as having consequences enforceable in law in South Africa (see, for example, *Daniels*; *Hassam*). The Court has recognized that the reason that such marriages have not been recognized was at least in part as a result of the discriminatory and demeaning attitude to such marriages (*Daniels*, at paras 19–20; *Hassam*, at para 33).

Finally, as in both Canada and England, the Court has faced at least one challenge based on section 9 relating to social security benefits. In this regard, it should be noted that section 27 of the South African Constitution provides that:

(1)   Everyone has the right to have access to –

...

(c) social security, including if they are unable to support themselves and their dependants, appropriate social assistance.

(2)   The state must take reasonable legislative and other measures, within its available resources, to achieve the progressive realisation of each of these rights.

Space does not permit a discussion of social and economic rights in the South African Constitution (see, for example, Bilchitz 2007; Liebenberg 2010). Suffice it to say that the intersection between the social and economic rights and section 9(3) is important. In the first case on this issue, *Khosa*, the Court had to consider a challenge to provisions of the Social Assistance Act 13 of 2004 which disqualified non-South African citizens from receiving certain social security benefits. The challenge was brought by an indigent group of people who had been granted permanent residence in the country and who would otherwise have been eligible for social grants in terms of the means test set for eligibility. The court held that the exclusion of permanent residents from social grants was not a reasonable way to achieve the realization of the right to social security and also constituted a breach of the right to equality. The Court noted that the effect of the order, on the figures provided by the government, would not increase the overall expenditure on social grants by more than 2%, while the denial of social grants to indigent people on the grounds of their nationality was materially harmful to the applicants and those similarly situated. The Court declared the legislative provisions excluding permanent residents from social grants to be invalid.

We can see that in *Khosa*, the Court was faced with similar questions to the Canadian Supreme Court in *Auton* and the United Kingdom Supreme Court in *R (on the application of RJM)*, yet the outcome was different than in those two cases. There are a range of possible reasons for this, a full discussion of which is beyond the scope of this chapter. One of the interesting questions to ask, however, is whether the entrenchment of social and economic rights in a Bill of Rights results in a higher level of scrutiny of social and economic rights legislation through the prism of the equality clause than where such rights are not entrenched.

6   CONCLUSION

The value of comparative analysis across legal systems is evident in the above account. We have seen that, despite the differences in text as well as historical and social context, courts in Canada, the United Kingdom and South Africa all face similar conceptual, methodological and institutional challenges in their adjudication of equality claims. In all three jurisdictions, courts have grappled with identifying the purpose that animates constitutional equality guarantees, and with using that purpose in interpreting and applying the guarantee. Courts in both Canada and South Africa have sought to use the concept of human dignity as a partial answer to the question, whereas this has not happened in the United Kingdom. Another conceptual question, particularly current in both Canada and the United Kingdom, remains the question of the role of comparator groups to equality jurisprudence. How important is the identification of a comparator group? And should courts focus on this question rather than what has been termed the 'justification' question, that is, is there a good and proportionate reason for the discriminatory rule or practice?

We have seen quite different methodologies, partly dependent on text, to the approach to equality claims. Both Canada and South Africa have adopted a detailed step-by-step test, while the United Kingdom, consonant with the approach of the European Court of Justice, has resisted the urge to develop a detailed test. The chapter has not sought to answer which of these approaches is to be preferred, but has rather sought to illustrate them.

Finally, it is clear that there are common questions of institutional role present in all three jurisdictions. Adjudicating equality claims, particularly in the context of social grants and other socio-economic issues, brings courts close to the allocation of budgets, a matter ordinarily reserved for the democratic arms of government. Developing a principled and predictive theory of judicial deference, which acknowledges the proper role of the democratic arms of government and protects fundamental rights, is an ongoing challenge.

The comparative analysis we have undertaken thus enables us to consider these recurrent conceptual, methodological and institutional issues from different angles. By doing so, we can identify and interrogate our own often unarticulated assumptions of the way to approach these issues. Here lies the real value of comparative legal study.

NOTES

1. The authors have endeavoured to ensure that this chapter reflects the case law in these jurisdictions as at 21 September 2009.
2. In 1991, the Civil Rights Act 105 Stat.1071 was enacted which codified the disparate-impact test established in *Griggs* (see 42 USC §2000e–2(k)(1)(A)(i)).
3. See Canadian Human Rights Act, RSC, 1985 c. H-6, which contains prohibitions against discrimination on the grounds of race, national or ethnic origin, colour, religion, age, sex, sexual orientation, marital status, family status, disability and conviction for which a pardon has been granted. See also the Alberta Individual's Rights Protection Act, RSA, 1980, c. 1–2; British Columbia Human Rights Code, RSBC, 1996, c. 210; Manitoba Human Rights Code, CCSM, c. H-175; New Brunswick Human Rights Code (RSNB, 1973, c. H-11); Newfoundland Human Rights Code (RSN, 1990, c. H-14); Northwest Territories Human Rights Act, SNWT,

2002, c. 18; Nova Scotia Human Rights Act (SN, 1991, c. 12); Ontario Human Rights Code, RSO, c. H-19; Prince Edward Island Human Rights Act (RSPEI, 1988, c. H-12); Quebec Charter of Human Rights and Freedoms (1981); Saskatchewan Human Rights Code, SS, 1979, c. S-24.1; and Yukon Human Rights Act, RSY, 2002, c. 116.

4. The exception is British Columbia which abolished its Human Rights Commission with effect from 31 March 2003. Complaints now proceed directly to the British Columbia Human Rights Tribunal.

5. The facts were that Andrews was a British citizen, permanently resident in Canada who had fulfilled all the requirements for admission to practise law in British Columbia, save that he was not a Canadian citizen. Citizenship was a requirement under section 42 of the Barristers and Solicitors Act (British Columbia). All the judges held that the citizenship requirement was in breach of section 15 and a majority held that it was unjustifiable under section 1 of the Charter. See also *Lavoie v Canada*, where the Supreme Court had to consider whether a requirement of citizenship for employment in the federal civil service was in breach of the Charter. By a majority, the Court held the requirement to be a justifiable limitation of section 15.

6. See *Miron v Trudel*, in which four of the nine judges held marital status to be an analogous ground. In *Nova Scotia v Walsh*, another case concerned with marital status, the Court was unanimous that marital status constituted an analogous ground under section 15.

7. See *Egan v Canada*, where eight of the nine judges held sexual orientation to be an analogous ground. This was confirmed in *Vriend v Alberta* (1998) 1 SCR 493, where the Alberta Human Rights Code was held to be in breach of section 15 for not prohibiting discrimination on the grounds of sexual orientation.

8. Seven judges originally heard the appeal, but only six participated in the decision: Dickson CJ and L'Heureux-Dubé J who concurred in the judgment of Wilson J finding section 42 to be an unjustifiable infringement of section 15; La Forest J who wrote a separate judgment but concurred in the majority result; and McLachlin J who dissented on the section 1 issue with whom Lamer J concurred.

9. Section 1 of the Canadian Charter of Rights and Freedoms provides that: 'The Canadian Charter of Rights and Freedoms guarantees the rights and freedoms set out in it subject only to such reasonable limits prescribed by law as can be demonstrably justified in a free and democratic society'.

10. A third case relating to equality, *Thibaudeau v Canada* [1995] 2 SCR 627 was also handed down on 25 May 1995, but the divergence between the judges in that case does not illustrate the divergence discussed here as sharply and we have chosen not to include it in our analysis.

11. See the useful summary at para 88 of *Law*.

12. Six other members of the Court concurred in their judgment (Binnie, LeBel, Deschamps, Fish, Charron and Rothstein JJ). The ninth member of the Court (Bastarache J), who wrote a separate concurring judgment on a different Charter provision, section 25, expressly confirmed his agreement with the revision of the *Law* approach to section 15 (*Kapp*, at para 77).

13. See, for example, McIntyre J's reasoning in *Andrews* (at para 8): Equality '... is a comparative concept, the condition of which may only be attained or discerned by comparison with the condition of others in the social and political setting in which the question arises'.

14. The decision in *Auton* in relation to the selection of a comparator was interestingly contrasted with the decision of the Supreme Court of Canada in *Martin v Nova Scotia* in Hogg (2007) at para 55.10(a).

15. For completeness, we should add that the Supreme Court of Canada held that the failure to provide for the behavioural therapy did not constitute a benefit conferred by law (*Hodge*, at para 47) and the question of the appropriate comparator, therefore, did not need to be dealt with. The Court chose to deal with it, nevertheless, because it raised a novel issue (*Hodge*, at para 47).

16. The institutional arrangements of the European Union are a complex topic on their own, beyond the scope of this chapter. A useful description can be found in Turpin and Tomkins 2007, at 278ff.

17. This directive has been consolidated into Directive 2006/54/EC of 5 July 2006 and was repealed with effect from 15 August 2009.

18. The Committee of Ministers of the Council of Europe approved Protocol 14 to the European Convention on Human Rights at its 114th Session in May 2004. The Protocol has now received 46 ratifications and entered into force on 12 May 2009. See the official Council of Europe website: http://www.conventions.coe.int/Treaty/Commun/ChercheSig.asp?NT=194&CM=8&DF=11/09/2009&CL=ENG, last visited on 11 September 2009. The Protocol is aimed at easing the burdensome case-load of the Court and deepening the independence of the judges by revising the applications process, amending the terms of office of judges. It also provides for the European Union to accede to the Convention. See the useful discussion in Greer 2005.

19. For example, in 2005 it received 41 510 claims, of which only 1036 were declared admissible. In the same year, the Court handed down 1105 judgments (of which 12 were Grand Chamber judgments). See Turpin and Tomkins 2007, at 266.

20. The provision has also been referred to as having a 'parasitic' quality (Harris et al 1985, at 463) and in a speech the former President of the European Court of Human Rights, Luzius Wildhaber, referred to the 'accessory nature' of article 14 (Wildhaber 2002, at 72).

21. See for details of the ratifications, the official website of the Council of Europe: http://www.conventions.

coe.int/Treaty/Commun/ChercheSig.asp?NT=177&CM=8&DF=11/09/2009&CL=ENG, last visited on 11 September 2009.

22. See the consideration of this provision by Lord Bingham of Cornhill in *R (Animal Defenders International) v Secretary of State for Culture, Media and Sport*, at para 37 and *R (Ullah) v Special Adjudicator*, at para 20.

23. A discussion of this interesting interpretive principle is beyond the scope of this chapter. See, however, the speech of Lord Steyn in *R v A (No 2)*, at para 44; and also in *Ghaidan v Godin-Mendoza*, at para 39; and the speech of Lord Nicholls in *Re S (Care Order: Implementation of Care Plan)*, at paras 37–40.

24. Section 4(5) of the Act provides that the following courts have the power to issue declaration of incompatibility: The House of Lords (the United Kingdom Supreme Court as of October 2009), the Judicial Committee of the Privy Council, the Courts Martial Appeal Court, in Scotland the High Court of Justiciary (though not when it sits as a trial court) and the Court of Session and in England, Wales and Northern Ireland, the High Court and the Court of Appeal.

25. See also *Hugh Jordan v. the United Kingdom*; and *Hoogendijk v the Netherlands*.

26. See, in particular, the following judgments in *Carson*: Lord Nicholls of Birkenhead at paras 2–3, stating 'for my part, in company with all your Lordships, I prefer to keep formulation of the relevant issues in these cases as simple and non-technical as possible'; Lord Hoffmann at paras 28–33; Lord Walker of Gestingthorpe at paras 61–4, stating 'I think the time has come to say that in cases on article 14, the Michalak catechism, even in a corrected form, is not always the best approach'; and Lord Carswell at para 97, stating '[t]hese questions can supply an admirable analysis for some cases, but can form a Procrustean bed if others are forced into their framework'. See also the speech of Baroness Hale of Richmond in *Ghaidan v Godin-Mendoza*, at para 134, where she noted the overlap between the different questions.

27. The approach echoes some of the criticisms that have been levelled at the Canadian jurisprudence.

28. Under the Fourteenth Amendment, differentiation on the ground of sex gives rise to an 'intermediate' level of scrutiny.

29. See also *AL (Serbia)*, at para 44, where Baroness Hale reasoned as follows: 'It is accepted that bright lines of this sort, even if they produce what appear to be arbitrary distinctions between one case and another, are often necessary and can be justified: see, eg the age rules in R *v* Secretary of State for Work and Pensions (sub nom R(Carson *v* Secretary of State for Work and Pensions) [2006] 1 AC 173)'.

30. See also *R (on the application of Clift) v Secretary of State for the Home Department*, at para 28, where Lord Bingham of Cornhill reasoned: 'I do not think that a personal characteristic can be defined by the differential treatment of which a person complains'.

31. In this regard, as well, it is interesting to note that section 1(a) of the Constitution entrenches 'the achievement of equality' as one of the founding values of the Constitution.

32. In *Prinsloo*, at para 25, the Court reasoned: 'In regard to mere differentiation, the constitutional state is expected to act in a rational manner. It should not regulate in an arbitrary manner or manifest "naked preferences" that serve no legitimate governmental purpose, for that would be inconsistent with the rule of law and the fundamental premises of the constitutional state. The purpose of this aspect of equality is, therefore, to ensure that the state is bound to function in a rational manner.'

33. 'Hate speech' is defined in that section as a publication that 'could reasonably be construed to demonstrate a clear intention to – (a) be hurtful; (b) be harmful or incite harm; (c) promote or propagate hatred'. This definition is based on section 16(2) of the Constitution which provides that the right to freedom of expression (entrenched in section 16(1)) does not extend to '(a) propaganda for war, (b) incitement of imminent violence; or (c) advocacy of hatred that is based on race, ethnicity, gender or religion, and that constitutes incitement to cause harm'.

34. Section 16 of the Act provides that every High Court is an equality court for its area of jurisdiction and that the Minister of Justice and Constitutional Development must designate certain magistrates' courts to function as equality courts (section 16(1)(c).

35. Section 8 of the interim Constitution provided as follows:

(1) Every person shall have the right to equality before the law and to equal protection of the law.

(2) No person shall be unfairly discriminated against, directly or indirectly, and, without derogating from the generality of this provision, on one or more of the following grounds in particular: race, gender, sex, ethnic or social origin, colour, sexual orientation, age, disability, religion, conscience, belief, culture or language.

(3) This section shall not preclude measures designed to achieve the adequate protection and advancement of persons or groups or categories of persons disadvantaged by unfair discrimination, in order to enable their full and equal enjoyment of all rights and freedoms.

(4) Every person or community dispossessed of rights in land before the commencement of this Constitution under any law which would have been inconsistent with subsection (2) had that subsection been in operation at the time of the dispossession, shall be entitled to claim restitution of such rights subject to and in accordance with sections 121, 122 and 123.

(5) Prima facie proof of discrimination on any of the grounds specified in subsection (2) shall be presumed to be sufficient proof of unfair discrimination as contemplated in that subsection, until the contrary is established.

36. This test is similar to the rational connection test applied in the United States as the least invasive form of scrutiny under the Fourteenth Amendment. It was first adopted in South Africa in the context of the equality guarantee in *Prinsloo's case*. The rational connection test imposed on legislation by section 9(1) is similar to the principle of rationality required of the exercise of public power arising from the constitutional value of the rule of law. See *Pharmaceutical Manufacturers*, at para 85; and see the discussion in Currie and de Waal 2005, at 243.

37. Like section 1 of the Canadian Charter, section 36 of the South African Constitution is a general limitations clause in which limitations of rights in terms of law of general application may nevertheless be justified. Section 36 provides as follows:

> (1) The rights in the Bill of Rights may be limited only in terms of law of general application to the extent that the limitation is reasonable and justifiable in an open and democratic society based on human dignity, equality and freedom, taking into account all relevant factors, including –
> (a) the nature of the right;
> (b) the importance of the purpose of the limitation;
> (c) the nature and extent of the limitation;
> (d) the relation between the limitation and its purpose; and
> (e) less restrictive means to achieve the purpose.
> (2) Except as provided in subsection (1) or in any other provision of the Constitution, no law may limit any right entrenched in the Bill of Rights.

38. See section 4 of the Act read with the definition of 'civil union' in section 1. That definition provides that: 'a civil union means the voluntary union of two persons who are both 18 years of age or older, which is solemnised and registered by way either of a marriage or a civil partnership…'.

39. See section 211(3) of the constitution which provides that: 'The courts must apply customary law when that law is applicable, subject to the Constitution and any legislation that specifically deals with customary law'.

40. Section 10 entrenches the right to respect for human dignity in the following terms: 'Everyone has inherent dignity and the right to have their dignity respected and protected'.

41. See also *Gumede*, where the Court had to determine whether it was unfair discrimination that a wife who had entered into a customary marriage was entitled to receive no property on the dissolution of that marriage while all of the property devolved on the husband. The Court held unanimously that the principle was unfairly discriminatory.

42. Section 211(2) provides that: 'A traditional authority that observes a system of customary law may function subject to any applicable legislation and customs, which includes amendments to or repeal of that legislation and those customs'.

REFERENCES

Books and Articles

Albertyn, Cathy and Beth Goldblatt (1998), 'Facing the Challenge of Transformation: Difficulties in the Development of an Indigenous Jurisprudence of Equality', *South African Journal on Human Rights*, 14, 248.

Allan, Trevor R.S. (2006), 'Human Rights and Judicial Review: A Critique of "Due Deference" ', *Cambridge Law Journal*, 65, 671.

Barker, Ernest (ed.) (1946), *The Politics of Aristotle, Book III: The Theory of Citizenship and Constitutions*, Oxford: Clarendon Press.

Bilchitz, David (2007), *Poverty and Fundamental Rights: The Justification and Enforcement of Socio-Economic Rights*, Oxford: Oxford University Press.

Brodsky, Gwen (2003), 'Gosselin v Quebec (Attorney-General): Autonomy with a Vengeance', *Canadian Journal of Women and the Law*, 15, 194–214.

Brownlie, Ian (1979), *Principles of Public International Law*, 3rd edition, Oxford: Clarendon Press.

Collins, Hugh (2003), 'Discrimination, Equality and Social Inclusion', *Modern Law Review*, 66, 16–43.

Cowen, Susie (2001), 'Can "Dignity" Guide South Africa's Equality Jurisprudence?', *South African Journal on Human Rights*, 17, 34–59.

Currie, Ian and Johan de Waal (2005), *The Bill of Rights Handbook*, 5th edition, Cape Town: Juta Publishers.

Davis, Dennis (1999), 'Equality: The Majesty of Legoland Jurisprudence', *South African Law Journal*, 116, 398.

Dworkin, Ronald (2000), *Sovereign Virtue: The Theory and Practice of Equality*, Cambridge, MA: Harvard University Press.

Edwards, Richard (2002), 'Judicial Deference under the Human Rights Act', *Modern Law Review*, 65, 859.

Fagan, Anton (1998), 'Dignity and Unfair Discrimination: A Value Misplaced and a Right Misunderstood', *South African Journal on Human Rights*, 14, 220.

Feldman, David (2002), *Civil Liberties and Human Rights in England and Wales*, 2nd edition, Oxford: Oxford University Press.

Fredman, Sandra (2002), *Discrimination Law*, Oxford: Oxford University Press.

Fredman, Sandra (2006), 'From Deference to Democracy: the Role of Equality under the Human Rights Act 1998', *Law Quarterly Review*, 122, 53.

Fudge, Judy (2007), 'Substantive Equality, the Supreme Court of Canada and the Limits to Redistribution', *South African Journal on Human Rights*, 23, 235.

Goldblatt, Beth (2001), 'Litigating Equality: the Example of Child Care', *Acta Juridica*, 8.

Greer, Steven (2005), 'Protocol 14 and the Future of the European Court of Human Rights', *Public Law*, 83–106.

Gretschner, D. (2002), 'The Purpose of Canadian Equality Rights', *Review of Constitutional Studies*, 6, 291.

Grosz, S., J. Beaston and P. Duffy (2000), *Human Rights: The 1998 Act and the European Convention*, London: Sweet and Maxwell.

Harris, D.J., M. O'Boyle and C. Warbrick (1995), *Law of the European Convention on Human Rights*, London: Butterworths.

Hogg, Peter W. (2005), 'What is Equality? The Winding Course of Judicial Interpretation', *Supreme Court Law Review*, 29 (2), 39–62.

Hogg, Peter W. (2007), *Constitutional Law of Canada*, 5th edition supplemented, looseleaf edition, Toronto: Carswell Legal Publications.

Kahn-Freund, Otto (1974), 'On Uses and Misuses of Comparative Law', *Modern Law Review*, 37, 1–27.

Kavanagh, Aileen (2004), 'The Elusive Divide between Interpretation and Legislation under the Human Rights Act 1998', *Oxford Journal of Legal Studies*, 259.

Klare, Karl (2008), 'Legal Subsidiarity and Constitutional Rights: A Reply to AJ Van der Walt', *Constitutional Court Review*, 1, 129.

Klug, Francesca (2007), 'A Bill of Rights: Do We Need One or Do We Already Have One?', *Public Law*, 701–19.

Laurie, Emma (2009), 'Judicial Responses to Bright Line Rules in Social Security: In Search of Principle', *Modern Law Review*, 72, 384.

Lester, Anthony (2000), 'New European Equality Measures', *Public Law*, 562.

Lester, Anthony, D. Pannick and J. Herberg (2009), *Human Rights Law and Practice*, 3rd edition, London: LexisNexis Butterworths.

Liebenberg, Sandra (2010), *Socio-Economic Rights: Adjudication Under a Transformative Constitution*, Cape Town: Juta Academic.

Liebenberg, Sandra and Michele O'Sullivan (2001), 'South Africa's New Equality Legislation: A Tool for Advancing Women's Socio-economic Equality?', *Acta Juridica*, 70–103.

Livingstone, Stephen (1997), 'Article 14 and the Prevention of Discrimination in the European Convention on Human Rights', *European Human Rights Law Review*, 26–34.

Martin, S. (2001), 'Balancing Individual Rights to Equality and Social Goals', *Canadian Bar Review*, 80, 299.

McLachlin, Beverley (2001), 'Equality: The Most Difficult Right', *Supreme Court Law Review*, 14, 17–27.

Mendes, E. (2000), 'Taking Equality into the 21st Century: Establishing the Concept of Human Dignity', *National Journal of Constitutional Law*, 12, 3.

Minow, Martha (1990), *Making All the Difference: Inclusion, Exclusion and American Law*, Ithaca, NY and London: Cornell University Press.

Moreau, Sophia R. (2006), 'Equality Rights and the Relevance of Comparator Groups', *Journal of Law and Equality*, 5, 81–95.

Reaume, D. (2003), 'Discrimination and Dignity', *Louisiana Law Review*, 63, 645.

Ruder, B., C. Faria and E. Lawrence (2004), 'What's Law Good For? An Empirical Overview of Charter Equality Rights Decisions', *Supreme Court Law Review*, 24 (2), 104–129.

Sheppard, Colleen (2004), 'Inclusive Equality and New Forms of Social Governance', *Supreme Court Law Review*, 24 (2), 45–76.

Tarnopolsky, Walter S. (1982), *Discrimination and the Law in Canada,* Totonto: Richard DeBoo Limited.

Turpin, Colin and Adam Tomkins (2007), *British Government and the Constitution*, 6th edition, Cambridge: Cambridge University Press.

Van der Walt, A.J. (2008), 'Normative Pluralism and Legal Anarchy: Reflections on the 2007 Term', *Constitutional Court Review*, 1, 77.

Van Dijk, P. and G.J.H. Van Hoof (1998), *Theory and Practice of the European Convention on Human Rights*, 3rd edition, The Hague: Kluwer Publishing.

Watson, A. (1976), 'Legal Transplants and Law Reform', *Law Quarterly Review*, 92, 79.
Watson, A. (1978), 'Comparative Law and Legal Change', *Cambridge Law Journal*, 37, 313.
Westen, Peter (1982), 'The Empty Idea of Equality', *Harvard Law Review*, 95, 537.
Wildhaber, Luzius (2002), 'Protection against Discrimination under the European Convention on Human Rights – a Second-Class Guarantee?', *Baltic Yearbook of International Law*, 2, 71–82.
Wintemute, Robert (2004), 'Sexual Orientation and the Charter', *McGill Law Journal*, 49, 1143.
Young, Iris M. (1990), *Justice and the Politics of Difference*, Princeton, NJ: Princeton University Press.

Other documents
617 House of Lords Official Report (5th Series) written answers col WA37 of 11 October 2000.

Judicial Decisions

Canada
Auton (Guardian, ad litem of) v British Columbia (Attorney General), [2004] 3 SCR 657
Benner v Canada (Secretary of State), [1997] 1 SCR 358
Egan v Canada, (1995) 2 SCR 513
Eldridge v British Columbia (Attorney-General), [1997] 3 SCR 624
Hislop v Canada, [2007] 1 SCR 429
Hodge v Canada (Minister of Human Resources Development), [2004] 3 SCR 357
Lavoie v Canada, (2002) 1 SCR 769
Law v Canada, [1999] 1 SCR 497
Law Society of British Columbia v Andrews, [1989] 1 SCR 143, 56 DLR (4th) 1
Martin v Nova Scotia (Workers' Compensation Board), [2003] 2 SCR 504
Miron v Trudel, (1995) 2 SCR 418
Newfoundland (Treasury Board) v Newfoundland Association of Public Employees (NAPE), (2004) 3 SCR 381
Nova Scotia v Walsh, (2002) 4 SCR 325
R v Kapp, [2008] 2 SCR 483
R v Oakes, [1986] 1 SCR 103
Thibaudeau v Canada, [1995] 2 SCR 627
Vriend v Alberta, [1998] 1 SCR 493

Europe
Abdulaziz, Cabales and Balkandali v United Kingdom Series A, No. 94, (1984) 7 EHRR 471
Bilka-Kaufhaus GmbH v Weber von Hartz, [1986] IRLR 317; [1986] CMLR 701
Botta v Italy (1998), 26 EHRR 241
Case relating to certain aspects on the use of languages in education in Belgium Series A no. 6, (1979) 1 EHRR 252
D.H. and Others v Czech Republic, [2007] ECHR 57325/00
Dudgeon v United Kingdom, (1981) 4 EHRR 149
Enderby v Frenchay, [1993] ECR I-5535, ECJ; [1994] 1 All ER 495
Fretté v France, (2004) 38 EHRR 21
Hoogendijk v the Netherlands, [2005] ECHR no. 58461/00
Hugh Jordan v the United Kingdom, [2001] ECHR no. 24746/94
Inze v Austria Series 1, no. 126
Kjeldsen, Busk Madsen and Pedersen v Denmark, (1976) 1 EHRR 711
Kowalska v Freie und Hansestadt Hamburg, [1990] ECR I-2591
Marckx v Belgium, (1979) 2 EHRR 330
Rasmussen v Denmark Series A, no. 87
Stec and Others v United Kingdom, (2005) 41 EHRR SE18

United Kingdom
AL (Serbia) v Home Secretary, [2008] UKHL 42; [2008] 4 All ER 1127
Ghaidan v Godin-Mendoza, [2004] UKHL 30; [2004] 2 AC 557
R v A (No. 2), [2001] UKHL 25, [2002] 1 AC 45
R (Animal Defenders International) v Secretary of State for Culture, Media and Sport, [2008] UKHL 15; [2008] 1 AC 1312
R (Carson v Secretary of State for Work and Pensions [2002] All ER 994
R (Carson v Secretary of State for Work and Pensions (HL) [2005] UKHL 37; [2006] 1 AC 137

R (on the application of Clift) v Secretary of State for the Home Department, [2006] UKHL 54; [2007] 1 AC 484
R (on the application of RJM) v Secretary of State for Work and Pensions, [2008] UKHL 63; [2009] 1 AC 311
R (Ullah) v Special Adjudicator, [2004] UKHL 26; [2004] 2 AC 323
Re P (A Child) (Adoption: unmarried couples), [2008] UKHL 38; [2009] 1 AC 173
Re S (Care Order: Implementation of Care Plan), [2002] UKHL 10; [2002] 2 AC 291
Wandsworth London Borough Council v Michalak, [2002] EWCA Civ 271, [2003] 1 WLR 617

United States of America
Griggs v Duke Power Company, 401 US 424 (1971)
McCleskey v Kemp, 481 US 270 (1987)
Ricci v DeStefano 129 S. Ct. 268, 174 L.Ed. 2d 490 (2009)
Washington v Davis, 426 US 229 (1976)

South Africa
Bato Star Fishing (Pty) Ltd v Minister of Environmental Affairs and Tourism and Others, 2004 (4) SA 490 (CC)
Bhe and Others v Magistrate, Khayelitsha and Others; Shibi v Sithole and Others; SA Human Rights Commission and Another v President of the Republic of South Africa and Another, 2005 (1) SA 563 (CC)
Brink v Kitshoff, 1996 (4) SA 197 (CC); 1996 (6) BCLR 752 (CC)
Daniels v Campell NO and Others, 2004 (5) SA 331 (CC)
Du Toit and Another v Minister of Welfare and Population Development and Others (Lesbian and Gay Equality Project intervening), 2003 (2) SA 198 (CC)
Geldenhuys v National Director of Public Prosecutions and Others, [2008] ZACC 21; 2009 (2) SA 310 (CC)
Gumede v President of the Republic of South Africa and Others, [2008] ZACC 23
Harksen v Lane, 1998 (1) SA 300 (CC); 1997 (11) BCLR 1489 (CC)
Hassam v Jacobs NO and Others, [2009] ZACC 19
Hoffmann v South African Airways, 2001 (1) SA 1 (CC); 2000 (11) BCLR 1211 (CC)
J. and Another v Director-General, Department of Home Affairs and Others, 2003 (5) SA 621 (CC)
Khosa and Others v Minister of Social Development; Mahlaule and Others v Minister of Social Development and Others, 2004 (6) SA 505 (CC)
KZN MEC of Education v Pillay, [2007] ZACC 21; 2008 (1) SA 474 (CC)
Minister of Home Affairs and Another v Fourie and Another, 2006 (1) SA 524 (CC)
National Coalition for Gay and Lesbian Equality v Minister of Justice and Others, 1999 (1) SA 6 (CC); 1998 (12) BCLR 1517 (CC)
Pharmaceutical Manufacturers Association of South Africa: In re: ex parte President of the Republic of South Africa, 2000 (2) SA 674 (CC)
Prinsloo v Van der Linde and Another, 1997 (3) SA 1012 (CC)
Satchwell v President of the Republic of South Africa and Another, 2002 (6) SA 1 (CC)
Shilubana and Others v Nwamitwa, [2008] ZACC 9; 2009 (2) SA 66 (CC)
South African National Defence Union v Minister of Defence and Others, [2007] ZACC 10; 2007 (5) SA 400 (CC)

Legislation

Canada
Alberta Individual's Rights Protection Act, RSA, 1980, c. 1–2
Barristers and Solicitors Act (British Columbia) RSBC, 1979, c. 26
British Columbia Human Rights Code, RSBC, 1996, c. 210
Canadian Charter of Rights and Freedoms
Canadian Human Rights Act, RSC, 1985, c. H-6
Manitoba Human Rights Code, CCSM, c. H-175
New Brunswick Human Rights Code (RSNB, 1973, c. H-11)
Newfoundland Human Rights Code (RSN, 1990, c. H-14)
Northwest Territories Human Rights Act, SNWT, 2002, c. 18
Nova Scotia Human Rights Act (SN, 1991, c. 12)
Ontario Human Rights Code, RSO, c. H-19
Prince Edward Island Human Rights Act (RSPEI, 1988, c. H-12)
Quebec Charter of Human Rights and Freedoms (1981)
Saskatchewan Human Rights Code, SS, 1979, c. S-24.1
Yukon Human Rights Act, RSY, 2002, c. 116

Europe
Directive 2000/78/EC of 27 November 2000
Directive 2006/54/EC of 5 July 2006
Employment Equality (Age) Regulations 2006
Employment Equality (Religion or Belief) Regulations 2003
Employment Equality (Sexual Orientation) Regulations 2003
Equal Pay Directive, Directive 75/117/EEC of 10 February 1975
Equal Treatment Directive, Directive 76/207/EEC of 9 February 1976
Equal Treatment in Goods and Services Directive 2004/113/EC of 13 December 2004
European Convention on Human Rights
Framework Directive on Equal Opportunities in Employment (October 2000)
Pregnant Workers Directive 92/85/EEC of 19 October 1992
Race Directive 2000/43/EC of 29 June 2000
Sexual Orientation (Goods and Services) Regulations 2007
Treaty of Amsterdam (1997)

United Kingdom
Disability Discrimination Act 1995
Equal Pay Act 1970
Equality Act 2006
Equality Bill 2010
Human Rights Act 1998
Race Relations Act 1976
Sex Discrimination Act 1975

South Africa
Civil Union Act 17 of 2006
Constitution of the Republic of South Africa, 108 of 1996
Employment Equity Act 55 of 1998
Promotion of Equality and Prevention of Unfair Discrimination Act 4 of 2000
Social Assistance Act 13 of 2004

27. The right to property

Tom Allen

Eminent domain – the power to take private property for public use – is an inherent aspect of sovereignty. However, the institution of private property would have little meaning if governments used their powers of eminent domain without restraint. Hence, most constitutions impose restrictions on eminent domain. These constitutional restraints can take a variety of forms, but the most common is the right to property.

1 THE FORM AND FUNCTION OF CONSTITUTIONAL PROPERTY CLAUSES

Constitutional property clauses tend to follow a common structure (Van der Walt, 1999; Mann, 1959; Daintith, 2004). Most provide that the government may only acquire property by a process laid down by law, for a public use or purpose, and on terms that provide the owner with compensation. These common elements provide the basis for the comparative study of right to property. Hence, much of the literature centres on several key questions: what is the meaning of 'property', as used in the property clause? What is a 'taking'? For what purposes may the state take property? And what level of compensation does the property clause require?

In addition to the scholarship based on these interpretive questions, there is a considerable body of writing that takes a more functional approach to the constitutional protection of property. It asks how a right to property affects the scope and impact of laws in specific areas, such as, for example, environmental protection (Adler, 2008), or housing and resettlement (Leckie, 2003), or transitional justice and the restitution of property (Posner and Vermeule, 2004; Macklem, 2005; Allen, 2007c). This body of scholarship raises a more general question: what is the general impact of a constitutional property clause?

It is often assumed that property clauses do have a significant impact on property. Indeed, the inclusion and form of a property clause is often one of the most contested issues in the drafting of new constitutions or constitutional amendments (Alvaro, 1991; Chaskalson, 1995; Choudhry, 2004). In recent years, some international financial organisations have put pressure on developing countries to enact property clauses, in the belief that property clauses make investment more secure and ensure the continuation of a market economy (Munro, 1972, pp. 156–62; Chaskalson, 1995). Plainly, there is an assumption that constitutional property clauses do make a difference, whether positive or negative. But is this the case? Some legal systems sustain the institution of private property and free markets without one. In Canada, and other former British colonies, the original form of constitutional protection for property was through executive and legislative review of laws affecting property, rather than a justiciable property clause. These forms of review did much of the work of a justiciable clause, but in a very different structure and subject to different forms of development and interpretation (Forsey, 1938). In Australia, the property clause only applies to the Commonwealth (federal) Parliament. It does not apply to the state legislatures, although states do have the power to acquire property; hence one might say that the constitutional protection is incomplete. Other jurisdictions have rights to property, but without the element of judicial review as it is understood in the United States. For example, in the United Kingdom, the Human Rights Act 1998 gives force to the European Convention on Human Rights and the property clause in the First Protocol to the Convention, but at the same time, sections 3 and 6 of the Act preserve Parliament's supremacy.

If states can sustain private property and market economies without a constitutional right to property that enables judicial review, what is the unique contribution of a right to property? Is there a risk of falling into the 'formalist trap', as Gregory Alexander (2006, p. 24) puts it?

> In the context of the property clause issue, the formalist trap is the assumption or claim that without constitutional protection, property rights are unlikely to enjoy the degree of security and stability that is necessary for a properly functioning liberal democracy as well as for an efficient free market economy. Stated differently, the claim, which frequently is left implicit in arguments about constitutionalizing property, is that the degree of legal protection that extant property holdings within a society enjoy is strongly affected by the existence or absence of a property clause in that country's constitution.

Alexander argues that the formal inclusion of a right to property does not guarantee any specific changes in actual status of property within the national system. It is necessary to take into account 'background nonconstitutional legal and political traditions and culture' (Alexander, 2006, p. 24). Other doctrines and principles can do the work of a constitutional right to property, provided that there is sufficient political support for property rights. Conversely, a right to property would have limited impact in a state with a very low commitment to property. Nevertheless, the constitutionalisation of property has considerable weight as a statement of commitment to private property and a market economy. That statement may, by itself, have an impact on investment. Similarly, constitutionalisation influences the form of the debate. For example, in the United States, the debate over the use of the power of eminent domain by private developers is framed in terms of the impact on individual property owners. However, in European jurisdictions, these concerns are often framed in terms of the need to avoid state aids that reduce competition; in other words, they are expressed in terms of protecting access to a European market (Allen, 2008).

2 THE SCOPE OF THE PROPERTY CLAUSE[1]

Constitutions vary in their descriptions of the interests protected by property clauses. The takings clause of the Fifth Amendment protects 'private property'. Constitutions of the former British colonies variously protect 'property',[2] 'property, movable or immovable', including every 'right over or interest in any such property'[3] or even 'property, movable or immovable, including an interest in, or in any company owning, any commercial or industrial undertaking'.[4] The European Convention on Human Rights refers to both 'possessions' and 'property', but without apparent distinction. Indeed, the official French version uses *biens* in the first sentence, *propriété* in the second, and then *biens* again in the third; the official English version uses 'possessions' in the first and second sentences and 'property' in the third sentence.

These clauses operate in systems that already have a reasonably well-established conception of private property. Hence, the scope of the constitutional clause is determined at least partly by the ordinary private law of property. By itself, this makes comparative work complex, as the meaning of private property varies from one jurisdiction to another. A further issue arises: does 'property' have a different meaning in constitutional law? In other words, does a property clause protect interests that are not recognised as property interests under ordinary private law?

A clear judicial statement in favour of this position was given by the German Constitutional Court in the '*Groundwater Case*'. The Court stated that the function of Article 14 of the Basic Law is 'to secure for its holder a sphere of liberty in the economic sphere and thereby enable him to lead a self-governing life' (58 BverfGE 300, 1989, p. 251). It concluded as follows:

> The concept of property as guaranteed by the Constitution must be derived from the Constitution itself. This concept of property in the constitutional sense cannot be derived from legal norms (ordinary statutes) lower in rank than the Constitution, nor can the scope of the concrete property guarantee be determined on the basis of private law regulations.

Accordingly, the conception of property in the Civil Code does not exclusively determine the scope of Article 14; both public and private considerations are relevant (58 BverfGE 300; Kommers, 1989, p. 251; Van der Walt, 2003, pp. 151–7; Mostert, 2002, pp. 233–4). Just how far each is relevant is a topic of continuing debate, but the key point is that Article 14 is seen as something other than an additional support for the entitlements of the Civil Code.

In relation to the South African Constitution, André van der Walt has argued that the emphasis on the values of open and democratic society based on human dignity, equality and freedom should inform the interpretation of the property clause, including the meaning of 'property' in that clause. Accordingly, the clause should not be wholly dependent on private property: 'an important part of the function of the new constitutional order was to free land and property distribution patterns from the shackles and restraints of apartheid, and actively to promote the establishment and maintenance of a more just distribution of property and of greater access to and security of tenure of land' (Mostert, 2002, p. 69). For example, Van der Walt argued that the Constitution provides an immediate guarantee for Africans whose customary rights to occupation were extinguished by apartheid, by creating 'a situation where those rights could again be recognised, not only by way of new land reform legislation, but also by simply giving those land rights the constitutional nod' (Van der Walt, 1997, p. 58; see also Michelman, 1981).

Courts in other jurisdictions have been more cautious. For example, courts generally reject arguments that constitutional rights to property provide access to resources for minimum subsistence, or to protect personal or communal identity, or to challenge laws that discriminate in respect of the capacity to acquire property. These functions, it seems, belong to other fundamental rights. The right to property is often raised in cases involving these issues, but usually by a property owner resisting a claim of access (*Syndicat Northcrest v Amselem*, 2004; *Port of Elizabeth Municipality v Various Occupiers*, 2005). In general, most courts treat the right to property as a right to maintain existing property holdings, rather than a right to have property.

A weaker version of the argument for the existence of a separate category of constitutional property holds that constitutional law does not create new forms of property, but it can recognise existing rights as constitutional property even if not recognised as rights of property in private law. For example, in many civilian jurisdictions, the interests of tenants are personal contractual interests, and yet the European Court of Human Rights has been willing to protect these interests under the Convention's property clause (*Iatridis v Greece*, 1999). Indeed, this is fairly typical: most courts treat contractual rights as a species of constitutional property. More controversial is the position in relation to rights conferred by public bodies: are permits, licences, and state benefits to be treated as constitutional property? In his article 'The New Property', Charles Reich put forward one of the best-known arguments in support of constitutionalisation (Reich, 1964). Reich observed that treating an interest as constitutional property provides the holder with greater security, and hence courts should decide whether the claimant has property by asking whether the claimant needs the security that the Constitution would provide. He maintained that this was the case with social welfare benefits, state-conferred licences, and other forms of government largesse. These interests are created under ordinary legislation; in that sense, they are not brought to life by constitutional law. However, constitutional law would provide judicial control over the legislature's power to withdraw or modify the interests (Reich, 1965).

While many courts have treated government benefits as property for the purposes of due process or procedural guarantees, they have been wary of applying Reich's argument in takings cases (Van der Walt, 2003, p. 23; Allen, 2000, pp. 153–60; Tani, 2008). The Supreme Court's reasoning in *Flemming v Nestor* (1960) is typical. The Supreme Court took the view that treating social welfare rights as property under the takings clause would limit the capacity of the legislature to change welfare scheme in response to changing economic and social conditions. That is, of course, precisely what Reich advocated, but courts have not been persuaded.

3 TAKINGS OF PROPERTY AND 'REGULATORY TAKINGS'

In many cases, it is clear that the individual holds 'property', but not whether there has been a 'taking of property'. Most constitutions work on the basis that a distinction can be made between takings and other forms of interference. A formal expropriation of ownership for public use is the clearest example of a taking; a prohibition on a narrow, specific use of property that still allows most beneficial uses would be an example of the latter. This question is important in all jurisdictions, but it is particularly important in the USA because an interference with property requires compensation if, and only if, it is a taking (*Eastern Enterprises v Apfel*, 1998). Other constitutional rules still apply to other interferences with property, with due process and the rule of law being the most obvious examples. However, those other rules do not necessarily require the state to provide compensation.

What types of regulation are regarded as takings? As a starting point, it is widely recognised that regulations that permanently appropriate all of the economic benefits of ownership should be treated as a taking, even if there is no formal acquisition of legal title (*Lucas v South Carolina Coastal Council*, 1992; *Sporrong and Lönnroth v Sweden*, 1983; *La Compagnie Sucriere de Bel Ombre Ltee v The Government of Mauritius*, 1995). There are specific exceptions made for public safety in cases such as the condemnation of dangerous property, but normally the state does not seek to enjoy the same or similar benefits of ownership from the property as the previous owner.

Two situations give rise to the most controversial cases. The first occurs when regulations leave the owner with legal title that still has some economic value; the second where the regulations are aimed at something less compelling than a direct threat to public health. Plainly, such cases require a balancing between public and private interests, but who should strike that balance? There are two opposing positions. One view is that the constitution should give the courts a broad power to decide each case by weighing any factors that the court thinks relevant, in whatever manner it believes appropriate. The alternative is to limit judicial discretion, by narrowly restricting the factors that a court may consider. For example, a constitution could provide that any regulation that reduces the market value of property by more than 80% should be treated as a taking. Or, it could state that any regulation that permanently limits the right to exclude others from entering land is a taking.

The takings clause of the US Constitution, as written, appears to be an example of the second approach. That is, the guarantee of 'just compensation' applies to every 'taking' of 'private property' for a 'public use': it appears that compensation is always payable if there is a taking, without any room for judicial balancing. There is a balance of interests, but the framers of the Constitution have already determined how the balance should be struck in every case.

This does not mean, however, that the American courts have rejected balancing in takings cases, as it has been introduced through the interpretation of 'taking' and 'private property'. In *Pennsylvania Coal Co. v Mahon*, Justice Holmes famously suggested that it is a question of degree: '[t]he general rule at least is, that while property may be regulated to a certain extent, if regulation goes too far it will be recognized as a taking' (1922, p. 481; Fischel, 1995; Friedman, 1986). In *Penn Central Transportation Company v New York City* (1978, p. 124), the Supreme Court stated that a takings analysis involves 'essentially ad hoc, factual inquiries'. Some factors would normally carry considerable weight, such as the economic impact of the regulation on the owner, the extent of the interference with 'investment-backed expectations', the purpose of the regulation, and whether there was a 'physical invasion' of the property.

The open-ended nature of *Penn Central* came under criticism from many scholars, who argued that undermined certainty to an unacceptable extent (Radin, 1988; Rose-Ackerman, 1988; Poirier, 2002). The Supreme Court has sought greater certainty by stating that certain types of cases do not involve the *Penn Central* test. So, for example, a regulation that deprives the owner of all economically viable use of the property would constitute a taking (*Lucas*, 1992). There is also the 'core rights' doctrine, by which the deprivation of certain fundamental rights associated with the property is a taking (Mossoff, 2003). In particular, the right to exclude is 'universally held to be a fundamental element of the property right' (*Kaiser Aetna v United States*, 1979, p. 179), and 'one of the most treasured strands in the owner's bundle of property rights' (*Loretto v Teleprompter Manhattan CATV Corp.*, 1982, p. 435; see also *Nollan v California Coastal Commission*, 1987, pp. 833–4). Accordingly, restrictions on the right to exclude are prima facie takings, and in such cases, there is no need to engage in the ad hoc balancing of *Penn Central* to determine whether compensation is required.

Some scholars argued that balancing should be rejected in virtually all cases. One of the best-known proponents of this position is Richard Epstein, who argued, in *Takings: Private Property and the Power of Eminent Domain*, that

> No matter how the basic entitlements contained within the bundle of ownership rights are divided and no matter how many times the division takes place, all of the pieces together, and each of them individually, fall within the scope of the eminent domain clause. (Epstein, 1985)

According to Epstein, any form of regulation that takes any right of property from the holder should be regarded as a taking that required compensation. Exceptions should only be made for regulations that fall within the scope of nuisance, as traditionally understood. As Justice Scalia put it in *Lucas v South Carolina Coastal Council*, such regulations must do no more than 'duplicate the result that could have been achieved in the courts – by adjacent landowners (or other uniquely affected persons) under the State's law of private nuisance, or by the State under its complementary power to abate nuisances … or otherwise' (*Lucas*, 1992, p. 1029).

The Epstein/Scalia approach has been subject to vigorous criticism (Grey, 1986; see generally Radin, 1988 and Poirier, 2002). This is at least partly due to the limited view of the role of the state that it supports. By allowing uncompensated regulation only in very narrow circumstances, it would restrict the powers of the state to an extent not seen in most countries. This is not a necessary consequence of the rejection of balancing: indeed, the adoption of balancing under the European Convention on Human Rights (discussed below) had the effect of expanding the protection for property (for a general discussion, see Stephen Gardbaum's discussion in Section 1 of his contribution to this volume). In any case, some scholars argue that the Epstein/Scalia view ignores a stream of American property law that incorporates ideas of social obligation (Underkuffler, 2004; Boyce, 2007). This view dominates the constitutional law of Germany, and arguably it has strong historic foundations in American constitutional law as well (Draeger, 2001; Alexander, 2003; Underkuffler, 2004). Others argue that balancing tests are appropriate and workable, or at least that attempts to be precise are unlikely to produce satisfactory results (Poirier, 2002). In any event, in *Palazzolo v Rhode Island* (2001) and *Tahoe-Sierra Preservation Council, Inc. v Tahoe Regional Planning Agency* (2002), the Supreme Court indicated that the *Penn Central* balancing test is still applicable in some cases.

The position in civilian jurisdictions, and under the European Convention on Human Rights, is quite different. To begin with, the civilian conception of property treats ownership as an indivisible and exclusive interest, and expropriation is normally reserved for the taking of ownership. Anything less, in formal terms, is regulation. Accordingly, the 'core rights' doctrine would not fit within this view, because the rights that collectively constitute ownership are distinct from ownership itself. There may still be a requirement to compensate for regulation, as these jurisdictions are more willing to accept the principle that regulation may require compensation. Conceptually, regulation is distinct from taking, but as compensation may be available for either, the distinction is not significant. For example, in *Chassagnou v France* (1999), the European Court of Human Rights found that laws that required landowners to allow hunters to enter their property did not amount to the European equivalent of a taking. As there was a permanent restriction on the right to exclude others, an American court would probably treat a similar regulation as a taking of property. That was not conclusive, however, as the Court of Human Rights still found that the hunting laws infringed the right to property as a violation of the balance that ought to be maintained between owners and the state.

A number of common law jurisdictions have also rejected the American 'core rights' approach, and implicitly the more radical views of Epstein and Scalia. A leading example is the judgment of the House of Lords in *Belfast v O.D. Cars* (1960), decided in relation to the property clause of the Government of Ireland Act, 1920. The Act conferred lawmaking powers on Northern Ireland, subject to the proviso that it did not have the power to 'take any property without compensation'. In *Belfast*, it was argued that the denial of permission to erect a building was a taking of property. Viscount Simonds rejected the argument that Epstein would make over twenty years later, as he stated that:

> anyone using the English language in its ordinary signification would ... agree that 'property' is a word of very wide import, including intangible and tangible property. But he would surely deny that any one of those rights which in the aggregate constituted ownership of property could itself and by itself aptly be called 'property' and to come to the instant case, he would deny that the right to use property in a particular way was itself property, and that the restriction or denial of that right by a local authority was a 'taking,' 'taking away' or 'taking over' of 'property'. (*Belfast*, 1960, p. 517)

The preference in most jurisdictions is for a balancing test, often in the form of the *Penn Central* test. In some jurisdictions, constitutions explicitly require balancing: the Constitution of South Africa is an example.[5] In others, it has been developed through judicial interpretation. The jurisprudence of the European Court of Human Rights illustrates the strength of this judicial preference for balancing, even in the face of a text that appears to exclude it. Indeed, it was the expectation of at least some of the signatory governments that there would be no judicial balancing. The right to property is as follows:

> Every natural or legal person is entitled to the peaceful enjoyment of his possessions. No one shall be deprived of his possessions except in the public interest and subject to the conditions provided for by law and by the general principles of international law.
>   The preceding provisions shall not, however, in any way impair the right of a State to enforce such laws as it deems necessary to control the use of property in accordance with the general interest or to secure the payment of taxes or other contributions or penalties.

There is no reference to compensation, or indeed to any kind of substantive balancing process. There is the reference to 'general principles of international law' in the second sentence. This was intended to preserve the rule of customary law that states cannot expropriate the property of aliens without compensation, but it was not intended to apply to expropriation from nationals (*Lithgow v United Kingdom*, 1986). Nevertheless, in the seminal case *Sporrong and Lönnroth v Sweden* (1982, para. 69), the Court stated that the first sentence of the clause contains a general principle of substantive fairness. This principle requires the state to maintain a 'fair balance' between 'the demands of the general interest of the community and the requirements of the protection of the individual's fundamental rights' in every case involving an interference with property. This applies to both regulation and expropriation, with the result that compensation may be payable for regulation, and is not necessarily payable for expropriation. There is a strong argument that this is contrary to the intentions of the signatories to the Convention, but it has not been challenged since *Sporrong* (Allen, 2010).

   The takings-regulation issue raises a final point. Many regulations that adversely affect one owner work to the advantage of another property holder. Some regulatory laws permit one private party to acquire the property of another by compulsion. This raises issues of the public use or interest behind the taking, which is discussed below, but even if that threshold is passed, there is still the question of substantive requirements of fairness or compensation. This creates the possibility that a right to property may have horizontal effect: in other words, it does not merely work vertically, against the state, but possibly against other private persons. Most states would treat the exercise of a delegated power of eminent domain as clearly within the scope of the property clause, but cases where property is taken under traditional private law are more difficult. Stephen Gardbaum addresses the idea of horizontality from a general perspective in his chapter in this work; how it would arise in property is suggested by the Constitutional Court's comment in the *Groundwater Case* that the constitutional conception of property is governed by values drawn from both public and private law. Van der Walt's argument suggests that the private law conceptions of property may also be governed by public and private values. To some extent, this has already been acknowledged in some jurisdictions. For example, the European Court of Human Rights has held that the right to property applies to rules of adverse possession (*J.A. Pye (Oxford) Ltd v The United Kingdom*, 2008) and the company law rules that enable a significant majority to acquire small 'holdout' shareholders in the event of takeover (*Bramelid v Sweden*, 1983).

4 PUBLIC INTEREST/USE IN TAKINGS

Constitutional property clauses normally provide that property may only be taken for a public use or in the public interest. In most jurisdictions, courts tend to defer to the legislature and executive on this issue. Even the taking of property for the use of a private person is permitted, so long as some benefit will ultimately accrue to the public. Hence, until recently, both the case law and legal literature on public use and interest has been quite sparse in comparison to the literature on property and takings.

The situation changed with *Kelo v City of New London* (2005). *Kelo* concerned a project for redevelopment, which the local government supported as economically beneficial to the larger community. However, the government did not acquire the land, but authorised a private developer to acquire and develop the land, with a view to an ultimate resale to another private owner. The owner argued that there was no public use, as required by the takings clause, because the developer acted for private profit; any public benefit was too remote to support the taking. However, by a 5–4 margin, the Supreme Court held that the taking was constitutional.

Kelo provoked a massive debate in the United States, on a number of different fronts. The delegation of eminent domain to allow one private person to acquire land from another is one key issue. The wisdom of 'economic regeneration' through indirect or direct subsidy is another. The case also raises questions about the fairness of displacing people from their homes, especially as this kind of regeneration tends to hit people who are not well-off. These issues arise in many countries, although the focus may be different (Azuela and Herrera, 2007). The *Kelo* debate is about property, but in many other jurisdictions, the focus falls on different aspects. So, for example, in Europe, the law of state aids prevents many of the practices that have been the focus of criticism in the United States. In the United Kingdom, there is nothing quite like the American 'property rights' movement, but then again, planning and competition laws prevent local governments from deriving any real financial advantage, even in the form of enhanced tax revenues, by assisting private development through cheap land assembly (Allen, 2008). There are still issues regarding the desirability of redevelopment, but they are not as charged with the *Kelo* concern that public power is being used for private profit.

Similarly, the international debate on the security of the home raises many of the concerns of *Kelo*, but without the focus on owners (Azuela and Herrera, 2007). For example, the scale of displacement caused by infrastructure and development projects in the developing world is a growing issue. The concern is not limited to property owners. A leading legal example is *Residents of Joe Slovo Community Western Cape v Thubelisha Homes* (2008), where the Constitutional Court of South Africa held that a community of about 20,000 residents could be evicted from public land scheduled for development. The case raises some of the issues of the American debate, as the value of displacing a community in the name of improvement was questioned. However, in *Joe Slovo Community*, the occupants were not homeowners, and their constitutional case turned on the right to housing contained in section 26 of the Constitution. The occupants did not succeed in stopping the evictions, but the Court did hold that the evictions could proceed only on the condition that the government provide the residents with 'adequate housing', and that 70% of the new housing units be reserved for the former residents.

From a comparative perspective, *Kelo* provides a reminder that the constitutionalisation of property does not necessarily elevate the protection for property. However, the focus on the right to property as the frame for the debate both raises similar issues while it also appears to give a different focus. The 'property rights' movement is, as the name suggests, largely about the treatment of property owners, rather than the market or about security of the home.

5   COMPENSATION IN TAKINGS CASES

Most constitutions explicitly guarantee compensation for takings, although they vary in the degree of detail on valuation and manner of payment. Some simply promise 'compensation',[6] or 'just compensation'[7] or 'just terms';[8] others go into considerable detail about matters such as the convertibility of the currency of payment and the speed of payment.[9]

In very general terms, there are two different approaches to compensation. The first holds that the purpose of compensation is essentially indemnification: compensation should restore the owner to their pre-taking position. William Blackstone famously asserted that, although the legislature may compel the individual to sell property, it can only do so 'by giving him a full indemnification and equivalent for the injury thereby sustained'.[10] Practical considerations may make it impossible to achieve a perfect balance. For example, it may be impossible to measure all intangible or subjective gains and losses. If so, it may be legitimate to rely on objective measures, and usually this is done by paying the market value of the property. Hence, true indemnification is rarely achieved. However, the key point is that it would not be legitimate to pay something less than the market value merely because the state is seeking to save capital for other purposes. Similarly, the individual's claim is based on ownership; it would not be legitimate for the state to pay less than the market value because other facts suggest that the individual was not morally deserving of full compensation.

The second holds that compensation should ensure that a fair or equitable balance is struck between public and private interests. Payment of the market value of the property would represent the fair or equitable balance, but there is discretion to pay something below the market value in some circumstances. There is no guarantee of full compensation in all cases. This might be expressed in terms of a social obligation inherent in property ownership, or possibly in terms of the pressing need for large-scale programmes involving matters such as economic restructuring, land reform or infrastructure development. Either way, full indemnification would not be expected in every case.

The most intense controversies over compensation have involved jurisdictions where the legislature seeks to apply the balancing model, but the courts support the indemnification model. For example, in the first twenty years after the adoption of the Constitution, the Supreme Court of India steadfastly maintained that compensation must seek to restore the property owner, or at least that compensation must provide a monetary equivalent for the lost property. Parliament amended the right to property on several occasions, but to no avail. For example, in *R.C. Cooper v Union of India* (1970), the Supreme Court held that the national-isation of the banks would be unconstitutional if compensation did not reflect the value of all the expropriated assets of the banks, including, in particular, the goodwill associated with those assets. At the time, the property clause stated that:

> No property shall be compulsorily acquired or requisitioned save for a public purpose and save by authority of a law which provides for the compensation for the property so acquired or requisi-tioned and either fixes the amount of compensation, or specifies the principles on which, and the manner in which, the compensation is to be determined and given; *and no such law shall be called in question in any court on the ground that the compensation provided by that law is not adequate.*[11]

One might have thought that the wording was sufficiently broad to allow expropriation without compensation for goodwill. There was no reference to market value, and the provi-sion appears to be designed to give Parliament the discretion to set compensation as it saw fit. Nevertheless, the Supreme Court held that 'compensation' would have little meaning if it did not counter-balance the entire economic loss.

Ultimately, the conflict moved beyond property to the responsibility for the Constitution itself, as the Court asserted that certain aspects of the property clause – including, apparently, the principle of indemnification – were beyond constitutional amendment. The interpretive issues were finally resolved in the fascinating case of *Kesavananda Bharati v State of Kerala* (1973), where, by a narrow margin, the Court ultimately ruled that Parliament's amending powers did not include the power to abrogate fundamental rights. By an equally narrow margin, it also ruled that the right to property was not a fundamental right. The Parliament subsequently amended the Constitution so as to remove the right to property from the list of fundamental rights (Dhavan, 1977, pp. 146–78; for recent developments, see Allen, 2007b and Dilal, 2008).

The position of the Supreme Court of India mirrors that of courts in many other common law jurisdictions. In the United States, the reference to 'just' compensation in the takings clause might suggest that there is some room for balancing, but the dominant rule is for market value compensation (Garnett, 2006). This is even true in Australia, where the Constitution only requires the Commonwealth Parliament to acquire property on 'just terms'. In *Nelungaloo Proprietary Limited v The Commonwealth* (1943, p. 569), Dixon J. of the High Court stated that 'Unlike "compensation", which connotes full money equivalence, "just terms" are concerned with fairness'; however, in *Georgiadis v Australian and Overseas Telecommunications Corporation* (1994, pp. 310–11), Brennan J., also of the High Court, declared that 'Unless it be shown that what is gained is full compensation for what is lost, the terms cannot be found to be just'. It appears that departures from the indemnification princi-ple must be clearly spelled out in the property clause.

One recent example is section 25(3) of the Constitution of South Africa, which was drafted in the light of the Indian experience. It provides that:

25(3) The amount of the compensation and the time and manner of payment must be just and equitable, reflecting an equitable balance between the public interest and the interests of those affected, having regard to all relevant circumstances, including
    a. the current use of the property;
    b. the history of the acquisition and use of the property;
    c. the market value of the property;
    d. the extent of direct state investment and subsidy in the acquisition and beneficial capital improvement of the property; and
    e. the purpose of the expropriation.

Unlike the Indian Supreme Court, the Constitutional Court has been willing to allow departures from the market standard (Van der Walt, 2005, 276–81). In *Du Toit v Minister of Transport* (2005, para. 36), the Constitutional Court stated that section 25(3) does not give market value 'a central role': 'Viewed in the context of our social and political history, questions of expropriation and compensation are matters of acute socio-economic concern and could not have been left to be determined solely by market forces'. It accepted that, in this case, compensation for the extraction of gravel for road construction could fall well below the market rate, on the basis that the public interest in developing infrastructure might be impeded if full market value were payable.

Section 25 was also influenced by the German constitutional approach. Article 14(3) of the German Basic Law requires compensation for expropriation, but also provides that 'compensation shall be determined by establishing an equitable balance between the public interest and the interests of those affected'. The Constitutional Court has stated that the 'equitable balance' would normally require market value compensation, but departures may be justified in special circumstances:

> An inflexible compensatory amount, which is related to the market value alone, is consequently foreign to the Basic Law. It is also not correct that the person deprived of property always 'must be given a full equivalent for what has been taken' by the compensatory amount. The legislator can provide for full compensation or a compensatory amount less than that, according to the circumstances. (*'Hamburg Flood Control Case'*, 1968, p. 24)

The German approach also appears to have influenced the European Court of Human Rights. As explained above, the text of the Convention does not refer to compensation, but the Court in *Sporrong* held that every interference with property must strike a fair balance between the owner's interests and the public and general interest. In *James v United Kingdom* (1986, para. 36), the Court stated that the fair balance would normally require compensation 'reasonably related to the value' of the property. In practice, this is generally presumed to be the full market value. However, the Court was careful to say that 'Article 1 (P1-1) does not … guarantee a right to full compensation in all circumstances, since legitimate objectives of "public interest", such as pursued in measures of economic reform or measures designed to achieve greater social justice, may call for less than reimbursement of the full market value'.

James concerned tenancy reforms; other cases have involved the nationalisation of major industries (*Lithgow*, 1986), tax reform (*National & Provincial Building Society v United Kingdom*, 1997), transitional justice (*Broniowski v Poland*, 2004; *Jahn v Germany*, 2005) and the protection of national heritage (*Kozacioğlu v Turkey*, 2009). These cases involve programmes that affect a large class of property owners. The primary concern appears not to be with the affordability of programmes, as in *Du Toit*, but rather with equality of treatment with other affected owners. With isolated takings pursuant to small-scale programmes, only market compensation would represent a reasonable sharing of the burdens. However, with very large-scale programmes, the sharing of the burden may be fair without market value compensation.

To date, the balancing approach has been invoked to justify compensation below the market value. I have argued that the adoption of the market value standard under the European Convention on Human Rights 'seems to abandon the idea that human rights should protect an area of personal choice, at least where the individual does not have the same desires, preferences or plans for their property as the community at large' (Allen, 2007a, p. 289). There may be some types of property that require additional connection, due to the nature of the individual's dependence on the asset. In the United States, the *Kelo* case raised questions about the adequacy of compensation for the expropriation of a family home. In practical terms, the costs of a forced move are likely to exceed the market value, and the individual loss is likely to be much greater than in the case of more fungible property. There is a movement in the United States to re-examine compensation principles for more personal assets, especially the home. Whether it is successful, and whether similar developments occur elsewhere, remains to be seen.

6   CLOSING OBSERVATIONS: THE COMPARABILITY OF TAKINGS LAWS

One important issue, rarely explored by comparative lawyers, is the relationship between international legal rules on takings and national constitutional law. International law includes customary principles regarding a state's right to protect its nationals and their property situated in other states. A multitude of bilateral and multilateral investment treaties add a further layer of protection for foreign investment. These treaties usually include provisions on takings and the regulation of property, with greater detail than customary law in relation to dispute settlement procedures and substantive issues concerning the amount and method of payment of compensation (Sornarajah, 2004). There is also the third category of international rules on takings, found in human rights treaties.

The key issue is whether these laws are sufficiently similar in their substance to justify a comparative analysis. They are certainly similar in their structure, as they deal with the legality and purpose of state action, and the amount of compensation that should be paid for property. If comparative law is valuable, why not compare these structurally similar rules of international law with each other, and with constitutional law? To some extent, I have already assumed that comparisons can be made, as I have drawn examples from the case law on the right to property in the European human rights system. However, as far as international law is concerned, I have been selective: I have not, for example, drawn examples from international investment law, although one might argue that they would be just as relevant. My choice reflects my belief that states draft human rights treaties with objectives that are broadly similar to the objectives of national constitutional law, but that they approach investment treaties with different objectives in mind. With human rights and constitutional law, there is a greater concern with individual autonomy for its own sake, than with the encouragement of specific uses of property that may contribute to economic growth. Of course, the pursuit of one objective may aid the achievement of the other, but it cannot be assumed that the two are equivalent. This view is certainly open to challenge (especially as I haven't defended it in any detail!), not least because it raises the problem of the 'formalist trap' that Gregory Alexander identified. But it does raise an interesting question for comparative lawyers: often, it is what we choose not to compare that is as important as what we choose to compare.

NOTES

1. This chapter is concerned with fundamental rights relating to takings of property, as opposed to fundamental rights relating to other forms of interference. Most constitutions that incorporate a takings clause also include a broader due process guarantee. The focus of the broader guarantee is usually procedural, although under some constitutions there may be a substantive element. The term 'property' may be used to define the scope of both of these rights, but its meaning may vary across them. See generally Van der Walt, 2003, pp. 1–39.
2. See e.g. Constitution of Australia, s. 51(xxxi); the Government of Ireland Act, 1920, s. 5; Constitution of Malaysia, Article 13; Constitution of South Africa, s. 25.
3. Constitution of Nigerian, s. 31(1) (as originally enacted).
4. Article 31(2) of the Constitution of India (as originally enacted).
5. Section 36.
6. See e.g. Article 14(3) of German Basic Law which requires 'compensation' for expropriation, and also states that 'Compensation shall reflect a fair balance between the public interest and the interests of those affected'.
7. See e.g. the Fifth Amendment of the Constitution of the United States.
8. Australia, s. 51(xxxi).
9. See e.g. Hong Kong Basic Law, Article 110: 'shall correspond to the real value of the property concerned at the time and shall be freely convertible and paid without undue delay'.
10. *Blackstone Commentaries* 135.
11. Article 31(2); emphasis added. The italicised words were added to the earlier version of Article 31(2) by the Fourth Amendment.

REFERENCES

Adler, Jonathan H. (2008), 'Money or Nothing: The Adverse Environmental Consequences of Uncompensated Land Use Controls', *Boston College Law Review*, 49, 301–66.

Alexander, Gregory S. (2003), 'Property as a Fundamental Constitutional Right? The German Example', *Cornell Law Review*, 88, 733–78.

Alexander, Gregory S. (2006), *The Global Debate over Constitutional Property: Lessons for American Takings Jurisprudence*, Chicago: University of Chicago Press.

Allen, Tom (2000), *The Right to Property in Commonwealth Constitutions*, Cambridge: Cambridge University Press.

Allen, Tom (2007a), 'Compensation for Property under the European Convention on Human Rights', *Michigan Journal of International Law*, 28, 287–334.

Allen, Tom (2007b), 'Property as a Fundamental Right in India, Europe and South Africa', *Asia-Pacific Law Review*, 15 (2), 193–218.

Allen, Tom (2007c), 'Restitution and Transitional Justice in the European Court of Human Rights', *Columbia Journal of European Law*, 13, 1–46.

Allen, Tom (2008), 'Controls over the Use of Eminent Domain in England', in Robin Paul Malloy (ed.), *Private Property, Community Development & Eminent Domain*, Aldershot: Ashgate Publishing, 75–99.

Allen, Tom (2010), 'Liberalism, Social Democracy and the Value of Property under the European Convention on Human Rights', *International and Comparative Law Quarterly*, 59, 1055–78.

Alvaro, Alexander (1991), 'Why Property Rights were Excluded from the Canadian Charter of Rights and Freedoms', *Canadian Journal of Political Science*, 24, 309–29.

Azuela, Antonio and Herrera, Carlos (2007), *Taking Land around the World: International Trends in the Expropriation for Urban and Infrastructure Projects*, Cambridge, MA: Lincoln Institute of Land Policy.

Boyce, Bret (2007), 'Property as a Natural Right and as a Conventional Right in Constitutional Law', *Loyola of Los Angeles International and Comparative Law Review*, 29, 201–90.

Chaskalson, Matthew (1995), 'Stumbling Towards Section 28: Negotiations over the Protection of Property Rights in the Interim Constitution', *South Africa Journal of Human Rights*, 11, 222–40.

Choudhry, Sujit (2004), 'The *Lochner* Era and Comparative Constitutionalism', *International Journal of Constitutional Law*, 2 (1), 1–55.

Daintith, Terence (2004), 'The Constitutional Protection of Economic Rights', *International Journal of Constitutional Law*, 2 (1), 56–90.

Dhavan, Rajeev (1977), *The Supreme Court of India: A Socio-legal Analysis of its Juristic Techniques*, Bombay: N. M. Tripathi Pvt. Ltd.

Dilal, Milan (2008), 'India's New Constitutionalism: Two Cases that have Reshaped Indian Law', *Boston College International & Comparative Law Review*, 31, 257–75.

Draeger, Tonya R. (2001), 'Property as a Fundamental Right in the United States and Germany: A Comparison of Takings Jurisprudence', *Transnational Lawyer*, 14, 363–400.

Epstein, Richard A. (1985), *Takings: Private Property and the Power of Eminent Domain*, Cambridge, MA: Harvard University Press.

Fischel, William A. (1995), *Regulatory Takings: Law, Economics, and Politics*, Cambridge, MA and London: Harvard University Press.

Forsey, E.A. (1938), 'Disallowance of Provincial Acts, Reservation of Provincial Bills, and Refusal of Assent by Lieutenant-Governors since 1867', *Canadian Journal of Economics and Political Science*, 4, 47–59.

Friedman, Lawrence M. (1986), 'A Search for Seizure: Pennsylvania Coal Co. *v* Mahon in Context', *Law & History Review*, 4, 1–22.

Garnett, Nicole Stelle (2006), 'The Neglected Political Economy of Eminent Domain', *Michigan Law Review*, 105, 101–50.

Grey, Thomas C. (1986), 'The Malthusian Constitution', *University of Miami Law Review*, 41, 21–47.

Kommers, Donald P. (1989), *The Constitutional Jurisprudence of the Federal Republic of Germany*, Durham, NC: Duke University Press.

Leckie, Scott (2003), 'New Directions in Housing and Property Restitution', in Scott Leckie (ed.), *Returning Home: Housing and Property Restitution Rights of Refugees and Displaced Persons*, Cambridge: Cambridge University Press, 3–61.

Macklem, Patrick (2005), 'Rybná 9, Praha 1: Restitution and Memory in International Human Rights Law', *European Journal of International Law*, 16, 1–23.

Mann, F.A. (1959), 'Outlines of a History of Expropriation', *Law Quarterly Review*, 75, 188–219.

Michelman, Frank (1981), 'Property as a Constitutional Right', *Washington & Lee Law Review*, 38, 1097–114.

Mossoff, Adam (2003), 'What is Property? Putting the Pieces Back Together', *Arizona Law Review*, 45, 371–443.

Mostert, Hanri (2002), *The Constitutional Protection and Regulation of Property and its Influence on the Reform of Private Law and Landownership in South Africa and Germany*, Berlin, Heidelberg and New York: Springer-Verlag.

Munro, Trevor (1972), *The Politics of Constitutional Decolonization: Jamaica 1944–62*, Mona, Kingston, Jamaica: Institute of Social and Economic Research, University of the West Indies.

Poirier, Marc R. (2002), 'The Virtue of Vagueness in Takings Doctrine', *Cardozo Law Review*, 24, 93–191.

Posner, Eric A. and Vermeule, Adrian (2004), 'Transitional Justice as Ordinary Justice', *Harvard Law Review*, 117, 761–825.

Radin, Margaret Jane (1988), 'The Liberal Conception of Property: Cross Currents in the Jurisprudence of Takings', *Columbia Law Review*, 88, 1667–96.

Reich, Charles (1964), 'The New Property', *Yale Law Journal*, 73, 733–87.

Reich, Charles (1965), 'Individual Rights and Social Welfare: The Emerging Legal Issues', *Yale Law Journal*, 74, 1245–57.

Rose-Ackerman, Susan (1988), 'Against Ad Hocery: A Comment on Michelman', *Columbia Law Review*, 88, 1697–711.

Sornarajah, M. (2004), *The International Law on Foreign Investment*, 2nd edition, Cambridge: Cambridge University Press.

Tani, Karen M. (2008), '*Flemming v Nestor:* Anticommunism, the Welfare State, and the Making of "New Property" ', *Law & History Review*, 26, 379–414.

Underkuffler, Laura S. (2004), ''ahoe's Requiem: The Death of the Scalian View of Property and Justice', *Constitutional Commentary*, 21, 727–55.

Van der Walt, A.J. (1997), *The Constitutional Property Clause*, Kenwyn, SA: Juta & Co.

Van der Walt, A.J. (2003), *Constitutional Property Clauses: A Comparative Analysis*, Cape Town: Juta & Co.

Van der Walt, A.J. (2005), *Constitutional Property Law*, Cape Town: Juta & Co.

Youngs, Raymond (1998), *English, French and German Comparative Law*, London: Cavendish Publishing Ltd.

Cases

Akkuş v Turkey, 1997-IV ECtHR 43

Belfast v O.D. Cars, [1960] AC 490

Bramelid v Sweden, 5 EHRR 249 (1983)

Broniowski v Poland, 2004-V ECtHR 1
Chassagnou v France, 1999-III ECtHR 21
Du Toit v Minister of Transport, CCT22/04 (2005)
Eastern Enterprises v Apfel, 524 US 498 (1998)
Flemming v Nestor, 363 US 603 (1960)
Georgiadis v Australian and Overseas Telecommunications Corporation, 179 CLR 226 (1994)
'Groundwater Case', 58 BverfGE 300 (1981) (D. Kommers, trans.), Durham, NC: Duke University Press (1989)
'Hamburg Flood Control Case', 24 BVerfGE 367 (1968) (R. Youngs, trans.), London: Cavendish Publishing Ltd.
   (1998)
Iatridis v Greece, 1999-II ECtHR 75
J.A. Pye (Oxford) Ltd v The United Kingdom, 46 EHRR 45 (GC) (2008)
Jahn v Germany, 2005-VI ECtHR (GC)
James v United Kingdom, 98 ECtHR (ser. A), para. 36 (1986)
Kaiser Aetna v United States, 444 US 164 (1979)
Kelo v City of New London, 545 US 469 (2005)
Kesavananda Bharati v State of Kerala, 4 SCC 225 (1973)
Kozacioğlu v Turkey, Appl. no. 2334/03, 19 February 2009 (GC)
La Compagnie Sucriere de Bel Ombre Ltee v The Government of Mauritius [1995] 3 LRC 494 (PC)
Lithgow v United Kingdom, 102 ECtHR (ser. A) (1986)
Loretto v Teleprompter Manhattan CATV Corp., 458 US 419 (1982)
Lucas v South Carolina Coastal Council, 505 US 1003 (1992)
National & Provincial Building Society v United Kingdom, 1997-VII ECtHR 2325
Nelungaloo Proprietary Limited v The Commonwealth, 75 CLR 495 (1943)
Nollan v California Coastal Commission, 483 US 825 (1987)
Palazzolo v Rhode Island, 533 US 606 (2001)
Penn Central Transportation Company v New York City, 438 US 104 (1978)
Pennsylvania Coal v Mahon, 260 US 393 (1922)
Port of Elizabeth Municipality v Various Occupiers, 2005 (1) SA 217 (CC
R.C. Cooper v Union of India, [1970] 3 SCR 530
Residents of Joe Slovo Community Western Cape v Thubelisha Homes, CCT22/08 (2008)
Sporrong and Lönnroth v Sweden, 52 ECtHR (ser. A) (1983)
Syndicat Northcrest v Amselem, [2004] SCC 47 (Can.)
Tahoe-Sierra Preservation Council, Inc. v Tahoe Regional Planning Agency, 535 US 302 (2002)

28. Socio-economic rights: has the promise of eradicating the divide between first and second generation rights been fulfilled?

Dennis M. Davis

On 16 December 1966, the International Covenant on Economic Social and Cultural Rights was adopted by the General Assembly of the United Nations.[1] The preamble to this Covenant proclaimed boldly that economic, social and cultural rights constituted a recognition that 'in accordance with the Universal Declaration of Human Rights, the ideal of free human beings enjoying freedom from fear and want can only be achieved if conditions are created whereby everyone may enjoy his economic, social and cultural rights as well as his civil and political rights'.

The Covenant became part of international law upon its entry into force on 3 January 1976. This ratification represented the possibility of a significant rupture of the traditional distinction between negative and positive rights or, using the phrase employed in the title to this contribution, the distinction between first and second generation rights.

Traditionally civil and political rights were seen as the provision of defences of the individual citizenship against excessive state control. But even these negative rights held positive implications. As Henry Shue[2] wrote, 'the complete fulfilment of each kind of right involves the performance of multiple kinds of duties'. In essence, every right, both negative and positive, contains three correlative duties, namely the duty to avoid depriving, the duty to protect from deprivation and the duty to aid the deprived. For example, the right to adequate food contains three duties, that is, the duty not to eliminate an individual's only available means of acquiring food, a duty to protect individuals against deprivation of their only available means of subsistence and a duty to provide the food for those unable to do so themselves. According to Shue, each socio-economic right created a correlative obligation of refraining from interfering as well as a duty to perform specific positive action.[3]

As to the concern for autonomy at the foundation of civil and political rights guarantees, Cecil Fabre has further argued that:

> Just as autonomy powerfully justifies constitutional civil and political rights, it also justifies assigning them social rights to decent income, education, housing and health care. Giving these resources to people is important because without them they would be unable to develop the physical and mental capacities necessary to become autonomous. If we are hungry, thirsty, cold, ill and illiterate, if we constantly live under the threat of poverty, we cannot decide on a meaningful conception of the good life, we cannot make long-term plans, in short we have very little control over our existence.[4]

It is possible to develop Fabre's argument further in order to justify the recognition of socio-economic rights, not only on the basis of dignity, but also on the principle of equality.[5] Even if this analysis eschews a definitive vision of a good life, a society committed to a concept of equality should strive to create enabling conditions for all members thereof in order to live a good life defined by their own perspectives. Thus, if a society recognises the equal importance of the life of each citizen, it must strive to guarantee to each being the necessary conditions for realising a life of some value.[6]

There is a further, related argument which contends that, by refusing to recognise second generation rights, members of society will not take a constitution seriously as the fundamental law of that society. A document which offers nothing to satisfy a citizen's most fundamental needs will invariably lack legitimacy.[7] A right to vote while destitute, or a right to freedom of speech while starving can hardly be considered to represent the exclusive constituent elements of a legitimate constitutional system.

The traditional distinction within legal culture between a negative right and a second generation, positive right, has proved to be far more resistant than the drafters of the Covenant might have expected. The recognition of socio-economic rights in domestic jurisprudence thus did not follow automatically upon the existence of the Covenant. Slowly, however, the artificial distinction between the positive and the negative has been blurred, as constitutional courts were confronted with the limitations of a strict negative rights jurisprudence.

For example, in 1972 the German Federal Constitutional Court held that the constitutional right to a free choice of occupation imposed a clear obligation upon universities to demonstrate that they had employed all available sources to maximise the number of places which were available for students.[8]

Similarly, during the 1970s the Indian Supreme Court began to develop a range of social rights drawn particularly from the expressly enshrined constitutional right to life by employing the Directive Principles of the Indian Constitution to expand the scope of the express provision. Thus, in *Bandhua Mukti Morcha v Union of India*,[9] the court interpreted the right to life in an expansive manner so as to promote the right to individual dignity. The court held that the right to life included adequate nutrition, clothing, shelter, facilities for reading, writing and expressing oneself in diverse forms, as well as the right to free movement and association with fellow human beings. This judgment followed upon a decision in which the Indian Supreme Court ordered the municipality to fulfil its statutory duties to provide water, sanitation and an adequate drainage system.[10]

By 1990 international jurisprudence had begin to evidence similar substance. General Comment 3 to the Covenant on Economic, Social and Cultural Rights included the key point that 'while the full realisation that the relevant rights may be achieved progressively, steps towards that goal must be taken within a reasonably short time after the Covenant's entry into force for the states concerned. Such steps should be deliberate, concrete and targeted as clearly as possible towards meeting the obligations recognised in the Covenant'.[11]

As this approach became influential in national jurisprudence, it was unsurprising that countries that witnessed dramatic democratic development during the 1990s, whether in Latin America, Eastern Europe or South Africa, incorporated social and economic rights into their constitutions and, whether expressly or by judicial law making, employed the approach set out in General Comment 3. It should be noted, however, that at the turn of the 20th century only first generation rights continue to enjoy universal appeal.[12]

The adoption in these constitutions of social and economic rights did not, however, meet with unanimous approval. Cass Sunstein characterised their inclusion as 'a large mistake, possibly a disaster'.[13] Sunstein contended that Eastern European countries in particular should develop their constitutions principally to produce two things, namely 'firm' liberal rights, such as free speech, voting rights, protection against abuse of the criminal justice system, religious liberty, protection from and the prevention of invidious discrimination, property and contract rights and, further, that the preconditions for a market economy should be guaranteed. Only in rare instances, where countries had market economies experiencing real growth yet neglected the poor, could a constitutional order benefit from including positive guarantees of rights such as a right to decent medical care or adequate nourishment.[14]

Reduced to its essence, the objections to including social and economic rights in these national constitutions rested on a question of the capacity of domestic courts to enforce these rights.

For Frank Cross, the enforcement of social and economic rights was particularly problematic because of a manifest judicial incapacity to enforce social and economic rights, arising particularly, from the indeterminacy of these legal guarantees as, for example, the right to minimally decent housing. Further, it is futile to rely on the judiciary to provide basic welfare for the disadvantaged, if the potential breaches are unwilling to do so.[15]

These criticisms must now be interrogated through the prism of a burgeoning domestic jurisprudence. The breath of the field imposes a necessary constraint on the range of that which can be examined in a single chapter. To this end, the objections to social and economic rights together with the judicial record over the past two decades will, for the purposes of this chapter, be tested against developments, primarily in South Africa, India and, to a lesser extent, Brazil.

1   THE SOUTH AFRICAN EXPERIENCE

The key social and economic rights which are protected in terms of the South African Constitution[16] are to be found in section 26(1) which entrenches the right of everyone 'to have access to adequate housing' and section 27(1) which provides for the right of everyone

> to have access to
>   (a) health care services, including reproductive healthcare;
>   (b) sufficient food and water; and
>   (c) social security including if they are unable to support themselves and their dependants appropriate social assistance.

Both sections qualify the right by the inclusion of a subsection which provides 'the state must take reasonable, legislative and other measures within its available resources to achieve the progressive realisation of each of these rights'. In addition to these sections, the Constitution entrenches social and economic rights for children, educational rights and social and economic rights for detained persons, including sentenced prisoners.[17]

From the outset, strenuous objections, such as those attributed by Cross and Sunstein, were raised about the inclusion of these rights. In its *Certification Judgment*, the Constitutional Court put an end to this dispute concerning the inclusion of social and economic rights in the constitution:

> It is true that the inclusion for socio-economic rights may result in Courts making orders which have direct implications for budgetary matters. However, even when a Court enforces civil and political rights such as equality, freedom of speech and the right to a fair trial, the order it makes will often

have such implications ... In our view, it cannot be said that by including socio-economic rights within a bill of rights, a task is conferred upon the Courts so different from that ordinarily conferred upon them by a bill of rights that it results in a breach of the separation of powers.[18]

Within its first five years, the court began to set out a framework for a South African social and economic rights jurisprudence, commencing with its key decision in *Government of the Republic of South Africa v Grootboom*,[19] In this case, Ms Irene Grooboom and some 899 squatters had been evicted from their informal homes which they had erected on private land which had been earmarked for formal, low cost housing. Many of the litigants had applied for subsidised low cost housing from the municipality and had been on the council waiting list for many years.

The key question for decision was whether the measures already taken by the state to realise the housing rights promised in terms of section 26 of the Constitution were reasonable. In considering the appropriate test for reasonableness, the Constitutional Court considered that it should not enquire 'whether other more desirable favourable measures could have been adopted or whether public money could have better spent'.[20] Rather, the court accepted that a measure of deference must be given to the legislature and, particularly the executive, to implement a proper housing program. However, the court insisted that the concept of reasonableness meant more than the assessment of simple statistical progress. Evidence was required to show that sufficient attention had been given to the needy and most vulnerable within the community, for they had to be considered as the priority in the development of any sensible and constitutionally valid housing policy.

In other words, those most desperately in need were the first group which the state was required to consider in the implementation of its housing policy in order for such policy to pass muster in terms of section 26 of the Constitution. Although invited to follow the approach of the United Nations Committee on Economic Social and Cultural Rights that there was at 'the very least a minimum essential level for each of the rights', the court concluded, '[i]t is not in any event necessary to decide whether it is appropriate for a Court to determine in the first instance the minimum core of a right'.[21]

The critical importance of the decision in *Grootboom* was that the court adopted an administrative law model to the adjudication of socio-economic rights jurisprudence. The court insisted that the impugned government programme be tested against the concept of reasonableness which, in essence, means that a policy is found to be reasonable, if those most desperately in need, are afforded sufficient attention and, further, that the programme involved the establishment and implementation by the state of a coherent, well-coordinated and comprehensive programme directed towards the progressive realisation of the right; in *Grootboom*, the right to adequate housing. However, in keeping with the administrative law model, the court has held 'the court considering reasonableness will not enquire whether other more desirable or favourable measures could have been adopted or whether public money could have been better spent ... It is necessary to recognise that a wide range of possible measures could be adopted by the State to meet its obligations'.[22]

The court's rejection of the 'minimum core approach' to sections 26 and 27 of the Constitution in favour of the administrative model has been the subject of considerable criticism, mainly because:

An enquiry into reasonableness does not place the vital interests of individuals at its core. Yet, it is difficult to find adequate reasons for including socio-economic rights in the Constitution without recognising that they are designed to protect the fundamental interest of individuals in having access to such essential goods as housing, food, and health care. Thus, the roots of the reasonableness approach do not clearly correlate with the purpose for specifically including socio-economic rights in the Constitution.[23]

Notwithstanding its narrow approach to the express social and economic rights enshrined in the constitution, the Constitutional Court has, on occasion, adopted a more active approach. This is best exemplified in its decision in *Khosa v Minister of Social Development; Mahlaule v Minister of Social Development*.[24] The case concerned the exclusion of permanent residents in South Africa from various social grants which were payable to citizens in terms of legislation which sought to deal with destitute citizens. The court held that a legislative exclusion of permanent residents, equally in need of support, violated both the prohibition of unfair discrimination in the Constitution and the right of everyone to have access to social assistance, provided in section 27(1) (c) of the Constitution. As a remedy, the court read the category of 'permanent residents' into the provisions of the statute governing the eligibility for social grants. The court confirmed that the purpose of the right of access to social assistance for those unable to support themselves and their dependants was to ensure that the basic necessities of life were accessible to all. It could be viewed as an expression of a constitutional commitment to the values of human dignity, freedom and equality.[25] In this manner, the court read the right of access 'to social security on everyone' to include permanent residents. Where the state had argued that the extension of social grants to permanent residents would impose an extremely high financial burden on the state, the court carefully examined the evidence placed before it by the state and concluded that the costs of including permanent residents in the system would only entail a small portion of the total costs of social grants.

The same progressive instinct guided the court in the *Modderklip* case.[26] In this case, the lack of affordability was held not to be a justifiable defence to access to shelter and the court refused to evict some 40 000 squatters, who had been illegally occupying private land, and had built shelters on this land. The court held that the state's failure to take reasonable steps to assist the landowner to vindicate his private property and, at the same time, avoid the large-scale social disruptions which would be caused by the eviction of 40 000 people, had raised the real possibility of a widespread violation of the rule of law as enshrined constitutionally in the right of access to courts.[27] It further held that the progressive realisation of the rights of access to housing or land for the homeless required 'careful planning', 'fair procedures' and 'orderly and predictable processes'.

In a novel remedy, the court required the state to compensate the landowner for the occupation of his property, thereby ensuring that the landowner's ownership was protected without evicting a large community of squatters until such time as alternative accommodation could be so provided by the State. The decisions in *Khosa* and *Modderklip* illustrate that the dominance of the reasonableness test did not prevent the court, on occasion, from vindicating rights of citizens and permanent residents as promised in the Constitution. In this way, the court imposed positive obligations upon the state to guarantee these rights.

A key question which has arisen, subsequent to the judgments in *Khosa* and *Modderklip*, is whether the court would, almost a decade after *Grootboom* and in the light of these later cases, reconsider its narrow administrative law model to the application of the provisions of sections 26 and 27 of the Constitution. This question has now been answered in the case of *Mazibuko v City of Johannesburg*.[28]

An application was brought by residents of one of the poorest suburbs of Soweto, Phiri, on behalf of all similarly placed residents. The applicants argued that the city's imposition of pre-payment water meters constituted an unfair means of economic regulation, aimed at restricting poor Soweto residents' water supply to an unreasonable free basic water quantity of 25 litres per person per day. Households which refused to change to a pre-payment water meter system were, as the only alternative, offered an outside tap with no connection to the water-borne sewage system. The applicants maintained that the limited access to free water and the institution of pre-paid meters which were the only means of applicants obtaining additional water was a policy in breach of section 27 of the Constitution.

The case was litigated through two courts before it reached the Constitutional Court. In the judgments of both the High Court and the Supreme Court of Appeal, the concept of a minimum standard for social and economic rights was accepted. Relying on the evidence of the applicants' expert, both courts accepted that a free supply of 25 litres of water per person per day did not pass the required constitutional standard. Further, the imposition of pre-paid meters, which would entail a cut-off of the water supply, unless the residents bought vouchers to finance further water beyond the free amount of water granted by the city, was struck down as constituting a discriminatory measure.

When the case was finally heard by the Constitutional Court, the court took the opportunity to confirm its initial approach to social and economic rights. It rejected the applicants' argument that the court should determine a quantity of water which would constitute a minimum content for the section 27(1)(b) right; that is, an argument which would establish a minimum core for social and economic rights. Based both upon its reading of the text and its conception of the role of the judiciary in the adjudication of social and economic rights, the court said the following:

> It was not expected, nor could it have been, that the state would be able to furnish immediately with all the basic necessities of life. Social and economic rights empower citizens to demand of the state that it act reasonably and progressively to ensure that all enjoy the basic necessities of life. In so doing, social and economic rights enables citizens to hold government to account for the manner in which it seeks to pursue the achievement of social and economic rights.[29]

The court insisted that the concept of reasonableness places 'context at the centre of the enquiry and permits an assessment of context to determine whether a government program was indeed reasonable'.[30] Perhaps more significantly the court then went on to say:

> It is institutionally inappropriate for a court to determine precisely what the achievement of any particular social and economic right entails and what steps government should take to ensure the progressive realisation of the right. This is a matter, in the first place, for the legislature and executive, the institutions of government best placed to investigate social conditions in the light of available budgets and to determine what targets are achievable in relation to social and economic rights.[31]

The court held that, if government does not take any steps to realise any of the social and economic rights, the court would then require the government to so act. If government measures are unreasonable, the court would similarly require that these policy measures be reviewed to meet the standard of reasonableness. The court confirmed that its standard for review would not have been met if government policy made no provision for those most desperately in need. Further, if the government adopts a policy with unreasonable limitations or exclusions from the benefits of the policy, the court may order these limitations or exclusions to be removed. Further, the obligation of the progressive realisation of the right imposes a duty upon government continually to review its policies to ensure that the achievement of the right is progressively realised.[32]

On this basis, the court found that the city's water policy had passed constitutional scrutiny. The free basic water allowance coupled with a further policy which granted indigents further free water was not unreasonable. In relation to 80% of city households, the free allowance was adequate, even on the basis of the applicant's case. Further, the amount provided by the city was based on a prescribed national standard for basic water supply. The city had adopted a flexible policy to comply with and even expand upon the national standard. Initially, indigent households were not afforded a further, free water allocation but, by December 2006, additional measures had been taken so that registered indigent households would receive an additional four kilolitres of free water per month. Accordingly, 'the record makes plain that the city was continually reconsidering its policy and investigating ways to ensure that the poorest inhabitants of the city gained access not only to water, but also to other services, such as electricity, sanitation and refuge removal'.[33]

Applying its reasonableness test to the contents of the city's water policy and the flexible nature thereof, the court found that the city had progressively sought to increase access to water for larger households who were prejudiced by the initial limit of free water. It had continued to review its policy regularly and undertaken sophisticated research to ensure that it met the needs of the poor who resided within the city limit.

For these reasons, the court held that the City had taken account of the poorest of the poor and had attempted to ensure that the right to water would be realised progressively over time. The judgment in *Mazibuko* has put an end to the debate about the use of the administrative model for social and economic rights in South Africa. Almost a decade after *Grootboom*, it appears that this approach is now entrenched in South African law.

2 INDIA

India has certain significant similarities to South Africa, most particularly, within this context, a constitution which was intended to transform Indian society and a legal culture, to a large extent, borrowed from its erstwhile colonial master, England. However, unlike South Africa, the Indian Constitution distinguishes between enforceable fundamental rights and non-enforceable Directive Principles of State Policy. While the preamble to the Indian Constitution reflects a commitment to ensure that all its citizens enjoy 'justice, social, economic and political; liberty to afford, expression, belief, faith and worship and equality of status and of opportunity',[34] the fundamental rights in the Constitution do not include enforceable second generation rights. In Part IV of the Constitution, there appears a list of Directive Principles of State Policy which correspond, significantly, to the provisions of the International Covenant on Economic, Social and Cultural Rights,[35] but which expressly are not binding rights.

Initially, during its first two decades, the Indian Supreme Court did not recognise any of the Directive Principles of State Policy as being legally enforceable.[36] Twenty years after its leading decision to this effect, in the so-called *Fundamental Rights Case*,[37] the court changed its approach and held that the fundamental rights in the Constitution and the Directive Principles were complimentary, neither part being superior to the other.

The manner in which the Indian courts have given social and economic substance to the fundamental rights contained in the Constitution is best illustrated by the approach adopted to article 21 of the Constitution. This section provides that no person shall be deprived of his life or personal liberty except according to procedures established by law.

In *Unni Krishanan v The State of Andhra Pradesh*,[38] the Supreme Court held that article 21 lay at the heart of the list of fundamental rights and that it was not merely a negative right. As a result, the scope of article 21 was expanded, such that many of the Directive Principles were now converted into enforceable fundamental rights. The expansion of article 21 can best be seen in the decisions to provide for the maintenance and improvement of public health, the provision of humane conditions in prison and the right to shelter and improvement of the environment.

The expansion of article 21 began with an emphasis on the importance of due process. Thus, in *Olga Tellis v Mumbai Municipal Corporation*,[39] the Mumbai municipality sought to evict pavement dwellers who had migrated from villages to the town and squatted on pavements living in atrocious conditions. The municipality contended that no person had a legal right to encroach on a footpath over which the public had a right of way. The pavement dwellers relied on article 21 to prevent their eviction from the pavements, arguing that an eviction would adversely affect their means of livelihood which could only be taken away or limited after compliance with a fair and reasonable procedure. The court accepted that a right to life guaranteed in terms of article 21 included the right to livelihood. It ruled that the evictions of persons from a pavement or a slum not only resulted in a deprivation of shelter but inevitably would lead to deprivation of a means of livelihood which would, in turn, result in a deprivation of life, in as much as the pavement dwellers were employed in the vicinity of their informal dwellings.[40]

After *Olga Tellis,* the court went further than relying upon a mere insistence of compliance with proper procedures before rights could be limited. In *Chameli Singh v State of Uttar Pradesh*,[41] the court expanded the scope of article 21 to enshrine the right of shelter. In so finding, the court said:

> Shelter for a human being, therefore, is not a mere protection of his life and limb. It is a home where he has opportunities to grow physically, mentally, intellectually and spiritually. The right to shelter, therefore, includes adequate living space, safe and decent structure, clean and decent surroundings, sufficient light, pure air and water, electricity, sanitation and other civic amenities like roads, etc. so as to have easy access to his daily avocation.

The development of the Directive Principles, read together with article 21, has led in the direction of the judicial enforcement of positive rights. This tendency was further confirmed in *Unni Krashana v State of Andhara Pradesh*,[42] in which the court imposed an obligation on the state to provide educational facilities on the basis of the right to live, which included the right to live with dignity. The rights that the courts have guaranteed by judicial interpretation are

1. Every citizen has a right to free education until he/she completes the age of 14 years;
2. Beyond that age, the state's obligation to provide education is subject to 'limits of the economic capacity and development' of the state.

Perhaps the most important judicial intervention in the past decade concerned the right to food. In 2001 a massive drought hit a number of Indian states. Climatic conditions exacerbated the already parlous position of millions of Indians, living in extreme poverty and without access to sufficient food. Notwithstanding widespread starvation, central government appeared to possess excess food grain in storehouses which had not been disbursed to the needy.

The agitation caused by this growing threat to life inspired public interest litigation in which the Peoples Union for Civil Liberties approached the Supreme Court in April 2001 for the enforcement of a constitutional right to food for thousands of families which were starving in certain Indian states.

The petition posed the question as to whether the right to life under article 21 of the Constitution included the right to food and accordingly, whether the State was not under a duty to provide the food, particularly in a situation of a drought, to those who were affected thereby and were not in the financial position to acquire sufficient food.

In recognising the right to food, the court said:

> In our opinion what is of utmost importance is to see that food is provided to the aged, infirmed, disabled, destitute women, destitute men who are endangered by starvation, pregnant and lactating women and destitute children especially in cases where they or members of their family do not have sufficient funds to provide food for them. In cases of famine, there may be a shortage of food but here the situation is that amongst plenty there is scarcity. Plenty of food is available but the distribution of the same amongst the very poor and the destitute is scarce and non existent leading to malnourishment, starvation and other related problems.[43]

The court granted an interim order on 28 November 2001, in which it directed all state governments and the Union of India effectively to enforce eight different food schemes designed to prevent starvation among the poorest of the poor. In particular, the Supreme Court directed state governments to 'implement a mid-day meal scheme (MDMS) for providing every child and every Government and Government Assisted Primary Schools with a prepared mid-day meal with a minimum content of 300 calories and 8–12 grams of protein each day of school for a minimum of 200 days. Those schools providing dry rations instead of cooked meals must within three months start providing cooked meals in all Government and Government Aided Primary Schools in at least half the districts of the state (in order of poverty) and must within a further period of three months extend the provision of cooked meals to the remaining parts of the State'.[44]

From the beginning of the 2002 academic year, primary schools in a number of states began to serve midday meals in compliance with the order. In a study of midday meals in Rajasthan, it was found that the scheme did not merely provide nutrition to school children, but resulted in a sharp increase in the enrolment of girls (36%) and the reduction in gender bias in school enrolment. Furthermore, daily attendance of children in the schools also increased and this change was attributed to the midday meals.[45]

3   BRAZIL

The Brazilian legal system differs considerably from those of both South Africa and India. It has been described as a hybrid of the North American and continental European legal systems.[46] Accordingly, the system of judicial view is structurally different to those of the other two countries examined in this chapter. It combines a concrete formal review of a kind examined earlier in this chapter, together with a continental European abstract form of review.

Of significance for this chapter is the constitutional provision in the Brazilian Constitution of healthcare which is enshrined as a right of all and hence a duty imposed upon the state.[47]

The Supreme Court has given content to the right to health and medical care by a judicial emphasis upon the constitutional right to life. In a case brought by an indigent woman suffering with HIV/AIDS, the court held that the right to life was 'a constitutional consequence inalienable from the right to life'. The court further held that 'the subjective public right to health represents an inalienable legal prerogative'. Accordingly, the state was responsible for the formulation and implementation of policies aimed at ensuring that there was universal and equal access for all persons to medical treatment, including for those suffering with HIV/AIDS, access to pharmaceutical, medical and hospital assistance.[48]

In a number of further decisions, the Superior Court of Justice has established that the right to health is a duty imposed upon the state which 'must ensure those in need not just any form of treatment but the most suitable and effective treatment capable of providing the patient with the greatest dignity and least amount of suffering'. Thus the medicine that is most effective and suitable for treatment must always be provided, even though it may not be prescribed in terms of the policy of a Ministry of Health.[49]

Notwithstanding the assertion of the states' obligation to guarantee a right to health, the justiciability of social rights has been qualified by the importance that must be given to budgetary resources. Thus, the Superior Court of Justice has found that, in terms of the Brazilian Constitution, 'no agency of authority can take on expenses without proper budget forecasting. Government agencies are bound by the allocation assigned in the budget for expenditure, whatever the nature, under penalty of committing misappropriation'.[50]

Significantly, within the context of this approach, the cases which have been most successfully litigated are individual claims as opposed to class actions, the strategy being that the courts are more likely to reject wide-ranging applications.

This development, however, should not be underestimated. As Hoffmann and Bentes[51] note:

> It is here that citizens have found formal remedies to inefficiencies of the health and education system and they have started using these remedies at a breathtaking rate. This of course testifies to an overall increase in rights consciousness and litigiousness and thus to a greater de facto accountability of public health and education authorities. Indeed, the fact that judicial actors are playing an increasing role in the administration of health and education policies has led to a slow but perceptible change in attitudes and practices of public administrators, more oriented towards preventing litigation in the first place by generating effective outputs.

4   CONCLUSION

The essential difficulty confronting advocates who wish to enforce social and economic rights by imposing direct obligations upon the state in terms of the express wording of the relevant clause is that there are a multitude of ways of realising these rights. Further, a decision to enforce socio-economic rights is one of great distributive complexity. This informs the argument, by scholars such as Sunstein, that in most cases, constitutional drafters should in fact avoid including such rights in national constitutions. As this review illustrates, however, these problems have not proved to be insurmountable obstacles. The courts in all three countries in this study have been careful not to encroach upon the budgetary prerogative of the legislature and the executive. To a large degree, the courts have employed a negative conception of rights to engage with entrenched socio-economic rights. In this way, they have imposed positive obligations upon the state, not by an innovative application of positive rights jurisprudence, but by utilising a legal culture with which they were familiar in order to fuse the negative and the positive. In this way, they have used their experience of enforcing negative rights to refrain from interfering with the government's rational and honest programme for realising social and economic rights. Only where there has been an absence of evidence which provides a plausible justification for either a programme or the absence thereof, have courts imposed duties upon the state. The jurisprudence analysed in this review indicates that courts have interfered to vindicate a constitutionally entrenched social or economic right, upon an absence of plausible evidential justification for government conduct.

The South African precedent is particularly illustrative. The court has eschewed the jurisprudence of a minimum core of rights, refusing therefore to set the exact requirements with which the state must comply. The court has instead employed the test of reasonableness, sourced in the familiar terrain of administrative law, to ensure that the state remains accountable to its citizens for the fulfilment of the enshrined social and economic rights, without encroaching on the policy prerogatives of the legislature and executive and, further, by being careful not to engage excessively in polycentric tasks, the consequences of which courts cannot possibly predict from the evidence provided by the parties. These limitations notwithstanding, the advent of social and economic rights has allowed citizens and residents to participate more effectively in those decisions which determine their lives and define, promote or constrain their own life goals. In this way, a legal culture predicated upon negative rights has also been, at least, partially transformed.

It may be argued that the story as set out in this chapter supports the approach that socio-economic rights are enforced so weakly by courts that the argument in favour of their inclusion cannot be justified; that is, little tangible benefit is obtained by the citizenry. However, the record reviewed indicates that these rights have potential to, at least, partially, transform a conservative legal culture. Judges become more responsive to the needs of the poor in the context of inaction or inadequate action from the state. Courts have thus given orders which reduce the effect of starvation, promote the rights of HIV/AIDS patients to obtain the necessary medication and, further, not only have protected the homeless from arbitrary eviction from shelter and informal housing but have compelled the state to take clear steps to ensure that permanent and viable housing structures should be made available to those most in need. Significantly, these achievements have taken place without an overreaching which encroaches unreasonably on the democratically sourced prerogative of other arms of state. Law may not transform a society if vibrant politics is absent, but it can temper injustice and help destabilise existing social and economic patterns which reproduce poverty and powerlessness.

NOTES

1. GA Resolution 2200A (XXI).
2. Shue, Henry. *Basic Rights* (1980) at 52.

3. See also Bilchitz, David. *Poverty and Fundamental Rights: The Justification and Enforcement of Socio-Economic Rights* (2007) at 90–91.
4. Fabre, Cecile. 'Constitutionalising social rights', 6 *The Journal of Political Philosophy* 263 at 267 (1998). See also Bilchitz at 67–9.
5. For a dignitarian account, see e.g. Nussbaum, Martha. *Frontiers of Justice: Disability, Nationality and Species Membership* (2006).
6. Bilchitz at 64.
7. Haysom, N.R.L., 'Constitutionalism, Majoritarian Democracy and Socio-economic Rights', 8 *South African Journal of Human Rights* 451 (1994).
8. Numerous Clausus 1 Case (1972) 33 Bverf GE 303.
9. AIR 1984 SC 802.
10. *Municipal Council Ratlam v Vardhaichand and others* AIR 1980 SC 1622.
11. General Comment 3 of the Committee for Economic Social and Cultural Rights: The Nature of States Parties Obligations (1990).
12. Elkins, Zachary and Tom Ginsburg. 'Constitutional Governance in Human Rights? The Reciprocal Relationship between Human Rights Treaties and National Constitutions' (unpublished paper, October 2009). However, the authors observe that there has been a moderate but noticeable shift after World War II in the recognition of second generation rights.
13. Sunstein, Cass. 'Against Positive Rights', in *Western Rights? Post Communist Application*, edited by A. Sajo (1996). Similarly, Cross called 'the reliance on positive constitutional rights … an ultimately misguided plan'. Cross, Frank. 'The Error of Positive Rights', 48 *UCLA Law Review* 857 (2001).
14. 'Against Positive Rights' in *Western Rights? Post Communist Application*, edited by Sajo (1996).
15. Cross at 887.
16. Republic of South Africa Constitution Act 108 of 1996. The operative provisions are to be found in section 26 and 27 thereof.
17. Section 28(1)(c) gives every child the right to basic nutrition, shelter, basic healthcare services and social services. A child is considered to be a person under 18 years. Section 29 includes the right of everyone to a basic education, including adult basic education. Section 35(2)(e) confers the right to conditions of detention that are consistent with human dignity, including at least exercise and the provision, at state expense, of adequate accommodation and nutrition, reading material and medical treatment.
18. The certification process involved the implementation of an agreement concluded between the African National Congress (ANC) and the National Party, being the white minority party which had governed during the apartheid area. This agreement was enshrined in the interim constitution passed by the then 'white' Parliament in 1993. It entailed requiring the Constitutional Court to certify that the draft constitution passed by the Constitutional Assembly, duly constituted after the first democratic elections, complied with 34 constitutional principles which had been agreed by the negotiators at the initial constitutional talks which had produced the interim constitution. *Ex Parte Chairperson of the Constitutional Assembly: In re Certification of the Constitution of the Republic of South Africa* 4 SA 744 (CC) (1996) at paras 12–19.
19. 2001 (1) SA 46 (CC).
20. At para 41.
21. At para 33.
22. *Grootboom* at para 41. See also *Minister of Health v Treatment Action Campaign* 2002 (5) SA 721 (CC). For a comprehensive narrative of the TAC case see Davis, Dennis and Michelle Le Roux. *Precedent and Possibility* (2008), chapter 7.
23. Bilchitz at 160. See also Liebenberg, Sandra. 'Needs, Rights and Transformation: Adjudicating Social Rights in South Africa', *Stellenbosch Law Review* 5 (2006); Roux, T. 'Understanding Grootboom – A Response to Cass R Sunstein', 12 *Constitutional Forum* 41 (2002).
24. 2004 (6) BCLR 569 (CC).
25. At para 52.
26. See also the Magistrate decision of the court in *President of the Republic of South Africa and Another v Modderklip Boerdery (Pty) Ltd* 2005 (8) BCLR 786 (CC).
27. Section 34 of the Constitution.
28. Unreported decision of the Constitutional Court 2009.
29. Para 59.
30. Para 60.
31. Para 61.
32. Para 67.
33. Para 94.
34. See the importance of the preamble as an interpretive tool in *B.S. Nakara v Union of India* (1983) 1 SCC 305 at 327.
35. See for example articles 45 and 47 which read thus: 'The State shall endeavour to provide early childhood care

and education for all children until they complete the age of six years' and '[t]he State shall regard the raising of the level of nutrition and the standard of living of its people and the improvement of public health as among its primary duties and, in particular, the State shall endeavour to bring about prohibition of the consumption except for medical purposes of intoxicating drinks and drugs which are injurious to health'.

36. See, for example, *The State of Madras v Champakan Doraiajan* (1951) SCR 525.
37. *Keshavananda Bharati v The State of Kerala* (1973) (4) SCC 225.
38. (1993) 1 SCC 645.
39. (1995) 3 SCC 545.
40. See also *Ahmedabad Municipal Corporation v Nawab Khan Gulab Khan* (1997) 11 SCC 121.
41. (1996) 2 SCC 549.
42. (1993) 1 SCC 645.
43. *Peoples Union for Civil Liberties (PUCL) v Union of India and others* WP (Civil) No 1964/2001.
44. Interim order 28 November 2001 PUCL, supra; *Peoples Union for Civil Liberties v Union of India* (2001) 5 SCALE 303.
45. Kothari, Janya. 'Social Rights and the Constitution', 6 *SCC Jour* 32 (2004).
46. See Hoffmann, F. and F. Bentes. 'Accountability for Social and Economic Rights in Brazil', in *Courting Social Justice*, edited by V. Gouri and D.M. Brinks (2018) at 101.
47. See articles 196 and 200 of the Constitution read together with article 6.
48. *Dina Rosa Vieira v Municipio De Porto Aegre*, discussed by Piovesan, Flavia. 'Chapter 9: Social Rights Jurisprudence: Emerging Trends and International Comparative Law', in M. Langford (ed.), *Social Rights Jurisprudence: Emerging Trends in International and Comparative Law* (2008).
49. Piovesan at 186.
50. Piovesan at 187.
51. At 141.

29. Comparative constitutional law and the challenges of terrorism law

Kent Roach

1 INTRODUCTION

Terrorism has been a main preoccupation for governments and courts since the terrorist attacks of September 11, 2001 (henceforth 9/11). The response of governments, legislatures, courts and international institutions to 9/11 provides a kind of horrible natural experiment of comparative constitutional law and scholarship in action. Book-length studies are starting to appear which examine on a comparative basis common constitutional themes in counter-terrorism law such as the limitation of rights (Sottiaux, 2008; Donohue, 2008) and the fate of non-discrimination norms (Moeckli, 2008). Comparative constitutional law as applied to terrorism is becoming an innovative, wide-ranging and challenging field.

Some of the most prominent scholarship has stressed that courts have generally deferred to the executive and legislative branches of government in circumstances of real or apprehended emergency such as those caused by terrorism. Building on this historical record, some scholarship has argued that courts should, for reasons of democratic legitimacy and institutional competence, defer to governments (Posner, 2006; Posner and Vermeule, 2007). In order to preserve the law from distortions caused by the exigencies of terrorism, others suggest that courts should avoid confrontations with governments and that governments should be allowed to act in an extra-legal manner (Tushnet, 2003; Gross, 2003). Some have even predicted that 9/11 would demonstrate the 'futility' of relying on a bill of rights enforced by courts (Ewing, 2004; Ewing and Tham, 2008), while others have stressed the 'limits on the judiciary' (Donohue, 2008: 20).

Despite such arguments, courts have not been particularly deferential in the post-9/11 era. For example, they have found major parts of American, British, Canadian and Indonesian anti-terrorism laws to be unconstitutional (Roach, 2004, 2009). The reasons for this increased judicial activism are speculative but intriguing. They may relate to the nature of 'weak form' (Tushnet, 2008a) or dialogic (Roach, 2001a) forms of judicial review, proportionality analysis (Beatty, 2005) and the migration of constitutional ideas (Choudhry, 2006), including 'anti-constitutional ideas' that may come from the United Nations Security Council (Scheppele, 2006). Some democracies, most notably Australia and India, lie outside of the pattern of increased judicial activism. This raises issues such as the importance of bills of rights (Williams, 2005) and the role of support structures (Epp, 1998) in encouraging judicial activism.

The legislative and executive responses to judicial activism in the counter-terrorism field also provide an important case study in the dialogue or interaction that occurs between courts and governments. Have constitutional norms done better in situations where courts are relieved of the burden of finality and does the dialogic nature of much modern judicial review help explain the surprising amount of post-9/11 judicial activism even in countries such as the United States not normally associated with dialogic review? (Roach, 2009). In contrast, have robust legislative and executive responses to courts marginalized constitutional norms so that the courts have emerged as only an 'irritant' to the repressive policies taken by governments and legislatures (Ewing and Tham, 2008; Resnik, 2010). By enforcing norms of legality and democratic authorization, have courts helped bring secret counter-terrorism activities into light and required wider legislative and democratic debate of such measures consistent with the idea that courts are well-suited to provoke democratic dialogue (Dyzenhaus, 2006)? In contrast, have courts imposed an elite and complex professional discourse on anti-terrorism laws that could be better resisted by popular constitutionalism (Tushnet, 1999) as manifested by grassroots protests against the American Patriot Act (Sidel, 2004)?

The terrorism context is also of interest because it underlines the transnational nature of much contemporary constitutional law. The counter-majoritarian difficulty identified by Bickel (1986: 16) remained at the heart of late 20th century constitutional law scholarship, but it focused exclusively on domestic courts and domestic legislatures. This difficulty has taken on a new dimension as the United Nations Security Council has emerged as a world legislator through Security Council Resolutions 1267 and 1373 and its critical role in compiling lists of terrorists (Scheppele, 2006). In a number of venues including the European Court of Justice, the new United Kingdom Supreme Court and the Federal Court of Canada, the listing of individuals said by the Security Council to be associated with al Qaeda or the Taliban have come under domestic constitutional challenge. The results of these cases fit into a new pattern of increased judicial activism in the face of anti-terrorism efforts. These cases, however, have the important twist that the activism responds to international as opposed to domestic mandates. Such engagements between domestic constitutional law and international law raise important questions about the potential pitfalls of continued dualism, which gives domestic constitutional regimes autonomy from international law (Meyers, 2008; Forcese and Roach, forthcoming).This autonomy can be used to allow domestic regimes to depart from international human rights norms, as the Canadian Supreme Court did when it contemplated exceptional circumstances that would allow deportation to torture (*Suresh v Canada* [2002] 1 SCR 3). But the same autonomy has been used in the more recent cases to nullify the domestic implementation of a UN intergovernmental and largely secret process for the listing of terrorists that has justly been labeled Kafkaesque (*Abdelrazik v Canada* 2009 FC 580 at para 53). These cases reveal the potential for overlapping and potentially clashing constitutionalisms at the international, regional and domestic levels. The international and transnational nature of the terrorism context may provide hints about how comparative constitutional law and its scholarship will likely evolve in the future.

Finally, the terrorism context provides an interesting case study about how legislatures and executives will interpret the constitution. Before 9/11, a number of commentators argued against the idea that courts should have an interpretative monopoly on the meaning of the constitution (Tushnet, 1999; Waldron, 1999). What does the post-9/11 experience with executive and legislative interpretations of the constitution demonstrate about the comparative ability of courts, governments and legislatures to interpret the constitution? Do the infamous American torture memos reveal the danger of self-interested constitutional interpretation? Or in contrast do they confirm the self-disciplining and self-correcting nature of the relevant interpretative community? How have legislatures and legislative committees performed in interpreting the constitution under the stresses of terrorism? Have they acted reasonably or have they disregarded rights and scapegoated unpopular minorities? More generally, how can constitutional norms be made meaningful with respect to the often secret counter-terrorism activities of the state and what does this indicate about possible evolution of the separation of powers (Dyzenhaus, 2006). Here again, the transnational context of counter-terrorism provides an important challenge to traditional and exclusively domestic understandings of constitutionalism.

2   TERRORISM AND THE OLD COUNTER-MAJORITARIAN DIFFICULTY

Much post-9/11 American constitutional scholarship stressed the case for judicial deference towards executive and legislative efforts to respond to emergencies such as that produced by the 9/11 attacks on the United States. This scholarship builds on a long tradition of academic debate about what Alexander Bickel famously coined the 'counter-majoritarian difficulty' (Bickel, 1986: 16) of an unelected court invalidating the actions of elected branches of government. Perhaps the most sophisticated and sustained case for judicial deference towards the counter-terrorism efforts of government was made by Eric Posner and Adrian Vermeule, who demonstrated that the pre-9/11 record in the United States reveals that courts have normally deferred to the executive and the legislature, especially in the midst of an emergency (Posner and Vermeule, 2007). They argue that courts should defer because they are institutionally incapable of appreciating the magnitude of the security threat, in part because they will not have access to secret intelligence. In their view, governments must make 'trade-offs' between liberty and security, 'policy should become less libertarian during emergencies and courts should stay out of the way' (ibid: 158). Similar points were made by Judge Richard Posner in his popular book 2006 *Not a Suicide Pact*. Judge Posner added to these arguments some support for an 'extralegal approach' which would allow the executive to respond robustly to emergencies 'by paying the political price of breaking the law' (Posner, 2006: 154–5).

The idea that the courts would not be an effective response to overreactions by the state to terrorism was also stressed by critical scholars on the left. Both Mark Tushnet (2003) and Oren Gross (2003; Chapter 19, this volume) argued for an extra-legal approach in large part to avoid damaging precedents such as the United States Supreme Court's *Korematsu* decision upholding the wartime internment of Japanese-Americans. Even traditionally liberal American scholars such as Cass Sunstein, Alan Dershowitz and Bruce Ackerman did not advocate for or rely on judicial defense of civil liberties in the wake of 9/11. Sunstein (2004) argued that judicial minimalism was especially warranted in the national security context. Ackerman (2004) accepted temporary internment as an attempt to restore public confidence after a second attack and stressed the role of Congress in providing safeguards. Dershowitz (2002) accepted the need to balance security for liberty to the point of contemplating torture warrants. With some exceptions (Cole, 2003; Sidel, 2004), elite American post-9/11 scholarship expected or counseled extensive judicial deference to governmental attempts to prevent terrorism.

The idea that courts would defer to governmental responses to 9/11 was not limited to the United States. In Canada and the United Kingdom, scholars did not initially hold out much hope that courts would resist anti-terrorism measures. Some stressed that post-9/11 legislative measures were shrewdly crafted with the minimum standards of the constitution in mind (Roach, 2001b). Others argued that the tradition of judicial deference to the executive in times of emergency would demonstrate the 'futility' of relying on court-enforced bills of rights (Ewing, 2004). Immediately after 9/11, the House of Lords deferred to an executive decision to deport a Pakistani-born Imam because he was alleged to have been involved in foreign terrorism even though a specialized tribunal with access to secret information had found that the Imam's continued presence did not constitute a threat to national security. Lord Hoffmann concluded the decision with a famous postscript that made the case for judicial deference by arguing that the executive 'has access to special information and expertise' in national security matters and more democratic legitimacy than the courts. 'If the people are to accept the consequences of such decisions, they must be made by persons whom the people have elected and whom they can remove' (*Secretary of State v Rehman* [2001] UKHL 47 at para 62). Such arguments, combined with the tenor of much influential scholarship, suggested that courts would defer to most post-9/11 counter-terrorism efforts. As will be seen, however, there has been a surprising amount of post-9/11 judicial activism.

3   THE NEW JUDICIAL ACTIVISM TOWARDS THE GOVERNMENT'S COUNTER-TERRORISM EFFORTS

Rehman was an administrative law case and it was not decided under the quasi-constitutional bill of rights, the Human Rights Act, 1998. The British government was soundly rebuffed by the House of Lords when it attempted to defend post-9/11 legislation derogating from the European Convention to allow indeterminate detention of non-citizens suspected of terrorism on the basis of the philosophy that an 'undemocratic' judiciary should defer to the elected government as articulated by Lord Hoffmann in *Rehman*. Accepting that there was a valid emergency, the House of Lords nevertheless held that the government had acted disproportionately and in violation of the equality rights of non-citizens. In the lead judgment, Lord Bingham did not accept the distinction that the Attorney General 'drew between democratic institutions and the courts. It is of course true that the judges in this country are not elected and are not answerable to Parliament ... But the function of independent judges charged to interpret and apply the law is universally recognised as a cardinal feature of the modern democratic state, a cornerstone of the rule of law itself' (*A (F.C.) v Secretary of State* [2004] UKHL 56 at para 42). Even Lord Hoffmann had a change of heart and went farther than the majority in also finding that the courts should not defer to the legislature's declaration of an emergency.

The House of Lords decision in this case drew on a number of strands in contemporary constitutional law. With reference to jurisprudence from the European Court of Human Rights as well as from the American and Canadian Supreme Courts, the Law Lords stressed that indeterminate detention of certain non-citizens suspected of involvement with terrorism was not a rational or proportionate response to pressing concerns about terrorism. These concerns were also subsequently validated by the European Court of Human Rights which affirmed the decision (*A. v United Kingdom*, 2009). The Court also stressed the equality rights of the non-citizens who would be subject to such a detention regime. Finally, the Court invoked the concept of 'democratic dialogue' (*A (F.C.) v Secretary of State* [2004] UKHL 56: para 42) and its remedy was a declaration of incompatibility. It was up to the elected government to decide how to respond to the decision.

Consistent with the thesis that weak forms of judicial review can produce the same effects as those based on traditional notions of judicial supremacy (Tushnet, 2008a), but also with an eye to the prospects of losing on further appeal in the European Court of Human Rights, the British government repealed detention without trial in response to the 2004 decision. In its place, the government enacted a new system that allowed control orders amounting to house arrest to be applied to citizens and non-citizens alike who were reasonably suspected of involvement with terrorism. The new legislation reflected the structure of the European Convention by providing for both control orders that derogated from the Convention and control orders that did not. So far, the government has only issued control orders that it claims do not derogate from rights. Although fewer than 50 control orders have been issued, they have been the subject of multiple decisions by the House of Lords and the European Court of Human Rights, many stressing the need to disclose more of the secret information held by the government in order to allow the detainees fairly to contest the control orders (*A v United Kingdom, Secretary of State v AF* 2009 UKHL 28). At the same time, the British government has not repealed control orders raising concerns that the court decisions may have helped legitimate elaborate and intensive regimes of preventive detention without trial (Ewing and Tham, 2008). At the same time, other scholars defend court decisions applying constitutional norms of legality, fairness, equality and proportionality as an important restraint on the most visible and controversial forms of the government's counter-terrorism policy (Dyzenhaus, 1996).

The United States Supreme Court has also asserted its role in supervising the detention of persons held at Guantanamo. In *Rasul v Bush* 542 US 466 (2004), it rejected the Bush administration's claims that habeas corpus and other forms of judicial review would not apply to the detention. Congress responded with legislation stripping courts of their habeas jurisdiction and devising a regime of truncated fair trial rights. In *Hamdan v Rumsfeld* 548 US 557 (2006), the Court refused to apply the jurisdiction-stripping provisions retroactively and concluded that the truncated process at Guantanamo designed to protect intelligence from disclosure violated both the Uniform Code of Military Justice and Common Article 3 of the Geneva Convention. This decision, like the House of Lords 2004 decision discussed above, is also consistent with the idea that constitutional courts are looking to international and transnational sources of law for inspiration and are prepared to take a bolder stance in situations where they are confident that their decisions need not be the final word. Congress responded to this decision with new legislation that clearly stripped habeas corpus jurisdiction in a retroactive fashion. In a 5:4 decision in *Boumediene v Bush* 128 S.Ct. 229 (2008), however, the Court finally asserted habeas corpus jurisdiction as a constitutional necessity, finding that the government had not satisfied the provisions in the American constitution for derogating from habeas corpus when required for public safety in times of rebellion or invasion.

The American Guantanamo decisions, combined with the British indeterminate detention and control order decisions, provide a fundamental challenge to the thesis advanced by Posner and Vermeule that courts should continue their traditional practices of deferring to the government on the proper response to terrorism. They signal increased judicial confidence in applying proportionality and equality norms to the state's security activities and an increased engagement between domestic constitutional norms and international sources of law. At the same time, all of these decisions deliberately left governments ample room to respond to the ruling of the courts and the American government even under the new Obama administration has not abandoned trial by military commissions and even detention without trial at Guantanamo. Although some American scholars argue that the courts have excessively interfered with the government's conduct of the war on terrorism (Posner, 2008), others suggest that the courts have done too little and only acted on narrow procedural margins (Martinez, 2008).

Judicial activism towards counter-terrorism measures has not been limited to Britain and the United States. The Supreme Court of Canada in the 2002 decision in *Suresh v Canada* [2002] 1 SCR 1 held that it would violate the Canadian Charter of Rights and Freedom to deport a suspected terrorist to a substantial risk of torture. The Court recognized the inviolable nature of the right not to be tortured under international law, but also opened the disturbing possibility that deportation to torture could be justified under domestic law in undefined 'exceptional circumstances'. This case reflects a continued dualism (Roach, 2005) that divides domestic and international law. The dualism in *Suresh* was used to justify possible domestic departures from international human rights standards, though no Canadian court has yet actually used the exception to allow deportation to torture. As will be seen below in cases involving domestic challenges to UN terrorist lists, dualism can also be used to impose domestic constitutional restraint on international crime control measures and targeted sanctions (Meyers, 2008).

In subsequent cases, the Canadian Supreme Court also held that immigration law procedures used to indeterminately detain non-citizens suspected of terrorism violated the constitution because they did not provide for adversarial challenge to the secret intelligence/evidence that the government submitted to the judge to justify the detention. The Court suspended its declaration of invalidity for 12 months to give the government time to respond (*Charkoaui v Canada* [2007] 1 SCR 350). The government's response was largely patterned after the British regime, which allows special advocates, or security cleared lawyers, to act on behalf of the detainees and to see secret information, but not to consult with the detainee after they have seen the secret evidence. The Canadian response demonstrates both the transnational nature of counter-terrorism law and the role that both proportionality analysis and dialogue can play in the Court's decision (Roach, 2009). At the same time, it is vulnerable to the critique that the Court has only nibbled at the margins of repressive measure and may have legitimated an unjust procedure of detention with trial (ibid, Ewing and Tham, 2008).

The Indonesia Supreme Court invalidated an attempt to apply emergency anti-terrorism law retroactively to the Bali bombers. The Court was divided 5:4, but the majority stressed both the international and domestic status of the prohibition on retroactive criminal offences. This decision played both to international norms and domestic debate about accountability for Suharto era abuses (Clarke, 2003). Despite this ruling, other parts of the law remain valid and some of the bombers have been convicted and executed under the ordinary criminal law. As in other parts of the world, constitutional decisions by the courts invalidated parts of terrorism laws, but were not necessarily the final word and did not stop other counter-terrorism activities.

Regional studies have a potential to isolate those constitutional features in somewhat similar states facing similar terrorist threats that may explain divergent responses to terrorism. For example, the Indonesian experience, which included democratic resistance to an initial draft terrorism law (Roach, 2004), can usefully be contrasted with that of the neighboring states of Singapore and Malaysia. In both countries, judicial decisions in the late 1980s that asserted the right of the judiciary to determine whether indeterminate detention was objectively justified were overturned by constitutional amendments that enshrined a subjective test requiring the judiciary to be more deferential to the executive (Hor, 2002; Lee, 2002). In Singapore and Malaysia, the constitution attempted to preclude more active judicial involvement by entrenching judicial deference to the executive's subjective views about the terrorist threat and repealing activist judicial decisions made in the late 1980s under the Internal Security Acts of both countries (ibid). In contrast, the Indonesian Constitution, especially after amendments made after the Suharto era, seemed to invite judicial activism. Other regional studies focusing on similarities and differences between responses to terrorism would also be helpful. For example, to what degree do countries in Europe converge and diverge in their response to terrorism? Can the convergences be explained by the effects of various forms of European Union guidance? Can the divergences be explained by the effects of different experiences with terrorism and/or different constitutional traditions and cultures? There is also a need to study regional responses in Africa, Asia and South America, regions which are often neglected in comparative work.

4   CONTINUED JUDICIAL DEFERENCE TO THE STATE'S ANTI-TERRORISM EFFORTS

Not all courts have invalidated counter-terrorism legislation when challenged. One of the great strengths of comparative constitutional scholarship is its ability to employ natural experiments to test the conditions that support various constitutional developments. One of the weaknesses in comparative constitutional law scholarship is that it too often focuses on advanced democracies and does not make enough use of natural experiments between countries with divergent conditions and histories.

The Indian Supreme Court upheld 2002 anti-terrorism legislation in a challenge brought by the People's Union for Civil Liberties (*People's Union for Civil Liberties v India* 2004 9 SCC 580). The Court stressed the importance of the objective of countering terrorism and the financing of terrorism including international support for such measures. The Court's ruling was affected by the global nature of the challenge to the entire law and the Court left some room for subsequent courts to find violations in specific cases. This raises the issue of how the support structure for constitutional litigation may affect the substance of constitutional rulings (Epp, 1998). The Indian Supreme Court also departed from the established nature of proportionality analysis by not emphasizing the question of whether the important objective of preventing terrorism could be accomplished by less restrictive means (Beatty, 2005; Roach, 2009). This question was particularly relevant with respect to provisions in the law that could facilitate torture by allowing police officers to take confessions as opposed to judicial officials. In any event, the government made a subsequent political decision to repeal the law, again underlining that courts often do not have the final word, especially with respect to politically salient issues such as terrorism.

Another understudied aspect of comparative constitutional law is the interaction between federalism and rights protection. The Indian Supreme Court in the above case held that the central government had jurisdiction to enact the terrorism law because of the transnational character of modern terrorism. The Australian High Court reached a similar conclusion when it held that the central government was justified in enacting a control order regime similar to that enacted in Britain (*Thomas v Mowbry* 2007 HCA 33). State counter-terrorism measures in Australia, India and the United States are understudied and more scholarship should be directed towards how federalism interacts with the protection of human rights and the treatment of minorities. For example, several Australian states have enacted their own control order regimes and applied them not only to suspected terrorist but organized crime such as motorcycle gangs.

The Australian experience with counter-terrorism law provides a fertile ground for comparison with other countries that unlike Australia have a national bill of rights (Williams, 2005). The High Court upheld control orders in Australia without placing the restrictions on non-disclosure of secret information to the detainee that have been seen in comparable British and Canadian cases (*Thomas v Mowbry* 2007 HCA 33). This as well as other measures that empower investigative detention and questioning by intelligence agencies support a thesis that Australia is an outlier among democracies (Williams, 2005). At the same time, however, Australia has adopted restrictions on speech that advocate terrorism that are similar to those adopted in the United Kingdom. Here the difference may not be so much the existence of a bill of rights but a cultural acceptance of limits on speech that diverge from an American free speech tradition which has not seen attempts to criminalize speech associated with terrorism. It would also be wrong to assume that constitutional restraints were totally absent in the Australian context. For example, investigative and prevention detention in Australia are deliberately not supervised by sitting judges but rather by prescribed authorities because of the fear of transgressing restraints on judicial powers (Roach, 2007). Even speech-based laws in Australia have to be evaluated against the implied freedom of political communication in Australia. Arguments have been made that the proscription of terrorist organizations and individuals in Australia infringes the implied freedom of political communication and the judicial power which prohibits bills of attainders that effectively make a person guilty of a crime (Tham, 2004). Future scholarship in this area should evaluate the role of bills of rights enacted in a number of Australian states and should compare the Australian response to terrorism with those of other democracies as a potential case study examining the effects of a bill of rights.

5   TERRORISM AND THE NEW TRANS-NATIONAL COUNTER-MAJORITARIAN DIFFICULTY

The United Nations Security Council has called on all states to enact counter-terrorism laws and in particular laws against the financing of terrorism in Security Council Resolution 1373 enacted under the mandatory provisions of Chapter VII of the United Nations Charter. The focus on terrorism financing also affirmed the pre-9/11 work of the UN under Resolution 1267, which attempted to identify individuals associated with al Qaeda and the Taliban, freeze their assets and prevent financial dealings with them. The Security Council and its terrorism committees have exercised robust legislative and executive functions. This invites constitutional analysis of the UN system itself. It also raises the prospect of counter-majoritarian difficulties both within the UN and between the UN and domestic states.

Within the UN, the Security Council is more powerful than the General Assembly and the UN's rights protecting bodies and has been characterized as 'an oligarch' (Forcese, 2007: 177). Others admit that the Security Council ignored human rights concerns in the immediate aftermath of 9/11, but suggest that it has become more sensitive to human rights criticisms both within and outside of the UN (Foot, 2007). In any event, the UN High Commissioner on Human Rights has repeatedly called on the Security Council's Counter-Terrorism Committee to pay more attention to international human rights in its work. The General Assembly representing all nations, unlike the Security Council, has stressed respect for human rights and the rule of law as an essential part of effective counter-terrorism strategies. It is tempting to conclude that the Security Council, dominated by its five permanent members, has functioned as the less transparent executive of the United Nations (Powell, 2005), while the General Assembly and the various rights protection bodies have functioned as the UN's weaker legislative and judicial branches. Important differences, however, are that the Security Council need not seek legislative authorization for mandatory and quasi-legislature measures such as the 1267 sanctioning process and Resolution 1373. In addition, the judicial branch of the UN lacks many of the powers of most domestic judiciary, including powers to review the effect of Security Council actions on individuals. These differences may help explain why the UN has been a source of 'anti-constitutional ideas' (Scheppele, 2006) in the migration of constitutional ideas about terrorism. The Security Council has also been able to work directly with domestic executives, for example by requiring them to implement various anti-terrorism measures through executive measures or through legislation that is sponsored by the executive (Forcese, 2007). Constitutional law scholars should increasingly apply constitutional analysis to the work of the UN and other transnational bodies.

Just as repressive domestic measures may eventually attract censure from international bodies, repressive international measures are starting to be challenged in domestic and regional forums. Such challenges demonstrate how the interaction between domestic and international law is not a one-way street. Although the traditional focus has been on how domestic law can look to international human rights norms for inspiration, current developments indicate how domestic due process norms can act as a restraint on international crime control measures such as the listing of those affiliated with al Qaeda and the Taliban. The domestic resistance has already influenced international institutions as the Security Council has through a series of recent resolutions, most recently Security Council Resolution 1904 (2009), attempted to reform its own process for listing terrorists to better comply with domestic and regional due process norms. As will be seen, however, these reforms have not persuaded domestic courts that the Security Council is domestically compliant with rights. Indeed, they may never do so in the absence of an effective judiciary within the UN that is open to individuals who are adversely affected by UN actions such as targeted sanctions. Even then, the problems of effectively challenging the secret intelligence that governments claim justify the listing will be great.

For the time being, it is domestic and regional courts that are making up for the judicial deficit within the UN and confronting the work of the Security Council. Domestic courts now face a double counter-majoritarian difficulty because they must evaluate the counter-terrorism work of both domestic executives and legislatures and the UN Security Council for compliance with rights. In 2006, Kim Lane Scheppele, 2006: 352 warned that 'comparativists who work solely within the nation-to-nation framework of "borrowing"... may well miss the way that international law enters our subject and alters it'. Scheppele presciently argued that the UN Security Council was a source of 'anti-constitutional' ideas to the extent that it was pushing states to freeze assets of suspected terrorists 'without any intervening domestic judicial process that could check either whether a suspected terrorist really is the person the [UN] Sanctions Committee believes him or her to be or whether the assets really belong to him or her' (ibid: 371). Several years after these comments, we are starting to see the 'anti-constitutional' product of the Security Council in the form of terrorist lists being indirectly but yet successfully challenged under domestic and supranational constitutional law.

The domestic push back so far has focused on the problematic process used by the UN Security Council and its 1267 committee to list terrorists. In *Kadi v Council of Europe* [2009] AC 1225, the European Court of Justice found that European Council regulations implementing the Security Council financing regime violated fundamental rights and should be annulled. The Court did not directly apply the European constitutional norms to the Security Council's activities. Nevertheless, it did so indirectly by noting that there was no effective judicial review at the UN level and that the delisting process remained an 'intergovernmental' process that did not provide the affected individual with even minimal information about the grounds for being listed as affiliated with al Qaeda or the Taliban (ibid: para 51). The Court went on to suggest that the obligations imposed by international agreements 'cannot have the effect of prejudicing the constitutional principles of the EC treaty' (ibid: para 285). This decision highlights the dynamic and transnational nature of comparative constitutional law in the terrorism context. Although the European Court of Justice claimed not to be directly evaluating the UN system, its ruling had that indirect effect. *Kadi* suggests that much of the work of both constitutional courts and scholars in the future may be to reconcile competing constitutionalisms at domestic, regional and international levels.

Not long after the *Kadi* decision, the UN system was indirectly put on trial in the Canadian case of *Abdelrazik v Canada* 2009 FC 580. Abdelrazick brought a claim against the Canadian government on the basis that it had denied him a right as a Canadian citizen under the Canadian Charter of Rights and Freedoms to return to Canada from Sudan. The Canadian government in its defense relied on the fact that he had been listed by the 1267 committee as a person affiliated with al Qaeda. The Court decided that Canada had violated his Charter right and successfully ordered that he be allowed to return to Canada. Although the Court found that the relevant international law properly interpreted did not deny a listed person the right to return to his or her country of citizenship, it also made clear that it was not blind to the lack of judicial and due process protections in the UN listing process. Zinn J concluded that under the regime 'the accuser is also the judge' and that the 1267 regime was 'a denial of basic legal remedies and is untenable under the principles of international human rights. There is nothing in the listing or de-listing process that recognizes the principles of natural justice or that provides for basic procedural fairness' (ibid: para 51). He also labeled the 1267 listing process as Kafkaesque given how the countries protected the intelligence behind the listing from disclosure. This case, combined with the Canadian case of *Suresh*, demonstrates how a dualist tradition has the potential to allow domestic courts to both judge and depart from international norms (Meyers, 2008). It also suggests that the interplay between international and domestic constitutional law is a two-way street and that domestic judges may be more willing to criticize the growing array of international crime control regimes for failing to meet the standards of either international human rights or domestic due process.

In early 2010, the newly named United Kingdom Supreme Court quashed two domestic orders introduced to implement various UN listing measures designed to freeze the assets of those associated with al Qaeda and the Taliban. The Court criticized the orders for going beyond the UN provisions by allowing freezing to be done on the basis of reasonable suspicion. At the same time, it also found that the orders were ultra vires the domestic United

Nations Act because the provisions applied automatically to all those on the UN list, including a person whom the United Kingdom had unsuccessfully attempted to have removed from the list (*Treasury v Ahmed* 2010 UKSC 2). Although it noted that the UN had made some improvement to the listing process, including the advent of an Ombudsperson, the UK Supreme Court endorsed the criticism of the UN listing process made by the Federal Court of Canada, stressing 'there is nothing in the listing or de-listing procedure that recognizes the principle of natural justice or that provides for basic procedural fairness' (ibid: para 80). The Court's reliance on both the European Court and Canadian decisions about the listing process underlines how quickly ideas can migrate between jurisdictions and gain a transnational momentum that would not be present from any one decision.

The United Kingdom decision, like the European and Canadian decisions, stressed domestic law even while it opined on the fairness of the UN listing procedure. For example, the UK decision stressed the importance of legality by noting that the impugned orders imposed severe hardships on individuals by unreviewable executive order. Consistent with the focus on proportionality in much constitutional law (Beatty, 2005), the Court stressed that both Australia and New Zealand had implemented similar international obligations through primary legislation (ibid: para 50). The Court also noted that the executive itself had a role in the UN Security Council's resolution and expressed concern that an unfettered domestic discretion to implement such resolutions 'conflicts with basic rules that lie at the heart of our democracy' (ibid: para 45). This decision suggests that international institutions will increasingly be evaluated from the perspective of domestic constitutionalism as they project their power into domestic spheres.

The dialogic nature of international law has traditionally involved various international bodies issuing judgments when domestic jurisdictions fail to comply with international human rights standards (Roach, 2005). The domestic listing decisions, however, suggest that dialogue can flow from the domestic to the international and the UN has taken steps to respond to *Kadi* and other criticisms of the 1267 listing process. These responses, including the creation of an Ombudsperson to facilitate delisting requests, were considered by the United Kingdom Supreme Court in *Ahmed*, but were still found to be wanting as measured by domestic due process standards, in large part because they do not provide an effective judicial remedy to the intergovernmental work of the committee. These decisions also suggest that questions of monism, dualism and tensions between competing constitutionalisms may increasingly occupy the attention of comparative constitutional law scholars. Some may see these cases as an example of a growing conflict between domestic and international constitutionalism that could place nations in breach of obligations to implement the mandatory 1267 regime (Fromuth, 2009). Others, however, see domestic courts filling a judicial challenge role that is not present in the UN (Cameron, 2003).

Divergences between the international and domestic legal orders should be examined as well as convergences. The rich array of legal sources that are increasingly readily available and used in domestic constitutional law will require domestic lawyers and scholars to become more familiar with international sources and processes. Comparative constitutional law may increasingly have a hybrid quality that reflects its multiple sources.

6 TERRORISM AND LEGISLATIVE AND ADMINISTRATIVE INTERPRETATION OF CONSTITUTIONS

Before 9/11, several influential scholars writing in the United States (Tushnet, 1999; Kramer, 2004), but also in other countries (Waldron, 1999; Manfredi, 2001), expressed concerns about judicial monopolies in interpreting the constitution. They expressed various degrees of support for the idea that legislatures in particular should be encouraged to act on their own interpretation of the constitution. The post-9/11 experience again provides a fascinating natural experiment in such endeavors.

The immediate post-9/11 response suggests that legislatures were prepared to interpret the constitution and act on that interpretation. In Canada, the government stressed that a massive new anti-terrorism act enacted within months of 9/11 reflected and complied with constitutional standards (Roach, 2001a). In addition, influential commentators within the Liberal government argued that the constitutional calculus should expand to recognize how the type of terrorism seen on 9/11 constituted a threat to an emerging new right to human security (Cotler, 2001). The Canadian government's use of the Charter has largely been successful and most of the Canadian decisions restraining or invalidating anti-terrorism law have involved older measures such as security certificates that were not drafted with the Charter in mind. In the United Kingdom, however, Parliament's implicit judgment that it had made a valid derogation from the European Convention in its legislation enacted immediately after 9/11 was decisively rejected first by the House of Lords in 2004 and then by the European Court of Human Rights in 2009. The ability of courts to review the proportionality of derogations and their effects on equality rights has emerged as a significant judicial power.

The terrorism context also allows for a comparison of the work of various legislative committees. In the United Kingdom, the Joint Committee on Human Rights has been particularly active in issuing reports in the anti-terrorism field, often calling on governments to abide by rule of law and other legal standards in the conduct of its counter-terrorism work (Hiebert, 2006; Hiebert, Chapter 17 this volume). The influence of this voice for human rights within government needs to be carefully evaluated, especially compared with that of the Intelligence and Security Committee which, unlike the human rights committee, hears secret information and reports directly to the Prime Minister. Just like courts, legislatures face dilemmas when deciding whether to evaluate the secret intelligence that may or may not justify anti-terrorism activities. Being privy to secrets comes at the price of silence about the secrets. At the same time, refusing to consider secret information may make both courts and legislatures vulnerable to criticisms that they are not properly informed about threat levels and the need to protect secrets.

The persistence of an unelected upper house in both Canada and the United Kingdom has the potential for revealing some of the effects of the prospect of standing for election on the performance of legislators on issues of human rights compliance. In the United Kingdom, the House of Lords has shown itself quite concerned with rights issues (Nicol, 2004) and the Privy Councilors who reported in 2003 laid much of the intellectual foundation for the House of Lords' decision a year later, declaring that indeterminate detention of non-citizens suspected of terrorism violated constitutional norms (*A (F.C.) v Secretary of State* [2004] UKHL 56). In Canada, there is also some evidence suggesting that unelected Senators are more willing to respond to the concerns of Muslim minority communities than elected legislators (Roach, 2008). In Australia, the heads of various review bodies were brought together to review anti-terrorism laws (Australia, 2006) and such quasi-independent watchdogs within the executive have been an important factor in other countries. Constitutional analysis can be turned inward on the work of the government and can reveal how values associated with the judiciary such as respect for the rule of law can find support within some parts of legislatures and governments.

Although there have been examples of post-9/11 legislative overreaching, few legislatures have scapegoated Muslim minorities in a way that many defenders of anti-majoritarian judicial review might have predicted. The American Patriot Act even contained an admittedly unenforceable sense of Congress re-affirming individual responsibility and deploring acts of discrimination against Muslim and Arab-Americans, even at the same time as massive immigration detentions were being used to respond to 9/11. Legislatures in Canada, the United States and the United Kingdom neither endorsed nor prohibited racial and religious profiling in the wake of 9/11. This is consistent with the thesis that the main threats to equality values came from the executive and not the legislature (Choudhry and Roach, 2003). Comparative constitutional law scholars have been perhaps too preoccupied with a counter-majoritarian difficulty that pits the unelected courts against the elected legislatures and have not focused enough on the role of the courts in supervising the executive.

The terrorism context underlines the need to focus more on the conduct of the executive, but the secrecy of both the conduct and justification of executive actions is a complicating factor. The extraordinary public revelation of the torture memos issued by the US Office of Legal Counsel provided a unique window into how the executive can interpret constitutional norms and then act on them (Greenberg, 2005). The torture memos can be interpreted as a graphic demonstration of the self-interested nature of constitutional interpretations that do not emanate from the independent judiciary. In contrast, some defenders of co-ordinate construction may argue that the memos themselves underline the importance of executive interpretations of the constitution as the first-order restraint on executive behavior. They can also point to the negative reaction to the memos as an example of a self-disciplining legal community. In any event, the counter-terrorism field provides an important window on legislative and executive constitutional interpretation in action.

The secrecy of many counter-terrorism activities raises the question of what institutions are necessary to apply constitutional norms to such activities or whether such activities should be allowed to operate in an extra-legal manner. Some in the American Congress were apparently briefed on various extra-legal activities such as the use of warrantless domestic surveillance by the National Security Agency but nevertheless were not able to go public. In Canada, disputes have emerged between Parliament's demands for documents relating to the treatment of Afghan detainees and governmental claims of secrecy.

Another challenge is the increasing integration of anti-terrorism activities within and among governments. Review agencies or Inspectors General that only have jurisdiction over one agency may find that effective review is impossible. In Canada, all government operations in relation to Maher Arar and other Canadian citizens held and tortured abroad were reviewed by the appointment of public inquiries conducted by sitting or retired judges with extraordinary mandates to examine the actions of all Canadian officials involved in the cases, including those in the security service, the police and foreign affairs departments. Even with such mandates, these inquiries encountered problems as the Canadian government resisted the disclosure of information claimed to be secret and the American and Syrian governments refused to co-operate with the inquiries (Canada, 2006). The Canadian public inquiries, as well as the use of judges to supervise parliamentary publication of secret documents relating to Afghan detainees, represent a creative hybrid of executive and judicial functions. Other hybrid institutions may be necessary to apply the rule of law to anti-terrorism activities (Dyzenhaus, 2006). Both counter-terrorism activities and their effective review challenge traditional and essentialist views of the separation of powers. They both may involve creative hybrids between legislative, executive and judicial powers and functions.

Even with such domestic innovations, however, the terrorism context reveals the glaring absence of an effective transnational mechanism of accountability. The Canadian public inquiries, for example, were frustrated by the refusals of the governments of Syria and the United States to participate in their processes. The terrorism context provides comparative constitutional law scholars with a glimpse of the grave challenges facing accountability and constitutionalism in a globalized transnational future.

7 FUTURE DIRECTIONS AND EXPANDED HORIZONS FOR COMPARATIVE CONSTITUTIONAL LAW SCHOLARSHIP

Comparative constitutional law scholarship needs to expand its horizons by examining countries beyond the usual Anglo-American axis. This work is starting in the terrorism field in large part because of the extensive experience that countries such as India and Israel have with terrorism. There is an instrumental tendency to look to such countries as a source for ideas and policies to combat terrorism, but they also provide a rich source for examining the impact of a country's experience with terrorism on its constitutional response to terrorism (Barak-Erez and Waxman, 2010).

The Northern Irish experience is also a particularly fertile field to examine not only the effects of measures such as special courts, detention without trial and attempts to regulate speech associated with terrorism (Donohue, 2008; Gross and ni Aolain, 2007), but also reforms that might make terrorism less attractive. There are also interesting similarities between the use of indeterminate detention under Internal Security Acts in Singapore and Malaysia and administrative detention in Israel's occupied territories. All of these forms of detention are based on British colonial legislation (Burch Elias, 2009: 107). The British influence is not only historical. Britain's Terrorism Act, 2000 and in particular its broad definition of terrorist activities served as a starting point as many countries enacted new anti-terrorism laws after 9/11 (Roach, 2006).

The Israeli experience with attempts to authorize or excuse torture arising out of the Landau commission (Kremnitzer, 1989; Kremnitzer and Seger, 2000) provides lessons that were too frequently ignored in the American torture debates. The same may be true of debates about targeted assassinations and administrative detention (Gross, 2007). The unsettling nature of 9/11 in many democracies has placed issues such as torture and indeterminate detention without trial back into the domestic mainstream where they had once been relegated to the colonial margins (Resnik, 2010). At the same time, however, the fallout from 9/11 will force scholars to resist simplistic distinctions between a liberty-loving West and a more communitarian and authoritarian East (Ramraj, 2002). Some countries with new or struggling democracies such as Indonesia and Hong Kong have resisted attempts to impose repressive new anti-terrorism laws (Roach, 2004).

A particular gap in the literature is the study of how Arab states have responded to terrorism (but see Welchman, 2005). Such studies might provide insights into some of the causes of al Qaeda-inspired terrorism. In addition, the treatment of terrorist suspects in countries such as Egypt and Syria also has a practical dimension given the rendering of terrorist suspects from established democracies to such authoritarian states. The full story of how constitutional and international rights norms have fared in countries such as the United States, the United Kingdom and Canada in the wake of 9/11 cannot be told without examining what happens in the prisons and military courts of Cairo and Damascus.

Another part of the expanded horizon for comparative constitutional law scholarship is the need to be more sensitive to the role that international and regional institutions play and the existence of potentially competing constitutionalisms at domestic, regional and international levels. The recent domestic cases on the UN's terrorist listing practices underline the two-way interchange and criticism that can emerge between international and domestic realms, especially when the dualism of the two forms of law is an accepted feature of the constitutional order (Meyers, 2008). Domestic courts may have to think through the counter-majoritarian difficulty at both domestic and international levels. Debates about the migration of constitutional and anti-constitutional ideas need to expand from the domestic into the international realm (Scheppele, 2006). The recent activism of international organizations in the terrorism field may make scholarship in this field a harbinger of things to come in other areas of constitutional law. Domestic courts may increasingly restrain and discipline other international crime control initiatives such as those targeting human trafficking and crimes against women, minorities, children and other vulnerable groups.

The claim that terrorism produces exceptional regimes needs to be critically evaluated in light of other constitutional developments. Judith Resnik (2010) has recently examined the American Guantanamo decisions in light of the broader American constitutional law relating to the availability of habeas corpus and detention conditions in America's prisons. She finds common practices of judicial restraint and tolerance for harsh conditions of confinements. James Forman Jr. also has related the war on terror with the war on drugs, which has produced super-maximum prisons and attacks on the authority of judges and defense counsel (Forman, 2009). Such insights reveal how domestic baselines may influence how far each country can challenge constitutional restraints in the terrorism context. Other work that integrates the study of anti-terrorism measures with other criminal justice measures is Lucia Zedner's important comparison of control orders with other preventive and civil measures used in British criminal justice, such as anti-social behaviour orders (Zedner, 2007). In Canada, scholars have also related terrorism activities to non-terrorist developments in the treatment of crime, including organized crime (Roach, 2001b) and immigration (Macklin, 2001).

The thesis of American exceptionalism should be examined in the terrorism context. To what extent has the high baseline of legalism in the United States (Kagan, 2001) influenced attempts to forge alternatives to the use of traditional criminal or military law? Although President Bush attempted to preclude all judicial review of Guantanamo, this only provoked hundreds of well-financed and sophisticated lawsuits and elaborate attempts both to legalize military commissions and to administer habeas corpus relief for Guantanamo detainees. The Patriot Act was criticized 'in apocalyptic terms' for expansion of existing search powers that are not uncommon in other democracies (Posner and Vermeule, 2007: 79). On the other hand, some of the most dramatic expansion of state powers in the United States occurred through actions that were not authorized in democratically enacted laws. One example is extraordinary rendition of terrorist suspects. Another example is the National Security Agency's domestic spying, which bypassed the Foreign Intelligence Surveillance Act (ibid: 81). This raises the question of the relation between American legalism and the frequent use and defense of extra-legal approaches in that country (Tushnet, 2003; Posner, 2006).

On the other hand, American exceptionalism also includes a robust free speech tradition that has allowed an unprecedented amount of secret information to leak into the public domain to the chagrin of those in the United States who advocate for an official secrets act and domestic security intelligence agencies found in many other democracies (Posner, 2006). American exceptionalism has resisted regulation of speech related to terrorism and the idea that democracy needs to be militant and repressive of anti-democratic ideas that have recently found favor in Europe (Roach, 2004). Recent incidents of home-grown al Qaeda-inspired terrorism will provide interesting challenges for the United States as it attempts to reconcile radicalization through the internet and religious teachings with its First Amendment traditions of free speech and free religion.

Although there is a danger of the narcissism of small differences, comparative constitutional law scholars should be interested in divergences among countries rather than convergences. Recent comparative studies have tended to stress convergences among countries, usually Britain and the United States, in their response to 9/11 (Moeckli, 2008; Sottiaux, 2008; Donohue, 2008). Future scholarship should examine divergences, including the impact of American exceptionalism, the role of bills of rights, different types of governmental systems and multiculturalism in the countries being studied. Increasing the number of countries studied will also increase opportunities for observing divergences as well as convergences (Roach, 2011).

The detection of divergences in each country's response to terrorism will require sustained engagement with the legal and political culture of each country studied. This approach may be a necessary antidote to simplistic comparisons that are sometimes encouraged by proportionality analysis. Comparative constitutional law is built into the least restrictive means analysis of proportionality analysis. For example, the special advocate regime was brought into being in Britain as a result of the European Court of Human Rights mistaken impression in *Chahal* ((1997) 23 EHRR 413) about the existence of a special advocate regime in Canadian courts. In turn, a special advocate regime was introduced in Canada in 2008 in large part because of the existence of the British special advocate regime, and special advocates have also spread to other jurisdictions, including New Zealand and Hong Kong (Ip, 2008). The more extensive British experience with special advocates also suggests that other countries may be embracing such innovations just as the British become more aware of their limitations (*A v United Kingdom* 2009). The comparative aspect of proportionality analysis can make the law very dynamic and facilitate the quick migration of constitutional ideas (ibid). At the same time, the pressures of litigation can obscure contextual differences between the responses of different countries to similar challenges such as the preservation of secrecy. Comparative constitutional scholars should be aware of the utility of comparisons in constitutional litigation, but they also need to be sensitive to place potentially facile comparisons into the broader legal, political and social contexts of each country (Lynch, 2008).

The terrorism context will also invite comparative constitutional law scholars to reflect on the influence of constitutional norms over a wide range of laws including immigration law, administrative law, criminal law, military law and international law. A full study of anti-terrorism law and policy challenges scholars to bring together many different parts of the law (Ramraj et al, 2005), It raises questions about whether all public law is unified by a common concern for constitutionalism (Dyzenhaus, 2006) or whether some areas of law are more resistant to the discipline of constitutional law (Macklin, 2001). The post-9/11 terrorism experience has educated many comparative constitutionalists about the resistance of immigration, military and even some forms of international law to rights claims. Comparative constitutional scholars should continue to use the fertile and important context of counter-terrorism to broaden their horizons with respect to both different sources of law and different countries to be examined.

REFERENCES

Ackerman, Bruce (2004), 'The Emergency Constitution', *Yale Law Journal*, 113, 1029–91.
Australia (2006), *Review of Security and Counter-Terrorism Legislation*, Canberra: Commonwealth Parliament of Australia.
Australia, Joint Committee on Intelligence and Security (2007), *Inquiry into the Proscription of Terrorist Organisations under the Criminal Code, September 2007*, Commonwealth Parliament of Australia.
Barak-Erez, Daphne and Waxman, Matthew (2010), 'Secret Evidence and the Due Process of Terrorist Detentions', *Columbia Journal of Transnational Law*, 48 (3), 1–58.
Beatty, David (2005), *The Ultimate Rule of Law*, Oxford: Oxford University Press.
Bickel, Alexander (1986), *The Least Dangerous Branch: The Supreme Court at the Bar of Politics*, New Haven: Yale University Press.
Burch Elias, Stella (2009), 'Rethinking "Preventive Detention" from a Comparative Perspective: Three Frameworks for Detaining Terrorist Suspects', *Columbia Human Rights Law Review*, 41, 99–234.
Cameron, Iain (2003), 'UN Targeted Sanctions, Legal Safeguards and the European Convention on Human Rights', *Nordic Journal of International Law*, 72 (2), 159–214.
Canada (2006), *Commission of Inquiry into the Activities of Canadian Officials in Relation to Maher Arar: Analysis and Recommendations*, Ottawa: Minister of Public Works.
Choudhry, Sujit (ed.) (2006), *The Migration of Constitutional Ideas*, New York: Cambridge University Press.
Choudhry, Sujit and Roach, Kent (2003), 'Racial and Ethnic Profiling: Statutory Discretion, Democratic Accountability and Constitutional Remedies', *Osgoode Hall Law Journal*, 41, 1–39.
Clarke, Robert (2003), 'Retrospectivity and the Constitutional Validity of the Bali Bombing and East Timor Trials', *Asian Law*, 5, 132.
Cole, David (2003), *Enemy Aliens*, New York: Free Press.
Cotler, Irwin (2001), 'Thinking Outside the Box: Foundational Principles for a Counter-terrorism Law and Policy', in Ronald J. Daniels, Patrick Macklem and Kent Roach (eds), *The Freedom of Security: Essays on Canada's Anti-Terrorism Bill*, Toronto: University of Toronto Press.
Dershowitz, Alan (2002), *Why Terrorism Works*, New Haven: Yale University Press.
Donohue, Laura (2008), *The Costs of Counterterrorism: Power Politics and Liberty*, New York: Cambridge University Press.
Dyzenhaus, David (2006), *The Constitution of Law*, Cambridge: Cambridge University Press.
Epp, Charles (1998), *The Rights Revolution: Lawyers, Activists and Supreme Courts in Comparative Perspective*, Chicago: University of Chicago Press.
Ewing, Keith (2004), 'The Futility of the Human Rights Act', *Public Law*, 829–52.
Ewing, Keith and Tham, Joo-Cheong (2008), 'The Continuing Futility of the Human Rights Act', *Public Law*, 668–93.
Foot, Rosemary (2007), 'The United Nations, Counter-Terrorism and Human Rights: Institutional Adaptation and Embedded Ideas', *Human Rights Quarterly*, 29 (2), 489–514.
Forcese, Craig (2007), 'Hegemonic Federalism: The Democratic Implications of the UN Security Council's "Legislative" Phase', *New Zealand Journal of Public and International Law*, 38 (2), 175–98.
Forcese, Craig and Roach, Kent (forthcoming), 'Limping into the Future: The 1267 Listing Process', *George Washington International Law Review*, 45.
Forman, James (2009), 'Exporting Harshness: How the War on Crime Helped Make the War on Terror Possible', *New York University Review of Law and Social Change*, 33, 331–74.
Fromuth, Peter (2009), 'The European Court of Justice Decision in Kadi and the Future of UN Counterterrorism Sanctions', 13 (20), American Society of International Law (ASIL) *Insights*, available at http://www.asil.org/insights091030.cfm.

Greenberg, Karen (ed.) (2005), *The Torture Papers*, New York: Cambridge University Press.

Gross, Emanuel (2007), *The Struggle of Democracy Against Terrorism: Lessons from the United States, the United Kingdom, and Israel*, Charlottesville, VA: University of Virginia Press.

Gross, Oren (2003), 'Chaos and Rules: Should Responses to Violent Crises Always Be Constitutional?', *Yale Law Journal*, 112 (5), 1011–134.

Gross, Oren and ni Aolain, Fionnaula (2007), *Law in Times of Crisis: Emergency Power in Theory and Practice*, Cambridge: Cambridge University Press.

Hiebert, Janet (2006), 'Parliament and the Human Rights Act', *International Journal of Constitutional Law*, 4 (1), 1–38.

Hor, Michael (2002), 'Terrorism and the Criminal Law: Singapore's Solution', *Singapore Journal of Legal Studies*, 30–55.

Ip, John (2008), 'The Rise and Spread of the Special Advocate', *Public Law*, 717–41.

Joint Committee on Human Rights, UK Parliament (2010), *Counter-Terrorism Policy and Human Rights (Seventeenth Report) Bringing Human Rights Back In*, London: The Stationary Office Limited.

Kagan, Robert (2001), *Adversarial Legalism: The American Way of Law*, Cambridge, MA: Harvard University Press.

Kramer, Larry (2004), *The People Themselves: Popular Constitutionalism and Judicial Review*, New York: Oxford University Press.

Kremnitzer, Mordechai (1989), 'The Landau Commission Report – Was the Security Service Subordinated to the Law, or the Law to the "Needs" of the Security Service?', *Israel Law Review*, 23 (2–3), 216–79.

Kremnitzer, Mordechai and Re'em Segev, Re-em (2000), 'The Legality of Interrogational Torture: A Question of Proper Authorization or a Substantive Moral Issue', *Israel Law Review*, 34, 509–58.

Lee, Therese (2002), 'Malaysia and the Internal Security Act: The Insecurity of Human Rights after September 11', *Singapore Journal of Legal Studies*, 56–72.

Lynch, Andrew (2008), 'Control Orders in Australia: A Further Case Study of the Migration of British Counter-Terrorism Law', *Oxford University Commonwealth Law Journal*, 8, 159–80.

Macklin, Audrey (2001), 'Borderline Security,' in Ronald J. Daniels, Patrick Macklem and Kent Roach (eds), *The Security of Freedom: Essays on Canada's Anti-Terrorism Bill*, Toronto: University of Toronto Press.

Manfredi, Christopher (2001), *Judicial Power and the Charter: Canada and the Paradox of Liberal Constitutionalism*, 2nd edition, Ontario: Oxford University Press.

Martinez, Jennie (2008) 'Process and Substance in the "War on Terror" ', *Columbia Law Review*, 108 (5), 1013–92.

Meyers, Daniel (2008), 'The Transatlantic Divide over the Implementation and Enforcement of Security Council Resolutions', *California Western International Law Journal*, 38 (2), 255–85.

Moeckli, Daniel (2008), *Human Rights and Non-discrimination in the 'War on Terror'*, Oxford: Oxford University Press.

Nicol, Danny (2004), 'The Human Rights Act and the Politicians', *Socio-legal Studies*, 24 (3), 451–79.

Posner, Eric (2008), 'Boumediene and the Uncertain March of Judicial Cosmopolitanism', *Cato Supreme Court Review*, 23–46.

Posner, Eric and Vermeule, Adrian (2007), *Terror in the Balance: Security, Liberty and the Courts*, New York: Oxford University Press.

Posner, Richard (2006), *Not A Suicide Pact: The Constitution in a Time of National Emergency*, New York: Oxford University Press.

Powell, C.H (2005), 'Terrorism and Governance in South Africa and Eastern Africa', in Victor Ramraj, Michael Hor and Kent Roach (eds), *Global Anti-Terrorism Law and Policy*, Cambridge: Cambridge University Press.

Ramraj, Victor (2002), 'Terrorism, Security and Rights: A New Dialogue', *Singapore Journal of Legal Studies*, 1–15.

Ramraj, Victor, Hor, Michael and Roach, Kent (eds) (2005), *Global Anti-Terrorism Law and Policy*, Cambridge: Cambridge University Press.

Resnik, Judith (2010), 'Detention, the War on Terror, and the Federal Court', *Columbia Law Review*, 110, 579–685.

Roach, Kent (2001a) 'The Dangers of a Charter-Proof and Crime-Based Response to Terrorism', in Ronald J. Daniels, Patrick Macklem and Kent Roach (eds), *The Freedom of Security: Essays on Canada's Anti-Terrorism Bill*, Toronto: University of Toronto Press.

Roach, Kent (2001b), *The Supreme Court on Trial: Judicial Activism or Democratic Dialogue*, Toronto: Irwin Law.

Roach, Kent (2004), 'Militant Democracy and Anti-Terrorism Legislation: Some Eastern and Western Comparisons', in Sajo, Andras (ed.), *Militant Democracy*, Utrecht: Eleven International Publishing (2004), 171–207.

Roach, Kent (2005), 'Constitutional, Remedial and International Dialogues About Rights', *Texas International Law Journal*, 40, 537.

Roach, Kent (2006), 'The Post 9/11 Migration of Britain's Terrorism Act 2000', in Sujit Choudhry (ed.), *The Migration of Constitutional Ideas*, New York: Cambridge University Press.

Roach, Kent (2007), 'A Comparison of Australian and Canadian Anti-Terrorism Law', *University of New South Wales Law Journal*, 30 (1), 53–85.

Roach, Kent (2008), 'The Role and Capacities of Courts and Legislatures in Reviewing Canada's Anti-Terrorism Law', *Windsor Review of Legal and Social Issues*, 24, 5–56.

Roach, Kent (2009), 'Judicial Review of the State's Anti-Terrorism Activities: The Post 9/11 Experience and Normative Justifications for Judicial Review', *Indian Journal of Constitutional Law*, 3, 138–67.

Roach, Kent (2011), *The 9/11 Effect: Comparative Counter-Terrorism*, New York: Cambridge University Press.

Scheppele, Kim Lane (2006), 'The Migration of Anti-Constitutional Ideas: The Post 9/11 Globalization of Public Law and the International State of Emergency', in Choudry, Sujit (ed.), *The Migration of Constitutional Ideas*, New York: Cambridge University Press.

Sidel, Mark (2004), *More Secure Less Free? Antiterrorism Policy & Civil Liberties after September 11*, Ann Arbor: University of Michigan Press.

Sottiaux, Stefan (2008), *Terrorism and the Limitation of Rights: The ECHR and the US Constitution*, Oxford: Hart Publishing.

Sunstein, Cass (2004), 'Minimalism at War', *Supreme Court Law Review*, 47–109.

Tham, Joo-Cheong (2004), 'Possible Constitutional Objections to the Powers to Ban "Terrorist" Organizations', *University of New South Wales Law Journal*, 27 (2), 482–523.

Tushnet, Mark (1999), *Taking the Constitution Away from the Courts*, Princeton: Princeton University Press.

Tushnet, Mark (2003), 'Defending Korematsu? Reflections on Civil Liberties in Wartime', *Wisconsin Law Review*, 273.

Tushnet, Mark (2008a), 'Dialogic Judicial Review', *Arkansas Law Review*, 61, 205–16.

Tushnet, Mark (2008b), 'The Political Constitution of Emergency Powers: Parliamentary and Separation-of-powers Regulation', *International Journal of Law in Context*, 3 (4), 275–88.

Waldron, Jeremy (1999), *Law and Disagreement*, Oxford: Oxford University Press.

Welchman, Lynn (2005), 'Rocks, Hard Places and Human Rights: Anti-Terrorism Law and Policy in Arab States', in Ramraj et al (eds.), *Global Anti-Terrorism Law and Policy*, Cambridge: Cambridge University Press.

Williams, George (2005), 'The Rule of Law and Regulation of Terrorism in Australia and New Zealand', in Ramraj et al (eds.), *Global Anti-Terrorism Law and Policy*, Cambridge: Cambridge University Press.

Zedner, Lucia (2007), 'Preventive Justice or Pre-Punishment? The Case of Control Orders', *Current Legal Problems*, 60, 174–203.

30. Legal protection of same-sex partnerships and comparative constitutional law

Nicholas Bamforth

In the past twenty years, courts and legislatures in many constitutional democracies have considered, but not always conclusively resolved, a cluster of questions concerning the law's treatment of sexual/emotional relationships between persons of the same sex (hereafter referred to as 'same-sex partnerships').[1] Along one dimension lie what might be described as substantive questions, concerning the content of the legal rights afforded to those in same-sex partnerships in the jurisdiction concerned; along another dimension lie what might be termed institutional questions, concerning the proper roles and powers of different state institutions in resolving the substantive questions. Both sets of questions are of a clearly constitutional, and more specifically constitutional law, character.[2]

A very basic substantive question is whether any form of legal recognition should be granted to same-sex partnerships, even to the extent of recognising their existence as a social phenomenon.[3] At this very basic level falls discussion of whether same-sex partners should have analogous rights to those enjoyed by unmarried opposite-sex partners, for example to succeed to tenancies, or to partnership-related employment or social security benefits.[4] A rather deeper-level, but analytically related, question is whether a formal legal status should be available to those in same-sex partnerships, whether such a status is described as marriage or civil/registered partnership and whether or not the accompanying legal rights and obligations are the same as or sometimes subtly different from those associated with opposite-sex state-recognised marriage.[5] A further question – albeit one which might be answered as part of a legislative or broadly drafted judicial determination concerning the formal legal status of same-sex partnerships – concerns the extent to which 'family-related' rights and obligations, for example relating to the ability to adopt or to retain custody of children, are to be recognised.[6] All these substantive questions can be seen as 'constitutional' for at least two reasons. First, they relate to what are seen as basic human entitlements, given that the rights to marry and to respect for one's intimate life are recognised in most jurisdictions as important human rights.[7] As UK Supreme Court judge Baroness Hale noted in relation to same-sex partnerships in *Ghaidan v Godin-Mendoza*, 'most human beings eventually ... want love. And with love they often want not only the warmth but also the sense of belonging to one another which is the essence of being a couple. And many couples also come to want the stability and permanence which go with sharing a home and a life together ... In this, people of homosexual orientation are no different from people of heterosexual orientation.'[8] Secondly, whether or not rights associated with same-sex partnerships are formally described as marriage- or intimate life-related, they tend also to be promoted in generally 'constitutional' terms: that is, by reference to constitutional values such as equality, autonomy or dignity.[9]

It should, however, be noted that while it is possible to separate out the different substantive questions in this analytical fashion, in practice they sometimes blur together. For instance, litigation which is ostensibly concerned with the availability of practical remedies for same-sex partners (most obviously, concerning access to similar employment- or social security-related benefits to those accessible to persons in opposite-sex partnerships) may be thought to involve or even turn on, implicitly, the adoption of some position concerning the desirability or otherwise of the legal recognition of same-sex partnerships. Furthermore, while some theorists have attempted – rightly – to impose clarity on the legal developments in a variety of jurisdictions by suggesting that debate about the formal legal recognition of same-sex partnerships tends to crop up rather later in the sequence of significant questions concerning the legal rights of lesbians and gay men than (for example) debate about whether there is a protected legal right for persons of the same sex to engage in consenting sexual activity with one another,[10] in practice the significance of this distinction has sometimes been diminished by the speed with which jumps have taken place from one debate to the other[11] and the fact that the same or very similar constitutional arguments have in fact been used in both debates to justify the adoption of liberal or conservative solutions.[12]

Institutional questions relate to the appropriate roles or activities of particular state institutions. In the context of same-sex partnerships, they include whether relevant substantive questions should be resolved by the courts or left to the legislature to pronounce upon (something going to the powers and respective spheres of competence of the institutions concerned), and how far comparative or international law arguments – as opposed to considerations local to the jurisdiction in issue – should be employed when deciding how to answer the substantive questions.[13] These are, again, classic questions of constitutional law, and as with the substantive questions, institutional questions can sometimes blur together in practice. Debates can arise in the same case concerning the analytically separate issues of the proper roles of courts and legislatures and the use of comparative and international law. In addition, as a practical matter, claims about the substantive treatment of same-sex partnerships can, as noted, sometimes follow quickly on the heels of judicial or legislative determinations that the decriminalisation of consenting sexual behaviour between persons of the same sex is constitutionally or politically necessary or appropriate, implying the existence of analogous judicial or legislative perspectives concerning the legitimate limits of judicial and/or legislative institutions' roles in both contexts. Finally, judicial answers to substantive questions concerning the legal rights of same-sex partners can often focus, in practice, on a blend of institutional and substantive issues which it may at first sight seem hard to separate.[14]

Given the high political profile which substantive and institutional questions concerning the law's treatment of same-sex partners have often assumed (sometimes due to the emotive nature, for many citizens, of the substantive issues involved), the constitutional significance – for the reasons just highlighted – of such questions, and the extent to which it is now common for courts and legislatures to use examples drawn from other jurisdictions when considering the law's treatment of lesbians and gay men (whether or not as members of same-sex partnerships) in their own jurisdiction,[15] it is unsurprising that debates concerning the legal rights of same-sex partners now play such a visible role within constitutional, and in turn comparative constitutional, law. With this in mind, the next section will highlight some recent examples, drawn from different jurisdictions, of constitutional analysis of the legal rights of those in same-sex partnerships. Later sections will consider three specific constitutional questions which have arisen: two institutional and one substantive. The institutional questions concern the roles to be played by courts and legislatures in recognising and protecting same-sex partnerships, and the use of comparative and international law arguments in that process. The substantive question concerns the extent to which claims for same-sex partnerships to be legally recognised and protected are to be balanced against opposing arguments based on the right to respect for particular religious beliefs.

1 SAME-SEX PARTNERSHIPS IN CONSTITUTIONAL DEBATE

At a concrete level, numerous examples may be found of plainly 'constitutional' cases focused on or with implications for the legal rights or status of same-sex partners. In Canada, the Supreme Court ruled in *Egan v Canada* that discrimination on the basis of sexual orientation in principle contravened the constitutional guarantee of equal protection and benefit of the law, plus equality before the law, found in section 15(1) of the Canadian Charter of Rights and Freedoms.[16] Nonetheless, the substantive claim made in the case – that a social security benefit should be available to those in a same-sex partnership on the same basis as it was available to an opposite-sex couple – was rejected, largely due to judicial deference to the legislature. More recently, however, the British Columbia and Ontario Courts of Appeal have ruled that the exclusion of same-sex couples from marriage violates section 15(1),[17] while the federal Supreme Court has accepted that the passage of a statute to allow for same-sex marriage would be consistent with that section.[18] Meanwhile, in South Africa, in a sequence of cases following the move to democratic rule, the criminalisation of gay sex,[19] the denial of immigration rights to same-sex partners of permanent residents,[20] and most recently – in *Minister of Home Affairs v Fourie* – the denial to same-sex couples of the right to marry,[21] have been found to violate (*inter alia*) the constitutional rights to dignity and equality. In these jurisdictions, claims to protection from discrimination on the basis of sexual orientation and for the judicial protection of same-sex partnerships (and, in South Africa, to freedom from unjust criminal prosecution for engaging in consenting sexual behaviour) have thus been based upon constitutional provisions guaranteeing the human rights of citizens.

In the USA, the position is a little more complicated. A claim relating to legal protection or recognition of same-sex partnerships has yet to reach the US Supreme Court, but in the *Goodridge* case the Massachusetts Supreme Judicial Court used the US Supreme Court's decision in *Lawrence v Texas*,[22] in which a state law criminalising consensual gay sex acts was found to violate the constitutional rights protected by the Due Process Clause of the Fourteenth Amendment to the federal Bill of Rights, to assist it in concluding that to deny same-sex couples access to civil marriage violated the dignity and equality guaranteed for individuals under the state constitution.[23] *Lawrence*, in turn, had built on the earlier Supreme Court decision in *Romer v Evans*,[24] in which the Equal Protection Clause of the Fourteenth Amendment was used to invalidate a state constitutional amendment which was found to display improper animus towards lesbians and gay men. Nonetheless, there has also been considerable legislative activity – including the amendment of state constitutions – concerning same-sex partnerships, generally instigated by opponents of the judicial recognition of substantive rights for those in such partnerships.[25] Thus, following the decision of the Supreme Court of Hawaii in *Baehr v Lewin* that it constituted impermissible discrimination in terms of the state constitution to confine marriage to persons of the opposite sex,[26] the federal Defense of Marriage Act 1996 sought to restrict the federal-level definition of marriage to a partnership of one man and one woman and allowed US states not to recognise same-sex partnerships where these had been recognised by other US states. The Hawaiian state constitution was also later amended to allow the right to marriage to be restricted to opposite-sex couples. The constitutionality of the 1996 Act has now been called into question by Tauro J in the United States District Court (Massachusetts) in *Gill and LeTourneau v Office of Personnel Management*, in terms even of the deferential federal 'rational basis' standard of review of legislation: a determination which may well generate further argument at federal level.[27] The District Court also questioned whether it was constitutionally appropriate for the federal legislature to seek to impose a definition of marriage upon state-level authorities. At a more micro-level, but also with possible implications for the interpretation of federal constitutional law, an extended process of judicial/legislative interplay has been seen in California following the state Supreme Court's recognition, in *In re Marriage Cases*, that courts must employ strict scrutiny when reviewing statutes which treated people differently on the basis of sexual orientation and that legislation confining marriage to persons of the opposite sex was unconstitutional in terms of the right to marry contained in the state constitution.[28] In the wake of this decision, a state-level referendum was triggered resulting in the amendment of the state constitution to confine the right to marry to opposite-sex couples in future cases. The amendment was upheld in the State Supreme Court in the face of a procedural and state constitutional law-based challenge relating to the method of its passage,[29] but was found as a substantive matter to contravene the federal Due Process and Equal Protection Clauses at United States District Court level in *Perry v Schwarzenegger*, a decision which – like *Gill and LeTourneau* – may generate further litigation at federal level (not least given Walker J's determination that the state constitutional amendment contravened both the Equal Protection and Due Process Clauses of the Fourteenth Amendment).[30] On a nationwide basis, attempts – which have not to date succeeded but may yet generate renewed political momentum – have been made to generate support for an amendment to the federal constitution to confine the definition of marriage to the union of one man and one woman.

Under the European Convention on Human Rights and Fundamental Freedoms, to which all European nations are signatories, claims concerning the legal status or protection of same-sex partnerships need to be made under one or more of Articles 8 (the right to respect for private and family life), 12 (the right to marriage) and 14 (freedom from discrimination in the enjoyment of other substantive Convention rights).[31] Apart from showing that the claim falls within the scope of the right in issue, a claimant would need to rebut any argument that the restriction in issue was proportionate and served a legitimate aim[32] and that it fell within the 'margin of appreciation' open to Convention states when making the initial assessment of whether there is a need to interfere with a Convention right.[33] The Court of Human Rights has been clear, in the context of Articles 8 and 14, that adverse treatment on the basis of an individual's lesbian or gay sexual orientation – if unjustifiable – violates that person's right to respect for private life (the first limb of Article 8), and may constitute impermissible discrimination, contrary to Article 14 coupled with Article 8.[34] The Court has also stressed that while Convention states enjoy a 'margin of appreciation' when determining the necessity of a restriction for a reason set out in Article 8(2), particularly serious reasons are needed for a restriction to pass muster where it concerns a most intimate part of a person's private life.[35] In this area, the 'margin' is therefore narrow.[36] Furthermore, where a difference of treatment in relation to the enjoyment of a Convention right is based upon the claimant's sexual orientation, it violates Article 14 in the absence of an objective and reasonable justification (in other words, if there is no legitimate aim or reasonable relationship of proportionality between the means employed and the aim being pursued).[37] Thus, the Court stressed in

Karner v Austria that 'differences based on sexual orientation require particularly serious reasons by way of justification'[38] and that states had only a narrow 'margin of appreciation' in this context.[39]

Most recently, the First Section Chamber of the Court noted in *Schalk and Kopf v Austria* that signatory states are not currently required to grant legal recognition to same-sex partnerships.[40] However, this is unlikely to be the last word on same-sex partnerships: for one thing, the case was not decided by the Grand Chamber, and for another the First Section Chamber repeatedly emphasised that the application of the Convention depended very strongly on the Court's interpretation of evolving social attitudes to same-sex partnerships among the signatory states.

In reality, *Schalk and Kopf* is a significant decision for three reasons. First, it departed from the Court's earlier finding, in its admissibility decision in *Estevez v Spain*, that 'long-term homosexual relationships between two men do not fall within the scope of the right to respect for family life' (that is, the second limb of Article 8).[41] The finding in *Estevez* rapidly came under pressure after it was announced in 2001. For example, in *Karner v Austria* the Court found that it *was* a violation of Article 14, coupled with Article 8, for the surviving partner in a same-sex relationship to be denied the right to succeed – where a heterosexual partner could do so – to the tenancy of the property the partners had shared.[42] This made it hard to see how the denial in *Estevez* that same-sex couples did not enjoy family rights when it came to claiming social security entitlements could easily be distinguished. The Court thus noted in *Schalk and Kopf* that 'since 2001', when *Estevez* was decided, 'a rapid evolution of social attitudes towards same-sex couples has taken place in many [signatory] States. Since then a considerable number of [signatory] States have afforded legal recognition to same-sex couples', while provisions of EU law (notably Article 9 of the Charter of Fundamental Rights of the European Union) – which play an increasingly important role for the Court of Human Rights when interpreting the application of the Convention – 'also reflect a growing tendency to include same-sex couples in the notion of "family" '.[43] In consequence, it was 'artificial' to maintain that a same-sex couple could not enjoy 'family life' for the purposes of the second limb of Article 8, with the relationship of a cohabiting same-sex couple in a stable *de facto* partnership (such as the litigants) plainly falling within that limb.[44]

Secondly, however, *Schalk and Kopf* did not seek, for the moment, to oblige Convention signatory states to grant legal recognition to same-sex partnerships. In relation to the litigants' Article 12-based claim that national law should have allowed them to marry as a same-sex couple, rather than enter into a registered partnership (an arrangement which, while generally similar to marriage in Austrian national law, contained important differences in relation to topics such as the adoption of children[45]), the First Section noted that while the institution of marriage had 'undergone major social changes since the adoption of the Convention', there was still 'no European consensus regarding same-sex marriage'.[46] While Article 9 of the EU Charter omitted any reference to men and women in defining the right to marry, it referred to the importance of national law in order to reflect the diversity of national provisions and to emphasise that the decision whether to allow for same-sex marriage lay with signatory states.[47] The First Section thus concluded that while the Court should no longer regard Article 12 of the Convention as being 'in all circumstances ... limited to marriage between two persons of the opposite sex' (thus reflecting Article 9 of the Charter), 'the question whether or not to allow same-sex marriage' remained one for national law.[48] The First Section also concluded that Article 14 coupled with Article 8 did not oblige signatory states to grant same-sex partners the right to marry.[49] While there was an emerging European consensus towards the legal recognition of same-sex partnerships, a majority of states did not yet provide such recognition. Since the area was one of evolving rights with no established consensus between signatory states, the states therefore enjoyed a 'margin of appreciation' in relation to when and to what extent legal rights were granted to those in same-sex partnerships.[50] Interestingly, the First Section drew attention, in reaching these conclusions, to the fact that it was not being called upon to examine whether a state's failure to grant *any* means of recognition for same-sex couples *at all* – that is, beyond a distinctive registered partnership scheme – would constitute a violation of Article 14 coupled with Article 8.[51] That issue therefore remains open.

Thirdly, as noted above, the First Section's conclusions rested very heavily on its reading of the emerging 'social consensus' within the signatory states, suggesting that – not least given the speed with which that consensus has appeared to change in recent years in Europe – it might be possible for a rather different decision to be reached in the future. Although the Court noted, when dealing with Article 12, that 'marriage has deep-rooted social and cultural connotations which may differ largely from one society to another' so that it 'must not rush to substitute its own judgment in place of that of the national authorities'[52] – classic 'margin of appreciation' reasoning – it also noted that there was *currently* (rather than permanently) no consensus regarding same-sex marriage[53] and that it could not be said that Article 12 might in all circumstances be inapplicable to a claim by same-sex partners.[54] In relation to Articles 14 and 8, the Court explicitly noted that 'one of the relevant factors' when it came to the 'scope of the margin of appreciation' may be 'the existence or non-existence of common ground between the laws' of the signatory states.[55] It was thus crucial that there was not *yet* a consensus among the signatory states,[56] although what would happen once a majority of signatory states granted legal recognition to same-sex partnerships was left unclear. In this light, it is interesting that the First Section chose to stress that states were *still* free – as opposed to free *per se* – to restrict access to marriage to opposite-sex couples.[57] In this regard, therefore, *Schalk and Kopf* provides an almost textbook illustration of the extent to which the Court's interpretation of key Convention rights can turn on its analysis of the 'margin of appreciation', something which often rests on its perception of whether there exists a consensus among signatory states concerning the legal treatment of the issue in question, especially when that issue is of a socially sensitive nature.[58] Legal recognition of same-sex partnerships would thus appear, in *Schalk and Kopf*, to have presented the First Section Chamber in sharp terms with a classic institutional question concerning the limits of the Court's powers.

Turning to child custody (albeit in cases involving a lesbian or gay individual rather than a same-sex couple), the Court of Human Rights has accepted that refusal to award custody of a child to a gay parent because of that parent's sexual orientation could not – without more – survive Article 14 scrutiny.[59] However, it has also accepted, perhaps puzzlingly, that 'protection of the family in the traditional sense' is 'in principle, a weighty and legitimate reason which might justify a difference in treatment' in appropriate circumstances,[60] and that 'the national authorities … should enjoy a wide margin of appreciation when they are asked to make rulings' about the suitability of a single gay man – by contrast with a single heterosexual – to adopt a child,[61] given the 'delicate' issues involved, the point that there was little common ground among the signatory states in this area and that the law appeared to be in a transitional stage.[62]

The United Kingdom is a party to the European Convention, and has brought the Convention into national law via the Human Rights Act 1998. At first sight, it may seem harder to conceptualise the legal rights of those in same-sex partnerships in constitutional terms within the UK, given that the country has no written constitution and no general concept of formally entrenched legislation.[63] The Civil Partnership Act 2004, which formally granted to same-sex partners just about all the legal rights available to opposite-sex married couples,[64] is thus a piece of legislation like any other. However, its provisions were justified during their passage by reference to deeper constitutional values, with Jacqui Smith MP, then Deputy Minister for Women and Equality, describing the legislation as a 'sign' of the government's 'commitment to social justice and equality'[65] and as being 'about equality'.[66] Furthermore, the Human Rights Act 1998 seemingly adds a constitutional tinge to judicial interpretations of the rights of those in same-sex partnerships.[67] Pursuant to section 3 of the Act, all legislation must be interpreted, so far as it is possible to do so, in the light of Convention rights, including Articles 14 and 8. Where legislation is incompatible with Convention rights, a court can only issue a declaration to this effect under section 4 of the Act, leaving Parliament to decide whether to amend the legislation, but given the generality of sections 3 and 4 and the significant role they have come to assume in judicial decision-making, one might well say that they are provisions of considerable constitutional importance.

This point might in turn be thought to support the argument that the Convention rights to which the 1998 Act gives effect in national law have come to assume a certain constitutional significance at national level within the UK. The power of Article 14, as read into legislation under section 3, has been powerfully demonstrated in *Ghaidan v Godin-Mendoza*. At Court of Appeal stage, Lords Justices Buxton and Keene characterised Article 14 as a right of high constitutional importance,[68] and accepted – as did the House of Lords when the case was appealed upwards – that same-sex partners must be treated on the same basis as opposite-sex partners in relation to the right to succeed to a statutory tenancy under the Rent Act 1977.[69] The House of Lords has also interpreted Article 14, in the *Carson* case,[70] as operating in a fashion akin to the equal protection standard in US law: that is, effectively in a constitutional fashion.[71] Both Lord Hoffmann and Lord Walker (with whom the rest of the House of Lords agreed) suggested that some grounds of discrimination – including sexual orientation – were more serious than others, and that a higher burden had to be met before they could be justified in terms of Article 14.[72] The relevant grounds of discrimination, for Lord Hoffmann, were those which *prima facie* appeared to offend against the modern notion of the respect due to an individual, and in such cases discrimination could not be justified merely on a utilitarian basis (by contrast with less serious grounds of discrimination which could be explained by a rational justification relating to the general public interest).[73] For Lord Walker, the more serious grounds were analogous to 'suspect classifications' in US constitutional law, being personal characteristics which an individual could not change and which particularly demeaned the victim when used as a basis for discrimination; severe scrutiny was called for in such cases, requiring very weighty reasons to be produced if the discrimination was to be justified.[74]

Various debates of relevance to particular jurisdictions have been mentioned in this section. What is key, for present purposes, is that litigation and legislative argument concerning the legal recognition and protection of same-sex partnerships may properly, in the jurisdictions concerned, be seen as constitutional in nature. With this general point in mind, the next three sections will consider some more specific constitutional questions posed by the discussion of same-sex partnerships.

2   THE ROLES OF COURTS AND LEGISLATURES

If it is accepted that same-sex partnerships deserve to be granted, in substantive terms, some level of legal recognition and protection, the question arises whether it is more appropriate for the legislature or the courts to do this (or to take the lead in doing it) in the jurisdiction concerned: a question which is clearly of an institutional nature.[75]

This question has been particularly important in the USA, where a bitter issue in political debate – at least, for opponents of legal rights for those in same-sex partnerships – has been the perception that such rights are emerging through the courts without the voices of elected legislators being fully heard. Part of the rhetoric used in the debates following the state supreme court decisions, mentioned in the previous section, in Hawaii and California thus related to perceived clashes between 'liberal' judicial decisions and the more socially conservative 'will of the people': leading ultimately to constitutional amendments in the states concerned.[76] Furthermore, arguments about the appropriate 'place' of courts have also arisen in strong terms within many of the cases concerning the substantive question of the rights to be recognised as existing in relation to those in same-sex partnerships, with the dissenters in *Goodridge*[77] emphasising the point with particular force (in so doing echoing the earlier dissents of Justices Scalia and Thomas at federal Supreme Court level in *Lawrence* on the issue of decriminalisation of consenting sexual activity between persons of the same sex[78]).

Nonetheless, despite noting that judicial deference was inappropriate where an important constitutional right – namely, equal access to marriage – was at stake,[79] Chief Justice Marshall sought in *Goodridge* to justify the state Supreme Judicial Court's decision as an exercise of its proper constitutional function: 'The Massachusetts Constitution requires that legislation meet certain criteria and not extend beyond certain limits. It is the function of courts to determine whether these criteria are met and whether these limits are exceeded … To label the court's role as usurping that of the Legislature … is to misunderstand the nature and purpose of judicial review [of legislation]. We owe great deference to the Legislature to decide social and policy issues, but it is the traditional and settled role of courts to decide constitutional issues.'[80] Furthermore, the Court was keen to allow the state legislature time to rectify the impugned legislation instead of striking it down immediately.[81] A similar strategy was evident in South Africa: Justice Sachs, emphasizing the importance of separation of powers and in spite of the strong normative weight that he had attached to the recognition of same-sex marriage, agreed in *Fourie* to postpone for a year the Constitutional Court's declaration of invalidity concerning the Marriage Act 1961's exclusion of same-sex couples, so as to give the legislature time to produce a constitutionally satisfactory solution.[82] One might perhaps also argue that, in Canada, a mirror-image process was in play: that is, one reason for the federal government's reference of its proposed same-sex marriage legislation to the Supreme Court was in effect – given its narrow Parliamentary majority at the time[83] – to pass a difficult decision about a socially contentious issue to a nationally respected institution that had long accepted responsibility for adjudicating upon the more sensitive aspects of citizens' constitutional rights unhindered by concerns about Parliamentary majorities or future general elections.

In the UK, judicial sensitivity to the constitutional significance and proper positioning of the boundary between sections 3 and 4 of the Human Rights Act is clear, even if there has been disagreement about the boundary's exact location.[84] In consequence, a court which sought, through section 3 interpretation, to give a statute (in Lord Nicholls' words) 'a meaning which departs substantially from a fundamental feature of an Act of Parliament is likely to have crossed the boundary between interpretation and amendment. This is especially so where the departure has important practical repercussions which the court is not equipped to evaluate'.[85] This was strongly evident in *Ghaidan*. Lord Nicholls stated that 'Parliament ... cannot have intended that in the discharge of this extended interpretative function the courts should adopt a meaning inconsistent with a fundamental feature of legislation. That would be to cross the constitutional boundary section 3 seeks to demarcate and preserve. Parliament has retained the right to enact legislation in terms which are not Convention-compliant.'[86] In a similar vein, Lord Rodger stressed the need for courts, when carrying out section 3 interpretations, to avoid 'crossing the border from interpretation to amendment'.[87] Constitutional concerns were also prominent in Lord Millett's dissent: 'The question' whether a section 3 interpretation was appropriate on the facts, he suggested, 'is of great constitutional importance, for it goes to the relationship between the legislature and the judiciary, and hence ultimately to the supremacy of Parliament. Sections 3 and 4 of the Human Rights Act were carefully crafted to preserve the existing constitutional doctrine, and any application of the ambit of section 3 beyond its proper scope subverts it. This is not to say that the doctrine of Parliamentary supremacy is sacrosanct, but only that any change in a fundamental constitutional principle should be the consequence of deliberate legislative action and not judicial activism, however well meaning.'[88] Aileen Kavanagh has suggested that one factor driving courts in determining where the practical boundary between section 3 reinterpretation and a section 4 declaration lies is the likelihood that the Westminster Parliament will in practice intervene to deal with the subject-matter (it is thus interesting to note that at the time *Ghaidan* was being litigated, Parliament was in the process of considering the proposals which resulted in the Civil Partnership Act 2004). Other factors include the court's characterisation of the subject-matter as more social (inclining the court not to intervene) or constitutional (inclining it to intervene).[89] All of these factors concern the limits of the appropriate constitutional role of the courts, and might be described as institutional in the sense set out above.

In the jurisdictions discussed, judicial decision-making concerning the legal recognition and protection of same-sex partnerships has thus acted as a focus for debate about the key institutional – and classically constitutional law – issue of the appropriate ambits of judicial and legislative decision-making.[90] Whether one regards judicial decision-making in this area as appropriate in normative terms will depend on whether one categorises the substantive questions involved as concerned with social policy rather than constitutional rights (itself a rather permeable distinction) and where one regards the appropriate limits of the judicial decision-making capacity as lying. Nonetheless, it deserves to be reiterated that in none of the cases discussed in this section have courts sought explicitly to challenge the authority of the legislature: in fact, often quite the reverse. In the UK, but also in the USA, the possibility of a political override of judicial decisions also remains in place (hence the campaigns for state-level and even federal constitutional amendments to bar same-sex marriage in the USA).[91] Furthermore, if the logic of the critics of court involvement in the recognition of legal rights for same-sex partners was to be applied strictly, it would – at least at face value – become somewhat difficult to see how one would not also need to support the dissenting judgments of Justices Scalia and Thomas in *Lawrence v Texas*, where they implied that while they might not favour moves to criminalise consenting sexual activity where this was not already the case, they believed that a decision to decriminalise was a social policy matter for the legislature rather than the courts.[92] This perhaps helps to further underline the point, made earlier, that while relevant substantive and institutional questions are analytically separable, they may sometimes blur together in practice.

3   COMPARATIVE AND INTERNATIONAL CONSTITUTIONAL LAW ARGUMENTS

It is now common to see arguments based upon comparative or international law used before legislatures and courts when they consider the substantive rights to be accorded to those in same-sex partnerships. Conservative jurists tend to respond to this development with hostility. Nonetheless, given the global availability of information, debate about the use of comparative and international material is likely to be ongoing.

Although *Lawrence v Texas* concerned decriminalisation of consenting same-sex sexual activity, rather than same-sex partnerships (a point which is also true of the High Court of Delhi's significant decision in the *Naz Foundation* case, where important use was again made of comparative authority[93]), it might be felt to provide useful pointers for the latter topic given the strong debate generated by the Supreme Court majority's use of comparative case law to help justify its conclusion that a state anti-sodomy statute was incompatible with the Due Process Clause of the Fourteenth Amendment and that its earlier, contrasting decision in *Bowers v Hardwick*[94] should be overruled. William Eskridge categorises *Lawrence* as 'the first time that the Supreme Court has cited foreign case law in the process of overruling an American constitutional precedent',[95] although non-US authority had been cited in other contexts. In his judgment, Justice Kennedy noted that the 'sweeping references' made in *Bowers* to 'the history of western civilization and to Judaeo-Christian moral and ethical standards' as a factor supporting anti-sodomy legislation 'did not take account' of contradictory authorities.[96] Of 'even more importance'[97] for Justice Kennedy was the decision of the European Court of Human Rights in *Dudgeon v United Kingdom*,[98] decided almost five years before *Bowers*, that the criminal prohibition of private consensual gay sex contravened the European Convention on Human Rights. Furthermore, '[t]o the extent *Bowers* relied on values we share with a wider civilization … [its] reasoning and holding … have been rejected elsewhere': the Court of Human Rights followed *Dudgeon* in later cases, and '[o]ther nations … have taken action consistent with an affirmation of the protected right of homosexual adults to engage in intimate, consensual conduct … [which] has been accepted as an integral part of human freedom'.[99] Justice Scalia, dissenting, challenged this use of comparative authority: 'Constitutional entitlements do not spring into existence because some [US] States choose to lessen or eliminate criminal sanctions on certain behaviour. Much less do they spring into existence … because foreign nations decriminalize conduct.'[100] Furthermore, 'The *Bowers* majority … rejected the claimed right to sodomy on the ground that such a right was not "deeply rooted in this Nation's history and tradition" '.[101] Justice Scalia also emphasised that it was 'dangerous' to use such *dicta*, since – citing Justice Thomas from *Foster v Florida* – ' "this Court … should not impose foreign moods, fads, or fashions, on Americans" '.[102] Eskridge thus notes, effectively in institutional terms, that 'country after country has recognized rights for gay people … without negative consequences for the body politic' and suggests that Justice Kennedy 'implicitly recognized' that this 'political experience' is 'instructive for the United States … Once other countries have accorded gay people … equal treatment without wrenching their pluralist systems, the price of denying gay people the same rights in the United States goes up and the arguments against equality grow shakier'.[103] This, in turn helped 'signal other countries that the Court is attentive to their norms and is a cooperative court'.[104]

At first sight, Justice Kennedy might appear to be treating *Bowers'* lack of fit with values the USA shared 'with a wider civilization' as a matter of empirical difference, in so far as he was measuring the prevailing opinion and showing that analogous constitutional provisions to those in *Bowers* had been interpreted differently elsewhere: most obviously, in *Dudgeon*. Eskridge thus suggests that 'the fact that *Bowers* had received a hostile reaction among judges in Europe' and in some 'traditionalist' US states 'provided a neutral reason' for the *Lawrence* majority 'to believe there was an emerging consensus that this precedent' had misread the 'libertarian traditions' of America and fellow democracies.[105] Eskridge notes, however, that Justice Kennedy must also have been engaged in a normative (or, in the terms used above, more substantive) exercise: 'The foreign precedents were both normative focal points, helping an American judge to evaluate the consistency of sodomy laws with fundamental and shared constitutional principles, and normative feedback, deepening concerns ... about the harmfulness as well as the incorrectness of *Bowers*'.[106] Meanwhile, Justice Scalia's reference to '*this Nation's* history and tradition' might at first look like an observation of fact, but the context and subject-matter suggest that the reference was playing a normative role. This substantive dimension is made explicit through Scalia's *openly* normative assertion that it was 'dangerous' to use non-US *dicta* which imposed 'foreign moods, fads or fashions' on Americans: something which might be summed up as 'Americans know best about American values and the constitution'.

Whilst, in analytical terms, debate about the use of comparative and international law material is thus clearly of an institutional nature – for it concerns the way in which key state institutions should go about making decisions about important substantive questions (and thus the nature and conduct of the role of those institutions) – *Lawrence* might also be felt, for the reasons highlighted, to provide a further illustration of the potential for overlap, in practice, between institutional and substantive questions.[107] Given the growing use of (in particular) comparative legal material, it seems very likely that such material will come to play a strong role in future discussions concerning the legal rights of same-sex partners, suggesting that similar constitutional points will play a role in that context.[108]

4 COMPETING RIGHTS

Returning to substantive questions, some litigants have sought to argue that judicial or legislative recognition of legal rights for same-sex partners poses a threat to their freedom to put into practice particular religious beliefs which are opposed to same-sex sexual activity and partnerships.[109] Such arguments assume that the law should maintain support either for religious beliefs in general or for a particular set of religious beliefs,[110] and also that relevant beliefs must – as a substantive matter – be given priority over competing rights-related claims, for example in relation to same-sex partnerships. The South African Constitutional Court thus acknowledged in *Fourie* that while for 'millions in all walks of life, religion provides support and nurture and a framework for individual and social stability and growth' and that religious belief 'has the capacity to awaken concepts of self-worth and human dignity' and 'affects the believer's view of society and founds a distinction between right and wrong',[111] it is one thing to allow religious believers freely to express their faith-driven views – and presumably, in applying them, to deny same-sex couples any religious celebration of their partnership – but quite another to use those beliefs as a basis for interpreting the constitutional rights of lesbians and gays, including the constitutional right to have their partnerships recognised by the state.

Arguments about the legal recognition or protection of same-sex partnerships help illustrate the broader clashes between claims that people should be free from discrimination on the basis of sexual orientation (including in relation to the legal recognition and protection of same-sex partnerships[112]) and claims that they should be free to act on the basis of religious beliefs which favour the adverse treatment of lesbians and gay men.[113] While this issue is clearly of a substantive nature, it is worth illustrating that it also has an institutional dimension. This is captured in Justice Sachs's assertion in the *Fourie* case that in an open and democratic society, 'there must be mutually respectful co-existence between the secular and the sacred. The function of the Court is to recognise the sphere which each inhabits, not to force the one into the sphere of the other. Provided there is no prejudice to the fundamental rights of any person or group, the law will legitimately acknowledge a diversity of strongly-held opinions on matters of great public controversy.'[114] Furthermore, 'The hallmark of an open and democratic society is its capacity to accommodate and manage difference[s] of intensely-held views and lifestyles in a reasonable and fair manner.'[115] While the major focus in this area, in analytical terms, is thus on substantive as opposed to institutional questions, the latter clearly still play a role.

5   CONCLUSION

This chapter has attempted to highlight, using examples drawn from a variety of jurisdictions, some of the key substantive and institutional questions which have arisen in discussions of the legal recognition and/or protection of same-sex partnerships: a topic which has assumed, for the reasons highlighted, visible political as well as deep-level constitutional significance in many jurisdictions. Furthermore, the fact that analogous substantive and institutional questions – often mixed in practice, even if analytically separable – can be seen to have arisen in this context in so many jurisdictions, potentially with reference to the case law of other jurisdictions, helps to underscore the topic's importance within the field of comparative constitutional law. It nonetheless deserves to be stressed that the levels of moral controversy and social disagreement surrounding the legal recognition and protection of same-sex partnerships vary as between jurisdictions: the more socially liberal atmosphere evident in many western European nations or in South Africa providing an obvious contrast, in this regard, with the greater social conservatism apparent in at least parts of the United States of America. This being so, while the topic provokes analogous constitutional questions in different jurisdictions and while case law examples can be used on a comparative basis, it is far from guaranteed that the various jurisdictions will, in material terms, necessarily recognise the same substantive legal rights as attaching to those in same-sex partnerships. This latter point often turns on the local interpretation and power of arguments relating to underlying values like dignity, autonomy and equality.

NOTES

1. The term 'sexual/emotional' relationships is defined in Robert Wintemute, *Sexual Orientation and Human Rights: The United States Constitution, the European Convention, and the Canadian Charter* (Oxford: Oxford University Press, 1995), pp. 6–9.

2. In *Thoburn v Sunderland CC* [2002] EWHC Admin 195, para [62], English Court of Appeal judge Sir John Laws categorised constitutional law as the body of law dealing with the powers of state institutions in general, including the respective spheres of competence of the legislature, executive and judiciary, and with rights of fundamental importance to the citizen. I employ this definition here, but should emphasise that I am sceptical about Laws LJ's associated argument that a distinction may generally be drawn in English law between 'constitutional' and 'ordinary' statutes, either generally or in terms of their properties.

3. A definitive, largely empirical, survey is Robert Wintemute and Mads Andenaes (eds), *Legal Recognition of Same-Sex Partnerships: A Study of National, European and International Law* (Oxford: Hart, 2001).

4. Key cases include *Ghaidan v Godin-Mendoza* [2004] UKHL 30, [2004] 2 AC 557 and *Egan v Canada* [1995] 2 SCR 513.

5. Key cases include *Goodridge v Department of Public Health* (2003) 798 NE 2d 941, *Reference Re Same-Sex Marriage* [2004] 3 SCR 698 and *Minister of Home Affairs v Fourie* (2006) 1 SA 524. For discussion of the UK position, see Nicholas Bamforth, ' "The Benefits of Marriage in All but Name?" Same-sex Couples and the Civil Partnership Act 2004' (2007) 2 *CFLQ* 133. As the European Court of Human Rights (First Section) noted in *Schalk and Kopf v Austria*, Application no. 30141/04, 24 June 2010, para [31]: 'The legal consequences of registered partnership vary from almost equivalent to marriage [in some jurisdictions] to giving relatively limited rights [in others]. Among the legal consequences of registered partnerships, three main categories can be distinguished: material consequences, parental consequences and other consequences' (see also paras [32]–[34], [87]).

6. See, for example, *Karner v Austria*, Application no. 40016/98, ECHR 2003-IX, (2004) 38 EHRR 24.

7. They are thus explicitly recognised in the European Convention on Human Rights: see Article 12 (right to marry and found a family); Article 8 (right to respect for private and family life). In the USA, they have been recognised by the Supreme Court as rights of fundamental importance: *Loving v Virginia* (1967) 388 US 1 (marriage); *Griswold v Connecticut* (1965) 381 US 479 (intimate private life). See also the California Supreme Court's use of a state-level right to marriage in relation to same-sex marriage: *In re Marriage Cases* (2008) 183 P. 3d. 384.

8. N.4 above, para [142]; see also *Goodridge v Department of Public Health*, n.5 above, 948 (Marshall CJ, *Halpern v Canada* (Attorney-General) (2003) 225 DLR (4th) 529, para [9].

9. See further Nicholas Bamforth, 'Same-sex Partnerships: Some Comparative Constitutional Lessons' [2007] *EHRLR* 47, 53–6. For practical examples, see *Minister of Home Affairs v Fourie*, n.5 above, esp. at paras [47], [48], [50], [60], [94], [103], [110], [114] (Sachs J). A court which recognises legal rights associated with same-sex partnerships is not only upholding deeper constitutional values but also protecting the interests of litigants at a more material level: for example, in relation to holding of and succession to property, custody of children, or immigration and freedom of movement. For further discussion, see *Goodridge v Department of Public Health*, n.5 above, 954-9 (Marshall CJ), 970–1 (Greaney J); *Minister of Home Affairs v Fourie*, n.5 above, paras [63]ff and [71]–[73], esp. [72] (Sachs J); Kees Waaldijk, 'Taking Same-Sex Partnerships Seriously – European Experiences as British Perspectives?' [2003] *IFL* 84, 84–5.

10. For example, Kees Waaldijk, 'Towards the Recognition of Same-sex Partners in European Union Law: Expectations Based on Trends in National Law', ch. 36 in Wintemute and Andenaes (eds), n.3 above, and 'Taking Same-sex Partnerships Seriously – European Experiences as British Perspectives?', n.9 above, 85–6, 91; Robert Wintemute, 'From "Sex Rights" to "Love Rights": Partnership Rights as Human Rights', ch.6 in Nicholas Bamforth (ed.), *Sex Rights: The Oxford Amnesty Lectures 2002* (Oxford: Oxford University Press, 2005), esp. pp. 187–97. Note also William Eskridge's discussion of 'three overlapping struggles' in the USA, the 'initial struggle' being to protect private gay spaces 'against spying and the intrusion of the police', 'second' and 'third' struggles being to assert control over the institutions of gay sub-culture and for equal gay citizenship: *Gaylaw: Challenging the Apartheid of the Closet* (Cambridge, MA: Harvard University Press, 1999), p. 15.

11. For a crucial example of the latter, see *Lawrence v Texas* (2003) 539 US 558. For discussion of a more negative UK counter-example to the notion of a 'smooth journey' from decriminalisation towards recognition of same-sex partnership rights – namely, the enactment of section 28, of the Local Government Act 1988 (since repealed) – see Waaldijk, 'Taking Same-sex Partnerships Seriously', n.9 above.

12. Examples from the case law might include, from the USA, *Lawrence v Texas*, n.11 above, if coupled with *Goodridge v Department of Public Health*, n.5 above, and, from South Africa, *National Coalition for Gay and Lesbian Equality v Minister of Justice (the 'Sodomy case')* (1999) (1) SA 6 when coupled with *Minister of Home Affairs v Fourie*, n.5 above.

13. See section 3, below.
14. See sections 2, 3 and 4, below.
15. See, e.g., *Naz Foundation v Government of NCT of Delhi*, High Court of Delhi, 2nd July 2009.
16. N.4 above.
17. In *EGALE Canada v Canada (Attorney General)* (2003) 225 DLR (4th) 472 and *Halpern v Canada (Attorney-General)*, n.8 above. Note also *Hendricks v Quebec* [2002] JQ No 3816 (SC).
18. *Reference re Same-Sex Marriage*, n.5 above.
19. *National Coalition for Gay and Lesbian Equality v Minister of Justice (the 'Sodomy case')*, n.12 above.
20. *National Coalition for Gay and Lesbian Equality v Minister of Home Affairs* (2000) (2) SA 1.
21. N.5 above.
22. N.11 above. Note Kennedy J's concern, in his majority judgment, to stress (at 578) that the decision was not concerned with partnership rights; note also O'Connor J's concurring judgment at 585; contrast Scalia J's dissent at 590, 601–2, 604–5.
23. N.5 above. For critical analysis of the use of state constitutions in litigation in the USA, see Gerald Rosenberg, *The Hollow Hope: Can Courts Bring About Social Change?* (Chicago: University of Chicago Press, 2nd edn., 2008), pp. 340 ff.
24. (1996) 517 US 620.
25. For general analysis, compare William Eskridge, *Equality Practice: Civil Unions and the Future of Gay Rights* (New York: Routledge, 2002) and Rosenberg, *The Hollow Hope: Can Courts Bring About Social Change?*, n.23 above, chs. 12 and 13.
26. (1993) 852 P. 2d. 44; see also *Baehr v Miike* (1996) 950 P. 2d. 1234.
27. Civil Action No. 09-10309-JLT, 8 July 2010; note also the 17 August 2010 stay of the decision pending appeal.
28. N.7 above.
29. *Strauss v Horton* (2009) 207 P3d 48.
30. No. C 09-2292 VRW, 8 July 2010; note also the 16 August 2010 stay of the decision pending appeal.
31. In those European Convention states which have signed up to Protocol 12, Article 14 may be pleaded without being tied to another Convention Article (e.g. Article 8). In those which have not, for example the UK, Article 14 applies only to discriminatory treatment in connection with the enjoyment of another Convention right.
32. See, for example, Jeremy McBride, 'Proportionality and the European Convention on Human Rights', in Evelyn Ellis (ed.), *The Principle of Proportionality in the Laws of Europe* (Oxford: Hart, 1999).
33. See *Handyside v United Kingdom* (1976) 1 EHRR 737, para [48].
34. *Dudgeon v United Kingdom*, Application no. 7525/76, (1982) 4 EHRR 149; *Norris v Ireland*, Application no. 10581/83, (1991) 13 EHRR 186; *Smith and Grady v United Kingdom*, Application nos. 33985/96 and 33986/96, (1999) 29 EHRR 493; *Lustig-Prean and Beckett v United Kingdom*, Application nos. 31417/96 and 32377/96, (1999) 29 EHRR 548.
35. *Dudgeon v United Kingdom*, n.31 above, paras [51]–[53]; *Smith and Grady v United Kingdom*, n.31 above, paras [87]–[89], [94]; *Lustig-Prean and Beckett v United Kingdom*, n.34 above, paras [80]–[83], [87].
36. *ADT v United Kingdom*, Application no. 35765/97, [2000] 2 FLR 697, para [38]; *Sutherland v United Kingdom*, Application no. 25186/94, para [57].
37. *Da Silva Mouta v Portugal*, Application no. 33290/96, ECHR 1999-IX, [2001] 1 FCR 653, paras [28]–[36]; *Frette v France*, Application no. 36515/97, ECHR 2002-I, [2003] 2 FCR 39, para [32].
38. Application no. 40016/98, ECHR 2003-IX, para [37].
39. N.6 above, para [41].
40. N.5 above.
41. Admissibility Decision no. 56501/00, ECHR 2001-VI. A further finding was that: 'despite the growing tendency in a number of European States towards the legal and judicial recognition of stable de facto partnerships between homosexuals, this is, given the existence of little common ground' an area in which signatory states 'still enjoy a wide margin of appreciation'. As is clear from the text, a 'margin of appreciation' of some width appears still to be in play in *Schalk and Kopf*.
42. N.6 above.
43. N.6 above, para [93]. See also paras [26]–[30].
44. N.6 above, para [94]. The Court did not address how it might treat those in a long-standing relationship which did not involve cohabitation.
45. N.6 above, para [23].
46. N.6 above, para [58].
47. N.6 above, para [60].
48. N.6 above, para [61].
49. N.6 above, paras [101], [108].
50. N.6 above, paras [104]–[109].

51. N.6 above, para [103].
52. N.6 above, para [62].
53. N.6 above, para [58].
54. N.6 above, para [61].
55. N.6 above, para [98].
56. N.6 above, para [105].
57. N.6 above, para [108].
58. For analysis of the constitutional controversies surrounding this approach, see Richard Clayton and Hugh Tomlinson, *The Law of Human Rights: Volume 1* (Oxford: Oxford University Press, 2nd edn., 2009), paras 6.52–6.55.
59. *Da Silva Mouta v Portugal*, n.37 above.
60. *Da Silva Mouta v Portugal*, n.37 above, para [40].
61. *Frette v France*, n.37 above, para [41]. On the facts, this clearly involved a difference of treatment based upon sexual orientation: see paras [32]–[33].
62. *Frette v France*, n.37 above, paras [41]–[42]. For an attempt to explain the distinction between the cases, see the joint partly dissenting opinion of Judges Bratza, Fuhrmann and Tulkens.
63. Although note the special procedural role of the Parliament Acts 1911 and 1949, as discussed by the House of Lords in *Jackson v Attorney-General* [2005] UKHL 56; [2006] 1 AC 262.
64. For analysis, see Bamforth, ' "The Benefits of Marriage in All but Name?" Same-sex Couples and the Civil Partnership Act 2004', n.5 above. Note also that the Equality Act 2010, s.8, protects civil partnership and marriage as prohibited grounds of discrimination within the contexts it covers.
65. HC Deb, 12 October 2004, col, 174.
66. HC Deb, 12 October 2004, col. 176.
67. For recent discussion, see Vernon Bogdanor, *The New British Constitution* (Oxford: Hart, 2009), esp. ch. 3; Aileen Kavanagh, *Constitutional Review under the UK Human Rights Act* (Cambridge: Cambridge University Press, 2009); Alison L. Young, *Parliamentary Sovereignty and the Human Rights Act* (Oxford: Hart, 2009).
68. *Mendoza v Ghaidan* [2002] EWCA Civ 1533 [2003] 1 FLR 468, paras [19] (Buxton LJ), [44] (Keene LJ). Note also Lord Mance's suggestion, in *Secretary of State for Work and Pensions v M*, [2006] UKHL 11, [2006] 2 WLR 637, para [136], that in addition to Article 14 'the United Kingdom already has … a developing body of common law authority underlining the importance attaching to fundamental rights, which surely include equal treatment'.
69. Although note the limitations to this, in respect of past discrimination, recognised in *Secretary of State for Work and Pensions v M*, n.68 above.
70. *R. v Secretary of State for Work and Pensions, ex p Carson* [2005] UKHL 37, [2006] 1 AC 173. See also the analyses of the undesirability of discrimination in *Ghaidan v Godin-Mendoza*, n.4 above, paras [9] (Lord Nicholls), [55] (Lord Millett).
71. However, as a comparison between *Ghaidan v Godin-Mendoza*, n.4 above, and *Secretary of State for Work and Pensions v M*, n.68 above, makes clear, given that Article 14-based claims must be tied to other, substantive Convention rights in United Kingdom litigation, in the partnership context the success of any discrimination-related claim depends upon how widely Articles 8 or 12 (the relevant substantive Articles) are interpreted.
72. Thus reflecting the Strasbourg Court's stance in *Karner v Austria*, n.6 above, para [37].
73. N.70 above, paras [15]–[17].
74. N.70 above, paras [55]–[58]. Note that Lord Walker was mistaken in his suggestion that sexual orientation was, at the time, recognised as a 'suspect classification' in US case law.
75. At a theoretical level, useful treatments of the issue can be found in: Bruce Ackerman, *We the People: Foundations* (Cambridge, MA: Harvard University Press, 1991); Ronald Dworkin, *Taking Rights Seriously* (London: Duckworth, 1977), *A Matter of Principle* (Oxford: Oxford University Press, 1985); John Hart Ely, *Democracy and Distrust: A Theory of Judicial Review* (Cambridge, MA: Harvard University Press, 1980); Janet L. Hiebert, *Charter Conflicts: What is Parliament's Role?* (Montreal: McGill-Queen's University Press, 2002); Larry D. Kramer, *The People Themselves: Popular Constitutionalism and Judicial Review* (New York: Oxford University Press, 2004); Lawrence Sager, *Justice in Plainclothes: A Theory of American Constitutional Practice* (New Haven: Yale University Press, 2004); Mark Tushnet, *Taking the Constitution Away from the Courts* (Princeton: Princeton University Press, 1999); Jeremy Waldron, *Law and Disagreement* (Oxford: Oxford University Press, 1999) and 'The Core of the Case Against Judicial Review' (2006) 115 *Yale LJ* 1346.
76. For critical analysis of the consequences, in this respect, of judicial decision-making about same-sex partnerships, see Rosenberg, *The Hollow Hope: Can Courts Bring about Social Change?*, n.23 above, pp. 5–6, 415–19, 435–6 (and, more generally, chs. 1 and 12 to 14).
77. N.5 above, Spina J (dissenting), 974, 977-8, Sosman J (dissenting), 982, Cordy J (dissenting), 983, 990–1, 998–1004.

78. Scalia J suggested that it was a matter for the legislature to resolve (n.11 above, 603–4); see also Thomas J (n.11 above, 605).
79. N.5 above, 965–6. Note also Walker J's finding at United States District Court level in *Perry v Schwarzenegger*, n.30 above, that those arguing for the constitutional recognition of same-sex marriage were not seeking a new right, but were instead enjoining the state to recognise the nature of their relationships as marriages as protected under the Due Process Clause.
80. N.5 above, 966. Kennedy J made an analogous point at US Supreme Court level in *Lawrence v Texas*, when he stated that the traditional legal principle of *stare decisis* should not be applied as if it was an 'inexorable command', and that particular care should be taken where a court was asked to overrule a precedent which recognised an important liberty interest (n.11 above, 577). Also interesting in this regard is Barak CJ's judgment, for the majority, in *Ben-Ari v Director of the Population Administration in the Ministry of the Interior* (HCJ 3045/05, 21 November 2006), where the Supreme Court of Israel accepted that same-sex couples who had been married abroad could be registered as married under the Israeli population registry legislation, but stressed that the more general question whether same-sex marriage should be recognised in Israel was for the legislature to decide.
81. See also the more deferential approach of the New Jersey Supreme Court in *Lewis and Winslow v Harris* (A-68-05, 25 October 2006).
82. N.5 above, Sachs J, paras [118], [124], [135]–[153], [158]–[161] (summarised by O'Regan J at paras [165]–[166]); note O'Regan J's dissent over this issue at paras [167]–[171].
83. Paul Martin's government lost office in the 2006 general election.
84. Compare, for example, *Re S* [2002] UKHL 10, paras [39]–[40] (Lord Nicholls); see also *R v A (No. 2)* [2002] 1 AC 45, paras [44] (Lord Steyn), [108] (Lord Hope), [162] (Lord Hutton); *R (Anderson) v Secretary of State for the Home Department* [2002] UKHL 46; *Bellinger v Bellinger* [2003] UKHL 21; Danny Nicol, 'Statutory Interpretation and Human Rights after *Anderson*' [2004] *PL* 274; Aileen Kavanagh, 'Statutory Interpretation and Human Rights after *Anderson*: A More Contextual Approach' [2004] *PL* 537, 'Unlocking the Human Rights Act: The "Radical" Approach to Section 3(1) Revisited' [2005] *EHRLR* 259 and, more broadly, 'The Elusive Divide between Interpretation and Legislation under the Human Rights Act 1998' (2004) 24 *OJLS* 259; Conor Gearty, *Principles of Human Rights Adjudication* (Oxford: Oxford University Press, 2004), pp. 52–3 and 'Reconciling Parliamentary Democracy and Human Rights' (2002) 118 *LQR* 248. Note, in English law, Stephen Cretney's argument that courts should be wary of decision-making concerning same-sex partnerships: *Same Sex Relationships: From 'Odious Crime' to 'Gay Marriage'* (Oxford: Oxford University Press, 2006), pp. 69–72.
85. *Re S*, n.84 above, para [40].
86. *Ghaidan v Godin-Mendoza*, n.4 above, para [33].
87. N.4 above, para [122]; see, more broadly, paras [112]–[118], [122]–[124].
88. N.4 above, para [57].
89. 'Statutory interpretation and human rights after *Anderson*: a more contextual approach', n.84 above.
90. A related but distinct issue might be felt to be the European Court of Human Rights' handling of the 'margin of appreciation' issue (see section 1, above) given its concern with the appropriate division between European-level judicial decision-making and national-level judicial and legislative decision-making.
91. See Rosenberg, *The Hollow Hope: Can Courts Bring about Social Change?*, n.23 above, chs. 12 and 13.
92. N.11 above. See further n.78 above.
93. *Naz Foundation v Government of NCT of Delhi* (2009), n.15 above. On the use of comparative and international law arguments in Indian jurisprudence, see Arun Thiruvengadam, 'In Pursuit of 'The Common Illumination of Our House': Trans-Judicial Influence and the Origins of PIL Jurisprudence in South Asia' (2008) 2 *Indian Journal of Constitutional Law* 67.
94. (1986) 478 US 186.
95. William Eskridge, 'Lawrence v Texas and the imperative of comparative constitutionalism' (2004) 2 *International Journal of Constitutional Law* 555, 555.
96. N.11 above, 572.
97. N.11 above, 573.
98. N.34 above.
99. N.11 above, 576–7.
100. N.11 above, 598.
101. N.11 above, 598.
102. N.11 above, 598, citing *Foster v Florida* (2002) 537 US 990 at 991.
103. N.95 above, 559.
104. N.95 above, 558.
105. N.95 above, 557.
106. N.95 above, 557.
107. A similar point might be made about the arguments of some academic opponents of *Lawrence v Texas*, n.11

above: see, for example, Steven Calabresi, '*Lawrence*, the Fourteenth Amendment, and the Supreme Court's Reliance on Foreign Constitutional Law: An Originalist Reappraisal', (2004) 65 *Ohio State LJ* 1096, 1106, 1122–3, Joan Larsen, 'Importing Constitutional Norms from a 'Wider Civilization': *Lawrence* and the Rehnquist Court's Use of Foreign and International Law in Domestic Constitutional Interpretation', (2004) 65 *Ohio State LJ* 1283, 1295. Contrast, however, Cass Sunstein, 'Liberty After *Lawrence*' (2004) 65 *Ohio State LJ* 1059, 1061.

108. For an example of the use of comparative authority by litigants, see *Schalk and Kopf v Austria*, n.5 above, para [48].
109. For a variety of such issues, see, generally, Nicholas Bamforth, Maleiha Malik and Colm O'Cinneide, *Discrimination Law: Theory and Context* (London: Sweet & Maxwell, 2008), chs. 8 and 9, pp. 745–8; David A.J. Richards, *Free Speech and the Politics of Identity* (Oxford: Oxford University Press, 1999).
110. See Baroness Hale's important discussion in *R (on the application of Begum) v. Headteacher and Governors of Denbigh High School* [2006] UKHL 15, esp. paras [95] and [96]. See also *R v. Secretary of State for Education and Employment, ex p. Williamson* [2005] UKHL 15, paras [15], [17] (Lord Nicholls). See also, in the UK, *R (AMICUS) v. Secretary of State for Trade and Industry* [1994] EWHC 869 (Admin) (for analysis, see Bamforth et al. *Discrimination Law: Theory and Context*, n.109 above, pp. 708–15, 718–20).
111. N.5 above, para [89].
112. For a legislative example from the UK, see the Equality Act 2010, s.8.
113. See, for example, *Trinity Western University v. British Columbia College Teachers* [2001] 1 SCR 772.
114. N.5 above, para [94].
115. N.5 above, para [95].

PART V

COURTS AND CONSTITUTIONAL INTERPRETATION

31. Judicial engagement with comparative law

Cheryl Saunders

1 INTRODUCTION

1.1 Rationale

Over a period of a decade spanning the turn of the 21st century, references to foreign constitutional experience appeared in a handful of decisions of the Supreme Court of the United States.[1] In *Atkins, Lawrence, Roper* and *Graham* the majority opinion referred to foreign law. In *Printz* and *Knight* the reference was confined to individual opinions.[2] The references played a variety of relatively minor roles in the reasoning processes of the Justices concerned (Tushnet 2005–6, p. 299). They nevertheless sparked considerable controversy, in the course of which the practice was criticised on grounds of both legitimacy and methodology.[3] The controversy served to highlight what Jackson has characterised as the 'engagement' of courts with foreign law, as a particular, practical application of comparative constitutional law (Jackson 2010). Judicial engagement with comparative law, which has also variously been described in terms of the migration of constitutional ideas (Choudhry 2006, p. 1), the importation of constitutional law (Dupré 2002, p. 267), constitutional borrowing (Friedman and Saunders 2003), cross-constitutional influence (Scheppele 2003, p. 296) or judicial dialogue (Harding 2003), is the subject of this chapter. Its inclusion in this volume can be justified on the basis that it represents a form of applied comparative constitutional law.

The debate in the United States in turn was a catalyst for examination of the extent to which courts elsewhere in the world refer to foreign law in the course of constitutional adjudication.[4] While there is much empirical work still to be done, it is already clear that practice varies dramatically, from states in which there is virtually no explicit reference to foreign law in the course of adjudication to those in which such references are common. It is also clear that change is under way in the sense that, as a generalisation, references to foreign law are becoming more frequent, although from an uneven base. And herein lies an equally compelling reason for the inclusion of this subject in a volume on comparative constitutional law. The engagement of courts with foreign law is itself a subject for comparative study. At one level the task is empirical. At others it calls for a sophisticated application of comparative method in order to understand why practice differs; how the phenomenon is perceived and understood in different jurisdictions; and whether concerns about usage are shared or are jurisdiction-specific.

This chapter is concerned with each of these dimensions of the subject. The remainder of this section explains the scope of the chapter and the range of cases on which it will focus. Section 2 identifies patterns of use of foreign law by the courts of different states and makes good the claim that it seems to be increasing. Section 3 examines the varying contexts in which constitutional adjudication occurs, as the basis for a series of hypotheses about why practice varies between states. Section 4 continues the focus on context by examining more closely the role that foreign law plays in judicial reasoning in those jurisdictions where the practice is found. The next two sections deal respectively with legitimacy and comparative method, as the twin objections that have been voiced to the use of foreign law. These parts show that objections based on legitimacy are more likely to be jurisdiction-specific than concerns about method, which are more generally shared. The final section draws some brief conclusions.

1.2 Scope

References to foreign law are more likely to be made, if they are made at all, by an apex court with jurisdiction in constitutional questions. While other courts sometimes refer to foreign law as well, this chapter will focus on courts at the peak of the judicial hierarchy or, where applicable, specialist constitutional courts. Otherwise, the chapter defines the subject broadly. It treats as relevant reference to any kind of foreign constitutional experience: a rule, an interpretation of a text, a practice, a mode of reasoning, or an institutional arrangement, to name some of the more obvious. It includes references to foreign law for any purpose, ranging from the provision of authority to decorative rhetoric. For reasons of accessibility, it is confined to explicit references to foreign law, in the opinion of the court or of individual justices, either in the body of the judgment or in supporting notes. It should be noted, however, that these do not exhaust the potential extent of the influence of foreign law, which may be unacknowledged or which may be canvassed in preparatory documentation rather than in the published reasons of the court.[5]

The chapter does not deal directly with references to international law. While in some jurisdictions, of which the United States is an example, attitudes towards the use of foreign and international law sources tend to be similar, in others the two are treated quite differently. The explanation lies in part in the different authoritative claims of the two bodies of law. In a monist legal system international law is part of the body of applicable law; in a dualist system, typically, treaty law, at least, is not and judicial recognition of international law may have implications for the separation of powers. One ironic consequence of this difference is that some jurisdictions that are less likely to refer to foreign law may readily refer to international law and vice versa.[6] For the moment, the difference justifies the distinction drawn here. In the longer term, however, the distinction is likely to become increasingly blurred as references to both foreign and international law proliferate in conditions of globalisation (Walker 2008, p. 373).

The distinction is challenged also by the existence of supra-national courts, of which the European Court of Justice and the European Court of Human Rights are paradigm examples. In the interests of consistency, in this chapter they are excluded from consideration of the practices of courts that lie in hierarchical relationship to them. From the standpoint of other states, however, supra-national courts have the same status as foreign courts and references to them are relevant for present purposes. It should be noted in passing that these courts also are of interest from the standpoint of judicial engagement with foreign law in at least two other ways, although neither is pursued further here. The first is that a supra-national court may itself engage in comparative constitutional law in order to resolve the questions before it.[7] The second is that courts that accept the authority of a supra-national court but do not themselves refer to foreign law may nevertheless be influenced by foreign law, filtered through decisions of the supra-national court (Poirier 2008).[8]

1.3 Cases

The analysis in this chapter will be illustrated by reference to a range of jurisdictions. The choice of these is influenced in part by availability of data and in part by the need to select cases that are reasonably indicative of world constitutional experience. For this latter purpose, selection is guided by a notional template, in order to ensure coverage of both common law and civil law legal systems and, within each, of both a range of regions and of constitutional systems in different stages of development. The common law states to which reference will be made are the United States, Australia, South Africa,[9] Singapore and Israel. These cover both the British and United States constitutional traditions, to the extent to which these can still be distinguished; span four geographic regions; and include both established and new constitutions with a variety of genealogical histories. The principal civil law jurisdictions are Germany, Argentina, Hungary, Taiwan and Japan. Again, these span several regions and include polities in a variety of constitutional circumstances, ranging from the established systems of Germany and Japan to the other three systems, each of which has emerged in relatively recent times from a period of authoritarian rule but which otherwise are quite different from each other.

It is important not to claim too much for this selection. In the first place, regional coverage is not complete, for reasons of lack of data.[10] Secondly, while, as I have argued elsewhere, a template along these lines has potential for inclusive comparative constitutional analysis, it remains to be tested (Saunders 2009). Even on the assumption that the template provides the basis for a generally appropriate jurisdictional spread, moreover, divergence between individual constitutional systems raises the possibility that particular factors will skew the outcomes in a particular case. Some attempt can be made to guard against this possibility by reference to other jurisdictions with broadly similar characteristics. Nevertheless, the conclusions drawn from this selection of cases need verification through ongoing research.

2 PATTERNS AND TRENDS

2.1 Use

Research on engagement with comparative constitutional law by courts reveals a wide variety of practice, ranging from polities in which courts never, or hardly ever, refer explicitly to foreign law in the course of constitutional adjudication and those in which such references are frequent. Of the cases selected for consideration in this chapter, those in the former category include Germany, with three references to foreign law over the 14 years from 1991–2005, justifying description of current practice as 'rare';[11] Japan, with no references to foreign law in majority opinions between 1990 and 2008 and only 11 in individual opinions (Ejima 2009, p. 28); and Taiwan, in which only four majority opinions, or 0.7% of the total, referred to foreign law between 1949 and 2008 (Chang and Yeh 2008).[12] At the other end of the scale is Australia, where research shows that foreign law was cited in the majority of constitutional cases decided by the High Court between 1998 and 2008;[13] South Africa, where foreign law has been cited in more than half of the 300 or so cases decided since 1994 (Bentele 2009, pp. 219, 227); and Israel, in which 18% of constitutional cases decided between 1994 and 2002 cited foreign law (Navot 2008) and such references have been described as 'extensive'.[14]

Occupying the middle ground is Hungary, where 10.12% of cases cited foreign law between 1999 and 2008 (Szente 2008);[15] Singapore, where citation of foreign law declined as the view that the Constitution should be interpreted within its own 'four walls' took hold but where, nevertheless, it has been characterised as 'very much the norm' (Ramraj 2002, p. 2020);[16] and Argentina, where a distinctive early pattern of authoritative citation of US law has been replaced by a more eclectic practice (Rosenkrantz 2003, p. 269). Probably, the United States should be included in this group as well. While the number of citations in recent years is small, the practice itself is long-established (Calabresi and Zimdahl 2005, p. 567).

On the basis of this data, common law states are more likely to cite foreign law in the course of constitutional adjudication and civil law states are less likely to do so. This conclusion can be strengthened by reference to the experience of other states. The apex courts in India and Canada, for example, make relatively frequent reference to foreign constitutional experience (Tripathi 1957, p. 319),[17] whereas the Constitutional Courts of Belgium and Austria do not (Poirier, 2008; Gamper, 2009, p. 155).[18] The line is far from bright, however. The United States and Singapore are common law states that show some signs of discomfort with references to foreign law, as also does, for example, Malaysia.[19] Argentina and Hungary, on the other hand, are civil law states in which courts periodically cite common law; and their number can be augmented by reference to, for example, Spain, Brazil and Indonesia (Guerra 2005, p. 567; Mendes 2009; Harjono 2010). Further, while the Constitutional Court of Germany now cites foreign law infrequently, the practice was once more common and Justice Bryde has observed that there are 'no fundamental objections' to it.[20] What seem likely to be multiple explanations for differences in practice will be sought in the next part, from consideration of the context in which constitutional adjudication occurs.

2.2 Increase

It is often claimed that the practice of referring to foreign experience in the course of constitutional adjudication is increasing.[21] In all probability such claims are correct. The substantial increase since 1990 in the number of states with new Constitutions and new Constitutional Courts is sufficient to raise the incidence overall.[22] The greater accessibility of foreign constitutional materials through information technology facilitates reference to them. The proliferation of international networks of jurists and scholars encourages transjurisdictional dialogue.[23] The internationalisation of constitutional law, especially in relation to human rights, is a further catalyst (Nijman and Nollkaemper 2007 p. 251, 257).[24] In some states, constitutional rights protection is accompanied by constitutional provisions that more or less explicitly authorise courts to refer to foreign experience. In South Africa the authority is clear and direct: in interpreting the Bill of Rights a court 'may consider foreign law' (s.39(1)(c)). Arguably, however, a requirement of the kind in section 1 of the Canadian Charter of Rights and Freedoms, which precludes limitations on rights that cannot be 'demonstrably justified in a free and democratic society', anticipates reference to foreign experience as well.[25] This is the likely consequence, also, of the appointment of foreign judges to a local court with constitutional jurisdiction.[26]

On the other hand, the movement is not all one way. As the examples of Germany, South Africa and Hungary show, the extent of reference to foreign experience may be greater in the early years of adjudication on a new Constitution, declining, although by no means disappearing, as the local jurisprudence becomes established. Other forces also may discourage foreign citation: the reaction against references to foreign constitutional experience in the United States and Singapore makes the point. It remains to be seen whether the debate in the United States prompts greater caution about foreign citation in other common law countries as well. There are some signs of emerging caution in Australia, although it too early to judge their significance.[27] It may also be that internationalisation is increasing the incidence of reference to international law at the expense of foreign law. There is some support for this hypothesis from Argentina, where the constitutional revision of 1994 incorporated nine international human rights treaties into the Constitution of Argentina, enhancing the status of international jurisprudence in the domestic court system (Levit 1998–9, p. 281).[28]

3   CONTEXT

Some of the differences between jurisdictions in their engagement with comparative law can be explained by reference to the context in which constitutional adjudication occurs, including the procedures for adjudication and local understanding of the nature of judicial review and constitutional interpretation. Context, thus understood, also throws light on the ways in which comparative experience comes to the attention of a court so as to be included in the formulation of judicial reasons. This section shows that there are features of the context for judicial review in common law and civil law legal systems that help to explain the differences between them in explicit engagement with foreign law. It also examines a range of other contextual factors that help to account for variations in the degree of engagement with comparative law between states within the same broad legal traditions.

3.1   Common Law

There are at least four characteristics of the common law that affect constitutional adjudication in common law states and assist in explaining the relatively easy engagement with foreign law by common law courts.

The first concerns the mode of reasoning by which the common law itself was and continues to be built. In this legal tradition, cases are decided by reference to earlier cases that are considered relevantly analogous;[29] principles are drawn from decided cases by a process of induction; future cases may be resolved by deduction from such principles, which nevertheless are flexible in their reach and application.[30] It follows that judges have some discretion in determining the law by which cases are resolved. Judicial discretion is constrained to a degree by the doctrine of precedent. On the other hand, the notion of binding precedent consolidates the position of judge as law-maker, albeit within limits that depend on cultural acceptance and may vary between jurisdictions. It also calls for a line to be drawn between precedents that are binding and those that are not. The latter are not ruled out of consideration if, in the circumstances of a case, they are considered persuasive (Glenn 1987, p. 261). This highly pragmatic *modus operandi* enables a common law court to draw on the experiences of other jurisdictions as well as its own. It enables a common law legal system to remain open to external influence without jeopardising its legitimacy from a domestic point of view.

This mode of reasoning, in turn, helps to explain the form of judicial decisions: a second, distinctive characteristic of the common law. At least at the appellate level, a common law judgment sets out in writing the facts of the case and includes relatively elaborate reasons that identify the legal issues, analyse the legal authorities on which the resolution of each issue rests and explain how the authorities are used.[31] Like the doctrine of precedent itself, the obligation to provide written reasons has developed over time and now performs several functions. Reasons help litigants to understand why the case was won or lost and, in the case of the latter, to accept the outcome. They effectuate common law method by providing some insight into what the case stands for and how it might be used in the future. They are a means for holding judges to account for the decisions that they make and the public power that they exercise. This function is enhanced by the assumption that each judge has the right and responsibility to give his or her opinion, in concurring or dissenting reasons, if joint reasons cannot be agreed. As the significance of the expectation of reasoned decisions grows, it has been argued that they represent a shift in the common law conception of legal authority from command towards justification.[32]

These first two characteristics provide a contemporary explanation for the engagement of courts with comparative law in resolving common law cases. No doubt the practice received considerable stimulus from the long period of colonialism in the 19th and early 20th centuries during which, at least within the British empire, the common law was regarded as a single legal system over which the Privy Council and the House of Lords presided, aided by their overlapping membership. This was also the period within which both the doctrine of precedent and the requirement for written reasons were consolidated. But more than half a century after most colonial ties effectively dissolved, causing the common law to fragment into distinct national legal systems,[33] this is no longer an adequate explanation for a practice that, if anything, has continued to expand.

An explanation of how and why courts engage with comparative law in common law cases does not necessarily explain references to foreign law in the somewhat different context of the construction and application of written constitutions. The extension of the practice to constitutional adjudication in most common law states can be attributed in part to the characteristics of constitutions themselves, which in turn affect the kinds of questions raised in constitutional adjudication. Many parts of most constitutions are expressed with a degree of generality. The types of issues raised are unlikely to be confined to questions of textual interpretation of the relatively straightforward variety found in connection with the application of many statutes. Constitutional issues are *sui generis* but the demands they place on courts have some affinity with those presented by the common law. The resulting tendency to apply the techniques of common law adjudication in constitutional cases when it seems useful to do so is further encouraged by the third of the characteristics of common law legal systems: that, typically, constitutional cases are determined by the courts that also administer the rest of the law, under arrangements sometimes described as diffuse review (Saunders 2007, p. 11). Many of the judges in such courts often have extensive practical experience in the common law.[34] The circumstances in which they carry out their tasks emphasise the interdependence of the Constitution and the rest of the legal system: indeed, a court often applies both the Constitution and other sources of law in resolving an ostensibly constitutional case. From this perspective, the engagement of common law courts with foreign law in the course of constitutional adjudication can be understood as a process of bringing to bear on a constitutional problem a set of techniques with which judges are familiar and which have worked effectively in broadly similar contexts.

A final, potentially relevant characteristic of a common law legal system is its reliance on adversarial procedures. Constitutional questions typically come before a court in the context of a concrete dispute, which requires judicial resolution and involves two or more parties as antagonists. The legal representatives of the parties present arguments that are designed to further the cause of their respective clients as far as possible, consistently with their overriding obligations to the court, which include a duty to disclose all relevant domestic law (Ipp 1998, pp. 63, 67). The court determines the case largely, if not solely, by reference to the arguments raised by parties or amici curiae.[35] For present purposes it follows that foreign experience enters judicial deliberations primarily through arguments that are put to a court by others, which in turn are expected to be reflected in its reasons.

It may be noted in passing that the practice of citation of foreign law has become enmeshed with a wider concern on the part of courts about the proliferation of domestic authority through information technology. Some of the resulting attempts to manage both are illuminating for present purposes. In 2001, a practice direction for England and Wales identified cases decided in other jurisdictions as 'a valuable source of law', which nevertheless 'should not be cited without proper consideration of whether it does indeed add to the existing body of law' (1 WLR [2001], p. 100). In Singapore also, a practice direction of the Supreme Court requires counsel citing foreign authority to ensure that it 'will be of assistance to the development of local jurisprudence' (Supreme Court Practice Directions [2007]). The former direction has been criticised on the ground that it paints 'an unsophisticated picture of legal argument'.[36] These developments suggest, however, that if the problem of the volume of authority is not resolved, it may have a further impact on judicial use of comparative law, which may affect the process of common law reasoning itself.

The variations between common law states in attitudes towards the use of comparative law, noted in the earlier section, can be attributed in part to differences in their legal arrangements, under the broad umbrella of the common law. In the case of the United States, for example, relevant differences might include the limited jurisdiction of the Supreme Court in resolving disputes by reference to the common law and the proliferation of precedents from multiple jurisdictions within the United States, which was a catalyst for the rise and partial fall of controversial no-citation rules.[37]

As debate in both the United States and Singapore suggests, however, opposition in common law states to the use of comparative law in constitutional cases also reflects a particular view of the Constitution as a distinctive instrument serving distinctively national needs. What is sometimes described as an expressivist view of the Constitution[38] may be triggered by textual considerations or by a range of other internal factors: in the United States these include contestation over originalism as the appropriate approach to constitutional interpretation and in Singapore they include a concern to preclude undue influence of what are claimed to be western values on the interpretation of the Constitution of an Asian state (Thiruvengadam 2009, pp. 114, 121). In its most extreme form, this view goes not merely to the methodology of judicial references to comparative law, but precludes its use.[39] In this event, it challenges the legitimacy of engagement with comparative constitutional law and will be taken up again in that context in section 5, below.

3.2   Civil Law

The corresponding characteristics of civil law legal systems differ in significant respects, which can be identified only at a general level, given considerable variations in both theory and practice between civil law states.[40]

First, the determination of legal questions relies to a greater extent on deduction from a written, legislated text as the source of the general law. On this basis, the role of the judge is more clearly delineated than in a common law system and the sources of legal reference are apparently more confined.[41] This form of positivism places a premium on legal certainty. Consistently with the conception of the role of a judge, moreover, there is no formal doctrine of binding precedent. In fact, the judicial function in civil law systems is much more complex and nuanced than this stylised account would suggest. Judges necessarily reach beyond legislated texts in search of solutions to legal problems that are not covered by them, in ways that demand creativity and potentially enhance the relevance of foreign legal experience.[42] Prior decisions are followed in the interests of consistency and fairness, to the point where they may be regarded as having normative force.[43] But the core assumptions about the role of a judge and the sources of law remain influential for present purposes. One consequence is a distinctive style of reasoning, which tends to draw on principle rather than on similarities and differences between particular factual situations and thus relies relatively little on analogy. This approach to the determination and application of law does not encourage fine distinctions to be drawn between judicial pronouncements that have normative force and those that do not in the form of the dichotomy either between ratio and obiter or between binding and persuasive authority.[44]

These features of civilian adjudication in turn affect the form and substance of judicial reasons for decision. Length and style differs between jurisdictions, from the brief and syllogistic decisions in the French tradition to the more discursive German judgments.[45] Typically, however, judicial reasons are formal, legalistic and 'magisterial' in tone.[46] In this case, practical as well as theoretical considerations inhibit reference to comparative experience. A civil law court also is more likely to deliver a single judgment, without opportunity for concurring reasons or dissents.

Again as a generalisation, these features of civilian judicial reasoning are less pronounced in constitutional adjudication. In part this is attributable to the nature of constitutions: their generality; the subject matter with which they deal; the expectation of longevity, whether realised or not. Ironically, difference in style is facilitated in this tradition by another feature more often found in civil law states: a specialist constitutional court, providing concentrated constitutional review.[47] Such courts may elaborate their reasons at greater length, in terms that are less legalistic and more explicitly oriented to principle. Multiple sets of reasons are more common and determinations are more likely formally to be binding on other courts, further encouraging persuasive reasoning. A different mode of appointment to courts of this kind ensures broader membership, which often includes a proportion of scholars with an interest and some expertise in comparative law.

Constitutional adjudication thus expands the opportunities for engagement with foreign experience. There are reports that such references are increasing, under the influence of internationalisation and globalisation, including the evolution of supra-national arrangements. One influential scholar, Peter Haberle, has suggested comparative law as an additional interpretative technique.[48] On the other hand, underlying theoretical assumptions, acquired habits of reasoning and established practices continue to limit explicit engagement with comparative law and to structure the way in which it occurs. Thus Bryde reports that 'the German Constitutional Court has developed a style of reasoning where it basically cites only its own precedents'.[49] And in Argentina, where references to decisions of the Supreme Court of the United States have been a long-established feature of constitutional jurisprudence, scholars express concern about the effects of a lack of training in 'the handling of precedents as a source of decisions' (Spector 2008, pp. 129, 130).[50]

The final characteristic, which also varies between states, concerns the process of litigation. Where constitutional adjudication is concentrated in a specialist court, access to review may be limited to specified public officials or to the presentation of a constitutional question by another court in which a constitutional issue has been raised over which it does not have complete jurisdiction. In the former case, review takes place in the abstract and the parties, such as they are, have a systemic interest in the outcome. Even in the latter, the Constitutional Court decides the question but not the concrete case. Again, there are signs of change: some decentralisation of judicial authority to deal with claims of unconstitutionality;[51] recognition of the rights of parties in the court below to present argument to the Constitutional Court;[52] adoption of procedures to enable complaints by individuals where infringement of constitutional rights is alleged.[53] Procedures born of an inquisitorial rather than an adversarial tradition nevertheless remain in place. These provide alternative avenues by which comparative experience may be introduced into the deliberations of the Court and reflected in its work. Where a rapporteur is assigned to prepare the case for consideration by the court as a whole, foreign constitutional experience may be taken into account in ways that do not appear on the public record: the *votum* prepared by a rapporteur for the German Constitutional Court is an example.[54] Inquisitorial procedures also enable a court to seek advice from experts on comparative experience in ways that would not be feasible in a common law appellate court.[55] In Taiwan, for example, the Constitutional Court may hold expert meetings in which scholars give their views on aspects of comparative constitutional experience relevant to a question before the court, at which the petitioners are not necessarily present (Constitutional Court of Taiwan 2010).[56]

Not all states that are broadly in the civil law tradition have specialist Constitutional Courts. The most common alternative is a system of diffuse review, typically influenced by the United States model. Of the cases singled out for special attention in this chapter, both Argentina and Japan fall within this category. As noted in the earlier section, however, the Supreme Court of the former engages freely with comparative law, while that of the latter does not. These examples therefore suggest that the choice of diffuse or concentrated review alone does not explain differences in preparedness to refer to foreign law.

Another obvious factor in play in the case of Argentina is its long fascination with the Constitution of the United States on which the Argentine Constitution of 1853 was modelled, leading to a practice of treating decisions of the Supreme Court of the United States as, effectively, binding (Miller 1997, p. 1483). This unusual reaction appears to have been prompted by a desire to fill a perceived gap in the available law in the aftermath of the adoption of a new Constitution in the interests of legal certainty, coupled with the prestige of the United States Constitution in 19th-century Latin America.[57] If this is correct, civil law values themselves are part of the explanation. The practice in Japan, on the other hand, lies closer to the traditional civil law norm and thus might be considered unremarkable. It has been suggested nevertheless that there are internal factors that explain the general passivity of the Supreme Court of Japan in judicial review, which include, for example, the influence of pre-enactment scrutiny by the prestigious Cabinet Legislation Bureau (Satoh 2008, pp. 603, 605).[58] Barriers to the accessibility of foreign case law, including language, may be part of the explanation as well.

There are considerable variations in explicit engagement with comparative law even amongst jurisdictions with a specialist constitutional court. The Constitutional Court of

Hungary offers an example from the cases in this study but the point could be illustrated also by other cases, including the courts of Spain and Indonesia. These may be explained in several ways that are not necessarily mutually exclusive. First, they may be a manifestation of a general tendency for procedures for constitutional review to converge in the conditions of globalisation and internationalisation that marked the turn of the 21st century, at least to the extent of providing more explicit reasons for decision. Secondly, such cases may also illustrate usage of comparative constitutional law in order to augment the authority of a new Constitutional Court and assist to establish its place in the constitutional order. Thus Dupré has argued that the importation of foreign constitutional experience in the early years of the Hungarian Constitutional Court was strategically important in establishing a new constitutionalism in a post-authoritarian state that was still using its old Constitution, albeit in amended form.[59]

3.3   Hypotheses

Examination of the context in which constitutional adjudication takes place suggests the following hypotheses.

First, there are features of the process of adjudication that, as a generalisation, are associated with common law and civil law legal systems respectively that assist to explain differences in the extent of explicit reference to foreign constitutional experience in judicial reasoning. Absence of citation of foreign law does not necessarily reflect the extent of foreign constitutional influence, which may be unacknowledged or to which reference may be made at other stages of the decision-making process, which do not always form part of the public record.

Secondly, reluctance to engage explicitly with comparative law may be attributable to characteristics of the legal system or may reflect the dominance of a particularistic view of the Constitution and thus of the relevance of comparative experience to interpreting all or parts of it.

Thirdly, there is a tendency towards some convergence of the conception of judicial review on grounds of constitutionality, which is contributing to an increase in explicit engagement with comparative law. The precise contribution that comparative law plays depends on the conventions of the local reasoning process.

Finally, courts in states that have recently undergone significant constitutional change may have a greater incentive to engage with comparative law, either to increase the authority of the new constitutional regime or as a source of guidance in interpreting the new Constitution as local jurisprudence develops.

4   THE CONTRIBUTION OF COMPARATIVE LAW

4.1   Precedential Value

In assessing the contribution of comparative law to constitutional adjudication it is convenient to deal with its status in the law of the jurisdiction concerned as a preliminary matter.

A rule represents law for those obliged by law to comply with it. Courts of an independent state are not legally obliged to comply with decisions of the courts of other states or with foreign constitutional rules. Rather, as Dupré has shown in relation to Hungary, a court that engages with foreign law voluntarily imports it, often adapting it in the process.[60] Foreign law is used to assist with the process of local decision-making and at best represents persuasive, rather than binding, authority. Its value depends on its substance rather than on the source from which it derives. This understanding of the precedential weight of foreign law is critical to the assessment of the legitimacy of reference to it and is potentially relevant also to consideration of comparative method.

It has been suggested that this dichotomy oversimplifies the problem because the boundary between binding and persuasive authority is not so clear-cut. Schauer has argued, for example, that the manner in which foreign law is used in practice often places considerable weight on the source paying relatively little attention to substance, at least in the sense of supporting argument (Schauer 2008, p. 1935). Conversely, precedents that are binding in theory can often be evaded in practice or, in extreme cases, overturned by courts of final jurisdiction. The perspective that sources of legal authority lie along a continuum suggests that the normative force of foreign law can be underestimated (ibid, pp. 1950–51). And, so the argument goes, even if the binding quality of authority is retained as the tipping point, the historical development of the doctrine of precedent shows that citation practice can sometimes harden into law (ibid, p. 1958).

As the previous section shows, from the perspective of global constitutional law, the line between binding and persuasive authority may be even finer than Schauer describes. Schauer is correct also that there are certain usages of comparative law that attach considerable significance to the source, in some instances to the exclusion of consideration of substance. Three examples may be given. First, in rare instances, the courts of one state may accept the decisions of a court of another as effectively binding. Historically, this was the case in Argentina, where the Supreme Court followed decisions of the Supreme Court of the United States, even when its own previous decisions suggested a different outcome.[61] It is clear that this practice was linked with the genetic relationship between the two Constitutions (Choudhry 1999, pp. 819, 838),[62] but it is possible to envisage circumstances in which the courts of one state have other incentives to automatically follow particular foreign law.[63] Secondly, source becomes critical in a different way where a court refers to foreign experience to demonstrate that, in practice, it is the norm, with the implication that it therefore should be followed. On at least some versions of this usage, what counts is the prevalence of the experience, or aggregate numbers, rather than individual substantive reasons for it. A range of examples of this kind of reasoning is provided in the opinion of the Supreme Court in *Roper v Simmons* (543 US [2005], p. 551), although the finding in *Roper* itself that the United States was the 'only country in the world that continues to give official sanction to the juvenile death penalty' was used only as 'respected and significant confirmation' of the Court's own conclusions (543 US [2005], pp. 551, 577, 578). Thirdly, in a closely related usage, a court may adopt a principle on the basis that it has universal application. In the case of Hungary, for example, human dignity was claimed as an element of 'modern' constitutions.[64]

These usages represent only a small proportion of the ways in which courts engage with comparative constitutional law. Reaction to them, when they are employed, is likely to depend on local conventions of judicial reasoning. A legal culture that is accustomed to deductive reasoning, for example, is more likely to be comfortable with a claim that a principle is universal than a culture used to the development of principles by a process of induction. The critical point for present purposes, however, is that, irrespective of the manner in which a court engages with foreign law, in no case is that law legally binding on the court concerned. In each case, the court has a choice whether to engage with foreign law or not. This distinction has consequences, including the following. Foreign law may lose its authority as a source, as local jurisprudence develops.[65] A foreign source may be freely adapted to local purposes.[66] An international legal consensus represents only a guide, although one which Waldron suggests may be more scientific and thus less susceptible to manipulation than reference to individual foreign jurisdictions (Waldron 2005–06, pp. 129, 144). The obligations of counsel to the court differ, in relation to the citation of foreign law.

4.2   Manner of Engagement

The manner in which foreign experience is used in constitutional adjudication is relevant both to assessment of legitimacy and to evaluation of methodology. This part focuses only on the practice of courts that make explicit reference to comparative law. Even within this group, however, practice varies dramatically. This section examines usage along several different axes: the broad purposes of recourse to foreign law; the role of foreign law in the reasoning process; the circumstances in which a court is likely to engage with foreign law.

It may be useful first to make some general observations about categorisation, both because of the diversity of the approaches that may be taken and because the difficulty of the exercise also offers insight into the manner in which courts collectively engage with foreign law. The controversy over engagement with foreign law that erupted in the United States in the 1990s prompted many attempts at categorisation in order better to understand this diffuse phenomenon. These came at the problem from a variety of perspectives, reflecting its multi-faceted character. Thus in an early contribution to the field, Mark Tushnet adopted an approach based on comparative methods, distinguishing between functionalism, expressivism and bricolage, subsequently elaborating the first two by distinguishing between normative universalism and functionalism on the one hand and simple contextualism and expressivism on the other (Tushnet 1999, p. 1226; Tushnet 2007). In another influential, early contribution, Sujit Choudhry identified three 'modes' of comparative constitutional interpretation as universalist, dialogical and genealogical,[67] each of which is directed to the rationale for judicial reference to comparative law, including the assumptions on which the practice is based. More recently, Vicki Jackson has proposed a categorisation based partly on the weight that courts accord to foreign law, distinguishing for this purpose between convergence, resistance and engagement (Jackson 2005, p. 109; Jackson 2010).

In one way or another, these and other categorisations that have been proposed[68] feed into an understanding of the purposes of recourse to foreign law. At the most general level, it is possible to identify at least two broad purposes that the practice serves. First, foreign constitutional experience sometimes is used in a functionalist manner to assist in resolving problems that appear to be shared, the answers to which might have universal or at least transnational application. For obvious reasons, foreign experience is more likely to be used in this way to resolve questions about rights, particularly where constitutional rights also are reflected in international norms, but this method of use can assist with the resolution of institutional questions as well.[69] Secondly, comparative constitutional law can assist constitutional self-understanding by, for example, providing new ways of thinking about old problems[70] or identifying dimensions of local experience that are distinctive by contrast with others.[71] It follows that exposure to foreign experience can perform a useful function whether it ultimately is applied or rejected. But these two broad purposes by no means account for all the instances in which courts make reference to foreign law. As the earlier examples of categorisation suggest, any schema that purports to cover the practice comprehensively is driven to providing for a 'catch-all' category. Tushnet's bricolage, Choudhry's dialogue and Jackson's engagement can also be seen in this light.[72]

Whatever the purposes of recourse to foreign law, it may play different roles in the reasoning process and be invoked at many different stages. Depending on the question for decision, for example, comparative law can assist in clarifying the nature of the problem or any aspect of it;[73] identifying options for the resolution of any of the issues before the court;[74] exemplifying the application of constitutional standards;[75] exploring the consequences of particular solutions;[76] confirming a tentative conclusion.[77] In any of these cases, some references to foreign law will have a more substantive effect on the outcome than others; from this point of view usage can be ranged along a spectrum between the constructive application of foreign law in legal argument to inspirational or cosmetic use.[78] References to foreign law are made not only to assist in the resolution of core questions before a court, which typically require decisions to be made about the interpretation and application of constitutional text and structure. They may be used also in the course of resolving a range of other questions that arise in the course of adjudication, including the determination of approaches to interpretation[79] and the formulation of remedies,[80] and the scope of the judicial role.[81]

Finally, it is possible to generalise, cautiously, about the circumstances in which a court is more likely to have recourse to comparative law. Empirical evidence suggests that new courts or courts dealing with new Constitutions are likely to engage with comparative law but that engagement will lessen, although not necessarily cease, as local jurisprudence becomes established. By extension, even established courts dealing with established constitutions may derive assistance from foreign constitutional experience in resolving questions to which local jurisprudence provides no clear answer. As in relation to the manner of use, so the timing of use also has attracted attempts at categorisation, with an eye to the United States debate (Marshall 2004, p. 1633; Sitaraman 2009, p. 32).[82] Typically, there is broad consensus that reference to foreign law may be helpful and appropriate where local law yields no clear answer but becomes increasingly problematic where local law is relatively settled and foreign experience diverges from it. Thus stated, this is merely an application of the obvious proposition that judges are bound by local law and that comparative law, by contrast, is an aid in the adjudicative process. Even in the more nuanced form in which they appear in the literature, however, such analyses are at best a rough guide, which cannot take adequate account of the multifarious purposes and methods that characterise the engagement by courts with comparative constitutional law.

5 LEGITIMACY

5.1 A Compound Question

Some criticisms of judicial engagement with foreign constitutional law question the legitimacy of the practice and thus challenge references to foreign law as a matter of principle. These criticisms are based on two different sets of considerations, which are not always clearly distinguished. One set concerns the role of a judge and thus depends on the conventions of the legal system in which the question arises. The other draws specifically on the character of Constitutions, including the particular problems of constitutional interpretation. At the margins, both shade into other aspects of the topic. The legitimacy of recourse to foreign law inevitably is dependent on the role that it plays in the judicial deliberative process. Even where judicial engagement with foreign constitutional experience is unquestioned in principle, its legitimacy in a particular case may depend on the adequacy of the comparative method employed by the court, in the light of the purpose for which foreign experience was used.

5.2   Concerns Derived from the Legal System

The legitimacy of judicial engagement with foreign law may be questioned in legal systems in which the traditional understanding of the role of the judge has a continuing inhibiting effect on the citation of authority and discursive judicial reasoning, despite changes in interpretive theory. Objection to citation of foreign law is less likely in legal systems in which the judicial task traditionally is expected to involve engagement with previous experience in order to determine and, within limits, to develop the applicable law.

Even in this latter situation, however, the legitimacy of engagement with foreign law depends on the degree of reliance on it. The example of Argentina, to which reference was made earlier, suggests that what is acceptable may vary between states and over time. Nevertheless, as a generalisation, foreign legal experience can be no more than persuasive and frequently will play an even less direct role in the reasoning process. Foreign law thus may be an aid, but local law is determinative and supplies the boundaries within which it is used. What this means in practice will depend on the question before the court, the degree of determinacy of local law and, perhaps, local understanding of the judicial role, but the general proposition is clear.

One of innumerable examples that might be given to illustrate the point is provided by the reasons of the Court of Appeal of Botswana in 2009 in upholding the constitutional immunity of a serving President from civil suit.[83] The Court referred to South African authority both to confirm the presumption to be applied in construing the section of the Constitution in question and to reject argument for a more purposive approach to align the Constitution with what the applicant claimed were democratic values. But the Court rejected an argument that it should consider constitutional experience elsewhere 'in order to determine whether the Botswana provision is too favourable to the President' in circumstances where the meaning of the Constitution was 'perfectly clear'. On this point also it referred to foreign authority, citing with approval the reasons of Chaskalson P in *Makwanyane*:

> In dealing with comparative law we must bear in mind that we are required to construe the South African Constitution, and not ... the constitution of some foreign country, and that this has to be done with due regard to our legal system, our history and circumstances, and the structure and language of our own Constitution. We can derive assistance from ... foreign case law, but we are in no way bound to follow it.[84]

Writing in the wake of *Roper* and in the context of the United States debate on judicial engagement with foreign law, Waldron has urged the need for a theory to explain the practice and assist in evaluating its use.[85] To this end, he has proposed a reconceptualisation of the notion of *ius gentium*, understood as a legal consensus between appropriate categories of nations on contemporary solutions to particularly 'intractable' problems, which might be used to guide the 'elaboration' of local law (ibid, pp. 135, 139, 145).[86] Waldron's theory is unlikely to have easy purchase in states where reference to foreign law is unexceptionable in principle and in which a theory that relies on broad-based international consensus does not in any event explain the actual usage of foreign law. His argument draws attention however to the distinctiveness of the United States within the common law legal family, sharing a preference for what Glenn calls 'affirmative ideas' with the civil law (Glenn 2007, pp. 249–50).

5.3 Constitutional Complications

In some states, considerations stemming from the character of a Constitution affect the attitudes that otherwise are taken towards engagement with foreign law. On one hand, the more general and enduring nature of a constitutional instrument encourages a mode of discursive reasoning that may involve explicit, if careful, reference to foreign law in states where, normally, this is not the practice. Conversely, courts in states where there is no objection in principle to engagement with foreign law may baulk at its use in relation to constitutional questions, as the examples of the United States and Singapore show.

In this latter category of states, engagement with foreign law in the course of constitutional adjudication may be resisted on three types of grounds.

The first points to the character of the Constitution as a compact between members of a national democratic community which, it is argued, should be interpreted and applied by organs of the community that in turn are accountable to the sovereign people.[87] This appears to be the objection to which Chief Justice Roberts referred during his confirmation hearing when, reflecting on a hypothetical reference by the Supreme Court to the decision of a German judge, he observed that: '... no President accountable to the people appointed that judge, and no Senate accountable to the people confirmed that judge; and yet he's playing a role in shaping a law that binds the people in this country'.[88] The straightforward answer to this objection, formulated in this way, is that it overstates the way in which foreign law is used.[89] National judges are not obliged to engage with foreign law. When they do so they are accountable for its use in the ordinary way, which includes published reasons for decision. The associated arguments that, while current use is acceptable it paves the way for practices that mandate reference to foreign law or that acknowledge its binding status, are difficult to take seriously in the absence of any sign that either is likely to occur.[90]

A second set of arguments against engagement with foreign law in the course of constitutional adjudication draws attention to the distinctive character of a national Constitution. Every Constitution is made for a particular national community even if, as is usually the case, it incorporates features from elsewhere. Typically, a Constitution not only creates institutions and provides a legal framework within which they are supposed to operate but responds to and reflects the circumstances of the state community in a myriad of ways that distinguish it from other Constitutions and give it a role in the expression of national identity (Frankenberg 2006, p. 439).[91] For these reasons, it sometimes is suggested that foreign law cannot provide a useful guide to local constitutional interpretation. Thus in *Stanford*, Scalia J rejected the relevance of foreign experience in determining whether the execution of juveniles offended the Eighth Amendment prohibition of 'cruel and unusual punishment' on the ground that 'It is American conceptions of decency that are dispositive'.[92] The rejection in Singapore of 'analogies drawn from other countries such as Great Britain, the United States or Australia'[93] can be understood in the same way. While this aspect of Constitutions is significant for constitutional comparison, it does not necessarily preclude reference to foreign law in principle but goes rather to the adequacy of comparative method and will be considered again in that context.

A third objection to judicial reference to foreign constitutional experience is linked to interpretive method. One of the most intractable and contentious problems in constitutional law is the approach that should be taken to the interpretation of an instrument that takes the form of a legal text but is written in general terms; which is intended to last for a long period of time; and which trumps some decisions of current democratic majorities. Those who would resolve this problem by relying on the meaning of the Constitution at the time of promulgation in accordance with a theory of originalism are less likely to accept the relevance of foreign experience after that date for the purposes of constitutional interpretation. Even on this basis, however, an original understanding may show that the Constitution was intended to evolve over time in a way to which foreign experience may be relevant[94] or simply that foreign experience was intended to be taken into account in the course of constitutional interpretation.[95] And, in any event, originalism is only one of a number of interpretive theories. Others, typically, allow for adaptation and change over time, in varying degrees and offer no objection in principle to engagement with foreign law.[96]

6   COMPARATIVE METHOD

6.1   Significance

From the perspective of global practice, the methodology that courts use in engaging with foreign constitutional experience is at least as important as the issue of legitimacy. As the discussion in the previous section showed, the legitimacy of citation of foreign authority by a court may depend on whether its approach is capable of taking adequate account of relevant distinctive features of both local constitutional arrangements and those of a foreign comparator. The practice of referring to foreign constitutional experience is growing, in terms not only of the number of jurisdictions that engage in it but also of the range of comparators on which courts draw. In many and perhaps most cases, the value of engagement with foreign law depends on the reliability of the methods employed.

In principle, engagement with foreign law in the course of constitutional adjudication raises all the standard problems of comparative law:[97] the rationale for the choice of comparators; the challenge of comparing like with like, excluding extraneous factors; the difficulty of adequately taking account not only of constitutional context but also of culture, helpfully defined by Cotterrell to include beliefs and values; tradition, including historical experience; material culture including levels of technological and economic development; and 'emotional attachments and rejections' (Cotterrell 2008). Further complicating the exercise is the possibility of genuine disagreement about where the balance lies in each case between two opposing realities: on the one hand, shared, if general, values, which make comparison potentially fruitful[98] and on the other, the inevitability of local difference, often in critical respects.[99] Nor is the situation stable: there are forces for both convergence and divergence operating on the constitutional systems of the world of the 21st century.[100] Differences may be enduring but in some instances represent a phase in the emergence of a common norm.[101]

There is a question, however, about whether the demands of comparative method are affected by the context of adjudication. The question has practical significance. Courts do not have the time nor, in most cases, the opportunity to engage in elaborate comparative study. Their methods must be adequate; but if the methodological demands of engagement with foreign law are claimed to be too great, the practice will be abandoned and its benefits lost. Justice O'Regan of the Constitutional Court of South Africa articulated the dilemma well: courts must avoid 'shallow comparativism' but to 'forbid any comparative review because of [the risks associated with comparative method] would be to deprive our legal system of the benefits of the learning and wisdom to be found in other jurisdictions'.[102] The rest of this section argues that what is adequate in a particular case depends largely on the purpose for which foreign law is used, the weight accorded to it in the deliberative process and the conclusions to which it is taken to lead. In the common law jurisdictions in which the practice is most securely established, adversarial procedure, the acceptance of multiple judicial opinions and the publication of reasoned judgments provide additional safeguards against error or misuse.

6.2 Choice of Comparators

Courts are relatively unlikely to engage in scientific selection of the jurisdictions to which they refer.[103] Relevantly, in jurisdictions where courts are dependent on the arguments of parties, advocates also are unlikely to do so, although there is anecdotal evidence of an obligation for advocates who raise a jurisdiction in argument to refer the court to all relevant jurisprudence in that jurisdiction of which they are aware.[104] The selection of jurisdictions nevertheless must be justifiable in the light of the purpose of the reference to foreign law and the claims based on it.

The point can be illustrated by examples. Claims of universality or prevalence, whether express or implied, require attention to the pool of relevant comparators. Thus Chief Justice Burger's claim in *Bowers*[105] that condemnation of homosexual conduct was 'firmly rooted in Judeao-Christian moral and ethical standards' was vulnerable to Justice Kennedy's response in *Lawrence* that there were foreign authorities within the same broad tradition 'pointing in the opposite direction'.[106] On the other hand, reference to foreign constitutional experience that is designed simply to show that there is another way of tackling a particular problem, or to identify a range of options, does not require the same attention to coverage. Examination by President Chaskalson in *Makwanyane* of decisions on the constitutionality of the death penalty in the United States, Germany, India and Hungary and by the European Court of Human Rights did not raise concerns on the grounds of case selection when the purpose was to explore the arguments for and against the death penalty in a range of courts that had already dealt with the question to assist in determining the meaning of South Africa's own constitutional provision.[107] Justice Breyer's famous reference to selected European federations in *Printz* would have served to illustrate his point that there are other federations in which the constituent units administer federal laws had he not overlooked the broader constitutional context in which the practice occurs, which undermined the utility of the example.[108]

In circumstances of these kinds, reference to a small number of cases in the manner sometimes pejoratively described as 'cherry-picking' can make a helpful contribution to the judicial reasoning process.[109] The potential for the practice to be misleading if there are examples from other relevant jurisdictions to the contrary, however, reinforces the need for the purpose of the reference to be explained and circumscribed.[110]

While the bases on which comparators are chosen varies between cases, judges and jurisdictions, it is possible to make some generalisations about use.

First, comparators sometimes are identified as a group, in order to claim common or at least prevalent practice. The claim may be based on empirical evidence but often is merely rhetorical. Examples include references to 'the overwhelming weight of international opinion' extrapolated from practice in all countries of the world;[111] 'modern constitutions';[112] and 'other great democratic societies'.[113] If used in isolation, this technique relies for its effect on weight of numbers and precludes nuanced examination of relevant differences between particular states. It tends to be associated with expectations of universality and for that reason to be understood as making greater demands for local compliance than many other forms of engagement with foreign law. On the other hand, a claim for the relevance of a practice because it is universal may be more acceptable in some legal cultures than analogical use of the constitutional experience of another state;[114] if it is empirically based, it also can be portrayed as more scientific than 'piecemeal' citation practice.[115]

Secondly, courts tend to refer to the constitutional experience of other states that are similar to their own in relevant ways. Language, legal system and shared constitutional assumptions are typically relevant factors; cultural context and economic development sometimes affect choice as well. Thus Australian courts refer primarily (although not exclusively) to experience in the United Kingdom, the United States, Canada and New Zealand; the Constitutional Court of Austria is likely to refer to German decisions, if it refers to foreign law at all (Gamper, 2009, p. 164); the Constitutional Court of South Africa refers to decisions from Canada, the United States, India and Germany, amongst others; and Anglophone African courts refer to decisions of South African courts. This pattern of behaviour has the practical advantage that it minimises the difficulties of adequately understanding foreign law, examined in the next section. As these examples suggest, similarity between jurisdictions sometimes is underpinned by genealogical or genetic relationships. While relationships of this kind also help to explain readiness to use foreign law, they serve primarily to identify a state or group of states that might be useful and accessible comparators.

Thirdly, it is apparent that a range of other factors also may be in play in selecting comparator jurisdictions. The prestige of a court in terms of the recognised quality of its jurisprudence is a significant factor, particularly in states in constitutional transition, as newly established courts seek to ensure respect for their own decisions.[116] The influence of the Constitutional Court of Germany in central and eastern Europe can be understood in part on this basis;[117] reference commonly is made to decisions of the Supreme Court of the United States for the same reason. In some courts, the underlying knowledge and expertise of the judges is a factor of a different kind. Chang and Yeh, for example, report a correlation between citation practice in the Constitutional Court of Taiwan and the country in which particular justices undertook graduate study.[118] While explicit citation of foreign law is relatively uncommon in Taiwan, it seems likely that this factor also has a more general effect on the deliberations of the Court.[119]

6.3   Substance and Context

A second group of methodological issues underscores the challenge for a court in adequately grasping the constitutional experience of another state so as to draw conclusions for its own. The difficulty may be less when the court is dealing with questions about constitutional rights, to the extent that values are shared and the outcome is somewhat less likely to be affected by other features of constitutional design that complicate institutional comparison.[120] Even in this context, however, there may be local cultural differences or institutional factors relevant to the conclusions drawn from foreign experience.[121] The difficulties of comparison potentially range from adequately understanding the law of another state through appreciating the interdependence of a particular experience with other aspects of the legal and constitutional system to evaluating any relevant impact of the cultural context from which the foreign experience arose. Conclusions drawn from references to foreign law may be flawed if relevant differences are overlooked.[122] If differences are exaggerated, on the other hand, the potential benefit of comparative insight is lost.[123]

As with the choice of comparator, the significance of these methodological considerations often depends on the purpose for which foreign experience is used. Depth of understanding is more important if substantial weight is placed on a particular foreign experience to provide or test a solution. Thus, in *Printz,* failure to take account of the structural design of the European federations was fatal to their relevance to assist in the resolution of a problem of United States federalism by showing that local administration of federal laws was a familiar practice elsewhere.[124] But even the somewhat softer, dialogic, use of foreign experience calls for a relatively sophisticated comparative method in order to explore the underlying assumptions of two constitutional systems so as to better understand one's own, in making interpretive choices.[125] Arguably, in these circumstances, no harm is done from the perspective of the quality of the final decision if the comparator jurisdiction is not fully understood. Nevertheless, a flawed understanding of foreign experience matters: the reasons of the court are less persuasive and the engagement with foreign law loses its educative value. And the same applies to the rejection of foreign experience on the basis of inadequate comparative analysis. In these circumstances, not only is the reasoning of the court unsound, but the opportunity for insight from comparative experience is lost.

As a generalisation, judges are equipped by their legal training to be conscious of legal context in identifying and evaluating authorities that may assist to resolve the case before them. This training serves them in good stead in making allowance for legal and constitutional difference in drawing on foreign constitutional experience as well. Their training equips them less well to identify wider contextual and cultural differences, which also are less likely to be drawn to their attention by the parties. Even so, it is not uncommon to find distinctions being drawn on the basis of considerations of these kinds.[126] Typically, the methodological hazards of engagement with foreign law are reduced by a tendency for judges to rely on familiar jurisdictions and to be wary of placing undue weight on foreign examples in the reasoning process.[127] The potential for error nevertheless further underscores the significance of transparency in explaining the relevance of foreign experience in published reasons.[128]

7   CONCLUSIONS

Constitutional ideas have never been confined by state borders. Judicial decisions on the meaning and application of Constitutions are one means by which fertilisation occurs. In the early part of the 21st century, variations in the extent to which national courts explicitly refer to foreign experience and in the manner in which they do so make this a case study in comparative constitutional law in its own right. Even in courts where explicit reference to foreign law is rare, evidence of engagement with foreign experience can often be detected in the jurisprudence of a court and is sometimes confirmed by extra-curial observations.

Explicit engagement with foreign constitutional experience is increasing, by reference both to the number of states in which the practice is used and to the variety of jurisdictions to which reference is made. This may be explained in various ways; the greater accessibility of foreign experience; some convergence of understanding of the role of a court in constitutional review; the incentives and opportunities provided by globalisation and internationalisation; growing acceptance of the benefits of transparency. The movement is not all one way, however. The usage is, properly, less where there is an established local jurisprudence on the question before the court or where features of local constitutional understanding are deemed to diminish the relevance of comparative experience. An additional factor, which may become increasingly significant in the future, is the volume of domestic precedents with which courts must deal.

Recent debate on judicial engagement with foreign law reveals two broad challenges to the practice. One, which disputes its legitimacy, can be met by the manner in which foreign experience is used. Despite the vigour with which this question has been canvassed in the United States, it has met with bemusement elsewhere. It seems unlikely that it can be sustained in the longer term.

But the debate on legitimacy has drawn attention to the second challenge, of the extent to which a court adequately understands the foreign experience on which it draws and makes sufficient allowance for relevant difference. Evaluation of the comparative methodology of courts is complicated by the variety of ways in which they use foreign experience, some of which involve aggregation and thus preclude consideration of difference and some of which make depth of comparative understanding less significant. On the other hand, in each case, the methodology employed must be adequate to the purpose, in order both to take advantage of the insight that foreign experience offers and to enhance the explanatory value of the reasons of the court.

Until recently, judicial reasoning received relatively little attention from the standpoint of comparative method. More critical scrutiny can be expected in the future, whether courts draw on foreign experience or reject it. The methodological bar need be set no higher than is necessary to obtain the benefit of foreign experience in the development of national constitutional jurisprudence and the resolution of national constitutional problems. Even so, it will call for reasoned attention to similarity and difference and precise articulation of how and why foreign law is used.

NOTES

1. *Printz v United States* 521 US 898 (1997); *Knight v Florida* 528 US 990 (1999); *Atkins v Virginia* 536 US 304 (2002); *Lawrence v Texas* 539 US 558 (2003); *Roper v Simmons* 543 US 551 (2005); *Florida v Graham* (2010). In a seventh case, *Grutter v Bollinger* 539 US 306 (2003), reference was made to international, but not foreign, law.
2. In both cases the opinion was that of Justice Breyer.
3. For a recent overview of the arguments, which also contains reference to the voluminous literature, see Mark Tushnet, 'When is Knowing Less Better than Knowing More? Unpacking the Controversy over Supreme Court Reference to Non-US Law' 90 *Minnesota Law Review*, 1275 (2006). What Tushnet characterises as theory based and expressivist criticisms both go to the issue of legitimacy; the concerns that he lists under quality control go to the issue of methodology.

4. Most notably, the International Association of Constitutional Law established a research group on The Use of Foreign Precedents by Constitutional Judges at the World Congress in 2007. The work of this group is expected to be published in 2011 as T. Groppi and M.-C. Ponthoreau (eds), *Constitutional Cross-fertilization: The Use of Foreign Precedents by Constitutional Judges* (London: Hart Publishing). See also Sir Basil Markesinis and Jorg Fedtke, *Judicial Recourse to Foreign Law* (New York: Routledge-Cavendish, 2006), with commentaries by jurists from South Africa, Israel, Germany, France, United Kingdom and the European Union.

5. Brun-Otto Bryde, 'The Constitutional Judge and the International Constitutionalist Dialogue', in Markesinis and Fedtke, op. cit., 295, 298.

6. France is an example of the former: compare the discussion of references to foreign law in Guy Canivet, 'The Practice of Comparative Law by the Supreme Courts', in Markesinis and Fedtke, op. cit., 309 and the discussion of the status of international law in Elisabeth Zoller, *Introduction to Public Law: A Comparative Study* (Leiden: Martinus Nijhoff Publishers, 2008), 222–3. Australia is an example of the latter, in which foreign law is used relatively freely but reference to international law is restricted: Cheryl Saunders, 'The Use and Misuse of Comparative Constitutional Law', 13 *Indiana Journal of Global Legal Studies* 37 (2006).

7. Christos L. Rozakis, 'The European Judge as Comparatist', in Markesinis and Fedtke, op. cit., 338, 351, describing the ECHR as 'par excellence, a comparatist court'.

8. Poirier refers by way of example to a decision of the Constitutional Court of Belgium, which referred to a decision of the ECHR, which in turn referred to decisions of Canadian and South African courts: CC 187/2005, 14 December 2005, referring to *Hirst v UK no. 2* ECHR (GC), 6 October 2005.

9. In reality South Africa has a mixed legal system, which also makes it a useful choice: Laurie W.H. Ackermann, 'Constitutional Comparativism in South Africa', in Markesinis and Fedtke, op. cit., 263, 268.

10. States with mixed systems of Islamic law are an obvious omission. Some insight into the potential for dialogue over the constitutionalisation of the Sharia, can be gleaned from Clark Benner Lombardi, 'Islamic Law as a Source of Constitutional Law in Eqypt: The Constitutionalization of the Sharia in a Modern Islamic State' 37 *Columbia Journal of Transnational Law* 81 (1998–1999).

11. Markesinis and Fedtke, op. cit., 77; the observation that the German Constitutional Court 'rarely cites … other courts', comes from Bryde, op. cit., 297.

12. Chang and Yeh report a much higher incidence of citation in individual opinions: 74, representing 13.4% of such opinions. The vast majority of these appeared in footnotes, rather than in the body of the text.

13. The data are on file with the author. They do not distinguish between the citation of sources that precede the enactment of the Constitution and those that come later; the incidence of citation of the latter nevertheless is high.

14. The quotation is from Aharon Barak, 'Comparison in Public Law', in Markesinis and Fedtke, op. cit., 287, 292.

15. These figures include references to the ECHR. Szente notes that the proportion of references is higher, at 22.32%, if certain categories of unlikely cases are excluded.

16. On the adoption of the four walls doctrine, see *Chan Hiang Leng Colin v Public Prosecutor* (1994) 3 SLR 662, 681, citing *Government of the State of Kelantan v Government of the Federation of Malaya* [1963] MLJ 355.

17. Adam M. Smith, 'Making itself at Home – Understanding Foreign Law in Domestic Jurisprudence: The Indian Case', 24 *Berkeley Journal of International Law* 218, 239 (2006) estimating reference to foreign law by the Supreme Court of India in an average 24.6% of constitutional cases between 1950 and 2004; Bijon Roy, 'An Empirical Survey of Foreign Jurisprudence and International Instruments in Charter Litigation', 62 *University of Toronto Faculty of Law Review* 99 (2004), 125, noting references to foreign law in 34 out of 402 Charter decisions of the Supreme Court of Canada between 1998 and 2003.

18. Poirier, op. cit.; Gamper (2009), 155.

19. *State of Kelantan v Government of the Federation of Malaya* [1963] MLJ 355.

20. Bryde, op. cit., 296. Markesinis and Fedtke, op. cit., identify 24 decisions of the German Constitutional Court citing foreign law between 1951 and 1974.

21. For example, Ran Hirschl, 'On the blurred methodological matrix', in Choudhry, *The Migration of Constitutional Ideas*, op. cit., 39, 42–43.

22. As a rough estimate, 91 new Constitutions or constitutional-type instruments for states and other distinct polities have come into force since 1990: Central Intelligence Agency, The World Factbook, https://www.cia.gov/library/publications/the-world-factbook/index.html (last visited 17 December 2009). Non-state polities included in these figures include Hong Kong and Macao.

23. See, for example, the World Conference on Constitutional Justice held under the auspices of the European Commission for Democracy through Law (the Venice Commission) in 2009: http://www.venice.coe.int/WCCJ/WCCJ_E.asp (viewed 1 January 2010).

24. As a result of this process, Peters has argued that national constitutions are now only part of a 'compound constitutional system' supplemented by international law. See Anne Peters, 'The Globalization of State

Constitutions', in J. Nijman and A. Nollkaemper (eds), *New Perspectives on the Divide between National and International Law* (New York: Oxford University Press, 2007), 251, 257.

25. Bryde, op. cit., suggests that in such cases the 'text of the national constitution cannot be understood without comparative analysis': 306.

26. For example, the Hong Kong Court of Final Appeal Ordinance 1997 authorises the Court to invite judges from other common law jurisdictions to sit on the Court as a member of the Court.

27. See the discussion in Adrienne Stone, 'Comparativism in Constitutional Interpretation', [2009] *New Zealand Law Review* 45, 51 ff, analysing the reasons of Heydon J in *Roach v Electoral Commissioner* (2007) 233 CLR 162.

28. On the continued citation to a wide range of foreign sources, however, see Jan Kleinheisterkamp, 'Comparative Law in Latin America', in Mathias Reimann and Reinhard Zimmermann, *The Oxford Handbook of Comparative Law* (Oxford: Oxford University Press, 2006), 262, 298.

29. For a sophisticated account of the role of analogy in the common law see Gerald J. Postema, 'A Similibus ad Similia: Analogical Thinking in Law', in Douglas E. Edlin (ed.), *Common Law Theory* (Cambridge: Cambridge University Press, 2007), 102, 116 ff.

30. The reasoning process is described in practical context by Lord Diplock in *Home Office v Dorset Yacht Co* [1970] AC 1004, 1058–60. For a description of the combination of 'principled, deductive analysis' with 'the inductive, empirical, case-by-case methodology' of Anglo-Saxon common law in the mixed legal system of South Africa, see Ackermann, op. cit., 265–6.

31. For a more comprehensive analysis see Zenon Bankowski, D. Neil MacCormick and Geoffrey Marshall, 'Precedent in the United Kingdom', in D. Neil MacCormick and Robert S. Summers (eds), *Interpreting Precedents* (Hants, England: Ashgate Publishing, 1997), 315, 321–3.

32. David Dyzenhaus and Michael Taggart, 'Reasoned Decisions and Legal Theory', in Edlin, op. cit., 134, 152.

33. Guy Canivet, 'The Practice of Comparative Law by the Supreme Courts: Brief Reflections on the Dialogue between the Judges in French and European Experience' in Markesinis and Fedtke, op. cit., 309, 315.

34. South Africa is an exception to the extent that it has a specialist Constitutional Court, with distinctive procedures for appointment and tenure. Other courts also can decide most constitutional questions, however, and the Constitutional Court engages extensively with the general law as raising 'issues connected with decisions on constitutional matters' (Constitution s.167(3)(b)) under a system in which 'all law … derives its force from the Constitution and is subject to constitutional control': *Pharmaceutical Manufacturers Association of South Africa; In re; ex parte President of the Republic of South Africa* 2000 (2) SA 674 (CC) [44], Chaskalson P.

35. Use of amici also varies between national legal systems: see for example Kirby J, reflecting on the relatively parsimonious Australian approach: 'Even if the practice in the United States is considered disharmonious with our legal system in this regard, the practice in England and Canada should not be', *Attorney-General (Commonwealth) v Breckler*, (1999) 197 CLR 83, 133.

36. Roderick Munday, 'Over-citation: Stemming the Tide', 166 *Justice of the Peace* 6 (2002), quoted in Catherine P. Best, 'Everything is Old Again: The Proliferation of Case Law and Whether There is a Remedy', 17 October 2007, http://legalresearch.org/docs/Proliferation_paper.pdf (viewed 2 July 2010).

37. Best, op. cit., 10–15. Best describes the adoption of 'no publication' and 'no citation' rules by both federal and state courts from the early 1970s, largely in the interests of efficiency, and their decline in the early years of the 21st century, in part in consequence of the easy availability of case law in electronic form. See now Fed. R. App. P. 32.1.

38. For early reference to expressivism in the context of comparative constitutional law see Mark Tushnet, 'The Possibilities of Comparative Constitutional Law', 108 *Yale Law Journal* 1225 (1999).

39. Neither originalism nor the 'four walls' doctrine in Singapore necessarily precludes engagement with comparative law: see respectively Tushnet, *Minnesota Law Review* (2006), op. cit. and Jack Tsen-Ta Lee, 'Interpreting Bills of Rights: The Value of a Comparative Approach', 5 *International Journal of Constitutional Law* 122 (2007).

40. On the error of treating civilian legal systems as unified, see D. Neil MacCormick and Robert S. Summers, 'Introduction', in MacCormick and Summers, op. cit., 1, 3.

41. For the distinction between closed or intrinsic and open or extrinsic methods of interpretation see Canivet, op. cit., 315–16.

42. Canivet, op. cit., 317. On 'elaboration and extension' of legislated law in Germany, see David P. Currie, 'Separation of Powers in the Federal Republic of Germany', 9 *German Law Journal* 2113, 2123–6 (2008).

43. D. Neil MacCormick and Robert S. Summers, 'Further General Reflections and Conclusions', in MacCormick and Summers, op. cit., 531, 532–3.

44. For a more detailed account of such differences, see MacCormick and Summers, 'Further General Reflections', op. cit., 536–40. On different kinds of distinctions drawn between potentially relevant precedents in Germany, see Robert Alexy and Ralf Dreier, 'Precedent in the Federal Republic of Germany', in MacCormick and Summers, op. cit., 17, 34 ff.

45. The contrast appears clearly from Michel Troper and Christophe Grzegorczyk, 'Precedent in France', in MacCormick and Summers, op. cit., 103, 109–10 and Alexy and Dreier, op. cit., 21.

46. In addition to the sources cited earlier, see Michele Taruffo and Massimo La Torre, 'Precedent in Italy', in MacCormick and Summers, op. cit., 141, 147.

47. For an analysis of the prevalence of such Courts within civil law member states of the European Union, see Victor Ferreres Comella, 'The European Model of Constitutional Review of Legislation: Toward Decentralization' 2 *International Journal of Constitutional Law* 461, 462–3 (2004).

48. Peter Haberle, 'Role and Impact of Constitutional Courts in a Comparative Perspective', in Ingolf Pernice, Julianne Kokott and Cheryl Saunders (eds), *The Future of the European Judicial System in a Comparative Perspective* (Baden-Baden: Nomos, 2006), 66, also reporting reference to the proposal by the Constitutional Court of Liechtenstein: at 72. The other four interpretative methods, identified by Savigny, are the grammatical, systemic, historical and teleological modes of interpretation: Joachim Ruckert, 'Friedrich Carl von Savigny, the Legal Method, and the Modernity of Law', *Juridica International* XI/2006.

49. Op. cit., 297–8.

50. Genaro Carrio, cited in Spector (2008), pp. 129–30.

51. Comella, op. cit., 463, who also analyses the consequential dichotomy between interpretation of a statute to attempt to preserve its constitutionality, which can be carried out by ordinary courts in some states, and the function of setting aside a statute, which is the preserve of a Constitutional Court: at 472–4.

52. Benito Alaez Corral and Abel Arias Castano, 'The Role of the Spanish Constitutional Court in the Judicial Review of Parliamentary Legislation', 15 *European Public Law* 597, 609 (2009), attributing this development in Spain to the requirements of article 9 of the European Convention on Human Rights.

53. The procedure exists in, for example, Austria, Germany and Spain.

54. Bryde, op. cit., 298.

55. Ibid, pointing to a German practice of asking 'comparative law institutes for expert advice on foreign laws'.

56. Wen-Chen Chang, contribution to a thread on 'Proactive Courts', Comp-admin-law Archives, September 2009.

57. Rosenkrantz describes this as 'the idea that a binding source of normative authority was needed in order to prevent the multiplicity of normative discourses that would emere in circumstances where no institution is yet able to provide authoritative interpretations ...': op. cit., 273. See also Miller, quoting Sarmiento: '... we will find ourselves with a case law to which no one will be permitted to say 'this is my opinion'': op. cit., 1526.

58. See also Yasuo Hasebe, 'Constitutional Borrowing and Political Theory', 2 International Journal of Constitutional Law 224, 237, suggesting that the Court's very conception of democracy also is a factor.

59. Op. cit., 277–8.

60. Op. cit., 274.

61. Rosenkrantz, op. cit., 273–6.

62. The influence of the Constitution of the United States on the Constitution of Argentina creates a genetic relationship in the sense employed by Choudhry, following Lou Henkin.

63. The aspiration of the post-communist states of central and eastern Europe to join the European Union is a possible example: for an implication of this effect, see Dupré, op. cit., 271.

64. Dupré, op. cit., 278.

65. As occurred in Argentina: Rosenkrantz, op. cit.

66. As with the case of human dignity in Hungary: Dupré, op. cit. See also the wide variations in the understanding and application of the principle of human dignity described by Christopher McCrudden, 'Human Dignity and Judicial Interpretation of Human Rights', 19 *European Journal of International Law* 655 (2008).

67. Sujit Choudhry, op. cit.

68. By way of examples, see Vicki C. Jackson, 'Narratives of Federalism: Of Continuities and Comparative Constitutional Experience', 51 Duke Law Journal 223 (2001); Sarah K. Harding, 'Comparative Reasoning and Judicial Review', 28 *Yale Journal of International Law*, 409 (2003); Joan L. Larsen 'Importing Constitutional Norms from a "Wider Civilization": Lawrence and the Rehnquist Court's Use of Foreign and International Law in Domestic Constitutional Interpretation' 65 *Ohio State Law Journal* 1283 (2004); Cheryl Saunders, 'The Use and Misuse of Comparative Constitutional Law', 13 *Industrial Journal of Global Legal Studies*, 37 (2006); Stone, op. cit.; Rosalind Dixon, 'A Democratic Theory of Constitutional Comparison', 56 *American Journal of Comparative Law* (2008) 947.

69. Tushnet (2007) distinguishes between comparisons involving rights and those involving institutional arrangements with his categories of normative universalism and functionalism respectively. On 'appeal to international standards' in connection with rights, from a German perspective, see Bryde, op. cit., 305–6, pointing in particular to the application of clauses restricting limitations on rights to those necessary in a 'democratic society'. For an illustration of engagement with comparative constitutional law in dealing with an institutional problem, see the decision of the Australian High Court in *Grollo v Palmer* (1995) 184 CLR 348, Brennan CJ, Deane, Dawson and Toohey JJ, referring to decisions of the Supreme Court of Canada, the Supreme Court of the United States and the European Court of Human Rights, in resolving the constitutionality of the conferral of authority to issue telephone interception warrants on federal judges in their personal capacity.

70. For confirmation, see Ackermann, op. cit., 278: '... in judicial problem-solving one can easily become trapped into a sort of tunnel vision, from which it is difficult to escape, or to see other or lateral answers'.

71. Choudhry, op. cit., 861 cites *Ex Parte Speaker of the National Assembly: In Re Dispute Concerning the Constitutionality of Certain Provisions of the National Education Policy Bill 83 of 1995*, 1996 (3) SALR 289 (CC) as an example of this usage (which he terms dialogical). The Court held that a national law could impose duties of implementation on provinces; the United States experience was irrelevant, in the face of fundamental differences in the assumptions on which the two constitutional systems were based.

72. Choudhry uses the concept of dialogical interpretation to refer to the use of comparative law to further self-understanding by identifying and comparing underlying assumptions as a basis for justifying subsequent interpretative choice: op. cit., 858. The multiple ways in which this might occur justifies its inclusion here. Jackson uses engagement as an umbrella to cover a range of non-binding uses of comparative law 'as a way of testing understanding of one's own traditions and possibilities': op. cit., (2005), 114. Bricolage simply involves judges using whatever comparative experience comes to hand when it seems 'appropriate': Tushnet (1999), op. cit., 1304.

73. For example, *Australian Capital Television v Commonwealth* (1992) 177 CLR 106, in which references to British, United States and Canadian experience helped a majority of the High Court of Australia to accept that restrictions on political advertising presented questions about representative democracy as well as about the scope of federal power over broadcasting.

74. *Executive Council of Western Cape Legislature v President of the Republic of South Africa* 1995 (4) SA 877 (CC), where the Constitutional Court examined different comparative approaches to the question whether power can constitutionally be delegated to the executive to make regulations that override the empowering statute.

75. Bryde draws attention to the potential use of foreign experience in measuring the proportionality of interference with constitutional rights standards, although he suggests that the German court would be likely to use foreign experience merely to raise a question about the law, which the state may (or may not) be able to resolve: op. cit., 305.

76. Thus, in *Hill v Church of Scientology of Toronto* [1995] 2 SCR 1130, the Supreme Court of Canada considered the consequences of the adoption of the 'actual malice' standard in the United States, concluding that it was undesirable in Canada on that ground.

77. *Roper v Simmons* 543 US 551 (2005).

78. The distinction is taken from Bryde, op. cit., 303–4.

79. The relevance of the federal character of the Constitution to interpretive method in the United States has influenced the Australian High Court in various ways over time: see *Austin v Commonwealth* (2003) 215 CLR 185.

80. *National Coalition for Gay and Lesbian Equality and Others v Minister of Home Affairs and Others*, 2000 (2) SA1 (CC), in which the Constitutional Court of South Africa examined decisions of courts in Canada, the United States, Israel and Germany in determining that it could read provisions into an otherwise unconstitutional statute in order to preserve its validity.

81. Barak, op. cit., 289.

82. Markesinis and Fedtke, op. cit., ch. 3.

83. *Motswaledi v Botswana Democratic Party* CACLB-053-2009, http://www.saflii.org/bw/cases/BWCA/2009/111.pdf (viewed 20 January 2010).

84. *S v Makwanyane* 1995 (3) SA 391 (CC), 415.

85. Waldron, op. cit.

86. Depending on the purpose, he suggests that the categories might be confined to 'civilized' or 'freedom-loving' countries: at 145.

87. Kenneth Anderson, 'Foreign Law and the US Constitution', 131 *Policy Review* 33, 49 (2005); see also Stone, op. cit., 56.

88. *Confirmation Hearing on the Nomination of John G. Roberts Jr to be Chief Justice of the United States*, 109th Congress 200-1, (2005). Roberts' actual hypothesis involved 'relying on a decision from a German judge about what our Constitution means'; this is, however, an implausible scenario.

89. Tushet (2006), op. cit., 1284–87.

90. Schauer, op. cit., 1948, 1958-9. See also Mark Tushnet, 'Referring to Foreign Law in Constitutional Interpretation: An Episode in the Culture Wars', 35 *University of Baltimore Law Review*, 299, 306–10 (2005), arguing that the conditions that are conducive to development of a 'slippery-slope' are not present in these circumstances, at least where courts that refer to foreign law make its role in their reasoning clear.

91. Frankenberg's identification of the 'layered narrative' of Constitutions provides helpful insight into the problem of comparison from this perspective. On the concept of expressivism, see: Tushnet (2007), op. cit., 10–15, also noting that an expressivist understanding of a Constitution is not necessarily shared even within the nation itself. And as Stone observes, states differ in the extent to which they claim or perceive an expressivist function for the Constitution: op. cit., 57.

92. *Stanford v Kentucky* 492 US 361, 369 (1989).

93. *Chan Hiang Leng Colin v Public Prosecutor* (1994) 3 SLR 662, 681.

94. For argument to this effect in relation to the Eighth Amendment to the Constitution of the United States, see

Tushnet (2006), op. cit., 1279. Constitutional provisions that permit limitation of rights by law to an extent determined by reference to the standards of a democratic society also fall within this category: section 1 of the Canadian Charter of Rights and Freedoms is an example; see also Bryde, op. cit., 305. Constitutions that can readily be understood in this way have become more prevalent with the incorporation of international human rights standards into constitutional texts.

95. The explicit authority to refer to foreign law in interpreting the Bill of Rights in section 39 of the South African Constitution is an example that is useful for this purpose also. It has been copied elsewhere: see s.32(2), Charter of Human Rights and Responsibilities Act 2006 (Vic). It is clear that in South Africa the provision was intended to encourage rather than to 'license' the courts to refer to foreign experience, which is an accepted practice that is not confined to the Bill of Rights: Ackermann, op. cit., 268.

96. On pragmatism, see e.g. Tushnet (2006), op. cit., 1280–84; on Australian 'modified originalism', see Stone, op. cit., 54; on the purposive approach prevalent in, for example, South Africa, see Ackermann, op. cit., 270.

97. For an overview of these in relation to comparative constitutional law see Cheryl Saunders, 'Towards a Global Constitutional Gene Pool', *National Taiwan University Law Review* 1–38 (2009).

98. Ackermann, op. cit., 274, referring to (at least the aspiration towards) a 'certain universally normative minimum core' of values; also Barak, op. cit., referring to the 'common fundamental values' of democracies and helpfully identifying the different levels of generality at which comparison might take place: 288.

99. This tension is a theme in much of the literature on this subject: see for example Tushnet (2007), op. cit. (normative universalism and contextualism); Jackson (2005), op. cit. (convergence and resistance); Sujit Choudhry, 'The Lochner Era and Comparative Constitutionalism', 2 *International Journal of Constitutional Law* 1, (2004) (universalism and particularism). It also has a dark side, which might be characterised as imperialism or hegemony and relativism.

100. Saunders (2009), op. cit.

101. Matthias Mahlmann, 'Theorizing Transnational Law – Varieties of Transnational Law and the Universalistic Stance', 10 *German Law Journal* 1325, 1328 (2009), illustrating the point by reference to the extension of the vote to women in Switzerland in 1971.

102. *N K v Minister of Safety & Security* 2005 (6) SA 419 (CC), 24–5.

103. See the principles of case selection for inference-oriented small-sample comparative studies outlined by Hirschl, op. cit., 47–63. Courts are not necessarily engaged in inference-oriented inquiry when they refer to foreign experience, but the principles are useful nonetheless. For an interesting argument that links the purpose of reference to foreign law with the possibilities of more scientific selection see Dixon, op. cit.

104. The point is based on discussions by the author with advocates in South Africa, Australia and the United Kingdom.

105. *Bowers v Hardwick* 478 US 186, 196 (1986). Chief Justice Burger's opinion was only a concurrence and on its face referred to moral, rather than legal, standards; nevertheless, it serves to illustrate the point.

106. *Lawrence v Texas* 539 US 558, 576–7 (2003), referring to *Dudgeon v United Kingdom* 45 ECtHR (1981).

107. *S v Makwanyane* 1995 (3) SA 391 [34], [26].

108. *Printz v United States*, 521 US 898, 921 (1997). For a critique of his contextual understanding see Daniel Halberstam, 'Comparative Federalism and the Issue of Commandeering', in Kalypso Nicolaidis and Robert Howse (eds), *The Federal Vision: Legitimacy and Levels of Governance in the US and the EU* (Oxford: Oxford University Press, 2001).

109. More pejorative still was Chief Justice Roberts' characterisation of the practice as 'looking over a crowd and picking out your friends': Confirmation Hearing, op. cit., 200–01.

110. *South African Broadcasting Corporation v National Director of Public Prosecutions* (2007) 1 SA 523 (CC), [25], [100] is an example of such a case, which also illustrates how adversarial argument and multiple judgments operate as a corrective. For an account of the debate on the use of foreign law in this case amongst the judges concerned, see Bentele, op. cit., 238–40. As that account also suggests, selectivity is an inevitable dimension of judicial reasoning at the level of an apex court and is not confined to the use of foreign law: ('Yes, we cherry pick all the time when we use authorities, foreign or domestic ...', quoting Justice Moseneke).

111. *Roper v Simmons* 543 US 551, 578 (2005); see also the examples cited from earlier cases: 'civilized nations of the world'; 'world community'; 'nations that share our Anglo-American heritage'. See also the reference in Makwanyane to practice in 'the countries of the world' based on a study by Amnesty International: [33].

112. Dupré (2002), op. cit., 278 (usage by the Constitutional Court of Hungary).

113. *Australian Capital Television Pty Ltd v Commonwealth* (1992) 177 CLR 106, 211, Gaudron J.

114. An inference drawn, for example, from Zoller, op. cit., 222–3, explaining the 'superiority of universal and humanistic values' in France.

115. Waldron, op. cit., 144–5.

116. Justice Kriegler of South Africa has referred to these as 'exemplary jurisdictions': *Bernstein v Bester* 1996 (2) SA 751 (CC) [133], cited in Ackermann, op. cit., 280.

117. Dupré (2002), op. cit., 278, in relation to Hungary.
118. Op. cit. They report that 87% of citations by Justices who had studied in Germany were from German courts and that 68.3% of those by Justices who had studied in the United States were from US courts. The correlation was less clear for Justices who had studied in Japan.
119. Chang and Yeh refer, for example, to the introduction of proportionality reasoning, due process of law and a political questions doctrine without express citation of foreign law: op. cit.
120. For characterisation of federalism as a 'package deal', for example, see Vicki C. Jackson, 'Narratives of Federalism: Of Continuities and Comparative Constitutional Experience', 51 *Duke Law Journal* 223 (2001).
121. See, for example, Tushnet's suggestion that the decentralisation of enforcement of the criminal law in the United States should be taken into account in comparing constitutional doctrine on hate speech in the United States with jurisdictions in which criminal law is centralised: op. cit. (2007), 10–11.
122. Although they may be useful nevertheless, as Bryde observed in relation to the famously flawed comparative conclusions of Montesquieu and Bagehot in their respective seminal works: op. cit., 304.
123. For criticism of judicial decisions in Singapore on this basis see Li-Ann Thio, 'Beyond the "Four Walls" in an era of Transnational Judicial Conversations', 19 *Columbia Journal of Asian Law* 428, (2005–06). The fine line between exaggerating difference and rejecting the relevance of foreign law altogether is identified in Adrienne Stone's analysis of the attitudes of the various Justices of the High Court towards Canadian and European authority in *Roach v Electoral Commissioner* (2007) 233 CLR 162: op. cit., 64–8.
124. *Printz v United States*, 521 US 898, 921 (1997), Breyer J.
125. Choudhry (2006), op. cit., 22–3.
126. Thus, for example, in *Ferreira v Levin NO* 1996 (1) SA 984 (CC), the Constitutional Court of South Africa refused to accept that the Constitution required self-incriminating evidence to be protected against derivative use, in accordance with United States authority, by reference to the disparity in the resources available to the prosecutorial systems in the two countries: Ackermann, op. cit., 275–6. See also *Hill v Church of Scientology of Toronto*, [1995] 2 SCR 1130, 1180, 1188, in which the Supreme Court of Canada declined to adopt the actual malice standard for defamation from the United States for Canadian law on the ground of social and political as well as legal and constitutional differences between the two states.
127. In relation to Canada, see Roy, op. cit., 130–34 (2004), estimating that most of the 60 references to foreign law by the Supreme Court of Canada in Charter cases between 1998 and 2003 were of a 'survey' nature or supported the Court's own conclusions and only one represented direct adoption of a foreign solution for resolution of an issue for Canada. See also Ackermann, op. cit., 274 ff; Bryde, op. cit., 305.
128. Canivet, op. cit., 325–7; also encouraging prudence; consciousness of the difficulty; and precision.

REFERENCES

Bentele, Ursula (2009), 'Mining for Gold: The Constitutional Court of South Africa's Experience with Comparative Constitutional Law', *Georgia Journal of International and Comparative Law*, 37, 219–240.

Calabresi, Steven G. and Stephanie Dotson Zimdahl (2005), 'The Supreme Court and Foreign Sources of Law: Two Hundred Years of Practice and the Juvenile Death Penalty Decision', *William and Mary Law Review*, 47, 743–909.

Chang, Wen-Chen and Jiunn-Rong Yeh (2008), 'The Use of Foreign Precedents in the Constitutional Court in Taiwan', a preliminary report to the IACL Research Group (copy on file with the author).

Choudhry, Sujit (1999), 'Globalization in Search of Justification: Towards a Theory of Comparative Constitutional Interpretation', *Indiana Law Journal*, 74, 819–98.

Choudhry, Sujit (2006), 'Migration as a New Metaphor in Comparative Constitutional Law' in Sujit Choudhry (2006) (eds.), *The Migration of Constitutional Ideas*, Cambridge: Cambridge University Press, 1–36.

Constitutional Court of Taiwan (2010), 'Procedure for Interpretation', http://www.judicial.gov.tw/constitutional court/EN/p02_01_02.asp (viewed 5 January 2010).

Cotterrell, Roger (2008), 'Law and Culture – Inside and Beyond the Nation State', *Retfaerd: Nordisk Juridisk Tidsskrift*, 31(4), 23–36.

Dupré, Catherine (2002), 'The Importation of Law: A New Comparative Perspective and the Hungarian Constitutional Court', in A. Harding and E. Orucu (eds), *Comparative Law in the 21st Century*, The Hague: Kluwer, 267–80.

Ejima, Akiko (2009), 'Enigmatic Attitude of the Supreme Court of Japan towards Foreign Precedents – Refusal at the Front Door and Admission at the Back Door', *Meiji Law Journal*, 16, 19–44.

Frankenberg, Gunter (2006), 'Comparing Constitutions: Ideas, Ideals and Ideology – Toward a Layered Narrative', *International Journal of Constitutional Law*, 4, 439–59.

Friedman, Barry and Cheryl Saunders (2003), 'Editors' Introduction', Symposium on Constitutional Borrowing, 1 *International Journal of Constitutional Law*, 177–80.

Gamper, Anna (2009), 'On the Justiciability and Persuasiveness of Constitutional Comparison in Constitutional Adjudication', *Vienna Online Journal on International Constitutional Law*, 3, 150–69.

Glenn, H. Patrick (1987), 'Persuasive Authority', *McGill Law Journal*, 32, 261–98.

Glenn, H. Patrick (ed.) (2007), *Legal Traditions of the World*, 3rd edition, Oxford: Oxford University Press.

Guerra, Luis Lopez (2005), 'Contribution to a Constitutional Court Judges Roundtable', *International Journal of Constitutional Law*, 3, 567–9.

Haberle, Peter (2006), 'Role and Impact of Constitutional Courts in a Comparative Perspective', in Ingolf Pernice, Julianne Kokott and Cheryl Saunders (eds), *The Future of the European Judicial System in Comparative Perspective*, Baden-Baden: Nomos.

Harding, Sarah (2003), 'Comparative Reasoning and Judicial Review', *Yale Journal of International Law*, 28, 409–64.

Harjono, Justice (2010), 'The Indonesian Constitutional Court', http://www.ccourt.go.kr/home/english/introduction/pdf/05.pdf (viewed 1 January 2010).

Ipp, D.A. (1998), 'Lawyers' Duties to the Court', *Law Quarterly Review*, 114, 63–107.

Jackson, Vicki C. (2005), 'Constitutional Comparisons: Convergence, Resistance, Engagement', *Harvard Law Review*, 119, 109–28.

Jackson, Vicki C. (2010), *Constitutional Engagement in a Transnational Era*, Oxford: Oxford University Press.

Levit, Janet Koven (1998–9), 'The Constitutionalization of Human Rights in Argentina: Problem or Promise', *Columbia Journal of Transnational Law*, 37, 281–346.

Marshall, Margaret H. (2004), ' 'Wise Parents do Not Hesitate to Learn from their Children': Interpreting State Constitutions in an Age of Global Jurisprudence', *New York University Law Review*, 79, 1633–56.

Mendes, Gilmar (2009), 'Constitutional Justice in Brazil', a paper submitted to the World Conference on Constitutional Justice, http://www.venice.coe.int/WCCJ/Papers/BRA_SupremeC_E.pdf (viewed 2 January 2010).

Miller, Jonathan M. (1997), 'The Authority of a Foreign Talisman: A Study of US Constitutional Practice as Authority in Nineteenth Century Argentina and the Argentine Elite's Leap of Faith', *American University Law Review*, 46, 1483–572.

Navot, Suzie (2008), 'The Use of Foreign Precedents by Constitutional Judges: Israeli Report', a preliminary report to the IACL Research Group (copy on file with the author).

Nijman, J. and A. Nollkaemper (eds) (2007), *New Perspectives on the Divide between National and International Law*, New York: Oxford University Press.

Peters, Anne (2007), 'The Globalization of State Constitutions', in J. Nijman and A. Nollkaemper (eds), *New Perspectives on the Divide between National and International Law*, New York: Oxford University Press, 251–308.

Poirier, Johanne (2008), 'The Use of Foreign Precedents by the Constitutional Court of Belgium', a preliminary report to the IACL Research Group (copy on file with the author).

Ramraj, Victor V. (2002), 'Comparative Constitutional Law in Singapore', *Singapore Journal of International and Comparative Law*, 6, 302–34.

Rosenkrantz, Carlos F. (2003), 'Against Borrowings and Other Nonauthoritative Uses of Foreign Law', *International Journal of Constitutional Law*, 1, 269–95.

Satoh, Jun-Ichi (2008), 'Judicial Review in Japan: An Overview of the Case Law and an Examination of Trends in the Japanese Supreme Court's Constitutional Oversight', *Loyola of Los Angeles Law Review*, 41, 603–27.

Saunders, Cheryl (2007), 'The Interesting Times of Louis Favoreu', *International Journal of Constitutional Law*, 5, 1–16.

Saunders, Cheryl (2009), 'Towards a Global Constitutional Gene Pool', *National Taiwan University Law Review*, 4, 1–38.

Schauer, Frederick (2008), 'Authority and Authorities', *Virginia Law Review*, 94, 1931–61.

Scheppele, Kim Lane (2003), 'Aspirational and Aversive Constitutionalism: The Case for Studying Cross-Constitutional Influence through Negative Models', *International Journal of Constitutional Law*, 1, 296–324.

Sitaraman, Ganesh (2009), 'The Use and Abuse of Foreign Law in Constitutional Interpretation', *Harvard Journal of Law and Public Policy*, 32, 653–93.

Spector, Horacio (2008), 'Constitutional Transplants and the Mutation Effect', *Chicago-Kent Law Review*, 83, 129–45.

Szente, Zoltan (2008), 'The Impact of Foreign Precedents on the Jurisprudence of the Hungarian Constitutional Court', a preliminary report to the IACL Research Group (copy on file with the author).

Thiruvengadam, Arun K. (2009), 'Comparative Law and Constitutional Interpretation in Singapore', in Li-ann Thio and Kevin YL Tan (eds), *Evolution of a Revolution*, Oxford: Routledge-Cavendish, 114-21.

Tripathi, Pradyumna K. (1957), 'Foreign Precedents and Constitutional Law', *Columbia Law Review*, 57, 319–47.

Tushnet, Mark (1999), 'The Possibilities of Comparative Constitutional Law', *Yale Law Journal*, 108, 1225–309.

Tushnet, Mark (2005–06), 'Referring to Foreign Law in Constitutional Interpretation: An Episode in the Culture Wars', *University of Baltimore Law Review*, 35, 299–312.

Tushnet, Mark (ed.) (2007), *Weak Courts, Strong Rights*, Princeton: Princeton University Press.
Waldron, Jeremy (2005–06), 'Foreign Law and the Modern Ius Gentium', Harvard Law Review, 119, 129–47.
Walker, Neil (2008), 'Beyond Boundary Disputes and Basic Grids: Mapping the Global Disorder of Normative Orders', *International Journal of Constitutional Law*, 6, 373–96.

32. Constitutional interpretation in comparative perspective: comparing judges or courts?[1]

Vicki C. Jackson and Jamal Greene

1 INTRODUCTION

Writing on comparative interpretive theory would seem to invite an association of particular interpretive approaches with the courts of particular countries. And in years past, one might well have felt comfortable embarking on the enterprise in this way, associating the US Supreme Court, for example, with common law methods of constitutional adjudication, the French Conseil Constitutionnel with a formalist and quite cryptic approach, and the German Federal Constitutional Court with a holistic teleological approach. Yet distinctions that in earlier times might have appeared large must now be tempered by noting considerable overlap in the approaches of different courts. Accordingly, this chapter will try to resist the temptation to focus only on how different approaches correspond to different national constitutional courts or legal cultures. In those countries that permit separate opinions and thereby facilitate the development of competing interpretive approaches within a single system, differences among individual judges may be as striking as differences across courts.

The increasing overlap in interpretive approaches may be an effect of globalization, reflecting the transnationalization of judicial discourses. But these areas of overlap may also be understood in other ways. First, as David Law suggests, they may be responses to the internal logic of constitutional review in more democratized polities, and the demands for justification of government action that the ideas of limited government and constitutionalism entail.[2] Second, the invocation of a range of justifications – beyond reliance on the 'plain meaning' of texts – that is found in constitutional court opinions today may reflect revised understandings of the meanings of language, under the influence of the deconstructive insights of postmodernism in elite intellectual discourses and popular culture in many countries of the world.[3] Third, the growing focus on human rights in international law, and on the notion of rights as a fundamental (though not necessarily universal) aspect of constitutionalism, may contribute to overlaps, if only because constitutional texts draw from a shared set of archetypes that invite cross-national comparisons and migrations of ideas and approaches. Fourth, as Mitchel Lasser suggests, there may be *procedural* effects of an increased focus on individual rights in constitutional adjudication, which may result in opening judicial processes up to a broader array of participants and to felt needs for reasoned responses to those participants' arguments.[4]

This chapter focuses on constitutional interpretation by courts in the United States, Canada, Australia, Germany, and France.[5] The first three are jurisdictions whose legal regimes grew out of the English common law; if there are differences among their high courts, they are particularly worthy of note given the many commonalities in their background legal traditions. The Federal Constitutional Court (FCC) of Germany is viewed by

many as the leading national constitutional court in Europe. The FCC has engaged in constitutional review for close to 60 years, developing a significant jurisprudence over that time.
The legal traditions of German law differ from those of the common law jurisdictions, and
for this reason similarities in constitutional interpretation, to the extent they exist, may be
quite revealing. France's Conseil Constitutionnel remains a distinctive institution that has
represented an important alternative to the *Marbury v Madison* concept that courts engage in
judicial review as part of their ordinary function of deciding what law to apply to resolve
disputes. The Conseil is, of the five, the only court that issues all of its opinions in a single
voice, without identifying authorship and without dissent; the absence of separate opinions
helps sustain a distinctive style.[6]

In any comparative study of courts, one must be careful to recognize the limitations
imposed not only by the countries selected but also by the materials to which one has access.
For the three common-law jurisdictions, the opinions of the courts, as well as scholarly
commentary, are readily available in English, but for Germany and France those not fluent in
the original language must rely on translations and on English-language scholarship, which
may be limited.[7] With these caveats acknowledged, the chapter proceeds as follows: section 2
describes several schools of constitutional interpretation whose approaches are reflected in
decisions in the five countries we have chosen to focus on. Section 3 discusses some distinctive aspects of the interpretive approaches of the five courts under study. Section 4 concludes
with some observations about the relationship of interpretive approach to substantive outcome.

2   INTERPRETIVE APPROACHES WRIT LARGE

Interpretive theory as a subject assumes a larger role in some jurisdictions than in others. It
has been a preoccupation of American legal scholarship for at least two generations. In
Canada, by contrast, debates center less on interpretive theory and more on substantive analysis and the possibilities of inter-branch dialogue, although in Canada (as in Australia) considerable attention has been given to the sources, and legitimacy, of unwritten constitutional
principles. The English-language literatures on constitutional review in France and Germany
also differ, with more focus on institutional questions about the French Conseil (is it a court?
how does it relate to the other French high courts?) and more focus on the jurisprudence of
the FCC.

At least three major categories of approaches to constitutional interpretation can be identified: historically focused positivist interpretation, where the court sees its task as giving
effect to a prior commitment made by the authoritative law giver; 'purposive' interpretation,
where the court gives effect to or implements the purpose or purposes of the constitution; and
'multi-valenced' approaches that draw on original understandings, purposes, structure,
history, values, and consequences to arrive at constitutional judgments. Justification in the
first approach is by reference to past decisions (by relevant public decisionmakers) embodied
in positive law, whether written or unwritten; justification in the second approach is by
reasoning about constitutional purpose; and justification in the last approach is eclectic, drawing from several sources, with some tendency to seek congruences among them.[8] Moreover,
constitutional courts will on occasion reason by self-expression or self-conception, by resort
to a sense of national ethos that cannot be fully captured by lines of text or something as functional as a 'purpose'.

Categories such as these, however, necessarily obscure important differences among approaches, and also obscure important overlaps between them. We thus offer a set of apparent antinomies, or oppositional approaches, within which constitutional interpretation operates, in an effort to illuminate, without reifying, important differences in emphasis. These antinomies, which are in some cases associated with one or another of the larger categories of interpretation, are discussed below.

2.1   Fixed or Evolving Meaning

An important divide among interpretive approaches across national courts, but especially in the United States and Australia, is between those who argue that constitutional meaning is fixed at a particular moment in the past and those who believe constitutional meaning is legitimately subject to evolving understandings. A famous statement of the US Constitution as a living instrument is found in *Missouri v Holland*. Justice Holmes, writing for the Court, announced:

> [W]hen we are dealing with words that also are a constituent act, like the Constitution of the United States, we must realize that they have called into life a being the development of which could not have been foreseen completely by the most gifted of its begetters. It was enough for them to realize or to hope that they had created an organism; it has taken a century and has cost their successors much sweat and blood to prove that they created a nation. The case before us must be considered in the light of our whole experience and not merely in that of what was said a hundred years ago.[9]

This evolutionary approach is perhaps foreshadowed by John Marshall's famous assertion in *McCulloch v Maryland* that 'it is a constitution we are expounding', and his implication that constitutions cannot frequently be amended; they must be understood 'to be adapted to the various crises of human affairs' that may arise in a future that cannot be clearly foreseen by their framers.[10]

A well-known statement of that principle in Canadian constitutional jurisprudence is found in the *Persons Case* of 1929, in which the Privy Council acknowledged that, although the Canadian constitution was, in form, a British statute, a different principle of interpretation applied when the 'statute' was a national constitution:[11]

> The British North America Act planted in Canada a living tree capable of growth and expansion within its natural limits. The object of the Act was to grant a Constitution to Canada. 'Like all written constitutions it has been subject to development through usage and convention.'[12]

Thus, the constitution as a 'living tree' takes on the impress of social understandings of its meanings, or exists in interaction with changing social understandings; yet, the metaphor implicitly acknowledges limitations on interpretive evolution that may arise from the text and (possibly) the need to distinguish between those areas in which meaning can change through interpretation and those in which a formal amendment through constitutionally specified processes is required. The 'tree', then, is rooted in an original text and legal tradition but capable of substantial, though not infinite, change over time through interpretation.[13]

In contrast to Canada's 'living tree' approach, 'fixed meaning' approaches play an important role in both Australia and the United States. Thus, Sir Owen Dixon, a Chief Justice of the High Court, was a leading proponent of what in Australia is understood as 'strict legalism', in which the words of the Constitution mean the same thing now as they did when adopted in 1900.[14] The approach is associated with a constrained role for the judiciary, assuring that judges' own preferences will not displace the law that was agreed to by authorized methods in the past. US Justice Antonin Scalia also favors an original meaning approach. He argues that both democratic principles and the need to constrain judicial discretion require that judges be limited to ascertaining what constitutional text meant when it was adopted; he has gone so far as to say that the purpose of a constitution is to 'obstruct modernity',[15] and has argued for and employed resort to 18th-century dictionaries as an aid to interpreting the words of the Constitution. Originalism in the United States is not only a legal approach to interpretation, but has become a subject of popular and political culture, including popular media and talk radio discourse.[16]

Although 'fixed' approaches are generally associated with more positivist historicism, a text may be intended and understood to authorize its own evolution over time. Originalists may recognize that, in theory, the original 'public meaning' of words that require courts to make moral judgments may develop over time,[17] but dominant originalist voices in the United States have tended to tie 'original meaning' to more specific original intentions.[18] Some jurists find a middle ground, in which the original commitments of the constitution are understood at a fairly general level. This practice is embodied in the Australian doctrine distinguishing between the unchanging 'connotation' of a constitutional provision and its 'denotation', a distinction explained by Jeffrey Goldsworthy as the distinction between the meaning of the words (connotation) and their intended applications (denotation):[19] the former is controlling for most Australian judges but not the latter.[20] This Australian distinction between two kinds of meanings has parallels with Ronald Dworkin's well-known distinction between legal concepts, designed to invoke moral qualities about law, and legal conceptions, or specific understandings of what a legal term means or how it applies.[21] A similar distinction was proposed some years later in the United States by Jack Balkin, in an essay in which he claimed to be an 'originalist' despite advocating an evolutionary approach to constitutional meaning,[22] thereby illuminating the practical permeability between ideas of fixed and evolving meaning, and between originalism and purposivism, discussed below.

2.2   Originalism, Textualism and Purposivism

Closely related to the divide over fixed versus evolving constitutional meaning is the debate over textualism, especially in its originalist forms, and purposivism in constitutional interpretation. For these purposes, one might distinguish between those who believe that interpreting the language of specific texts will provide answers to at least a significant array of constitutional questions, and those who believe that constitutional questions, whether about texts or structures and their implications, can only be resolved by reference to broader purposive or teleological understandings. But one must also distinguish textualists from originalists; textualists might believe that answers to constitutional questions may be derived from the words of the constitution, but may not (logically) be committed to interpreting those words by reference to a point in the past, rather than their contemporary meaning. Most textualists, at least in the United States, employ originalist methods focused on the intentions of the drafters or the 'public meaning' of the words as they would have been understood at the time of ratification.

Originalist textualists may believe that most legal issues are resolvable by reference to prior public choices embodied in the text; or they may believe that only some issues can be so determined (those subject to what Keith Whittington and Randy Barnett refer to as 'interpretation'), while other issues cannot be resolved by reference to the words of the text and must be subject therefore to constitutional 'construction' (i.e., interpretive development based on non-textual materials).[23] Such originalists may be committed to specific understandings of text but may not believe that the Constitution's meaning is entirely fixed, in areas legitimately open to 'construction'. Other 'moderate originalists' are willing to distinguish, as noted above, between the original meaning of words, which cannot change, and their expected application, which can. On this view, even if the equal protection clause of the Fourteenth Amendment was not understood at its enactment to apply to gender discrimination, in the 20th century the equal protection clause has been properly understood – in its original meaning, though not its intended application – to do so.

Purposivists differ in emphasis, framing questions of original understanding at a high level of generality and often seeking coherence in the constitutional system as a whole. Moderate originalism can shade into a more purposive approach, which is committed to the idea of interpreting the constitution so as to advance the overarching purposes of the instrument understood as a basic charter of good government and government under law.

A wide range of purposes may be attributed to different clauses of a constitution or to a constitution as a whole: some purposivists may be 'clause-bound', focusing only on certain parts of the constitution; others may advance a general theory of the value a constitution is most designed to protect, be it the German Constitutional Court's commitment to human dignity, or, in the United States, 'active liberty' for Justice Stephen Breyer, or representative democracy on the influential view of John Hart Ely.[24] Others may see the purpose of a constitution as that of preserving traditions (or in Justice Scalia's memorable phrase, 'obstruct[ing] modernity'), thereby collapsing purposivism into a kind of historicism. For still others constitutions may be seen as transformational, evoking a dichotomy expressed by some scholars as 'restorative' versus 'redemptive'.[25] Debates over the transcendent purpose of the constitution may reflect competing visions of national self-conception (or 'ethos'), whether, for example, as pluralist versus assimilationist or as libertarian versus egalitarian.

Aharon Barak is one of the leading theorists of purposive interpretation in law, arguing that judges should interpret a constitution according to 'the objectives, values, and principles that the constitutional text is designed to actualize'.[26] On his account, the 'subjective' intent of the framers of the constitution is relevant but not 'decisive'; its 'influence diminishes' over time. Because a constitution's 'purpose is determined by the needs of the present, in order to solve problems in the future', the 'objective purpose' of the constitution prevails over past understandings, though the latter may help 'in resolving contradictions between conflicting objective purposes'.[27] Purposive interpretation, he argues, is most consistent with the role of a constitutional court judge in a democracy – to preserve democracy; to bridge gaps between law and society's changing needs; and to advance the 'values and principles that the constitution seeks to actualize', which represent a 'social consensus at the core of the legal system' derived from the constitution's text and history as well as from the history of its people.[28]

Proportionality analysis might be understood as a purposive approach to interpretation, even though some of its proponents contrast proportionality with 'interpretive' approaches. As elaborated in Canada and Germany (as well as elsewhere), proportionality analysis is at its core concerned with justifications of government action, justifications which must be consistent with constitutional purposes. Canadian legal scholar David Beatty has described proportionality as 'the ultimate rule of law', the fundamental purpose of constitutionalism.[29] On this account, the purpose of constitutionalism is to restrain and regulate government action in accordance with universal standards of fairness. Whatever the government's purposes, they can only be achieved through means rationally designed to effect the goal, and in ways that minimize their intrusion on other important values of the society.[30] Greater intrusions on individual choices require greater justifications on this model. Beatty argues that most constitutional courts rely on this methodology (though expressed in different terms) and praises the method as 'neutral' in that it does not specify the values of society but only the relationship between those values and the means chosen by the government to advance them.[31] Robert Alexy, a German constitutional theorist, also defends proportionality as an essential tool by which the competing principles of a constitution are reconciled; Alexy views constitutional law as primarily made up of principles that require optimization of a value, rather than of rules that specify particular conduct as in or out of bounds. Proportionality is the way in which competing principles can be optimized.[32]

Whether proportionality is viewed as an underlying principle of constitutional law, or rather as an interpretive approach that permits reconciliation of different values, it is worth noting that despite its ubiquity the specific form it takes may vary from country to country.[33] And, even where the formulation is roughly similar, as for example between Canada and Germany, how the test is applied may differ.[34]

2.3   Single-valenced vs. Multi-valenced Interpretation

Multi-valenced interpretive theories embrace textualism and purposivism, precedent and history, as well as concern for constitutional values and pragmatic concerns for consequences. Among US constitutional theorists, David Strauss and Ernest Young offer differing versions of 'common law constitutionalism', and Philip Bobbitt argues that US constitutional interpretation is grounded in six modalities of argument. Some scholars suggest that multi-valenced interpretive approaches are in a sense self-legitimating; this is what courts deciding constitutional cases in common law and other jurisdictions do, and have done. Other justifications focus on the tendency of such factors, especially if weighted towards precedent, to be conservative in the Burkean sense of slowing the pace of constitutional change while still allowing for improved understanding, either in deference to the wisdom of the past or with a humility that cautions incrementalism. Still others argue that the range of factors that can be considered has the advantage in a pluralist, democratized society of offering a range of forms of persuasion, thereby inviting a broad set of views into the process of constitutional interpretation.[35] Multi-sourced interpretive approaches raise concerns for other jurists about the potential for unconstrained discretion absent clear priorities and weights for the different sources.

Unlike originalism, or particular purposive theories, multi-valenced interpretation is not confident of the existence of single right answers, and may in some cases view a range of answers as constitutionally tolerable or plausible. Multi-valenced interpreters tend to spend less time focusing on methodology and more time assessing how the various sources within the interpretive canon ought to be weighted or understood together in particular cases. Even those who theorize a priority for the different sources, like Richard Fallon, acknowledge that in practice factors nominally ranked low may in fact drive analysis.[36] Reliance upon multiple sources of interpretation is a feature not only of decisions by the US Supreme Court but also of many of the world's constitutional courts.[37] Examples of multi-valenced opinions may be found in the German Constitutional Court,[38] the Australian High Court,[39] and the Canadian Supreme Court;[40] multiple considerations also appear to influence, even if they are not as overtly reflected in, the French Conseil Constitutionnel's decisions.[41]

2.4 Formalism and Rules; Functionalism, Flexibility and Standards

Debates over fixed versus evolutionary constitutional interpretation, or between originalism and purposivism, correspond, though not exactly, to another set of debates, between more formalist approaches to adjudication and more flexible approaches, or between rules as compared to standards in implementing constitutional principles. More formalist approaches, on this account, are efforts to constrain judicial choices; as Frederick Schauer explains, the existence of a rule counts as a reason for a decision, even if the reasons underlying the rule might support a different decision. Rule-bound decisionmaking promotes predictability and stability, Schauer says, by 'forc[ing] the future into the categories of the past'.[42] Decision according to rule is said not only to enhance predictability but also to reduce errors made by other decisionmakers charged with applying doctrine or law; whether it is desirable may depend on a contextual evaluation of the likelihood of error if decisionmakers are free to reach an all-things-considered optimal judgment or are bound to apply a rule without regard to the reasons for it. The advice-giving requirements of *Miranda v Arizona* may be seen as an example of the articulation of a constitutional rule, to constrain the all-things-considered judgments of police and prosecutors.

Rule-bound formalism may be contrasted with more contextual judgments, whether these result from applying proportionality analysis on a case-by-case basis (even if proportionality as an approach might sometimes support creation of a rule), or from the articulation of other 'standards' for resolving particular kinds of questions. Kathleen Sullivan has famously contrasted the jurisprudence of 'rules' with the jurisprudence of 'standards',[43] describing the difference thus:

> [R]ules reflect the rationalist and positivist spirit of the codifiers and standards the pragmatic spirit of the common law judges. The Justices of rules are skeptical about reasoned elaboration and suspect that standards will enable the Court to translate raw subjective value preferences into law. The Justices of standards are skeptical about the capacity of rules to constrain value choice and believe that custom and shared understandings can adequately constrain judicial deliberation in a regime of standards.[44]

Rules are often associated with categorical approaches, standards with more flexible balancing or with judicial efforts to reach 'fair' or reasonable results.

2.5 Deference, Majoritarianism and Autonomous Legal Values

Central to any theory of constitutional interpretation is an understanding of the role of a court in a democracy: if judicial review is authorized, what role, if any, does judicial deference to political actors play? What weight should be accorded the constitutional views of legislative majorities? How 'majoritarian' should interpretive theory be – should judicial understandings be open to normative influence from social movements, as reflected either in legislation or in changing public opinion? Or should interpretive theory emphasize more the role of independent judicial judgment about legal values in securing the constitutional bases for democratic government, under law, to function?

Majoritarianism may influence interpretive approaches in different ways.[45] On one account, if a constitution is silent on an issue, that means it is up to the democratic process and legislative majorities to decide free from judicially enforceable constitutional constraints; so Justice Scalia in the United States has frequently argued. On the other hand, the theory of popular constitutionalism affords changing popular understandings a significant role in changing the understood meaning of the Constitution that can be enforced by courts; it may or may not be associated with deference to legislatures.[46] Much of the Australian Court's interpretive approach is informed by a sensibility viewing the legislature as the primary guardian of rights; yet when issues are understood to arise under constitutional text, 'strict legalism' has strong elements of autonomy from current popular views. Canadian opinions can likewise be found that debate the relationship of the court to legislative decisionmaking.[47]

All democratic constitutional systems need to maintain a balance between the court's role as an independent decisionmaker and the need for law, including constitutional law, to maintain a connection with the society in which it functions.[48] Some systems address this need through interpretation, whether by allowing substantial room for legislative judgment or through evolving interpretation informed by changing social understandings. In other systems, as discussed below, formal amendment has been a more frequent instrument of constitutional change. Still others provide mechanisms short of amendment that permit legislative response to or override of judicial decisions,[49] though in Canada, whose Section 33 override provision was hailed as a major constitutional innovation, it is not at all clear that the override has influenced the Court's interpretive autonomy or deference to legislatures.

2.6   Amendments, Positivism and Suprapositive Constitutionalism

In all of these jurisdictions, interpretive theory might be thought to require an account of the limits of legitimate interpretation, of when a constitutional change would require an amendment as compared to an interpretive shift. Little of the scholarship on interpretation is explicitly framed in these terms, and in many systems there are areas in which either interpretation or amendment might be available to address the same issue. In France, amendments have on recent occasions been adopted when a law, or a proposed treaty, is found inconsistent with the existing constitution;[50] Donald Kommers has commented that in Germany, 'judicially imposed remodeling of the Basic Law' would be regarded as inconsistent with a 'constitutional Rechtsstaat'.[51] In the United States, amendment as a vehicle for constitutional change is infrequent. Amendments face high procedural hurdles; some view amendment as a normative rupture to be avoided; and interpretation by the Court has often accommodated social change. Barry Friedman has gone so far as to claim that the events of 1937 amounted to a decision by the people that henceforth, the Constitution could be altered by judicial interpretation provided the Court stayed 'within the mainstream of popular understanding'.[52]

One further divide should be mentioned, and that is between those courts willing to apply standards not clearly expressed in the constitution to review the validity of formal constitutional amendments and those that are not. The difference is one not merely about interpretation but about judicial power, and the very idea of constitutionalism. But the difference is also reflected in the scope of legitimate *interpretive* claims about what a constitution stands for. Thus, in Germany, the Basic Law is interpreted as standing for a 'never again' principle, to prevent the reappearance of a Nazi-like regime. The 'eternity clause' of Article 79 makes aspects of the Basic Law unamendable, and Article 20 authorizes resistance, if necessary, to efforts to abolish the constitutional order. The eternity clause provides a positive basis for the German Court to hold amendments to the Basic Law unconstitutional; but the Court has also invoked principles of natural law or justice, principles that *'precede'* the constitution, in discussing the possibility of unconstitutional amendments.[53] On the other hand, the presence of an explicit unamendability clause (for example, Article 89 of the French Constitution) is not necessarily sufficient to generate judicial enforcement of limits on amendment, even in the hands of a court capable of creativity in interpreting constitutional instruments.[54] A court's willingness to engage in substantive review of amendments may well depend both on the presence or absence of a textual basis for deeming some matters unamendable, and on the prevailing conception of the 'pouvoir constituant', or power to engage in constitution-making, and its relationship, if any, to principles outside that formal process.

3   INTERPRETIVE APPROACH AND NATIONAL COURTS

Having identified a series of interpretive contests that may transcend national lines, we now identify some differences in interpretive approach among some leading national constitutional courts. The effort here is not to describe the most typical interpretive approach in each court, but rather the most nationally distinctive approaches to interpretation. The German Court will be considered here as an example of highly purposive reasoning, based on a view of the Constitution as a principled document to be interpreted holistically while still enabling pragmatic accommodations to go forward. In contrast, the US Court's justices are, as a whole, more inclined to what Ely criticized as 'clause-bound' interpretation than to attempting to bring the body of constitutional law into a principled and coherent whole; they are also more concerned with original understandings than are their counterparts in many other jurisdictions. The Canadian Supreme Court illustrates that constitutional interpretation in a common-law system need not be characterized by a focus on originalism, just as the Australian Court suggests that originalism has many variants and is not a made-only-in-the-USA phenomenon. Perhaps the 'most different' approach to interpretive discourse among our examples is found in the decisions of the French Conseil Constitutionnel, with its sparse and often cryptically syllogistic reasons set forth as if a logical deduction from legal materials. With these five countries we hope to illustrate both basic points: that there are distinctive approaches that we can identify within each of these courts, but that the areas of overlap are also significant.

3.1   Germany

The German Constitutional Court's commitment to developing an 'objective hierarchy of values' under the Basic Law bespeaks an effort to achieve coherence across constitutional areas. Its commitment to human dignity as the pervasive constitutional value is significant, especially because human dignity is one of the unamendable provisions of the German Basic Law protected by the so called 'eternity clause' of Article 79; the constitutional text here might be understood to commit the interpreters to a broadly purposive or teleological approach. The Court's recent decision finding invalid a statute (enacted after the 9/11 attacks in the United States and a threatened air attack on Frankfurt in 2003) authorizing the shooting down of hijacked civilian aircraft, as inconsistent with the human dignity of its innocent passengers, is an example of the power of this normative value in the highly teleological German jurisprudence.[55] In addition to other constitutional problems with the law, the Court found that by authorizing the sacrifice of the innocent passengers' lives, the state violated the fundamental principle of human dignity and the right to life: 'What is thus absolutely prohibited is any treatment of a human being by public authority which fundamentally calls into question his or her quality of a subject, his or her status as a legal entity ... by its lack of the respect of the value which is due to every human being for his or her own sake'.[56] Indeed, the Court wrote, to shoot down a plane with helpless passengers and crew:

> ignores the status of the persons affected as subjects endowed with dignity and inalienable rights. By their killing being used as a means to save others, they are treated as objects and at the same time deprived of their rights; with their lives being disposed of unilaterally by the state, the persons on board the aircraft, who, as victims, are themselves in need of protection, are denied the value which is due to a human being for his or her own sake.[57]

Although in many other of its opinions the German Court has engaged in proportionality analysis, or balancing, as a basic interpretive approach to reconciling and maximizing competing constitutional values,[58] in this part of this opinion respect for human dignity appears as something of an absolute barrier to government action.

The importance of human dignity and reasoning from that commitment as a transcendent, almost prepolitical value, is likewise suggested by the Court's analysis in a case finding life imprisonment without parole to contravene human dignity:

> The free human person and his dignity are the highest values of the constitutional order. The state in all of its forms is obliged to respect and defend it. This is based on the conception of man as a spiritual-moral being endowed with the freedom to determine and develop himself. This freedom ... is not that of an isolated and self-regarding individual but rather [that] of a person related to and bound by the community. ... [T]he state must regard every individual within society with equal worth.[59]

For these reasons it 'is contrary to human dignity to make persons the mere tool of the State'; in respect of punishment, the state needs to 'guarantee the minimal existence ... necessary for a life worthy of a human being', which makes it 'intolerable' to deprive a defendant of his freedom 'without at least providing him with the chance to someday regain this freedom'.[60]

If particular constitutional values play an important role in the highly purposive forms of German interpretation, other factors, including original understandings, play a lesser role. Indeed, in the Life Imprisonment case, the Court wrote that 'original history' and the ideas of the drafters were not of decisive importance, as opposed to improved understandings of the value of human dignity and better insights into the effect of life imprisonment on prisoners.[61] While the enactment history of the Basic Law plays a lesser role than do original understandings in US jurisprudence, its consideration is not entirely ruled out by the conventions of German constitutional discourse, as in references to the need to break from the Nazi legacy in interpreting the right to life in the first German Abortion Decision, referenced below.[62] Also, not unlike the common law jurisdiction courts, the FCC cites its own jurisprudence as an important source of authority,[63] and as discussed further below, considers the pragmatic consequences of interpretive choices in reaching decisions as well.

3.2   United States

US Supreme Court decisions often begin with either a recitation of a prior precedent, as framing the question, or a statement of the facts and procedural history of the case, rather than with a basic constitutional value or principle. Reference to precedent may reflect the degree to which the Court's common law background influences interpretive approach so that prior cases and their doctrine are treated as a part of the 'constitutional law' with at least some *stare decisis* effect. Perhaps the strongest statement of this position is found in *Cooper v Aaron*, where the Court, in an opinion signed by all nine members, wrote, 'the interpretation of the Fourteenth Amendment enunciated by this Court in the *Brown* [*v. Board of Education*] case is the supreme law of the land', under the Supremacy Clause of Article VI.[64] In practice, however, it is not clear that prior case law constrains the Court any more than prior German cases constrain the FCC. The recent decision in *Citizens United v Federal Election Commission*,[65] striking down restrictions on corporate political campaign expenditures, is a dramatic illustration of the degree to which strict *stare decisis* is rejected by many justices, since the Court had to overrule two prior decisions to reach the conclusion it did. The Court's attention to 'facts' is also probably related to its common law tradition, and the influence of interpretations of the 'case or controversy' limits of Article III as precluding advisory opinions and substantially limiting standing (for example, of legislators or taxpayers). But at the same time, one may question how significant the facts of each case actually are, given the Court's increasing sense of itself as an 'Olympian', law-announcing rather than error-correcting body.[66]

Each of the interpretive approaches described in section 2 can be found in some opinions of some justices of the US court, though the United States is less likely to produce constitutional opinions that frame their reasoning within constitutional first principles or values. *Brown* was predicated on a willingness to re-understand the significance of public education in the American democracy and the social meaning of segregation (in ways that would not be entirely unfamiliar to the contemporary Canadian Court).[67] The decision in *Lawrence v Texas*, holding that a state law criminalizing same-sex sodomy was unconstitutional under the Due Process Clause, drew on other cases to articulate the principle of a right to develop intimate relationships in the private sphere, while considering as well European law and changes in state law.[68] But there are opinions written in the US Supreme Court that would be quite rare, if not unheard of, in other leading constitutional courts.

Perhaps the most notable recent example is the decision in *District of Columbia v Heller*, striking down a DC law prohibiting the possession of handguns. The majority adopted a remarkably historical perspective to interpreting part of the Second Amendment's text, while eschewing attention to original purposes in interpreting the Amendment's implications for the regulation of weapons. In brief, the majority reasoned that the 'preamble' of the Second Amendment, asserting the importance of 'well-regulated' militias to a 'free State', did not constrain the meaning of the so-called 'operative clause' providing that the right of the people to keep and bear arms shall not be infringed. The Court abandoned specific-applications originalism in discussing the possible scope of this right,[69] but nonetheless the 40-plus pages in the majority opinion and the more than 35 pages in dissenting opinions devoted to arguments about intended meanings in the 18th and 19th centuries is something few other courts would produce.

3.3   Australia

As discussed above, 'legalism' – in the sense of 'strict devotion' to the words in the Constitution as they were understood in 1901 – is a distinguishing feature of Australian constitutional interpretation. *Stare decisis* is regarded in Australia as a part of 'strict legalism', rather than being an inconsistency to be either tolerated out of necessity or rejected, as some US originalists treat precedent viewed as inconsistent with original understandings.[70] Australian opinions on the whole seem to place Australia in the 'multi-valenced' camp of jurisprudential tendencies.[71] 'Strict legalism' is a commitment to the original meaning of the text, together with consideration of precedent, but in practice the Court has shown some willingness to depart from the original meaning in the face of changed understandings or circumstances, along with a willingness by many justices to consider foreign or international law.[72] The 'multi-valenced' character of the Australian High Court's interpretive approach is reinforced by the Court's seriatim opinion practice.

At another level, much of Australia's constitutional jurisprudence is informed by a self-consciousness about the deliberate omission of a bill of rights and a concomitant reliance on parliamentary decisionmaking.[73] In *Al-Kateb v Godwin,* the Court by a 4–3 vote rejected a challenge to the constitutionality of an alien's continued detention under a federal immigration statute.[74] The statute under which the alien was detained required that the federal government remove an unlawful alien and detain the alien until removal; the alien in question was a stateless person who could not be removed to another state and thus faced a seemingly indefinite period of detention. Rejecting the argument that insofar as indefinite detention was authorized it was a form of punishment that could only be carried out under the judgment of an Article III court, the majority judges reasoned that the detention was not imposed in order to punish but rather to be able to carry out the national government's powers to expel unlawful aliens. Judges in the majority placed considerable weight on parliamentary decisionmaking. Justice McHugh, for example, wrote that the power belonged to parliament and that the remedies, if any, for misuse of those powers lie elsewhere:

> If the Parliament of the Commonwealth enacts laws that direct the executive government to detain unlawful non-citizens in circumstances that prevent them from having contact with members of or removing them from the Australian community, nothing in the Constitution ... prevents the parliament doing so. For such laws, the parliament and those who introduce them must answer to the electors, to the international bodies who supervise human rights treaties to which Australia is a party and to history. Whatever criticism some – maybe a great many – Australians make of such laws, their constitutionality is not open to doubt.[75]

In the face of the majority's reliance on a broad scope for parliamentary power, the dissenting justices relied primarily on statutory grounds to find the continued detention ultra vires. Chief Justice Gleeson, for example, would have found the continued detention not authorized by law, based in part on a fundamental principle of 'legality', which requires courts not to assume without a clear statement that legislation was intended to intrude on certain human rights, including liberty.[76] Resort to statutory interpretation as a basis for finding invalid executive action may reflect not only the understandable hesitation of courts to adopt a more confrontational stance than necessary in matters involving foreign affairs,[77] but also the Australian tradition of parliamentary democracy as the principal protector of rights.[78]

As is true in the United States, different justices on the Australian Court have offered significantly different approaches to interpretation. Some argue that the Australian Constitution should be a 'living force',[79] in contrast to the more dominant commitment to 'legalism', in which (as noted above) the constitution's words are understood to mean the same thing now as when they were first adopted. On the whole, the Australian case law may be characterized as giving somewhat greater weight to the text, as originally understood, than do US cases on the whole, while also paying attention to and being influenced by many of the factors discussed in the US, German, and Canadian cases, including 'structural principles and implications', which may be unwritten, and 'policy' concerns of 'justice, utility and good government'.[80] Until quite recently, the detailed legislative history of the Constitution was not referred to in High Court opinions, but this has begun to change.[81] The Court's new willingness to resort to the constitution's legislative history to shed light on original understandings and purposes might be understood to reflect a less literal approach to Australian 'legalism', and in any event evinces a more complex multi-sourced interpretive approach.[82]

Just as interpretive approaches in the United States have been thought to vary with the period of time presided over by different Chief Justices (e.g., the 'Warren Court' as opposed to the 'Rehnquist Court'), Australia's High Court has been viewed as having somewhat varying interpretive postures in the different time periods associated with its Chief Justices. During the Mason Court in particular, observers perceived a significant openness to revised understandings of precedent and constitutional requirements.[83] In one case, *Street v Queensland Bar Ass'n*, the Court overruled a case decided just 16 years earlier. The issue was whether one state could impose a residency or primary practice requirement for bar admission under section 117 of the Constitution, which prohibits state discrimination against out-of-staters. In seven separate opinions, the Court unanimously reached the judgment that prior interpretations of section 117 had been unduly narrow, and that the reach of its ban on discrimination needed to be read more broadly in light of the overall constitutional purpose of building a unified country.[84] Several justices explicitly discussed the impact of modern developments on constitutional meaning, expressing concerns, for example, about not 'fossilizing' the Constitution.[85] An evolutionary approach to interpretation emerges, then, even within the 'legalistic' traditions of the Australian High Court. While observers have noted some movement back towards older approaches since Chief Justice Mason stepped down in 1995, the Court's approach remains firmly ensconced in the multi-valenced traditions of common law constitutionalism.

3.4 Canada

In Canada, the impact of the 'living tree' metaphor has extended from cases involving interpretation of the older, more structural constitution provided by the 1867 Constitution Act to the rights provisions in the 1982 Charter of Rights.[86] Canadian judicial discourse is marked by an interesting absence of disagreement on interpretive methodology; disagreements tend to focus more on substantive differences among the justices' evaluations of relevant constitutional values and their implications for the case at hand, including different evaluations of the degree of deference owed the legislature in the application of the agreed-on doctrinal tests. In *R v Keegstra*, for example, a closely divided Court upheld a statute prohibiting public hate speech directed at certain vulnerable groups. Both the majority and the dissent accepted and applied the same doctrinal formulation of proportionality analysis under Section 1. Where they disagreed was in its application, including disagreement over the consequences and effects of having such a law.[87] In another case affirming national legislative power to define marriage to include same-sex couples, the Court characterized its approach as one of 'progressive interpretation' that 'accommodates and addresses the realities of modern life'.[88] The text of Charter Section 1 may be regarded as an opening for fairly broad-ranging inquiries into what 'can be demonstrably justified in a free and democratic society' – language that invites consideration of the lessons of history and experience both in Canada and in other 'free and democratic' societies.

Indeed, Canada's jurisprudence illustrates the interpretive impact of the 'limitations clauses' now found in many domestic constitutions with respect to certain fundamental rights. Section 1 operates as a 'salvage' clause that permits laws found to infringe on protected rights to be upheld provided that they meet its requirements.[89] Those requirements have been developed in an elaborate jurisprudence of proportionality, involving an initial determination of whether the purpose of the legislation is itself compatible with a free and democratic society. If so, a three-step test (of rationality, minimal impairment, and proportionality as such) are applied to evaluate the statute as a means towards that end. The Canadian approach, some suggest, has contributed to a more purposive and expansive understanding of rights themselves, in contrast to the US approach of bundling analysis of the rights and the government interests involved.[90] In both systems, however, there are concerns for proportionality, albeit expressed in different terms.[91]

3.5   France

France is a somewhat problematic but nonetheless interesting comparative case. It is problematic, first, because there is disagreement whether to view the Conseil Constitutionnel as a court or as a distinctive political organ (in the words of some, a third legislative chamber). The problem arises in part because, as a formal matter, the Conseil's jurisdiction to review laws could until very recently be exercised only before the law was promulgated by the President.[92] Second, French judicial opinions are notably terse and cryptic; to understand and situate them it is helpful to read academic notes and analyses, not widely available in English,[93] as well as the legal commentary offered by the Conseil's Secretary-General. Moreover, although the Conseil Constitutionnel has begun translating some decisions into English, the original references to the Conseil and the government's replies, which are also publicly available, are not translated into English. For those (like us) with only rudimentary French, the selective availability of the Conseil's decisions and in particular of the associated commentary provides only limited access to what, within the French legal community, may be understood as the Conseil's interpretive approaches. Much of the literature in English, finally, is concerned less with interpretive theory or approach than with institutional, or subject-specific, concerns. Comments in this section are therefore particularly cautious and limited.

The discursive style of the Conseil Constitutionnel is somewhat similar to that of the two French supreme courts, the Cour de Cassation and the Conseil d'État.[94] The style of those courts has received extensive attention in the scholarly literature. It is in form syllogistic, beginning with a 'Whereas' or 'Having regard to' or 'Considering' clause. As Michel Rosenfeld has written,

> In the French style, the court 'speaks' the law or the constitution in the name of the Republic as an indivisible whole. In contrast, in the US common law context, judges 'make' or infer or construct

the law. ... by a process of interpretation, accretion, experimentation, argumentation and trial and error ... [I]n the French model, the rule-of-law republic speaks with one voice regardless of the actual difficulties presented by the constitutional issue at stake.[95]

The brevity and opacity of the published decisions of all three of these courts has been widely noted, and limits efforts to discern an interpretive approach from their words standing alone.

A 1971 decision of the Conseil Constitutionnel, sometimes referred to as France's *Marbury v Madison*,[96] was made up of only four brief 'In light of' clauses, each identifying a different source of law, followed by six terse numbered paragraphs.[97] Nonetheless, it resulted in a very dramatic expansion of understandings of the controlling constitutional texts and of the controlling sources of constitutional law. It not only found a law enacted by parliament to be inconsistent with individual rights, but it did so on the basis of the seemingly indeterminate (and potentially expansive) concept of the fundamental principles of the laws of the republic, which the Conseil said were incorporated into the present constitution by preambulatory references. The 1971 decision found such a fundamental principle by reference to a 1901 statute that was not itself characterized as part of the constitution. In prioritizing the principles of one statute enacted 70 years earlier over the challenged statute, just passed by the parliament, the Conseil offered no underlying reasoning in its published decision, however much the decision may have drawn from earlier decisions by the Conseil d'État,[98] or been discussed in internal memoranda and meetings.[99] As Alec Stone said, 'The entire text of the famous 1971 decision on freedom of association . . . contains only six "considerations," sentence-like assertions about what the law is.'[100] The 1962 Referendum decision, in which the Conseil found it lacked jurisdiction to review the legality of a referendum to change the constitution, consists of only five 'consideration' paragraphs, taking less than two pages in the Recueil reports.[101] In 1970 a scholar described the 'laconic' decisions of the Conseil Constitutionnel as simply a 'decision on the facts' that 'a given enactment. . . is or is not [permissible] and no light is thrown on the principle if any, behind the decision'.[102] While this may go too far, the brevity and cryptic nature of the Conseil's decisions can make it difficult to characterize its interpretive approach.[103]

Yet the Conseil Constitutionnel's opinions since the 1980s have been, on the whole, less laconic than its earlier years;[104] they offer justifications, though not full defenses of their positions, in ways that permit some greater insight into interpretive approaches. Recent decisions reveal, for example, concern in some areas with proportionality;[105] implicit awareness of comparative constitutional law and attention to the jurisprudence of the European Court of Human Rights across an array of issues;[106] and rare but occasional references to the Conseil's own prior case law. Implicit references to prior case law appear through use of language from the prior opinions.[107] In many cases, reasons for the judgment responsive to the arguments raised are given, though they are not necessarily fully explained.[108] Indeed, in his 2008 book, John Bell, another leading scholar of the Conseil Constitutionnel, noted that the decisions of the Conseil are not as brief as those of the Cour de Cassation and Conseil d'État, and that the Conseil now makes an effort to be accessible to the press.[109]

The French interpretive approach, as revealed in the published decisions, remains distinctively syllogistic, sparsely written as if the reasons are plainly adduced from the listed sources of law. And yet, the creativity and judgment involved in identifying the sources of French constitutional law belie the apparent constraint of the positive theoretical framing.[110] The incorporation of fundamental principles identified in the laws of the republic, noted above, was a major expansion. In later cases, the Conseil distinguished such principles from mere 'traditions', not of constitutional value,[111] in a move that emphasized the degree of historical, social and cultural judgment entailed in identifying those principles. The effort to reconcile sometimes quite divergent values, for example, on property rights in the 1789 and 1946 constitutional instruments,[112] plainly requires judicial choice. The Conseil has also developed the doctrine of 'constitutional objectives', derived from more modern legislation, and relied on these to invalidate subsequent legislation, as in a series of cases on concentration of press ownership.[113] The decisions of the Conseil can be taken to show how a positivist, formalist interpretive discourse may nonetheless draw on multiple sources, and contribute to an evolutionary body of court-made jurisprudence.[114]

Thus, on the Conseil, reasons are given, but often not explained; contrary readings are left unexplored; and univocality reinforces an apparent formalism. By rooting the constitution in sources from many different periods in the past, as well as in statutes of the Third Republic, however, the Conseil has increased its flexibility to adapt the constitution to changing circumstances; at times it has shown little hesitation to invalidate major statutes, seemingly accepting the possibility that amendment will follow.[115] (Perhaps the jurisdiction regularly exercised under Article 54, to determine whether treaty ratification requires a constitutional amendment, helps normalize amendment.[116]) Some scholars characterize the Conseil's role as that of channeling political disagreement into a procedure (amendment) that requires more compromise across party lines.[117] With a significant change in jurisdiction authorizing referrals of challenges to enacted statutes in individual cases from the Conseil d'État and the Cour de Cassation, the trend towards more justificatory reasoning on the face of the opinions may well become more intense, as the Conseil forms relationships with individual litigants, and as the impact of transnational discourses and decisions on constitutional law grows.

4   CONCLUDING REMARKS: INTERPRETIVE APPROACH AND SUBSTANTIVE OUTCOME

All of the dominant interpretive approaches have a range of indeterminacy in their applications. And all successful constitutional courts must maintain a relationship of trust with legal elites and with the population sufficient to induce compliance with unpopular decisions in their polities; thus all are responsive at times to broader currents of thought and opinion in ways not always captured by interpretive method. We briefly illustrate these two points below with reference to the Second Amendment in the United States and the German Court's decisions on abortion.

In *Heller*, the Court effectively overruled a nearly 70-year-old precedent, *United States v Miller. Miller*, in rejecting a Second Amendment challenge to one of the first federal firearms control statutes, explained its reasoning in ways that strongly suggested that the Amendment was limited to the protection of the existence of armed state militias.[118] It was so viewed for decades in legislative bodies, which enacted gun regulations, and in the lower federal and state courts. Nonetheless, a movement spearheaded by, inter alia, conservatives in the National Rifle Association in the 1970s, and the Reagan election in 1980, led to a body of government reports and scholarship that argued that the Amendment should be read to protect an individual right to bear arms, whether or not connected to state militias in their current form.[119] In *Heller*, the Supreme Court declared unconstitutional a District of Columbia law that banned the possession of handguns by most persons in the District. Reading the Second Amendment in a deliberately non-purposive way, the Court treated its opening or 'prefatory' clause as irrelevant to its 'operative' force. Textualism was thus placed at war not only with purposivism but with itself.[120] The degree to which the majority was prepared to discount *stare decisis* in the wake of 70 years of regulation in reliance on *Miller* was startling and not entirely acknowledged by the Court.[121]

For present purposes, what is worth noting is the degree to which the principal *dissent* argued the original understanding of the Amendment (to protect militias and to protect arms bearing only in connection therewith). Justice Stevens vigorously contested the majority's analysis of what the framing generation understood, invoking examples of regulations of firearms and ammunition of the late 18th century. The conflicts over what the 'originalist' sources showed tends to support the suggestion that much of the emphasis on originalism reflects less a commitment to a particular method of legal interpretation than a phalanx of positions tied together by political and cultural understandings;[122] it also lends credence to Reva Siegel's argument that what the Court now perceives as the core meaning of the Second Amendment was constructed through the social and political movements of the 1980s and 1990s.[123] Given the conflicting mounds of evidence amassed in the majority and dissenting opinions, and the overruling of prior precedent, originalism as an interpretive method is plainly not predictive – by itself – of the result.[124]

We turn now to an example from the German Constitutional Court. As noted above, central to the German Court's interpretive approach is the foundational character of human dignity and the right to life in the objective ordering of values. Yet application of these norms may well be influenced by more pragmatic considerations and may change over time, as the movement from the Court's first decision on abortion to the second illustrates. In the first Abortion Decision, the German Court found unconstitutional a liberalization statute that would have authorized abortions in the first 12 weeks of pregnancy, following counseling. Although the statute was defended as promoting unborn life, on the theory that if more women went for counseling they would decide to continue their pregnancies, the court emphasized the individual character of the (fetal) right to life and the value of human dignity, suggesting that to give 'unrestricted power of disposition' to pregnant women to terminate early pregnancies was inconsistent with those values.[125] The Court specifically rejected the consequentialist argument that 'developing life would be better protected through individual counseling of the pregnant woman than through a threat of punishment', asserting that 'the weighing in bulk of life against life which leads to … the destruction of a supposedly smaller number in the interests of the preservation of an allegedly larger number is not reconcilable with the obligation of an individual protection of each single concrete life'.[126]

In the second German Abortion Decision of 1993, reviewing the legislation that emerged after the reunification of East and West Germany, the Court appeared to retreat from this position. The abortion question was one of the most divisive in the negotiations between the two Germanies; indeed, the reunification agreement allowed both parts of Germany to maintain their own abortion law regime for a period of two years. When the compromise legislation was before it in 1993, the Court took a very different view of approaches that relied on counseling, without third party evaluation, for an early decision to abort. As Gerald Neuman described the Court's reasoning, because pregnancy often could not be perceived in the first trimester, '[a] system that elicited the cooperation of the woman therefore had a greater chance of success in preventing abortion than a system that antagonized her and prompted evasion', and the 'threat of criminal punishment and the subjection of the woman to third party evaluation of her need for an abortion had proved antagonizing'.[127] In this passage, then, we see a distinctly more consequentialist view of how the value of human dignity was to be served than we saw in the First Abortion Decision – or in the later decision on shooting down airplanes, discussed earlier. Might the Court have been willing to tolerate this as a pragmatic accommodation on a highly divisive issue? Whatever the motivation, one can see on this issue that, even in a court that highly values coherence and purposivism in the interpretation of the Basic Law, there is some degree of indeterminacy in the application of its interpretive method to individual cases.

In choosing only five countries to examine, we have necessarily limited the inferences we can draw about constitutional interpretation across the world's courts. Still, as these examples make clear, leading constitutional courts, like the judges that populate them, operate within and are constrained by distinctive interpretive traditions but at the same time display considerable interpretive overlap. The differences within courts and their scholarly communities may well be as significant – if not more so – as the differences across courts.

NOTES

1. We would like to thank Donald Kommers, Gerald Neuman and Mark Tushnet for helpful comments on an earlier draft.
2. See David S. Law, 'Generic Constitutional Law', 89 *Minnesota Law Review* 652 (2005).
3. Vicki C. Jackson, 'Multivalenced Constitutional Interpretation and Constitutional Comparisons: An Essay in Honor of Mark Tushnet', 26 *Quinnipiac Law Review* 599, 601–04, 637–47 (2008).
4. See Mitchel de S.-O.-l'E Lasser, *Judicial Transformations* 20–22, 27, 299–305 (2009); see also Donald L. Horowitz, 'Constitutional Courts: A Primer for Decision Makers', 17 *Journal of Democracy* 127 (2006) (noting that judicial review has grown in importance 'largely to enforce guarantees of human rights'); cf. Miguel Schor, 'Mapping Comparative Judicial Review', 7 *Washington University Global Studies Law Review* 257 (2008) (situating the rise in judicial review in the context of citizen rights demands manifested in their bringing claims before courts).
5. For a useful discussion of case selection, see Ran Hirschl, 'The Question of Case Selection in Comparative Constitutional Law', 53 *American Journal of Comparative Law* 125 (2005). Note also that our analysis is trained on *judicial* constitutional interpretation; we do not here address interpretation by other institutional actors within the constitutional systems under study.
6. Cf. Mitchel de S.-O.-l'E. Lasser, *Judicial Deliberations* 27–60 (2004) (noting the bifurcation between the public presentation of a terse single judgment and the rich but hidden internal discourse of the French Cour de Cassation).
7. As the case selection indicates, we read mostly English. Many of the decisions of the FCC are available in translation on the court's website, and helpful English-language legal analysis is also available from scholars such as Donald Kommers. See, e.g., Donald P. Kommers, *The Constitutional Jurisprudence of the Federal Republic of Germany* (1997). Likewise, the Conseil Constitutionnel has placed translations of some of its opinions on its website, and many of its decisions have been explored by scholars writing in English. See, e.g., John Bell, *French Constitutional Law* (1992); Alec Stone, *The Birth of Judicial Politics in France* (1992). That said, partial translations of opinions reflect translators' decisions about what is most important, and even where full translations are available on judicial websites, the choice of cases may reflect the courts' own views of the cases' importance. That selection effect may limit the representativeness of the interpretive methods observed. Moreover, important differences in interpretive approach might be glossed over because of the limits of translation.
8. See Richard H. Fallon, Jr., 'A Constructivist Coherence Theory of Constitutional Interpretation', 100 *Harvard Law Review* 1189 (1987).
9. 252 US 416, 433 (1920).
10. 17 US (4 Wheat.) 316, 407, 415 (1819). See also *Marbury v Madison*, 5 US (1 Cranch) 137, 176 (1803).
11. Just as Holmes implied, in *Missouri v Holland*, that there are 'words' and then there are 'words that are a

constituent act', the Privy Council observed that 'there are statutes and statutes'. *Edwards v. Att'y-Gen. for Can.*, [1930] AC 124, 136 (PC 1929) (appeal taken from Can.).

12. *Edwards,* [1930] AC at 134 (quoting Sir Robert Borden, *Canadian Constitutional Studies* 55 (1922)).
13. See Vicki C. Jackson, 'Constitutions as Living Trees? Comparative Constitutional Law and Interpretive Metaphors', 75 *Fordham Law Review* 921, 954 (2006).
14. See Owen Dixon, 'Swearing In of Sir Owen Dixon as Chief Justice (Apr. 12, 1952)', in (1952) 85 CLR xi, xiv (Austl.) ('There is no other safe guide to judicial decisions in great conflicts than a strict and complete legalism'); see also *Singh v Commonwealth*, (2004) 222 CLR 322, 338 (Austl.) (Gleeson, CJ) (explaining that constitutional interpretation is based not on current understandings but on 'the contemporary meaning of the language used in 1900').
15. Antonin Scalia, 'Modernity and the Constitution', in *Constitutional Justice under Old Constitutions* 315 (Eivind Smith ed., 1995).
16. See Jamal Greene, 'On the Origins of Originalism', 88 *Texas Law Review* 1, 11 (2009).
17. See, e.g., David C. Gray, 'Why Justice Scalia Should be a Constitutional Comparativist – Sometimes', 59 Stanford Law Review 1249 (2007); Mark Tushnet, 'When is Knowing Less Better Than Knowing More? Unpacking the Controversy over Supreme Court Reference to Non-U.S. Law', 90 *Minnesota Law Review* 1275, 1279–80 (2006).
18. Greene, *supra* note 16, at 9–10 (discussing Justice Scalia's views).
19. See *Street v Queensland Bar Ass'n*, (1989) 168 CLR 461, 537–8 (Dawson, J) (discussing 'denotation' and 'connotation' of constitutional terms); Jeffrey Goldsworthy, 'Originalism in Constitutional Interpretation', 25 *Federal Law Review* 1, 20 (1997) (arguing that a distinction between 'enactment' and 'application' intentions is an aspect of 'moderate originalism').
20. See, e.g., *King v Jones*, (1972) 128 CLR 221, 229 (Barwick, CJ); *Eastman v R*, (2000) 203 CLR 1, 40–47 (McHugh, J).
21. See Ronald Dworkin, *Freedom's Law: The Moral Reading of the American Constitution* 76 (1996); Ronald Dworkin, *Taking Rights Seriously* 134, 136–7 (1977) (arguing that judges should consider constitutional terms like 'equality' not as specific conceptions of rights but as 'appeals to moral concepts'); see also *In re Wakim; Ex parte McNally*, (1999) 198 CLR 511, 552 (McHugh, J) (drawing a parallel between Dworkin's concept–conception distinction and Australian doctrine).
22. Jack M. Balkin, 'Abortion and Original Meaning', 24 *Constitutional Commentary* 291 (2007) (distinguishing original meaning from original expected application and arguing that there is a false dichotomy between originalism and living constitutionalism).
23. See Randy E. Barnett, *Restoring the Lost Constitution* 120 (2004); Keith Whittington, *Constitutional Construction* 2 (1999).
24. Stephen Breyer, *Active Liberty* (2006); John Hart Ely, *Democracy and Distrust* (1980).
25. See Balkin, *supra* note 22, at 301; Greene, *supra* note 16, at 81.
26. Aharon Barak, *Purposive Interpretation in Law* 190 (2005).
27. Id. at 191.
28. Id. at 238.
29. David M. Beatty, *The Ultimate Rule of Law* (2004).
30. Many jurisdictions use a four-part test, the first aspect of which is to assure the legitimacy of the government's purpose; assuming that there is a legitimate purpose, the inquiry proceeds to consider the suitability or rationality of the means chosen; whether the means are necessary towards the goal, or minimally impair the right; and whether the intrusion can be justified by the government's goal of beneficent effects. See *R v Oakes*, (1986) 1 SCR 103, 139.
31. Beatty, *supra* note 29, at 160–61. For critical examination of this claim, see Vicki C. Jackson, 'Being Proportional About Proportionality', 21 *Constitutional Commentary* 803 (2004).
32. See Robert Alexy, *A Theory of Constitutional Rights* 67 (Julian Rivers trans., 2002).
33. See generally Jacco Bomhoff, 'Balancing, the Global and the Local: Judicial Balancing as a Problematic Topic in Comparative (Constitutional) Law', 31 *Hastings International and Comparative Law Review* 555 (2008).
34. See Dieter Grimm, 'Proportionality in Canadian and German Jurisprudence', 57 *University of Toronto Law Journal* 383 (2007) (suggesting that Canadian proportionality analysis focuses on the second step, minimal intrusion, while German proportionality analysis focuses on both minimal impairment and on the weighing of the harm to constitutional values against the nature of the government's purpose).
35. See Ernest Young, 'Rediscovering Conservatism: Burkean Political Theory and Constitutional Interpretation', 72 *North Carolina Law Review* 619, 624 (1994) (advocating constitutional interpretation grounded in the 'gradual, evolutionary development of traditional constitutional principles in a manner similar to the common law'); David A. Strauss, 'Common Law Constitutional Interpretation', 63 *University of Chicago Law Review* 877 (1996) (arguing that a common law approach accords with current US practice and provides the best justification for that practice); Philip Bobbitt, *Constitutional Fate* 3–119 (1982) (sketching six distinct, self-legitimating

'modalities' of US constitutional interpretation); Jackson, *supra* note 3, at 642 (arguing that multi-valenced interpretation 'makes it more likely that a wide array of claimants will be able to join in constitutional interpretation').

36. Fallon, *supra* note 8, at 1246.
37. See Jeffrey Goldsworthy, 'Conclusions', in *Interpreting Constitutions: A Comparative Study* 321, 325 (Jeffrey Goldsworthy ed., 2006).
38. See Jackson, *supra* note 13, at 929–32 (discussing the multi-sourced approach of the FCC in the first German Abortion Decision).
39. See *Roach v Electoral Comm'r*, (2007) 239 ALR 1 (Gleeson, CJ) (discussing, inter alia, precedents of the Supreme Court of Canada and the European Court of Human Rights, and constitutional text, history, and purpose, to invalidate the disenfranchisement of all prisoners regardless of sentence length); see also *SGH Ltd. v Comm'r of Taxation* (2002) 210 CLR 51, 75 (Gummow, J) ('Questions of construction of the constitution are not to be answered by the adoption and application of any particular, all-embracing and revelatory theory or doctrine of interpretation.').
40. For invocation of text, precedent and purpose, see *Labatt Breweries of Canada v AG Canada*, [1980] 1 SCR 914 (invalidating national beer labeling rule). For the Canadian Court's willingness to depart from original understandings, see *Reference re Section 94(2) of the Motor Vehicle Act (British Columbia)*, [1985] 2 SCR 486.
41. According to Professor Lasser, the French high courts consider a much broader range of material and perspectives in their internal deliberations than are reflected in their opinions. Although he has studied principally the Cour de Cassation (and to some extent the Conseil d'État), a similar pattern likely exists in the Conseil Constitutionnel. See *infra* note 99. On the range of foreign and international sources considered by the Conseil, see Olivier Dutheillet de Lamothe, 'Judges' Roundtable', 3 *International Journal of Constitutional Law* 550 (2005).
42. Frederick Schauer, 'Formalism', 97 *Yale Law Journal* 509, 537, 542 (1988).
43. Kathleen Sullivan, 'Foreword: The Justices of Rules and Standards', 106 *Harvard Law Review* 22 (1992). The rules-standards debate is a feature of US interpretive discourse; related debates are found as well in other jurisdictions. See, e.g., Stefan Sottiaux and Gerhard van der Schyff, 'Methods of International Human Rights Adjudication: Towards a More Structured Decision-Making Process for the European Court of Human Rights', 31 *Hastings International & Comparative Law Review* 115, 117–21 and nn. 5, 18 (2008) (citing sources); Peter McCormick, 'Blocs, Swarms, and Outliers: Conceptualizing Disagreement on the Modern Supreme Court of Canada', 42 *Osgoode Hall Law Journal* 99, 105 (2004) (contrasting 'formalism' with 'contextualism'); Paul Horwitz, 'Law's Expression: The Promise and Perils of Judicial Opinion Writing in Canadian Constitutional Law', 38 *Osgoode Hall Law Journal* 101, 132 (2000) (describing formalist 'tests' for ascertaining Section 2 violations).
44. Sullivan, *supra* note 43, at 27.
45. See Roger P. Alford, 'In Search of a Theory for Constitutional Comparativism', 52 *UCLA Law Review* 639, 674 (2005) (distinguishing 'structural' and 'interpretive' majoritarianism); see also Ely, *supra* note 24.
46. Both 'gun rights' and the anti-abortion rights movement have been identified as examples in the United States of popular mobilizations in support of constitutional change. See Reva B. Siegel, 'Dead or Alive: Originalism as Popular Constitutionalism' in *Heller*, 122 *Harvard Law Review* 191 (2008); Robert Post and Reva Siegel, 'Roe Rage: Democratic Constitutionalism and Backlash', 42 *Harv. C.R.-C.L. L. Rev.* 373 (2007). On legislative deference, compare, e.g., *District of Columbia v Heller*, 128 S. Ct. 2783, 2852 (2008) (Breyer, J, dissenting) (advocating deference to legislatures in seeking a balance between gun rights and gun control), with *Stenberg v Carhart*, 530 US 914, 920 (2000) (Breyer, J) (striking down Nebraska's prohibition on an abortion procedure, notwithstanding argument for deference to the state legislature, *id.* at 1017–18 (Thomas, J, dissenting)).
47. See, e.g., *Health Services & Support v B.C.*, 2007 SCC 27, 161–4 (Deschamps, J, dissenting in part) (canvassing cases to argue that a 'contextual' approach to proportionality analysis may lead to greater or lesser deference to the legislature depending on circumstances); *R v Morgentaler*, [1988] 1 SCR 30, 132 (McIntyre, J, dissenting) (arguing for deference to Parliament's abortion regulations).
48. See Victor Ferreres Comella, *Constitutional Courts and Democratic Values* (2009).
49. See generally Stephen Gardbaum, 'The New Commonwealth Model of Constitutionalism', 49 *American Journal of Comparative Law* 707 (2001); Mark V. Tushnet, *Weak Courts, Strong Rights* 23–42 (2007).
50. See Susan Wright, 'The French Conseil Constitutionnel in 1999', 6 *European Public Law* 146, 147 (2000) (describing several constitutional amendments made in 1999 to promote 'Europeanization', to allow participation in the International Criminal Court, and to permit affirmative legislation on behalf of women's equality in elective office). The Conseil has jurisdiction to review proposed treaties before they are ratified. See Constitution of France, 1958, Article 54 (explaining that a proposed treaty found inconsistent with the constitution may be ratified only after the constitution is amended).
51. Donald Kommers, 'Germany: Balancing Rights and Duties', in *Interpreting Constitutions, supra* note 37, at 171 (noting that formal amendment is 'a principal mode of constitutional change', with amendments in the prior decade of 25 articles and 44 clauses).

52. Barry Friedman, *The Will of the People* 196 (2009).
53. BverfGE 1, 14 (1951) ('There are constitutional provisions that are so fundamental and to such an extent an expression of *a law that precedes even the constitution* that they also bind the framer of the constitution, and other constitutional provisions that do not rank so high may be null and void, because they contravene those principles'), translated in Gary Jeffrey Jacobsohn, 'An Unconstitutional Constitution? A Comparative Perspective', 4 *International Journal of Constitutional Law* (I•CON) 460, 477 n. 58 (2006) (emphasis added); cf. Sudhir Krishnaswamy, *Democracy and Constitutionalism in India: A Study of the Basic Structure Doctrine* (2009) (describing the 'basic structure' doctrine, under which the Indian Supreme Court has declared unconstitutional certain duly enacted constitutional amendments). For a more general discussion of the possibility of 'suprapositive' constitutional norms, see Gerald L. Neuman, 'Human Rights and Constitutional Rights: Harmony and Dissonance', 55 *Stanford Law Review* 1863 (2003).
54. See Ferreres Comella, *supra* note 48, at 105-06 (stating that the Conseil Constitutionnel has made clear that it lacks power to review constitutional amendments and noting the availability of amendment as 'a crucial ingredient' to justify judicial review in French scholarly discourse); see also Susan Wright, 'The Self-Restraint of the Conseil Constitutionnel', 11 *European Public Law* 495, 496 (2005) (noting that the Conseil recently rejected a challenge to the constitutionality of an amendment in a decision with 'only three recitals'). On the Conseil's implicit rejection of the idea of 'supra-constitutionnalité' in connection with Maastricht Treaty challenges, see Bruno Genevois, Conseiller d'État, 'Le Traité sur l'Union européenne et la Constitution révisée: A propos de la décision du Conseil constitutionnel n° 92-312 DC du 2 septembre 1992', RFDA 1992, p. 937, para. II (A) (2)(B). We thank Denis Baranger for helpful discussions and for bringing the Genevois article to our attention.
55. 1 BvR 357/05 (First Senate, 2006), available at http://www.bverfg.de/entscheidungen/rs20060215_1bvr035705en.html.
56. Id. ¶ 119; see also id. at ¶ 35 ('The state may not protect a majority of its citizens by intentionally killing a minority.').
57. Id. ¶ 122.
58. See, e.g., 1 BvR 2150/08 (2009) (upholding criminal statute penalizing public assemblies glorifying Naziism that disturb the public peace) (English-language press release available at http://www.bverfg.de/en/press/bvg09-129en.html). In the Shoot Down case, the Court also noted the great uncertainty that would accompany any targeted shooting down of a plane, which might be read to suggest a form of proportionality analysis in play. 1 BvR 357/05, ¶ 123.
59. Kommers, *supra* note 7, at 307–08 (translation of Life Imprisonment case).
60. Id. at 308.
61. Id. at 307.
62. See Jackson, *supra* note 13, at 929–30.
63. In the Shoot Down case, for example, the court referred to its past decisions elaborating the guarantee of human dignity and the fundamental right to life. 1 BvR 357/05, ¶¶ 117–19.
64. 358 US 1, 18 (1958).
65. 130 S. Ct. 876 (2010).
66. Arthur Hellman, 'The Shrunken Docket of the Rehnquist Court', 1996 *Supreme Court Review* 403, 432–3; see Edward A. Hartnett, 'Questioning Certiorari: Some Reflections Seventy-Five Years After the Judges' Bill', 100 *Columbia Law Review* 1463 (2000).
67. Compare *Brown v Bd. of Educ.*, 347 US 483 (1954), with *Vriend v Alberta*, [1998] 1 SCR 493 (finding unconstitutional a provincial antidiscrimination law that failed to prohibit discrimination based on homosexuality).
68. 539 US 558 (2003).
69. Indeed, the Court applied the Amendment to handguns, which were not in common use at the time of ratification. See Jamal Greene, '*Heller* High Water? The Future of Originalism', 3 *Harvard Law and Policy Review* 325, 337 (2009) (referring to the majority's 'evolving standards of self-defense' test).
70. See Greene, *supra* note 16, at 16–17, 49 n. 335, 61.
71. See Michael McHugh, 'The Constitutional Jurisprudence of the High Court: 1989–2004', 30 *Sydney Law Review* 5, 8–9 (2008) (calling Australian constitutional interpretation a 'house of many rooms' that relies on text, structure, history, precedent, and policy considerations); see also Leslie Zines, 'The Present State of Constitutional Interpretation', in *The High Court at the Crossroads: Essays in Constitutional Law* 224, 234–8 (Adrienne Stone and George Williams eds., 2000) (concluding that the Court displays no 'general pattern' or interpretive direction).
72. There are occasional assertions that specific sources are ruled out. See, e.g., *Al-Kateb v Godwin*, (2004) 219 CLR 562, ¶ 66 (McHugh, J) ('[T]his court has never accepted that the Constitution contains an implication to the effect that it should be construed to conform with the rules of international law.'). Yet Justices of quite different ideological approaches have comfortably invoked foreign law for or against various propositions. See generally Cheryl Saunders, 'The Use and Misuse of Comparative, Constitutional Law', 13 *Indiana Journal of Global Legal Studies* 37, 53–61 (2006); cf. Adrienne Stone, 'Freedom of Political Communication,

the Constitution and the Common Law', 26 *Federal Law Review* 219, 220 (1998) (criticizing the Mason Court for being unduly influenced by the US approach on free speech issues).

73.   The Australian Constitution has only a small number of provisions concerning individual rights at the federal level. See Australian Constitution ch. I, pt. 5, § 51 (xxxi) (right to just terms in the event of a taking); id. ch. III, § 80 (right to jury trial); id. ch. V, § 116 (right to religious freedom). In 1988, a proposed constitutional amendment to extend those rights to the states was overwhelmingly rejected. Goldsworthy, 'Devotion to Legalism', in *Interpreting Constitutions*, *supra* note 37, at 110. In 2009 a national commission recommended Australia's adoption of a Human Rights Act. See www.humanrightsconsultation.gov.au.

74.   *Al-Kateb v Godwin*, (2004) 219 CLR 562.

75.   Id. ¶ 48; see also id. ¶ 298 (Callinan, J) ('It is a matter for the Australian Parliament to determine the basis on which illegal entrants are to be detained. So long as the purpose of detention has not been abandoned, a statutory purpose it may be observed that is clearly within a constitutional head of power, it is the obligation of the courts to ensure that any detention for that purpose is neither obstructed nor frustrated.').

76.   Id. ¶¶ 19–21 (Gleeson, CJ) ('The possibility that a person, regardless of personal circumstances, regardless of whether he or she is a danger to the community, and regardless of whether he or she might abscond, can be subjected to indefinite, and perhaps permanent, administrative detention is not one to be dealt with by implication.'); see also id. ¶¶ 118–40 (Gummow, J) (concluding that the statute did not authorize detention once it became clear that there was no reasonable prospect for removal, though also finding that the act would be unconstitutional if it applied); id. ¶ 144 (Kirby, J) (agreeing with Justice Gummow's statutory analysis). Relying on ultra vires review rather than individual rights adjudication to maintain the rule of law, as the Australian High Court also did, for example, in *Australia Communist Party v Commonwealth*, (1951), 83 CLR 1 (invalidating a law dissolving the Communist Party), might correspond to a similar tradition within French jurisprudence. See Lasser, *supra* note 4, at 68–70 (describing 'legality' review (including ultra vires) in the Conseil d'État as a typically French practice that is now under assault from an emphasis on individual rights).

77.   Compare, e.g., *Zadvydas v Davis*, 533 US 678 (2001) (applying the canon of constitutional avoidance in a case involving a statute authorizing alien detention).

78.   Even when the High Court took its first, cautious steps towards protecting an implied individual right to political communication, in *Australia Capital Television Pty Ltd. v Commonwealth*, (1992) 177 CLR 106, and *Nationwide News Pty. Ltd. v Wills*, (1992) 177 CLR 1, the justices justified the decisions by reference to the traditions of parliamentary democracy. See, e.g., *Nationwide News*, Id. at 48 (Brennan, J) ('Freedom of public discussion of government . . . is not merely a desirable political privilege; it is inherent in the idea of a representative democracy.'); see also id. (Deane, Toohey, JJ) ¶ 19 ('[T]here is to be discerned in the doctrine of representative government which the Constitution incorporates an implication of freedom of communication of information and opinions about matters relating to the government of the Commonwealth.').

79.   See Michael Kirby, 'Constitutional Interpretation and Original Intent: A Form of Ancestor Worship?', 24 *Melbourne University Law Review* 1, 11 (2000) (approving of Andrew Inglis Clark's argument that the Australian Constitution must be 'made a living force' and arguing that present understandings of the Constitution's meaning should control interpretation today). See also Adrienne Stone, 'Australia's Constitutional Rights and The Problem of Interpretive Disagreement', 27 *Sydney Law Review* 29, 41–2 (2005).

80.   Goldsworthy, *supra* note 73, at 128, 131–3.

81.   Goldsworthy, *supra* note 73, at 124; see *Cole v Whitfield*, (1988) 165 CLR 360, 385 (rejecting past practice and allowing use of convention debates to ascertain the meaning of constitutional text). The Court's earlier refusal to cite to constitutional convention debates was thought to be consistent with legalism, rooted in the English common law tradition of ignoring extrinsic evidence of statutory meaning.

82.   See, e.g., Jeremy Kirk, 'Constitutional Implications (II): Doctrines of Equality and Democracy', 25 *Melbourne Law Review* 24, 27 (2001) (treating *Cole* as illustrating the difference between originalism as orthodox textualism and originalism as 'intentionalism', the latter of which permits 'some resort to extraneous materials'). The Court itself was careful to describe its changed practice as improving its understanding of the original meaning of the words used in the Constitution, but not to substitute for that meaning the subjective intentions of the Constitution's drafters. See *Cole*, 165 CLR at 385. For other discussions of *Cole* among Australian scholars, see, e.g., Michael Coper, 'Critique and Comment, Concern About Judicial Method', 30 *Melbourne University Law Review* 554, 568–9 (2006); Kirby, *supra* note 79, at 10; McHugh, *supra* note 71, at 10.

83.   For a description of the Mason years (1987–95) and those that followed, emphasizing continuities in interpretive method, see McHugh, *supra* note 71. For a different perspective, see Jason L. Pierce, *Inside the Mason Court Revolution* (2006).

84.   *Street v Queensland Bar Ass'n*, (1989) 168 CLR 461 (overruling *Henry v Boehm*, (1973) 128 CLR 482 (Austl.)). Section 117 of the Australian Constitution provides, 'A subject of the Queen, resident in any State, shall not be subject in any other State to any disability or discrimination which would not be equally applicable to him if he were a subject of the Queen resident in such other state.' Commonwealth of Australia Constitution Act, 1900, § 117.

85. *Street*, 168 CLR at 518 (Brennan, J); see also id. at 566 (Gaudron, J) (writing that prior decisions interpreting section 117 'do not reflect recent developments within the field of anti-discrimination law', and noting both Australian and American legal sources); id. at 531 (Deane, J) (asserting that conditioning the right to practice law on residency or primary practice in a state violates section 117, 'in the context of modern circumstances in this country including the existence of a unitary system of law administered in the various States and Territories by both national and State courts').

86. For invocation of the living tree metaphor in a case involving the structure of the judicial powers established in the 1867 Constitution Act, see, e.g., *Re Residential Tenancies Act, 1979*, [1981] 1 SCR 714, 723 (Dickson, CJ) ('A constitutional reference is not a barren exercise in statutory interpretation. What is involved is an attempt to determine and give effect to the broad objectives and purpose of the Constitution, viewed as a "living tree" ...'). For a recent Charter case invoking the living tree, see *Canada v Hislop*, [2007] 1 SCR 429, 467–8 (referring to the living tree in discussing retroactive or prospective remedies for Charter violations).

87. *R v Keegstra*, [1990] 3 SCR 697, 759–87 (Dickson, CJ); id. at 848–65 (McLachlin, J, dissenting).

88. *Reference re Same-Sex Marriage*, [2004] 3 SCR 698, 710.

89. *R v Morgentaler*, [1988] 1 SCR 30, 73.

90. See, e.g., Kent Greenawalt, 'Free Speech in the United States and Canada', 55 *Law & Contemporary Problems* 5, 10 (1992) (noting Canada's 'expansive approach to what counts as freedom of speech'). Some argue that both section 1 and the notwithstanding clause, section 33, enable an intergovernmental 'dialogue' between Canadian courts and provincial and national parliaments. See Peter W. Hogg and Allison A. Bushell, 'The Charter Dialogue Between Courts and Legislatures (Or Perhaps the Charter of Rights Isn't Such a Bad Thing After All)', 35 *Osgoode Hall Law Journal* 75 (1997); see also *Vriend v Alberta*, [1998] 1 SCR 493, 565 (Iacobucci, J) (agreeing with Hogg and Bushell that 'the Charter has given rise to a more dynamic interaction among the branches of governance'). For conflicting views, see, e.g., Christopher P. Manfredi and James B. Kelly, 'Six Degrees of Dialogue: A Response to Hogg and Bushell', 35 *Osgoode Hall Law Journal* 513 (1999).

91. Cf. Stephen Gardbaum, 'The Myth and Reality of American Constitutional Exceptionalism', 107 *Michigan Law Review* 391 (2008) (arguing that the structure of rights in the US is not that different from those in Canada or European countries, even if the content is).

92. Louis Favoreu, the French constitutionalist, has treated the Conseil Constitutionnel as fundamentally a judicial body, a court. See Louis Favoreu, *Constitutional Courts* 14, 83–92 (trans. Alain Levasseur and Roger Ward) (2001); see also Alec Stone Sweet, 'The Politics of Constitutional Review in the United States and France', 5 I•CON 67 (2007) (discussing Favoreu's work). On the other hand, Professor Stone Sweet concluded in his influential book that the Conseil was better viewed as a third legislative chamber. Stone, *supra* note 7; see also John Bell, *French Legal Cultures* 240 (2008) (noting Stone's 'less provocative analogy' to a 'legal advisory body'); but cf. Alec Stone Sweet, 'Judicialization and the Construction of Governance', 32 *Comparative Political Studies* 147, 176 (1999) (Conseil 'reinvented itself as a court'). Effective March 2010, the Conseil Constitutionnel is authorized to exercise jurisdiction over concrete constitutional complaints concerning enacted statutes, upon referral by either the Conseil d'État or the Cour de Cassation. The possibility of hearing individual complaints, and to statutes already enacted, marks a significant expansion of the Conseil's jurisdiction, one highly likely to lead to other changes, in both procedure and jurisprudence, that will support those who have viewed it as essentially a court. See generally Lasser, *supra* note 4 at 299–305. The Conseil Constitutionnel held its first ever public hearing in May 2010. See Conseil Constitutionnel Website, http://www.conseil-constitutionnel.fr/conseil-constitutionnel/francais/a-la-une/juin-2010-la-publicite-des-audiences-au-conseil-constitutionnel.48374.html.

93. The English-language section of the Conseil Constitutionnel's website refers to but does not appear to include press releases or official and other commentary found in or through the French section. See http://www.conseil-constitutionnel.fr (including a 'Documentation Publications' section); http://www.conseil-constitutionnel.fr/conseil-constitutionnel/root/bank_mm/anglais/saisinen.pdf (noting preparation of press communications and drafting of commentary on decisions). The Recueil des décisions du Conseil Constitutionnel has included very brief English case summaries since 1990.

94. The Cour de Cassation is the court of last resort in criminal and private civil cases; the Conseil d'État is the highest court for review of administrative action.

95. Michel Rosenfeld, 'Comparing Constitutional Review by the European Court of Justice and the US Supreme Court', 4 I•CON 618, 635 (2006).

96. *Comparative Constitutional Law* 594 (Vicki C. Jackson and Mark Tushnet eds., 2nd edition 2006).

97. See Decision No. 71-44 DC, 16 July 1971, Journal officiel, 18 July 1971, p. 7114, Recueil, p. 29.

98. See Burt Neuborne, 'Judicial Review and Separation of Powers in France and the United States', 57 *NYU Law Review* 363, 386–7 (1982) (discussing a 1956 decision of the Conseil d'État finding that a refusal to issue a permit for formation of a political group was inconsistent with fundamental principles of the laws of the republic under the 1946 constitution and thus had to be clearly authorized by legislation).

99. Lasser, writing about the Cour de Cassation, has argued that to look only at the published decision is to ignore

the legitimacy conferred by virtue of the much broader gauged, purposive internal reasoning processes that the judges engage in, Lasser, *supra* note 6, at 47–62, and through academic commentary and explication, *id.* at 31–40. Stone has said that the Conseil Constitutionnel has adopted the 'decision-writing style' of French judges (Stone, *supra* note 7, at 97), a style that may obscure important, and internally acknowledged, interpretive sources and influences.

100.   Stone, *supra* note 7 at 97.
101.   Decision No. 62-20 DC, 6 November 1962, Journal officiel, 7 November 1962, p. 10778, Recueil, p. 27.
102.   Barry Nicholas, 'Loi, Règlement and Judicial Review in the Fifth Republic', [1970] *Public Law* 251, 269-70.
103.   Indeed, Burt Neuborne, who constructed an interpretive theory for the Conseil's early decisions as based on a structural concern with allocation of decisionmaking, sensitive to whether the law in question touched on fundamental principles, acknowledged that some of the same decisions could be read as more substantively driven; Neuborne, *supra* note 98, at 384; the opacity of the decisions left open alternative interpretive understandings. On the Conseil's role in the separation of powers, see Bell, *supra* note 92, at 203–4 (describing aggressive Conseil enforcement of the quite limited powers of the legislature in enacting the budget).
104.   See Stone, *supra* note 7, at 101 (documenting growth in the average number of 'considerations' or justificatory paragraphs in Conseil opinions between the early 1970s (average of 5–7) and mid 1980s (average of 13–42)).
105.   See Bell, *supra* note 7, at 145–6 (noting use of proportionality principles in reviewing penalties).
106.   Olivier Dutheillet de Lamothe, 'European Law and the French Constitutional Council', in *Comparative Law before the Courts* (Guy Canivet, Mads Andenas, and Duncan Fairgrieves eds., 2004); De Lamothe, *supra* note 41, at 551–5 (noting, inter alia, the impact of ECHR decisions on the Conseil's jurisprudence on freedom of speech in an information society and stating that, even when the Conseil 'derives its inspiration from the decisions of foreign courts, [it] does not refer to them explicitly'); see also Marie-Pierre Granger, 'France is "Already" Back in Europe: The Europeanization of French Courts and the Influence of France in the EU', 14 *European Public Law* 335 (2008).
107.   See John Bell, 'French Constitutional Council and European Law', 54 *International & Comparative Law Quarterly* 735, 740 (2005) (describing a 'rare case' of citing its own previous decisions in deciding on the character of the primacy of EU law). On implicit reference through repetition of prior language, see Alec Stone Sweet, *Governing with Judges* 145 (2000).
108.   Thus, in Decision No. 2008-562, 21 February 2008, rejecting a constitutional challenge to an act pertaining to post-sentence preventive detention, the Conseil not only summarized the challenged statute, but briefly summarized the parties' arguments against the constitutionality of post-sentence detention. The Conseil then responded to those arguments, albeit briefly. See, e.g., *id.* ¶ 16 (explaining that because it is limited to persons sentenced to more than 15 years for a short list of serious crimes, and provides for a re-evaluation of dangerousness over a period of six weeks no later than one year prior to their date of release, the statute provides 'suitable guarantees that post sentence preventive detention will be reserved solely for persons who are particularly dangerous'). See also Bell, *supra* note 92, at 229 (describing the 1993 Asylum case, CC Decision No. 93-325 DC, 13 August 1993, Recueil, 224, as the Conseil's 'longest ever decision', in which 'the Conseil set out some basic principles to the effect that the legislator had to respect the freedoms and fundamental rights recognized to all people on French territory, whether they were citizens or not').
109.   Bell, *supra* note 92, at 219.
110.   Lasser has observed the impact of considerations of equity and the public good in the deliberations of the Cour de Cassation and Conseil d'État, see Lasser, *supra* note 4 at 75–9, 119, 289; *supra* note 6, at 59, considerations which might also play an unacknowledged role in the Conseil Constitutionnel's reasoning.
111.   Bell, *supra* note 7, at 71.
112.   For discussion see Bell, *supra* note 7, at 176–87; Stone, *supra* note 7, at 140–72.
113.   Bell, *supra* note 7, at 171–2; see also Bell, *supra* note 92, at 202–03; Stone, *supra* note 7, at 193.
114.   See also Christian Joppke and Elia Marzal, 'Courts, the New Constitutionalism and Immigrant Rights: The Case of the French Conseil Constitutionnel', 43 *European Journal of Political Research* 823, 834 (2004) (describing development of constitutional right of asylum).
115.   See Bell, *supra* note 92, at 226–30, 199–200 (describing constitutional amendments in response to Conseil decisions on affirmative measures towards gender equality, the right of asylum, and ratification of the Maastricht Treaty); see also Susan Wright, 'The French Conseil Constitutionnel in 1999', 6 *European Public Law* 146, 147 (2000) (stating that the constitution 'is now being amended with such regularity that the situation is described as a "little worrying" by the Conseil itself'). But cf. Alec Stone Sweet, 'The Politics of Judicial Review in France and Europe', 5 I•CON 69, 88 n. 53 (2007) (describing the constitutional revision with respect to the asylum law as the only 'important instance').
116.   See, e.g., Decision 98-408 DC OF 22 January 1999 (Treaty laying down the Statute of the International Criminal Court), available at www.conseil.constitutionnel.fr (under 'caselaw', subheading 'constitutional review as regards treaties and international agreements'). See also *supra* note 50.
117.   Bell, *supra* note 92, at 228; Ferreres Comella, *supra* note 48, at 105 (describing Favoreu's 'switchman' analogy).

118. *United States v Miller*, 307 US 174, 178 (1939) ('In the absence of any evidence tending to show that possession or use of a "shotgun having a barrel of less than eighteen inches in length" at this time has some reasonable relationship to the preservation or efficiency of a well regulated militia, we cannot say that the Second Amendment guarantees the right to keep and bear such an instrument.')
119. See Siegel, *supra* note 46, at 202–25.
120. As Reva Siegel points out, the second part of the opinion – which indicates the scope of permissible regulation of arms-bearing – is in complete opposition to the purpose of protecting state militias. See id. at 200 ('[T]he majority imposes restrictions on the kinds of weapons protected by the Second Amendment that the majority concedes would disable exercise of the right for the amendment's textually enunciated purposes.')
121. The majority discounted the authority of *Miller* for, among other reasons, failing sufficiently to engage the historical sources. See *Heller*, 128 S. Ct. at 2814–15; see also Jamal Greene, 'Selling Originalism', 97 *Georgetown Law Journal* 657, 683–6 (2009) (summarizing *Heller*'s multiple layers of devotion to originalism). However, the *Miller* Court did in fact discuss the original purpose behind the Second Amendment, which, it argued, should be read in conjunction with the militia clauses of Article I and the Framers' concern to prevent development of a standing army. *Miller*, 307 US at 178–9 (specifically referring to 'the debates in the Convention, the history and legislation of Colonies and States, and the writings of approved commentators'). The *Heller* Court also argued against reliance on *Miller* because the respondent did not appear in the case, but Justice Stevens's dissent responded: 'as our decision in *Marbury v Madison*, ... in which only one side appeared and presented arguments, demonstrates, the absence of adversarial presentation alone is not a basis for refusing to accord stare decisis effect to a decision of this Court'. *Heller*, 128 S. Ct. at 2845 (Stevens, J. dissenting) (citing academic work by Professor Susan Low Bloch).
122. See generally Greene, *supra* note 121, at 8–18; see also id. at 84 ('The rhetoric upon which originalist arguments rely ... is driven by a narrative about the American ethos.').
123. Siegel, *supra* note 46, at 194.
124. A more interesting aspect of the case is the majority's reliance on debates around enactment of the Fourteenth Amendment after the Civil War, which, some might argue, shifted the meaning of the Amendment towards a more individual rights-oriented understanding. See *Heller*, 128 S. Ct., at 2809–11.
125. 'West German Abortion Decision: A Contrast to *Roe v. Wade*', 9 *John Marshall Journal of Practice & Procedure* 605, 652–3 (1976) (Robert E. Jonas and John D. Gorby trans.).
126. Id. at 650, 655.
127. See Gerald L. Neuman, '*Casey* in the Mirror: Abortion, Abuse and the Right to Protection in the United States and Germany', 43 *American Journal of Comparative Law* 273, 282 (1995).

33. Docket control and the success of constitutional courts

*David Fontana**

I   INTRODUCTION

In a chapter about comparative constitutional law, it might be surprising to start off this chapter with a mention of Alexander Bickel. Bickel was no doubt one of the landmark figures in American constitutional law. Writing in 1980, John Hart Ely called him 'probably the most creative constitutional theorist of the past twenty years'.[1] But exporting some of Bickel's ideas about American constitutional law can actually inform our understandings of comparative constitutional law as well. Bickel's observation that the power of courts to do nothing – to avoid deciding constitutional cases entirely by declining to grant certiorari and hear a case in the first place – can greatly enhance the success of these courts, is an observation that can help us understand much of the success and failure of various courts deciding constitutional cases around the world, even beyond the United States Supreme Court. This judicial power to decide not to hear a case is a power that I will reference as the power of 'docket control'. It is not just a significant power for the United States Supreme Court, but for all courts deciding controversial constitutional cases.

There are many reasons why giving courts the power of docket control can contribute to their success. Deciding what cases to decide permits a court to issue the right decisions at the right times, what this chapter calls 'issue timing'. A court can avoid encountering an issue until the country is ready to discuss the issue, and perhaps ready to resolve the issue in the manner the court is contemplating – or the court can decide to avoid the issue altogether because the issue is too polarizing for the court to encounter. As part of this 'issue timing' is what this chapter calls 'legitimacy timing', meaning giving the court the power to decide what to decide allows courts both to initially create and then later maintain their legitimacy, even in situations when political forces might not support the specific outcome ordered by the court. Courts create and maintain their institutional legitimacy by giving political forces and the public time to adjust to a newer style of institution – a judicial institution – deciding leading issues of the day. But there is also a quantitative benefit to docket control, one related to legitimacy timing and the general politics surrounding courts. Giving courts docket control permits them to limit the sheer number of major issues they are deciding, which permits them to avoid excessive political fights, and gives them an agenda control power that allows them to compete on more equitable terms with the other branches of government, which do have agenda control.

Part of the argument of this chapter, then, is that courts deciding constitutional cases benefit from having the power to set their agenda – but also that docket control is an indispensable part of courts exercising this agenda-setting power. There are certainly other options that courts have at their disposal to enjoy some of the same agenda-setting powers that docket control gives courts. Indeed, these are some of the same options that Bickel mentioned. Courts can decide cases on technical grounds, as Bickel suggested. Courts can decide cases on substantive grounds, but do so narrowly, a position most famously associated in the United States with Cass Sunstein.[2] There are many other options courts have to avoid deciding constitutional cases in a broad and controversial manner.[3]

Certainly, as this chapter will discuss, other courts deciding constitutional cases beyond just the United States Supreme Court have experimented with these options. But all of these other ways of giving courts agenda-setting powers share the same limitation: even though they involve courts in deciding constitutional issues in a less controversial fashion, they still involve courts in deciding constitutional issues. The power of docket control gives courts the power to avoid constitutional issues entirely, and the politics of that can often be better for courts.

This chapter should be considered an intellectual down payment on a larger project about the role that docket control plays in contributing to the success of constitutional courts. Because it is merely a down payment, and because of the structure of these chapters, my arguments will be mostly illustrative, drawing on helpful examples to highlight some of the dynamics that make docket control such a powerful contributor to the success of constitutional courts. Later work will make the same argument and probe these examples in greater detail, using more traditional large- and small-sample research design in different places.

For the purposes of this chapter, as well, I adopt an inclusive definition of the 'success' of constitutional courts – meaning the ability of the constitutional court to have their decisions enforced, their legitimacy respected and their political relevance ensured. As Ran Hirschl has noted, the 'success' of an element of a constitution can be hard to define,[4] and more precise definition must await additional papers exploring docket control. Also for the purposes of this chapter, I will use the phrase 'constitutional review courts' to describe any high courts deciding constitutional cases. There are, of course, courts like the United States Supreme Court which decide constitutional as well as other cases, and courts like the German Federal Constitutional Court which exclusively decide constitutional cases – and this phrasing of 'constitutional review courts' is meant to communicate some shared dynamics about the politics of constitutional review facing both generalist supreme courts and specialized constitutional courts.

2   THE CURRENT REALITY OF DOCKET CONTROL

With the proliferation in literature about comparative constitutional law, there is now much literature about differences in institutional design among many constitutional review courts. But, to this point, there is almost no literature about differences in docket control rules. This is a substantial part of the reason why the explanatory power of these differences in docket control rules has been neglected. As it turns out, even though the assumption is that constitutional courts have no control over their dockets and supreme courts do, many forms of constitutional review courts have substantial powers of docket control.

2.1   A Scholarly Oversight

There is very little scholarship about docket control and constitutional review courts, along two dimensions, one factual, the other analytical. First, while there is much literature about the sorts of dimensions along which the structure of constitutional courts around the world vary, there is almost no discussion of variations in docket control as one of the dimensions of variation. The usual presentation of institutional variations focuses on a few topics. As Lee Epstein, Jack Knight and Olga Shvetsova have phrased it, courts differ in terms of (1) 'who has the power to engage in judicial review',[5] (2) 'when can judicial review occur',[6] (3) 'can judicial review take place in the absence of a real case or controversy',[7] and (4) 'who can initiate disputes'.[8] But there are additional – and, this chapter will argue, consequential differences – in the docket control process among courts, and scholars have not studied comprehensively the different docket control structures in place around the world.[9] As an initial problem, then, there is simply very little aggregated information about the realities of docket control from which to draw conclusions.[10]

Without this simple factual information available, then, it is unsurprising that the explanatory powers of docket control rules are ignored. Part of the reason for missing the analytical power of docket control differences is because the core question that institutional differences in docket control might help to answer – what makes constitutional courts succeed or fail – is a question that scholars rarely ask in the first place. There is a substantial literature about the 'origins of dictatorship and democracy',[11] the variables that might lead to the creation of democratic regimes. There is also a substantial literature on democratic failures, headlined by Juan Linz's contribution and the literature it spawned.[12] When it comes to the rise and fall of constitutional courts, though, the literature is more asymmetrical. There are several different explanations for the creation of constitutional review courts,[13] but very little literature about conditions under which the creation of constitutional courts leads to their eventual and durable success. This chapter offers an initial explanation as to part of the reason why constitutional review courts succeed, one deriving from institutional structure: the power of courts to decide what cases they hear in the first place can help create a politics of constitutional review that assists constitutional review courts.

2.2   Docket Control as Common Institutional Practice

The conventional wisdom, to the extent scholars have studied docket control, seems to be that supreme courts have broad discretionary jurisdiction and constitutional courts simply have 'no discretionary jurisdiction'.[14] As Kim Lane Scheppele has written, the assumption is that 'constitutional courts do not typically have formally recognized discretionary powers to choose which cases they will decide'.[15] Constitutional courts are supposed to be 'anti-Bickelian'[16] in the very little power they have to 'do neither' and supreme courts are supposed to be Bickelian. The actual practice of the most successful constitutional review courts, regardless of their structure, is actually quite informed by Bickel's ideas of the importance of the power to decide not to decide.

It is certainly the case that in many countries with supreme courts, those supreme courts have broad powers over their docket. Since 1988 the Supreme Court of the United States has had almost complete control over what cases to hear on appeal.[17] The Supreme Court of Canada heard 900 appeals over the past ten years, and less than 20 percent of those cases were heard as part of the Court's mandatory jurisdiction, with the rest subject to broad discretion by the Court in terms of what cases it wants to hear.[18] The Supreme Court of India is granted, by the Constitution of India, control over what cases it can hear.[19] The Supreme Court of Israel, particularly when heading petitions as the High Court of Justice (HCJ), has some discretion in deciding what cases fully to adjudicate and decide.[20]

Despite the conventional wisdom, though, constitutional courts in addition to supreme courts have broad control over the cases that they want to hear. Consider the German Federal Constitutional Court (FCC), the 'most active and powerful constitutional court in Europe'.[21] The FCC can hear constitutional claims either by abstract review, concrete review, or by the filing of a constitutional complaint. Abstract review cases must be brought by specified members of the government.[22] It is difficult for the FCC to avoid deciding these cases, but as a practical matter there have only been on average less than three a year brought to the FCC – and because of consolidation and other procedural details, the FCC has only decided about half of these abstract review cases.[23]

Concrete review cases are cases where a lower court not entrusted with jurisdiction over constitutional cases finds that there might be a constitutional problem in the course of addressing other legal claims.[24] The FCC can decline to hear these cases because it only need hear these cases if the case presents major implications for lower courts and the FCC is convinced of the unconstitutionality of the action, rather than simply harboring doubts.[25] The number of concrete review cases under Art. 100 (1) of the Basic Law is substantially lower than the number of constitutional complaints as well, so combined with the FCC's discretion not to hear these cases, they constitute a tiny part of the docket of the FCC.[26] As an empirical matter, the overwhelming majority of cases are brought to the FCC as constitutional complaints – a full 96 percent of the caseload of the FCC, by one count.[27] The FCC only grants review in less than 1 percent of the constitutional complaints it receives.[28]

The same institutional structure and constitutional review court docket control is true of many of the world's other constitutional courts. In Hungary, the very active and quite powerful constitutional court only decides a case as the whole court if a statute is being reviewed.[29] If the challenge is to an administrative regulation, then the case is disposed of by a three-judge panel.[30] Because of this and other docket control rules, in its first three years the Constitutional Court of Hungary considered about 6000 petitions and only published between 200 and 300 decisions each year.[31] In Brazil, much of the recent success of the court has been related to Constitutional Amendment 45, which permits the Supreme Federal Court to decline to hear a case if it does not present an issue of general importance.[32]

3 WHY DOCKET CONTROL MATTERS

3.1 The Explanatory Power of Docket Control

3.1.1. The timing of constitutional review

Part of the reason why having control over the cases that it hears can contribute to the success of constitutional review courts has to do with timing. Docket control permits a constitutional review court to address a constitutional issue when the timing is right for the court successfully to intervene to decide that issue – what I will hereinafter call 'issue timing'. Docket control also permits a constitutional review court to address a constitutional issue at a time – and, as discussed later, at a pace – that allows the court to create and ensure its own legitimacy (what I will hereinafter call 'legitimacy timing'). As compared to other means of avoiding constitutional controversies, docket control leads to a political dynamic that better assists constitutional review courts.

There are many reasons why a constitutional court might want to avoid deciding a particular constitutional issue altogether, or might want to avoid deciding a constitutional issue until the timing is right. We start with a simple statement: not all constitutional issues that constitutional review courts decide are created equal. A decision on the Dormant Commerce Clause in the United States, for instance, does not have the same salience – or the same judicial politics dynamic – as a case involving abortion.[33] Some constitutional issues presented to courts might be so polarizing that a judicial decision on the issue could generate more political toxins, either forever or at a particular time, than the court could manage. By deciding a case, the constitutional review court would be taking sides on the issue, which would inflame passions on the losing side so much that it could lead to a dangerous political dynamic.

Not only would deciding a case related to the issue generate a firestorm from the losing side, but the nature of the debate between the competing sides might present a 'clash of absolutes'.[34] Therefore, not only would a judicial decision on the issue be viewed as incorrect by the losing side, but also it might be viewed as immoral or manifestly unjust. The other branches of government might also decide to avoid this polarizing issue for the same reasons that the constitutional review court does, which, as discussed later, would create problems for the constitutional review court if it does not have the identical power to avoid issues.

In the American system, a good example of the Supreme Court using its power of docket control to avoid entering a polarizing political debate entirely was its decision to deny certiorari to hear cases related to the constitutionality of the Vietnam War.[35] The legitimacy – and therefore, in part – the constitutionality – of the Vietnam War was an intensely polarizing issue,[36] but the Court never decided a case that directly addressed the constitutionality of the Vietnam War.[37] If the American Supreme Court had in fact addressed the constitutionality of the Vietnam War, it would have survived, because of the support it enjoys. In countries where the constitutional review courts occupy a more precarious position, deciding a polarizing case at all, at any point in time, could lead to the destruction of the court.[38]

In other situations, courts avoid deciding a polarizing issue for some time, until the political timing is more conducive. Although *Brown v Board of Education* was intensely polarizing at the time it was decided by the United States Supreme Court,[39] if a case like that had been presented to the Supreme Court and decided before then, the Supreme Court could have been seriously damaged. With not just an unsympathetic South and therefore part of Congress, but an unsympathetic President and all of Congress, who knows what might have happened if *Brown* had been decided years earlier.[40]

Other constitutional review courts that have experienced success likewise either avoided entirely or delayed deciding polarizing constitutional issues. In Israel, the Supreme Court of Israel has three roles, but in one of them it sits as the High Court of Justice (HCJ), with the power to decide what petitions fully to adjudicate.[41] The Israeli Supreme Court decided explicitly as early as 1969 that judicial review of some sort was authorized,[42] but it did not decide many major cases until years later. For years and years cases were brought to the HCJ questioning the legality of different military actions in the occupied territories – and for years and years the HCJ largely declined to decide these cases, with some exceptions.[43] During this time, the HCJ tended to 'impose strict limitations on the ability of litigants to raise political issues in court'.[44]

It was not until 1979 that the HCJ decided a number of major cases related to the occupied territories.[45] Part of the reason for this had to do with the changing political climate in Israel, making the timing better for the HCJ just as it was for the American Supreme Court deciding

Brown in 1954; and part of it was, as discussed later, because enough time had passed for the HCJ to establish a degree of core legitimacy ('legitimacy timing'). After these 1979 decisions, the HCJ issued other occasionally consequential decisions, but it was not until the 1990s when it started to issue many major decisions – and, by that time, the Israeli Supreme Court in general was wildly popular and seen as deeply legitimate, even while other branches of government (except the army) were not.[46]

More recently, many of the world's most successful constitutional review courts waited several years – until the politics of the situation had cooled off some – before deciding major cases related to the responses by the political branches to the events of September 11. The High Court of Australia issued its first major decision in 2007.[47] The FCC in Germany declined to hear several cases,[48] and did finally address a case related to the European Arrest Warrant in 2005.[49] The House of Lords issued its first major decision in 2004.[50] The Supreme Court of India issued its first major decision in 2004.[51] The United States Supreme Court did not decide its first cases until it decided three of them in 2004.[52]

Another reason why docket control can contribute to the success of constitutional review courts is a notion related to the idea of issue timing, what I will call 'legitimacy timing'. If issue timing is about the importance of the court deciding the right issue at the right time *for the issue*, then legitimacy timing is about the court deciding the right issue at the right time *for the court*. A constitutional review court might want to wait to decide an issue until the timing is right, and the timing might never be right. But the time must also be right for the court, and where the constitutional review court sits in the public and political dynamic of the country.

A preliminary concept must be addressed. Constitutional review courts might enjoy two different genres of support. One genre, 'specific support', refers to the support for a constitutional review court because of support for the particular decisions issued by that court.[53] Another and more challenging form of support that constitutional review courts might benefit from is called 'diffuse support'. Diffuse support is 'a reservoir of favorable attitudes or good will that helps members to accept or tolerate outputs to which they are opposed or the effect of which they see as damaging to their wants'.[54] It is agreeing to disagree; the support that courts enjoy from members of the public or political figures who disagree with particular decisions but agree with the court's ability to make them, and therefore support the fundamentals of the constitutional review court even after that court issues a specific decision with which they disagree.

Most courts, even in established democracies, do not enjoy diffuse support in the eyes of most of the population.[55] For most courts then – since most courts have to survive simply on specific support – deciding an issue that leads to any meaningful disagreement or political backlash can be dangerous. The mandatory portions of the dockets of the German FCC and the Supreme Court of Canada provide good examples. In Canada, although the docket of the Supreme Court is largely discretionary,[56] the Supreme Court must hear reference cases brought to it by the political branches, unless there is some tangential jurisdictional issue.[57] This has brought the established Canadian Supreme Court into political trouble when it had to deal with issues such as the *Quebec Secession Reference*.[58] In then-West Germany, the FCC in its early years accepted very few cases involving meaningful constitutional disputes – indeed, of all of the cases filed before it in 1955 using the constitutional complaint procedure, only one case was admitted and decided by the FCC.[59] But then the FCC faced an abstract review challenge to German participation in some of the defense treaties of the new European government,[60] a case that the FCC was of course obligated to decide.[61] Ultimately, this situation might have helped the FCC, but in the short term it put the new FCC in a precarious position because it involved it in a major political battle of the day – and the FCC had no choice but to decide these cases.[62]

Particularly when the constitutional review court is new, and trying to transition from having simply specific support to enjoying a deeper legitimacy in the society, docket control is crucial. Early on during the existence of a constitutional court, political coalitions or the general public might not be ready for the constitutional court to decide cases. As a newer institution, the exercise of power by the court (even if it is just to decide the case on technical as opposed to substantive grounds) might seem alien to these political coalitions or citizens, and therefore more threatening. Moreover, it is often the case that the constitutional court might be staffed by judges tainted from their associations with previous autocratic regimes.[63] It is not surprising, then, that courts that have been in operation for some time seem to be more popular than courts in operation for a shorter period of time, even controlling for other factors.[64]

At first, then, when the court is only supported if the outcomes of its decisions are supported, then the court can decide to hear cases that will not antagonize the public, perhaps even by focusing on lower salience issues to create a reservoir of support and trust from the public. Since a series of specific decisions that the public supports can lead to the creation of diffuse support and a stronger foundation of support for the court,[65] over time the court can then grapple with more controversial and complicated issues as it builds diffuse support.

Many of the most successful constitutional courts have used this strategy, with great success. For one example of this strategy, consider the Constitutional Tribunal of Poland. The Tribunal started its operations in 1985, and was granted the power of judicial review in 1986.[66] At first, the Tribunal functioned simply as an administrative court, reviewing what the executive could do by decree.[67] The Tribunal simply policed the process of lawmaking, not the ultimate substantive acceptability of laws. Eventually, though, starting in 1989, the Tribunal started to review the substantive constitutionality of statutes.[68] Many of the targets of its constitutional invalidations were the surely unpopular laws from the old Communist regime.[69] Later, the Tribunal started to decide cases related to the major constitutional issues of the day. In 1991, for instance, the Polish Constitutional Tribunal invalidated an important pension reform statute.[70]

The more established Western constitutional courts adopted a similar strategy when the power of constitutional review was first established. Many forget that the United States Supreme Court was in operation for 14 years before it decided *Marbury v Madison*,[71] and it had three Chief Justices before it had John Marshall. During that time, the Court avoided major constitutional disputes. As William Michael Treanor put it, the 'Court upheld the one substantive congressional statute that it examined, and it did so even though there was a very strong argument that the statute ran afoul of constitutional text'.[72] The Court instead addressed the constitutionality of congressional statutes dealing with jurisdictional as opposed to substantive issues, and even then had very few cases of that sort.[73] In France, it was thirteen years after the creation of the Constitution of the French Fifth Republic before the French Conseil Constitutionnel clearly stated that constitutional review was authorized by the French Constitution.[74]

3.1.2   The quantity of constitutional review

Part of legitimacy timing has to do not just with what cases are being decided and when, but *how many* cases are being decided. Deciding too many cases can be damaging to established and secure, as well as new and vulnerable, constitutional review courts. Constitutional review courts deciding many cases are creating many losing parties, meaning many political enemies and many political battles. In order to fight these battles, the court is at a severe disadvantage; deciding many cases will create political criticism that simply exceeds the available sources of political support that the court can use to fight back, and also is difficult for courts to handle because of the institutional disadvantages created by less discretionary agendas for courts and more discretionary agendas for political actors. In a system with a stable constitutional court, that might lead to a significantly weakened court; in a system with a fragile constitutional review court, this might lead to the elimination of the court altogether.

It should not be surprising, then, that many of the major constitutional review courts around the world fully decide just a small number of cases per year. The Supreme Court of the United States decides about 80 cases a year by full opinion, and less than half of these involve constitutional issues.[75] The Supreme Court of Canada decided 74 cases last year.[76] The Italian Constitutional Court decides about 500 cases per year.[77] The French Conseil Constitutionnel decides about 100 cases per year.[78] The Russian Constitutional Court decides about 211 cases per year.[79] Part of the success of the newer constitutional review courts in Central and Eastern Europe is because they spent their earlier years deciding only about 50 or so cases.[80]

There is a very simple reason why permitting constitutional review courts to avoid deciding many cases helps them: quantity negatively correlates with quality. There is good reason, including some experimental evidence,[81] to believe that reasoning affects the legitimacy of constitutional review courts, so more time might mean better reasoning and more legitimacy. The more cases a court has to decide, the less convincing its decisions will be, and it would simply be impossible for constitutional review courts to decide all or many of the cases they are faced with given the sheer number of those cases. Particularly with constitutional review courts first trying to establish themselves – and prove that they are legal as opposed to political bodies – quality legal reasoning might be important, and the sheer number of cases these courts face[82] makes docket control therefore crucial.

But the politics of high volume constitutional courts might present an even bigger obstacle. The more cases that the court decides, the more enemies the court will be making, because the more parties the court will be ruling against. Many of these enemies might be politically inconsequential, or politically consequential but aggrieved about an issue of such low salience that these enemies cannot use the court decision successfully to attack the court. In Hungary, for instance, the mostly successful Hungarian Constitutional Court decided many controversial cases in its earlier years.[83] By 1995, the Court had issued so many constitutional decisions that the number of political enemies conspiring against the Court had grown. The Court invalidated 26 provisions of an important law to reduce the economic impact of the Hungarian welfare state, and angered factions in the government attacked the Court for the first time.[84]

Not just are more enemies created to fight against, but with more cases decided, the political tools that courts can use to fight for their interests are reduced. Jeffrey Staton and Georg Vanberg have written convincingly about how constitutional courts can use the power of publicity to convince other branches of government to comply with court decisions.[85] Staton and Vanberg are writing mostly about constitutional review courts that are not in dire straits,[86] where the support for courts is higher than for political institutions. In those situations, by drawing attention to court decisions, these courts compel the other branches to implement the decision because political actors do not want to ignore a public which both likes the constitutional court and is aware of what the constitutional court has said those other branches of government should do. Courts cannot equally publicize all decisions, and courts do not necessarily have many members of their staff. Courts can only issue so many press releases,[87] write so many opinion essays, be interviewed on television so many times. If the constitutional review court is forced to decide many cases, that means that some of its decisions might be politically vulnerable because the court won't be available to take the political steps to protect those decisions.

Regardless of whether the constitutional court is popular or not, though, any court needs a 'support structure' to implement their decisions.[88] After constitutional review courts issue decisions, there must be other actors in place to implement and enforce and support their decisions. Even after the constitutional review court issues its decision, for decisions not to be undermined there must be other groups who 'have coordinated research, facilitated the exchange of ideas and generated publicity around ... agendas'.[89] A constitutional review court issuing many decisions might simply overburden the support structure. This is particularly true in countries with smaller support structures, where the constitutional review courts might need the assistance of the support structures even more. For instance, in Costa Rica only 9 percent of citizens are involved in civil society activities, and in Colombia 8 percent – with the comparative number in the United States being a substantially larger 27 percent.[90]

Docket control can be crucial to constitutional review courts not only to help them fight political enemies effectively, but also to help them fight fairly. Legislatures and executives generally face few constitutional constraints on their agenda for a particular year. Constitutions include many negative restrictions on what the political branches are permitted to do. Even with the increasing spread of positive obligations that the political branches face, these obligations generally require minimal action on the part of the political branches and do not compel their agenda in any meaningful manner. Positive obligations might be vague. As Mark Tushnet has described it, they might be merely 'declaratory rights'.[91] The Constitution of Ireland mentions 'Directive Principles of State Policy',[92] but states that these are simply 'intended for the general guidance of the [Parliament]'.[93] Constitutional rules providing simply 'general guidance' do not mean that the Parliament of Ireland has much in the way of a compelled agenda.

Sometimes these rights might be what Tushnet calls 'weak substantive rights',[94] such as the command in the Constitution of South Africa that '[t]he state must take reasonable legislative and other measures, within its available resources, to achieve the progressive realisation of this right'.[95] Again, the political branches need not do much to comply with this obligation, and even if the government must act, often this can be delegated to administrative officials rather than something that must be addressed directly by the legislature or high-ranking executive officials. If positive obligations are more concrete, commanding a specific result (the Constitution of Mexico, for instance, guarantees that '[f]or every six days of work a worker must have at least one day of rest'[96]), these might be self-executing and not require much time or effort on the part of the political branches.

The contrast with a constitutional review court with limited or no docket control should be clear. Even if political branches faced constitutionally compelled agendas, these agendas would be simply to focus on issues. By contrast, constitutional review courts can be compelled to focus on these issues, as well as or perhaps by focusing on specific petitions brought by individual parties. As a practical matter, of course, constitutions tend not to compel political branches to do anything in the first place.

Agendas are also not fixed – if a problem or a complaint is not solved by one branch of government, then it might need to be solved by another branch. It is often the case that political branches of government might manipulate the constitutional review courts to serve their own political agenda. One facet of this might be what Keith Whittington has observed, whereby judicial review is encouraged and furthered by political actors wanting to avoid controversial issues and therefore pass them on to courts.[97] Another facet might be politicians using courts to gain attention for their own causes[98] – but without having to resolve these causes through their own, singular, heroic but potentially risky political actions. Either way, if political actors can manipulate the agenda of courts, they might well do so; and this puts courts at a disadvantage if they do not have the capacity to control their agenda as well. In other words, then, if the design is to create some semblance of equity between the branches, docket control is a must.

3.2 Imperfect Alternatives to Docket Control

As mentioned earlier, there are certainly many tools that constitutional review courts have to avoid deciding entirely a polarizing issue, or to wait before deciding polarizing issues.[99] But, even with those tools at its disposal, the power to decline to hear a case entirely occupies a special position. The decision not to hear a case can be more politically innocuous than deciding a case, but on secondary grounds. One reason is the 'clash of absolutes' logic described earlier. If any action related to these issues is highly consequential and morally tinged, then deciding a case, even on tangential grounds, could be more morally offensive and politically provoking than simply avoiding an issue altogether.

This is because, in many ways, deciding a case on tangential grounds is still deciding the case, while declining to hear the case altogether is practically and legally different. There are certainly many examples of constitutional review courts using tangential grounds to decide cases as a means of avoiding the core substantive issues. The Hungarian Constitutional Court in its first years decided its first abortion case on the grounds that the abortion rules were passed not through statute but through regulation.[100] The Russian Constitutional Court ruled on the constitutionality of the war in Chechnya by looking at whether the rules and process leading to the commencement of wars were followed, not whether the actual war itself was constitutional.[101] The sorts of concerns similar to the legitimacy timing concerns mentioned before surely played a part in the nature of these decisions – vague decisions or decisions ordering weak remedies pose less risk of non-compliance and therefore less of a threat to the legitimacy and power of the constitutional review court.[102]

While these are welcome tools for constitutional review courts to have at their disposal, having the power not to decide a case in the first place is also important – and different. If a constitutional review court decides to hear a case, there will be full briefing of the case, discussions of it in law schools and law journals, coverage of the case in newspapers, and debate about the issue among political figures. It is often only later that stakeholders know the constitutional review court will decide the case on tangential grounds, so all of the heat and intensity generated by the process leading to a substantive constitutional decision is generated by the process leading to a tangential decision. One study of the debates leading to decisions by the Israeli Supreme Court found '[t]he greatest portion of media coverage for political petitions does not refer to final court decisions but rather to earlier phases of the process: threats, the issuance of petitions, and most notably court proceedings while the petition is still pending'.[103] By contrast, if the constitutional review court declines to hear the case in the first place, that whole process and publicity and attention is eliminated before it even starts.

In part because of this different amount of pre-decision attention, there is a different political dynamic following a decision not to hear a case as compared to a decision on a tangential ground. Decisions by constitutional review courts not to decide cases rarely generate newspaper attention, and rarely generate political attention.[104] By contrast, decisions about major constitutional cases can generate much attention. When the HCJ in Israel decided their first series of major cases related to the occupied territories, one of the major newspapers printed these decisions verbatim over four pages in the newspaper.[105]

In this way, decisions not to hear a case impose no direct political costs on constitutional review courts, since they are decisions made with no attention, and therefore little oversight or accountability. The constitutional system – more generally and longitudinally – might suffer by the incoherence and lack of clarity that results from inaction by the highest constitutional review court in a country. The constitutional review court might suffer gradually, systematically from these results. But these costs are more diffuse and gradual. By contrast, decisions by constitutional review courts to decide a case on tangential grounds generate more attention and more immediate and tangible risk. If the HCJ had decided a case related to the occupied territories in any way, regardless of how technical, it would have made front-page news. A decision not to decide receives far less attention.

3.3   The Dangers of Docket Control

The sorts of powers and opportunities for success presented by docket control discussed above also carry with them some obvious dangers. Deciding when to decide might be an action constrained very little by law, and controlled very much by political judgment. This is precisely the sort of judgment that constitutional review court judges might have in low amounts, while the actors they are competing against have it in greater amounts. The danger, then, created by docket control is the danger created by granting a more overtly political power to a formally legal branch of government.

But this danger is not merely theoretical. There are several examples of constitutional review courts miscalculating in their use of their docket control, and paying a severe price for it. The early failures of the Constitutional Court of Russia after the dissolution of the Soviet Union are a good example of this. In December 1991, the new Court went into operation, with Valery Zorkin as the Chairman of the Constitutional Court.[106] The Court had enormous discretion about what cases to hear. It received about 1700 complaints in its first year.[107] Most of the complaints were rejected by the Registry of the Court, but a small number went forward and were submitted to one of the specialized divisions of the Constitutional Court.[108] These specialized divisions would then prepare a report, the Court would deliberate about this report and decide whether to move forward with the case based on this report, and if it did decide to go forward, Zorkin would assign the case to a particular Justice to lead the Court's discussion and decision on the case.[109]

In less than two years, the Zorkin Court used this discretion to issue 20 decisions invalidating exercises of executive or legislative powers, including cases involving controversial issues related to banning the former Communist Party or taking over media outlets.[110] At the same time, the Court did little to decide cases that would receive broad and cross-cutting support from the public. It decided very few cases related to human rights, deciding only six cases on these issues in its first 16 months.[111] Most members of the Court insisted that the Court focus on the political crisis between the new President Boris Yeltsin and the Duma and not on the human rights concerns faced by average citizens.[112] It should not be surprising, then, that a poll in January 1993 found a meager 10 percent of the population trusted the Russian Constitutional Court – while 23 percent trusted the President.[113]

Eventually, then, this Court was abolished.[114] The Court that was created to replace it eliminated much of the docket control that the previous Court had enjoyed. The previous Court could reject a petition if it considered review of the case 'inadvisable';[115] the new Court seems to have fewer screening standards.[116] Even under the new regime, though, the Russian Constitutional Court does not have to fully adjudicate all cases brought to it. Between 1994 and 1999, the Court received about 15,000 petitions, and about 98 percent were dismissed by the Secretariat of the Court.[117] That left 300 cases brought to the full Court, and the Court decided only 39 of those fully on the merits.[118]

While there are reasons to believe that constitutional review courts will constantly make mistakes in their use of docket control, there are also reasons to believe these mistakes are not fundamental or crucial. Constitutional review court judges do not come from purely legal backgrounds. Constitutional review court judges in all sorts of constitutional democracies are appointed by political officials. In the United States, Supreme Court Justices are appointed by the President with the advice and consent of the Senate.[119] In France, the members of the Conseil Constitutionnel are appointed one-third by the President, one-third by the President of the National Assembly and one-third by the President of the Senate.[120] The basic logic is essentially the same across all constitutional democracies: the appointing individuals are elected, and so the judges they appoint are likely to be tied to, and not entirely unaware of, the political process. However technical appointment and promotion might be in some lower courts in some countries, appointments to constitutional review courts are almost always political in part.

After their appointments, constitutional review courts are not entirely unaware of the political situation surrounding the constitutional issues presented to their courts. Constitutional review courts are facing thousands upon thousands of petitions every year. The Supreme Court of the United States receives about 7000 petitions per year.[121] In Argentina, the Supreme Court receives 26,000 petitions per year. The Supreme Federal Court in Brazil in 2001 had 110,771 petitions filed before it.[122] These petitions – the stories they present, the lower court decisions they embody – serve as information to the constitutional review court about how different constitutional issues are faring in the general public, and in the political system. Constitutional review does not just generate outcomes, it provides information to constitutional review courts.[123]

Of course, there were concerns voiced in response to Bickel's initial articulation of the benefits of docket control decades ago. These concerns were largely normative in a theoretical as opposed to an actual way. Gerald Gunther, in his famous response to Bickel's arguments, criticized Bickel for his lack of devotion to principle.[124] Beyond that, according to Gunther, by declining to hear cases, the Supreme Court was not offering reasons in the first place, so there was very little candor about what was transpiring.[125] Gunther's concerns are conceptually valid, but as mentioned before, denials of cases receive virtually no public or political attention. The reality, then, of a political actor or the public finding the lack of principle or lack of candor troubling are quite slim.

There might also be a concern that empowering constitutional review courts to avoid constitutional cases will lead to even more 'underenforced constitutional norms'[126] than is necessary. Indeed, the underenforcement of constitutional rights by constitutional review courts can weaken these courts sometimes just as much as the overenforcement of rights can.[127] I will have more to say about this in other writings on docket control, but for now it is worth noting that this is part of the reason that other courts have taken up the cause of protecting constitutional rights. In the years before the Canadian Supreme Court intervened in issues related to September 11 – and indeed even since then – the lower courts have issued many decisions protecting constitutional rights.[128] The same has become true even in countries where only constitutional courts are supposed to protect constitutional rights, but other courts have found ways to issue decisions that have the same effects of protecting constitutional rights. These decisions all exist outside of the major national politics that both precedes and follows decisions of the highest constitutional review courts.

4   CONCLUSION

The burgeoning literature on comparative constitutional law has led to a burgeoning literature on constitutional design. The institutional structures put in place in constitutions, according to this emerging area of scholarship, might play a substantial role in the later emergence of this constitutional order. The predictable elements of constitutional design have been studied at length: whether to create presidential, parliamentary or semi-presidential regimes; the terms of constitutional court judges; and so on.

But, at the end of the day, no institutional structure turns out to be more important for the judicial branch created by a constitution than the control given by that constitution and related documents to the courts created. It is almost universal for political actors to receive control not just over the decisions they make, but of the issues they decide to focus on in the first place. Likewise, giving courts – particularly constitutional review courts – the ability to decide what to decide proves crucial to the success of these courts. A court empowered to set its agenda is a court that can avoid excessive political conflict and ensure maximum compliance. For new courts and old courts alike, then, there is no issue more important than an issue that appears to be the most simple: the content and structure of the docket of the court.

NOTES

*   For comments on this chapter, my thanks to Rosalind Dixon, Tom Ginsburg, Daphne Barak-Erez, Barry Friedman, Chip Lupu, Micah Schwartzman, Kim Lane Scheppele, Brad Snyder, Amanda Tyler and David Zaring.
1.   Hart Ely, John. *Democracy and Distrust: A Theory of Judicial Review* (1980) at 71. See also Schmidt, Benno. *History of the Supreme Court of the United States: The Judiciary and Responsible Government 1910–21*, Part 2 (1984) at 722 (labeling Bickel as 'the most brilliant and influential constitutional scholar of the generation that came of age during the era of the Warren Court').
2.   See Sunstein, Cass R. *One Case at A Time: Judicial Minimalism on the Supreme Court* (1999); Sunstein, Cass R. 'The Supreme Court, 1995 Term – Foreword: Leaving Things Undecided', 110 *Harvard Law Review* 4 (1996).

3. See Katyal, Neal. 'Judges as Advicegivers', 50 *Stanford Law Review* 1709–22 (1998) (summarizing different options courts have at their disposal).
4. See Hirschl, Ran, 'The "Design Sciences" and Constitutional "Success"', 87 *Texas Law Review* 1353–72 (2009).
5. Epstein, Lee, Jack Knight and Olga Shvetsova, 'The Role of Constitutional Courts in the Establishment and Maintenance of Democratic System of Government', 35 *Law & Society Review* 117, 121 table 1 (2001) (discussing which courts have the power to exercise constitutional review, and contrasting the diffuse American system with the concentrated European system).
6. Id. (contrasting the American system, where constitutional review takes place after a law goes into effect and the European system, where courts have that power as well as the power to review laws before they go into effect).
7. Id. (contrasting American standing rules with the more tolerant abstract review culture of European courts).
8. Id. (contrasting American rules limiting lawsuits to parties with standing to more tolerant and permissive European rules). For additional institutional features that have been discussed – and contrasted between countries – see, for instance, Horowitz, Donald L. 'Constitutional Courts: Primer for Decision Makers', 17(4) *Journal of Democracy* 125, 128 (2006) (listing the same institutional features, but also referencing variations in judicial appointment and tenure and the effects and reversibility of judicial decisions), Tushnet, Mark. 'Marbury *v* Madison Around the World', 71 *Tennessee Law Review* 251, 252–7 (2004) (listing the same institutional features, and adding variations in judicial independence).
9. The information available in academic articles is generally presented as an informational afterthought, rather than as a key institutional feature relevant for analytical purposes. See, e.g., Scheppele, Kim Lane. 'Guardians of the Constitution: Constitutional Court Presidents and the Struggle for the Rule of Law in Post-Soviet Europe', 154 *University of Pennsylvania Law Review* 1757, 1769 n. 29 (2006) (describing docket-control style procedures in Russia and Hungary).
10. Part of the reason for the dearth of information is because even though the power to decide which cases to hear is enormously important, and seems to be a decision of constitutional-level importance, it is often a decision reflected not in constitutional text but rather in statutory text. See, e.g., Heun, Werner. 'Access to the German Federal Constitutional Court', in *Constitutional Courts in Comparison: The US Supreme Court and the German Federal Constitutional Court*, edited by Ralf Rogowski and Thomas Gawron, 125–57 (2002) (describing statutory changes affecting the docket control of the German Federal Constitutional Court). And however difficult it is to do comparative constitutional research, comparative statutory research might be even more difficult.
11. See Moore, Barrington. *Social Origins of Dictatorship and Democracy: Lord and Peasant in the Making of the Modern World* (1965).
12. For Linz's arguments, see Linz, Juan J. 'Presidential or Parliamentary Democracy: Does It Make a Difference?', in *The Failure of Presidential Democracy: Comparative Perspectives*, edited by Juan J. Linz and Arturo Valenzuela, 5–44 (1994). For some notable responses to Linz, see Przeworski, Adam, Michael E. Alvarez, José Antonio Cheibub and Fernando Limongi. *Democracy and Development: Political Institutions and Well-Being in the World, 1950–1990*, at 50–51 (2000); Stepan, Alfred and Cindy Skach 'Constitutional Frameworks and Democratic Consolidation', 46 *World Policy* 1 (1993) (gathering data to contrast pure presidentialism with pure parliamentarism in Latin American and Eastern European countries).
13. For the major arguments, see Ginsburg, Tom. *Judicial Review in New Democracies* (2003); Hirschl, Ran. *Towards Juristocracy: The Origins and Consequences of the New Constitutionalism* (2007).
14. Comella, Victor Ferreres. 'The Consequences of Centralizing Constitutional Review in a Special Court: Some Thoughts on Judicial Activism', 82 *Texas Law Review* 1705, 1713 (2004).
15. Scheppele, Kim Lane. 'A Comparative View of the Chief Justice's Role: Constitutional Court Presidents and the Struggle for the Rule of Law in Post-Soviet Europe', 154 *University of Pennsylvania Law Review* 1757, 1769 (2006).
16. Comella, supra note 14, at 1713.
17. See Judiciary Act of 1925 (43 Stat. 936). It was only after changes in 1988 that the Supreme Court could decline to hear appeals from state supreme courts challenging the constitutional acceptability of state statutes. See 42 USC §§ 1252, 1254(2) (repealed 1988).
18. See Supreme Court of Canada, *Bulletin of Proceeding: Special Edition* (2009).
19. India Constitution, Art. 132 (stating that the High Court must 'certify that the case involves a substantial question of law as to the interpretation of this Constitution' before the Supreme Court will accept the case for review). See also India Constitution, Art 133(a) (stating that in civil cases there must be a 'substantial question of law of general importance'); Art. 133(b) (stating that in civil cases it must be 'in the opinion of the High Court [that] the said question needs to be decided by the Supreme Court').
20. Yoav Dotan has explained the process:

> A petition to the HCJ can be written by the layman, and at no stage of the proceedings is representation by a lawyer required. Any person who has reason to believe that a particular public agency denies her legal

rights may petition the Court and apply for an order nisi. A single judge reviews the petition. The judge may order a preliminary hearing before three justices to take place, requesting the respondent to supply the Court with a concise statement as to the reasons and background for the relevant government action. Alternatively, the judge may order an issue nisi, requiring the respondent to appear in court and show why a particular action should or should not be performed. A full hearing before three judges would then be held before the Court reaches its full decision.

Dotan, Yoan. 'Judicial Rhetoric, Government Lawyers, and Human Rights: The Case of the Israeli High Court of Justice During the Intifada', 33(2) *Law and Society Review* 319, 323 (1999).

21. Kommers, David. 'The Federal Constitutional Court in the German Political System', 26 *Comparative Political Studies* 470, 470 (1994).
22. German Basic Law, Art. 93(1).
23. See Landfried, Cristine. 'Judicial Policy-Making in Germany: The Federal Constitutional Court', 15 *Western European Policy* 50, 51 (1992).
24. German Basic Law, Art. 100(1).
25. See, e.g., Heun, supra note 10 at 128.
26. Abstract and concrete review combined make up 2.03% of FCC cases, http://www.bundesverfassungsgericht. de/organisation/gb2008/A-I-1.html.
27. Cases September 7, 1951–December 31, 2008, available at http://www.bundesverfassungsgericht.de/ organisation/gb2008/A-I-1.html.
28. See Kommers, Donald P. *The Constitutional Jurisprudence of the Federal Republic of Germany* 23 (2nd edition, 1997).
29. Scheppele, supra note 9, at 1770 n. 29.
30. Id.
31. Id. at 1780. See also id. at 1785 (noting that the Constitutional Court issued 1871 decisions in its first nine years).
32. See De Santa Cruz Oliveira, Angela Jardim. 'Reforming the Brazilian Supreme Federal Court: A Comparative Approach', 5 *Washington University Global Studies Law Review* 99, 100 (2006).
33. See, e.g., J. Mitchell Pickerill, *Constitutional Deliberation in Congress: The Impact of Judicial Review in a Separated System*, 67 (2004) (discussing the different politics of high versus low salience constitutional issues).
34. See, e.g., Laurence H. Tribe, *Abortion: The Clash of Absolutes* (1992) (discussing the uncompromising and absolute language used by those involved in the constitutional debate over abortion).
35. See, e.g., *Mora v McNamara*, 387 F.3d 862 (DC Cir. 1967), cert. denied, 389 US 934 (1967); *Orlando v Laird*, 443 F.2d 1039, 1043–4 (2d Cir. 1971), cert. denied, 404 US 869 (1971).
36. See, e.g., King, Michael. 'Assimilation and Contrast of Presidential Candidates' Issue Positions', 41 *Public Opinion Quarterly* 515 (1977).
37. The Supreme Court did decide First Amendment and other cases related to the Vietnam War, but nothing related to the core, polarizing issue about the War's legitimacy. See, e.g., *Greer v Spock*, 424 US 828, 838 (1976) (deciding about speech rights on military base); *Cohen v California*, 403 US 15, 26 (1971) (upholding First Amendment rights of protester who put words 'Fuck the Draft' on the back of his jacket).
38. In later papers about the importance of docket control, I will expand in greater detail and therefore be more exacting about the relationship between the precise status and success of the court and its precise docket control rules.
39. See, e.g., Klarman, Michael J. 'The Puzzling Resistance to Political Process Theory', 77 *Virginia Law Review* 747, 817 n. 309 (1991) (noting that support for school integration hovered below 50 percent).
40. See, e.g., Justice Douglas memorandum (January 25, 1960), reprinted in Melvin I. Urofsky, *The Douglas Letters* 169 (1987) (noting Frankfurter's statement made at Court conference that in the 1940s he would have found 'segregation in the schools . . . constitutional because "public opinion had not then crystallized against it" ').
41. See Dotan, Yoav and Menachem Hofnung. 'Legal Defeats, Political Wins: Why Do Elected Representatives Go to Court?', 38 *Comparative Political Studies* 75 (2005).
42. See Klein, Claude. 'A New Era in Israel's Constitutional Law', 6 *Israel Law Review* 376 (1971).
43. Shamir, Ronen. ' "Landmark Cases" and the Reproduction of Legitimacy: The Case of Israel's High Court of Justice', 24(3) *Law and Society Review* 781, 785 (1990). (noting that 'the overwhelming majority of these petitions were removed, compromised or settled in one way or another' and that only 65 petitions reached adjudication and were published as HCJ decisions).
44. Dotan and Hofnung, supra note 41 at 85.
45. See Shamir, supra note 43, at 795.
46. See Barzilai, Gad. 'Judicial Hegemony, Polarization of Parties, and Social Change', 3 *Politika* 31–51 (1988); Barzilai, Gad. 'Courts as Hegemonic Institutions: The Israeli Supreme Court in a Comparative Perspective',

at 23, in *Israel: The Dynamics of Change and Continuity*, edited by David Levi-Faur, Gabriel Sheffer, and David Vogel (1999).

47. See *Thomas v Mowbray*, (2007) 233 CLR 307. See also Lynch, Andrew. 'Australia's "War on Terror" Reaches the High Court', 32 *Melbourne University Law Review* 1182, 1182–3 (2008) (stating that 'the importance of the decision … is indisputable.').

48. See Kost, Timo. 'Mounir El Motassadeq – A Missed Change for Weltinnepolik?', 8 *German Law Journal* 443 (2007).

49. See Nohlen, Nicholas. 'Germany: The European Arrest Warrant Case', 6 *International Journal of Constitutional Law* 153 (2008).

50. See *A and others v Secretary of State for Home Affairs*, [2004] UKHL 56.

51. See *People's Union for Civil Liberties v Union of India*, 2004 9 SCC 580.

52. See *Hamdi v Rumsfeld*, 542 US 507, 510 (2004); *Rasul v Bush*, 542 US 466 (2004); *Rumsfeld v Padilla*, 542 US 426 (2004).

53. See, e.g., Friedman, Barry. 'Mediated Popular Constitutionalism', 101 *Michigan Law Review* 2596 (2003) ('Specific support is driven by agreement with particular policies, it is a measure of whether a person thinks an institution is doing a good job in terms of policy output.').

54. See Easton, David A. *A Systems Analysis of Political Life* (1965) at 273.

55. See Gibson, James L., Gregory A. Caldeira and Vanessa A. Baird, 'On the Legitimacy of National High Courts', 92 *American Political Science Review* 343, 349 (1998).

56. See supra 18.

57. See Brown, Henry S. and Biran A. Crane, *Supreme Court of Canada Practice*, part 1, chapter 2 (2007).

58. [1998] 2 CSR ¶¶ 9–15.

59. See Heun, supra note 10, at 161.

60. See Vanberg, Georg. 'Establishing Judicial Independence in West Germany: The Impact of Opinion Leadership and the Separation of Powers', 32 *Comparative Policy* 333, 342 (2000).

61. See supra note 21.

62. Id. at 342–8.

63. See Ferejohn, John E. 'Constitutional Review in the Global Context', 6 *New York University Journal of Legislation & Public Policy* 49, 51 (2002).

64. Gibson et al., supra note 55, at 355.

65. See Durr, Robert H., Andrew D. Martin and Christina Wolbrecht. 'Ideological Divergence and Public Support for the Supreme Court', 44 *American Journal of Political Science* 768 (2000).

66. Brzezinski, Mark F. and Leszek Garlicki. 'Judicial Review in Post-Communist Poland: The Emergence of a Rechtsstaat?', 31 *Stanford Journal of International Law* 13, 13 (1995).

67. See Schwartz, Herman. 'Eastern Europe's Constitutional Courts', 9 *Journal of Democracy* 100, 102–03 (1998).

68. Id.

69. Gibson, James L. and Gregory A. Calderia. 'Defenders of Democracy? Legitimacy, Popular Acceptance, and the South African Constitutional Court', 65 *Journal of Policy* 1, 2 (2003).

70. See Bugaric, Bojan. 'Courts as Policy-makers: Lessons from Transition', 42 *Harvard International Law Journal* 247, 263 (2001).

71. 5 US (1 Cranch) 137 (1803).

72. Treanor, William Michael. 'Judicial Review before Marbury', 58 *Stanford Law Review* 455, 541 (2005).

73. Id. at 541–2.

74. CC decision no. 71-44DC, July 16, 1971.

75. See Starr, Kenneth W. 'The Supreme Court and Its Shrinking Docket: The Ghost of William Howard Taft', 90 *Minnesota Law Review* 1363, 1369 (2006).

76. Supreme Court of Canada, *Bulletin of Proceeding: Special Edition* (2009).

77. Oliveira, supra note 32, at 130–31.

78. Id. at 133 table 6.

79. Trochev, Alexi. 'Less Democracy, More Courts: A Puzzle of Judicial Review in Russia', 38 *Law and Society Review* 513, 514 (2004).

80. See Smithey, Shannon Ishiyama and John Ishiyama. 'Judicial Activism in Post-Communist Politics', 36 *Law and Society Review* 719, 723 (2002).

81. See Farganis, Dion. 'Does Reasoning Matter: The Impact of Opinion Content on Supreme Court Legitimacy', available at http://papers.ssrn.com/sol3/papers.cfm?abstract_id=1434726.

82. The Supreme Court of Argentina has in recent times faced around 26,000 cases per year. See Helmke, Gretchen. 'The Logic of Strategic Defection: Judicial Decision-Making in Argentina under Dictatorship and Democracy', 96 *American Political Science Review* 291 (2002). The Supreme Federal Court has faced around 110,000 in the recent past. See Oliveira, supra note 32, at 100.

83. See Scheppele, supra note 9, at 1772–90.

84. See id. at 1781–2.
85. See Staton, Jeffrey. 'Constitutional Review and the Selective Promotion of Case Results', 50 *American Journal of Political Science* 98 (2006); Vanberg, Georg. 'Establishing Judicial Independence in West Germany: The Impact of Opinion Leadership and the Separation of Powers', 32 *Comparative Politics* 333 (2000).
86. Staton is talking mostly about Mexico, and Vanberg is talking about West Germany.
87. Staton, supra note 85, at 98 ('An exhaustive search of all European and American high, constitutional or international court websites suggests that 71% of these courts issue press releases summarizing at least some of their resolutions.').
88. See Epp, Charles R. *The Rights Revolution: Lawyers, Activists, and Supreme Courts in Comparative Perspective* (1998) (discussing the existence of a 'support structure' as crucial to the judicial development and protection of individual rights in Canada, India and the United States).
89. Southworth, Ann. 'The Rights Revolution and Support Structures for Rights Advocacy', 34 *Law & Society Review* 1203 (2000) (reviewing Epp, supra note 88).
90. See Wilson, Bruce M. 'Institutional Reform and Rights Revolutions in Latin America: The Cases of Costa Rica and Colombia', 2 *Journal of Policy in Latin America* 59, 66 (2009).
91. Tushnet, Mark. 'Social Welfare Rights and the Forms of Judicial Review', 82 *Texas Law Review* 1895, 1898 (2004).
92. Art. 45, Constitution of Ireland, 1937.
93. Art. 45, § 1, Constitution of Ireland, 1937.
94. Tushnet, supra note 91, at 1902.
95. South African Constitution, § 26(2).
96. Mexico Constitution, Art. 123.
97. See Whittington, Keith. 'Interpose Your Friendly Hand: Political Supports for the Exercise of Judicial Review by the United States Supreme Court', 99 *American Political Science Review* 583 (2003).
98. See Dotan and Hofnung, supra note 41.
99. See supra note 3.
100. Scheppele, supra note 9, at 1770.
101. Id. at 1770–71 n. 32.
102. See Staton, Jeffrey K. and Georg Vanberg. 'The Value of Vagueness: Delegation, Defiance and Judicial Opinions', 51 *American Journal of Political Science* 504, 515 (2008).
103. Dotan and Hofnung, supra note 41, at 98.
104. See Levinson, Sanford. 'Strategy, Jurisprudence and Certiorari', 79 *Virginia Law Review* 717, 717–18 (1993) (reviewing H.W. Perry, Jr., *Deciding to Decide: Agenda Setting in the United States Supreme Court*).
105. Shamir, supra note 43, at 795–96.
106. See Hausmaninger, Herbert. 'Towards a "New" Russian Constitutional Court', 28 *Cornell Journal of International Law* 349, 350 (1995).
107. Id. at 354.
108. Id.
109. Id.
110. Id. passim.
111. Id. at 354.
112. Id.
113. Epstein, Knight & Shvetsova, supra note 5, at 144.
114. See Hausmaninger, supra note 106, at 366.
115. See Law on the Constitutional Court of the RSFSR, Vedomosti RSFSR, Issue No. 30, Item No. 1017 (1991), translated in FBIS-USR-91-029, September 10, 1991, at 69, p. 14.
116. See Constitutional Law on the Constitutional Court, SZ RF Issue No. 13, Item No. 1447 (1994), translated in FBIS-SOV-94-145-S, July 28, 1994, ch. XII.
117. See Epstein et al., supra note 5, at 122 n. 6.
118. Id. See also Scheppele, supra note 99, at 1769 n. 29 ('In practice, because of the huge press of cases, however, courts have to find a way to triage their decisions. The Russian Constitutional Court separates cases into first impression cases (postanovlenia) versus mere elaborations (opredelenia). Postanovlenia require formal briefing, oral arguments, and plenary sessions of a senate of the court. Opredelenia are decided on the basis of the initial submissions and are generally written by one judge as rapporteur, with the decision then voted on in a full plenary session of the Court, without full oral argument.').
119. US Constitution, art. II, § 2 ('The President ... by and with the Advice and Consent of the Senate, shall appoint ... Judges of the supreme Court, and all other Officers of the United States.').
120. France Constitution art. 56.
121. See Epstein, Lee, Jeffrey A. Segal, Harold G. Spaeth and Thomas G. Walker, *The Supreme Court Compendium: Data, Decisions, and Developments* 71–6, table 2-2 (2nd edition, 1996).

122. See Oliveira, supra note 32, 100.
123. See Rogers, James R. 'Information and Judicial Review: A Signaling Game of Legislative-Judicial Interaction', 45 *American Journal of Political Science* 84 (2001).
124. See Gunther, Gerald. 'The Subtle Vices of the "Passive Virtues" – A Comment on Principle and Expediency in Judicial Review', 64 *Columbia Law Review* 1 (1964).
125. Id. at 24–5.
126. See Sager, Lawrence Gene. 'Fair Measure: The Legal Status of Underenforced Constitutional Norms', 91 *Harvard Law Review* 1212 (1978).
127. The failures of the Tribunal of Constitutional Guarantees of Costa Rica to decide major cases, and the damage it did to that court, are good examples of this dynamic. See Dargent, Eduardo. 'Determinants of Judicial Independence: Lessons from Three "Cases" of Constitutional Courts in Peru (1982–2007)', 41 *Journal of Latin American Studies* 251, 263–4 (2009).
128. See, e.g., *Khadr v Canada (Prime Minister)*, [2009] FCJ No. 893 (CA); *Canada (Attorney General) v Ribic*, [2005] 1 FCR 33 (FCR 2003); *Canadian Security Intelligence Service Act (Can.) (Re)*, [2009] FCJ No. 1153 (FCC 2009); *Almrei (Re)*, [2009] FCJ No. 1 (FCC 2009); *Amnesty International Canada v Canada (Canadian Forces)*, [2008] FCJ No. 356 (FCC 2008).

Index

abortion, and autonomy and dignity 441–58
  in constitutional adjudication 461, 465, 466,
    615–16
  Germany 448–55
  Ireland 442–5, 452–5
  US 443, 445–8, 452–5
Abranches, S. 222
Ackerman, B. 96–7, 230, 234, 251, 340, 346,
    347, 352, 353, 534, 565
Ackermann, L. 591, 592, 594, 595, 596
Adler, J. 504
Afghanistan 80–82, 84–6, 88, 89, 91
Agresto, J. 301
Ahdar, R. 423
Ahronot, Y. 169
Ajzenstat, J. 164
Al-Ali, Zaid 77–95
Albania 48, 50
Albert, R. 234, 301
Albertyn, C. 494
Aleinikoff, A. 164, 166, 391
Alesina, A. 118
Alexander, G. 189, 352, 505, 509
Alexander, L. 303
Alexy, R. 389, 390, 391, 592, 604, 617
Alford, R. 418, 618
Allan, J. 312, 459
Allan, T. 488
Allars, M. 245
Allen, Tom 189, 504–18
Alonso García, R. 275
Alston, P. 74, 400
Alter, K. 276
Altman, D. 222
Alvarez, J. 63, 193, 196, 198
Alvaro, A. 504
Amar, A. 98, 360, 417
Ambwani, S. 104
amendment rules *see* constitutional amendment
  rules
Amorin Neto, O. 222, 226, 228
Andenaes, M. 563
Anderson, G. 200, 201, 202
Anderson, K. 594
Anderson, L. 365
Andrews, W. 230
Anghie, A. 172
Ankut, P. 53

Appleton, S. 457
Arato, A. 22, 34, 51
Argentina
  bilateral agreements and fair and equitable
    treatment 196, 199
  CMS 196, 199
  court docket control 635
  dispute resolution 193
  judicial engagement with comparative law
    574, 578–9, 581, 584
  legislative and executive powers, separation
    of 235
  presidential democracy and decree power
    228–9
  Simon 67–8
  state responsibility in past human rights
    violations 65–6, 67
  transitional justice 66–8
Arjomand, S. 436
Aroney, N. 358
Aronson, M. 247
Arsu, S. 75
Asimow, M. 248–9
Aspinall, E. 378
Atiyah, P. 242, 243, 244, 251
Attwood, B. 101, 102
Aung, T. 22
Austin, G. 122
Australia
  Al-Kateb v Godwin 610
  birthright citizenship 151–2, 153–4, 164, 165,
    166, 167
  Chu Kheng Lim v Minister for Immigration
    144–5
  citizenship and constitutional text 144–5
  citizenship definition 149–50, 163
  citizenship rights 144–5, 158–9
  constitution endurance 115
  constitutional amendments 97, 98, 99, 100,
    101–2
  constitutional interpretation 601–2, 605, 606,
    610–11
  constitutional temperance campaign 21
  court docket control 629
  dual citizenship 153–4, 155
  dual nationals, restricted rights of 156
  freedom of expression 408, 412–13, 419
  gender-constitutional analysis 21

immigration and detention 610
and indigenous communities 101–2
judicial engagement with comparative law
    573, 588
judicial review 304, 312
legislative and executive powers, separation
    of 246–7
mandatory referenda voting 50
non-citizens 157
notwithstanding clause and bill of rights
    302–3
parliamentary systems in common law world
    242–7
power to remove cases 100
private individuals, effects on 393
property rights 505, 513
reproductive rights 29
terrorism law 538–9, 542, 543–4
Victorian Charter of Rights and
    Responsibilities 100
Austria 407, 463, 555–6, 574, 588
Axelrod, R. 213
Ayres, A. 369
Azuela, A. 511

Backer, L. 84
Baer, S. 169
Bagaric, M. 459
Baines, B. 31, 32
Bakan, J. 164–5
Balkin, J. 101, 602, 617
Bamforth, Nicholas 551–67
Banazak, K. 27
Bankowski, Z. 592
Banks, A. 22, 34–5, 46, 47, 376
Bannon, A. 44, 50, 52, 53
Banting, K. 52
Barak, A. 287, 416, 591, 594, 595, 603
Barak-Erez, D. 161, 165, 168, 169, 545
Barber, B. 39
Barendt, E. 406, 408, 409, 415
Barker, E. 473, 474
Barnett, R. 603, 617
Barrionuevo, A. 235
Barron, D. 195
Barros, R. 13
Barsh, R. 179
Bartlett, K. 32, 35
Barzilai, G. 352, 638–9
Basedau, M. 263
Bates, J. 459
Bateup, C. 317
Baun, M. 3
Baxi, U. 193
Baylis, E. 362

Beatty, D. 189, 391, 532, 538, 542, 603–4, 617
Beauvais, J. 193, 195
Beck, U. 201
Been, V. 193, 195
Belgium 115, 485, 486, 574
Bell, J. 247, 251, 613, 616, 620, 621, 622
Bendor, A. 350
Benomar, J. 38, 43, 44, 52, 53
Bentele, U. 573, 595
Benvenisti, E. 66
Berkowitz, D. 119
Berman, P. 191
Bermeo, N. 366
Best, C. 592
BeVier, L. 414
Bhargava, R. 139
Bickel, A. 270, 272, 317, 533, 534, 624–5, 635
Bieber, F. 377
Bilchitz, D. 495, 530
bills of rights *see* constitutional experimentation
    and bills of rights functionality
Bingham, T. 93
Blackstone, W. 512
Blasi, V. 415
Blendon, R. 251
Blount, Justin 38–56
Bobbitt, P. 604, 617–18
Bogdanor, V. 565
Bohmer, M. 66
Boix, C. 115
Bolivia 193
Bollinger, L. 415, 417
Bomhoff, J. 617
Booth, W. 235, 236
Boralevi, L. 1
Borchard, E. 199
Bork, R. 414
Bosnia
Bosnia v Serbia 59, 72
    collective presidency 376
    constitutional drafting 82–4, 85, 87, 89, 91
    veto powers of ethnic groups 82–4
Bosniak, L. 164, 169
Botswana 584, 587
Boudreaux, D. 98
boundaries *see* citizenship and constitutional
    boundaries
Bourdieu, P. 192, 197
Boyce, B. 509
Bracey, C. 459
Bradley, A. 300, 315
Bragyova, A. 43
Brancati, D. 369, 371, 377
Brazil
    amnesty case and transitional justice 62

consultation process 47
court docket control 627, 635
judicial engagement with comparative law
  574
presidential democracy and decree power
  226, 228
socio-economic rights 527–8
Brennan, G. 3
Brennan, W. 301
Breslin, B. 44, 120, 130
Brewer-Carías, A.-R. 265, 268
Briffault, R. 360
Brodsky, G. 478
Bronitt, S. 167
Brookfield, F. 172
Brown, H. 639
Brown, L. 247
Brown, N. 437
Brownlie, I. 483
Brubaker, R. 366
Brunner, G. 50
Bryce, J. 194
Bryde, B. 574, 578, 591, 592, 593, 594, 596
Brzezinski, M. 639
Buchanan, J. 3, 104
Bugaric, B. 639
Buhaug, H. 378
Buhler, S. 152, 165, 166, 167
Buitrago, M. 22
Bull, T. 122
Bunce, V. 367
Burch Elias, S. 545
Burke-White, W. 200
Burma 22
Bushell, A. 301, 312, 313, 332, 621
Bussani, M. 2
Butler, A. 308, 310, 389
Butler, P. 308, 310
Byrnes, A. 302

Cachard, O. 469
Cairns, A. 159, 168
Calabresi, S. 241, 250–51, 567, 574
Calderia, G. 639
Camen, U. 94
Cameron, I. 542
Cameron, J. 301
Campbell, T. 311, 312, 316, 415
Canada
  abortion rights 458
  bicameralism 310
  bill of rights 300–301, 302, 305–10
  birthright citizenship 151, 152
  citizenship and constitutional text 145–6,
    406

citizenship definition 149–50, 163
citizenship rights 145–6, 158, 159
constitution endurance 115
constitution and political parties 257–8
constitutional amendment rules 97, 105
constitutional amendment rules, and power to
  remove cases 100
constitutional interpretation 601, 605, 606,
  611–12
constitutional and ordinary jurisdiction,
  interplay of 292–4
court docket control 626, 629, 631, 636
criminal activity and freedom of expression
  409
dual citizenship 155, 157
emergency provisions 337, 341
equality and discrimination 475, 476–81, 488,
  493
equality, and inquiries undertaken 477–8
equality and internal relevance test 477
federalism 245, 341, 358, 362, 368–9
Figueroa 257
freedom of expression 408–13, 415–18
gender-constitutional analysis 21–2, 25
general limitations clause 328, 331
human dignity in constitutional adjudication
  460, 464, 465, 478–9
immigration law 537
indigenous peoples and constitutional law
  170–76, 182–5
international investment and law, effects of
  194
judicial engagement with comparative law
  574, 588
judicial review 192, 300–301, 302, 312, 313,
  326–7, 330–31
legislation invalidation costs 309
limitations clause 389
Newfoundland 481
non-citizens 152, 157
notwithstanding clause in and bill of rights
  300–301, 302, 309, 325, 327–8,
  330–31
Oakes 328, 390, 410, 411, 481
parliamentary systems in common law world
  244–6
principle of proportionality 390
private individuals, effects on 393, 395
property rights 504–5
proportionality analysis 328, 603–4
religion and multicultural accommodation
  431–2
same-sex partnerships 477, 553, 558, 612
social security schemes and equality
  480–81

sovereignty, state acquisitions of 172–3
terrorism law 533, 534–5, 537, 540, 542, 543,
    544–5, 546
Canivet, G. 591, 592
Cappelletti, M. 268, 278, 280, 281, 282, 294
Capps, P. 464
Carey, J. 39, 116, 216, 218, 227
Carozza, Paolo G. 459–72
Carrio, G. 593
Carroll, S. 35
Case, M. 24, 25, 30
Casey, J. 352
Cass, D. 190
Castano, A. 593
Cederman, L. 370
Chad 44
Chang, H. 195
Chang, W. 573, 588, 593
Chappell, L. 27
Charlesworth, H. 27
Charters, Claire 170–88
Chaskalson, M. 504
Cheadle, H. 394
Cheibub, José Antonio 115, 120, 211–33
Chemerinsky, E. 392
Chernykh, S. 217, 219
Chesterman, S. 94
Chile 62, 115, 431
China 423
Chinkin, C. 27
Choudhry, Sujit 3, 106, 190, 315, 356–84, 411,
    418, 504, 532, 544, 571, 581–3, 594, 595
Cisar, E. 237, 239, 240, 242, 248
citizenship and constitutional boundaries 143–69
    Australian constitutional text 144–5, 158–9
    birthright citizenship 150–52
    Canadian constitutional text 145–6, 158, 159
    citizen coordination, and constitutional
        endurance 116
    citizen involvement 98, 103, 107
    citizenship definition 148–50, 163
    and citizenship law, divergent approaches
        148–62
    comparative approaches, challenges for
        162–3
    dual nationality 152–6
    dual nationality, differential rights for 156–7
    and government policing 39
    Israeli constitutional text 147–8
    naturalization rights 150–51, 152
    non-citizen categories 157–8
    responsibilities 490
    and text of national constitutions 144–8
    US constitutional text 146–7, 158, 159–60
civil law 247–8, 268–9, 577–80

Clark, D. 2
Clarke, R. 537
Clay, K. 119
Clayton, C. 3
Clayton, R. 565
coalitions *see under* legislative-executive
    relations
Cohen, F. 171
Cohen, J. 63
Cohen-Eliya, M. 391
Cole, D. 352, 353, 534
Cole, P. 162–3, 169
Coleman, C. 31
Colker, R. 457
Collier, P. 378
Collins, H. 474–5
Colombia 115, 431, 632
common law 242–7, 509–10, 575–7
Commonwealth Human Rights Initiative 40–41
comparative perspective *see* constitutional
    interpretation in comparative perspective
Congleton, R. 105, 108, 121
Connell, R. 192
constitutional amendment rules 96–111
    amendment functions 97–102
    and amendment irrelevancy 101
    and amendment substitutes 100–101
    and basic constitutional rules 97–8
    cautionary approach 102–4
    citizen involvement 98, 103, 107
    comparative difficulty of 104–8
    and constitutional age and length 106
    and democratic pressure 98–9
    and democratic self-government 102
    evidentiary value 98–9
    and exceptional forms of law-making 96–7
    future research 107–8
    interpretation of 99–100
    and judicial interpretation 98–101, 105, 108
    and minority rights protection 103
    path dependency difficulty 106
    and political competition 102, 106, 107
    power to remove cases 100
    ratification process and legislative approval
        103–4, 105–6
    and scale of state legislature 106
    and sovereignty, popular 98
constitutional boundaries *see* citizenship and
    constitutional boundaries
constitutional drafting and external influence
    77–95
    Afghanistan case study 80–82, 84, 85, 88, 91
    Bosnia case study 82–4, 85, 87, 91
    and democratic governance rights 85
    and differences of opinion 88

disagreement categories 86–8
double standards, perceived 90
and fundamental rights 84
and gross violations of fundamental rights
    86–7
interaction patterns 84–8
international best practice disagreements 87–8
and international monetary system 85, 87–8
Iraq case study 78–80, 84, 85, 87–8, 91
and judicial independence 85, 87
normative values, influence of 88–91
presidential system 81–2, 88
reach and limitations of 84–5
sovereignty and principle of non-interference
    89–90
and threats to peace 90–91
veto powers of ethnic groups 82–4
and women's rights 78–9, 81, 86
constitutional endurance 112–25
    case studies 120–22
    and citizen coordination 116
    consequences of 114–16
    constitution-specific institutions 113
    and design features 118
    and financial shocks 117
    future research 120
    history of 115, 117–18, 120–22
    observed patterns 117–20
    and public policy language 118–19
    reasons for 112–14
    and regime type 115, 119–20
    regional effects 118
    and rent-seeking 114, 116–17
    and self-enforcement theory 116–17
    and social and environmental change 113,
        118
    and stability 113–14
    and subnational units 119
    theories 116–17
    and written constitution 119–20
constitutional experimentation and bills of rights
    functionality 298–320
    and bicameralism 310
    and compatibility requirements 306–7, 312
    consequences of failing to comply 309
    future research 308, 310
    intra- and inter-institutional reflection on
        justification of legislation 312
    judicial power, effectiveness of limits on 312
    and judicial review 300–301, 303–5, 311–13
    legislation invalidation costs 309
    legislation scope or effects, altering
        interpretation of 311
    legislative and judicial judgment, relationship
        between 311–13

legislatures in rights judgment, role of
    305–11
and notwithstanding clause 300–303, 309
parliamentary committees, specialized,
    argument for 310–11, 312
parliamentary rights model 299–303, 304–10,
    311–12
reconsideration of bill of rights functionality
    303–5
and risk assessment 307
constitutional identities, formation of 129–42
    and bounded fluidity 132–3
    concept of constitutional identity 129–31
    and constitutional disharmony 130, 131–40
    and constitutional text 131–2
    and cross-national similarities 130
    dissonance dynamics 133–7
    and experience 129–30
    and extra-territorial intervention 136–7
    historical reference points 131–3, 135, 137,
        139
    internal and external disharmonies, balance of
        137–40
    and political balance 133–4
    and secularism 133–4, 136, 138–40
constitutional interpretation in comparative
    perspective 599–623
    amendments, positivism and suprapositive
        constitutionalism 606–7
    Australia 601–2, 605, 606, 610–11
    Canada 601, 605, 606, 611–12
    deference, majoritarianism and autonomous
        legal values 605–6
    fixed meaning approach 601–2
    France 605, 607, 612–14
    functionalism, flexibility and standards
        605
    Germany 605, 606–8, 615–16
    and human dignity 607–8
    interpretive approaches 600–607
    living tree approach 601, 611
    and national courts 607–14
    originalism, textualism and purposivism
        602–4, 607
    proportionality analysis 603–4, 607
    and reference to precedent 609
    rule-bound formalism 605
    single-valenced vs. multi-valenced
        interpretation 604–5, 610
    and substantive outcome 614–16
    US 601, 602, 604, 605, 606, 609, 614–15
constitutional and ordinary jurisdiction, interplay
    of 278–97
    acoustic separation, ideal and allure of
        279–82

acoustic separation under full-scale
transformative constitutionalism 284–9
Canada 292–4
compromised regimes, examples of 289–94
and constitutional supreme tribunals (CSTs)
279, 280, 281–2, 284–5, 288–9
and constitutional types 282–3
detached reviews of statutes 287–9
doctrinal control and adjudication 281, 288–9
functional and methodological differences
280
Germany 289–90
judicial ministries and need for differing
talents and skills 280–81, 288–9
and political resistance 281–2
private-law integrity and parallel legal
systems 285–7
and real effect demand 283
separation, standard case for 280–82
South Africa 286–7, 290–92
substantive constitutional effect, competing
demand for 282–4
substantive constitutional norms, concrete
effectuation of 283–4
and substantive guarantees 279, 284–5
constitutional rights, structure and scope of
387–405
first and second generation rights 400
and fixed tiers of review (US) 391
future research 396
indirect horizontal effect 394–5, 397
internal and external limits 388–90
and judicial review, weak-form 401
liberal, vertical position 392
limits, conceptions of 388–91
negative and positive rights, differences
between 396–402
and principle of proportionality 390–91
private individuals, effects on 392–3, 394–5
and property rights 400
protective rights 397, 398, 399
and public-private division 392
scope and substantive content, connections
between 395–6
social and economic rights 396–401
vertical and horizontal effect 391–6
welfare rights 397, 398, 401
constitutional supreme tribunals (CSTs) 279,
280, 281–2, 284–5, 288–9
Conway, D. 366
Coper, M. 620
Cornell, D. 60
Corral, B. 593
Corwin, E. 351
Costa Rica 29, 632

Cotler, I. 352–3, 543
Cotta, M. 230
Cotterrell, R. 586
Cottrell, J. 50, 52, 80
courts
European Court of Human Rights *see*
European Court of Human Rights
and national constitutional interpretation
607–14
role of, same-sex partnerships 558–60
specialized *see* specialized constitutional
courts, rise of
and terrorism law, challenges of 532–3,
534–8
see also judicial headings
Cowen, S. 494
Cowley, M. 235
Cram, I. 415
Crane, B. 639
Craven, M. 401
Crawford, B. 367
Crawford, J. 59
Creighton, D. 351
Cretney, S. 566
Crock, M. 164
Croissant, A. 229
Cross, F. 250, 358, 360, 401, 521
Cruz Villalón, P. 266, 270
Currie, D. 242, 246, 249, 263, 289, 400–401
Currie, I. 406, 409, 499
Cusack, T. 40
Czech Republic 259, 485

Dahl, R. 35, 100, 116
Dahlrup, D. 29
Daintith, T. 400, 402, 504
Dan-Cohen, M. 294
Dana, D. 195, 202
Daniels, R. 360
Dann, P. 89
Dargent, E. 641
Dauvergne, C. 168
Davis, Dennis M. 283, 401, 494, 519–31
Dawood, Y. 415
De Lamothe, O. 618, 622
De Mello, L. 93
De Mello, S. 94
De Raadt, J. 53
De Swaan, A. 213
De Waal, J. 406, 409
Deakin, S. 361
Deheza, G. 222
democracy
deliberative, and participation in
constitutional design 40–41

and freedom of expression 414
governance rights, and constitutional drafting
   85
inclusive, and secession 370
militant, and transitional justice 58
pressure, and constitutional amendment rules
   98–9
self-government, and constitutional
   amendment rules 102
and specialized constitutional courts, rise of
   270–71
Democratic Republic of the Congo (DRC) 49
Denning, B. 96, 97, 98, 100, 101
Dershowitz, A. 534
design *see* participation in constitutional design
devolution *see* federalism, devolution and
   secession
DeVotta, N. 369
Dezalay, Y. 192, 197
Dezso, M. 43
Diamond, L. 92
Dillon, J. 195
DiMaggio, P. 3
discrimination *see* equality
Dixon, O. 617
Dixon, Rosalind 1–15, 34, 96–111, 313, 332,
   389, 401, 593, 595
Dobrowolsky, A. 23, 31
docket control and success of constitutional
   courts 624–41
   clash of absolutes 628, 633
   and court support structure 632
   dangers of docket control 634–6
   declining to hear cases 633–4, 635–6
   and discretionary jurisdiction 626–7
   and fairness 632
   imperfect alternatives 633–4
   institutional practice, common 626–7
   and institutional variations 626
   and judge appointments 635
   and judicial review 627–30
   legitimacy timing 629–33
   and operational age of court 630
   and political enemies 631–2
   and political involvement 633, 634
   power of docket control 627–33
   quantity of constitutional review 630–33
   scholarship view 625–7
   and support, diffuse and specific 629
Dolzer, R. 195, 199–200
Donoho, D. 94
Donohue, L. 532, 545, 547
Dorsen, N. 57, 165
Dotan, Y. 637–8, 640
Douglas, Z. 198

Draeger, T. 509
drafting *see* constitutional drafting and external
   influence
Dreier, R. 592
Driedger, E. 304
Dumont, F. 350
Dunn, F. 199
Dunoff, J. 76, 191
Dupré, C. 461, 467, 571, 580, 581, 593, 595, 596
Durr, R. 639
Duverger, M. 218
Dworkin, R. 414, 416, 455, 475, 565, 602, 617
Dyer, B. 247
Dyzenhaus, D. 533, 534, 536, 545, 548, 592

East Timor 43, 89
Easton, D. 639
Eberle, E. 290
Ebrahim, H. 48
economic rights *see* socio-economic rights
Ecuador 53, 194
Edwards, R. 488
Egypt 436–7, 546
Eisenmann, C. 268
Eisgruber, C. 102, 103
Ejima, A. 573
Elazar, D. 357, 358, 359
Elgie, R. 217
Elias, J. 67
Elkin, S. 202
Elkins, Z. 12, 38, 46, 51, 52, 96, 102, 106, 112,
   114, 116–19, 202, 262, 530
Ellingwood, K. 236
Elliott, M. 312
Elster, J. 3, 41, 42, 44, 45, 51–2, 53, 98, 102,
   103, 193
emergency regimes 334–55
   and augmented extraordinary powers 341
   authority to declare emergency 339–40
   checks and balances 342–3
   counter-emergency measures and targeting
      outsiders 343
   declaration ratification 340
   dispersed emergency regulation 347
   emergencies, definition of 336–9
   emergency classification 338–9
   emergency provisions in constitutional
      documents 335–44
   enforcement duration 340
   and entrenchment of emergency powers
      346–7
   and executive branch of government, role of
      343, 344, 345, 346–7
   and federalism 341
   inherent emergency powers 343–4

and institutional power sharing 339–40
and judicial review 341–2, 347
and legislature 341, 342–3, 345–7
models of accommodation, abuse of 348
normalcy and emergency, distinctions
     between 349
and public reassurance 345–6
Roman dictatorship as prototype 334–6
state of emergency, effects of declaring
     340–42
state of emergency, and suspension of rights
     and freedoms 340–41
and suspension of constitutional provisions
     341–2
Emerson, T. 414, 415
Emiliou, N. 391
Epp, C. 315, 532, 538
Epstein, H. 93
Epstein, L. 352, 626, 637, 640
Epstein, R. 508–9
equality 473–503
     affirmative action programmes 475
     and appropriate comparators 479–81
     balancing model and compensation 513–15
     Canada 475, 476–81, 488, 493
     citizens and private associations,
          responsibility of 490
     comparability of takings laws 515–16
     comparability test 477–8, 486–7
     conception of 473–6
     core-penumbra test 487
     discrimination not on listed ground 493–4
     differential treatment discrimination 478,
          482–8
     and differentiation 474
     discriminatory impact of division 474–5
     European Court of Human Rights, Article 14
          483–9
     and family law 494–5
     and human dignity 464, 478–9, 494
     and individuals, focus on 474
     and inequality, entrenchment of 474
     inequality and group disadvantage 475–6, 492
     and internal relevance test 477
     non-citizen rights and terrorism law 535
     problems with principle of 474
     proportionality analysis 494
     and same-sex partnerships, legal protection of
          553, 557
     and separation of powers 481
     and social security schemes 480–81, 484,
          487–8, 495
     South Africa 489–96
     and subsidiarity principle 491
     UK 482–9, 557

and unfair discrimination 492–3
     see also gender as imperative of design
Erdei, A. 468
Erdos, D. 300, 315
Erk, J. 365
Eskridge, W. 99, 100, 560, 561, 563, 564, 566
Estrada, M. 235, 236
Esty, D. 360
Ethiopia 84, 362, 423
ethnic groups 82–4, 356–7, 363–7, 372–5
     see also indigenous peoples
Europe
     constitutional identity and international
          governance 137
     constitutional influence in Bosnia 82–3, 89
     Eastern 50, 368
     emergency provisions 337
     militant democracy 58
     reconciliation and accession processes 70–71
     rights-based legislation, challenges to 308–9
     transitional justice and transformation of
          constitutionalism 68–72
     see also individual countries
European Court of Human Rights
     abortion rights 442, 443–4
     Article 14 and equality 483–9
     constitutional rights and principle of
          proportionality 390–91
     equality and discrimination 483–9
     formation of 482–3
     freedom of expression 409, 463
     human dignity concept 459, 462, 463, 464
     legislation along ethnic lines 70–71, 72, 93
     and political party bans 260–61
     property rights 505, 507, 509, 510, 511, 514
     Protocol 12, ratification of 484
     religious freedom 424, 428–9
     same-sex partnerships 489, 554–6, 560, 561
     Sejdic and Finci v Bosnia and Herzegovina
          70–71, 72, 93
     special advocate regime 547
     as specialized court 275
     terrorism law 535, 536, 547
European Court of Justice 243, 482
     as supranational court 275, 276
     and terrorism 533, 540, 541, 542
Evans, C. and S. 303, 310
Ewing, K. 300, 310, 315, 532, 533, 535, 536,
     537
executive powers *see* legislative and executive
     powers, separation of;
     legislative–executive relations
experimentation and bills of rights *see*
     constitutional experimentation and bills of
     rights functionality

expression, freedom of *see* freedom of
expression
external influence *see* constitutional drafting and
external influence
Ezer, T. 459, 462

Fabre, C. 311, 519
Fachiri, A. 199
Fagan, A. 494
Falconer, Lord 306
Fallon, R. 391, 604, 616
Farber, D. 352, 361
Farganis, D. 639
Favoreu, L. 278, 281, 294
Fearon, J. 378, 380
federalism, devolution and secession 356–84
    and autonomy 360
    basic assumptions 363–4
    central institution design and future research
        376
    classical federalism 357–63
    comparative studies 361
    and confederations, differences between 358
    and consociationalism 374–5
    constitutional court design 376
    court role 361–3
    criticism of 360–61
    definition of federalism 357–9
    democracies, inclusive, and secession 370
    devolution and decentralization, differences
        between 358
    and emergency regimes 341
    and ethnic groups and minority nationalism
        356–7, 363–7, 372–5
    executive president role 375
    future research 370, 372–80
    and gender as imperative of design 25–8
    and judicial references to foreign law 362
    local government in post-conflict situations,
        and future research 377–8
    natural resources and post-conflict settings,
        and future research 378–80
    and new global constitutional order 191
    parliamentary and presidential government,
        choice between 375–6
    post-conflict federalism 363–80
    power-sharing at the centre and future
        research 374–6
    quasi-federalism 358–9
    reasons for federalism 359–61
    referendums on regional autonomy and
        natural resources 379–80
    regional borders and future research 372–4
    and regional political identities, shaping
        367–8, 371–2, 377

secession, argument on likelihood of 370–71,
    374
secessionist sentiment, claimed dampening of
    365–7, 371, 376
self-government and secession, likelihood of
    369–70
and terrorism law 538–9
and unitary state, advantages over 360
federalism, post-conflict
    and constitutional structure 373, 374
    evidence 368–72
    failure of 368
    success of 368–9
    theoretical debate 364–8
Fedtke, J. 591, 594
Feeley, M. 358, 360
Feldman, D. 455, 467, 486
Feldman, N. 90
Ferejohn, J. 98–103, 105, 106, 109, 267, 270,
    274, 639
Ferreres Comella, Víctor 265–77, 278, 279, 281,
    282, 284, 288, 289, 290, 294, 331, 352,
    593, 618, 619
Figueiredo, A. 226, 228, 230
Figueiredo, R. 361
Fiji 119
Fine, S. 202
Finer, S. 189
Finkel, J. 315
Finkel, S. 39
Finland 218
Finn, J. 350
Fischel, W. 202, 508
Fisher, L. 301, 317
Fishkin, J. 41, 46
Fiss, O. 392, 412
Flaherty, M. 248
Fligstein, N. 189
Fontana, David 2, 624–41
Foot, R. 540
Forbath, W. 98, 108
Forcese, C. 533, 539
Forman, J. 546
Forsey, E. 505
Fox, G. 93
Fox, R. 35
France
    assertive secularism 423
    constitutional amendments 98, 605, 607,
        612–14
    constitutional endurance 119
    constitutional policy making 224
    court docket control 630, 631
    human dignity in constitutional adjudication
        460, 461, 464–5

legislative and executive powers, separation
of 247–8
legislative review 267
parliamentary supremacy 332
property rights 509
referendum defeats and women's interests
22–3
semi-presidential system 218, 219
Franck, T. 93, 94, 352
Frankenburg, G. 198
Franklin, D. 3
Frantz, L. 410
Fredman, S. 473, 474, 475, 484, 488
freedom of expression 406–21
categories and balancing 410–11
comparative conceptions 413–19
and constitutional text 406–7
coverage and protection 407–10
and criminal expression 408–9
and democracy 414
and expressive conduct 408
flag desecration laws 409
guarantees, application of 411–13
horizontal and vertical application 412–13
judicial comparative analysis 415–17
limitations on expression 409–10
and mistrust of government 414
philosophical foundations 413–14, 415,
416–17
and political expression 414
and pornography 416, 417
positive and negative application 411–12
proportionality test 410, 411
speech, concept of 407–9
structure of freedom of expression principle
407–11
and terrorism law 539, 543, 544–5, 547
values in constitutional systems 415–18
Freidenvall, L. 29
Friedman, B. 100, 270, 317, 360, 571, 606,
639
Friedman, L. 118, 448, 508
Friedman, Nick 473–503
Fritz, N. 351
Fromont, M. 265, 267
Fromuth, P. 542
Frosini, J. 265
Frug, G. 195, 202
Fudge, J. 25
Fukasaku, K. 93
Fuller, L. 137
Furley, O. 42
future research
constitutional amendment rules 107–8
constitutional endurance 120

constitutional experimentation and bills of
rights functionality 308, 310
constitutional rights, structure and scope of
396
federalism and central institution design 376
federalism, devolution and secession 370,
372–80
local government in post-conflict situations
377–8
natural resources and post-conflict settings,
and future research 378–80
power-sharing at the centre and federalism
374–6
regional borders, and federalism 372–4
specialized constitutional courts, rise of
272–3
terrorism law, challenges of 539
Fyfe, R. 460, 464

Galadima, H. 378
Galbraith, J. 94
Galbraith, P. 372
Gallagher, M. 50
Galli, G. 40, 42, 43, 44
Galloway, D. 146, 150, 165, 166, 167
Gamper, A. 574, 591
Ganev, V. 349
Gardbaum, Stephen 109, 189, 266, 298–300,
306, 332, 387–405, 411–13, 418, 511,
618, 621
Garlicki, L. 273, 279, 282, 284, 290, 294, 295,
639
Garran, R. 26
Garth, B. 192, 197
Gathii, J. 49
Gavison, R. 162, 169
Gawron, T. 265
Gearty, C. 566
Geiringer, C. 177
gender as imperative of design 19–37
and comparativism 33
and entrenchment 32
equality rights 23–5
and executive promotions 32
and federalism 25–8
and gender quotas 28–9
history of 20–26
and hortatory asymmetry 24
and international norms 27–8
and jurisprudence 20
participatory factors 23
political cooperation and federal relations 27
and recalibrated symmetry 24
and reproductive rights 29–31
sexuality and human dignity 464

supremacy clauses and federalism 28
whole-constitution approaches 31–3
see also equality; same-sex partnerships, legal
    protection of
Genevois, B. 619
George, R. 460
Germany
    abortion rights 448–51, 466, 615–16
    Classroom Crucifix 428
    constitution and political parties 254, 255,
        256–9
    constitutional amendments 104, 338
    constitutional interpretation 605, 606–8,
        615–16
    constitutional and ordinary jurisdiction,
        separation of 289–90
    constitutional rights, internal limits 389
    court docket control 627, 629–30
    electoral thresholds 259
    emergency provisions 337–8, 341, 348
    flag desecration laws 409
    freedom of expression 408, 409, 412, 415,
        417, 418
    gender-constitutional analysis 22
    human dignity in constitutional adjudication
        460, 461, 462, 463, 465, 466, 615
    internal parliamentary rights of minor parties
        and independent officeholders 258–9
    judicial engagement with comparative law
        573, 574, 578, 585, 588
    legislative review 267
    Ludin 429–30
    Lüth 289–90, 393, 394, 412
    party autonomy rights 261
    political party bans 260
    private individuals, effects on 393, 394, 395
    property rights 506, 509, 511, 514
    proportionality analysis 604
    protective rights 398, 399
    religious freedom 428, 429–30
    reproductive rights 29–30
    socio-economic rights 520
Getches, D. 185
Ghai, Y. 3, 40, 41, 42, 43, 44, 45, 50, 52, 80, 366
Gibbs, W. 92
Gibson, J. 639
Giersch, J. 50, 52
Gill, S. 192–3
Gillespie, C. 230
Gillman, H. 3, 196
Ginsburg, R. 447, 457
Ginsburg, Tom 1–15, 38, 39, 49, 50, 52, 53, 104,
    112–25, 196, 265, 270, 272, 274, 281,
    283, 315, 530, 637
Glanz, J. 92

Glendon, M. 454
Glenn, H. 139, 575, 585
globalization *see* new global constitutional order
Goldblatt, B. 494
Golden, A. 350
Goldfarb, S. 27
Goldsmith, J. 352
Goldsworthy, J. 84, 299, 300, 617, 618, 620
Goldwin. R. 22
Gonzalez, L. 230
Gordon, B. 22
Goretti, M. 228–9
Gouldman, M. 157, 167
Gover, K. 181
government
    benefits as property 507
    and cabinet control 225
    executive branch of, and emergency regimes
        343, 344, 345, 346–7
    freedom limitation by 464–5
    mistrust of, and freedom of expression 414
    policing by citizens 39
    and political parties *see* political parties and
        constitutionalism
    state action and accountability 57–8
    state responsibilities, and transitional justice
        64–8
    see also parliamentary systems
Gözler, K. 332
Grady, M. 235
Granger, M. 622
Grant, E. 464
Grant, T. 85
Gray, D. 617
Greenawalt, K. 407, 408, 409, 415, 416, 438,
    621
Greenberg, K. 544
Greene, Jamal 599–623
Gretschner, D. 478
Grey, T. 509
Griffin, M. 85, 87, 90
Griffin, S. 97, 98, 107
Griffiths, A. 359
Grimm, D. 280, 289, 290, 410, 412, 417, 617
Grindle, M. 358
Grodin, J. 96
Grofman, B. 230
Groppi, T. 265, 267, 591
Gross, E. 545
Gross, Oren 334–55, 532, 534, 545
Grosz, S. 485, 487
Grzegorczyk, C. 593
Guarnieri, C. 271
Gudridge, P. 353
Guerra, L. 574

Guiraudon, V. 157, 167
Gunther, G. 635–6, 641
Gunther, R. 52
Gurr, T. 363, 364, 366
Guzman, A. 199

Haberfeld, S. 38, 46
Haberle, P. 578
Habermas, J. 73, 75–6, 191, 391
Hachhethu, K. 53
Hacker, J. 249
Haggart, R. 350
Halberstam, D. 359, 362, 595
Hale, H. 364, 373–4, 376
Halmai, G. 396
Hamilton, A. 239, 240, 250, 336, 361
Hammons, C. 118–19
Hansen, R. 153, 167
Hardin, R. 116
Harding, S. 571, 593
Harjono, Justice 574
Harris, J. 459
Hart Ely, J. 352, 411, 414, 565, 607, 624
Hart, H. 38
Hart, V. 23, 31, 38, 39, 43
Harvey, P. 350
Hasebe, Y. 593
Hatchard, J. 51
Haussman, M. 27
Hausmaninger, H. 640
Havemann, P. 185
Hayo, B. 115, 119–20
Haysom, N. 92, 530
Hayson, N. 379
Hellman, A. 619
Helmke, G. 639
Henkin, L. 455, 459
Herrera, C. 511
Heun, W. 637, 638, 639
Heymann, P. 352
Hiebert, Janet L. 298–320, 543, 565
Hilbert, A. 456
Hindelang, S. 199
Hirschl, Ran 23, 30, 133, 135, 192, 315, 377,
        422–40, 591, 595, 616, 637
Hirst, P. 191
Hoeffler, A. 378
Hofnung, M. 638, 640
Hofstadter, R. 262
Hogg, P. 165, 202, 242, 244–5, 246, 251, 301,
        312, 313, 332, 350, 417, 474, 478, 621
Holden, R. 105–6
Holló, A. 468
Holmes, S. 3, 64, 102, 104, 262
Honduras 235–6

Hong Kong 408, 409
Hooja, R. 377
Hor, M. 538
Horowitz, D. 3, 40, 51, 372–3, 374, 375, 616,
        637
Horowitz, H. 392
Horwitz, P. 618
Howell, W. 229
Howse, R. 74, 76, 190, 358
Huang, T. 215
Huber, J. 224–5, 226, 227, 228
human dignity in constitutional adjudication
        459–72
    and abortion 461, 465, 466, 615–16
    aircraft security 607–8
    and assisted suicide 461
    community poverty and vulnerability 463
    and constitutional interpretation 607–8
    and equality 464, 478–9, 494
    and foreign court decisions 466–7
    and freedom limitation by governments
        464–5
    fundamental rights, protection of 466–7
    multiple meanings 460–65
    multiple uses 466–7
    prison detention and punishment 462–3
    and sexuality 464
    and social status and social roles, value of
        463
    sources of term 462, 464
    warnings over use of 467–8
Hume, Nathan 356–84
Hungary
    constitutional elite-level negotiations 42–3
    court docket control 627, 633
    human dignity in constitutional adjudication
        460, 461, 463–7
    judicial engagement with comparative law
        574, 580, 581
Hunt, M. 396
Huntington, S. 40, 53
Huscroft, G. 304, 308, 313
Hussain, N. 353
Hwang, W. 226
Hyre, J. 240

Iceland 218
Immergut, E. 121
India
    constitutional amendments 103, 104, 122
    constitutional endurance 118, 122
    constitutional identity 132, 135, 137–40
    court docket control 626, 629
    federalism 358–9, 362, 369, 373
    Fundamental Rights Case 525–6

Golaknath v State of Punjab 104, 122
human dignity in constitutional adjudication
    463, 464, 466
judicial engagement with comparative law
    574, 588
judicial review 331
mid-day meal scheme (MDMS) 527
property rights 104, 122, 513
religious freedom 433–5
reproductive rights 29
same-sex partnerships 560
secularism 138–40
social and economic rights 398
socio-economic rights 520, 525–7
S.R. Bommai v Union of India 141–2
terrorism law 538
indigenous peoples 170–88
    Canada 170–76, 182–5
    and comparative constitutional scholarship
        185–6
    constitutional comparisons, fundamental
        173–82
    and future constitutional trends 184–5
    and human rights norms 182–3
    influences on 170–72
    and international law 183–4
    New Zealand 170–73, 176–9, 182–5
    and settler population size and power 171
    sovereignty and state acquisitions 172–3
    US 170–73, 179–85
    see also ethnic groups
Indonesia 537, 538, 545, 574, 580
institutional involvement 191, 312, 339–40, 376,
    546, 626–7
Inter-American Court of Human Rights 62,
    64–6
International Criminal Court, and transitional law
    63, 64
international law
    best practice disagreements 87–8
    and indigenous peoples 183–4
    and legislative and executive powers,
        separation of 243
    and new global constitutional order
        199–200
    and transitional justice and transformation of
        constitutionalism 59
investment rules 193, 194–8
Ipp, D.A. 577
Iran 436
Iraq
    constitutional drafting 78–80, 84, 85, 87–8,
        91
    election polarization 44
    and federal powers 79–80

gender-constitutional analysis 34
and international monetary system 85, 87–8
judicial independence 87
natural resources and post-conflict federalism
    379
protection of fundamental rights 84
referenda 80, 379–80
women's rights 78–9, 86
Ireland
    abortion rights 431, 442–5
    constitutional identity 133, 135
    constitutional rights, private individuals,
        effects on 392–3
    court docket control 632
    emergency provisions 342
    freedom of expression 412
    religious freedom 430–31
    reproductive rights 29, 30, 442–5
    social and economic rights 398
    X Case 431, 442, 445–6
Irving, Helen 19–37, 149, 159, 166, 168
Ishiyama, J. 639
Israel
    Bavli 435
    birthright citizenship 152
    citizenship rights 147–8, 160–62, 163, 168,
        169
    constitutional identity 135
    constitutional rights and principle of
        proportionality 390
    constitutional text and citizenship 147–8
    court docket control 626, 628–9, 633–4
    dual citizenship 155–6
    dual nationals, restricted rights of 156–7
    emergency provisions 338
    freedom of expression 415
    human dignity in constitutional adjudication
        459, 463, 466
    human dignity and corporal punishment 459,
        462
    immigration 147–8
    judicial engagement with comparative law
        573
    judicial review 192
    non-citizens 157–8
    religious freedom 435
    reproductive rights 30
    terrorism 545
Issacharoff, S. 102, 263
al-Istrabadi, F. 34
Italy 267–8, 274, 399, 428–9, 631

Jackson, J. 190
Jackson, P. 377
Jackson, R. 352

Jackson, Vicki G. 32, 33, 143, 164, 169, 202,
    236–7, 241–2, 295, 331, 362, 391, 410,
    416, 418–19, 571, 582–3, 593, 595–6,
    599–623
Jacobsohn, Gary J. 104, 129–42, 425, 433, 619
Japan
    election of delegates 42
    emergency provisions 349
    freedom of expression 415
    gender-constitutional analysis 22
    judicial engagement with comparative law
        573, 579
    judicial review 332
    social and economic rights 399
Jennings, S. 75
Joerges, C. 189, 191
Johnson, S. 92
Jones, M. 226
Joppke, C. 168
judicial engagement with comparative law
    571–98
    and accountability 585
    adversarial procedures and common law,
        reliance on 576–7
    binding and persuasive authority, fine line
        between 581
    cases considered 573
    and categorisation 582–3
    and character of national constitution 585–6
    choice of comparators 587–8
    and civil law 577–80
    and common law 575–7
    comparative law contribution 580–83
    comparative method 586–9
    comparative purpose 589
    comparators identified as group 588
    concerns derived from legal system 584–5
    and constitutional amendment rules 98–101,
        105, 108
    and constitutional characteristics 576, 578
    constitutional complications 585–6
    context of adjudication, significance of 586–7
    court experience and likelihood of
        engagement 583
    diffuse review system and civil law 579
    and freedom of expression 415–17
    increase in 574–5
    and information technology 577
    interpretive method 586
    judicial independence 85, 87
    judicial power, effectiveness of limits on 312
    and jurisprudence quality 588
    and legal context 589
    and legislative and executive powers,
        separation of 243–4

    and legitimacy 583–6
    litigation process and civil law 579
    manner of engagement 582–3
    mode of reasoning and common law 575
    patterns and trends 573–5
    precedential value 580–82
    and problem resolution 583
    scope of argument 572
    single judgments and civil law 578
    and state similarities 588
    study hypotheses 580
    and substance and context 588–9
    supra-national arrangements and civil law
        578–9
    talents and skills, need for differing 280–81,
        288–9
    and terrorism law 532–3, 535–9
    use of 573–4
    and written constitution 575–6, 578
judicial review
    and constitutional experimentation 300–301,
        303–5, 311–13
    and docket control *see* docket control and
        success of constitutional courts
    and emergency regimes 341–2, 347
    references to foreign law, and federalism 362
    and specialized constitutional courts, rise of
        270–71
    see also courts; legislation headings
judicial review, rise of weak-form 321–33
    and constitutional rights, structure and scope
        of 401
    development of weak-form review 327–30
    future speculations 330–31
    general limitations clause 328, 331
    and incompatibility declaration 324, 329–30
    interpretive mandate and statutory bills of
        rights 323–4, 330, 331
    and judicial-legislative dialogue 326–7
    and notwithstanding clause 325, 327–8,
        330–31
    and parliamentary and legislative sovereignty
        limitations 322–3
    parliamentary supremacy and strong-form
        review 321–2, 326, 330
    reasonable disagreement and amendment
        process 322–3
    and responsibility of legislators 325–6
    rights-vetting 322–3
    rights-violations 324, 331
    specialist knowledge 325
    types of review 323–6
    and written constitution 321

Kagan, R. 546

Kahana, T. 315
Kahn, P. 137
Kahn-Freund, O. 473
Kalven, H. 410
Kane, S. 379
Kang, J. 34
Kant, I. 191
Karli, M. 39, 40
Katalikawe, J. 42
Katyal, N. 637
Katz, S. 137
Kaufman, A. 22
Kavanagh, A. 488, 559, 565, 566
Kay, R. 112, 392
Kazakhstan 149
Keith, A. 202
Keller, H. 275
Kelly, J. 104, 105, 108, 308, 310, 311, 313, 316,
    317, 621
Kelsen, H. 38, 268, 278, 289, 290, 294, 295
Kelsey, J. 192, 197
Kennedy, D. 190, 192
Kenya 50, 64, 433
Khamsi, K. 196
Kimber, C. 361
Kincaid, J. 359
King, M. 638
Kingsbury, B. 200
Kirby, M. 620
Kirk, J. 620
Kissane, B. 133
Klaaren, J. 165
Klare, K. 283, 284, 491
Klarman, M. 638
Klein, C. 638
Klein, E. 468
Kleinheisterkamp, J. 592
Klug, F. 300, 316, 484
Klug, H. 48, 137
Klusmeyer, D. 164, 166, 169
Knopff, R. 315
Koh, H. 351, 352
Kolo, A. 199, 202
Kome, P. 22
Kommers, Donald P. 3, 262, 263, 266, 350, 412,
    428, 441–58, 506, 606, 616, 618, 619, 638
Koplow, D. 250
Korea 399
Koskenniemi, M. 191
Kosovo 90
Kost, T. 639
Kothari, J. 531
Kramer, L. 301, 305, 543, 565
Krehbiel, K. 230
Kremnitzer, M. 545

Kretzmer, D. 161, 165, 168, 468
Krisch, N. 200, 201
Kristinsson, G. 218
Kritz, N. 43, 47, 48
Krotoszynski, Ronald J. 234–53, 350, 406, 415
Kühn, Z. 280, 281, 282, 288, 289, 295
Kumm, M. 189, 191, 266, 276, 294, 387, 388,
    391, 396
Kuru, A. 423, 425
Kymlicka, W. 143, 162–3, 164, 169, 171, 182,
    363, 365, 366, 431

La Torre, M. 593
Lahav, P. 349
Lajala, P. 378
Lake, D. 118
Lake, M. 166
Landfried, C. 267, 638
Langton, R. 416
Larsen, J. 241, 250–51, 567, 593
Lasser, M. 599, 616, 618, 621–2
Lasswell, H. 347
Latin America
    emergency provisions 336–7, 339–40
    see also individual countries
Laurie, E. 488
Lauterpacht, E. 193, 197, 199
Lauvaux, P. 225
Laver, M. 213, 230
Law, D. 10, 13, 169, 201, 332, 391, 599
Law, S. 457
Lazare, D. 427
Le Roux, M. 530
Le Roy, M. 469
Leckie, S. 504
Lee, J. 592
Lee, P. 460
Lee, T. 538
Leff, C. 367
legislation
    and emergency regimes 341, 342–3, 345–7
    invalidation costs 309
    and judicial judgment, relationship between
        311–13
    review, and specialized constitutional courts
        266–71, 272
    rights judgment, role of, and constitutional
        experimentation 305–11
    role of, same-sex partnerships 558–60
    scope or effects, altering interpretation of 311
    and terrorism law, challenges of 543–5
    see also judicial headings
legislative and executive powers, separation of
        234–53
    and international obligations 243

and judicial enforcement 243–4
parliamentary systems in civil law world
    247–8
parliamentary systems in common law world
    242–7
and risk of tyranny 239–40
US model of strict separation 237–42
US model of strict separation, original
    understanding 239–40
legislative-executive relations 211–33
    agenda power and decision-making process
        224–6
    and coalition formation 213–14
    coalition government 222–4
    coalitions and presidentialism 214–15, 216,
        222–4
    confidence vote and package vote, difference
        between 225
    earlier studies 212–19
    and government and cabinet control 225
    and legislative organization 221–2
    minority governments, conflict and
        presidentialism 215, 216, 224
    minority governments in parliamentary
        democracies 221–2, 224
    parliamentary democracies 212–14, 215,
        221–2, 224
    and partisanship 226–7
    and party discipline 225–6
    presidential democracies 214–16, 217, 224
    recent studies 220–29
    and restrictive legislative procedures 224–5
    semi-presidential democracies 216–19
    standing committees 222
    strong presidents and decree power 226–9
    unilateral action and delegation theories
        227–8
Legrand, P. 169
Leigh, I. 352, 423
Lemont, E. 49, 52, 53
Lenagh-Maguire, Niamh 143–69
Lenoir, N. 29
Le Roy, K. 3
Lessig, L. 96, 103
Lester, A. 483, 484
Levinson, S. 96, 97, 98, 101, 108, 116, 141, 352,
    427, 640
Levit, J. 67, 75, 575
Levy, J. 361
Lewis, B. 136
Lewis, C. 279, 291, 292
L'Heureux-Dube, C. 249, 250
Liberia 115
Liebenberg, S. 494, 495, 530
Lijphart, A. 22, 366, 374, 375

Limongi, Fernando 115, 211–33
Linz, J. 214–16, 222, 223, 230, 234, 375,
    626
Lipset, S. 52, 53
Lipson, C. 199
Livingstone, S. 484
Llorente, F. 399
Loewenstein, K. 350
Lombardi, C. 591
Londregan, J. 226, 229
Longaker, R. 353
Loomis, D. 350
Loughlin, M. 35, 200
Loveman, B. 350
Lucas, L. 25
Lukitz, L. 22
Lustgarten, L. 352
Lutz, D. 34, 35, 96, 97, 102, 105, 106
Luxembourg 115
Lynch, A. 547, 639

McAllister, M. 455, 461
McBride, J. 564
McCahery, J. 361
MacCormick, N. 592
McCormick, P. 618
McCrudden, C. 460, 466, 467
McGarry, J. 366, 379
McGinnis, J. 190
McHugh, M. 619, 620
McHugh, P. 171, 184, 185, 186
MacIntyre, A. 133
MacKinnon, C. 26, 457
Mackintosh, J. 315
Macklem, P. 504
Macklin, A. 546, 548
McLachlan, C. 197, 199
McLachlin, B. 473, 477, 479, 480
MacLennan, C. 316
Madison, J. 51, 102, 107, 239–40, 241, 250, 343,
    360
Mahlmann, M. 466, 468, 595
Mahoney, R. 417
Maine, H. 2
Mainwaring, S. 214–15, 230
Majeed, A. 359
Malaysia 537–8, 545, 574
Mallat, C. 94
Manfredi, C. 97, 104, 105, 108, 313, 543, 621
Mann, F. 504
Manning, C. 378
Mansbridge, J. 39, 107
March, J. 3
Marcos, M. 1, 2
Marilley, S. 101

Markesinis, B. 591, 594
Markovits, I. 22
Markus, A. 101
Marshall, M. 583
Martin, S. 478
Martineau, R. 119
Martinez, J. 537
Marx, H. 350, 351
Mathew, G. 377
Mathews, J. 390, 391
Mattei, U. 2
Mayhew, D. 230
Meierhenrich, J. 133
Meiklejohn, A. 414
Mejía Acosta, A. 222
Melnitzer, J. 199
Mendes, E. 478
Mendes, G. 574
Mendez, F. 52, 361
Merrill, T. 195, 202
Merritt, D. 360
Mexico 115, 118, 195–7, 632
Meyers, D. 533, 537, 540, 546
Michelman, Frank I. 35, 266, 278–97, 393, 396, 506
Micronesia 119
Mill, J. 414
Miller, A. 351
Miller, J. 579
Miller, R. 185
Minow, M. 475
Mittelman, J. 192
Moe, T. 230
Moeckli, D. 532, 547
Moehler, D. 39, 42, 49, 52
Moffett, M. 235
Monopoli, P. 32
Moon, G. 459, 460
Moore, B. 637
Moore, R. 42
Moreau, S. 479
Morgan, M. 22
Morris, D. 455
Morton, F. 313, 315
Mostert, H. 506
Mount, S. 410
Movsevian, M. 190
Munday, R. 592
Munro, T. 504
Murphy, W. 97, 104
Murray, C. 19, 22, 24

national
    constitution, and judicial engagement with
        comparative law 585–6

courts, and constitutional interpretation
    607–14
systems, development of, and globalization
    192–3
Navot, S. 148, 165, 406, 409, 573
Negretto, G. 112, 118
Nehru, J. 139
Nepal 43–4, 376
Netherlands 22–3, 115, 336, 398–9
Neuborne, B. 104, 621, 622
Neuman, G. 399, 455, 469, 619, 623
new global constitutional order 189–207
    bilateral agreements and fair and equitable
        treatment 196, 199–200
    constitutional critiques 192–5, 198
    constitutionalist interpretation, arguments
        against 198–201
    constitutionalist projects 190–92
    dispute resolution and investment treaties
        193–4, 198–9
    domestic law and minimum standard
        treatment 199–200
    and federated institutions 191
    general international law and international
        investment law, relationship between
        199–200
    global administrative law and international
        investment law, relationship between
        200
    international investment law and national
        constitutional law, similarities between
        194–5, 196–7
    and international trading system 190
    and interstate competition 197
    investment rules regime 195–8
    and investment treaties 193, 194–5
    and national systems, development of 192–3
    takings rule and investment 193, 195–6,
        197–8, 199
    and thick constitutionalism 191
    and thin constitutionalism 191
New Zealand
    bill of rights 301–2, 306, 308, 309, 310
    constitution endurance 115
    constitutional change 172
    constitutional rights, private individuals,
        effects on 393
    expressive conduct 408
    judicial power 312
    judicial review 192, 304, 312, 328–9, 331
    notwithstanding clause and bill of rights
        301–2
    terrorism law 542, 547
New Zealand, indigenous peoples
    and constitutional law 170–73, 176–9, 328

and future constitutional trends 184–5
and human rights norms 182–3
and international law 183–4
and state acquisitions of sovereignty 172–3
Treaty of Waitangi 173–5, 177–8, 184–5, 328
Newton, N. 179
Newton, S. 191
Neyer, J. 189, 191
Ní Aoláin, F. 349, 352, 353, 545
Nicaragua 72
Nicholas, B. 622
Nicol, D. 310, 311, 543, 566
Nicolaïdis, K. 190, 358
Nigeria 372–3, 379, 433
Nijman, J. 574
Nikolenyi, C. 217
Nimmer, M. 389, 411
Niño, C. 75, 215
Niskanen, W. 116
Nohlen, N. 639
Nollkaemper, A. 574
Norchi, C. 94
Norman, W. 163, 164, 169
Norris, P. 35, 375
North, D. 3, 195
Norton, A. 112, 133, 136
Norway 88, 115, 428
notwithstanding clause 300–303, 309, 325,
    327–8, 330–31
Nowak, J. 425, 427
Nowrot, K. 94
Nussbaum, M. 29, 530

O'Brien, D. 93
O'Connell, R. 464
O'Donnell, G. 215
O'Leary, B. 366, 372, 379
Oliveira, A. 638, 639, 641
Oliver, D. 332
Olivetti, M. 265, 267
Olsen, J. 3
O'Mahoney, A. 118
Ordeshook, P. 116
ordinary jurisdiction *see* constitutional and
    ordinary jurisdiction, interplay of
O'Regan, Kate 473–503
Osiatynski, W. 401
O'Sullivan, M. 494

Paine, T. 44
Palmer, G. 300, 306, 328
Palmer, M. 176, 177
Pardo, J. 3
Parikh, S. 361
parliamentary systems

in civil law world 247–8
committees, specialized 310–11, 312
in common law world 242–7
democracy *see* democracy
and legislative sovereignty limitations 322–3
presidential 214–16, 217, 224, 375–6
rights model, and constitutional
    experimentation 299–303, 304–10,
    311–12
supremacy and strong-form review 321–2,
    326, 330
see also government; political parties and
    constitutionalism
participation in constitutional design 38–56
autocratic referenda 50–51
'better citizens' claim 39
Cherokee Nation of Oklahoma 45–6, 48, 49
constituent assembly-based reform model
    44–5
and decisive consultation 47–9
and deliberative democracy 40–41
election exceptions 42–3
elections 41–2
elite-level negotiations 42–3
and government policing by citizens 39
justification of 39
legislature-based reform model 44
and majoritarianism 43–4
negotiation and agreement problems 40
and polarization 44
political approach to consultation 46–7
and public consultation 46–9
and public oversight 51–2
and ratification 49–51
referenda 49, 50–51
reform model choice 44–5
and representation 41–6
and self-interest 40, 51–2
technical approach to consultation 46
and textual coherence 40
transparency, self-interest and arguing 51–2
uncertain benefits of 40
Pasquino, P. 267, 270, 274, 352
Pateman, C. 35, 39
Peabody, B. 307
Pederzoli, P. 271
Pegoraro, L. 265
Pelikan, J. 427
Pelletier, G. 350
Peppin, P. 350
Perea, J. 249
Pereira, C. 227–8
Perry, M. 131, 300, 311
Persson, T. 115
Peru 192

Peters, A. 202, 592
Petersmann, E. 76, 190, 199
Petter, A. 313
Philippines 192, 197
Phillipson, G. 394
Pickerill, J. 307, 638
Pildes, Richard H. 254–64, 388, 391
Pillard, C. 305
Piovesan, F. 531
Pitkin, H. 130, 131
Poirier, J. 572, 574
Poirier, M. 198, 508, 509
Poland 44, 514, 630
political parties and constitutionalism 254–64
    approach to consultation 46–7
    ballot access and campaign financing 256–8
    bans on political parties 259–62
    and constitutional law 256–62
    constitutional texts 255–6
    and docket control 631–2, 633, 634
    electoral thresholds 259
    internal parliamentary rights of minor parties
        and independent officeholders 258–9
    and jurisdiction resistance 281–2
    override of judicial decisions, same-sex
        partnerships 559
    party autonomy rights 261–2
    political balance, and constitutional identities
        133–4
    political competition 102, 106, 107, 256–9
    regional variations 255–6
    see also government; parliamentary systems
Ponthoreau, M. 591
Popper, K. 352
Porat, I. 391
Portugal 336
Posner, E. 10, 103, 104, 119, 273, 353, 504, 532,
    534, 538, 546
Posner, R. 353, 532, 534, 547
Post, R. 12, 133, 416, 618
Postema, G. 592
Powell, C. 540
Powell, W. 3
presidential system 214–16, 217, 224, 375–6
Prince, P. 167
Pritchard, A. 98
property rights 504–18
    balancing test 510
    and common law jurisdictions 509–10
    compulsory takings 510–11
    constitutional property clauses, form and
        function 504–5
    and constitutional rights, structure and scope
        of 400
    government benefits as property 507

scope of property clause 505–7
takings cases, compensation in 512–15
takings of property and regulatory takings
    507–11
takings, public interest/use in 511–12
and tenants' interests 507
proportionality principle 390–91, 410, 411, 494,
    603–4, 607
Pryles, M. 165
Przeworski, A. 116, 117, 637
public participation 46–9, 51–2, 345–6, 392

Quick, J. 26
Quint, P. 409, 415

Radin, M. 508, 509
Ramos, F. 265
Ramraj, V. 545, 548, 574
Rao, N. 460, 467
Rasch, B. 105, 108
Ratner, S. 193, 197, 198
Raunio, T. 218
Rawls, J. 98, 103
Raz, J. 112, 129, 135, 191
Reaume, D. 478
Redish, M. 237, 239, 240, 242, 248, 414
referenda 49, 50–51, 379–80
regional
    effects, and constitutional endurance 118
    institutions, and terrorism law 546
    political identities, and federalism 367–8,
        371–4, 377
    variations, and political parties 255–63
    variations, and specialized constitutional
        courts 267–8
Rehnquist, W. 352
Reich, C. 507
Reimann, M. 359
religion and comparative constitutional law
    422–40
    assertive secularism 423–4
    atheist state 423
    church–state separation, but denominational
        pre-eminence 430–31
    jurisdictional enclaves 433–5
    multicultural accommodation 431–2
    and public education 425–9
    and reproductive freedoms 431
    separation as state neutrality 424–7
    state and religion relations, models of 422–37
    strong religious establishment 435–7
    and terrorism law, challenges of 543–4
    weak religious establishment 427–30
Renderos, A. 236
Resnik, J. 26, 533, 546

Reubenfeld, J. 457
Revesz, R. 360, 361
Reynolds, A. 40
Reynolds, H. 166
Richards, D. 567
Richardson, B. 185
Richardson, J. 352
Riggs, F. 230
Riker, W. 213, 357, 358, 359, 361, 366
Riles, A. 2
Rimalt, N. 469
Rinken, A. 290
Rishworth, P. 299, 300, 304, 306, 315, 406
Rittich. K. 190, 192
Rivera-Perez, W. 396
Rivers, J. 391
Roach, Kent 301, 312, 352, 532–50
Robinson, D. 42
Rodrik, D. 194, 195
Roeder, P. 365, 367–8, 369, 374, 375
Rogers, J. 641
Rogowski, R. 265
Romania 259
Romer, T. 224
Roper, S. 217
Rosamond, B. 192
Rose-Ackerman, S. 201, 508
Rosenberg, G. 305, 564, 565, 566
Rosenblum, N. 262
Rosenfeld, M. 35, 169, 415, 612–13
Rosenkrantz, C. 574, 593
Rosenthal, H. 224
Rosenthal, P. 350, 351
Ross, M. 378, 380
Rossiter, C. 349, 350, 351, 352, 353
Roth, B. 93
Rotunda, R. 425, 427
Rousseau, D. 265, 267
Roy, B. 591, 596
Rozakis, C. 591
Rubenfeld, J. 140, 141, 391
Rubenstein, Kim 143–69
Rubin, B. 81
Rubin, E. 250, 358, 360
Rubio, D. 228–9
Rubio-Marin, R. 31, 32
Ruckert, J. 593
Ruder, B. 478
Ruru, J. 185
Russell, P. 93, 120, 185, 186, 301, 305, 316
Russett, B. 352
Russia 22, 374, 631, 633, 634–5
Rwanda 47, 63, 73–4, 90
Ryder, B. 431

Saban, I. 469
Sabato, L. 116
Sachs, J. 566
Sadurski, W. 263, 265, 270, 281, 282, 284, 287,
    288, 294, 295
Sager, L. 98, 101, 102, 103, 109, 565, 641
Sajó, A. 131, 266, 401
Salisbury, R. 40
same-sex partnerships, legal protection of
    551–67
    and child custody 556
    comparative and international institutional
        law arguments 560–61, 587, 609, 612
    competing rights 561–2
    and constitutional debate 553–7
    courts and legislatures, roles of 558–60
    and equality 553, 557
    political override of judicial decisions 559
    and sexual activity laws 560–61
    and social consensus 556
    substantive and institutional questions 552–3
    see also gender as imperative of design
Samuels, K. 38, 39, 46, 51, 52
Sandrino, G. 196
Santos, B. 192, 197
Sartori, G. 218, 234
Sathe, S. 433
Saudi Arabia 437
Saunders, Cheryl 3, 396, 571–98, 619
Scaff, L. 40
Scanlon, T. 414
Schabacker, E. 94
Schauer, F. 303, 407, 408, 410, 411, 414, 416,
    418, 581, 594, 605
Scheinin, M. 401
Scheppele, K. 5, 13, 401, 532, 533, 540–41, 546,
    571, 626, 637, 638, 639, 640
Schill, S. 200
Schmeiser, D. 350
Schneiderman, David 189–207
Schofield, N. 213, 230
Scholtz, C. 186
Schor, M. 616
Schuck, P. 164
Schumpeter, J. 102
Schwartz, B. 240, 250
Schwartz, H. 265, 639
Schwartzburg, M. 113
Scolnicov, A. 286, 287, 435
Scott, C. 74
Scott, Z. 377
Scully, T. 230
secession *see* federalism, devolution and
    secession
secularism 133–4, 136, 138–40

Seger, R. 545
Seidman, G. 22
Selassie, B. 22
Serbia 59, 72
sexuality *see* same-sex partnerships, legal
    protection of
Seychelles 50–51
Shachar, A. 30, 147–8, 151, 158, 165, 166, 167,
    432
Shamir, R. 638, 640
Shany, Y. 66
Shapiro, D. 361
Shapiro, I. 74
Shapiro, M. 3, 295
Shaw, M. 199
Sheppard, C. 478
Shepsle, K. 222, 230
Shiffrin, S. 415, 416
Shue, H. 519
Shugart, M. 216, 218, 227
Siavelis, P. 226
Sidel, M. 533, 534
Siegel, R. 98, 457, 615, 618, 623
Simeon, R. 19, 52, 96, 104, 107, 366
Singapore 537–8, 545, 574, 575, 577, 585
Sitaraman, G. 583
Skach, C. 115, 120, 211, 215, 230, 375, 637
Skeet, C. 22–3
Skold, M. 240
Slaughter, A. 243, 276
Smiley, M. 61
Smith, A. 591
Smithey, S. 639
social security schemes *see* welfare
socio-economic rights 519–31
    Brazil 527–8
    constitutional rights, structure and scope of
        396–401
    and domestic jurisprudence 520–21
    due process, importance of 526
    education 526
    food rights 527
    foundations 519–20
    housing rights 522–3, 526
    India 520, 525–7
    minimum core approach 522–3
    public health provisions 526, 528
    second generation 520
    social assistance access and permanent
        residency 523
    South Africa 521–5
    water charges 524–5
Solomon, P. 120
Solum, L. 166
Sommeregger, G. 395

Sornarajah, M. 199, 200, 515
Sottiaux, S. 532, 547, 618
South Africa
    amnesty cases 61–3
    citizenship definition 149
    constitutional amendment rules, and power to
        remove cases 100
    constitutional amendments 98, 103, 104, 107,
        133
    constitutional identity and international
        influences 137
    constitutional and ordinary jurisdiction,
        separation of 286–7, 290–92
    constitutional rights, limitations clause
        389–90
    constitutional rights and principle of
        proportionality 390–91
    constitutional rights, private individuals,
        effects on 393
    consultation process 47–9
    court docket control 632
    emergency provisions 338, 340, 346
    equality and discrimination 489–96
    equality and family law 494–5
    equality and social security schemes 495
    expressive conduct 408
    Grootboom 35, 74, 399, 401, 459, 463, 522–3
    human dignity in constitutional adjudication
        459, 463, 464, 465, 466, 467, 492, 494,
        495–6
    human dignity and corporal punishment 462
    and international monetary system 85
    Joe Slovo Community 512
    judicial engagement with comparative law
        573, 574, 584, 587, 588
    judicial review 192
    Khosa 459, 464, 495–6, 523
    Khulumani 62
    land rights 61
    Mazibuko v City of Johannesburg 523–5
    Modderklip 523
    Promotion of National Unity and
        Reconciliation Act 60
    property rights 61, 506, 512, 513–14
    recalibrated gender symmetry 24
    reproductive rights 30, 31
    same-sex partnerships 469, 494, 553, 558,
        561–2
    social and economic rights 74, 399, 401,
        521–5
    transitional justice and transformation of
        constitutionalism 60–63
    Treatment Action Campaign 399, 401
    Truth and Reconciliation Commission (TRC)
        60, 61, 62

sovereignty
  limitations, and weak-form judicial review 322–3
  popular, and constitutional amendment rules 98
  and principle of non-interference 89–90
  and state acquisitions, indigenous peoples 172–3
Soviet Union *see* Russia
Spain
  constitutional design process 52
  emergency provisions 338, 340
  judicial engagement with comparative law 574, 580
  same-sex partnerships 555
  social and economic rights 398
specialized constitutional courts, rise of 265–77
  activism of constitutional courts 271–3
  and civil law 268–9
  constitutional reading and legislature, gap between 272
  definition 265
  and democracy 270–71
  and expertise 269–70
  future research 272–3
  and interpretive decisions 274
  and judicial review 270–71
  and legal certainty 268–9
  and legislative review, centrality of 266–71
  and mixed models of constitutional review 273
  and ordinary courts, tensions between 273–4
  possibility of specialization 266
  post-authoritarian regimes and democracy 270
  and regional variations, additional 267–8
  and supranational developments 274–6
  supranationalism and erosion of constitutional courts 275–6
  see also courts
Spector, H. 579
speech, freedom of *see* freedom of expression
Spiewak, P. 44
Spiro, P. 150, 164, 166
Spitz, R. 291
Spolaore, E. 118
Stanhope, J. 304, 317
Starr, K. 639
Stasavage, D. 53
state of emergency *see* emergency regimes
Staton, J. 631, 640
Stepan, A. 115, 120, 211, 215, 230, 358, 359, 361, 366, 375, 637
Stewart, R. 361
Steytler, N. 377

Stith, C. 361
Stone, Adrienne 406–21, 592, 595, 619–20, 622
Stone, Alec 3, 247, 613, 616
Stone, G. 101
Stone Sweet, A. 189, 191, 198, 265, 267, 272, 275, 278, 281, 282, 289, 294, 295, 307, 308, 390, 391, 620, 622
Stopford, J. 199
Strange, S. 199
Strauss, D. 96, 99, 100, 101, 604, 617
Strauss, P. 248
Straw, J. 316, 317
Strom, K. 221–2, 224, 225
Strossen, N. 417
structure and scope *see* constitutional rights, structure and scope of
Stuntz, W. 352
Suberu, R. 379
Sudan 88, 89, 379
Sullivan, K. 24, 97, 103, 106, 605
Summers, R. 242, 243, 244, 251, 592
Sunder, M. 86, 90
Sunstein, C. 3, 35, 51, 104, 196, 250, 352, 400, 401, 402, 411, 412, 520–21, 534, 567, 625, 636
Sutter, D. 114, 116–17
Sweden 115, 121–2, 510, 511, 514
Switzerland 50, 115, 342, 398
Syria 546
Szente, Z. 574

Tabellini, G. 115
Taggart, M. 592
Taiwan 573, 579, 588
Takii, K. 2
takings rule
  investment and globalization 193, 195–6, 197–8, 199
  and property rights 507–15
Tani, K. 507
Tarnopolsky, W. 476
Tarr, G. 359
Tartter, J. 51
Taruffo, M. 593
Tate, N. 3
Taylor, G. 279, 286, 289, 290, 291, 292, 293
Teitel, Ruti 3, 57–76
Teivainen, T. 192
Tenofsky, E. 350
terrorism law, challenges of 532–50
  and anti-constitutional ideas 532
  and constitutional interpretation 533–4
  control orders 536, 540–42
  and counter-majoritarian difficulty 534–5
  and court/government dialogue 532–3, 534–8

and criminal law 546–7
deportation to torture 533, 537
and detention without trial 535, 536–7, 545, 546
equality rights of non-citizens 535
exceptional regimes, production of 546
federalism and rights protection, links between 538–9
and freedom of speech 539, 543, 544–5, 547
future directions 545–8
future research 539
Guantanamo Bay detention 536–7, 546
and immigration law 537
and international and regional institutions 546
and judicial activism, new 532–3, 535–8
judicial deference to state anti-terrorism efforts, continued 538–9
legislative and administrative interpretation of constitutions 543–5
listing of terrorists 533, 540, 541–2, 546
and racial and religious profiling 543–4
search powers 546–7
and secret intelligence 543, 544–5, 547
special advocate regimes 547
and torture 536–7, 544, 545
transnational counter-majoritarian difficulty, new 533, 539–42
Teubner, G. 191
Thailand 49
Tham, J. 532, 533, 536, 537, 539
Thayer, J. 305, 311
Thio, L. 596
Thiruvengadam, A. 566, 577
Tiebout, C. 360
Tilly, C. 165
Tocqueville, A. 194
Toft, M. 364
Tomkins, A. 482, 497
Tomlinson, H. 565
Torres Pérez, A. 276
Trachtman, J. 76, 191, 197, 202
transitional justice and transformation of constitutionalism 57–76
accountability of actors beyond the state 61
amnesty cases 61–3, 66, 67
and changing constitutional self 59–63
contemporary constitutionalism as law of peoples 70–72
Europe 68–70
and future legislation 72–3
and human rights 60–61, 64–8, 70–71
and inclusiveness and consociationalism 60–61
and international law 59
and militant democracy 58
and reconciliation and accession processes 70–71
self-amnesty law 66
self-determination and political equality 70–72
and state action and accountability 57–8
state responsibilities, evolving understandings of 64–8
tribunalization and state responsibility evolution 63–4, 67
Treanor, W. 630, 639
Tribe, L. 58, 129, 146, 202, 353, 455, 638
Triga, V. 52
Tripathi, P. 574
Trochev, A. 639
Troper, M. 270, 593
Tsebelis, G. 40
Tullock, G. 3, 104
Tully, J. 34, 194
Turkey
constitutional identity 133–4, 136
political party bans 260–61
property rights 514
secularism 133–4, 136, 424
transitional justice and transformation of constitutionalism 69–70
Turpin, C. 482, 497
Tushnet, Mark 10, 43, 57, 96, 132, 169, 190, 237, 241–2, 248, 266, 271, 278–9, 283, 285, 290, 293–5, 299–301, 305, 311, 321–33, 352–3, 394–7, 399, 401, 413, 532–4, 536, 543, 547, 565, 571, 582–3, 590, 592–6, 617, 632, 637

Uganda 42, 64
Uhr, J. 310–11
Uitz, R. 266, 279, 396
UK
bicameralism 310
bill of rights 302, 306, 307, 308, 310, 329–31, 484–5, 505, 535, 556–9
Constitution, alleged lack of 482
court docket control 629
equality and discrimination 482–9, 557
equality and social security schemes 484, 487–8
and European Convention on Human Rights 482–7
European Court of Human Rights, Article 14 485–6, 488–9
expressive conduct 408
gender-constitutional analysis 22
human dignity in constitutional adjudication 461, 463, 464

judicial engagement with comparative law 577, 588
judicial power 312
judicial review 304, 312, 329–30, 331
legislation invalidation costs 309
legislative and executive powers, separation of, and judicial enforcement 243–4
notwithstanding clause and bill of rights 302
parliamentary systems in common law world 242–4
private individuals, effects on 393
property rights 505, 509–10, 511, 514
Protocol 12, non-ratification of 484
religious freedom 428, 430
same-sex partnerships 551, 556–7, 558–9, 560, 561
Shabina Begum 430
specialized parliamentary committees 310
Taff Vale 329
terrorism law 330, 534–6, 540–41, 542, 543, 545, 547
Ullrich, D. 455
UN
    accreditation process 87
    constitutional influence 79–80, 81, 89
    International Covenant on Economic Social and Cultural Rights 519
    sovereignty and principle of non-interference 89, 90
    terrorism legislation 533, 539–42, 546
Underkuffler, L. 509
US
    abortion rights 443, 445–8, 461
    Afghanistan, constitutional influence in 82, 89
    Afroyim v Rusk 155
    Alien Tort Act 62
    bilateral agreements and fair and equitable treatment 196
    birthright citizenship 151
    Black Codes 165
    Bosnia, constitutional influence in 82–3
    Cherokee Nation of Oklahoma constitutional design process 45–6, 48, 49, 179
    citizenship definition 148–9, 163
    citizenship rights 146–7, 155, 158, 159–60
    conscription exemption and religious belief 426–7
    Constitution of California revisions 96
    constitution and political parties 255
    Constitutional amendment rules, and power to remove cases 100
    Constitutional amendments 20–21, 98, 99, 100, 104, 105–6, 107

Constitutional amendments, and amendment substitutes 100–101
constitutional endurance 115, 119, 120–21
constitutional identity 136, 140–41
constitutional interpretation 601, 602, 604, 605, 606, 609, 614–15, 628
constitutional text and citizenship 146–7
constitutional rights, external limits, lack of 389, 396
constitutional rights and fixed tiers of review 391
court docket control 626, 628, 629, 630, 631, 632, 635
court support structure 632
criminal activity and freedom of expression 409
Dillon's Rule 195
dual citizenship 154–5, 157
Due Process Clause 99, 100, 553, 554, 609
emergency provisions 341, 343–4, 347
Equal Protection Clause 99
Equal Rights Amendment 21, 23
equality 26, 474, 553
federal citizenship 146–7
federalism 26, 358, 362
fixed tiers of review 391
flag desecration laws 409
freedom of expression 407–8, 409–11, 412, 413, 414, 415, 416, 418, 539, 547
gender-constitutional analysis 20–21, 23–4, 26
Hamdi v Rumsfeld 160
Heller 614–15
human dignity in constitutional adjudication 459, 461, 462, 465
indigenous peoples and constitutional law 170–73, 179–85
investment treaties and takings rule 193, 195, 197–8, 508, 509
Iraq, constitutional influence in 79–80, 85
judicial engagement with comparative law 574, 575, 577, 579, 581, 584–5, 587, 588, 589
judicial review 270, 305, 307
Kelo 511–12, 515
Lawrence v Texas 459, 553, 558, 559, 560, 587, 609
legislative and executive powers, separation of 235, 237–42, 248–50
Myers v United States 250
non-citizens 158, 160
parliamentary sovereignty, limitations on 322–3
party autonomy rights 261–2
presidential democracy 214–16, 217

presidential democracy and decree power
  228–9
property rights 198, 507, 508–9, 511–12, 515
religious freedom 424–7
reproductive rights 29, 30, 443
Roe v Wade 29, 443, 444, 445–7
same-sex partnerships 553–4, 557, 558, 559,
  560–61, 587, 609
Slaughterhouse Cases 99, 147, 160, 165
social and economic rights 400–402
standing committees 222
Sudan, constitutional influence in 88
tax exemptions and religious belief 427
terrorism law 59, 160, 534, 536–7, 544,
  546–7
United States v Morrison 26, 28, 35, 100
Vietnam War 628
Violence Against Women Act 26, 35
Webster v Reproductive Health Services 447
Wisconsin v Yoder 426

Valenzuela, A. 215, 230
Vallinder, T. 3
Van den Hauwe, L. 113–14
Van der Merwe, D. 286
Van der Schyff, G. 618
Van der Walt, A. 189, 284, 491, 504, 506, 507,
  511, 514
Van Dijk, P. 486
Van Harten, G. 194, 198, 200, 202
Van Hoof, G. 486
Van Roozendaal, P. 230
Vanberg, G. 272, 631, 639
Vargas, J. 196
Venkatachaliah, M. 142
Venter, F. 12
Vermeule, A. 101, 106, 273, 353, 504, 532, 534,
  546
Vermeulen, E. 361
Verney, D. 121
Vickers, J. 27
Vile, J. 96, 97, 98, 100, 101
Vile, M. 240
Voigt, S. 3, 39, 40, 46, 51, 52, 115, 119–20
Volcansek, M. 3, 267
Volokh, E. 409
Von Staden, A. 200
Vrachnas, J. 164

Waaldijk, K. 563
Wade, W. 243
Wadham, J. 302
Wagner, R. 117
Wälde, T. 199, 202
Waldrep, C. 165

Waldron, J. 332, 416, 533, 543, 565, 582, 584–5,
  595
Walker, N. 35, 190, 191, 192, 572
Walter, B. 364, 378
Walters, M. 172, 174
Warwick, P. 213
Watson, A. 473
Watts, R. 357, 358, 359, 360, 361, 364
Waxman, M. 545
weak-form judicial review *see* judicial review,
  rise of weak-form
Webber, J. 389
Weiler, J. 58, 70, 191, 197, 202, 275
Weiler, P. 301
Weiler, T. 245–6
Weill, P. 153, 166, 167
Weingast, B. 39, 116, 120–21, 222, 230, 360,
  361
Weinrib, L. 189, 298, 417
Weiss, L. 194
Welchman, L. 546
welfare
  rights 397, 398, 401
  social security schemes and equality 480–81,
    484, 487–8, 495
Wells, C. 352
Wennmann, A. 379, 380
Westen, P. 474, 475
Westin, A. 249
Wheare, K. 357, 358–9, 360, 361, 364
Wheeler, N. 94
Whitaker, B. 50, 52
Whitman, J. 417, 460, 463
Whittington, K. 135–6, 603, 633
Whitty, N. 29
Whyte, J. 301
Widner, J. 40, 41, 42, 43, 44, 47, 48, 50, 52, 53
Wild, P. 193, 197
Wildhaber, L. 485
Wilkinson, T. 236
Williams, G. 302, 306, 316, 415, 416, 532, 539
Williams, J. 193, 199
Williams, R. 119
Williams, S. 22, 24, 29, 31
Wills, G. 249, 252
Wimmer, A. 379
Wintemute, R. 473, 563
Winterton, G. 97
Wolff, S. 365
World Court, *Bosnia v Serbia* 59, 72
World Trade Organization, dispute settlement
  190, 193–4
Wright, S. 618, 619, 622

Yeh, J. 573, 588

Yoo, J. 352
Young, A. 312, 565
Young, E. 96, 604, 617
Young, I. 33, 475
Yugoslavia 59, 64, 68–9, 75

Zagrebelsky, G. 274
Zaum, D. 90, 94

Zedner, L. 546
Zeidler, W. 285, 287, 289, 290
Zelaznik, J. 222
Zimdahl, S. 574
Zines, L. 619
Zohar, N. 96
Zoller, E. 591, 595
Zumbansen, P. 201